D0212179

WITHDRAWN
From Toronto Public Library

DICTIONARY
OF
BRITISH
CHILDREN'S
FICTION

0915-70360

DICTIONARY OF BRITISH CHILDREN'S FICTION

Books of Recognized Merit

N–Z

ALETHEA K. HELBIG

AND

AGNES REGAN PERKINS

Greenwood Press
New York • Westport, Connecticut • London

Library of Congress Cataloging-in-Publication Data

Helbig, Alethea.
   Dictionary of British children's fiction : books of recognized
   merit / Alethea K. Helbig and Agnes Regan Perkins.
      p. cm.
   Includes index.
   ISBN 0–313–22591–5 (set)
   ISBN 0–313–27239–5 (v. 1 : lib. bdg. : alk. paper)
   ISBN 0–313–27240–9 (v. 2 : lib. bdg. : alk. paper)
   1. Children's stories, English—Dictionaries. 2. Bibliography—
Best books—Children's stories. 3. Authors, English—Biography—
Dictionaries. I. Perkins, Agnes. II. Title.
PR830.C513H4 1989
823'.009'9282—dc19   88–17788

British Library Cataloguing in Publication Data is available.

Copyright © 1989 by Alethea K. Helbig and Agnes Regan Perkins

All rights reserved. No portion of this book may be
reproduced, by any process or technique, without the
express written consent of the publisher.

Library of Congress Catalog Card Number: 88–17788
ISBN 0–313–22591–5 (set)
ISBN 0–313–27239–5 (v.1)
ISBN 0–313–27240–9 (v.2)

First published in 1989

Greenwood Press, Inc.
88 Post Road West, Westport, Connecticut 06881

Printed in the United States of America

The paper used in this book complies with the
Permanent Paper Standard issued by the National
Information Standards Organization (Z39.48–1984).

10 9 8 7 6 5 4 3 2 1

CONTENTS

Preface   vii

Abbreviations   xv

The Dictionary   1

Index   1421

PREFACE

The *Dictionary of British Children's Fiction: Books of Recognized Merit* contains 1,626 entries on such elements as titles, authors, characters, and settings based on 387 books published from 1678 to 1985. Like the two earlier companion volumes, *Dictionary of American Children's Fiction, 1859-1959: Books of Recognized Merit* and *Dictionary of American Children's Fiction, 1960-1984; Recent Books of Recognized Merit*, it is intended for the use of everyone who is concerned with children's literature in any way: librarians, teachers, literary scholars, researchers in comparative social history, parents, booksellers, publishers, editors--those to whom literature for children is of vital interest professionally or personally. A later reference will deal with award-winning books in Canada, Australia, New Zealand, and English-speaking countries of Africa and Asia. Periodic updates are planned.

We have long been aware of the need for such references, and a volume dealing with fiction from the British Isles was part of our plan from its inception. The response to the American volumes has shown that the need and interest which we had perceived is indeed real. Although we realized from the first that we could not include all the thousands of novels published for children, we hoped to present the best and those most representative of each period, and to do so, of course, we needed to consider the many fine books written by British authors.

Rather than depend upon our own subjective judgment about which books are best or most significant, we have included those books that have won or been finalists for major awards in children's literature, using the award lists in *Children's Books: Awards & Prizes* published by the Children's Book Council. We have not included translations or any strictly regional awards, nor those issued by organizations to their members only. We also excluded those given to books chosen by children, since the selection of books made available to the children who are polled is necessarily limited. For this book we have relied mainly upon the British: the Carnegie, the Whitbread, the Guardian, the Young Observer, and the Children's Rights Workshop Other awards. We have also included books by British authors appearing on lists that consider both American and British books, for example, the *Boston Globe-Horn Book* Award and the Children's Literature Association Phoenix Award.

Some books that clearly have become important as literature for children, however, were published before awards were given or were overlooked at the time of their publication by editors and award committees. Others, although perhaps of less-than-award quality, have become popular or have come to be considered standard novels that should be part of any representative collection for young people. We have, therefore, added several other lists that include both British and American books: the *Choice* magazine list of children's books for an academic library (1974, 1978, and 1983 editions); the lists of classics, both early and contemporary, published by *Horn Book* magazine; May Hill Arbuthnot's choices in *Children's Books Too Good to Miss* (1963, 1966, and 1979 editions); and the Children's Literature Association Touchstones. We have also included a type that has become increasingly important among books for young people, mysteries which have been nominated and selected as winners of the Edgar Allan Poe Award. Altogether, we have drawn books from twenty-one award and citation lists. A compilation of lists appears in the front matter.

While *Dictionary of British Children's Fiction* is not a history of children's literature or even of fiction for children, these many inclusions have given us a broad spectrum of the fiction recognized for merit by a wide variety of experts in children's literature. The awards reflect contemporary critical attitudes toward books for young people. Of course, the selections on various lists result from the application of somewhat different criteria, since the purposes of the awards vary. Although the selection committees all want to provide interesting, well-written books for children, some place more emphasis on social or spiritual values, like the Other, Christopher, and Child Study awards, and others on entertainment, like the Edgar Allan Poe Award.

Because our study is of fiction and not of illustration, we have not included fiction in picture book form, since the texts of such books can seldom stand alone and their analysis requires a consideration also of the illustrations. Somewhat arbitrarily, we have set 5,000 words as a minimum; most books need at least that number to develop a story that can work without pictures. Books of more than 5,000 words are included, even if the illustrations are very prominent.

Collections of short stories also require a different sort of analysis and plot summary from novels. Episodic books with the same characters in each chapter, like A. A. Milne's Pooh books, are included. Books of unconnected stories are not, even if technically they are fiction. Retellings from the oral tradition are included if the material has been developed like that in novels. A few books by Australian, New Zealand, American, and Indian authors have been included when they have won British awards.

In our author entries, we have focused on what in the author's life is most relevant to children's literature and to the particular books in the *Dictionary of British Children's Fiction*. Although several other published sources give biographical information for authors, none considers all the authors whose books are in our study. Having the information in the same volume is not only of convenience for researchers; it is of particular value for those areas where libraries are on limited budgets and do not own the other publications.

In presenting our entries we have tried to follow an arrangement that will be convenient for a variety of users. Entries are of several types:

A. Title entries. These consist of bibliographical information, including the American title if it is different from the British, and the publishers, the British title listed first even though the book may have been first published in the United States; the sub-genre to which the work belongs; the setting in time and place; a plot summary incorporating the plot problem (if any), significant episodes, and the denouement; a brief literary critical evaluation; sequels, if any; additional entries not mentioned in the summary, if any; and awards and citations in abbreviated form. A list of the complete names of the awards and citations appears in the front matter. Entries vary in length. Length in itself does not indicate the importance or quality of a book, since plots can be summarized more briefly and critical judgments stated more succinctly for some books than for others. Most readers will be acquainted with the terms we have used for sub-genres, but a few terms may need some explanation. By realistic fiction, we mean books in which events could have happened some time in the world as we know it, as opposed to an imaginary or fantastic world, and not necessarily that the action is convincing or plausible. Historical fiction includes those books in which actual historical events or figures function in the plot, as in *The Silver Sword* and *The Namesake*, or in which the specific period is essential to the action and in which the story could not have occurred in any other time, as in *The Iron Lily* and *The Eagle of the Ninth*. Books that are merely set in the past we have called period fiction.

B. Author entries. These consist of dates and places of birth and death, when available; education and vocational background; major contribution to children's literature; significant facts of the author's life that might have a bearing on the work; titles that

have won awards; frequently titles of other
publications, usually with brief information
about them; and critical judgments where they
can safely be made.

C. Character entries. These include physical and
personality traits for important, memorable,
or particulary unusual characters who are not
covered sufficiently by the plot summary, and
focus on such aspects as how they function in
the plot, how they relate to the protagonist,
and whether the characterization is credible
and skillful. Characters are classified by
the name by which they are most often referred to or by the name by which the protagonist refers to them, e.g., Uncle Andrew Ket-
terly; Caxton, William; Red Queen; Smaug. The
name is also cross referenced in the index
under other most likely possibilities. If the
character's surname does not often appear in
the story, it will usually not appear in the
index; when it is included, it is usually as
a family name: Clock family, Dunham family,
etc. If the plot summary gives all the significant information about characters, as
with many protagonists, they are not discussed in separate character entries. All
major characters, however, are listed in the
index.

D. Miscellaneous entries. These include particularly significant settings and elements that
need explanation beyond mention in the title
entry.

Every book has title and author entries.
When a book has different American and British
titles, the complete entry appears under the
British title, but the book is also listed under
the American title, with a reference to the
British title. Unhyphenated two-word surnames
are treated similarly. Entries are in alplabeti-
cal order for convenience. Asterisks indicate
that the item has a separate entry elsewhere in
the book. Accompanying entries do not duplicate
one another. While a book's title entry gives
the plot summary and a critical assessment,
other entries provide additional information to
give a more complete understanding of the book.

Publishers' names have been abbreviated; a full list appears in the front matter. Similarly, the list of awards and their abbreviations appears at the front of the dictionary. A list of the books classified by awards appears in the index. The index also includes all the items for which there are entries and such items as cross references, major characters for whom there are no separate entries, specific place settings, settings by period, and such items as themes and subjects, books of first-person narration, unusual narrative structures, significant tone, authors' pseudonyms, illustrators, and genres.

The majority of the early classics for children and many of the strongest books in recent years are British. We have treated the American books in separate volumes from the British simply for convenience. Together they make up one large, significant, and cohesive body of literature in the English language. Most of the best books are eventually published in both England and the United States, and the children who read them are often oblivious of their origins, or accept foreign terminology and customs as naturally as those of an unfamiliar part of their own country, indeed often relishing unusual points of view and settings.

Some aspects of British fiction for children stand out. In the first place, many of the earliest novels on the British lists, and even some published in the twentieth century, were not originally intended for children, but have been widely read by them. *Pilgrim's Progress*, *Gulliver's Travels*, and *Robinson Crusoe* were adopted by children before imaginative literature was published for them. The works of Dickens and Tolkien's *The Fellowship of the Ring* are shared by young people, even though written for adults.

Fantasy has dominated British children's fiction. With a very few exceptions, all the major English-language fantasies for children are British and have come to be considered masterpieces of world literature, books that every educated person should know. Whereas in realistic fiction, children's literature has frequently borrowed from that for adults, in fantasy, children's literature has made a major contribution to imaginative writing. In recent

years, books of fantasy, although proportionate-
ly fewer in number, have continued to dominate
the British children's literature scene in quality, and many of the fantasies of the last two
decades are outstanding for their inventive concepts and their daring and skillful style.

At the same time, historical fiction has
been a less frequent but nevertheless strong
genre, coming into its own in the 1950s. It is
impossible to consider British historical fiction without thinking of such major figures as
Rosemary Sutcliff, Hester Burton, C. Walter
Hodges, and Barbara Willard, although others
have also made significant contributions. Settings range over the world and from ancient
times almost to the present, with a number of
fine World War II books having emerged twenty or
more years after the event, an interesting
literary phenomenon. Typically, the historical
novels reflect sound, accurate research that is
skillfully melded with interesting plots to
produce powerful stories. The result is that
British historical fiction has a solidity which
makes the books memorable.

Like historical fiction, realistic fiction
has appeared throughout the list, but only since
1960 has it led numerically. The influence of
Arthur Ransome, who wrote holiday adventures in
the 1930s, persisted for a long time, and
British writers were slower than Americans to
exploit social concerns. While some recent
novels have entered the realm of the gritty,
urban working class, the most memorable examples
of realistic fiction seem to be based on the
authors' own childhoods and have the genuineness
of lived experience, for example, *A Sound of
Chariots* and *A Long Way from Verona*.

An interesting aberration appears with the
works of Joan Aiken and Leon Garfield, which are
melodramatic, exaggerated representations of
their periods. Their convoluted structures,
playful use of conventions, and style full of
wit, irony, and humor produce entertainment with
unusual depth.

Overall, British children's fiction is
rich. It offers a great many examples of strong,
subtle characterizations and mature themes,
developed without didacticism. Plot structures
are often complicated, and style is frequently

sophisticated and demanding. It is safe to say that many of the best books remembered from the twentieth century, as with earlier periods, will be British.

As university teachers of literature for children and young adults for more than twenty years and as people trained in the study of literature as literature, we are dedicated to the idea that books for children must be judged by the same criteria as those for adults, keeping in mind, of course, that children are the intended audience. Our critical comments, therefore, judge each book as imaginative literature, not on other values, regardless of the particular emphasis of the award or list for which it was chosen.

As with the companion volumes on American children's novels, we ourselves have read every book included in *Dictionary of British Children's Fiction: Books of Recognized Merit* and have done all the research and writing in this volume. We have had some valuable assistance from a variety of sources. We wish to acknowledge the help of Eastern Michigan University and the Josephine Nevins Keal Fund with leaves and grants and to express our appreciation to the Eastern Michigan University Library and the Ann Arbor, Michigan, Public Library for the use of their extensive collections. Specifically, we thank Marcia Shafer of the Ann Arbor Public Library Youth Room and her staff for their encouragement and aid in research, Brian Steimel and his colleagues of the Interlibrary Loan Department of Eastern Michigan University Library for their invaluable help in obtaining obscure books, and Jennifer Striker for her expert assistance with computer programming.

ABBREVIATIONS

PUBLISHERS

Abelard	Abelard-Schuman Ltd.
Alden	Alden Press
Allen & Unwin	Allen & Unwin (Publishers) Ltd.
Allied Pub.	Allied Publshers, Private, Ltd., India
Allman	Allman & Son (Publishers) Ltd.
American Humane Ed.	American Humane Education Society
Anderson	Anderson Press
Angus	Angus & Robertson Ltd.
Appleton	Appleton-Century-Crofts
Arrowsmith	J. W. Arrowsmith Ltd.
Arts Council of Northern Ireland	Arts Council of Northern Ireland
Atheneum	Atheneum Publishers
Atlantic/Little	Atlantic Monthly Press in association with Little, Brown & Co.
Baker	J. Baker
Barker	Arthur Barker Ltd.
Barnes	A. S. Barnes & Co., Inc.
BBC	BBC (British Broadcasting Company) Publications
Beaufort	Beaufort Books Inc.
Bell	Bell and Daldy
Benn	Ernest Benn Ltd.
Bentley	Robert Bentley, Inc.

Blackie	Blackie & Son Ltd.
Blackwell	Basil Blackwell, Publisher Ltd.
Bles	Geoffrey Bles
Blond	Anthony Blond
Bobbs	Bobbs-Merrill Co. Inc.
Bodley	The Bodley Head Ltd
Boni	Boni and Livewright
Bradbury	Bradbury Press
Brockhampton	Brockhampton Press
Browne	Browne & Nolan
Burgess	W. F. Burgess
Burnham	T. O. P. Burnham
Cambridge U. Press	Cambridge University Press
Cape	Jonathan Cape Ltd.
Capricornus	Capricornus Press
Carey	Carey, Lea & Blanchard
Cassell	Cassell Ltd.
Century	The Century Co.
Chapman	Chapman and Hall Ltd.
Chatto	Chatto & Windus. The Hogarth Press.
Chetwood	W. Chetwood
Children's	Children's Press International
Civil and Military Gazette	Civil and Military Gazette
Colburn	H. Colburn
Collins	Wm. Collins Sons and Co. Ltd.
Constable	Constable Young Books
Cosmopolitan	Cosmopolitan Press Ltd.
Covent	Covent Garden
Coward	Coward, McCann
Criterion	Criterion Books
Crowell	Thomas Y. Crowell Co.
Crown	Crown Publishers Inc.
Daldy	Daldy, Isbister
David	David and Charles (Holdings) Ltd.
Davies	Peter Davies Ltd.
Day	The John Day Co.
Delacorte	Delacorte Press
Dennis Dobson	Dennis Dobson
Dent	J. M. Dent & Sons Ltd.
Deutsch	Andre Deutsch Ltd.
Dickson	Dickson and Thompson
Dobson	Dobson Books, Ltd.

Dodd	Dodd, Mead & Co.
Doran	G. H. Doran
Doubleday	Doubleday & Co. Inc.
Duckworth	Gerald Duckworth & Co. Ltd.
Duell	Duell, Sloan & Pearce
Dutton	E. P. Dutton & Co., Inc.
Edling	T. Edling
Eel Pie	Eel Pie
Elder	Elder & Co.
Elm Tree	Elm Tree Books
Elsevier	Elsevier-Nelson
Evans	Evans Brothers Ltd.
Eyre	Eyre & Spottiswoode (Publishers) Ltd.
Faber	Faber & Faber Ltd.
Farrar	Farrar, Straus & Giroux, Inc.
Fortune	Fortune Press
Funk	Funk & Wagnalls Co.
Gay Men's Press	Gay Men's Press
Gill	M. H. Gill
Gollancz	Victor Gollancz Ltd.
Greenwillow	Greenwillow Books
Grosset	Grosset & Dunlap, Inc.
Hamilton	Hamish Hamilton Ltd.
Harcourt	Harcourt Brace Jovanovich, Inc.
Harrap	Harrap Ltd.
Hawthorn	Hawthorn Books
Heinemann	William Heinemann Ltd.
Hill	Hill & Wang, Inc.
Hind Pocket Books	Hind Pocket Books, India
Hodder	Hodder & Stoughton Ltd.
Holiday	Holiday House, Inc.
Holt	Holt, Rinehart & Winston
Horn Book	The Horn Book, Inc.
Houghton	Houghton Mifflin Co., Inc.
Howe	Gerald Howe, Ltd.
Hurst	Hurst and Blackell
Hutchinson	Hutchinson Publishing Group Ltd.
Hyperion	Hyperion Press Inc.
India Book House	India Book House
Indiana U. Press	Indiana University Press
International	International Publishers Co., Inc.
Jack	T. C. & E. C. Jack, Ltd.

Jarrold	Jarrold & Sons Publishers Ltd.
Joseph	Michael Joseph, Ltd.
Kampmann	Kampmann & Company, Inc.
Kaye	Kaye & Ward Ltd.
Kenedy	P. J. Kenedy
Kestrel	Kestrel Books
Knopf	Alfred A. Knopf, Inc.
Lane	Allen Lane
Laurie	T. Werner Laurie, Ltd.
Lawrence	Lawrence & Wishart Ltd.
Lea	Lea and Blanchard
Lippincott	Lippincott & Crowell, Publishers
Little	Little, Brown & Co.
Lodestar	Lodestar Books
Longman	Longman Group Ltd.
Lothrop	Lothrop, Lee & Shepard Books
Lovell	Lovell, Coryell & Company
Lutterworth	Lutterworth Press
Macdonald	Macdonald & Co., Ltd.
Macmillan	Macmillan Publishers Ltd.
MacRae	Julia MacRae Books
Macrone	J. Macrone
Maunsel	Maunsel & Co.
McDowell	McDowell Obolensky
McGibbon	McGibbon & Kee
McGraw	McGraw-Hill Publishing Co.
McKay	David McKay Co. Inc.
Meredith	Meredith Corporation
Merrimack	Merrimack Publishing Corp.
Methuen	Methuen, Inc.
Michael Joseph	Michael Joseph Ltd.
Miller	J. Garnet Miller Ltd.
Morrow	William Morrow & Co.
Motte	Benj. Motte
Muller	Muller, Blond & White Ltd.
Murphy	J. F. Murphy
National Foundation for Educational Research	National Foundation for Educational Research
Nelson	Thomas Nelson Publishers
Newnes	Newnes Books

Norton	W. W. Norton & Co., Inc.
Novello	Novello
Nutt	E. Nutt
Oliver	Oliver & Boyd
Orient Longmans	Orient Longmans, India
Osgood	James R. Osgood & Co.
Oxford	Oxford University Press
Page	L. C. Page
Pantheon	Pantheon Books, Inc.
Parents	Parents' Magazine Press
Parrish	Max Parrish & Co., Ltd.
Pelham	Pelham Books Ltd.
Penguin	Penguin Books Ltd.
Peterson	T. B. Peterson and Brothers
Phillips	S. G. Phillips Inc.
Philomel	Philomel Books
Phoenix	Phoenix House Publications
Pitman	Pitman Publishing Ltd.
Ponder	N. Ponder
Prentice	Prentice-Hall Inc.
Putnam	G. P. Putnam's Sons
Rand	Rand McNally & Co.
Random	Random House, Inc.
Rebman	Rebman Ltd.
Redding	Redding & Co.
Religious Tract Society	Religious Tract Society
Reynal	Reynal & Hitchcock, Inc.
Rex Collings	Rex Collings
Robert Bentley	Robert Bentley, Inc.
Routledge	Routledge & Kegan Paul PLC
Roy	Roy Publications
Samson Low	Samson Low, Marston, Low, and Searle
Saunders	Saunders & Ottley
Scholastic	Scholastic Book Services
Scribner	Charles Scribner's Sons
Seabury	Seabury Press, Inc.
Secker	Martin Secker & Warburg Ltd.
Seizin	Seizin Press
Sheed	Sheed & Ward Ltd.
Sidgwick	Sidgwick & Jackson Ltd.
Small	Small, Maynard & Co.
Smith	Smith, Elder & Co.
SPCK	Society for Promoting

	Christian Knowledge
Stacey	Tom Stacey
Stanley Paul	Stanley Paul & Co. Ltd.
Stein	Stein & Day Inc.
St. Martins	St. Martin's Press Inc.
Stockwell	A. H. Stockwell, Ltd.
Stokes	Frederick A. Stokes Co.
Stone	Stone and Kimball
Strahan	Strahan & Co., Publishers
Taylor	W. Taylor
Thacker	Thacker and Spink
Ticknor	Ticknor & Fields
U. of London	University of London
U. S. Book	United States Book Co.
Vanguard	Vanguard Press
Van Nostrand	C. Van Nostrand Co.
Viking	The Viking Press, Inc.
Walck	Henry Z. Walck, Inc.
Walker	Walker Books Ltd.
Ward	Ward Lock Ltd.
Warner	P. L. Warner
Washburn	Washburn Press
Watts	Franklin Watts, Inc.
Wells Gardner	Wells Gardner, Darton & Co.
Wheaton	Wheaton Publishing
Wiley	John Wiley & Sons, Inc.
Winston	John C. Winston Co.
World	World Book Co.
World's Work	World's Work Ltd.

THE DICTIONARY

N

NAIDOO, BEVERLEY, South African teacher and writer, who came to England at the age of twenty-two to study at the University of York. She has since taught in elementary and secondary schools. *Journey to Jo'burg** (Longman, 1985; Lippincott, 1986), her first book of fiction, received the Other Award. It tells of the difficult and disappointing trip of two black South African children, a girl and her younger brother, to Johannesburg to fetch their Mma, who works as a domestic there, to help their ill baby sister. The idea for the book rose out of discussions at meetings of the Education Group of the British Defense and Aid Fund for Southern Africa. The book is sociological in orientation and coincides with the group's purpose of raising the consciousness of the world to the suffering caused by apartheid and of working for a free, nonracial society. With the same group she has also published *Censoring Reality* (1984), an examination of nonfiction books on South Africa for young readers.

NAMEON (*Mr. Moon's Last Case**), dwarf who falls asleep in a derelict lifeboat and finds himself in the world of humans and who, after a series of adventures during which he is pursued by persevering detective Mr*. Reginald Moon, finds the boat made of oak which returns him to his dimension. Often frightened to the point of panic, he is also often quite clear-headed and makes the most of his unusual size and appearance, as when he paints himself like the human conception of a leprechaun and does a wild dance in the cinema for the schoolchildren of SPLOT, his way of convincing them that another world really does exist. He has large, coarse-skinned hands, weather-beaten features, a broken nose, a child-sized, chunky body, and eyes like those of a child "gazing out from behind an ancient mask." He is amazed but not awed by the marvels he experiences in the human world.

THE NAMESAKE (Hodges*, C. Walter, ill. author, Bell, 1964; Coward, 1964, historical novel set in East Anglia and Wessex in the ninth century. Narrated by Alfred the One-Legged, also known as Alfred* Dane-Leg, in his old age, it starts back at Thornham monastery, where he was taken as a young child after being injured in a Danish raid and having his leg amputated. When he is about ten, the Danes come again, in great force, kill the pious King Edmund, and burn the monastery. Alfred escapes with the old monk Githo, the only one who can read, and the mad monk Esdras*, who takes with him two blood-stained arrows from Edmund's body. For a while they join a band of people dispossessed by the Danes, eventually coming to Cambridge, to the monastery at Bedford, where Githo becomes ill. There Alfred has a dream that his crutch is taunting him, and a voice seems to say in his head that he will master his misfortune only if he takes what he holds in his hand and shows it to his namesake. He finds his hand, supporting him against the roof post, is on an old horse harness with Christian symbols on the ancient metal parts. The only other Alfred he has heard of is the brother of the King of Wessex, later known as Alfred* the Great. When Githo dies, Alfred and Esdras set out to find the army of the West Saxons. They are on the outskirts of the battles where the Wessex men make their initial victories and are in the camp of King Ethelred before the victorious battle of Ashdown, when Alfred of Wessex leads the men in place of the king, his brother, who insists on waiting to hear mass first. There, while Esdras enters the battle like a berserker, charging with his cross of arrows aloft, young Alfred watches from a distance, is surprised by a Dane, and by a fluke is able to grab the man's lance and overcome him. When the villagers would have killed the man, Alfred insists that he be allowed to live if he will be baptized. At Prince Alfred's household in Wantage, the smith makes young Alfred a wooden leg from the Dane's spear. When he tries to give the harness to Lord Alfred, he can think of no reason, and he is ashamed and takes it back. The prince suggests that he stay and learn to read, since he has as much need of scholars as of fighting men. As the fortunes of war turn against the West Saxons, Prince Alfred must take on more of the leadership, since Ethelred is ill and does little but pray. At Easter, directed by the voice of his crutch, Alfred Dane-Leg again takes the harness and, carrying it to Prince Alfred, falls, only to be raised by the prince and to put the harness over his head. The next moment word comes that Ethelred is dead and that Alfred is king. Alfred buys time by making an agreement with the Danish leader Halfdan that in return for a large sum of gold the Danish will not invade Wessex. Halfdan himself keeps the agreement, since he has East Anglia and Mercia, but his follower Jarl Guthorm* goes to Halfdan's brother, Hubba Ragnarsson, in Ireland, and makes plans for a joint attack on Wessex. King Alfred plays a clever game: he keeps his army from engaging directly with the Danes while holding them in a small area of the coast at Wareham (where Hubba's many ships join them) and attacking their foraging parties until they are short of supplies. By chance, Alfred Dane-Leg, who has become a secretary to the king, is captured and happens to be found by the Dane whose life he earlier saved, Torgils* Auk. Guthorm becomes interested in him, thinking he is King Alfred's son, so he is spared to be a hostage. Finally the Danes are starved out, and Alfred agrees to let them leave if they swear an oath not to attack Wessex again. Alfred Dane-Leg and three other hostages learn from Torgils's woman, a Christian who fears to be with oath-breakers, that Guthorm and Hubba plan treachery, meaning to sail and march off to Exeter and then attack the West Saxons again. They try to get word out to the king, but two are killed and the third arrives too late.

Alfred Dane-Leg and the woman, with her baby, escape from Wareham and reach Saxon soldiers. The army is trying to block the entrance to Wareham Water with ships and rafts and balks of timber to keep Hubba and his huge force from joining Guthorm at Exeter, but the bad weather breaks and Hubba sails before the barricade is in place. While the two Alfreds watch from a hilltop, the Danish ships set out. A sudden gale wrecks almost the entire fleet before their eyes. After nearly starving in Exeter, Guthorm is allowed to leave with the bedraggled remains of his army. The vivid details give a strong sense of the period and make the history which is played out in the book seem fascinating. The first-person narration is interrupted frequently by passages and chapters in third person and even first person from another character's point of view, a technique that overcomes the awkwardness of everything having to be experienced by the protagonist but that diminishes the feeling of conviction and weakens the sense of the story being told by Alfred Dane-Leg in his old age. While young Alfred is a sympathetic character, history takes precedence to his development. The sequel is *The Marsh King*. Carnegie Com.; Fanfare.

NAN (*The Silver Curlew**), imperious and "very, very, very old" nurse and housekeeper of Nollekens*, King of Norfolk. Her insistence on new linens leads to the story's problem and Doll's predicament with the Spindle-Imp*. Doll must spin flax into yarn or lose her "noddle," says King Nollekens. Since Doll can't spin, she accepts the help of the Spindle-Imp, who demands her and her baby as the price. Nan consistently treats Nollekens like a little boy and jealously retains her perogative as ruler in fact if not in name of the King's household.

NANCE PRICE (*A Likely Lad**), old woman in the village shop who takes in Willy* Overs, thinking he is her long dead son, Joey. Although she realizes for brief periods that he cannot be, her mind is so confused that she keeps slipping back into believing he is her son, for whom she has kept a bed ready for years. Her shop is so cluttered and dirty that the job of cleaning it and putting it in order almost defeats Willy, especially as Mrs. Price complains that she'll never be able to find anything if he moves it. Because Joey was a poacher and a such a troublemaker that he had to be bribed to emigrate to Australia, where he died, the earl has not arranged for anyone to care for the old woman or given her a place in his almshouses until Willy takes up her cause.

NANCY (*The Fox in Winter**), district nurse in a Cornish village. Tough minded and practical, she works hard at a job with minimal rewards and refuses to let herself be manipulated by her many demanding patients, but she also treats them with humor and genuine affection. When her daughter, Frances*, becomes involved in taping the memoirs of Tom* Treloar, she frequently warns her not to let the old man dominate her time, though she does carry his messages to "the maid," as he refers to Fran. Although she doesn't go to the funerals of most of the old people she has been caring for and seems callous when she remarks that through the "good luck" of a death there is an opening in the hospital, she admits to her daughter that in the night she sometimes weeps for her old patients.

NANCY (*The Owl Service**), crotchety housekeeper of the English family living in the Welsh countryside house in which the action of the novel occurs. One of the book's most interesting figures, she is the mother of Gwyn*, the boy who is attracted to Allison*, who is the daughter of the house and whose mother opposes their friendship. Nancy was once also part of a love triangle. Long before the novel begins, she was Huw* Halfbacon's sweetheart but left him for Bertram, who owned the house now belonging to Allison and her family. In retaliation, Huw tampered with the brakes of Bertram's motorcycle just to plague him a bit, but Bertram crashed to his death on the mountain. Nancy despises Clive* because she feels he doesn't measure up to Bertram. She is often surly and hard to get along with. The more she attempts to get Gwyn to stay away from Allison and Huw, the more he wants to cultivate them. She serves as a foil for Margaret* Bradley, her mistress and

Allison's mother.

NANCY AND NORA SHOUTER (*Which Witch?**), comic figures, twin witches of Todcaster who compete for the hand of Arriman the wizard. They work at the Todcaster Central Station, whose passengers and trains they hate. They also hate each other and bicker constantly, often fighting over their chicken familiars. Nancy's black magic trick involves producing a bottomless hole. She does this dramatically, then argues and scuffles with Nora over familiars, and Nora falls into the hole.

NANCY BLACKETT (*Pigeon Post**; *Swallows and Amazons**), elder of the Amazons who challenge the Swallows to a mock war on the lake and then become fast friends with them. The eldest of the whole group of youngsters, she is referred to as a "wild young one" by her mother and is given to expressions like "Shiver my timbers!" She doesn't do anything very unconventional, however. In *Swallows and Amazons* she is captain of the *Amazon* and in *Pigeon Post* she leads the expedition to find gold. While she doesn't appear in *We Didn't Mean to Go to Sea**, she is referred to frequently. She is not called by her real name, Ruth, because she likes to play pirate and her uncle has said that pirates are ruthless.

NAN GRAHAM (*The Battle of Wednesday Week**), Nicole Ann Graham, 16, a fair-minded, motherly girl, the eldest of the Grahams. She uses Southern American terms of endearment, in imitation of her dead mother. Her best scenes involve making the red blouse for Charlotte* Lattimer and driving to Fort William for more fabric, an action that the Lattimer children resent because they feel she has brought shame on the family by driving when she knows it is illegal for her to do so and by being brought home by a policeman. She helps to rescue Lucy* Graham when the children are stranded on the school bus during the terrible storm. Here Nan's ability to drive comes in handy, a situation that seems contrived.

NANNY TRANTER (*The Way to Sattin Shore**), grandmother of Kate*, Ran*, and Lenny* Tranter,

discovered by them in the course of the novel.
She lives in a cottage in the village of Sattin
not far from where the Tranters live, but
because of a family rift they have been unaware
of her existence. She writes the note in violet
ink to Granny* Randall which evidently informs
Granny and Kitty* Tranter that Fred, Kitty's
husband, has returned to Sattin. Since the
reader knows only what Kate discovers, the
reader never learns whether or not Kitty
attempts to contact him, but probably she does
not, nor is it ever clear whether or not Nanny
knows the part Arnold West played in Bob
Tranter's death by drowning. Nanny is a pleasing
but enigmatic figure, a foil to Granny Randall.

NAN OWLAND (*A Grass Rope**), older sister of
Mary*, eldest child of the owners of Lew Farm in
the Yorkshire hills, perhaps twelve or thirteen.
She attends Thornton Grammar School, where Adam*
Forrest is Head Boy, and is very self-conscious
in his presence and embarrassed when she thinks
Mary is being overly forward. Her attitude
contributes some humor to the story. She is
responsible and helps about the farm in many
ways. She tends to be very practical and cares
little about such things as fairies, but she
plays along with Mary's fancies because she is
very fond of her little sister.

NARNIA (*The Magician's Nephew**; *The Lion, the
Witch and the Wardrobe**; *The Horse and His Boy**;
*Prince Caspian**; *The Voyage of the "Dawn
Treader"**; *The Silver Chair**; *The Last
Battle**), mythical land created by the
magnificent lion, Aslan*, which various human
children from England visit and which is ruled
by a series of monarchs, whom the children
assist in different ways. Narnia has its own
peculiar system of time, which seems much
faster than Earth time. In physical appearance
Narnia is much like Earth, with rivers, hills,
cliffs, and vegetation, and is part of a set of
countries in a world bounded on one side by an
ocean. It lies in a valley between mountain
ranges and provides a home for humans, animals
of forest and field (some talking), and beings
from Greek and Norse belief, like Dryads,
Fauns, Satyrs, Hags, Dwarfs, Gnomes, Giants, and

Wer-Wolves. Aslan determines who shall enter
Narnia and how long they shall stay, and
eventually brings Narnia to an end. It is
succeeded after a terrible battle between good
and evil by the real Narnia, a splendid land of
which the first Narnia was a mere shadow. The
reader learns more about Narnia as the series
proceeds, and the developing landscape adds a
dimension of enjoyment to the novels.

NAT MARLOWE (*When Shakespeare Lived in Southwark**), Fortunatus, son of the playwright
Christopher Marlowe, who becomes the companion
and sworn brother of Miles Francis. With his red
hair, slight build, and quick tumbler's body,
Nat is described as "elfin" and as looking like
a fox. A cocky, impudent, mercurial boy, he is
more worldly wise than Miles, having lived in
and around the playhouses since the death of
his father in his infancy. He is, however, less
able to cope with the real adversity they
encounter and does not have the steady moral
outlook that keeps Miles from succumbing to the
life in the thieves' den. His bragging almost
costs him the chance to become one of the
queen's chosen entertainers, the Children of the
Chapel, but he is loyal to Miles when he might
have advanced his own fortunes by parting from
him.

THE NATURE OF THE BEAST (Howker*, Janni,
MacRae, 1985; Greenwillow, 1985), realistic
novel of a working-class boy in a Lancashire
mill town when unemployment hits the area,
evidently in the late twentieth century. The
first-person narrator, Bill* Coward, about fourteen, lives mostly with his father, Ned* (Noel),
sometimes with his grandfather, Chunder (Charles
Ernest), in Long Moor Lane, West Haverston,
where they occupy separate houses because, both
having fiery tempers, they fight too much when
they live together. Bill's mother never got
around to marrying Ned and, years earlier, left
their infant with him and took off for Canada.
It is a rough life, but the boy likes it until
the Stone Cross Mill, where Ned works and
Chunder has worked since he was thirteen,
closes. This stuns the local people, except for
Jim* Dalton, father of Bill's best friend,

Mick*, who has been the union steward and has
tried for years without much success to rouse
the workers to reality. At first the workers
occupy the mill in a sit-down strike, but when
they get a letter from the company saying that
if they go home for a week there will be
negotiations, they celebrate. Bill, sensing
trouble, runs through the rain to the mill and
arrives just in time to see his history teacher,
Oggy* (Mr. Oglethorpe), sitting on his father,
who is drunk and has apparently just smashed
the windshield of a boss's white Mercedes. Oggy
takes them home, and the next day Ned remembers
none of it, but Bill is ill with pneumonia.
Before the week is up, they discover that the
company has secretly removed all the essential
machinery from the mill so it will do the
workers no good to occupy it. Ned has been
visiting a friend, Dancer Smith, who travels
with a circus, mainly because Smith's sister Sal
has caught his eye, and returns to report that
the circus is on the rocks and probably has no
permits for the big cats. Chunder has turned his
attention to the chickens he keeps, not quite
legally, on his allotment, to which he has added
a hen named Alice to raise fighting cocks. He is
devastated when he discovers that some large
animal has savaged and killed all his chickens,
including Alice. This is the first of a series
of killings of livestock, both poultry and
sheep, near Haverston and up Hardale. Most of
the local people think it is a dog, or several
dogs, but there are reports of people sighting
another creature. Ned leaves for Scotland,
hoping to find work, and Bill is downcast and
furious at his father for leaving without him
and at Chunder for letting him go. When a
newspaper offers 500 pounds for a picture of
what is now being called the Haverston Beast,
Mick talks Bill into swiping Oggy's camera and
heading up Hardale to try to find the creature.
By a quirk of chance, they actually come upon
the animal in the dark and Bill takes a couple
of pictures, but the newspaper editor scoffs at
them and refuses to pay. Bill, whose temper is
slower to rouse than his father's and
grandfather's but is even stronger, goes almost
berserk. He sets out with just his air rifle to
hunt the beast, realizing that it is a black

panther from the circus, which was released when
they could not pay for a permit. After a day of
stomping around hunting, he heads back home only
to see police cars around his house. He turns
back toward Hardale and, gradually hearing
something padding after him, runs terrified into
the marsh and peat of Aggerton Moss. He is
caught up to his thighs in the muck when the
panther springs and lands where it is sucked
into the muck as it struggles and slowly drowns.
Bill, using his air rifle as a lever, is finally
able to pull himself out and stumble and crawl
to the village of Kirby Haverston. There the
villagers care for him and summon Chunder, but
no one believes his story, and when a man shoots
a Doberman, they assume that it was the
Haverston Beast. Two weeks later, Chunder tells
him that his father is in prison, having gotten
into a fight and hit a policeman. At school the
next day, he is hunting for Oggy to explain to
him about the camera when he hears the teacher
talking to a social worker, trying unsuccessfully to persuade her to let Bill stay with
Chunder rather than put him in an institution
or foster care. Bill takes his air rifle and
sets off for the hills above Hardale, where he
vows to turn into the Haverston Beast himself.
The title has at least three possible
applications, referring either to the panther,
the social-economic system which has savaged the
lives of the mill workers, or to Bill's fury,
which is slow to rouse but formidable when
pushed too far. The three Coward men are
convincingly drawn and memorable, as is the
whole gritty community struck by the tragedy of
the mill closure. Bill's voice as the narrator
is believable and interesting, and the pace is
tense and suspenseful. Scenes stick vividly in
the mind: the mill workers celebrating and
rioting in the rain, Ned gently caring for Bill
when he has pneumonia, the terrifying struggle
in the muck of the marsh. Carnegie Highly Com.;
Fanfare, Whitbread.

NECTAN (*The Stronghold**), strong chief of the
Boar people, husband of Anu, a man no longer
young but still physically strong and
intellectually vigorous, father of Clodha*,
whose husband-to-be, Niall*, will be the next

chief, and of Fand*, foster-father of Coll, the
protagonist of the novel and developer of the
stronghold. A stubborn man, Nectan seems locked
in fruitless disagreement with the head Druid,
Domnall*, for mastery of the tribe. He realizes
that what started as a dispute over policy
toward the Romans develops into a power struggle
and fortunately has the resilience and good
sense to keep his head and avoid personal and
tribal disaster by choosing the right moment to
allow Coll to build his stronghold. At the end,
he abdicates in favor of Niall and sends Coll
out to teach the other tribespeople how to build
strongholds to defend themselves against the
Romans. As a character, he wins the reader's
sympathy from the outset. He is a real-seeming,
vigorous leader who faces tremendous odds in
governing and saving his people.

NED BYRNE (*The Green Bough of Liberty**), youngest in the family at Ballymanus, County Wicklow,
Ireland, and therefore assigned to stay and
protect the women when his older brothers join
the rebellion of 1798. At eighteen, Ned is the
tallest and strongest of the brothers and the
least studious. He is full of enthusiasm for the
war and chafes at his less active part in it. He
is also full of sexual longings, mostly for
Ellen Kennedy, and this causes conflict with the
strict Catholic teaching that rules his
conscience. After he has seen the brutal realities of war, he is sickened and is particularly
bothered that he drove a pike through the belly
of a young man just his age, whom he thinks was
the son of General Dundas. The low points of his
experience are in the dungeon, where he fights
the other prisoners like an animal for the
meager food, and in his emotional visit to
Billy* the night before his brother is to be
hanged. By the time the English seize Ballymanus, he has matured enough to accept the inevitable and look forward to the birth of his son
and, perhaps in the far future, the eventual
freeing of Ireland.

NED COWARD (*The Nature of the Beast**), Noel,
father of Bill* and son of Chunder*. A rough
mill worker and a heavy drinker, Ned has never
married but has raised his son, with some help

from his father, after the boy's mother left the infant on his hands. He and his father both have fiery tempers and blaze away at each other when they are together too much, but they band together against any outside criticism or trouble. After the mill closes, Ned goes off to see a woman traveling with a circus, and his son muses on how it would be to have a woman in the family and remembers the way his friend Mick* Dalton's mother, a woman of some education and social standing, sometimes looks at Ned with more than casual admiration. At the end, Ned goes to prison for two years for hitting a policeman in a fight in Glasgow.

NEIL RAMSAY (*The Thursday Kidnapping**), second child, an imaginative twelve-year-old. A great reader, Neil becomes an expert on one subject at a time, the current interest being falconry. Although he knows that he frequently scares himself by letting his imagination run away with itself, he cannot always control it, and when he starts to think that Bart may have been kidnapped for political purposes, he elaborates upon the idea until they are all thoroughly convinced. He is the first one to get the story off his mind, being able to tell Freddy as they are putting away the baby's bath, and though he is in tears, he finds it a great relief and Freddy's calm acceptance of the story comforting.

NELL HENCHMAN (*Castors Away!**), 12, only daughter of Dr.* William Henchman and twin of Tom*, with whom she is very close. Since she has been used to spending a lot of time with her brothers and is strong-minded, she does not get along well with her Aunt Julia Henchman, who has been taking care of her widower brother's household since his wife died and who seems determined to make a lady of Nell. Nell and Betsy* Farr, the new maid, become very close friends. Nell is inclined to be impetuous and impractical, and Betsy often fills her in on the way things must go. Nell is encouraged to use her mind in unconventional ways by her teacher, Monsieur* Armand, and, at the very end of the book, when the author relates quickly what happens to the various Henchmans after the story is over, the reader learns that Nell marries John Paston, a friend of her brother Edmund* and also a medical student. John admires her spirit and individualistic ways, and the new couple emigrate to the New World. Nell is a convincing, well-drawn figure.

NELLY STAGG (*Fathom Five**), madam of Garmouth's most notorious brothel, to whom the Maltese take Sheila* Smythson when she has been playing a tart in the Low Street bars. Nelly realizes that Sheila's father, a town councillor, will seize the opportunity to put her out of business if he uses the kidnap charge, and she willingly agrees to Sheila's proposal to help find the spy for Chas* McGill in exchange for Sheila's silence to the police. On Chas's subsequent visits to her, she tells him that she was a World War I widow with three children when she went into the business, and that she has grandchildren whom she seldom sees. She is a real power in Garmouth, able to control the toughest elements, but she is evidently murdered by Sven*, who thinks she has discovered his identity. She is a stock figure of the good-hearted whore.

NESBIT, E(DITH) (1858-1924), born in Kennington in London; author of many novels and poems, who thought her best work was her poetry for adults but whose reputation rests on her humorous, episodic novels of realism and fantasy for the young. Of these, the best make up two sets: the four books about the six irrepressible Bastable children: *The Story of the Treasure Seekers** (Unwin, 1899; Stokes, 1899), the book that made her a household name and appears in Children's Classics, *Choice*, and the Children's Literature Association Touchstones list, *The Would-be-goods* (Unwin, 1901; Harper, 1902), *The New Treasure Seekers* (Unwin, 1904; Stokes, 1904), and *Oswald Bastable and Others* (Wells Gardner, 1906; Coward, 1960); and a family-fantasy trilogy of magic adventures: *Five Children and It** (Unwin, 1902; Dodd, 1905), which is listed in Children's Classics and *Choice*, *The Phoenix and the Carpet* (Newnes, 1904; Macmillan, 1904), and *The Story of the Amulet* (Unwin, 1906; Dutton, 1907). Both sets are considered classics of their genres. Nesbit was one of six chil-

dren, a tomboy whose childhood exploits with her
older brothers formed the basis for her most
convincing realistic stories. Her father, who
conducted an agricultural college in London,
died when she was four. She was educated in
France and Germany, as well as in England, and
spent her teens in Kent, where she told stories
to neighbor children and wrote verse. Her first
poem was published when she was seventeen. At
twenty-one she married Hubert Bland, a
journalist of ill-health, uncertain finances,
and philandering ways, who was one of the
founders of the Fabian society of Socialists and
friend of Bernard Shaw, among other literati of
the day. She wrote to support their Bohemian
establishment in Lewisham Road and their family
of five children, turning out romances or humor,
short or long, whatever would sell; her work was
undistinguished in quality but saleable. In the
mid-1890s, she was asked to contribute sketches
of her childhood to the *Girls' Own Paper*,
enjoyed doing them, and proceeded to write *The
Treasure Seekers*, using her memories for the
Bastables' escapades, too. First published as
separate stories, these appeared in book form at
Christmas in 1899, and E. Nesbit had found her
niche in the literary world. The very true-to-
life stories of Oswald and siblings led to some
two dozen more books, most from stories
originally serialized in *Strand Magazine*.
Though one of her less satisfactory books in
structure and style but conceptually attractive
to the young, *The Railway Children* (Wells
Gardner, 1906; Macmillan, 1906), also remains
popular today. It concerns a family down on
their luck, who go to live near a railway line.
Wet Magic (Laurie, 1913; Coward, 1937), about
the adventures of some children and a mermaid,
was her last full-length book for the young. Her
husband, who had gone blind, died in 1914, and
she was forced to take in roomers and accept a
government pension in order to maintain her
home, Well Hall in Kent, to which they had moved
in 1899 and which was the prototype of the Moat
House in the Bastable books. In 1917, she
married again, more happily this time, to Thomas
Terry Tucker, a marine engineer and old family
friend, who persuaded her to write further
stories. They were published posthumously, but

nothing else she wrote achieved the permanency, in particular, of her Bastable novels. These of all her books seem the least dated. She understood what children like and how they act and was unusually apt at capturing both in words. She also wrote under the names E. Bland and Fabian Bland.

NESSIE MORTIMER (*Noah's Castle**), Agnes, 17, eldest child and older daughter of Norman, called Father*, and May, called Mother*. Nessie is pretty, sensible, and spirited but a little more modern than Father thinks suitable. She often talks back to Father, who is tactless, domineering, and certain his way is best, or mumbles asides to protest his ideas or ways of treating members of the family, in particular, his arrogant manner toward Mother. She moves out to live with the Timpsons, her boyfriend's family, when Father informs her that he expects her to accept the invitation of Mr*. Gerald Bowling to attend the theater. She thinks, correctly, that Mr. Gerald is a "dirty old man." After she moves out, she remains on good terms with everyone else in the family.

NETTY BELLINGER (*A Pattern of Roses**), young cousin of Miss* May Bellinger and niece of old Brimstone Bellinger, the Edwardian vicar. For unexplained reasons, Netty has come to live for two or three years at the vicarage, where she meets Tom* Inskip, the village boy to whom Miss May is giving drawing lessons. Netty is bold and a bit naughty, inclined to flirt with Tom without considering the consequences to him. After his death, we learn from Miss May's letter, she changes, becomes a World War I nurse, and never marries. Tim* Ingram first knows of her from the picture he finds drawn by Tom, which is imperfect but catches her personality. Rebecca* visits her in her confused and ill old age and gets clues that help her unravel the mystery of Tom's death.

NIALL (*Master of Morgana**), 16, protagonist, brother of Ruairidh, whose near-fatal fall from the bridge over the chasm near the seashore fishery while grappling with Murdo, the surly, red-haired fisherman, precipitates the story.

Niall is certain that Murdo has tried to kill his brother and sets out to learn the truth. He naively trusts one-legged Long* John MacGregor, who turns out to be the villain and head of a salmon poaching ring, rightly distrusts Murdo, and wrongly distrusts the bald-headed man. Niall is a combination of innocence, local wisdom, and practical know-how, a loving son to his mother, at odds with his supercilious, younger sister, Morag, and a little sweet on her friend, Catriona. He is a rather typical adolescent youth, impetuous and sharp eyed, who succeeds by luck, pluck, and daring, and who is pretty much the same at the end of the story as he was at the beginning. Niall is glad Long John gets away at the end, for ironically he truly likes and admires the clever thief for overcoming his disability, demanding respect from his men, and triumphing (illegally) over the landholders.

NIALL (*The Stronghold**), brave and sensible youth of about twenty, member of the Boar people's ruling Council, best friend of Coll, betrothed of Clodha*, and as Clodha's husband destined to be the next chief of the tribe. He realizes that the tribe cannot survive long if they continue to lose adults at the same rate they have been. He sees the importance of Coll's scheme to build a stronghold and believes it is feasible. Along with Coll, he realizes that Taran* is dangerous to the tribe, but, since he believes in law and order, he goes along with Nectan's* decisions. Similarly, he refuses to openly oppose Domnall's* decree that Fand* must be sacrificed, since to do so would be blasphemy. He is a brave fighter and performs valiantly against the Romans when they attack and the effectiveness of the stronghold is at stake. He serves as the decoy to lure them into a position where the Boar people can annihilate them. As a character, he is interesting even though he lacks the distinctiveness of Taran, Coll, or Clodha.

NICHOLAS AND THE WOOLPACK. See *The Wool-Pack.*

NICHOLAS FETTERLOCK (*The Wool-Pack**), only son of the well-to-do wool merchant Master* Thomas

Fetterlock, about fourteen years old. He proves that his father has not violated Staple* regulations. Usually respectful and obedient, Nicholas also has a mind of his own, and is fun-loving and occasionally mischievous. He is pleased to discover that Cicely* Bradshaw, to whom his father has betrothed him, likes to enjoy life and do things, and the two get on well immediately. Predictably, Nicholas grows more responsible as the story proceeds.

NICHOLAS LATTIMER (*The Battle of Wednesday Week**), 16, Charlotte* Lattimer's older brother. He is a fun-loving youth, not very outgoing, inclined to be bookish in speech and pompous in manner when he is unsure of himself or under tension, almost as though he were playacting. At Robert Graham's orders, he takes charge when the children are left to work out their diffi- culties. Like the others, he wavers in his attitude toward the merging of the two families, but he eventually even calls Nan* Graham sister and compliments her on her driving, which is quite a mature thing to do, considering how envious he is of her having a driver's license and a car of her own in America.

NICKLESS, WILL (1902-   ), born in Brentwood, Essex; illustrator, painter, and lecturer. He was educated at St. Martins School of Art and has illustrated numerous books, in addition to his own. He started work at fourteen, at eighteen joined an advertising agency and then a paper, *The Motor*, for which he made technical drawings for both editorial and advertising departments. He left that position to become a freelance illustrator, which he has been ever since, for books, magazines, and advertising in many forms. He paints and has had a number of exhibitions, and has a small private press on which he prints limited editions of his own poems. A series of his antiwar etchings was reproduced in *The New Leader* in 1939. He has also lectured on the illustration of Dickens's novels. Among the several books he wrote is *Owlglass** (Day, 1966), an animal fantasy with something of the comfortable, men's club atmo- sphere of *The Wind in the Willows** by Kenneth Grahame*. Others include *The Nitehood* (Oliver,

1966) and *Molepie* (Baker, 1967). He has made his
home in Sussex, where he has indulged in such
diverse hobbies as making violins and violas, an
astronomical telescope, and model locomotives.

NICK WILLOW (*Carrie's War**), younger brother of
Carrie*, nine when the book starts. A beautiful
child with deep blue eyes and fair hair, Nick is
something of a baby, but he is also greedy and
manipulative and not nearly as honest as Carrie.
He is also less concerned with how people feel,
but he is very fond of Auntie* Lou, and when he
finds out that she is planning to run off and
marry her American soldier, he keeps the secret
even from Carrie so that Mr.* Evans won't find
out, realizing that Carrie is not as good at
lying as he is. Throughout their year in the
Welsh town, he steadfastly hates Mr. Evans,
while Carrie's emotions vacillate from hatred to
fear to pity. At Druid's Bottom he is the only
one who understands much of Mister* Johnny's
Gotobed's speech, though sometimes he just
pretends to understand.

NICKY GORE (*The Devil's Children**), Nicola,
twelve-year-old who joins the Sikh group after
the Changes have turned the English to a violent
hatred of machines. Because she has been badly
hurt by her separation from her family, Nicky
deliberately hardens herself and tries not to
become emotionally involved with the Sikhs and
particularly does not want the women, who are
overprotective of their own children, to mother
her. Several times she does rash or adventurous
things to assert her independence until one of
the uncles cautions her that, if she influences
the Sikh children to disobedience, they will
have to send her away. In the end it is clear
that she has become very much attached to the
Sikhs, but she is also strong enough to be able
to leave them to search for her own parents.

NICKY NICHOL (*The Machine Gunners**), Benjamin,
son of a well-to-do naval captain in whose vast
neglected garden the youngsters build their
machine gun emplacement and underground bunker.
A timid, nervous boy, smaller than his
classmates, he has been terrorized by Boddser
Brown, and he gladly accepts the protection and

companionship offered by Chas* McGill in exchange for the use of his garden. A sensitive child, he is very much ashamed of his mother's drinking and sleeping with the officer billeted in their house, and he misses his father, who has been killed in action. When a bomb strikes the house, he is in the fortress but is assumed dead along with his mother and the sailors who live there, and, afraid of being sent to a Home, stays there with Clogger* Duncan, the tough red-haired boy, who pretends that he has gone home to Glasgow. Rudi* Gerlath, the German flyer whom they capture, is more afraid of tense, jumpy Nicky than of Clogger and is much relieved when he can get them to uncock his Luger and put the safety catch on. Nicky is the one who leads Rudi through the streets full of panicky people expecting the invasion, pretending Rudi is his deaf-and-dumb father, and gets him to the boat. Before Rudi leaves, Nicky tells him that he wishes he were his father.

NIGHTBIRDS ON NANTUCKET (Aiken*, Joan, Cape, 1966; Doubleday, 1966), humorous, complicated melodrama that purports to be historical, set on the high seas and in Nantucket in the 1830s. Resourceful, sharp-witted Dido Twite, who is either eight, nine, or eleven, awakens aboard the whaler *Sarah Casket* after a ten months' sleep, during which she has been cared for by capable ship's boy, Nate Pardon, who has kept her alive on molasses and whale oil. Dido had been found floating unconscious on the North Sea, having escaped from the burning *Dark Dew* at the end of *Black Hearts in Battersea**. At the time of rescue, the *Sarah Casket* was in hot pursuit of a great pink whale on the orders of the captain, the gloomy, pious, obsessed Quaker, Jabez Casket. At first the voyage proceeds uneventfully. Dido makes friends with the captain's shy, fearful daughter, Dutiful* Penitence, later called Pen, and enjoys the company of Nate, who sings amusing sea chanteys. Dido's curiosity is aroused when she spies a mysterious veiled lady hiding in the blubber room and notes the furtive behavior of the disagreeable first mate, Mr. Slighcarp, who, among other peculiar actions, is startled when Nate's bird, Mr. Jenkins, spouts sentiments in

favor of King James. Nate informs Dido that the
mate favors Bonnie Prince Georgie of Hanover for
the throne. At the Galapagos Islands, the
captain learns that Rosie* Lee, the pink whale,
has been sighted off Peru and takes off after
her. After a frantic chase, the ship puts in for
supplies at New Bedford, Massachusetts, and the
captain leaves the girls in the care of his
sister, Aunt Tribulation, whom Pen has not seen
since she was three. Mungo the donkey picks them
up and takes them to the captain's farm where
strangely no one greets them, and the place is
cold and dark. They discover Aunt Tribulation
upstairs in bed, half-invalided, according to
her, by rheumatism. Cold and domineering, for
days she burdens them with housekeeping duties
and work about the farm, berating and punishing
them for even minor infractions of her orders.
Sharp-eyed Dido notes suspicious occurrences,
among them, Aunt Tribulation's occasional un-
characteristic spryness, a mysterious visitor,
footprints in the attic, and a locked door. Sent
out to hunt a lost sheep, the girls are
separated by a sudden fog, and Pen encounters a
sad-faced, monkey-like, bald, pidgin-English-
speaking German who calls himself Professor
Breadno and is an expert on firearms and explosives. Plot entanglements build. The captain and
Nate turn up, having been shipwrecked and
rescued by Rosie and deposited on the Nantucket
shore. The captain is demented by his experiences and proves unhelpful at the time, but Nate
suspects a Hanoverian conspiracy. It comes out
that Aunt Tribulation is an imposter, being in
reality Miss Letitia Slighcarp (of *The Wolves
of Willoughby Chase**), sister of the mate. Both
are involved in a Hanoverian scheme to construct
an enormous cannon so powerful it can propel
shot across the ocean and kill the King of
England. If they succeed, the kickback of the
gun will drive Nantucket Island into New York
Harbor, a fearful catastophe. When the other
conspirators, who lurk on the island pretending
to be ornithologists, kidnap Dido and Nate,
Pen, who under Dido's tutelage has developed
latent resources of character, drugs Aunt Trib
and bribes Professor Breadno with molasses candy
to stall on his calculations, it having been
learned that the conspirators deceived him about

their intentions. Pen and the local mayor, Doctor Mayhew, aghast at the threat to Nantucket, locate Dido and Nate, held captive in a lighthouse. The good group, with the captain's senses restored, decide that the plot can best be foiled by disposing of the gun. Nate lures Rosie to shore with sweet songs, they hitch Rosie to the gun, and she accommodatingly pulls it into the sea, Aunt Trib astride the chassis angrily attempting to cut the towrope. The real Aunt Trib then turns up, having been at sea with her new husband and now calling herself Aunt Topsy. Pen goes to live with her, Rosie returns and frolicks around the *Sarah Casket*, and homesick Dido joyfully sails for England, her responsibilities toward the no-longer feckless Pen discharged and her debt to Captain Casket paid. Aiken hijinks her way through numerous Gothic conventions, a large cast of absurd characters, and pleasingly overblown incidents. The humor is many-faceted, employing also clever diction, dialogue, and allusion. Later books about Dido are *The Cuckoo Tree* and *The Stolen Lake**. Choice.

NIGHT FALL (Aiken*, Joan, Macmillan, 1969; Holt, 1971), mystery-suspense novel set in London and Cornwall in which the main action takes place in 1968. When her mother, a divorced Hollywood actress, dies in an auto accident, Meg Frazer, 9, is shipped off to England to live with the physician father she has not seen since she was very small. Finding her father cold and distant, the servants resentful and unsympathetic, and school unsatisfying, lonely Meg begins having a recurring nightmare about a closed room and swaying face that becomes more frequent and terrifying as she enters her teens. Her closest friends are the Barnard children, who live near by, gregarious Polly and imperious George, and her mother's sister, understanding Aunt Venetia, who gives her a cat, Hodge, which becomes a dear pet and deep comfort to the unhappy child. When she is nearly nineteen and a budding portrait painter, Meg wins an art scholarship to Paris which her father insists she refuse. On the rebound from this disappointment, Meg accepts a proposal of marriage from George, now a rising young stockbroker. The dreams worsen as the

engagement flounders, and Aunt Venetia suggests
that Meg travel to Penleggen on the rocky coast
of Cornwall where, when she was five, Meg
suffered a broken leg and concussion from a fall
down the cliff. Accompanied by Hodge, Meg checks
in at the local inn, the Trevelyan Arms, begins
to meet residents of the isolated, decaying
village, and, while exploring, enters a quayside
cottage which she quickly realizes is the
setting of her swaying-face dream. She soon
learns that the cottage is the site of the
unsolved murder of invalid Gerald Trevelyan, the
twin brother of the wealthiest man of the
district and owner of most of the village land,
Mark Trevelyan. She learns Gerald was slain on
the very day Meg suffered her childhood
accident. Then Toby Trevelyan, idealistic young
engineer and son of the murdered man, confides
to her his plans to revitalize the village by
attracting light industry, much as his father
had hoped to do in plans that were vigorously
opposed by Mark. Several disturbing incidents
leave Meg fearful for her safety. The sketch she
makes of the face from her dream disappears from
her portfolio. Fortunately Hodge is able to
dispatch a huge rat that has been locked in her
car while she is parked on the cliff overlooking
the village. The boat in which she and Toby
sightsee runs out of gas and is almost wrecked
on the rocks. On her last night in the village
(the innkeeper having mysteriously refused to
rent her a room any longer), Mark invites her to
dinner at his mansion on the cliff. As soon as
she meets him, Meg recognizes his face as the
one in her dream and realizes that Mark murdered
Gerald. At the time, she herself, injured in a
fall from the cliff, lay in the cottage on the
shadowed windowseat, unseen by the murderer,
while her mother went to fetch help. When she
informs Mark that she knows he killed his
brother, he has his handyman put Hodge in a
dangerous place on the cliff, hoping to use
Hodge to buy her silence. Meg undertakes a
daring rescue, pelted all the while by stones
Mark flings at her. Toby arrives just in time,
Uncle Mark suffers a heart attack brought on by
the shock and strain of events, and Toby and Meg
realize they are in love. Though characters and
incidents are conventional and the plot moves

unevenly to a rushed and melodramatic conclusion, Meg tells her story with an ominous
tone that early enlists the reader's emotions.
The intensity builds and results in a highly
suspenseful psychological thriller. Poe Winner.

*THE NIGHT OF THE COMET, A COMEDY OF COURTSHIP
FEATURING BOSTOCK AND HARRIS.* See *Bostock and
Harris; or, The Night of the Comet.*

THE NIGHT WATCHMEN (Cresswell*, Helen, ill.
Gareth Floyd, Faber, 1969; Macmillan, 1969),
light, suspenseful fantasy set in the town of
Mandover, England, one March in the late 1960s.
Lonely, bored Henry*, perhaps ten, just released
from the confinement of a month's illness and
yearning for adventures, encounters in the park
early one morning a middle-aged tramp, amiable,
communicative Josh*, and his impatient, suspicious brother, Caleb*. The two have spent the
night in the park and carry all their possess-
ions in wheelbarrows. They say they must "tick"
the town before nightfall; otherwise it means
the "night train" for them. Intrigued, Henry
strikes up a friendship with them, shares their
meals, and gradually picks up information about
them. Pretending to be workmen, they have dug a
hole under the railroad bridge that spans both
road and canal, placed a "danger--workmen" sign
over it, and pitched beside it a kind of
tent-hut in which they intend to live while
"ticking," that is, getting the sense of the
area, and accumulating information for a book
Josh is writing. Henry learns they are "do-as-
you-pleasers," independent spirits who have come
"Here" from a mysterious "There" on a night
train that they can summon by whistle if in
danger. They are also night watchmen on the
alert for villains called Greeneyes, who can see
well only at night, are blinded by sunlight, and
seek to learn the secret whistle, board the
night train, and travel to There. Not long after
they have set up camp, Caleb suspects a Greeneye
may have found them, and soon Henry bumps into a
man with intense green eyes. "Night train," says
the realistic Caleb, but, when they discover the
railroad tracks are cold and realize they cannot
summon the night train, Henry suggests throwing
the villains off the track by moving camp to the

railroad near his house the next day, when the
Greeneyes can't see well. He helps them do it,
using a mirror to blind a Greeneye he spots
along the way. Caleb and Josh plan to eat dinner
early that night (Henry is invited) and whistle
for the train at sunset, exactly 7:18. Although
he's been told it's too dangerous for him to
stay around when they leave, Henry is eager to
see the night train because that will prove all
this has been real, and comes up with an idea to
help them. He packs a rucksack with a lamp and
fireworks, eats dinner with the night watchmen,
puts a piece of night-train-decorated cake in
his pocket for later, and bids his friends
farewell. In the exciting climax, he shines his
lamp about in the darkness, spotting hundreds of
Greeneyes, and, as the train pulls in, sets the
flares ablaze, completely baffling the enemy and
enabling his friends to board. Josh and Caleb
pull him on, too, putting him off when the
threat of danger is past, and they presumably
continue on their way to There and safety. On
the way home, Henry wonders if indeed the
watchmen were real. He wants to prove to himself
that they were, but the cake has fallen from his
pocket, the tree they planted when they filled
in the hole could have been planted by someone
else, and his mother has told him that old Mr.
Seaton complained because Henry flashed a mirror
in his eyes. Henry concludes that even if he
can't prove the men existed, the memory of them
will always be "as real to him as the fingers on
his own hand." Every word counts in this
carefully crafted, skillfully paced story. After
a slow beginning, in which Cresswell establishes
Henry as an imaginative, intelligent, indepen-
dent-thinking lad and introduces the eccentric
tramps, the tempo picks up and suspense
intensifies, gripping the emotions to the very
last page. Characters are well drawn, the
interplay between the two brothers is engagingly
humorous, and Henry's acceptance of the tramps
and their plausibly detailed story about There
and the Greeneyes actualizes them and their
problems and gives the fantasy conviction.
Carnegie Com.

NIKABRIK (*Prince Caspian**), surly, suspicious
Dwarf of Narnia*, who with the Dwarf Trumpkin*

and the Badger Trufflehunter rescues Caspian*
after he has fallen from his horse while
searching for Old Narnians. Nikabrik insists
that they kill Caspian because he's a Telmarine, but is dissuaded from the deed by
Trumpkin and Trufflehunter. He joins in the
activities against Miraz, but proves very
troublesome when things go against the Old
Narnians. After they blow Susan's* horn and help
is slow in arriving, he enlists a Hag and a
Wer-Wolf to prepare black magic against the
Telmarines. Nikabrik and his cohorts are killed
by Peter*, Edmund*, and Trumpkin. He is an
interesting but obvious character and serves as
a foil for loyal Trumpkin.

NINA CARRINGTON (*Fire and Hemlock**), big, plump,
loud friend of Polly* Whittacker, whom Polly
admires for her bold, madcap disposition. As
they grow older, Nina goes from one enthusiasm
to another, starting the superstition club at
school, dying her hair odd shades, and
eventually turning her attention to the pursuit
of boys. Nina is one of the people whose memory
of the first five years of Polly's acquaintance
with Tom* Lynn has been erased.

THE NINE LIVES OF ISLAND MACKENZIE (Moray*
Williams, Urusla, ill. Edward Ardizzone, Chatto,
1959; *ISLAND MACKENZIE*, Morrow, 1960), fantasy
set on a tropical island at an unspecified
time, starring an independent and self-assured
cat. When a typhoon wrecks the pleasure cruiser
Marigold, Mackenzie, the cat belonging to Captain Jupiter Foster, escapes from the first
mate, who is trying to save him, and swims to
the nearest island, pursued by eight hungry
sharks. A competent and self-sufficient cat,
Mackenzie gets along well but is lonesome and is
overjoyed to discover that one passenger has
also been cast up on the island. Unfortunately,
his fellow castaway is Miss Mary Pettifer, a
woman whose devotion to the bachelor captain has
been tempered only by her strong dislike of
cats. Mackenzie's first overtures toward her are
met by nuts, that she shies at him with great
accuracy. She even goes so far as to try to
drown him in her knitting bag. She repents,
however, and later saves him from mermaids who

try to lure him to Davy Jones's locker with the story that Captain Jupiter is waiting for him there. Mackenzie repays this by saving her from savages, who are diverted into capturing him and putting him in their cooking pot. Miss Pettifer, her face painted with purple fruit juice, scares them away. As they leave, however, they set the jungle afire, and the two castaways huddle together in a cave. With all the tidal pools fouled with ash and the jungle fruit burned, they face starvation. Just then they are rescued by Captain Jupiter, who has been sailing the islands searching for his lost passenger and has been attracted by the fire. Miss Pettifer, now much attached to Mackenzie, whom she has called Em (being unable to remember his name), agrees to marry the captain, and the three then will live happily together. The light story is given substance and humor by the two assertive characters who become dependent upon each other after their initial mutual dislike. Most of the story is told from Mackenzie's point of view, revealing him to be strong-willed and intelligent, though rather old-fashioned in his ideas of propriety and honor. Fanfare.

NJIMBIN (*A Little Fear*), a gnome, sly, cunning, and as ancient as the land itself, who has lived for time out of mind among the ridges, woods, and swamp near the cottage that old Mrs.* Tucker has inherited from her brother. Once the Njimbin had made a good living off the land, but the coming of humans changed his way of life and made hunting harder. When Mrs. Tucker arrives, he has been living quite comfortably in the fowlhouse a short distance from the cottage. When she decides to keep hens, the Njimbin sets out to drive her away, plays tricks upon her, and either tricks or persuades the indigenous creatures, frogs, ants, rats, and so on, to help him. At the end, he gets his way and she leaves, but his victory is an ironic one because the reader last sees the old woman preparing to burn down the filthy old fowlhouse before she goes.

NOAH (*The Moon in the Cloud**), presented as a kind, good-hearted old man, often irritatingly righteous, occasionally drunk, and somewhat of a figure of fun among the tribes of Israel who live near him. They respect him, however, because he is thought to be an oracle of the Lord* God. Even though the tribespeople regard his pronouncements as ravings, they feel they should for safety's sake treat them with respect. Even though he realizes that Ham* has taken advantage of Reuben, Noah is righteous to a fault and firmly refuses to alter the Lord's command that only members of his own family may board the ark until he is specifically commanded by the Lord to take Reuben and Thamar. Mrs. Noah thinks Noah's communications from the Lord are indigestion.

NOAH'S CASTLE (Townsend*, John Rowe, Oxford, 1975; Lippincott, 1976), realistic novel, fantasy only in that events are projected into the future. It takes place one school year in a city in the English Midlands at a time when runaway inflation, record unemployment, soaring prices, and worsening shortages of food, fuel, and other necessities have resulted in a break- down in law and order and intense social unrest. Father*, Norman Mortimer, a compulsive, author- itarian, bullheaded manager of a chain shoe- store, stuns his family one Sunday in September by announcing that they are moving to another home. He has purchased a big, old Victorian house on the Mount, a once elite, now seedy section of the city. Submissive Mother*, May Mortimer, and their children, rebellious Agnes, called Nessie*, 17, sensible Barry*, 16, the narrator, conscientious Geoff, 15, and protected Ellen, 10, find the new place strange, cold, forbidding, and much too big for them, more like a fortress or castle than a home, and not at all what its name, Rose Grove, implies. Father's motives in purchasing it gradually become apparent. He refuses to allow visitors, under- takes all the marketing, once Mother's pre- rogative, and spends hours shut up in the always locked basement, hammering and sawing with the assistance of Geoff, who is closest to him of all the children. Curious, Nessie and Barry investigate and discover that Father has turned the basement into an immense pantry, stocked with foods and other necessities intended to tide the family over until better times arrive.

As the country's economic situation worsens outside, tension mounts inside the Mortimer house as gradually each member of the family comes into conflict with Father. When Father decides to have Peggy, the family dog, put down to save money, Terry Timpson, Nessie's boyfriend, takes her, but Ellen, now also forbidden to bring home school friends, goes into a decline and becomes withdrawn and wan, unable to eat. Nessie's and Mother's problems with Father revolve around the presence of elderly, imperious, sharp-minded Mr*. Gerald Bowling, who once owned Father's store. At first flattered by Mr. Gerald's attention and later intimidated by him, Father allows his former employer to move in. Nessie leaves to get away from Mr. Gerald's unwanted attentions, moves in with the Timpsons, and is angrily disowned by Father. Fed up with the extra work and with being treated like a maid, Mother also moves in with Terry's family, taking Ellen with her. Barry, who has become friends with Wendy Farrar, a schoolmate whose mother is dying of malnutrition, is caught between loyalty to Father and a growing social consciousness. Over Father's protests he takes food to the Farrars and then becomes a volunteer with Share Alike, a social welfare organization for which Father's assistant manager, Cliff* Trent, also works. In spite of food riots, vandalism, and government edicts against hoarding, Father maintains that his only obligation is to his family. When a blackmarketer threatens Father, Barry realizes that something must be done. He realizes also that, although he loves his father, he can no longer support his selfish motives. He arranges with Cliff to turn Father's supplies over to Share Alike, but on the night they come to cart the food away, vandals also arrive, a fight breaks out, and the place is soon a shambles. Father, who has donned his World War II uniform and oiled his gun in readiness for an attack, shoots at the looters. Geoff, loyal thus far, turns on his father, calling him a madman, and Norman Mortimer finds himself alone in his efforts to maintain his food supply. The next day Mother comes back because Father needs her, bringing Ellen with her, although Father still insists he did the right thing. Spring returns to the city, carrying with it the hope that the general economic situation and circumstances in the Mortimer household will improve. Even though things turn out as expected, this is a first-rate suspense story. Fine social and economic details make the hypothetical future of deprivation and struggle for survival all too real. The novel is also an excellent portrait of a near-psychotic personality and his effect on those around him, as well as a provocative exploration of the moral and practical implications of a father's obligations to his family. Fanfare.

NOBODY'S GARDEN (Jones*, Cordelia, ill. Victor Ambrus, Deutsch, 1964; Scribner, 1966), psychological problem novel set in London in 1948, not long after the end of World War II. Tactless and talkative, Hilary Toft, 12, is often ridiculed by the other girls at school, and, although she is unquelled by their scorn, she determines that the shy new girl, Bridget Sanders, 12, will be her friend. Even though the headmistress, after asking the girls to be especially kind to this orphan, has put her into the charge of the model student, Catherine Newland, Hilary tags along on the way home and gets herself invited to tea by Bridget's aunt. When Hilary asks Bridget to tea in return, the aunt accepts for her, and although the girls have little in common beyond an interest in reading, they become companions, mostly because Hilary thinks of Bridget as an acquisition and is willing to go to considerable trouble rather than give her up. Bridget almost never volunteers conversation and answers only in monosyllables, but gentle, perceptive Mrs. Toft is able to bring her out a bit. Since Bridget's only enthusiastic response, subdued as it is, has been about gardens and in suggesting that Hilary borrow *The Secret Garden*, Hilary sets out to find a garden they can secretly cultivate among the bombed-out house sites still uncleared in their neighborhood. At first discouraged, she at last finds what she wants in late winter at one of the old houses on Campden Hill near Holland Park. Although the gate in the wall is scrawled, "Whoever enters here *never* comes out again!" Hilary finds a spot where the wall is partly

broken, climbs over, and discovers the remains
of a large estate yard that has run wild for
years, the house having been ruined in the
bombing. Together the girls explore it, Bridget
surprisingly and knowledgeably taking the lead
and insisting that they clear space and plant
flowers before they go off to spend spring
holidays, for which she is to join the Tofts, at
the home of Hilary's grandmother, Mrs. Fisher.
In the country, Bridget relaxes and begins to
blossom. Mrs. Fisher gives the girls seedlings
and cuttings from all the plants they ask for
and, more importantly, persuades Mrs. Toft not
to question them about it, pointing out that
girls should be allowed some secrets from their
mothers. Back in London, Bridget's unresponsiveness has begun to annoy her aunt and the others
at school, and their sympathy wears away, but
Hilary defends her, even though she is a little
shocked to learn that Bridget has been playing
truant and forging her excuses. When Bridget is
discovered swiping biscuits for the garden's
secret larder, her aunt explodes and threatens
to turn her out, Bridget confesses to Hilary
that she was on German-occupied Guernsey during
the war; that after her widowed mother was
seized and executed by the Germans, she ran away
from their farm tenants, the Champignons; that
since the war she has already run away from two
aunts; and that she intends to run away from her
Aunt Sanders. Hilary persuades her not to go,
hoping that her mother will take Bridget to live
with them, but Mrs. Toft treats her story as
alarmism, though she secretly worries. Some
days later, when Mrs. Sanders, driven almost
frantic by Bridget's unresponsiveness, explodes
again, Bridget leaves, takes the cookies from
the tin in the garden, and sets out to get to
the country where she hopes to get a job in a
garden and to be independent. At the station she
sees the police, is afraid they are after her,
slips out and starts to walk, becomes confused,
and finally goes into a church to rest and falls
asleep there. When she wakes, a long supressed
memory surfaces of friendly Michel Champignon,
the tenants' oldest son, tricking her into
revealing that they have a forbidden radio and
then selling the information to the Germans.
Horrified that she betrayed her mother, she has

been haunted by this guilt and has refused to trust anyone. After sobbing a long time, she leaves the church and finds her way back to the garden. In the meantime, Hilary has been questioned by Mrs. Sanders and the police and has revealed nothing, but her mother realizes that she knows of a possible hideaway. After the others leave, they go with a flashlight to the garden, hunt everywhere, and are just giving up when Bridget returns. Although she hides from them, Mrs. Toft seeks her out, lets her tell the story of the Guernsey incident, assures her that she is not responsible for her mother's betrayal, and persuades her to come and live with them. The novel succeeds mainly because of the strong characterization of both girls and of Mrs. Toft and Mrs. Sanders, both unusually well developed and believable for adults in books for young people. Although sensitive Bridget is the central character of the action, straightforward, bumbling Hilary is so good-hearted that she captures the reader's affection. Fanfare.

NOEL (*Kept in the Dark**), at fourteen the eldest of the three children who come to stay with their grandparents and must cope with David*, their sinister half cousin. A quiet, responsible boy, Noel is ashamed of being too good. He is sensitive enough to be suspicious of David from the start but in the end is the one most willing to admit that the young man may genuinely have been looking for family love and security.

NOEL BASTABLE (*The Story of the Treasure Seekers**), ten-year-old third son in the large and lively Bastable family, twin of Alice*, and the poet of the family. He has a delicate chest and gets sick easily. All the children, and Alice in particular, look out for his health. He likes books and stories and is the artistic one in the family. Oswald* remarks that Noel is disgustingly like a girl sometimes, being easily intimidated, but on the whole the others seem to feel he's a plucky little chap. He is an interesting, winning figure and serves as a good foil for the other boys.

NO END TO YESTERDAY (Macdonald*, Shelagh, Andre Deutsch, Ltd., 1977), searing girl's-growing-up

story set in Streatham, London, near Brixton
Hill and Brockwell Park, mostly in the 1920s.
Marjory* Bell, ten when the story starts, knows
almost nothing about her life before she came to
live with her grandparents when she was two, but
she is aware of the derogatory remarks and snide
comments made about her mother, Greta, and she
is haunted by a recurring nightmare of a bear in
an apron climbing the stairs toward her. It
requires all her determination to keep her
spirit from being extinguished by life in Gran*
Bell's house (which is never referred to as
belonging to gentle Grandad). She hates Gran, a
tight-lipped Irish woman who firmly dominates
her ten grown children, all either resident at
home, living nearby, or visiting frequently--six
daughters shaped in her own image, and four
dutiful sons, who in Gran's eyes can do no
wrong--and she recognizes, without understanding
why, that Gran hates her. Marjory's father,
Henry*, works in Watford but comes every
weekend, to be told of Marjory's misbehavior
during the past week and to show a very
perfunctory interest in her accomplishments.
Most of the family follow Gran's lead in
deploring Marjory and predicting that she will
go bad like her mother--including Auntie* Molly
and Auntie Ada, who still live at home; Auntie
Ellie, who lives with her weak husband and
tattle-tale daughter, Susie, in the third-floor
apartment; Uncle Arthur and Auntie Liza; even
Uncle Bertie, who likes to pat the fannies of
his older nieces; and Auntie Flora, who comes in
for her share of criticism because she spends
"poor Bertie's" money on fashionable clothes.
Marjory has a few supporters: Uncle Ron, the
joking youngest of Gran's sons, who still lives
at home; Auntie June, the only daughter-in-law
who dares to talk back to Gran; her cousin
Archie, 15, son of Arthur, who makes her a
dollhouse; and mostly her cousin Teddy* Bell, a
few months her junior, son of Bertie and Flora,
who shares her hatred of Gran and plans
elaborate ways to murder her, one of which they
almost manage to carry out. She is also treated
kindly by her Jewish friend from school, Keziah
Hope, and Keziah's parents, who invite her to
their Sabbath dinners. Her love is turned almost
entirely to Grandad, who raises roses and sees

no wrong in anyone, and to the dogs and other
animals of the household, and she harbors a
secret desire to become a veterinarian. The
story pictures events until Marjory is almost
seventeen: the time Daddy brings a girlfriend
home and Gran, with her daughters' help, snidely
destroys the relationship; the romance of Uncle
Ron and the girl Marjory has seen him with in
the park, which seems destined for an elopement
known only to Marjory but which ends with Ron's
sudden death; Marjory's bout with diptheria,
nearly fatal because Gran has refused to call a
doctor and has treated her with frequent doses
of epsom salts; Gran's refusal to let her retake
the scholarship exam for high school, which
thwarts her aspirations to study veterinary
medicine; a wonderful week at Yarmouth with
Auntie Flora and Teddy. The most devastating
occurrence is when Auntie Molly misses some
money and suspicion falls on Marjory. To her
horror, it is found in her "treasure box" when
Gran searches. She is confined to her room for
days. When Daddy has been told and he summons
the entire family to hear her apology, she
refuses to admit the theft and is in deeper
disgrace. The worst part of the incident is that
when it is finally discovered that Auntie Ada,
angry because Molly has once again stolen an
admirer from her, is the real thief, Marjory is
simply allowed to return to meals, with no
explanation or apology. Unable to go to high
school, Marjory wins a scholarship to a domestic
science college (not what she wants to do but
better than nothing), and when she excels in
cookery, she is hired by a noble family to help
direct their kitchen in Scotland. The young
people of the family treat her as almost an
equal, and after the son admits that he's been
warned not to get romantically interested in
her, she has to fight off his forceful attempt
at seduction. Daddy brings home another young
lady, a spirited girl named Dolly Hawthorne, who
neatly stands up to Gran and the catty aunts;
their mutual support is Marjory's first real
communication with her father, and she is
delighted when he marries Dolly. There are good
scenes at school, both Christ Church and the
domestic science college, but the emphasis is on
the family relationships. Every chapter strongly

evokes the atmosphere of suspicion, nagging
disapproval, and repressive morality of Gran's
house. Throughout, Marjory is tormented by
innuendos and mean references to her mother,
whom she has always assumed is dead but has
never dared ask about. When, at Dolly's
insistence, her flapper cousin, Nora, tells her
the real story, that her mother ran off with
another man while her father was in France in
the war, and left Marjory with a huge, filthy,
tenement woman (the bear of her nightmare), she
is stunned to learn that her mother is still
alive, and she is terribly hurt and furious that
her family has all known and kept it from her.
Each chapter is introduced by a short scene,
usually in dramatic form, of Marjory in later
life, mostly the 1950s, so we learn that, as
Auntie Junie has predicted, when a man comes
along who really shows her some love, she falls
for him although he is already married; that her
father throws her out; and that it is nearly
fifteen years before Dolly can bring about a
reconciliation and Marjory can take her own
daughters to meet their grandfather. The number
of characters skillfully developed is unusual,
with the focus on Marjory, the tough-minded
survivor of this psychologically abusive childhood. Whitbread.

NOLLEKENS (*The Silver Curlew**), also called
Nolly, King of Norfolk, a simpering, spoiled,
willful young man of twenty-one. He is a gentle
caricature of English royalty, somewhat
slow-witted, impulsive, childish, self-indulgent, and indulged. He has a double nature--
sometimes overly good, warm, and anxious to
please, and then throwing tantrums and pestering
the servants in such unreasonable ways they
threaten to quit. His nature for the day
depends on which foot he puts out of bed first.
Nan*, his "very, very, very old" nurse and
housekeeper, occasionally makes him stand in
the corner until he comes to his senses. He
loves Doll very much, and he is proud of their
baby, which he persists in thinking is a boy. At
the end, he takes responsibility for the
predicament Doll and the baby are in--that the
Spindle-Imp* may claim them--because Doll says
she accepted the Imp's help since she was afraid

of Nollekens's temper (which is not entirely true). Doll sensibly forgives the king and says what he did was just due to his double nature.

NORDY BANK (Porter*, Sheena, ill. Annette Macarthur-Onslow, Oxford, 1964; Roy, 1967), realistic adventure novel with fantasy, animal, and growing-up story aspects. Bronwen Owen, about twelve, and five other boys and girls camp out for two weeks in the Shropshire Hills on Nordy Bank, the site of an ancient Iron Age Fort. Ordinarily gentle and good-natured, Bron becomes unfriendly, argumentative, and aloof as some dark shadow from the past impels her to do and say things that are not typical of her. She seems to have a memory that is not hers and an unusual knowledge of Iron Age ways. When an escaped army Alsatian dog, half-starved, comes to the camp for food, she drives it away angrily, torn by feelings of pity and fear for the huge, hungry, wolf-like creature. Three times she drives it off before conquering her dislike for the animal, removing its muzzle, and offering it food. Though nervous and hostile toward everyone else, Griff attaches himself to the girl, who gradually becomes her previously amiable self. Although Bron's mother protests, arrangements are made for Bron to keep the dog and board him with the family of Margery Furness (another camper, a dog lover, and Bron's best friend), whose family raises Dalmatians, after he has been retrained as a pet and until Bron's family finds a home where they can keep pets. Bron takes him to the dog reform school in Bristol, and, after several months, is pleased to have Griff returned to her, docile and gentle, shorn by skillful retraining of his aggressive tendencies. Then another problem arises. Bron's father has been transferred to Paris, and, after some thought, Bron decides to give up Griff. Her parents, however, decide that she shall live with the Furness family until they return to England, enabling Bron to keep the dog she loves so much, and her best friend, Margery, as well. The plot is uneven and un- focused, and the conclusion in particular is unconvincing and unsatisfying, but the sense of place on Nordy Bank is very strong, allusions to *Warrior Scarlet** and history add depth, the style is pleasing, and the dialogue seems real. The story starts very slowly, and until it settles on Bron's relationship with Griff it seems just another Arthur Ransome*-like adventure story. Except for Bron and Margery, the children are almost interchangeable, and adults are types or are necessary for the plot. The episode in the training school seems deliberately informative. Carnegie Winner.

NORMAN CLOUGH (*Hell's Edge**), Yorkshire schoolboy of almost sixteen who assists Ril* Terry in reclaiming the Common land enclosed by the ancestor of Celia* Withens, Sir George Withens, in the early nineteenth century. Norman is a proud, abrupt boy, who jumps to conclusions, particularly involving Ril, who he at first thinks is stuck-up because she has been attending an exclusive girls' school in the south of England. He likes math and science and doing things with his hands. He is a decent sort, a rough diamond, who deplores the sharp, less than honest business tactics of Roy Wentworth, the car salesman for whom he occasionally repairs cars. He quits working for Roy because he doesn't want to abet the man's sharp dealing. He also has a strong spirit of adventure, and this together with his deep moral sense motivates him to help Ril. At the end he decides to try for the university. Norman is an interesting and likeable, if type, figure.

NORTON, MARY (1903–   ), born in London, the daughter of a surgeon descended from Edmund Spenser; actress, author of fantasies for children, and playwright. She grew up near Leighton Buzzard, Bedfordshire, in a big, old house much like that in her Carnegie-winning novel, *The Borrowers** (Dent, 1952; Harcourt, 1953). Her ambition was to become an actress, and, her convent schooling concluded, she joined the "Old Vic" Shakespeare Company in London for a year, studying under Lillian Baylis. She married Robert Charles Norton, who came of an old and prominent shipping family, in 1927, and moved to Portugal, where her four children were born and where she began writing. The Great Depression hit the family's finances hard, and, when World War II began, her husband enlisted in the British Navy, and she returned with her family to work in England. For two years she served in the War Office and then moved with her children to a rented house in Connecticut while she worked with British Purchasing in New York. She wrote on the side to augment her income. Back in London, she published her first book in 1943 after completing it during air raids, *The Magic Bed-Knob* (Hyperion). About three children and a loveable, elderly spinster studying to become a witch and their adventures with an old bed, it and its sequel, *Bonfires and Broomsticks* (Dent, 1947) were partly based on stories she had told to her children. The books were lively and imaginative; they caught on, and were later published in a combined, revised edition entitled *Bedknob and Broomstick* (Dent, 1957; Harcourt, 1957). *The Borrowers* established her as a leading writer for children. Gently humorous, actualized by careful and plentiful detail, it tells of pencil-sized people who live under the floor of an old Georgian country house and take what they need to survive from the "human beans" above them. One of the most honored books in children's literature, in addition to the Carnegie Medal, it appears in Fanfare, *Choice*, *Books Too Good to Miss*, Children's Classics, the Children's Literature Association Touchstones, and the Lewis Carroll Shelf list. The idea for it came from Norton's childhood, when she and her brothers and friends played out stories with china dolls and delighted in imagining things from their near-the-floor perspectives. Four full-length novels continue the Borrowers' adventures, which are essentially accounts of the very human search for survival and security: *The Borrowers Afield** (Dent, 1955; Harcourt, 1955), *The Borrowers Afloat** (Dent, 1959; Harcourt, 1959), *The Borrowers Aloft** (Dent, 1961; Harcourt, 1961), all in Fanfare and *Choice*; and *The Borrowers Avenged** (Kestrel, 1982; Harcourt, 1982), listed in Fanfare. There is also one short story about them: *Poor Stainless* (Dent, 1971; Harcourt, 1971), a *Choice* selection. In 1975 she published *Are All the Giants Dead?* (Dent; Harcourt), about a boy who finds himself in Cinderella's land and seeks to free a princess from an evil spell. *Bedknob* was made

into a motion picture starring Angela Lansbury
and Roddy McDowall, and *The Borrowers* was made
into a television special starring Eddie Albert
and Judith Anderson. Norton has also written
plays for stage and radio. She has made her
home in Ireland and North Devon.

NO WAY OF TELLING (Smith*, Emma, Bodley, 1972;
Atheneum, 1972), novel of suspense set in Wales
in the last third of the twentieth century. When
a snowstorm threatens to isolate Amy Bowen and
her grandmother at Gwyntfa, their remote
cottage, they are not worried. Granny has plenty
of supplies, Amy (apparently eleven or twelve)
has reached home from school with some
difficulty but no real problems, and their
nearest neighbor, Tom Protheroe, has stopped
while driving his sheep down to check on their
welfare, leaving a leg of mutton in case their
larder should be short. That night, however,
they are astonished when a huge man comes to
their door, blunders in without speaking, seizes
the mutton, the blankets from Amy's bed, and a
hurricane lamp, and then stumbles out again into
the storm. The next day Amy realizes that the
stranger has spent the night in their woodshed
and has taken the hatchet. She also discovers
four of Protheroe's five missing ewes huddled
around a haystack up the hill and brings them to
her grandmother's shed, also hauling on her
homemade toboggan the baled hay to build a
sheltering wall and to feed them if the storm
should continue. To their further surprise, two
men on skis show up, question them about
strangers, and search the area. Amy is attracted
to one of them and, assuming they are police, is
confused when Granny does not mention the man of
the previous night. Later she takes her toboggan
and slides down to an abandoned farm, Tyler's
Place, where she thinks she has seen a light,
and she finds the huge man, badly injured, and
the last missing ewe. After they have fed him
and dressed the bad gash in his arm, Amy draws a
picture to indicate the two skiers, since he
appears not to understand English. He jumps up
and leaves, only to return and write a long
letter in a foreign language, which Amy promises
to post. After he has disappeared again, the two
skiers return, announce that they are staying,

demand food, and give their names as Chief Inspector Catcher of Scotland Yard and Mr. Nabb. Gradually the old woman and the girl realize that they are not policemen and that their earlier visitor, a sailor named Bartolomeo* Cordoba, has some information that makes him a threat to the men. After a day of being held captive in their own house and becoming more and more convinced that they will not live through the experience, Amy sneaks out the window, takes her toboggan, and heads for Dintirion*, the Protheroe home, going the "short way over the top," which is a dangerous path that goes by Billy Dodd's Dingle, a narrow ravine into which sheep often have slipped. She gets away, but snow has changed the path so much that her toboggan goes over the edge, and she is thrown into the ravine. Bartolomeo, seeing from a distance, comes to her rescue, helps her back to the path, and heads her toward Dintirion, while he goes back to rescue Granny. A sudden renewal of the storm almost kills her, but young Ivor Protheroe, her classmate, finds her and gets her to his house on his pony. The skiers turn out to be Viguers and Harris, two international terrorists for hire; Bartolomeo has seen a South American diplomat killed, and his letter contains the information that will avert a war; and finally, the Protheroe men and the local police find Bartolomeo protecting Granny from the terrorists. The suspense and the scenes of struggles through the snow are vivid, and although the plot involves an international intrigue that is never entirely explained, it is a well-crafted story, plausible and convincing. The characters of Amy, Granny, and Bartolomeo are well developed. Boston Globe Honor; Carnegie Com.

O

OCCUPIER (*Carbonel, The King of the Cats**), the young actor who buys the witch's steeple hat as a costume for his act. He is somewhat cross when the children ask for the hat, but his friend and fellow performer, Molly, comes up with a compromise: that he loan the children the hat once they have found the cauldron and the Silent Magic spell. His real name is Bill, but the children call him the "Occupier" because they got his address from an advertisement he dropped that had been sent to "Occupier." The hat helps them break the spell that keeps Carbonel* from returning to his kingdom.

ODO THE PLOWMAN (*The Writing on the Hearth**), Stephen's dead mother's second husband. A surly laborer who kept her children reluctantly after his wife died, he decides to marry Lys*, Stephen's sister, to a man much older than she. When Lys runs away to avoid the marriage, Stephen searches for her and locates her at Meg's* hut, where he loses the copy he has made of Dame* Alice's letter. Thus the plot "pot" begins to boil.

O'FAOLAIN, EILEEN (GOULD), born in Cork; Irish writer of some dozen books of fantasy and retellings from Irish oral tradition for children. Her fantasies include *The Little Black Hen: An Irish Fairy Story** (Random, 1940), which was named to the *Horn Book* Fanfare list. It tells of how two children, Garret and

Julie, help their friend, old Biddy Murphy, a
storyteller, recover her fairy hen after the
fairies claim her. In *Miss Pennyfeather and the
Pooka* (Random, 1946), fairies steal Miss
Pennyfeather's Mickey Joe, who is a fairy horse,
or pooka, and the same two children help her
save him. This story won critical approval for
its "fresh and sparkling" diction. These and
similar fantasies skillfully improvise on Irish
folklore and have a strong Irish flavor in
atmosphere and style but seem arch and old-
fashioned by today's standards, which call for
more careful plotting and stronger characterization. Less dated are her retellings, in
particular the spirited *Irish Sagas and Folktales* (Oxford, 1954; Walck, 1954), which
contains stirring versions of stories associated
with Cuchullin, the Children of Lir, Deirdre,
and Finn. She also edited *Children of the
Salmon, and Other Irish Folktales* (Longman,
1965; Little, 1965), another book that remains
good to read. Among her other publications are
High Sang the Sword (Oxford, 1959), *King of the
Cats* (Morrow, 1942), and *Miss Pennyfeather in
the Springtime* (Browne, 1946). She married Sean
O'Faolain, Irish writer of fiction, biography,
and criticism, and the couple lived near Dublin.

OGGY (*The Nature of the Beast**), Mr. Oglethorpe,
Bill* Coward's history and English teacher. The
only teacher the boy can stand and the only one
who sees any potential in him, Oggy is resigned
to his frequent absences and only sporadic
interest in doing his homework. His most
frequent comments are, "Aw, what the hell," and,
when Bill does an occasional fine bit of work,
"You're a dark horse, Coward." An avid photographer and local historian, he has been taking
pictures at the mill when the workers start to
celebrate what they think is a victory in their
sit-down strike, and he sees Ned* Coward, drunk,
smash the windshield of a boss's white Mercedes.
When Bill arrives, afraid his father will be out
of hand, Oggy is sitting on Ned and, with
Bill's help, gets him away from trouble and
home. At the end he does not want to press
charges over the stolen camera, and he tries to
persuade the social worker that to separate
Bill and his grandfather, Chunder*, will break

both their hearts.

OLD BEAK AND CLAWS (*Owlglass**), owl whose full name is the Hon. Richard William Strix Flammea de Striges. Because of failing eyesight, he nearly attacks one of the club members hurrying to the meeting, and the animal community, which accepts the need of predators to hunt, is galvanized into action by this shocking violation of the code that protects members on meeting night. When Brock, the badger, calls to inform him of their plan to provide him with eyeglasses, the owl is touched by their consideration, and he shows himself a creature of considerable learning by introducing Brock to the use of the microscope and the telescope, which he focuses on the Great Nebula in Orion. A club member who doesn't attend often, he comes to the next meeting to thank the animals, brings a couple of kegs of cider and assorted bottles, and tells "The Story of the King, the Hermit, and the Two Robins." The attitude of the other animals toward him is both protective and respectful, that of younger, more active members of a male social group toward a much admired and rather feared older man who is getting beyond his best years.

OLD DA (*A Stranger Came Ashore**), Robbie Henderson's grandfather and very close friend. He tells Robbie stories from Scottish oral tradition, including that of the Great Selkie. Because he has steeped the boy in the folklore of the region, Robbie soon becomes suspicious of Finn Learson, and this leads to his accumulating evidence against Finn and saving his sister's life. Very early in the story, Old Da becomes suspicious of Finn and asks him pointed questions, which alert the reader and Robbie to Finn's real identity. Story interest then lies not in discovering who Finn is but in how Robbie will prevent Finn from achieving his objective of luring Elspeth away.

OLD DOG, NEW TRICKS (Cate*, Dick, ill. Trevor Stubley, Hamilton, 1978; Elsevier, 1981), short, humorous, realistic novel of family life set in a declining mining town in northern England as seen from the point of view of the son, Billy, a

perceptive, observant boy of ten or twelve. When
Grandma brings home a dog from the Royal Society
for the Prevention of Cruelty to Animals booth
in Durham market, nobody in the family is
pleased. Steven, who is married to Billy's
sister, Sandra, says that "it would win first
prize in any Ugly Competition," and Dad says
she'll "be a nuisance." Grandma notes that the
dog "only needs training," but the dog, named
Dot, proves "daft as a brush," knocks things
over, jumps on people, runs off when called, and
generally causes trouble. Billy observes that
nobody loves it, spends time with it, or gives
it positive attention. Then normally genial Dad
grows distant and irritable, and Billy learns
that the mine in which he works is about to
close. Steven, who also works in the mine, quits
and moves his family to Barnsley, Yorkshire,
where he soon finds work in the pits. Dad
doesn't want to move, but he doesn't want to
learn a new job either. He says that, like Dot,
he's too old to learn new ways. Once Dad becomes
unemployed, nerves fray. Then Mr. Murray, the
new neighbor Billy's mam refers to disparagingly
as "him next door" because he is always
borrowing things, tells Dad about a job driving
a van. Dad declares he'll never be able to learn
to drive, "not in a month of Sundays," but with
Mr. Murray's help he succeeds in under a month,
gets the job, and smiles for the first time in
weeks. He even borrows the van and drives the
family to Steven and Sandra's house for a
satisfying visit. By Christmas, Billy finds
things at home better than before, because Dad
no longer has to work shifts and is ready and
willing to try to train Dot. Though the sentence
structure is uncomplicated and vocabulary easy,
the book never sounds like a reader. It presents
a warm, low-keyed, unsentimental picture of a
loving, working-class British family. Characters
are realized with bold strokes, and even Dot the
dog has individuality, being something more than
just a metaphorical counterpart to Dad. The
dialogue seems spoken by real people and reveals
character very effectively. One of a series
about Billy and his family. Other.

OLD GUIDO (*The King's Goblet**), aging gondolier
who sees a magazine article about an art

collection in Chicago which boasts one of a pair of goblets blown in the sixteenth century for the King of Navarre and who writes to the collector, telling of the goblet's mate in a poor glass blower's home in Venice. Guido is found dying, evidently from overexertion, by Aldo* Gambadello, but is unable to tell the boy the story. After Aldo has used Guido's gondola and it has been wrecked, he finds that the old man has willed it to him.

OLD JOHN (Cregan*, Mairin, ill. Helen Sewell, Allen, 1937; Macmillan, 1936), talking animal fantasy set once upon a time in Ireland, which improvises on Irish folklore. Old John, a kindhearted Irish shoemaker, loves the animals that live with him: Kruger*, a Kerry blue terrier, Nanny, a goat, and Circin Rua, a little red hen. He befriends a small white cat, Bainen, who is really a fairy doctor. Bainen has assumed the appearance of a cat to escape from a wicked dwarf, Gruaga. The fairy lives on with Old John and the animals in her cat form to protect them from the evil dwarf. The dwarf, who hates Old John because he shelters the fairy, changes himself into a fish, allows himself to be hooked by the old man, and then viciously bites him in the wrist, inflicting what threatens to be a mortal wound. Kruger sends Colm*, a pigeon which has joined the household, to fetch Bainen, who heals the old man. In retaliation, Gruaga kidnaps Bainen and holds her captive in the tower of his castle high on Blue Mountain. After Colm locates her, Kruger and his friend, Bonzo the sheep dog, fail in a brave attempt to free her. Kruger than suggests that Old John enlist the aid of the Prince of Gleann na Nean, since they have rescued from the wicked dwarf the white donkey, Achilles, that belongs to the prince's daughter, Princess* Fionuala. After a terrible battle, the prince's archers take the castle and rescue Bainen, but the dwarf gets away. Bainen suggests that Old John seek help from the fairy queen in breaking Gruaga's power. The queen provides a tiny pair of red and blue boots, just the dwarf's size, which Colm deposits at a strategic place. Gruaga finds the boots, puts them on, and discovers to his dismay that his feet will only carry him away from Old

John and his animal friends. The little household has been freed from him forever. Gaelic terms and the cadence of Irish speech contribute much of the interest and help create physical and psychological setting in this consistently entertaining but inconsequential tale in which the reader is never in doubt that good will eventually win out. The plot meanders along accumulating folktale-like incidents and characters. Ample sprightly conversation, and a chatty, lighthearted storytelling attitude keep the tempo up in spite of numerous digressions and some stories within the larger story. The animals speak to one another and interact with humans, but only Old John can understand what they say. Fanfare.

OLD UNCLE (*The Song of Pentecost**), patriarch of the Harvest Mice, a two-faced, crotchety, chronically complaining old fellow, who often offers unsolicited advice and constantly demands special treatment because he has tender paws. He adds humor and some tension to the story. When the chips are down, he rises above his selfish need for attention and fights just as hard as anyone else. Normally, however, he is the thorn in Pentecost's* side.

OLD WILLIAM (*The Stone Book**), Mary's uncle and Father's* brother. He is a weaver who plies his trade in his room in the family cottage, with whom Mary communicates by mouthing words over the clatter and bang of his loom, whose stooped form bears his product to market, and who sings hymns to the accompaniment of Father's ophicleide. It is his dilapidated, long-unused loom that provides some of the wood for young William's sled generations later in *Tom Fobble's Day**, the last book in the series, a story feature that helps to unite the books through showing symbolically how the generations are tied together in small, seemingly insignificant ways.

OLD WOMAN (*The Kelpie's Pearls**), the disgruntled, hard-fisted, old Scottish woman who lives down the way from Morag* MacLeod's place and is Torquil's* unsympathetic guardian. Although apparently a misanthrope, she also exemplifies the attitude of the crofters of the region, who think Morag is a witch. Ironically, although she dislikes and fears Morag (partly because Morag has befriended Torquil), her statement that Morag was weeping as she passed by on the black horse provides the main evidence that Morag was indeed not a witch.

OLWEN (*The City of Frozen Fire**), Princess of Quivera, fictional kingdom in South America. Olwen is the daughter of Prince Madoc's brother, who was Governor of Cibola and was killed, along with his wife and son, when that city was captured by the convicts. She is an expert shot with the bow and arrow and soon becomes equally good with Tops's gun. Although their communication is hindered by having to be carried on in Latin, she and Tops (both of whom dislike Aeneas) soon become friends. Self-confident and uninhibited, she leads the way in many of their adventures and chooses in the end to leave the medieval culture of Quivera for nineteenth-century England.

ONE IS ONE (Picard*, Barbara Leonie, Oxford, 1965; Holt, 1966), historical novel set in the early fourteenth century in England. As a child, young Stephen* de Beauville is a misfit in the castle of his father, Robert, Earl of Greavesby, in Yorkshire. A sensitive boy, he is tormented by his cousin Edmund, just a year older than he is, by his half brothers and half sisters, both older and younger (his father's present wife is his third), and by his two full sisters, all of whom taunt him for his apparent cowardice and in particular for his fear of dogs. One day when he is ten, out of pity he asks the huntsman for the runt of a litter, a puppy that ordinarily would be drowned. Immediately regretting his request, he decides to lose the pup, but when it falls and actually is in danger, Stephen climbs down a dangerous cliff to save it and, now committed to the animal, names him Amile; soon they are inseparable. Earl Robert has long since decided that Stephen should be a monk, and when the boy is thirteen arranges that he enter the Benedictine Abbey of Richley. Before he goes, Stephen has Amile killed rather than give him to his insensitive half brother. At the abbey

Stephen, by far the youngest novice, is bored
and inattentive until he is sent to help the
crusty old artist, Brother* Ernulf, where he
learns to mix paints, draw, and develop his
natural talent, but because he is never praised,
he has no idea how talented he is. With no
religious inclination and a fierce desire to
prove his family wrong, he runs away and, nearly
starving and being attacked by a mob for
stealing a loaf of bread, he is rescued by a
good-natured knight, Sir* Pagan (Paine)
Latourelle of Worchestershire. Sir Pagan
recognizes his superior breeding and education
and takes him to his home at Lower Avonden,
where they become great friends and Sir Pagan
teaches Stephen the martial arts neglected in
his childhood. Stephen finds that Sir Pagan,
unlike his own father, is a supporter of King
Edward II, and when the king is taken prisoner,
the knight makes an unsuccessful attempt to
rescue him. Later, betrayed by a mercenary named
Ranulf, Sir Pagan is seized in an inn and
hanged, but he first saves Stephen's life by
accusing him of being the betrayer. Crushed by
the loss of his first real friend, Stephen
becomes ill and is nursed and put to work by an
innkeeper's wife in Gloucester. There he is seen
in the street by his uncle, Bartholemew Boncourt, Earl of Manningfield, the elder brother
of his mother, who has heard rumors that the boy
was associated with Sir Pagan. Earl Bartholemew
takes him to his castle in Berkshire, where he
serves as a squire. When he is nineteen, he
catches sight of Ranulf, follows him, and in a
duel with daggers, kills him. When political
changes make life in England uncomfortable, Earl
Barholomew sets off to make a pilgrimage to the
Holy Land, taking Stephen in his retinue. When
he is twenty-one, Stephen is knighted and soon
finds himself headed for the Scottish wars. On
the way he delivers a message for his uncle at
the home of the FitzAmory family and, his own
squire having been called away and the
FitzAmorys' son, Thomas*, a spoiled, troublesome
boy, having just been sent home in disgrace
from the castle where he had been in training,
Stephen is persuaded to take the boy on as his
squire. He deals with the boy's faults patiently
and wins his unswerving loyalty. Earl Robert is

also with the army in Scotland, and when they meet, he bids Stephen come home to visit and meet his new stepmother, wife number four. At Greavesby Castle, Stephen is treated with respect or tolerance by most of his former tormentors, but Edmund challenges him to a jousting duel. Stephen is diffident until he sees how much it means to Thomas that he win, and he unseats Edmund without great difficulty. Returning from a renewed Scottish campaign, Thomas falls ill, and Stephen stays with him in the home of a bitterly resentful Scottish woman, who helps nurse him for smallpox. After Thomas dies, Stephen reassesses his life and returns to Rickley Abbey, where he is welcomed for his talent, and Brother Ernulf, now almost blind, turns over to him the completion of his manuscript of the Gospels. In the main, this is a story of the difficulties of one who does not conform to the accepted pattern of his society, and the theme, that one must follow one's own way even if it differs from the norm, is stated both explicitly and implicitly. Stephen is well characterized, and his final decision is believable. Details of the social and political life of the early fourteenth century are richly reported. The novel covers a long sweep of years, and plot tension is evidenced only in scenes scattered throughout, but interest in Stephen's development is sufficient to keep a reader continuing through the quieter narrative and descriptive portions. Carnegie Com.; Choice; Fanfare.

ON THE EDGE (Cross*, Gillian, Oxford, 1984; Holiday, 1985), realistic novel of mystery and suspense with detective story aspects, involving ten days of terrorist activity in England one recent August. The uncomplicated linear plot shifts back and forth from a captive youth and his kidnappers to one girl whose persistence eventually frees the boy. Liam, called Tug*, thirteen-year-old son of investigative reporter Harriet Shakespeare, returns to his home somewhere in London one Sunday morning feeling exhilarated from his usual demanding exercise run. As he enters the house, he is grabbed and carried off by the Free People, a revolutionary group dedicated to abolishing the family as a

social institution. They take him to the Derbyshire countryside 160 miles away and confine him
in isolated Black Clough Dale cottage near Ashdale Great Edge. In return for his release, they
demand that the government set up community
homes for all youth under the age of sixteen.
Tug's arrival at two o'clock in the morning is
witnessed by Jinny* Slattery, 13, who happens
to be in the area reluctantly helping her
father, Gypsy Joe, a farmer and jewelry craftsman, poach hare. Her curiosity aroused, Jinny
sets out to discover whether there is any
connection between the three occupants of the
cottage, the striking golden-eyed woman she
calls the Hare-woman* (and who is given no other
name in the story), the unpleasant, frightening
man who calls himself Doyle*, and the black-
haired youth they say is their simple-minded
son, Philip, and the missing youth. She concludes there is indeed a connection and enlists
the help, first unsuccessfully of Mr. Hollins,
the local constable, and then of his eighteen-
year-old son, Keith, in releasing Tug. Knocked
out in the kidnapping, Tug wakes up in the
cottage with people who are unfamiliar to him
but insist they're his parents, and for a time
he is unsure of who he really is. Gradually,
however, bits and pieces of his life with
Harriet, whom he calls Hank, return to memory,
and in spite of their efforts to intimidate him
and bend his will to theirs, he gathers his
wits, smuggles out a note pleading for help,
and systematically sets about retaining his
sense of self by separating out his former from
his present existence and by making lists of
his personal features and attributes, including
such tangible items as pulse rate, to which he
can refer when the psychological going gets
tough. Things come to a head when Jinny and
Keith phone Tug's mother with the information
that Tug is at the cottage. She brings the news
that the terrorists plan to strike a symbolic
blow at the concept of the family (probably) by
bombing the royal family and will kill Liam if
the bombing coup doesn't come off. A carefully
laid plan to release Tug fails, and matters so
fall out that the terrorists take Jinny hostage,
too, and head for the Edge, where they give Tug
the opportunity to do as a final act the one

thing he most wishes before they shoot him. He chooses to engage in his greatest pleasure, running, and Jinny's quick thinking in a tense moment enables the authorities to take the kidnappers. The book's title applies not only to the physical setting but also aptly encapsulates the story's chilly atmosphere, and protagonists and readers are kept in a state of anxiety throughout. More than an exciting suspense story, however, the book looks at interpersonal relationships within the family unit, examines the nature and purpose of terrorism--"to puzzle and tease and make people *think*....Playing mind games...."--and draws an ironic picture of the terrorists. Bitter social misfits, they are antifamily crusaders who create a family to confine their hostage and protect themselves from the society which is their prey. Their pseudofamily contrasts interestingly with the Slattery, Hollins, and Shakespeare families, the Shakespeare a happy and effective one-parent organism, the others in contrasting stages of function. The Slattery family ironically seems the most effective at bringing up children, although regarded by the community as abnormal, while the Hollins family, which enjoys a higher level of social acceptance, seems only marginally effective at meeting the psychological needs of the children. The Hare-woman and Doyle are rounded and convincing in their misanthropy, self-delusion, and self-destructiveness. Both Tug and Jinny are appealing protagonists who grow in self-understanding and self-confidence as a result of their experiences. Poe Nominee.

OOMPA-LOOMPAS (*Charlie and the Chocolate Factory**), the 3,000 workmen in Willy* Wonka's Chocolate Factory. They are a pygmy tribe he has brought from Africa, where they lived in trees and were in danger of being eaten up by jungle animals. Mr.* Willy Wonka says he has saved them from extermination. Now they work making his chocolates and other exotic and delicious concoctions in exchange for all the cacao beans they want. They are shown as a carefree, always smiling, energetic little people, who beat on drums, dance around, and sing long nonsense songs that comment on events as the novel goes along, like a kind of Greek chorus. They are intended as comic characters, and, indeed, the whole book is an extended comic strip, but, considering modern attitudes toward ethnic groups, the way they are depicted is a literary embarrassment.

OPIO (*Black Samson**), protagonist of the novel and nephew of the war leader, Magere*. He is known as Opio the Fish, because as a young child he stumbled onto a huge mudfish and rode the creature downstream to where his people were driving fish into their basket traps. As he grows up, his greatest talent is as a story-teller. Opio is brave and strong, but because he has some modesty and moderation in these things, he acts as a foil to Magere*, whose excesses bring disaster to him and his people.

ORDINARY JACK: BEING THE FIRST PART OF THE BAGTHORPE SAGA (Cresswell*, Helen, Faber, 1977; Macmillan, 1977), lighthearted, domestic real-istic novel set in and near a rambling estate in the present-day English countryside. Jack Bagthorpe, 11, is the only underachiever in the large, talented, eccentric Bagthorpe clan, in which everyone but Jack has several "strings to his bow." Because he is fond of Jack and wishes to take his too self-satisfied relations-by-marriage down a peg, Uncle* Parker hatches a Plan of Campaign by which Jack will be elevated in the eyes of his family by being made to appear to be a Prophet or Phenomenon. The Plan of Campaign, which, at Uncle Parker's instruc-tions, Jack dutifully records in his notebook and hides in his room under a stack of comics, consists of several stages, worked out care-fully by Uncle Parker as the novel progresses. In the first phase, Uncle Parker tells Jack to Act Mysteriously, that is, receive Messages, hear Voices, experience Visions, and Make Pronouncements, chief of which is that a Man in a Lavender Suit will arrive Bearing Tidings. This latter, of course, turns out to be Uncle Parker in garish new garb, returning from the village with news that the Danish housemaid Mrs. Bagthorpe has engaged will soon report for duty. The next stage consists of Two Prongs, in the first of which Jack employs props secured from the local Mysteries shop (tarot cards, crystal ball, incense, dowsing rods, and so forth), while in the second, Jack utters Certain Key Words and Phrases. As this nonsense goes on, in an ironically parallel story, Jack seeks to boost the self-esteem of his hound dog, Zero*, regarded by the family as a useless lamebrain, in particular, by teaching the dog to fetch. Gradually, the family begins to take notice of Jack, and Zero, too, and to attribute to them greater worth. Jack's apparent Visions and Manifestations rattle them, and they actually begin to think he may have prophetic powers. Jack finds shaking the family up quite enjoyable. Things come to a head with Prong Three (undertaken to produce "diversity," according to Uncle Parker), in which Jack Mutters about a Giant Red and White Bubble descending from the clouds and a Great Brown Bear. These arrive at a picnic Uncle Parker gives for Rosie* Bagthorpe's ninth birthday out in the meadow. A great balloon appears over the trees carrying two brown bears that scatter cards proclaiming Jack a Prophet. At that moment, Mr.* Bagthorpe, who had taken to the house in a huff, appears with Jack's notebook, and the game is up. After everything quiets down, Jack is praised for his boldness and invention, and the Bagthorpes seem a little more charitable toward one another. Jack feels less ordinary than before, and both he and Zero have earned the status of equals in the household, for the time being at least. While this craziness transpires, other members of the family have been up to assorted hijinks, and some commotion is always happening: Rosie painting Grandma* Bagthorpe; Mrs. Bagthorpe writing her Agony Columns; Mrs. Fosdyck, the housekeeper (termed "the hedgehog" by Mr. Bagthorpe), generally worrying about property and appearance and gossiping in the village about the ridiculous crew she works for; Uncle Parker living up to his reputation for driving recklessly and being an "idle devil"; little Daisy* Parker setting fires; William* Bagthorpe falling for the Danish housemaid; and Mr. Bagthorpe striving withal to produce his television scripts on a tape recorder. Even though the strained plot outruns itself, events rollick along, and the amusement level stays high. Most of the book is dialogue, consisting largely of disjointed conversations, interruptions, non sequiturs, traded insults, sardonic taunts, and literal misunderstandings. Numerous ironies underscore the slapstick, and there is much implied commentary on contemporary family life, but most of the comedy is just plain fourth-grade humor. Characters are one-dimensional, identifiable only by their names and idiosyncratic features, altogether a hyperbolically idiotic crew in a constant state of simmer. Sequels. (Grandpa* Bagthorpe; Tess* Bagthorpe) Choice; Fanfare.

OSKAR STANISLAWSKY (*The River at Green Knowe**), eleven-year-old displaced Polish boy sent by the Society for the Promotion of Holidays for Displaced Children to spend his vacation in the old house at Green Knowe. A leggy boy with a large appetite, he is Miss Sybilla* Bun's favorite. His most individual adventure is when he shrinks to mouse size to make himself a nest and then enjoys it so much that he wants to stay in it all night, though the other two worry that the cat might get him.

OSWALD BASTABLE (*The Story of the Treasure Seekers**), eldest son in the large and lively Bastable family, he tells the story of how the six children search for treasure to restore the fallen fortunes of their house. He is the most fully revealed of the children, showing himself to be imaginative, moralistic, self-congratulatory, intelligent, bossy, evasive, and proud-- he shows many characteristics, and is one of the most interesting narrators in literature for the young.

OSWALD TUBBS (*Tumbledown Dick**), brother of Dick Birkinshaw's mother, a stage magician in music halls and vaudeville. A dapper little man, he is currently unemployed and living with Dick's paternal Uncle Henry* Birkinshaw, whose wife, Maria, insists that Tubbs put on a "coarse apron" and help with the washing up, a blow to his self-esteem. At the Christmas party, he wears an evening suit with a black cape lined with crimson silk and charms the Lady Mayoress, who is very fond of conjurers.

THE OTHER PEOPLE (McNeill*, Janet, Chatto, 1973;
Little, 1970), realistic novel set in Sunny Bay,
an English seaside town, in the mid-twentieth
century. Kate* Lucas, 13, has been sent to the
run-down Sea View Guest House owned by her Aunt
Poppy while her mother honeymoons with her new
husband. Although at first she is terribly ill
at ease, she gradually becomes involved with the
other guests: Dilys Darlington, a middle-aged
woman who writes poetry; her nieces, beautiful
Rose, to whom boys swarm like flies, and the
less attractive Marni, both fifteen; elderly Mr.
Tweedle and his solicitious wife, with his pills
and shawls and special diets; the Blunt family,
who usually stay at the far swankier Hotel
Splendide, including Mrs. Blunt, her athletic
husband, and their unhappy son, Richard*, who is
about Kate's age; and Mr. J. L. S. Smith, whom
Kate nicknames the Mad* Hatter. She also is
curious about the strange house with blinds
drawn and curtains pinned together that stands
between the Sea View and its view of the sea.
Rose and Marni first encourage and then snub her
as they go off with boys. She comes upon Richard
forcing himself to dive off high rocks beyond
the beach and learns that he is unable to dive
off the high board at the pool in the presence
of his domineering father. With Marni,
temporarily dumped by Rose, Kate goes to the
Kooky Kapers Koncert on the Esplanade and to her
amazement and embarrassment recognizes the Mad
Hatter despite his red wig and dark glasses as
the pianist and comedian. She has begun to
realize that he has something to do with the
mysterious house, where, exploring with Richard,
she has found a dolls' house in the conservatory
and has seen Aunt Poppy leave a basket of food
at the door. When Aunt Poppy collapses from
overwork, Kate puts together the pieces she has
puzzled out and calls at the house, demanding
that the reclusive man she finds release Aunt
Poppy from the burden of caring for him, even
though she was for many years his housekeeper,
so that she can sell her property to the Hotel
Splendide and retire from the overtaxing job.
She learns that he has shunned people since his
fifteen-year-old daughter was drowned, an

accident that could have been prevented if she had not stopped to talk with a local boy. When Rose goes to look for a motorcyclist boy from home and is caught by the tide in the same place where the other girl drowned, Kate sounds the alarm, and Richard and the Mad Hatter risk their lives to save her. It becomes apparent that the Mad Hatter is the rejected son of the recluse and that the boy to whom his sister was talking was Kate's father at fifteen. Although the complex relationships provide most of the action, the main story concerns Kate's awakening to an understanding of the other boarders and her own emerging sexuality and her beginning to come to terms with her mother's new marriage and the new house and life this will mean for her. While the novel seems slow in starting and the boarders somewhat bizarre, the reader's interest and sympathy grow with Kate's. The second-rate resort setting is well handled. Fanfare.

THE OTHERS (*A Sound of Chariots**), term commonly applied to Bridie McShane's older sisters: Nell, Moira, and Aileen. Nell is the nonacademic one. She likes pets and always has several animals around. The children resent Nell's bossiness even before their father, Patrick*, dies, and, when she quits school to take care of the house after Patrick's death, they refuse to behave for her, and she has a hard time with them. Bridie has some misgivings about the way they treat her. The other two sisters are good students, and Mrs. Mackie encourages Bridie to emulate them.

THE OTHER WAY ROUND (Kerr*, Judith, Collins, 1975; Coward, 1975), realistic historical novel set during the World War II years in London, sequel to *When Hitler Stole Pink Rabbit**. Having come to England on the possibility of Papa's* film script being produced, Anna*, Max*, and their parents are in even greater financial straits than before. Totally impractical and unable to speak Englsh, Papa continues to write anti-Nazi articles and pieces about Berlin as he knew it, few of which find publishers. Mama* has a job as a social secretary that pays very little. Anna and Max have both gone to schools tuition-free. Max has won a scholarship and now goes to Cambridge. Anna has gone to a school that taught her very little and now is living with American family friends, the Bartholomews, to save the cost of a room in the Hotel* Continental, where her parents live. The war approaches. Anna, now fifteen, decides she must get a job, and the Relief Organization for German Jewish Refugees provides tuition to a secretarial school. She spends one marvelous weekend at Cambridge, where Max's friends are congenial and admiring and Max is about to shine in his exams. Then the Germans invade Holland and Belgium, England enters the war, and Max, along with Papa's cousin Otto and a number of distinguished professors, is interned as an enemy alien. The Bartholomews return to America, and Anna goes to live with her parents at the Hotel Continental. Because she deliberately does not read newspapers or listen to the radio news, she hardly notices Dunkirk and other events of importance. They visit old friends, Dr. Rosenberg and his wife, and Anna realizes to her horror that Papa has requested and received poison to use on himself and Mama in "an emergency." Through the efforts of Max's old headmaster and a letter Mama writes to a newspaper, Max is released and goes to teach at his old school. Air raids become a regular event, and the Rosenbergs, who have moved to the country, insist that Anna should come to live with them. They prove to be sheltering an oddly assorted group of quarrelsome relatives and friends, and Anna soon returns to London and school. When she applies for jobs where her language ability would be useful, she is rejected because she is not British-born. She finds a place with the Honorable Mrs. Hammond, Colonel of the British Red Cross and manager of volunteer women who knit and sew for the armed forces, and she earns enough to support herself. The Hotel Continental is hit by a bomb, and the owner moves her refugees to a house in Putney. Anna, now eighteen, starts a night-school art class, falls in love with her instructor, John Cotmore, a man of about forty who is separated from his wife. When he talks of making love, she naively thinks he means kissing her, and he gallantly refrains from pressing his desires, but she is crushed and humiliated when she finds he is soon living with Barbara, one of the art students. Papa has a stroke, from which he recovers. As the war ends, Anna wins a scholarship to art school, and she and Max realize that they are thoroughly English but that their parents will never really fit in; consequently, their dependence on Mama and Papa has been reversed and the situation is now the other way round. Although a quiet book, it gives a moving and often funny picture of the life of refugees in England during the war. The characters, even minor figures, are memorable, and Anna's first love and disillusionment are sympathetically described without sentimentality. Although less dramatic in events, it is a stronger book than its predecessor. Fanfare.

OUT OF THE MINES. See *The Bonnie Pit Laddie*.

THE OVERLAND LAUNCH (Hodges*, C. Walter, ill. author, Bell, 1969; Coward, 1970), historical novel detailing the heroic efforts of the Lynmouth lifeboat crew to answer a distress signal from a floundering ship, based on a real incident on the Devonshire coast on the night of January 12, 1899. Derry Larkins, 13, a stableboy, is feeling left out because his friend, Billy Pritchard, 16, seems to have outgrown him, calls him "young 'un," and has just been admitted to the crew of the lifeboat *Louisa*, of which his older brother is second coxswain. When a distress signal comes from the *Forest Hall*, a three-masted full-rigged ship, Derry seizes the opportunity to run with Billy's muffler, which his worried mother finds he has left behind. In the resort town, in winter, half the town's inhabitants turn out to watch the lifeboat set off, but the storm is so severe that it is clear it cannot be launched from Lynmouth. Since the telegraph lines are down, so no other lifeboat can be summoned, the coxswain, Jack Crockham, decides to haul the thirty-four foot boat overland to Porlock Weir, some fourteen miles over rough, narrow roads, where there is enough shelter to make launching possible. Derry is sent up Contisbury Hill to fetch the eighteen horses from the Blue Boar Inn, and then is told to come along to mind a "vexy" mare which takes to him. The

schoolmaster, Mr. Alfred Nathaniel Stringston,
assures Derry's mother that he will keep an eye
on the lad, and the procession starts off for
the longest night's work most of the men have
ever experienced. The boat is seven feet six
inches wide and the carriage wider than that,
and in many places the road is narrower, so that
the men must knock down walls to get through. In
Ashton Lane, about half way to Porlock, they
have to take the boat off the carriage and haul
it laboriously on skids, while the lightened
carriage is pulled around over the sodden moor.
In the more open country, the fierce storm blows
out lanterns and makes going extremely
difficult. At the very entrance to Porlock, the
lane narrows so much that they have to chop the
corner off a house to get past. Ten and a half
hours after they set out from Lynmouth, they
launch the *Louisa* from the harbor at Porlock
and are able to help the distressed vessel to
the Welsh coast. Derry and Mr. Stringston have
breakfast at the inn and go back to Lynmouth,
with Derry sleeping in the signalman's cart.
Their relationship is enriched by a conversation
before the storm, in which Derry tells the
schoolmaster about his memories of the Greek
myths from school, about Ooly-Sees (Ulysses)
and Yolus (Aeolus) and Pozzidon, and how he
fancies that these characters are still active
when the sea gets high. A later scene shows them
meeting in 1927, when Derry is the proprietor of
a garage near Lynton. Derry's son is a
solicitor, and his daughter is at university,
studying classics; he still treasures the book
of Greek myths the schoolmaster gave him after
their experience together in the storm. The
essentially single-incident story gets its
strength from the details of the fight to haul
the lifeboat across the moor, a step-by-step
description that evokes the cold and the driving
rain and the tremendous effort put in by the
dedicated men. Characters are convincing, though
not highly developed. A preface gives the story
of the actual incident and lists the names of
the historical lifeboat crew. A map helps
greatly to show the route and the problems.
Fanfare.

OVER THE HILLS TO FABYLON (Gray*, Nicholas

Stuart, Oxford, 1954; Hawthorn, 1970), lighthearted fantasy set in the marchen kingdom of
Fabylon at an unspecified time in the past.
Fabylon is "a city with magic." It is under an
entailed protective spell by which, when danger
threatens, the king can shut his eyes and count
to five, and the whole city vanishes to the far
side of the mountains where there is a flat
space that is just the proper size to hold it.
King Francis of Fabylon is a sensible monarch,
though inclined to be nervous, in particular
about his three children: the much-loved
Rosetta, 16, a dark-haired, blue-eyed beauty who
has many suitors but who is not yet ready to
settle down; Conrad, the crown prince, who is
black-haired, green-eyed, tall, handsome, overly
serious, and always calm and cool; and Alaric, a
handsome, golden-eyed, red-haired, inquisitive,
fun-seeking youth, who falls in love with every
pretty girl he meets. The novel is loosely
constructed, its many lively episodes given
tenuous unity by two concerns, neither of which
arouses much tension. One, about the efforts to
learn the city's spell by a bad-tempered, woods
witch and a surly, black sorcerer named Ancel,
whose familiar is a comic "thing" named Blackie
that likes to drink ink, has more promise for
suspense but fades out as the other concern, the
matter of Rosetta's many suitors, becomes more
prominent. The time span lasts from March to
December. In the spring, Princess Rosetta, who
likes to go on excursions in disguises, which
really fool no one, leaves the palace for the
pleasures of the countryside. She sips water
from a magic well and is given a wish, which she
uses to summon a flying horse. On the horse, she
and a handsome, young shepherd named Bracken
rescue a lamb that a marauding eagle has carried
off. Later, Prince Torquil comes courting her
and gives a magic, love-inspiring handkerchief
to Bobbette, the laundry maid, with instructions
to place it among Rosetta's things. The plan
goes awry, and he falls in love with Bobbette,
who accepts him. Other suitors come, too, and
are rejected, among them, arrogant Prince Martel
of the Fenlands, who is approved on practical
grounds by Conrad but dismissed unceremoniously
by Rosetta, who happens at the time to be under
a laughing spell. Worried that the Fenlanders

might decide to wage war against Fabylon because of the way she treated their prince, Rosetta goes on a shopping trip, has adventures with the city's tame bears, Beavis and Bedelia, and gets lost in an underground glowworm cave, from which she is rescued by the local cats, whose king is Courteney, the palace tom. When six more princes seek her hand, she takes the suggestion of her old nurse that she send them on quests to prove themselves. She instructs them to find what she has lost but doesn't tell them what it is. Bracken, the shepherd, hears of the challenge, goes into the dangerous mountains where he is rescued by a huge, comic monster, the Blodsnap, and returns with a jam tart for her. He himself being what she has lost and wants most, she chooses him for her husband. One week before their betrothal party scheduled for Christmas Eve, the Fenlanders declare war, and the King is ready to pronounce the moving spell when it is discovered that Corrie, the Captain of the King's Cavalry, is missing. Conrad, whose rigidity has mellowed through the experiences he has undergone in the story, insists he will not abandon his friend. When Corrie turns up, he announces that he has learned that the thousands of lights they thought represented approaching soldiers are really fireflies and that somehow the Fenlanders have learned about the trans-mountain refuge and have gone there to wait for King Francis to move the city. The king decides to leave Fabylon in place and let the Fen-landers sit in the snow as long as they please. Rosetta and Bracken are betrothed at a beautiful ball and plan to live on a big farm that the king has given them as a wedding gift. Other episodes concern the feckless Corrie, a pleasant, likeable youth who has a way of arousing Conrad's ire for his bumptious ways. In an amusing episode, he takes as a riddle Con-rad's remark that Corrie is too stupid to know how many beans make five and seeks help from the witch, who sends him against a pitiful, loathly worm. His dog, Wanda, who is really his mother enchanted, gets Conrad to rescue him. In still others of the book's fifteen chapters, the romantic Alaric seeks ice for his ill father and falls in love with an ice maiden, but, as usually happens with his love affairs, he promptly forgets her when he gets home. Alaric and Rosetta have an unusual adventure on the lake near the city, where on a magical island they discover a nautical-speaking old sea chest and visit a kingdom on the bottom of the lake. Conrad has separate adventures, too, in one accidentally putting a spell on Wanda. To undo it, he scales the sides of the city's big, old cathedral, inside of which he encounters various beings, among them a gargoyle who offers to be his dog. Conrad returns home humbler and happier. There are enough episodes, action, and dialogue, as well as talking cats, stags, griffins, magical doors, rhymes, and spells--the paraphernalia and conventions of the folk tale appear in profusion--along with coincidence, near encounters, and narrow escapes, subtle humor and overt comedy for several books. Characters are one-dimensional types, interesting but flat and unchanging except for Conrad, whose dynamism is totally predictable. The device of the moving castle is original and inventively worked out. The tone is good-natured and the style playful, high-spirited, and unpatronizing, with a pleasing veneer of courtesy. Interest flags three-quarters of the way through, however, because there simply is too much of the same sort of thing. The whole is entertaining but somewhat old-fashioned, since today's taste demands a tighter structure for suspense. Carnegie Com.

OWAIN (*Dawn Wind**), Roman-British boy who loses his father and brother, the whole of his family, in the last fight against the Saxons at Aquae Sulis and, after living in the deserted city of Viroconium with the beggar girl, Regina*, for most of a year, becomes a thrall on a Saxon farm in order to get care for her when she falls ill. Repeatedly Owain agrees to stay on at Beornstead to help the Saxon family, even when he has gained his freedom. He is a figure of endurance and devotion to honor, rather than great deeds or physical courage, and, because he sees beyond his enmity to view his Saxon master and his family as people in need of his help, he is a symbol of the hope for eventual reconciliation.

OWL (*The Song of Pentecost**), morose recluse who

lives in an oak tree on Lickey Top, the area
Snake* deceitfully assures the Harvest Mice that
the Owl will be happy to share with them. Owl
has become a recluse because he thinks he
murdered his own brother, a mystery solved when
the Cockle-Snorkle* Bug lets slip the information that the so-called murder was really an
accident. Owl so loved his brother-to-be that he
overpolished the egg and broke it, thus killing
the unhatched chick. The Cockle-Snorkle has
cruelly and deliberately not enlightened the
Owl of the true facts surrounding his brother's
death, thus subjecting the old bird to a
lifetime of anguished guilt.

OWLGLASS (Nickless*, Will, ill. author, Day,
1966), whimsical animal fantasy set in Sussex in
an unspecified but relatively modern time. When
Harris*, the rat, rashly cuts across an open
field on his way to his club meeting, he
narrowly escapes fatal attack from Old* Beak and
Claws, the owl more properly called the Hon.
Richard William Strix Flammea de Striges. This
incident concerns everyone in the club: the
host, Brock*, also called Meles-Brock, the
badger; Popghose* the weasel; Pointz the
hedghog; Mink; and the other members, all of
whom agree that the owl would never have done
anything in such shockingly bad form unless,
perhaps, his sight were failing. Harris, Mink,
and Popghose are appointed as a delegation to
call on their distinguished neighbor and make
tactful inquiries, taking a gift that has been
donated by the badger: a silver trophy from a
cockfight in the shape of a spike to be attached
to a cock's leg. This deputation is graciously
received by the owl, who admits that his
eyesight is not what it once was. To help their
admired friend and to protect themselves from
attack, Popghose thinks of a plan: he will ask
the jackdaws, clever thieves, to fetch pairs of
spectacles from the Others until they find a
pair that provides the necessary correction for
the owl. Although jackdaws are only marginally
acceptable as social acquaintances, Popghose
contacts his friend Corky and persuades him that
it is in the jackdaws' best interests to insure
that the owl can see what he's hunting.
Thereafter, the village people develop an

amazing tendency to mislay their eyeglasses. Old Beak and Claws works out a system. He puts two shoe boxes at his doorstep, one marked "in" and the other "out"; he then tries each new pair from the "in" box in a series of test flights, and when they prove unsatisfactory, leaves them in the "out" box. When he discovers a pair that actually increases his vision, he pitches all the others into the "out" box, ties it up, and deposits it at Brock's doorstep with the word "EUREKA" scrawled across the top. Unable to interpret this, the friends ask Foxy* Williams at the next club meeting, who confirms their guess that the owl has found what he needs. Brock and Popghose make a sign in a field with pocket handkerchiefs saying "STOP NOW" to call off the jackdaws' thievery of spectacles, but they cannot get their cooperation to return the unnecessary pairs. The next day the sexton at the local church finds a shoebox in the church porch. Already irritated by the blowing leaves and a gumboil, he gives the box a good kick, jumps upon it, then punts it right to the feet of the clergyman, one of those who have lost their spectacles recently. The sexton loses his job, and the reverend gentleman quietly burns the evidence, now smashed beyond repair. Reminiscent of *The Wind in the Willows**, the book has a literary style and is somewhat formal, with a mock serious tone. The animals' club is patterned on Victorian men's clubs, with rigid but unwritten protocol, rituals of punch making, and storytelling. Stories by Harris, Popghose, Old Beak and Claws, and Brock are included, all with considerable humor, and although they interrupt the main plot, the whole story is so relaxed that the intrusion is not annoying. Illustrations by the author are in the style of Ernest Shepard. The characters are well delineated, and descriptions of food and drink are particularly detailed. Fanfare.

THE OWL SERVICE (Garner*, Alan, Collins, 1967; Walck, 1968), fantasy set in a valley in contemporary Wales not far from Aberystwyth. The novel improvises with skillful invention upon the Celtic myth of Blodeuwedd*, the maiden created of flowers by the wizard Gwydion, who proves unfaithful to her husband and is turned into an

owl. Three present-day teenagers are brought by
their families to a big, old Welsh countryside
house, where they find themselves unwittingly
reenacting the old legend. Two of them, the
English youths Allison* and Roger*, have come to
Wales on holiday. Their parents, Margaret* and
Clive* Bradley, have just married, and the newly
formed family is learning how to get along
together. Helping about the place is Welsh-born
Gwyn*, a teenager of high career aspirations,
who is attracted to Allison at the outset. His
mother is Nancy* the housekeeper, and both he
and Nancy have an ambiguous and uneasy relationship with the seemingly slow-witted handyman,
Huw* Halfbacon, who is a permanent resident of
the valley. Tension builds immediately. Gwyn
discovers in the attic over Allison's room a
set of dishes bearing a decorative band which
might be either flowers or owls. Allison feels
strangely compelled to trace on paper the
elusive pattern, which comes out as owls that
always disappear once she has drawn them. Then
Roger discovers by the river a boulder with a
hole bored through it, which is called the Stone
of Gronw and associated locally with the myth.
Roger takes pictures of the boulder and the view
from it and discovers peculiar shadows in the
prints that imply that people invisible to the
naked eye were present on the landscape when he
snapped the shutter. Cracks appear in the
pebble-dash (stucco) of the billiard-room wall,
revealing the painting of a woman made of
flowers, the lady of the legend. Huw makes
obscure remarks about a lady who is coming and
darkly cautions Gwyn against "making Allison
owls when she wants to be flowers." As the
friendship between Gwyn and Allison grows,
parental opposition on both sides increases,
too. Allison breaks appointments with Gwyn because she wishes to avoid trouble with her
mother. Gwyn becomes increasingly defensive because he knows that it is his Welshness and
lower social status they object to. The
incipient friendship between Roger and Gwyn goes
sour, too, since Margaret in particular and
Clive in support of her attempt to separate Gwyn
and Allison. Things come swiftly to a head after
Gwyn and Allison meet one afternoon on the
mountain and Gwyn confides to her his aspira-

tions, among others, his attempts to improve his
speech by using records. Allison inadvertently
mentions this to Roger, who taunts Gwyn with it.
Deeply hurt by what he feels is Allison's
betrayal, Gwyn runs away to the mountains. He is
fetched back by Huw, who tells the boy that he
has it within his power to halt the curse that
haunts the valley, which says that the ancient
story will be reenacted in each generation. He
tells Gwyn that such triangular associations
have persisted in his family; that he himself
was part of such a triangle with Nancy; that
Nancy left him for Bertram, former owner of the
house that now belongs to Allison, inherited
through her father; that he, Huw, had brought
about Bertram's death by tampering with the
Englishman's motorcycle; and that he is Gwyn's
true father. He also tells Gwyn to give Allison
a certain owl pendant. Then Roger uses a
screwdriver to open the door to the stable,
whose key Nancy had thrown into the river, and
there discovers Bertram's motorcycle, a large,
carefully preserved stuffed owl, and ranged
around it the many small paper owls Allison had
copied from the table service. All have been
carefully placed, but no footsteps leading to
any of these objects are visible on the very
dusty floor. Nancy angrily makes a tremendous
scene, smashing the large owl and scattering
feathers all about. She announces that she is
leaving and insists that Gwyn accompany her,
though it is dark and stormy, but they soon
return because downed trees block the road. When
Gwyn bitterly refuses to give the pendant to
Allison, Huw places it about her neck. She
falls in a faint, strange red scratch marks
appearing on her face and feathers clinging to
her clothing. Huw tells Gwyn that he can break
the power by comforting Allison, but the boy
adamantly refuses. Roger, ashamed and needing to
set the record straight, confesses that only
he, not Allison, had ridiculed Gwyn's aspirations, but Gwyn rejects his apology. Roger
brushes the feathers away from Allison and
speaks gently to her, telling her that she is
flowers, not owls. The scratches gradually fade
from her skin, and the book concludes with the
feathers disappearing and flower petals spreading their fragrance throughout the room. This

is a very sophisticated book, almost all dialogue, high in atmosphere, and skillful in
characterizations. Since the action starts in
medias res and proceeds in a direct line from
there, close and attentive reading is necessary
to understand the background, characters,
setting, and plot. The reader must be alert for
inferences and sensitive to subtle juxta-
positions. Fantasy aspects blend Gothic conventions and old-story magic: objects that
disappear, the isolated house with a history,
strange lights, a sealed room, and the like, and
it is easy to believe that forces more powerful
than human passions are at least partially
responsible for events. Gwyn is the best developed of the artfully foiled figures and the one
who early wins sympathy. The conclusion may not
be emotionally satisfying to those on his side;
it suits the story intellectually, however,
given the social context. Questions remain. Are
we to assume that Roger and Allison will become
a couple? Has Roger's sudden compassion halted
the ancient power, or can only Gwyn keep it from
continuing, since he is, according to Huw, the
next indigenous lord of the valley? Will
letting Roger win Allison stop the power, and
are we to assume that Gwyn will do so? This rich
and compelling novel enjoys near-classic
status. Carnegie Winner; Choice; Fanfare;
Guardian.

P

PAPA (*The Other Way Round**; *When Hitler Stole Pink Rabbit**), distinguished anti-Nazi Jewish writer who escapes from Germany in 1933 when Hitler comes to power, father of Anna* and Max*. A brilliant but impractical man, he once spends almost all the family's meager funds on a sewing machine that doesn't work and gets his money back only because his friend, a French woman, goes with him and assertively threatens the store owner. Although he loves Paris, he moves the family to England in hope of selling a movie script, but he does not learn English and remains an outsider. A gentle, understanding man, he accepts his problems with detachment, contrasting with his much younger volatile wife. Before the end of World War II he suffers a stroke, from which he recovers, though his health remains fragile.

PAPA ANDREAS (*The Lark on the Wing**), elderly musician who has been a vocal teacher for Kit* Haverard's mother and who becomes Kit's instructor. He is a man of principle and insists on a long, careful grounding in fundamentals before he allows a student to sing publicly. He is very fatherly to Kit, whom he calls by her mother's name, Janey.

PAPA DOCTOR (*Marassa and Midnight**), little, enigmatic, old leader of the Haitian black slaves. Himself the slave of a "good" master, he is the healer of the slaves, their doctor. He enlists Midnight to the cause of rational revolution, telling the boy to keep his ears and eyes open about revolutionary activities and pass along information to any messenger who says, "I come by Whydah roads!" and "I speak for the Feraille!" "Whydah roads" refers to the port in Africa through which the blacks were sold, and Feraille is the second half of the name of the Haitians' god Ogoun, his name "as it was known in the golden time of peace," according to Papa Doctor. In the novel, the term Feraille also refers to Papa Doctor. Marassa and Midnight have romantically believed that they are princes, the sons of the King of Dahomey, but Papa Doctor says that is not so. He knows this by their long, thin feet, which mark them as members of his own family, which is not royal. They are cousins of a sort to him.

A PARCEL OF PATTERNS (Paton Walsh*, Jill, Kestrel, 1983; Farrar, 1983), historical novel set in the village of Eyam in Derbyshire in the plague year of 1665. Though the daughter of a prosperous contractor for the lead mines, Mall* Percival, 16, keeps a small flock of sheep, the descendants of one given her by Thomas* Torre of Wardow when, as a lass of eight, she helped him save the ewe in difficult labor. In tending the sheep she has come to know and love Thomas, a matter her mother suspects and approves of, but they hesitate to tell her father. Plague comes to Eyam in a packet of patterns cut in sackcloth. A tailor has ordered them for Catherine* Momphesson, the new parson's wife, who, being of the Restoration faith, does not think it a sin to wear pretty clothes as most of the villagers, trained by the now-deposed Puritan Parson* Thomas Stanley, do. At first no one says the name of the illness that kills the tailor so suddenly, but soon others die, and Eyam has to admit that plague has struck the village. Parson Stanley preaches that it is God's will and punishment for sins. Parson* William Momphesson advises fresh air, staying away from houses of sickness, and burning the blankets of the victims, but both men themselves visit the sufferers, as does Catherine. Mall's friend, Emmot Sydall, has confided that she is in love with Thomas's cousin, Roland Toree of Middleton.

They have become betrothed, but the sickness keeps the young couple apart. Mall refuses to let Thomas come near her for fear of contagion. Emmot sickens and dies, and both Mall and her mother help tend her, though Mall's father tries to keep them from going where there is illness. Eventually he hears that his long-estranged sister is dying, and he visits to make his deathbed peace with her. From this contact he, too, becomes ill and soon dies. Mall's mother, no longer having any will to live, also becomes a plague victim. Mall, unable to keep Thomas from trying to see her, has sent word by her old playmate, Francis Archdale, that she has died, thinking that will keep him away. Distraught at this news, Thomas breaks the self-imposed quarantine of Eyam, saying he would rather die than go on living apart from Mall. By this time there are few able-bodied men left in the village, so he becomes the grave digger, his first grave being for Catherine. Soon Mall's mother dies, and Parson Stanley insists that Thomas and Mall be married immediately to avoid sin or scandal. There follows a brief period of great happiness for both, even in the midst of such deep sorrow. Soon, however, Thomas becomes ill. His death leaves Mall in shock, so that she hardly realizes that, after more than a year, the plague has run itself out, and Eyam, once a village of 350, of which 267 have died, is at last free of contagion. Francis, long in love with Mall, begs her to marry him and go to the New World, even though he knows she still loves Thomas. To rid herself of the terrible memories and sorrows, she writes this first-person account, intending to leave it behind as a charm to rid her of the horrors and let her start a new life. Although the simple, moving romance of Thomas and Mall is fictional, the facts of the plague year of Eyam are historical. Well-drawn minor characters and vivid details combine to give a compelling picture of the period when Puritan-trained villagers were suddenly faced with a new attitude toward religion and life-style, and of the terrible suffering caused by the plague. The language, with a suggestion of dialect, is convincingly used in the voice of the young but intelligent protagonist. Fanfare.

PARSON THOMAS STANLEY (*A Parcel of Patterns**),
Puritan minister who has lost his place with the
restoration of King Charles II but remains in
the village of Eyam, still leading the people in
prayer though forbidden to preach, and reminding
them constantly of the sinfulness of the new
ways. When the plague strikes, he visits the
sick and uses his influence to make the
villagers swear not to leave so that the illness
will not spread through the district. Although
he considers the illness God's will and
punishment for sin, he joins the new parson in
trying to help and comfort the afflicted.

PARSON WILLIAM MOMPHESSON (*A Parcel of Patterns**), new minister sent by the Restoration
church to Eyam in 1665. An intelligent, gentle
man, he does not send the old parson away as
he is supposed to, but rather lets him live
within the village where he is a constant
reminder to the people of the Puritan faith.
William has a lovely young wife and two little
children, but when plague comes, he visits the
sick and tries to comfort the bereaved, knowing
all the time that they have never really accepted him. Not a fanatic, he tries to lead the
people back gradually to the less austere
church, but to many he seems to exemplify the
sins of frivolity and idolatry.

PATON WALSH, JILL (GILLIAN BLISS PATON WALSH)
(1937-   ), born in London; educator and
novelist. She attended St. Michael's Convent,
North Finchley, London, and St. Anne's College,
Oxford, earning a diploma in education and an
M.A. degree in English. For several years she
was an English teacher at Enfield Girls Grammar
School, Middlesex, and has been a member of the
Permanent Visiting Faculty of the Center for
Study of Children's Literature at Simmons
College, Boston. She was also the Whittall
Lecturer at the Library of Congress in 1978. Her
novels are varied in type--historical fiction,
modern stories, fantasy, and science fiction--
and in style, and six have been included on
the *Horn Book* Fanfare list, as well as receiving
other honors. Her first book, *Hengest's Tale*
(Macmillan, 1966; St. Martin's, 1966), is about
the mid-fifth-century ruler of Kent. *Fireweed**

(Macmillan, 1969; Farrar, 1970), a story of the bombing of London in World War II, has been named a Contemporary Classic. Dealing with the same period is *The Dolphin Crossing* (Macmillan, 1967; St. Martin's, 1967), telling the story of Dunkirk. Reaching further back in history are *A Parcel of Patterns* (Kestrel, 1983; Farrar, 1983), based on a real incident during the plague year of 1665 when a village voluntarily quarantined itself to keep disease from spreading, and *The Emperor's Winding Sheet* (Macmillan, 1974; Farrar, 1974), dealing with the fall of Constantinople in 1453, which won the Whitbread Award and was named to the Carnegie Commended list. During World War II she lived for two years in Cornwall, which provides the setting for two stories of a girl growing up, *Goldengrove* (Macmillan, 1972; Farrar, 1972) and its sequel, *Unleaving* (Macmillan, 1976; Farrar, 1976), which won the *Boston Globe-Horn Book* Award. She combines the modern with ·the historical in her fantasy *A Chance Child* (Macmillan, 1978; Farrar, 1978), in which an abused boy from modern times goes back to share and surmount the abuse of child labor in the late eighteenth century. *The Green Book* (Macmillan, 1981; Farrar, 1982) is a brief, futuristic story of a community that emigrates to a distant planet. Paton Walsh has also written books in the Long Ago Children's Book Series, including *Crossing to Salamis* (Heinemann, 1977), *The Walls of Athens* (Heinemann, 1977), and *Persian Gold* (Heinemann, 1978).

PAT PENNINGTON (*Pennington's Seventeenth Summer*; *The Beethoven Medal*), also called Patrick or Penn, big, surly, aggressive, and musically talented boy who fights his way out of school, into jail and prison, and finally onto the concert stage. He conflicts with and leaves his lower-class parents, his father a brutal ex-convict and his mother an insensitive shrew, who have done only one supportive thing toward his future and that was to give him piano lessons. Pat rebels against authority in the form of parents, schoolmasters, and police, but he has great musical sensitivity and the potential for genuine love and even tenderness. Except in physical activity and music, he is insecure and ill at ease. Although adults usually find Pat sullen and antagonistic, girls recognize and are drawn to his animal vitality. His choice of Ruth* Hollis for a girl friend is mostly the result of chance and of her crush on him, but her stubborn devotion, even after he has been sent to prison, gives him strength and wakes a gradual love in him after she has become pregnant and they are married in *Pennington's Heir* In *Marion's Angels*, he is beginning to be successful and suffers conflicts between the demands of his career and his family.

PAT PIERSON (*The Watch House**), friend and steady companion of Timmo* Jones. A cheerful, unpretentious girl, she introduces herself to Anne* Melton as "Fat Pat," though she is only plump, and explains that she is not Timmo's girlfriend because he is "off sex." She shares Timmo's interest with Anne without apparent jealousy, though she is reluctant to let him hypnotize Anne because of her own experience with Timmo's tricks. At one point, she tries her skill at being a medium with tumbler writing, and the glass is propelled with such force that it shatters, gouging the oak window frame and, having struck a glancing blow to her head, raises a large goose egg. Her main role is to listen to Timmo in his various crazes, act as his sidekick and support, and bring him down to earth again when possible. She has more sensitivity to people than Timmo has and, unlike him, she treats Anne more as a friend than as an interesting phenomenon.

PATRICK MCSHANE (*A Sound of Chariots**), father of Bridie and the main influence in her life. He dominates the novel even after he dies. An Irishman taken as a prisoner of war by the Germans in World War I, he becomes acquainted with Agnes* Armstrong through a Red Cross prisoner-of-war correspondence program. The two fall in love by mail, and over the protests of her family they marry when he comes home. Although he is a staunch liberal who feels that laws should be passed to keep the rich from exploiting the poor, while Agnes is considerably more conservative owing to her Presbyterian upbringing, the two love each other very much and have a satisfying marriage. They are respected by their neighbors, even though Patrick gets thrown out of village meetings for his Marxist views. He is a strong-minded, outspoken, and idealistic man, yet is practical enough to fight for what he believes about social justice and is ready always to go to the aid of friends and neighbors when they are in need. His death changes the family's life dramatically.

PATTEN, BRIAN (1946–   ), born in Liverpool, Lancashire; editor and writer of poetry and fiction for adults and children. His best known book for young readers is *Mr. Moon's Last Case** (Allen, 1975; Scribner, 1976), which was nominated for the Edgar Allan Poe Award. A witty, lighthearted, picaresque fantasy novel, it sports with private-eye conventions and at the same time explores attitudes toward the new and different. He was educated at Sefton Park Secondary School in Liverpool and has worked as a journalist, gardener, and newspaper vendor. He was a reporter for *Bootle Times* and for the English underground poetry magazine, *Underdog*, both in Liverpool. Now a full-time writer, he has published mainly for adults, and these books are largely collections of poems, including *Little Johnny's Confession* (Allen, 1967; Hill, 1968), *The Mersey Sound* (Penguin, 1967), and *Notes to the Hurrying Man* (Allen, 1969; Hill, 1969). Though intended for adults, much of his poetry is readily understood and appreciated by children. For children, he also wrote *The Elephant and the Flower: Almost Fables* (Allen, 1970), *Manchild* (Covent, 1973), *Two Stories* (Covent, 1973), *Emma's Doll* (Allen, 1976), *The Sly Cormorant and the Fishes* (Kestrel, 1977) (which is an adaptation of Aesop's fables), a book of story poems, and several plays for radio, stage, and television, among them *The Ghost of Riddle Me Heights* (produced in Birmingham, 1980). He received the Eric Gregory and the Pernod awards for poetry, both in 1967.

A PATTERN OF ROSES (Peyton*, K. M., ill. author, Oxford, 1972; Crowell, 1973), fantasy set in an English country village, partly in the present day and partly in the last years of this

century's first decade. The parallel stories are
held together by boys who live in the same room,
both with unusual artistic ability and both
attracted to girls with similar qualities. Tim*
Ingram (Timothy Reed Ingram), 16, convalescing
from glandular fever, is not a rebel, but he is
weary of his mother's constant manipulation and
is revolted by his parents' expectation that he
will follow his father in the advertising
business. A builder blocking up a chimney in his
room, the old cottage around which his parents
have built a modern, suburban-style house, finds
an old biscuit tin, covered with a design of
roses and containing a drawing, crude but
powerful, signed TRI, 17 February, 1910. Tim has
a strange sensation of seeing the boy who drew
them, which is stronger than a mere whim of
imagination. Their shared initials intrigue him,
and he is startled to find a gravestone of a
fifteen-year-old in the churchyard with the same
initials and the death date of 18 February,
1910--just one day after the drawing. In front
of the stone grows a purple rose. Piqued by
curiosity and a sense of kinship, he goes
through church records with the vicar's angry,
red-haired daughter, Rebecca*, whom he at first
considers "a dog" but gradually comes to like
and admire. Together they discover the story of
Tom* (Thomas Robert) Inskip, with Rebecca doing
most of the research and Tim actually experiencing some of the events in Tom's short life. A
dreamy boy, Tom incurs the wrath of the new
vicar, "Brimstone" Bellinger, by his inattention
when the dignitary visits the local school, but
Miss* May Bellinger, the vicar's lame daughter,
takes an interest in his drawings which are on
display. Later, after he has left school and
starts working for Mr. Pettigrew, the local
landowner, Miss Bellinger offers to give him
drawing lessons so he will not waste his "God
given talent," an idea that seems as strange to
him, a working-class boy, as it does to his
father, but his mother insists that he accept
the offer. At Bellingers he meets Miss May's
young cousin, Netty* Belllinger, and falls
hopelessly in love. Netty teasingly encourages
him, and one lovely spring day, seeing him
chopping sugar beets, entices him to leave his
job and come walk with her and her dog, Mermaid.

They have a lovely, innocent stroll in the woods, pick primroses, and hold hands, until Mr. Pettigrew rides up and Tom, terrified of being caught truant from work, runs off. He gets the sack, and village gossip distorts the incident to the rape of Netty and an attack on Pettigrew. Miss May, however, sorts out the truth and gets him his job back. He doesn't see Netty again until February 18, when the fox hunt passes him at the edge of the lake and he sees the fox cut across the thin ice. When the dogs follow, Mermaid among them, and crash through, Netty begs him to save her dog. He tries, is caught on the cracking ice, and drowns. Tim's story, though primary, is simpler. Under the influence of Rebecca and Tom's spirit, he rejects his parents' plans for him, refuses to go back to school, gets a job with the local blacksmith, and realizes that he can live simply and happily and, with luck, build a life more useful and satisfying than his father's. The strength of the book lies in its strong characterization and skillful interweaving of the two stories, with the 1910 period particularly well evoked. The parallels are close--the two girls, the two Christmas parties, the similar drawings, the Feburary 18 afternoon on the ice--but varied enough to be interesting. The fantasy element is not contrived but rather seems intrinsic to the present-day story, and the detective work Rebecca does is all easily within plausibility. Contemporary Classics; Fanfare.

PAULA MARTIN (*The Summer People**), sister of Philip* and the one who brings to an end Philip's and Sylvia's secret romances. Paula is in conflict with her father, who doesn't want her to learn to drive a car or continue with her education. She takes driving lessons on the sly and eventually goes into teacher training in spite of his opposition. She is bitter about having to take care of her little sister, Alison, and help her mother about the house when her parents don't require Philip to do similar tasks. Her bitterness erupts in angry tirades occasionally and finally leads to her breaking into the bungalow when Ann and Philip are together, Alison in tow. Alison, 7, babbles to her mother about being with Ann and Philip, and thus their secret gets out.

PAULA RIGG (*Bilgewater**), matron of the dormitory where Bilgewater's father is housemaster
and the nearest thing to a mother that the girl
has. Fiercely protective of all her charges,
Paula has been confident that Bilgie is not
retarded, as most of her early teachers have
assumed, and has determinedly read to her during
the many years when she was unable to learn to
read. She treats Bilgie much as she does the
boys, with humor and a no-nonsense practical-
ity--"Beware of self-pity!" is her dictum--but
she knows when the homesick new boys need
special attention, and she is a dynamo of action
in a real emergency. She is strikingly good-
looking, young for her job, and adored by everyone in the school, though she is not an educated
woman and she speaks with a broad Dorset accent.
It is only when Miss Bex sets out to capture
Bilgie's widowed father that Paula first leaves,
then returns, routs her rival, and marries the
unworldly man.

PAUL FAIRFAX (*The Plan for Birdsmarsh**), dreamy,
worrying fourteen-year-old who happens to own
the old smack, *Swannie*, and who is pushed into
making it fit for sailing by his friend, Gus*
Roper, and into using it for testing an inflatable survival suit invented by his brother,
Chris*. Paul is not particularly interested in
sailing, having used the old boat mostly as a
place to get away by himself, but he has a deep
feeling for the land and a love of working with
animals. Convinced that he is stupid, awkward,
and cowardly, Paul has difficulty asserting
himself and cannot make his parents understand
his deep love for Birdsmarsh as it is and the
way the idea of it being commercially exploited
violates his whole being. After the accident
that leaves him floating in the North Sea for
thirty-three hours, Paul becomes subdued and
more mature, and while he still cares strongly
for Birdsmarsh, he is able to face the prospect
of its change without the agony he formerly
felt.

PAUL HUNTER (*The Girl in the Grove**), boy who is
much involved with the spirit of Laura*

Seccombe, which wanders the grove and the old
manor house near his home. In his early childhood Paul was a victim of polio, which affected
his growth and has left him with a limp when he
is tired. Paul has a chip on his shoulder among
his contemporaries, and he resents the money-
getting drive of his father, particularly the
burning down and grubbing up of woods near his
orchards. At the same time, Paul is genuinely
concerned about the spirit girl, Laura, who was
so little loved in her life that she now wanders
the manor house and the grove looking for
friends. He has figured out that the romance of
his grandmother, then a nursemaid to Laura, and
Laura's older brother, Charles, may well have
resulted in the birth of his father, though his
grandmother was already married to John Hunter
before her son was born. Paul is originally rude
to Jonquil* Darley but eventually helps her to
see that the marriage of his father and her
mother will make their parents happier and will
not be disastrous for the two young people.

PAULINE (*A Chance Child**), half sister to
Creep*, younger than her brother Christopher*
and far less eager to find Creep and bring him
back. She tells Christopher that she doesn't
want a brother who isn't one really, always
sniveling and smelly, and she tries to deny to
him and herself that Creep ever existed. She is
more clearly aware than Christopher, however,
that their own father left the family when he
came home after a long absence and discovered
Creep, and she is more afraid of talking to the
Welfare and the Cruelty people for fear of
getting their mother into trouble. She
accompanies Christopher on his expeditions to
try to find their half brother, but she tires
easily and complains, being ambivalent about
their quest.

PEAGREEN (*The Borrowers Avenged**), Peregrine
Overmantel, the Borrower youth who helps the
Clocks after they have moved to the Old Rectory
to get away from Mr.* and Mrs.* Sidney Platter,
in particular by giving them his old quarters
behind the windowseat after he moves to the
aviary above the larder. He likes to read, is
affected in speech and manner but is honest

enough to admit he's a snob, and has a gentle, sideways smile. He was lamed in a fall from the mantel when he was a little boy and doesn't like the outdoors and active pursuits. He reads a lot, especially poetry; paints; writes poems of his own; is engaged in writing his family history; and teaches Timmus to read and write. He is inventive and comes up with building ideas that Pod* capably implements for making the Clocks' new quarters more liveable and that please Homily* greatly. Arrietty* is the first Clock to see him, and he remains her special friend. One of the most interesting and best-developed figures in the series about the Borrowers, he serves as a foil for Spiller*. He appears only in the last of the six books, and the reader is left to wonder whether or not he and Arrietty may discover a romantic interest in each other.

PEARCE, (ANN) PHILIPPA (1920-   ), born in Great Shelford, Cambridgeshire; editor, script-writer, producer, and author of novels and short stories of fantasy and realism for children. She grew up in the village of Great Shelford, where her father operated the local water mill. Great Shelford and the surrounding territory provided landscape and color for most of her books. She attended Perse Girls' School and received her degrees with honors in English and history from Girton College, Cambridge, in 1942. From 1945-1958, she wrote and produced scripts both original and adapted on historical and literary subjects for the BBC; from 1958-1960 she was assistant editor in the educational department of Oxford University Press; and she was children's editor for Andre Deutsch, Ltd., in London from 1960-1967. In 1963, she married Martin Christie (a fruit grower) who died in 1965, and had one daughter. She began to write for children in the early 1950s, while she was recovering from tuberculosis. *"Minnow" on the Say** (Oxford, 1955; as *The "Minnow" Leads to Treasure*, World, 1958), her first novel, which tells of some boys' adventures treasure hunting on a river, draws heavily on her memories of her own childhood and home turf. Though it seems conventional today, it caught on and was commended for the Carnegie Award and named to

Fanfare and the Lewis Carroll Shelf. She followed this with *Tom's Midnight Garden** (Oxford, 1958; Lippincott, 1958), a time fantasy some critics have deemed the masterpiece of the late twentieth century. The engrossing story of a lonely boy who at night has adventures in a garden not there during the day, it won the Carnegie Medal and appears in *Choice*, Fanfare, the Children's Literature Association Touchstones, Lewis Carroll Shelf, *Books Too Good to Miss*, and Contemporary Classics. Although none of her other books can match the reputation of *Tom's Midnight Garden*, several others have won critical approval: *A Dog So Small** (Constable, 1962; Lippincott, 1963), a sensitive, genuine-seeming story of a boy's yearning for a dog of his own (in Fanfare); *The Battle of Bubble and Squeak** (Deutsch, 1978), about a family's squabbles over a pair of gerbils (in *Choice*, commended for the Carnegie, and winner of the Whitbread); and *The Way to Sattin Shore** (Kestrel, 1983; Greenwillow, 1983), about how a girl's curiosity about her father is whetted by the disappearance of his tombstone from the local graveyard (commended for the Carnegie). Pearce has also published several collections of short stories, edited an edition of Hans Christian Andersen's tales, and written the stories for several picture books, among them the recent Bunnykins series of talking rabbit fantasies published by Viking and Greenwillow.

PEGGY BLACKETT (*Pigeon Post**; *Swallows and Amazons**), younger of the two Amazons who have a mock war with the Swallows and then become friends in a series of holiday adventure novels. Peggy is mate of the *Amazon* and one of the older group in *Pigeon Post*, but is not individualized much except as being a chatterer.

PENNINGTON'S LAST TERM. See *Pennington's Seventeenth Summer*.

PENNINGTON'S SEVENTEENTH SUMMER (Peyton*, K. M., ill. author, Oxford, 1970; *Pennington's Last Term*, Crowell, 1971), realistic psychological novel of the conflicts of a lower-class boy at odds with all authority, who happens to have a remarkable gift as a pianist. Big, pugnacious Pat* Pennington, 16, also called Penn, is a hoodlum to the local police, a good-for-nothing to his parents, and a sore trial to his schoolmasters at Beehive Secondary Modern, except for Mathews, the games master, who appreciates his aggressiveness at soccer and his skill at swimming, and old Mr. Crocker, called "Dotty" by the boys, who struggles to bring out his unusual musical talent. The headmaster, Mr. Stacker, longs for the day when Pat will leave school, and his form master, Marsh, called "Soggy" by his pupils, is a petty tyrant who is determined to prove his authority over the boy. Pat already has a police record, having been blamed for shoplifting actually done by his rival, Smeeton, a pimply weasel of a boy who contends with Pat for the ownership of a nearly rotten smack that they sometimes take out to putter about the river but mostly use as a clubhouse and an excuse for fights. After a midnight set-to that ends with Pat being blamed for defacing a white Jaguar on which Smeeton has written rude words with tar and a reprisal attack by Pat on Smeeton and three of his henchmen in broad daylight, Pat is let off with a warning by the older policeman, Sergeant West, and becomes a prime target for the eager young police constable, Mitchell. At school, Mr. Crocker has arranged with the other teachers, who are glad to get rid of Pat, that he will spend most of his days practicing for the Open Solo Pianoforte competition at the Northend music festival, but Pat is more interested in the social evening for parents and friends. He has been commandeered to accompany most of the performers and to lean on his diffident friend, Bates*, to sing, the problem being that Bates will launch into his lovely rendition of folk songs accompanied by Pat on the harmonica only when well primed with beer. At school Marsh decides to make an issue of the boy's long hair, setting a deadline for a haircut. The afternoon of the concert, Smeeton tricks Bates and Penn into entering a deserted sail loft and then locks them in, intending to leave them there until they have missed the concert and brought everyone in school down on them. Penn waits until the tide has risen, then takes a run across the loft and leaps into the water, having to clear a fifteen-foot concrete wharf. He lets Bates out, runs him home, swipes his father's motorcycle, and gets to the school on time. The other boys overdo the beer they are feeding Bates on an empty stomach, and Pat swipes the brandy from the school first aid room to revive him. The concert is a smashing success, climaxed by Pat's discovery that a girl named Sylvia, a folksinger whom he admires, has come to hear it, but just as he is about to get into conversation with her Marsh grabs him by the back of the neck and steers him into the headmaster's office, where Constable Mitchell is waiting. Pat tells the truth about the loft, which Mitchell clearly does not believe, but since he doesn't have a license, he says his father ran him up to school on his cycle. When he gets home his father beats him up for taking the cycle but sticks up for his story to the police, who are investigating a motorcycle theft during the afternoon. The next day Mitchell takes Pat back to the loft, thinking he has trapped him in a lie, and even though the tide is not as high, Pat repeats his daring leap and then scornfully turns his back and walks home. Since Pat has not cut his hair, he has been barred from sports. After he swims anyway, winning the meet for the team, he gets it cut to save the games master's job, but insists on sending an insolent message to Marsh. The day before the music competition, which Pat has decided to skip so that he can play for Sylvia and Bates at a folk festival, he rigs a bucket of liquid manure and other foul ingredients over the door and trips it when Marsh walks through. Marsh gives him six heavy cuts with the cane on each hand, even when reminded by another student that Pat is to play in the competition. That makes Pat change his mind and decide to play there after all, just to show Marsh, but because Mitchell has found that he rode without a license (enough with his prior record to send him to reform school), he takes off with Bates in the smack to stay out of the way. Mr. Crocker's wife hails them as they set off, worried because her husband went fishing the night before in his outboard motor boat and hasn't come back. They promise to look for him, and they find him way out, collapsed in his boat from a heart attack. They run aground trying to get near him, and can't get him into their smack, nor can Pat get into Crocker's boat since he is too heavy and there is not enough clearance. At Pat's insistence, Bates gets into Crocker's boat and rows him back up river, while Pat tries unsuccessfully to get the motor started in the smack. He then resigns himself to ending his life there as the smack breaks up but is picked up by a yawl. In scruffy borrowed clothes he comes into the competition when it is nearly over, pleads for a chance to play, and, rising to the occasion under adversity, performs far better than he ever has before, and wins. To his astonishment, Sylvia has left the folk festival early and come to hear him. They go to her house, and her insensitive mother insists that he play for them. He plays and plays and plays, releasing all his pent-up emotion, until all the family has gone to bed. When he arrives home in the morning, a Professor* Hampton calls at the house, insists that Pat play for him, gives him an impromptu music test, and then accompanies him and his father, along with Bates, who has turned up, to the police station. Professor Hampton, who has been visiting in the flat above that of Sylvia's family, has heard the three hours of steady playing the night before and now persuades Sergeant West that, if the charges are dropped, he will take Pat in hand, get him a scholarship at a music college, and teach him personally. Although his good fortune is rather more than believable, the novel is powerful in characterizing Pat and making the reader share his inarticulate rage at the petty tyranny and injustice perpetrated by most of the adults in his life. Other characters are well realized, and some of the scenes, among them that of tipsy Bates trying to turn pages for Pat at the concert and those of the infighting in the school staff room, are very funny. Fanfare.

PENTECOST (*The Song of Pentecost**), title given to the leader of the Harvest Mice of Pentecost Farm. The second Pentecost explains that the term means Spring Festival and represents hope. Three mice bear the title in the story. The first is an old, tired mouse, who is worried

that the mice may not be able to survive the
hard times that urban encroachment has brought.
He strikes the bargain with Snake* in which the
mice will help Snake regain his Oily Green Pool
from wily Cousin* Snake in return for Snake
helping them to find a new home on Lickey Top.
He tends to ramble in his thinking and speech
and is relieved when he is eased out of his
position of leadership by a younger mouse. The
new Pentecost has from birth been considered an
oddity, since he has one inky black eye and one
that is blue as a cornflower. A sensible,
courageous fellow, good at planning and conflict resolution, he leads the expedition to its
destination, where he is accidentally slain by
two boys out hunting the red Fox* of Furrowfield. He is replaced by the third Pentecost, a
small mouse with misshapen ears who makes up
rhymes and enjoys poetry with Fox. His ears became misshapen because he didn't wash them as
the Old Aunts told him to when he was young. The
sawdust packed into his ears to keep him from
going deaf when the mice were in Woodpecker Wood
blended with the dirty wax and had to be drilled
out by a woodpecker.

THE PEPPERMINT PIG (Bawden*, Nina, Gollancz,
1975; Lippincott, 1975), story of one eventful
year in the life of the Greengrass family, which
they spend in Norfolk in the very early twentieth century. Events are seen mostly through the
eyes of Poll*, 9, who, having been banished
beneath the table for bad manners and having
fallen asleep there, wakes to overhear her
parents deep in a discussion she doesn't fully
understand. She does grasp that her father, a
coach painter, has admitted to stealing money
from the firm and, now unemployed, is going to
go to America to seek his fortune. Not until
later does she understand her mother's
bitterness nor the references to "the old man,"
though she does figure out that the real thief
is the son of Mr. Rowland, the owner, and she
has to agree with her brother Theo*, ten and a
half, that their father has long wanted to go
to America and may be seizing this good chance.
Poll and Theo, along with their mother, Emily*,
their sister, Lily, 14, and their brother,
George, 15, move to Norfolk to live on the

charity of their father's two older sisters,
Aunt* Sarah, thin, high-minded headmistress of
the local school, and Aunt* Harriet, merry,
red-faced teacher of the infants. Though Poll
has pale yellow hair and an angelic face and
Theo is delicate looking, smaller than Poll with
big, innocent blue eyes, they both have an
appetite for bloodthirsty stories, and Poll has
a strong will and a stubborn temper. Despite
such inconveniences as no longer having a maid
or indoor plumbing and their mother being forced
to return to her premarriage occupation of
dressmaking, Poll adjusts quickly and soon loves
the small town life. Theo has a harder time,
mainly because of Noah Bugg, a boy about his age
but much bigger, who torments him for being a
runt, yet he is not pleased when Poll takes his
side and attacks Noah. Noah's mother, Marigold,
makes snide remarks transparently disguised as
sympathy about "poor Emily" and, referring to
Father, says that "blood will out," a remark
that Poll broods over. To Poll, the most
important element in their Norfolk life is
Johnnie, the "peppermint pig," a runt piglet
Mother buys from the milkman for a shilling and,
on sudden impulse, pops into a pint beer mug on
the table. Johnnie becomes a house pet, clean
and usually well behaved, following the children
everywhere like a dog only with more brains than
a dog. When he eats up all the hot cross buns
set out to rise and Mother banishes him to the
hen house, Poll is so angry that she sets out
without permission to see her friend, Annie
Dowsett, child of a poor, scraggy family that
lives a long way out of town. Coming home she
loses her way and is almost run down by the mail
coach which she, terrified, thinks is the ghost
coach said to haunt Bride's Pit. This experience
has two results: having plumbed the depths of
terror, Poll no longer fears anything ordinary
and, having tended Annie's sick infant brother
and played with the three-year-old, who
afterward dies, Poll contracts scarlet fever and
is critically ill for weeks. In the meantime,
Noah has seen Theo steal an egg from the market
and blackmails him, threatening to tell Aunt
Sarah. Theo pays him with bits from a box of
gold leaf scraps, which Father had brought home
from the coach company and which Theo, with his

clever but overimaginative mind, says is the reason for Father losing his job, a story he half believes himself, even though Mr. Rowland, having discovered the truth, has called to apologize. This tortured relationship changes at the fair, when Theo, having grown during the year, attacks Noah and then thinks he has killed him, a fear that Poll shares, though Noah proves to be faking. Another mystery is cleared up when Poll discovers a tramp in Aunt Sarah's summer house and then learns it is Grandpa Greengrass, who deserted the family years ago but comes back occasionally for a handout and whom Father was shielding when he said he had stolen the Rowland money, since Grandpa had been in the office that day. For Poll, the tensions and disasters of the year are summed up when she comes home from school and finds that Johnnie has been sent to the butcher. Although Aunt Harriet has already bought her a puppy, which she names Mac, Poll is so stunned that she can't eat for days and faints at the sight of the carcasses in the butcher's window. George, who has always been a sympathetic older brother, finally interests her in buying a collar and leash for Mac and pays her for each small quantity of food she is able to force down. Even after she can eat again, Poll is afraid to look ahead, being sure that Father will never return since "blood will out." When he does come back and asks her what has happened during the year, the only thing she can think to say is, "Johnnie's dead," and the distance he has been from family concerns is indicated when he doesn't have any idea who Johnnie was. Point of view is so skillfully handled in the novel that the reader understands weaknesses, strains, and conflicts in the family which Poll only senses vaguely and which Theo, with his convoluted thinking, distorts. The characterization of all the Greengrass family and of many of the village people is sharp and keeps the novel interesting despite a seemingly meandering plot. The total effect is a far more moving book than the usual loss-of-a-pet story. Choice; Fanfare; Guardian.

PERDITA (*The Witch's Daughter**), orphan daughter of a foreign woman believed to be a witch. Raised by old Annie MacLaren at isolated

Luinpool, Perdita is thought to have second sight and is shunned by the other children of the island. Because Mr. Smith, for whom Annie keeps house, insists on as little contact as possible with other people, Perdita has not been sent to school and is shy and half-wild when the Hoggart children come to the island; she is not afraid to approach Janey* Hoggart only because Janey is blind. Perdita is so ignorant that she thinks the diamond she has been given is pretty glass. In some ways she is tough and calculating but at the same time she is vulnerable and yearns to have love and learning.

PETER AND WENDY (Barrie*, James, ill. F. D. Bedford, Hodder, 1911; Scribner, 1911), also called *Peter Pan* and *Peter Pan and Wendy*, classic story of the little boy who refused to grow up and of the children who have adventures with him in the Neverland. In the Darling family, the children, Wendy*, John, and Michael, have for their nurse a prim Newfoundland dog named Nana. Although she is a real treasure, Mr. Darling is afraid the neighbors think it odd, and when she shames him by discovering that he has poured his medicine into her bowl when he supposedly was taking it bravely as an example to Michael, he chains her in the yard before he and Mrs. Darling go out to dinner; consequently, there is no one watching in the nursery on the fateful night. It is not the first night Peter* Pan has come into the nursery. In fact, on a previous occasion Nana caught his shadow just as he flitted out the window, and Mrs. Darling folded it neatly and put it into a drawer. Now he has returned with his fairy companion, Tinker* Bell, to find the shadow, and Wendy wakes to see him sitting on the floor, crying because he can't stick it back on with soap. Wendy sews it on for him and tells him the end of "Cinderella," the first part of which he has overheard her mother telling. When she suggests that she could tell lots of stories to him and the Lost Boys with whom he lives, he teaches her and her brothers to fly, and they start out for the Neverland, "second to the right, and straight on till morning." As they approach the island they become separated, and Tinker Bell, jealous of Peter's attentions to Wendy, flies on ahead and tells the Lost Boys that the Wendy bird is coming and that Peter wants them to shoot it. Tootles, the boy always least successful at adventures, sees his opportunity to shine and fires an arrow. Wendy flutters to the ground. Fortunately she is not dead, so they build a little house around her and adopt her for their mother. In the Neverland, the Lost Boys, children who have fallen out of their prams when their nursemaids are looking the other way, are chased by the pirates, led by the villainous and elegant Captain* Hook, who in turn are followed by the redskins of the Piccaninnie tribe. The redskins are hunted by wild animals, the last being a gigantic crocodile, which, having swallowed a clock, ticks as it goes. This gives warning to Captain Hook, who fears it above all other things since in a previous fight Peter Pan cut off the pirate's right hand (now replaced by a vicious hook) and tossed it to the crocodile, which, having acquired the taste, now follows patiently, wanting more of the pirate leader. With Wendy acting as mother and her brothers joining the Lost Boys, the Darling children settle into Neverland life, living in the home under the ground, which each one enters by his special hollow tree, swimming in the lagoon, and joining in the many adventures. In one adventure, which is related in detail, the pirates capture the Indian princess, Tiger Lily, and leave her bound on Marooners Rock, but Peter saves her, winning the gratitude of the redskins, who thereafter guard the entrances to the home under ground. Although Wendy sometimes has a twinge of uneasiness about her own parents, all goes well until Peter tells her of his own attempt to go home, only to find the window shut and another baby in his mother's arms. Immediately Wendy marshals John and Michael to return to London, and when the other boys protest, she invites them all to come and live with the Darling family. Only Peter declines, but he proudly arranges to have Tinker Bell lead them back. Even as they prepare to leave, however, the pirates have attacked and all but wiped out the redskin tribe, and as each boy and Wendy emerges from the home underground, the pirates capture them and carry them off to their ship. Peter,

feigning indifference to their leaving, stays
below and defiantly leaves his medicine undrunk
when he falls asleep. Captain Hook, entering the
tree that Slightly, who drank too much water
and swelled, whittled larger than the others,
finds Peter asleep and foully drops poison into
his medicine. Wakened by Tinker Bell, who tells
him of the capture, Peter springs up to go to
the rescue, but first repents and starts to
drink his medicine. Tinker Bell intervenes and
drinks it first, then almost dies, but is saved
by Peter's appeal to all the children who are
dreaming to clap if they believe in fairies.
They create a strong applause that saves her
life. Then Peter sets off to the pirate ship,
which he boards by ticking like the crocodile,
thereby so terrifying the pirates that he is
able to cut the bonds of the boys and Wendy. In
a swashbuckling fight most of the pirates are
killed, and Peter defeats Captain Hook in hand
to hand combat and forces him to jump off the
ship into the jaws of the crocodile, which has
stopped ticking because the clock has run down.
They sail the pirate ship to the mainland,
return to the nursery, and receive a heartfelt
welcome from Nana and Mr. and Mrs. Darling, who
are more than happy to adopt all the boys, all
except Peter, who refuses to grow up and flies
back to the Neverland, with Mrs. Darling's
promise that Wendy can return each year for one
week of spring cleaning. After two years,
however, he forgets to come for her until she
is grown up with her own daughter, Jane, who
flies off with Peter at spring cleaning time, as
years later, Jane's daughter, Margaret, does.
The idea of flying off to a life of adventure
is naturally appealing to children, but what
individualizes the novel is the style, aimed at
least as much at adults, with author asides,
clever satirical passages, and deliberately arch
comments. Some of these, like Mr. Darling's
insistence on living in the dog kennel to
expiate his guilt (and his pride in the
admiration this engenders), seem to many critics
too cute, and some of the concepts are rather
dated, but there are also genuinely funny
situations and telling wit and irony. Books Too
Good; Children's Classics; Choice.

PETER BEAUMARCHAIS (*We Couldn't Leave Dinah**), sober French youth, 15, whose mother was German. He informs Caroline* and Mick* Templeton that his father, whom they have dismissed as a tiresome, fussy, little traitor, works for the Germans only because the Germans have threatened to torture their relatives who are still in Germany and is really a double agent working for the British against the Germans. Peter and the children work out an elaborate system of signals whereby he uses fishing rods to inform them of his efforts to find an escape for them to England.

PETER BECKFORD (*The Grange at High Force**), mechanically inclined youngest son of the rector of All Saints Church in Darnley. It is Peter who has designed the ballista that Guns* Kelly and Admiral* Sir John Beauchamp-Troubridge help the boys to test, and it is Peter's unsuccessful repair of the brakes on his bike, the Yellow Peril, that causes the accident leading to their first acquaintance with the Admiral. During the book he purchases an ancient tricycle, repairs and paints it, and transfers to it the many gadgets from the bike. He then christens it the Yellow Peril II.

PETER BERESFORD (*Thursday's Child**), dreamy, bookish orphan whose "borrowing" of three novels precipitates the escape from St. Luke's. Although he is ten, just the same age as Margaret* Thursday, he seems in many ways younger since he lacks her imagination and drive. What he minds most about the orphanage is that there are no books and no time to read. After Margaret discovers that he has taken the books from Mr. Windle's library and insists that he leave a note to the schoolteacher asking her to return them for him, he typically keeps out *Bleak House* because he has not finished reading it. On the canal he tries hard but does not have the stamina to be a legger and, being naturally frail and run-down from lack of food, he faints on the tow path. At the theater he is a miserable failure as an actor, but he does quite well selling tickets.

PETER CLEVERTON (*The Far-Distant Oxus**), one of

the six children who participate in the "expeditionary force" down the Oxus to the sea during summer holiday. A pleasant boy, he is almost indistinguishable from Anthony*, whose age he is, except that he is the builder of the group, their acknowledged architect and carpenter.

PETER DYSON (*A Grass Rope**), about eleven, son of the owner of Unicorn Inn in the Yorkshire hills. He has just sat for examinations for Thornton Grammar School and so is somewhat in awe of Adam* Forrest, the school's Head Boy, when Adam first arrives to paint the inn, but he loosens up later on. A mixture of qualities, he is sometimes an earnest boy yet at other times overly casual. He dearly loves his hound, Hewlin, which is a descendant of the hound that, story has it, refused to be enticed by magic into Yowncorn Yat, and which Peter often addresses as "honey" and amusingly confuses with the original hound. Peter employs the local dialect, half believes the legend, and advances the story considerably when he decides in the middle of the night to blow the horn that Adam has removed from the inn signboard. On the fringes of most of the action, he is nevertheless an important figure in the plot.

PETER MCNAIR (*The Team**; *Prove Yourself a Hero**), competent, cheerful son of a slave-driving horse dealer, who becomes an expert rider and trainer. In the earlier *Fly-by-Night*, Mr.* McNair sells the pony that Peter has trained, loves, and has been promised for his own, and Peter, deeply disturbed, leaves home and is sent to live with the family of Ruth* Hollis as a foster son while he sees a psychiatrist. His father's marriage to a comfortable Italian woman makes his home more endurable, and Peter returns but continues to be in conflict with his father in *The Team*, in which he trains and rides the unmanagable Sirius against his father's orders. In *Prove Yourself a Hero*, he is with Jonathan* Meredith when the wealthy boy is abducted, and he is designated by the kidnappers to deliver the ransom money. He comports himself with courage and cleverness, and he understands how Jonathan's strained relationship with his mother has brought on his feelings of guilt after his return as well as his subsequent nightmares. It is Peter who suggests the solution, to find the kidnappers and "prove yourself a hero." In a later book, *Free Rein*, Jonathan runs away from school to Peter, who is now working at his brother's horse training farm, and together they leave to camp out in a derelict house so they can train a difficult horse for the Grand National. Although a broken collar bone prevents Peter from the ride, which has been his single-minded goal, he remains for the most part good-natured and makes some progress toward becoming a professional jockey, which has always been his ambition. In his lack of worry about his family's expectations, his nonintellectual casualness about school, and his ability to put failures philosophically behind him, Peter serves as a foil for Jonathan.

PETER PAN (*Peter and Wendy**), boy who can fly. He lives with fairies and the Lost Boys in the Neverland and refuses to grow up. Peter is brave and clever, but also cocky, self-centered, and inconsistent, quite likely to forget a friend or an adventure. He is distinguished by having all his first teeth, a quality that makes all females want to mother him, though Wendy* Darling, Tiger Lily the redskin princess, and Tinker* Bell the fairy, all seem to want something more from him than the love of a respectful son. He is the epitome of childhood, which author James M. Barrie* sees as "gay and innocent and heartless."

PETER PAN. See *Peter and Wendy*.

PETER PAN AND WENDY. See *Peter and Wendy*.

PETER PEVENSIE (*The Lion, the Witch and the Wardrobe**; *Prince Caspian**; *The Last Battle**), the adventurous, take-charge, eldest of the four Pevensie children, which include Susan*, Edmund*, and Lucy*, and one of the major figures in the Narnia* series. He becomes High King in Narnia after the defeat of the White Witch, Queen* Jadis. Peter is an open and honorable boy, who in *The Lion, the Witch and the Wardrobe* owns up to Aslan* that he may have been partly at fault for Edmund's defecting to the Witch since he was bad-tempered with his brother. Peter draws first blood in the struggle against the queen, when he slays the queen's terrible Wolf, which has attacked Susan. Aslan knights him on the spot. In *Prince Caspian*, he is the nobly speaking High King who assumes leadership, proving his worth as a political leader and warrior. A fine aspect of his characterization is that Lewis* portrays him both as boy and as king without compromising either role by cuteness or contrivance. Peter plays a small part in *The Last Battle*, the concluding book, where he appears as one of the Seven Kings and Queens of eternal Narnia, assisting Aslan in small ways and commenting with Lucy on events of the termination of Narnia as they occur. He seems older now and more mature in attitude. It is learned that he and the others have died in a railway accident and will stay permanently in Aslan's realm.

PETER POSSIT (*The Circus Is Coming**), twelve-year-old boy who runs away with his younger sister to an uncle in a circus rather than go to an orphanage. Peter is very bright but has been educated by ignorant tutors and has been taught to consider himself superior, so he has a hard time adjusting to the new schools and the new life. Naturally argumentative, he clashes with the other circus children and with his uncle, Gus* Possit, but he makes a real effort to change and is hurt when Gus continues to be annoyed with him and when the circus girls refer to him as "Little Lord Fauntleroy." His natural affinity for horses saves him, and he becomes a skilled rider in a single season.

PETER SIMPSON (*Moses Beech**), 17, runaway who lives with independent old Moses* Beech for nine months and learns much about country life, self-reliance, and love. Peter's father has lived mostly on the dole, expecting his wife to work at an unregistered job which will not be reported to the welfare people but for which she will be underpaid. He has insisted that Peter leave school and get a job, presumably to help support him, even though the boy does well in school and is unable to find employment. Peter

has left home largely in frustration and in an
effort to make something of himself and be
different from his father. His friend Susan*
Bailey points out that he resembles his father
in his stubbornness. Town-bred, Peter has never
imagined a life without television, movies, fast
foods, and the crowded slums where he was
raised, and at first he has difficulty adjusting
to the loneliness and simplicity of Moses*
Beech's cottage. In his relationship with
Moses, Peter finds his first positive role
model, and in his relationship with Susan, his
first real love. At the end of the book he has
lost both, but he has gained some self-
confidence and self-respect.

PETER'S ROOM (Forest*, Antonia, Faber, 1961),
Christmas holiday adventure of the Marlow family
featured in *Falconer's Lure* and a number of
her other school and vacation stories. As the
younger members of the large family return from
boarding school to Trennels, the Marlows' farm,
Peter, 14, often called Binks by his sisters, is
the first to arrive and discovers a room full of
junk over the old shippen, or cow shed, which is
now used to store wood and coal. Among other
treasures he finds as he cleans out the rubbish
is a trunk full of the old farm records,
including a letter about a sixteen-year-old
Marlow named Malise in 1645, who had just left
the Puritan family to fight for the Royalists.
He also finds an assortment of weapons which he
hangs on the walls. Although he has thought of
it as his own hide-out, it is soon shared by his
sisters, Ginty (Virginia), almost fifteen, the
twins, Nicola and Lawrie, 13, and their friend
from the next farm, Patrick Merrick, 15.
Continued heavy snowfall keeps them from riding,
even though Ginty has been given a fine new
horse, Catkin, for her coming birthday, Patrick
has his own hunter and allows Nicola to use his
old pony, Buster, and Peter is allowed to ride
the farm saddle horse. They gather in Peter's
room around the fireplace, roast potatoes and
chestnuts, and get to talking about the Bronte
family, about whom Ginty must do a school
project, and the imaginary countries of Gondal
and Angria that the Brontes invented. They
decide to "do their own Gondal," making up and

acting out a romantic, swashbuckling story in which Lawrie is Jason, the young king of Exina, and the others are members of the Palladian Guard, sent by the wicked Regent ostensibly to escort the king on a mission to his cousin in Angora but actually into an ambush designed to kill the king. Peter takes the name of Malise, Patrick becomes Rupert, most daring of the officers, Ginty is his great admirer and friend, Crispian, and Nicola is Nicholas. Except for Nicola, who goes along with the game rather self-consciously, they get more and more wrapped up in the story, each one thinking out other parts of the history of his character and beginning to feel the story as more real and certainly more interesting than the other holiday activities. They are interrupted by two major events, the Twelfth Night dance at the Merricks' and, with the weather breaking, the first fox hunt of the new year. Despite a good deal of discussion and contrivance about suitable dresses for all six girls, the only major occurrence at the Merrick's party is that Patrick and Ginty lock themselves into the chapel of the lavish house and "Gondal" a bit on their own, a scene in which Ginty becomes Rosina, daughter of the Regent, who is in love with Rupert. The hunt is described in detail, mostly from the point of view of Nicola, though there are bits through the eyes of Peter, who is not as good a rider as he wishes and gets a broken collar bone in a fall, and Lawrie, who must rent a riding academy hack and feels very put upon. They return as soon as possible to Peter's room and the game, in which Rupert betrays the others rather than face torture when captured, then, discovered in his treachery, puts a pistol to his own head. At that point, Nicola, sensing that the game has gone too far, protests and strikes the pistol from his hand with her sword. The ancient weapon, one Peter had hung on his wall, knocks against the table and fires, breaking a window and startling the others out of their make-believe. Nicola refuses to go on with the story, and Peter follows suit, telling the others to get out, that he no longer wants to share his room, though actually he is disaffected with the character of Malise since he has discovered that the real Malise was a traitor in the English Civil War. Lawrie, the one who has enjoyed the acting more than any of the others, is heartbroken, but Ginty and Patrick, pulled back from the verge of a romantic episode, philosophically decide to go riding instead. The three older Marlow girls, Karen, who is at Oxford, Rowan, who runs the farm, and Ann, who is kindly and scorned by the others, are in the fringes of the action but play no important roles. The point of view changes throughout, being mostly Peter's in the early part of the book and shifting to Ginty and Patrick for much of the story, though occasionally becoming that of Lawrie or Nicola, who, having spent the previous summer falconing with Patrick, is hurt that Ginty, the prettiest of the Marlow girls, now is Patrick's main interest. The Gondal episodes are cleverly inserted in italic type, interrupted by discussions and arguments by the youngsters, and are more compelling than the realistic main story. Information about the Brontes is provided, though too much and clumsily, and the family interplay often becomes tedious, but as a study of how the creative process takes hold and seems to run itself and control its authors, the novel has an interesting central theme. Carnegie Com.

PEW (*Treasure Island**), blind pirate who appears, wearing a great green shade over his eyes and nose and a huge old tattered sea-cloak with a hood, at the Admiral Benbow Inn and gives the black spot to Billy* Bones. Jim* Hawkins, the narrator, says, "I never saw in my life a more dreadful-looking figure." Long* John Silver says that Pew spent 1,200 pounds in a year and then for two years he was starving-- begging, stealing, and cutting throats--and still starving. Although he is run down and killed by the revenue men in the fifth chapter, he is mentioned frequently, and his memory haunts the book.

PEYTON, K. M. (KATHLEEN WENDY PEYTON) (1929-), born in Birmingham, Warwickshire; artist, teacher and novelist. She attended Wimbledon High School and Manchester Art School, graduat- ing with an Art Teacher's Diploma in 1951. She

taught art at Northampton High School and has
illustrated several of her own novels. She has
written under her maiden name, Kathleen Herald,
and her pseudonym comes from her collaboration
in her earliest novels with her husband, Michael
Peyton. Among their works is *Windfall** (Oxford,
1962; as *Sea Fever*, World, 1963), a story of
fishing boats and sailing competitions in the
late nineteenth century. Her interest in sailing, acquired from her husband, is also reflected in books she wrote alone, among them *The
Maplin Bird** (Oxford, 1964; World, 1965), set in
the mid-nineteenth century on the Sussex coast,
*The Plan for Birdsmarsh** (Oxford, 1965; World,
1966), a modern story of a fight against the
commercial development of coastal land, and
*Thunder in the Sky** (Oxford, 1966; World, 1967),
about the sailing barges that carried supplies
to France during World War I. Peyton's best-
known novels, however, are concerned with horses
and fox hunting, particularly the Flambards
books: *Flambards** (Oxford, 1967; World, 1968),
*The Edge of the Cloud** (Oxford, 1969; World,
1970), *Flambards in Summer** (Oxford, 1969;
World, 1970), and *Flambards Divided* (Oxford,
1981; Philomel, 1982). The second of these, *The
Edge of the Cloud*, which won the Carnegie Medal,
is primarily about the early development of aviation just prior to World War I. Her two books
that fall most into the pattern of the "pony
club books," though excellent examples of the
genre, are *Fly-by-Night* (Oxford, 1968; World,
1969) and *The Team** (Oxford, 1975; Crowell,
1976), which tell of Ruth* Hollis's single-
minded determination to own a horse and to
compete in the pony club events despite her
family's lack of interest and funds for the
sport. Ruth appears again as girlfriend and
finally wife in the Pennington series, *Pennington's Seventeenth Summer** (Oxford, 1970; as
Pennington's Last Term, Crowell, 1971), *The
Beethoven Medal** (Oxford, 1971; Crowell, 1972),
and *Pennington's Heir* (Oxford, 1973; Crowell,
1974), but the focus is shared by Pat* Pennington a big, surly, and extremely talented boy
who makes his way from school to prison to the
concert stage, with many difficulties along the
way. Both Pennington and Ruth appear again in
Marion's Angels (Oxford, 1979), but the emphasis

there shifts to Marion Carver, an intense, imaginative child with a passionate interest in a crumbling medieval church near her home. This habit of bringing characters from one book into another is exhibited again in *Prove Yourself a Hero** (Oxford, 1977; World, 1978), a story of the kidnapping of Jonathan* Meredith, a character from *The Team*. Jonathan is also the protagonist in *A Midsummer Night's Death** (Oxford, 1978; Collins, 1979), a murder mystery set in a boarding school, and its sequel, *Free Rein* (Oxford, 1983; Philomel, 1983). In a different vein, *The Right-Hand Man* (Oxford, 1979) is about a swashbuckling Georgian coach- man. In a rare dip into fantasy, Peyton in *A Pattern of Roses** (Oxford, 1972; Crowell, 1973) tells the story of two artistic boys who live in the same room some sixty years apart, the modern boy experiencing many of the events that occurred to the other one generations before he was born. All her novels are distinguished by vivid descriptive writing and believable characters. Five of them have been commended for the Carnegie Medal, ten have been included in the *Horn Book* Fanfare lists, *A Pattern of Roses* has been named a Children's Classic, and *Prove Yourself a Hero* is on the Junior High Contemporary Classics list. She has also writ- ten a biography of Fred Archer, the jockey, *Dear Fred* (Bodley, 1981; Philomel, 1981).

PHAEDRUS (*The Mark of the Horse Lord**), gladia- tor known as Red Phaedrus who wins his wooden foil, and therefore his freedom, by killing his only friend among the men of the arena. At first so aimless and uncertain of himself that he panics, gets drunk, and lands in jail, he grows and develops in character as he impersonates Midir* of the Dalriadains, although for a while he plays the part mostly for the reckless sport of it. At first he is able to convince the people that he is Midir by relying on the information the real Midir has drilled into him and by falling back on the swagger he developed for the arena. Gradually the rights and needs of the people become so important to him that he forgets he is not the rightful king and leads them in their war with the Caledones with real dedication and purpose. His relations with his wife, Murna*, also develop from dismay at the idea of marrying her, to cool indifference, to curiosity, and finally to deep love. In the end he does what the true king must do in times of trouble to his people and sacrifices himself for their good.

PHILIP D'AUBIGNY (*Knight Crusader**), young noble born in Outremer, as the Normans call the Holy Land, who loses his father in battle with the Turks, is prisoner for four years in Damascus, escapes, serves with Richard* I in his attempt to retake Jerusalem, and travels with his forces to England, where he claims ancestral lands in the Welsh Marches. An impulsive boy, Philip learns self-control when he serves as secretary and servant during his imprisonment. He remains surprisingly modest despite gaining great recognition for his outstanding feats of valor.

PHILIP HOLBEIN (*The Robbers**), nine-year-old who has always lived with his grandmother and talks in the quaintly grown-up way of a child raised among educated adults. When he is forced to live with his father, whom he scarcely knows, and a new stepmother, he is polite and well behaved but makes mistakes because the rules are different from those he knows. A child of strong emotions, he loves his grandmother, his stepmother, his new friend, Darcy* Jones, and Darcy's black sister-in-law, Addie*, admires Darcy's brother, Bing*, and hates his own self-centered father. His intelligent but naive view of fairness shows up the shallowness of the conventional attitudes of right and wrong.

PHILIP MARTIN (*The Summer People**), protagonist of almost seventeen who secretly carries on a summer romance with Ann* Tarrant but eventually marries Sylvia Pilling, daughter of his father's business partner. Philip is respectful of his father but is often at odds with him, most recently because his father refuses to buy him a sailboat. He is occasionally on the outs with his older sister, Paula*, who, he acknowledges, is indeed put upon by their chauvinistic father, and readily goes along with Sylvia's idea that they pretend to be sweethearts while pursuing other romances. Philip tells his story fairly honestly and informs the reader that he knows his relationship with Ann can come to nothing because she is not of his social class. While he admits Ann excites him sexually and he necks with Brenda Fox in the back of a car at her provocation, he resists getting sexually involved with Ann. Although he is not an unfeeling snob, he tends to be passive and takes Paula's informing on him too much in stride. He is likeable and just complex enough to remain interesting, however, and his narrative serves well to give the reader the sense of the mores of the time and of a last idyllic summer before World War II changes things forever.

PICARD, BARBARA LEONIE (1917-   ), born in Richmond, Surrey; folklorist, short story writer and novelist. She was educated at St. Katharine's School, Wantage, Berkshire, and has had a distinguished career as a reteller of myths and hero tales. Her well known collections include *Tales of Norse Gods and Heroes* (Oxford, 1953), *Tales of the British People* (Ward, 1961; Criterion, 1961), *Hero-Tales from the British Isles* (Ward, 1963; Criterion, 1963), and similar volumes of French, German, Persian, and Celtic tales, as well as retellings of *The Odyssey*, *The Iliad*, and the stories of King Arthur, Rama, and William Tell. She has also published a number of books of short stories, all in the folktale tradition but literary tales of her own invention, including *The Mermaid and the Simpleton* (Oxford, 1949; Criterion, 1970), *The Lady of the Linden Tree* (Oxford, 1954; Criterion, 1962), *The Faun and the Woodcutter's Daughter* (Oxford, 1951; Criterion, 1964), and *The Goldfinch Garden: Seven Tales* (Harrap, 1963; Criterion, 1965). Her novels have all been historical, the best known being *Ransom for a Knight** (Oxford, 1956; Walck, 1967), the story of a journey undertaken by a fourteenth-century ten-year-old girl from Sussex to Scotland to ransom her father and brother. Others include *Lost John** (Oxford, 1962; Criterion, 1963), a story set in the late twelfth century about an outlaw who resembles a realistic Robin Hood, and *One is One** (Oxford, 1965; Holt, 1966), the story of an artistic boy who is a misfit in his fourteenth-century family and who escapes from the monastery where he has been sent, finds adventure and recognition, and returns at last to the contemplative life. Two of these works were commended for the Carnegie Medal and all three are included on the *Horn Book* Fanfare lists. Picard also edited the *Encyclopaedia of Myths and Legends of All Nations* (Ward, 1962).

THE PIEMAKERS (Cresswell*, Helen, ill. W. T. Mars, Faber, 1967; Lippincott, 1968), humorous fantasy set in the village of Danby Dale, England, in the pre-Industrial Revolution days of cottage industries, candles, and carriages. The Rollers are piemakers, proud craftsmen of large, crusty meat pies, pungent with herbs and succulent with rich meats: steady, hardworking Arthy*; acerbic, status-conscious Jem*, his wife; and their ten-year-old daughter, Gravella*, who shrewdly observes the action and sometimes affects it. At book's opening, Arthy has received a coveted commission from the king to bake a pie that will feed 200 people. He uses the king's own recipe, which his brother and piemaking rival, Crispin of Gorby Dale, supplies him, and ironically produces his first failure--too much pepper. Jem is sure Crispin engineered the disaster to embarrass his brother, but Gravella thinks she may have copied out the recipe wrong. At any rate, to save face, Arthy engages in arson, burning up both bakehouse and pie before anyone else discovers the mistake. He then falls into a depression and refuses to bake any more, upsetting Jem and worrying even Gravella. Then a king's messenger comes to town and makes an important announcement. The king has declared a contest: to the maker of the best and biggest pie shall go a prize of One Hundred Guineas and the right to carry the Royal Coat of Arms above his door. As the Rollers ponder the implications of this in a customary family conference, a delegation of townsmen arrives at the door. They urge Arthy to enter the contest, pledging support and suggesting he make a pie big enough for 2,000 people. Arthy rejoices in the prospect, and preparations begin. The whole village participates, converting Farmer Leary's barn into a bakehouse, assembling ingredients for Arthy's

own special Standard Meat Recipe, and even
commissioning a blacksmith upriver to fashion a
pie dish which they then float down the Dan,
disguised as a boat. On the day of the contest,
a carnival atmosphere pervades Danby Dale.
Sixteen beautiful pies from as many villages
decorate the meadow just outside Farmer Leary's
barn, displayed grandly on trestles. After the
king has tasted each of them, the Danby pie is
rolled out from the barn. So huge it takes all
the strength of twenty men to move it, it is
immediately declared the winner and deemed a
"miracle under that blue sky, standing among
the grass and clover like some enormous fruit.
It was seen and yet impossible to believe."
Being true craftsmen, Jem and Arthy subsequently
discuss how they might have made it better.
Gravella notices how enthusiastically her
father contributes ideas to the discussion and
happily realizes that Arthy is "back in
piemaking again." The details of the family
business are worked out with precision, and the
author never resorts to sentimentality or undue
tension to maintain the plot. The characters are
a skillful blend of realism and caricature. The
humor, both low-keyed and very funny, stems
naturally from character, action, and real-
sounding conversation. Gravella's perceptive
insights into her parents' behavior contribute
to the amusement, though her observations would
probably have more appeal to adults than to
children. Although the author's invention and
meticulous attention to detail give the book
its flavor of actuality, clever authenticating
touches appear also in the preface and epilogue.
There, tongue-in-cheek, the author claims that
certain artifacts verify her tale, among them an
oblong duckpond that can be seen on the Danby
Dale green. She maintains this is the very pie
dish Arthy used. Choice.

PIERS MEDLEY (*The Iron Lily**), master of
Mantlemass*, brother of Richard*, and true
father of Lilias Godman. Unlike his brother, who
acts quickly, Piers is more thoughtful and
introverted. He lost his wife many years
before, just after his prim, over-religious
daughter Catherine was born. Piers dreams of
rebuilding the stud line for which the family

had once been famous and which came to an end years previously when Ghylls Hatch, the stable farm, burned. He and his ward, Robin, spend hours poring over the Mantlemass stud book and planning how to reassemble the herd. At the end, repulsed in his efforts to enclose a particular area now considered a forest common as a pasture for his horses, he and Robin decide to rebuild Ghylls Hatch, which is where Robin and Ursula will live when they marry. Piers's great capacity for charity can be seen by his having taken into his home Robin and Robin's sister, Lucy, even though they were the children of the man whose actions led to the death of Piers's wife.

PIGEON POST (Ransome*, Arthur, ill. author, Cape, 1936; Lippincott, 1937), sixth in a series of twelve holiday adventures about the Walker and Blackett families, this one set in the lake country in the early 1930s. Roger* and Titty* Walker, coming by train to stay at Beckford, the Blackett home on the lake, receive a pigeon basket at a station some ten miles from their destination with instructions to loose the bird immediately and bring the basket on. Thus, they are involved even before their arrival in the new schemes of Nancy* Blackett, and when they do arrive they find their older siblings, John* and Susan*, Nancy's sister, Peggy*, and the two Callum children, scientific Dick and imaginative Dorothea (who entered the Swallows and Amazons series in the fourth book, *Winter Holiday*), all camping in the Blackett yard and ready to start a mining company, determined to find the gold rumored to be on High Topps and thereby to tie down their roving uncle, Captain* Flint (Jim Turner), to mining in the area. First, they consult an elderly resident, Slater Bob, whom they find in an old digging getting slates, and learn they will have to camp at some distance from the lake to be able to search for the workings he describes. Some of them go on an expedition to find a farm where they can get milk; others row into Rio to get supplies; and Dick concentrates on rigging a bell that will sound in the house when a pigeon arrives so that they can send messages home by pigeon-post. Mrs. Blackett, busy with workmen remodeling her

house, distractedly sees them off to the only
camp they could arrange, right in the orchard of
the Tyson farm, where, because of drought, Mrs.
Tyson will not even let them do their own
cooking and hovers constantly. They have left at
Beckford a box arranged for an Aardvark they
believe Captain Flint is sending them, although
he has referred to it only as Timothy. They feel
compelled to hurry since a stranger whom they
call "Squashy Hat" is staying at a nearby farm
and seems to be seeking the same gold they are
after. In the next couple of days the young
people make two significant discoveries: Titty
finds she has some ability as a dowser and
discovers a spring upon the Tor, which allows
them to move up to a camp made by charcoal
burners, and Roger stumbles upon the old
diggings that seem to be the gold mine described
by Slater Bob. With tremendous energy they dig,
grind up, and pan the ore, trying to get enough
to make an ingot to show Captain Flint. Dick
designs and the others build a blast furnace,
powered with the bellows from the Blackett
fireplace. While the older ones work on this,
the younger ones lurk and keep track of Squashy
Hat. When they see him appear out of an old
tunnel, they explore it and, following it along,
hear it collapse behind them. Dick points out
calmly that they can follow Squashy Hat's
footprints and get out wherever he got in. They
travel right through the mountain and come out
where Slater Bob is working. From him they learn
that he has been talking to Squashy Hat. With
very little time left, they construct the blast
furnace and keep it working through the night
until the bellows break. Hopefully, they open
it, only to find that the crucible has broken
and the metal disappeared. Disturbed and feeling
guilty, Dick takes the remaining pinch of dust
and bicycles to Beckford where he thinks that he
will prove the metal is gold by seeing if it
will dissolve in aqua regia. He is interrupted
by Captain Flint, returned from South America,
who shows him that what he has thought is gold
is really copper. In the meantime, careless
picnickers have started a brush fire. Titty,
Roger, and Dorothea, sleeping in camp, awaken to
the smoke, send off a pigeon with a message,
"Fire Help Quick," and then fight the spreading

blaze. Nancy, John, Peggy, and Susan are in the mine when they notice Squashy Hat resting nearby and then see the fire. They save him by taking him into the mine while the fire passes over, then run across the smoking ground to the camp. At Beckford, the pigeon message galvanizes Captain Flint, who calls the local fire fighters, then with Mrs. Blackett and Dick drives madly to the nearest point to the camp. When the fire is out and Mrs. Tyson, who thinks they started it, is placated, Captain Flint introduces them to Squashy Hat. He turns out to be Timothy, a mining friend from South America, who has been searching High Topps for the copper they have found. The story has many implausibilities, notably why any mother as concerned as Mrs. Blackett that the children have fresh milk every morning and get to bed at proper times would be unconcerned at their wandering unsupervised over an area known to be pocketed with old mining diggings and even exploring crumbling tunnels. The characterization depends mostly upon knowing other books in the series. Carnegie Winner.

PIGLET (*Winnie-the-Pooh**; *The House at Pooh Corner**), very small and timid friend of Pooh* Bear and Christopher* Robin. Piglet lives in a home which bears the sign, "TRESPASSERS W," which he believes is short for his grandfather's name, Trespassers William. Although fearful, Piglet often joins Pooh in his more daring adventures, like hunting the Woozle and trapping the Heffalump, and he bravely takes the place of Roo, who is kidnapped by Rabbit, and courageously lets Pooh and Owl hoist him on a pulley to the letter box (located in the ceiling after Owl's house has blown down), so that he can squeeze through and summon help. Pooh makes up his longest hum about Piglet, with a verse that starts, "O gallant Piglet (PIGLET)! Ho!" Under its influence Piglet does a Noble Thing, giving up his home to Owl and going to live with Pooh.

PILGRIM'S PROGRESS (Bunyan*, John; original title: *The Pilgrim's Progress from This World to That Which Is to Come . . .*, Ponder, 1678; cited edition abridged by Mary Godolphin, ill. Robert

Lawson, pub. Lippincott, 1939; Godolphin text originally pub. McLoughlin Bros, 1884), classic fantasy novel about the journeys of a man named Christian and his wife to The Celestial City of Zion, or, as obvious Christian allegory, about the progress of the soul toward everlasting life. The story is in two parts, both related by "I," presumably the author, who reports the adventures of Christian and his wife as he sees them in several dreams. Christian, dressed in tatters, battered by life, and burdened by sins, cries out for help in saving his soul and escaping from The City of Destruction before it is consumed by fire. Evangelist advises him to seek The Wicket Gate, where he will be given instructions for his salvation. Christian sets out amidst the wails of loved ones and friends, with a great load of sins on his back and a comforting and exhorting Book in his hands. On the plain outside the City, he is intercepted by two men, Obstinate and Pliable, who have been sent by neighbors and family to fetch him home. He resists their entreaties and persuades Pliable to accompany him. They fall into the Slough of Despond, where Pliable, true to character, soon gives up and turns back, but Christian ploughs doggedly onward through the mire, and is assisted out by a man named Help, who tells him the Slough is composed of human doubts and fears. He meets good-looking, persuasive Mr. Worldly Wiseman from the town of Carnal Policy, who suggests he consult Legality, or Legality's son, Civility, but Christian finds the path to where they live too steep and the flames en route too fearful. Evangelist says these men are false guides but that the man at the Gate will forgive Christian for being enticed by them since he is a person of good will and love. At The Wicket Gate, Christian states his case to the gatekeeper, Good-will, who tells him he must bear his load until he arrives at the place of Deliverance. Farther on he comes to the house of Mr. Interpreter, who shows him a painting of Christ and gives him more instruction, after which he continues on a route hemmed in on each side by the high wall of Salvation. When he arrives at a tall cross with a tomb at its foot, Christian's load of sins falls into the mouth of the tomb, and he is finally and gratefully freed of that burden. Three Bright Ones strip off his rags and dress him in a new robe, put a protective mark on his face, and give him a scroll bearing a certain seal. He next encounters three sleeping, chained men, Simple, Sloth, and Presumption, seeks to help them but fails and then meets Formalist and Hypocrisy, who have attempted to short-cut the route to Zion and failed. He drinks of the Spring of Life, climbs the Hill of Difficulty, meets Timorous and Mistrust, who are too fearful to continue on the quest for Zion, and takes a nap in a cave, after which he discovers he's lost his scroll and must return to the cave to recover it, scolding himself all the while for his sloth. He comes to a great house called Beautiful which is guarded by two wild beasts and a man named Watchful. Here he is instructed by four maids, Discretion, Prudence, Piety, and Charity, and sleeps the night in a room called Peace. Before he departs the next morning they show him such blessed artifacts as the rod of Moses and Jael's nail, give him a sword and coat of mail, and escort him to The Vale of Humiliation. Here he is beset by the winged monster, Prince Appolyon, whom he had once served and who attacks him, demanding he again give allegiance. After a half-day's hard struggle, Christian is sorely wounded but dispatches the creature with one lucky, well-placed blow, then is healed of his hurts by leaves provided him from the tree of life by a disembodied hand. He next passes through the Valley of the Shadow of Death, a place of drought and pits where no man dwells and where he meets two struggling men who complain of evil men who have no laws, but Christian defiantly proceeds anyway, drawn sword in hand, past quags and ditches and encouraged by a voice, saying, "Though I walk through the valley...." Once out, he is soon joined by a good man whose name is Faithful. The two come to a town called Vanity, where a fair is in progress and whose wares are vain and void of worth, a place of fools and rogues who taunt and jeer the travelers, beat and cage them, and submit them to numerous tribulations. Faithful is tried in the court of Lord Hategood, testified against by Envy, Superstition, and Pick-thank, and is judged

guilty by twelve jurors, among them Mr. Malice,
Mr. No-good, Mr. Enmity, and Mr. Cruelty. His
life ended with scourge and stake, Faithful is
taken up by car and steeds to The Celestial
City, accompanied by melody of harp and lute.
Christian breaks free and is joined by a new
companion, Hopeful. At Christian's suggestion
they turn aside into By-Path Meadow, where they
get lost and arrive at Doubting Castle, whose
lord is Giant Despair. He imprisons them in his
dungeon for three days without food and water
and beats them, hoping to drive them to the sin
of suicide, but Hopeful keeps up their spirits,
and Christian discovers in his pouch a key named
Promise by which they unlock their prison and
escape. They next come to The Delectable
Mountains, which are owned by Immanuel, the Lord
of the Hill, a place rich in fruits and green-
ery. They are greeted, helped, and encouraged
by four shepherds, Knowledge, Experience,
Watchful, and Sincere. The shepherds take them
to the tops of the hills Error, Mount Caution,
and Clear, for instructive purposes, and warn
them not to sleep on The Enchanted Ground.
Proceeding, Christian and Hopeful deplore the
lack of understanding of a brisk youth they meet
named Ignorance, and at a fork in the road they
are led astray by Flatterer and caught in a
net. Once released, they resist the urge to
sleep on The Enchanted Ground and arrive at the
sweet Land of Beulah, where the birds sing all
day long, the sun shines day and night, and they
have splendid views of Zion, whose brightness
and magnificence cause them to fall ill of
sheer joy. They are met by two white-robed men
with shining faces, who tell them they must now
cross the deep stream that circles the City, and
they do so keeping in mind Christ's words that
he will accompany all those forced to cross
deep streams in life. After that, they walk up
the hill to Zion with ease and speed, led by
the two men, are met by hosts of saints, and,
upon entry, are clad in golden robes. At that
point, having had a glimpse of the bliss that
awaits Christian and Hopeful inside Zion, the
speaker awakens wistfully from his dream. In
Part II, which is less well known, the author
dreams again, this time of the salvation of
Christiana, Christian's wife, to whom a messen-

ger appears one day bearing a note from
Christian exhorting her and their four sons to
join him in Zion. Having dreamed that he is in
bliss, she resists the pessimism of Mrs. Timorous about the journey, remains steadfast in her
resolve to depart, and is accompanied at the
beginning by helpful, kind-hearted, young Mercy,
whom she engages as maid. The six pass through
the Slough of Despond without incident and
arrive at the immense field gate, where Mercy,
who has been afraid that she will be thought too
bold in joining the wayfarers, is also accepted
by the Lord of the gate. He feeds them and sets
them on the right path. They proceed, Christiana
singing a hymn, but encounter bad men who refuse
to let them continue. They are rescued by men
from the gate lodge, among them Reliever, come
to the house of the Interpreter, where they are
met by Innocent, a maid who announces their
arrival with great joy. After they have been
instructed in Christian piety, given food and
robes white as snow, and marked by signs that
identify them, they leave singing hymns and
preceded by the courageous knight, Great-heart.
To reach the house named Beautiful, they must
toil up a great hill, and James, the "least of
the boys," gives way to tears, but knows that
downhill leads to death and remains steadfast in
his resolve. As they travel, they discuss
Christian's experiences, the story of his
journey having reached them before they left
home. Great-heart protects them from beasts of
prey that threaten them and courageously slays
Giant Grim with a single blow for blocking the
King's highway. At the lodge whose gateman is
Watchful, they are given hospitality, that night
Mercy dreams of arriving at Zion, and they are
encouraged by Prudence, Piety, and Charity.
After a week, the fair Mercy is wooed by Mr.
Brisk, but, advised by the three maids that he
thinks too much of the things of this world,
rejects his suit. Then Matthew, another of
Christian's sons, falls ill of fruit he ate as
they entered the lodge Beautiful, and Mr. Skill
says the fruit is evil because it belongs to
Beelzebub. Some special pills, which cure only
those who express grief for their sins, save the
youth, and the party continues, adding Prudence
and Piety to their company. They pass through

The Vale of Humiliation, are encouraged by the pious song of a shepherd boy, are frightened by a great roaring animal, and are surrounded by a fell mist. They are entertained by generous Gaius and instructed by moralistic verses made up by him and his friend, Honest. They stay here some years; Matthew weds Mercy, and James weds Gaius's daughter, Phebe. After taking a sad leave, they depart, encountering more frights and fears before coming to Vanity Fair, where a Mr. Mnason houses them and tells them the townsmen regret executing Faithful and have reformed. They live here for some years, and Christian's other two sons, Samuel and Joseph, marry Mr. Mnason's daughters, Grace and Martha. After Great-heart helps the townsmen kill a huge snake that has attacked the place, they take their leave and travel through The Delectable Mountains, defeat the Giant Despair, and pull down his terrible house, freeing his prisoners, Mr. Despondency and his child, Much-afraid. They resist the lure to sleep at The Enchanted Ground, try to wake Heedless and Too-bold, and rest in the Land of Beulah, eating of the fruit from its bountiful boughs. A messenger brings a note for Christiana from the Lord of The Celestial City, welcoming her to the Lord's throne in ten days' time. The messenger indicates that at that time she will die. Rejoicing that her trials will soon be over, Christiana summons her family about her, exhorts them to lives of faith and good works, and looks forward to entering the world of everlasting love and truth. Her last words, as she enters The Celestial City, are "I come, Lord, to be with Thee." This shortened version is about one-fifth the length of the original version. It retains all the better-known incidents and cuts away most of the moralistic and religious material. For the most part, events are easy to follow. Sometimes antecedents and references are not clear, but the book is an exciting, fast-moving, and even occasionally quite dramatic tale of adventure and conflict. This is especially true in Part I; Part II often seems repetitous and slower in tempo. The style is Biblical, and some Biblical quotations are included. The intensely serious and pious tone is both relieved and enforced by humor of irony, wordplay, parody, and character. Part II is more joyful than dramatic, as befits the saving of Christian's once-reluctant wife, and her entry into Zion provides a visually vivid and emotionally appealing grand climax to the tale. Robert Lawson's black and white illustrations make this edition especially attractive. They help with characterization, clarify incidents, add comedy and conflict, and enhance the old-time flavor. The map on the end-papers lends an air of reality to proceedings. Children's Classics.

PILLING, ANN, writer and anthologist. Some of her work has been published in picture books, including *The Friday Parcel* (Blackie, 1986) and *No Guns, No Oranges* (Heinemann, 1986). With Ann Wood, she has compiled *Our Best Stories: A Collection of Stories Chosen by Children* (Hodder, 1986). Her *Henry's Leg** (Viking, 1985), an amusing mystery story about a boy whose love for junk gets him into a bizarre robbery case, was winner of the Guardian Award. Other titles by Pilling include *The Year of the Worm* (Kestrel, 1984) and *The Big Pink* (Viking, 1987).

PING (*The River at Green Knowe*; A Stranger at Green Knowe*; An Enemy at Green Knowe**), whose whose real name is Hsu. Displaced Chinese boy from the border country of Burma, he spends summer holidays at Green Knowe. He has velvety black eyes and a rare but charming smile and is neat, polite, and rather formal. In *The River at Green Knowe* he is nine years old, younger than Ida* Biggin and Oskar* Stanislawsky but grown up for his age. In *A Stranger at Green Knowe*, a year later, he is the main human protagonist, and his fascination with the gorilla Hanno* is the major plot element. In *An Enemy at Green Knowe*, he has become a regular holiday resident of Green Knowe and goes to school with Tolly* during the term. He has an air of the inscrutable East about him. When he was six, his settlement was burned and raided, and with another child he wandered through the jungle and tiny villages, begging and eating berries, until a Buddist monk took them to a shelter and he was eventually sent to England. At the end of *An Enemy*, his father has been

found   and is   coming with   Tolly's father   from
Burma.

PINKS RIDLEY   (*Castaway Christmas**),   younger
sister,   ten   and a   half,   of   Miranda*   and
Lincoln*,   who   with   them   is   marooned   in   a
deserted   cottage   in   Somerset   at   Christmas.
Although   her main   concern is   having a   joyful
Christmas,   with presents,   cards, and   parents,
she   does   her   share   of   the   work   while   the
children   are   at   Little   Topsails.   Several
important   episodes   occur   because of   her,   in
particular,   finding   the   chickens and   rescuing
the   Hunters. Miranda   and   Lincoln care   deeply
for   her and   are protective   of her.   She wears
glasses and is very   feminine. She owes her name
to   a bowl   of clover-scented   pinks that   stood
near her mother's bed when   she was born. She is
a type   figure, the "cute" little   sister, sweet
and immature for her age.

PIP (*Great Expectations**), Philip Pirrip, orphan
boy who lives   with his   terrible-tempered sister
and   her kindly,   simple husband,   Joe* Gargery,
the blacksmith.   Pip's life is an example of how
false   expectations   can   ruin   a   young   person.
Originally he was happy at the prospect of being
apprenticed to Joe,   but   after   he   spends some
time   at   Miss*   Havisham's   house   and   meets
beautiful Estella*, he desires something higher,
and when   he is   told that   he is   to be   made a
gentleman,   he begins to lead an idle,   extravagant life   and to be   ashamed of honest   Joe and
his   village   background.   He does   retain   some
decency and shows this   by secretly arranging to
buy a place in a   company for his friend Herbert
Pocket,   but   it   is not   until his   hopes for   a
fortune are   completely   dashed   that   he understands how   badly he has acted.   His concern for
his   crude,   brutal   benefactor,   the   fugitive
convict,   Magwitch*--even after   he has   decided
not to   benefit further by the   man's money-- is
further evidence of his essential soundness.

PIPPIN TOOK (*The Fellowship of the Ring**), Peregrin, youngest and,   originally, smallest hobbit
of the fellowship, cousin   of Frodo* Baggins and
Merry*   Brandybuck. Pert and impulsive, Pippin
causes   trouble   more   than   once,   notably   by

dropping a stone into the well in the Mines of Moria, thereby waking the orcs and possibly the Balrog in the depths, and again, after the drowning of Isengard, picking up the Palantir, the crystal of far-seeing, which is thrown at them from the tower, and later by looking in it and facing Sauron. When he and Merry are captured by orcs and carried toward Isengard, he is responsible for their escape and also for leaving his elven brooch on the trail as a sign to his friends who are following. Later, in Gondor, he pledges his service to the stern Lord Denethor, steward of the city, and when Denethor's mind cracks and he tries to have both himself and his son Faramir burned alive, Pippin gets help to save the gravely ill Faramir. Throughout, Pippin is unquenchably cheerful, and in the end, because of the drink given him and Merry by the Ents, he grows to an almost unprecedented size for a hobbit.

THE PLAN FOR BIRDSMARSH (Peyton*, K. M., ill. Victor C. Ambrus, Oxford, 1965; World, 1966), realistic novel set in the mid-twentieth century in a village on the English coast north of Colchester. Birdmarsh, the name of both the village and the Fairfax farm, has been bypassed by progress so that the individual fishermen, like Gus* Roper's father, make a bare living and there seems no future for their sons. This is the way Paul* Fairfax, dreamer and bird lover, wants it to stay, so that he can take over his father's seafront farm, working with the animals and roaming the muddy tidal flats he loves. Sidney* Peacemaker, a doctor from London and president of the East Coast Smack Preservation Society, also hopes to keep Birdsmarsh as it is, so that he can keep his *Pheobe* in the local harbor in peace, but well-financed speculators approach Mr. Fairfax, planning to put in a hotel and marina and offering him far more for his land than it is worth for farming. Gus and Paul, both fourteen or fifteen, get Sidney's help to refurbish the old smack, *Swannie* (really *Swan Song*), which was built in 1910, left to the Fairfaxes by an uncle, and claimed by Paul as a den. Gus is more interested than Paul, wanting passionately to sail and fish and knowing that instead he must drop out of school and be apprenticed as a garage mechanic, a job his drunken father considers promising. When they are ready to try it out, Paul's brother, Chris*, arrives from Cambridge with an invention he has been working on, an inflatable survival suit he calls "Charlie" which is to be used as a life-saving device and which he wants to test secretly. In their first trial, Chris is hit by floating timber and almost drowns. The boys get him back on board and hail the *Woodwind*, the only other nonworking boat of Birdsmarsh harbor, whose owner, Peter Winnington, gives Chris artificial respiration and after an agonizing time brings him around. Late the next night Paul sees Winnington rowing in from *Swannie* and suspects from the smoke smell that he has been in the cabin, examining the suit. He offers to take Chris on the *Woodwind* for a twenty-four hour test of the suit, however, and Paul goes along, though he hates the thought of it. While he is resting in the cabin, he hears Chris yell and rushes out to find the *Woodwind* sailing away from Chris, who is in trouble. Winnington brings her around, and they pick up Chris, but Paul suspects some sort of complicity between Winnington and his uncle, Willy Warner, who is also on board. Chris, discouraged by the suit's failure, which he can't explain, goes off with a friend to Bavaria. In the meantime a hearing has been held to oppose the marina plan and attended mainly by retirees from London and bird lovers like Sidney. Angry, Gus speaks up for the marina, which he hopes will create jobs, and the gulf widens between him and Paul. Nonetheless, they continue to fix up *Swannie* and sail it in the race for gaff-rigged boats. When their patched sail begins to split, Paul has to take over the tiller while Gus mends it, and because of his awkwardness, *Swannie* loses to *Pheobe*. Gus is furious and, having to go to work in the morning, leaves Paul to bring the boat home alone the next day. Paul misses the tide, gets caught in a fog, hits a buoy, and sinks *Swannie*. He has just time to climb into Chris's suit, which has been roughly repaired and stowed on board. For thirty-three hours he drifts in the North Sea. Chris, now thinking things over in Bavaria, realizes that Paul's misgivings about Winnington were justified, and

he hurries home to check further. When he
confronts them with his evidence, both
Winnington and Warner tackle him, hold him down,
and give him an injection to keep him quiet
while they clear out. Gus, worried also about
Paul's suspicions, alerts the local police. By
the time a helicopter picks up Paul, the police
have intercepted the two men making their getaway on *Woodwind* with a load of industrial secrets which they are selling to foreign powers.
Stealing the plans for Charlie had just been an
incidental sideline. Released from the hospital,
Paul is surprised at the contrite attitude of
both Gus and Chris. Although the plans for
building the marina at Birdsmarsh have gone
through, somewhat modified, and he still hates
the idea, his experience has matured him and
put things into perspective enough so that he
can face the reality without great pain. While
the plot about the stealing of the suit is
plausible, the main interest is in the psychology of the various characters, each of whom is
interested in his own future and somewhat
blinded to that of the others. The characterization is strong, as are the scenes of sailing and
of Paul's isolated ordeal in the water. Carnegie
Com.; Fanfare.

PLOWMAN, STEPHANIE (1922-   ), teacher and historical novelist. She received a B.A. degree in
history at the University of London in 1944,
returned in 1948 for graduate study, and earned
a Ph.D. degree in 1950. She has taught in
England, South Africa, and Ghana, and was the
Gulbenkian Research Fellow at Lucy Cavendish
College, Cambridge, from 1969 to 1972. Among her
novels for young people are two about classical
Greece, *The Road to Sardis* (Bodley, 1965;
Houghton, 1966), about the war between Athens
and Sparta and the decline of democracy, and *The
Leaping Song* (Bodley, 1976), about Athens in her
glory, covering the period from Marathon to
Salamis, when the Persian fleet is destroyed.
Her most noted books are two set in Russia, in
the period before and during the revolution:
Three Lives for the Czar* (Bodley, 1969; Hough-
ton, 1970) and *My Kingdom for a Grave* (Bodley
Head, 1970; Houghton, 1971), solid and demanding
novels told from the point of view of a young

man who is an intimate of the royal princesses and whose cosmopolitan family foresees the downfall of the monarchy. Both were named to the *Horn Book* Fanfare lists. She has also published a biography of Nelson for young people and a play for adults. Her books have been frequently commended for their thorough research.

POD CLOCK (*The Borrowers**; *The Borrowers Afield**; *The Borrowers Afloat**; *The Borrowers Aloft**; *The Borrowers Avenged**) a steady, hardworking, philosophical man, fond father of Arrietty* and loving and indulgent husband of Homily*. Skillful at his trade of borrowing, which he has developed to an art, he is an excellent provider. Though he can stand up to Homily's nagging demands for more comforts and conveniences, he usually gives in to her and gets the items she wants, difficult though it may be for him now that he is getting older. His greatest fear is of being "seen" by humans, and he has developed a sixth sense that tells him when one is about. He is a stickler about Arrietty's keeping strictly to the rules of borrowing. Pod is an engaging, well-developed character, who asserts himself increasingly as leader and chief decision-maker as the series progresses. His good sense and insistence on obedience to his orders, for example, are instrumental in getting them safely out of the attic of Mr.* and Mrs.* Platter. At the end, he seems content to let Arrietty do more of the borrowing and to return to cobbling and other handicrafts.

POLL (*The Silver Curlew**), Doll's sister and Mother Codling's youngest child. She is garrulous, quick-tongued, and obnoxiously curious, and she argues a good deal with King Nollekens*. She is also intensely loyal to Doll; warm-hearted in her treatment of Doll, the injured Silver Curlew, and the baby; and extremely brave and determined in facing the evil powers of the Witching Wood to learn the true name of the Spindle-Imp*.

POLLAND, MADELEINE A(NGELA CAHILL) (1918-   ), born in Kinsale, County Cork, Ireland; librarian and historical novelist. She grew up in Herfordshire and attended Hitchin Girls' Grammar School there. During World War II she was a member of the Women's Auxiliary Air Force on the south coast of England, and for periods both before and after the war she was assistant librarian at Letchworth Public Library in Herfordshire. Her writing career, which includes about thirty books of fiction, eight of them for adults, began after her children were in school. Most of her books for children have been historical novels with such diverse settings as Ireland, China, Viking Denmark, Norman England, medieval Scotland, Moorish Spain, and ancient Crete, but some reflect modern life, among them *A Family Affair* (Hutchinson, 1971), which is set in contemporary Denmark. Among her historical novels are *To Kill a King* (Hutchinson, 1970; Holt, 1971), about a plot to assassinate William the Conqueror, and *The Queen's Blessing** (Constable, 1963; Holt, 1964), about Margaret*, Queen of Scotia and wife of Malcolm* III of Scotland, both set in the eleventh century. Works set in earlier periods include *To Tell My People** (Hutchinson, 1968; Holt, 1968), set in southern Britain and Rome in the first century, B.C., and *Beorn the Proud** (Constable, 1961; Holt, 1962), about a ninth-century Irish girl captured and carried to Denmark by Viking raiders. *Children of the Red King** (Constable, 1960; Holt, 1961) is about the son and daughter of Cormac*, King of Connacht, in the early thirteenth century. Also with an Irish background is *Deirdre** (World's Work, 1967; Doubleday, 1967), a fictionalized retelling of the ancient and tragic tale of romance. Four of her novels have been named to the *Horn Book* Fanfare lists, and *To Tell My People* has been included on the *Choice* magazine list of children's books for an academic library. Her stories have strong plot lines with enough historical background to make the adventures convincing.

POLL GREENGRASS (*The Peppermint Pig**), child whose angelic looks hide an assertive nature and stubborn will. She has "a soft, rosy face and long hair the color of duckling's down," but she is frequently naughty and can swear like a trooper--hardly the turn-of-the-century image of a sweet little girl. She also has a sharp understanding and, despite her lack of knowledge about family problems and tensions, a clearer picture of their troubles than does her brother Theo*, who is about a year and a half older. During the year they live with their aunts in Norfolk, she has a good time, despite her worry about the possibility of going to the workhouse, her grief at the necessary death of their pet pig, and her fear, which the reader sees is not unfounded, that her father will never return to the family from America.

POLLY PLUMMER (*The Magician's Nephew**), friend of Digory* Kirke, who is present with him when Aslan* creates the land of Narnia*. She is a brave, sensible, thoughtful child of about ten, not as interested in finding out new things as Digory is but still curious and courageous in meeting situations. She tries to anticipate difficulties; for example, she realizes they need to mark the pool that will take them back into their world because all the pools in the Wood between the Worlds look alike. She is cautious, obedient, and responsible and thinks Digory ought to obey the sign they find in the world of Charn and not strike the bell beside it. They argue, but he strikes it anyway, bringing Queen* Jadis to life, and thus is responsible for the presence of evil in Narnia. Polly forgives him later, does what she can to rectify matters, and accompanies him in his quests. Polly is a pleasing, multifaceted figure who often influences the action. She appears briefly in *The Last Battle** as Lady Polly, with Digory and five others who make up the Seven Kings and Queens of Narnia, along with other figures from the previous books.

POLLY WHITTACKER (*Fire and Hemlock**), imaginative girl who gets drawn into a series of otherworldly adventures after she wanders by accident into a funeral at Hunsdon House and meets Tom* Lynn. Polly explains to Tom that what she likes best is "making things like heroes up with other people, then being them," and that is essentially what their relationship becomes, though the spell laid upon Tom is that whatever they make up becomes true in some bizarre and usually dangerous way. A highly intelligent and bookish girl, Polly takes the name of "Hero" for herself and then tries to live up to it, playing vigorous games and fighting at school, boldly confronting new situations, and even trying to overcome her embarrassment when she feels she is making a fool of herself. It is through this last weakness and her compassion that Laurel* entraps her, making her promise to forget Tom because, Laurel tells her, he has cancer and only a short time to live, and her devotion is making him uncomfortable. Her love for Tom in the end forces her to renounce him.

POLYNESIA (*The Story of Doctor Dolittle*; *The Voyages of Doctor Dolittle*), wily old parrot who first teaches Doctor* Dolittle the languages of animals. Being nearly 200 years old, Polynesia has had many experiences, including sailing with pirates and knowing people of many nations and degrees, both high and low, and she has acquired much wisdom and practical good sense. It is Polynesia who manages the escape of the doctor and his crew from imprisonment in Jolliginki, summons the Black Parrots to defeat the Bag-jagderags on Spidermonkey Island, and works out a way for the doctor to escape the job of being king. After the first voyage she remains in Africa, but she returns to England shortly after the doctor and Tommy Stubbins meet. It is she who first suggests that Tommy become the doctor's assistant. Somewhat cynical, scornful of many of the other animals, patronizing toward Tommy and Bumpo*, she is devoted to Doctor Dolittle and uses her considerable wits to protect his interests.

PONY CRAY (*The Lark on the Wing*), Ursula, leader of the trio of Quaker girls who have been friends from childhood and who live together in a London flat as they become women. Inclined to be bossy, Pony is often impatient with or scornful of Kit* Haverard and treats her rather contemptuously at boarding school, but she remains a friend and even refrains from trying to get Bob Hardcastle's attention when she knows he is in love with Kit. She is studying medicine.

POOH BEAR (*Winnie-the-Pooh**; *The House at Pooh Corner**), also known as Edward Bear and Winnie-the-Pooh, Bear of Very Little Brain, the favorite companion of Christopher* Robin. Pooh is distinguished by a genial, modest temperament, a large appetite for honey and other sticky treats, particularly when he is feeling a little "eleven-o'clockish," and an ability to compose poems or "hums" on almost any occasion. Although he can't read, like Rabbit, or spell (even incorrectly, like Owl), and although he admits he does not have much brain, Pooh often comes up with the most ingenious and sensible ideas. It is he who thinks of using an empty honey jar for a boat in the flood and of riding in Christopher Robin's umbrella to rescue Piglet. He invents the game of Poohsticks, discovers the North Pole while rescuing Roo from the stream, and, after Owl's house blows down, he figures out a way to get Piglet up to the letter box on the ceiling, so that he can run for help. Pooh goes through life with a pleasant lack of worry and is a good and faithful friend, particularly to Piglet. Pooh is also a character in A. A. Milne's* two books of verse for children, *When We Were Very Young* and *Now We Are Six*.

THE POOL OF FIRE (Christopher*, John, Hamilton, 1968; Macmillan, 1968), third novel in the Tripods science fiction trilogy, also known as the White Mountains series, which are set 100 years in the future mostly on the continent of Europe. In this book, Will and his cohorts free the world of the tyranny of the Masters. Will tells this story, as he tells the others, in unemotional, factual fashion, beginning with his return in the company of Beanpole (Jean-Paul Deliet) from the City of Gold and Lead, one of the Masters' three great metropolises. He has learned that, with the help of a spaceship from their motherland in outer space, the Masters intend to take over the earth, rendering its atmosphere habitable for them and thus annihilating all human life. Since the ship will arrive in about four years, Julius and his ruling council take time to lay plans carefully to destroy the Masters' Cities before it arrives. Henry is dispatched to the westernmost of the Cities, the one located on the isthmus between the two continents of the Western Hemisphere. Beanpole leaves for the research laboratory, where good use can be made of his mechanical aptitude, and Will (soon joined by Fritz, who has managed luckily to escape from the City of Gold and Lead) becomes a recruiter for their cause in southern Europe and northern Africa. On their return months later, Will and Fritz are dispatched to a castle on a promontory overlooking the northern sea, which they discover is one of several laboratories that the insurgents have developed and is Beanpole's workplace. They learn that Beanpole and others have recovered a good deal of the technology, such as electricity and radio, lost when the Masters conquered the earth a century earlier. Beanpole and Julius enlist their help in capturing a Master. After a couple of unsuccessful attempts to lure a Tripod into a pit trap, Will paints himself and his horse green and thus attracts the curiosity of a Tripod who is subsequently trapped. The Master within, Ruki, is imprisoned in a specially epuipped underground room in the castle. Interrogation proves fruitless in gaining useful information, but a breakthrough comes when Ulf, the hard-drinking barge captain now chief of the castle guard, mischievously pours a little schnapps into Ruki's food, and Ruki is rendered unconscious for six hours. The insurgents realize they now have a tool for overcoming the Masters: alcohol. Three separate parties are sent, one to each of the Masters' metropolises, with instructions to penetrate the City, manufacture alcohol, and mix it with the Masters' water supply. Will and others, with Fritz as their leader, travel to the City of Gold and Lead. The details by which they conduct their dangerous enterprise are worked out in precise, clear, and suspenseful detail. Using scuba equipment, they enter the City by the river that flows through it, set up the distillation machinery, make the alcohol using materials available in the City, locate the water purification room, dispose of the Masters in charge, dump their product, disable the City's power unit (known as the Pool of Fire), breach the golden wall to let in the outside

atmosphere (thus killing the inebriated
Masters), and rekindle the fire to activate the
machinery by which they can open the outer doors
and get out of the City--all this seems real and
believable. The suspense is gripping because the
boys are under severe time constraints and labor
against overwhelming odds. The City breached,
they return to headquarters to discover that,
while the City in the East has also fallen to
the insurgents, that in the West, which was
Henry's quest, still stands. With one and a half
years remaining before the Masters' spaceship
arrives, Julius orders an attack on the western
City with newly developed flying machines, but
the Masters jam the electrical systems, and the
invasion fails. The next attempt, by lighter-
than-air balloon, proves successful. Of the
dozen launched, most go astray, some dump loads
of explosives on the green dome without effect,
but Henry courageously and resourcefully lands
his balloon on the City's carapace. He carefully places his load of explosives for greatest
impact and dies as the whole dome goes up in a
billow of green air. The novel concludes some
two years later with a conference of nations
high in the White Mountains where the struggle
for freedom led by Julius had begun years
before. Dissension breaks out over leadership
of the international union, and the conference
disbands in heat, but Will, Beanpole, and Fritz
(an Englishman, a Frenchman, and a German
respectively), decide optimistically to devote
themselves to trying to get people to live
together in peace and take satisfaction in
knowing that they have helped the world achieve
liberty from the long oppression of the Masters.
While some scenes have power--that in which the
Tripods hunt down men for the entertainment of
cheering, bloodthirsty crowds; the capture of
the Tripod; the disabling of the Pool of Fire;
and breaching the dome, where the heavy inner
air expels with such force that one of the
insurgents is sucked out to a swift death on the
rocks below--and the conflict is clear, this
book seems more contrived, less cohesive, more
preoccupied with technology, and less exciting
than its predecessors, *The White Mountains** and
*The Pool of Fire**. The concluding scenes, in
the nature of an epilogue, are message-laden.

Taken together, the three books have great power to move the emotions in a superficial way. They are less concerned with technology than is typical for the genre, however, and as trilogy they are only partially successful since the last book depends upon the first two for its impact. Choice; Stone.

POOP NEWCOMBE (*Emma Tupper's Diary**), beautiful but weak-brained young lady staying with the McAndrew family when Emma* visits. So called because of the resemblance to "nincompoop," she is always pleasant but has limited comprehension. She has been taken in by Major McAndrew because she was being used by a gang of shoplifters, was arrested, and was sent to prison, although she is unable to comprehend the wrongness of what she was doing. One of the duties of the McAndrew youngsters is to keep her away from shops, where she will revert to old habits. She idolizes Major McAndrew and especially likes Emma because the girl calls her "Miss Newcombe" instead of "Poop."

POPGHOSE (*Owlglass**), clever weasel who thinks up the plan to get spectacles for Old* Beak and Claws. Although he is unable to read, as some of the other animal club members can, Popghose has a retentive memory and considerable ingenuity, as well as an acquaintance beyond the usual social circles of his class, which enables him to enlist the aid of the common jackdaws. At the club meeting, he tells "The True Story of How a Great Western Railway Got Its Broad Gauge," a story that goes back to a favor one of his ancestors did for William the Conqueror.

A POPPY IN THE CORN. See *Sisters and Brothers.*

PORTER, SHEENA (1935-   ), born in Melton Mowbray, Leicestershire; writer of fiction for preadolescents. After attending King Edward VII Grammar School, she received her diploma from Loughborough College School of Librarianship in Leicestershire in 1956. She was for eight years a librarian in Leicester City Library and children's librarian for Nottinghamshire County Library and Shropshire County Library, and for two years editorial assistant at Oxford Univer-

sity Press in London. Her first novels were
published while she was still working full-
time. While on holiday once, she met an author
and editor who encouraged her to write, and the
result was *The Bronze Chrysanthemum* (Oxford,
1961; Van Nostrand, 1965), a mystery-detective
story. Two more novels followed in rapid
succession. In 1964 came *Nordy Bank** (Oxford,
1964; Roy, 1967), for which she received the
Carnegie Medal. It combines aspects of adventure, girl's-growing-up, and animal stories and
was praised especially for its evocation of
place. Several children on holiday in Shropshire
find a half-starved Alsatian dog, and important
decisions must be made. The central problem is
strong, and local color provides much interest,
but the plot moves inconsistently and occasionally seems made-to-order and too instructive of
animal training. In 1964 she made writing her
main occupation, and subsequently published
several other novels which varied in content
from her previous ones, including *The Hospital*
(Oxford, 1973), about mental illness; *The
Scapegoat* (Oxford, 196>), about stepmother
problems; and *The Valley of Carreg-Wen* (Oxford, 1971), about environmental concerns. Her
novels are unsensational stories of adventure
and family relationships and are undemanding in
content, style, and structure for their intended
audience of later elementary and preteens. She,
her artist husband, Patrick Lane, and their two
daughters have lived in Shrewsbury near the
Welsh border.

PRICE, SUSAN (1955-   ), born in Round's Green,
Staffordshire; writer of fiction and short
stories for middle-grade and early adolescent
readers. Her father was an electrical motor
technician, and she grew up in an industrial
area and attended Tividale Comprehensive School.
Her family life and her various jobs from
1973-1979, in a bakery, supermarket, hotel,
warehouse, and museum, produced a strong identification with the working class. She has said
she writes for working-class children, and
social expose and creating awareness of working-
class concerns play a large part in her
writing. She received the Children's Rights
Workshop Other Award for her second book,

Twopence a Tub* (Faber, 1975), a historical novel about an unsuccessful coal pit strike in 1851, which gives an exceptionally vivid picture of the miners' problems. Before that she published *The Devil's Piper* (Faber, 1973; Green-willow, 1976), about a troublesome leprechaun. Later, she wrote *Sticks and Stones* (Faber, 1976), a contemporary father-son story; *Home from Home* (Faber, 1977), a contemporary novel about the friendship between a youth and an elderly woman; *Christopher Uptake* (Faber, 1981), set in Elizabethan times; and *From Where I Stand* (Faber, 1984; Faber, 1984), about prej-udice against Pakistani in English schools. She has also published two books of short stories, *Ghostly Tales* (Ladybird, 1987) and *Here Lies Price: Tall Tales and Ghost Stories* (Faber, 1987); a book of retellings of traditional ghost stories, *Ghosts at Large* (Faber, 1984; Faber, 1984); and two more novels, *In a Nutshell* (Faber, 1983) and *The Ghost Drum* (Faber, 1987; Farrar, 1987). She was writer in residence at North Riding College of Education in Scarborough in 1980.

PRINCE CASPIAN: THE RETURN TO NARNIA (Lewis*, C. S., ill. Pauline Baynes, Bles, 1951; Macmillan, 1951), fantasy novel of war, adventure, and righting of old wrongs set in the mythical land of Narnia*, second published and fourth in time order in the series. One year after *The Lion, the Witch and the Wardrobe**, the four Pevensies, Peter*, Susan*, Edmund*, and Lucy*, are sitting in a railway station, awaiting the train to take them to school. They feel a sudden, strong wrench and find themselves back in Narnia. They are surprised to discover that evidently many years have passed since they ruled there as kings and queens, because their castle, Cair Paravel, lies in ruins, and trees and vines grow where none were before. From their former treasure house, they take the magical gifts they received from Father Christmas on their previous trip. Shortly thereafter, Susan's splendid marksmanship with her magical bow and arrow enables them to rescue a Dwarf, whom two soldiers are holding prisoner in a rowboat and are about to drown. In a long story of four chapters within the longer story, Trumpkin* the

Dwarf updates them on the history of Narnia and explains how he came to be in such sore straits. Many years before, aggressive humans from the west, the Telmarines, invaded Narnia. They killed many Narnians, including talking beasts, Dwarfs, and Fauns, silenced others, and drove many into remote areas. The present king, Miraz, has usurped the throne from his nephew, Caspian*, a youth whose life was endangered when a son was born to Miraz. Caspian's tutor, Doctor* Cornelius (himself half dwarf), helped the lad escape to the Old Narnians in the hills and forests. Two Dwarfs, feisty Trumpkin and surly Nikabrik*, and a Badger, Trufflehunter, took him in and introduced him to others of the Old Narnian kind of talking creatures. In danger of attack from Miraz, the Old Narnians took refuge inside Aslan's How, the great mound that was erected over the old Stone Table that was Aslan's* special place during the Golden Age of the children's reign. Bottled up in their lair and defeated in almost every sortie, they blew Susan's magical horn (which somehow had come into the possession of Doctor Cornelius; he gave it to Caspian, who blew it, causing the wrench that brought the Pevensies back to Narnia). Trumpkin was dispatched to the coast to greet whatever help might arrive from that quarter and had been captured by two of Miraz's men. Story told, the four and Trumpkin hurry to Aslan's How by boat and on foot, not without some difficulties, and with the help of Aslan, who first reveals himself to Lucy, they arrive to find that Nikabrik, grown impatient, has resorted to witchcraft in the effort to defeat Miraz. Nikabrik and his minions slain, Peter challenges Miraz to single combat, and, when it appears Peter will be victorious, the Telmarines prove treacherous, and full battle is joined. The Awakened Trees, restored to rights by Aslan's arrival, turn the tide, and the Telmarines surrender in terror. Aslan then rights old wrongs, joy ensues in the form of Bacchanalian revelry, Caspian is made king, and those Telmarines who so choose, as well as the four Pevensies, are sent back to their respective dimensions through a special door Aslan constructs for the purpose. The characters are well drawn, and the plot moves quickly through plenty of excitement, action, and conflict. Scenes stand out--Doctor Cornelius and Caspian on the tower under the stars as Cornelius apprises Caspian of Old Narnian problems, the Pevensies in the treasure-house nostalgically rejoicing in old times, the dramatic rescue of Trumpkin, the vividly described and lighthearted pastoral meeting of Caspian and the Bulgy Bears and other charmingly created and named woodland beings, and Aslan restoring the tail of the feisty mouse, Reepicheep*, after the little fellow's countrymen assert they will cut off theirs if he must remain tailless. Those scenes in which Aslan returns strike false notes, since there seems to be no reason why he should appear only to Lucy and put Lucy in the awkward position of having to persuade her siblings to her way of thinking without proof. Similarly, those scenes of the revels where Lewis brings in Bacchus and the Maenads seem incongruous and melodramatic, and the door concept seems lame and contrived. The clear-cut conflict makes this one of the most cohesive books in the series, and, like the others, it has a warm and affectionate tone that contributes to its charm and helps outweigh its faults. Choice; Fanfare.

PRINCE DAVID (*The Whispering Mountain*), David James Charles Edward George Henry Richard Tudor-Stuart, Prince of Wales, sometimes called Prince Deio. While on a hunt in Wales, he is attacked by three wild boars and wounded. Owen finds him, and Arabis* Dando tends his wounds. Tom* Dando dies of the gunshot Lord* Malyn intended for the prince. A gently comic and likeable caricature of British royalty, Prince David speaks with a heavy Scots dialect. He wears a tartan kilt, a prune-colored velvet hunting-jacket, and a hat with three white feathers held in place by a diamond as large as a walnut. He likes to live well. Although inclined to be blustery and speak in bursts of words, he is a sincere and kindly man who aids the good side against the wicked lord.

PRINCE PRIGIO (Lang*, Andrew, Arrowsmith, 1889; the edition cited by the selection committee was illustrated by Robert Lawson and published by Little, Brown, 1942), humorous fantasy set in the imaginary kingdom of Pantouflia at an unspecified time, which plays with the pattern and motifs of the marchen. After a long-hoped-for son is born to imperious, impatient King Grognio and his practical and unimaginative Queen, his mother refuses to believe in fairies and hence does not invite them to the baby's christening party. One hundred attend anyway, all dressed in green, and bestow splendid, magical gifts upon little Prince Prigio, except for the last one to arrive. A cross old thing, she spitefully announces her gift to him, a trait of character, "My child, you shall be *too* clever!" All the fairy gifts, except the last one, of course, the queen immediately stores away in a room at the top of the castle, and no one pays any attention to them for many years. Prince Prigio grows up to be handsome, learned, and exceedingly clever. He is also very much disliked, because he is so clever that he is always right in his facts and is conceited and tactless about correcting people who happen to be wrong. Though the queen is proud of his intellectual capability, his father dislikes him more and more, and, to make family matters worse, the king grows to fear that Prigio will overthrow him and usurp his throne. He decides to get rid of his son by sending him against the terrible Firedrake that is scorching the countryside and creating an unbearable heat wave, but Prince Prigio refuses to go because he has read old stories and knows that the youngest son always triumphs in such quests. The king is compelled to send Alphonso, his youngest son, and then Enrico, the middle son, against the monster. When neither returns and both are presumed dead, the angry king terms Prince Prigio "quite unendurable," and orders the entire court to pack up and move to Falkenstein, a city some weeks' journey away by carriage. Alone and servantless in the palace, Prigio searches the empty castle looking for food and clothing and discovers in the garret the fairies' discarded gifts, among them seven-league boots, a magical carpet, and an invisible cap, which he uses, at first not knowing, of course, that they are magical. Humorous misadventures follow when he puts on the boots and cap and wishes himself in a

Gluckenstein eating house, where he is invisible
to everyone but doesn't know it, overhears
disparaging remarks made about him, and learns
that his subjects think he is conceited. He
meets the English Ambassador, Lord Kelso, and
falls in love with his beautiful daughter, Lady
Rosalind. She is the only person who feels his
cleverness is a misfortune and not his fault.
Prince Prigio declares he will present her with
the horns and tail of the Firedrake. Making use
of several magical objects, Prigio finds the
Firedrake and eggs on the dragon and a very cold
monster named the Ramora to fight each other.
The Ramora kills the Firedrake and then expires
with the effort. With a magical sword of
sharpness, Prince Prigio hacks off the head and
tail of the Firedrake, returns to the ambassador's palace where he hides the articles under
his flying carpet but then discovers to his
dismay that the ambassador's butler has found
them and ridden off to the king to claim the
reward the king had posted for the items. There
is also by now a bounty on Prigio's person.
When the practical queen refuses to accept the
fact of the Firedrake, in spite of the head and
tail, Prigio flies off to the Firedrake and cuts
off its hoofs to prove his deed to the king and
claims both rewards. He refuses, however, to
marry the Lady Molinda, Alphonso's former
sweetheart, who is part of the reward. This so
infuriates the king that he threatens Prince
Prigio with the gallows unless he finds his
absent brothers and returns with them alive.
Another fairy gift enables Prigio to get out of
this predicament. With magic water from the
Fountain of Lions, he revivifies the ashes of
his brothers, who were burned to death by the
Firedrake, and brings them back to court. When
the stubborn king goes back on his promise to
restore Prince Prigio to crown princeship,
Prigio threatens to revive the Firedrake in
retaliation. The king capitulates speedily and
apologizes publicly. The three princes are
married, each to his chosen sweetheart. After
the honeymoon, Rosalind suggests that Prigio use
his magical wishing cap to wish himself no
cleverer than others so that everybody will like
him. He agrees, then privately changes his mind.
He makes a wish that is slightly different from

the one she suggested. He wishes that he will seem no more clever than other people. As a result, he becomes the most popular prince and best-loved king in the history of Pantouflia. The author improvises on his source material in sprightly, self-conscious style, with tongue-in-cheek humor, occasional high-sounding vocabulary, a few underhand shots, here and there some winks at the adult audience, and a few footnotes to "verify" the truth of things. The characters and incidents are familiar from folktale, though they are given more individuality than their oral tradition counterparts would have. Prigio is better developed than the hero of folktale, being three-dimensional, a scholar, party-lover, dutiful, cheerful, impatient, callous, as well as quick of mind and conceited about his intellectual advantages. He changes gradually, if expectedly, and first shows concern for the feelings of someone else when Lady Molinda mourns the loss of Alphonso. When he falls in love with Lady Rosalind, "something seemed to give a whirr! in his brain," and he comes to believe in fairies and in the fairy gifts. After that, the cleverness the old fairy gave him and the gifts of the other fairies combine with his bad qualities of pride and stubbornness to ensure his triumph. The whole is a deftly written and entertaining bit of fluff, whose author appears to enjoy his rollicking romp through the conventions of old story. Lawson's comic drawings enhance the humor. Sequels. Fanfare.

THE PRINCESS AND CURDIE (MacDonald*, George, ill. James Allen, Chatto, 1883; Lippincott, 1882), sequel to *The Princess and the Goblin**, set about a year later when the Princess Irene is nine and Curdie fourteen. Since the princess has gone to live with her father the king in Gwyntystorm, Curdie has returned to his work in the mines and has come to doubt her stories of her great-great-grandmother in the tower of her palace, whom he has never been able to see. One evening he shoots a white pigeon but then repents and rushes to the now vacant castle with the injured bird, climbs to the tower room, and at last sees the grandmother, who appears first as a withered old woman and later as a

beautiful young queen. After several other
trials, including thrusting his arm into a fire
of roses which gives him the power to tell the
true nature of man or beast by the feel of its
hand, the grandmother directs Curdie to go at
once to Gwyntystorm and do whatever needs to be
done. He sets off as directed, and that night on
a lonely heath he is at first terrified, then
relieved to be joined by Lina, a weirdly shaped
beast he has seen in the grandmother's room and
whose paw feels like the hand of a child. As
they go through a forest, Lina collects
forty-nine other strangely shaped creatures who
serve as an escort and turn back when they
emerge from the woods. As Curdie and Lina enter
Gwyntystorm, whose people are mostly suspicious
and unfriendly, two dogs attack them and are
killed, one by Lina and one by Curdie's mattock.
The people are angry, but too frightened of Lina
to attack Curdie, and at last he is taken in by
a woman named Debra and her little granddaughter, Barbara, who live in a simple, thatched
cottage. The next morning Curdie is arrested,
taken to a dungeon, and locked up there with
Lina. With his mattock, which he has managed to
retain, he breaks a hole in the floor through
which he can see water a long way below. Using
the rope with which he was bound, he lets
himself down, sees that he can swing himself
over into an opening on one side of the cave
below and manages to get Lina down with him.
They follow a passage up into the wine cellar of
the king's palace. There they see the king's
butler carefully rinse a flagon with wine
several times before he drinks from it and then
refill it with wine from a different cask. Lina
scares him away with her fearful howl, so that
Curdie is able to get the key to the cellar.
Later they creep up, find most of the staff
drunk and asleep, and, after getting some food,
make their way up to the king's chamber, where
they find the king very ill and Irene sitting by
him. She knows Curdie at once, and by watching,
concealed, in the chamber he is able to see that
the doctor is giving the king poisoned wine and
denying him good, wholesome food. Curdie, with
Lina's help, is able to substitute good wine and
smuggle in some plain bread, so that the king
recovers enough to refuse to sign the document

brought to him the next day by the lord
chamberlain, which is actually a new will,
though presented as a routine paper. When the
doctor next appears and tries to administer
poison to the king, Lina crunches one of his
legs. Curdie, with Irene's concurrence, sends
Lina to the forest to bring the weird beasts,
but first he gives the servants a chance to
repent by sending a message to them through a
loyal housemaid that if they confess and change
their wicked ways they will be spared. Only one
page boy goes to Irene's side, while the others
mock and revile her. At Curdie's command, the
beasts drive all the evil servants and court
officers out and imprison the main ringleaders
in their rooms, while also cleaning the filthy
castle. As they wait for the king to regain his
strength, Curdie brings Debra to the palace to
cook for him, and the presence of innocent
little Barbara aids in his recovery. In the
meantime Curdie's father, Peter, has become
uneasy about him, tries to find the grandmother,
and failing, starts for Gwyntystorm, where the
wicked men, still planning to overthrow the
king, have invited an unfriendly neighboring
monarch to march in and take over. In a sort of
night vision, Curdie sees the grandmother
burning the king in her fire of roses, and the
next morning he is fully recovered. With the one
faithful courtier, Sir Bronzebeard, the colonel
of the guard, the loyal housemaid and page, the
princess riding her white pony, and the band of
Uglies (as the princess calls the beasts), the
king and Curdie set out to meet the attacking
army. As things begin to go badly for them,
Peter arrives, as does a great cloud of pigeons
which fly in the faces of the attackers,
directed by the housemaid who turns out to be
the grandmother in disguise. The king again
takes command, revitalizes the people, and rules
wisely. Curdie discovers that the rock on which
the castle stands contains gold, Peter leads the
mining of it, which finances the kingdom, and
Curdie and Irene eventually are married. The
story has frequent moralizing passages and an
overall improving tone, with mystical elements
like the painful but redeeming fire of roses,
but the ugly beasts and the routing of the
faithless servants are lively elements in an

old-fashioned fantasy still popular with many readers. Children's Classics; ChLA Touchstones; Choice.

THE PRINCESS AND THE GOBLIN (MacDonald*, George, ill. Arthur Hughes, Strahan, 1872; Routledge, 1871), fantasy set in an unnamed kingdom where Princess Irene, 8, lives in a castle on a mountain cared for by Lootie, her rather foolish nurse. Her father the king visits occasionally. One day the princess finds a strange stairway to a tower room where she discovers an old woman spinning, who says she is Irene's great-great-grandmother and that she keeps pigeons. Lootie believes none of Irene's story when she returns, and Irene cannot always find the room again, but when she does she finds the old woman sometimes young and beautiful, sometimes very large, and sometimes small. On the same mountain lives Curdie, 12, son of Peter, a miner. Once when Irene and Lootie stay too late on the mountain and are threatened by the goblins who live in its depths, Curdie meets them and scares away the goblins by singing defiantly impertinent songs while he escorts the little princess home. Later, one night when he stays late in the mine to earn extra money for a gift for his mother, he discovers that the goblins are plotting some treachery, but he does not realize at the time that they are planning to capture Irene and marry her to their goblin prince. He continues to watch and to try to discover their plan, and eventually is captured. Irene, visiting her grandmother in the tower, is given a ball of extremely fine thread, the result of the old woman's spinning, and told she must follow it, although it is invisible to others. Guided by her hand upon the thread, she goes up the mountain, enters the mine, and rescues Curdie. Afterwards she takes him to see her grandmother, and he is angry because he sees nothing but a bare room and thinks she is mocking him. Curdie's mother chides him for his behavior and tells of her unusual experience of seeing a strange, moonlike globe that led her to safety on the mountain, though no one else could see it. Curdie is unable to see Irene to apologize, but he keeps a careful watch and just as the goblins, who have tunneled under the castle,

break through and try to kidnap the princess, he
is able to spread the alarm and avert the
disaster. The king arrives and wants to reward
him by taking him into his service, but he
decides to stay with his parents. The story has
a mystical, allegorical tone, and stops
frequently for author asides about goodness,
true nobility, and beauty. Curdie and his
parents are salt of the earth, good and honest
in every way; Irene is good and beautiful and
trusting; the grandmother seems to be goodness
personified. Devotees of MacDonald usually
treat this work as inferior to *At the Back of
the North Wind**, but it has a more interesting
story line and is probably more popular with
children, though now appearing very old-
fashioned in its approach to fantasy and in its
moralizing. ChLA Touchstones; Choice.

PRINCESS FIONUALA (*Old John**), aged seven, only
daughter of the Prince of Gleann na Nean, who
sickens after her beloved white donkey,
Achilles, disappears. The little girl is lying
at death's door when Old John arrives at the
castle with news that the donkey has been
kidnapped by the wicked dwarf, Gruaga, and that
he knows how the animal can be saved. In
gratitude, the prince promises to help Old John
any time he needs him. The prince later sends
his archers to rescue Bainen at Old John's
request.

PROFESSOR HAMPTON (*Pennington's Seventeenth Sum-
mer**; *The Beethoven Medal**), elegant, confident
music teacher who overhears Pat* Pennington play
and takes him on as a pupil and disciple,
coolly talking the local police sergeant out of
a charge that might have sent the boy to reform
school, getting him a scholarship to a London
music college, and generally dominating and
directing his life. When Pat is sent to prison,
he keeps in touch and does what he can to see
that the boy can continue his practice, and he
takes Pat into his own house when he gets out.
He dislikes Ruth* Hollis because she distracts
Pat from his music, and he is barely polite to
her when they are together, although later he
comes to have a grudging respect for her. In
Pennington's Heir (Oxford, 1973; Crowell, 1974)

after Ruth becomes pregnant and Pat agrees to
marry her, the professor cuts him off
completely, but when Pat breaks his hand and
Ruth calls Professor Hampton to get the name of
a specialist, he comes immediately, takes Pat to
the doctor in his imperious way, and insists on
paying the bill for treatment. A man of about
forty-five, extremely sure of himself professionally and socially, he is not able to understand Pat's inbred antagonism to authority or
his need of an occasional release from the
rigors of musical study.

PROVE YOURSELF A HERO (Peyton*, K. M., Oxford,
1977; World, 1978), adventure novel but more importantly a psychlogical study of a kidnapping
and the resulting trauma to the victim, set in
England in modern times. Two old friends from
Pony Club days, Jonathan* Meredith and Peter*
McNair, both sixteen, having met casually during
a brief holiday from Jonathan's boarding school,
are riding their bikes home from town when a
plumber's van passes them, then stops, and a man
sticks his head out of the window and asks the
way to Ravenshall Court, Jonathan's posh home.
Explaining that a water main has burst in the
stable yard and the local plumber is busy, the
man suggests that Jonathan put his bike on the
roof and hop in to give directions. Peter, whose
father is a horse dealer, envies Jonathan the
lift and thinks nothing more of the incident
until Mrs.* Meredith calls late that evening,
wondering if Jonathan might be at his house and,
hearing Peter's story, almost immediately says
she will call the police. As soon as he enters
the van, Jonathan is overpowered, bound,
blindfolded, driven for some time, changed to
another vehicle, and forced in a cramped
position into a life-raft case from a sailboat,
in which he loses consciousness. When he wakes
he is on a yacht, evidently in a sailing race
across the North Sea, in the company of three
well-educated young men who call themselves
John, Paul, and Ringo, and one less educated
Irishman who is called Jamie and whose job is to
guard him. In spite of being drugged and
blindfolded most of the time, Jonathan is able
to learn that Jamie knows something about horses
and must be from the vicinity, since he knows

Mrs. Meredith's horse Florestan; that the boat has almost had a collision in the harbor in Holland with the yacht *Jago*, owned by one of his father's friends; and that if the ransom of 500,000 pounds is not paid as specified, he will be dropped overboard somewhere in the North Sea. There is a long, tense period when the message of the payment does not come on the wireless, as expected, during which Jonathan keeps himself well under control, but after they learn that the ransom has been paid and they near port, he panics at being put back into the life-raft case and actually asks to be drugged again so he will be unconscious when he is carried ashore. In the meantime, his sister, Jessica, 13, has received by phone the ransom demand which specifies that the money will be delivered to a lonely crossroads at midnight by the boy, alone and on foot, who was with Jonathan when he was abducted. Unfortunately Peter has injured his ankle and can't walk, but it is decided that he will ride Sirius. To his surprise, the man coming to pick up the ransom also arrives on horseback, takes the money cheerfully, and rides away across the fields. Peter gives him a head start and then follows, doing some expert jumping in the dark (a dangerous undertaking with his injured ankle), and manages to summon the police to the spot where the man changed from horse to van and to capture the horse, which proves to have been stolen from a local woman. Jonathan wakes to find himself in a woods with no sign of his captivity except a yellow blindfold, which he has already identified by the smell as a horse's leg bandage. He makes his way home and is able to tell the police his story, but he keeps to himself the fact that he asked for the drugs, feeling terribly ashamed of his weakness and guilty that he didn't try to make some kind of disturbance as they came off the boat to cause the apprehension of his abductors. He also sees that now that he is safely home, his very competitive and domineering mother resents having been bilked out of so much money and, as Jessica has rightly predicted to Peter, blames Jonathan for not somehow escaping. Back at boarding school, Jonathan starts having nightmares of being forced into the life-raft case

that are so severe that he wakes screaming and
disturbs the school. His mother, who is
summoned back from Switzerland to take him home,
briskly decides that what he needs is hard work
to keep his body so tired that his mind won't
cook up dreams and arranges that he go to
McNair's as a stable hand. Although Mr.* McNair
is a hard driver and the work is gruelling,
Jonathan rather likes it because he is away from
his mother and Peter is working with him. Part
of his job is to ride Florestan at the local
point-to-points, in training for the Wembley
Open, and at one contest he sees a horse with
three yellow leg bandages and one white one. At
the next race, having come in second to Peter
and therefore failed before his watching mother,
he goes off alone, hears the voice he knows is
Jamie's, and impulsively ducks into his horse
trailer. When they arrive at the isolated farm
where Jamie is groom for some wealthy man's
horses, Jamie is more scared than Jonathan. He
pulls a gun but then offers Jonathan a cup of
tea laced with whisky, and becomes quite
friendly. Carefully, Jonathan gets the information that Jamie has not yet been paid for the
job and suggests that his parents would pay him
a lot more for the address of the kidnappers,
who are now in Australia. Jamie gives him an
envelope with the address on it, but then the
police, alerted by Peter, pull into the yard,
and Jamie, thinking he has been betrayed, shoots
Jonathan in the lower back. At the hospital,
Jonathan tells Peter about the address in his
back jeans pocket, but ironically his mother has
asked the hospital aide to burn the bloody
clothes. Jonathan does remember enough of the
address to give the police a lead to catch the
kidnappers. Although he is badly injured and
will not be able to ride for a long time,
Jonathan is at peace, having heard Jamie's
admiration for his courage and knowing that he
has done something toward getting his abductors
brought to justice and his mother's money back.
More importantly, he has earned his mother's
respect. Although the action of the plot is
fast-paced and intriguing, the main interest is
in the conflict between imperious Mrs. Meredith
and Jonathan, who resists in a passive but
stubborn way. Both have appeared in an earlier

book, *The Team**, and Jonathan is the main pro-
tagonist in a sequel, *A Midsummer Night's
Death**. Fanfare; Junior High Contemporary
Classics.

PSAMMEAD (*Five Children and It**), the Sand-fairy
that the four children, Cyril*, Anthea*,
Robert*, and Jane*, find in a sand pile in an
abandoned gravel pit and who reluctantly grants
them wishes that bring them humorous adventures.
At first the children think the Psammead is a
rat or a snake. It is brown, furry, and fat,
with a tubby body like a spider's and long furry
arms and legs. Its hands and feet are like a
monkey's, its eyes stick out on long horns like
a snail's, and it can move them in and out like
telescopes. It can be cross and crotchety and is
easily irritated. It doesn't like water and came
to live where it is now, once the back of a
beach well away from the water, in the days of
the dinosaurs, a time which it clearly remembers and thinks preferable to today. At first,
since it is out of practice at granting wishes,
it must push itself up and strain to make the
wishes come true, but later it seems to do them
so effortlessly that the granting seems to be
merely a matter of thought. The Psammead (pro-
nounced Sammyadd) is a convincing, inventive,
likeable character.

PUDDLEGLUM (*The Silver Chair**), a frog-like man
of loquacious tongue and pessimistic disposition
who accompanies Eustace* Scrubb and Jill* Pole
on the expedition to find and free Prince
Rilian*, Caspian's* kidnapped son and heir.
Puddleglum has a surface comedy that obscures
the substance of his character. His tongue
chatters away about impending doom, but his mind
is sharp. He is ever willing to do his part and
is brave, plucky, and even cunning. He is one
of the most admirable and memorable characters
in the series, along with the courageous mouse,
Reepicheep*.

Q

QUEEN JADIS (*The Magician's Nephew**; *The Lion, the Witch and the Wardrobe**), beautiful, fierce, ambitious, strong, very tall witch, who is present when Aslan* creates Narnia* in *The Magician's Nephew*. She represents evil. In *The Lion, the Witch and the Wardrobe*, she is referred to as the White Witch and calls herself Queen of Narnia. Between *Nephew* and *Lion*, she has taken over the country, imposing her cruel rule upon the inhabitants, terrifying all of them and subverting many good ones, turning opponents to stone statues in her palace coutryard and imprisoning many. She has also caused it to be always winter and never Christmas. In the climactic scenes, Aslan kills her, and the Pevensie children, Peter*, Susan*, Edmund*, and Lucy*, replace her as monarchs of Narnia and bring goodness and justice back to the land. In *Lion*, the children learn from Mr. Beaver that the Queen is descended from Lilith, a jinn who was the first wife of Adam in the Bible. On her other side she comes from the giants. Thus she has no human blood but is half jinn and half giant. There is a comic aspect about her that relieves her villainy, and the reader never doubts that she will be defeated.

THE QUEEN OF THE PHARISEES' CHILDREN (Willard*, Barbara, MacRae, 1983), period novel set in and near a large forest somewhere in England not long after the execution of Charles I. Sim Swayne, "half tinker, half pedlar," is loving

husband to golden-haired, black-eyed, light-
voiced Moll, whom he calls Queen of the
Pharisees (fairies) and often addresses as "my
lady," and wise and caring father to obedient,
earnest Will (Willow), 12, and Will's younger
sisters, helpful if stubborn Delphi and
"scarcey-witted" Fairlight. The half-starved,
tattered family, which once had three more
children, wanders about, begging and stealing
such essentials as milk for wizened and increasingly weaker baby son, Star, and hauling their
meager worldly goods, brooms, and a few other
saleable wares in a little cart pulled by their
old horse, Brownie. They have never had a
settled home since Sim feels cooped up under a
roof, and they are used to being rejected and
reviled, but the children feel loved and wanted
by their parents and are very close to one
another. Sim takes the family to a secluded area
deep in the forest, intending to winter there in
ruins of some sort. Ruffians attack and steal
the cart, Sim's only protection against a
possible charge of vagrancy and the main means
of the family's meager livelihood. They live for
a time in a burned-out manor house, doing odd
jobs for blind, old Goody Nye who lives nearby
in return for milk from her goats. After she
dies and Star continues to decline, they decide
to take advantage of an offer made them earlier
by kind and charitable Widow Tester to live in
her barn. Widow Tester, however, plans to marry
widower John Penfold, a cold, hard man who
covets the goats the family brought with it from
Goody Nye's and has them arrested and tried as
vagrants. Sim is imprisoned, and Moll and the
children are parceled out to various parishes.
Star dies in the cart in which they are hauled
away. The story now focuses on Will, who falls
into the hands of a parson, Mr. Hazelwood, whose
piety is deep but practical and humane. He and
his wife treat the boy kindly, giving him time
to grow used to what they see is a very
different and frightening way of life, respect-
ing his loss of family, and recognizing the
intelligence they realize is there under the
dirt and bad grammar. The parson also seems to
feel that the lad has been sent as a replacement
for his own recently deceased son. As soon as
the snow allows, he rides to town to try to help

Sim and discovers that the tinker has broken jail. Sure that his father will return to the forest glade where the children thought their mother danced among the Pharisees, Will, though plagued by feelings of guilt, runs away, intending to go there and join his father. He gets sidetracked and discovers Delphi, plump and happy in a nearby parish. She says that their mother has run away and Fairlight has drowned. Dispirited, Will returns to the parson's house, is again treated with love and compassion, and is baptized by the parson, who begins to instruct him in letters, behavior, and proper speech. At summer's end, the Hazelwoods are visited by Mrs. Hazelwood's sister's family. Since Mr. Godley is interested in archaeology, Mr. Hazelwood tells him about some old coins that Will had once mentioned that the Swaynes saw in the forest, and then Will tells him about the ruins. Mr. Godley thinks they might be Roman, and Mr. Hazelwood organizes the three into an expedition there. Will finds the family's hidden storeroom empty and knows that his father has come and gone. That evening, as the little party is about to return to the Hazelwoods', Will breaks away, and in the golden sunset, runs widdershins around the family knoll, and then, as though by magic, he sees Sim returning with a cart, with Moll beside him. Will runs joyfully to greet them and discovers to his dismay that his mother has lost all memory of her children. He learns that Sim, who has earned another cart working for an iron foundry, is devoting all his time to caring for her, now and forever Queen of the Pharisees. Will realizes there is no longer any place in their lives for him and that he must make his own way in the world. He also sees the advantages of returning with Mr. Hazelwood, continuing to live as his ward, and gaining some education. The novel is rich in both its picture of the period and its appeal to the emotions. The Swayne family is warmly and lovingly created, and a social system that makes criminals and outcasts of such struggling and well-meaning if unlettered human beings is put on trial and found guilty. The true goodness of the Hazelwoods stands out in stark relief to the self-righteousness and avarice of John Penfold and his court clerk brother, Robert, who subvert the system to their own ends. The author builds Will's dilemma of loyalty gradually until it becomes painfully real for the reader, and the boy's final realization that he must take care of himself first of all seems completely appropriate. Whitbread.

THE QUEEN'S BLESSING (Polland*, Madeleine A., ill. William Stobbs, Constable, 1963; Holt, 1964), historical novel set in Northumbria and Scotland in 1070-1073. Merca*, 11, and her little brother, Dag*, 6, have become waifs in Wearmouth after the killing of their parents and the burning of their homestead by the troops of Malcolm* III of Scotland, who has led a revolt against William the Conqueror in an attempt to put Aedgar, a Saxon, on the throne, and has been betrayed by a Northumbrian earl. They see Malcolm greet the Princess Margaret*, Aedgar's sister, and when Dag's precious shell rolls to the feet of the advancing party and he rushes out to retrieve it, they are saved from immediate slaughter only by the intervention of the gentle princess. They are taken, along with other homeless people who have been rounded up, on Malcolm's march north to Dunfermline. The strongest refugees are quickly sold off for slaves, and the two children, being among the last, are finally given at two for the price of one to a mean-spirited Scottish woman. Through nearly a year they toil, underfed, overworked, abused, and in rags, until the sound of Christmas bells startles Merca out of her stupor, and the realization that Dag does not remember Christmas awakens her determination to escape. When they do make their break, they are almost retaken but are allowed to escape by the woman's meek husband. The next night they wander onto the campsite of a vagabond who feeds them, then, having drunk too much, tells Merca he is Thomas the Knife, an assassin by profession, with an ambition to kill a king. This information arouses in Merca a determination to get enough gold to have Thomas kill Malcolm. Though Thomas sets them on their way south, they get turned around and, after some days of walking, Merca collapses in the road just as a band of horsemen approach. Among them are Mary, lady in waiting to Margaret, who is now Malcolm's queen, and her brother, Dougal, who take them to Dunfermline where the queen has a few pauper children she is bringing up as her own. Added to this group, Dag flourishes, but Merca retains her hatred of Malcolm and even of Margaret because she is his wife. When she tries to steal some gold to buy Thomas's services and is caught, she is forgiven. When the Normans invade Scotland and Malcolm goes off to war, she hopes he will be killed, but instead he comes to a peaceful agreement. Hoping that change will banish what she perceives as unhappiness in Merca, Queen Margaret includes her in the group to accompany the royal couple on a tour of the western part of their country. When Merca spots Thomas among the soldiers in the group, she is elated, thinking now her hopes for Malcolm's death will be realized. She is troubled by Margaret's obvious love for her husband and Malcolm's tenderness to his wife, but she puts these out of her mind. On the island of Iona, the farthest and most isolated point on their trip, she wakes in the middle of the night and sees a figure slip into the tent of the king. Her scream wakes the king before the dagger reaches him, and, though slightly wounded, Malcolm kills Thomas and is both astonished and grateful that Merca has saved his life. As she realizes that this is what she wished to do, Merca's hatred and misery slip away, and she allows herself to feel safe and happy for the first time in three years. The two children and their plight dominate the story, with the historical background, the picture of Dunfermline, and the life of the eleventh century all integral but subordinate. The misery of the abused children is well evoked, and Merca's fierce protectiveness toward Dag is convincing. The horrors of war and the destructiveness of vengeful feelings are strong thematic elements. Fanfare.

QUENTIN SYKES (*Archer's Goon**), father of Howard* and Awful*, whose failure to produce the quarterly 2.000 words starts the family's involvement in the intrigues of the seven wizards that control the city. Quentin is balding and has a paunch. He is a teacher of

English at the local Polytechnic, and when he
asserts himself , he can quell a disgruntled
student, a roomful of angry people, or even his
daughter, Awful, but not his wife, Catriona. At
first Quentin refuses to write the words because
he resents being pushed around, but after he
hears Archer* say that he wants to farm the
world, he stands on his refusal as a matter of
principle. In the end, because of what Archer
has done to the typewriter, he can cause things
to happen by writing them, and in this way he
controls the scene in which the three eldest
wizards are lured into the spaceship and shot
off to a distant star. Howard/Venturus never
tells him that his quarterly words were really
just a red herring and a way of being repaid for
adopting Howard by being freed of taxes. Quentin
is a comic but ultimately admirable figure.

R

RACHEL ANSEL (*Twopence a Tub**), daughter of a tough Dudley, England, nailer or iron founder. She is nice looking but not particularly pretty. What attracts Jek Davies to her is her peacefulness. She has a calm air and a strength of character that remind him of Annie Woodall, the wife of Jim Woodall the Union Man, or president of the Union local, who seems the antithesis of his own termagant mother. Rachel has a congenitally deformed right hand and thus is excused from working in the foundry along with her father's two wives and the other children. She likes to read, and ironically is reading about King Arthur when Jek visits her house. She encourages him to think of the miners' strike as part of the larger cause for human rights. At the end of the book, the reader anticipates that some day the two will marry.

RAHERE (*The Witch's Brat**), actual historical founder of the hospital at the Church of Saint Bartholomew the Great in Smithfield, London. In the novel he appears first as the King's Jongleur or jester, a tall, sardonic man with black hair and bright grey eyes. The second time he comes to the New Minster he has become an Austin, or Augustinian, canon, having suffered greatly from the death of the crown prince and most of the young men of the court who have drowned in a ship on which they had requested Rahere to accompany them. Finding the life of a churchman still lacking in meaning, he has made a pilgrimage to Rome, caught a fever there, and almost died. When he recovered, he vowed to start a hospital for the poor in London, and he has had a vision in which Saint Bartholomew directed him to build it in Smithfield and to get King Henry I to donate the land by also building a church, since Henry is stingy but pious. He is pictured as a man of kindness, unusual perception, and ironic humor.

RANSOME, ARTHUR (MITCHELL) (1884-1967), born in Leeds, Yorkshire; novelist, critic and journalist. He attended Old College, Windermere, and Rugby .College, Warwickshire; he started to study science at Yorkshire College (now Leeds University) but left shortly. He worked as an office boy at Grant Richards, publishers, in London and as an assistant at Unicorn Press, but in 1903 he left to become a freelance writer, a ghost writer, and a publisher's reader. In 1905 and 1906 he was assistant editor for the magazine *Temple Bar* in London, and he moved to Russia in 1913. During World War I he was a correspondent for the *Daily News* and *The Observer*, and during the 1920s, he was a correspondent in Russia, Egypt, and China. For many years he was a columnist for the Manchester *Guardian*. Although for adults he wrote one novel, a book of short stories, and sixteen other volumes of biography, autobiography, and criticism, and translated and edited others, he is mostly remembered now for his twelve books of fiction for children, starting with *Swallows and Amazons** (Cape, 1930; Lippincott, 1931), in which two families of young people sail Lake Windermere, where he spent summers until he was thirteen and his father died. Two Callum children, scientific Dick and imaginative Dorothea, are added in *Winter Holiday* (Cape, 1933; Lippincott, 1934). The other books carry on with the same characters in various groupings. Five, including *Pigeon Post** (Cape, 1936; Lippincott, 1937), a Carnegie Medal winner, are set in the lake country; others, like *We Didn't Mean to Go to Sea** (Cape, 1937; Macmillan, 1938), have settings further afield. These novels are credited with changing the pattern of realistic fiction in England from highly unlikely stories of smugglers and coiners to the "holiday adventure," which could reasonably happen and which employs believable details of everyday life, but they also have been criticized for slowing the transition to books about less privileged children who attend public-supported schools and face real problems of society. *Swallows and Amazons* is on the Children's Literature Association Touchstone list. Ransome's sailing stories draw from his own experience in the lake district and later sailing the Baltic in his own ship. He also wrote the story of Aladdin in verse and a number of other kinds of books for children, including *Old Peter's Russian Tales* (Jack, 1916; Stokes, 1917). He was awarded honorary degrees from the University of Leeds and the University of Durham, and was named Commander, Order of the British Empire.

RANSOM FOR A KNIGHT (Picard*, Barbara Leonie, ill. C. Walter Hodges, Oxford, 1956; Walck, 1967), historical novel of a young girl's journey that starts in Sussex and goes to Scotland in the year 1315. Like everyone else at Little Merton, Alys de Renneville, 10, has believed the report that her father, Sir Robert, and her older brother, Robin, 14, were killed in the fighting at Bannockburn. Then a wounded knight is thrown from his horse at the gate to their manor, and Alys, along with Lady Ermengarde, her father's cousin who runs the household, and Sely, her old nurse, tends him and sits with him. For a brief period, when she is alone with him, he is lucid, and he gives her a message from her father that she is to arrange a ransom of 100 marks to be sent to Angus MacAngus of Glengorman, near Perth, who is holding both Sir Robert and Robin prisoner. The knight then lapses into delirium, and even when he recovers enough to be coherent he can remember nothing of his past. Alys can convince neither Lady Ermengarde nor her father's overlord, Baron Walter FitzGilbert, that this is not a tale she has invented in her desire for her father's safety. She enlists the help of Hugh, 14, the son of a serf who was foster brother of Robin and his best friend, and with great difficulty she takes the jewels left by her mother and a bag she thinks contains gold coins from her cousin's locked chest, and

together they start out on Blanche, her favorite
horse. The journey is long and, in the tradition
of the quest pattern, they run into various
obstacles and aids. The bag turns out to have
only a few silver coins of small denominations.
When they stop at a nunnery, the abbess, Lady
Matilda, suggests that they rest for a few days
and insists on locking up the jewels, secretly
sending word to Little Merton. Alys manages to
steal back her jewels, and they escape but are
almost taken prisoner by a wicked innkeeper in
Southwark, where they are saved by a young man,
Nicholas Fletcher of the Skinners Fraternity of
Corpus Christi, who takes them to his mother's
home in London, shows them the sights, including
King Edward the II and Queen Isabella, and
arranges for them to travel to Oxford with a
scholar friend, Adam Maynard. Adam arranges an
escort for them to Nottingham with Master Simon
Yonge, a wool merchant, who lets them watch
their first play at Coventry but is set upon by
thieves and knifed soon afterwards. When it is
apparent that he will recover but that it will
be a slow process, Alys gets a tavern letter-
writer to pen a note to him, and she sets off
again with Hugh. At Nottingham they go to the
home of Master John Bridgford, a business
acquaintance of Master Yonge, whose spoiled
daughter, Cicely, 14, takes a liking to Alys,
mostly because Alys can help her with the
embroidered hanging her mother insists she
finish before her impending marriage. Craftily,
Alys charges her a gold penny for her needlework
and another for teaching her the elements of
French, but Cicely's fiance shows his attraction
for Alys, Cicely becomes jealous and insulting,
and Alys and Hugh move on. Not long after that,
Hugh sprains his ankle severely, and they wait
for three weeks in the crowded one-room cottage
of Widow Magot, along with her fifteen
children. As they come near to the border, they
find burned farms and high prices, and they
soon have no more money. Alys tries begging,
with little success, but the wife of a grumbling
cobbler takes them in for three weeks while Alys
regains some of her strength and Hugh works for
his food at an inn. As they cross the Aln River,
they must pass through a village where there is
plague, and when Alys becomes ill on the snowy

moor, Hugh is sure she has contracted it. A one-armed farmer lets them stay in a cow stall, though his shrewish wife objects, and he leaves them water and bread at a distance every day. Prodded by Hugh, the farmer finally admits that he might get some medical aid from Maudlyn the witch, who comes to help mainly to spite the farmer's wife. While Alys gradually recovers from pneumonia, Blanche has a foal, which Hugh treasures but knows they must leave behind. Maudlyn pronounces a strong curse on the family if they sell the horses before the youngsters return to claim them. Though he has let Alys lead in every way, Hugh now insists that they must sell something from the bag of jewels, but when they select the simplest gold ring, the silversmith, sure that they are thieves, raises a hue and cry against them. They are saved by three traveling jugglers and dancers, cutpurses on the side, who conceal them in a cart. Nan, the acrobat, gets a look at the jewels, and thinks Alys a very clever thief, but when one of the men steals them, Nan steals them back and sends Alys and Hugh on their way. From this point on they get various kinds of help, and though they fear the Scots, they are mostly well treated and even escorted by Tammas, the son of a Scot farmer, to Dunkeld, fifteen miles north of Perth. At the castle of Angus MacAngus, Alys boldly approaches the high seat where the Scottish lord has just dined, and demands to see her father before she gives up the ransom. The reunion with her father and brother, who have been well treated, is joyous. Admiring Alys's spirit, Lord MacAngus refuses to take the jewels and halves the ransom demand, saying he will wait for the rest. A week after they have started home, they run into Baron Walter also bringing the ransom, the wounded knight finally having recovered his memory and convinced the residents of Little Merton that Sir Robert is alive. When they stop to pick up Blanche, Sir Robert gives the foal to Hugh, and at home Lady Ermengarde decides to retire to a nunnery and leave the household management to Alys. Alys is rather high-handed, and Hugh is somewhat simple, but characterization is not the strong point of the novel, which shows a great deal of careful research into the period. Many of the adventures

have an instructive tone. The appearance of the
king and the various stories of his extravagance
and the murder of his friend the Earl of Warwick
are included without any real connection to the
rest of the novel, and an author's note at the
end gives further historical information. The
plot is weakened by the appearance of Baron
Walter as they start home, since presumably he
would have ransomed the two de Rennevilles
without the arduous trip by Alys and Hugh.
Carnegie Com.; Fanfare.

RAN TRANTER (*The Way to Sattin Shore**), Randall
Tranter, about fifteen, named for his mother's
family. The eldest son in the Tranter family,
brother of Kate* and Lenny* and son of Kitty*,
he has grown away from the family, works during
the day, takes night classes, and has a
girlfriend with whom he spends a lot of time. It
is he who tells Kate the family history that
sends her to the village of Sattin and to Sattin
Shore. Their father contacts him by putting a
note in his alarm clock, and thus he is the
first of the children to learn the truth, that
their father is alive and has returned to
Sattin. Ran has many sides--a youth with
romantic inclinations, competitive elder brother
grappling with the younger, solicitous elder
brother caring for the little sister, happy
family member flipping pancakes, and secretive
teenager. Next to Kate, he is the book's most
appealing figure.

RAOUL (*Three Lives for the Czar**), French uncle
of Andrei* and Alix* Hamilton who is an
emissary from the French army to the Russian and
tries vainly to persuade the generals and the
nobles to upgrade the army, particularly to
mechanize and to invest in artillery, before
World War I. A "razorish" young man, he is
dashing, well-educated, literary, and of great
practical understanding, but he can be nothing
more than a bystander as the countries he loves,
France, Austria, and Russia, move blunderingly
toward war.

RAT (*The Wind in the Willows**), the Water Rat
who becomes friend to Mole* and in whose home
Mole lives when he comes to the riverbank. Rat

is friendly, genial, generous, and sensitive; he
is well liked by all the riverbankers, and
writes poetry in his leisure time. He is also
brave, level-headed, and considerate. When Mole
has gone off to the Wild Wood alone, Rat does
not hesitate to set off to his rescue. When
Toad* describes the joys of taking to the road
in a gypsy caravan, Rat is skeptical. When Mole
comes upon his old home one winter night, Rat is
kind enough to help him find it and to praise it
while setting about making it habitable,
realizing that Mole loves it however shabby it
is. Rat's only real moment of weakness comes
from his overactive imagination when he meets
the Sea Rat and is almost talked into leaving
for foreign ports and strange coasts. Mole
counteracts this strange seizure by grappling
with his friend, sitting on him until he seems
calmer, and finally inducing him to try his hand
at writing a poem again.

RAVENSGILL (Mayne*, William, Hamilton, 1970;
Dutton, 1970), realistic novel of family and
neighborhood life with mystery and detective
story aspects set for a few weeks in the
mid-1900s, perhaps in the 1950s, among the Yorkshire hills and moors, in which a grammar-
school boy's persistence results in putting to
rest a long-standing conflict between two
related families. The setting of hills,
streams, river, reservoir, and isolated farms
plays an unusually strong role in both present
and historical events in the story. A letter to
Wig, the old hired man at the Chapmans' farm,
New Scar House, brings news of the death of the
policeman who, fifty years earlier, was professionally interested in Lizzie White, the chipper, eccentric old Grandma* at Ravensgill farm
over the hill and beyond the reservoir. Both
Wig and the Chapmans' Gran, Lizzie's estranged
cousin, write the news to Ravensgill, Wig to
his brother, Tot Tuker, the old hand there, and
Gran to Lizzie, the latter requesting Lizzie to
come home and prompting Lizzie to pack her
bags. Though the letters' contents are not
divulged to him, comments arouse the curiosity
of inquisitive, orphaned Bob* White, about
fifteen, who then, on purpose and by luck,
pieces together the jigsaw of an old family

scandal, partly with the help of chubby Judith
Chapman who is his age and whose curiosity has
similarly been whetted by obscure remarks and
the "shushing" of family members. After a
near-fatal swim in the nearby gill (river), Bob
finds a portion of Gran's letter on the hillside
and then goes home only to collapse from shock
and thus keep Grandma from departing. Recovered,
Bob goes to the local police station, where he
learns that one Abraham Dinsdale had died at
Ravensgill under suspicious circumstances, and
that the case was never closed. He then pursues
other leads to old newspaper files, from which
he learns that his grandfather, Clifford Patrick
White, was accused of killing Dinsdale, the
Chapmans' great-grandfather, whose badly bruised
body was found in the gill. White escaped, with,
it was thought, Lizzie's help, and disappeared,
never to be seen again. Bob realizes that the
Chapmans are in some way involved and confides
in Judith. The two eventually discover that
Abraham Dinsdale was killed by the water and the
rocks of the same river Bob almost died in.
Dinsdale was pursuing White, who had married
Lizzie Dinsdale without his consent. When White
fled from the police, he took refuge in an
underground tunnel, which the two youths also
discover, and later died there. Since circumstances imply that White did not murder Dinsdale, a Chapman ancestor, the two families are
reconciled, but after the initial glow no one
feels that there has been much change in their
lives. It might even have been just as well, as
was suggested several times to Bob and Judith
by older members of their families, to have
allowed bygones to remain bygones. The understated, almost cryptic style, the numerous
similar names, many obscure allusions to past
events, and the abrupt switches in scene from
Ravensgill to New Scar and, hence, in point of
view, call for careful, close reading. Details
of the scandal come out gradually, discovered
pretty much by the reader as Bob and then Judith
uncover them, although Bob's experiences in the
river and tunnel leading into it serve as a
clear foreshadowing of the conclusion and
explanation of what happened to Dinsdale. What
happened to White is not clear. What caused his
death, and how much did Lizzie know about that

and the supposed murder? How much did Tot, who was in love with Lizzie, know, and what was his role in the old story? The flagstone in the yard, uncovered by Tot, bears White's name and birth and death dates. Tot says he could have testified to White's innocence but was never asked. This is a consistently suspenseful story, here and there relieved by humor, generous with local color, and well paced. The main characters are roundly and convincingly drawn, and the antagonism between Bob and Mick Chapman, which erupts in a rural rumble, seems appropriate. A map would help. Fanfare.

READY, MASTERMAN (*Masterman Ready**), wise, knowledgeable, staunch, Bible-quoting old seaman of sixty-four, who insures the survival of the Seagrave family after their ship is disabled in the south seas on the way to Australia and they are cast ashore on a desert isle. Although his name symbolizes his character and he is composed of all such finer qualities as patience, perseverance, piety, respect for authority, kindness, prudence, selfless devotion, and love of God, he never seems priggish or unreal. The author skillfully weaves the story of Ready's life as a long story within a story into the tapestry of the adventure story. Marryat never lets Ready's life history get in the way of the seriousness of the castaways' situation. Here and there during the rainy season Ready tells the Seagraves how, in his early teens, he ran away from a loving mother to satisfy a long-held ambition to go to sea; survived imprisonment, abuse, and numerous vicissitudes; and returned to England wiser and contrite only to discover that the Mr. Masterman, for whom he had been named, has died and willed his fortune elsewhere (thinking Ready dead), leaving the youth without financial resources. Ready subsequently spent his life as a seaman before the mast. His premonition that he might die on the island comes true. There is enough adventure and action in Ready's account to fill another novel. It serves not only to deepen his characterization and provide moral instruction for young minds, but also adds quite a few thrills to an already thrill-filled novel and heightens the suspense. Much of Ready's life story parallels that of the author.

REBECCA (*A Pattern of Roses**), youngest daughter
of the new "with it" vicar, who becomes involved
with Tim* Ingram's interest in the story of the
Edwardian boy, Tom* Inskip. Angry, resentful of
the missionary zeal of her parents and siblings,
and scornful of the advertising success of Tom's
parents, Rebecca is a complex character, waspish
yet vulnerable, decisive yet insecure. A bright
girl who wants to be a probation officer, she
takes the lead in the research to discover Tom's
story. She has blotches of freckles and a great
mop of fuzzy, ginger-colored hair. It is not
until he has begun to become attached to her
that Tim realizes that she looks much like the
drawing he has found of Netty* Bellinger, done
by Tom more than sixty years earlier.

RED JAK (*The Writing on the Hearth**), scarred,
surly miller on the Thames near Ewelme, who
bridles with anger every time he must assist
anyone of importance to navigate past his mill.
He gives Stephen lodging in return for labor
after Stephen leaves his stepfather's house and
later is prevented from overturning Duchess
Eleanor's barge only by Stephen's quick action.
If Red Jak had succeeded, the Earl* of Suffolk
would have suffered political as well as social
embarrassment, because the mill stands on his
land.

RED QUEEN (*Through the Looking-Glass**), chess
piece that Alice* rescues from the ashes of
Looking-Glass House and that later becomes
person-sized. The Red Queen screams a lot, is
curt and blunt, and bosses Alice around. She
drags Alice along in a mad race, explaining,
"Now, *here*, you see, it takes all the running
you can do, to keep in the same place. If you
want to get somewhere else, you must run at
least twice as fast as that!" Alice confides to
her her desire to become a queen herself. After
Alice achieves the eighth square and becomes a
queen, the Red Queen and the White* Queen hold a
party for her, during which the Red Queen is
especially hard on Alice, pushing her around
verbally and physically until Alice seizes hold
of the tablecloth and terminates the scene. The

Red Queen shrinks to chess-piece size and Alice
grabs her, shakes her, and wakes to find she's
shaking her black kitten. The Red Queen is
distorted into caricature like most of the
book's characters and is one of the most
disagreeable of the lot.

RED SHIFT (Garner*, Alan, Collins, 1973; Macmillan, 1973), novel set in Cheshire, England,
in three time periods--late twentieth century,
mid-seventeenth century during the English Civil
War, and the early second century after the
loss of the Roman Ninth Legion. The three
stories are told concurrently, with shifts back
and forth in time without transition, and are
parallel in many ways, mainly in that each tells
the love story of a young man named Thomas (or
Macey*, a diminutive of Thomas in the earliest
tale), who is tormented by mental imbalance and
subject to visions or fits, and a girl who is
more stable psychologically. They also share a
talisman, a stone ax used by Macey, cared for
and cemented into his house by seventeenth-
century Thomas* Rowley, and sold to a museum by
twentieth-century Tom*. In the modern story, Tom
lives claustrophobically in a house trailer with
his army sergeant father and his dreadful,
mean-minded mother and carries on his relationship with Jan*, who is studying nursing in
London, by meeting at Crewe station and roaming
the area, eventually settling upon Barthomley
church and the old quarry, once a sacred place,
on the nearby hill, Mow Cop. Theirs is a
tortured love, complicated by their separation,
by Tom's spiritual self-flagellation, and by the
suspicions of his parents. In the earliest
story, Macey and his mates, remnants of the
destroyed Ninth Legion, decide to "go tribal,"
first razing a village to get proper clothes and
weapons, and to convince the local tribe, the
Cats, that they are rivals, the Mothers. After
they destroy the village, they find one girl
survivor, whom they gang rape and hamstring but
keep to serve them. Only Macey, in whom they are
able to induce a sort of berserker's fit,
refrains from attacking the girl, and only he
becomes close to her and escapes the death that
she causes the others by poison. Ironically, she
carries the child of her attackers, the only

link of the Roman Ninth Legion to the future. In the Civil War story, the massacre of Barthomley, a historical occurrence in which men, women, and children who sought sanctuary in the church were murdered, is the main action. The story is of the love of Thomas Rowley for Margery, who has also been sought by a neighbor, Thomas Venables, now one of the attackers. In a fit induced by the parson's son, John* Fowler, now leader of the local revolutionists, Thomas fires the shot that triggers the massacre of the king's forces. Because of his love for Madge, Thomas Venables helps her and the wounded Thomas escape to Mow Cop, where they find a sanctuary. The stories are told almost entirely in dialogue in scenes which slide into one another, very much as a film shifts scenes. This technique, with complete lack of explanations and formal transitions, makes the novel difficult; a second reading clears up most obscurities, though some knowledge of British history is assumed. The theme seems to be that establishing genuine communication through love is extremely difficult but of paramount importance. The title comes from the physical principle known as the Doppler Effect, in which the colors of approaching sound waves change to red as they pass the observer and begin to recede in the distance. This is a novel rich in nuance and allusion, difficult but rewarding. Choice.

REEPICHEEP (*Prince Caspian**; *The Voyage of the "Dawn Treader"**), one of several delightfully named talking animals of Narnia* that contribute to the action, among them Pattertwig the Squirrel, Glenstorm the Centaur, Clodsley Shovel the Mole, and Hogglestock the Hedgehog. Bigger than an ordinary mouse (over a foot high), Reepicheep is spirited and martial, carries a tiny rapier at his side, sports a long, crimson feather projecting jauntily from a thin gold headband, and twirls his whiskers like a mustache. In *Prince Caspian* he fights valiantly for the Old Narnians against Miraz, is wounded and healed by Lucy's* cordial, and loses his tail, which is later restored by Aslan*. In *The Voyage of the "Dawn Treader"*, he has a good deal of difficulty at first with Eustace*, who

teases him and abuses him physically. During the
trip, Reepicheep remains consistently over-
assertive and aggressively valiant. It is not
known whether or not he meets Aslan after he
leaves Edmund*, Lucy, and Eustace*. Reepicheep
is a thoroughly engaging figure, one of the most
memorable of the series. He makes a brief, final
appearance in the concluding book, *The Last
Battle*, where he is bright-eyed, chipper, and
dapper, having entered eternal Narnia. He
welcomes Tirian*, Jill, Eustace, and the rest of
the Seven Kings and Queens of Narnia into
Aslan's everlasting realm with his usual
courteous manner and aplomb.

REES, DAVID (BARTLETT) (1936-   ), born in London; teacher, author, critic. He attended King's
College School, Wimbleton, from 1946 to 1954,
then Queens' College, Cambridge, where he
received his B.A. degree in 1958 and his M.A. in
1961. For five years he was a schoolmaster at
Wilson's Grammar School, London, then head of
the English department at Vyners School,
Ickenham, Middlesex, for several years. As a
child during World War II he was evacuated to a
remote farmhouse on the north coast of Devon,
and because of his happy memories of the period,
he returned in 1968 to Devon where he has lived
most of the time since, becoming a lecturer at
St. Luke's College in Exeter and later at the
University of Exeter. In the early 1980s he
taught at California State University at San
Jose for a year and lived in San Francisco. He
is married and has two sons. The first of his
more than twenty books of fiction for children
was *Storm Surge* (Lutterworth, 1975), a story of
floods on the east coast of England. He was
awarded the Carnegie Medal for his World War II
novel, *The Exeter Blitz* (Hamilton, 1978;
Elsevier, 1980), and the Other Award for *The
Green Bough of Liberty* (Dobson, 1979), about
the 1798 rebellion in Ireland. Among his other
novels that have received critical attention is
The Milkman's on His Way (Gay Men's Press,
1982), which has been described as a "very
explicit and often painfully moving" account of
a homosexual adolescence. As a critic he is
noted for his book, *The Marble in the Water:
Essays on Contemporary Writers for Children and*

Young People (Horn Book, 1980). He has also written a novel for adults.

REEVES, JAMES (JOHN MORRIS REEVES) (1909-1978), born at Harrow-on-the-Hill, London; for more than forty years a prominent man of letters. Though he was best known for his numerous poems, critical essays, and anthologies for adults, he also published many books for juveniles, most of them an outgrowth of his great love for folklore and old legends. Named to the *Horn Book* Fanfare list by the magazine's editors, *The Cold Flame** (Hamilton, 1967; Meredith, 1969) is a witty and inventive improvization of "The Blue Light" from the Brothers Grimm. It was written as a novel for adults, but rejected by publishers for that audience and eventually issued for children. In addition, Reeves published books of short stories and several other novels of magic and fantasy, including *The Strange Light* (Heinemann, 1964; Rand, 1966), a time fantasy in which a girl enters a violet-atmosphered storybook land of people who will soon become characters in novels, and *The Path of Gold* (Hamilton, 1972), which is based on the Grimms' "The Water of Life." Also for young readers, he retold English folktales, the exploits of Don Quixote, stories from the Bible, fables of Aesop, and the tale of Odysseus, among other renditions from oral tradition, and edited anthologies of prose and poetry. He published for children nine books of original poems, of which the best known are *The Blackbird in the Lilac* (Oxford, 1952; Dutton, 1959) and *Prefabulous Animiles* (Heinemann, 1957; Dutton, 1960). His poetry has been praised for its unforced music, clear imagery, and variety of subject, rhyme, rhythm, and mood. During World War I his parents moved from London to Buckinghamshire, where he went to school. He received his M.A. with honors in English from Jesus College, Cambridge, in 1931, and taught in schools and training colleges for teachers until 1952. He began to write poetry about 1920 and published his first book, *The Natural Need* (Seizin; Constable), poems for adults, in 1935. Numerous other books followed, even after the onset of glaucoma in 1946 prevented him from reading. The first of his many books for children came out soon thereafter, entitled *The Wandering Moon* (Heinemann, 1950; Dutton, 1960), also verse. Retired from teaching, in 1951 he became general editor of the Heinemann Poetry Bookshelf series and, in 1960, general editor of Unicorn Books. He also wrote plays, contributed extensively to magazines and newspapers, and was a broadcaster and lecturer. The brother of children's novelist Joyce Gard, he married, had three children, and lived in Lewes, Sussex.

REGINA (*Dawn Wind**), beggar girl who has returned to Viroconium after the Saxon destruction of the city and whom Owain* finds living in the ruins. Despite her rags, she is something of a beauty, with very black hair and dark eyes fringed with long lashes. Though dirty, unkempt, and terribly undernourished, Regina is not just a waif. She is a girl of considerable spirit and ingenuity, and she is shown to have a real appreciation of beauty in her love of the birds, particularly the blue tit, and her delight in the blue flames of the burning olive wood box.

REG WHITTACKER (*Fire and Hemlock**), father of Polly* who is divorced from her mother, Ivy*, early in the book. Polly thinks for a long time that her mother's comments on his weakness of character and inability to face reality are just part of Ivy's own moody and suspicious nature, but when Polly goes to stay with him she realizes that he has not even had the nerve to tell his wife, Joanna, that his daughter is coming or that she plans to live there. To save them all from shame, Polly pretends that she has come just for a couple of nights, but she is disillusioned and has no desire to see Reg again.

THE RELUCTANT DRAGON (Grahame*, Kenneth, ill. Ernest H. Shepard, Holiday, 1938), tongue-in-cheek literary tale originally part of Grahame's autobiographical *Dream Days* (Lane, 1898) as a story told to the narrator and his sister Charlotte by his friend the circus man. The shepherd and his wife, Maria, have a little son much given to reading and particularly versed in tales of giants and heroes, so that when a dragon shows up in the neighborhood, it seems

sensible that the Boy should climb up to its
cave to interview him. The dragon explains that
it has never enjoyed rampaging and devouring
damsels, like the other young dragons, and
confesses somewhat shyly that it plans to
settle down and make up verses. The Boy explains
politely but frankly that it will never do,
since the dragon is an enemy of the human race,
a role which the dragon denies. Although they
become friends and spend many pleasant evenings
together, with the dragon telling stories of
old, old times, the villagers become frightened
and send for St. George. The Boy, though tempted
by the prospect of watching a good fight,
rushes off to warn the dragon, who refuses to be
worried, telling the Boy, "You'll be able to
arrange something. I've every confidence in you,
you're such a *manager*." The Boy finds St. George
alone at the inn and explains the situation. St.
George realizes that he has been overly
credulous in believing the villagers' tales of
wrongs but feels it would be quite against the
rules just to go quietly away. He does, however,
walk up to the dragon's cave to confer with the
beast. At first the dragon threatens to climb
back into the far recesses of its cave and wait
for a few years, but St. George appeals to its
artistic sensibilities and persuades it to put
on the appearance of a good fight. The next day
the Boy joins the villagers assembled near the
cave to watch the contest (with bets running six
to four on the dragon), and they put on such a
good show that he fears the dragon, ramping and
breathing fire, may get carried away and forget
the bargain, or that St. George may vanquish the
beast and feel compelled to cut off its head,
but in the end the dragon gives him a big wink
and lets St. George lead it tamely to the
banquet in the village. The dragon makes the Boy
promise to see it home afterwards, but, with
the responsibility having been transferred to
the Boy, it eats until it drops off to sleep.
Finding the Boy crying with frustration, St.
George prods the dragon awake, shames it into
motion, and takes one arm while the Boy takes
the other, and they set off up the hill
together. With urbane language and gentle humor,
Grahame plays with the variation on the old hero
tale in a slight but charming story which, with

the Shepard illustrations, holds up apart from
its original setting. Lewis Carroll.

RENVOIZE, JEAN (1930-   ), born in London; publisher and writer, mostly for adults. Daughter
of an artist, she was educated in England, has
worked in publishing, being a director of
Maurice Temple Smith, Ltd., and Book Representation, Ltd., and is married to a publisher. Her
novel, *A Wild Thing** (Macmillan, 1970; Atlantic/
Little, 1971), which was named to the *Horn Book*
Fanfare list, was written as an adult book and
published for adults in England but for
adolescents or young adults in the United
States. The idea for it came from the news
reports of an orphan boy about twelve whose
bones were found on a Scottish hillside and who
was identified by his dental condition. She
changed the main character to a sixteen-year-old
girl. Among her other novels are *The Masker*
(Secher, 1960) and *The Net* (Stein, 1973). Two
of her nonfiction books are studies in the
problems of domestic violence, *Children in
Danger: The Causes and Prevention of Baby Battering* (Routledge, 1974) and *Web of Violence: A
Study in Family Violence* (Routledge, 1978).

THE RESCUERS (Sharp*, Margery, ill. Judith
Brook, Collins, 1959; ill. Garth Williams,
Little, 1959), talking-animal fantasy. At the
request of the Prisoners' Aid Society, a world-
wide organization of mice devoted to bringing
cheer, comfort, and assistance to prisoners
everywhere, Miss Bianca, a pretty, pampered,
ermine-white mouse who lives in a porcelain
pagoda in the embassy and is the pet of the
ambassador's son, Boy; Nils, a staunch Norwegian
sailor mouse; and Bernard, an earnest and
practical pantry mouse, set out to rescue a
Norwegian poet imprisoned in the infamous
dungeon of the terrible Black Castle, located a
month's journey away in a vast and barren
desert. The trio hitches a ride in a country
wagon carrying foodstuffs for the jailers and
prisoners, where they hide among some flour
sacks. After the three adventurers arrive at the
prison, their chief adversaries are the cruel,
fat jailer, who has decorated his walls with
impaled butterflies, and his overstuffed,

equally heartless cat, Mamelouke. The three mice set up housekeeping in a hole behind the wainscoting of the jailer's cigar-strewn living room and form a branch of the society, electing Miss Bianca chairwoman and Bernard secretary. They hold frequent meetings to discuss problems and make plans. Miss Bianca, who is also a poet, often contributes brief verses expressive of their feelings and hopes. Nils and Bernard go on expeditions about the castle and give close attention to Miss Bianca's safety and comfort. Days pass before they learn where the prisoner is and get him safely out. Miss Bianca, who has never learned to fear cats, cannily abstracts the information from Mamelouke that every New Year's Day the jailers have bilious attacks from overeating the night before and are unable to work. Then Bernard and Nils discover a water gate overlooking the river, an excellent escape route. On New Year's Day, Bernard climbs up the jailer's inert body to secure the keys with which the prisoner then opens his cell door. The four sneak out the water gate and fall in with some raft people who take them to safety. The Prisoners' Aid Society decorates the three comrades for extraordinary valor and even dedicates a new award in their honor. Miss Bianca returns to her beloved Boy, Nils and the poet go home to Norway, and Bernard returns to his pantry and eventually becomes secretary of the society. Bernard and Nils are flat characters, the villains are caricatures, and Miss Bianca is a charming and somewhat precious heroine. The plot never delivers on its promise for suspense, the author's somewhat condescending tone keeps the reader at arm's length, and the conclusion seems foreshortened. The details of the setting are very good, and the Prisoners' Aid Society is an inventive notion. The book carries the conviction of real-life situations where prisoners have made pets of mice. Carnegie Com.; Choice; Fanfare.

THE RETURN OF THE TWELVES. See *The Twelve and the Genii.*

RHODES (*Brother in the Land**), former physical education teacher who becomes the chief guerrilla leader in Masada, the resistance group that Danny* Lodge joins. A man who loves activity and violence, he is good at his job of seizing vehicles and supplies from the soldiers, but he is constantly at odds with Sam Branwell*, Masada's leader, because he wants to exclude many of the refugees while Branwell sees that their camp must be open to all in need. After their garden is discovered to be worthless because of radiation, Rhodes leaves with some of the other men and vehicles, supposedly to find supplies but actually with no intention of returning. Danny and Kim* Tyson encounter him later as a member of a motorcycle gang terrorizing the survivors, and Kim kills him.

RICHARD BLUNT (*The Other People**), unhappy boy who, along with his parents, is staying at the Sea View Guest House when Kate* Lucas spends her holiday there. Something of a pawn between his mother, who takes every opportunity to point out the inferiority of Sea View to the Hotel Splendide, where they stayed previously, and his father, a physical fitness enthusiast, Richard feels that he is a failure and is surly to Kate because she understands him. When she finds him diving from the high rocks, she realizes that he is practicing to live up to his father's expectations, yet he fails in his father's presence. In the climactic episode, he helps save Rose from drowning when the rising tide cuts her off and justifies himself by his bravery.

RICHARD MEDLEY (*The Iron Lily**), brother of Piers*, and, as it turns out, uncle of Lilias Godman, the wife of Grover Godman* and the mother of Ursula. He has a humped back, and, when he visits Froreden foundry hoping to buy it, Lilias notices the deformity and suspects he may belong to the same Medley family she is seeking. Richard boldly stands up for her against the forest men when they come to wreck her foundry at Strives Minnis because she has hired laborers from Wales. He is a "man coming up to fifty or so, curly-haired, once dark now crisply grizzled. He had a strong, keen face but a smile of great gentleness." Although Piers is master of Mantlemass*, Richard is the man of action there.

RICHARD OF GLOUCESTER (*The Black Arrow**), leader of the forces for York, who afterwards becomes King Richard III. In the novel, he is depicted as about seventeen, a fanatic, extremely brave and skilled at swordsmanship but without human sympathy or compassion. Although he is referred to as "Crookback" and he mentions his own deformity, he is not shown to be unsightly or crippled, only pale and distorted by his obsessive emotion.

RICHARD I OF ENGLAND (*Knight Crusader**), historical figure whom Philip* d'Aubigny meets in Outremer where he is leading the crusade to recapture the Holy Land. Richard is pictured as decisive, acting with impatient grace and suppressed energy, and possessing a strong sense of humor.

RILIAN (*The Silver Chair**), Prince of Narnia*, Caspian's* son, kidnapped by the evil Queen of Underland, or Deep Realm, to be her puppet king when she captures Narnia. Eustace* Scrubb and Jill* Pole meet him when he rides on Ettinsmoor as the Dark Knight with the queen in her aspect as the Lady of the Green Kirtle. Later they regard him as a silly, foppish fool until they come to see that such behavior is part of the spell she has placed on him. They realize that when he sits on the silver chair, he becomes his true self.

RIL TERRY (*Hell's Edge**), Amaryllis Terry, 15, schoolgirl who is instrumental in returning the commmon land taken over by the Withens family to the city of Hallersage, or Hell's Edge. A capable girl and mature for her age, with a well-developed sense of responsibility, she oversees her father's life and runs the household, making sure that he is comfortable and not interrupted in his work. Before the Terrys moved to Hallersage in Yorkshire, she had been attending an exclusive girls' school and is a little snobbish about that. She likes history and literature and writes poetry in her spare time, though she does little of this after coming to Hallersage. At first she doesn't think she'll ever fit into her new environment. After Celia* Withens has her accident and it seems the battle for the common is lost, Ril travels back to Bellhampton. To her surprise, she discovers that in just a few weeks she has grown away from her old friends and has gotten caught up in the lives of Norman*, Hilda, and others in Hallersage and is glad to return to Yorkshire. Ril is an interesting and likeable figure, even if a type.

THE RIVER AT GREEN KNOWE (Boston*, L. M., ill. Peter Boston, Faber, 1959; Harcourt, 1959), third in a series of fantasies set at Green Knowe, an old English house that was already standing at the time of the Crusades. Dr.* Maud Biggin, a scientist who believes that there were giants in prehistoric times, has rented Green Knowe for the summer with her friend, Miss Sybilla* Bun. Seeing that there is much room to spare, and to keep Sybilla (who loves to cook) happy, she invites her niece, Ida* Biggin, and two displaced children to spend the holidays with them. The Society for the Promotion of Holidays for Displaced Children sends Oskar* Stanislawsky, 11, from Poland, and Hsu, 9, also known as Ping*, a Chinese boy from Burma. Ida, 11, but small for her age, likes the boys immediately, and the three start off in a canoe to have adventures on the river, unhampered by the two women, who think children, like kittens, have only to be fed and turned out, and they will take care of themselves. The children come upon a hermit, formerly a London bus driver who came on holiday to an island in the river to get away from people and stayed for years. One night, on another island, they encounter a herd of flying horses. In one episode, when they have been watching a mouse build a nest and are trying to imitate it Oskar shrinks to mouse size and builds such a well-crafted nest that he wants to stay in it, but after a night in his own bed he resumes his original size. After a heavy rain, not realizing that the river is in flood, they are borne far downstream in the canoe and come upon an island inhabited by Terak, a young giant, and his discontented, nagging mother. Because his father was hoaxed into a circus, Terak's mother thinks that the worst fate is to be laughed at, but when the children laugh *with* Terak he enjoys it and decides to be a clown. They are rescued by an official launch, whose men don't even see the giant, taking him for a tree or some other natural phenomenon. The children bring with them a tooth Terak recently lost. Because they have promised not to betray him, the children cannot tell Dr. Biggin about their find, but they do plant the tooth on the gravel drive where she finds it. She uses it to startle a group of scientists meeting for lunch at Green Knowe, and the meeting ends in a shouting match, which satisfies Dr. Biggin. Their last adventure with magic begins when they find a manuscript in a bottle, a confession of Piers Madely, Vicar of Penny Sokey, written in 1647 and telling of a fearful and unbelievable thing he saw. It is written mostly in Latin which they cannot read, but there is an ink drawing of what they recognize as Green Knowe with the full moon appearing to rest on the point of the roof and entitled "The Island of the Throning Moon." At first they think it refers to another island, but when they are out on the river in the moonlight, they realize it must be the island of Green Knowe itself. As the full moon reaches the peak of the roof, the house seems to have changed to one built of rushes, and they witness a wild dance of primitive men wearing headresses of antlers. Later, when they see a notice of a circus coming with a grand new star, Terak the Giant, they earn money to take Dr. Biggin, telling her it is an expression of their gratitude and thinking it will be a marvelous discovery for her. Although she is properly appreciative of the circus, she dismisses Terak as a "wonderful fake." The two adults at Green Knowe are little more than caricatures, and the children are far less well-developed than those in the earlier books of the series, though Ping does stand out as an individual. The adventures on the river have little connection with each other so the effect is episodic. Each individual adventure, however, is realized with intense clarity and strong sensory appeal so that the bizarre elements are believable. Scenes of the river in moonlight and even in a heat wave are memorable. Choice.

THE ROAD TO CAMLANN (Sutcliff*, Rosemary, ill.

Shirley Felts, Bodley, 1981; Dutton, 1982), last
of a three-volume retelling of the Arthurian
legends, following *The Sword and the Circle:*
King Arthur and the Knights of the Round Table
and *The Light Beyond the Forest: The Quest for*
the Holy Grail. It tells of the treachery of
Mordred and the death of Arthur, King of
Britain, following closely the story as told by
Mallory, but filling out character, including
motivations, and adding details of setting and
action that make the book seem a novel in the
modern sense. The book starts with two episodes
not directly part of the final tragedy but
related to it in that both tell of rescues of
Queen Guenever by Sir Lancelot. The first
episode is the tale of the feast given by
Guenever for twenty knights, including one Sir
Pinel who has long carried a blood feud against
Sir Gawain and his brothers. Because Gawain's
love for apples is well known, Guenever has
provided a bowl of apples for him, and, at the
oblique suggestion of Arthur's son Mordred, Sir
Pinel has poisoned one. When another knight
takes the first apple and dies, his cousin,
again goaded by Mordred, cries that it is poison
by the queen, and Lancelot fights to prove her
innocence in a Court of Honour. In another episode, Guenever, riding a'Maying with an escort
of unarmed men, is kidnapped by Sir Meliagraunce, who has long loved and coveted her.
One of the young squires gets word to Lancelot,
who rides to Meliagraunce's castle, has his
horse shot from under him, and, since his armour
is too heavy to walk in, gets a ride in a cart,
like a felon going to execution, and saves her.
The rest of the book tells of Mordred's scheme
to bring down Arthur by revealing the guilty
love between Lancelot and the queen, a revelation that, once made public, the king may no
longer ignore but rather must treat with the
laws he has imposed upon the land. Sutcliff does
not deny the physical love between the two, as
many retellers do, nor yet does she hedge, as
Mallory does, but rather treats it as a natural
problem that Lancelot, at least, fights against
without success. She has him go of his own free
will to the queen's chamber when Arthur is away
from court, though warned by his cousin Sir
Bors that Mordred and his half brother Agravane

are watching his actions closely. There they
are surprised, he fights his way out, and the
queen is taken and condemned to be burned at
the stake. Lancelot rescues her at the last
moment, but in so doing kills Sir Gaheris and
Sir Gareth, two good knights and beloved
brothers of Gawain, who goads Arthur to set
seige to Lancelot's castle. Lancelot finally
agrees to leave the country and return to
Benwick, in France, but Gawain insists that
Arthur follow with his army. There word comes
that Mordred, who has been left behind, has
seized power, spread lies that both Arthur and
Lancelot have been killed, proclaimed himself
High King, and tried to marry Guenever to
solidify his claim on the throne. Arthur returns
with his army, meets Mordred and his forces at
Dover, and drives them westward to the plains
of Camlann, where, to spare the country more
bloodshed, he proposes a truce. As he and
Mordred are signing the treaty before their
assembled armies, all tensely fearing treachery,
an adder bites one of the knights, who
thoughtlessly draws his sword to slay it. At the
sight of a drawn weapon, chaos breaks out and a
terrible battle follows, in which Arthur kills
Mordred but simultaneously gets his own death
wound from his son. He is helped to a small
chapel by Sir Lucan and Sir Bedivere, both of
whom are wounded. Sir Lucan dies, but Arthur
begs Bedivere to take his sword Excaliber, which
came from the Lady of the Lake, and cast it into
the water. Twice Bedivere goes and cannot bring
himself to discard the beautiful weapon, but the
third time he throws it far out into the lake,
and an arm clothed in white samite catches it by
the hilt, brandishes it three times, and draws
it down below the water. Then, at Arthur's
bidding, Bedivere helps him to the water's edge,
and a barge containing three women glides up and
takes the king to Avalon where, he says, he will
be healed of his grievous wounds and will return
at the hour of Britain's greatest need. Sir
Lancelot, learning of Mordred's treachery in a
letter from the dying Gawain, comes with his
army back to England, but is too late. He finds
Guenever in a convent and Bedivere and the
former archbishop now hermits. He joins them, as
later Sir Bors does also, to found a brotherhood

at what is now Glastonbury. The passing of
Arthur is a deeply moving story even in its
barest presentation, and Sutcliff has added just
enough description and detail to emphasize the
tragic human aspects without destroying its
dignity. Of the many retellings of the Arthur
stories, it is certainly one of the most
approachable, true to the early sources, and,
with the first two volumes, complete. Boston
Globe Honor; Junior High Contemporary Classics.

THE ROBBERS (Bawden*, Nina, Gollancz, 1979;
Lothrop, 1979), realistic novel of family
relationships set in London in the 1970s. Philip* Holbein, 9, has always lived with his
Grandmother* Holbein in the castle apartment
given her by the queen because her husband had
been a famous general, and he knows his father,
Henry*, only from infrequent visits and from
watching him on television, where he is a news
correspondent. When his father arrives with a
new wife, Maggie*, while he is at school, Philip
is not much concerned about having missed them
until he learns that he must go to their house
in London for the week of the Easter holidays.
At first he protests but, aware that it upsets
his grandmother, he agrees and tries to remember
all that she has cautioned him about being
cooperative and less outspoken. In London he is
surprised that his father and Maggie laugh at
almost everything he says seriously. The first
morning he thinks he sees a thief coming into
the garden but discovers it is a boy a little
older than he is who is looking for tadpoles.
This lively, talkative, red-haired boy, Darcy*
Jones, shows him the boats and locks on the
canal, which runs behind their garden, and takes
him home for breakfast where he meets Darcy's
pregnant black sister-in-law, Addie*, and his
father. He also learns that Mr. Jones is badly
crippled by arthritis and that Darcy's brother,
Bing*, has a stall selling antiques in the
market. When he gets home, his father is furious
that he went off without telling them, and in
the ensuing discussion it comes out that he is
with them not just for the holiday but
permanently. Shocked, he almost admits that his
grandmother has not told him the truth, but out
of loyalty he covers for her and agrees to try

it for a term. School brings troubles when he
innocently explains that he lived in a castle,
and two bullies take offense and start torment-
ing him. He escapes for several days but is
waylaid on his way home and almost drowned in
the canal before Darcy shows up and saves him.
After that they become close friends, and when
summer holidays come Grandmother asks Darcy to
spend them at her castle with Philip. Bing
drives them down, and on the way they stop at
the early dawn "market," where dealers inspect
goods in the back of trucks with flashlights and
make deals in whispers. The boys' wonderful time
with Grandmother, who discovers and starts to
train Darcy's fine singing voice, is interrupted
when Addie appears to take Darcy home because
Bing has been arrested as a receiver of stolen
goods. Back in London, Philip skips school to go
to court with Darcy where they see Bing plead
guilty and get a sentence of six months in
prison. Frantically worried over what will
become of Addie, the coming baby, and crippled
Mr. Jones, Philip persuades Darcy to go caroling
with him and collect money. They do fairly well
until they try the house next door to Philip's,
where a fat man invites them in, orders them to
sing for his toadlike mother, and "rewards" them
by showing them valuable trinkets. Insulted by
such treatment and enraged by how little all
their work will do to solve the family's
financial problems, Darcy proposes getting into
the house via Philip's balcony and taking just
one thing of value. Since only Philip can get
through the tiny unlocked window, he squeezes
into the upstairs room, looks around, absent-
mindedly puts an ivory chess piece into his
pocket, then opens the French door and sets off
an alarm. The boys scramble back to their own
balcony and into Philip's room, and when the
police come, the chess man proves their guilt.
Philip's father is furious, forbids him to see
Darcy again, and makes plans to send him to
boarding school. Philip gets off with a
talking-to from the police, but, because he is
older and has a questionable family, Darcy has
to go to court. Philip again skips school in the
rain, and meets Addie, who takes him to a
restaurant while Darcy sees the probation
officer. There Philip's father, angry and

insulting to Addie, finds him and takes him
home. His grandmother, alerted to the trouble,
is waiting and, to Philip's surprise, is angry
not at him but rather at her son, his father.
Before she takes him back to the castle with
her, she and Philip call upon the Joneses, where
she shows real sympathy for Addie, defuses Mr.
Jones's anger, asks that Darcy visit them again,
and suggests that with her connections she may
be able to help Darcy get a scholarship to train
his beautiful voice. His father is pleased, but
Darcy says he will have to help Bing when he
gets out of prison. The strength of the book is
in the characterization of Philip, his relatives, and the whole Jones family. The reader
sees events through Philip's eyes and through
his emotions, which are deep and genuine. The
irony of his clear-eyed view of right and wrong
compared to that of the adults gives some depth
to the simple plot. Fanfare.

ROBERT (*Five Children and It**), second son and
third eldest of the children who discover the
Psammead* which grants them wishes that bring a
week's exciting and humorous adventures. Robert
is a lively boy who likes to play practical
jokes and often acts before he thinks. He
figures most prominently in the episode in which
he becomes a sideshow giant at the fair and the
one where the White House becomes a castle and
is besieged. In the giant episode, he has
preciptiously attacked the baker's boy as a
prank and has been soundly trounced. In anger he
wishes he were bigger than the baker's boy, and
the Psammead grants his request. In the castle
episode, he has a humorous and, to him, scary
encounter with knights. He draws on what he has
learned from reading historical romances for
what to say to them and how to act with them. He
is an interesting character, funny and earnest
by turns.

ROBERT KERRIDGE (*Time of Trial**), able young
medical student, who boards with the Pargeters
while going to school in London. His father is a
well-to-do country physician, whom Mr.* Pargeter
had once aided in his youth. The romance between
Meg and Robert is low-keyed, and Robert gives
no real indication of how seriously he feels

about her (a defect of the plot), until the end
of the story, when he declares his intentions,
first to his parents and then to Meg. When
Robert secures a position with a renowned
physician, he at last feels financially able to
ask Meg to marry him. A plaster figure, he is a
"prince charming" type.

ROBERT MYHILL (*Handles**), Erica Timperley's
lumpish, undisciplined cousin, whose principal
characteristic is his rudeness. Erica, from
whose point of view Robert is mostly seen,
thinks he is lazy and inconsiderate, simply
"afraid of straining anything; fingers, feet,
mind, even...." He seems constantly to be
building traps for creatures, mostly cater-
pillars, according to some elaborate plan he
has in mind which seems overly complicated and
never works. Auntie* Joan requires Erica to
help her about the house and yard but never
makes Robert do so, a matter of concern and some
resentment to the girl. It is obvious to the
reader that Robert is indulged and exhibits an
unrestrained feeling of male superiority. He
serves well as a foil for Erica. The reader
likes her even more for having met him.

ROBIN DUFFIELD (*Dogsbody**), younger cousin of
Kathleen* O'Brien, the only one in the family
who really likes the girl. Robin is bullied and
influenced by his older brother, Basil*, so his
support of Kathleen and Sirius is not
consistent, but he is genuinely fond of them
both, and when Kathleen has left with the dog
and his family know only that she is with
someone named Smith, he patiently calls all the
Smiths until he finds one who doesn't tell him
he has the wrong number and then goes to that
address, wanting to stay with her and Sirius
instead of with his parents. Because she knows
she must take him home, Kathleen promises to
give up her possibility of freedom with Miss*
Smith and to go back to the Duffields, but this
plan is interrupted by the Wild Hunt. Robin's
request to the Master of the Hunt is that he be
given one of the puppies he has seen in the
underworld.

ROBIN HOOD (*Bows Against the Barons**), presented

in the novel much less romantically than in the
legends. He is a notorious outlaw who leads a
band of outlaws that live deep in Sherwood
Forest in clearings and caves that penetrate far
into the hills. Some of his men have wives and
children with them. Robin is no longer young,
is of mysterious background, has a sense of
humor but is usually very serious, refuses to
be called chief, and promotes a grand scheme for
uniting the commoners to break the power of the
barons and churchmen who have been exploiting
them. Dickon sees Robin as a "man for the
people," one who can help them gain God-given
rights against the cruel, selfish oppressors.
Robin's plan fails for lack of numbers, and he
dies at the end of the novel.

ROBINSON, (WANDA) VERONICA (1926-   ), born in
Jersey, Channel Islands, the daughter of a
teacher; children's librarian, author of novels
for middle readers and up. She attended Jersey
College for Girls and from 1946-1981 worked as a
children's librarian in Jersey, Kent, Worcestershire, and London. She published an
article in the *London Times* when she was nineteen but no novels until *The Captive Isle* (Dent)
in 1960, which reflects her own experiences
during the German occupation of Jersey in World
War II. *David in Silence** (Deutsch, 1965; Lippincott, 1966), a problem novel about a deaf
boy, grew out of her work with the deaf and
echoes her own childhood memories of being
unable to express herself. It is listed in
Choice. She also wrote for young readers *The
Willow Pattern Story* (Oliver, 1964) and *Delos*
(Deutsch, 1980), a futuristic science fiction
novel of travel in space. A sculptor, she has
exhibited in Mall Gallery, London, and at
Hampstead Arts Council shows.

ROBINSON CRUSOE (Defoe*, Daniel, W. Taylor,
1719-1720), fictitious account credited with
being the first English novel, originally titled
*The Life and Strange Surprizing Adventures of
Robinson Crusoe, of York, Mariner: Who Lived
Eight and Twenty Years All Alone in an
Un-inhabited Island on the Coast of America,
Near the Mouth of the Great River Oroonoque;
Having Been Cast on Shore by Shipwreck, Where-in*

*All the Men Perished But Himself. With an
Account How He Was at Last Strangly Deliver'd by
Pyrates.* In 1651, against his father's advice,
Robinson Crusoe, 18, goes to sea in a ship
bound from Hull to London which founders in a
storm near Yarmouth. Undeterred, he goes by land
to London and sails for Guinea. On the second
trip to Africa he is captured by Turkish pirates
of Sallee, where he is a slave for two years
before he escapes with a slave boy, Xury, and is
picked up by a Portugese ship bound for Brazil.
There he becomes a plantation owner and a slave
holder, and after four years, in 1659, he goes
on a ship to Africa to trade for more slaves.
This vessel, which carries fourteen men besides
the master, the ship's boy, and Crusoe, hits a
storm and is wrecked, with all lost except
Crusoe, who is washed up on an island near the
mouth of the Orinoco River in what is now
Venezuela. To his great good fortune, the ship
does not immediately sink but lodges against
some rocks near enough so he can swim to it,
build a raft of pieces of the mast and other
lumber, and transport a large amount of usable
salvage to the shore. After thirteen days, in
which he makes eleven trips by raft, the weather
changes and breaks up the remainder of the ship,
though some useful things are washed ashore
afterwards. With ingenuity and much hard work,
he builds himself a fortification in front of a
cave and for fifteen years lives with no sign of
human life. During this time he has some
setbacks: an earthquake and hurricane destroy
part of his cave, he gets malaria and nearly
dies, and he makes a canoe so large and far from
water that he cannot move it. He also has some
strokes of luck: grain and rice that he threw
out, thinking it spoiled by rats, sprouts and
affords him the seed for further crops, his
illness restores his interest in religion, which
he finds a great comfort, and he is able to
capture some young kids and start a domesticated
herd of goats. By trial and error he learns to
cook, sew, and do some carpentry, even building
a smaller boat and getting it to sail, though
the first time he launches it he is nearly swept
out to sea by the current. After fifteen years,
he is stunned to see a footprint on the shore.
For two years he improves his fortifications,

knowing that the natives on the mainland nearby
are cannibals. In his twenty-third year on the
island he finds a cave, where he leaves supplies
to use as a last hideaway in time of need, and
he sees savages at a distance on the shore,
evidently cooking and eating their captives.
During the next year, he sees a ship in distress
and risks the dangerous trip in his canoe to try
to rescue survivors, but finds it deserted
except for two dead men and a nearly starved
dog, which he brings to the island. In his
twenty-fifth year, a party of cannibals land on
his island, and he is able to rescue one of
their captives, a young man about twenty-six,
dark, with straight black hair and without
Negroid features. He calls the man Friday,
teaches him English and religion, and makes him
his servant. For three years they live amicably
until another party of cannibals lands, and they
are able to save two of their victims, one of
whom turns out to be Friday's father. The second
man is a Spaniard, one of seventeen survivors
from the ship Crusoe had visited three years
before who have been living a miserable and
destitute life with Friday's people. After
increasing the amount of land in grain so that
the island can support more people, Crusoe sends
Friday's father and the Spaniard to the mainland
to bring the other survivors to the island.
Before they arrive, an English ship anchors
nearby and a company of mutineers lands,
planning on going pirating after marooning the
captain, the mate, and a passenger. Crusoe and
Friday manage to save these three men and, with
clever tactics engineered by Crusoe, to lure
more of the mutineers to the island, separate
the real rascals from those willing to be loyal
to the captain, and then retake the ship. In all
his dealings with other people, Crusoe is
careful to assert his authority and to get
assurances that he will be neither turned over
to the natives nor to a Spanish colony, since he
fears the Inquisition. On December 19, 1686,
after more than twenty-eight years on the
island, Crusoe departs, leaving his island to
the survivors of the Spanish ship and a few
mutineers considered too dangerous to take on
again as crew. In England he finds most of his
family dead and his financial position shaky, so

he goes to Portugal, sells his plantation in Brazil, which has been well managed and become quite valuable, and heads back to England by land. In the Pyrenees Mountains his party is attacked by wolves and narrowly escapes. In a brief narrative summary, he tells of his marriage, his setting up of his nephew as captain of a ship, and of his return to his island, but he leaves the details for another book. The first-person narration is completely convincing, in somewhat antiquated but straightforward language and so meticulously detailed that it is hard to believe the author did not experience any of the adventures related. He undoubtedly got the idea for the novel from the story of Alexander Selkirk, who was rescued from an island off the coast of Chile, but Selkirk, who had been put on the island at his own request and remained there only four years, was evidently neurotic and quarrelsome and not at all the practical, ingenious, rational Englishman par excellence that has made Robinson Crusoe a favorite character for nearly three centuries. Books Too Good; Children's Classics; Choice.

ROD COOPER (*The Great Gale**), young American airman who, though he cannot swim, dons a rubber suit and picks up refugees during the great flood at Reedsmere, taking them to safety at Reedsmere Hall in a rubber dinghy that he pushes through the water. Fortunately he is tall and lanky enough for his feet to touch ground beneath the water. The party on the Saturday after the flood is in his honor. Rod's prototype in history, the author explains in an afterword, was "Airman Reis Leming, who on the night of January 31, 1953, rescued twenty-eight people from the roofs of their bungalows at Hunstanton. For this act of courage he was awarded the George Medal. Like Rod Cooper he used an inflated rubber dinghy and, like my hero, he could not swim."

RODDY MCANDREW (*Emma Tupper's Diary**), Roderick, 14, clever younger brother in the Highland family that Emma* Tupper is visiting during her school holidays. Gifted with a wild imagination, Roddy can carry on spontaneous fantasies with ease, and he can (and does) needle his older brother, Andy*, just to watch him lose his temper. Roddy's weakness is a fear of climbing down from heights or even moderate distances, a weakness that he must overcome with real fortitude when he and Emma are caught in the creatures' cave.

ROGER BRADLEY (*The Owl Service**), son of Clive* and stepbrother of Allison* whose mother, Margaret* has just married Clive. Though there is tension between Roger and Allison at times, he is also attracted to her, and as this attraction grows, the tension between Roger and Gwyn*, the Welsh housekeeper's son, also grows. Roger's class consciousness comes out as the story goes on. Roger taxes Gwyn about his Welshness, but then apologizes at the end when he realizes that Gwyn blamed Allison for what Roger had in fact said. Roger promises to grow into the stereotypical Englishman of means.

ROGER WALKER (*Pigeon Post**; *Swallows and Amazons**; *We Didn't Mean to Go to Sea**), youngest of the Swallows, the four Walker children who camp on Wildcat Island and have a mock battle with the Amazons. Just seven in *Swallows and Amazons*, he is still considered something of a baby by his older siblings and is both mothered and bossed by Susan*. To Titty* he is more of a companion, falling in naturally with her imaginative play and willingly going with her in what the others consider a fruitless search of the small island, where they actually do find Captain* Flint's sea chest, hidden there by robbers. In *Pigeon Post* he is more adventurous, being the one who actually finds the old digging for which they have all been hunting and also the one who leads the exploration of the old mine tunnel that collapses behind them. In *We Didn't Mean to Go to Sea* he is nine and has been influenced by a friend at school to become interested in engines and so takes charge of greasing and starting the motor. Always hungry and more lively and natural than the others, he is perhaps the most believable of the four.

ROSIE BAGTHORPE (*Ordinary Jack**), youngest of

the Bagthorpes, at eight already an overachiever with "several strings to her bow," among them swimming, at which she easily beats Jack, and painting. During most of the novel she is trying to complete a portrait of Grandma* Bagthorpe to replace the one Daisy* Parker burned up at Grandma's birthday party. The picture is eventually finished by Atlanta, the Danish maid.

ROSIE LEE (*Nightbirds on Nantucket**), large pink whale that Captain Jabez Casket seeks like a man possessed. The whale is described as "just about like a great big strawberry ice" and "like a pink blancmange in the breakers." When she was a tiny calf, Captain Jabez Casket found her washed up on the beach and put her back into the sea. Henceforth, whenever he hears that someone has sighted her, he takes off immediately to try to find her and has spent years in fruitless search. Rosie plays a large part in foiling the Hanoverian scheme to kill King James and put Bonnie Prince Georgie on the throne by pulling the gun out to sea. It seems that all along Rosie had been searching for the captain. When he was following her she was following him. The allusion to *Moby Dick* is obvious.

ROSIE RUGGLES (*The Family from One End Street**), mother of the large and close Ruggles family; a laundress. She is a loving wife and mother, hardworking, excitable, and resourceful with clothes and limited funds. She has a romantic streak that reveals itself especially in the names of her eldest daughter, Lily Rose (her real first name of Carnation fell away), and Peg, named for Princess Margaret Rose. Rosie is always conscious of appearances and tends to be a bit smug toward her neighbors.

ROS MACBRIDE (*An Island in a Green Sea**), former college teacher of Gaelic literature, 27, who returns to his native island in the Outer Islands of Scotland (Hebrides) to recover from a World War I wound. He takes a close interest in the Gilbride family, helping them in various ways, and in Isobel* Darroch's work among the islanders in preparation for her book. Although Mairi hopes that he will marry Isobel because she thinks he would make a perfect husband for the young Englishwoman, he is love with Mairi's sister, Jean, and the story's end sees them married. He and Isobel exemplify the virtues of education for Mairi.

THE ROUGH ROAD (MacPherson*, Margaret, ill. Douglas Hall, Collins, 1965; Harcourt, 1965), realistic novel of an abused boy set on the Isle of Skye in the mid twentieth century. Until he meets Alasdair* MacAskill, Jim* Smith's life has mostly consisted of being bored in school, where he is lazy and troublesome, and of being overworked, neglected, and abused by his foster parents, Sarah* and Donald Bruce, and Donald's brother, Finlay. At thirteen, Jim is tall, thin, dark, poorly dressed, and always hungry. At the cattle sale he and his friend Tom Mackenzie are sent to help Alasdair herd his new cattle to the Brae, an isolated farm beyond Udale where the boys live. Later the boys help Alasdair haul his household goods up from the shore, and he invites them to come back. At first Jim is shy, but he soon is there every time he can get away, playing truant and doing a great deal of work that Alasdair takes for granted and at the same time learning a good deal about cattle. When the Bruces, mean-spirited, penny-pinching people, find he has not been going to school, they beat him, even though they often keep him out to work for them, and when he runs off, they start a search for him by blaming Alasdair, then Murdo (Tom's father), when he is found in Mackenzie's barn. Murdo escorts him home and gives the Bruces some straight talk but doesn't effect any major change. Jim is hurt and furious when he learns that Alasdair has gone off for the holidays leaving the cattle in the care of Alec John Macdonald, a neighboring boy, and when Jim discovers Alec John running the cattle as he plays cowboy, he knocks the younger boy in the swamp, threatens him, then makes a deal: Alec John can get the pay but Jim will look after the cattle. Alasdair returns to find Jim in his house, cooking a rabbit to leave for Alasdair's supper, and they make peace. Since the cattle graze on forestry land, Alasdair has promised to keep them out of the young trees, and he soon comes to depend upon Jim to head them off on Sundays when he comes to help. Jim learns a

great deal about the cattle, and he twice acts
in emergencies that show his responsibility. At
Easter he comes looking for Tom and discovers
Effie Mackenzie, Tom's mother, alone and in
pain. Jim runs across the moor several miles for
the doctor. The next fall Alasdair flatters
Donald until he agrees to let Jim help with the
three-day drive of the cattle to the ferry at
Kyle on the way to the market at Dingwall, an
agreement Sarah opposes. Jim is delighted with
the hard work, but when they get to the ferry a
run-away heifer knocks Alasdair against the
causeway. After he is taken unconscious to the
hospital, Jim must go on alone with the cattle
on the ferry, then the railway to Dingwall, and
handle them at the sale. Since he has no money,
he doesn't know how to eat or where to sleep,
but a man from Skye finds him by the roadside
and takes him in. When he returns to Udale with
presents for the Bruces and a new bicycle pump
for Tom, Sarah abuses him, scornfully dumps her
gift of chocolates on the floor, and tries to
ruin the pump. Jim grabs it, and Sarah trips
over a pot and falls, bloodying her nose. Jim
flees and eventually is found and arrested at
Brae, when the police are brought by Alasdair,
who believes Donald's story that Jim has tried
to kill his foster mother. Crushed at this
betrayal, Jim refuses to defend himself, and it
is not until Murdo's testimony at the hearing
that the real story of the Bruces' treatment of
Jim comes out. Contrite, Alasdair finds Jim a
temporary home with Mary Martin, an old school
friend of Alasdair's, as well as a good job with
cattle near Dingwall. At first Jim does not
trust any of them, but the confidence of Tom and
Mary win him over to a new try. The characterizations of Jim, the Bruces, and particularly
Alasdair are strong, and the picture of the
tensions in the small community is interesting
and believable. Fanfare.

ROWLANDS, JOHN (*The Grey King*), steady,
capable, kindly Welsh shepherd, friend of Bran*
Davies, who helps Will* Stanton awaken the Six
Sleepers. When the Dark rises, he chooses to
give up his wife, Blodwen, whom he dearly
loves, so that Bran can assist the Light. He is
an interesting figure, if a type.

RUDI GERLATH (*The Machine Gunners**), German flyer who becomes a prisoner of six youngsters in their underground bunker which they have built to house their machine gun. No hero, having been shot down Rudi is mostly interested in surrendering to some army unit and spending the rest of the war in a nice, safe military prison camp, but he is afraid of being captured by civilians, who might be brutal, having had their houses wrecked and their friends killed by the German bombers. He is extremely uneasy in the bunker as long as the English children keep guarding him with his Luger, mostly because he knows it could go off by accident and is sure someone might be hurt by a ricocheting bullet. When they want him to repair their machine gun, he is reluctant, knowing it is not a safe plaything, and he agrees only on the condition that they get a boat for his escape, confidently expecting that they will be unable to do so. After some time together, they become good friends, and he teaches them German words and songs. On the night of the invasion alarm he goes off in the boat, hoping to meet the German navy waiting off shore, but after he gets out of the harbor and doesn't find them, he turns around and comes back to England. In the end he is wounded by Clogger's wild shot with his Luger, but he is not killed.

RUSKIN, JOHN (1819–1900), born in London; art critic and sociological writer. Of Scottish descent, he had an oppressive childhood in a strict evangelical family and was educated by tutors and at a day school at Cumberwell. He later attended King's College, London, and Christ Church College, Oxford, where he won the Newdigate Prize for Poetry. His university career was interrupted by illness, his health having always been delicate, but he returned and was graduated in 1842. From early childhood he always drew and wrote, and his enthusiasm for the paintings of the artist Joseph Turner started his career as a critic. Volume I of his first book, *Modern Painters* (Smith, 1843), created almost a revolution in taste; it was followed by two other volumes and by *The Seven Lamps of Architecture* (Smith, 1849; Wiley, 1849), in which he associated artistic and moral

values, as he did in *The Stones of Venice*
(Smith, 1851; Wiley, 1851). His interest then
turned from art to economics, and he worked for
social reforms and gave away the fortune he
inherited from his father. He later taught as
holder of the Slade professorship in fine art at
Oxford. He wrote his literary tale, *The King of
the Golden River** (Smith, 1850; Wiley, 1860),
now listed as a Children's Classic, which expresses a Wordsworthian reverence for nature, at
the request of Effie Gray in 1841 and married
her in 1848, but the marriage was never
consummated and was annulled about three years
later. Throughout his life he suffered periods
of mental illness. His style is now considered
overly elaborate, but he is credited with having
influenced the Victorian sensibility toward
interest in art, socioeconomic questions, and
preservation of nature.

RUSTY ROBERTS (*Sea Change**), fellow apprentice
to Cam* Renton, an easygoing, sloppy boy, easily
led by the more intense Cam. Although at first
less resentful of the first mate, Andy*, Rusty
wants to keep on with their fake poltergeist
after Cam has decided to discontinue the hoax.
In the Caribbean port of Boca del Sol, Rusty
thoughtlessly enters the old fort and stumbles
over the gun of the sleeping guard at the gate,
and so is instrumental in getting himself and
Cam arrested.

RUTH BALICKI (*The Silver Sword**), 13, eldest of
the Balicki children, sister of Edek* and
Bronia* and fellow-refugee of Jan*, who, with
the others, makes her way from war-torn Poland
during World War II to join the Balicki parents
in Switzerland. The author describes her in the
cliche, "born teacher." Ruth organizes refugee
children into a school, which she maintains
until early in 1945 when the Balickis leave for
Switzerland. She remains a maternal type,
mothering the children throughout. She can be
assertive, and her ability to speak up and push
demands results in their getting help on a
number of occasions and always wins her
admiration. She is the only person who can "get
through" to Jan on a continuing basis. He likes
and respects her as he does no one else, perhaps

because she is always loving in her firmness.
Mostly she controls him with gentle persuasion
or positive assertion; only in desperation does
she resort to the force of a stick. She is the
children's strong leader as well as nurturer.
Immediately on the children's arrival in
Switzerland and reunion with their parents, Ruth
reverts to early childhood in her behavior. She
gradually recovers her self-confidence and
eventually becomes a teacher. She is central to
the story, but is not as interesting a figure as
the excitable, unpredictable Jan.

RUTH HOLLIS (*The Team**; *The Beethoven Medal**),
intense, dedicated teenager who first appears in
Fly-by-Night (Oxford, 1968; World, 1969) and
in later books becomes a hardworking, determined
wife and mother. Despite her self-doubt, she
single-mindedly pursues her goals to acquire and
train her difficult horses and then to be part
of the Pony Club, and, with even greater mental
anguish and insecurity, she becomes part of the
life of Pat* Pennington, a friend who is every
bit as unrestrained and complex as her half-wild
ponies. She faces the many crises in her
relationships with inner trauma but considerable
courage. In *Pennington's Heir* (Oxford, 1973;
Crowell, 1974) she becomes pregnant after a
single episode of love making on the day of
Pat's release from prison. Though married under
a cloud, living in crowded conditions with
almost no money, and knowing she takes second
place to music in Pat's mind and affections, she
is nevertheless happy. In *Marion's Angels* (Oxford, 1979), she resents the demands Pat's musical career makes on his time and attention, but
but she and Pat are reconciled, at least temporarily.

S

SALLY STUDDARD (*The Wind Eye**), six-year-old sister of Beth* and daughter of Bertrand*, who has a crippled hand as a result of a severe burn she suffered when she was two. Because her father is afraid people will flinch from the sight of it, he has her wear a glove, which makes it itch in warm weather. Sally is the first one to see St. Cuthbert and the only one to spend any time in close contact with him. He carries her on his shoulders and shares his old bread and onions with her. He makes her go out to a rock where a bird has dropped a fish and bring it to him, though she thinks it is too big to manage with her one hand, and then to return half of it to the bird. Then she notices that her hand is cured. The twentieth-century doctor has no explanation, and her father is infuriated, feeling that it is some sort of trick. Her stepbrother, Mike* Hendrey, comes up with the most logical solution, that St. Cuthbert affects those who want something very much, as Sally wants a good hand, Beth wants her father to survive, and Michael wants Beth saved.

SALLY TINKER (*The Weathermonger**), younger sister of Geoffrey* who, with the support of the French army intelligence, returns to England to ferret out the cause of the Changes, which, over the last five years, have turned the country into a fanatically anti-machine culture which has adopted the dress and attitudes of the Middle Ages. Sally is a staunch little girl, practical and surprisingly clever in emergencies. Because she has learned Latin for the past five years in school, she is the only one who can converse with Merlin and explain to him that he has been drugged.

SAM GAMGEE (*The Fellowship of the Ring**), rustic hobbit who has been gardener for Frodo* Baggins and insists on going along as his servant when Frodo leaves The Shire. Sam is practical and matter-of-fact, but he has listened to the tales of old Bilbo* Baggins and has a great desire to see elves. Through the long adventure he also reveals that he has learned his letters from Bilbo along with many of Bilbo's songs and poems and that he even makes up poems himself. When Frodo decides he must go off by himself to Mordor, Sam guesses his intent and follows, so in the last part of their great journey the two hobbits travel together, and a number of times Sam is instrumental in saving Frodo or the ring from disaster. Back in The Shire, Sam marries Rosie Cotton and has thirteen children, one of whom marries Pippin* Took's son. Sam's chief role is that of faithful retainer, but stylistically he also serves to bring the high-flown language back solidly to earth and make the fantasy more realistic.

SAMUEL PONTIFEX (*Up the Pier**), gruff, testy, elderly gatekeeper at the pier Carrie* visits in Llangolly, Wales. In his youth, Samuel ran away from the pier, coming back after twenty years to discover all the Pontifexes gone and things dramatically changed. When George's* family arrives, Gramper's* spell having gone awry, Samuel (also known to the family as Sam'el) sees an opportunity to be part of a family again and sets out to keep Gramper from spelling the Pontifexes back to their own time. This is Samuel's way of recapturing the past. He appears to have magical powers also, but they prove to be less strong than Gramper's.

SANDRA THOMPSON (*Gumble's Yard**; *Widdershins Crescent**), sister of Kevin* and niece of Walter*, described by her brother as serious-minded, self-reliant, and capable. A practical, matronly girl, she is good at peacemaking and trouble-shooting and holds the family together by her careful management of the few resources they have. She is small and thin, has straight hair and gray eyes and a sharp but honest face, and seems old beyond her years, probably because to survive she has had to grow up fast. She and Kevin have lived with Walter and Doris* since their parents died some time before *Gumble's Yard* begins, and long enough for her to realize that she and Kevin must look out for themselves and Harold* and Jean*, since Walter and Doris are not reliable. By the end of *Widdershins Crescent*, she is beginning to show a romantic interest in Dick* Hedley, a steady, earnest boy much like herself in character. Sandra is a clearly drawn, credible, likeable figure.

SANDY HARDCASTLE (*The Edge of the Cloud**), flying instructor and stunt pilot who becomes the best friend of William* Russell. A cheerful, easygoing fellow, Sandy is much more sensitive to Christina* Parson's emotions than Will is, and he understands that she must make a great effort to control her fears when Will is flying and even more when he expects her to fly with him. Sandy is much in love with Dorothy* Saunders, but he knows that she is seeing other men. He is killed in a dual exhibition he and Will put on.

SANTA POSSIT (*The Circus Is Coming**), orphan who with her brother, Peter*, runs away to live with their Uncle Gus* Possit, who is a clown in Cob's Circus. More adaptable than Peter, Santa fits into the circus life sooner, but she suffers at the misunderstanding between Peter and Gus and worries about what will happen to them at the end of the tenting season. She keeps trying to think of ways to make them indispensable to Gus, most of which backfire and cause him to be annoyed. Given acrobatic lessons by Gus's partner, at first she doesn't practice, but when she does she shows a natural aptitude.

SARAH BRUCE (*The Rough Road**), abusive foster mother of Jim* Smith, who regularly underfeeds and berates the boy and who eggs on her husband and his brother to beat him. Like the men, she

is mean-minded and suspicious, unwilling to help
neighbors even at no cost to herself, but she
also seems to have a touch of insanity and
hatred beyond the callousness and greed of her
husband and his brother. When Jim brings her a
gift of chocolates from his trip to Dingwall,
she deliberately spills then on the floor and
stamps on them, then tries to ruin the bicycle
pump he has brought for his friend Tom. At the
hearing she insists wildly that she wants
obedience, not gifts, and though it was she who
attacked Jim, she says he tried to kill her. At
the end she has left her husband, and it remains
a mystery both why she took Jim in the first
place and why she has gone now.

SARAH CODLING (*"Minnow" on the Say**), girl of
eleven when her father, Jonathan* Codling,
leaves to join the British army to fight the
Spanish Armada in 1588. Before he left,
Jonathan hid the family treasure and taught
Sarah the rhyme that indicated its location. She
later recited the rhyme to her mother, who wrote
it down, along with the story of Jonathan, but
who never found the treasure. This story and the
rhyme came down in the family to Miss* Codling
and her father, Mr.* Codling, and when her
nephew, Adam*, and David* Moss hear about it,
they set out to find the treasure. Sarah later
married into the Ashworthy family. Mr.* Andrew
Smith (really named Ashworthy-Smith) and his
daughter, Betsy*, are her descendants and
rightful owners of part of the treasure.

THE SCARECROWS (Westall*, Robert, Chatto, 1981;
Greenwillow, 1981), novel that slides between
realism and horror fantasy dealing with the
emotional trauma a boy suffers when confronted
with his mother's sexuality and second marriage,
set in Cheshire in the mid 1970s. Simon* Wood,
13, first "lets the devils into his head" the
evening after a visitors' day at his boarding
school when a bully in his dormitory makes snide
fun of his mother. Like a berserker he loses
consciousness, and he wakes to find the bigger
boy badly beaten, blubbering in terror. From
that time on Simon suffers a growing fear of his
own rage, so that when his widowed mother shows
up at the next parents' day with Joe* Moreton, a

"yob" who is clearly not her social equal, he is filled with dread, both of what the bully will say in the class-conscious school and of what he may do in retaliation. Fortunately, that night, when he is just about to succumb to the devils, Tris* la Chard, a larking schoolmate who is not afraid of anything, deflects the sneering remarks and saves Simon from his own fury. The idea of Joe, a big, good-natured, rich, talented caricaturist and serious artist, being with his upper-crust mother sickens Simon, so that he gets drunk at the art exhibit showing Joe's drawings and is less than civil when his mother drives up to school to tell him that she plans to marry Joe. At the holidays, Simon goes first to stay with Nunk, his father's friend in the paratroopers, whom he admires greatly, but, when he must go, insists on hitchhiking to the home in Cheshire, Mill House, where his mother and little sister, Jane*, are living with Joe. There, nursing his hate and taking every opportunity to be disagreeable, Simon makes them all miserable and suffers greatly himself, particularly after he discovers that through a hole in his closet floor he can hear his mother and Joe discussing him and making love in their bedroom below. The only time he and Joe come close to an understanding is when Simon finds a starving cat and three kittens, one with an eye infection, in the old mill across a huge turnip field, and his stepfather backs his insistence that the kitten be treated instead of being put to sleep. This incident is not enough to make Simon willing to be part of the happy family gathered in the living room each evening, and he sulks in his room, resenting their cosiness which excludes him. To get revenge, he arranges his father's uniform and kit in their bedroom while they are out, putting everything in the exact position he remembers his father doing. The resulting shock to his mother snaps Joe's patience, and from that point on they are acknowledged enemies. Simon has been strangely attracted to the old mill, which has not been worked for more than thirty years but where he finds three coats and hats still hanging and a feeling of being watched. From the old gardener Tom Mercyfull, he learns the grisly story from the World War II era, when the miller's body was found, caught underwater in the mill wheel, murdered by his wife and her lover. In his hatred for Joe, Simon tries to call up the spirit of his father, killed in the Middle East, but instead seems to call up the ghosts of the three people from the mill, who appear as scarecrows in the turnip field. As they move nearer each day, he frantically tries to ward them off, even sitting at the window all night with his father's loaded pistol, which Joe has to take away from him by force. The threat withdraws temporarily when Tris appears, having been asked to visit by Simon's mother, who hopes his cheerful antics will distract her son, but soon Simon feels that even Tris is on Joe's side. In a climactic scene, on a night when Joe, Jane, and his mother are playing monsters, Simon lets the three ghosts from the mill into the house, and Tris, who seems to understand their threat, tells him that only he can destroy them. To save his mother, Simon rushes across the turnip field, climbs up in the old mill, and turns the lever to start the water streaming through. The resulting strain on rotten timbers and ungreased machinery makes the whole structure collapse, just seconds after Simon flees it. Then he destroys the three scarecrows, one for his mother, one for Jane, and, after some hesitation, one for Joe, before he falls unconscious among the turnips. They find him there in the morning, evidently now free from the destroying presences of the mill spirits and his own furies. The psychology of Simon's overattachment to his mother and his father's memory can be read as resulting in a hallucination of threatening, moving scarecrows in a psychosis brought on by the boy's growing sexual awareness, but since Tris also sees the scarecrows move and feels their threat, it seems instead to be a horror fantasy. Simon is not a likeable boy, but his feeling of loss and betrayal is made very real, and his final brave effort to save his family redeems him. The adults, who are baffled and unhappy living with the resentful boy, are particularly well drawn. Boston Globe Honor; Carnegie Winner; Contemporary Classics; Fanfare.

SCHLEE, ANN (CUMMING) (1934-   ), born in

Greenwich, Connecticut; writer of historical novels and science fantasy. The first eleven years of her life were spent in the United States with American grandparents. At the end of World War II, she went for two years to Cairo, Egypt, where her father was stationed, then spent two years in Downe House, an English boarding school, and later attended Sommerville College, Oxford, where she received her B.A. degree in 1956. She lived with her parents in various parts of Africa, among them western Sudan, Khartoum, and Ethiopia. For two years, she taught in an American school for girls, but after her marriage and the early childhood of her four children she started writing novels, choosing unusual places and little-known incidents in English history as backgrounds for for her books for older children. *The Strangers* (Macmillan, 1971; Atheneum, 1972) is an adventure story culminating in the capture of Tresco in the Scillies Islands by the Parliamentary fleet in 1651. *The Consul's Daughter* (Macmillan, 1972; Atheneum, 1972) concerns the siege of Algiers in 1816. *The Guns of Darkness* (Macmillan, 1973; Atheneum, 1974) is a strong and moving novel of the fall of the Emperor Theodore of Abyssinia, told through the perceptions of a half-Abyssinian, half-English girl. *Ask Me No Questions** (Macmillan, 1876; Holt, 1982) is a horrifying yet tender story of systematic starvation and other abuse in a school for workhouse children in the 1840s, based on a well-documented incident. It was an honor book for the *Boston Globe-Horn Book* Award and was named to the Fanfare list. She departed from historical setting in the futuristic novel, *The Vandal** (Macmillan, 1979; Crown, 1981), which posits the deep-seated power of the survival of ritual in a society of almost complete mind control. It is a winner of the *Guardian* Award and was commended for the Carnegie Medal. More recently she has published novels for an adult audience, including *Rhine Journey* (Macmillan, 1980; Holt, 1981) and *The Proprietor* (Holt, 1983).

SCREAMING HIGH (Line*, David, Cape, 1985; Little, 1985), mystery thriller set in London and Amsterdam, concerning a brilliant teenaged trumpeter, an international school music

competition, and a sinister drug smuggling ring.
The narrator, Nick Sanders, 15, hears someone
screaming in the park, investigates, and discovers it is a black kid known as Ratbag playing a
trumpet. From that time Nick is tied to Ratbag,
whose real name is Paulie Mountjoy, a strange,
scruffy, abstracted kid who, he discovers,
lives in a coal cellar with his mother, both
having escaped from his father, who has become
an abusive drug addict and from whom he has
acquired the trumpet. Since his mother thinks he
has pawned the trumpet, Ratbag has to play in
secret, and Nick finds himself persuading
Skinhead (Mr. Skindle) the band director to let
Ratbag try out on a school trumpet, and later
to pretend to get the original trumpet out of
hock. Skinhead almost immediately recognizes
Ratbag's unusual talent, natural, though the boy
cannot read music, and soon plans his whole
band program around his trumpet solos. The band
wins the local competitions, then the regionals,
until they become the national champions and go
to Amsterdam for the international play-off.
Ratbag is still a loner, but he thinks he needs
Nick with him, and they team up with a
classmate, Sammy, a little kid with big glasses,
who loves to manage things, and together they
take a tour of the city. The band takes third
place the first day but gets knocked into fifth
place on the second, though Ratbag attracts a
good deal of attention. That evening Nick,
Sammy, and Ratbag go out looking for Dixieland
jazz and get scooped up by a bunch of university
students, who get Ratbag to play, buy the boys
drinks, and take them to a private home, one of
the old houses of the wealthy that line the
canals. When they get back to the hostel,
Skinhead tells Ratbag that the famous trumpeter
Julius van Bergh, wants him to return to
Amsterdam in a month to try out for a
scholarship. Back in London, Ratbag discovers
that his trumpet has been taken and another one
substituted. The case looks right but feels
wrong, and they discover that the lining is
filled with plastic bags of heroin. When the
police question them, Sammy remembers two
things: he saw someone switching Ratbag's
trumpet case for a similar one just as the
baggage was to be loaded on the bus, and he

switched it back;   later he thought he saw a man
taking   something   from   the   locked   baggage
compartment while they were   at a rest   stop,   a
man   he   had   seen   twice   before,   once when   he
pushed   into a   back room   at the   travel agency
that had   booked their tour,   and again   when he
was hunting   for the   bathroom at   the Amsterdam
home   the night   before.   The police figure   out
that this is   a clever scheme worked   out by the
travel agency   to get   drugs through   customs by
substituting a drug-filled case   for that of one
of the   players in Holland and   retrieving it at
the rest   stop in   England.   Nick and Ratbag are
recruited   by   a   narcotics agent   from   Holland
named Groot to try,   when they   are in Amsterdam
again,   to find the   house where they   went with
the students and thereby   finger the main source
of a large drug trade.   They do hook up with the
students again and return to the house, but they
are suspected,   bound, and   locked in   an attic.
Ratbag has been knocked out and drugged,   but he
is able to   get his bonds off   and release Nick,
who then figures out a daring escape by means of
a hook on a rope attached to a block and tackle,
by   which the   old merchants   of past   centuries
lifted cargoes from their   ships to store in the
attics   of   their   houses   and   which   has   been
resurrected and put to use to lift the shipments
of drugs to this attic. They let themselves down
on the   rope but   have to swing   out to   avoid a
barge   moored below,   with   the whole   operation
under pressure   of time   since they   figure they
will   be dealt   with as   soon as   the drugs   are
shifted.   Nick drops safely into the   canal, but
Ratbag   hits   the   edge   of   the   barge   and   is
paralyzed except for   one arm.   Nick pulls   him
through the dark canal,   hiding in the shadow of
boats   while their pursuers   hunt by   both power
boat and car,   and   finally hauls him, half dead,
to   a   landing   stage.   Nick,   himself   terribly
weakened,   stumbles   along   the   canal-side   and
flags down a police car.   The headquarters for a
large narcotics   ring, with computer   records of
all   the small   dealers,   is   discovered in   the
subsequent   raid.   Ratbag   has   missed   the
scholarship,   but after an operation and   a long
recovery,   he becomes   a fantastically successful
jazz and rock star, his greatest success being a
recording   and   video called   "Screaming   High."

Though full of implausibilities, the story has a fast pace and, in the escape scenes, strong suspense. Background information about the old houses in Amsterdam and the music the band plays is added in a pedestrian style. Poe Nominee.

SEA CHANGE (Armstrong*, Richard, ill. M. Leszczynski, Dent, 1948; Bentley, 1956), realistic sea novel telling of a voyage from Liverpool to the Caribbean and back, presumably in the mid-twentieth century, though it could be earlier, as neither World War is mentioned. Cam* Renton, 16, joins the steamship *Langdale* as an apprentice after a year on another vessel. He and his fellow apprentice, red-haired Rusty* Roberts, are tired of deckhand work, which they think will not teach them the skills they need to become officers. They believe that the first mate, Andy*, has a grudge against them and decide to attack his weakness, superstition, by pretending there is a poltergeist that whistles "Shenandoah" while he is on watch. After a couple of daring night trips through the ship's vitals to whistle from unlikely positions, they have the whole crew jittery. Then Andy puts Cam to work tallying cargo, so that he cannot get ashore in the Caribbean ports, a move that reawakens his antagonism. In Boca del Sol he asks Andy if he can go ashore and gets permission only to stretch his legs on the jetty. There Rusty persuades him to go "just around the corner." Soon they are climbing to the old fort high above the town. Rusty stumbles over the sleeping guard's gun, Cam knocks the knife out of a startled soldier's hand, and both boys find themselves imprisoned in a thick-walled cell. Alarmed that the *Langdale* will leave before anyone realizes where they are, they overcome their jailor and break out, only to meet their captain who persuades the commandant to let them go and drop the charges. Chastened by the experience, the boys stop complaining and dig into their work, studying together with the help of the second mate in the evenings. On the return trip they are put on regular watches as they have wanted all along, and it seems they will have a good trip home until they run into an abandoned ship, the *Arno*, which has been rammed by another vessel

and   left to sink but is surprisingly still
afloat.   A skeleton crew led by Andy and
including Cam board her and decide to try to
take her to port, since her diesel engines are
undamaged. With a heroic effort they patch her
hole, and, with both Andy and the third mate
injured, Cam takes over the navigation, and they
manage to bring her into Falmouth. Details of
the two vessels and the life and work aboard
ship give the setting authenticity and make the
plot plausible, though this one voyage has a
multitude of problems, including a threat from a
hurricane and a fire in the coal supply. There
is an earnestness about the story and the
descriptions of the boys' attitudes that seems
like   the   boarding   school   stories   of   the
pre-World War II period. Cam's character change
is rather clumsily handled, and most of the
sailors are types. Carnegie Winner.

SEA FEVER. See *Windfall.*

SEB LEROY (*Fire and Hemlock**), Sebastian Ralph
Perry Leroy, son of Morton* Leroy and stepson of
Laurel*. Polly* Whittaker first meets him at the
funeral at Hunsdon House when she is ten and he
is fourteen, and not long afterward, when she
confronts him for trailing her, he warns her to
have nothing to do with Tom* Lynn. Later, when
he is going to Wilton School, he begins to
pursue her, an attention she finds both flatter-
ing and annoying. After her memories having to
do with Tom are erased, Seb meets her again,
starts pursuing her again,   and eventually
becomes engaged to her, though her feelings are
always ambivalent. He is handsome and wealthy
but very self-centered; Polly's friend Fiona
calls him Marmaduke, and both she and Granny*
Whittaker dislike him. In the end it is clear
that he has been using Polly and trying to
counter her influence on Tom's fate not by
harming her physically, as his father has, but
by subverting her affections and urging her to
spy on Tom. Polly also realizes that he has
always been afraid of his fate if Tom escapes,
since it means that Morton will die and Laurel
will take Seb as her new king.

SEED (*John Diamond**), dwarf who runs a primitive

elevator at Foxes Court, London. Maliciously
envious of anyone of normal height, he torments
William even as he helps the boy, charging him
for all his services but refraining from robbing
him even when the opportunity arises.

SEEDY SAM (*Black Beauty**), a miserable, shabby
London cab driver, who in a long speech
complains bitterly about the long hours, low
pay, and inhumane treatment he receives from his
employer. He dies of overwork and poor diet. An
obvious type, he illustrates some contemporary
social problems.

SEFTON, CATHERINE (MARTIN WADDELL) (1941-   ),
born in Belfast, Northern Ireland; author of
novels for adults and children, some published
under his own name and some under the pseudomyn
of Sefton. He has worked and lectured for the
Arts Council of Northern Ireland, as well as
holding various jobs book selling and junk
dealing. He has written radio plays, edited (as
Martin Waddell) *A Tale to Tell: Stories by
Young People from Northern Ireland* (Arts Council
of Northern Ireland, 1982), and published six
thrillers for adults, several about a character
named Otley, the first being *Otley* (Hodder,
1966; Stein, 1966), which was made into a movie
in 1969. Most of his books for children under
the name Waddell are light stories for boys,
designed for amusement. As Sefton, he has
written family stories and ghost stories, among
them two for younger children, *The Ghost and
Bertie Boggin* (Faber, 1980), about Bertie, too
small to play with his older siblings, who finds
a ghost for a best friend, and *The Emma Dilemma*
(Faber, 1982), a fantasy in which a fall and a
bump on the head produces a second Emma who is
transparent and flickery around the edges. Most
of the fantasies and ghost stories involve a
trauma or change in a child's normal life which
creates an oppportunity for the supernatural. In
The Back House Ghost (Faber, 1974; as *The
Haunting of Ellen: A Story of Suspense*, Harper,
1975), a teenaged girl is haunted by a ghost who
seems to be asking for her help. Another fantasy
In a Blue Velvet Dress: Almost a Ghost Story
(Faber, 1972; Harper, 1973), features a book-
loving girl who survives a vacation without a

single book with the help of a ghost in a blue
dress. Both are set in Northern Ireland, as is a
more realistic novel, *Island of the Strangers*
(Hamilton, 1983; Harcourt, 1985), which concerns
the trouble in a village when a school group
from another district camp on a nearby island.
His *Starry Night: A Novel** (Hamilton, 1985),
which won the Children's Rights Workshop Other
Award, is about a girl living on the border
between Northern Ireland and the Irish Republic.
His novels have a strong sense of place, evoking
the Irish temperament and customs as well as the
physical setting and lilt of the speech.

SEFTON OLDKNOW (*The Chimneys of Green Knowe**),
spoiled, arrogant brother of blind Susan*, ten
years older than his sister. Even his father
knows that Sefton is reckless and irresponsible,
but he doesn't know that Sefton is heavily in
debt to the corrupt manservant, Caxton*, and
that he has been involved with Caxton in
catching boys and selling them to the press
gangs as forced recruits for the navy. With his
vain and silly mother, Sefton ridicules his
religious grandmother, his upright father, his
friend Jonathan* Morley, the parson's son, and
his blind sister, and he particularly likes to
torment Jacob*, the little slave boy bought to
be a companion to Susan. Sefton views Caxton's
apparent death in the fire with relief, since it
wipes out the possibility of blackmail and
assures that he will not be brought to account
for his extravagance and crimes.

SELINA PLACE (*The Weirdstone of Brisingamen**),
neighbor of Gowther and Bess Mossock and enemy
of Colin and Susan. She is a big woman with
incongruously thin legs and no neck, bird-like
in appearance and movements, who lives in St.
Mary's Clyffe, a big house on the edge of a
cliff, where she keeps her hounds, three wolf-
like dogs. The children discover she is really a
witch called the Morrigan, who practices black
magic and can shape-change. She and Grimnir are
their principal adversaries. An obvious character with no depth who combines folkloric
elements, she epitomizes evil in the story.

SELINA SEYMOUR (*The Maplin Bird**), dissatisfied,

pouting daughter of the wealthy woman for whom
Emily* Garland becomes a housemaid. Bored with
the stultifying social life imposed by her
domineering mother, Selina wants to be useful
and become a teacher or a nurse. When Emily's
brother, Toby*, breaks his leg, her mother
directs Selina to care for him, thinking that
this will cure her of her desire to be a nurse.
Though shocked at first to be asked to wait upon
a "common" boy, she soon demonstrates that she
is an efficient and devoted nurse. In the end
her mother allows her to go to Queen's College
in London. Her character is contrived, serving
as a foil for Emily, who drudges in a back-
breaking job through necessity.

SELJUK OF RUM (*The Whispering Mountain**), a
round, fat, bright-eyed, overdressed Ottoman who
has come to Wales to search for a lost colony of
his people, the tribe of Yehimelek*. These
"Children of the Pit" or "Pit People" were
talented gold miners and craftsmen who were
brought as slaves 2,000 years earlier by the
Romans to mine gold in the Welsh mountains. The
Seljuk believes they made the Harp* of Teirtu.
Fullsome in speech as well as in dress and
figure, he talks a lot and often repeats
himself, using synonyms liberally for emphasis.
Though exaggeratedly comic, he is a very
likeable character.

THE SENTINELS (Carter*, Peter, Oxford, 1980;
Oxford, 1980), historical novel about British
efforts to halt the slave trade to the Americas
set in 1840 in England, Africa, and mostly on
the high seas off northwest Africa. Three
simultaneous journeys, one involuntary, come
together to produce the story. A Yoruba farmer
and trapper, Lyapo*, kidnapped by two Dahomeys,
is sold to a cross-eyed Mandingo slave dealer,
who conveys him and a canoeload of other
captured tribespeople downriver to the coast and
sells them to an American slaver, callous, cruel
Kimber, captain of the *Phantom*, which has just
arrived on a slaving voyage from Baltimore. At
the same time in England, a concerned, dutiful
relative secures for newly orphaned John
Spencer, 15, a post as "gentleman volunteer" on
the HMS *Sentinel*, commanded by religious,

humane, Scots-born Captain James Murray*. The
Sentinel has been assigned to antislavery patrol
with the West African Squadron in the Bight of
Benin southeast of Freetown, Sierra Leone, the
area in which the *Phantom* operates. Murray and
his lieutenant, Brooke*, mold the sailors,
called the Sentinels because of their ship, into
a smoothly operating fighting collaborative, and
they have a couple of minor engagements before
encountering the *Phantom*. Although seasick,
frightened, and bumbling at first, Spencer is
willing and proves an apt student under the able
instruction of Murray, who takes a special
interest in him. The other men also admire the
boy's mettle and respect him, and he soon earns
a midshipman's commission and wears proudly the
gleaming silver dirk of his rank. Emotion runs
high when the *Sentinel* sights and hails the
Phantom homebound for Carolina, loaded with a
cargo of human filth and misery consisting of
180 men, 50 women, and 30 children, among them
Lyapo, chained together like swine and jammed
into the slave deck. Kimber decides to fight,
and a bitter battle ensues in which both ships
sustain severe damage. Kimber limps for the
African coast, since his water hold is empty,
and lies up in a secluded lagoon. Superior
seamanship and some luck enable the Sentinels to
find and capture the ship. Things so happen that
Spencer, though inexperienced, is the only
officer that can be spared. Murray puts him in
charge of the *Phantom*, assisted by some experienced seamen. They are to take the *Phantom* to
Freetown, Sierra Leone, where the crew will be
charged with piracy since Kimber fired upon a
patrol ship. All goes well until the *Phantom* is
intercepted by another slaver, the *San Felipe*,
commanded by the notorious Portuguese Captain Da
Silva. The Sentinels arm the slaves, including
Lyapo, and beat off the enemy, but they sustain
damage to the fo'c'sle that enables Kimber and
his men to stream from the hold. All the
Sentinels are massacred except Spencer, who is
knocked overboard by a blow to the head. Lyapo
rescues him, hauling him into the ship's jolly-
boat, and against incredible odds the two make
it to the African shore where Lyapo's knowledge
of how to live off the land keeps them alive
until they are rescued by British seamen about

two months later. The *Sentinel* in the meantime
has continued patrolling and with the help of
another warship, the *Esk*, bottles up five loaded slavers in the Mono River. One, the *Dolphin*,
proves especially troublesome, and, as the men
are throwing their human cargo overboard, the
Esk commander rams the slaver. The Sentinels
swarm aboard the *Dolphin*, and a revenge-massacre
follows. The battle over, Spencer arrives and is
reunited with his fellows. The *Sentinel* proceeds with the four slave ships to Freetown. The
men are proud of their feat and look ahead to
fine bounties for their several months' work.
Spencer is dispatched to England as a witness
against the *Phantom*, Lyapo decides to stay in
Africa and take advantage of the British offer
of free land, and Murray leaves to take the
Sentinel on a barracoon (slave stockade) raid
along the Gallinas River. In an epilogue set
five years later, the reader learns that Murray
has been beached because of a change of political parties in England; his first lieutenant,
Brooke, is now a captain; the *Sentinel* has been
shipwrecked off Java; Lyapo has a new family and
is prospering; Kimber and his crew were released
on technicalities; and Spencer, now regarded as
a fine, upcoming, young officer, is about to
stand for lieutenant. The author looks ahead and
sees the work of the *Sentinel* as the prelude to
a great upheaval that is to come, and the book
concludes with Spencer's reflecting that "some
good did come from it [the men's valiant
efforts] in the end." A first-rate adventure
story with a stark and dramatic setting, the
author's occasional lapses into melodrama and
overwriting do not diminish the power of the
effectively counterpoised scenes, the rich picture of the period's abuses and heroic moments,
and the large cast of interesting characters, a
few of whom, like the British governor at
Freetown, were actual minor historical figures.
The reader is shown good views of life on a
well-run warship and differing attitudes toward
the slaves, the slave trade, and the ship's
responsibilities. The author's style is energetic and vibrant. Participial phrases and sentence fragments often introduce scenes, pulling
the reader quickly into the action, and the
occasional use of the present tense gives

urgency to the episodes. Although the principal figures on the good side are rounded, the slavers, whether African or white, are mostly avaricious, inhuman types, and Kimber is over-drawn as a pre-Civil War "ugly American," cigar-smoking, ungrammatical in speech, blas-phemous, crude, and cruel, the black-hat antithesis of the good but more credibly charac-terized Murray. Guardian.

SERAPHINA (Harris*, Mary K., Faber, 1960), boarding school story set in the 1950s in Medborough, a town in the Midlands. When her grandmother, with whom she has always lived, dies, Seraphina Brown, 13, sometimes called Fenny, goes to live briefly with the large, comfortable Richards family next door, but when one of the Richards boys comes down with measles, she is shipped off to live with her Aunt Edna, who has a hairdressing shop in Medborough but lives in Pennyford, a village twelve miles out. Aunt Edna is very busy, neat, and precise, and is far from thrilled to have Seraphina dumped on her hands, partly because it disrupts her life and partly because she has no use for Seraphina's mother, who left the child as an infant and has not been heard from since. After lonely weeks of summer holiday at Clovelly, Aunt Edna's immaculate and cheerless house, Seraphina is relieved when her aunt discovers that the school at Medborough has a small boarding facility attached and arranges that Seraphina will live there. The first night at the boarding house Seraphina refuses to be adopted as best friend by boring Jenny or to be intimidated by Lydia Dukes, who wears glasses and makes sarcastic and critical remarks as she watches Seraphina unpack, but, goaded by Lydia's questions, she does make the mistake of saying that her mother, about whom she really knows nothing, is an explorer in Central Africa. The headmistress, Miss Graham, is friendly and dis-cerning and very much in control, both in the school and in the house. A number of the girls in the dormitory with Seraphina are well de-defined: Sarah, who is only eleven and seldom speaks to anyone but Lydia since her mother was killed in an accident the previous term; Ann, who Seraphina realizes is the nicest girl and

whom she doesn't like but thinks she should;
Philippa, who looks like a policeman and sings
hymns "very thoroughly"; but her best friend is
almost at once Stephanie Ayrton, a day girl she
met briefly in the grocery store before the term
started. Disorganized Stephanie gets off immediately on the wrong foot with the new
form-mistress, Miss Jason, who is something of a
martinet. When Miss Graham allows Seraphina to
go to Stephanie's house for tea, she discovers
that the girl is trying to do all the housework
for herself and her music-teacher father, her
mother having left when she was three and the
interim housekeeper having departed to be
married. Seraphina, who excels almost cumpul-
sively at school and is extremely organized and
neat, tries to help and manages to insult
Stephanie. Their friendship survives, however,
and at half term she invites Stephanie to tea at
Clovelly, then, ashamed of her aunt's linoleum
floors and plastic flowers, takes her instead
to the Copper Kettle Tea Room, run by Aunt
Edna's friend, Lillah Leek, a mousey woman with
a sharp nose who has tried to be friendly but
from whom Seraphina has kept aloof. When
Stephanie discovers her reasons, she laughs, and
they are closer than before. Seraphina's main
problem at the boarding house is that she gets
no mail from her mother and, goaded by Lydia's
frequent mention of it, is forced to expand her
stories of Africa until she has a tangled web of
deceit. As her birthday approaches, the girls
are excited to see what she will be sent. She
tries to solve the difficulty by buying herself
a wood carving of a leopard at a junk shop,
wrapping it, begging an African stamp from the
matron who collects stamps for the mission, and
placing it with the morning mail. Although she
feels guilty, her birthday is a success, with a
gift of her grandmother's watch from Aunt Edna
and a cake from Miss Leek. Then Stephanie gets a
bad case of flu, Miss Graham calls to see how
she is, surveys the disaster of the girl's
housekeeping, tactfully talks to her father, and
arranges that they hire a housekeeper. She also
allows Seraphina to go see her friend, since it
is Stephanie's birthday. Shocked that she has no
gift to take, Seraphina tries to sell the
leopard back to the junk shop only to discover

that Lydia is there, being the niece of the owner, and having known all along about her deception. When she takes the leopard as a gift to Stephanie, however, and admits the whole story, her friend is not only delighted with the leopard but thinks the bond between them is stronger because they both have mothers who have deserted them. At the boarding house, also, Seraphina makes a clean breast of her deception, and though the girls are annoyed at being tricked, they are also forgiving. In the meantime they have been practicing for a production of Shaw's *St. Joan*, in which Miss Jason has cast Stephanie as the lead, recognizing that the girl has real acting talent, with Miss Jason's love of literature and desire for a good performance overcoming her annoyance at Stephanie's continual tardiness and clumsiness. Although Stephanie sings beautifully, Miss Graham will not allow her to take part in both the play and the annual carol concert and then, after she has been so ill, decides that even the play will be too taxing for her. At the carol concert, for which Stephanie is still ill, a foreign woman shows up, is scornful of the lead singer, and, too late to explain, Seraphina discovers she is a famous music teacher who has come to hear Stephanie. Aunt Edna also arrives and, having heard from Miss Graham about the African stories, gives Seraphina a good dressing-down and tells her the truth about her selfish mother. Totally disappointed, ashamed, and embarrassed, Seraphina manages to face Miss Graham to ask permission to see Stephanie again and arrives to find her friend in rapture because the foreign teacher has located her, listened to her sing, and so impressed her father that she will be allowed to go to Rome to study voice. Seraphina now can assume the part of St. Joan, for which she was the understudy, with a clear conscience. She also agrees gratefully to work in Miss Leek's tea shop before Christmas so she can earn money to visit the Richards family for part of the holiday, and, since she is the top girl scholastically, she hopes Miss Graham will eventually persuade Aunt Edna that she should go to college instead of becoming a hairdresser. The rigid rules of the school, in which the girls must have permission to be on their own even for a few minutes and which make Seraphina's effort to buy and send herself a present so difficult, seem strange by American standards even of the 1950s, but the personalities in the novel are well defined and Seraphina, as the first-person narrator, has a convincing voice, though Stephanie is a more compelling character. The strains and worries about relationships, both in and out of school, are made interesting. Carnegie Com.

SERGEANT SAMWAYS (*Danny, The Champion of the World**), the local constable who happens to ride up on his bicycle just as Victor Hazell and William*, Danny's father, are arguing over who owns the pheasants. Sergeant Samways's manner of speaking, apparently cockney, is his most outstanding trait. Danny says the Sergeant has a "funny habit of sometimes putting the letter *h* in front of words that shouldn't have an *h*" and taking away "the *h* from words that should have begun with that letter." The sergeant appears to be slow of thought but actually sizes up situations quickly. He puts himself firmly on the side of William, Danny, and Doc Spencer when Hazell gets pushy and starts to throw his weight around. Samways informs Hazell that the land-owner will have to prove that the birds belong to him and that he can do that by driving them back onto his land. Danny suspects that the sergeant helps guide the birds to Hazell's Rolls Royce, which they promptly foul. The reader never fears that the sergeant will fail to be the protagonists' ally.

SERRAILLIER, IAN (LUCIEN) (1912–   ), born in London; teacher, editor, and author of novels, plays, verse, and retellings for children and young people. His most highly regarded novel is *The Silver Sword** (Cape, 1956; Criterion, 1959), which was commended for the Carnegie Medal, received the Boys' Clubs of America Junior Book Award, and has been translated into many languages and serialized on television and radio. Based on case histories of actual happenings, it tells of the World War II flight to Switzerland of a family of Polish refugee children. Critics have called his seven other novels commonplace adventures in comparison, among them *Flight to Adventure* (Cape, 1947) and *There's No Escape* (Cape, 1950; Scholastic, 1973), both about mountain climbing. After attending a school near Hampstead Heath, a preparatory boarding school in Sussex, and Brighton College, he received his M.A. from St. Edmund Hall, Oxford, in 1935. He started to read classics, then switched to English, and was a teacher and headmaster in public and private schools in Gloucestershire, Worcestershire, and Sussex. Although his ambition was to become a writer, he wrote only in his spare time until 1962, but he had already been publishing since the mid-1940s. His first publications were a book of poetry, *The Weaver Birds* (Macmillan, 1944; Macmillan, 1945) and an adventure novel, *They Raced for Treasure* (Cape, 1946). More novels and some twenty books of verse followed, among them *Happily Ever After* (Oxford, 1963) and *The Ballad of Kon-Tiki and Other Verses* (Oxford, 1952). He published many more poems and stories, some original and some retellings. He is also highly regarded for his retold legends, for which he goes to the original sources. Some are in verse, like *Beowulf the Warrior* (Oxford, 1954; Walck, 1961) and his versions of the Robin Hood and the Green Knight stories. Others are in prose, like his well-known series on the Greek heroes Perseus, Theseus, Jason, Daedalus, and Heracles. His retellings are cogent and lucid, and amply satisfy his intention of reinterpreting the old tales to meet the literary needs of a new generation. He has adapted tales from Shakespeare and Chaucer in a format for slow readers, produced the librettos for musicals, and is founder and editor with his wife, Anne, of the New Windmill Series of fiction, travel, and biography for schools, published by Heinemann Educational Books, Ltd. Highly respected for his large and varied contribution to literature for the young, he has lived in a 300-year-old house on the South Downs in West Sussex not far from the sea.

SETH-SMITH, E(LSIE) K(ATHLEEN) (1883-   ), born in Wonersh Guilford, Surrey; author of historical novels for older children and biographies of religious subjects. She married

Arthur Frederick Murrell, a schoolmaster, in 1921, and some of her books for adults were published under the name of Murrell. They had two daughters and lived at East Grinstead, Sussex. Many of her books, especially those of the 1920s, were published by the Central Board of Missions, Society for Promoting Christian Knowledge, for instance, *The Firebrand of the Indies, a Romance of Francis Xavier* (SPCK, 1922; Macmillan, 1922), *St. Hugh of Lincoln, 1140-1200* (SPCK, 1923), and *St. Boniface, A.D. 679-755* (SPCK, 1924), but even in her earlier years she wrote historical novels like *A Son of Odin: A Tale of East Anglia* (Jarrold, 1909), which is set in England in 861. Her novels for older children are all historical, starting with *When Shakespeare Lived in Southwark** (Harrap, 1944; as *Vagabonds All*, Houghton, 1966), the story of a boy who runs away and joins traveling actors. Among her other titles are *At the Sign of the Gilded Shoe* (Harrap, 1955), *The Black Tower* (Harrap, 1956; as *The Blacktower*, Vanguard, 1957), and *The Fortune of Virginia* (Harrap, 1960). Her first tale was published when she was eighteen, and her last, *Jonah and the Cat* (Harrap, 1967), when she was eighty-four.

THE SEVENTH RAVEN (Dickinson*, Peter, Gollancz, 1981; Dutton, 1981), novel of terrorism and suspense set in St. Andrew's Church, Kensington, England, in the last third of the twentieth century. Since the age of nine, the first-person narrator, Doll* Jacobs, 17, has been an actor in the annual Christmas opera, a sophisticated musical production acted and sung by children for an adult audience. This year she has become a sort of girl Friday to the production staff, known as the Opera Mafia, which includes her cellist mother and the parents of her boyfriend, Adam Slim. Limited to a cast of 100, the opera is a big event in this upper-class, educated area, and the cast is already full when the son of the ambassador from Matteo, Juan O'Grady, insists on taking part. Under pressure, the mafia decide he can be a seventh raven in this story of Elijah, Ahab, and Jezebel. The boy turns out to be a bristly macho young Latin, full of his own sense of worth and concerned with his honor, but his bodyguard,

Ferdy, keeps him in line and also becomes   very
popular with   the   staff   and with   the   other
children, even learning a tricky guitar part for
practices before the professional guitarist can
join the company. The mafia represents the whole
spectrum of British political attitudes,   from
ultraconservative Mrs. Banks to Mrs.* Dunnitt,
who has been a communist and always participates
in Amnesty International demonstrations. Just as
the dress rehearsal, for which the children get
into their costumes and makeup at a number of
houses near the church, is about to start, a
group of four terrorists bent on kidnapping Juan
shoot Ferdy and invade the church. Unable to
single out Juan in the confusion, they are
nearly persuaded by calm young Queenie Windsor
that he isn't among them, and they are almost
ready to leave when the police descend and
surround the church. Stuck with 100 children
and twenty or so adult hostages, these amateur
terrorists are disconcerted but determined. They
are led by Danny*, an ex-drama teacher. The
others are Al*, a priest, Chip*, a half-American
former student activist, and Angel*, the only
real peasant Mattean, a truly dedicated revolutionary terrorist woman. Doll is chosen to be
held at gun point at the church door in the
glare of the police and television spotlights
while Mr. Slim, who speaks Spanish but has a bad
heart, translates the negotiations with the
police. Doll also must accompany the terrorists
in a search for the missing Juan, who they think
has been hidden, though all the English adults
and children realize that he has been disguised
by quick-thinking Mrs. Dunnitt as a handmaiden
of Jezebel. Even a child-by-child examination
fails to identify him, mainly because several
children simultaneously wet their pants at the
moment he is in the spotlight, unintentionally
distracting Danny's attention. On the second
afternoon, the terrorists decide the children
should perform the opera for them, and it goes
poorly but without major hitches until Angel
suddenly grabs the handmaiden everyone has been
trying to ignore and pulls off Juan's headdress.
Still, even with the boy in their hands, the
terrorists cannot leave the church and, because
the children are continually guarded by one
hidden, gun-toting Mattean, the police dare not

attack. To pass the time, Danny, with his dramatic flair, sets up a "trial," using Mrs.* Jacobs as the accused to stand for British citizenry, with Mrs. Dunnitt, ironically, as her advocate, Danny as prosecutor, and Angel as the judge. Al, as a witness, gives an impassioned description of the torture and imprisonment of political prisoners by the rightist Mattean government, and Mrs. Dunnitt, and, surprisingly, Mrs. Jacobs, give strong rebuttals defending the rule of law, however clumsy, and the value of music and art. At the end, Angel, always the revolutionary, declares Mrs. Jacobs guilty and starts to shoot. Chip, appalled, rushes up to stop her, leaving the children unguarded, and the police, who have waited for this opportunity, shoot from the windows and capture the four Matteans. Full of suspense and fascinating detail, the story also manages to pose the political questions in a dramatic and nondidactic way without belittling their importance or reaching a facile conclusion. The result neither justifies nor completely condemns the attitudes and actions of the terrorists. The tone of the first-person narration is completely convincing as the voice of a bright seventeen-year-old girl. Fanfare.

SEVERN, DAVID (DAVID STORR UNWIN) (1918-   ), born in London; author of a wide variety of books for children and adults. He attended Abbotsholme School, Derbyshire, and a school in Germany, and in 1938 became an editorial assistant at the League of Nations Secretariat in Geneva. The son of publisher Sir Stanley Unwin, he gravitated toward the publishing world and worked for Unwin Brothers, printers, in Woking, Surrey, in 1939, for Basil Blackwell booksellers in Oxford in 1940, and served as a member of the production department at George Allen & Unwin, publishers, from 1941 to 1943. For children he has written more than twenty-five books, the early ones, published in the 1940s, being straightforward adventure stories and domestic adventures. In *Dream Gold* (Lane, 1949; Viking, 1952), he switched to fantasy, a story about two boys who share an identical dream which takes them into a tale of piracy and treasure among the Pacific islands. *Drum-*

beats (Lane, 1953), is a time fantasy, with an African drum being the catalyst that transports the children to an African expedition of thirty years earlier. Two of his books for younger children are *Foxy-Boy* (Bodley, 1959; as *The Wild Valley*, Dutton, 1963), in which a little girl befriends a wild boy brought up by foxes, and *The Wishing Bone* (Allen, 1977), in which children get caught in a fort which grew from a model built by one of them. Some of his novels are even set in the American West, like *Jeff Dickson: Cowhand* (Cape, 1963). *The Girl in the Grove** (Allen, 1974; Harper, 1974) is a skillfully handled fantasy-mystery novel for older children and was a nominee for the Edgar Allan Poe Award for the best juvenile mystery. Severn has also written nonfiction for children and novels for adults.

SEWELL, ANNA (1820-1878), born in Great Yarmouth, Norfolk; daughter of Isaac, a bank manager, and Mary Sewell, a poet; died at Old Catton near Norwich; writer of *Black Beauty: The Autobiography of a Horse** (Jarrold, 1877; as *Black Beauty: His Grooms and Companions* by Am. Humane Ed., 1890), probably the most famous animal story of all time. A protest against cruelty to animals, in particular horses, it was enormously successful in persuading people to adopt more humane treatment of animals and resulted in the establishment of a home for horses. She was reared in a strict Quaker household and educated privately. At fourteen, she twisted her ankle while running during a rainstorm. The injury was not treated properly, and she was lame for the rest of her life. She maintained a cheerful disposition, drove her father to work each day in pony and chaise (developing thereby a strong love for horses), and oversaw the house for her increasingly busy mother. Except for a year spent in unsuccessful physical therapy in Germany, she lived at home and with her mother established the Working Man's Evening Institute at Wick in Gloucestershire, teaching classes three nights each week for local miners and laborers. From 1871 on, she was confined to the house and, as her disability worsened, she began writing *Black Beauty*, "its special aim being to induce kindness, sympathy, and an understanding treatment of horses." *Black Beauty* is the imaginary story of a high-bred horse, willing, able, and accustomed to kind treatment, who meets hard times after his legs are ruined by a drunken groom, becomes a cab and cart horse, and eventually falls into the hands of three gentlewomen who appreciate his virtues. Sewell died only a few months after the novel came out but lived long enough to see that it was successful. Though contrived, sentimental, quaint, and moralistic in style, it engages the emotions from the outset and is today considered a classic. It is still a favorite with children and has gone to more than twenty editions, been translated into many languages and been made into several movies. The only book Sewell ever wrote, it appears in Children's Classics.

SHAKY FRICK (*The Battle of St. George Without**; *Goodbye, Dove Square**), Charlie Frick, World War I veteran who was once gardener for a wealthy woman of Dove Square and at her death inherited a bequest to care for her Pekinese dogs, the Duke and the Duchess. Injured in the war, he has a sort of palsy that has given him his nickname. As a self-appointed watchman, he patrols the grounds of St. George's Church and sends regular reports to the bishop. He becomes the only adult ally of the children who want to save the church. Two years later, he is discovered by Matt* McGinley and Madge* living unauthorized in one of the abandoned houses of the square. He retains a childhood admiration for Miss* Queenie Harrison, and there is some hint that they may join forces after his hideout is destroyed in a fire.

SHARP, MARGERY (1905–   ), born in Salisbury, England; novelist for adults. She achieved popularity in children's literature for her first two novels for young readers, the humorous, talking-animal fantasies, *The Rescuers** (Collins, 1959; Little, 1959), named to Fanfare and *Choice* and recommended for a Carnegie Medal, and *Miss Bianca** (Collins, 1962; Little, 1962), selected for Fanfare and *Choice*. Grandiloquent, tongue-in-cheek, and inventive in central concept, they tell of the adventures of an elegant, white lady mouse named Miss Bianca and her valiant and practical cohort, the pantry mouse Bernard, with the Prisoners' Aid Society, an association of mice whose purpose is to free all those whom the mice feel have been wrongly incarcerated. Further exploits of the daring and resourceful pair appear in *Miss Bianca in the Salt Mines* (Heinemann, 1966; Little, 1966), *Miss Bianca in the Orient* (Heinemann, 1970; Little, 1970), and *Miss Bianca in the Antarctic* (Heinemann, 1970; Little, 1971), and in *Bernard the Brave* (Heinemann, 1976; Little, 1977) and *Bernard into Battle* (Heinemann, 1979; Little, 1979). The Miss Bianca and Bernard stories have gone into foreign language editions, and *The Rescuers* was made into a motion picture. Sharp was raised in Malta and educated at Streatham High School in London and Bedford College at the University of London, from which she was graduated with honors in French. She published her first poem while in high school, continued to write poems as "fillers," and made writing her profession upon receiving her degree. She married Geoffrey L. Castle, an army major, and has made her home in London. Beginning in 1930, she wrote two dozen novels for adults, several of which became very popular. Some were made into movies, among them, *The Nutmeg Tree* (Barker, 1937; Little, 1937), *Cluny Brown* (Collins, 1944; Little, 1944), and *Britannia Mews* (Collins, 1946; Little, 1946). She has been praised for her dry humor, economical style, and skill with farce. She has also written plays and short stories for adults and has contributed frequently to leading magazines.

SHASTA (*The Horse and His Boy**), a youth, ostensibly the son of a cruel fisherman named Arsheesh in the country of Calormen, south of Narnia*, who is revealed as Cor, twin of Corin and true son and heir of warm and merry King Lune of Archenland. When Shasta overhears the man he has assumed is his father dickering to sell him to a Calormene warrior and discovers that the warrior's horse, Bree*, is a talking animal from Narnia, Shasta decides to run away on Bree to Narnia. In the process, he becomes instrumental in preventing the Calormenes from launching a surprise attack on Archenland and

Narnia. Over the months of the journey, he becomes more self-confident, less self-en-
grossed, and more worthy of the title of prince.
On one occasion, he even bravely goes to the
aid of Aravis*, the girl with whom he is
traveling, when she is attacked by a great lion,
which he later learns is Aslan*. Shasta is an
interesting figure who changes predictably.

THE SHEEP-PIG (King-Smith*, Dick, ill. Mary
Rayner, Gollancz, 1983; *BABE: THE GALLANT PIG*,
Crown, 1985), warm, affectionate farmyard
fantasy of a pig who finds a place for himself
as a sheep herder. When Farmer Hogget wins a
piglet at the fair by correctly guessing its
weight, he takes it home, and his sheepdog, Fly,
mothers it along with her four pups as she
teaches them how to behave on the farm. He
proves to be a remarkably quick learner, and
Hogget, a kindly man of few words, lets him have
the run of the place with the others. When the
puppies are sold off, the pig, whom Fly calls
Babe, proposes that he become a sheep-pig, and
Fly, whom Babe calls Mum, humors him by teaching
him the basic commands and letting him practice
by herding the ducks. While she is out with the
sheep, he makes friends with an old ewe that
Hogget is treating for foot rot. Ma, as he calls
her, tells him that all sheep resent the rude,
harrying ways of "wolves," as they call sheepdogs, and explains that if anyone would ask them
politely, as he does, they would be only too
glad to obey. This advice proves invaluable a
short while later, when Ma is back with the
flock and Babe seizes the opportunity to visit
them after Hogget and Fly leave in the Land
Rover. He arrives just as sheep rustlers are
rounding up the flock and herding them into a
cattle truck. When Ma explains to him what is
happening, Babe rushes furiously to the front of
the flock, jumps onto the tailgate, and begs the
"dear, sensible sheep" to come no nearer. As the
rustlers and their sheepdogs try to catch Babe,
he dives between the nearest pair of legs and
starts such a commotion that the rustlers drive
away in panic. Mrs. Hogget, a woman of many
words, tells her husband the story and declares
that, like it or not, after the way the pig has
saved their flock she intends to keep him as a

pet and not butcher him. Hogget just smiles. The
next day he tries giving the pig a few simple
commands and is amazed at how well he handles
the sheep. Gradually, Babe takes over most of
Fly's duties, to the satisfaction of the mother
dog who is glad to retire from hard work. Hogget
even takes Babe along with Fly to watch the
local sheepdog trials. When Fly realizes that
her boss actually has competition in mind for
Babe, she starts him on an exercise and diet
program to build up his strength and speed. He
is doing his early morning run when he comes
upon the flock being worried by two sheep-killer
dogs. In fury, Babe attacks and drives away the
astonished dogs, then turns to find that the
dogs have downed old Ma, who is not badly
wounded but still dies, apparently of a heart
attack. When Fly and Hogget find Babe bending
over Ma, with blood on his snout, they both jump
to the conclusion that he has turned into a
sheep-killer. Hogget is about to shoot the pig
when his wife answers the phone and calls out
the news about two sheep-worrying dogs in the
area. Fly finds out the truth by humbling
herself to ask the sheep politely what happened.
When she discovers that Hogget is planning to
enter Babe in the Grand Challenge Trials, she is
worried that with strange sheep her foster son
will not be successful. Again she goes humbly to
the sheep and gets from them the password, a
verse that they assure her will make the
unfamiliar sheep listen to Babe. At the trials,
Hogget has listed his entry as "Pig," but he
keeps Fly with him and Babe in the car until the
last moment. The judges are astonished but can
find nothing in the rule book disqualifying a
pig. At first, even with the password, it takes
Babe some time to explain the situation to the
sheep, but then, while farmers from all over the
United Kingdom stand in the rain to watch and
Mrs. Hogget watches on the television at home,
Babe takes his little flock through a flawless
performance to win the highest score ever
awarded. Tall, quiet Farmer Hogget's kindly
reserve, when contrasted with his comfortably
round wife's garrulousness, provides much of the
humor of this good-natured novel, but all the
way through there are clever touches that make
it appeal not only to middle-grade readers, for

whom it presents no difficulty, but also to a more sophisticated audience. While it does not have the depth of theme of *Charlotte's Web*, with which it inevitably will be compared, it is not imitative and has a charm of its own. Boston Globe Honor; Fanfare; Guardian.

SHEILA SMYTHSON (*Fathom Five**), upper-crust girl who becomes interested in Chas* McGill and joins in his spy-hunting activities. Daughter of a nervous mother and a preoccupied father, she is neglected despite her wealth and privileges. When she is confronted by the madam of the brothel, Nelly* Stagg, her self possession allows her to make a deal, and she is able to stand up to the police with the same cool confidence, but her parents send her away to a strict boarding school where her mail is censored. Through Audrey* Parton she engineers a meeting with Chas on a train, as she returns to boarding school from a vacation, and at the very end he receives a letter from her, evidently smuggled out of the school, but it is clear that their romance cannot outlast the separation.

THE SHEPHERD (*A Sound of Chariots**), the man who rescues Bridie McShane in the vivid scene in which she falls into the pile of lambs' tails and bloodies herself while seeking violets for her mother's birthday. With great tenderness, he picks her up and takes her home to his wife, who cleans her up and feeds her. Because of this terrifying experience, Bridie sees her mother as self-centered and unloving and detaches herself from Agnes* emotionally until she is in her mid-teens.

SHERE KHAN (*The Jungle Books**), lame tiger from near the Wainganga River, twenty miles from the Seeonee Hills where Mowgli* wanders into the den of Mother and Father Wolf. Because he is denied what he thinks is his rightful quarry--the man cub--that night, he becomes an implacable enemy to the boy and incites the resentment that drives Mowgli from the wolf pack when he is about eleven or twelve. Shere Khan is something of a coward, being scared away from the wolves' den by Mother Wolf and shown at the water hole during the drought to have been killing man.

After Mowgli has gone to live in the village,
the wolves bring him word that Shere Khan is
hunting him, and he works out the plan to trap
the tiger in a ravine where he can be trampled
by the stampeding water buffalo.

THE SHIELD RING (Sutcliff*, Rosemary, ill. C.
Walter Hodges*, Oxford, 1956; Walck, 1962),
historical novel set in the Cumberland Fells in
the last quarter of the eleventh century,
dealing with the resistance of the descendants
of the Vikings to the Normans, who are trying in
vain to conquer that area of the British Isles.
When her family is killed and their home,
somewhere south of Lancaster, is burned by the
Normans, Frytha, not yet five, is brought by her
father's shepherd, Grim, far north to the
stronghold of Butharsdale, a community of
Northmen swollen by refugees from Saxon areas
ravaged by the invaders. There she is raised in
the family of the Countess Tordis and Jarl
Buthar, along with Bjorn, an orphan two years
older than she, who has Celtic blood from a
far-off grandmother in Wales. Bjorn is the
foster child of Haethcyn, the harper of Saxon
origin, and clearly has in his nature the music
lacking in the Northmen. During their childhood,
the Normans under Red William advance in such
great numbers that Buthar reluctantly proposes
making peace with them and sends his right-hand
man, Ari Knudson, under the green bough of truce
to seek terms. When the Normans attack with the
bodies of Ari and his four companions bound to
spears as standards, the defending Northmen are
enraged and fight as never before. The weather
comes to their aid with a terrible storm, a Helm
Wind that seems sent by the gods to breed panic
among the Normans and avenge the torture death
of Ari. This encounter inspires not only an
unshakable resolve to hold out among the Northmen but also a secret doubt in imaginative Bjorn
(known only to Frytha) of whether he would be
able to hold out under torture and not reveal
the hidden ways into Butharsdale that keep the
community safe from attack. At not yet fifteen,
Bjorn joins the War-band, and Haethcyn gives him
his father's sword and a ring with a dolphin cut
in a flawed emerald, an heirloom that has come
down from his far-off Welsh grandmother. Frytha,

like the other girls of Butharsdale, has also
been trained as an archer and to use a dirk
should need arise. Through all the off-again,
on-again fighting of the next few years,
Butharsdale keeps a secret trade with Ireland
for grain and other necessaries, using a tavern
keeper as their intermediary. When Bjorn goes in
to pick up new Irish harp-wire for Haethcyn's
harp, the Sweet Singer, he overhears Norman
men-at-arms arguing and pointing out that the
next attack on Butharsdale must be from the
north. On the basis of this warning, Buthar has
his men destroy the only road from the north and
build a new road into Rannardale, a road leading
into a trap, which comes to be called the Road
to Nowhere. Several years later, the Normans
have gathered a huge force and made new
outposts, and an attack from the north seems
imminent. Bjorn volunteers to get into the
Norman camp as a harper to gain information,
taking the Sweet Singer with him. Chopping off
her hair and dressing as a boy, Frytha follows
him, and together they make their way into the
camp, gain most of the information they need,
and are ready to make a getaway when they are
summoned to the pavilion of Ranulf Le Meschin,
the commander, to entertain him. There a squire
with whom Bjorn once had hand-to-hand combat
recognizes his ring, and their disguise is
penetrated. Hoping to get more information about
the Butharsdale defences, Ranulf has a torch
held to Bjorn's harping hand, but the boy holds
fast under torture. Frytha then is seized, and
her great fear is not that she will give way
under the flames but that Bjorn will, as he
watches her suffer. Just then a band of Northmen
attack, and Bjorn and Frytha are bound and left
for later torture. They manage to escape to the
attackers, to give their valuable information to
Buthar, and to help in the great ambush at
Rannardale in which the overwhelmingly larger
Norman force is destroyed. Bjorn, who has been
fighting one-handed, survives, but back in
Butharsdale he collapses and remains ill a long
time. Frytha nurses him, and by the time he is
well again the community at Butharsdale is
breaking up, the people going back to their own
home places, now safe again with the Normans
defeated so decisively. Bjorn and Frytha, with

Grim, plan to go to his father's holding, Bjornsthwaite, to clear the long-neglected land and make a new start. The plot, based on historical fact, is compelling, but the main interest is in the strong characters, particularly sturdy, determined Frytha and sensitive, self-doubting Bjorn. The setting, crucial to the story, is well evoked, with its towering crags, deep dales, and fiercely changeable weather, as well as the domestic scene of the Viking descendants in Butharsdale. The title refers not only to the physical setting, but, more importantly, to the ring of trust on which the Northmen depend. Carnegie Com.

SHINE (*Archer's Goon**), female wizard who farms crime. She is dark and vastly fat, dressed all in tight black leather, and utterly unprincipled. She controls burglars, bank robberies, and gangs of hoods through a series of television screens. She almost gets both Howard* and Awful* Sykes under her power by invading their minds with thoughts of the excitement of ordering gangsters around and racing off in getaway cars. Although she intends to hold them hostage to force Quentin* to write the words for her, she is tricked by Torquil* and the Goon* through her desire to get Archer* in her control.

SHOT-IN-THE-HEAD (*John Diamond**), rat-like street boy who attempts to burn the tenement and is allowed to escape by William Jones though the dwarf, Seed*, is demanding that he be bashed with the poker. In return, Shot-in-the-Head saves William when the pack of boys sets on him and takes him to his hideaway--a shack made of old clothes and covered over by boards, on the roof of a slum building. In the pockets of the clothes he keeps his treasures--watches, brooches, snuff boxes, rings, and buckles--which he has acquired by the "snick and lurk," that is, by picking pockets. Rather simple-minded, he values them for their shine rather than their intrinsic value and seems to exist mainly by the theft of food and what is given him for caring for a neighbor's baby. When he follows William to his country home he leaves his treasure behind, and the boys draw maps and make plans to retrieve it.

SIDNEY PEACEMAKER (*The Plan for Birdsmarsh**), London doctor devoted to sailing and particularly to antique boats. He is the president of the East Coast Smack Preservation Society, which is the butt of much local humor. A cheerful, tweedy type, he is aware of the amusement he produces, but he is so fond of the quiet and peace of Birdsmarsh that he continues to keep his old boat, *Phoebe*, there and works ineffectually against the commercial exploitation of the place. He helps the boys get the *Swannie* sailing by contributing a couple of old sails and giving them advice and at the end suggests that the sunken smack might be salvageable.

SID PARKER (*The Battle of Bubble and Squeak**), eldest child in the Parker-Sparrow family, brother of Peggy and Amy Parker and son of Mrs.* Sparrow. A responsible, well-brought-up boy, he is unable to tell his mother how much the gerbils mean to him because the family has obviously never learned to communicate feelings of this sort. He stands up to his mother over the gerbils, even daring to cheek her about them, but she blatantly overrides his pleading. Because she makes him feel powerless over something so important to him, he dashes a jar of grease to the floor in the larder as a sign of defiance while she is out of the house. After school and before she returns from work, when he discovers that his stepfather, Bill* Sparrow, has not taken the gerbils back to the pet store as Mrs. Sparrow had demanded, Sid hastily cleans up the mess in order not to antagonize her further and to influence her to think more favorably about the animals. Sid learns perseverance and patience. It is easy to like and sympathize with him in his struggles for his gerbils.

THE SILVER BRANCH (Sutcliff*, Rosemary, ill. Charles Keeping, Oxford, 1957; Walck, 1959), second in a trilogy of historical adventure novels set in Roman Britain, this one in the last decade of the third century, telling of the fall of Carausius, self-proclaimed Emperor of Britain, and of the efforts to defeat his

murderer, Allectus, who seizes control. Junior
Surgeon Tiberius Lucius Justinianus, known as
Justin*, newly arrived in Britain, runs into
young Centurion Marcellus Flavius Aquila, called
Flavius, and discovers they are distant cousins,
both descended from the Marcus* Flavius Aquila
of *The Eagle of the Ninth**. Quiet, stammering
Justin and outgoing, red-haired Flavius become
fast friends, and on an early morning hunting
expedition in the marshes they make the startling discovery that Allectus, finance minister
to the Emperor Carausius, is meeting secretly
with a Saxon. They are able to follow and
capture the Saxon, bring him back to the fort,
and give the news directly to Carausius, who
interviews them in front of Allectus. To their
surprise and horror, Carausius does not seem to
believe them, and the Saxon, with whom they hope
to back up their story, is discovered to have
been poisoned. They are posted to a remote
station on the Great Wall, but again they are
surprised that not only are they allowed to stay
together but both are promoted, Flavius to
command a cohort and Justin to be surgeon for
the same cohort. Flavius whips the disgruntled
unit into shape, and Justin wins the friendship
of Evicatus, an outcast from a Dalraid tribe, by
treating his infected wolf bites. Evicatus, with
whom they go hunting, tells them that Allectus
is making plans to take over Britain and has
enlisted the support of the Picts, agreeing to
help them wipe out the Dalraids once he is
emperor. Out of loyalty to his people, Evicatus
takes a message, jointly signed by Flavius and
Justin, to Carausius, but he is waylaid, and the
message is taken. He manages to get word to
Justin and Flavius, who realize that their hours
are numbered if they stay. Together the three
travel south, only to learn on the way that
Allectus has murdered Carausius and taken power
even before they sent the message. Evicatus
turns back to the north, but Justin and Flavius
head for Calleva, where they secretly visit
Flavius's formidable old Aunt Honoria, who
strips off her valuable bracelets to pay their
passage to Gaul. As they are inquiring cautious-
ly about possible passage, they meet Paulinus, a
little, rotund man, who turns out to be the
unlikely head of a loose band of resistance

agents dedicated to smuggling legionnaires and
others loyal to Carausius to Gaul to join
Constantius, the Roman commander there. Paulinus, observing their spirit and intelligence,
suggests that they might rather stay and work
with him. At first they refuse, but at the last
minute they change their minds and become
deeply involved in the underground movement,
which grows rapidly. In attempting to help a
young Centurion named Anthonius who has
incurred the displeasure of Allectus, Justin
inadvertently leads a spy to the headquarters of
Paulinus in the rear of a ramshackle deserted
theater. Although most of them escape by crawlng
beneath the rafters of the old theater, Paulinus, unfit for such acrobatics, deliberately
walks into the midst of the guards who are
firing the building and is killed. Flavius and
Justin jointly take over the band and move it to
the farm that belongs to Flavius, the one
started some generations before by Marcus
Aquila. Over the next months, their band grows
as defectors from the legions under Allectus,
farmers who have lost their homes to his
raiding bands of Saxon mercenaries, and other
dissidents join, among them Pandarus, a gladiator who has won the wooden foil that means freedom but who can't bear the dullness of ordinary
life, and Evicatus, who comes from the north.
On an expedition to Calleva to buy weapons,
Justin and Flavius come upon Saxon mercenaries
beating up little Cullen*, a British slave who
was known as Carausius's Fool or "hound," a
strange fellow who carries an unusual musical
instrument shaped like a branch with silver
apples, each of which has a different tone when
struck. They manage to get him away from that
particular band of Saxons, then lead a wild
chase through back alleys and courtyards until
they get to the home of Aunt Honoria, where they
hide in the hypocaust, the heat vents under the
floor, while the Saxons search the house.
Afterwards they have two important surprises:
Cullen extracts from the hollow tube of his
silver branch a letter written by Carausius to
Justin and Flavius, to be delivered to them if
he should die, saying that he had believed them
and sent them away to protect them from the
revenge of Allectus. The second surprise is a

bundle they pull from beneath the floor, the mortar holding the stones of its secret hiding place having crumbled, which contains a battered, wingless eagle, the same that Marcus and his uncle had buried there several generations previously. This becomes the standard for the band of the sixty-odd mounted men they take to join Constantius when his forces land in Britain. They take part in the major battle with the forces of Allectus, some six miles south of Calleva, then turn back to try to save the town from the looting, pillaging remnants of the mercenary troops. Although too late to keep them from Calleva, they manage to defend the basilica in the Forum, where many of the townspeople are seeking refuge, and to hold out until reinforcements come, even though the building burns almost over their heads, and the eagle is buried when the roof crashes in. Evicatus is killed, as is Pandarus, but Cullen survives and vows to follow and serve Justin and Flavius when they are accepted into the forces of Constantius and posted to duty again in the north. Most of the novel is told from the point of view of Justin, the less confident and more sensitive of the two young men and the more interesting character. Although the plot depends on a number of coincidences, the vivid scenes and the sense of the times are so strong that this is hardly noticeable. Suspense is high, with intrigue and action in plenty, but there is also quiet speculation about the nature of loyalty, the attachment of a man to his physical surroundings, and what constitutes true heroism. The history of the period is made clear without slowing the pace. Third novel in the trilogy is *The Lantern Bearers**. Carnegie Com.; Choice; Fanfare.

THE SILVER CHAIR (Lewis*, C. S., ill. Pauline Baynes, Bles, 1953; Macmillan, 1953), fantasy of magic, adventure, and a search for a missing person, sixth in order of events and fourth published of the novels set in the mythical land of Narnia*. When Eustace* Scrubb, introduced in *The Voyage of the "Dawn Treader*"*, and Jill* Pole, a classmate, are plagued by bullies at their horrible, progressive school, Experiment House, Eustace calls upon Aslan* for help, and they manage to escape from the schoolyard through a normally locked gate in the school-yard wall. They meet Aslan in Aslan's Mountain, a beautiful, in-between world, where he orders them to seek Caspian's* lost son, Prince Rilian*, gives Jill specific but obscure instructions for finding the youth (which they persistently muff throughout, thus causing the ensuing adventures to occur), then blows them into Narnia. They arrive to discover that seventy years have elapsed in Narnian time since the events in *The Voyage of the "Dawn Treader"*. King Caspian, now old and despondent over the loss of his son, has just left on a voyage to eastern waters in hopes of finding Aslan for advice about the succession to the throne. A talking Owl, Glimfeather, takes them to Lord Trumpkin*, Caspian's deaf, old Dwarf Regent, who orders them put up at Cair Paravel and then bears them to the Parliament of Owls, where another owl tells them the story of how Prince Rilian disappeared ten years earlier after he had encountered a shining, green woman, who was obviously evil, at the very place where his mother had recently been slain by a wood-serpent. The owls carry them to the region of the Marsh-wiggles, where the gloomy, loquacious frog-man Puddleglum joins them as helper and guide, and following Aslan's instructions, they head northward for the Ruined City of the Giants, camping out along the way, a difficult and hazardous journey of about two weeks. They cross the River Shribble and the barren and rocky Ettinsmoor and meet a Dark Knight and the Lady of the Green Kirtle, who tells them they will be welcomed at the Giants' city of Harfang and entertained at the Autumn Festival soon to come. They eagerly hasten onward, anticipating revelry and creature comforts. They are welcomed cordially but then are dismayed and frightened to learn that they are destined to be on the Giants' menu at the festival. They escape from the* city just in time, hurry to the Giants' Ruined City, which they were supposed to find but bypassed mistakenly, fall through openings there into the Underland, are taken ever deeper by the Warden of the Marches of Underland, the gnome Mulugutherum, through sets of caverns of claustophobic atmosphere, exotic vegetation, and weird lighting, until they arrive at the queen's castle, where they meet the Black Knight again. He ridicules their quest and their conscientious persistence and then informs them that he suffers from a strange enchantment. A frenzy comes upon him regularly, during which he must be bound to a silver chair and severely restrained despite his repeated pleas for release. The frenzy upon him, bound to the chair, the youth begs them to release him, and they persistently refuse. When he calls upon Aslan's name, however, a sign by which they were to recognize the lost prince, they realize the Dark Knight is Rilian and cut his bonds. They slay the queen by turning her magic back upon her. They learn that she is the Lady of the Green Kirtle and has been employing gnomes called Earthmen to dug tunnels by which she can invade Narnia and put Rilian on his own throne as her puppet king. The little party escapes to the Overland just as the Deep Realm of the Underland begins to break up under the impact of rising waters. They burst out of the Underland at the very place where Fauns, Dryads, and other Narnian creatures are engaged in the moonlight festival, the Great Snow Dance. They return joyfully to Cair Paravel just as Caspian puts in from his unsuccessful voyage. He blesses his son and dies. Aslan uses a special thorn to restore him to life and grants Caspian's wish to see the children's world just once by blowing them all into Experiment House, where they beat the school children thoroughly with whips and swords and cause such a commotion that reforms are made, and it becomes a worthwhile school for children to attend. Caspian returns to his own dimension, Rilian buries him and ascends the throne, and Jill and Eustace remain friends at the school where they can now be comfortable and learn the right things. Jill and Eustace are interesting protagonists, much like their Pevensie counterparts, Peter*, Susan*, Edmund*, and Lucy*. They bicker and complain just enough to make them seem real and keep the pot boiling. The resourceful if pessimistic Puddleglum steals the show. He is physically interesting but never made grotesque or cute, and provides good character ballast. The remaining figures are clear good or evil types but still

interesting; the concepts of the Underland and
the planned invasion are inventive; and the
kidnapped prince aspect improvises skillfully
on folklore. The punishment ending seems forced
and cutely melodramatic, but there is never a
dull moment in the rest of the story. ChLA
Touchstones; Choice.

THE SILVER CURLEW (Farjeon*, Eleanor, ill.
Ernest Shepard, Oxford, 1953; Viking, 1954),
lively, lighthearted fantasy of magical happenings embellishing the old English folktale of
"Tom Tit Tot," adapted from a play of Farjeon's
called *The Silver Curlew*. Events are set in
Norfolk near the sea at an undisclosed time but
before the Industrial Revolution. Among the six
children of Mother Codling, a hardworking miller's widow, are four adult yokel sons, Abe, Sid,
Dave, and Hal; a lazy daughter, Doll, 18, who
loves dumplings; and one warmhearted, overly
curious daughter, Poll*, 12, who is always
asking questions. When Poll fetches flounder for
her mother's dinner, she and Charlee* Loon, a
dour fisherman, who makes up little ditties and
plays tunes on his whistle, rescue the Silver
Curlew, a magical bird with silvery plumage and
ivory beak and claws, from an ugly black animal
of some sort that has come out of the Witching
Wood. Poll takes the injured bird home and
nurses it. Doll, who refuses to spin and dreams
of eating all the dumplings she can hold,
devours the entire batch of a dozen that Mother
Codling has prepared for family dinner, eating
them as they are still baking. At the palace,
imperious Nan*, old nurse and housekeeper for
willful, spoiled King Nollekens*, announces that
the palace linen closet needs replenishing,
laments the lack of good spinners nowadays, and
tells Nollekens it's time he got married. He
says he'll find and marry the best spinster in
the land. While he's searching, he overhears
Mother Codling deplore Doll's eating the twelve
dumplings, is allowed to think she's talking
about Doll's spinning, and announces that he'll
marry Doll and make her Queen of Norfolk if she
can spin three huge farm carts of flax in a half
hour's time; otherwise he'll chop off her head.
Alone in the kitchen, Doll cries with despair
but then notices a little black man-like

creature with a long black tail pop out of the
hearth. He says he's the Spindle-Imp* and offers
to spin for her. He says he'll return in one
year's time, at which point she must guess his
name, or he'll claim her for himself. Practical
Doll agrees, Nan is delighted with the yarn, the
king makes Doll his queen, and all in his
household soon love her dearly for her easygoing
nature and sweet disposition. Almost a year
passes, and the palace thrills to the birth of a
baby princess, whom down-to-earth Doll calls
simply Joan. Then Nollekens informs Doll that
the linen closet needs replenishing. She must
spin the new flax or lose her "lovely noddle."
Again in despair, Doll weeps, and again the
Spindle-Imp turns up, saying she must guess his
name. Nine times she guesses with no success.
Then unexpectedly the Imp gives her three more
guesses, provided she will wager the baby, too.
Now in even deeper trouble, Doll confides her
peril to Poll, who sets out to learn the Imp's
name and save her sister and the baby she loves
like her own. She discovers the Silver Curlew's
wing has mended and she can fly, and on the bird
she is wafted away on a cloud of moonshine to
Charlee, who informs her that the Imp is the
evil power that rules the nearby Witching Wood.
Disguised in the skin of the ugly black creature
that had attacked the Curlew, Poll bravely
enters the wood, followed surreptitiously by
Charlee. She falls in with the Imp's Queer
Things, who take her to the Imp's cook,
Spider-Mother, a witch-like creature also called
Rackney. The creatures think Poll is the dead
Queer Thing, call her Runton, and force her to
guess a riddle and dance, during which her
disguise becomes undone and both she and Charlee
are captured and bound to trees by spider webs.
In malicious triumph, the Imp capers about and
croaks a little verse that contains his name,
Tom Tit Tot, and then rushes away to the palace
to claim his prey. To the rescue comes the
Silver Curlew, who with burning twigs melts the
spiderweb bonds and releases Poll and Charlee.
Back at the palace, grand preparations for the
baby's christening occupy the attention of
everyone except Doll, who despairingly blurts
out her tale of woe. Surprisingly, Nollekens
admires her even more when he realizes how many

dumplings she put away without a stomach ache.
The Imp turns up, all try unsuccessfully to
bribe him to leave without Doll and the baby,
and Nollekens wastes all but one of the guesses.
Just as the Imp is about to grab the baby, Poll
appears and near exhaustion gasps the true name.
The Imp immediately expires in a "bang and a
flash and a fizzle," leaving behind only a black
smudge on the palace carpet, and Doll and baby
Joan are safe. The baby's christening is a
marvelously grand affair, attended also by four
fairy godmothers with superlative gifts, the
Morning Fairy, the Noontide Fairy, the Twilight
Fairy, and the Midnight Fairy. The last is a
lady of "exquisite loveliness," "as light as a
moonbeam," the Silver Curlew bird now restored
to her proper form as the Lady in the Moon. She
is accompanied by Charlee Loon, now in his
proper form as the Man in the Moon. They spread
their wings and rise into a sky glittery with
stars. That night, the sea shell Charlee gave
Poll and that she keeps under her pillow sings
to her the magical story of the Man and Lady's
romance, separation, and reunion as Poll falls
asleep. The tone is intimate and chatty, and the
voice of the author as storyteller can be heard
clearly throughout. The story is written in a
skillful if self-conscious style, full of wordplay, puns, and repetition for effect. Dialogue, much of it patter and colloquial,
abounds; characters are added to the basic tale;
the king, the mother, and Nan in particular are
caricatured; and many incidents project a comic
opera atmosphere. Doll and Poll emerge as the
most sympathetic characters, and the only ones
the reader can identify with, Doll for her quiet
strength and Poll for her pluck; and the
Spindle-Imp is a deliciously wicked villain. The
peasant themes of the triumph of common sense
and courage in the face of great adversity
balance out the magical elements and make
palatable the addition to the basic story that
of the Curlew and fisherman and their ill-fated
romance as Man and Lady in the Moon. Their story
seems tacked on, however, underdone, and sentimental, an incongruous and unnecessary accretion
to an already entertaining adaptation. Fanfare.

THE SILVER SWORD (Serraillier*, Ian, ill. C.

Walter Hodges*, Cape, 1956; Criterion, 1959),
historical novel of five years in World War II,
that begins in Poland and follows the varying
fortunes of the Polish Balicki children, Ruth*,
13, Edek*, 11, and Bronia*, 3, and their
waif-friend, Jan*, who is of undisclosed age but
perhaps ten, as they journey across Europe to
seek the Balicki parents in Switzerland. The
book opens in 1941 when Joseph* Balicki, their
schoolteacher father, escapes from a German
prison camp in southern Poland. He returns to
Warsaw to find his Swiss-born wife, Margrit, has
been taken to Germany for slave labor, his house
exploded to rubble, and his children gone and
presumed dead. While examining the rubble, he
discovers a five-inch-long paper knife in the
shape of a silver sword, which he had once given
to Margrit as a birthday present. He also
notices a small, ragged boy with a bony gray
kitten watching him intently. When the boy, Jan,
declares the house is his "pitch," or area of
salvage, Joseph tells him he intends to journey
to Switzerland to the home of his wife's
parents, where the family had once agreed to
meet if separated. He gives Jan the little
sword, on condition that if Jan ever sees the
three missing children, he must inform them of
where Joseph has gone. The novel then backtracks
to pick up on the children's lives, connecting
with events at the point when Margrit was seized
by German storm troopers. The children escape
before the Germans bomb the house. They live on
the other side of the city in a cellar during
the winter and in a hollowed-out oak tree in the
country during the summer. Self-reliant Edek
assumes the role of provider, and maternal Ruth
that of homemaker and nurturer. They live by
their wits, theft, and luck, until Edek is
caught smuggling and taken for slave labor.
Months pass, and the book glosses over the tough
time Ruth must have had maintaining herself and
little Bronia. One day in early 1945, after the
Russians liberate Poland, Ruth, who has been
conducting school for some twenty refugee
children, finds Jan lying half-starved outside
the cellar, a feisty rooster beside him. She
happens to see the little sword and learns from
him of her father's plans. With the help of a
friendly Russian soldier, she learns Edek is in

a transit camp in Posen, and she, Bronia, and
Jan, who attaches himself to them, decide to
make for Switzerland, a long, hard journey
walking and hitching rides. They travel first to
Posen, where they happen upon Edek in a soup
kitchen, tubercular and malnourished; his
ill-health remains a continuing problem. They
live on handouts and sometimes "borrow" or
"organize" others' property to their own
advantage. Jan in particular is a clever thief,
and he has an affinity for animals that proves
to their advantage when he takes in hand Bistro,
a chimp that has escaped from the zoo, and gets
100 marks as a reward. As they travel they
encounter hordes of refugees and returning
soldiers; it seems all Europe is on the move.
Out of the Russian zone and into American
territory by mid-June, they are held up
temporarily when Jan gets caught and is
incarcerated for altering railroad signals so
trains can be raided. They are befriended
briefly by a Bavarian farmer, Kurt Wolff*, who
speeds them on their way down the Falken River.
When their canoes founder, they are picked up by
a Polish-American soldier, Joe Wolski, and
transported by army truck the remaining sixty
miles to the very crowded Red Cross camp near
Lake Constance opposite Switzerland. Problems
continue. They must prove they have relatives
awaiting them before they may enter Switzerland.
Coincidentally, Herr Wolff has sent ahead the
silver sword they have left behind, along with
his written account of the children's story, and
Joseph has written to the superintendent to
inquire about them. They barely survive a final
obstacle: a sudden, violent storm on the lake.
Their reunification with their father and mother
(who has been found by the Red Cross in a
concentration camp) is joyful. Time, medicines,
and family love heal their wounds, and even the
severely psychologically scarred Jan becomes
better adjusted. Joseph and his family become
involved in developing an international children's village for war waifs. Although the
reader sees many instances of the ravages of
war--leveled towns, cold, hunger, thousands of
homeless (in particular children), and inhu-
manity--the predominant tone is hopeful. The
emphasis is on survival through love, per-

severance, and cooperation. The children also find many people who seem sincerely interested in helping them, former enemies as well as allies, and they see that war turns some people into monsters but that good people can be found everywhere. Characters are drawn in bold strokes, and there are many exciting scenes. Jan's escapades seem in keeping with his antisocial nature as presented, but the storm scene seems anticlimactic and gratuitous. Coincidence plays a strong role in events, but the author's unemotional tone makes it acceptable, along with a note at the beginning that the book is based on true happenings. The story belongs mostly to strong, indefatigable, undauntable Ruth. The Bavarian farmer stands out, Americans are not idealized, and the most interesting character is the unpredictable Jan. The silver sword is a symbol throughout of hope and courage and serves also as a means of identifying the children. Carnegie Com.

SILVESTER (*The Dancing Bear**), slave boy and bear ward who sets out to find and ransom his friend and mistress, the Lady Ariadne*, who has been carried off by a raiding Hun. Although from the first he uses his cleverness to try to hide the girl in the bear cage and continues to make intelligent decisions throughout the story, he retains the mentality of a slave, preferring to take orders unquestioningly, until after the death of Antonius*, when he discovers that the man was not the Roman he pretended to be but a descendant of a Greek slave. Ariadne points out to him that it is not the manumission paper that she signs with her seal that makes him free but his change of mental attitude, and he assumes the role of a Byzantine noble, now owner of Antonius's Roman tower in Slavic lands. Part of him continues to long for the busy city, with its disputatious, noisy population, to which he can never return, though he knows that Ariadne is far happier in her new life.

SIMON (*Black Hearts in Battersea**; *The Wolves of Willoughby Chase**), gooseherd who in *The Wolves of Willoughby Chase* enables Bonnie and Sylvia to escape from cruel Mrs. Brisket's charity school in Blastburn, helps to bring wicked Miss Slighcarp to justice, and is rewarded by the offer of an art school education in London. Simon plays a larger role in *Black Hearts in Battersea*, where, while in London pursuing his art studies, he helps foil a plot to put Bonnie Prince Georgie of Hanover on the throne. In the process of defeating the conspirators, Simon discovers that in reality he is noble, being the son of the Duke of Battersea's brother who died in the Hanoverian Wars. He also learns that he has a sister, Sophie*, a girl whom ironically he had met while both were at the Poor Farm, where he had been taken at the age of three after he was found wandering in a village. He had simply been left in the village by Buckle, a Hanoverian conspirator, who then passed off his own son, Justin, as the Battersea heir. At the age of eight, Simon ran away from the Poor Farm to Willoughby Chase, where in *Wolves* he lives in a cave and keeps geese. In *Black Hearts*, Mr.* and Mrs. Abednego Twite call him Thingummy.

SIMON (*The Ghost of Thomas Kempe**), friend of James* Harrison, about James's age of ten. They strike up an acquaintance after James's family moves to East End Cottage in Ledsham. Simon wears glasses and looks like an "amiable gargoyle." He is a carefree sort and a realist, who goes along with James's story of the ghost not because he believes in the ghost, something he never comes around to doing, but simply because he's polite and accommodating. He gives James information about things that go on in Ledsham. He serves as foil to both James and Arnold* Luckett.

SIMON WOOD (*The Scarecrows**), tense, tormented boy who cannot accept his mother's second marriage and is sometimes possessed by "devils" that drive him into a berserk-like rage. Simon idolizes the memory of his father, a paratrooper killed in the Middle East, who was a man addicted to action, fast cars, and dangerous challenges, evidently unable to feel real emotion. Something of a prig and a snob, Simon also is horrified at the idea of his mother as a sexual being and deeply resents his stepfather, Joe* Moreton, particularly because Joe comes from a social level far beneath that of his upper-crust parents. Underneath his disagreeable aloofness, however, Simon longs for his mother's love, and Joe is right when he perceives the boy as lonely.

THE SINGING CAVE (Dillon*, Eilis, ill. Richard Kennedy, Faber, 1959; Funk, 1960), adventure novel set on the island of Barrinish off the coast of Connemara, Ireland, in the first third of the twentieth century. Young Pat has been saved from apprenticeship to the tailor by his grandfather, Mick* Cooney, who has taken the boy to be his companion and heir. Together they have a fine time, for the old man is as willing as the boy to leave farm chores to fish or sail their hooker to Spain. When Pat is saving a straying bullock from the cliff edge during a storm, he hears a deep ringing sound which he realizes must come from the cave known as the Singing Cave. Both he and his grandfather suffer terrible impatience until the weather calms enough so that they can take their currach to visit the cave. There they discover that part of the rear wall has broken out to reveal what looks like a great grillwork, which is evidently man-made. Pat squeezes through one of the spaces and in the light of his candle makes an astonishing discovery, a Viking boat containing a skeleton and a game made of a peg board and a pattern of beautifully carved ivory wolf heads. Pat shows the game to his grandfather, who persuades him to leave it with the Viking skeleton. The next day they hitch up the horse and go off to the other end of the island to tell of their find to Mr.* Allen, the most educated man in the area. To their dismay, he makes light of their discovery, implying that Pat has invented the tale and assuring them that in his own books he has written that the Vikings never came so far west in Ireland. The next morning, Pat visits the cave and finds the grillwork broken out and the Viking and his boat missing. His honest, innocent grandfather mourns that Mr. Allen will think him a liar, but Pat realizes that Mr. Allen must be responsible and enlists his friend Tom Joyce to help discover the truth. From a chance remark of simple-minded old Johnny Gill, they realize that the Viking

was moved the previously evening, and that night
they trail Mr. Allen to a ruined house where he
meets Big Dan Moloney, captain of the lobster
boat *Saint Ronan*, who loads several boxes onto
an ancient cart and takes them to his cabin.
Leaving a message for Pat's grandfather, the
boys stow away in the hold above the lobsters,
where they are found by Louan*, the Breton
boatman, who hides them out for a while and,
when Big Dan discovers them, insists that they
be treated well. Big Dan angrily commands Louan
to stay and guard them on the *Saint Ronan*
while they are in his home harbor of Kerronan.
Humiliated, Louan disobeys, takes them to his
home, then helps them trail Big Dan, whom they
overhear making a deal with the mayor to
"discover" the Viking in their local cave. Louan
and the boys beat them to the cave, take the
boxes, and are picked up by Pat's grandfather in
his hooker. They sail home, chased by the *Saint
Ronan*, and arrive in the middle of the annual
sports day. They manage to hide the boxes under
the platform in the sports field and watch the
currach races in which their man, quiet Lord*
Folan, beats even loud-mouthed Rooster Hernon,
his continual rival. Suddenly all the spectators
are diverted by the word that Lord's cattle are
loose and in danger of going over the cliff. The
boys, racing down the shore and climbing the
bank, are able to head off the cattle only to
see them driven back by Mr. Allen and his
housekeeper. When the cattle make one last
stampede, the ground over the Singing Cave
collapses, and Mr. Allen falls in. Lord and
Rooster team up with Pat and his grandfather to
save him, but, during all this diversion, Big
Dan, trying to load the boxes, has in fact set
them adrift in a currach. With the hooker, Pat,
his grandfather, Tom, Lord, and Rooster go out
to rescue the currach. Pat gets into the little
boat, and saves the game, but, with the approval
of the others, he gives the Viking and his boat
a sea burial. The adventure is fast-paced and
convincing, but the strength of the book lies in
the characters, particularly the lively old
grandfather and the many well-drawn minor
characters, and in the picture it gives of life
of the period on the far western Irish islands.
The first-person narration uses dialectal turns

of speech that give a feel for the language and the ways of thought of the people with both humor and sympathy. Fanfare.

SIR DANIEL BRACKLEY (*The Black Arrow**), guardian to Dick* Shelton and abductor of Joanna* Sedley. An intriguer and a turncoat, Sir Daniel is the epitome of the worst among the nobles of the period, a man without compassion, willing to sell his loyalty for a chance of preferment while at the same time hedging his bets by secretly dealing with the other side. Although it is not entirely clear who actually killed Dick's father, Sir Daniel is certainly responsible and has been adding to his wealth by taking the lands that are rightfully Dick's. When his side seems to be losing, he is not above fleeing, once disguised as a leper, once as a pilgrim.

SIR JOCELIN DE COURCY ROHAN (*Children of the Red King**), Norman holder of Androhan Castle in early-thirteenth century Connacht. Pictured as a man of great kindness and sensitivity for his time, he treats Grania* and Fergus*, children of King Cormac*, his adversary, not as hostages but as his wards. Through his gentle spirit he eventually achieves his ends, through he must anger King John to do so.

SIR OLIVER OATES (*The Black Arrow**), priest in the household of Sir* Daniel Brackley, who has been tutor to Dick* Shelton. A man clearly afraid of Sir Daniel, he swears to Dick that he had nothing to do with the death of his father, but it is clear that he is doing so at Sir Daniel's command, and his manner indicates that he is committing perjury. Later he tells Dick that he did, indeed, lead his father to the ambush where he was killed, but that he did it unwittingly. More weak than evil, he does not betray Dick and Lawless* in the chapel before the marriage but does point them out when Lord Shoreby has been shot. In the end, he is the only one of Jon* Amend-All's intended victims to survive.

SIR PAGAN LATOURELLE (*One Is One**), wealthy, generous knight of Worchestershire, who takes in

Stephen* de Beauville and teaches him the skills
of combat. Though lighthearted and even frivolous in appearance, Sir Pagan has a strong loyalty to King Edward II and is hanged as a result
of an attempt to rescue the king from captivity.
With quick wit and kindness, he accuses Stephen
of having betrayed him, and even attacks him
physically, thereby assuring that the soldiers
will let Stephen go rather than hanging him
along with Sir Pagan.

SIR RALF THE RED (*Lost John**), popular name for
Sir Raoul de Farrar, the outlaw who leads a band
that robs rich and poor alike, and seldom,
though occasionally, shares any loot with the
needy, but who is the realistic prototype for
the legendary Robin Hood. Mercurial in temper
and heartless to his victims and enemies, Sir
Ralf is a charismatic leader and soon becomes a
hero to John* Fitzwilliam, who, when captured,
is spared so he can act as squire to Sir Ralf.
Having killed his wife for warning her brothers
that he planned to attack them, Sir Ralf can't
stand the sight of his son, Alain, who resembles
his mother, and he treats the boy badly. In a
not entirely believable final action, he throws
himself over John's body to receive a spear
thrust himself and save the boy.

SIR RANDOLPH GRIMSBY (*Midnight Is a Place**),
Lucas* Bell's guardian, and, at the book's
beginning, the owner of the mansion called
Midnight Court and the major sweatshop in
Blastburn, Murgatroyd's Carpet, Rug, and Matting
Manufactury. Sir Randolph detests children,
snarls at the servants, drinks heavily,
neglects the mill, and is so deeply in debt
from gambling that he cannot meet the taxes. He
sets fire to Midnight Court so that the tax
people won't get it and then walks into the
flames himself to end his life. At the book's
conclusion, it is revealed that he cheated at
the bet by which he won the house and mill from
his friend Sir Denzil* Murgatroyd.

SIR SIMON MONTPELIER (*Which Witch?**), the ghost
of Darkington Hall, whom Arriman the wizard
yearns to raise and whom Belladonna (really
Terence* Mugg) brings back to life. Sir Simon

was a sixteenth-century nobleman who murdered
his seven wives and who walks the earth
groaning with guilt and striking his forehead
with a "plashing sound." At the end, raised and
real again, he goes off with Madame* Olympia,
whose five husbands disappeared mysteriously.
The reader is left to imagine what happens next.

SISTERS AND BROTHERS (Weaver*, Stella, Collins,
1960; *A POPPY IN THE CORN*, Pantheon, 1961),
realistic novel set in North Cornwall in the
mid-twentieth century, concerning the difficulty of fitting into a strange family as a
teenager. When the Clare children, Laurence,
about fourteen or fifteen, and his younger
sister, Anna*, twelve or thirteen, learn that
their adopted cousin, Teresa* Giselli, is coming
to live with them, Anna is at first delighted to
have a poor orphan for a sister, but when Teresa
arrives, competent, reserved, more mature and
possibly even older than Anna, only little Ben,
six or seven, a strange, detached child, really
likes her. Unexpectedly, Dr. and Mrs. Clare go
to America, leaving the family at Whitebear farm
in the care of the nurse-housekeeper Tucker, who
breaks her leg on a day trip to London. Left to
themselves, the teenagers argue but manage,
mostly because of Teresa's practical skill, but
the money left for them runs low, and Teresa
shoplifts food from the local store. Laurence
gets a job at a nearby farm, which makes him
feel grown up and helps financially, but Anna,
jealous and confused, alternates between fits of
temper and remorse, and Teresa often slips away
to Lanzion, the elaborate house of the recently
deceased Mrs. Meneot, where Ellen Pearl, the old
lady's companion and servant, has taken a fancy
to her. There, amidst articles of great wealth,
she steals a rather crude little pottery figure
of a man riding a camel as a gift for Laurence,
unaware that it is a valuable ancient Chinese
treasure. When Anna is told by the storekeeper
that things have been missing after Teresa has
been there, she doesn't know what to do, but
shortly afterwards she and Laurence are able to
save the storekeeper's daughter who is caught in
an outgoing tide, and the woman assures them
that she will say no more. Teresa, able to
manage Ben better than his siblings can,

discovers him after a storm riding what she
fears is a washed-up floating mine, and she
lures him away from it just before it explodes.
The theft from Lanzion having been discovered,
Teresa runs away, gets lost, and finds herself
back at Lanzion House where she is locked up by
the housekeeper but rescued by understanding
John Meneot, nephew of the former owner, who is
crippled from war combat. By strange coincidence
he has been hunting for her, having known her
Italian father, a Resistance worker, during the
war, and having promised him to try to find his
French Jewish wife and child who were taken to a
concentration camp. Anna and Ben arrive and
later Laurence, and reconciliations take place
all round. Despite a rather slow pace, the book
is absorbing because of good characterization
until the end, where the coincidences and
moralizing mar it. Fanfare.

SLEIGH, BARBARA (DE RIEMER) (1906-1982), born in
Acock's Green, Worcestershire, the daughter of
an artist; teacher and author of radio plays,
novels, and short stories of fantasy and magic
for children. After graduation from St.
Catherine's School in Bramley, Surrey, she
attended art school in Birmingham and received
her art diploma from Clapham High School Art
Teacher's Training College in London in 1928.
After teaching art in high school in Staffordshire and lecturing at Goldsmiths' Teacher
Training College in London, she became an
assistant on the "Children's Hour" program for
BBC-Radio from 1932-1935, retiring to become a
freelance broadcaster, radio writer, and writer
of fiction. In 1935, she married David Davis,
also a freelance broadcaster for BBC, and the
couple had three children. In addition to
writing many radio plays, she published anthologies of legends, an edition of *The Wind in the
Willows** by Kenneth Grahame* (Hodder, 1983),
books of short stories like *The Singing Wreath
and Other Stories* (Parrish, 1957) and *West of
Widdershins* (Collins, 1971; as *Stirabout
Stories*, Bobbs, 1971), and stories for picture
books, among them *Grimblegraw and the Wuthering
Witch* (Hodder, 1978) and *Charlie Chumbles*
(Knight, 1977). Her chief claim to fame in children's literature came with her first pub-

lished book for young readers, *Carbonel, The King of the Cats** (Parrish, 1955; Bobbs, 1957), a lighthearted fantasy of magic and talking animals starring a large, black, strong-minded tom named Carbonel. Listed in *Choice*, it was followed by *The Kingdom of Carbonel* (Parrish, 1959; Bobbs, 1960) and *Carbonel and Calidor* (Kestrel, 1978). She also wrote the novels *The Seven Days* (Parrish, 1958; Meredith, 1968), in which each one of the Day children proves his similarity to his twin in the old rhyme, "Monday's child...," and *Jessamy* (Collins, 1967; Bobbs, 1967), a time-slip fantasy in which an orphan emerges from the closet of an old mansion into the world of 1914. For adults she wrote her autobiography, *The Smell of Privet* (Hutchinson, 1971).

SMAUG (*The Hobbit**), vast, red-golden dragon which some three centuries before has invaded the Lonely Mountain, driven out the dwarfs, and taken their treasure for his own. Wicked and wily, he smells out Bilbo* Baggins and engages in riddling talk with him, learning more than the hobbit* intends and realizing from something he says that the dwarfs must have come from Laketown. Bilbo is able to flatter him into showing his underside, which is encrusted with jewels so that it is protected against arrows except in one bare spot where the diamonds have worn off. A thrush takes news of this vulnerable spot to Bard, and when the dragon attacks the town, Bard is able to shoot an arrow directly into that spot and slay the huge creature.

SMITH (*Smith**), twelve-year-old pickpocket in eighteenth-century London who steals a document from an old man who is murdered immediately afterwards and who thereby becomes involved in a convoluted plot of intrigue and betrayals. Skillful and quick ("a rat was a snail beside Smith"), the boy is intelligent but illiterate, and his quest for learning so that he can decipher his prize leads him to a job as groom in the home of a blind magistrate, to being accused of the murder and locked in Newgate Gaol, and eventually to a modest fortune and a secure place in the world. Though cynical and tough, Smith has an innate compassion which contrasts with the unfeeling justice admired by his magistrate friend. He also has a clear-eyed view of human nature that sees through much of the hypocrisy of position and sham gentility.

SMITH (Garfield*, Leon, ill. Anthony Maitland, Constable, 1967; Pantheon, 1967), Dickensian period novel set in eighteenth-century London, starring clever, scruffy, undernourished Smith*, 12, a pickpocket of great speed and dexterity whose chance selection of a country gentleman as his victim leads to a maze of threats and betrayals before he finds a secure place for himself in the world. After lifting the contents of the gentleman's pocket, Smith ducks into a doorway and witnesses with terror the murder of the old fellow by two men in brown and sees a man with a limp join them to search the body. After mingling with the crowd and escaping, Smith sees that his prize is a document--evidently valuable enough to be murdered for--which he cannot interpret, being illiterate. Only to Miss* Bridget, 23, and Miss* Fanny, 19, his sisters with whom he lives, does he show the paper, but they can read no more than he can, though they would be quite willing to steal it from him or betray him for a few shillings. He tries to persuade a number of acquaintances, both in prison and out, to teach him to read, but they refuse, so he carries the precious document inside his shirt undeciphered. He is about to show it to his idol, Lord* Tom, a highwayman who frequents their room in the cellar of the Red Lion Tavern, when the landlord tells him that two men in brown are looking for him. Knowing that they will slit his throat if they catch him, Smith runs, leading them a three-hour chase in bitter weather through London's back alleys and grimy courts, finally eluding them but fearing to go home. In an unfamiliar part of the city, he literally bumps into a blind man, Mr.* Mansfield, magistrate, and leads him to his home in Vine Street, where the old man asks him in for a meal and to spend the night. Although Miss* Mansfield, his daughter, is horrified at the sight of the dirty, unkempt child, she pretends to her father that she is pleased to help Smith, and soon he is installed as an assistant groom in their

household, with Miss Mansfield teaching him to
read. This fulfills his desire ironically, since
the document has been taken along with his
filthy sheets by the housemaid, who thinks it is
one of Mr. Mansfield's legal papers and locks it
in his study. Before he can find a way to
retrieve it, Smith is accused by Miss
Mansfield's admirer, an attorney named Mr.*
Billing, of being the boy he saw kill the old
gentleman, a Mr. Field of Prickler's Hill. Mr.
Mansfield, though grieved, thinks that justice
must be served, and Smith is taken off to
Newgate Gaol. There he finds the whole prison
much interested in the impending hanging of the
famous highwayman, Dick Mulrone. Smith is
visited by his sisters and Lord Tom, but more
frequently by Mr. Billing, all of whom, particularly Billing, try to get him to give up the
document or to tell them where it is hidden.
Meg, the housemaid at Vine Street, comes to see
him, and he rouses from his despair to persuade
her to retrieve the document for him. but she is
not successful. To Smith's amazement, Mr.
Billing proposes a plan of escape for him
through the narrow ventilator shaft which,
connecting with other shafts, leads to the roof
of the prison and which he can reach when
Billing has bribed the guard to unlock the
grating in the large general room where he is
housed. Smith has nearly reached the top when he
sees the outlines of the two men in brown ready
to grab him as he emerges on the roof. In
horror, he loses his hold and careens down a
different shaft into the prison chapel. At its
door, he joins the crowd come to hear the last
sermon to Dick Mulrone, among them his sisters.
Miss Bridget lifts her hoop skirt and conveys
Smith out of the prison beneath it. In the
meantime, Smith has learned that Mr. Mansfield
intends to take the document without reading it
to its addressee, an attorney at Prickler's
Hill, and that Billing knows his intention. Lord
Tom, whose place of business is the Finchley
Common, takes Smith to Bob's Inn to intercept
Mr. Mansfield's coach, but before it arrives,
Smith sees Lord Tom in conversation with the two
men in brown and realizes that he has been
betrayed by his friend. Smith flounders out into
the snowstorm, reaches the coach, and is able to

pull the blind magistrate out of it and down into the snowdrift before the highwaymen accost it. Then silently he leads the bewildered magistrate through the snowstorm, not daring to speak for fear he will be handed over to the law again. Before they finally reach the shelter of a cottage, however, Mr. Mansfield guesses and Smith admits that it is he, and that night the magistrate breaks his own stern code of justice by giving Smith the document and asking him to read it aloud. It contains nothing of value, in itself, but has a note that Mr. Field had made a terrible discovery, which he intended to carry with him to his grave. In a suspenseful final scene at Prickler's Hill, it is revealed that the lame man is Field's ne'er-do-well son, Jack, who has been egged on by Billing to have his father killed, thinking the document is a key to his fortune. His father, having thought Jack dead, had discovered his evil actions. The men in brown, Billing, and the lame man all converge on the cemetery, where Smith and Mr. Mansfield are hiding. When they are discovered, Smith does not run away, since he cannot make himself leave the blind man helpless. In the nick of time, Lord Tom appears and redeems himself by shooting one of the men in brown, Jack Field, and is himself shot dead by Jack Field. Under the statue where Jack used to play as a boy, they find buried the old gentleman's fortune, a portion of which is awarded to Smith. He sets his sisters up in a house on Golden Square, but goes himself to live as Mr. Mansfield's companion. The story has a breakneck pace, with tense scenes and melodramatic flourishes. Besides following the conventions of the eighteenth century novel, rich in language and labyrinthine plot, it skillfully enlists the reader's sympathy for an initially unsavory hero. Scenes of the filthy area of London around St. Paul's and Ludgate Hill, as well as in Newgate Gaol, are strongly sensory, particularly in smell, and the biting cold of Smith's nights in the streets and on Finchley Common is equally vivid. The novel also unsentimentally demonstrates the theme that blind justice must be tempered with compassion. Boston Globe Honor; Carnegie Com.; Choice; Phoenix.

SMITH, EMMA (1923-   ), born in Newquay, Cornwall; author of a limited number of skillfully
handled books for children and adults. For
children she has written two books about a
charmingly practical guinea pig, *Emily: The
Story of a Traveller* (Nelson, 1959; as *Emily,
the Travelling Guinea Pig*, McDowell, 1959) and
Emily's Voyage* (Macmillan, 1966; Harcourt,
1966), in which Emily leaves her boring brother
and once again journeys to distant places and
adventures. For older children she has written
Out of Hand (Macmillan, 1963; Harcourt, 1964), a
holiday adventure and family story which deals
with the conflict between a group of children
and their straightlaced spinster cousins who
attempt to impose repressive standards of conduct during a summer vacation. A much more
chilling and tense story is told in *No Way of
Telling** (Bodley, 1972; Atheneum, 1972), a
thriller set during a blizzard when the isolated
farmhouse where a girl and her grandmother live
is invaded first by a huge, seemingly insane
foreign man and then by two sinister skiers who
seem to be chasing him, a novel which was
commended for the Carnegie Medal and named a
Boston Globe-Horn Book honor book. Her adult
novels include *Maiden's Trip* (Putnam, 1948),
which won the Rhys Memorial Prize, *The Far Cry*
(MacGibbon, 1949; Random, 1950), which won the
James Tait Black Memorial Prize, and *The
Opportunity of a Lifetime* (Hamilton, 1978;
Doubleday, 1980).

SMOKY HOUSE (Goudge*, Elizabeth, ill. C. Walter
Hodges*, Duckworth, 1940; ill. Richard Floethe,
Coward, 1940), fantasy set in the early third of
the nineteenth century in the idyllic seacoast
village of Faraway in England's West Country, "a
part of the world so beautiful that the people
who live in it are always happy." Trouble comes
in the person of a long, lean, sad-eyed Fiddler,
who so intrigues the villagers that they urge
him to remain in Faraway, partly for his
entrancing music and partly for the therapy they
are certain their peaceful village can offer the
unhappy man. He settles into Smoky House, the
local inn, with earnest, respected John
Treguddick, landlord; his five children, brave,
capable, pretty Jessamine, 17, plain, shy, good

Genefer, 13, Tristram and Michael, 12 and 10,
described as "just boys," and Jane, 8, a tiny
terror; and their beloved animals, the helpful
mongrels Spot and Sausage, rescued by John as
puppies from an insensitive master, and
Mathilda, the dour and resourceful donkey, which
all converse in human speech to one another but
never with humans. For a little while after the
Fiddler's arrival life continues much the same.
Angels visit the children's beds, hovering about
their bedposts after prayers each night, while
the Good People, tiny pointy-eared fairy beings
who inhabit the hills, fields, and woods near
by, gratefully perform Jessamine's housekeeping
chores in return for the milk she always leaves
them. During the day, the children tidy the
manor house of the local squire, a jolly young
man of whom all the villagers are fond. Only the
dogs and Mathilda are uneasy; they alone
recognize the Fiddler for the evil villain he
really is--Mathilda's former master, who beat
her and from whom she was rescued by Jane's
special angel after Jane had prayed for a
donkey. Things come to a head one moonlit night
about a week after the Fiddler comes when a ship
anchors in a secluded cove and the animals
discover the Fiddler in the squire's cellar
nosing about his stock of French wines. They
drive the Fiddler away, trail him, discover he
is a spy whose task is to ferret out those who
receive goods smuggled in from France, and
realize that he has summoned the local Red-Coats
to catch the villagers while they unload the
ship. That same evening, the children are as-
tounded to discover in the inn The-Man-with-
the-Red-Handkerchief, the local legendary good
bad man who steals from the rich, gives to the
poor, and is said to have the power to cure
minor ailments and perform little miracles.
Instead of shooting them, he unmasks himself and
is revealed as the squire, and they learn that
he is the leader of the village smugglers who
call themselves the Brotherhood of Free Traders. The children also learn that contraband is
stored in a room hidden behind the inn fireplace, and that the Fiddler is onto things.
Jessamine summons the Good People to move the
contraband before the Red-Coats come, and
Michael and Tristram help the smugglers,

comprised of all the village tradesmen and the
Parson, to unload the ship and stow the
contraband in a hidden pool. Then Good People
with fish-tails, who live in the sea, tow the
ship away. When Red-Coats arrive, neither ship
nor contraband remains as evidence of wrongdoing
in either inn or cove, and when the Fiddler
insists that the squire be arrested anyway, the
squire announces that he is the local justice of
the peace and will not arrest himself. The
village men feel that the Fiddler should be
imprisoned, but the squire is convinced that the
Fiddler is basically a good man who can be
reformed by good treatment and association, and
the reader learns via the music the Fiddler
plays that he became a misanthrope after the
death of his beautiful wife and children in a
plague. In compromise, he is given a prison cell
in the church tower made comfortable for him
with books and furniture, a circumstance that so
touches the man that he lives there in joy and
happiness, playing at weddings and christenings
and parties of all sorts and engaging in Free
Trading by night, in fact becoming the cleverest
Free Trader of them all. Everyone but Jane
either turns over a new leaf or lets his or her
good points shine forth, including the squire,
who in particular becomes very humble and
soft-hearted and, most of the time anyway,
adopts Jessamine's suggestion of helping the
poor by attending to his manor and sharing its
produce instead of stealing. He proposes to
Jessamine, who accepts because she has loved him
all along, and the Good People soon bring them
four fat and dimpled babies, who were discovered
lost among the lilies and which they raise quite
happily. Though slow and even tedious at times,
with description and authorial comments, once
the plot problem is introduced, the pace picks
up. The tone is jolly if condescending and
occasionally arch, the theme of goodness
triumphing cannot be missed, overshadowing
abounds, and the author's skill with detail
often gets away from her and obstructs the
story, but the resource of the children and
animals to solve problems exerts a certain
quaint charm, and the book has interest
especially as an artifact. Fanfare.

SNAKE (*The Song of Pentecost**), long, thin, olive green reptile with yellow ear muffs. When the story starts, Snake is mourning the death of his father, who quite literally knotted himself to death. Naive and innocent in the ways of the world, Snake is cheated out of his inheritance, Oily Green Pool, by a slick-talking con artist, who insists he is Snake's Cousin*. Cousin says Snake's father willed the pool to him, and his claim is verbally upheld by a lying Frog*. Evicted by Cousin, Snake wends his way to Pentecost* Farm, where he joins the Harvest Mice. They agree to help him get his pool back, but never completely trust him. He is badly injured battling Cousin for the pool but is gullible enough to agree to share the pool with Cousin. Snake then goes back on his promise to help the mice find a home on Lickey Top. When last seen, Snake appears to be paying for his treachery, since Cousin is throwing him around the pool in his special "boomerang chuck," to the accompaniment of Snake's despairing cries.

SNEEZEWORT (*The Little Grey Men**), youngest of the three gnomes, but still older than Julius Caesar if Caesar were alive. Unlike most gnomes, he lacks whiskers. A follower, he relies on Baldmoney* and Dodder* to make decisions. He often gets hiccups. Like the others, he is just a step away from the Disney kind of character, momentarily interesting but too distorted for comic effect to be memorable.

SONGBERD'S GROVE (Barrett*, Anne, ill. N. M. Bodecker, Collins, 1957; Bobbs, 1957), amusing, lively, realistic novel of family and neighborhood life set in the early 1950s in a slum area of London. Because housing is short, the Singer family, Mr. William Singer, a draftsman, Mrs.* Dora Singer, and their thin, red-haired, owl-glassed son, Martin*, about twelve, have been waiting seven years for a flat of their own. Their enthusiasm for No. 7 Songberd's Grove is only slightly diminished by finding the complex rundown, dingy, and abused by vandals. They settle in cheerfully, and Mrs. Singer, a chronic cleaner, scrubs and polishes, hoping that through her heroic efforts the place will meet the approval of fussy Aunt Emmeline, Mr.

Singer's sister, with whom and Uncle Alfred they
have been living for seven years at their place
called Emandalf's. Then Martin discovers that
Lennie* Byre, a teddy boy who lives at No. 1, is
perhaps fifteen, and affects barrel jackets,
pipe-stem trousers, and long hair, has set up a
sort of dictatorship, tyrannizing the neighborhood and forcing younger children, among them
Mudface, Trevor, and Rusty, to carry out
spiteful and destructive acts. Martin courageously refuses to fall in line and joins forces
with Geneva*, a black-haired, gypsy-like girl of
fiery disposition, who lives upstairs with her
ex-Spanish dancer mother, La* Golondrina, and
who has become a prisoner in the house because
she, too, has defied Lennie. Martin and Geneva
want to turn the row into a pleasant place and
begin with the walled garden attached to
Martin's end of the complex. They tidy it up
and do some planting, and Martin discovers a
sculptured stone face that they set up in a
special way as a kind of mascot or monument.
When Lennie discovers their activities in the
garden and sets his junior thugs onto them,
they flee down to the canal, where in a once-
splendid pillared white mansion they encounter
John* Pollard, a painter, and John* Pim, an
architect, who help them get safely home. While
they are gone, Lennie vandalizes the garden and
steals the face. Things between Lennie and the
children come to a head when the Singers decide
to paint their front door in preparation for an
impending visit from Aunt Emmeline. Their
redecorating stimulates similar behavior from
the other tenants and angers Lennie, who has
also begun to lose his hold on the junior thugs
because of Martin and Geneva's defiance. He
enlists the aid of teddy boys, older thugs from
an adjoining neighborhood, in attacking Martin
and Geneva, who have been guarding the newly
painted doors, and a hilarious but very
serious, no-holds-barred, free-for-all battle
ensues. Geneva jumps on a bike and summons help
from John Pollard. At the same time,
coincidentally, arrive Lord* Simon Vigo, the
trustee of the Serrat Estate, of which
Songberd's Grove is a part, and John Pim, whom
Lord Simon has engaged to implement the restoration of those parts of the estate that have

historical architectural significance, among
them, Songberd's Grove. The teddys depart
hastily, and Lennie takes on Lord Simon,
executing a masterful blow and a fancy sidestep
that Lord Simon recognizes as a trademark of
Lennie's deceased father, Basher, a boxer whom
he particularly admired, and he invites Lennie
to work out at his club. Area "small fry"
previously bullied by Lennie, who have raided
Lennie's closet for a football he took from
them, produce the stone face, which is just the
one needed to complete the fractured stonework
over the door of No. 7. The face is that of
Nicholas Songberd, a once-eminent architect,
which explains the peculiar spelling of the name
of the complex. The Singers are dejected by the
ruined state of the door but learn by telegram
that Aunt Emmeline will not be visiting because
Uncle Alf has the flu. Some weeks later Aunt
Emmeline arrives to find photographers and
newsmen flocking about and a party in progress
celebrating the restoration of Songberd's Grove.
Good things have happened. Lennie's hold on the
area has been broken, and, in connecting subplots, La Golondrina is to marry her lost
sweetheart, who has also turned up, and Mr.* Tom
Triplett, the distracted, friendly, elderly
tailor who occupies a first-floor room, has
renewed his old acquaintance with Lord Simon and
will sew again for him. Martin and his parents
are happy in refurbished, peaceful Songberd's
Grove. This account of youths succeeding where
adults cannot or will not catches the interest
early and holds the attention throughout, even
though some events seem quite unlikely, such as
fat La Golondrina shedding within a couple of
weeks enough weight to become "fragile" and
agile and be able to dance ballet again. Martin
is a plucky youth, easy to like, who sees early
on that you have to stand up for your rights
even though you may get hurt, and that
capitulation serves the best interests of
neither the enemy nor the vanquished. He
triumphs by wit, good sense, courage, and some
luck. He has a warm and understanding
relationship with his parents, in particular
with his mother, whose desire to impress Aunt
Emmeline he sees as appropriate simply because
she wants it and he wants her to be happy. The

many characters are easily identifiable types,
adults are eccentric, and some lean toward
caricature, like La Golondrina and Lord Simon,
but all, even Lennie, are handled sympathetically. The book's central irony is that
the adults are unaware of Martin's struggles
with Lennie. They are aware of the vandalism and
property abuse but are unaware of the potentially bitter conflict for supremacy in
Songberd's Grove. More than mere conflict
between a bully and couple of "straight kids,"
the book also looks at styles of mothering and
the kinds of children produced by such parents,
with implied and sometimes explicit social
comment but without seeming didactic. Mothers
and offspring serve as obvious foils. Lennie's
overprotective mother has turned him into a
spoiled bully, and Geneva's mother is so
ineffectual and obsessed with her career that
Geneva has taken on the role of mother in their
home, while Martin's mother tends to be fixated
on housewifely tasks, trusting him to do the
right thing. The tone is intimate, inviting, and
good-natured, the style is detailed, scenes are
vividly depicted, events move fast, and the
result is pleasant if dated entertainment.
Carnegie Com.

SONG FOR A DARK QUEEN (Sutcliff*, Rosemary,
Pelham, 1978; Crowell, 1979), biographical novel
about Boudicca (Boadicea), queen of the Iceni, a
British tribe who in 60 A.D. led the most nearly
successful revolt against Roman domination in
Britain. Since little is known about this dynam-
ic woman or her people except through obviously
prejudiced Roman records, Sutcliff pictures
Boudicca as the Royal Woman, Goddess on Earth,
of a matrilineal people, basing her assumptions
on archeological and mythological studies. The
story is narrated by Cadwan, the Queen's Harper,
who has known Boudicca since her birth and who
has a favored position among the Iceni and is
therefore present and close to the queen at all
major events. Boudicca's mother dies when the
child is four, and her father is killed when she
is fifteen. Her husband has been chosen two
years earlier by Merddyn, chief of the Oak
Priests. He is Prasutagus, Iceni on his mother's
side but son of the chieftain of the neighboring

Parisi. With the death of her father, Boudicca
must be married at once so that the Iceni will
have a king, a move she can't refuse but resists
by placing her father's sword down the center of
the marriage bed and vowing not to let her
husband cross it until she bids him. Prasutagus,
however, proves to be a patient and thoughtful
king, and when he is badly injured in a horse
stampede, Boudicca is deeply concerned and soon
puts away the sword. Their first child is
Essylt, the Royal Daughter, blond and soon tall
like her mother, proud, and good at weapon
sports at which Iceni women are trained. Their
second child is Nessan, another girl but small,
dark, muscial, and very close to Cadwan
emotionally. The happy time of their early
childhood is shadowed by the coming of the
Romans and the summons to Prasutagus (since Rome
does not recognize the primacy of a woman) to
come and swear allegiance to Claudius, the
Roman emperor, who has come personally to
Britain. The Iceni are named a free state,
paying a yearly tribute in gold, horses, and
young men to serve in the Auxilliaries. For a
while this situation continues, but soon the
governor orders the tribes along the border to
turn in their weapons. Prasutagus agrees,
reluctantly and bitterly, and life goes on among
the Iceni, with Duatha, a childhood companion,
selected as mate for Essylt at the Choosing
Feast when she is fifteen. When, shortly
afterward, Prasutagus dies of pneumonia, the
Roman Procurator, Decianus Catus, arrives with
an order from Nero, who is now emperor, that
since the Iceni have no king and no male heirs,
they will be absorbed into the Province of
Britain. At the evening meal at which the
insulting official insists that Boudicca and her
daughters eat with him, the escort commander
makes a pass at Essylt, and Duatha leaps the
table and knifes him. Immediately there is
chaos; the Royal Daughters are raped and
Boudicca is stripped to the waist and publicly
whipped. With this excuse, the Romans drive off
the horses and take most of the free men and
women as slaves. Thus provoked by what is not
only insult but also sacrilege to the Iceni,
Boudicca restrains her followers until she can
organize all the outlying Iceni and neighboring

tribes, even their old enemies, the Catuvellauni who have suffered under the Roman yoke. She seizes the opportunity when the governor of Britain is in the west destroying a native priesthood on the Island of Mon to sweep southward with her war host to destroy the Roman city of Camulodunum. When the city has been sacked and burned, she has the captured women taken to the sacred grove and, insisting that representatives from all the tribes attend so that they will all be involved and therefore cannot defect to the Romans, sacrifices them in some unspecified horrible way. The tribal host then sweeps on to Londinium, which has been abandoned by Roman forces, and leaves it ravaged and burning. The governor, however, has escaped. With a force much smaller than that of the tribes, he meets them and, in a terrible, bloody battle, defeats them largely by superior tactical skill. Cadwan trades his harp for a sword and tries to reach Nessan, but, finding her dead, pulls her body beneath a burning wagon so it will be cremated and not desecrated, then turns to find Boudicca, who is badly wounded, and to join with a few other Iceni to take her back to their home place, a terrible journey that lasts many days. There Boudicca's old nurse, one of the little dark people that predate the Iceni in the area and are skilled in poison, has already brewed her the Sleep-Drink. The queen downs it with dignity and goes to her own chamber to die. Cadwan, himself wounded, is left to record the story before he also dies. Boudicca's history is interrupted at intervals by letters from a young Roman Tribune, Gaius Julius Agricola, on the staff of the governor of Britain, to his mother in Massilia, rather awkwardly giving the Roman view of the situation. While the story of Boudicca is absorbing and the background of the tribal ways of the Iceni is convincingly created, the novel suffers as fiction by being tied to the tragic and hopeless biographical facts. Of the characters, Prasutagus, the king whose zeal is tempered by pragmatic thoughtfulness, is the most interestingly developed. Other.

THE SONG OF PENTECOST (Corbett*, W. J., ill. Martin Ursell, Methuen, 1982; Dutton, 1983), tongue-in-cheek, talking-animal fantasy set recently in the Lickey Hills in the English Midlands, in which various small animals help a large extended family of Harvest Mice find a new home. The city has spilled over the rich cultivated land of Pentecost Farm, destroying the homes and livelihood of the mice who have been living there. They agree to help a gullible young Snake* recover Oily Green Pool, the home he has lost to a bogus Cousin* Snake, in return for his help in finding a new place for them to live. They set out under the leadership of earnest young Pentecost* Mouse, accompanied by Snake; a lying Frog*, now reformed, the one whose lies enabled Cousin to work his scam; and Little Brother, a gentle water vole who yearns for a new home with a succulent apple tree. The little group has mildly suspenseful, action-filled adventures as they make their way over the countryside. The terrain gives them some problems, and other problems come from animals along the way, but they triumph over all adversities with courage, tooth and claw as ncessary, and good fortune. They must cross Great Green River, where Snake ferries most of them over on his back, must repel in a bitter battle an attack from Ruffian mice, a renegade pack that tries to enslave them, and must pack their ears with sawdust to avoid going deaf from the din of the drilling in Woodpecker Wood before arriving at Oily Green Pool. Once there, they are dismayed to see Frog revert to previous form and tell two stories, supporting both Snake's and Cousins's claims to the pool. Snake challenges Cousin to mortal combat and is well on his way to being decisively licked by that unscrupulously dirty fighter when Pentecost declares the battle a draw. Cousin has a sudden change of heart (later shown to be sham) and suggests that he and Snake share the pool. The selfish Snake is so happy to be back in his home that he reneges on his agreement to help the mice to the destination he himself had proposed, the knoll called Lickey Top where a recluse Owl* lives. The little party presses on anyway. The crafty red Fox* of Furrowfield, impressed by Pentecost's determination and charitable nature in releasing him from a trap (a sham entrapment), creates a diversion that enables the refugees to get through Weasel Woods safely. When they arrive at Lickey Top, the Owl proves inhospitable. A conniving orange Cockle-Snorkle* Bug, a double-dealer bent on mischief, has turned the Owl against the mice. In an unguarded moment, however, the Cockle-Snorkle makes a mistake and informs the mice that he knows the Owl is innocent of the crime of murdering his brother, a burden of guilt that has weighed heavily on the Owl's soul since childhood. The mice convey the information to the Owl, who gratefully agrees to let them settle in a small part of his property provided they keep the place neat and tidy. The trip has elevated Pentecost's self-esteem considerably, but ironically it is to short advantage for the Harvest Mice. While out on the hillside Pentecost observes Fox emerge from Weasel Woods and runs out happily to greet his friend, since the conniving Cockle-Snorkle had told the mice that Fox was dead, and dies of a bullet some boy hunters had intended for Fox. The mice choose a new Pentecost, a pert but promising young mouse. The plot never flags and supports the themes of courage and charity: one must be ready to fight against overwhelming odds and treachery to protect one's own and to be "my brother's keeper for better or for worse." Though there is some suspense, interest comes more from the enjoyment of individual episodes and from the distinctively created characters than from speculating on the outcome. Some slapstick, ample punning and parody in narrative and dialogue, and several caricatures of well-known types contribute to the light, pointed, but never bitter or caustic humor. Clever shifts keep the story from becoming cliched, and the vantage point remains consistently that of the little animals. Sequels. (Old* Uncle) Whitbread.

SOPHIE (*Black Hearts in Battersea**), maid to the Duchess of Battersea. She learns in the course of foiling the Hanoverian conspirators that she is Simon's* sister and also a Battersea. The first hint that she is gentry appears when it is noted that she bears a likeness to a figure in the Battersea heirloom painting. It comes out that she is the daughter of the Duke of Battersea's brother, who was killed in the

Hanoverian Wars. Buckle, the Duke's retainer and
Justin's tutor, abandoned her in the forest and
left Simon in a nearby village when they were
not much more than babies. He then passed off
Justin, his own son, as the son of the dead
brother, intending eventually to kill the duke
and thus seize the fortune. Sophie is loyal and
quick-thinking. She several times saves the
lives of the duke and duchess by making good use
of the duchess's tapestry, for example, suggesting it serve as a rope when the theater catches
fire, blocking the doorway with it when wolves
attack the glass-burner's cottage, and covering
the hole with it when Buckle's shot punctures
the getaway balloon.

SOPHIE HATTER (*Howl's Moving Castle**), eldest of
the three Hatter sisters and therefore, according to folklore tradition, the least likely to
succeed. Being resigned to this fact, she does
not realize that she has some powers of magic
and that she has been endowing the hats she
trims with special qualities by talking to them
as she sews. This "meddling" has earned her the
wrath of the Witch of the Waste, who casts a
spell changing her into an old woman. Sophie,
always practical, is glad that she seems to be a
vigorous old woman and is quite relieved to
discover that she is no longer embarrassed to
speak her mind. At the castle she says she is
the cleaning woman, and she sets forth with
energy and tart comments to reform the filthy
and disorganized establishment. Although she
often seems to have done just the wrong thing,
her bumbling usually occurs because she doesn't
realize her powers, and in the end she is able
to save both Howl* and his fire demon Calcifer*.

SORRY CARLISLE (*The Changeover: A Supernatural
Romance**), Sorensen Carlisle, 16, son of
Miryam*, grandson of Winter*, and friend and
eventual sweetheart of Laura* Chant. A self-
deriding youth, he is quick with a quip. At
school he appears as an almost exemplary
student, polite, well-organized, satisfactory in
his studies, and a good athlete. At home he
affects a different appearance, wearing a black
dressing gown or caftan and many rings and
seeming altogether less good, Laura thinks, than

at school. Laura discovers he is much less self-assured than he seems. When nervous or ill at ease, he stammers. He has trouble accepting his witch nature, but at the story's end he has come to terms with himself. He decides to devote himself to ecological causes and takes a position as a trainee for the wildlife service. After Laura becomes a witch, Sorry and Laura are able to communicate telepathically. Sorry sensibly warns her against vindictiveness in dealing with Carmody Braque*. He is an intelligent, well-drawn figure whose character becomes more intelligible to the reader and understandably changes as he associates with Laura. Through her his human side grows and hence also his abilities as a witch.

A SOUND OF CHARIOTS (Hunter*, Mollie, Hamilton, 1973; Harper, 1972), realistic novel of family life set in Scotland some years after World War I, in which a girl copes with the death of a much-loved father, comes to a greater under-standing and appreciation of her mother, and pursues her ambition of becoming a writer. Bridie (Bridget) McShane is the fourth daughter and second youngest of the five children in the warm, close, working class family of Patrick* and Agnes* McShane, who live in veterans' housing in a village near the Firth of Forth. The novel, told in third person from Bridie's point of view, begins with Patrick's death when Bridie is nine, and then, in the first half, flashes back to when she is five and shows how a special relationship develops between father and daughter. Bridie much prefers her fun-loving, idealistic, iconoclastic father to her strongly Calvinist mother. A strong-minded Irishman with a keen sense of social justice, he champions the rights of the poor against the landlords, while Agnes's upbringing impels her to support authority and take things as they are. The novel traces Patrick's decline in health from an unspecified wound received in World War I, reveals how he encourages Bridie to stick up for her rights and be proud and fearless, and describes things they do as a pair and with the family. When Mrs. Mackie, the headmistress, informs Patrick that Bridie has potential as a student and writer, he encourages her to develop

her talents and even suggests that she write a
novel. While her sisters (called The Others*)
deride her literary efforts, Bridie persists,
though she keeps the novel secret even from her
father. She develops a very sharp eye for
details of action and character and begins to
view things from the outlook of one who will
later choose the exact words to set her ideas
down on paper. In March Patrick is found
unconscious by the roadside and is taken to the
military hospital. He recovers enough to take
the children on an outing by the sea but dies a
week later. The last half of the book describes
how the family copes with Patrick's death. For a
while Bridie has nightmares and develops a
morbid curiosity about the afflictions of the
veterans who live on the street. Mother
experiences a crisis of faith, almost giving in
to her grief. Bridie reacts to what she sees as
her mother's weakness and cuts herself off
emotionally from Agnes for many years. Agnes
works as a maid, does laundry for the gentry,
and spends long hours away from hone, Nell, the
eldest of The Others, drops out of school to run
the house, and the children must learn to cope
with problems and one another without their
tired, overworked mother's advice. The girls
pick berries to earn money, and Bridie has a
paper route. Continuing to enjoy words, she
tells stories to the younger children at school,
savoring the language and visualizing with
pleasure the situations she describes. Mrs.
Mackie encourages her to try for the academic
prizes won previously by her older sisters, but
Bridie concentrates on English. Old Mr. Miller,
a local lover of literature, shares his books
with her and introduces her to the poet Andrew
Marvell, whose line "Time's winged chariot
hurrying near" (from which the novel's title
comes) encapsulates her own fears of mortality
and motivates her to try her hand at poetry. She
enters secondary school, her sisters variously
find employment, and only Bridie and her
brother, William*, remain at home with Agnes.
Bridie begins to see her mother as an individual
and to appreciate what Agnes has done for the
family, and the two are reconciled. Her teacher
Dr.* McIntyre describes her poetry as "innocent
wisdom" and encourages her to continue to write

even though her schooling must end. She leaves for a position in her grandfather's business and arrives at Grannie's house in Edinburgh with a poem in her mind, waiting to be inscribed in her own small poem book. Bridie has come to terms with herself and life. This is a solid, convincing, ambitious story of a girl's growing up. More a book of character, interpersonal relationships, and scenes than of plot, it excels in showing how Bridie grows and changes through her ties with her father and her contacts with neighbors and teachers, but the figure that dominates the entire story is Patrick. The tone is objective yet sympathetic. Some humor comes from irony and from Bridie's young-old way of looking at things. Conversation carries the ring of real life. The reader gets some sense of life in the village and the problems of the times, deriving in particular from the war and the class structure. Themes involve perseverance, striving for a goal, developing one's unique talents, and the importance of family and friends and of standing up for one's beliefs. (Miss* Dunstan; Mr.* Purves; The Shepherd*) Child Study; Choice; Contemporary Classics; Fanfare.

THE SOUND OF COACHES (Garfield*, Leon, Kestrel, 1974; Viking, 1974), rollicking period novel of a boy who comes to manhood among the coachmen, innkeepers, barmaids, and actors of eighteenth-century England. *The Flying Cradle*, a stage coach on the London-Chichester run, pulls into the midpoint, the Red Lion at Dorking, on a stormy night, carrying among its passengers a young woman far advanced with child who clutches a barber's box. That very night she gives birth to a boy, kisses her infant son, indicates the box and says, "His father's. Keep it for him, please," and dies. Inside the box, Mrs. Roggs, the innkeekper's bewildered wife, finds a gentleman's dueling pistol and a cheap pewter ring set with an imitation emerald, but no indication of the identity of either parent. The four other passengers, moved by the drama of the occurrence, take up a collection for the infant and settle, after much discussion, on Sam for his name, but they and the Roggses are aston-ished when the coachman, called Chichester

after the road he drives, and his guard, who
turns out to be his wife, announce that they
will "shoulder" the child. Temporarily they
leave him at The Red Lion, where Mrs. Roggs
arranges for a wet nurse, but as soon as spring
comes they take the baby between them on the
coach and so his peripatetic life begins, London
to Chichester, Chichester to London, with
Dorking always the halfway point between them.
The Chichesters are a very fond but silent
couple, and Sam gets most of his knowledge of
life from Joe the cellarman, who was pot boy the
night Sam was born and contributed a shilling to
the collection. It is Joe who shows him a stone
in the graveyard that says "Mary Arundel,"
Arundel being the town where his mother boarded
the coach and Mary the stonemason's invention;
tells him that his "other pa" was hanged, and
starts his vivid nightmares; creates the
situation by which Sam is given his pistol,
which he admires extravagantly to Chichester's
consternation; takes Sam to his first play along
with Joe's girl, Milly, barmaid at The White
Horse, on whom Sam gets his first childish
crush; and gives him a dipperful of wine on
which he gets wildly drunk, all by the time he
is eight years old. Because the wine has made
him very sick, Mrs. Chichester for the first
time stays with Sam in Dorking, letting the
osler go in her place as guard, and on that run
the coachman is shot by a man who wishes to
board the already loaded coach and is crippled
for life. In the years that follow, Sam and his
mother still ride the coach with a variety of
drivers, leaving Mr. Chichester at Dorking. The
embittered coachman drags himself around the inn
on crutches and refuses to say anything about
the man who shot him. When Sam is sixteen he is
allowed to drive the coach without his mother
aboard, but while showing off for a girl he
drives too fast and wrecks it. Mr. Chichester
hurls his crutch through the window at Sam and
shouts at him to get out. With the money from
the collection taken up the night he was born
and carefully saved by Mr. Roggs, Sam goes to
London, takes up lodgings at a small, seedy inn,
The Bunch of Grapes, and calls on his
benefactors, as the other passengers of that
fateful night have always been called at The Red

Lion and who have continued to send him highly inappropriate gifts. They all sentimentally remember the night, but they are unprepared to help out a sixteen-year-old in need of a position in life. Utterly discouraged, Sam hangs around The Bunch of Grapes and The Shakespeare's Head tavern in Covent Garden, attracted to the area because his mother had asked about the place when she boarded the coach. His only friend is Jenny, the maidservant at The Bunch of Grapes, who, having examined his luggage, seen the pistol, and counted his money, has decided that he is a gentleman in disguise. They become acquainted with Daniel Coventry, a down-on-his-luck actor well soaked in port wine, who picks up from something Jenny says that Sam has some money and proposes, with many fancy phrases and much flattery, to train Sam for the stage for thirty pounds. Practical Jenny sees his offer for what it is and berates Sam, but to no avail. He leaves with Mr. Robinson's traveling company, completely stagestruck and thinking Coventry the greatest man to walk the boards. During the next months with the seedy company, Sam learns differently, seeing that among the petty, vindictive actors Coventry stands out only by being cleverer and more self-centered. After a rare and truly generous gesture by Coventry, Sam discovers the man going through his belongings hunting for his other money and coming upon his pistol, which the actor recognizes as the mate to his and therefore the one he left about seventeen years before with some girl in Arundel. Horrified and furious at Coventry's casual memory of the affair, which does not even call up a name or an appearance, Sam nurses a murderous hatred which, surprisingly, transforms his acting from a rote speaking of lines to a real presence on stage. Hoping somehow to justify his going on the stage, which he knows the Chichesters think a low profession, he hangs on with the company until it is headed for Dorking. In some agony of indecision about whether he dares go with them, he leaves his barber's box containing the pistol and ring, along with all his money, for Jenny at The Bunch of Grapes. He joins the company but keeps out of sight while the stage is set up in the yard of The Red Lion and the audience assembles,

with his parents in the front row. Though he
fears that clever Coventry will use all his
stage tricks to eclipse him and make him look
like a fool, Sam does his best and is amazed
that the older actor seems almost unable to say
his lines and acts as if he were under a spell.
Actually, Coventry has seen the coachman in the
front row and realizes that it is the man he
shot some years before. Chichester recognizes
his attacker and with great generosity of heart
restrains himself from pointing him out,
realizing what he has suspected from the pistols
and Sam's growing resemblence to Coventry that
the actor must be Sam's real father. Sam gives
the performance of his life, is received with
joy by the Chichesters, and thinks that Coventry
is showing rare tact by disappearing immediately
after the last curtain. A few days later the
coach jolts into Dorking, among the passengers a
young woman clutching a barber's box--but this
time it is Jenny, who has thought Sam left his
things to pay her off and is determined that he
will not get away with it. She is astonished to
be greeted warmly by Sam and his mother and even
the old coachman, and the book ends with her
about to give birth to Sam's first offspring.
The story has much the tone of eighteenth-
century novels, with melodramatic action, ironic
humor, and memorable characters, all told in
language laced with telling metaphor and vivid
description. It is divided into three parts,
each one as long as many novels for children,
and it has a large cast of eccentric figures,
all described with a sardonic attitude that is
not altogether sympathetic to them (even to
Sam) but makes them convincing despite the
obvious coincidences upon which the plot
depends. Choice.

SOUTHALL, IVAN (FRANCIS) (1921-   ), born in
Canterbury, Victoria, Australia; author of many
books of both fiction and nonfiction for young
people and adults. He attended Chatham State
School, Mont Albert Central School, and Box Hill
Grammar School. In 1941 he served with the
Australian Army and from 1942 to 1946 with the
Royal Australian Air Force, where he was awarded
the Distinguished Flying Cross. For a few years
before World War II he was an engraver for the

Melbourne *Herald and Weekly Times*, but since
1948 he has been a full-time writer, producing
some twenty books of fiction, nine of
nonfiction, and one screenplay for children, and
six novels, a book of short stories, and at
least ten works of nonfiction for adults. His
early books for children were highly romantic
adventure stories featuring Squadron Leader
Simon Black of the RAAF, starting with *Meet
Simon Black* (Angus, 1950) and later published in
eight volumes as *Simon Black in Peril* (Angus,
1951-1962). With *Hills End* (Angus, 1962; St.
Martin's, 1963), about a town destroyed by a
flood, and *Ash Road* (Angus, 1965; St. Martin's,
1966), about a forest fire, he started a new
pattern in which a group of young people are
confronted with a catastrophe and muddle
through, using more sense than most of the a-
dults in the situation. *Bread and Honey* (Angus,
1970; as *Walk a Mile and Get Nowhere*, Bradbury,
1970) is an initiation story set on a small-town
holiday when a boy meets a strange nine-year-old
girl, and, under pressure, thrashes the henchmen
of the local bully. He won the Carnegie Medal
for *Josh** (Angus, 1971; Macmillan, 1972), an intense story of a boy's nearly disastrous visit
to his great-aunt in the town founded by his
great-grandfather and still dominated by the
man's memory. It also was named to the *Horn Book*
Fanfare list and to the list of Contemporary
Classics. Many critics consider his most successful book to be *Let the Balloon Go* (Methuen,
1968; St. Martin's, 1968), a story of a cerebral
palsy victim who achieves his great desire to
climb a tree, in which Southall's tone of almost
frantic tension suits the situation better than
in other books. He has been the foundation
president for the Knoxbrooke Training Centre for
the Handicapped in Victoria. For his writings,
he has received many honors, including the
Australian Writers Award in 1974 and membership
in the Order of Australia in 1981. Four of his
novels for young people have won the Australian
Book of the Year award and four others have been
named as Commended. They have been translated
into many languages.

SPILLER (*The Borrowers Afield**; *The Borrowers
Afloat**; *The Borrowers Aloft**; *The Borrowers*

Avenged), Borrower youth whom Arrietty* first
meets while fetching horse hair from a hedge in
The Borrowers Afield and who becomes the good
friend of the Clocks. A skillful hunter with bow
and arrow and a fearless forager, he aids them
by bringing them food and other items and plays
a major role in their efforts to find a home.
Without him they would not have survived. He
also is a good friend to the Uncle* Hendrearys.
He has a brown face, black eyes, and tousled
dark hair and dresses in animal skins that Aunt*
Lupy fixes for him. He is a master at
concealment and can melt into any background,
appearing and disappearing at will. A loner who
lives wild in hedgerows, he doesn't like
questions. He navigates streams in a boat he has
built out of an old wooden knife box, caulked at
the seams with beeswax and dried flax, but for
shorter trips he uses the battered lid of an old
tin soapbox. An orphan whose full name is
Dreadful Spiller, on occasion he stirs Homily's*
maternal instincts. A "man's kind of youth," he
gets on well with Pod*, too. For a time he
arouses Arrietty's romantic inclinations, but he
never reciprocates. He is one of the
best-developed and most interesting characters
in the series and serves as a foil for
Peagreen*.

SPINDLE-IMP (*The Silver Curlew*), the little,
black evil power of the Witching Wood, whose
real name is Tom Tit Tot and who demands Doll
and later also her baby, Joan, as the price for
spinning flax into yarn for Doll Codling so that
she can marry King Nollekens* of Norfolk and not
be beheaded by him. Though overdrawn, the
Spindle-Imp is an engaging villain. He is
malicious, conceited, and without compassion. He
also has a comic side, being a ball of energy
who speaks with a broad country dialect and
typically "puffed and...strutted and twirled
his long tail" and "sneered and jeered and
fleered." Though Poll* Codling unsuccessfully
tries to trick him into revealing his true name,
he later gives it away in a premature burst of
triumph: he "swung his tail over his arm and
capered round her, croaking, 'Tom Tit Tot!/ Tom
Tit Tot!/ Nimmy-nimmy-not/ My name is TOM TIT
TOT!'" When Poll speaks his true name, he simply

expires in a flash, and the only trace left of him is a black smudge on the carpet.

SPRING, (ROBERT) HOWARD (1889-1965), born in Cardiff, South Wales, and died in Falmouth, Cornwall; journalist, novelist and playwright. He attended local schools in Wales until he was eleven and later studied in evening classes. At twelve he joined the staff of the *South Wales Daily News* as a messenger boy and later became a reporter. He worked as a reporter for the *Yorkshire Observer* from 1911 to 1915 and for the Manchester *Guardian* from 1915 to 1931. For the next seven years, he was literary critic for the London *Evening Standard*, after which he became a freelance writer. During World War I he served with the British Army Intelligence Service in France. His best known book is *O Absalom!* (Collins, 1938; as *My Son, My Son!* Viking, 1938), a novel for adults which became a best-seller, but *The Houses in Between: A Novel* (Collins, 1951; Harper, 1952) was also popular, becoming a Book-of-the-Month Club selection. His three-volume autobiography, *Heaven Lies about Us: A Fragment of Infancy* (Constable, 1939; Viking, 1939), *In the Meantime* (Constable, 1942), and *And Another Thing...* (Harper, 1946), was republished as *The Autobiography of Howard Spring* (Collins, 1972). His first books for children, *Darkie & Co.* (Oxford, 1932) and *Sampson's Circus* (Faber, 1936), were written for his sons, but the only one widely known in the United States is *Tumbledown Dick: All People and No Plot** (Faber, 1939; Viking, 1940), which is just as its subtitle suggests, a series of rollicking episodes set in Manchester with sharply drawn characters but no central plot organization. Spring also wrote plays for adults.

SQUEAK WILSON (*"Minnow" on the Say**), Philip Wilson, called Squeak because he is a little pip-squeak of a man. A handyman and ne'er-do-well, he once was fired by Mr.* Codling for drunkenness. After he drank up the four jars of rose wine that Mr. Codling had made, Mr. Codling then refilled them, putting the Codling treasure into one, and hid them under the water tank under the roof, intending not to open the wine and reveal the treasure until he could celebrate the return of his son, John, from World War II. After John was killed, the bottles stayed there, until, in cleaning out for the auction that Miss* Codling is planning, Squeak finds them, gets drunk again, and takes the one with the treasure home, from where Miss Codling eventually retrieves it. Squeak goes into a depression, apparently over the dilemma of what to do with the treasure that he shouldn't have in his possession.

SQUIRE TRELAWNEY (*Treasure Island**), local gentry who buys and outfits the *Hispaniola* for the trip to find the buried treasure. A tall man, over six feet, and broad in proportion, with "a bluff, rough-and-ready face, all roughened and reddened and lined in his long travels" and very black eyebrows that "moved readily, and...gave him a look of some temper, not bad...but quick and high." He is garrulous and susceptible to the flattery of Long* John Silver, and he soon gives away all the secrets of the proposed trip and is therefore indirectly responsible for the pirate band coming on board. He takes along his two personal servants and his gamekeeper, all of whom are killed on the island, but he is himself valuable to the group of honest men, being very brave and a crack shot.

STAN SOWTER (*A Likely Lad**), beefy, bullying cousin of Willy* Overs. Stan's ambition is to be a commercial traveler (salesman) like his father. Because his family lives in a better neighborhood, he lords it over his Overs cousins and sneers at Willy for his meekness and bookish ways. Although he is full of bravado, he clearly is afraid of his father, and when George* Overs says that Stan's mother acts afraid of her husband, his cousin's reaction shows that he has hit the mark. For years he has been dragged by his father to see Auntie* Maggie Chaffey, in hope that she will leave her money to the boy. The family is then dumbfounded to learn that the money has all been destroyed by the dogs.

STAPLE (*The Wool-Pack**), the large and influential organization of wool growers and wool merchants to which Nicholas* Fetterlock's father belongs. Headquartered at Calais, the Staple fixes prices and makes rules that everyone engaged in the wool trade must obey. When Staple officials discover evidence that seems to indicate that Master* Thomas Fetterlock has been violating their procedures, they imprison him, but Nicholas's letter saying that Leach and the Lombards are smuggling Fetterlock wool out of England comes in time to free him, and he proves himself innocent of wrongdoing.

STARR (*The Member for the Marsh**), schoolboy, David Rosley's companion in the Harmonious Mud Stickers, the club's secretary. He is flat-faced and inclined to be surly, a touchy sort. Kitson* says it's because he won't wear his spectacles. He is the son of a well-off farmer, whose land lies near that of Mr.* Tuckee and will benefit from Mr. Tuckee's drainage. Starr wants David to keep tabs on what's going on in the marsh, ostensibly because the boys want things to be all right in the imaginary land of Chorasmia, as they call the marsh, but also because what affects the marsh affects the Starrs. David isn't sure he likes Starr but is always deferential to him as well as to the other two boys. Starr is the cook of the group and prepares a fine dinner with a chicken from his farm. He is a well-drawn, rounded figure.

STARRY NIGHT (Sefton*, Catherine, Hamish Hamilton, 1986), girl's growing-up story set in Northern Ireland, very near the border with the Republic, covering a few days in recent times during which a teenager becomes aware of family relationships that have been hidden from her and begins to realize that she can be independent and determine her own destiny. Kathleen Fay, 14, lives at the family farm, Kiltarragh, with Mammy, as she calls old Mrs. Fay, and her two unmarried older daughters, Rose, 29, and Teresa, more than thirty. Frank, 40, the eldest, lives in a rented house down the lane with his wife, Carmel, and their three-year-old daughter, Imelda, but Frank works the farm and takes direction from his mother. The younger son, Mike, is a builder in England, but returns whenever he is out of work. Kathleen's awakening to the realities of her family begins when a blue Maxi rattles up to their house and Mammy shoos her off down to the lake with Imelda, for whom Kathleen is a somewhat resentful, unpaid babysitter. Annoyed at being kept out of a secret and intensely curious, Kathleen invents and rejects a number of theories to explain the mystery. Seeing that both Mammy and Frank are upset and angry, she thinks at first that Carmel, who signs on for unemployment compensation in the North and then goes over the border to work three days a week, has been caught by the authorities. This would not make Kathleen sorry. Everyone in the family except Frank distrusts Carmel and envies her television set, telephone, car, and pretty furniture, and they are scornful of her fussiness about cleanliness and nice ways of speaking. Talking to her friend, Ann O'Connor, from Belfast, who spends summers with her aunt on the farm across the lake, Kathleen realizes that all the neighbors and probably Ann, too, knows what is going on, and she reacts defensively to Ann's suggestion that she needn't be stuck at Kiltarragh all her life, to become a farmer's wife or a stiff old maid like Teresa, but rather might come to Belfast and take teacher's training. When Mike comes home and brings her a travel clock for a gift, she thinks he might be suggesting that she return to England with him, and she considers the idea but rejects it, wanting to hold fast to the place she knows and to have all the family living together, with Carmel perhaps departing to go her own way. When she finds Rose, who has always been especially tender to her, weeping, she asks straight out what has been going on, but Rose puts her off, saying she will explain it all soon. For a short while she thinks Rose may have cancer or some other incurable disease, until she takes a good look at her and realizes that Rose is pregnant. Mike, trying to be helpful, breaks a large hole in the wall to make a window for Kathleen's room, an improvement long promised but never accomplished by Frank, and then, expanding it to fit the window frame he has acquired, damages the whole roof. Kathleen must sleep on Carmel's sofa until repairs can be made. There she answers the phone call that routs Frank out to the

police station in the middle of the night to
rescue Mike, who has beaten up Sean Begley to
defend Rose's honor. While they wait, Carmel
angrily tells her how the family looks from her
point of view, how they all expect Frank to work
for them before his own wife and child, and how
it feels to be kept an outsider even after four
years of marriage. When Kathleen asks Carmel
straight out whether Begley is the father of
Rose's baby, Carmel says he is, and adds, "But
not your daddy, pet." Stricken, Kathleen locks
herself in the bathroom and later hides in the
hay barn, trying to sort out her own feelings,
pain at the realization that she is a bastard,
shame that the neighbors have all known for
years, outrage that no one in the family has
told her, and embarrassment that she hasn't
figured it out long ago. The next day Rose
leaves with Begley in the rusted Maxi in a wild
scene with Mike trying to beat him up again,
Frank preventing him, and Mammy, always a
partisan for Mike, attacking Frank; Carmel takes
Kathleen to talk to Rose, who tries to persuade
her to come live with her and Begley in his
cottage at the scrap yard; Ann, about to leave
for Belfast again, tries to convince Kathleen
that she must be her own person and not let
Mammy control her as she has controlled all the
others; and Kathleen begins to question her
certainties about her family and outsiders, her
hatred of the British and Protestants, and even
the evilness of abortion and contraception, and
to decide to direct her own life whether she
leaves or stays at Kiltarragh. The end is open
but hopeful, since Kathleen has grown in understanding and determination. The hostility of
the Irish Catholics to the soldiers who are
omnipresent in the border area is an interesting
aspect, but the novel's strength is in the
picture of the family relationships and the
astute characterization of the main figures. Ann
is a useful functionary, but Mammy, who dominates her grown children, hates and distrusts
doctors, and keeps even Kathleen in thrall by
making her the only person who can treat and
dress the abcess on her leg, yet is also a great
one for hugging and loving, is well drawn. So
are nun-like Teresa, who, because of Mammy's
opposition, years ago gave up her chance to

marry and go to Australia with the man she loved; irresponsible Mike, his mother's favorite, who has never really broken away even though he lives in London; and patient, slow Frank, surviving the conflicting demands by a sort of passive resistance. Perhaps the strongest character, aside from Kathleen, is careless, loving Rose, who used to tell Kathleen stories of a wonderful dream world, always starting, "One starry night ...," a pattern that Kathleen has continued in stories for Imelda. Kathleen's failure to figure out her own background, even though Daddy was dead before she was born and had been in a hospital nearly a year before his death, is convincing, as is her anguish at having to give up her own dream world to face reality. Other.

STEPHANOS BULGARICOS (*The Emperor's Winding Sheet**), eunuch of the bedchamber for Constantine*, last emperor of the Roman Empire of the East. Stephanos is able to speak Latin as well as Greek, and therefore he is able to communicate with Vrethiki*, the English boy who becomes part of the emperor's retinue in the last months before the fall of Constantinople. Through Vrethiki's questions and Stephanos's patient answers, much of the historical background of the story is told, but the eunuch is a strong characer, much more than a device in the novel. Although Vrethiki is horrified to learn that Stephanos, who showed promise of being clever as a young boy, was castrated by his own father and sold into slavery, Stephanos points out that it was his only chance to be educated and to rise in the world and that there are worse fates. He is absolutely devoted to the emperor, and though fond of Vrethiki, he turns on him in fury when the boy troubles Constantine by begging to be allowed to go free. In the last days of the defence of the city, he throws himself in front of the emperor to shield him from the debris of a cannon shot and is killed. Many times he is kind to Vrethiki and spares him pain if it causes no inconvenience to his master, and he admits to the boy that, though he no longer envies men who love girls or have wives, he does sometimes wish he could have a son.

STEPHEN DE BEAUVILLE (*One Is One**), retiring, sensitive son of a fourteenth-century earl, a boy who is considered a coward by his family and assigned to a monastery, from which he escapes. Even as a young child, Stephen has been fascinated by color and has enjoyed drawing, finding peace and happiness in using his talent. Although life in the monastery suits him in some ways, he has a fierce desire to prove himself to his family by becoming a knight. As he achieves this goal and even bests his cousin Edmund in front of the assembled family, he sees the shallowness of the satisfaction this gives him. Grieving over the loss of his squire, Thomas* FitzAmory, and still wounded by the loss of his great friend, Sir* Pagan Latourelle, Stephen tries to draw and through his love of art is drawn back to the monastery, the only place to practice such skills during this period.

STEPHENS, JAMES (1882-1950), born in Dublin, Ireland; poet, novelist, playwright, short-story writer, and reteller of traditional Irish tales. An ardent nationalist and champion of the working people, he became one of the more popular personalities of the Irish renaissance in the early part of the twentieth century. He grew up in poverty and educated himself by reading. He taught himself stenography and was working in an office when his writing attracted the admiration of author A.E. (George William Russell), who encouraged the young man and helped him become better known. Stephens's great interest in the once oral tales of Ireland is evident in much of his work. *Deirdre** (Macmillan, 1923; Macmillan, 1923), his fiction-alization of the poignant, exciting, and originally oral story of the beautiful, tragic heroine of Ulster, was the first of a pro-jected, but never completed, reconstruction of Irish saga. *Deirdre* earned him the Tailteann Gold Medal in 1923 and appears on the *Horn Book* Fanfare list. He published poetry, *Insurrections* (Maunsel, 1909; Macmillan, 1917), and a novel, *The Charwoman's Daughter* (Macmillan, 1912; in the United States as *Mary, Mary*, Boni, 1917), which first appeared in serial form; he then won the Polignac Prize in 1912 for *The Crock of Gold* (Macmillan, 1912; Small, 1912), a fantasy novel that is probably his best known work. After that he became a full-time writer, producing publications regularly until the 1930s, when he published only occasional poems. He was a good friend of James Joyce in the 1920s, moved to London in 1925, and lectured annually in the United States in the 1930s. From 1937 to his death, he lectured on poetry for BBC-Radio. An authority on Gaelic Art, he was assistant curator of the Dublin National Gallery. He was much interested also in folk music and was an active Sinn Feiner working hard for the formation of the De Valera government. During World War II, however, he openly expressed disapproval of Ireland's neutral stance. He married and had two children. Among his books of poetry are *The Hill of Vision* (Maunsel, 1912; Macmillan, 1912) and *Green Branches* (Maunsel, 1916; Macmillan, 1916), and for children he published a collection of traditional stories, *Irish Fairy Tales* (Macmillan, 1920; Macmillan, 1920), that was illustrated by Arthur Rackham. His prose work is imaginative in a deep and moving way, and his poems are musical, varied in form, simple and effective in diction, skillful with dialect, and witty. He also wrote on prose, poetry, and public affairs, and some of his imaginative writings have been reissued many times.

STEVENSON, ROBERT LOUIS (BALFOUR) (1850-1894), born in Edinburgh and died in Samoa; essayist, poet, and novelist. A sickly child, Stevenson grew up in a heavily religious household, attended Edinburgh Academy, and studied engineering, at his father's insistence, at Edinburgh University. He switched to law and was admitted to the Scottish bar in 1875. He had by then become an atheist, and his interest had turned to writing. Between 1876 and 1882 he contributed to *Cornhill Magazine*, London, and in 1880 he married Fanny Osborne, thereby acquiring two stepchildren, one of whom was Lloyd Osborne, who afterwards became a writer and for whom Stevenson's most famous book, *Treasure Island** (Cassell, 1883; Roberts, 1884), was originally written. Throughout his life Stevenson suffered from lung disease, and moved frequently looking for a better climate, living in California,

Switzerland, France, Bournemouth, England, and finally in the South Seas, where he died of a cerebral hemorrhage. For adults he wrote many short stories, several plays, thirteen books of verse, many books of essays, travel, criticism, and letters, and seven novels, among them *The Strange Case of Dr. Jekyll and Mr. Hyde* (Longman, 1886; Scribner, 1886), a story often read by young people. His *A Child's Garden of Verses* (Longman, 1885; Scribner, 1885), is considered one of the classic collections for children. Besides *Treasure Island*, a gripping tale of pirates and a sailing voyage which is a touchstone for all adventure stories, he wrote several other novels for young people, including *Kidnapped** (Cassell, 1886; Scribner, 1886), set in Scotland and dealing in part with the Jacobite movement, its sequel, *Catriona* (Cassell, 1893; as *David Balfour*, Scribner, 1893), and *The Black Arrow** (Cassell, 1883; Roberts, 1884), a historical adventure set during the War of the Roses. Except for *Catriona*, these have all been named Children's Classics, and *Treasure Island* is also listed in the Arbuthnot *Children's Books Too Good to Miss*, the Children's Literature Association Touchstones, and the *Choice* Magazine selection of children's books for an academic library. Stevenson's novels rise above others of the same genre in their excellence of style and their inclusion of memorably equivocal characters, notably Long* John Silver and Alan* Breck Stewart.

STEWART, A(GNES) C(HARLOTTE), born in Liverpool, Lancashire; author of a dozen problem, domestic, and mystery novels for older children and young adults. She and her sister grew up in a seaside town in Cheshire. The family moved in her teens to Kent, where she developed her love for animals and gardens. She was educated privately, married Robert Stewart, a mechanical engineer, and had one daughter. The Stewarts made their home in Scotland, a locale that figures largely in her stories. She began writing after her daughter left for boarding school, and her novels reflect her interests and the places she knows, but are more concerned with what happens to the characters inside than with incident or setting. She frequently develops place as part of character and pairs a child character with an adult, showing the influence on the child of the developing relationship with the older person. She often exploits a mystery angle. In *The Boat in the Reeds* (Blackie, 1960; Bradbury, 1970), a nine-year-old boy finds a boat and keeps it secret until he meets a mysterious man who knows about boats. In *Dark Dove* (Macmillan, 1975; Phillips, 1974), Margaret, a sixteen-year-old Scottish girl, must contend with her dour father's intimations that disaster will strike and forms a relationship with the local laird. In *Ossian House* (Blackie, 1974; Phillips, 1976), an eleven-year-old city boy inherits his grandfather's estate in Scotland and must cope with hostile relatives there. In *Falcon's Crag* (Blackie, 1969) and its sequel, *Biddy of Craigengill* (Blackie, 1979), Biddy grows to understand her Scottish relatives as she comes to love Craigengill itself. In *Silas and Con* (Blackie, 1977; Atheneum, 1977), a ten-year-old boy, abandoned by his mother and abusive stepfather, sets out through the wilds of Scotland to find a new home accompanied by a stray dog. There is a strong mystery element in *Elizabeth's Tower** (Faber, 1972; Phillips, 1972), an Edgar Allan Poe nominee, where a girl, unpopular because she is bossy, finds friendship and understanding with a lame stranger involved with foreign spies. The years Stewart lived near Liverpool provided the background on trains for her novel *The Quarry Line Mystery* (Faber, 1971; Nelson, 1973), about a disappearing freight train.

A STITCH IN TIME (Lively*, Penelope, Heinemann, 1976; Dutton, 1976), quiet, realistic novel with fantasy aspects set in the contemporary period on the seacoast of England, a story less of action than of a girl's growing understanding of herself and her relationship to others around her. Maria Foster, 11, is small for her age, shy, and introverted, the only child of a precise-minded, firm, highly confident father and a proper, self-assured mother, who love her but keep her at arm's length. In her loneliness and uncertainty about herself, Maria often makes up conversations with objects, such as the gas

pump when they fill up the car, or the cat that
lives in the old Victorian house the Fosters
rent on the seacoast for the summer holidays. As
the days go by, Maria gains in self-respect and
gradually learns to asert herself. Shortly after
they arrive she develops an interest in the
fossils of the region, books about which she
discovers in the old house and in the apartment
of their landlady, Mrs.* Shand, and she makes
friends with Martin Lucas, the eldest of the
horde of children belonging to the vacationers
next door. Martin, a self-assured and manipulative but not devious boy, shares her enthusiasm for fossils, and her association with
him, outings with his family, getting to know
Mrs. Shand, and pursuing her curiosity about
Harriet, a girl her own age who in 1865 worked
on the heirloom sampler that now belongs to Mrs.
Shand and who once lived in the cottage they
have rented, all help Maria to come out of
herself. She investigates simple clues about
Harriet, whose swing and dog she fancies hearing
(or perhaps does hear), whose rusted, buried
swing she finds and with Martin's help repairs,
and whom she eventually fears may have come to a
violent end. She (and the reader to a lesser
extent) is surprised and relieved to learn that
Harriet's dog, according to Mrs. Shand, and not
Harriet herself, fell victim to the shifting
coastal sands. The book is chiefly memorable for
Lively's accuracy at catching Maria's feelings
and reactions about people and situations. The
mystery seems designed to hold the reader, the
action scenes seem distant as though seen
through a telescope, and the characters are
shallow if individualized. Except for Maria, no
one changes, and even Maria develops predictably. The theme of time as a continuum seems
well supported by plot, tone, and narrative
motifs. Choice; Fanfare; Whitbread.

THE STOLEN LAKE (Aiken*, Joan, Cape, 1981;
Delacorte, 1981), fantasy novel in the Dido
Twite series which mingles melodrama, mystery,
and adventure-story aspects in an ostensibly
historical setting. The ship carrying Dido back
to England after *Nightbirds on Nantucket** is
diverted to Roman America, apparently Brazil, on
a mission of state. Captain Hughes, a capable,

efficient, solicitous gentleman, has been ordered to offer his services to Queen Ginevra of New Cumbria, who is having trouble with the neighboring kingdom of Lyonesse, ruled by King Mabon. Because the queen is said to enjoy the company of young girls, Captain Hughes takes Dido with him when he leaves for the royal city of Bath Regis with his steward, Mr.* Holystone, and his officers. At the port city of Tenby, perceptive Dido immediately catches the air of tension. Signs advertise for lost children; people seem suspicious of newcomers. Excitement breaks out as Dido is kidnapped by the two seamstresses that Captain Hughes has engaged to prepare appropriate attire for her (women later exposed as evil-doers in the queen's pay), rescued by a mysterious bard named Bran (who pops in and out of the story at advantageous points to help set things to rights), and travels upriver with her friends by ship and rackety-pack railroad through forests infested with threatening riders and ferocious creatures to Bath Regis high in the Andes. Beautiful, aging, hard-eyed Ginevra lives in a lavishly appointed, constantly revolving palace. She informs her guests that King Mabon has accused her of abducting his daughter, Princess Elen, and has in retaliation stolen the lake, Arianrod, on which the barge bore her husband, Artaius (Arthur of British legend), to his final resting-place and which she and her followers, 1,000 years earlier, transported to the New World as blocks of ice. She wishes Captain Hughes and his men to restore the lake so that Artaius may return as predicted in legend. She instructs Dido to impersonate Elen and takes Hughes hostage, imprisoning him in her royal dungeon. Dido and friends set out for Lyonesse, bearing with them on a litter Mr. Holystone, who has fallen ill with a mysterious malady. Adventures build as Dido discovers in the dry lake bed the sword, Culibrun, which, when placed in Holystone's hand, restores his memory. They discover imprisoned in a cave in the mountains Elen, who had indeed been kidnapped by the queen, one more in the series of young girls abducted as sacrifices to maintain the queen's youth and beauty; Dido and Elen are captured by the queen and Elen escapes on a friendly leopard, Hapiypacha; and Dido is rescued in the very nick of time by Captain Hughes, who has invented a lighter-than-air machine while in prison. All good forces then converge upon Bath Regis, where the queen welcomes Holystone (revealed as Artaius), confesses to her crimes of child abduction, and, when repudiated by Holystone, flies into a rage and rushes into her palace, which then begins to revolve at a tremendous rate and apparently kills her. At that very moment, the volcano overlooking the city erupts, necessitating an immediate evacuation. Dido and friends flee on the racketypack railroad, leaving Holystone (Artaius) to rule and heal the breach between New Cumbria and Lyonesse and eventually marry Elen. Except for pert, irrepressible, knowing Dido, the characters represent good or evil or influence action as required in proper Dickensian fashion. The elaborate, fast-moving plot spins along with dramatic abandon to its roaring climax with a profusion of villainous deeds, unexpected complications, hairbreadth escapes, a rapidly expanding cast of motley figures, and an absolutely impertinent improvisation on Arthurian tradition. The whole conglomeration is made amazingly acceptable by the author's meticulous attention to details and skillfully maintained tongue-in-cheek tone. Far more outrageous and somewhat less credible than the predecessors about Dido, it is still jolly good reading. Fanfare.

THE STONE BOOK (Garner*, Alan, ill. Michael Foreman, Collins, 1976; Collins, 1978), short, loosely plotted, realistic period novel of family life, involving a Victorian father and daughter, first in a series of four books that "form a saga tracing four generations of a working class family in Chorley, a small town in Cheshire, England." Young Mary's Father* is a self-respecting, highly skilled stonemason, who is currently putting the finishing touches on the steeple of the village church. After checking on Old* William, Father's brother, who is busy as always at the loom in his room in the family cottage, Mary treks to the church to take Father his baggin (lunch). Father invites her to climb up to where he is working, and in time to the friendly, encouraging tap of his hammer, she conquers her fear of falling and staunchly maneuvers herself up the ladder's dizzying steepness. Once up, she sits proudly astride the golden weathercock that tips the summit and surveys the village below that her father has had so much a part in creating. As her father rotates the cock in the wind, she shouts at the top of her voice, "Faster! Faster!...I'm not frit!," and bangs her heels on its golden sides. All the while, her father's whoop of joy echoes across the countryside. Mary yearns to learn to read and have a prayer book to carry to chapel like her friends Lizzie Allman and Annie Leah, who use theirs to press flowers in. Father points out to her that learning to read would not be appropriate and then takes her under the hill into the stone quarry, telling her to follow the malachite strain as far as it leads her. All by herself, deep into the layers of earth, Mary walks carefully and wonderingly and just as bravely and trustingly as she climbed the ladder, until she arrives at the end of the track and sees Father's stonemason's mark on the wall, faint and black, next to a drawing of a great, shaggy bull, and on the muddy ground beneath, hundreds of thronging footprints. When she returns, Mary learns that her journey has taken her to where her ancestors trod and that she has glimpsed secrets of the world's history that only stone can know, of eons gone by dating back to the great flood. Father then hones for her a prayer book of a sliver of stone bearing a pattern of fronds and encloses it within blue-black calfskin, another book of stone, one she can hold as well as read. The story is notable for its sharp characterizations; its powerful, tidy style, which employs dialect judiciously, respects the reader's intelligence, and doesn't lay everything out; its warm, understanding relationship between father and daughter; the keen sense it conveys of Mary's fear and exhilaration (so strong one fairly holds one's breath) as she scales the ladder and whirls atop the gleaming cock, and for the glimpse (expanded in later books) it gives of pride in hand crafts and village attitudes and ways. Choice; Fanfare.

STORM FROM THE WEST. See *The Battle of Wednesday Week.*

THE STORY OF DOCTOR DOLITTLE (Lofting, Hugh, ill. author, Cape, 1920; Lippincott, 1920), fantasy starting in the town of Puddleby-on-the-Marsh in England but largely concerned with a voyage to Africa "when our grandfathers were little children," presumably in the first third of the nineteenth century. Doctor* John Dolittle has gradually lost his practice because he cares more for animals than humans. When, at the suggestion of the Cats'-Meat-Man, he becomes an animal doctor, he does well because his parrot, Polynesia*, a wise old bird, teaches him to speak the language of the animals, but his sister, Sarah, who has been keeping house for him, leaves in a huff. His animals take over the housekeeping duties, but money for food becomes critically short. Then Chee-Chee* the monkey gets a message via swallow from his cousin in Africa that a terrible sickness is killing the monkeys there. The doctor borrows a boat and money and sets off with Polynesia, Chee-Chee, Jip his dog, Dab-Dab the duck, and Gub-Gub the pig, led by the swallow who brought the news. Although their ship is wrecked and they are captured by the King of Jolliginki, Polynesia is able to trick him into letting them escape to the edge of Jolliginki, where the monkeys make a "Bridge of Apes" by holding hands, which the others use to walk across the deep gorge. In the land of the monkeys, Doctor Dolittle vaccinates all the healthy monkeys and cures the others with the help of the lions, the leopards and the antelopes, which he presses into service as nurses. To reward him, the monkeys capture the rarest animal of all, the two-headed pushmi-pullyu and persuade it to go home with the doctor to help him earn money to pay for the voyage. On their return trek across Africa, they are again captured by the Jolliginkis and escape only because the king's son, Prince Bumpo* Kahbooboo, reads romantic fairy tales and thinks he could marry the Sleeping Beauty if he were only white. The doctor concocts a basin of medicine that temporarily removes the pigmentation from his face, and with the help of thousands of

swallows pulling the ship, the doctor and his
animals get away, only to find at their first
stop that the rats are leaving because their
ship is unseaworthy and will sink. After a
number of other adventures including pirates
and a rescue of an eight-year-old boy and his
uncle, they return to England where the doctor
shows the pushmi-pullyu for sixpence admission
and earns enough to pay his debts. The story is
written with a matter-of-fact simplicity that
has charmed generations of readers. Doctor
Dolittle himself is wise but unpretentious and
unworldly, a genuinely good man who treats
other living creatures with respect, and his
main animals have well-defined characters.
Unfortunately, the book employs terms for blacks
used at the time of its writing that are now
considered offensive and, a more serious fault,
treats the Jolliginki royal family as comic
characters, Prince Bumpo's gullible desire to be
white being questionable to modern tastes. Later
books in this series are less subject to these
criticisms. Lewis Carroll.

THE STORY OF GRIZEL. See *Girl with a Lantern.*

*THE STORY OF THE TREASURE SEEKERS: BEING THE
ADVENTURES OF THE BASTABLE CHILDREN IN SEARCH OF
A FORTUNE* (Nesbit*, E., ill. Gordon Browne and
Lewis Baumer, Unwin, 1899; Stokes, 1899),
amusing, realistic, episodic family novel set in
London at the turn of the century. The six
motherless Bastable children--maternal Dora*,
the eldest; Oswald*, the next eldest and a young
gentleman; practical Dicky*, at eleven the
businessman of the family; Alice* and Noel*,
ten-year-old twins; and H. O.* (Horace
Octavius), the eight-year-old tagalong--live
with their cheerful and patient father and
slovenly housekeeper, Eliza, in a big, old house
in Lewisham Road. Since their father's business
is not doing well, the children set out "to
restore the fallen fortunes of the ancient house
of Bastable." One of them (eventually revealed
as Oswald) tells the story of the "different
ways we looked for treasure" and how they "were
not lazy about the looking." Each venture is
proposed by one of the children in turn, and
most are drawn from the books they have been

reading. None nets them much money, but all are
lively, interesting, and good reading. They
begin by digging for buried treasure in their
backyard, Dora's idea, and pusillanimous
Albert-next-door is almost covered by a sudden
cave-in. His author uncle (who represents to the
children the ultimate in adults, being patient,
mildly indulgent, understanding, and imaginative) helps dig him out and in the process
happens to "discover" two half-crowns for them.
Next, one of the children (Oswald forgets
which) proposes they become detectives and solve
a crime. They stake out the house next door,
where Alice has seen a strange light at night
even though the people are supposed to be
vacationing. They are disappointed and somewhat
embarrassed to discover that the family has only
pretended to be away so that the neighborhood
won't think they are too poor for a holiday.
Noel proposes to make money by selling poems he
has written and by marrying a princess. He and
Oswald take the train to inner London to the
Daily Recorder office. They have tea and
conversation with the editor, who buys several
of Noel's poems and later runs them in a feature
story about the children. Then, coincidentally,
the children meet a prim and proper little girl
in Greenwich Park and play princes and princesses with her, only to discover later that
they have been playing with the fifth cousin of
Queen Victoria herself. On Guy Fawkes Day they
try H. O.'s idea of becoming bandits, capture
Albert-next-door, who snivels and whines
throughout his captivity, and hold him until he
is ransomed for eight pence by his uncle.
Albert's uncle then proposes they publish a
newspaper, which consists mostly of a collab-
oratively written story and nets them two
shillings, also from Albert-next-door's uncle.
They borrow seed money from a G. B. (Generous
Benefactor), a professional moneylender named Z.
Rosenbaum, and, at Oswald's request, set out to
rescue a gentleman from deadly peril in hopes he
will make them his heirs. Finding none, they
deliberately distress one. They set their dog,
Pincher, on an old man who is crossing the
heath. He happens to be Lord Tottenham, a
distinguished member of Parliament, to whom,
after the scheme comes out, they apologize and

with whom they become good friends. Dicky's way
of restoring their fortunes involves answering
an ad to become salesmen for Castilian Amaroso
wine, a plan that backfires when they attempt to
sell some to a local clergyman, who happens to
be a staunch teetotaler. They seek gold (Alice's
idea) with an umbrella divining rod, a procedure
carried out with great pomp and circumstance,
and find a shiny, bright half-sovereign under
the upstairs floorboards. Ironically, the family
fortunes are restored by the children without
design. An Indian uncle, an elderly relative of
their mother, comes visiting. Thinking he must
be from North America and hence poor, the
children unselfishly and innocently share their
own meal with him and give him money. Actually
well-off and influential, he secures financing
for their father's business and is so impressed
by the children's generosity and good behavior
that he invites them all to come and live with
him in his big house. The book ends at that
point, and the children's adventures while
living with the Indian uncle occur in *The
Would-be-goods* and *The New Treasure-Seekers*. One
of the first and still considered among the best
of its kind, the book enjoys the status of a
classic. Its style is breezy, conversational,
and filled with the kind of detail of observation and action that appeals to the young.
The characters are exceptionally well defined
for this genre, and it is easy to distinguish
each from the others both in action and in
speech. The adventures are typical of the things
children left to their own devices will do, and
the point of view is unerringly that of happy,
intelligent, active youth. This book has worn
well and seems dated today only in details of
dress or custom. Children's Classics; Choice;
ChLA Touchstones.

STRACHAN, IAN, born in Altrincham, Cheshire;
writer, actor, and radio and television producer. He first appeared in a Children's Hour
play for the BBC and spent several years working
in repertory theaters in various parts of
Britain. He has also worked in television and
more recently as a producer on BBC-Radio in
Stoke-on-Trent. His first book, *Moses Beech**
(Oxford, 1981), which won the Young Observer

Teenage Fiction Prize, is the story of a runaway city boy who hides out with a reclusive old man and learns to appreciate country life and to have respect for himself as well as for the old man's independence. It is set in an isolated area very like the valley in Staffordshire where Strachan makes his home.

THE STRANGE AFFAIR OF ADELAIDE HARRIS (Garfield*, Leon, ill. Fritz Wegner, Longman, 1971; Pantheon, 1971), high-spirited farce set in nineteenth-century Brighton, centering on events at Dr. Bunnion's Academy. When James Brett, a thin, depressed youngish man, lectures on ancient Rome to his dozen rumpled students, aged twelve or thirteen, eleven are listening only for the dismissal bell, but Harris*, the one Mr. Brett most dreads, is attending avidly, particularly to the story of Romulus and Remus. After school, Harris divulges his plan to his loyal and admiring follower, Bostock*: to kidnap and expose his infant sister, Adelaide, and to watch to see what animal will arrive to nurse her, all, of course, in the interests of science. Their abducting of Adelaide coincides with a walk on the Downs by Ralph Bunnion, handsome son of the proprietor of the academy, and Tizzy Alexander, pretty daughter of the arithmetic master, with Tizzy anticipating with a little fear and much eagerness being swept off her feet by Ralph and Ralph intent on making another conquest to add to his impressive list. By the time they get to the secluded grassy spot surrounded by thorn bushes, Tizzy is bored with talking only about Ralph and not about her, and Ralph is annoyed that she doesn't seem sufficiently impressed by his stories of the hearts he has broken. Just as he launches himself at her with anger and lust, she sees the baby and leaps forward, forgetting romance in her maternal feelings. They arrive back at the school in a disheveled state, Ralph with his face scratched by the turf and Tizzy cooing over the baby she carries. Major Alexander immediately assumes the worst and challenges Ralph to a duel over the honor of his daughter. Dr. Bunnion, horrified at the thought that scandal might harm his school and, to a lesser degree, that Ralph, whom he hopes to marry to

the sister of a boarder from a titled family,
might be killed, sends his son off to leave the
infant at the church door and asks Mr. Brett to
act as a second for Ralph. The same evening,
Major Alexander asks Mr. Brett to serve as his
second, and the history master who despises
both Ralph and the major, as well as Dr.
Bunnion, finds himself unable to refuse either
of them. Mr. Brett is staying on at the school
only because he has fallen deeply in love with
Tizzy, to whom he has been giving ancient
history lessons in exchange for her mother
mending his laundry. In the meantime, Bostock
and Harris, having trailed Ralph and Tizzy back
to the school, learn that the baby is to be
deposited at the church door. They go to pick
her up but unfortunately choose a different
church, and the baby they find there is
definitely not blond little Adelaide but rather
a dark-haired male gypsy infant. They nonetheless place this baby in Adelaide's crib. From
this point in the story the complications
multiply. Dr. Harris hires an inquiry agent,
Mr.* Selwyn Raven, a sinister character with a
club foot who stumps tap-thump, tap-thump
through the story working out an elaborate (and
entirely incorrect) network of guilt, at the
center of which he places Mr. Brett. Bostock and
Harris, discovering that Adelaide is in the
infant ward at the poorhouse, ply the keeper's
wife, Mrs. Bonney, with contributions which she
spends on brandy. In the end, the duel is
avoided because Mr. Brett, responsible for
making arrangements, has named two different
places to the two principals and then has left
town with Tizzy on their way to a life together
in the New World. Bostock and Harris, having
finally found Mrs. Bonney so inebriated that she
doesn't notice them, retrieve Adelaide and
return her to her own crib. It has just been
vacated by the gypsy baby, which Mr. Raven has
taken and deposited at the doorstep of the
family he has deduced (incorrectly) to be
responsible for it. He leaves town, congratulat-
ing himself on having prevented a murder which
he alone assumed was imminent. The intricate
plot is full of misunderstandings and coincidences, peopled by a rich set of caricatures, all
gamboling through the story in hilarious

confusion. Garfield's style employs frequent and unusual figures of speech and an ironic tone that adds greatly to the humor. The treatment of the inquiry agent is a satire on the Holmesian sort of detection, but enjoyment of the story does not depend on a knowledge of these earlier stories. Fanfare.

THE STRANGER (Weaver*, Stella, ill. Genevieve Vaughan-Jackson, Collins, 1955; Pantheon, 1956), holiday adventure with mystery-story aspects set in Ireland in the mid-twentieth century. Edmund, probably about fifteen, and Emily Tennant, much younger, have come to the village of Ballymurry for the first time to visit Aunt Lucy, the elder sister of their father who was killed in World War II. Aunt Lucy lives in Cloughfin, a small house that was attached to the estate of Donarink, which has been owned by their family for generations, where she, their father, and his younger brother, Hugh, grew up. Although most of the local people welcome them, speak to Edmund as "sir," and refer to his sister as "Miss Emily," the youngsters are rudely warned off, when they explore and come across the empty house of Donarink, by a strange-looking, evidently retarded man named Matt Heffernan, whom Aunt Lucy has allowed to stay on as caretaker. Later they learn two startling facts: that Donarink, which must be inherited by the eldest son, actually belongs to Edmund, and that the local people have been losing geese and other fowl with no sign of foxes or dogs. When they borrow Mike Moriarty's donkey for a hike in the mountains and leave it tethered before they scramble up the highest point, it has disappeared by the time they return for it. Since Mike is a small farmer, a fisherman's guide, and a handyman who badly needs the beast, they feel very guilty and search diligently for it, for they know that neither their aunt nor their hard-up mother, who works as a secretary in London, can afford to replace it. Bridget Flynn, their cook, takes them to see her aunt, who was nurse to three generations of Tennants and is now 106 years old but still has "all her senses." The old woman, who also is said to have second sight, tells Edmund she has seen him before, the night his great-uncle died as a

child, and she gives him a mysterious message,
"What was lost in Lissnanowl will be found again
in Coomagraw." Searching maps and asking local
people, they can find neither of the names, but
they think the mountain where they lost the
donkey may be connected to the first by an old
legend, so they return there. From a point of
rock they see the camp of a tinker named Tizer
Lee, and they sneak down to examine his donkeys.
The tinker's wife tries to trick them into
buying one of her donkeys, but a boy who lives
with the tinkers, Tim Curtin, tells them
secretly that Mike's donkey is tied up at the
old stone hut called Lugnascatha, where there
are ancient standing stones and natural lime-
stone caves. Trying to take a shortcut to get
there, Edmund and Emily get thoroughly lost,
finally come out at a small lake, see a house on
the other side, and row a boat they find on the
shore across to get help. To their dismay, the
house is empty and a ruin, but they come upon a
stranger who says he has been reaping corn for
the master and, after various enigmatic
statements about signposts of the mind, tells
them they will find the donkey in the stable at
their home and advises them to go through a
little wood to get there. Though they are many
miles from home, they take his advice and come
upon Mike and the professor he guides in
fishing, who takes them home in his car. To
their great disappointment, the donkey is not at
Cloughfin, but realizing that the stranger may
have meant Donarink, they go there the next
morning, get into the house, where there is
evidence that someone has been living, and from
an upstairs window see the tinkers, Matt
Heffernan, and another man loading fowl and
produce from the tinker's cart to an automobile.
Edmund realizes that this is how the tinkers
dispose of their stolen goods, and when they
have left he finds the donkey, but later when he
tries to talk to Mike about his suspicions he
gets only a blank response. The next morning he
gives Emily the slip, goes back to Donarink, and
manages to get to a place where he can see into
the walled garden, which is full of an
astonishing array of well-tended fruit trees and
vegetables. He gets back to Cloughfin in a
terrific rain, learns that Emily is gone, and

finds a scrawled note suggesting that she will find treasure in the caves of Lugnascatha. Since she was angry to have been left behind and since they both long for treasure to fix up Donarink, he knows she must have gone there, and he and Colum, Mike's son, take ropes and lanterns and head for the caves, though Colum partially believes the local legends that they are haunted and is far from eager to enter them. They discover that the recent rain has brought down a landslide that has blocked the entrance, but Colum knows another way in, and they make a long and gruelling trek through the labyrinth of passages before they come upon Emily and Tim Curtin, who has broken a leg. He admits that Tizer told him to direct them into the cavern, but he also says that he hates Tizer and wants to leave him. They find another way out quite easily, and while Colum goes for the donkey to carry Tim down, the stranger appears to them again, gives them food, and helps them rid their minds of the greed for treasure which has led them to such difficulties. The next day they go again to Donarink and talk to the man they saw there, who turns out to be Matt Heffernan's brother Jim, an old friend of their father and of Mike. He has been hiding out at the place, having gotten into trouble in America and feared the police were after him, a fear played upon by Tizer. The children's mother and Uncle Hugh arrive from England, Edmund tells them he wants to stay and farm at Donarink with Jim Heffernan's help, and they decide that they can all live there without modern conveniences or servants. The story ends with a village dance being held in the big room at Donarink and most of the local people volunteering to work for Edmund, so that he will still be in some ways the young squire despite having no fortune. The characterization is minimal. Emily's age is hard to guess. She is very babyish in her dialogue and her attitudes, yet she is old enough to hike a long day with her brother and end up some eleven miles from home. The story has some good scenes, particularly in the cave, but there is ambiguity about the social structure. Edmund worries about how the English landlords in the past were extravagant, then turned the Irish, including the Moriarty family, out of their

homes if they couldn't pay rent, but he accepts
the deference of the local people as his natural
due, and the author seems to agree with him.
Still, it would be a lively enough adventure if
it were not for the intrusion of the stranger, a
supernatural figure not necessary to the plot,
which brings a jarring moralistic note that is
not convincing either as realism or fantasy.
Fanfare.

A STRANGER AT GREEN KNOWE (Boston*, L. M., ill.
Peter Boston, Faber, 1961; Harcourt, 1961),
fourth in a series of books about Green Knowe,
the only one which is not a fantasy. Ping*, now
about ten, on a field trip to the zoo with other
displaced children, sees the gorilla, Hanno*,
and falls in love with the magnificent beast.
Ida* Biggin writes to Mrs.* Oldknow, suggesting
that she invite Ping to spend the holidays at
Green Knowe, and, since Tolly*, her great-
grandson, can't come to her, the old lady takes
up the suggestion. As Ping is on the train to
Green Knowe, he sees newspaper stories saying
that the gorilla has escaped from the zoo.
Though they had not met previously, Ping and
Mrs. Oldknow get on famously, and Ping spends
his solitary time largely in the bamboo thicket
beyond the garden, an almost impenetrable area
that is a bird sanctuary and gives the house
privacy from the fields. Ping and Mrs. Oldknow
follow the story of the gorilla in the newspaper
and on the radio and are both pleased that he is
not immediately caught. Ping builds himself a
hut of bamboo in the thicket and enjoys himself
immensely, but he begins to feel that someone is
watching him. News reports say that it is
thought that Hanno was shut by mistake in a van
and may have then escaped along the highway that
runs near Green Knowe. Ping, dozing in his hut,
wakes to see a foot and to find that the
orange he had is now scattered orange peel. He
is both delighted and terrified and, though
bursting to tell Mrs. Oldknow, knows he must
keep Hanno's presence a secret. Desperately, he
takes food from the kitchen and whole rows of
vegetables from the garden to satisfy Hanno's
huge appetite. The gorilla accepts him,
evidently considering him a young gorilla, and
Ping is torn between pride and fear that Hanno

will reveal himself and be caught. When the
local police and a major, a big game hunter,
come to search the area, Ping lies to lead them
off the track, and Mrs. Oldknow displays her
rare temper at the persistence and rudeness of
the police. The morning after a terrific storm,
knowing the thicket is to be searched, Ping goes
there and shows Hanno the way over a tree
fallen across the moat into the garden. While
they are eating breakfast, Mrs. Oldknow sees
Hanno and is almost as fascinated as Ping,
though she realizes that he can't stay and
urges Ping to go tell the keeper, who has been
summoned, before someone shoots Hanno. A cow,
scared by the crowds of onlookers, charges Ping,
and Hanno, protecting his little gorilla, takes
her horns and flips her over. The major with the
police shoots him. Ping tells the whole story to
the keeper and, though grieved, is glad that
Hanno doesn't have to go back to captivity.
Hanno is a remarkably real character, described
in strong sensory detail so that his size and
power are almost overwhelming and his deftness
and agility amazing. One can smell his slghtly
smoky body odor and feel the different textures
of hair on various parts of his body. This
concrete detail makes an unlikely situation
plausible. Ping is an individualized character,
and his friendship with Mrs. Oldknow is warmly
convincing. Carnegie Winner; Choice; Contemporary Classics; Fanfare.

A STRANGER CAME ASHORE (Hunter*, Mollie, Hamilton, 1975; Harper, 1975), fantasy of suspense
set in the early nineteenth century among the
fisherfolk of the Shetland Islands. The story
revolves around the Scottish legend of the Great
Selkie, the bull seal who is king of the seal
people. He is said to be able to cast aside his
sealskin and come ashore as a handsome young
man, and in that guise to lure a mortal maiden
away to his undersea kingdom. The novel begins
on a stormy night when a stranger comes to the
door of fisherman Peter Henderson and his wife,
Janet. The stranger says he is Finn Learson, a
shipwrecked sailor, the only survivor of the
Bergen, which has foundered on the rocks just
off shore. A charming, handsome young fellow,
Finn soon becomes part of the social and work

life of the village and courts Elspeth, 17, the
Henderson's pretty daughter. The Hendersons'
dog, Tam, however, takes a strong dislike to
Finn; the man's odd smile and occasional strange
behavior bother Robbie Henderson, about twelve,
and Old* Da, the venerable grandfather, is
suspicious, too. Not long after Finn arrives,
Old Da falls ill, and on his deathbed he
whispers a warning to Robbie not to trust the
newcomer. Robbie, from whose standpoint the
story is told, sees mounting evidence that Finn
is the Great Selkie. Among other indications,
omens predict that Elspeth will marry a rich
man and then die; Finn seems magically to lead
astray officers of the Press Gang when they land
unexpectedly, searching for men to impress into
the British fleet; and Finn's flesh has the
same warm feel that the hides of baby seals
have. Everyone else likes Finn, except, of
course, Nicol Anderson, Elspeth's beau, but even
he rejects Robbie's suspicions and tells the
boy to mind his own business. When Elspeth
declares that she will choose between Finn and
Nicol on the last day of the Yule holidays,
Robbie realizes that there is no time to waste
and sets about enlisting help to save his
sister. He consults Yarl* Corbie, the dour old
schoolmaster, who proves a valiant and
knowledgeable ally. Convinced Finn is the Great
Selkie, they search diligently for his skin,
find it, and hide it. They then arrange with
Nicol to control the festivities during the
guisers' (mummers) dances on the night Elspeth
will announce her decision. Things so fall out
that Robbie breaks up a terrible fist fight
between Nicol and Finn just as Finn is getting
the best of Nicol. Robbie shouts out that he
knows where the skin is. Finn chases Robbie
toward the sea, to a place where Yarl Corbie
attacks the Selkie man, blinding him in one eye.
Finn retrieves his skin and returns to the sea.
Now minus one eye, he will never again be able
to come on land as a handsome youth and lure
maidens away to their doom. Though not well
developed in personality, Robbie serves to keep
the reader interested. Most characters are clear
types, but Old Da clings to the memory as an
individual and Yarl Corbie holds surprises. The
book is mostly plot, and almost everything for

predicting the outcome lies open to view. In firm control of her story material, the author moves events along evenly and surely to the tense and exciting climax, after which she brings the reader down smoothly and gently, all the while sustaining the flavor of an oral storytelling situation. Celtic speech and beliefs and details of physical landscape and the fisherfolk way of life help also to ground events in reality and create credibility. The result is a well-above-average mystery-thriller. Books Too Good; Boston Globe Honor; Choice.

STREATFEILD, (MARY) NOEL (1895-1986), born in Amberley, Sussex; prolific author for both children and adults. The daughter of an Anglican clergyman, she attended school at St. Leonard's on Sea, Sussex; Laleham School, Eastbourne, Sussex; and the Academy of Dramatic Art, London. During World War I, she made munitions at Woolwich Arsenal, and during the 1920s, she was an actress in England, South Africa, and Australia. For adults she published seventeen novels as Streatfeild, twelve as Susan Scarlett, and three plays, as well as her three-volume autobiography, A Vicarage Family (Collins, 1963; Watts, 1963), Away from the Vicarage (Collins, 1965; as On Tour, Watts, 1965), and Beyond the Vicarage (Collins, 1971; Watts, 1972). For children she published thirty-seven books of fiction, several plays, and fifteen books of nonfiction, among them The First Book of Ballet (Watts, 1953; Ward, 1963) and The First Book of England (Watts, 1958; Ward, 1963). Her Ballet Shoes* (Dent, 1936; Random, 1937), illustrated by her sister, seems quaintly dated today, but was original in the 1930s, one of the first novels to treat the trials and hard work of a career seriously. It was followed by a number of other well-researched novels about working children, including Tennis Shoes (Dent, 1937; Random, 1938), The Circus Is Coming* (Dent, 1938; as Circus Shoes, Random, 1939), which won the Carnegie Medal, Curtain Up (Dent, 1944; as Theater Shoes; or, Other People's Shoes, Random, 1945), and White Boots (Collins, 1951; as Skating Shoes, Random, 1951). Her later books departed from the career story pattern. Thursday's Child*

(Collins, 1970; Ramdom, 1970) is the story of an orphan set in Victorian times, using many of the conventions of the novel of that period. *When the Siren Wailed* (Collins, 1974; Random, 1977) is a story set in wartime England of German air raids. After World War II, Streatfeild became a leading figure in the British children's book world. Although her plots often depend upon unlikely coincidences, her novels are realistic about the sorts of lives they explore and about how children think and feel.

STRIDER (*The Fellowship of the Ring**), Ranger who meets the four hobbits* at the inn at Bree and who becomes their leader to Rivendell. Really Aragorn, son of Arathorn and rightful king of Gondor, he is also called The Dunadan (or Man of the West), Numenorean, and Elessar, Isildur's heir. Far older than other men since he comes from a line that includes the half-elven people, he appears to be a young man, very wise in the paths of Middle-earth and particularly the country around The Shire, which he has patrolled for many years. When Gandalf* is lost in the Mines of Moria, Strider takes over as leader of the fellowship, but he worries that he is making the wrong decisions. To the others, he is always courteous and even gentle, and in Gondor he is shown to have the power of healing in his hands. His great feat in the war is to rouse the spirits on the Paths of Dead, those who broke their oath to fight against Sauron in ancient times and cannot rest until they have fulfilled their promise. He is a great warrior and a truly noble man, the one character based on the usual concept of the hero type from the oral tradition.

A STRONG AND WILLING GIRL (Edwards*, Dorothy, ill. Robert Micklewright, Methuen, 1980), episodic novel based on the early life of the author's aunt, who started in domestic service at the age of eight in Teddington in the 1880s. The eldest in a family that eventually includes ten children, Nan is small and has gone to school only rarely, but she is a bright girl and a hard worker, already quite competent at eight. The vicar's wife, who had been one of her

mother's charges when she was a nursery maid,
suggests that she could earn something giving "a
little extra assistance" at houses with only one
regular maid. Since her father is out of work
and another baby is on the way, her mother
agrees, and Nan starts her first paid jobs,
going out to several houses before light to
start fires, scrub steps, and do other tasks
that must be finished before eight in the
morning. Her first problem comes at the
Vicarage, where the cook scolds her for mud on
the steps even though she has cleaned them
thoroughly and it has not rained for days.
Suspecting that the penny postman, who often
teases her, is playing a trick, she hides
beneath the stairs with a bucket of water until
she hears footsteps going up, then jumps out and
swooshes the water upward, only to discover that
she has drenched the boots of the visiting
bishop, a naturalist who has been out hunting
specimens by the river. This is typical of her
attitude: she works hard without complaint, but
she expects fair treatment and is ingenious at
getting even when she has been misused. Her
first live-in job, when she is ten, is in
Richmond for two old maids, where she helps the
cook and the other maid, Orphan Alice, 15, who
proves a good friend. It is 1887, the year of
Queen Victoria's Golden Jubilee. The girls are
excited to see all the other houses decorated
with flags and bunting and disappointed when the
two ladies say they are going to London for the
celebrations and will not waste money to
decorate their house, even if it is in a
prominent spot on the hill. The girls are
outraged when their employers lock them into the
house so they will "be quite safe" while they
are gone. Unable to get out, even to watch the
festivities, Alice delves in old trunks in the
attic and finds relics of an American visit the
two ladies made when they were girls. Together
she and Nan climb out the attic window to the
roof and hang out their bit of color, bright
scarves and shawls and cushion covers, all
strung on a clothes line with a flag in the
center, red, white, and blue (and American,
though the girls do not know it), flanked by two
big double bags of orange-colored flannel, which
they do not recognize as bloomers. Although

their decoration attracts a lot of attention, they think it is all admiration because they are locked in and cannot open the door. Nan has a number of other jobs before she is fifteen; she works for old Miss Ellum, who is tormented by neighborhood boys until Nan captures one of them and locks him in the cellar; for Mr. Button, a retired head coachman, who foils his greedy daughter's plans to take over his home by marrying the widow that owns a nearby public house; for a "Boheemymum" photographer and his wife, where her employer takes a picture of Nan's three younger siblings who have come over to play and she is humiliated to discover has published it as "London beggar children"; for a young lady who lends her to help with the Church Sunday School Treat, where she discovers that the Verger's wife sets aside for her own use all the nicest goodies donated and Nan, with the cooperation of two gentry children, manages to hide and serve the delicious pink cakes she has brought and to discover and serve all the Verger's wife's secret hoard. She also helps out temporarily at a Day Academy for Young Ladies, where the bad behavior and meanness of the girls shocks her, and for a titled family, whose penny-pinching and grasping ways earn her scorn. When she is fifteen she goes to Miss Johnson's at Twickenham, where she stays for twenty-six years. In her first year there, she discovers a "Useful Boy," Dick Mason, at the house next door. He is nearly starved, being expected to exist on his employers' leftovers and to sleep in a bitterly cold, empty stable. When he grows weak they turn him out, but he returns and hides in the stable, having nowhere else to go. Nan smuggles food out to him but soon realizes that he is really ill. She confesses to Miss Johnson, who immediately takes charge, summons a doctor and a policeman, moves the boy into her own guest room, and sits holding his hand all night as he dies. Nan relates her adventures in colloquial but not highly dialectic language, with spirit, practical good sense, and a good deal of humor. Though she details a life that seems shockingly exploitive by modern standards, she does not feel sorry for herself or ask for sympathy. Her picture of the high standards and love in her own crowded home is reassuring.

Other.

THE STRONGHOLD (Hunter*, Mollie, Hamilton, 1974; Harper, 1974), historical novel set for one year in the first century B.C. among the Boar people, a Celtic tribe in the Orkney Islands off Scotland, and which proposes a fictional explanation for the massive, circular, tower-like structures made of stone found there and in northern Scotland and known to archaeologists as "brochs." From the time he was five, when Roman slave hunters sailed in and killed his father, carried off his mother, and broke his hip, permanently laming him, Coll, now eighteen and the foster-son of the chief, Nectan*, has yearned to find a way to build a stronghold to protect his people against these foreign predators who periodically raid the coast. Although he has devised a clever scheme for building one of stone in this treeless region, Coll shares his hopes and plans only with his foster-sisters, Clodha* and Fand*, with Niall*, Clodha's betrothed, who is destined to be the next chief (since with this tribe succession passes through the chief's daughters), and, later, with Bran*, his own younger brother, now in training as a Druid. Since the tribe has been decimated of adults by repeated raids, some sort of action is imperative, but Domnall*, Chief Druid, and Nectan differ on procedures, the former counselling open and determined resistance, the latter opting for prudent flight whenever the watchmen sight raiders on the horizon. What begins as a policy disagreement over defensive tactics between the two leaders evolves into a power struggle between church and state, as it were, and intense bitterness results. After the arrival of Taran*, a young man who says he was kidnapped by the Romans thirteen years earlier and taken to Gaul where he escaped, and who ingratiates himself into Domnall's favor, the disagreement intensifies, soon embroiling the entire tribe and two neighboring tribes who also look to Domnall as religious leader. One night Niall and Coll trail Taran to a tryst with Domnall near the circular formation of stones known as the Druids' Ring. They spy on the meeting and learn from Bran, who lives with Domnall, that

Domnall is scheming with the Raven and Deer
tribes, which are hostile to the Boar, to ally
with the Boars under Taran's leadership. They
also learn that Taran's ambitions exceed local
proportions, that he proposes to become leader
of all the Celtic tribes of the region. Coll
describes his stronghold plan to Nectan, but
Nectan rejects the idea. In an attempt to
retain leadership over his courage-worshipping
people, Nectan fights a wild boar singlehandedly
and triumphs, but immediately Domnall counters
the victory by threatening to withhold passage
to the Otherworld, the Celtic world of the dead,
from Nectan's people unless the tribe agrees to
fight the Romans when they arrive, and the
tribe, thoroughly intimidated, readily acqui-
esces. Domnall then commands that Fand be
sacrificed at Beltane (May 1, the festival of
the god Belanos) to atone for their rebellion
against him. Nectan is forced to accept Taran as
a new member of the ruling Council, but
stipulates that marriage to Clodha and continued
membership in the Council will depend on the
success of the proposed alliance. Nectan then
agrees to let Coll build a stronghold, but at
some future time when it seems more appropriate
to embark on the venture. Coll schemes to save
Fand's life, carefully planting seeds of
suspicion in the mind of a rigid old Councillor,
Ogham, that Fand may not be a virgin and hence
is unsuitable for sacrifice. At the last moment,
in a very tense scene, Bran takes the kinfe-blow
intended for Fand and dies in her stead. Coll is
put on trial for sacrilege--for despoiling a
virgin to be sacrificed and for attempting to
circumvent the will of the gods. It is decided,
after Nectan's eloquent defense of Coll, that
Coll is to be spared to provide a means of
protection for the tribe, and work commences on
the long-awaited stronghold. If the stronghold
proves effective, Coll will be allowed to live.
In spite of the obvious uncertainty, Coll is
elated; he is on the way to realizing his dream.
He need no longer be ashamed of his lameness
among a people who value valor and physical
strength. The construction proceeds feverishly
but carefully, and, when next the Romans arrive,
the Boars easily repel the attack. When Taran
shows his true colors and turns traitor by

shouting out in Latin instructions to the
attackers by which they may defeat the Boars
while pretending that he is cursing them,
Domnall gets the proper drift, and Clodha,
herself a brave warrior, kills him. Coll decides
to capitalize on Taran's treachery to entrap the
Romans, and another exciting attack scene
ensues. The power of the attackers is broken,
and at the end Niall and Clodha are about to
marry and succeed to tribal leadership. Coll and
Fand look forward to a good life together, and
he anticipates helping other settlements construct strongholds for their defense. A strong
theme--that physical and ideological survival
may depend upon innovation and coopera-
tion--excellent characterizations, a tightly
knit, action-filled plot, and a vigorous style
produce a dramatic and exciting book. The
several struggles--between Boars and Romans,
between Nectan and Domnall, between Taran and
Coll and Niall, and that within Coll himself,
among others--result in steady tension. Even the
less important characters stand out, like young
Ibar, the boy who leads the white bull that
carries Fand to the sacrifice, flattered to help
Coll save Fand, and the women characters have
unusual dimension. The reader sees more than one
side even with the negative characters of Domnall and Taran, who never lapse into typical
story-book villainy. Like Coll's personal
problem and the tribal problem, probable
history and story mesh perfectly, and the reader
is left remembering vivid scenes of the times
that would naturally be shown to make the story
work--conversations at night in Nectan's Dun,
the battle with the boar, the Council meetings,
the preparations for sacrifice--and gets a good
sense of the way the people live and their
customs and traditions--the recreations, the
forehead Boar marks, making spears at peat
fires, ritual cursing before fighting, and the
acceptance of women as leaders and fighters, to
specify a few. Coll's recurring daydreams of
the terrible attack in which he was crippled
give dimension and urgency to his hopes for a
stronghold, and his lameness provides additional
impetus for his aspiration. He cannot hunt and
fight like the other men, but he can use his
head and prove his worth to the tribe that way.

He grows in self-esteem and develops the ability to command. Though he changes less than does the tribe and Domnall, he learns that innovation comes hard and that custom and tradition are not to be taken lightly. They must be respected and, if properly exploited, can be the means of needed change. This is a rich and memorable novel, a story of unusual depth and power. Carnegie Com.; Choice; Fanfare.

STUART, MORNA (1905-   ), born in India; author, teacher and scriptwriter. A member of the fifth and last generation of a family whose first member arrived in India with the British army at the end of the 1700s, she attended St. Michael's School, Oxford, and received her M.A. degree from St. Anne's College, Oxford. After tutoring in English, history, and mathematics for seven years, she became an educational scriptwriter for the BBC and the Nigerian BC from 1937-1962. During World War II, she served as a Civil Defense Warden and as an incident officer's clerk for the Belgravia Relief Control Team (1943) and the Flying Squad (1944). She married M. R. Nicholas and has made her home in Essex. She contributed poems and book reviews to such periodicals as *Cornhill Magazine*, *Observer*, and *Church Guardian*. Her novel *Marassa and Midnight** (Heinemann, 1966; McGraw, 1967), about black twin slave boys who become involved in the Haitian movement for independence, was commended for the Carnegie Award. She also wrote *Traitor's Gate: A Historical Play in Three Acts* (Collins, 1939), about Sir Thomas More; and her poem, "Michael Angelo's Confession of Faith," was set to music for baritone solo, chorus, and orchestra (Novello, 1935). Other publications include *Children of Aries* (Blackwell, 1925), *Night-rider* (Barker, 1934), and *Till She Stoop* (Barker, 1935).

STUMPS (*The Twelve and the Genii**), one of the twelve toy Napoleonic soldiers that Max discovers in his attic and that once belonged to the Bronte children. Stumps, once Frederic Guelph, Duke of York, has a history that is "long, complicated and shrouded in mystery." He makes his way back to the attic from the kitchen, where Max feeds the soldiers, by climbing up the creeper attached to the Morley house. This gives the soldiers their idea for how to escape and also the mode of entry to the nursery at Haworth.

THE SUMMER AFTER THE FUNERAL (Gardam*, Jane, Hamilton, 1973; Macmillan, 1973), realistic novel set in modern England and detailing the emotional disarray in a family in the first months after the clergyman father dies. Although the point of view skips sometimes to Sebastian, 17, or Beams (Phoebe), 12, it is mostly concentrated on their sister, Althene Price, 16, a beautiful, intelligent, accomplished girl whom grown-ups (except a few mothers of other girls) have always considered the ideal daughter. She is a favorite at school, shows great self-possession and poise, and has spent her holidays in attending her old father (who was seventy when she was born), reading with him and taking long walks over the moors deep in conversation. The book starts with his funeral where the reader gets a glimpse of the silent rebellion they all feel against their self-centered and domineering mother, known as Dodo. Since the family has to vacate the rectory in six weeks after his death, she has refused to have any of her children help her and has imposed the girls on friends and acquaintances and agreed that Sebastian shall go to a retreat at a Buddist monastery in Scotland suggested by one of the masters at his school. Beams, who is an ugly, near-sighted, ill-mannered girl, but highly intelligent, has been sent to stay with the family of a school mate whom she dislikes, the Padshaws, a hearty sailing family who find her disagreeable and begin to shun her. Through her own writing we learn that she was thought retarded by all but her father until she was nine, when the psychiatrist to whom she was taken found she liked music and tricked her into reading the labels. It also is apparent that she is hurt and vulnerable, and devoted to Athene. Sebastian, it turns out, is really at the Society of Saint Matthew, an Anglican Community for Men, with his friend Lucien. He is worried, he tells Father Ignatius, about sin, specifically about whether it is a sin to be glad that his father, whom he detested, is dead. He despises the way women, especially older, unattractive women, doted on his father and how he responded to their adoration. The main focus, however, is on Athene, who is being juggled around among various unwilling friends of her mother. She goes first to Auntie Posie Dixon, a plump, wealthy, rather simple-minded woman who spends her summers at Crag Foot, an expensive hydropathic hotel in York. On the surface polite, considerate, and contented, Athene is in inner turmoil, full of sexual yearnings and sure that she is somehow Emily Bronte. At Crag Foot, quite by accident, she sees a boy she thinks is Heathcliff, but he disappears. From there she goes on to stay with Sybil Bowles, a teacher who is living at a seaside community with her fellow teacher and constant friend, Primrose Clarke. Miss Clarke, deep in gin, is far from welcoming, and Athene flees with her suitcases in the rain, finally ending at the cottage of an artist, Basil, who takes her in, feeds her, draws her, and, when she gets a bit hysterical, puts her to bed. Afraid of the sexual interest she sees in him, she abandons her luggage and leaves in the early morning via a rope ladder that her mother has sent with her to be delivered to her sister Boo, a matron at the school Sebastian attends. Wondering frantically whether she could have been raped in her sleep, Athene makes her way to her Aunt Boo's school, which is empty except for a youngish man named Henry Bell who is grading exam papers. Aunt Boo is at a Red Cross conference and her apartment is locked, but Henry, at first at a loss what to do with her, suggests she might sleep in one of the dormitories. She spends several peaceful days with him, helping him with the papers and only half understanding his growing attraction to her. When he insists that they celebrate her birthday by an expedition to Haworth, she is delighted, and as they are looking at Emily's room, just after he has confessed that he loves her, a friend of Auntie Posie barges up, asks Henry about his wife, and recognizes Athene. The romantic illusion shattered, they bicker on the way home, but make up just before they arrive at the school, and it seems they will spend the night in each other's arms until they find that

Aunt Boo has returned. All this time, letters from Mrs. Price detail her manipulations to control the movements of all her family, to impose shamelessly on her friends, and to find a new situation for herself. At her direction, they all gather at the station near the rectory, the Padshaws thankfully getting rid of Beams; Sybil and Primrose grimly delivering Athene's luggage along with the resort hotel waitress to carry it; Posie, who has brought her chauffeur to drive the whole family to stay in her home temporarily; Sebastian and, briefly, Lucien; and Aunt Boo, who has been driving Athene back but has somehow mislaid her. They find Athene clinging to the flagpole on the church tower, locked from the inside, that faces the rectory. They think she is going to jump and hold a blanket like a net to catch her as she swings back and forth and looks with amazement at them dancing below. When she realizes they all care about her, she comes down and breaks into weeping for the first time. The book ends with one of Mrs. Dixon's letters to Posie, telling about how all three children flatly refused her marvelous idea that she stay on at the rectory as housekeeper for the new vicar and insisted that she take the offered job as a residence hall directer at Manchester University. Athene has given up her boarding school, enrolled in the local high school, and lives with her mother. Athene is quite changed, speaking her mind and saying that Manchester is going to make them all less fancy. The story, which is essentially that of Athene's journey from romanticism to reality, deftly skips from one manifestation of sex to another--Athene's near encounters, the implied lesbian relationship between Sybil and Primrose, Sebastian's righteous disgust at the women swooning over his old father--all masked by more acceptable behavior. Mrs. Dixon is shown through her letters to be a pretentious and obnoxious woman, and the one false note seems to be that Athene, however changed she might be, would choose to live with her. The characterization, even of minor figures, is sharp. Boston Globe Honor; Choice.

THE SUMMER BIRDS (Farmer*, Penelope, ill. James

J. Spanfeller, Chatto, 1962; Harcourt, 1962),
fantasy of magic set in a village in England
about the time the book was published. The two
Makepeace sisters, standoffish, responsible
Charlotte*, 12, and active, gregarious Emma, 10,
live with their Grandfather Elijah, whose latest
interest is astrology, and his lazy, unconcerned
housekeeper, Miss Gozzling, in big, old Aviary
Hall. Charlotte feels excluded by the children
at school, who call her "prig" because she
dislikes dissension, keeps to the rules, and
always tries to smooth things over. On the way
to school one morning, she and Emma meet a
strange, bird-like boy with a freckled face,
chestnut red eyes, and a remote, wild manner.
Invisible to the other school children, the boy
first teaches Charlotte to fly, then the next
day Emma, and later little Maggot Hobbin, who is
parentless and living with a great-uncle who
pays no attention to her. Over the next two
weeks, the boy teaches the other children to fly
one by one, but refuses to teach their teacher,
Miss Hallibutt, because he says she is too old.
After school lets out for the summer, wet
weather sets in for two weeks, but on the first
clear, moonlit night, the boy gathers the
children for a midnight gala (it is Emma's idea
to have food). Strife breaks out between the boy
and bossy Totty Feather over control of the
group. Charlotte suggests an old-fashioned
tournament to decide the issue. The children
choose sides, a battle ensues, and the conflict
culminates in a single-combat struggle between
the two boys. The bird boy wins, and the rest of
the summer is filled with glorious days of
flying adventures. When only one day of vacation
remains, the boy leads the children back to the
shore of the lake where they first enjoyed the
excitement of flight together. He commands them
to fly away with him to a special place he
knows, saying he is the last of an almost
extinct species of birds. If he can find
children to return to his island with him, his
bird-lord, the fiery Phoenix, will allow his
kind to continue. The children, including Emma,
would like to leave as they see life with him as
a welcome release from parental and school
restraints, but Charlotte stoutly speaks out.
She convinces the children that going with the

boy would be wrong and would cause much harm and sorrow. Finally, only lonely, unhappy Maggot accompanies the boy. In spite of their joyful summer together, the children return to their separate interests and again refer to Charlotte as a "prig," leaving her feeling as isolated as before. A skillful blend of reality and fantasy, the story moves slowly, almost tediously at times, but presents a good psychological study of the way children behave toward one another in a group. The language is vivid and sensory and the atmosphere appropriately dreamy, but the bird imagery is so extensive that the conclusion seems overforeshadowed. The characters are flat or indistinct, except for Charlotte, who grows and changes as the story moves on. As she flies and experiments with her new ability, she becomes more sure of herself, and her new forcefulness and assertiveness win through at the critical moment. Emma is also convincing as the rebellious younger sister, but the bird boy is too obvious and too enigmatic, and any reader even a little familiar with old stories can predict what he is and what will eventually happen. The climax scene in which Charlotte confronts both the bird-boy and the children reveals with accuracy and makes universal the personal existential dilemma of a child like Charlotte: no matter what she does she will look bad in the eyes of those with whom she would most like to look good, her peers. Carnegie Com.; Choice; Fanfare.

THE SUMMER PEOPLE (Townsend*, John Rowe, ill. Robert Micklewright, Oxford, 1972; Lippincott, 1972), realistic novel of family life, friend-ship, and romance, covering about three and a half weeks' time in August of 1939. Three families, the Foxes, the Pillings, and the Martins, all long-time friends, customarily holiday together at Linley Bottom, a sleepy fishing village on the English coast. Rodney Fox, 18, follows closely events on the con-tinent, certain that war is imminent and that call-up lies ahead for him. Paula* Martin, also eighteen, acerbic and somewhat man-hating, spends most of her time helping her mother and caring for her little sister, prattling Alison. Philip* Martin and pretty, lively Sylvia Pilling share the same birthdate, are almost seventeen, and are regarded as a matched pair by the families. The two secretly pursue separate summer romances, each with someone their families would regard as unsuitable. At Sylvia's suggestion, they pretend to spend their time together. Sylvia keeps company with sturdy, good-looking Harold Ericson, a fisherman's son, and Philip meets clandestinely with Ann* Tarrant, the daughter of the local hotel receptionist, who is frail because she is recovering from pleurisy. Sylvia and Harold meet variously, but Philip and Ann "play house" sedately and chastely in an empty bungalow situated on the tip of the cliff overlooking the sea. They openly play games with each other, sometimes speaking and behaving formally, at other times being childishly silly and frivolous. First Brenda Fox, 15, who is sweet on Phil, and then Rodney and Paula see through the scheme. Angry because she thinks Philip is treated with favoritism because he is a boy and has simply been evading his share of domestic responsibility, Paula informs on Phil and Sylvia. Then Sylvia learns that Harold has joined the Navy and intends to spend his last few days before call-up with a male friend, and the two quarrel. Realizing that Britain will soon be embroiled in the war against Hitler, Mr. Martin decides that the family must return to the city so that he can get his clothing manufacturing firm ready for the war effort. Philip attends Harold's farewell party and tipsily makes his way across the cliff to the bungalow where he spends a last night, again chastely, in bed with Ann. Though they reiterate their love for each other, both know that nothing will come of it. With morning a portion of the cottage slips symbolically into the sea, and the youths go their separate ways. Philip tells the story in first person and present tense, a mode that keeps the narrative from lapsing into nostalgia or becoming saccharine and recreates with remarkable clarity the more innocent era of class consciousness and sexual propriety just before World War II. Prefacing and following the account are italicized letters from Philip thirty years hence to his son, Stephen, and Ann's daughter, Carolyn, who coincidentally are planning to marry. In the letters we learn that Philip and Sylvia eventually marry and that Ann emigrates to Australia. The author treats the romances with respect and delicacy and intersperses headlines and comments about the war judiciously to produce the sense of a pleasant last interlude, to point up both holiday larks and youthful pretensions and spats, and at the same time to foreshadow the inevitable domestic storm. Parents and even the spoiler Paula are drawn with sympathy and understanding, and the seaside setting of crumbling shore and collapsing cottages is well integrated with the plot. Fanfare.

SUN HORSE, MOON HORSE (Sutcliff*, Rosemary, ill. Shirley Felts, Bodley, 1977; Dutton, 1978), historical novel set in the first century B.C., concerned with the making of the White Horse of Uffington on the Berkshire Downs. Lubrin Dhu is the third son of Tigernann, the Chieftain of the Iceni, a tribe of horse breeders. He is younger by two years than the twins, Brach and Corfil, and different from them in temperament, being quieter and more thoughtful, and in appearance, having some of the look of the Old People, the smaller, darker race the Iceni have displaced and sometimes interbred with. When Lubrin is five years old, his sister, Teleri, is born, a cause of great rejoicing in the matriarchial society where chieftainship goes to whoever marries the Woman of the Clan. At the feast celebrating her birth, Lubrin, already trying to capture things he sees and feels in pictures, is drawing the music of the harper with charcoal on the hearth stone when Corfil deliberately walks across his lines to scuff them out. In fury, Lubrin attacks him and is soon being pummelled by both twins, when suddenly Dara, son of Drochmail, comes to his aid. They are separated like squabbling puppies, but from that day on Lubrin and Dara are closest friends, going together to the boys' house when they are nine, serving and learning there for seven years, and passing through the manhood ceremonies together. In the first autumn of his manhood, Lubrin's mother dies, and, according to the custom the priest, Ishtoreth of the Oak, having taken the

sacred drink and dreamed, announces who shall
marry Teleri to become Lord of the Woman of the
Clan and therefore the next chieftain: Dara, son
of Drochmail. This puts some distance between
the friends, but for two years it matters little
since Teleri cannot be married before she is
fourteen. At the wedding feast, news comes that
the Attribates, the sun-worshipping people to
the south, are approaching with a war host. As
the men with their chariots prepare, Lubrin
protests when Tigernann orders him to stay
behind, until his father tells him quietly that
one son of the chief must stay and that he
cannot trust either of the twins for this hard
job, in case the Iceni are overcome by the much
more numerous Attribates. In the ensuing battle,
the Attribates demolish the Iceni warriors and,
despite fierce defense capture the dun, rounding
up the few survivors as slaves. Cradoc, the war
lord and now the chieftain, chooses Lubrin to be
the spokesman for the Iceni, knowing he is the
chieftain's son and not realizing that it is
Dara, husband to the Woman of the Clan, who is
the rightful leader. Dara, who has been badly
wounded but survives, backs Lubrin up, and
through the long, hard winter they work as
slaves, with most of the wounded, the old, and
the very young dying from the hardship. One day
Cradoc sees Lubrin drawing, and later, bored
with his harper's songs, sends for him to draw
horses to amuse him, threatening to kill other
Iceni if he refuses. It is Cradoc who has the
idea of carving a huge horse into the chalk
mountainside to mark the frontier of the
Attribates. Lubrin bargains with him, agreeing
to find a way to do it if, when it is done and
he finds it good, Cradoc will allow the remnants
of the Iceni to leave with enough stallions and
brood mares to raise a herd in a new place.
Lubrin climbs a tree that was his refuge as a
boy, picks the Dragon's Hill as the site, and
imagines the lines that the horse must take.
Cradoc allows him the services of the Iceni he
needs to stake out the lines with oxhides and
birch stems, and they work long and hard, but
Lubrin is not satisfied. Finally, back in his
tree, he realizes two things: the horse must not
be stationary but must be a running horse,
moving with the line of the hills, and there

must be an appropriate sacrifice to give life to the god-horse he is making, and that sacrifice must be his own life. He redesigns the horse. His people, aware of his intentions, follow his directions though they avoid stepping in his shadow or touching him, and when it is finished, Cradoc is satisfied, but more importantly, Lubrin himself knows it is right. He watches his people leave, less than 200 of all the Iceni remaining. Dara, the only one who dares touch Lubrin, embraces him. The next day Lubrin walks proudly to the place of sacrifice on the horse's head, knowing that though it may be the sun horse of the Attribates, it is also the moon horse of the Iceni, and that while his death may insure the success of the Attribates' horse runs, it will also be a sacrifice to Epona the horse goddess for the survival of the Iceni. The brief novel is moving and told with poetic simplicity. It follows what is known from archeology and mythology about the Iceni, and it also gives a convincing feeling of the life and beliefs of a world more than 2,000 years ago. Fanfare.

SUSAN BAILEY (*Moses Beech**), farmer's daughter who becomes friend and lover of runaway Peter* Simpson, the boy staying with reclusive Moses* Beech. Susan is extremely far-sighted and must wear thick glasses, but otherwise she is a very good-looking blonde. Her father, who always wanted a boy, is determined that she shall marry a farmer, someone who can carry on the farm, and so is insisting that she go to agricultural college where she will meet the right sort of young man. Susan is interested in Commercial Design and rather likes the idea of living in town. Peter is really the first boy she has ever been attracted to, just as she is his first love, and she does as much as he does to further their relationship. When she mistakenly thinks she is pregnant and her father calls the police to return Peter to his parents, Susan clear-sightedly realizes that their romance is at an end, even though Peter keeps hoping that they may someday get together again.

SUSAN OLDKNOW (*The Chimneys of Green Knowe**), blind daughter of a sea captain, who has been treated like an invalid, almost like a prisoner, until her father, Captain* Oldknow, brings little black Jacob* to be her companion. Very bright and perceptive, Susan knows more about what goes on in the house than its seeing occupants, since many of them treat her as if she were retarded and talk freely in front of her. With Jacob's help she learns to feed herself, to climb trees fearlessly, to run about the garden, and to know the world around her. When she grows up she marries Jonathan* Morley, who has been her tutor.

SUSAN PEVENSIE (*The Lion, the Witch and the Wardrobe**; *The Horse and His Boy**; *Prince Caspian**), practical, cautious, elder sister of the four Pevensie children, which include Peter*, Edmund*, and Lucy*. She is a peacemaker and keeps their well-being and safety in mind. As a queen in Narnia*, like the other children she becomes regal and speaks nobly. In *The Lion, the Witch and the Wardrobe*, along with Lucy she witnesses Aslan's* humiliation and death and is present the morning of his resurrection. In *The Horse and His Boy*, she is the sweet-tempered, beautiful Queen of Narnia over whom Rabadash of Calormen goes to war. Susan can fight, run, and ride as hard as any boy and is an excellent archer, yet she is also very feminine. In *Prince Caspian*, she assists her siblings in restoring Prince Caspian to his throne. At the end of the series, in *The Last Battle**, she does not take a place as one of the Seven Kings and Queens of Narnia. The reader learns from conversations among the other children that Susan "is no longer a friend of Narnia," and even refuses to believe in the reality of their adventures there. Jill* scornfully remarks that Susan is interested only in "nylons and lipstick and invitations. She always was a jolly sight too keen on being grown-up."

SUSAN POOLEY (*The Devil on the Road**), wife of Derek, who owns the barn in which John* Webster shelters and where he becomes caretaker. Susan is warm, middle-aged, friendly, and sensible. She is not from Suffolk originally, and she is particularly interested in the small animals of

the area, so she and John share a curiosity
about what his cat, News, brings him from her
hunting. She is clearly not a part of what John
comes to think of as the plot to keep him at the
barn, and she gets more and more worried at her
husband's involvement. When her husband finally
explains to her what is going on, she leaves him
and tries to warn John to go while he still can.
Later she returns, but the worry has aged her
and affected her appearance.

SUSAN WALKER (*Pigeon Post**; *Swallows and Amazons**; *We Didn't Mean to Go to Sea**), next to
eldest of the four Walker children who are the
main characters in a series of twelve holiday
adventure novels. A domestic, maternal type,
Susan is in charge of most of the cooking and
clean-up in all the stories and is so
responsible that the mothers consider that all
is well as long as she is part of the group.
Overburdened with conscience, she is pictured
rather unsympathetically in *We Didn't Mean to
Go to Sea*, when she gets nearly hysterical at
the idea that they are breaking their promise
not to leave the harbor and almost insists on
various courses that would certainly bring
disaster. With perhaps unconscious psychology,
she is shown to be terribly seasick until it is
clear that they cannot take any other course and
then recovers and steers well for a large
portion of the night. Her characterization seems
more dated than others in the series and may
annoy modern readers.

SUTCLIFF, ROSEMARY (1920-   ), born in West
Clanden, Surrey; one of the best historical
novelists of the twentieth century. Her early
life is told in moving detail in her autobiographical *Blue Remembered Hills: A Recollection*
(Bodley, 1983). When she was three, rheumatic
fever left her crippled, and she has triumphed
over physical handicaps and an overprotective
mother to lead a full life and become a prolific
author, producing more than thirty novels and at
least a dozen retellings of the stories of such
heroic figures as Cuchulain, Finn MacCool,
Beowulf, and Robin Hood, as well as her three-
volume retelling of the Arthurian legends in *The
Sword and the Circle: King Arthur and the*

Knights of the Round Table (Bodley, 1981; Dutton, 1981), *The Light Beyond the Forest: The Quest for the Holy Grail* (Bodley, 1979; Dutton, 1980), and *The Road to Camlann** (Bodley, 1981; Dutton, 1982). Also from the Arthurian legends is *Tristan and Iseult** (Bodley, 1971; Dutton, 1971), told in a fictionalized version, as is her novel for adults, *Sword at Sunset* (Hodder, 1969; Coward, 1970), the story of King Arthur as he might have been historically, a Roman-British leader against invading Saxons. She has also drawn partly on legend, partly on history in her *Song for a Dark Queen** (Pelham, 1978; Crowell, 1979), which tells the story of Boadicea, Iceni queen who led a revolt against the Romans. Her earliest novels, like *Brother Dusty-Feet** (Oxford, 1952), while accurate in history, have little character development, but with the publication of her Roman trilogy, *The Eagle of the Ninth** (Oxford, 1954; Walck, 1961), *The Silver Branch** (Oxford, 1957; Walck, 1959), and *The Lantern Bearers** (Oxford, 1959; Walck, 1959), she became recognized as a major historical novelist. With only a few exceptions, her fictional works all are set in the British Isles and cover periods from the prehistory of *Warrior Scarlet** (Oxford, 1958; Walck, 1958), set about 900 B.C., and *Sun Horse, Moon Horse** (Bodley, 1977; Dutton, 1978), in the first century B.C., up through the English Civil War. Like the Roman trilogy, *The Mark of the Horse Lord** (Oxford, 1965; Walck, 1965), which won the first Children's Literature Association Phoenix Award, is set during the Roman occupation, but concerns conflicts in the tribes of what is now Scotland. *Dawn Wind** (Oxford, 1961; Walck, 1962) starts with the last battle in which Roman-British forces fought the Saxons and tells of a boy who becomes a slave in a Saxon household. *Knight's Fee** (Oxford, 1960; Walck, 1960) and *The Shield Ring** (Oxford, 1956; Walck, 1962) both occur shortly after the Norman invasion, and *The Witch's Brat** (Oxford, 1970; Walck, 1970), a lesser but still interesting work, is set during the medieval period. *Blood Feud** (Oxford, 1977; Dutton, 1977), though it starts in Britain, follows the Vikings to Constantinople. In *Frontier Wolf* (Oxford, 1980; Dutton, 1981), she returns to the end of the Roman period in Britain. Her novels have been praised for having passion, insight, and depth, and for giving the feeling of the period with telling details and suitable language. Among her themes are the triumph of the maimed or handicapped hero and the continuity of history and of peoples. Among her many awards, besides the Phoenix, are the *Boston Globe-Horn Book*, the Other, and the Carnegie Medal. Ten of her novels have been commended or highly commended by the Carnegie award committee, five have been named to the *Horn Book* Fanfare lists, one is on the Lewis Carroll Shelf, and one is listed as a Junior High Contemporary Classic. Although her major recognition has been for her writing, Sutcliff is also a skilled painter of miniatures, having been educated in the Bideford School of Art in Devon and being a member of the Royal Society of Miniature Painters.

SVEN (*Fathom Five**), Norwegian sailor who has been rescued from the Loften Islands where he has been in a slave labor camp, and now is the hand on Dick Burley's tug boat, the *Hendon*. He seems much more interested in Chas* McGill's story of the spy than does Dick, and later gives Cem* Jones the key to his boat, so both boys trust him completely. After escaping from the Maltese, Chas* goes to Sven with his whole story and almost rows with him to the boat, but the engineer comes along and the two men leave in a hurry. Later, Chas realizes that Sven, who proves to be the real spy, was planning to drown him that night. When Chas thinks Dick must be the spy, he goes to Sven, who takes him to the *Hendon* and then does nearly drown him. Later, when Chas has a chance to finger Sven and realizes that Sven knows it, he resists, partly because he knows Sven will be in a detention camp for the remainder of the war anyway, partly because he thinks of the nice pregnant girl, with whom Sven was living, and partly because he is more disgusted with the snobbish local politicians and police than he is angry at Sven.

SWALLOWS AND AMAZONS (Ransome*, Arthur, ill. Helene Carter, Cape, 1930; Lippincott, 1931), holiday adventure novel set in 1929 in the Lake District of England. Having waited two weeks

for an answer from their father to their excited
letters, the four young Walkers, teenagers John*
and Susan*, Titty*, ten or eleven, and Roger*,
7, are delighted by his telegram: BETTER DROWNED
THAN DUFFERS IF NOT DUFFERS WON'T DROWN, which
gives them permission to sail the *Swallow*, a
dinghy that goes with Holly Howe, lakeside farm
where they are summering, and to camp on the
island they have seen from the nearby hill,
which they call the Peak of Darien. Their mother
makes them tents--canvas held by ropes tied to
trees and weighted down by pockets filled with
rocks--and bags filled with hay for mattresses,
helps them collect supplies, of which the tea
kettle is most often mentioned, and makes
arrangements for them to row to a nearby farm
for milk and other fresh food each morning. At
the island they find signs of previous campers
but take over for themselves, discover a secret
harbor for their boat, and are well settled
before their mother is rowed out to check on
them. Their adventures begin when another sailboat, the *Amazon*, runs up a skull-and-crossbones
flag as it passes the island. They follow it to
the northern end of the lake, past the village
they call Rio. The next day the pirates, who
turn out to be the Blackett sisters--Nancy*
(really Ruth), older than John, and Peggy*,
about John's age--come secretly to the island,
seize the camp while the Walkers are out, and
then call for a parley. They propose that they
make a treaty of offense and defense, joining
together against the natives (particularly their
Uncle Jim Turner, whom they call Captain* Flint
and who lives on a houseboat in a nearby bay)
and that they have a war between the Swallows
and the Amazons, to be won by whoever can
capture the other ship. Since, as they have
learned from the farm woman, they have been
wrongly accused of meddling with the houseboat,
the Swallows are happy to form an alliance
against Captain Flint, who is writing a book
about his travels and has been ignoring his
nieces. John works out a plan to capture the
Amazon by lurking at the north end of the lake
near the Blackett boathouse until dusk, when
the Blackett girls will think they must have
sailed back, then seizing the boat and sailing
home in the dark. This requires Titty staying at

their camp, now named Wildcat Island, to light a
beacon lantern and to put up two leading lights
in the secret harbor so they can get home in the
dark. The Amazons, however, have foreseen some
such trick and have lured the Swallows up the
river where they live, meanwhile hiding the
Amazon in the reeds, and have then sailed to
Wildcat Island to hide out until the Swallows
are back, planning to seize the *Swallow* in the
night. Titty sees the Amazons in the camp,
realizes the situation, and boards and rows the
Amazon away in the dark. John discovers that he
can't sail among the islands at the northern end
of the lake in the dark, so he, Susan, and Roger
spend the night in the *Swallow*, while Titty
anchors near a small island and sleeps in the
Amazon. She is startled to hear a boat nearby
and to overhear two men hiding something on
the island. The next morning the Amazons admit
defeat and plan the joint attack on the
houseboat. In the meantime the houseboat has
been robbed, and they are suspects, but, after
the Amazons explain to their uncle that the
Swallows are good sorts, they storm the
houseboat, make Captain Flint walk the plank,
and then share a fine feast he has prepared.
Titty insists she has heard the robbers in the
night and with Roger goes to the little island
where she was anchored and discovers Captain
Flint's sea chest which contains his typewriter
and the movie-script he has been writing all
summer. Gratefully, he gives her his parrot, and
they all plan to meet for further adventures
next summer. Modern readers may bridle at the
tone, with children and adults all pretending in
such a jolly fashion, and at the way the girls
are expected to do all the cooking and clean-up,
and even older readers may find it curious that
a mother of five (there is a two-year-old
sister, Nicky) has to get permission from an
absentee husband in the navy in foreign parts
before allowing the youngsters to sail or to
camp. Only Titty and, to some extent, Roger, are
developed as rounded individuals. Still, the
story is full of genuinely child-like touches,
and the night sailing episode has considerable
excitement. This is the first of a series of
twelve and is credited with turning realistic
fiction in Britain to new, more believable

stories. ChLA Touchstones; Choice.

A SWARM IN MAY (Mayne*, William, ill. C. Walter
Hodges, Oxford, 1955; Bobbs, 1957), subtly
humorous, realistic novel of school life
covering one week in May perhaps in the 1950s.
John Owen, called Owen, a Cathedral Singing Boy
of about twelve, returns to the Canterbury Choir
School in Kent from his native Wales after
holidays to discover to his chagrin that he is
the new Beekeeper, the former one having
developed mumps. Although the Cathedral has kept
no bees for four hundred years, the traditional
position carries some ceremonial importance. It
falls automatically to the youngest boy, who
performs certain duties on the Sunday after
Ascension Day. He must sing an introit and speak
set Latin passages in response to the bishop, in
return for which he receives five shillings.
Since he dreads singing a solo and doesn't want
to make the effort to learn the Latin, Owen
defers to the next youngest boy, Iddlingley, who
is not too keen on the job either, and thus
brings upon himself the scorn of Mr. Ardent, the
shrewd, observant, and sometimes acid-tongued
Head Master, who maintains that the boys should
shoulder whatever responsibility comes their way
without complaint; of Mr. Sutton, called Brass
Button from the scientific equivalent of his
initials, the elderly and no-nonsense Latin
Master; and now and then of the boys, among
them, Iddlingley, of course, the more scholarly
Madington, the often put-upon Dubnet, and Head
Chorister Trevithic, a quick, clever, capable,
adventurous youth from Cornwall, who simply
expects his schoolmates to take hold and do
things. Much of the novel is taken up with
descriptions of such daily activities as meals,
lessons, recreation, and singing practice. It
shows the horseplay among the boys and the
banter and verbal sparring both among them and
between them and the adults in vivid detail that
conveys a good sense of what life is like for
the boys when the holiday is not yet quite over
and school not yet begun in earnest. It also
helps to establish Owen's character as a
likeable, intelligent, sometimes forgetful,
lazy, and willful youth and makes believable
what eventually transpires. While on a trip to

the tower storage room to get Owen's Welsh dictionary from his trunk, Owen and Trevithic hear the music of the Beekeeper's Introit in a certain area even though they feel sure that it is not then being played by Dr. Sunderland, the portly, congenial Choir Master, who puffs a lot when he speaks, whom the boys often make fun of behind his back and affectionately call Tweedledum, and whom Trevithic teases gently to his face. Later, inspired by an old legend that there is a Beekeeper lost in the Cathedral, shut in by mistake, when, during the reign of Henry VIII, Prior Tollelege refused to keep bees any longer and sealed up the bee room, the boys and Dubnet investigate and discover a small room at the head of a spiral staircase in which lie remains of the old Prior's beehives. Owen also finds a key connected to a chain and on the chain a round, white ball that exudes a strangely pleasant odor when warm. Invited to Dr. Sunderland's house to see his "family" of bees, some of which are swarming, Owen is struck by how much a good swarm costs (ten pounds) and keeps a small swarm from leaving the Choir Master's place, first, by singing to them, and, then, by allowing them to cling to the little white ball, which has an unusual attraction for them. Now interested in bees, Owen helps Dr. Sunderland make candles for the coming ceremony, and then gets the idea of re-enacting the ancient ritual in which the Beekeeper brings the bishop a swarm. He enlists the aid of Trevithic and Dr. Sunderland in gathering the old wax and making a candle and of Madington and Mr. Sutton in learning the Latin. He practices the Introit and singing alone in the Cathedral to build up his confidence. When Ascension Sunday comes, the ceremony goes beautifully, the bees swarming eagerly around the little, white globe. Owen receives the promised five shillings in pay, the bees are taken to the little room, the legend gains new life, and Owen's pride in self and reputation with fellows and masters is restored. Some details are left open: why have the boys heard the Introit in that area, and what is the little ball made of? The strength of this slowly starting story lies in its strongly pictorial style, which is rich with color and makes it easy to visualize situations, and in the interpersonal relationships and authentic-sounding conversation. Biblical and classical allusions add texture and support the setting and characters, and Owen's change in attitude toward his unwanted position seems well motivated. Sequels. Fanfare.

SWIFT, JONATHAN (1667-1745), born in Dublin, Ireland, of English parents; clergyman, political satirist, author of the literary masterpiece *Gulliver's Travels** (Motte, 1726), originally titled *Travels into Several Remote Nations of the World, by Lemuel Gulliver.* Originally intended as a scathing adult satire on human foibles in general and English ways and politics in particular, the novel appealed also to child readers, who especially enjoyed the portions about the diminutive Lilliputians. The book has been widely translated and gone to many editions, and, as reissued in condensed versions, it appears on the Children's Classics list of important books for young readers. After graduating from Trinity College, Dublin, Swift became secretary to the distinguished statesman, Sir William Temple, until 1699. He was ordained in the Church of England in 1694 and held pastorates in Ireland, visiting England and gaining influential friends there during that time. He became highly involved in the religious and political life of the times and wrote a vast number of articles, tracts, and books in defense of the Tories and against the Whigs. A very effective political apologist, he did a great deal to mold public opinion of his day. Queen Anne made him Dean of St. Patrick's Cathedral in Dublin in 1713, a post he held for the rest of his life. While Dean, he wrote *Gulliver Travels* and became a champion of the Irish people. An ambitious man, he never attained the heights he coveted in the church, and he died embittered, ill in body and mind. He left his estate for founding a mental hospital and is buried in St. Patrick's. The next most famous product of his prolific pen is "A Modest Proposal," a caustic, tongue-in-cheek essay in which he suggests that Irish babies would be better off killed and eaten than grow up and live in poverty under English rule. Among his many other writings for adults are *A Tale of a*

Tub (Nutt, 1704), a satire about three brothers who battle over their father's estate, and *The Battle of the Books* (Nutt, 1704), in which library books wage war on one another as scholars often do.

SWINDELLS, ROBERT E(DWARD) (1939-   ), born in Bradford, England; teacher and writer. He served in the Royal Air Force from 1957 to 1960 and worked as a copyholder, advertising clerk, engineer, and printer before receiving a teacher's certificate from Huddersfield Polytechnic in 1972. Before becoming a full-time writer in 1980, he taught elementary school for several years in Bradford. Among his books for young adults are *When Darkness Comes* (Hodder, 1972), *A Candle in the Night* (David, 1974), and *World-Eater* (Hodder, 1981). Among his books for younger children are *Voyage to Valhalla* (Hodder, 1976), *The Ice-Palace* (Hamilton, 1977), *The Very Special Baby* (Prentice, 1977), *Dragons Live Forever* (Prentice, 1978), *The Weather-Clerk* (Hodder, 1979), and *A Ghost Ship to Ganymede* (Wheaton, 1980). His novel *Brother in the Land** (Oxford, 1984; Holiday, 1985), a grim postnuclear holocaust story, was named to the Highly Commended list by the Carnegie Award committee and won the Other Award. He has also edited *The Wheaton Book of Science Fiction Stories* (Wheaton, 1982) and translated four books by Gunilla Bergstrom, which star a character called Alfie Atkins.

SYBILLA BUN (*The River at Green Knowe**), friend and companion of Dr.* Maud Biggin who stays with her at Green Knowe and cooks for her and the three children. A little, round woman who wears many strings of beads, she is mainly interested in food and her greatest happiness is seeing it eaten. Although Ping* is the most polite of the children and always insists that they must get back in time for meals, Oskar* Stanislawsky is Sybilla's favorite because he eats the most.

T

TABITHA PALMER (*The Haunting**), Barney's older sister, a brown, round child who always has something to say and who considers everybody's business her own. She is an aspiring writer and jots down in her notebook whatever she thinks might provide material for her projected masterpiece novel. Her bossiness and curiosity are a trial to the family, and her stepmother, Claire, gently tries to rein her in. She is bouncy and lively, and she sincerely cares about her family. She is the first one to discover that something special is going on with Barney, and she takes it upon herself to help him. She exemplifies the theme of acceptance.

TAHLEVI (*The Moon in the Cloud**), fat, philosophical tomb robber, whom Reuben meets in prison and who befriends Reuben. He suggests that Reuben play his flute to entertain the prisoners and take their minds off their wretchedness. Thus Tahlevi is instrumental in getting Reuben out of prison. Reuben's musical ability brings him to the attention of the King*. This eventually also leads to Tahlevi's own release from confinement. On the day he is to be executed, things so fall out that Reuben returns the favor by helping Tahlevi to get away safely. They hide for a while among the pyramids with Tahlevi's friends. Tahlevi declines Reuben's offer to take him back to Israel, convinced that the flood will only be local and will not destroy Kemi. Since Tahlevi is an "artist" at picking pockets and stealing, the reader has little doubt that Tahlevi will return to his former occupation after Reuben departs for Israel.

THE TALES OF OLGA DA POLGA (Bond*, Michael, ill. Hans Helweg, Penguin, 1971; Macmillan, 1973), episodic, talking animal fantasy set in an English suburban home in the late 1900s. Olga da Polga, a pretty, proud, romantic guinea pig with "devil-may-care" rosettes in her brown and white fur and a "gleam in her eye, which set her apart" from others of her kind, is certain that adventures lie in store for her. After she is bought by Karen Sawdust and her family, Olga experiences even more excitement than she had hoped for. The Sawdusts provide a tidy, roomy cage for her in their grassy back yard, and Karen paints Olga's name over the door after Olga writes the appropriate letters in the dust of the floor. The excitement begins when Olga gives a sharp nip in the tail to the family's black cat, Noel, sending him scurrying into a tall pine tree from which he must be rescued by the Fire Brigade. She later spins a tale for Noel to explain why guinea pigs lack tails: their Peruvian ancestors sacrificed theirs to provide a rope for a prince to use in saving his beloved from the tall tower in which she has been imprisoned. Olga also makes friends with Graham the turtle and Frangio, an Argentine hedgehog. On an "off day," she explores Frangio's thicket, his "Elysian Fields," where briars tangle up her fur, and she gets caught in the rain. She wins a prize at the local pet show, not for being the best or prettiest guinea pig there, but for being clearly the fattest one. In a whimsical mood, she starts a rumor that the sun has changed places with the moon, later ironically to frighten herself by believing her own foolish story. She suffers a fall and is nursed back to health inside Karen's house, where she is treated in the royal fashion to which she believes she is entitled and where she is entertained by television, on which she sees a dancing sugar-plum fairy that she emulates to show she has recovered. Her several months of lighthearted adventures conclude at Christmas time, when Father Christmas brings her

a new bowl with her name on it. These uncomplicated, humorous, fast-moving episodes about a
pampered, conceited household pet offer
innocuous amusement for early readers. Some
humor derives from slapstick and some from
stituation, while some depends on wordplay or
misunderstanding, and some seems directed at
adults. The animals converse with one another
but not with humans, though they can understand
the humans' speech. The style is more polished
than in most books for this age group, and the
tone is warm and affectionate. Some situations
seem strained for effect and occasionally the
attitude seems precious. The black-and-white
line drawings recall Ernest H. Shepard's and
support the impression that the book reflects
the work of A. A. Milne*. Sequels. Choice.

TALKING IN WHISPERS (Watson*, James, Gollanz,
1983; Knopf, 1984), chilling, realistic novel of
the oppression and inhumanities perpetrated by
the military regime that seized the government
from Allende in Chile in 1973. After nearly ten
years of ruthless control by the forces of the
president, General Zuckerman, elections are to
be held. The book starts at the rally for Miguel
Alberti, the Silver Lion, the opposition
candidate who promises a return to democratic
principles. On the way home, the car of Juan
Larreta and his musical group, Los Obstinados,
who have performed at the rally, is shot at and
forced off the road by soldiers of the CNI, the
dreaded secret police. The guitarist, Horatio
Rivera, is killed, and Juan is taken into
custody, but Juan's son, Andres*, 16, is thrown
clear and escapes in the dark. He is picked up
by Beto* and Isa*, twin performers of a
traveling puppet show, Marionetas de los
Gemelos, who manage to get their old van through
the brutal crackdown shooting and tanks to the
remains of a half-ruined mill which is their
home. They learn that Alberti has been
assassinated and the government has blamed the
communists. Andres makes his way across Santiago
with great risk and difficulty to his home,
where he finds troops sacking the house and
burning all the family's belongings in a street
bonfire. He tries then to find Horatio's family
and to alert the other members of Los Obstinados

that Juan was taken alive, although the papers
have reported that both he and Andres died in
the "accident." Some of the homes are abandoned
and gutted; at others he finds people afraid to
speak to him, but one suggests, in a whisper,
that Juan may have been taken to the National
Stadium. Outside the stadium gate, he stands at
the edge of a crowd watching the arrival of
truckloads of prisoners being brutally treated.
Among them he spots Braulio Altuna of Los
Obstinados, a man who stands out because he is
very tall. Heedless of the danger, Andres fights
his way through the crowd toward Braulio and is
aided by an American cameraman, who captures on
film the scene of Braulio being clubbed by a
soldier's rifle butt. Then, as an officer spots
the American, he shoves the camera into Andres's
hands and shouts that his name is Don Chailey,
just before he is beaten to the ground. Andres
takes the camera back to the mill, and the twins
help him get it to Diego Rosales, a printer who
has been crippled by the CNI and whose shop was
wrecked, but who has maintained a secret dark
room. There they discover that the film has even
more incriminating evidence on it: a clear
record of the Junta officer shooting Alberti.
Since Diego has dismantled his press and stored
pieces of it with various friends, the three
young people agree to try to get the parts
together so that he can print the evidence.
Their elaborate plan is to have each of the
friends, contacted separately, bring his
portions of the press to the Central Station in
Santiago and leave them in storage lockers,
dropping the keys along with small change into
Isa's helmet as she puts on a street puppet show
near the entrance. Andres, dressed as a porter,
will then collect them and take them to Beto's
waiting van. With many complications and near
misses they drive off but then realize they are
being followed. As they get to a wooded area
they speed up, then slam on the brakes, and drag
the bags of press parts out, and Beto and Isa
pull out again to lead their followers away,
leaving Andres to hide the bags, then find his
way to a seminary where he can get shelter. On
the way he witnesses the mass execution of
prisoners, including Don Chailey, by a small
pond, and at the seminary, where he is taken in

by Father Mariano, he sees the priest smuggle in a wounded man during the night and then fetch a doctor. Later as soldiers raid the seminary and beat up Mariano, Andres escapes over a wall, only to be captured outside. He is taken to the dread House of Laughter, the secret headquarters of the CNI, where he is questioned and tortured. When his captors are distracted by more important matters, he is dumped into a ditch in the countryside. In the meantime, Isa has contacted an American newsman who is making inquiries about Chailey and has given him copies of the pictures. A poor farmer and his little daughter, at great risk to themselves, take Andres into their van to the San Miguel market, for the sake of his father who was an idol to the oppressed poor. There he sees the twins performing their marionette show and, though scarcely able to walk, he stumbles with the help of the little girl into their van. An epilogue tells of the opening of the Two Hemispheres Cup soccer match, at which, among the crowds, two young people distribute copies of photographs that have simultaneously appeared in American newspapers, photographs incriminating the ruling Junta in the death of Alberti and related atrocities. Unrelenting details of beatings, torture, and brutal murders make this an uncomfortable book to read, although the end is probably more hopeful than the political situation in Chile warrants. There is no effort to disguise the partisan point of view or the outrage that the author feels. Characters are not highly developed, but the action is fast-paced and, if the reality of the situation did not demand that it be taken seriously, the novel might be read as an exciting adventure story. Carnegie Highly Com.; Other.

TAPKESOS (*Black Samson**), Nandi woman who marries Magere* in order to learn his secret vulnerability. A beauty far beyond the best of the Joluo women, she is said to have refused all other men, wanting only Magere, the leader of her people's enemies. Shunned by the jealous Joluo women, she plays the part of a happy and devoted wife, continually urging Magere to retell the stories of his triumphs until he bores his friends. As soon as she has learned the secret that he can be harmed by an attack on his shadow, she returns to her people where she is honored as a hero.

TARAN (*The Stronghold**), arrogant, clever, cruel, power-hungry youth of about twenty-one who becomes Domnall's* ally in attempting to cement an alliance between the Boar people and the neighboring hostile tribes of Raven and Deer. He arrives one day alone in a small boat. He says he was formerly of the Boar people, and was captured and enslaved by the Romans when he was eight. He says he killed his Gallic master and escaped to come home. It comes out that his story is a pack of lies and that he is determined to use Domnall to gain power over all the tribes purely to satisfy his own ambition. Coll and his friends, Clodha*, Fand*, and Niall*, and his brother, Bran*, know what Taran has in mind because Bran has been observing Taran's movements and overheard conversations between the youth and Domnall. Taran is superstitious and sets great store by the carnelian stone that Clodha smashes. When it is decided that the gods wish Coll to live in order to complete his stronghold, Taran reacts with anger, reveals his lust for power, and is cursed by Domnall with a spell on his sword hand. When he realizes that Coll's stronghold will successfully repel the Romans, he treacherously attempts to help the Romans defeat the Boar people and is slain by Clodha. He is a complex, ambivalent villain, one for whom the reader feels both dislike and sympathy.

THE TEAM (Peyton*, K. M., ill. author, Oxford, 1975; Crowell, 1976), horse novel set in a village in East Anglia in the modern period, a sequel to *Fly-by-Night*. Ruth* Hollis, now fourteen, continues her intense interest in horses and determination to succeed as a rider despite her family's lack of interest and money for the sport. Having outgrown Fly-by-Night, her first pony, she attends an auction and spots a horse she is sure is Toadhill Flax, the difficult pony Peter* McNair trained and loved, and which his father heartlessly sold. Though the horse has been underfed and badly treated, Ruth impulsively borrows money from her brother Ted and buys

Toad. It seems at first that she has bought
nothing but trouble. Her conscience bothers her
when she sells Fly to an insensitive man for
his daughter, who is a bad rider. Toad eats more
than the smaller pony, and Ruth, with no help
from her family, has constant financial worries.
Peter still covets Toad, and when Ruth refuses
Mr.* McNair's generous offer to rebuy him, the
comfortable friendship with Peter seems doomed.
Worst of all, Ruth is almost unable to manage
Toad. Nonetheless, she perseveres with some good
advice and moral support from Thea Parker, 16,
an experienced rider new in the neighborhood.
Ruth is both scared and thrilled to be chosen
for the Pony Club team by the D.C. (district
commissioner), wealthy, imperious Mrs.* Meredith, along with Thea and Peter and Jonathan*
Meredith, the D.C.'s reluctant son. As the
youngest and least experienced rider, Ruth
suffers qualms at her first meet with Toad, but
does so well that, to her consternation, she
must have a jump-off with Peter. Against his
father's orders, he is riding a wild, almost
uncontrollable pony called Sirius, which bolts
and throws Peter at the triple-bar jump. Peter
suffers a concussion, but before he passes out
he begs Ruth to keep his father from shooting
Sirius. Ruth takes the horse to her house and
manages to persuade Mr. McNair that to destroy
Sirius might affect Peter's recovery, and he
agrees to put the horse out to pasture
temporarily. At the next meet, when Ruth is
suddenly ill and Peter's mount is injured, Mrs.
Meredith has him ride Toad, and Ruth is crushed,
but she puts up a brave front. The culmination
of the year for the team is the Area Trials.
Ruth has known for some time that Peter has been
skipping school and secretly riding Sirius, but
even she is surprised when she discovers that
Peter and Jonathan have substituted Sirius for
the more tractable mount in the horse box. Mrs.
Meredith is furious but is so competitive that
she goes along with the plan rather than
withdraw the team. Ted waylays Mr. McNair until
Peter can start off. His careful training of
Sirius pays off when he takes individual winner
honors. Ruth, expecting to be low man and
therefore not counted, finds she is very
important when Jonathan goes down, and she has

an excellent round. The team wins, Jonathan has a broken collar bone but nothing worse, and Mrs. Meredith comes up with a good buyer for Fly-by-Night, who is up for sale again. Descriptions of the jumps and the meets are vivid and compelling, but the book's strength is in its characterization, particularly of intense, self-conscious Ruth, stubborn Peter, autocratic Mrs. Meredith, and wry, sardonic Jonathan. Ruth appears again in the Pennington series and some of the characters reappear in *Prove Yourself a Hero** and *A Midsummer Night's Death**. Fanfare.

TEDDY BELL (*No End to Yesterday*), Marjory's irrepresible cousin, who is a few months younger than she is and her most constant companion in the family. Son of Auntie Flora and Uncle Bertie, Teddy lives a few doors away from Gran's house, close enough to share in most of the mischief for which Marjory is punished. Frequently, Auntie Flora, who loves to dress up and show off her new clothes, takes both children with her as an excuse to get away and meet friends, presumably men with whom she is flirting. On one memorable occasion, the black monkey at the zoo deliberately urinates on her new outfit, an accident Teddy foresees and keeps Marjory from warning her against. Like Marjory, he hates Gran, and he comes up with various diabolical schemes to murder her, the most nearly accomplished being to loosen the screws on the rod that holds the stair carpet, figuring that it will slip and catapult her down the steep, third-floor stairs. Before this happens, however, he sees Grandad, whom they both love, has second thoughts, and retightens the screws, to Marjory's mixed relief and disappointment.

TERENCE MUGG (*Which Witch?**), the abused orphan befriended by Belladonna, who turns out to be the long-awaited replacement for the wizard Arriman Canker. A foundling baby, he was taken to the Sunnydene Children's Home in the most dismal part of Todcaster, where the Matron christened him. She dislikes him intensely, because he is sickly and plain and she can't make him whimper or beg. Belladonna rescues him and cures his pet earthworm, Rover, which Matron has injured, thus earning Terence's devotion. At Darkington Hall, Terence soon blossoms, his mud-colored eyes brightening and his limp hair taking on new life. His eyeglasses perch on the end of his nose at a jaunty angle. He proves smart and resourceful. When the reader is told that his eyes never actually fill with tears, the reader suspects he is the wizard predicted by the fortune teller, because never weeping is also one of Arriman's characteristics.

TERESA GISELLI (*Sisters and Brothers**), adopted cousin who comes to live with the Clare family in North Cornwall. Having been in a concentration camp, where her French Jewish mother died, during her early childhood, and then separated from the servant girl, Germaine, who cared for her, and sent to an orphanage, she was spotted by the Clares' flighty Aunt Sylvia, who enjoyed having a pretty child to show off but provided no genuine emotional support. She is eventually taken in by the family of her adopted father's brother, but the girl feels that she does not fit, like a poppy in a corn field. Insecure though apparently competent and mature, she thinks she may prove herself by managing when the teenagers are left on their own. She steals food from the store to eke out the household money which the others have wasted. In the end she is accepted by the others and, from John Meneot, learns something of her brave Italian father, who was killed in the French Resistance movement, and that she has a grandmother still living.

TERRAPIN (*Bilgewater**), Tom Terrapin, student at St. Wilfrid's who, for reasons unknown to Bilgewater, stays at school during holidays and so has seen more of the girl whose father is his housemaster than have most of the boys. As a young boy he is odd looking, with a gargoyle face and unkempt, very pale, straight hair, and is he described by Bilgie as an albino ape, but as he grows older she sees him as looking Arthurian. When, by sheer coincidence, she comes to half-ruined Marston Hall, at night, cold, wet, and badly frightened, and finds that he lives there alone except for a huge, crafty, crude housekeeper, he gets her dry clothes and

hot soup and for the first time tells her
something of his background. His mother was of a
high-class family but was tubercular and wild;
his father was a pierrot, an entertainer in the
tent theaters of the beaches, whom he scarcely
knew but admired extravagantly; his grandmother,
who had lived at the hall until her death a year
before, had found him unattractive and shipped
him off to boarding school. He is described by
Bilgie's father as perhaps the most gifted
student of classics he has ever had, and by
himself as unstable. It is clear that he is in
love with Bilgie, though she has never suspected
it, and is deeply hurt by her rejection and her
insistence that she return to the Roses' home.
It is rather hard to believe that he elopes with
Grace Gathering. In the epilogue set years
later, we discover that Grace has long since
departed and that he has turned Marston Hall
into an experimental theater.

TERRY CHAUNTESINGER (*The Lark on the Wing**),
young singer whom Kit* Haverard first meets at
her Kitson cousins' home at Gramercie. Terry has
had to defy his father by switching from the
study of architecture to music and changing from
the Anglican church to Quakerism, and in his
rebellion he is something of a role model to
Kit. Red-haired and emotional, he is frequently
upset by Kit's failure to stand up for her
rights against her cousin, Laura* Haverard, and
by her friendship with Felix Hardcastle, a
reaction that Kit fails to understand as
jealousy. Terry is a student of Papa* Andreas.

TESHOO LAMA (*Kim**), devout holy man from Tibet,
to whom Kim* O'Hara attaches himself as *chela* or
disciple. An elderly Oriental with an ivory
yellow face, he dresses in many folds of dingy
stuff like horse blanketing and carries only a
wooden rosary, an openwork iron pen-case, and a
begging bowl, but he is a man of financial
resources, formerly Abbot of Such-zen, and when
he decides to pay for Kim's schooling, he can
command the funds without question. Ostensibly a
Buddhist, he is really without interest in creed
or cast but calls himself a follower of the
Middle Way, seeking the River of the Arrow,
which, when the Lord Buddha tested the bow that

none might bend, gushed forth where the arrow touched earth and which washes away all sin. A man of great simplicity, gentle and untainted by baser emotions, he struggles against his love for Kim, fearing it is worldly desire, but rationalizes that the boy is sent to aid him in his search for Enlightenment. He is a portrait of a genuinely good man.

TESS BAGTHORPE (*Ordinary Jack**), Jack's elder sister, 13, the only one of the immediate family who encourages him not to think of himself as a failure because he has no particular accomplishment of which he can boast. She says he may be a late bloomer, like Einstein. Except for Uncle* Parker, she is the only character supportive of Jack, and even she does not help much, being too occupied with her own concerns. She wishes to learn Danish and is very pleased when Mrs. Bagthorpe hires a Danish maid. Like all the Bagthorpes except Jack, she has "several strings to her bow," that is, several areas in which she is proficient.

THEODORE TEWKER (*Tulku**), son of the missionary at the Settlement of the Congregation of Christ Jesus in China, which was destroyed by rebel Boxers in 1900. Theo joins Mrs.* Daisy Jones, an eccentric Englsh botanist, and her guide, Lung, a young Chinese poet, and they finally make their way to the Tibetan monastery of Dong* Pe, where Mrs. Jones's unborn child by Lung is believed to be the new incarnation of the Tulku. Theo is torn between his fundamentalist Christian background, which condemns the rough language and easy morals of Mrs. Jones, and his growing fondness and admiration for her. While he resists the "heathen" Buddhist teachings he must translate, he comes gradually to see their power and to understand something of the life of the monastery.

THEO GREENGRASS (*The Peppermint Pig**), brother of Poll*, about eighteen months older than she but smaller and more delicate. He has big, innocent blue eyes and is thought to be subject to chest infections, so that Aunt* Sarah knits him pink undervests and he suffers agonies when he must wear them. Theo is clever and imaginative, and he twists things in his tortuous mind in ways that baffle and confuse straightforward Poll. Noah Bugg's blackmail is, in a way, partly Theo's fault, and he himself sees that it has become a sort of game to them both. Even after he has grown bigger than she, Poll feels protective toward him, and in a moment of insight she sees that Theo will always be lonely and that she'll always have to look after him, no matter how angry she may get with him.

THE THIRD EYE (Hunter*, Mollie, Hamilton, 1979; Harper, 1979), realistic novel of family and village life with mystery and girl's growing-up story aspects set in Ballinford, West Lothian, Scotland. On February 14, 1935, Jinty (Janet Beatrice) Morrison, 14, sits in the office of the Procurator Fiscal with her Mam*, Jean, and two neighbors, Archie* Meikle, the gnome-like, swarthy blacksmith, and Lord Garvald, son of the Earl of Ballinford, waiting to give evidence in the earl's recent death of a fall from a local landmark, Temple Rock. As she waits to be called, Jinty thinks back over the last three years and recalls events that led up to the earl's apparent accident. Three main problems occupy her mind: the matter of the Ballinford doom, whereby no eldest son ever succeeds to the title; the mystery of the parentage of her eldest sister, Meg*; and the increasingly strained relationship between Mam and Meg and also her second sister, Linda*. She recalls how she overheard a heated conversation between the "bad old Earl" and the vicar in the churchyard during which she had the sense of some strange power within the man and realized that she herself is fey and can see and sense things others cannot. She also recalls how she learned soon after from Archie of the Ballinford doom and noted how protective the earl was of his only son and heir. She recalls how Meg asked permission of Mam to attend the annual kirn, or harvest dance, at Ballinford barn and was refused but ran off anyway, only to return shortly with the horrible news that a Paddy (Irish worker) woman was dying for lack of medical help while giving birth to a baby on the ground floor as the dancing proceeded directly above. She recalls how horrified she, Jinty, felt that the earl should ignore the woman's plight. When all three girls are punished by being confined to the village for Meg's action, they go for walks in the woods, where they encounter Toby, the blind son of the earl's factor. When Toby dies, Jinty sees a different earl, a man sincerely moved by the grief of another man's loss of a son. She learns at the same time from her father how after World War I the earl gave him a job when he couldn't find one anywhere else. Still another facet of the earl's personality appears, showing him as a man with a deep respect for tradition, when he arranges for an anvil marriage, a wedding in the smithy conducted by Archie with all the village attending, between Miss Carson, the village teacher, and Tom Meikle, Archie's son. At the same time, tension between Mam and the older girls grows, as Mam puts more pressure on them to achieve in school so that they can get out of the village, go to the university, and make something of themselves. Meg, however, has fallen in love with Dave Ferguson, son of the earl's chauffeur and a budding mechanic. A terrible scene ensues after church one Sunday, when Dave asks permission to marry Meg and Mam belittles him. The two older girls apply themselves to their schoolwork, as Mam wishes, but shut her quite effectively out of their thoughts and personal lives away from the house. The winter Jinty is thirteen, Mam gets her a job as weekend kitchen maid at Ballinford Hall, where she earns the approval of all the supervisory personnel and the earl for her industry and discretion. Meg and Linda pass their Higher exams, making Mam proud but then announce to her that they do not intend to go on to the university. Linda, making use of Jinty's good relationship with the earl, has gotten a letter of reference from the earl for a manager trainee job in his hotel chain, and Meg still wishes to marry Dave Ferguson. In an angry scene, Meg announces she's going to have Dave's baby and has been married to Dave in an anvil marriage, and Linda, in support of her sister and to hurt Mam, announces that she has proof that Meg was born out of wedlock. Mam kicks Linda out, and, when Mam refuses to honor the anvil marriage, Meg walks out. Tension continues

in the Morrison house for many months, and Jinty
is lonely without her sisters. The climax occurs
at Lord Garvald's twenty-first birthday party, a
swank affair for all the village held on the
ice-covered lake, with skating, dancing, curl-
ing, and feasting. Needing to be alone, Jinty
goes into the woods, where the earl soon joins
her, somewhat inebriated and needing to talk.
He rambles on about having to break the doom to
secure Garvald's future. He sees that this can
be done in only one way—by committing suicide
and making his death seem an accident. The earl
makes Jinty promise never to tell anyone what
they have talked about. The frame story ends
with Jinty responding appropriately to the
Fiscal's inquiries, and the earl's death is
ruled accidental, to the relief of the entire
village. Another problem concludes with the
earl's death, too. In the waiting room, Mam has
time to sort things out, and on the way home she
relents and visits Meg. At the end, Jinty
realizes that the earl has for years dominated
the village and will do so for years to come,
but she is quietly comfortable with the way
things have turned out. She realizes that she
herself is more an observer than a doer, but is
at peace with the outcome of her third-eye
revelations. This is essentially the story of
two contrasting yet similar parents, possessive,
overprotective, and self-sacrificing, the one a
village woman of little financial means but
great courage and endurance, the other the
wealthy, self-indulgent earl, who regards
himself and is regarded by the villagers almost
as a feudal lord. These two are bound together
by family circumstances and by their great love
and ambition for their children. Jinty grows up
credibly and is a warm and convincing protagonist, sometimes an astute and at other times a
bewildered onlooker, an occasional affector of
the action, candid in her reactions. Tom
Meikle, Archie's Viking-blond, well-read son,
forebearing Dave Ferguson, Mrs. Torrie, the
gap-toothed village woman who imagines she's
pretty and loves to trip the light fantastic
with the earl at his parties for the village,
blind Toby, for whom Jinty paints pictures with
words—even less important characters are drawn
with a life-giving pen. The third-person

narration is tightly focused from Jinty's point of view, almost like first-person, producing a strongly intimate tone. The book is a good story, offering plenty of conflict and human interest. It also projects a rich picture of village life, with such cherished old customs as the village funeral, the harvest kirn, the shoot, Prize Day at school, the anvil wedding, and the harvest with the hare hunt and the corn dolly. It is an era in transition, however, with the advent of mechanical technology that will soon render such traditional methods as smithying obsolete. Fanfare.

THOMAS (Burton*, Hester, ill. Victor G. Ambrus, Oxford, 1969; *BEYOND THE WEIR BRIDGE*, Crowell, 1970), rich, substantial historical novel set in southeastern England from 1651 to 1667, the turbulent times following the defeat of Charles II Stuart at the Battle of Worcester, and focusing on the persecution of the Quakers and the great plague that decimated London. The loose plot revolves around three youths, playfellows of seven when the novel begins: brash, competitive Richard Holder, whose Roundhead officer father died of a fever during the Cromwellian war; timid, scholarly Thomas Egerton, whose father is a dispossessed Royalist officer; and spirited Richenda Bemmerton, whose real father, also a Roundhead, was killed in battle and who serves as the catalyst in their relationship. Since their parents have long been friends, the three children develop great affection for one another. When Richard's cold, selfish mother abandons him to the care of a servant while she goes off to London and he develops smallpox, Mrs. Bemmerton takes Richenda and drives over immediately by coach to make sure everything possible is being done for him. After they return to their estate at Benfield, Sir James Egerton, a burly man of action who despises his son for his gentle ways, gives in to Thomas's requests to learn Latin and asks Mr. Bemmerton to prepare him for grammar school. For some months thereafter, Richenda and Thomas are happy schoolfellows, the clever Thomas progressing at a rapid pace and much ahead of Richenda, who is proud of his ability. Times become hard for Richard, whose mother marries again, this time a dismal Presbyterian widower called Philip Drew, who discovers the boy is unschooled, calls him a dolt, and packs him off to Wittendon Free Grammar School, where he makes uninspired progress in Latin and continues the close friendship with Thomas, now a schoolmate. Richard has a lively curiosity and soon draws unfavorable attention to himself by often posing questions which in those days were considered unanswerable, such as where birds go in the winter. During the school years, Richard spends holidays with the Bemmertons. Thomas often rides over to join them, and good times (and sometimes quarrels, too) ensue, but always the children feel that they belong together. In their mid-teens, things begin to change. Sir James's finances become critical, and he is unable to send Thomas to Oxford. Richenda's parents decide to marry her to a youth from the north. Richard matriculates at Oxford, but, upset about Richenda and feeling his oats, he gets involved with demonstrations on behalf of the Free Parliament and the return of the king and is soon dismissed from Oxford and disinherited. Sorry and determined to mend his ways, he travels to London and apprentices himself to Dr. Boteler, a physician who admires the youth's questing mind. Richenda, who has fallen in love with Thomas, refuses to go through with the arranged marriage, and the Bemmertons return to Benfield. On the way back, their coach meets with an accident, and Mr. Bemmerton is injured. He is nursed to health by the historical Quaker leader, Margaret Fell, whom they admire so much they adopt her religion and soon convert Thomas. About two years later, Richard, who has prospered intellectually and emotionally under Dr. Boteler's skillful and demanding but fair instruction, decides to visit his friends. He discovers Thomas's home deserted and Thomas, who has had smallpox, living with the Bemmertons. Enraged at finding them all Quakers, a sect Londoners consider fanatical troublemakers, he returns bitterly to Dr. Boteler, who voices the current hostility toward the Quakers by insisting they are confusing whim with conscience and compromising the country's welfare by refusing to swear allegiance to the king. Political unrest mounts with the king's return. The

Royalists sate their thirst for revenge on
Roundheads, and sectarians like the Quakers come
under increasing suspicion. Along with some
4,000 other Quakers, the Bemmertons and Thomas
are arrested and imprisoned, and several years
of persecution follow for them. Eventually
Thomas returns after months in Newgate, pale and
gaunt but even more loving in attitude and more
steadfast in his conviction that the Quaker
sufferings will help make posterity free.
September of 1664 sees him and Richenda married
in the new little Quaker meeting house. They
work hard to restore the estate at Maplehampden, now his by inheritance, and to win
back the affection of the servants and retainers, who distrust Quakers. The year 1665 brings
plague to London and deaths by the thousands.
Richard and Dr. Boteler labor valiantly to
combat a disease only dimly understood. In
ministering to Quaker patients, Richard
develops respect and admiration for their
loving and caring ways during great adversity.
Thomas feels called by God to assist stricken
Quakers and leaves for London, soon to be
followed by Richenda, now pregnant. Thomas
catches the disease and dies, with Richard in
attendance, and Richenda gives birth to a son.
Richard returns to Maplehampden the following
May, where he woos Richenda "with an exquisite
patience--born of love" and with a new
gentleness and understanding born of the
suffering and sorrow he has experienced.
Richenda has changed, too; she is more ready to
accept life as it comes and appreciate what she
has. The following year, his apprenticeship
complete, Richard returns to marry Richenda,
help her run Maplehampden, and serve the people
of the area as their physician. The story is
romantic but never sentimental. Although the
plot pieces fall together predictably, the
narrative never fails to hold the interest. The
three main characters are roundly sketched and
change believably. While most other characters
exist to serve the plot and are hardly more than
names, some minor figures do have life: gentle
Isaac Bemmerton, stern Dr. Boteler, cruel Mr.
Drew, and the briefly seen Francis Norton,
Richenda's intended, who is just as frightened
about marrying her as she is him. Here and there

little family mysteries are inserted, and there is some humor. Details of everyday life and information about the social, economic, and political problems of the day are worked naturally into the tapestry of the story. Especially vivid without being sensational are the plague and persecution scenes. In fact, the book's outstanding feature is the author's skill at so convincingly blending the youths' personal lives with the times. Boston Globe Honor.

THOMAS FITZAMORY (*One Is One**), undisciplined boy whom Stephen* de Beauville takes on as a squire after he has been twice sent home in disgrace from the castle where he has been in training. After gradually improving in manner, Thomas attacks another squire and nearly beats him to death with a mallet. For some time he will give no explanation for his behavior, but it finally comes out that Thomas is defending Stephen's honor when the squire has repeated that he betrayed his knight who was afterwards hanged for treason. After Stephen explains the situation, Thomas becomes his strongest supporter. On their return from the Scottish campaign, Thomas dies of smallpox.

THOMAS HEYWOOD (*When Shakespeare Lived in Southwark**), actual Elizabethan actor who is guardian to Nat* Marlowe. At the death of the playwright Christopher Marlowe, Heywood and the head of his acting company discover that Marlowe has left an infant son, and when the mother dies, Heywood takes on the responsibility for the boy, though he realizes he is a poor person to be a guardian. At the end of the story, Heywood is in debtors' prison, playing cards with the other prisoners who can afford to be separated from the common herd, and there he gallantly receives Mistress Adams, who is searching for Miles.

THOMAS REEVES (*The Islanders**), about sixteen when the story begins, brother of Molly*, son of Dick and Hester, and soon-to-be brother-in-law of Adam* Goodall. A sensitive, fearful youth, he is somewhat looked down upon because he doesn't like the sea and fears heights, both necessary for survival on Halcyon* Island. He

eventually teaches himself to read from Charlie*
Herrick's books, and the reader learns in an
afterword that he journeys to the mainland and
becomes a professor. He appears in most of the
scenes as one of the "good guys."

THOMAS ROWLEY (*Red Shift**), only survivor of the
massacre at Barthomley church in the English
Civil War, allowed to live by his rival, Thomas
Venables, who is among the attackers, for the
sake of his wife, Madge or Margery. Subject to
fits or visions, he is considered odd and
simple-minded by his compatriots. When he first
finds the stone ax, buried some twelve centuries
before by Macey*, he recognizes it as a talisman
of power and wants to smash it and give each of
the men a piece, but Madge prevents him. In the
end he cements it into their house on Mow Cop.

THOMAS SMITH (*The Warden's Niece**), eldest of
the three boys who live next door to the Warden
and whose lessons Maria* Henniker-Hadden shares.
Thomas, at thirteen, feels quite superior to the
other youngsters and is inclined to act lofty,
though in the middle of an adventure he is as
much a child as the others. He is scheduled to
enter Rugby at the end of the summer, and he
frequently tries to lord it over Joshua* and
quell James* by referring to this school. At
first he is scornful of Maria, but he responds
to her admiration and eventually comes to
approve of her spirit.

THOMAS TORRE (*A Parcel of Patterns**), young
shepherd who loves Mall* Percival of Eyam during
the year of 1665-1666 when plague strikes the
village. Thomas first meets Mall when she is
a child of eight, when he seeks her help in
turning a lamb in its mother's womb, since it is
being born wrong and his hands are too big. He
give her the lamb and with that starts her small
flock and eventually a romance. After Eyam has
voluntarily quarantined itself, he repeatedly
tries to see Mall, and she stubbornly refuses to
meet him, for his own safety. Finally, she sends
word that she has died, hoping to discourage
him, only to have him come into Eyam to catch
the disease rather than live on without her.
They have a brief but extremely happy marriage

before he contracts the illness and dies.

THORIN OAKENSHIELD (*The Hobbit**), leader of the thirteen dwarfs who employ Bilbo* Baggins as a burglar to help them retrieve their home and treasure in the Lonely Mountain from Smaug*, the dragon that drove them out some three centuries earlier. Thorin is a very important dwarf, inclined to be slightly pompous, but he starts out sensibly offering Bilbo one fourteenth of whatever treasure they recover and funeral expenses, if necessary. As they approach the mountain, the lure of the treasure begins to get a hold on his mind, and by the time they have been captured by the elves in Mirkwood, he is so greedy and suspicious that he refuses to tell them what the dwarfs are doing there, and so they are held in the dungeons until Bilbo contrives their escape. Later, after Smaug has destroyed Laketown and the men seek some of the treasure to rebuild their town, Thorin is so stubborn that he holes up in the mountain and sends for his relatives from the Iron Hills, expecting to wage war against both men and elves. Because Bilbo gives the Arkenstone of Thrain to Bard, leader of the Laketown men, as a bargaining chip and because Thorin covets the Arkenstone above all else, he agrees to meet with the men and is therefore able to become an ally in the Battle of the Five Armies, in which he is killed.

THE THREE BROTHERS OF UR (Fyson*, J. G., ill. Victor G. Ambrus, Oxford, 1964; Coward, 1966), episodic historical novel, very strong in the sense of the times, set 4,000 years ago in ancient Ur on the Euphrates in the Land Between the Two Rivers, or Mesopotamia. At the center of the story are the three young sons of Teresh the Stern, a respected merchant and trader and a grim father: Shamashazir, 14, the eldest, whose greatest wish is to leave the mathematics academy, at which he is learning the skills necessary to run the family business, and join his cousin Serag, who directs caravans to the dangerous White Mountains; Naychor, 12, the jealous, troublemaking middle son, who appreciates good craftsmanship; and Haran, 10, good-hearted if impulsive, naughty, and disobedient, whose curiosity creates the book's main problems and brings them into contact with the story's other main character, Uz, a half-starved, abused, fearful slave who works as a donkey boy and has great skill at sculpting, pottery, and carving. Having played hookey from school, Haran decides to try to buy his way back into his teacher's good graces with a gift of gold and barters a blanket to Jerah the Camel Driver for a nugget. Uz, Jerah's son, is to deliver the nugget to Haran that night at Haran's house. While the exchange is being made, Naychor maliciously spies on Haran, "captures" Uz, and delivers him to Teresh as a thief. Loyal to Haran, Uz keeps mum, says he's the son of Illi Silli the Image Maker, whom he much admires, and, after a complicated series of events, is bought by Illi Silli to work as a pottery boy. Uz is delighted with the arrangements. No longer is he beaten and starved, and he is doing what he has longed to do, work with images and pots. The next major plot complication develops out of Haran's wish to have his gold piece made into a lion's head. Although Teresh arranges for a leading craftsman in gold to fashion it, the boys want Uz to do the job and eventually maneuver things so that Uz carves the wooden lion upon which the craftsman overlays the gold. The resulting piece is so beautiful that Teresh agrees to include it among his wares on the next trading trip. The story's last major problem grows out of Haran's curiosity about how the Teraphim (the Teresh family's special household god) consumes the food the worshippers offer him. The image gets broken, and, while Teresh is away on a business trip, the boys, their sister Dinah, 11, and Uz contrive with the help of Illi Silli's beautiful and high-spirited wife, Mushinti, to smuggle Uz into the Teresh house, where he fashions a clay replica of the Teraphim. That night Dinah carefully carries it on her head, accompanied by the boys, to Illi Silli's shop, where it is fired. Later Naychor gets the new Teraphim home safely without their father knowing and also disposes of the broken original. Teresh is impressed by the good sense with which Shamashazir has acted as head of the family in his absence and assures him that the Teraphim has informed him that it is all right for Shamashazir to go on the next caravan trip, and Serag and Shamashazir depart. Haran soon confesses to his father about the Teraphim, and that produces another problem. Teresh worries that Shamashazir has left under an evil omen. The story ends abruptly at that point, and the author promises a sequel about the adventures of Shamashazir on the trip. Fyson relies heavily on summarized narrative, often seems more interested in getting across information about the period than in promoting the story, and she occasionally falls into an instructive or condescending tone ("At least we should call it a small bridge nowadays--a very small bridge indeed..."; "but it was a real prayer to God in spite of being whispered to an image"). The loose plot starts slowly and sometimes plods, but there is sufficient action and suspense to hold the interest, and scenes of family life are lively and warm. Humor lightens the didacticism, for example, when Naramea, the elderly magistrate who is a dinner guest when Naychor drags Uz in and denounces him as a thief to embarrass Haran, conducts the interrogation without patronage, as seriously and patiently as any court case; when spunky, spoiled little Sarah, 8, to whom Haran has entrusted his nugget, refuses to turn it over to Teresh because that would be breaking a sacred agreement; and especially when Haran in fear and trembling politely asks the Teraphim how he eats, attempts to feed him, and succeeds in pouring porridge and honey all over the statue and then in breaking it. The book's strengths lie in its clear if typed characterizations and vivid views of ancient life--scenes in school, home, market, quay, chapel, potter's shop, bakeshop, and traversing the crowded streets; customs of personal hygiene; dining with family and friends; slavery; religious practices and beliefs--a wealth of such information makes the book a rich and substantial picture of the period. The style is appropriately Biblical. The sequel is *The Journey of the Eldest Son**. Carnegie Com.

THREE LIVES FOR THE CZAR (Plowman*, Stephanie, Bodley, 1969; Houghton, 1970), historical novel

set mainly in Russia in the years from 1894 to
1914. Told in first person by Andrei* Hamilton,
who was born in 1894 and is a member of the
Russian nobility though of Scottish ancestry on
his father's side and French-Austrian descent on
the side of his mother, Avoye*, the story also
has many third-person scenes, quotations from
diaries, letters, and documents from the period
leading up to the fall of the Czar. The three
lives sacrificed are those of Andrei's father,
Alesha* (Alexander), who is killed by an assassin's bomb thrown at the Grand Duke Serge, uncle
of the Czar, whom he is accompanying, his
sister, Alix* (Alexandra), who dies at twelve
from wounds incurred when an assassin bombs the
home of "Uncle" Peter Stolypin, Chairman of the
Council of Ministers, where she is attending a
children's party, and Stolypin, shot down at a
theater performance, evidently with the complicity of the secret police. From the point of
view of wealthy, educated, prominent nobles who
visit the Imperial Family but are also
"foreign" and spend much time in France and
Austria, the major events of the two decades are
shown: the coronation of Czar Nicholas II, the
disastrous war with Japan, the misunderstood
march of the peasants led by Garpon which is met
by army gunfire at the Narva Gate in 1905, the
convening of the First Duma (or parliament) in
1906, the hope for Russia under the courageous
leadership of Stolypin, the gradual drift toward
fatal international policy, and the actual
declaration of war in 1914. Most of the events
are pictured as the result of personalities: the
Czar's ineffective, fatalistic attitudes, the
Czarina's combination of cold, Puritanical
upbringing as Queen Victoria's granddaughter and
her hysterical religious fervor, the hemophilia
that afflicts the young prince Alexei, the
malign influence of Rasputin, the Holy Man from
Siberia, the intriguing court officials, and the
amibitious generals. Andrei and Alix are among
the few children ever invited to play with the
royal princesses, whose austere life, deprived
of normal comforts and of contact with learning
and the outside world, is commented on frequently with shock and pity by the cosmopolitan Hamilton family. Olga, the eldest, pictured as an
intelligent, promising girl, is a great friend

of Alix, and Andrei is one of the few boys or young men with whom she has any contact. Andrei's father and his Uncle Raoul*, his mother's younger brother, who is with the French army and is often detailed on missions to Russia, try vainly to persuade the military that artillery and transportation will be decisive in future wars and to promote modernization of the army. Andrei's grandfather, Alain* Duc de Saint Servan-Reze, a French Duke, and a frequent visitor to Russia, sees the irony and futility in the views of the Czar and most of the officials and speaks out bluntly, but is not heeded. Andrei, an officer in the cavalry at the end, faces the prospect of war with no heroic hope. This is a dense and serious book, full of names, dates, places, and incidents from history, all told with a sense of foreboding in a style reminiscent of the great Russian novels. It is difficult to believe these are not personal records of a period the author lived through. Though long and demanding, the story is never boring. The reading skill required and the interest seem on an adult level, though the chief protagonist is a young person. For children able to read the novel, it offers a haunting picture of the life in the upper levels of society and power in Europe in the first part of the twentieth century. The sequel is *My Kingdom for a Grave)*. Fanfare.

THREE TIMES SEVEN (*Up the Pier**), the spell which brings Carrie* into the Pontifexes' dimension, where she and they are invisible to the rest of the world. It is activated by stepping seven times in succession on every third plank in the wooden flooring of the pier. Later, when they have reflected on how easily Carrie picked up the spell, the Pontifexes change the spell to Seven times Seven. Kitchener*, however, informs Carrie of the change so that she can continue to visit them.

THROUGH THE LOOKING-GLASS, AND WHAT ALICE FOUND THERE (Carroll*, Lewis, ill. Sir John Tenniel, Macmillan, 1871; Macmillan, 1871), episodic dream fantasy, often-quoted and frequently cited sequel to *Alice's Adventures in Wonderland**, in which the seven-and-a-half-year-old Victorian

child has further unsettling and sometimes
exciting adventures in Wonderland. Alice* sits
sleepily curled up in the great armchair before
the fire, musing on the antics of her small
black kitten and speculating on chess and the
Looking-Glass House in the mirror over the
mantel. She falls asleep and finds herself
behind the mirror in the untidy room, where
chess pieces lie scattered about. After rescuing
the Red King and Red* Queen pieces from the
ashes, she decides to investigate this intriguing new world. It takes her some time to
discover that the countryside is laid out like a
chessboard and that things work backwards. The
loose plot revolves around Alice's efforts to
become a Queen (she starts as a Pawn) and her
relations with the various, mostly unaccom-
modating and eccentric characters she meets,
many of which are drawn from nursery rhymes.
The Live Flowers she converses with in the
garden by the house are uncharacteristically
obstreperous for flowers, and in order to meet
the Red Queen, now grown person-sized, Alice
must walk away from her. After a strenuous race
with the Queen holding fast to her hand ("it
takes all the running *you* can do, to keep in the
same place...," says the Queen), Alice has a
brief train ride with some bossy and vociferous
animals and then finds herself sitting under a
tree conversing with a Gnat the size of a
chicken, a patience- and logic-straining, pun-
filled discussion about Looking-Glass Insects
like the Snap-dragon-fly and the Rocking-horse-
fly. As in the first book, Alice has problems
with identity; seldom do her encounters
alleviate her difficulties with who and what
she is, and these remain among her chief
problems. Wandering in a wood, she comes upon
two fat little men with arms entwined; they are
cantankerous and irascible Tweedledum* and
Tweedledee, mirror-image twins, who persist in
contradicting one another. They ignore her
requests for directions through the wood, engage
her in a breathtaking dance, and Tweedledee
recites "The Walrus and the Carpenter," one of
several parodies that adorn the book. They lead
her to the Red King and inform her that she's
only a part of his dream, and end up battling,
because Tweedledum says Tweedledee has spoiled

his new rattle. Their scuffle ends when an
ominous crow flies over, casting a dark cloud
over the wood and creating a wind of hurricane
force. Alice catches a shawl being blown by and
then encounters the White* Queen to whom it
belongs. Alice helps the unkempt, flustered
chess-piece-grown-large to tidy herself. Their
conversation, about how things happen backwards
and believing in impossibilities ("Why, sometimes I've believed as many as six impossible
things before breakfast," remarks the Queen)
amuse and perplex Alice. After a sudden gust of
wind blows the Queen across a little brook,
Alice watches her change into a woolly Sheep in
a shop, whose shelves seem empty when Alice
examines them and full when she doesn't. She
buys an egg which gradually enlarges into the
character of Humpty* Dumpty. In an episode that
plays on the proverb of pride going before a
fall, Alice and sharp-tongued, supercilious
Humpty discuss the meanings and usage of words
("When I make a word do a lot of work like
that," said Humpty Dumpty, "I always pay it
extra.") and un-birthdays, and he explains what
the words mean in the poem "Jabberwocky." Their
conversation terminates when crowds of soldiers
pour tumbling through the forest. They belong to
the White King, who also has two strange
messengers, Hatta and Haigha (the Mad* Hatter
and the March* Hare from the first book). Alice
then observes the Lion and the Unicorn fight for
the crown and becomes the object of intense
scrutiny as the Unicorn and Haigha discuss her
nature. After drums drive them out of town, she
meets a gentle, befuddled White* Knight, who
keeps falling off his horse, shows her various
impractical inventions, and ushers her to a
brook, across which Alice discovers that she has
a crown on her head and realizes she is now the
queen she yearned to be. The Red and White
Queens hold a party for her with about fifty
guests of animals, birds, and flowers, during
which events become so bizarre that Alice
declares she can't stand them any longer, seizes
the tablecloth with both hands, and sends
everything on it crashing to the floor. She
grabs the Red Queen, who has shrunk to little
doll-size, shakes her, and awakens to find she
is shaking the small black kitten. The book

concludes with Alice speculating about whose dream it all was, the Red King's or her own. Scenes are less defined than in the first book and slip and slide into one another like movie scenes, a technique that emphasizes the dreaminess of Alice's experiences and supports the theme of exploring the nature of dreaming. Other themes and meanings from the first book appear, too, including growing up, the nature of living, and identity. Sources of humor, like zany characters, logic, slapstick, parody, wordplay, and non sequiturs, to name a few, are much the same. All characters show distortion into caricature or extreme eccentricity, except Alice, who remains rational and provides unity. She is the only figure with whom the reader can identify, being the representation of conventional logic and order in a world that seems to be completely irrational. The white figures generally treat Alice better than do the red ones, but she is perplexed, offended, or bewildered by almost every one she meets, which may reflect the author's perception of how children view grownups. Of the several poems, the mock-heroic ballad "Jabberwocky" is one of the most famous nonsense verses in world literature and has contributed such words as "galumphing" and "chortle" to the English language. Many speeches are also famous (the Red Queen's "When you've once said a thing, that fixes it, and you must take the consequences"; the White Knight's "It's a plan of my own invention"; the Unicorn's "If you believe in me, I'll believe in you. Is that a bargain?"), and Humpty Dumpty's notion of celebrating un-birthdays has become commonplace. Although less original in concept and not as loved as *Alice's Adventures in Wonderland*, the book is an apt sequel and has garnered enough avid followers to be deemed a classic fantasy of English literature. Books Too Good; Children's Classics; ChLA Touchstones; Choice; Fanfare.

THUNDER AND LIGHTNINGS (Mark*, Jan, ill. Jim Russell, Kestrel, 1976; Crowell, 1979), realistic novel of family and neighborhood life set in the late twentieth century in a village in Norfolk, England, and involving a friendship between two schoolboys. When Andrew* Mitchell,

about twelve, and his amiable, rather messy
family, his mother, a former librarian, his
father, a computer specialist, and his baby
brother, Edward, move into Tiler's Cottage in
the countryside, Andrew is immediately struck by
the openness of fields and sky and by the
roaring of planes overhead that come from the
RAF airfield not far away. Somewhat of a loner
because his family moves frequently, Andrew soon
strikes up a friendship with another isolated
child, a schoolmate named Victor* Skelton, who
is fascinated with airplanes, particularly the
Lightning, a fighter of importance in World War
II, but who is thought by teachers and fellow
pupils to be slow and unable to learn. Andrew
discovers that Victor is very knowledgeable
about planes and enjoys sharing information
about them, which he does in an authoritative
tone and without his usual country accent. The
two boys play with the models with which he has
decorated his room, visit the RAF airfield to
watch the planes take off and land, among other
jaunts about the area, and begin, at Andrew's
suggestion, a project on planes for Victor to
hand in at the holiday's end. When Andrew
learns that the Lightning planes are to be
retired from service, he fears that Victor will
take the news badly, and clumsily but
considerately tries to soften the blow, only to
discover that Victor, used to hard knocks, feels
that the Lightnings are going out in glory and
sees beauty in their replacements, the
Spitfires. Offsetting the growing friendship
between the two youths are scenes of family
life. Andrew's home is warm and inviting;
conversations are free and prolific, with a kind
of organized untidiness that comes from
involvement the rule. At Victor's house, little
is said, Victor's mother cherishes an immaculate
house, and his father is distant and a television addict. The brutality that underlies
their coldness comes out when Victor's mother
clobbers him because Andrew has accidentally
dropped a freshly laundered sheet. The plot line
is simple, but Andrew's growing appreciation and
understanding of his new friend keep the story
interesting. The author's style is understated
and employs striking and robust imagery:
"Victor's father was...reading the paper with a

frown that went up and down his forehead like a
venetian blind." "The house was long and low,
lurking behind the bushes with its head down."
The day "already looked worn out, like five
o'clock in the evening at eight o'clock in the
morning." There is much humor, particularly in
the dialogue, where wordplay and punning occur
frequently, and the sense of place comes through
strongly, as does Victor's isolation. Andrew's
concern for Victor is very convincing and makes
him seem real and likeable. Carnegie Winner.

THUNDER IN THE SKY (Peyton*, K. M., ill. Victor
Ambrus, Oxford, 1966; World, 1967), historical
novel of the sailing barges that carried coal
and munitions from England to France during
World War I. In 1914, both Sam Goodchild, 15,
and his brother, Gil, 17, get new skippers for
the barges where they work as mates when their
old skippers enlist in the army, as their older
brother, Manny, 24, also a barge skipper,
already has done. Gil gets a man named Harry
Finch, who soon proves to be a drinker, as his
boss on the *Trilby*, and Sam gets the dreaded
Bunyard, an older man known as a driver, on the
Flower of Ipswich. They also find that they will
no longer be in the coastal trade but will start
crossing to Calais, carrying at first coke and
later munitions. Crossing the channel means a
third hand is necessary, and the *Flower* picks up
a boy named Albert, an agreeable fellow with a
tubercular cough. At first both Sam and Albert
are suspicious of Bunyard, who is said to have
a German wife and who is scornful of the blind
patriotism that has infected the country. They
discover that on their trips to Calais he sends
them below to sleep, then meets and talks with a
French trawler. Sam stays awake, spies on the
meeting, and sees a package thrown from the
trawler to the barge. When he confronts Bunyard
with his suspicions, the older man shows him
four bottles of cognac which the French captain
insists on giving him for having once aided him
in trouble. Sam is disgusted with Gil, whom he
sees now and then at loading or in Calais, for
not enlisting and for being in love with Agnes
Martin, a girl from their village of Battles-
bridge, who goes out with other men in his
absence, but he also notices that Gil is acting

as skipper most of the time while Finch does
less and less. Something Bunyard has started to
say, then stopped, has made Sam and Albert
suspicious about the big French fishing trawler,
La Notre Dame de Calais, and when the captain,
named Jules, leaves it in Calais, they follow
him to a small cafe called Chez Jules. Sam has
reason to suspect that Gil is dealing with
Jules, and, trying to find something out by
getting into the walled back yard, he is
captured, beaten, tied securely, and dumped in
an upstairs room. Although Gil later secretly
releases him, he is chased and narrowly gets
back on the *Flower* just as she is pulling out.
Despite ribs broken by Jules, Sam takes the
wheel in a rough sea and soon realizes that the
Notre Dame is chasing them. Bunyard thinks at
first that it is a good-natured rivalry, but
when the *Notre Dame* starts firing on the
Flower, they sail in dead earnest and escape
only when an English aircraft appears, assesses
the situation, and strafes the trawler, forcing
it to turn back. While the *Flower* is in Ipswich
for repair and Albert in the hospital for a head
wound, Sam goes home. There he confronts Gil,
who is also home, and who admits to having taken
messages for Finch to Jules, in order to have
more money to court Agnes, until he has become
so implicated that he can't quit. Sam, torn by
conflicting loyalties, decides he must get
advice from Manny, and the next time they are in
France he takes off and walks to Bethune, where
he has heard that Manny's Royal Engineers are
stationed. There he experiences the horrors of
trench warfare, though his genial guides assure
him it is a quiet night, before he finds Manny
badly wounded and unable to talk to him. Nearly
desperate, Sam decides to try once more to talk
to Gil and finds the occasion when they are both
loading in England again. Sam warns him that he
intends to tell Bunyard, and when Gil doesn't
answer, he carries out his threat. Bunyard is
sympathetic and offers to talk to Gil himself.
He is able to do so when the Naval Patrol stops
a whole line of barges, all carrying munitions,
and they have to wait out the next tide. He and
Albert wait while the others talk in the
skipper's quarters, and they watch an enemy
Zeppelin which has been bombing trying to escape

the antiaircraft guns. As Gil and Bunyard return to the deck, they all realize that the *Trilby* has been hit and is on fire. Gil jumps into the boat, rows to the *Trilby*, and tries to put out the fire, while Finch and the other hand escape in the rowboat. Realizing that if the munitions catch fire, the whole row of barges will blow up, Gil gets the anchor up and sails the barge out into open water while all the other barge men watch. She is well clear of the other vessels when she explodes. Sam goes home to tell his mother and learns that a soldier who has seen Manny has reported that he is expected to live and to be sent home for recovery. He also finds a letter to Gil, telling him where to report, and realizes that Gil has tried to solve his problem and atone by enlisting. Sam takes the letter and, despite his horror of the war he has seen in France, uses Gil's name and reports for duty in his stead. The story has plenty of action, with a strong picture of life aboard the barges and the hardships and heroism of such sailing. Characterization is not as strong; since one sees the action from Sam's point of view, one never quite understands Gil's character and has only Sam's hero worship by which to judge Manny. Although the scenes of the front in France are vivid, the episode seems dragged in awkwardly and the spying is never explicit enough to be totally convincing. Carnegie Com.

THUNDER OF VALMY (Trease*, Geoffrey, ill. John S. Goodall, Macmillan, 1960; *VICTORY AT VALMY*, Vanguard, 1961), historical novel set just before and during the early part of the French Revolution, mostly in Paris. One cold day in the famine winter of 1784, imperious, elderly, fat Madame* de Vairmont, a renowned portrait artist, visits the inn in the village of Valaire and notes the remarkable ability of ragamuffin Pierre Mercier, 12, to catch character in charcoal. She takes him home to the Argonne to her "iced-cake" cottage, as Pierre, who tells the story, describes it. She trains him to be her helper and teaches him social graces and the rudiments of painting. Much traveled and knowledgeable, she also introduces him to the radical thinking of the period. When her old friend, the cold, hard Marquis de Morsac*, requests that she paint his daughter, Angelique, Madame refuses, but she persuades Morsac to hire Pierre to paint his niece, Pauline. Pierre moves into the Morsac chateau, where he is treated shabbily by everyone including, ironically, the servants, because he is peasant-born. Pierre and Pauline, who is a Morsac poor relation, become good friends, and the work goes well until one day Morsac overhears the revolutionary ideas Pierre shares with the girl, slashes the painting, and orders Pierre beaten and thrown out. Pierre tramps home to Madame's cottage where he learns that two of Madame's friends, Father Gamain and Monsieur Legrand, local priest and chemist respectively, have been chosen as deputies to the convention of the States-General. This meeting of the three estates will soon be held at Versailles by decree of Louis XVI because the country is near bankruptcy. Madame, Pierre, and Madame's most faithful retainers leave for Paris, Madame at the age of seventy as happy as a girl of seventeen because she is sure the convention will be making important history. In Paris they live at Madame's apartment in the palace of the Tuileries and in a hotel in Versailles. Pierre has a good view of the grand procession of dignitaries when the deputies convene. At Versailles he encounters Pauline, who now lives in the area since Morsac is also a deputy and has moved his family to the capital. Pierre and Pauline resume their friendship, which blossoms into a low-keyed romance that is declared late in the novel. When Morsac discovers that they are seeing each other, he confines the girl to his apartment. Pierre contrives to visit her disguised as a priest but is captured and remanded to the Bastille by Morsac's *lettre de cachet*, the means by which court favorites can imprison whomever they wish without benefit of trial. Pierre arrives in the vicinity of the Bastille on July 14, 1789, just after the Parisian mob has stormed the infamous prison and killed the governor. The revolution begun, mob rule prevails and riots become widespread. The Morsacs flee to England, without Pauline, because she had been sent back to the Morsac chateau outside Valaire. Since peasants are rising all over France and burning the

houses of the nobles who have oppressed them,
Pierre rides on horseback the 120 miles to his
home village to make sure she is safe. He
arrives just as the local mob, which includes
his own brother Jean, is preparing to burn the
chateau, and in a series of exciting scenes he
manages to get into the chateau, find Pauline,
and confront Jean and the mob. In the nick of
time Pauline engineers their escape through a
secret door. They return to Madame in Paris,
and for many weeks the city is racked by plots
and counterplots. After Louis XVI and Marie
Antoinette are apprehended while attempting to
flee the country and then imprisoned, war
breaks out with Austria and Prussia. The mob
seizes City Hall in August of 1792, Madame's
maid, Berthe, falls victim to a stray shot, a
terrible loss for the old woman, and ironically
Madame gives refuge to Morsac who is on the run.
Pauline and Madame return to the Argonne, but
Pierre joins the National Guard and takes part
in the important battle at Valmy in September of
1792 in which the French repel the Prussian
invaders. The book ends with Pierre and Pauline
planning to be married, Madame assuring Pierre
that he will be able to make a good living as
an artist in postwar France, and Pierre looking
forward to a bright future. Except for Madame,
who is memorably depicted as a strong, intelligent, and independent woman, all characters,
even Pierre, are clear types or necessary for
the plot. Morsac is the stock political
villain, and his spoiled, selfish daughter
serves as a convenient foil for sweet, virtuous
Pauline. The author puts across the most
important issues and gives a good sense of the
turmoil of the times. He shows the hatred of the
peasants for the nobles, the callousness of the
upper classes, and the ironic ambivalence of
servants who hate the nobles they serve and yet
take pride in serving them, and such events as
Bastille Day, the convening of the States-
General, and Louis's speech refusing sufficient
reform are well drawn. Pierre's involvement
with historical events and contact with such
revolutionary figures as Mirabeau, Danton, and
Robespierre seem appropriately limited. Although history and story are poorly knit,
occasionally melodrama takes control, and Pierre

seems privy to information that he could not be
expected to know since he is recounting events
as they occur, the novel presents a consistently interesting and substantial if superficial picture of a complex and turbulent
period. Fanfare.

THE   THURSDAY   KIDNAPPING (Forest*, Antonia,
Faber, 1963; Coward, 1965), realistic novel set
in the London suburb of Hampstead concerning the
terrible day for the four Ramsay children when
the baby they are caring for disappears. Ellen*
(often called Len), 13, is a very responsible
young person who starts the day with a paper
route, then prepares breakfast for her father,
herself, and her siblings, and usually gets them
off to school while her mother sleeps in. Their
household is shared by a Hungarian refugee
couple, Freddy (Ferenc) and Marika Kodaly and
their year-old baby, Bart (Bartholomew), a
comfortable arrangement since Freddy works with
Father in a top-secret laboratory and they all
adore him and Bart and get along moderately
well with Marika. On the particular Thursday,
Mother and Marika are spending the day shopping,
leaving Ellen in charge of Bart and Neil*, 12,
Jamie* (Jamesina), ten and a half, and Bobbin*
(Robert), 9, with a list of groceries and
sundries to purchase and directions to see that
Jamie and Bobbin get off to a party in the
afternoon decently clean and dressed. As soon as
Ellen is left in charge, she efficiently
reorganizes the lunch menu to what each of them
likes best and divides the shopping into four
lists, so they can get it out of the way in a
hurry and have time to stop at the library. Two
unusual things occur before they reach the
library: in the grocery store Jamie sees their
neighbor, Kathy* Fisher, who is about Ellen's
age, shoplifting and even being caught and made
to pay for her last item, an event so shocking
Jamie can hardly believe it; and Bobbin, tired
of being criticized by the older ones for
repeating that Kathy stole his bow and arrow,
dashes off across the street alone, creating a
minor traffic jam. When the others take far
longer in the library than she thinks is fair,
Jamie, who is watching Bart, leaves him in the
carriage, intending to dash in and exchange her

book in a hurry, but takes longer than she
expected. While Bart is alone, Kathy comes along
and pretends to a passing woman that it is her
baby brother. Caught out in a web of lies she
has spun, she furiously resents the woman and by
extension the Ramsays for creating the
occasion, and she decides to pay everyone back
by taking Bart home with her, since she has
often wanted to play with him. When the Ramsays
emerge from the library to find Bart missing,
they at first rush wildly along the streets
looking for him until Ellen collects her wits
and marches them off to the police station.
Ellen, with Jamie weeping and Neil gamely trying
to help, explains their problem to the police,
though they are embarrassed at not knowing what
either their father or Freddy does for a living.
Then they go sadly home and are astonished to
see the carriage at the back of their own
garden. Not waiting to check further, Ellen
immediately calls the police, but then discovers
that Bart is not in the carriage. Neil, a
bookish and imaginative boy, suggests that Bart
might have been kidnapped for political reasons,
in exchange for information Freddy might have
and, expanding on the idea, begins to think that
if the police know, they may deport Freddy and
Marika as bad security risks. Ellen seizes on
this as an excuse not to telephone and change
her story again to the police, and when a
foreign-sounding man phones, asks for Freddy,
and will not leave his name, they become
convinced. Just then they discover that Kathy's
dog, a fatuous spaniel, is in their house with
one of Bart's mittens. Sure that he will track
the kidnappers, they put him on an old leash and
rush off in what to them is a daring rescue but
to the spaniel a marvelous chance for an
unaccustomed run. In a squabble between Neil and
Bobbin, the dog gets away and races across the
busy street with both Bobbin and Jamie after
him, oblivious to the screech of brakes and the
crash of metal. Ellen and Neil are left to view
with horror the three-car pileup and see the
motorcycle rider lying with one leg broken.
Ellen, heavily motivated by conscience, insists
on confessing to the traffic police what caused
the accident. Dismally they return home, only to
run into Miss Lambert, a nosy neighbor, who

warns them that Kathy is not a reliable baby-sitter and that they should collect Bart from her at once. Astonished and full of rage, they descend on Kathy's house and are met by a series of lies about the baby being her cousin Adam, her grandmother being sick, her father resting, and others. Unable to push their way in, they boost Jamie through the bathroom window so she can undo the bolts on the door. Since she can't reach them, she uses an umbrella, is discovered by Kathy, and in the skirmish the door's window is broken. This is just the first of a series of disasters that make a shambles of the Fisher living room before Mrs. Fisher enters. Ellen is not surprised that she is furious and blames them, but she is horrified that Mrs. Fisher seems to dislike her own daughter and then tries to bribe them to lie about the events so her husband will not find out. With what dignity they can muster, they take Bart and go home, give him his bath, realize that they have missed the party, and try to think of how to explain the afternoon to their parents. Neil manages to get Freddy aside and tell him the story and is extremely grateful that, with his usual calm acceptance, Freddy is not upset, but they are just summoning up courage to tell their parents when a policeman arrives. Ellen lets him in with relief, thinking that they will at least get all the explanations over at once. The story is rather slow in starting and, since the reader knows all the time that Kathy is the kidnapper, there is no suspense about who took the baby, but the sick fear and worry that the four children experience is so well evoked that, once Bart is found to be gone, the story moves at a rapid and gripping pace. Kathy is a thoroughly disagreeable yet pitiable girl, and each of the Ramsay youngsters is clearly differentiated and convincingly portrayed. The grown-ups do not come off as well, but since the whole book is seen through the eyes of the children, predominately Ellen, this is not a major flaw. Carnegie Com.

THURSDAY'S CHILD (Streatfeild*, Noel, ill. Peggy Fortnum, Collins, 1970; Random, 1970), realistic novel set in Staffordshire in the first decade of the twentieth century, starring an orphan who, like Thursday's child in the old rhyme, is destined to go far. Margaret* Thursday was so named by the rector because she was found as a newborn infant on the steps of the church on a Thursday, in a basket with three of everything, and all of the very best quality, and a note saying, "This is Margaret, whom I entrust to your care. Each year fifty-two pounds will be sent for her keep and schooling." The rector, a bachelor, has arranged that she live with the elderly Cameron sisters, local gentry, where she is cared for by the servant, Hannah, and raised with a strong sense of her own importance. Each year until she is ten, the promised money is found in the church, but that year the rector has discovered a note in the baptismal font saying, "No more money for Margaret." Because the Cameron women have fallen on hard times and are in poor health and Hannah is overworked, the rector decides that Margaret must be sent to St. Luke's, an orphanage recommended by the archdeacon as an "exceptionally pleasant place." St. Luke's proves to be just the opposite. Margaret is immediately spotted as a potential trouble-maker by Miss Jones, the rigid and disagreeable assistant to the Matron, an assessment concurred in by the cruel and evil Matron, who takes the nice clothes Hannah has provided for her and puts her in the uncomfortable and archaic costumes of nearly a century earlier which are still worn by all the orphans. Margaret has made three friends on the trip to the institution, Lavinia* Beresford, 14, and her two brothers, Peter*, 10, and Horatio*, 6. The two brothers are to be at St. Luke's, and Lavinia is sent to be the scullery maid for the Countess of Corkberry, where she hopes to be allowed to walk the four miles to see her brothers on every other Sunday. Before she leaves, she asks Margaret to look after her brothers, a charge that Margaret takes very seriously. Despite the meager food, discomfort, hard work, and severe punishments, Margaret keeps up her spirits and does her best to help the boys. A few bright spots occur. Lady Corkberry allows Lavinia to visit her brothers, but because she is afraid that her brothers will be treated more unkindly if there are inquiries about the orphanage, Lavinia says nothing of the conditions there.

The cook suspects and passes word to the
housekeeper and thence to Lady Corkberry, who
is already interested in Lavinia because she
speaks and acts in such a refined way for a
servant and because her husband thinks she
looks much like the daughter of Lord Delaware,
an Irish friend, a girl who eloped with a groom
and was completely cut off by her family. When,
after a rare treat of tea with the archdeacon's
brother, Margaret finds that Peter, a compulsive
reader, has "borrowed" three books from the
library, she realizes that he could be arrested
and decides that they must run away. She plans
and directs their escape and takes them to the
stables at Sedgecombe Place, the Corkberry
estate, because Jem, the youngest groom, has
jokingly told her he'll help her if she wants to
run away. When she shows up in his room over
the stables, Jem is terrified that she will
cause him to lose his position and solves the
problem by taking them to his parents, who run
a canal boat and happen to be tied up nearby.
Jem's mother, Ma Smith, takes the children in,
dyes the boys' fair hair, and provides old
clothes for all three. For some time the
children gamely take turns at legging, leading
the horse along the bank, a job Margaret really
likes and the boys find far superior to the
orphanage, until Peter, always frail, faints
from exhaustion and exposure in the rainy
weather. Ma Smith and her husband, the captain,
take them to the captain's sister, Ida
Fortescue, an actor in a traveling tent company.
They plan that they can get Ida to take the two
boys, who are handsome and speak with upper-
class accents, and they will keep Margaret.
Taking her promise to Lavinia literally,
Margaret refuses to be parted from the boys, and
the Fortescues are persuaded to take all three.
In the meantime, word has gotten out that three
orphans have escaped, although Matron has
forbidden any mention outside the home, the
police find Margaret's nightgown, which she had
discarded in the canal, Lord Corkberry has
fetched Lord Delaware from Ireland, having been
convinced by a look at Horatio that the
Beresfords are his friend's grandchildren, and
the local people, who have long suspected that
all is not right at the orphanage, have "rough

musicked" the Matron, surrounding the place at night and beating on pots and pans to shame her and show their disapproval. Much shaken by this treatment, she and Miss Jones do not argue when Lady Corkberry dismisses them both. At the theater, the Fortescues plan to add *Little Lord Fauntleroy* to their repertoire, but Peter is a dismal failure at acting. When Margaret tries to help him, they discover that she is a natural actor, and with her hair dyed with peroxide, she takes the part of Cedric in the play and is a smashing success. That very night, Lord Corkberry and Lord Delaware, having traced the children through Jem, come with Lavinia and the Smiths to the theater. There is an emotional meeting of Lord Delaware with his grandchildren, whom he proposes to take to live with him in Ireland. When he asks Margaret to join them, however, she refuses, insisting that she will make her own way and become famous as an actress. The mystery of her own origin and the money left in the church is not solved. Most of the situations and characters are stereotypes and the central reunion of the Beresfords and their grandfather depends on an unlikely coincidence. The plot elements like the escape from the cruel orphanage have a surefire appeal, however, and the details of lives of servants in wealthy homes of the period and of canal boaters are interesting. Margaret is a spunky protagonist and, as a child given to self-dramatizing, is believable. Choice.

TIM CHARLTON (*Danger at Black Dyke**), friend of Geordie* Bickerson and Hamish* MacLeish and a cofounder and member of the society of Mithras. His father has let the boys use the old farmhouse called Black Dyke for the society's headquarters. Tim has lots of energy and is totally dedicated to the society. He readily defers to Geordie's wishes. He understands Geordie's need to be in control of things and acknowledges his superior resource and wit.

TIME OF TRIAL (Burton*, Hester, ill. Victor G. Ambrus, Oxford, 1963; World, 1964), historical novel set in London and then in an English seacoast village in 1801–1802 against the background of the wars with France. Blunt-speaking,

protected Meg (Margaret) Pargeter, 17, learns
to face adversity and to sort out her values
during her father's imprisonment and her
rejection by the family of the young man she
loves and hopes to marry. Meg, her impractical,
idealistic bookseller father, Mr.* Pargeter,
her older brother, John*, and Robert* Kerridge,
a young medical student who boards with the
Pargeters, live in Holly Lane over the family
bookshop, which is the gathering place for local
intellectuals. When the ramshackle tenement at
the foot of Holly Lane collapses from disrepair, Mr. Pargeter adopts little Elijah*, the
sole survivor of the ruin, and composes "The New
Jerusalem," a manifesto in which he advocates
that property be administered by local parishes
so that everyone may have decent, appropriate
housing. He is arrested, tried, and convicted of
sedition and libel, but, because Dr.* Kerridge,
Robert's respected physician father, speaks on
his behalf, his sentence is less severe than
expected. He is remanded to Ipswich Gaol for six
months. Dr. Kerridge arranges for Meg, Elijah,
and their housekeeper, Mrs.* Neech, to stay
while the bookseller is in prison in a cottage
in the doctor's home village of Herringsby on
the coast not far from Ipswich. The last half
of the novel concentrates upon Meg's romance
with Robert, a match strongly opposed by the
status-conscious Kerridges. A small mystery
develops when a customs officer is found slain,
and gradually Meg becomes aware that the village
is the center of an extensive smuggling operation. Events reach a climax when British
soldiers, of which John is now a captain,
encircle the region and a mighty storm alters
the coast and exposes the smugglers' hidingplaces. Robert informs his parents of his
intention to marry Meg in spite of their
disapproval, and the book ends with the newly
married couple receiving loving congratulations
from Mr. Pargeter. The first half of the book
has more interesting intellectual substance than
the second part, and the book's strong romantic
emphasis seems intended to appeal to adolescent
girls. Except for Meg and her father,
characterization is shallow. The two fathers
present quite obvious contrasts, as do Robert
and John. The farm family who befriend Meg and

whose daughter, Lucy* Moore, becomes Meg's confidant, serve as foils to the Kerridges, and, like them, never come alive as real people. While the smuggling is historically accurate, Meg is too much on the fringes of what goes on in that part of the book for it to have much impact on the reader. The conversation carries conviction, small details of setting provide interest and add considerable texture, and Meg's experiences mature her predictably. Left unanswered is the question of whether or not Dr. Kerridge heads the smuggling ring. Carnegie Winner; Choice; Fanfare.

TIM INGRAM (*A Pattern of Roses**), Timothy Reed Ingram, 16, present-day boy whose parents have purchased an old cottage in an English village and have built a modern house around it, more enthusiastic about the idea of country living than the actuality. Tim has been out of his boarding school for a term with glandular fever, and the change, plus his involvement with Rebecca* and with Tom* Inskip's story of some sixty years before, changes him from passive acceptance of his parents' expectation that he will go to Oxford, enter his father's firm, and become an advertising executive. He asserts his individuality, refuses to go back to school, and gets a job with a local blacksmith. Tim's greatest interest is in drawing, and he sees the possibility of a future business designing iron work for houses and churches.

TIMMO JONES (*The Watch House**), Timothy, highly intelligent boy just ready to start at the University, who takes an interest in the Watch House and Anne* Melton's problem with its ghosts. Eccentric in both actions and dress, Timmo at first arouses the suspicions of Prudie, but the fact that he is son of the doctor and his quick, expert repair of her refrigerator convert her, though she continues to try to get him to cut his long hair. Typically, Timmo turns his full intellectual energy to one thing at a time, exploring it intensely, then dropping it as quickly and moving on. He depends on his friend Pat* Pierson to handle personal relationships for him, though he can be charming when he thinks of it. A rationalist, he fights against believing in the presence of the ghosts and in the efficacy of exorcism but ends up admiring Father da Souza and trying to find some logical explanation for the occurrences at the Watch House.

TIMUR VEN (*Children of the Book**), young recruit in the Twenty-eighth Orta of the Turkish Janissaries, the infantry. He is personal servant to the unit's commander, Colonel Vasif*, whom he respects, admires, fears, and wants very much to please. A devout Muslim, he looks forward to battle for the sake of personal glory and pleasing Allah by killing the despised Christian infidels. Once his unit is in the trenches doggedly pursuing the siege and the mortality rate escalates, however, Timur begins to question the meaning of what the Turks are doing. He feels the war is "burning away not dross and leaving gold [as Vasif had told him], but burning away the gold and leaving dross, robbing men of their humanity and their souls and leaving them mere animals." He comes finally to wish it were just all over and done with. He sustains a wound killing his first Austrian valiantly and is rewarded with a fine Damascus silk uniform, a sword inlaid with gold, and full rank as a Janissary. He is invited to serve at headquarters with Kara Mustafa, but declines, preferring to stay with Vasif and his war comrades. He dies in the battle that breaks the siege, on September 12, 1683.

TINKER BELL (*Peter and Wendy**), sexy fairy who accompanies Peter* Pan to the home of the Darlings and who lives in the home underground in the Neverland, having a private apartment the size of a birdcage recessed in the wall, an exquisite boudoir with bedspreads varied according to what fruit blossom is in season. Tinker Bell is vain, jealous, and spiteful, and inclined to pinch any girl who attracts Peter's attention. She falsely tells the Lost Boys that Peter wants them to shoot Wendy* and cries when Wendy lives. She is genuinely devoted to Peter, however, and risks her own life by drinking his poisoned medicine so that he won't die.

TINY TIM CRATCHIT (*A Christmas Carol**), youngest

of the poor but loving family of Ebenezer*
Scrooge's clerk. A crippled child who must walk
with a crutch and be supported by an iron frame,
he is nevertheless sweet-tempered. He says he
hopes the people in church saw him, because "it
might be pleasant to them to remember on
Christmas Day, who made lame beggars walk and
blind men see." It is he who gives the
much-quoted toast, "God bless us, every one!"
Although treated rather sentimentally, he is one
of the favorite characters from the classic
Christmas story.

TIRIAN (*The Last Battle**), King of Narnia*,
descendant 200 years later of Prince Rilian* of
*The Silver Chair**. A youth of some twenty years,
he is broad shouldered and muscled and has a
fearless and honest face. He loves and respects
the land of Narnia and its creatures and does
his best to combat the evil unleashed by Shift
the Ape. He appears mainly as a brave and
capable warrior and fine strategist. He speaks
in high diction. He wins the reader's sympathies at the onset, because of his conscientious attitude toward his duties, and,
later, because of his heroism against what prove
to be overwhelming odds and his strong faith in
Aslan*.

TIR NAN OG (*Marassa and Midnight**), the name
Marassa calls the captain who rescues him. The
captain is the means by which Marassa is
reunited with his twin brother, Midnight. The
captain sings a song in which the words Tir nan
Og appear, and, at first, Marassa thinks he's
saying Ti nan Ogoun, Son of Ogoun. Ogoun is the
war god of the blacks of Haiti, and, since the
captain has red hair and carries a rapier and
Ogoun likes red and machetes, the boy connects
the two. Later the captain tells Marassa that
Tir nan Og, or Land of Heart's Desire, which is
the Celtic mythological otherworld, is the name
of his lost estate in Scotland, and the boy
decides to call him that. The symbolism seems
labored.

TITTY WALKER (*Pigeon Post**; *Swallows and Amazons**; We Didn't Mean to Go to Sea**), next to
youngest of the four Walker children who are

featured in a series of holiday adventures. An imaginative child, she seems to have more literary knowledge than either of her older siblings. In the crucial adventure of *Swallows and Amazons*, she stays on Wildcat Island by herself and manages to seize the *Amazon* and row it away thereby winning the mock battle for her side. She also finds the sea chest that has been stolen from Captain* Flint's houseboat. Her role in *Pigeon Post* is less important, although she takes a lead in fighting the fire. In *We Didn't Mean to Go to Sea*, she is overcome by a terrible headache (perhaps brought on by the fear she senses in her older brother and sister) and is resting in the bunk through the worst of their near disaster.

TITUS CARVER (*Jeremy Craven**), Jeremy's Uncle Titus. He takes Jeremy from an orphanage in England, declaring that he is the brother of Jeremy's dead mother, an assertion which is possibly true but never substantiated in the story. Why Titus should bother with the boy at all provides some suspense and is never satisfactorily explained. He evidently plans to use the lad as eyes and ears in promoting his gunrunning enterprise, and possibly other illegal activities as well. Fat and overbearing, he can be vulgar, cruel, and unconcerned about the feelings and wishes of those around him, in particular, the Mexicans, for whom he has some liking but little respect. He considers them ignorant and inferior. His main concern is making money, and he does this in any way he can. On the other hand, he can be generous to a fault, especially with Jeremy, of whom he seems genuinely fond but not to the point where he allows his feelings for Jeremy to interfere with the chance to make money. Jeremy understands the old man's need for someone to love him and has compassion for him, in spite of the way Titus uses him. Titus is a complex, interesting figure.

TIZZY RUSSELL (*Flambards in Summer**), originally Thomas Mark Bugg, illegitimate son of Mark* Russell by Violet Wright, whom Christina* Parsons Russell adopts, thinking Mark is dead. Though not yet six when he comes to Flambards,

Tizzy is already much like his father, dark haired, daring, and truculent, with a great love for horses. He is also insecure and vulnerable, having been unwanted by his mother and stepfathers. His genuine love for Christina and for his uncle, Dick* Wright, give hope that he may turn out to be a less self-centered and more compassionate person than his father.

TOAD OF TOAD HALL (*The Wind in the Willows**), wealthiest of the riverbankers, with a good heart but little good sense. Generous and well-meaning but also boastful and thoughtless, Toad is loveable but a trial to his friends, mainly because of his series of obsessions, the most destructive of which is a passion for motorcars. In his troubles with the law and his various escapes, he is always extremely pleased with himself, not reflecting that he has brought his troubles on himself. After his friends have helped him regain Toad Hall, he plans a banquet at which he will give a speech, recite a poem, and sing a song composed by himself, but Rat* and Badger* take him firmly in hand, point out that his speeches are nothing but self praise and vanity, and make him promise to forego the entertainment he has arranged. Reluctantly, Toad agrees, but before the guests arrive he dresses in his best, stands before a semicircle of empty chairs, bows, and sings his song very loudly to his imagined enraptured audience. After that he appears to be reformed, an appearance that a reader may well question.

TOBY GARLAND (*The Maplin Bird**), 16, fisherman brother of Emily*, who is used by the gentleman smuggler, Adam* Seymour, and nearly destroyed as a result. A good boy, though inclined to be impetuous and wild, Toby takes part in Adam's schemes partly for the badly needed money and partly for the love of sailing. The experience of almost being wrecked in their attempt to reach France and of being arrested sobers him, and in the end it appears that, with Emily's steadying influence, he will show maturity.

TOBY OLDKNOW (*The Children of Green Knowe**), Toseland, one of a long line of Toselands in the family, about thirteen or fourteen when he died

in the   Great Plague   of 1665.   He is a   hero to
Tolly*   because he   wears   a sword   and has   the
marvelous horse, Feste*,   and he naturally leads
the other two spirit   children who still inhabit
the   old   house   at   Green   Knowe.   His   main
individual   adventure   related by   old Mrs.*
Oldknow   is riding   Feste through   the flood   to
fetch the   doctor for   his sister,   Linnet*, who
had   a high   fever.   Toby planned   to become   a
soldier.

TOLKIEN,   J(OHN)   R(ONALD)   R(EUEL)   (1892-1973),
born in   Bloemfontein, South Africa;   scholar of
Anglo-Saxon and Germanic   linguistics and author
of   some   of   the   best-loved   fantasy   of   the
twentieth   century.   Tolkien   was   brought   to
England in 1895,   attended King Edward's School,
Birmingham, St. Philip's School, Birmingham, and
Exeter College, Oxford, where he was awarded his
B.A. degree in 1915 and his M.A. in 1919. During
World War I,   he served   as a lieutenant   in the
Lancashire Fusiliers. In 1919 and 1920 he was an
assistant on the Oxford English Dictionary, then
taught at   the University   of Leeds   until 1925,
when he returned to Oxford where he taught until
his retirement in 1959. He received many awards,
including   honorary   degrees   from   University
College, Dublin,   the University   of Nottingham,
Oxford   University,   and   the   University   of
Edinburgh, and being named a fellow of the Royal
Society of Literature and Commander in the Order
of the British Empire.   His work   on   *Beowulf* is
credited with starting a complete reappraisal of
Old English literature   and of the Saxon culture
in England,   and his *Tree and Leaf*   (Allen & Unwin, 1964; Houghton, 1965),   a study of fantasy,
is considered   a major critical work.   It is for
his   fantasies themselves,   however, that   he is
best remembered, particularly *The Hobbit** (Allen
& Unwin,   1937;   Houghton, 1938), which,   among
other   honors,   has   been   named   a Children's
Classic,   a   Children's   Literature   Association
Touchstone, and   a Children's   Book Too   Good to
Miss, and   its three-volume sequel,   *The Lord of
the Rings*, made   up of   *The Fellowship of the
Ring** (Allen & Unwin, 1954; Houghton, 1954), *The
Two Towers* (Allen & Unwin, 1954; Houghton, 1955)
and *The Return of the King* (Allen & Unwin, 1955;
Houghton,   1956). Although   the   first was   pub-

lished for children and the sequel for adults, they are read by all ages and are both essentially quest stories. *The Hobbit* tells the tale of Bilbo* Baggins, a hobbit* who signs on with an expedition of dwarfs to regain their mountain kingdom and treasure from a dragon and introduces, somewhat incidentally, a ring of great power. The second concerns the much longer, more dangerous, and darker journey of Bilbo's cousin Frodo* to return the ring to the place of its forging and thereby to save the world from evil. Tolkien also wrote several minor fantasies, including *Farmer Giles of Ham** (Allen & Unwin, 1949; Houghton, 1950) and *Smith of Wooton Major* (Allen & Unwin, 1967; Houghton, 1967). At his death he left unfinished a long work dealing with the mythology of his fantasy world, Middle-earth, which was later edited by his son Christopher and published as *The Silmarillion* (Allen & Unwin, 1977; Houghton, 1977). A strong interest in Tolkien's fantasies developed in the 1960s, some fifteen years after they were published, especially on college campuses, until Tolkien became something of a cult figure; today the works are still popular and widely read, and they are credited with renewing an interest in other fantasy.

TOLLY (*The Children of Green Knowe**; *The Chimneys of Green Knowe**; *An Enemy at Green Knowe**), whose real name is Toseland, boy who spends holidays with his great-grandmother at her house that dates from the Middle Ages. In *The Children of Green Knowe*, at perhaps eight, he meets three Oldknow children from the seventeenth century who died in the Great Plague. In *The Chimneys of Green Knowe*, at nine, he gets to know Susan* Oldknow, blind daughter of a late-eighteenth-century sea captain, and Jacob*, the black slave boy the captain bought in Barbados and brought home to be a companion to his daughter. Somewhat older in *An Enemy at Green Knowe*, he and Ping* help old Mrs.* Oldknow thwart the evil machinations of a woman involved with black magic. Tolly is a solitary and sensitive little boy, very imaginative and responsive to the old lady's affection. He has been less than happy at boarding school and is shy and uncomfortable with his stepmother, who now has gone to Burma with his father. In *An Enemy at Green Knowe*, with Ping for a friend, he is much more confident but seems less an individualized character.

TOLLY DORKING (*Black Jack**), Bartholomew, a draper's apprentice who becomes involved with a huge ruffian revived from the gallows and with a girl thrown from a coach on her way to the madhouse. Tolly is naive but intelligent, and when he stumbles upon the seedy traveling fair he sees it a haven for himself from Black* Jack and a possible place of cure for Belle* Carter, since Dr. Carmody believes his Elixer of Youth will produce medical wonders of all kinds. Tolly is a victim of his own contending emotions. Besides fear of Black Jack, he longs for admiration rather than scorn from the great hoodlum, and besides his dread of being caught as caretaker for a madwoman, he is soon deeply in love with Belle. Tolly credits all his knowledge and decent impulses to the influence of his uncle the sea captain and mentions this relative so often that Belle and others begin to ridicule him, but in the end it is the uncle who carries them away in his ship to a new life.

TOM (*Red Shift**), twentieth-century boy about ready for the university, suffering separation from Jan*, the girl he loves, who is studying nursing in London. He is driven to mental imbalance by the obtuseness of his sergeant-major father, a weak man egged on by his wife to assert his authority, and his small-minded mother, who objects to Jan and who outrageously reads and then hides Jan's letters to Tom and whose suspicions that they are sexually active push them to the act. Tom, a highly intelligent boy, finds refuge in words and quotes continually. He also finds refuge in his caravan (house trailer) home by wearing stereo earphones with no tapes and without plugging them in. His inability to cope with his own emotions finally seems to destroy his relationship with Jan.

TOM ASS; OR, THE SECOND GIFT (Lawrence*, Ann, ill. Ionicus, Macmillan, 1972; Walck, 1972), lighthearted fantasy set in the late Middle Ages in England. Tom, clever youngest son of Farmer

John, idles his time away, sure that when he is
ready his ideas will make him great and famous.
An elf-woman, critical of his attitude, grants
him one gift: whatever he begins at sunrise
shall be sufficient to the day. To the surprise
of both Tom and his family, he starts a small
job for his mother at sunrise and works hard at
it all day, several days in a row. Realizing
what is happening, he decides to leave home to
seek his fortune, as he has long planned. When,
on the first day, he again meets the elf-woman
and upbraids her for the inconvenient gift, she
calls him a Great Fool and grants him a second
gift: he shall be whatever his future wife
chooses to make of him. Shortly thereafter, he
meets a girl, singing and spinning and watching
the sheep. She introduces herself as Jennifer,
and in the ensuing conversation about his first
gift, she immediately sees its possibilities and
calls him "a great donkey." Before she can
blink, he is changed into a fine, grey ass.
Realizing that she has been somehow involved in
his change, Jennifer practically decides to
stay with him, and the girl and the donkey start
on their travels together. Their first lengthy
stop is with a farmer and his wife, where they
both work so well that they are urged to stay,
but clever Jennifer asks only that they be
allowed to glean after the field has been
harvested, and since whatever Tom starts at
sunrise lasts all day, they get many bags of
grain from a seemingly nearly empty field.
Jennifer sells it and starts Tom at dawn
counting the money, again an all-day job. With
this nest egg, they start off again. Jennifer
is smart enough to use the gift sparingly but to
good purpose, when they enter the employ of a
weaver and later Master Welford, a wool
merchant in London. Although Master Welford
cannot take a woman seriously in business,
Jennifer persuades him that a reclusive man
from her home county, Tom Ass, deals in fabrics
but hates to meet people and has asked her to
act as his agent. Reluctantly, Welford takes on
her business. Each night she weaves a short
piece of fabric and at dawn Tom starts rolling
it up so that by evening he has a considerable
length. With the business sense Tom picks up on
his wandering about town, they prosper and, in

the next six years, buy several ships and a farm. Merchants from the Hanseatic League fear the rivalry of this mysterious Tom Ass, and the king, who needs to borrow money, has Jennifer picked up and secretly brought to him to find out how to get in touch with this possible source of loans. In defending Tom Ass to a scornful Privy Councillor, she insists her master is a gentleman, generous and wise. When she returns home, she finds the donkey is once again Tom in human form, much improved by her description and his experiences. They marry, and the elf-woman calls to take away her gifts before they should turn to harm. The story cleverly uses the folktale pattern combined with realistic detail in a tone that is never serious yet has several strong themes: he who deals with magic had best be ready to take care of himself; one sometimes becomes what others think of him; and cleverness is useful only when accompanied by work and practical good sense. Fanfare.

TOM DANDO (*The Whispering Mountain**), Arabis's* father and Owen's friend. He is a traveling barber and poet and when first met is so deeply involved in composing a long poem about King Arthur that he only speaks on Wednesdays, Fridays, and Sundays. After the poem is finished, he livens up and sings lustily at the top of his voice every song and hymn he can remember. He tells Prince* David about Lord* Malyn's wickedness, and the prince agrees to have the marquess arrested. The prince likes Tom's poem so much he decides to have it published. Tom and Arabis travel about the countryside in a covered wagon pulled by a sturdy, very intelligent horse named Galahad.

TOM FOBBLE'S DAY (Garner*, Alan, ill. Michael Foreman, Collins, 1977; Collins, 1979), realistic, short, period novel of family and neighborhood life set during the blitz of World War II, last in The Stone Book Quartet, a "saga tracing four generations of a working class family in Chorley, a small town in Cheshire, England," and, like its predecessors, telling of a momentous day in a youth's life. On Lizzie Leah's Hill, William, perhaps ten, grandson of Joseph*, the smith of *Granny Reardun** and *The

Aimer Gate*, is "Tom Fobbled" by Stewart Allman
of his makeshift sledge (although William
insists Tom Fobbling is legal only for marbles),
which Stewart then wrecks. William accepts its
loss gamely, goes home to the village, and stops
at the shop of Grandad (Joseph), who is busy at
his bench. Grandad burns identification marks on
William's clogs against air raids, noting the
irony that he usually puts such marks on
farmers' milk cans; oils the boy's clogs so they
won't collect snow; and reminisces about the
Boer and Kaiser Bill's wars and family history.
He makes two long, thin strips of iron, fits the
irons to wood, and then, after tidying his
bench, closes the shop, saying, "Fifty-five
years....Did you not know it was me last day?"
The two go to his house, where Grandad finishes
the new sled using wood from the dilapidated
loom that once belonged to Old* William, young
William's great-great-grandfather's brother.
Young Wlliam goes to the potato hogg (storage
pit), where among the potatoes he discovers his
great-great-grandfather's Macclesfield pipe,
prompting Grandad to more reminiscences, this
time about the sturdy old stonemason, Robert
(Father*). Back on Lizzie Leah's hill that
evening, with air-raid sirens screaming the
approach of German bombers, William impresses
Stewart Allman and company with the craftsmanship of the sledge and with his own bravery
and skill in gliding at precarious speed from
the very topmost layer of the mighty hill, a
dizzying height the others have never
attempted. While on the sledge he has a very
strong feeling that he is not alone but rather
part of a "line through hand and eye, block,
forge and loom to the hill. He owned them all;
and they owned him." He returns to discover
Grandad upstairs in bed surrounded by neighbors,
apparently the victim of stroke or heart attack.
William announces to the fierce, urgent blue
eyes, still intense with intelligence, that the
sled's a "belter," and knows his Grandad
understands. William returns to Lizzie Leah's
Hill, confident that the line to the past has
strength to hold. Like the previous three books,
this one leaves much unsaid, relying on the
reader to pick up on subtle inferences and make
the right connections, a happy change from the

many late-twentieth-century books that spell
everything out. Mostly simple sentences make
little use of figurative language and much use
of repetition, giving the whole work a poetic
rhythm and projecting a sense of tidiness and
completion. This book, while also entire in
itself, rounds out the series, binding the books
together by repeating motifs and settings,
adding information about the family, showing how
times have changed in the village and yet have
not, and projecting a strong sense of physical
setting. It is a pity that the four books were
not joined into one long novel to tell in a
continuous story the family and village history;
as four separate books, they seem slighter than
they really are. Choice; Fanfare.

TOM GOODENOUGH (*The Borrowers**; *The Borrowers
Afield**), boy with the ferret, who observes
Pod*, Homily*, and Arrietty* Clock leaving
Firbank Hall in the first book and who later
saves them from the gypsy, Mild* Eye, and takes
them to the cottage where he lives with his
gamekeeper grandpa. There, Arrietty tells him
the story of the Clocks' journey to Parkin's
Beck in search of the Uncle* Hendrearys; and
some seventy years later, himself now the
gamekeeper, he still lives in the cottage which
has come by right of inheritance to Mrs.* May.
Now an old man with bright, dark, strangely
luminous eyes, a secret smile, and a reputation
as the bigest liar in five counties, he passes
the story along to Kate, who writes it down
years later for her four children. As a
character Tom is more interesting as an
enigmatic old man, who may or may not be telling
the truth, than he is as a boy, although, when
a boy, he is sharp-minded and quick-acting
enough to significantly affect the Borrowers'
lives.

TOM HENCHMAN (*Castors Away!**), 12, Nell's* twin,
middle son in the family, a boy who tends to be
irresponsible and loves excitement. He longs to
join his uncle, Simon Henchman, captain of the
Pericles, but his father, Dr.* William Henchman,
refuses to give his permission until Tom can
demonstrate sufficient maturity to stay out of
silly scrapes. During the difficult hours the

Henchmans work to save James* Bubb's life, Tom behaves most admirably, and, when Uncle Simon sends for Tom, Dr. Henchman allows him to leave. This happens at a most felicitous point in the plot, since Tom's departure enables the children to get James out of England and away from the military authorities, and probably to save his life again. Tom serves on the *Pericles* as powder boy during the battle of Trafalgar. He is dismayed and shocked to discover that war brings a kind of excitement and adventure quite different from what he imagined. Despondent for some time after the engagement and his return to England, he gradually regains his characteristic buoyancy of spirit, and eventually he returns to the *Pericles* and a life at sea. What happens to him in the story is predictable but appropriate to the situation.

TOM INSKIP (*A Pattern of Roses**), Thomas Robert Inskip, village boy in Edwardian England who reappears to a present-day boy, Tim* Ingram, when Tim finds Tom's drawings in the chimney of the old cottage around which his parents have built a modern house. Tom has unusual ability as an untrained artist, but his ambitions are limited. He expects to work on Mr. Pettigrew's farm as his father has done, and the lessons Miss* May Bellinger insists on giving him seem strange and pointless, although he enjoys drawing. Even his love for Netty* Bellinger is tempered by his realization of its hopelessness. As Miss May says at the end, he has "a sweet nature," demands "very little," and accepts what he has with "perfect spiritual grace." He is just short of his sixteenth birthday when he is drowned.

TOM LONG (*Tom's Midnight Garden**), English youth who is very unhappy at having to stay with his childless Aunt* Gwen and Uncle* Alan Kitson while his brother, Peter, recovers from the measles. About twelve, Tom is coolly polite to the Kitsons' awkward advances. When he discovers the garden, he at first thinks they have been lying to him about its existence. Later he seeks to keep his knowledge of it secret from them because he is sure they would not understand. A persistent boy, he researches

Hatty* Melbourne's time period and holds his own in discussions with dogmatic Uncle Alan. He writes detailed letters home to Peter about his midnight adventures in the garden with Hatty that are so vivid and convincing that Peter even joins the two in the Ely tower during the skating episode. Tom is a convincing, likeable figure.

TOM LYNN (*Fire and Hemlock**), cellist with the London Philharmonic who befriends Polly* Whittacker when she stumbles by accident into the funeral at Hunsdon House and who becomes her companion in a series of fantasy adventures in which he is Tan Coul, a hero, and Polly is his assistant. He was an orphan when Laurel* first found him, sent him to Wilton school, then married him. He asserted himself to become a professional musician and divorced her, but she clearly still has power over him at the time when he gets to know Polly. Together they make up hero adventures, most of which come true in bizarre ways. He realizes that he needs Polly to escape the fate Laurel has projected for him, but he tries at the same time to protect her by taking along a girlfriend, Mary Fields, by getting the other members of the quartet to write his letters to her, and by sending her books that will warn her of what lies in store. In the end it seems that his brother, Charles, was Laurel's first choice and that he bargained with her, giving her Tom in exchange for his own freedom. Charles has been hiding out for nine years, disguised as Mr. Piper, an ironmonger, with his wife Edna acting as his sister and his son Leslie as his nephew. In the ordinary world Tom has become quite a famous cellist, and his Dumas Quartet is one of the leading chamber music groups. Nearsighted, with fine, pale hair, he seems quite old to Polly when she is a child, but after she is nineteen and sees his picture, she realizes that he is young. Though mild-mannered, he has a tough, stubborn streak that has made it possible for him to escape from Laurel.

TOM MOORHOUSE (*A Chance Child**), about nine, workhouse orphan bound to be apprenticed to the brutal miner, Bill Greenwood. As Greenwood's

butty, he has not only been overworked and
beaten, but his master has also stuck him in the
bottom with his pick, wounding him more than
once. After running away from the mine with
Creep*, he works for some time in the pottery, a
job that requires him to run constantly from the
potter's shop to the drying kilns with the plate
molds, stack them in the heat of the kiln, and
run back, from before light to after dark, until
the constant change of temperature makes him
ill. Although he accepts help from Blackie*, he
is unfeeling in rejecting her fantasy that they
might be married some day, saying bluntly that
his girl must have a pretty face. Though older
than Creep and Blackie and in some ways callous,
he reveals that his own secret fantasy has been
to have a mother who would care for him. When he
gets the chance to work in a better mine than
the first one, he parts from the other two
children without regrets. His is a real name and
case drawn from the Parliamentary Papers.

TOMMY SEAGRAVE (*Masterman Ready**), naughty,
mischievous lad of six, who with his parents,
Mr*. and Mrs*. Seagrave, his brother William*, a
younger brother and sister, their black nanny,
Juno*, and their seaman-friend, Masterman
Ready*, survives on a desert isle. His will-
fulness and disobedience provide some humor,
often cause trouble, and create opportunities
for the author to instruct young readers in
right and wrong behavior. Sometimes Tommy's
misdeeds merely discomfit Tommy himself, as when
he eats castor-oil beans and fools around with
a crawfish. Sometimes they have more serious
consequences, for example, when he loses the
thimble in the soup, steals eggs, fires the
musket and kills a pig, and, in particular, when
through laziness he drains the stockade keg of
water rather than fetching it as instructed,
thus depleting the entire supply and indirectly
causing Ready's death. Tommy likes to eat and
craves attention and praise. He seems young for
six since he often refers to himself as Tommy
and is more pettish, sulky, and silly than most
boys of that age. He is an overdrawn figure,
almost to the point of caricature.

TOM OAKLEY (*Good Night, Mr. Tom**), reclusive

church caretaker, past sixty, who becomes fond of the sickly, timid evacuee child billeted with him during World War II. Having retreated from village society nearly forty years earlier after the death of his beloved wife, Rachel, and his infant son, Tom has become known as being short-tempered and difficult, but he shows surprising patience with William* Beech, who vomits most of his meals at first, wets the bed regularly, and has arrived with no clothes except the thin set he wears. Tom's involvement with Willie draws him back into village life, and he surprises his neighbors by volunteering as a fire warden, making an air-raid shelter, and taking over the carol directing when the regular organist is called up. Later, Tom's concern at not hearing from the boy drives him to go to London, where he discovers Willie abandoned and nearly dead. His practical good sense tells him that the boy will not recover in the hospital or a children's home, so he kidnaps him and takes him back to Little Weirwold. In the end he adopts William.

TOM'S MIDNIGHT GARDEN (Pearce*, Philippa, ill. Susan Einzig, Oxford, 1958; Lippincott, 1958), fantasy that explores the concept of time. Young Tom* Long, a mid-twentieth-century English boy of about twelve, is sent to stay with his Uncle* Alan and his Aunt* Gwen Kitson, while his brother, Peter, recovers from the measles. Disappointed because he cannot spend his summer holidays playing games and climbing trees with Peter as they had planned and irritated at having to stay with childless relatives he hardly knows, Tom soon discovers adventures of such pleasure that, when the time comes to go home, he begs to stay on with the Kitsons. The adventures begin with the erratic striking of the old grandfather clock that stands in the hallway of the Kitsons' apartment house and which lures the boy on a midnight prowl. To Tom's amazement, he discovers behind the house a lovely Victorian garden where only an alley and walls exist during the day. Subsequently, throughout his summer's stay with the Kitsons, each night Tom exercises his unique ability to go back in time into the garden, where he plays with a little girl, lonely, high-spirited Hatty*

Melbourne, who grows progressively older as the seasons change and years go by in the garden. An orphan, she lives in the large rambling house, in Tom's time remodeled into flats, but in her time the comfortable dwelling of the aunt whose ward she is and who treats her like a charity child, and three lively, patronizing boy cousins, all older than she. Hatty can see Tom and converse with him, although she thinks he is a ghost, and he is visible also to animals and to Abel the gardener, who at the beginning thinks he's a devil. Abel continues to harbor suspicions about Tom's intentions even when Tom desperately inquires about Hatty's condition after she falls while they are building a tree house. As Hatty grows older, her interests broaden. She forms a romantic attachment with young Barty Bartholomew, who, in the last scenes in the garden portion of the novel, gives her and Tom (invisible to Barty) a lift home in his gig after Tom and Hatty have skated down-river. Though Tom is present, Hatty's attention lies elsewhere, and she no longer even sees him. On the night before he is to go home to his family, Tom tries once more to enter the garden but discovers that it is no longer there. In his anguish, he screams Hatty's name, which attracts the attention of the elderly landlady, Mrs. Bartholomew. Tom learns she is the Hatty of his midnight adventures, grown up and now the owner of the apartment house where the Kitsons live. What she has dreamed at night of her past life, Tom has experienced with her in her former garden, in a unique blending of time and experience that subtly conveys the message that all time and experience coexist. Slow-starting and mostly subdued throughout, the story never-theless builds in dramatic intensity to a properly foreshadowed and convincing conclusion. Tom and Hatty are especially well drawn, but even such minor figures as the boy cousins, the wispy, scuttling maid, Susan, and Tom's well-meaning but inept relatives emerge as distinct individuals. Conversation is idiomatically con-vincing in both periods, and customs, clothing, and behavior are equally typical. Detailed descriptive passages make the garden vividly real. Suspense arises from the reader's concern about whether, once in the garden, Tom will be

able to get back home, and then, after he has
become deeply involved in the fantasy world,
whether he will be able to continue associating
with Hatty, and how long their innocent,
carefree relationship can continue. The symbolism of the garden and depths of thought and
meaning that will be detected by more astute or
mature readers in no way detract from the
surface story, which is gripping in itself, but
create resonances of significance that make it
even more powerful. Books Too Good; Carnegie
Winner; ChLA Touchstones; Choice; Contemporary
Classics; Fanfare; Lewis Carroll.

TOM TRELOAR (*The Fox in Winter**), Cornish farmer
who clings to his independence and his isolated
farm where he was born and where he eventually
dies at ninety. After Frances*, the teenager who
helps him tape his memoirs, comes to know him,
she realizes that he has a strong temper and a
fierce desire to get his own way, and she knows
that he demands more of her time and attention
than he has any right to, but she also enjoys
his humor and his great appreciation of his
coastal land. He has dignity, intelligence, and
understanding of the power of language, and she
becomes fascinated with the stories of his life
as a boy and a young man, watching seals and
birds along the coast, salvaging from wrecked
ships, and exploring the abandoned tin mines.
His story of wooing his wife, Lettie, by mail
after her family moved to South Africa and his
tenderness to her, even after she has become
senile and seldom knows him, are moving.

TONY BOYD (*Gumble's Yard**; *Widdershins
Crescent**), curate of St. Jude's Church, not far
from the Jungle*, who acts as friend and advisor
to the Thompson children. He is young, tall, and
thin and wears glasses. A man of courage and
principle, he can use his fists as well as his
head and doesn't let his emotions get in the way
of doing what is right. Ironically, it may have
been his request that Mr. Widdowson hire Walter*
Thompson that led to Walter's downfall. Even
though at the end of *Widdershins Crescent*,
Walter is in jail and Kevin* no longer attends
school and works at a job to support the family,
Tony thinks the children have risen above the

difficulties of their environment and have a better future ahead of them. In *Gumble's Yard*, Tony courts Kevin's English teacher, Sheila, and in *Widdershins Crescent*, he marries her. She is a warm-hearted, caring young woman, who helps the younger children. They seem a well-matched couple.

TORGILS AUK (*The Namesake**), Danish soldier who is captured by Alfred* Dane-Leg and who agrees to become a Christian when Alfred makes the villagers spare his life. As soon as the Danes get the upper hand again he renounces his new religion, but when he captures young Alfred near the Danish camp, he tries to square accounts by letting him get away, though he does take his horse. Alfred is captured anyway. Later, when Torgils finds young Alfred lying bound in the sheep pen, he gives orders that his hands be untied so he can eat in comfort and later has him brought to his own house. Knowing that Guthorm* has an interest in using the boy, Torgils keeps him, tied up at first, later put to work. When Torgils discovers that his woman has given away the plans by Guthorm to break his oath, he at first seems likely to kill both her and Alfred, but he is distracted and simply beats her with his saddlebag instead.

TORQUIL (*Archer's Goon**), wizard who "farms" music, sports, and shops. Addicted to fantastic costumes, earrings, and turbans, he is quite good-looking when not made up, being tall with curly hair. Because Catriona Sykes is a music supervisor, he tries to get at Quentin* through her, threatening her job and plaguing her with a cacophany of bands, television singing, and other noise which assaults her sensitive ears. Although he is one of the good wizards, glad to get rid of the evil and ambitious older three, he is the most mecurial one and is dangerous when angry.

TORQUIL MACVINISH (*The Kelpie's Pearls**), Scottish orphan boy of twelve who becomes Morag's* friend, because she generously and understandingly gives a home to his pets when the Old* Woman with whom he lives refuses to accept them. Torquil is the only character who sees both sides of Morag's predicament. He understands why she is so distressed by the sightseers and the rumors that she is a witch, but he also sees why people think she is a witch. He reassures Morag that in calling up the storm she has been acting out of unselfish motives and not out of malice. He eventually goes to live with the Naturalist, who encourages his interest in animals and birds, and the reader is pleased that he no longer has to live with the disgruntled Old Woman.

TO TELL MY PEOPLE (Polland*, Madeleine, ill. John Holder, Hutchinson, 1968; Holt, 1968), historical novel set in the first century B.C. in southern Britain and in Rome. Lumna, 13, despises her crude, filthy family and the village set on a stagnant lake in a deeply forested area and cut off from any contact with other people. When she was younger, an old woman of the village who came from some other place told her of a wider world of sunshine, more advanced people, and even gods that her own small tribe has forgotten. Scorned by her brutish family as a dreamer, she retreats for peace to a hilltop refuge, entered by lifting a cleverly engineered stone and following an underground passage. There she comes upon a Roman scouting party led by the gentle tribune, Durus Velanius, mapping the country for Caesar's army. Durus prevents the centurion, Flavius, from immediately killing her and scares her by telling her, through his Belgian boy slave, Cassilus, that they are gods and that she will die if she tells of them. The next day she follows her father, the chief and the only one who cares about the refuge, as he goes to oil the entrance stone. Although she dares not tell him of the Romans, she has her first conversation with him and learns that he, too, had listened to the old woman and has wondered about the world beyond their immediate vicinity. Before she has digested this knowledge, he is killed by a Roman spear, and she is taken captive by the Romans and put to work cooking, a skill Cassilus lacks. After several days she begins to realize that they are really men and to listen to the tales Cassilus tells of Rome, where he was taken as a slave when he was a small child. In a break in the rainy weather, Lumna learns the secret of the terrifying flashing lights she has seen: they come from the signaling device of a polished piece of metal sending code messages by reflecting sunlight from the tops of hills and tall trees. The message tells the scouting party to return to the ships immediately, and Durus, realizing that this means they will be leaving Britain, tells her how to get back to her lake and lets her go. Instead she trails the Romans, comes to a British hill fort, tells the people there what she knows, and inadvertently causes them to ambush a corn-cutting cohort. Seeing this from a distance and thinking she has caused the death of the first people to be kind to her, Lumna stumbles off in panic and is captured to be one of the 6,000 slaves Caesar has ordered to be sent after him to Rome. There Cassilus, on an errand for Durus, sees her in the slave market and gets his master to buy her. She proves to be an intelligent and skillful slave, changing so fast that Cassilus, who is much attracted to her, feels resentful, but when she realizes that Caesar is returning to Britain, she enlists Cassilus's help and travels, disguised as a boy, with Durus's baggage. In Britain she makes her way back to her tribe, hoping to tell them that resistance is useless and of the good things that will come of contact with Rome, but they not only laugh at her, they also accuse her of her father's murder. She quickly proves this accusation foolish, but she cannot make them listen to her and has to watch while they ambush and kill Durus, Flavius, and Cassilus. Alone, she starts off toward Caesar and the sea. This is a far from hopeful ending to a grim tale. The main interest is in the gradual awakening of Lumna's mind and her wrestling with the ambiguous feelings she has toward the Romans and toward her own people. The native Britons are pictured as people without emotional ties or dignity, a questionable interpretation, but as a picture of two cultures colliding, the story is compelling. Choice.

TOTTIE PLANTAGANET (*The Dolls' House**), wooden Dutch doll about seven years old for all of her 100 years of existence, since she was purchased for a farthing in the mid-nineteenth century. Tottie is made of good solid wood, and neatly jointed at the hip and shoulders, with a round head and glossy painted hair. A doll of good sense and firm convictions, she has a calm voice and a comforting personality.

TOWNSEND, JOHN ROWE (1922-   ), born in the industrial city of Leeds, Yorkshire; journalist, critic, and author of novels highly regarded by critics and popular with adolescents. After his education in Leeds Grammar School, he served in the Royal Air Force until 1946 and then received his B.A. and M.A. degrees from Emmanuel College, Cambridge. He worked for many years as a reporter and editor for major newspapers and then in 1969 began to concentrate on writing and lecturing, acting as part-time children's books editor for the Manchester *Guardian*. He has since lectured in the United States, Australia, and Japan, as well as in England; served for several summers as a member of the faculty at Simmons College in Boston; and was honored as the May Hill Arbuthnot Lecturer in Atlanta, Georgia, and Anne Carroll Moore Lecturer in New York City, both in 1971. Eight of his some dozen and a half novels, all of them realistic fiction, have won awards or citations. Two were recommended for the Carnegie Award, *Hell's Edge** (Hutchinson, 1963; Lothrop, 1969), a mystery-detective story set in an industrial town in Yorkshire, and *The Intruder** (Oxford, 1969; Lippincott, 1970), a novel of suspense set somewhere on the coast of northern England and praised for its skillful integration of setting and story. Townsend's most decorated book, *The Intruder*, was also a *Boston Globe-Horn Book* Winner, won the Edgar Allan Poe Award, and was named to *Choice*, Contemporary Classics, and Fanfare. Appearing in *Choice* are *Gumble's Yard** (Hutchinson, 1961; as *Trouble in the Jungle*, Lippincott, 1969), Townsend's first novel and also a Fanfare selection, and *Widdershins Crescent** (Hutchinson, 1965; as *Good-Bye to the Jungle*, Lippincott, 1967), the first two in a series set in an inner-city slum in northern England and known as Townsend's Jungle* Trilogy. The series concludes with *Pirate's Island* (Oxford, 1968; Lippincott,

1968). Also on the Fanfare list are *The Summer People** (Oxford, 1972; Lippincott, 1972), which tells of the rocky course of some teenagers' holiday romances just before World War II; *Dan Alone** (Kestrel, 1983; Lippincott, 1983), about an abused and neglected inner-city boy's search for his father; *Noah's Castle** (Oxford, 1975; Lippincott, 1976), set in a future of runaway inflation and severe shortages; and *The Islanders** (Oxford, 1981; Lippincott, 1981), an adventure-survival story set on the island of Halcyon somewhere on the high seas, which also won the Christopher Award. Townsend broke ground in realistic fiction for later elementary-grade and adolescent readers, writing about ordinary and working-class children in tough situations sympathetically and not voyeuristically. Themes that recur include friendship, the search for identity, and differences between the social classes, and the development of settings and characterization are strong points. He has also written novels of science fiction: *The Xanadu Manuscript* (Oxford, 1977; as *The Visitors*, Lippincott, 1977) and *King Creature, Come* (Oxford, 1980; as *The Creatures*, Lippincott, 1980); edited a poetry anthology, *Modern Poetry* (Oxford, 1971; Lippincott, 1974); and published *Written for Children* (Miller, 1965; Lothrop, 1967) and *A Sense of Story* (Longman, 1971; Lippincott, 1971), revised and reissued as *A Sounding of Storytellers* (Kestrel, 1979; Lippincott, 1979), major books of criticism. His recent novels include *Tom Tiddler's Ground* (Viking Kestrel, 1985; Lippincott, 1986), a middle-grade adventure story, in which five children unravel a mystery about a decrepit canalboat and its hidden treasure, and *Downstream* (Walker, 1988; Lippincott, 1987), about a teenager who falls in love with his teacher. Townsend and his family live in England.

TRAVELERS BY NIGHT (Alcock*, Vivien, Methuen, 1983; Delacorte, 1985), modern, realistic novel of two children who rescue an aging circus elephant destined for the slaughter house. When Peachem's Circus goes bankrupt and cannot even finish out the season, Charlie* Marriot's Uncle Bert and Auntie Annie, with whom he has lived since a road accident killed his parents when

he was five, find a job with circus relatives
in America, and arrange that Charlie and their
daughter, Belle*, both twelve, will live with
Auntie May in Worthing and go to a regular
school for the first time. First they all go to
Goosebeak Farm, near Bradnam, the circus's
rented winter quarters, where they disband
gradually until only the two youngsters and the
aging animal trainer Danny Murphy and his three
elephants remain. Mr. Murphy has arranged with a
European circus to take two of the beasts, but
Tessie, with her scarred ears, is too old and
disfigured to be taken, even as a gift. Mr.
Murphy keeps the news of Tessie's inevitable
fate from Belle, since the elephant has been a
great favorite of the girl and a comfort to her
since she scarred her own face in a fall from a
high wire. Then Mr. Murphy has a stroke, and,
when they learn the truth, Belle devises a plan
to kidnap Tessie and take her to Blanstock
Safari Park, some 100 miles away, and enlists
Charlie's faithful though reluctant help. With
some clever acting, they convince the slaughter
house that the plan has been changed and
persuade the Goosebeak Farm family that the
elephant has been picked up while they were
distracted with other problems and that their
Auntie May has arranged that they meet her
immediately and take a barge trip before school
starts. Previously they have been giving secret
"private performances" along the road of their
Star Spinner tumbling act of Cosmo the clown and
Christobel the ballerina, begging and saving the
money in a fund for plastic surgery to repair
Belle's face. With this money they have bought
supplies for their trip. They have a plan of
sorts: to get to Yald Forest, cross it, keeping
Tessie concealed by moving only at night, and
somehow get her inside the safari park without
those in charge knowing. Charlie, more practical
than Belle, realizes that the plan is full of
holes. The first day they stay, as arranged, in
a derelict barn. Exhausted and tense, they
quarrel, and when Charlie wakes he discovers
that Belle has gone, leaving him a note saying
she will do it alone. After frantically trying
to find her, he goes on to the entrance to Yald
Forest, where he waits all night for her. In the
meantime she has become lost and weary and has

even partially overcome her fear of heights,
which has plagued her since her high-wire
accident; when she finally appears where he
waits, she is riding Tessie. They bumble on,
encountering various difficulties. In the dark
they stumble upon a group of boys camping with a
scout or school master, and the next morning a
friendly hiker stumbles upon them. The greatest
threat comes from a group of young hoodlums
living like Robin Hood, stealing from campers
and hikers and living in hideouts in the forest.
They capture Charlie and take the money, but
Belle, cleverly demonstrating her control over
Tessie, terrorizes them into returning it and
giving up their knives. Impressed by her nerve
and even by her scar, their leader, Flick*,
volunteers the band's help to get across the
forest, which the boys know thoroughly. A
dissident among them, Jerry, cuts the elephant
loose, however, and deserts, going to the
newspaper office in a nearby town to sell the
story. By the time he returns with a young
reporter they have found Tessie, posted
lookouts, and are able to escape without being
seen, though Tessie leaves an unmistakable trail
through the trees and brush. When they come to a
fence, the tough boys see no way to get the
elephant across, and they abandon the circus
children without a qualm. Belle gets Tessie to
step across dextrously, and they move on, hiding
in the daytime in a rhododendron swamp and
crossing a dangerous bog at night. In the
meantime, the newspaper editor has followed
leads, determined that the story is true, and
alerted the London papers. When they arrive at
the safari park, pretending to drive an escaped
elephant before them so that the gatekeeper will
allow them in, they run into a barrage of police
and reporters with cameras, and they weep,
thinking their hard journey has ended in
failure. The publicity, however, has caught the
public's imagination, and the Duke of Blanstock
is glad to have this new attraction and even
welcomes the children to do their Star Spinner
act during school holidays. At school Belle puts
on an act of bravado about her scar and is
immediately popular. The bizarre adventure is
made plausible by close attention to detail.
Characters are well delineated. Belle, who, like

the ballerina in their act, treats devoted Charlie imperiously, is shown as vulnerable when she tries to hide her scarred face or quails at heights. Charlie, cautious, worried, and sensitive, is also well characterized. The young hoods are less believable, but minor characters like the owners of Goosebeak Farm, whose friendliness cools with the fortunes of the circus, are convincing. Fanfare.

TRAVERS, P(AMELA) L(YNDON), (1906-   ), born in Queensland, Australia; writer best known for her highly popular Mary Poppins books. She was educated privately and in the 1920s and 1930s was an actress, a dancer, and a journalist, being a regular contributor to the *Irish Statesman* in Dublin. During World War II she worked for the British Ministry of Information in the United States and in the 1960s and early 1970s was Writer in Residence at Radcliffe College, Cambridge, Massachusetts, Smith College, Northampton, Massachusetts, and Scripps College, Claremont, Calififornia, and has frequently been a featured speaker at conferences and conventions. She was also named an officer in the Order of the British Empire. Her first book for children, *Mary Poppins** (Howe, 1934; Reynal, 1934), an episodic fantasy starring a prim, no-nonsense nanny with magical powers, has remained popular for more than fifty years and has been listed as a Children's Classic and included in *Children's Books Too Good to Miss*. It has been followed by a number of sequels: *Mary Poppins Comes Back** (Dickson, 1935; Reynal, 1935), *Mary Poppins in the Park** (Davies, 1952; Harcourt, 1952), *Mary Poppins Opens the Door** (Davies, 1944; Reynal, 1943), and *Mary Poppins in Cherry Tree Lane* (Collins, 1982; Delacorte, 1982). There are also *Mary Poppins from A to Z.* (Collins, 1963; Harcourt, 1962), an alphabet book with pages of text each using a letter, frequently alternating with pages of illustration, and *Mary Poppins in the Kitchen: A Cookery Book with a Story* (with Maurice Moore-Betty, Collins, 1977; Harcourt, 1975). Among her other books for children are *I Go by Sea, I Go by Land* (Davies, 1941; Harper, 1941), about two English children who are evacuees to the United States in World War II; *The Fox in the Manger* (Collins,

1963; Norton, 1962), in which the fox gives the
Christ Child the gift of his cunning; and *Friend
Monkey* (Collins, 1972; Harcourt, 1971), which is
based on Hanuman, the monkey lord of Hindu myth.
A book that combines folktale with literary
tale is *About the Sleeping Beauty* (Collins,
1977; McGraw, 1975), which includes five
versions of the Sleeping Beauty tale from the
oral tradition, with notes about the origin or
discovery of each story, plus her own literary
version, resulting in an unusual and interesting
introduction to the study of comparative folklore. She has also written a number of nonfiction books for adults.

TREADGOLD, MARY (1910-   ), born in London;
editor and writer of domestic, mystery, and
adventure novels for children. She was educated
at Ginner-Mawer School of Dance and Drama,
Challoner School in London, and St. Paul's
Girls' School and received an honors M.A. in
English from the University of London in 1936.
In the early 1930s, she was an editor with
Raphael Tuck and then went with William
Heinemann of London from 1938 to 1940 as their
first children's book editor. From 1941-1960,
she was a producer and literary editor for BBC
in London. She was one of the early writers of
pony novels, working out the idea for her first
one while sheltering from an air raid in her
garden during the war. She was sure she could
do better than the novels that were being
submitted to her for publication. This book, her
first published novel, won the Carnegie Medal.
Entitled *We Couldn't Leave Dinah** (Cape, 1941;
as *Left till Called For*, Doubleday, 1941), it is
a story of adventure, intrigue, and children on
their own during the German occupation of the
fictitious Channel island of Clerinel, in which
ponies are important but not the main subject.
Its sequel, *The "Polly Harris"* (Cape, 1949; as
The Mystery of the "Polly Harris", Doubleday,
1951), finds the same brother and sister in
London involved in a chase to capture smugglers.
Although she wrote a dozen novels after *We
Couldn't Leave Dinah*, none achieved its
popularity or critical stature. Some others of
her books are *No Ponies* (Cape, 1946), a
mystery-adventure set in the south of France

just after World War II; *The Winter Princess*
(Brockhampton, 1962; Van Nostrand, 1964), about
the friendship between a group of children and
an old woman at Hampton Court; *Maids' Ribbons*
(Nelson, 1965; Nelson, 1967) and the books about
Patty, *Elegant Patty* (Hamilton, 1967) and *Poor
Patty* (Hamilton, 1968) for younger children; and
the Heron series, in which children have adventures at a riding school: *The Heron Ride* (Cape,
1962), *Return to the Heron* (Cape, 1963), and
Journey from the Heron (Cape, 1981). For adults
she wrote *The Running Child* (Cape, 1951), a
novel.

TREASE, (ROBERT) GEOFFREY (1909–   ), born in
Nottingham, son of a wine merchant; novelist and
writer of nonfiction for adults and older
children. He grew up in Robin Hood's city and
wanted to be a writer from his early years. He
produced a magazine at thirteen, edited his
school magazine, and at sixteen wrote a play
that was school-produced. After Nottingham High
School, he entered Queen's College, Oxford, on
a Classics scholarship but dropped out after a
year. For several years thereafter he led a
hardscrabble existence in London, holding jobs
as a social worker in the East End slums, as a
freelance writer of articles and publicity, and
as a teacher in a prep school. In 1933, at age
twenty-four, he married and also became a
full-time writer. His first novel came out the
next year, *Bows Against the Barons** (Lawrence;
International). Considered one of his best books
and named to *Choice*, it is an exciting, action-
filled historical adventure that blends an
actual fourteenth century insurrection of
peasants with details from the Robin* Hood
legends and portrays the outlaw as a
revolutionary in the peasants' struggle for
their rights. Subsequently Trease pioneered in
historical fiction for youth, producing over the
next five decades some sixty novels, most based
on history, in addition to books of nonfiction,
plays, short stories, and four novels and
similar writings for adults. In addition to
Thunder of Valmy* (Macmillan, 1960; as *Victory
at Valmy*, Vanguard, 1961), a Fanfare book about
the French Revolution from the standpoint of
ordinary people, some of his best known stories

are *Cue for Treason* (Blackwell, 1940; Vanguard, 1941), set in Shakespeare's time; *The Hills of Varna* (Macmillan, 1948; as *Shadow of the Hawk*, Harcourt, 1949), about Erasmus; *The Barons' Hostage* (Phoenix, 1952; Nelson, 1975), set during the thirteenth century Barons' War; and *Word to Caesar* (Macmillan, 1956; as *Message to Hadrian*, Vanguard, 1956). In the late forties, he began writing books about modern teenagers, among them *No Boats on Bannermere* (Heinemann, 1949; Norton, 1965) and *The Maythorn Story* (Heinemann, 1960). His nonfiction for children includes biographies of Walter Raleigh, Mozart, Byron, and D. H. Lawrence, and two collections about English monarchs. He translated two books by Rene Guillot, introducing the noted French writer to English children. His books for young readers have been translated into a dozen languages. Although his historical books may seem structually naive and quaint and instructive today, they still amply satisfy his main objective of entertaining with a good story. His list for adults is also imposing, and includes a book of poetry, *The Supreme Prize and Other Poems* (Stockwell, 1926), and *Tales Out of School: A Survey of Children's Fiction* (Heinemann, 1949), one of the earliest attempts to define the role of the children's writer and to look at children's books from a literary perspective. In World War II he served in the infantry and the Army Educational Corps in India. He has made his home in Worcestershire.

TREASURE ISLAND (Stevenson*, Robert Louis, Cassell, 1883; Roberts, 1884), adventure novel set in the eighteenth century in England, aboard ship, and on an imaginary island probably in the Caribbean where the main characters search for buried pirate gold. For Jim* Hawkins, son of the proprietor of the Admiral Benbow Inn in Black Hill Cove on the west coast of England, events start with the arrival at the inn of an old buccaneer, Billy* Bones. Finding the place isolated, with infrequent visitors, Bones settles in for months, drinking large amounts of rum, calling himself "the captain," and terrorizing the local people with rough songs and stories of sea fights. He pays Jim to keep on the lookout and warn him if a seafaring man with one leg should appear, but instead it is a pale, tallowy man named Black Dog who arrives and asks for his mate Bill, and later a blind man named Pew*, who gives the old buccaneer the "black spot," the pirates' ultimatum, that cause Billy Bones to collapse and die of a stroke. Jim's father having recently died, Jim and his mother go through Billy Bones's sea chest, where Mrs. Hawkins insists on counting out exactly what he owes her from the bag of coins. Before she is finished they are interrupted. They hide nearby and see a band of pirates ransack the inn until they are scared away by revenue officers. Jim takes a packet sealed in oilskin, which he picked up to square the account as he and his mother fled, to Dr.* Livesey, the local physican and magistrate, at the hall of Squire* Trelawney, and the three open it, finding a map showing where treasure has been buried. Squire Trelawney buys and outfits a ship, the schooner *Hispaniola*, and soon the three gather, along with the squire's gamekeeper, Tom Redruth, and two of his other servants, at Bristol, where the squire has been assembling a crew with the help of a tavern keeper, a one-legged ex-sailor named Long* John Silver. At the tavern, Jim catches sight of Black Dog, but the pirate runs out, and Long John makes such a show of trying to have him apprehended that Jim's suspicions are quieted. Captain Smollett, a stern, sharp-looking man, protests the way all the crew know what should be secret and insists that the arms and powder be shifted and other precautions be taken. One night on the voyage, on which Jim is cabin boy, he climbs into the nearly empty apple barrel and overhears Long John, who is the ship's cook, talking to one of the younger seamen, clearly revealing that the men are almost all from the crew of the dead pirate Captain* Flint, and that after the treasure has been found they will mutiny, seize the treasure, and kill the men loyal to the captain. Just as land is sighted, Jim is able to tell the squire, the doctor, and the captain of his discovery. To avert an immediate mutiny, Captain Smollett allows the men an afternoon on shore, and Jim climbs into a boat to go along. On the island he gives Long John the slip, but later hears the

death cry of one honest man and sees Long John
kill another. Running in panic, he comes upon
Ben* Gunn, a ragged, demented creature who was
marooned on the island three years earlier. Ben,
who was on Flint's ship when the treasure was
buried, suggests a bargain with the squire and
tells Jim where his homemade boat is hidden.
While Jim is on the island, the other loyal men
move as many supplies and guns as they can to
the old stockade, leaving the ship to the
pirates. Jim joins them there, and they fight
off a pirate attack in which the captain is
wounded. Bored and restless, Jim sneaks out of
the stockade, determined to find Ben Gunn's
boat. When he does, he impulsively acts upon
another idea and cuts the *Hispaniola* loose, a
job that takes him far out of the harbor and
nearly swamps his lopsided coracle, but at the
last minute he is able to board the erratically
sailing ship where he finds that the two men
left on guard have fought. One is dead and the
other, Israel Hands, who was Flint's gunner, is
wounded. Hands, pretending friendship, directs
Jim in getting the ship under control and into a
harbor on the far side of the island, but as
soon as the ship is beached, he starts after Jim
with his knife. Jim scrambles up to the
crosstrees, and, when Hands throws his knife and
pins Jim's shoulder to the mast, the boy
involuntarily shoots both his pistols and
watches the gunner plunge into the water, dead.
Feeling pretty cocky and proud of himself, Jim
returns to the stockade only to find that the
pirates are now in charge there and have the
treasure map. Long John, clearly trying to play
up to both sides, saves him from the other
pirates, saying they need a hostage, although
first they give Silver the black spot marked
"deposed," a notice of a mutiny he subsequently
talks them out of. The next day all five
remaining pirates as well as Long John, leading
Jim by a rope, set off to find the treasure. At
one point the supersitious men are almost scared
off by the voice of Ben Gunn imitating Flint,
but Long John rallies them, and they come to the
spot where the treasure was buried, only to find
an empty pit, Ben Gunn having found and
transported the gold and coins to his cave.
Furious, the pirates turn on Long John, but a

shot by Dr. Livesey, who is hiding nearby, kills one and Long John kills another, sending the rest fleeing. The good characters accept Long John back among them conditionally and, with Ben Gunn and the treasure, sail away, leaving the three remaining pirates marooned. In the South American port where they go to get more crew, Long John escapes, taking with him a large bag of coins. Jim is the narrator for most of the story, though Dr. Livesey fills in about events that occur in Jim's absence. Though no objectionable language appears, even by Victorian standards, the dialogue gives the impression of the natural speech of rough and foul-mouthed pirates. The style is vivid and the plot tightly knit and exciting, but what makes the story stand far above other adventure novels of the period is the characterization of Long John Silver, a villain absolutely ruthless and unscrupulous but also charming and likeable. The novel is one of the most famous and best-loved adventure stories of all time. Books Too Good; Children's Classics; ChLA Touchstones; Choice.

TREASURE OF GREEN KNOWE. See *The Chimneys of Green Knowe.*

TREECE, HENRY (1911? 1912?-1966), born in Wednesbury, Staffordshire; schoolmaster, editor, poet, novelist, and writer for later elementary-grade and teen readers, best-known in literature for children for his historical fiction. He grew up with a strong sense of history, nourished by books of history and anecdotes from his family's past. His father could trace his lineage back to 1573 in Nottinghamshire, where his family continued to live on the same bit of land in Sherwood Forest. His mother's people came from Wales to work in the iron foundries in the English Midlands. Their experiences provided the basis for his adult novel *The Rebels* (Gollancz, 1953). He was an indifferent student but won a scholarship to Birmingham University and received his diploma in education in 1934. He worked ked at odd jobs and then became a teacher and headmaster at various schools and colleges. He maintained his connection with education until his death, except for the years he spent in the Army and the Air Force

Intelligence during World War II. He began to write while at the university, continued while teaching, and published his first book, *38 Poems* (Fortune) in 1940. In the late thirties, he became friends with prominent poets like T. S. Eliot and Dylan Thomas and started a literary movement called the "New Apocalyptic," coediting three anthologies of poems, and more came later. He edited magazines and made collections of poetry for Bodley Head during the war, and afterward he went into radio. He published an adult novel in 1952, *The Dark Island* (Gollancz; Random), which was set in Celtic Britain, and nine more followed. He continued to publish fiction and verse for adults until his death. He developed a strong interest in writing for children, and, beginning in 1954, he wrote mostly for a young audience, producing altogether over a fifteen-year period thirty-two books of fiction (almost all of them novels), plays, and books of nonfiction. He wrote a set of mystery-adventure novels, including *Desperate Journey* (Faber, 1954), *Ask for King Billy* (Faber, 1955), *Killer in Dark Glasses* (Faber, 1965), and *Bang, You're Dead!* (Faber, 1966), but won greatest critical approval for his historical novels. Of these, his two Viking trilogies are the most highly regarded. The first features Harald Sigurdson, who grows to maturity during the series: *Viking's Dawn** (Lane, 1955; Criterion, 1956), set at the beginning of the Viking period, overflowing with color and action, and named to *Choice*; *The Road to Miklagard* (Lane, 1957; Criterion, 1957); and *Viking's Sunset* (Bodley, 1960; Criterion, 1961). The second set is for somewhat younger readers and consists of *Horned Helmet* (Brockhampton, 1963; Criterion, 1963), *The Last of the Vikings* (Brockhampton, 1964; as *The Last Viking*, Pantheon, 1966), and *Splintered Sword* (Brockhampton, 1965; Duell, 1966). These and other Viking stories reflect Treece's familiarity with Snorri Sturluson and the Norse sagas both in story content and in style. Other books of fiction are *The Children's Crusade* (Bodley, 1958; as *Perilous Pilgrimage*, Criterion, 1959), *The Windswept City* (Hamilton, 1967; Meredith, 1968), about Troy, and his last work, posthumously published as *The Dream Time** (Brockhampton, 1967; Meredith, 1968), a Stone Age story that was highly commended for the Carnegie Award and named to Fanfare. He also wrote radio plays and features and made many appearances on radio and television. He was preoccupied with crisis times in history and presented past events unromantically, clearly, and succinctly.

TREGARTHEN, ENYS (1851-1923), born in Cornwall, England; storyteller and writer. Although confined to her room from the age of sixteen when an illness left her crippled, she became a writer and was widely known as a storyteller. In the 1880s and 1890s she wrote more than a dozen books and in the early 1900s published three collections of stories: *The Piskey-purse: Legends and Tales of North Cornwall* (Wells Gardner, 1905), *North Cornwall Fairies and Legends* (Wells Gardner, 1906), and *The House of the Sleeping Winds and Other Stories, Some Based on Cornish Folklore* (Rebman, 1910). Her tale using the Cornish setting and dialect, *The Doll Who Came Alive** (Day, 1942), was found in manuscript among her things after her death and, edited by Elizabeth Yates, was published in the United States. Yates also edited a collection of Tregarthen's stories, *Piskey Folk: A Book of Cornish Legends* (Day, 1940).

TRIS LA CHARD (*The Scarecrows**), lively, clowning schoolmate of Simon* Wood and the only one able to deflect Simon's psychotic rage and fears. Son of a tomato farmer on the island of Jersey, Tris is not vulnerable to the snide bullying of the class-conscious boys at school or to the threat that Simon feels from the scarecrows and the old mill. Still, he alone understands Simon's fear and seems to see the scarecrows as Simon does, as the spirits of the adulterous inhabitants of the mill, though whether he feels their enmity himself or only as Simon's hallucination is not clear. As a self-confident, well-balanced boy, he serves as an obvious foil to overwrought Simon.

TRISTAN AND ISEULT (Sutcliff*, Rosemary, ill. Victor Ambrus, Bodley, 1971; Dutton, 1971), retelling and novelization of the ancient Celtic legend of Tristan, which later became part of the Arthurian cycle. Set in Cornwall, Ireland, and Brittany in the premedieval period, the novel follows the old story in most ways but omits the love potion drunk by mistake by the two principals, and thereby makes their love depend upon human attraction and not on magic. At sixteen, Tristan, son of the king of Lothian, travels with his friend and tutor, Gorvenal, to Cornwall. They pose as merchants, and come to the Royal Stronghold of Tintagel, home of his uncle, King Marc, where they join the king's warriors and Tristan is soon recognized as foremost among them. When a mighty Irish champion known as the Morholt seeks to enforce an old treaty and demands that one-third of all the children born in Cornwall since the last tribute was paid be given up to become slaves in Ireland, Tristan volunteers to meet him in single combat to settle the claim. He slays the Morholt, leaving a fragment of his sword in the Irish champion's skull, but is himself sorely wounded and lies near death for a long time. Finally he begs King Marc to have him set in a boat and pushed out to sea, where he will either die or by some strange adventure be cured. The skiff drifts to Ireland, where the king's daughter, Iseult, has great skill in healing. At her direction, but without their ever meeting, Tristan is treated by her serving women and returns to Cornwall. There King Marc is pressured by his nobles to take a wife. As a delaying tactic, he says he will marry only the woman who has hair like that he has seen dropped from a swallow's beak, a flaming copper red. Tristan sets out to find such a woman. Their ship having been blown onto the Irish coast, he and his men again pose as merchants and learn that the countryside has been beset by a terrible dragon and that the king has promised his daughter's hand to anyone who can slay it. Tristan sets off for this adventure and, after a great combat, destroys the beast and cuts out its tongue; then, severely wounded, he crawls away to a stream and loses consciousness in the shallow water. The king's steward, whom the Princess Iseult loathes, has followed him and, coming upon the dead dragon, cuts off its head, returns to the court, and claims his prize. With her handmaiden Branigan, Iseult steals away to

the site of the   conflict and finds Tristan. The
women   bring him   back and   nurse him   secretly.
Although Iseult realizes, when she burnishes his
sword and finds that   the bit broken out matches
that   taken   from   the   Morholt's   skull,   that
Tristan   has   been   an   enemy   to   Ireland,   she
carefully preserves the   dragon's tongue to back
his   claim of   having killed   the dragon   and is
relieved   when   the   steward's claim   is   proven
fraudulent. She is distressed, however, to learn
that   Tristan will   take her   as bride   for King
Marc instead of for himself.   On their trip back
to Cornwall a storm   forces them to take shelter
on the   Welsh coast. There Iseult   confesses her
love to   Tristan and,   though he   foresees great
trouble,   he   spends   the   night   with her.   In
Cornwall, married   to King Marc, who   loves her,
she   behaves circumspectly   for   some time,   but
eventually   she and   Tristan   give   in to   their
passion again and are   seen by another nephew of
Marc, the jealous Andret. He warns Marc, and the
lovers   are   discovered   together.   Marc   takes
Iseult back, but banishes Tristan from court. In
spite of   Gorvenal's urging that they   leave the
country, Tristan stays not far off, and when the
royal party moves to the country for the summer,
he   contrives to   send messages   to Iseult,   who
then steals   away to   be with him.   Andret again
watches and   warns Marc,   but Tristan and Iseult
realize that they are   being spied upon from the
branches of a tree,   and they   deflect suspicion
by acting as though   innocently wronged by Marc.
He begs   their forgiveness and   restores Tristan
to his   place at court, but Andret still watches,
and this time Marc catches them in bed together.
Both are   sentenced to   death,   Tristan by being
broken on the wheel   and Iseult by fire. Tristan
is   able to   evade   his   captors, return   before
Iseult is burned, and, bribing a leper to change
clothes with him,   approaches the stake and begs
the   king to   sentence Iseult   to life   with the
lepers instead of to death by fire.   They escape
to a deserted part of   the kingdom and, with the
faithful   Gorvenal,   live   happily   for   several
years.   Then the king takes a notion   to hunt in
that area,   and they   are discovered.   Marc goes
quietly to their hut and finds them sleeping. He
exchanges   his sword   for   that   of Tristan   and
leaves   his hunting   glove   on Iseult's   breast.

Realizing that this means she will be forgiven,
Tristan insists that they go back to court.
Tristan is again banished, but before they part,
Iseult gives him a ring by which he can call her
to him at any time. Some time later, Tristan and
Gorvenal come to the aid of King Hoel in
Brittany, and as a reward Tristan is given
Hoel's daughter, Iseult of the White Hands, for
his wife. Although she loves him dearly and her
brother Karherdin becomes his close friend,
Tristan cannot forget Iseult of Cornwall. He
persuades Karherdin to go with him to Cornwall,
where he secretly sees Iseult again, but through
a misunderstanding she rejects him. He returns
to Brittany, able at last to love his wife. Some
time later he accompanies Karherdin on an
expedition to see the woman who, as prince and
now king, Karherdin has long loved, although she
is married to another noble. They are pursued on
their homeward journey and, greatly outnumbered,
are cut down, leaving Karherdin killed and
Tristan deeply wounded. At the point of death,
he sends a messenger with the ring to Iseult of
Cornwall, begging her to come and heal him. He
warns the messenger to change his black sail for
a white one if Iseult has forgiven him and come
to heal him. His wife, however, overcome by
jealousy, tells him that the approaching sail is
black, and he dies before Iseult of Cornwall
reaches him. She demands to approach the body
ahead of his wife, and lying down beside him,
dies of a broken heart. The novel departs from
the traditional legend more in style than in
content, with increased emphasis upon motiva-
tion, feelings, and realistic details to produce
a very readable version of the tragic love
story. Some of the trappings of the Middle Ages
have been dropped so that attention centers on
the psychological struggle rather than upon the
jousting, religious ceremonies, magic, and
pagentry of Arthurian retellings. Boston Globe
Winner; Carnegie Com.; Fanfare.

TRON (*The Blue Hawk**), novice priest of the hawk
god, Gdu, who upsets the ritual of the King's
Renewal by taking the hawk meant for sacrifice
and thereby starts a series of events that leads
to the breakdown of the absolute power of the
priests. Since Tron was the thirty-third child

born in his village since the last priest was
taken, his father was forced to sell him at the
age of one year to the priests, and he has been
brought up knowing nothing but the temple life.
After his taking of the hawk and his encounter
with the king, Tron sees himself as two people,
one the obedient priest trainee, still deeply
religious and shocked by deviations from strict
ritual, and a second who responds to the freedom
of hunting with his hawk and to the friendship
offered by the king. In the end, since he
believes the gods have left, it is clear that he
will not be going back to the discipline of the
temple, and it is implied that he will follow
the king.

TROUBLE IN THE JUNGLE. See *Gumble's Yand.*

THE TROUBLE WITH DONOVAN CROFT (Ashley*,
Bernard, ill. Fermin Rocker, Oxford, 1974),
realistic novel of family and school life
revolving around an emotionally disturbed child
and set for about a month in London in the late
1960s or early 1970s. Acquiring a foster child
named Donovan Croft, a ten-year-old black boy of
Jamaican descent, spells trouble for the white
Chapman family: Ted, the forthright, sturdy,
workingman father; Doreen, the practical housewife; and especially for Keith, who is also
ten, tall, fair, active, usually obedient and
respectful, well-liked by his mates and
teachers, and resourceful. Even before Donovan
arrives, sharp-tongued Mrs. Parsons next door
reveals her antiblack bias. When the social
worker brings him, Donovan won't get out of the
car until Keith entices him out with Fluff, his
baby guinea pig. When Keith takes him to school
the next day and introduces him to his
schoolmates as his foster brother, Keith's chums
Dave and Tony react with jealousy and cut Keith
out of their games. When Donovan, who either
can't or won't speak, doesn't answer roll call,
Mr.* Henry, the teacher, shouts at him, strikes
him, and calls him a "stupid black idiot."
Donovan runs away from school, and, while
teachers and pupils search diligently, makes his
way home and takes refuge in the guinea pig's
shed. When days pass and Donovan still doesn't
communicate but just stands or sits dejectedly

and hangs his head, logic and the school
psychologist lead the sensible and loving Chapmans to see that Donovan has retreated into an
inner world because he feels rejected and
abandoned by his mother, who has returned to
Jamaica to nurse her dying father, and his
father, who has had to put him in foster care
because his job leaves him no time to care for
Donovan. Several weeks pass during which
teachers and the foster family take extra pains
to help the boy feel comfortable and wanted. He
does fairly well at his schoolwork, and at home
he performs responsibly at simple tasks like
taking care of Fluff, making his bed, and
washing dishes, but he still does not talk or
show emotion. All this is especially hard on
Keith, who takes a brotherly attitude toward
Donovan and regrets the loss of his old chums. A
major breakthrough occurs when Mrs. Parsons
scolds Donovan for entering her yard to retrieve
Fluff. Keith comforts Donovan, unintentionally
and ironically using almost the same words that
Mrs. Croft used to use, and Donovan responds
with a slow nod. Gradually a bond develops
between the two boys, but Donovan remains mute.
Then the Chapmans learn that Donovan's favorite
football (soccer) team will be playing the
Chapmans' favorite team. Mr. Chapman gets
tickets for the match and invites Mr.* Croft.
Their hopes that the excitement of the game and
the presence of his father will enable the boy
to shake off his despondency are dashed,
however. Though obviously involved in the
action, Donovan utters not a single word, not
even at the most critical moment of play. After
the game, as they are leaving the grounds, a car
almost runs Keith down. Donovan's shout of
warning, the first words the boy has spoken
since he arrived at the Chapman house, saves
Keith's life. The trauma dissolved, Donovan
slowly begins to relate to family and
schoolmates and even to express his opinions in
words. The omniscient point of view allows the
reader to learn how teachers, parents, and Keith
see Donovan as well how Donovan views himself.
Though Donovan behaves stereotypically, his
thoughts individualize him, and it is through
them that the reader learns that his father and
mother argued violently before the mother's

departure, an incident overheard by the boy and frightening to him. The school scenes are rich with activity and with the interplay of personalities in and out of class and among staff as well. Mrs. Parsons exists for the sake of the plot and is the least convincing character, Mr. Croft seems too ineffectual, and the car which threatens Keith appears too fortuitously. Keith experiences anxiety and frustration typical of a well-brought up boy from a loving family. The author creates the moment well, employs an unusual amount of figurative language for this kind of story, and depicts with skill and sympathy, and without didacticism and sentimentality, some diffi- culties of meeting the needs of children with special problems. (Mr.* Roper) Other.

TROY PALMER (*The Haunting**), Barney's elder sister, a dark, bony, silent child, who does well in school and is fanatically neat and well-organized. Unknown to the family (but not unexpected to the reader), she has magical powers inherited through her dead mother from her Great-Grandmother* Scholar, talents that she has tried to use to good ends. For example, she has been conjuring up playmates for Barney to relieve his loneliness, but the rest of the family thinks they are figments of his imagination. Though she proves to be a witch, the family accepts her and continues to love her, exemplifying one of the novel's themes. She becomes friends with Great-Uncle* Cole Scholar, also a magician.

TRUMPKIN (*Prince Caspian**; *The Silver Chair**), feisty, persevering, and faithful Dwarf who assists Caspian* in gaining his rightful position as King of Narnia*. He, the Dwarf Nikabrik*, and the Badger Trufflehunter rescue Caspian after he has fallen from his horse while fleeing from Miraz. Trumpkin prevails against Nikabrik's suggestion to kill Caspian because he is a Telmarine and hence can't be trusted. The Dwarf is one of the leaders after the Old Narnians retreat to Aslan's* How, and he willingly undertakes the mission of going to the coast to see if help has arrived there. After the Pevensies rescue him from drowning, he plays a strong role in getting them all back to the stronghold. Edmund* terms him Dear Little Friend, and subsequently the Pevensies often call him D.L.F. for short. Though he never appears in *The Voyage of the "Dawn Treader"**, the reader learns that Trumpkin is acting as Caspian's regent while Caspian sails in search of the seven exiled lords. He is an engaging, strongly drawn figure and serves as a foil for the surly Nikabrik, who resorts to easy answers and dubious morality. In *The Silver Chair*, he appears as the Regent, an old man, hunched, deaf, peppery, and irascible in disposition but with the self-confidence born of gentle authority and still true as steel to his master and friend, King Caspian the Tenth.

TUG SHAKESPEARE (*On the Edge**), Liam Shakespeare, son of Harriet Shakespeare, a well-known London investigative reporter, whom Tug calls Hank and to whom he feels very close. Tug is kidnapped by the Free People, who hold him hostage in an effort to get the British government to set up community schools for youth under sixteen. His captors are Doyle* and the Hare-woman*, who ironically conduct a kind of brainwashing exercise to get him to think of them as his parents and thus control him. Tug clarifies his relationship with his mother at the same time as he works out how he must relate to his captors and thinks through his priorities. It is the solid relationship that he has with his mother, who has taught him to be self-sufficient and helped him to have a good self-image, that enables him to win through in this difficult time. When first seen, Tug is running, pushing himself to the limits of his endurance for the intense psychological satisfaction the experience gives him. The scene gives the reader insights into Tug's character and skillfully foreshadows and balances the conclusion. Serving as Tug's foil is Jinny* Slattery, who frees him and saves his life.

TULKU (Dickinson*, Peter, Gollancz, 1979; Dutton, 1979), historical adventure novel set in China and Tibet in 1900, at the time of the Boxer rebellion. Theodore* Tewker, 13, son of the missionary at the Settlement, a mission of

the Congregation of Christ Jesus, flees at the
attack by the rebels and is the only survivor.
Dazed and numb, he joins Mrs.* Daisy Jones, 39,
an eccentric English woman who is a botanist,
and her guide, a young Chinese poet named Lung.
Together they manage to cross the Yangtze River,
aided by a helpful Chinese ex-official,
P'iu-Chun, who also gives them a map of the area
leading to Tibet. In the mountains they are
ambushed by bandits in league with their
porters, but Mrs. Jones shoots some of them, and
the original party of three escapes, coming at
last to an idyllic valley where she discovers an
unknown lily. She also tells Theo, who has been
horrified by her rough language and her use of
cosmetics but has come to like her, about her
colorful past, including her love affair with
wealthy Monty German, who taught her botany, and
about his family who have taken in their
illegitimate child, arranged a marriage for
Monty, and are now paying her to stay out of
England for ten years. With mixed feelings, Theo
realizes that Lung and Mrs. Jones have become
lovers. Their idyll is destroyed when the bandits discover them, and they flee to a bridge
made only of ropes across a chasm, where they
meet Tibetan Lama Amchi and his entourage, who
drive away the bandits, help them across the
bridge, and take them to the almost inaccessible
monastery at Dong* Pe. The lama reveals that he
has believed Theo is the new incarnation of the
Tulku of the Siddha Asara, comparable to the
Dalai Lama, but decides it is rather the unborn
child of Mrs. Jones and Lung. Theo is pressed
into service as interpreter as the lama
initiates Mrs. Jones into Buddhist beliefs, and
he also tries to learn Tibetan from Achugla,
formerly Major Price-Evans, who has become a
monk and whose English old-boy manners mix
strangely with a tolerant and accepting attitude
toward all beliefs. Though the three hope to
escape and Lung makes a plan with a dissident
monk, Mrs. Jones, who has become impressed by
the beliefs of the lama, decides to stay. Lung
attempts to shoot the lama, is put under a
mind-control spell, and is released only when
Mrs. Jones demands it as a condition of her
staying. In the last chapter, Theo calls upon
Monty German, giving him news of Mrs. Jones,

delivering a bulb of the new lily, and declining his offer of help, saying he will return to Bluff City, headquarters of the Congregation. The adventure is exciting throughout, but more impressively, the religious beliefs, both Christian and Buddhist, and the characterizations of the disparate people are made believable and moving. Carnegie Winner; Fanfare; Whitbread.

TUMBLEDOWN DICK (Spring*, Howard, ill. Steven Spurrier, Faber, 1939; Viking, 1940), story accurately described in a subtitle, "All People and No Plot," set in Manchester and nearby Cheshire in the 1920s. Because his mother has influenza and he is to stay with his father's brother Henry* until she recovers, Dick Birkinshaw, 12, son of a market gardener, starts with his father in a pre-dawn winter morning for the Manchester Smithfield market behind the patient old horse, Uncle Arthur. This begins a couple of wonderful weeks for him, full of new people and places. While he is waiting on the wagon, he sees a line of automobiles pull up and a group of stylishly dressed people get out and begin to tour the market. Boylike, he tags along and soon is walking right beside the Lady Mayoress, wife of the Lord Mayor of Manchester. When the men catch her under the mistletoe and roguishly insist that she kiss someone, she soundly kisses Dick, and then gets into conversation with him, takes him to breakfast and for a tour of the refrigeration system, and before they part suggests that Dick call at City Hall to get a ticket to a Christmas party she is giving. When he returns, Uncle Arthur and the wagon are gone. Dick is soon found, however, not by his father but by Uncle Oswald* Tubbs, his mother's brother, an unemployed stage magician, who, it turns out, has been living with Uncle Henry and Aunt Maria. Uncle Henry's shop sells small animals of all descriptions, but his love is for his fish, which he guards jealously, hating to sell to anyone who doesn't understand and feeling deeply about their care. When another conjurer is injured and Uncle Oswald is called upon to take his place, he makes Dick part of his act, reenacting their first meeting when Dick was selling flowers and lemonade in front of his house. At the end, when Dick is

supposed to run off stage, he gets confused and
tumbles into the orchestra, hitting his head on
the base drum and making a big hit with the
audience, who think it is part of the act.
Exploring Tib Street, where Uncle Henry lives
behind his shop, Dick meets Tom Figgis, son of a
wealthy owner of many market stalls, and Alf
Eckersley, a former soldier of World War I, who
ostensibly works for Tom's father but actually
spends most of his time at Rosies', an eating
house run by Hyman Rose, or at "Guvnor's kip," a
sort of flophouse run by Alf's father, a street
beggar who dresses like a gentleman down on his
luck and wears an enigmatic sign reading "Last
Chance." Dick and Uncle Oswald, invited to
supper at the kip, meet a variety of street
hawkers and beggars, including Larry the Loon,
who laughs wildly until people pay him to go
away, and Gentleman* George, who tells of a
scheme to bilk clergymen by appealing to their
sympathy. Dick, with his uncle, goes caroling
with an assortment from this crew; he persuades
Tom Figgis to choose an aquarium for his
Christmas present; he and Uncle Oswald go to the
town hall and are given tickets by the Lady
Mayoress; at her party he wins the fancy dress
contest by going as an aquarium; on Christmas,
his aunt and uncle take him home, where he finds
his mother recovered and gets his first set of
skates; he meets Gentleman George, actually the
son of the new clergyman, and learns that he has
been masquerading as a down-and-outer to get
material for a book; and he tries his skates
and, tumbling down as usual, knocks himself out.
A letter from his agent offers Uncle Oswald a
job, again as a substitute, but this time on a
long tour to Africa and Australia. Dick goes to
see him off at Liverpool, and meets some of the
cast of the review, and he sees New Year in at
Albert Square with his parents, who have come to
take him home. Plotless but lively, the book
conveys the sense of wonder the boy feels and
his uncritical enthusiasm for the odd characters
he meets, and it gives a strong sense of
Manchester during that period. Fanfare.

TUPPENNY STANDISH (*The City of Frozen Fire**),
Penelope, young aunt of Tops. After nursing
Prince Madoc, she insists on joining the

treasure hunting voyage, threatening to marry a local suitor if she is left behind and thereby winning the consent of her brother, who dislikes the man, and of Sir Richard Gayner, who hopes to marry her himself. She records the adventure in a series of needlepoint chair covers, each depicting an important event, and thereby giving the designation to any vivid place, person, or incident as "very chair-seat." Her name comes from her childhood objection to being called Penny, insisting that she is worth a great deal more.

THE TURBULENT TERM OF TYKE TILER (Kemp*, Gene, ill. Carolyn Dinan, Faber, 1977), humorous, episodic, realistic novel of school and neighborhood life set recently in a town in England. Life during the last term of Tyke Tiler, 12, at Crickelpit Combined School is filled with unfairness, according to Tyke, who tells the story. Most problems revolve around Tyke's efforts to help a classmate, angelic-looking, slow Danny Price, who suffers from a speech defect and light fingers. When Tyke tries to make things right after Danny steals a ten-pound note from the purse of Miss Bonn, a teacher, Tyke gets caught and hauled into the Headmaster's office. On the way out, Tyke literally bumps into sour Mrs. Somers and must stay after to write lines for the "old ratbag," but Danny is taken home for tea by Miss Bonn, who wants to have a "cozy chat" with him. When Danny discovers a "skellinton" in the river nearby, probably a murdered man they think, Tyke helps him recover some bones. Danny gets house points at school, but Tyke gets covered with smelly muck--and finds more trouble, this time at home. When Tyke's Dad runs for Council and asks Tyke to deliver campaign leaflets for him, the two children lose them in the river and then attempt to compensate by picking up those of his opponent and throwing them in the river, too. Interspersed throughout are scenes of Tyke's relationships with Martin Kneeshaw, the son of Tyke's Dad's opponent, who is often the object of Tyke's flailing fists; with prissy Linda Stoatway; with "Miss," the beautiful new student teacher; with Mr. Merchant, Tyke's "Sir," or regular teacher, who has written a history of the school; with Chief Sir, or Headmaster, whose long words Tyke struggles to comprehend; and with Beryl and Spud, older siblings whom Tyke feels their mother favors unfairly, especially Spud. Tyke's greatest attempt to help Danny results from Tyke's fears that Danny will not score high enough on the upcoming Verbal Reasoning Test to get promoted to the Comprehensive School with his classmates. Tyke swipes a test from Chief Sir's office, figures out the answers with help from sister Beryl, and coaches Danny, who passes satisfactorily. Ironically, Tyke does so well, too, that the Headmaster urges enrollment in a school for the gifted, an idea that Tyke's father rejects as elitist. When Mrs. Somers's watch turns up missing, Danny is accused of theft and runs away. Tyke discovers him in the old paper mill the two have fitted up as a hideout, persuades Chief Sir that Danny is innocent because he can't tell time, and reveals Martin Kneeshaw and his pal as the real thieves. The end of the term finds Danny "fantastic as Galahad" in the class play about King Arthur. On the last day, Tyke emulates an ancestor by scaling the school roof and ringing the old bell, but tumbles precipitously to the ground and ends up in the hospital with broken bones and a concussion. The fall was occasioned by Mrs. Somers shouting Tyke's detested first name, Theodora, and thus the reader learns that exuberant, irrepressible Tyke is a girl. In the last chapter, appended as a postscript, Mr. Merchant reports that Tyke confessed to cheating on the exam and says that he wrote down for her the story of Tyke's turbulent term as she related it to him. The author exhibits great skill at creating credible school life; at catching the children's boisterousness, romanticism, attitudes towards teachers, and enjoyment of rowdy jokes; at making up dialogue that is accurate and clever with repartee; and especially at getting inside the head of loyal, resourceful, often wrongheaded, if good-hearted, Tyke, and presenting things unerringly from her point of view with warmth, sympathy, and ironic good humor. Carnegie Winner; Other.

THE TURF-CUTTER'S DONKEY GOES VISITING (Lynch*,

Patricia, ill. George Altendorf, Dent, 1935; *THE DONKEY GOES VISITING*, Dutton, 1936), fantasy set in Ireland, presumably in the early twentieth century, sequel to *The Turf-Cutter's Donkey*. Eileen, Seamus, and their parents accept an invitation to visit Uncle Miheal, who lives on an island with Aunt Kathleen and their fat, spoiled, red-haired son, Liam. On the way, Eileen runs into her friends, the leprechaun and Fluffy Tail the squirrel, and promises to send them an invitation to join her. Toward evening, Eileen leads Long Ears, the donkey, on a "short cut" that ends in a hole where the cart is wrecked. Unable to go further, the family camps and the children, hunting for wood, run into the hero, Finn, and his followers, who, with the help of the leprechaun, mend the cart. Seamus is tempted to leave with Niam of the Golden Hair for the Land of Youth, but warned by Oisin and reminded of home by a song, he resists the spell. At the island, they find that Aunt Kathleen is sharply critical of Eileen but thinks that greedy Liam can do no wrong. Eileen writes an invitation to the leprechaun, which is taken by Rose, her cat, and the leprechaun arrives and sets up house in a cave at the end of the garden. Eileen takes some tarts Liam has set aside for himself, gives them to the leprechaun, and is accused of theft by Liam, but is forgiven by Aunt Kathleen. The three youngsters set off to buy toffee in the village, but Liam, seeing his mother making treacle pudding, turns back. Seamus and Eileen are trapped in a strange prison made of hardened paper created by the Wise Woman of Youghal, who has posed as the toffee shop woman. Liam, sent to take the treacle pudding to his father and uncle, eats it on the way, then hides from the spider sent by the leprechaun in an empty, unwashed treacle barrel, which starts to roll, crashes into the prison room, and frees Eileen and Seamus. The threat from the Wise Woman is not over, however: she contrives to get the children in a curragh, then throws a magic net around it, and sets an eagle on them; but they are aided by the spider, the squirrel, and finally the Silver Airman, who is able to tug the boat to shore. The white pig accompanying the airman falls out and follows them to the

farm. That evening a blind ballad singer turns
up, and all three children and Long Ears become
involved in an adventure on One-Tree Mountain in
which the boys hold off the evil forces sent by
the Wise Woman while Eileen accompanies the
ballad singer. With the leprechaun and the
airman, who returns, Eileen and Seamus enter a
door in the mountain, but Liam is afraid.
Wandering around the mountain in the dark, he
comes on the Tinker band and is held for a while
but escapes on Long Ears, who is rushing by. At
home he finds Seamus and Eileen, but they act
strangely, and when Eileen can't sing with the
Tinker Chief, they are shown to be changelings
and fly away. The children's mother, going to
seek them, is carried across the bay by a
mermaid and meets them returning. Chasing
Blackie, Liam's puppy, Seamus and Eileen fall
into a cave, where, in a busy workshop, a
leprechaun is making shoes. Eileen tries on a
pair that dance her all around the island. In
the meantime Seamus gets out of the cave and
helps a rebel chased by Redcoats to find another
cave. When the mist clears, they have all
disappeared, but Eileen reappears, exhausted,
and can finally rest, having worn out the
dancing shoes. In the rebel's cave they find the
silver stolen long ago from Aunt Kathleen. In
the final episode, Captain Cassidy of the turf
barge and his man, Tim, come to the island on
Tim's brother's lorry. Eileen and Seamus go to
meet them, and Tim, determined to see the whole
island, wrecks the lorry on the side opposite
from Uncle Miheal's farm. A huge horse appears,
they all climb on his back, and he carries them
to the shore. They all jump off but the Captain,
who is carried into the water. The others wait
around miserably and finally find the captain's
cap on some steps leading to the water. There
they meet a mermaid and a salmon, which asks for
the captain's cap, but Tim wisely substitutes
his own cap. The mermaid says the captain wants
to stay, but Eileen gives her a thimble and
Seamus gives her his knife. The captain returns
angry at first, since he had been a king in the
other world. Uncle Miheal gives the family a
pony and cart, so the captain and Tim can ride
home with them. The fantasy seems to have no
consistency or principle of control; characters

unrelated to each other or to the rest of the
story suddenly appear and take part in the
action with no explanation. Although some of
them come from Irish mythology, the Silver
Airman would not appear to do so, and others act
rather differently from their traditional roles.
Overall, the story is confusing and, since the
fantasy has no rules or limitations to give the
plot tension, it is dull. Fanfare.

TURNER, PHILLIP (WILLIAM) (1925-   ), born in
Rossland, British Columbia, Canada; Anglican
priest, teacher, and novelist. The son of a
clergyman, he returned from Canada to England
at the age of six months. He received his B.A.
degree from Worcester College, Oxford, in 1949,
and his M.A. in 1962. From 1943 to 1946, he
served in the Royal Naval Volunteer Reserve. He
attended Chichester Theological College, Sussex,
from 1949 to 1951, was ordained, and served as
parish priest in Leeds, Sussex, and Northampton.
For five years in the 1960s, he was head of
religious broadcasting for the BBC Midland
Region, then became a teacher at Droitwich High
School, Worcestershire, and later chaplain at
Eaton College, Buckinghamshire. Since 1975, he
has been a part-time teacher at Malvern College,
Worcestershire. His writings are varied: he has
published thirteen plays for adults, four
mystery novels under the pseudonym Stephen
Chance, all starring Septimus, a retired London
detective now a country parson, and at least a
dozen books of fiction for children under his
own name. Most of this last group are holiday
adventures, full of comedy and set in the
Yorkshire Dales from the seaport of Darnley
Mills inland to the hills and open moors. Among
these are *Colonel Sheperton's Clock* (Oxford,
1964; World, 1966) and *The Grange at High
Force** (Oxford, 1965; World, 1967), which
received the Carnegie Medal. These feature the
same three boys, and both have elements of
mystery stories. Some critics have been more
enthusiastic about his stories set in the same
location in former generations, among them the
three that concern a narrow-guage railway that
runs through the area: *Steam on the Line*
(Oxford, 1968; World, 1968), *Devil's Nob*
(Hamilton, 1970; Nelson, 1973), and *Powder Quay*

(Hamilton, 1971).

TWEEDLEDUM AND TWEEDLEDEE (*Through the Looking-Glass**), chubby, zany, irascible mirror-image twins, two of several nursery rhyme figures that appear in the novel and two of the book's most famous characters. Alice* approaches them for directions through the forest. In response to her query, Tweedledee recites the parody, "The Walrus and the Carpenter," which is followed by a brief discussion of the relation between intentions and actions. The brothers are at odds with each other, Tweedledum's favorite expression being, "Nohow," and Tweedledee's favorite being, "Contrariwise." They inform Alice she's not real but instead only a part of the Red King's dream. When Tweedledum discovers that Tweedledee has broken his new rattle, the two agree to have a battle. They arm themselves in blankets, tablecloths, coal scuttles, kettles, and the like. Alice considers them rude, selfish, and foolish.

THE TWELVE AND THE GENII (Clarke*, Pauline, ill. Cecil Leslie, Faber, 1962; *THE RETURN OF THE TWELVES*, ill. Bernarda Bryson, Coward, 1963), fantasy about anthropomorphized toys set in the mid-1900s in a rural area of Yorkshire not far from Haworth, the Bronte family home. Under the floorboards of the attic of the old farmhouse his family has just moved into, Max* Morley, 8, discovers a dozen toy Napoleonic soldiers. As he plays with them, he finds that they come alive and that each has a distinct personality. At 140 years old, Butter Crashey is their patriarch and spokesperson. Stumps* has had a long and varied career, while the Duke of Wellington, Sneaky, Parry, and Ross are kings; Monkey, Tracky, and Cracky are agile midshipmen; and the rest are Cheeky, Bravey, and Gravey, who is serious and pessimistic. A close-knit group, they care a good deal about one another and have a history of precarious and exciting adventures, of which Max learns as the story unfolds. He learns, too, that they once belonged to four Genii, who protected them, and that they regard him as their present-day Genii. He speaks to them in formal speech, and they address him quite formally in return, referring to him as Genii

Maxii. He lets his older sister, Jane, in on his secret, and she, too, becomes a Genii. A visit from the local parson, Mr. Howson (whom Jane, a lover of *Jane Eyre*, privately refers to as Mr. Rochester), a Bronte fan, brings the first hint that the soldiers might once have belonged to the four Bronte children. Suspense builds when Seneca Brewer, an American professor, offers 5,000 pounds for lost toys called the "noble Twelves, the Young Men beloved of Branwell and his sisters," and the Morley family and others begin to suspect that Max's soldiers may be the genuine Bronte items. Philip, Max's older brother, who likes money, informs the professor about the soldiers, and the professor makes plans to visit the Morleys. A reporter shows up, keen on a story. All this distresses Max, who fears for the safety and sensibilities of his soldiers. From reading *The History of the Young Men*, Branwell Bronte's account of the adventures of the toys, Max concludes that they are indeed the Bronte pieces and were somehow transferred to the farmhouse from Haworth. Butter Crashey overhears the news about the professor's impending visit and mobilizes the Twelves to leave. They climb down the creeper that clings to the house, find an old skate of Max's, which they use as a carriage, and embark upon a hazardous and adventure-filled journey across the countryside toward Haworth. Max and Jane help them along. Philip discovers what is going on, and, conscience-stricken, joins the effort. The soldiers suffer a shipwreck and are attacked by a rabbit, and Butter Crashey is captured by a farmer, among other disasters and difficulties, before the children, helped by Mr. Howson and under cover of night, drum the Twelves in appropriate military fanfare (Philip's idea) into the former Bronte nursery at Haworth, now a museum, safe and sound where they belong, where the original four Genii had played with them and made up exciting exploits for them. Parts of the story seem to take place only in Max's imagination, but most of the fantasy has others who witness the soldiers' activities, and all of it is written with such conviction, ingenuity, and careful attention to details of character, setting, and action, underpinned with just enough information about the Brontes, that the reader has no doubt it all happened as described. There is some humor, as well as plenty of action and suspense, and family relationships seem true. Biblical allusions provide texture and point up the themes of respect and concern for others. Carnegie Winner; Choice; Fanfare; Lewis Carroll.

TWOPENCE A TUB (Price*, Susan, Faber, 1975), historical novel about an acrimonious, unsuccessful coal miners' strike about 1850 in the central English town of Oldbury. Events are seen from the vantage point of eighteen-year-old Jek (Jechonias) Davies, son of a collier and a collier himself since the age of ten. His large family suffers from deep poverty, their sparsely furnished, one-bedroom, company-owned shack barely large enough to accommodate the five surviving children and their parents, once-pretty, self-pitying Reenee and short, tough Dewi. They are all undereducated, malnourished, and inadequately clothed, and emotional and physical abuse are common in the family. While out with his cousin Shanny (Thomas) Shannon clearing Shanny's poaching traps, an enterprise that provides the numerous Shannons with meat, a food which the other miners seldom taste, the two youths learn of impending strikes in neighboring collieries, then return home to discover that their own Wild Horse ('Oss) Pit comrades have held a union meeting and voted to strike. The miners are demanding twopence per tub of · coal, one penny more than they've been getting. Jek welcomes the news, since he has been for strike action all along, but the conflicting opinions he hears confuse him. Religious Grandpa Ellis, his mother's father, insists that striking violates God's laws about authority, and the pragmatic Shannons argue that there's no possible way the miners can win, that time and the main cards are on the side of the owners. The Gaffer, or manager, of the mine, who openly despises the colliers and thinks they're wasteful, spending money on such foolishness as schooling, gives the miners a chance to change their minds, then sacks Jim Woodall, their union man (president), and has him evicted from his company-owned house. Some of the miners, called blacklegs, go back to work, but most stay out

for an increasingly acrimonious and financially
difficult sixteen weeks. Food and fuel become
very scarce. Jek and Shanny decide to try to
earn money by stealing coal from tips (refuse
piles), and selling it to iron founders, called
nailers, in Dudley. They open a tip, and, when
other miners continue their work, four are
buried in a cave-in probably brought on by
torrential summer rains. This accident
effectively breaks the strike. Since funeral
expenses have drained the union treasury, the
miners vote to go back to the pits. The Gaffer
cuts the men's wages by a quarter, a measure he
asserts is economic and not punitive. Jim
Woodall is not rehired, and he and his family
leave to seek work elsewhere. Jek's feelings
remain mixed. He resigns himself to working
weeks of six fourteen-hour days for the next
twenty years, until he is forty, the age at
which most of the miners die. The memories of
the past few months fester in his mind, however.
He sees no way out of the poverty and no relief
from the drudgery except Sunday visits to
Rachel* Ansel, a nailer's daughter he met in
Dudley, who has encouraged him to regard the
miners' strike as part of a greater cause. Sober
in tone and bleak in atmosphere, this account of
a noble effort that failed is seldom lightened
by humor or hope. The Davies family taken as a
whole are not pleasant people. Jek's affection
for his little sister Nellie, who, since she has
survived to the age of four can now be safely
loved, stands out amidst the interpersonal
strife in this troubled family. The miners as a
whole are hard on one another, and yet the
reader's sympathies lie firmly with the Davieses
and the other miners, so strong a case does the
author build on their behalf against the owners,
suggesting that their poverty and brutishness
are the result of the owners' greed and
oppression. Characters are well-realized:
confused and eventually defeated Jek; earnest,
sensible, pathetic Jim Woodall; Jim's counterpart the self-indulgent, self-righteous Gaffer;
the sanctimonious vicar, who attempts to use
religion to keep the miners under the control
of the owners; the bookstall owner who gives
Jek the newspaper carrying the story of the
strike, which Jek can't read because he's

forgotten what little learning he had; and
stubborn Grandpa Ellis, who at eighty still has
not learned not to argue. The plot is skillfully
constructed to maintain interest. The reader
sees all too well the hardships of the miners'
way of life, the puny, ramshackle dwellings that
are allowed to go to ruin by the mine owners on
the excuse that the miners won't take care of
them anyway, the community outhouse, entire
families sleeping in their shack's single
bedroom, or some out on the hills because there
is no room in the house--social comments well
blended into the plot. The author also creates
scenes well, depicting the strike vote, the
Gaffer's ultimatum, the Gaffer eating a rich
dinner in luxurious surroundings, the miners
eating oatmeal while seated on the floor or on
crates with their few dishes also on crates, the
miners pushing aside drying clothes while they
are trying to eat or sloshing through ankle-deep
water that flows through the house when it
rains, the bitterly ironic sermon at the funeral
in which the vicar asserts that the miners'
deaths are God's punishment for the strike--
vivid scenes that severely indict a system that
keeps workers in bondage on the pretext that it
is for their own good. Extensive use of dialect.
Other.

U

UNCLE ALAN KITSON (*Tom's Midnight Garden**), Tom*
Long's uncle, with whom he stays while his
brother, Peter, is quarantined with measles.
Uncle Alan is easily irritated, doesn't understand children, and, when he tries to explain
something to Tom, just overloads the boy with
words. He represents well-intentioned, unimaginative, unaware adults.

UNCLE ANDREW KETTERLEY (*The Magician's Nephew**),
arrogant, ambitious uncle of Digory* Kirke. A
very tall, thin man with a sharp nose, extremely
bright eyes, and a mop of tousled, gray hair, he
seems less evil than stupid, with his badness
arising rather from ignorance and cupidity than
from the desire to cause trouble. He learned
from his godmother the magic that enables him to
fashion the green and yellow rings that take
people in and out of other worlds. As the book
starts, he has been conducting experiments using
guinea pigs, because he is too pusillanimous to
use the rings on himself, to try to determine
whether or not there really are other worlds.
He first tricks Polly* Plummer into going, and
then Digory, his nephew, follows Polly to bring
her back. When he falls in love with evil Queen*
Jadis, he acts very silly, and the more he tries
to please her the more she despises him and the
sillier he becomes. When Aslan* creates
Narnia*, Uncle Andrew is terrified by the
creatures there but still intrigued by the
commercial possibilities of this new land. He

may represent materialism and immoral scientific exploration. He is too comic a figure for the reader to take his villainy seriously.

UNCLE BEN (*The Watcher Bee**), brother of Kate's* mother, who married her Aunt* Beth, the sister of her father, after Kate's parents both died during her infancy. Though Uncle Ben and Aunt Beth were friends when they were young, he admits that they probably would not have married if had not been more convenient for a couple to bring up Kate. Uncle Ben has never liked farming, so he has rented his family house and farm and devoted his attentions to his orchard and his rose garden, which he cares for devotedly. Despite Aunt Beth's dominating personality and sharp tongue, the two are mostly amicable until Lucy* Denham-Lucie returns, bringing her airs and charm and reopening old wounds. Kate notes that Uncle Ben presents roses to Lucy and her daughter, Zoe* Vardoe, with a gallantry she has not seen before, and, after some particularly acerbic comments by Aunt Beth, he admits that he was one of Lucy's lovers when they were young and that she rejected him because she felt he would never go far in the world. Driven to rebellion by his memories, he builds himself a hut at the far end of the garden and moves his books and easy-chair, and finally his bed there, to Aunt Beth's dismay. In many ways he and Kate have always teamed up in self-protection against Aunt Beth's sharpness.

UNCLE CHACHA RAHMTA (*The Devil's Children**), one of the sons of Daya* Wanti, father or uncle to most of the Sikh children. Though fat, he is very quick and brave, and in the battle with the robbers he kills their leader and fights alone against three mounted hoodlums until Gopal* joins him. Before the Changes he was a checker at a warehouse and a champion squash player and had learned judo to defend himself against racially intolerant fellow workers. When Nicky* Gore tries to knife Kewal* for starting the bus, Uncle Chacha Rahmta clubs her aside and is concerned afterwards lest he has injured her.

UNCLE CHARLIE (*Granny Reardun**; *The Aimer*

Gate*), Joseph's* half brother. He is a baby in a bassinet in *Granny*, whom Joseph pushes full-tilt down the hill while playing the cornet. Charlie grows up to be cheerful and outgoing and inclined to boisterousness, a strong, hearty man who affectionately addresses Robert, his nephew, as Dick-Richard. He is a professional soldier, apparently, who shows a particular concern for Faddock Allman, a paraplegic from the Boer War, and who takes pride in his craft of soldiering as did his ancestor Robert in stonemasonry and his half brother, Joseph, in smithying. When Robert says he might like to become a soldier, Charlie says the boy's not got the "flavor for soldiering." Charlie is killed in World War I, the reader learns in *Tom Fobble's Day**, the last book in the series known as The Stone Book Quartet.

UNCLE EBENEZER BALFOUR (*Kidnapped**), miserly younger brother of David* Balfour's deceased father. He lives in a decaying manor, parts of which have never been completed, eats almost nothing but thin oatmeal, and exists with a bare minimum of fire and candles. Terrified of losing the estate of Shaws to its rightful heir, he tries first to force David into a fatal accident, then arranges for him to be kidnapped and sold as a slave by the captain of the brig *Covenant*. Because he and David's father both loved the same girl and she chose David's father, he made such a fuss that his brother left Shaws to him and became a village school-master. A spoiled boy, he has become a contemptible and pitiable old man.

UNCLE HADDEN (*The Warden's Niece**), Warden Henniker-Hadden of Canterbury College, Oxford University, to whom his niece Maria* runs away from school. Uncle Hadden has no idea of how people usually act to little girls and treats her with vague courtesy, as he might a grown woman living in his home. Often at meals he is so abstracted that he doesn't speak, and he doesn't seem to notice that she is too shy to start a conversation. After the escapade when she and two of the Smith boys go off to Jerusalem House with the new housemaid's uncle, she is afraid he is very angry, as his housekeeper, Mrs. Clomper, has told her, but she is so concerned for the new maid that she writes him a note, explaining that it was not Lizzie's fault. His answering note, which she fears will tell her she must return to school and that Lizzie has been dismissed, suggests only that the young maid be given an extra half-day off to compensate for this one, which was rather spoiled. He is quite oblivious to any problems created by having a child in the house except when Mrs. Clomper complains, and then his response is unexpectedly mild. When Maria's accomplishments with Greek and her original research do come to his attention, he is delighted.

UNCLE HAROLD SOWTER (A Likely Lad*), loud, bullying commercial traveler, husband of Willy* Overs's Auntie Kitty. Beefy and bug-eyed, with ham-sized hands and straddling legs, he shouts in good humor and in anger and does all he can to make the Overs look inferior. His wife and his two daughters cower when he is displeased, and even his stolid son, Stan*, is clearly afraid to cross him. He regularly drags Stan to see his wife's Auntie* Maggie, confidently hoping that she will leave her money to the boy, and he would have been furious to learn that she changed her will in Willy's favor if it were not that the money has been destroyed before she dies.

UNCLE HENDREARY (The Borrowers Afield*; The Borrowers Afloat*; The Borrowers Avenged*), husband of Aunt* Lupy and relative of the Clock family, Pod*, Homily*, and Arrietty*. He is not a strong figure and is easily controlled by his wife. He is thin and has a straggly beard. After the Clocks come to live with the Hendrearys, he resents sharing the borrowing duties with Pod, and Pod goes back to cobbling. Hendreary has trouble coping with problems.

UNCLE PARKER (Ordinary Jack*), Russell Parker, Jack Bagthorpe's uncle by marriage. His wife is Jack's Aunt Celia, a poet and potter just as eccentric as the rest of her family but considered by them a typically gifted Bagthorpe. Uncle Parker and Aunt Celia live at The

Knoll not far from the Bagthorpe house. Uncle Parker has "something to do with stocks and shares," rises early in the morning to jog, makes lots of phone calls, and terrifies everyone by his reckless driving. He incurs the dislike of Grandma* Bagthorpe by driving down and killing her pet cat, Thomas, and he and Mr.* Bagthorpe trade insults on every occasion. Uncle Parker informs Jack that he works hard at being an "idle devil" and sets out to help Jack improve his image among the clan.

UNCLE PETER MYHILL (*Handles**), Erica Timperley's dull uncle, father of lumpish Robert*, husband of her Auntie* Joan, her mother's sister, with whose family Erica is sent on holiday by her mother. Since Erica's brother was going on vacation with friends, Mum Timperley thought Erica would be pleased to go on holiday, too, and arranged the occasion with Auntie Joan without consulting her daughter. Erica tries to make the best of the situation. Among other problems, she has difficulty understanding Uncle Peter, whose main recreational interest is television. Reception is extremely poor, with the picture being of various garishly horrid colors, but Uncle Peter seems to have adjusted to the low quality and resists any suggestions for improvement. His obsession is the peacock from the gentleman farm up the way. Every morning he gets up early to shoot the creature, but he always misses. His wayward shots wake Erica every morning and provide some comic relief. Going into Polthorpe to get his jump leads brings Erica into contact with Elsie* Wainwright and the pleasure of his motorcycle shop. Uncle Peter serves as a fine foil for Elsie*.

UNCLE RON BELL (*No End to Yesterday**), Gran's* youngest son, a great joker, who still lives at home and teases Marjory* but is more sympathetic to her than are other family members. Several times he has brought prospective girlfriends home for inspection only to have Gran and his sisters find them unsuitable. Marjory shares a secret with him because she has seen him with his present girlfriend, Rosalie, when she was walking the dogs in the park. Later, after they have broken up, she is instrumental in bringing them together again, and he confides in her that they plan to be married secretly before Gran can interfere again. Unfortunately, his sudden illness and death destroy the plan.

UNCLE RUSSELL (*Flambards**), owner of Flambards, half brother of the deceased mother of Christina* Parsons, whom he expects to have marry his older son, Mark*, so that her inheritance can prop up the decaying estate. A man of violent temper, his single passion is fox hunting, a sport at which he unfortunately was crippled so that he cannot ride at all or even get about easily on crutches. He has turned to drink, and bullies his servants and his sons, particularly William*, whom he scorns for his fear of riding. In the next two books of the trilogy, *The Edge of the Cloud** and *Flambards in Summer**, he does not appear, but his person-ality still affects the characters. He refuses his permission to Will and Christina, who are both under twenty-one, to marry, so they have to wait until his death. He leaves nothing to Will, and his debts are so great that Mark must sell Flambards, ironically giving Christina the chance to buy the place.

UNCLE TURNER (*John Diamond**), brother of William Jones's mother. A large, bulky man with a bullying face, he always greets William by pinching the boy's cheek between his knuckles and then berating him for sniveling. "Give him to me for six months," he often suggests, "and you won't know him!" It is largely because Uncle Turner accuses him of stealing his dying father's watch that William runs off to London.

UNDER GOLIATH (Carter*, Peter, ill. Ian Robbins, Oxford, 1977; Oxford, 1979), historical novel set mostly in Belfast, Ireland, from early spring to fall in 1969 and concerning the hostilities between Protestants and Catholics. Alan Kenton, a Protestant, who tells the story, concludes through first-hand experience how savage, deeply rooted, and unreasonable is the hatred of the two factions for each other. In a frame story, Alan, on duty with a British army peacekeeping force stationed in a hilly, desert

area near a refugee camp, probably in the Middle
East, discovers the body of a red-haired soldier
killed accidentally in a mortar blast, realizes
it is a youth he knew years before in Belfast,
and tells the story of their relationship to the
Medical Officer. This narrative makes up the
bulk of the novel. Alan, 13, lives in a seedy,
working-class section of Belfast with his Dad, a
quiet immigrant from England who works as a
riveter in the shipyards, which are dominated by
an immense crane known almost affectionately as
Goliath, and who insists that his family not get
involved in sectarian activities. The rest of
the family includes his usually understanding
Mam; his hardworking, sensible older brother,
Billy, a strong union man who maintains that low
wages, poor working conditions, and lack of jobs
form the root of the strife; and his little
sister, Helen. An occasional visitor is brash
Uncle Jack Gowan, Mam's brother, a greengrocer
and ardent Orangeman (or Ulsterman, that is, a
Protestant partisan). The action starts when
Alan, to satisfy a long-held ambition, goes down
to the Old Sash Lodge of the Loyal Order of
United Orangemen and proposes himself as a
member of Mr. Mackracken's drum and fife Walking
Band, hoping to be chosen to play the lambeg,
the big old Irish drum. Doughty, zealous
Orangeman Mackracken gives him a fife instead,
which dims his ardor somewhat. Alan notes with
characteristic irony that his parents and Billy
greet "the news of his musical career without
rapture," an attitude that discomfits him. Uncle
Jack quite predictably is elated with what he
takes as Alan's decision to show his true
colors, that is, his zeal for the Protestant
cause. Shortly thereafter, while on delivery
rounds, Uncle Jack and Alan spot a beribboned,
red-haired bagpiper of about Alan's age, a youth
from St. Malachi's band, the Fenian (or
Catholic) counterpart of Mackracken's group. At
Uncle Jack's suggestion, Alan razzes the youth
roundly. Later, the boys meet face to face on
the street, exchange insults heatedly, agree to
fight out their animosity, meet in the cellar of
an abandoned stable at the edge of the park,
battle to a draw, and then make up and smoke
companionably together. They also discover a gun
hidden behind a loose panel in the stable

cellar. For weeks, after band practice, the two
meet surreptitiously in the cellar, playing with
the gun, chatting, smoking, and generally
enjoying each other's company. Alan observes
that, except for his blaming the social and
political problems on the Orangemen, Fergus is
much like himself. He even visits Fergus's home,
where he notes that their home-life compares to
that of the Protestants. Trouble breaks out: the
water reservoir in the Protestant sector and
post offices are bombed. Tempers flare as each
side blames the other for the trouble.
Protestant and Catholic neighbors refuse to
speak to each other. Then two bandsmen bullies,
Cather and Packer, discover that Alan and Fergus
are meeting and accuse Alan of being a spy. Alan
tries to drop the band, caught between their
threats and his parents' disapproval of his band
association, especially since the band will soon
be "walking" (marching) for the Glorious Twelfth
of July, the anniversary of King William's
victory over King James and a red-letter day for
the Ulstermen. Alan pleads lack of money for a
uniform since his father has recently suffered a
broken leg in an accident and has been
hospitalized, but Mackracken insists he play and
gives him a uniform. Alan marches, at first with
apprehension and then, to his surprise, with the
exuberance of the occasion, but a family row
follows. Alan falls out with Fergus over the
gun, which they have decided to get rid of and
find gone. Each thinks the other has taken it,
and they part in heat. Alan drops out of the
band, and in the fall turns his attention to
raising pigeons with a mated pair given him by
an understanding next-door neighbor, Mr. Black,
in whom Alan has confided his troubles.
Sectarian hostility increases, and events reach
a predictable climax one night while Alan is on
his way home from Uncle Jack's store. He gets
caught by rioting Catholics, but unexpectedly
and fortuitously Fergus turns up and speaks up
for him, and then disappears into the night. In
the epilogue part of the frame story, Alan says
that he had only a couple of glimpses of Fergus
subsequently. He also says that later his father
died, that Billy emigrated to Australia, and
that he himself joined the army, ironically as a
bandsman, after being unable to make a decent

living in Belfast. He suspects that Fergus enlisted for the same reasons. He confesses to feeling "rage at the waste and folly of it all," anger with people like Mackracken, Gowan, and Fergus's father who perpetuate the "borders" of sectarianism that "divide the hearts of men" so that they must continue to live under its overwhelming and murderous terror, in "the shadow of Goliath." Though the book's theme is bleak--hatred persists because people want it to--the author's skillful use of irony keeps the story from becoming morbid or preachy, and Alan's narrative, which focuses on domestic matters to show how easily the young become enmeshed in the traditional rivalry, contains many light moments. Some scenes, such as that in which old Popeye struts his stuff to show the bandsmen how to walk, are quite funny. Characters are easily recognizable types, but they are individualized and interesting, and Alan's comments on the situation avoid didacticism because they seem true to his adolescent point of view. That the two boys should never again encounter each other on the streets strains credulity but supports both the theme and the plot. Carnegie Com.

UNLEAVING (Paton* Walsh, Jill, Macmillan, 1976; Farrar, 1976), sequel to *Goldengrove*, told in two time frames, alternating between a summer when Madge Fielding is perhaps seventeen, three years after the first book, and a summer when she is Gran, with her own daughter and son-in-law visiting with their children. The earlier story starts when Madge returns for her grandmother's funeral and learns that Golden-grove, the house on the Cornwall coast, has been left to her, much to the disgust of her father, who is there with his son, Paul. Her headmis-tress, who wants her to apply for Oxford, sug-gests that she rent the house for a philosophy reading party from the university which she could also attend. Because her mother will not set foot in Goldengrove nor allow her daughter to go there by herself, Madge sees this as an opportunity to get back to the place she loves, and she agrees. The group is composed of undergraduates and two professors and their families, Mr. and Mrs. Jones, who have three

young   children,   and   Professor   and   Mrs.
Tregeagle, who have   a   son, Patrick, about
Madge's age, and   a mongoloid daughter, Molly.
After   the first   shock of   seeing Molly,   Madge
plays   with   her kindly   and   wins Patrick's
approval for that and for showing him the way to
get out onto the roof from the attic room he has
been given   next to hers.   Together they go down
to the small private beach, where the sea three
times washes   up a bottle to Madge, even after
she has   thrown   it far   out.   The philosophy
sessions   are   highly intellectualized,   and
Madge's occasional commonsense comments seem out
of place. She is thrown more and more into the
company of Patrick, an angry, intense boy who
plays the piano and rejects philosophy, and does
both passionately. The undergraduates are mostly
uninteresting to Madge, although there is nice
Mathew Brown, a dark, stocky boy, and tall, fair
Andrew Henderson, who always climbs and hikes by
himself. After a week Paul comes, and though he
finds   Patrick "a   nutter,"   the   three of   them
spend   time together   and   with Jeremy Stevens,
their   old fisherman friend,   who has sold his
boat and given up going to sea but promises to
try to   borrow one   to take them   to the
lighthouse.   Several   incidents   show   Patrick's
fierce protectiveness toward Molly and his anger
at his   father, who   seems unable to see   the
retarded   child as   really human.   Patrick   also
tells Madge of his fury at the doctor who did
not   let Molly   die when   she was   ill the   year
before. For the last weekend a picnic is planned
at Godrevy Point, not right at the top of the
cliff   but   in   a   sheltered   spot some   distance
down.   There is a discussion of the soul, with
Professor Tregeagle holding   forth on how pure
intellect   is   the   immortal   part   and how   a
person's soul resembles his body. Into the group
stumbles Molly, with one of the Jones girls
following her, mimicking her awkward walk and
drooling, as Patrick watches, aghast. Then Molly
smiles and clearly   repeats the phrase her
brother has   taught her,   "Cogito ergo sum."
Shocked,   the group   breaks off   the discussion,
and Patrick takes Molly for a walk up to the top
of the cliff. Following him, Madge and Paul see
her go near the edge. Patrick stretches out his
arm, and Molly falls. The entire group watches

as the lifeboat crew tries to recover the body,
a tricky maneuver among the rocks and the heavy
surf, and Jeremy is killed in the attempt. Paul,
an uncomplicated, straightforward boy who would
never lie, tells the police that he saw Patrick
try in vain to grab Molly when she got too near
the edge. Madge, who saw Patrick push Molly to
her death, lies, saying she saw the incident
just as Paul did. In the next few days, waiting
for the inquest, Patrick is in agony, thinking
himself damned and enduring horrible guilt, not
for Molly, whom he deliberately saved from
growing up to suffer the contempt he knows she
could feel, but for Jeremy, the unexpected
victim of his action. Madge comforts him and
persuades him not to tell the truth at the
inquest, for his mother's sake. Though Paul
tries to persuade her to make a break from
Patrick, she knows she loves him and is already
tied to him by his need for her. In the later
story, it becomes clear that Madge married
Patrick, who has died some years earlier, and is
now entertaining her daughter's three children,
as well as Paul's daughter by a second
marriage, Emily, a girl about the age Madge was
the summer of the reading party, who has arrived
with a young man, a long-haired undergraduate.
Much of what happens echoes what happened or was
discussed in that long-ago summer. At one point,
Madge comes upon Emily and her young man asleep
in the summer house, nude and in each other's
arms. She looks at them calmly and fondly,
thinking that Paul would not like it, that he
has become stuffy about such things, as is her
daughter, Harriet. Cleaning out a space for her
friend in the attic, Emily comes upon the bottle
from the sea which Madge has saved all these
years. The oldest grandchild, Peter, 8, wrestling with the philosophical question of death,
says he can't see the point of life if it just
has to end that way, and Madge, thinking of the
Yeats poem, tells him to clap hands and sing.
His little sister, Beth, 4, who seems to be a
Madge in embryo, dances around them, clapping
and caroling. The novel handles the philosophical discussions and questions deftly, without
any didactic tone, and makes the unfeeling
intellectual game the professors and students
are playing contrast with the real emotional

applications, as when Madge realizes that she is compromising the truth to save Patrick and his parents and using a bad means to achieve a perceived greater end. Character is more important than action in the story, with Paul and Mathew serving as foils for intense, self-flagellating Patrick. Molly is treated realistically, without sentimentality. The structure is demanding, since it is not clear at first that Madge and Gran are the same person. As in *Goldengrove*, the story has a sensitive, delicate style told entirely in the present tense. Boston Globe Winner; Choice; Fanfare.

UP THE PIER (Cresswell*, Helen, ill. Gareth Floyd, Faber, 1971; Macmillan, 1972), fantasy of magic and shifts in time set in the seaside town of Llangolly, Wales, the first two weeks in October of 1971. On the first of the month, the evening train from London brings Carrie*, 10, and her mother to stay with Aunt Ester at her small private hotel until Carrie's father, who has a new position, can find them a place to live. On the same train arrives the Pontifex family, two men, a woman, and a boy, who quickly make their way on foot to the old, fog-shrouded pier that juts out into the ocean and is now only a tourist attraction. The next day, bored and lonely, Carrie investigates the pier and meets gruff, disgruntled Samuel* Pontifex, the gatekeeper, who is the last of the large family that once lived and worked on the pier. Once off the tarmac and onto the wooden flooring of the oldest part of the pier, Carrie encounters the other Pontifexes, a boy, Kitchener*, and his parents, Ellen* and George*. With them is Gramper*, or Ponty, a magician whose wayward spell has transported them fifty years into the future from their proper year of 1921. Since Carrie has accidentally discovered the Three* times Seven spell, she has been brought into their dimension and become visible to them and they to her. Carrie soon warms to the unfortunate family, whom Samuel has put up in a rude kiosk. Over the next ten days she visits them often and shops for their needs, making life more bearable in particular for worried, upset Ellen. Tension mounts as Samuel tampers with Gramper's spell making equipment in hope of keeping them in Llangolly indefinitely so he will have a family of his own again. Gramper falls into a depression and despairs of ever producing effective spells again. After Gramper informs Carrie that she alone has the power to return them to their proper time, Carrie realizes that she must sacrifice her pleasure in their company and wish them back home in order to break Samuel's hold on them. She leaves the pier to find her father waiting for her with the news that he has found a home where the family can be together again. That night she dreams that her desire to see the Pontifexes safely home triumphs over Samuel's desire to keep them, and the Pontifexes are set free. At the end, the reader is left somewhat in doubt about whether or not the events really happened. Perhaps the Pontifexes were figments of Carrie's imagination, the result of her loneliness and wishful thinking, or possibly they were Samuel's memories come alive. Though Carrie seems a bit mature and serious for ten, and the wily, authoritative Kitchener, through whom she learns about what has happened to the family, is a bit immature for twelve, the characters are well-defined and convincing. After a slow, almost plodding start, the pace accelerates and results in a first-rate suspense story that ably supports the significant themes of time as a continuum and the importance of unselfishness and the family. The style is deceptively simple, and the reader must pay close attention to catch the subtleties of plot and character. Carnegie Com.; Fanfare.

USAMAH IBN-MENQUIDH (*Knight Crusader**), aging Emir whom Philip* d'Aubigny serves during his captivity in Damascus. A real historical character, Usamah wrote the story of his ninety and more years, memoirs that have survived and been translated into English.

V

VADIR CEDRICSON (*Dawn Wind**), bitter, emotionally twisted neighbor of Beornwulf. He is a man
with a club foot who rides with great skill. He
comes upon Owain* on his land the night Teitri,
the white foal, is born, and he shows an
unusual gentleness and great interest in the
colt, coming often to Beornstead just to look at
him as he grows, as if he somehow senses that
his destiny is linked to that of the horse.
Vadir's cruel streak is shown when he watches
his dogs killing Owain's Dog and does nothing to
stop the fight, seeming in fact to enjoy it. He
seizes every opportunity to taunt Owain for
being a thrall and for having come out alive
(presumably the only one on the British side)
from the battle at Aquae Sulis. On the night of
the wedding of Beornwulf's daughter Helga, he
first notices Helga's younger sister Lilla, and
in the bride-race he cuts in front of Horn,
Lilla's friend and intended husband, to sweep
the girl up on his horse and carry her on the
wild ride. Lilla is very much afraid of him, and
when he asks for her in marriage, the news is
kept from her brother, Bryni, who already hates
Vadir and is impulsive enough to carry out his
early threat to kill him. Vadir brings on his
own death when, in the drawing of straws to
settle the quarrel between himself and Bryni at
the king's feast-fire, where fighting is forbidden, he draws the long straw, which means he
must put his life into some hazard. He chooses
to ride Teitri, the God's Horse, who has never

been ridden, thereby committing both a rash act of courage and a sacrilege.

VAGABONDS ALL. See *When Shakespeare Lived in Southwark.*

THE VANDAL (Schlee*, Ann, Macmillan, 1979; Crown, 1981), futuristic fantasy set in a world that has rejected violence and even meat eating in exchange for a drink that causes a loss of memory after three days. Essential information for jobs and so forth is programed into a computerized Memory that retains and retransmits only what is deemed necessary. Paul Simonds, 16, has committed the unthinkable wrong of burning the sports pavilion of his Estate (housing complex) in an effort to fight against what he has perceived as darkness taking over the world, but which was actually a brief power failure. As an "amendment," the psychiatrist, Dr. Palmer, assigns him two hours a day of work with a Mrs. Ellie Willmay, a "sick" woman in a substandard area of the Ackroyden Estate, adjacent to his own. There he finds a strange situation, an unhappy woman, her laconic daughter Sharon, about his age, a couple of younger children, and two sympathetic neighbors. Mrs. Willmay is said to like to read but only glances at the books he has been told to take her. The strangeness of the people, who also have a caged parrot, unheard of in the society, both disturbs and intrigues Paul. He discovers that his own estate also has a substandard area, where he finds a group of little boys with a "guy," a stuffed figure, chanting, "Remember, remember, the fifth of November." The word "remember" is meaningless to Paul, but he recognizes it as what his senile great-great-grandmother from "Pre-Enlightenment" days was trying to say when she saw the fire. Against the rules, he has written an account of the fire on a scrap of paper and retained it, though the memory has been blotted from his mind by the Drink which is taken with ceremony every day. One day he returns to Mrs. Willmay's and finds her gone, reported by her friend. The parrot has been freed by Sharon. Inexplicably, Paul feels the need to find and destroy the bird, which he does in a wild scene followed by a line of younger boys singing about killing a wren on St. Stephen's Day. Relieved of his work and of school as a result, Paul discovers a plant growing in a crack in the asphalt and for some days shields it from the sight of the street cleaners, aided by a girl who appears and tells him her name is Sharon. When the plant is destroyed, Paul goes berserk, leading a group of boys in a wild run through buildings, over walls, at last onto a highway. He finds himself in a hospital with Dr. Palmer, who tells him that he will be sent away, ostensibly to a symposium on futurism. Actually, he is sent to a slave labor camp for those who are unable to give up the deep emotions of old times. On the bus with him is a girl whom he does not remember, but who is Sharon. She is dropped at a work center before he is. There he enters a sort of feudal work group, the Reapers, who harvest grain grown in vast domes that control the weather. As his memory returns (without the Drink) he recognizes Mrs. Willmay as the cook. The work is gruelling, but it has meaning, and he is happier than before, but as he develops he comes to see that there is no reason not to escape. The leader of his group, Lord, tells him escape is possible, that there are clusters of escapees somewhere to the west. He and Sharon, whom he has helped her mother find, plan to leave together. When he discovers that the main Lord, their top slave-master, is really Dr. Palmer, he realizes the depth of the control, and he makes a last gesture of protest by firing the dome. As he and Sharon leave, they see other domes burning in the distance, a tribute to the strength of the human spirit to resist tyranny. The depth of the response of human psyche to certain folk elements--ceremonial fires, songs, pathways, and rituals--is another rather curious theme. The horror of a populace with no ability to remember is skillfully handled, growing gradually through the novel. Paul is a rounded character, and the other characters are more interesting than in many science fantasy novels. Carnegie Com.; Guardian.

VASIF, COLONEL (*Children of the Book**), tough, hard-bitten, fatalistic commander of the Twenty-eighth Orta of the Turkish infantry (Janissaries), that participate in the siege of

Vienna. He is called Corbaci, which means
colonel, by his men. He is a *Devshirme*, one of
the Christian children who "in the old days, the
Turks had taken from Christian families to be
brought up as Muslims and Janissaries, knowing
no father but the Sultan, no family but the
army, and no fear except the fear of Allah. It
was that which perhaps accounted for the very
un-Turkish blue eyes which glittered in Vasif's
weatherbeaten face." A devout Muslim, he prays
at all the appointed times, even during battle.
He is a Turkish soldier's soldier, a man who has
spent his life in the army, knows his trade,
and gives everything to it. He is hard on
himself, his men, and his personal servant,
young Timur* Ven, whom he lashes with tongue and
cane into always putting service first. As the
siege wears on, he becomes almost "super-human;
immune to fatigue, wounds, disease, death
itself...." In the last battle, on September 12,
1683, he puts Timur in the rear, hoping thus to
save the boy's life. This poignant, unexpected
act shows that he is capable of loving and
letting his love affect his behavior positively.
He dies in the same battle.

VERNEY, (SIR) JOHN (1913-   ), born in London;
painter, illustrator, and novelist. He attended
Eton and Christ Church College, Oxford, where he
received a B.A. in history in 1935. During
World War II he served in the North Somerset
Yeomanry, Special Air Force, in the Middle East
and Europe, and was awarded the Legion d'Honneur
in 1945. In 1959 he was created Second Baronet.
His paintings have been displayed in group shows
at the Royal Society of British Artists, London,
and at other galleries, and he has illustrated
books, among them a number of novels by Gillian
Avery*. Besides two novels and several books of
nonfiction for adults, he has written lively
novels for young people in which the children
are involved in adult affairs and help with the
solutions, among them *Friday's Tunnel*
(Collins, 1959; Holt, 1966) and *February's Road*
(Collins, 1961; Holt, 1966), both concerning the
large Callendar family in Sussex and both
commended by the Carnegie award committee.
Among his other books for children are *Seven
Sunflower Seeds* (Collins, 1968; Holt, 1969),

about a plot to fix the Grand National Steeplechase and to edge Britain into the Common Market, and *Samson's Hoard* (Collins, 1973), a story concerning local elections, a treasure hunt and conservation.

VERUCA SALT (*Charlie and the Chocolate Factory**), the second obnoxious child to win a ticket to Willy* Wonka's Chocolate Factory. She is the pampered, willful daughter of rich parents who induge her every whim. Her father buys hundreds of Wonka candy bars until Veruca finds one with a ticket. Inside the factory, she gets the stubborn notion that she wants one of the squirrels that open Mr.* Wonka's walnuts (he uses squirrels because they never break the nuts while shelling them). She grabs one and is attacked by the other squirrels in retaliation and thrown into the garbage chute. She and her parents, who rescue her, go home covered with garbage. Like the other bratty children, she is a caricature.

VICTOR SKELTON (*Thunder and Lightnings**), Norfolk youth who becomes friends with Andrew* Mitchell after the Mitchell family moves to the country. Victor maintains a sunny disposition in spite of his uncomfortable home and school situations. His classmates and teachers regard him as backward, and he can barely read and write. No one but Andrew knows he is an expert on planes and can speak knowledgeably and authoritatively about them. His surly mother keeps an immaculate house, insisting on such cleanliness that the boys tiptoe through the place in order not to soil her spotless floors. An exceptionally thin child, Victor wears his dark hair long, has big ears that stick out through his hair, and he usually wears several sets of clothes at the same time. Victor likes to bike, enjoys playing with his guinea pig and wheeling Andrew's baby brother, Edward, in his pram, and especially likes to watch planes taking off and landing at the RAF airfield near by. He seems not particularly bothered about his lack of success in school or his uninviting house, and the resiliency he displays when he learns that his favorite planes are being retired is perhaps born of the necessity to face hard knocks alone. As a character, he offsets Andrew well.

VICTORY AT VALMY. See *Thunder of Valmy.*

VIKING'S DAWN (Treece*, Henry, ill. Christine Price, Lane, 1955; Criterion, 1956), historical novel of a voyage of Northmen on the North Sea around the year 780 A.D. at the beginning of the Viking period. Events are seen mostly from the vantage point of adventurous young Harald Sigurdson, who is probably in his mid-teens. After the death of their master, an old Norse farmer, frees them from their pledge of service, Harald and his cautious, realistic father, Sigurd, make their way to the coast and join determined, charismatic Thorkell Fairhair, sometimes called Skullsplitter and likened to the god Balder, who is preparing to take the maiden longship *Nameless* on a treasure-seeking voyage. A motley crew accepts the knucklebones of service to Thorkell: the stooped, round-shouldered old Finn, Gnorre, called Nithing because he has been outlawed for murder; the massive, blackhaired, bearskin-clad Aun Doorback, who speaks up for Gnorre; Horic Laplander, the magic-maker, who can summon favoring winds and whose dancing creates illusions of whatever wild creatures he wishes; the contentious Wolf Water-hater, Thorkell's sidekick, a tall, thin redhead, who constantly scratches because he refuses to wash and who carries a deadly mace of bog oak; and some thirty-five others of mercurial temperament, strong arms, and sturdy backs. Last to come is the arrogant Dane, Ragnar Raven, tall, swarthy, and tattooed on forehead and cheekbones. He is Thorkell's blood-brother, who insists on joining even though his presence creates an unlucky number. When Sigurd suffers a broken leg in the launching and must remain at home, his accident is considered blood payment to the gods for the launching and also restores the crew to its previous count. Just before sailing, Harald overhears Ragnar plotting to take over the ship, information he later conveys to Thorkell, who seems already to have suspected that his friend may prove disloyal. Since Sigurd broke a limb in his service, Thorkell acts as Harald's father

during the trip, but the other men all look out
for the youth, too, since this is his first
voyage. The journey brings good times, warm sun,
fair winds, stories, and songs, but untoward
happenings soon outbalance the trip's pleasant
aspects. Not long out, they encounter a wrecked
longship, which they ironically hope is not a
harbinger of their future, and the crew begins
to divide among itself, with some, including
Harald, favoring Thorkell, and others considering Ragnar the better man to head a treasure
hunt. Off Scotland they take a Pictish ship at
heavy cost in men and for no gain in treasure,
and Harald experiences his baptism in battle.
He is both terrified and amazed by the fray and
the realization that the handsome Thorkell is a
berserk, a special warrior who loses control
during battle and fights like a madman,
inspiring great terror in his foe. The crew then
accepts the hospitality of another Pict, Feinn,
with whom Thorkell makes a blood-oath of
friendship. Harald kills his first man when
Ragnar treacherously raids Feinn's treasure
house during the night, and the *Nameless* crew
must fight their way back to their ship.
Supplies run short, they must forage for food, a
storm snaps the mast and they are forced to row
to make progress, they run out of water, Harald
falls ill of a fever--the hardships mount.
Better fortune meets them temporarily when they
put in at Olaf's steading in the Orkneys. Harald
is nursed to health by Olaf's wife, and Olaf's
three stout sons and some cousins join the crew,
welcome additions to their now sorely depleted
manpower. Dissension grows, however, and when
Thorkell goes blind from the bitter winds that
rake the islands, almost all the men side with
Ragnar, who takes command when next they sail,
this time for the coast of Ireland where Ragnar
wants to raid monasteries. On the way they
capture a holy ship manned by monks, whose
treasure they sieze and one of whom, John, a
calm, patient man, they take with them. The ship
soon runs aground, and they are captured by the
band of cutthroats headed by Leire, a vicious
pirate, and his henchman, the monstrous Aurog,
and imprisoned in the underground stronghold in
his Dun. Ragnar and his partisans escape, but
are soon captured and slaughtered to a man. The

rest are publicly whipped into unconsciousness
and returned to the dungeon. The whipping
miraculously restores Thorkell's eyesight, and
he leads the effort to dig out of the dungeon,
as its plank doorway adjoins a kind of tunnel.
They accomplish this feat with more speed than
seems credible given the circumstances of the
beatings and lack of food. Aun holds up the
archway of the door just long enough for the
others to get out and dies when it collapses on
him. The others flee to the shore, clamber into
one of Leire's curraghs, and put out to sea
where the flimsy craft splinters on a spar. All
perish except Harald, whom John has saved from
drowning and who is found in the water near
death and rescued by a Danish ship. Returned to
his village in Norway and hailed as a hero,
Harald looks forward to more adventures on
future voyages. Although the pace is uneven, the
dramatic scenes at Leire's and on the sea seem
rushed, and the author's knowledge of Viking
life and ethic sometimes gets in the way of the
narrative, this is a top-notch adventure story.
It also evokes a splendid sense of the
hardiness, courage, and recklessness of the
early Vikings and the cruelty, pomposity, and
nobility of their era. The themes that events
reveal a person's worth and that real courage
lies in meeting with a good heart whatever comes
arise quite naturally from the story. The
characters are types and too much alike to keep
straight, but the understated style with its
terse, laconic dialogue, and language sounding
like proverbs, and economy of description
supports the period well. This is the first of a
trilogy about the adventures of Harald
Sigurdson, its sequels being *The Road to
Miklagard* and *Viking's Sunset*. Choice.

VILA: AN ADVENTURE STORY (Baylis*, Sarah, Bril-
liance, 1984), strongly feminist novel set in an
unspecified time in a Slavonic area along a
deep, swift, and much-feared river. In the village where Nina, 14, and Masha, 15, live, it
is believed that any woman who ventures into the
water will be captured by the Rusalka or water
witch and becomes a witch herself. When Masha
slips from the wooden washing platform, Nina
unthinkingly throws herself in after her friend,

and both are carried far down the river clinging
to branches and trees washed out in the flood.
Borne finally to the shallows, Nina stumbles
out, discovers Masha not far away, manages to
revive her, builds a fire, removes and dries
their clothing, and falls asleep with a strange
sense of security despite being in the forest
where the women of the village never venture.
The next day, after struggling for hours through
almost impenetrable brambles, the girls are
rescued by a young woman named Vila dressed in
men's hunting attire, which they consider sinful
for a woman to wear. She takes them in the first
boat they have ever seen to a village on a lake
further down the river and introduces them to
her companion, Ania, and Ania's two-year-old
son, Stepan. They are accepted without question
by the other villagers, who lead a life of great
freedom, each doing what he or she likes best,
with no predefined roles for men and women. Many
are refugees from other villages, like Ania, who
was driven out for becoming pregnant, and
Saskia, a woman from their own village who fell
in the river as a young child, was rescued and
returned to her own village by the lake people;
there the men decided she must be a witch to
have survived and threw her back into the river.
Rescued again by her friends, who had waited to
see what would happen, she was taken to the lake
village and has survived but is reclusive, being
emotionally scarred by the terrible experience.
Masha, who is artistic, fits in easily, delighted by the freedom of design and use of color in
the lake village, but Nina mourns for her
mother, Dunya, and her old life, until Vila
agrees to take her back to try to let Dunya know
she is still alive. Ania and Masha insist on
coming along, and as they travel upriver they
come upon two of Masha's brothers, Tomilin, 13,
a sensitive boy who strongly believes Masha has
survived and is hunting for her, and Vanya, 18,
who has been sent along by their father to watch
over his brother. Tomilin is delighted to find
them and to hear about the lake village, but
Vanya is resentful and suspicious. Vila leads
them all to a strange clearing in the forest
where she calls upon the Mati, an ancient woman
who lives in a tree house and seems to have more
than normal understanding. The Mati gives advice

and one of her exquisite carvings to each of
them, but, before they leave, a group of village
men hunting Tomilin and Vanya appear, shoot an
arrow into the throat of the Mati, who has tried
to distract them, and capture Vila. The others
escape. Tomilin and Masha are taken to the lake
village by two of the forest people, strange
unkempt creatures who seem to be relatives of
the Mati, where they gather several volunteers
to help rescue Vila. Nina and Ania press on to
the village, where they are able to contact
Dunya, who, it is revealed, helped Vila escape
years before when she was a child bride of an
abusive pedlar. A huge pile of brush around a
stake has been constructed, the punishment
having been predetermined before the trial, at
which a priest from another village presides.
Vila is, of course, convicted of being a witch,
partly on Vanya's testimony, but just as the
brush around the stake is being lit, the church
and several homes burst into flames, having been
set afire by the forest people. In this
distraction, Ania climbs on the burning pyre,
frees Vila, and they escape. Vanya leaps into
the water to join them and is rescued and taken
to the lake village, as is Dunya, who has calmly
left her husband and many sons to join Masha in
the new, freer life. The story, though not
fantasy, contains many implausible elements: a
river so swift and deep that it sweeps the girls
many miles in a few minutes, yet has rapids
through which a canoe can be paddled swiftly
upstream; a network constructed by the forest
people of plank and rope bridges through the
tops of the forest trees right to the village
edge yet unsuspected by the village men who hunt
in the forest; Vanya's sudden decision to give
up his position in the village and join the
free-thinking lake people. Occasionally the
style is clumsy and employs cliches. Nevertheless, the novel is written with intensity and
has an energy that carries a reader along to
share the characters' anger at the mistreatment
of women in this superstition-laden society.
The idea of the Rusalka comes from Slavonic
folklore. Other.

THE VILLAGE BY THE SEA: AN INDIAN FAMILY STORY
(Desai*, Anita, Heinemann, 1982; Allied

Publishers, India, 1983), quiet but moving novel
of a family living in poverty in the village of
Thul in modern India and of the changes that
industrialization of their area promises for
their lives. Lila*, the eldest, has left school
because her mother is ill and her alcoholic
father earns little and drinks that little up
each night. She tries to care for their home,
her bedridden mother, and her two little
sisters, Bela and Kamal, and to stay out of the
way of her drunken father. Her brother, Hari*,
one year younger than Lila, has also left school
and tries to help out by clearing space for a
garden, catching a few fish with his net, and
climbing for coconuts to sell in the market,
but their combined efforts scarcely keep the
family from starvation. Occasionally they earn a
little money by running errands and doing odd
jobs for the de Silvas, a wealthy Bombay family
whose vacation house, *Mon Repos*, is just across
the creek from their hut. The point of view
alternates between that of Lila, who toils
stoically but with little hope, and that of
Hari, who is humiliated by the low status to
which they have fallen and who dreams of ways he
might change their fortunes. Rumors of a huge
fertilizer factory to be built along their coast
bring hopes of jobs which his friends
anticipate, and he joins their talk somewhat
skeptically, fearing that labor for all the good
jobs will be imported to their area. When he
polishes Mr. de Silva's car, the man gives him
his Bombay address and suggests that he will
give the boy a job if he ever gets to Bombay.
One day after their mother has become much worse
and their little dog, Pinto, has been poisoned
by neighbors angry that their father has not
repaid a drinking debt, Hari hears an impassioned speech about the harm that the chemical
factory will do to the village, ruining the
fishing, the crops, and the whole way of life of
the area. Hari joins the men from their village
and from nearby towns who go in their fishing
boats to Bombay to protest to the government.
After the rally, at which they are surprised to
hear an educated Bombay man, Sayyid Ali, support
their protest, Hari does not follow the others
back to the boats; he has decided to stay in
Bombay and get a job, although the traffic,

lights, and violence of the city terrify him.
He finally makes his way to the high-rise
apartment building where the de Silvas live, but
a scornful servant tells him they have left that
day for Thul and sends him on his way. Afraid to
go out into the streets at night, Hari hangs
around the lobby of the building until the night
watchman, a kindly sort, spots him and takes
him to the Sri Krishna Eating House of Gowalia
Tank, the lowest of the poor restaurants in
Bombay, catering to beggars, coolies, and cart-
pullers. There the proprietor, Jagu, gives him
a meal and a job helping the two other boys who
toil around the clock in the heat and fall to
sleep exhausted on the benches in the kitchen.
Hari cannot communicate with the boys, who are
suspicious and unfriendly and speak a different
language, and Jagu is a silent man, though fair
and kind in his way. The village boy finds life
confined to the eating-house stifling and is
desperately homesick until he meets Mr.
Panwallah, the old watchmaker in the shop next
door, who suggests that he sleep in the park and
starts to teach him to repair clocks and
watches when business is slow at the Sri
Krishna. In the meantime, their mother becomes
so much worse that Lila prepares to go to the
nearest town to describe her condition to a
doctor and try to get medicine. Before she takes
this unprecedented step, the de Silvas return to
Mon Repos and agree to take the mother to the
hospital, which is free, and to pay for her
medicines and let Lila work to repay them. When
her father returns, drunk, and finds his wife
gone, he is furious, berates Lila, smashes the
water pots, and stumbles off to the town
hospital. To everyone's surprise, he stays
there, not drinking, living on the hosital
veranda where he can hear his wife call if she
needs him. With him out of the way, the three
girls get along better than they ever have
before, working for the de Silvas and then, to
their delight, for the friend of Mr. de Silva,
Sayyid Ali, who comes to stay at *Mon Repos* all
through the monsoon, when the wealthy family
goes away. The monsoon season is a nightmare in
Bombay. The torrential rains keep everything
wet, the streets become mudholes, Mr. Panwallah
becomes ill, and Hari is deeply depressed. One

night he hears on a customer's radio of the fishing boats from Thul being lost in a storm. The news brings back to him his love of his village and his family, and he decides to go home. No ferries run during the rainy season, however, and Jagu will not release him from his job until *Dwali*, the Hindu festival of lights. When he does go back to Thul, with presents for his sisters and his carefully hoarded earnings, he learns that his mother has greatly improved with medicine and good food, and he goes to the hospital to fetch her home. His father, now sober, seems old and gray, and for the first time Hari feels pity for him instead of hatred. When he visits Sayyid Ali to thank him for employing the girls, he finds it is the same man who addressed the rally. He confides in Sayyid Ali his plans to start a poultry farm so that he will be in a position to sell eggs and chickens to the many workers who will come to Thul with the fertilizer factory, and eventually to start a watch-repairing shop. The gentleman compliments him on his willingness to adapt and predicts that the family will survive. The story is plausible and the main characters believable, but the strength of the book lies in the descriptions of life in both Thul and Bombay, seen from the point of view of the two young village adolescents, of both the hardship and the beauty of their lives and that of the many people, both poor and well-to-do, whom they come to know. Guardian.

VIOLET BEAUREGARDE (*Charlie and the Chocolate Factory**), bratty, bossy, insolent child who always chews gum. She is the third of the obnoxious children to win a ticket to Willy* Wonka's Chocolate Factory. On the tour, she grabs some blueberry gum, although Mr.* Wonka tells her the product has not yet been perfected. She chews it, turns blue, and puffs up like a giant blueberry. After the tour she returns home, dejuiced to her appropriate size but still blue in the face. As a character, she is distorted for comic effect and is a caricature like the other terrible children.

VIPONT (FOULDS), ELFRIDA (1902-   ), born in Manchester, Lancashire; professional singer and

novelist. She was educated at Manchester High
School for Girls and at The Mount School, York.
During World War II she was headmistress at the
Quaker Evacuation School, Yealand Manor,
Lancashire. She was trained and performed as a
professional singer, and many of her books
reflect her interest in music. For adults, she
wrote one novel and several books of nonfiction,
mostly about Quakerism. She has also written as
E. V. Foulds, her married name, and as Charles
Vipont. For children, she has published more
than twenty books of fiction, four plays, and
about a dozen books of nonfiction, some of them
about religion or music, and several biographies, among them those of Margaret Fell, Henry
Purcell, Charlotte Bronte, George Elliot, and
Jane Austen. Her best known novels are those
about the Quaker Haverard family, *The Lark in
the Morn* (Oxford, 1948; Bobbs, 1951), *The Lark
on the Wing** (Oxford, 1950; Bobbs, 1951), which
won the Carnegie Medal in 1951, *The Spring of
the Year* (Oxford, 1957), and *Flowering Spring*
(Oxford, 1960). Among her other books for young
people is *Terror by Night: A Book of Strange
Stories* (Hamilton, 1966; as *Ghosts' High Noon*,
Walck, 1967), a group of stories of second sight
and supernatural happenings.

THE VOYAGE OF THE "DAWN TREADER" (Lewis*, C. S.,
ill. Pauline Baynes, Bles, 1952; Macmillan,
1952), fantasy of magic and high adventure
involving quests, fifth in time and third
published in the series about the mythical land
of Narnia* and the magnificent god-lion, Aslan*.
One year in real-world time after restoring
Caspian* to the throne in *Prince Caspian**,
Edmund* and Lucy* Pevensie are visiting their
disagreeable cousin, Eustace*, in Cambridge.
The three are sitting in Lucy's room one day
staring at a picture of a dragon-prowed, Narnian
sailing ship, when they are suddenly pulled into
the waves surrounding it. They are fished out of
the water and taken aboard the *Dawn Treader* by
Prince Caspian, who has been King Caspian the
Tenth for three years in Narnian time. Leaving
Trumpkin* as regent, Caspian has embarked on a
long and hazardous voyage to the east in search
of the seven lords his usurper uncle, Miraz,
had exiled beyond the Lone Islands. Accompanying

Caspian is the bold and outspoken warrior mouse, Reepicheep*, whose ambition is to sail to the very eastern end of the world, where Aslan is rumored to live. The first part of this episodic plot focuses mainly on complaining and fretful Eustace, who becomes increasingly difficult and bad-tempered. At the Lone Islands, Caspian, the children, and Reepicheep go ashore for a lark. They are captured by a slaver named Pug, and Caspian is sold, as it happens, to one of the lords he seeks, Bern, with whose help he disposes of the lazy and corrupt governor, Gumpas, secures the release of his companions, and puts Pug out of business. Leaving Bern as Duke of the Lone Islands, they push east, are battered by a terrible storm for many days, and put in at another island for water and repairs. To get out of work, Eustace goes off by himself, and in one of the series' most memorable passages, enters a dragon's lair, falls asleep atop the dragon's treasure, and awakens as a dragon, all this without realizing what is happening, because, the author tells us, Eustace hadn't read the right books. The group later concludes that the body of a dead dragon near the lair is what remains of another lost lord. The adventures increase in number from this point, but they are less developed, tend to become repetitious, and could in most instances be interchanged. The wanderers just manage to evade the coil of an immense Sea Serpent and survive another terrible storm, putting ashore then at an island where they discover a pool whose water turns whatever touches it to gold. Within the pool they can see the body of a third lord, now a statue of gold. Aslan's appearance keeps the party from succumbing to greed and, restored to their senses, they leave the island they call Deathwater behind and sail on. Semicomic scenes ensue at the next island stop when they encounter an invisible people, the Monopods or Dufflepods, whose lord, a magician named Coriakin, has enspelled them for disobedience. The disembodied voices persuade Lucy to consult the magician's magical book and restore them to visibility. The appearance of Aslan's face keeps Lucy from being tempted to try other potentially harmful spells. Later, as the group is about to sail into a dark mass on the horizon, they rescue from the water a tattered and terrified man, another exiled lord, who warns them away, informing them that the island they approach is the Island of Dreams come true. They find the three remaining lords on the next island stop, asleep at a banquet table, and are told by the lord of the island, Ramandu, a retired star, that the Sleepers can be awakened if the travelers sail to the end of the world and leave one of their party there. From there they enter a region where the air and water are very clear and bright. Under the ocean's surface they can see the country of the Sea People, and when they drink the water they feel strong and content and have no desire for food. They sail through a sea of white lilies until the water becomes so shallow the ship can go no further. Caspian wants to take the ship's boat and continue on with Reepicheep. He insists that the others turn back and that he is abdicating his royal responsibilities to Trumpkin, but when he sees Aslan's angry eyes before him, he changes his mind. The three children and Reepicheep continue in the ship's boat, and Caspian puts about to return to Narnia. At the End of the World, Reepicheep gets into his own little coracle and disappears over a great wave. The three children land, walk on to where it seems the sky meets the earth, and see a white Lamb, who tells them that this is not the way into Aslan's country for them and then is metamorphosed into Aslan himself. He tells them that Lucy and Edmund will never return to Narnia again, because they are too old now, and that they must learn to know him by another name. With a sudden rending of the blue wall of atmosphere around them and a terrible white light, the children find themselves back in Cambridge, with Eustace startlingly improved in temperament and behavior. In spite of an overextended plot, lapses into sentimentality and contrivance, a too-obvious message and symbolism, and a lame conclusion, the book has much to commend it. It offers more adventure than most in the series, adds dimensions to the reader's understanding of Narnia, and has a good-natured tone that is very attractive. Aslan appears less than in the previous books, here

being more of a moral than an actual guide. The
most interesting episodes--the entry, Pug and
Bern, and the reformation of Eustace--take up
the first half of the book, leaving the rest of
the adventures crowded into the last half. The
beginning of the novel is slow and more adult in
appeal, since Lewis appears occupied with
commenting on progressive education and contemporary parenting. ChLA Touchstones; Choice.

THE VOYAGES OF DOCTOR DOLITTLE (Lofting*, Hugh,
ill. author, Cape, 1923; Lippincott, 1922),
second in a series of fantasies with a home base
at the town of Puddleby-on-the-Marsh in England,
this one set in 1839. Told in the first person
by Tommy Stubbins, 9 1/2, the cobbler's son,
this introduces Doctor* John Dolittle, the
physician who can talk with animals, five years
later than the first book, after he has had many
voyages and has become a famous, though not a
wealthy, naturalist. Tommy, wanting the doctor
to treat a squirrel with a broken leg, finds him
by accident, bumping into him in the rain, then
going to his comfortable but unconventional
house to get his clothes dried. Fascinated by
the cheerful, unpretentious doctor and his
household of animals, which is managed by the
efficient duck, Dab-Dab, Tommy soon becomes his
assistant and is taught the animals' languages
by the parrot, Polynesia*. He is at the trial of
Luke the Hermit when the doctor translates the
evidence of Bob, Luke's bulldog, the only
eyewitness to a murder of which Luke is wrongly
accused, and he is part of the crew that
includes Polynesia, Jip the dog, and Chee-Chee*
the monkey, on the voyage to Spidermonkey Island
off the coast of South America, the place where
the world's other great naturalist, Long Arrow,
son of Golden Arrow, was last seen, according to
Miranda, the Purple Bird-of-Paradise, who
brought the news. Bumpo* Kahbooboo, Crown Prince
of Jolliginki, who is now attending Oxford,
decides to take a holiday and go with them. At
Monteverde, where they put in for supplies
because a stowaway has eaten so much, Doctor
Dolittle makes a wager with the promoter of
bullfights that if he can outperform the chief
matador, all bullfights will be discontinued.
Then, with the help of the bulls, with whom he

has conferred in their language, he puts on a marvelous show, while Bumpo, who has learned about side bets at Oxford, replenishes their fortunes. Further along on the trip, they catch a small fish, a Silver Fidget, which speaks some English having once been in an aquarium. The fidget advises the doctor that he may be able to learn the language of the shell fish, as he wishes to do, from the Great Glass Sea Snail, if he can find the creature. Later their ship is wrecked, a circumstance that worries the doctor very little, and the pieces of wreckage are pushed together and then on to Spidermonkey Island by helpful porpoises. There Doctor Dolittle discovers a very rare Jabizri beetle, with a picture message written in blood on a dried leaf tied to its leg. He rightly inter-prets it as a message from Long Arrow saying that he and his companions have been trapped in a cave by a landslide. Led by the beetle, they find the cave, dig under the slab of rock that blocks the opening, and release the Indians. At the Popsipetel Indian village, they learn that the humans and vegetation are all suffering because the island, which is floating, has drifted too far south into Antarctic regions, and the people have never known fire. Doctor Dolittle makes fire with a bow and drill, teaches the Indians to use it, and gets whales to push the island back to the tropic regions. Then the other tribe on the island, the Bag-jagderags, attack, and although Bumpo and Long Arrow battle side-by-side with the doctor, they are almost overcome until Polynesia recruits millions of Black Parrots from the mainland, who fight by grasping the hair and ripping bits from the edges of ears. The Indians of both tribes are so impressed that they join forces and insist that Doctor Dolittle become their king. At his coronation, the great shouts and cheers dislodge the hanging stone at the edge of an old volcano so it crashes through the hollow airspace in the island's center and causes it to settle, fortunately in water not deep enough to cover the island. At the secret suggestion of Polynesia, the Great Glass Sea Snail, which the doctor is treating because the island came to rest on its tail, offers to carry them back to England. The story, though narrated by Tommy,

has the same matter-of-fact simplicity as the
first book (*The Story of Doctor Dolittle**), with
the added advantage of a young protagonist. The
treatment of Bumpo, while amusing because the
black prince uses long words and malapropisms,
is not offensive, being more affectionate than
contemptuous. The wildly imaginative adventures
always have a seeming logic. First published in
the United States, the novel won the second
Newbery Medal. Children's Classics.

VRETHIKI (*The Emperor's Winding Sheet**), so
called because when he falls into the garden at
Mistra he keeps saying "Bristow," the name of
his English home, which the Greek-speaking
retinue of the emperor interpret as "Vrisko,"
meaning "find," and which they change to
Vrethiki, which means "lucky find," although his
real name is Piers Barber. Because of his
father's death, his uncle has found him a place
on a ship, the *Anna,* which has been wrecked,
and after clinging to a spar for some thirty
hours he has been picked up by pirates, who so
badly mistreat him that his mind rejects the
memory. He has escaped and made his way over
mountains to Mistra, where, desperately hungry,
he climbs a tree to get at an unripe orange and
in his dizziness falls at the feet of
Constantine*, then Despot of Morea. He is
pressed into service--slavery, really--because
his presence at the moment when Constantine is
offered the crown can be used to seem to fulfil
the prophecy in the dream of Plethon that as
long as one who is near at that moment remains
at the emperor's side, the city will not fall, a
prophecy that neither the emperor nor the boy
believe but which is important to the common
people. Although his age is not given, he cannot
be more than eleven or twelve, since even after
about two years in Constantinople he is still
spoken of as a child and is not expected to
wield a sword or join in the defence of the
walls. A blond, blue-eyed English boy, he stands
out among the Greeks and Near Easterners even in
a city full of every race and nationality.
Although he has not been much of a student at
home, he has enough Latin to communicate with
Stephanos*, the body slave of the emperor, and
he gradually picks up enough Greek to understand

much of what is going on, though he can never
really talk to Constantine, whom he grows to
admire and love.

W

WALL OF WORDS (Kennemore*, Tim, Faber, 1982),
realistic episodic novel of family life set
recently in London. Plunged into the events, the
reader needs time to discover that two main
problems confront the Tate family: first, why
Kerry*, 8, suffers from a phobia toward school,
and second, how to make ends meet while Mr*.
Tate is away completing his long-projected novel
on Russia. Character revelation initially
catches the reader's attention and contributes
much of the interest throughout the book. July
holidays from school have just started, and
Kim*, at thirteen the eldest of the four Tate
girls and the one from whose vantage point most
events are seen, looks forward to enjoyable
outings with Kerry, her favorite sister. During
the school year, Kerry comes down with various
illnesses whenever she must go to school, where,
though apparently bright, she seems unable to
achieve in even the smallest way. Numerous
visits to psychologists and endless tests
haven't helped find a solution at all. When Mrs.
Tate loses her job because Wilshire's store
shuts down her department, Kim sets out to pick
up a little money, and with the help of David*
Holder, 14, who lives next door, she does odd
jobs, one of which is walking McCluskey, an
accommodating English sheepdog, for Mrs.
Hanrahan, Kim's form mistress at school, a task
that turns out to be a permanent summer job. Kim
also agrees to go with her mother to talk with
still another psychologist, whose conversation

with Kim goes in circles, and who, it turns out,
has no more sense of what might be wrong with
Kerry than have the many previous experts. Kim
also visits her father at his apartment, where
she discovers that he has quit his job and sold
the family car for money to live on. She gets on
poorly with her stage-struck, golden-haired
little sister, Anna*, 7. Reproved by her mother
for her churlishness, she contritely makes the
Grand Gesture and suggests that Anna ring up the
local radio station, which has been advertising
for young talent to serve as Kidsline present-
ers, and apply for the position. Anna does and
is accepted at a good salary and what becomes a
continuing Saturday morning job. Kim takes Kerry
with her on her regular visit to Mrs.
Hanrahan's. Their conversation results in Mrs.
Hanrahan suggesting that Kerry's inability to
read and write and her general clumsiness may
be due to dyslexia, a malady from which fortuitously the teacher also suffers and with which
she has managed to cope without her colleagues'
knowledge. The girls are disappointed to learn
that Mrs. Tate, whose family had been well off,
has sold the family jewels which the Tates have
all along relied upon as their insurance
against really bad times. Frances, eleven and
the domestic one of the girls, reacts by
complaining to Kim about what she sees as her
father's irresponsibility, an attitude that Kim,
who has always felt very close to and protective of her father, resents. Luckily Mrs.
Tate gets a job at the new Sports Centre. She
then visits her husband and discovers that he
hasn't even begun to write his novel. She
returns to confide in Kim that she has put up
long enough with what she sees as her husband's
immaturity and lack of incentive to support his
family and will probably seek a divorce. At the
end, the reader knows that Kim accepts the
break, even though it hurts, and that Kerry is
overcoming her handicap. Although also a
convincing girl's growing-up story, this
loosely and limply plotted story essentially
looks at family relationships, at how important
it is for all members of a family to be loved
and appreciated for what they are and at how
important it is for all to contribute to the
welfare of all. It is also about pluck--not

giving up--and about facing facts. Kim's concern
for her sister, her longing for her father, and
her blindness   toward his   real   nature are
convincing in view of her character as presented
and make her and the others seem like actual
people. The home atmosphere is warm and
inviting, and conversation is free and prolific.
There is much humor, some of it best appreciated
by adults, in the dialogue between the girls,
which accurately   mirrors   the   fads   and
pretensions of everyday family life and where
wordplay and punning abound, and especially in
those passages where the author looks at things
pointedly but without   malice from   Anna's
self-centered point of view. The author's wit,
verve, and sympathy for everyone, including the
father, keep the book from becoming just another
expose of contemporary family life or another
treatise on dyslexia. The short scene in which
Anna reads aloud verse obituaries from the
newspaper while Kim searches through the yellow
pages   to determine   whether   or not   Mrs.
Hanrahan's husband is a funeral director and
Mrs. Tate attempts to instill in the girls a
sense of propriety toward death and grief is a
gem of ironic hilarity. The title refers to a
graffiti wall the girls pass while walking the
dogs and also to the facts that Kim has refused
to face ("...the writing's been on the wall..,"
says Mrs. Tate, near the end). Carnegie Com.

WALSH, JILL PATON. See Paton Walsh, Jill.

WALTER THOMPSON (*Gumble's Yard*; *Widdershins
Crescent*), father of Harold* and Jean* and
uncle of Kevin* and Sandra*, for whom he has
been guardian since their parents died, some
time before *Gumble's Yard* begins. He has been
living with Doris* and the children in a rundown
place in the Jungle*, since his wife left him,
also before the first novel begins. He is a
shiftless spendthrift, who is too lazy to go to
work regularly, wastes his meager pay on ale and
horses, and being weak and easily led is often
on the edge of the law. Although he has many
faults and doesn't take care of the children,
the reader likes him and doesn't want to see
him jailed, which is what happens to him at the
end of *Widdershins Crescent*. Walter appears

more often in *Widdershins Crescent* than in *Gumble's Yard*, but he produces the plot problem in both books.

WANDERLUST (*Mr. Moon's Last Case**), stray mongrel that Mr*. Reginald Moon finds curled up on the passenger seat of his car when he is in the village of Penmoor hunting for Nameon* the dwarf. A small dog, Wanderlust has ears that are over-large for his body, which is covered with a mass of curls that give him a disheveled look. Mr. Moon names him Wanderlust, because the dog is "preoccupied with rabbit-holes and ditches," "investigated places he should not investigate," like backyards, and "seemed to have a built-in radar system that led directly to bones." Wanderlust is instrumental in helping Mr. Moon find Nameon, in particular when he swipes a bone from the Lewsbury Cathedral museum. Mr. Moon recovers the bone, and, not wanting the Cathedral people to discover that Wanderlust had taken it, wraps the dog in a newspaper he finds nearby and carries him to his car. In the car he opens the newspaper, which happens to be the edition carrying the story that the leprechaun might be in Steelborough and which sends Mr. Moon to that city and the conclusion of his search for the dwarf.

THE WARDEN'S NIECE (Avery*, Gillian, ill. Dick Hart, Collins, 1957), story of a Victorian girl who starts her adventures in 1875 by running away from her oppressive boarding school to Oxford, where her uncle is Warden of Canterbury College. Maria* Henniker-Hadden, 11, has no intention at first of staying with her Uncle* Hadden, intending to return to her great-aunt in Bath, but she has only enough money for a ticket to Oxford, and she cannot bear to stay at school, where the geography mistress has promised to make her wear a sign saying "Slut" for her messy map of Europe. When she arrives bedraggled and very damp in the middle of a rainstorm, Uncle Hadden tells her that her aunt has just died and calmly sends her to have a warm bath and go to bed. The next day, when she confesses to him that she'd like to learn Latin and Greek and be a professor at Oxford, he is startled and pleased and immediately decides that a girls' school, of which he disapproves, is not a place to get a good education and that she must live with him and be tutored with the family next door, the three sons of Professor Smith. The rest of the book tells of how Maria, a timid and proper little girl, gets into one daring scrape after another trying to prove to Uncle Hadden that she is promising as a scholar so he will not send her back to school. Although his housekeeper, Mrs. Clomper, who is protective of his time and energies, considers her a trial and she has never before even talked to boys, she soon finds her life full of interest with the Smith brothers, Thomas*, 13, who is lofty and often imperious, Joshua*, 11, who is gentle and nervous, and James*, 8, who is loud and outrageously naughty. Since their regular tutor is called away by a family emergency, they are taken over by the Reverend Mr.* Copplestone, an immensely tall and unconventional clergyman. Lessons with Mr. Copplestone are as eccentric as his appearance and his other behavior. He regularly bribes James with money and promises of exhibitions of bull-fighting techniques, which make a shambles of the Smith schoolroom, and he skips around in history to any period where he can get a good argument going. On an expedition to Jerusalem House, the large manor and estate of the Fitzackerley family not far from Oxford, he asks so many questions and takes so many notes that the possessive caretaker, Miss Hickmott, is most annoyed and is even irritated at the children, who are more interested in a drawing labeled "Unknown Boy" than in the proper portraits of gentlemen. When Thomas asks if it isn't clear that the boy is a Fitzackerley, she nearly evicts them. Some days later, while playing "Truth or Dare?," Maria dares Thomas to go to Jerusalem House and break in, and when he takes the dare, the three older children hitch a ride with the new housemaid and her farmer uncle in his cart, get into the Jerusalem House grounds, sneak up close to the house, and, frightened at someone coming out the door, hide at the foot of a wall. Maria sees an inscription carved on the stone, "20 July 1654" with the initials, "S.StG.F." and the message, "Begone, ye foul traitors." They return without mishap to a great row from Mrs. Clomper and the Smith

parents, which reduces Maria to misery but which
the boys shrug off. Maria, who has been doing
very well in Latin and Greek, hits a spell when
she can't remember anything, and is thoroughly
afraid that her uncle will send her back to
school. When a friend of Uncle Hadden mentions
that there is a book on the Fitzackerleys in
"the Bodley," which she learns is the Bodleian
Library, she decides to do some original
research on the unknown boy, whom she suspects
is Stephen St. George Fitzackerley, son of the
Ninth Lord. On her walk with Mrs. Clomper, they
escape from a mad bull into a door and up a
stairway, where Mrs. Clomper faints. Maria runs
for help and finds herself in the Bodleian.
Since someone else has rescued Mrs. Clomper and
taken her home in a cab, Maria seizes the
opportunity to ask for the book about the Fitzackerleys, and the library head, the Protobibli-
otecarius Bodleianus, thinking that the warden
has sent her, has the oath administered to her
and the book fetched, though the library is
ordinarily open only to members of the college.
Her further research entails another visit to
Jerusalem House, where she and Mr. Copplestone
walk in by a back door uninvited and are thrown
out at the orders of Miss Hickmott, and another
visit to the Bodleian, where she sees her uncle
and the librarian in conversation and escapes by
crawling up the long reading room under the
tables past the legs of the reading scholars.
The regular tutor having returned, Mr. Copplestone calls to say goodbye and as a parting gift
hands Maria a paper that he has casually stolen
from a professor working on the Fitzackerley
papers. It proves to be a letter from the Ninth
Lord Fitzackerley to his son, Stephen. When
Maria conquers her embarrassment to return the
letter to the scholar, he produces other letters
of the period that show that the Ninth Lord, a
Royalist, had fled to France, leaving Stephen
at Jerusalem house with his tutor, and that,
word having come that Cromwell's men are about
to arrive at the house, Stephen and his tutor
have also fled. Having solved the mystery,
except to learn what had eventually happened to
Stephen, Maria finds no one much interested, the
Smith boys being bored with the subject and Mr.
Copplestone having left for Bolivia. When summer

holidays come, the Warden suggests that perhaps Maria would like to join him in a visit to an old friend in Kent. There, on an expedition by pony cart to look at graveyards, her uncle finds the stone of Stephen Fitzackerley, who died in a fall from his horse just two days after he carved his message on the wall at Jerusalem House, obviously during his attempt to escape to France, and was buried in his uncle's churchyard in Kent. In the friendly atmosphere of the pony trap, Maria is able to tell Uncle Hadden the whole story, including her escape from the Bodleian and her trespassing at Jerusalem House. He is impressed and suggests that she rather than he give the talk that his hostess has promised to the Kentish Historical Association and for which he had hoped to find inspiration during their graveyard visits. The story is kept interesting and credible by the deft characterization, particularly of Maria who wants to be good and to conform but is daring in her efforts to escape boarding school and, later, reform school, to which she fears she is destined after her adventures with Mr. Copplestone. The setting in Victorian Oxford is exact and believable, and the book is full of sly humor. Some of the characters, notably Mr. Copplestone and the Smith boys, reappear in later novels by Avery. Carnegie Com.

WARRIOR SCARLET (Sutcliff*, Rosemary, ill. Charles Keeping, Oxford, 1958; Walck, 1958), historical novel set on the South Downs in the Bronze Age of Britain, about 900 B.C., exploring the psychological experience of failure according to the customs of the tribe. Although he has always had a withered right arm, it is not until he is nine years old that Drem* realizes, from overhearing the scornful comments of his grandfather, Old Cathlan, and his mother's defensive replies, that the condition may keep him from becoming a warrior on the Men's side and, therefore, an adult member of the tribe. Hurt and furious, he runs off into the forest, where he is found near morning by Talore, a highly repected hunter of the tribe who lost one hand on a wolf hunt. Admiring the little boy's fierce courage and feeling a kinship because of their handicaps, Talore points out

that a one-armed man can be skilled with the
spear and promises that when Drem has made his
wolf-kill, the ritual test for membership in the
Men's side, he will stand with Cathlan as the
boy's sponsor. When Talore's dog, Fand, has
half-wolf puppies, the hunter offers Drem the
best male if he pays for it with a bird he has
killed himself. Partly by chance, Drem is able
to spear a magnificent white swan, almost as big
as he is, and soon he and the puppy, which he
calls Whitethroat, are inseparable. The only
other person Whitethroat will go to is Blai*,
the orphan daughter of a travelling smith, whose
mother died at her birth in the village and who
has been taken in by Drem's mother, not as a
slave or even a servant, but not quite as a
daughter either. At eleven, Drem leaves his
home bothy to live for four years with the other
males his age in the Boys' House, training to
become warriors and hunters of the tribe. On his
first day, he is taunted by Luga, whose father
wanted Whitethroat as a puppy and who has
resented Drem ever since. Drem lashes out with
his one fist, and in the ensuing melee finds
Vortrix, the chieftain's son, fighting at his
shoulder, an incident that starts a lifelong
friendship and blood-brotherhood between the
two. In Drem's third year in the Boys' House,
the king dies, and at the funeral the new king
averts an ugly quarrel between Drem's chieftain
and another man by declaring that they shall
fight it out with dogs rather than dirks. When
Whitethroat is chosen as one of the dogs, Drem
knows that, though he is big, strong, and loyal,
he is no fighter and would be killed by the mean
cur pitted against him. Impulsively Drem jumps
forward and, pointing out that the boys, the New
Spears, are called the Hounds of each chieftain,
suggests that he will fight any New Spear of the
rival tribe. Despite his handicap, he holds his
own in the single combat with dirks until both
boys are badly wounded and the king stops the
fight. After the four years of training, the
boys draw lots to see in what order they will
hunt wolves for their individual kills. Drem's
turn comes last. They track a large, wily dog
wolf to his den, but at the moment he leaps,
Drem steps on a sharp root, misses his timing by
a second, and goes down under the animal. Before

he can think, Vortrix jumps in and stabs the
wolf, saving Drem's life but condemning him to
the status of a failure, no longer a member of
the tribe, unable to join the Men's side or even
to live in the village. He goes off to the hills
to the Half-People, the little Dark People and
their mixed descendants who are older in the
area than their conquerors, the Bronze people of
Drem's tribe, and who keep the sheep for the
tribe. There, enigmatic old Doli, who has been
his friend since Drem was a child, teaches him
with patience, but he still belongs to neither
tribe nor Half-People. In the winter, when Vortrix comes up with the warriors of the Wolf
Guard, he tries to talk with Drem, but there is
a gulf between them. In a sudden bad storm, Drem
comes to the sheep fold to find that Doli has
gone out after a stray sheep. Drem, with
Whitethroat, follows him, finds him collapsed
near the sheep, sends Whitethroat back to get
the Wolf Guard, and drags Doli and the sheep to
a sheltered spot where he has some chance of
defending them. The wolves attack, and Drem
kills the leader just as Whitethroat and the
Wolf Guard arrive, but he is badly wounded. When
he wakes, days or weeks later, he is once again
in his home bothy and his mother is weaving for
him the Warrior Scarlet, the cloth that can be
worn only by the initiated of the Men's side.
Vortrix explains that he discovered from the
scars on the hide that the wolf Drem slew was
the same he had missed a year before. The
council has considered and decided, with the aid
of an opinion by the tribal priest, that the Sun
God has sent Drem a second chance. He is
initiated and at the Beltane celebration, when
young couples leap over the fire to ensure
fertility, he takes Blai to jump with him, now
understanding how she has always been an
outsider and seeing that they belong together.
In this emotionally moving novel, the sense of
failure and rejection is made devastatingly real
through the experiences of both Drem and Blai.
Although the ending is hopeful, it is clear that
both young people have suffered and are
psychologically scarred by having lived outside
the warmth of tribal acceptance and approval.
The picture of life in the Bronze Age tribe,
based on archeological and mythological studies,

is convincing, and even the coincidence of the slain wolf is made to seem plausible. Carnegie Com.; Choice; Fanfare.

THE WATCHER BEE (Melwood*, Mary, Deutsch, 1982), novel of a girl growing up in a Midland village not far from Sheffield in the 1920s and 1930s. Taking the metaphor from her childhood misinterpretation of a poem her uncle quotes, "Let me a partaker, not a watcher be," Kate* thinks of herself as a watcher bee, humming and fumbling around the edge of the action, never really part of it, never really belonging. Even her family does not quite fit the conventional pattern. An orphan whose father died as a result of World War I and whose mother died in the flu epidemic, she has always lived with her Aunt* Beth, her father's sister, and her Uncle* Ben, her mother's brother, who married to make it convenient to bring her up. Her life is intertwined from infancy with that of Charlie*, the boy next door. In early childhood, Kate and Charlie are inseparable; then they go through the normal antagonisms between boys and girls, but they are thrown together again when they finish the village school and Kate wins a scholarship to Fulford High School, which she has always thought of as the "Hockey School." Charlie's parents think more education might be good for him, so he, too, attends school in Fulford, unwillingly, and the two bicycle together to Welham Station, then take the ten-mile train ride to Fulford. Although Kate has been a prize student in the village and considered very clever, she does not do well at Fulford, being slow at math, not very good at Latin, and hopeless at hockey. Even the headmistress, Isa Ibald (called by the girls the Great Orb) criticizes her for lacking esprit de corps, and she is uncomfortably conscious of her height, her beanpole figure, and her school uniform, which shows where the hems have been let down. Her out-of-school education about life and love proceeds in a series of incidents. Accompanying her aunt, who is a registrar, to Orbin Old Hall where old Sir George has just died, she briefly walks out onto the snow-covered terrace and watches a young man playing with a child and a dog. Although the encounter is hardly more than that--he assures her that the dog will not bite and smiles at her--she feels that she has entered another world, and she falls in love with this young Sir George St. Orbin, or with the romantic idea of him. A more earthy view of love and life comes when she sees Charlie rolling in the hay with Ivy Holt, a girl from a scraggy poor family in the village. An even more jolting series of incidents occur during what they afterwards call "Zoe's summer," when they are both nearly fifteen. Charlie's mother rents her front rooms to Lucy* Denham-Lucie, a woman who taught with Aunt Beth and Kate's mother when they were young but who left the village to have an illegitimate child. Now a widow, she returns with her nineteen-year-old daughter, Zoe* Vardoe, who is not well, evidently from having suffered a self-induced abortion. Lucy sweeps into the village and into their lives with stylish clothes, lavish decoration for Granny's old rooms, theatrical posturing, and condescending advice, exposing a new world to Kate, who has been brought up with the careful, sensible, inflexible attitudes of Aunt Beth, and opening old wounds for both her aunt and her uncle. Zoe, Charlie, and Kate are thrown together frequently, but it is soon apparent to Kate that Charlie worships Zoe, who teases and leads him on, with Kate once more the watcher bee. Before too long, Lucy has a follower, a man from Sheffield who seems to have a lot of money and whom Charlie calls The Undertaker. Zoe goes off with her mother to visit him for a month, and when they return they announce, to everyone's astonishment, that he and Zoe are engaged. Charlie is devastated, and Uncle Ben is surprisingly sympathetic to him. It is only after they have departed for the wedding in Sheffield that Charlie's mother, who has overheard loud quarrels between Zoe and her mother, comes out with a startling conclusion: Zoe is not being forced into the marriage against her will, but has deliberately taken the man from her mother in order to have control of the money in the family. Some months later, when a card comes from Lucy to Aunt Beth, she and Uncle Ben have words, and he admits for the first time that he and Lucy were lovers when they were young. When Kate excitedly decides

that this makes Zoe her cousin, her uncle denies
it, saying grimly that he was not the only man
with whom Lucy went bicycling in the moonlight.
Charlie confides in Kate that he is going to run
away long enough to be expelled from school,
which he hates. Kate finds him in the woods
quite near their homes and brings him food
several times, but she doesn't tell, and he
sticks it out until it is certain that he won't
be accepted back into school. He is sent off to
work on a farm in Lincolnshire. In matriculation
exams for the university, Kate does not do well
and is relegated to a teacher training college.
Hating the idea of being an ordinary teacher,
she applies for a position in a language school
in Brussels and is accepted. Although her aunt,
her principal, and a representataive of the
County Education Committee all pressure her to
change her mind, she stubbornly sticks to her
choice. She hasn't enough money to get there,
and her aunt refuses to help. A long period of
tension is broken in a strange way. The nearby
woods have been taken over by the Ministry of
Defense and fenced, but she and Charlie have a
way in via some loosened boards. One night,
restless and thinking she hears an odd noise,
Kate slips a coat on after her bath and
investigates, stumbling on a body just outside
the fence. She drags the man to a hut her uncle
has at the bottom of the garden, gives him
mouth-to-mouth resuscitation, strips off his wet
clothes, and tries to warm him against her body.
They are discovered there by her aunt, who is
horrified at what appears to be a wild sex orgy.
Her uncle calls the police, hushes up Kate's
part in the rescue, and the man is taken away,
never to be heard of again, but the incident
somehow breaks the tension in the family, and
Aunt Beth helps Kate prepare to leave for
Belgium, even though, in 1938, European politics
make it a risky endeavor. Before Kate leaves,
she and Charlie walk in the woods once more, the
last time she ever sees him since he is joining
the air force and is later shot down. Kate is
prepared at last to jump into life as a
partaker, not a watcher. The novel, rather long
by recent standards, is full of wry observation,
amusing scenes, and sharp characterization,
giving a genuine feel to the picture of time,

place, and people. The first-person narration is
handled skillfully. Only the events near the end
of the rescue of the near-dead man seem extraneous and not fully integrated into the rest of
the novel. Young Observer.

THE WATCH HOUSE (Westall*, Robert, Macmillan,
1977; Greenwillow, 1978), fantasy concerning a
ghost that inhabits the old Watch House of the
Volunteer Life Brigade, set in the 1970s in
Garmouth, a name the author uses in several
books for Tynemouth on the North Sea coast.
Anne* Melton, a teenager, is taken from her
father's home and dumped for the summer by her
shallow, officious mother with her old nanny,
Prudie, who was also the mother's nanny and who
now lives with her brother, Arthur* Prudie, in
Brigade Cottage in Garmouth. Bored and lonely,
Anne escapes Prudie's suffocating attention by
helping Arthur in the Watch House, which stands
on the headland above the wide mouth of the Gar
and which has become a cluttered repository for
a miscellanea of flotsam picked off the sands.
Though it served a vital purpose when it was
founded in 1870 and for many years thereafter,
the Life Brigade with its breeches buoy has been
made nearly obsolete by two long piers, which
break the force of the waves before they crash
onto the rocks called the Middens, and by the
modern inventions of radar and rescue helicopters. Arthur, the Watch House caretaker, drives
a two-wheeled cart pulled by a bad-tempered
Galloway pony. Visiting the priory graveyard,
Anne meets two young curates, Father Fletcher of
the High Church of England, and Father da Souza,
an American of the Church of Rome, who are both
intensely bored with their duties in Garmouth.
Dusting curios in the Watch House, Anne is
astonished to find writing in the dust, "AN
HELP," repeated with variations even in the
glass case which hasn't been opened for years.
Anne faints, but Arthur dismisses it casually
as the work of "the Old Feller," though he is
more disturbed when the door of a glass case is
shattered by a very large, heavy skull falling
from the inside. When Anne is nearly drowned
and pulled from very shallow water by Arthur,
Prudie suggests writing to Anne's mother to come
fetch her, and Anne, desperately not wanting to

return to her mother's incriminations and her mother's lover, Uncle Monty, who can't keep his hands off the girl, announces that she has met Father Fletcher, who has invited her to the youth club, and Prudie is mollified, thinking Anne will meet people her own age and stop mooning around the Watch House. After an initially miserable time, Anne meets two people at the youth club disco, Timothy Jones, known as Timmo*, the long-haired boy who runs the tape deck, and his friend Pat Pierson, a nice plump girl who explains that she is Timmo's companion and not his girlfriend. Timmo, who is something of an eccentric genius, becomes interested in the Watch House, appeases Prudie's suspicions about his hair and odd clothes by fixing her refrigerator, and incorporates Anne with Pat into his threesome. Mr. McGill, the solicitor who serves as secretary of the Brigade, asks Anne to write a guidebook to the Watch House collection, and gives her some unpaid professional information about her rights in the marital conflict between her parents. Timmo starts hypnotizing Anne, and each time he does, she relives something from the life of the Old Feller, whom she has identified as Henry Cookson, the actual founder of the Life Brigade. In one of the dust messages Anne has been warned to "Ware Hague," whom they identify as Major Scobie Hague, drowned "while attempting the mercy of rescue" in 1854 and who, since he was "of gigantic stature," Anne is sure was the original occupant of the skull in the Watch House. Anne realizes she is somehow caught up in a conflict between two spirits, the Old Feller, of whom she feels protective, and Hague, who is terrorizing the Old Feller. Under hypnotism Anne relives the experience of the Old Feller at the wreck of the *Hoplite*, when he was ten years old and witnessed the death of Major Hague, who attempted to swim ashore with a line and was murdered by wreckers looking for spoils. Since the last face Hague saw was that of the little boy, to whom he cried out for help, the Old Feller spent his lifetime trying to placate the ghost and has continued after death. In an attempt to end the harrassment, Timmo tries to bury the skull in the graveyard at night, only to have it dug up by a dog and deposited on the

Watch House doorstep in the morning. Having incurred the enmity of Hague, they now suffer a series of near disasters, including narrowly escaping being buried under a fall of the cliff near the Watch House, which kills Arthur's pony which was grazing above. Putting clues together, Timmo realizes that the money Hague was trying to save when he swam ashore must be buried beneath the putting green at the edge of a sandbank. Anne, fearing they are in real danger, enlists Father de Souza, who has been investigating on his own and knows that Hague was really a criminal, cashiered from his regiment and sought for murder. They perform an impromptu exorcism on the sand, with the last-minute help of Father Fletcher, and lay the spirit of Hague to rest. Anne, waiting behind when the others leave, sees the Old Feller again and encourages him to go on beyond this world at last. Some days before this, Anne's mother has reappeared, expecting to collect Anne to come back to London with her, but the girl refuses, citing Uncle Monty's advances as a reason, and Prudie, shocked, has backed her up and written to her father. At the end, her father, his business crisis resolved, comes to get her. Hague's money, which was stolen by the wreckers but carefully replaced by the Old Feller, goes to the Watch House to shore up the sea wall, and Timmo has arranged for Arthur to buy cheaply a Galloway pony "needing a good home." There is a good deal of speculation, mostly from Timmo and Father da Souza, about how ghosts get their power through the fear of the people they haunt, and how the Old Feller, who was only mildly troublesome and treated lightly by the Watch Brigade, grew in power through Anne's loneliness and fear. The logical explanation and the powers of the two priests are not entirely convincing, but the story has the spookiness essential to a good ghost story and a group of interesting, if rather eccentric, characters. The scenes that Anne relives by hypnotism are particularly vivid. Fanfare.

THE WATER-BABIES: A FAIRY-TALE FOR A LAND-BABY (Kingsley*, Charles, Macmillan, 1863; Burnham, 1864), fantasy of magic, transformations, and talking animals, set first in a "large town in

the North country" of England and then on and in
the water of various streams and seas. While
Tom, a filthy, abused, thieving, illiterate
chimney sweep of ten, and his cruel master, Mr.
Grimes, are on their way to clean chimneys at
the mansion called Harthover Place, they
encounter a tall, handsome, dark Irishwoman who
delivers a warning that sets the novel's tone
and predicts its outcome: "Those that wish to be
clean...will be; and those that wish to be
foul...will be." At Harthover, Tom loses his way
in the hall's maze of chimneys, tumbles into the
room of Sir John's pretty little daughter,
Ellie*, and, in a great fright, flees precipitously for ten miles over the moors to the
valley of Vendale. There a kindly schoolmistress
gives him food and a hay bed in an outhouse. Tom
comes down with a fever, longs to be cool, hears
church bells, yearns to be clean so he can
enter the church, goes to a nearby brook to
wash, and falls asleep. He is taken into the
waters by the fairies, whose queen is the
Irishwoman, and is changed by them into a
water-baby. His pursuers find only a "black
thing in the water," say it is Tom's body, and
bury it in the local churchyard. Tom awakens as
a 3.87902-inch-long water-baby, amphibious,
gilled, and clean for the first time in his
life. The remainder of the novel consists of
his adventures underwater as he, first, strives
to discover other water-babies, second, learns
to behave himself, and, third, seeks to join
Ellie in the beautiful place where she goes on
Sundays. Tom explores his new environment and
soon learns to converse with the water creatures
with whom he gets along variously. At first, he
mistreats some for sport, but soon he reforms. A
big sea otter gives him trouble, but the water
fairies turn themselves into dogs and chase the
rude creature away. Tom follows the otter to the
salmon river, where he witnesses a poaching.
Attacked by the keepers, one poacher, who turns
out to be Mr. Grimes, falls into the river and
drowns. Tom continues downstream to the sea,
where he sits on a buoy for many days without
seeing any of his kind, though a conceited old
lobster, among others, informs him the water-
babies exist. After Tom helps the lobster escape
a lobster-pot, he discovers a water-baby, who

greets him warmly and informs him that he has
arrived in the water-baby area and that there
are dozens around. Their home is St. Brandan's
Isle (called Atlantis by Plato, says the
author), and they were taught first by the saint
and later by the fairies. The great fairy is
Mrs. Bedonebyasyoudid*, an ugly woman who
punishes Tom when he misbehaves, as he still
does frequently. Also important is her sister,
pretty Mrs. Doasyouwouldbedoneby*, who comforts
and cuddles him when he repents. After he
invades Mrs. Bedonebyasyoudid's cupboard and
gobbles up all the sweets, he becomes prickly
and ugly like her and is instructed in how to be
good by the most beautiful little girl he has
ever seen, sweet Ellie, who has died of a fall
and become a water-baby, too. She recognizes him
as the chimney sweep who accidentally invaded
her room and teaches him for seven years, during
which he becomes increasingly envious of her
because she goes to a beautiful place on Sundays
that she says is worth all the rest of the world
put together. He becomes cross and mischievous
when informed by the fairies that the way to get
to Ellie's Sunday place is to go where he does
not like to go, do what he does not like to do,
and help someone he does not like. He is certain
that the fairies wish him to seek and rescue Mr.
Grimes. He resists but then relents when Ellie
fades away and he can no longer see her. The
remaining two chapters of the total of eight
depict Tom's progress to find Mr. Grimes in the
Other-end-of-Nowhere. He is assisted by a large
number of unusual creatures, with whom he has
mildly suspenseful adventures, among them, the
last of the Gairfowl, who sits on the
Allalonestone, recites a nursery rhyme, and
sends him to Mother Carey, whose children are
petrels, and a molly bird named Hendrick Hudson.
At his destination, he sees various striking
sights, including all the little people of the
world writing all the little books in the world;
the center of Creation; and Gotham, the Pantheon
of the great Unsuccessful, where the wise men
live. Puzzled and frightened, he finally arrives
at a great building where he sees surly, dirty
Mr. Grimes stuck fast in a chimney. Determined
to help Mr. Grimes, Tom tells him about the kind
schoolmistress who helped him and discovers that

she is Mr. Grimes's mother. Mr. Grimes weeps heartily for his numerous past misdeeds, which include abandoning his mother, and his tears wipe away the soot and crumble the chimney mortar, cleaning him and releasing him from his imprisonment. He is sent to Mount Etna to sweep the crater there by the fairies, whom Tom realizes now are really just one being, composed also of the Irishwoman and Mother Carey. The journey successful, Tom returns to St. Brandan's Isle and Ellie. Both he and she are grown up now, he is allowed to go home with her on Sundays, and he eventually becomes a great man of science. In a "Moral" attached as an epilogue and addressed to "my dear little man," the author lightheartedly announces that children should never throw stones at efts, should always do their lessons, and should remember that this has all been "a fairy-tale, and only fun and pretence; and, therefore, you are not to believe a word of it, even if it is true." It is hard to identify with any character, since the reading interest focuses on the exotic nature of Tom's surroundings, which are described with elaborate, affectionate, romantic detail and occasional humor. Though inventive in concept, the plot is simply a series of sequential, almost suspenseless episodes, which go rapidly downhill in interest after Tom's metamorphosis and which patently afford the author an excuse for offering moralistic and Christian comments, philosophical or judgmental observations (many of them "inside" and intended for adults), and nature study, passages which are sometimes quite lengthy and hold up the meager plot for long periods. The conclusion is rushed and cluttered, the author's voice is always in evidence, and the tone is often coy or arch. Some portions have a dream-like quality, but most are grounded in the reality of the carefully described world of nature. One of the earliest fantasies for young readers, the book enjoys the status of a classic, but judged by today's standards for novels, it seems dated, lacking in unity, often tedious with extraneous detail, and very didactic. Children's Classics; Lewis Carroll.

WATERSHIP DOWN (Adams*, Richard, Rex Collings, 1972; Macmillan, 1974), long, serious, talking-animal fantasy involving physical and ideological survival and set recently from May to October on the Berkshire Downs. One moonlit night, motivated by the premonitions of danger of Fiver*, a small, intuitive rabbit, and led by steady, unassuming Hazel*, a bigger yearling, about a dozen male rabbits, disorganized, and sundry in temperament, leave comfortable Sandleford Warren and head south to look for a new home. They make for the distant hills Fiver insists must be their destination. The linear plot proceeds with some expected problems from the terrain (crossing the Enborne River), humans (guns and cars), animals (crows and foxes), and the need for food and shelter, and some important unexpected ones as well. The first major threat to their existence as a group occurs when, as they are digging shelters on a sunny meadow just over the Enborne, a large, sleek, aristocratic rabbit named Cowslip invites them to join his warren. The weary and bedraggled crew debates in characteristic democratic fashion the propriety of this move and decides to accept. Though they find the secretive atmosphere of the warren disquieting, they appreciate the hospitality, good food, and commodious quarters and are tempted to stay on until they realize that the rabbits' easy living depends upon a nearby farmer's largesse, given in exchange for periodic snarings. When Bigwig*, a sturdy fighter, is caught by a wire and severely wounded, his companions dig him loose, and all depart urgently, adding to their number a large buck named Strawberry. He decides to accompany them because he has recently lost his mate to the farmer's snare and, like them, has decided freedom in the wild is preferable to a good life bought at so high a price. He proves useful as a fighter and scout later on. The group ascends, at Fiver's direction, the rolling hill called Watership Down, finds a pleasant beech hanger, and, although digging is really does' work, constructs a secure and comfortable warren with a large central meeting place they call the Honeycomb, an endeavor that demonstrates effectively how adversity has melded them into an organized cooperative under Hazel's sensible leadership. At this point they are joined by two survivors of the Sandleford

Warren, Holly*, the former captain of the warren
Owsla, or peace force, and Bluebell, a clown of
quick wit and ready tongue. Holly relates the
long and emotional tale of the gassing and
slaughtering of the Sandleford rabbits when the
area was razed for urban development. The
rabbits' next major problem involves the need
for does; males alone cannot make a warren. They
learn from Kehaar, a seagull Hazel has
befriended, that there is a large warren to the
south and decide to send an expedition there
under the leadership of Holly to ask for does.
While they are gone, "in a spirit of happy
mischief" and jealous because the others felt
that as Chief Rabbit he was too valuable to
embark on the dangerous quest to the other
warren, Hazel takes malleable but brave little
Pipkin to nearby Nuthanger Farm to "liberate"
some tame does. Eventually, they succeed in
getting two, but Hazel is badly hurt by a bullet
and only restored to his friends through Fiver's
clairvoyance. Holly and party return unsuccessfully after some harrowing experiences at
Efrafa, a totalitarian warren, whose dictator-
leader, General* Woundwort, not only refused
their request for does but sought to impress
them into his closed society. Although Holly
insists the idea is utter folly, Hazel sets out
for Efrafa with most of the Sandleford rabbits
for another try. The clever Blackberry having
devised a scheme that involves Kehaar, they
send Bigwig into Efrafa. He represents himself
as Thayli, a renegade looking for a permanent
home. He soon becomes an Owsla officer, links up
with a dissident and brave doe named
Hyzenthlay, and under cover of a sudden
thunderstorm and protected by Kehaar, leads out
ten does. The return trip is harrowing and
involves among other excitements a nick-of-time
escape from General Woundwort and his forces and
a punt ride down the River Test. They arrive
back at Watership much the worse for their
journey and settle in safely, only to discover
shortly that Woundwort has trailed them and
intends to do battle over the does. There
follows a hard, bitter struggle for survival.
Woundwort viciously and systematically sets his
rabbits to burrowing into the warren. While the
redoubtable Bigwig heads the defense effort,

almost losing his life in a one-to-one showdown
with Woundwort, Hazel, Blackberry, and Dandelion, all good runners, head off to Nuthanger
Farm, where Hazel releases the watchdog by
gnawing through his rope. The dog soon catches
the scent and sight of the other two rabbits.
They lead him a ferocious chase back to the
warren where he plunges into the attacking
rabbits and effectively routs them. Captured and
injured by a farm cat, Hazel is rescued by Lucy,
the farmer's little daughter, who enlists the
aid of the local doctor in returning Hazel by
hrududu (the rabbits' term for a motorized
vehicle) to his natural environment. He returns
to a safe and relieved warren, which, with its
epic struggle for survival now won, grows
prosperous. Though anthropomorphized into clear
human types, the rabbits remain rabbits, and
their life on the run and in warren is clearly
depicted. They have dimension and vitality. They
are living beings caught up in the life-and-
death realities of subsistence, procreation,
self-defense, love, hate, compassion, mischief,
and ideology. Adams early wins the reader's
confidence that he knows rabbits, and he keeps
the point of view unerringly theirs in spite of
numerous digressions with information and
comments, some of them preachy, about the
relative virtues of men and animals and about
ecological concerns. Even the unrabbit-like
behavior of crossing the Enborne on a plank and
piling into a punt are made plausible by the
author's skill in getting inside the heads of
the rabbits and making their feelings and
concerns real. Adams invents a rabbit language,
proverbial expressions, mythology, religion, and
customs, all of which serve the function of
enlarging upon the rabbits' world and the plot
and are not merely decorative. He overwrites
almost every scene, but length and density here
contribute to belief. False notes appear with
the mouse and sea gull, who speak in Italian
and Middle Eastern dialects respectively, but
even the several lengthy "rabbit myths," related
mostly by Dandelion, who serves the rabbits as
tribal storyteller, point up important episodes
and add to the reality of the rabbit world, even
if they do hold up the action. The setting is
vividly described; trees, flowers, weeds, wind,

rain, sand, and mire all can be seen and felt as though one were right there with the rabbits; and there is enough humor to keep matters from becoming too stark. This combination of nature study, ethics, politics, philosophy, and good story, if seriously flawed, has still become a classic of the late twentieth century. Carnegie Winner; Choice; Fanfare; Guardian; Maxi.

WATSON, JAMES (1936–   ), born in Darwen, Lancashire; teacher, journalist, and novelist. He received his B.A. degree from the University of Nottingham in history in 1958 and served for the following two years in the British Royal Army Educational Corps. Later he taught English for the British Council in Milan, Italy, was a journalist and art critic for the *North East Evening* Gazette in Middleborough, Yorkshire, and served as educational officer and director of educational literature for Dunlop County, London. Since 1965, he has been a lecturer at West Kent College at Tunbridge Wells, Kent. Among his novels are *The Bull Leapers* (Gollancz, 1970; Coward, 1970), set in Crete, a fictionalized reconstruction of the tale of Theseus and the Minotaur, and *The Freedom Tree* (Gollancz, 1976; David, 1986), a story of the Spanish Civil War with a strong anti-Fascist stance. His chilling novel of political oppression and torture in Chili, *Talking in Whispers** (Gollancz, 1983; Knopf, 1984), received a Highly Commended rating by the Carnegie award committee. He has also authored a radio play, *Gilbert Makepeace Lives!* and a research work, *Liberal Studies in Further Education—An Informal Survey* (National Foundation for Educational Research, 1973). Watson has been active in arts and social causes, being a member of the Tunbridge Wells No-Censorship Committee, treasurer of the West Kent College Film Society, founder-secretary of the Teeside Film Club, a member of the Purcell Recorder Consort, and founder of a local arts cooperative.

THE WAY TO SATTIN SHORE (Pearce*, Philippa, ill. Charlotte Voake, Kestrel, 1983; Greenwillow, 1983), quietly suspenseful realistic mystery novel with detective-story aspects set from February to July recently in the English village of Ipston near the sea. Kate* (Catharine Alice) Tranter, about ten, gives little thought to her father, until sharp-tongued, domineering Granny* Randall, with whom the Tranters live, gets a mysterious and disturbing letter written in violet ink, the gravestone bearing her father's name disappears, and her brother Ran*, who is about fifteen, informs her that the family had once lived in the village of Sattin, that they used to have an Uncle Bob, that according to Granny their father died in a drowning accident, that this happened on the very day Kate was born, and that after the incident Granny had brought them to live with her in Ipston. Soon realizing that the tombstone really commemorates her uncle, Kate sets out to put together the jigsaw puzzle of her family history. Her quest involves several long bike rides alone and with Ran to Sattin, where she discovers her shy, sweet Nanny* Tranter, and to Sattin Shore, the drowning site on the estuary, where she encounters the strange, intimidating Arnold West, proprietor of the local fruit farm. Mildly Gothic conventions ensue as the story picks up gradually in intensity: Kate spies eerie eyes in a mirror one time when she is alone in the house, eyes she later learns belong to her father, who has quietly returned to Sattin and stealthily entered the Randall house to leave a message for Ran in his son's alarm clock; Syrup, Kate's much-loved, vagabond tomcat, mysteriously gets locked in the loft (attic); and they learn that a suitcase in the loft contains a pillow-case-full of banknotes and, very surprisingly, belongs to Granny. Kate, Ran, and their brother Lenny*, about twelve, meet their father and make friends with him, and the adults in their own ways also make peace with him, except for Granny Randall, who adamantly refuses to accept him. Fred Tranter and his brother, Bob, did not get on well. Fred fled after Bob's accidental drowning because he was afraid of gossip, since Bob had once been romantically interested in Fred's wife, Kitty*, and because he felt intimidated by his mother-in-law, who seized the opportunity to drive a wedge between Fred and her only child. At the end, the children are pleased to get to know their father and Nanny

Tranter, and all except Granny Randall (and probably Ran) expect to emigrate to Australia, where Fred has been working. This skillfully crafted and distinctively written story of family animosities and ghosts laid to rest engages the emotions early and remains engrossing to the very end. The reader stands beside Kate throughout and shares her perplexities and discoveries. The third-person limited point of view is so tightly focused it gives the effect of first-person narration and thus intensifies the story's dramatic value. The author plays fair with the reader with the mystery and withholds none of the puzzle pieces. Kate's courage and resourcefulness develop gradually out of her need to clarify her own identity and satisfy her curiosity, and what she does is more believable because she doesn't set things to rights. She merely discovers what is going on, and the outcome depends upon what the adults choose to make of their lives. The author draws scenes well, the tone is quietly expectant, the style is richly sensory, humor is employed judiciously, and the characters are individually created, the most memorable being malevolent Granny Randall, manipulative, possessive, and vindictive to the end, when she tries to buy Fred off. Her malign influence is symbolized by the "beam of darkness" that emanates from her room and through which everyone who enters the house must pass. A good deal of texture adds interest and enhances the mystery: frequent mention of puzzles; references to and playing with names and initials; the three stories of the house that echo the levels of the mystery; the carefully foiled characters; the tiffs between Ran and Lenny that echo those of the previous generation's brothers; and the meandering cat, whose disposition and behavior humorously parallel Kate's own personality and actions and whose wanderings actually advance the plot, among others. The book is a perceptive look at relationships within a troubled family as well as a top-notch, never sensationalized mystery. Carnegie Com.

THE WEATHERMONGER (Dickinson*, Peter, Gollancz, 1969; Little, 1969), futuristic fantasy set in England in a period five years after the country

has returned to a preindustrial state and
adopted a medieval attitude in dress, manners,
and laws. Geoffrey* Tinker wakes to find himself
out in Weymouth Bay on the ruins of an old pier
with the tide coming in and a crowd of oddly
dressed men armed with spears and pitchforks
lining the shore. A girl of eleven beside him
tells him she is his sister, Sally*, whom he
remembers as a six-year-old, and that they are
being drowned as witches. He has been caught
with the magneto from their boat, the *Quern*,
and she has been drawing pictures of cars,
motors, and other now forbidden mechanical
objects. Geoffrey, who has been weathermonger
for the community, though he remembers nothing
of the last five years, creates a dense fog. He
swims, towing Sally, to the *Quern*, which he has
secretly kept in good running order, and starts
it, and they escape and sail to France, landing
at Morlaix. There they are taken to Monsieur
Pallieu, who is in charge of refugees, and
General Turville, Inspecteur du Departement, who
grill them, and then arrange for them to return
to England to try to ferret out the causes for
the antimechanical Changes, which have isolated
the country from the rest of the modern world.
They are taken to an automobile museum at
Beaulieu Abbey, where their owner had cocooned
his precious antique cars in plastic foam before
fleeing to France. There, with the help of two
young refugee men who accompany them, they steal
a 1909 Rolls Royce Silver Ghost and attach a
battering ram to the front of it. Geoffrey and
Sally start north toward the Welsh border,
encountering hostility whenever they see people
and having some narrow escapes but no real
trouble until a freak storm approaches. Geoffrey
tries to counter it with some weathermongering
of his own, but it overpowers him, destroys the
car, and leaves him unconscious, while Sally
tries to fend off the curious villagers, who
think he has called up the storm to destroy the
hated machine. One of the onlookers, who is more
astute than the others, sees through their act
and introduces himself as an ousted weathermonger from Norwich also seeking the source of the
Changes, which may be caused by a rumored
Necromancer in Wales. With Geoffrey's money,
the weathermonger buys two horses and a

bad-tempred pony for Sally, and they start out.
The next morning Geoffrey and Sally find that
one of the horses, Geoffrey's purse, and the
weatherman are all gone. Eventually they come to
a virgin forest out of which rises the
Necromancer's castle, to which they are welcomed
somewhat distractedly by the Seneschal,
Willoughby Furbelow. From Furbelow's incessant
and disconnected chatter they gather that he was
a pharmacist who happened on the place where
Merlin is imprisoned and, to bind his power to
do good, has been addicting him to morphine.
Now, in drugged confusion, the wizard has
extended his power incoherently over the whole
country. Geoffrey makes a spell for freezing
weather which causes Furbelow to slip and break
his leg, and Sally, in Latin she has learned in
school, explains to Merlin that the morphine is
poison and that he has become its slave. He
tells them to go, and the shudders of his
withdrawal cause a terrible storm that wrecks
the castle and buries Merlin's underground
chamber in tons of rubble. The next day the
general arrives by helicopter, and as they ride
toward Weymouth they see people trying to repair
rusty tractors and other machines. The idea of
the Changes and the details of a world gone
fanatically back to the Middle Ages are ingenious and fascinating. The trip in the Rolls
Royce and the discovery of a drugged Merlin are
clever but far less believable. The book has an
oddly ambivalent attitude toward mechancial
things. The antimachine age is clearly dominated
by superstition and vicious bigotry, yet the
last sentence is ironic: "And the English air
would soon be reeking with petrol." Companion
novels are *The Devil's Children** and *Heartsease*. Choice.

WEAVER, STELLA, author of two books for children
in the late 1950s and early 1960s which were
cited on the *Hornbook* Fanfare list of the best
books of the year. *Sisters and Brothers**
(Collins, 1960; Pantheon, 1961) is set on the
Cornish coast, a story of the difficulties a
teenager, a newly orphaned adopted cousin, has
in fitting into a close family. It was named an
honor book in the New York *Herald Tribune*
Children's Spring Book Festival. *The Stranger**

(Collins, 1955; Pantheon, 1956), a more complicated but probably less successful novel, is
set in Ireland, a story of two children visiting
relatives there who discover that the boy is
heir to a large but neglected estate which he
cannot afford to claim and repair. It involves a
mysterious stranger, a fantasy or legendary
figure, who appears and helps set things right.

WE COULDN'T LEAVE DINAH (Treadgold*, Mary, ill.
Elisabeth Grant, Cape, 1941; *LEFT TILL CALLED
FOR*, Doubleday, 1941), realistic animal novel
and adventure story set on the fictitious
English Channel island of Clerinel at the
beginning of World War II. Until the Germans
occupy the little island that is now theirs by
the fall of France, Caroline*, 13, and Mick*
(Michael) Templeton, 14, English children who
regularly holiday there, look forward to
continued frolics with their horses, Dinah and
Punch, and other members of the Clerinel Pony
Club. Left behind in the confusion of the
evacuation, they plan to continue to live in the
family home, Point House, only to discover that
it has been taken over by the Germans for their
headquarters. Peter* Beaumarchais, 15, president
of the Pony Club, whose father the children
learn is a double agent, hides them in the Pony
Club cave meeting-place until he can arrange for
them to be taken to England. While at the cave,
they discover in the nearby cove an oil-cloth
packet containing a secret message in code.
After Mick breaks the code, they become involved
in helping Monsieur Beaumarchais discover
information about the impending German invasion
of Britain, activities that find Mick at German
headquarters disguised as a stableboy and teaching the German commandant's granddaughter,
Nannerl, to ride Dinah; Caroline captured by the
Germans and then released by little Nannerl,
whom Caroline initiates into the club; Mick
discovering the salient information; and the
children evacuated just before the RAF bombs the
German invasion barges. The narrative is fast
moving and has plenty of child-pleasing, coven-
tional detail like codes, secret signals,
sleuthing, children on their own, hiding places,
and club activities. The conflicts are clear-
cut, intrigue abounds, and the plot is so

skillfully constructed that interest never flags. Implausible in retrospect, typical "unreal realism," the whole thing seems convincing while one is immersed in it because of the generously described main characters and well-fleshed-out incidents. The setting is vivid, the evacuation absorbing, and the children are well drawn and individualized. Other characters are types, and the little German girl is especially unconvincing. The horses play their part in events, though they are not the main item, but the meaning of the title is obscure. Sequel. Carnegie Winner.

WE DIDN'T MEAN TO GO TO SEA (Ransome*, Arthur, ill. author, Cape, 1937; Macmillan, 1938), seventh in a series of twelve holiday novels about the Walker family and their friends, this one starting at Pin Mill on the Orwell River near Harwich Harbor, where the Walkers are staying while waiting for their father, Naval Commander Ted Walker, to return from China, where he has been stationed for some years. Roger*, Titty*, Susan*, and John*, now nine to possibly fifteen or sixteen, become friends with an older boy, Jim Brading, who has just finished school and is soon to enter Oxford. When he invites them to spend a couple of days on his little cutter, the *Goblin*, their mother agrees with the stipulation that they do not leave the harbor and that they phone in daily and return in time for tea on the third day, since their father's arrival is imminent. Mrs. Walker and the youngest child, Bridget, about four, see them off, and they sail down the river, see Shotley, call their mother, spend a night afloat, swim in the morning, and sail out as far as the Beach End buoy, where they lose the wind. To keep from drifting out to sea, Jim starts the motor, and they just make it to the shelf at Felixstowe before running out of fuel. They anchor, and Jim, with the fuel can, rows ashore in the dinghy, the *Imp*, and catches a bus to a nearby garage. Although he expects to be back in about ten minutes, the Walkers wait hours, first expecting him back momentarily then, as the fog moves in, realizing that he won't be able to find them until it lifts. Although they are lonely, they believe they are safe as long as they bang on the frying pan at intervals and Roger plays his penny whistle to warn off any moving craft until they realize that with the turn of the tide their anchor chain is too short and they are drifting. Frantically, John tries to pay out chain and loses the whole thing overboard. He and Susan try to set the other anchor with rope, but it doesn't catch, and as they pass the Beach End buoy they realize that they are being swept helplessly out to sea. To get some control, John puts up sail and steers a southeast by east course which he can see by Jim's charts is the only way to avoid the shoals. Susan is almost hysterical with worry over breaking their promise, and she also becomes violently seasick. Titty gets a terrible headache and has to lie down. The lifting of the fog is followed by heavy rain and strong wind. When they try to turn around, the wind is too strong for them, and even Susan admits that they have to keep going until the storm dies down. John realizes that they must reef the sails. He creeps out with a lifeline attached to his middle, and, while Susan steers, he manages the tricky maneuver, although he is almost swept overboard. The scare and the realization that they can't turn back immediately seem to cure Susan of her seasickness, and Titty's headache leaves. They sail on quite optimistically, even managing to show a signal light with a large torch shining through a red plastic plate to get a steamer to alter course and avoid them. Susan insists that Titty and Roger go to bed, and she herself falls asleep trying to keep John company. Later, when he is falling asleep, she takes over and steers through the night. Just before dawn, they see searchlights from land and realize that their best bet is to go on, find a harbor, and wire home. Among the flotsam from the storm they find a kitten clinging half drowned to a chicken coop; they rescue it and name it Sinbad. As they approach land, not knowing where they are, they sight a pilot ship and run up their flag to signal for a pilot. Because they are afraid to tell anyone that they are alone, John sends the other three down to the cabin to make noise like a party, while he plays the role of ship's boy. The pilot, fortunately able to speak a little English, takes them in to harbor at Flushing. As they pull in, they meet a Nederland Steamer just taking off, and John sees his father on deck. Just as the pilot discovers they are alone, a motor launch pulls up, and their father climbs aboard, having jumped from the steamer at the last minute. He straightens everything out with the pilot, who quite admires John. He then wires their mother, takes them all on shore for a meal and to buy wooden shoes and a doll for Bridget, and, fortified with fuel and charts, sails them back home. They discover that Jim has been hit by a truck and was unconscious in the hospital and only now has escaped and begun to look for his boat. The story is superior to the other books in the series in having a real adventure rather than a make-believe situation. The trip across the North Sea by night in the storm is vividly described and genuinely gripping. John is the main hero. Susan comes across as spineless and emotional, especially in the early part of the trip, and Titty and Roger have lesser roles than in some of the other books. The entrance of their energetic, macho father is a deus ex machina that detracts from the realism of the thrilling trip itself. Fanfare.

THE WEIRDSTONE. See *The Weirdstone of Brisingamen.*

THE WEIRDSTONE OF BRISINGAMEN: A TALE OF ALDERLEY (Garner*, Alan, Collins, 1960; *THE WEIRDSTONE*, Watts, 1961), exciting, adventurous fantasy involving magic, witchcraft, and elements from Norse and Celtic mythology and Arthurian legend and lasting for six months in the mid-twentieth century. The story begins in late spring when Colin and Susan, a brother and sister of about twelve and ten whose parents are abroad, come to Highmost Redmanhey farm at Alderley Edge, Cheshire, to stay with stalwart, practical Gowther Mossock and his warm and kindly wife, Bess, once their mother's nurse. The children are soon embroiled in a battle against evil forces striving to take over the world. One day, while exploring the great hill known as the Edge, they encounter the white-bearded wizard named Cadellin*. He takes them inside the Edge where, in the cave called

Fundindelve, they observe a company of knights lie sleeping. Cadellin tells them the Sleepers await the time when he will rouse them and send them forth against the malice of the evil Nostrand, the Great Spirit of Darkness, who was banished by the King of the Sleepers to the Abyss of Ragnarok, where presumably he still lives. The magic that binds the Sleepers is Firefrost*, the Weirdstone of Brisingamen, but, since Cadellin has lost Firefrost, the Sleepers are in great danger of being called forth and defeated by their enemies. Shortly after encountering Cadellin, Susan notices that the center stone of her bracelet emits a light similar to that in Fundindelve. The stone Susan calls the Tear was given to her mother years ago by Bess. An heirloom in Bess's family, the Tear is also called the Bridestone and is very old. On their hurried way to consult Cadellin about the stone, the children get lost in a sudden fog. A huge, hooded, man-like figure they later learn is Grimnir*, or the Hooded One, materializes out of the mist and takes the bracelet from Susan. They soon discover that he and a neighbor of the Mossocks, Selina* Place--who is really the Morrigan, a shape shifter and the chief witch of the evil morthbrood--are conspiring to master the power of the stone for their own devious ends. The children bravely enter Selina's house, steal the stone from where the witch has been preparing black magic with it and escape through a cupboard in her kitchen that exits into an elevator which takes them down into the ancient copper mines that underlie the area. There ensues a long and precarious flight involving feats that defy gravity and reason. Susan is captured by goblins, who serve the witch and Grimnir, and is rescued by two good dwarfs, Fenodyree* and Durathror*; then she, Colin, and the dwarfs observe the moot at which the morthbrood devise their evil plans. They have terrible battles with swarts, evil beings that also serve the witch and Grimnir, but Fenodyree and Durathror's magic swords, Widowmaker and Drynwyn respectively, and their great courage and perseverance prevail. After traversing pools of ooze, climbing up and down mazes of shafts and tunnels, and enduring stagnant silences,

they reenter the light, and the dwarfs escort
the children home. They enlist Gowther in their
enterprise to get the stone to Cadellin, and the
five make a harrowing journey of several days'
length across the countryside before meeting up
with Cadellin. They keep to the trees,
undergrowth, and running water for protection,
doing their best to avoid the evil forces, which
are disguised in hikers' garb and include even
neighbors Gowther has long known and trusted.
With Fenodyree in the lead and Durathror
bringing up the rear, swords bared, and with
Gowther's superior knowledge of the terrain
proving invaluable, they especially avoid birds,
since birds carry tales to the Morrigan. They
are beset by the terribly cold fimbulwinter,
which has been called up by an ice giant, and
suddenly find themselves on a floating island in
Redesmere Lake, the Isle of Angharad Goldenhand,
the Lady of the Lake, who, as they dream,
provides them cloaks against the cold and gives
Susan a protective bracelet of white metal. A
strange, dark rider, Gaberlunzie, carries them
all through a particularly dangerous point with
six on his one horse, and two clever foxes
obliterate their tracks so that the Morrigan's
vile hounds lose their scent. Once at the iron
gates at the entrance to Fundindelve, they are
attacked by flocks of vicious birds and the
morthbrood pours in, 500 svarts strong.
Fenodyree suffers a broken sword arm and cannot
fight, but Durathror rises up with the aid of
his eagle cloak and fights valiantly. Finally he
is so severely wounded he must bind himself in
an upright position to a pillar, where hordes of
swarts assail him until he dies. A crow takes
Firefrost from him, and then Grimnir snatches it
from the crow but is slain by Cadellin, who
discovers to his great sadness that Grimnir is
his own brother, Govannon, who had gone bad. He
uses Firefrost against Selina Place and the
remainder of the wicked hordes, banishing them
to the Abyss of Ragnarok and ensuring the safety
of the Sleepers and the world for years to come.
This take-off on Arthurian legend exudes
exictement and a good sense of danger. Incidents
are overly numerous and follow one another in
rapid order after a gripping start but usually
are flimsily motivated and could easily be

interchanged in sequence. Similarly, characters are numerous and not individualized. Susan and Colin, the protagonists, could easily trade places, and the others are mostly familiar types, good or evil as needed. Style is vigorous but often cliched in expression. Cadellin and the dwarfs speak in high diction, Gowther in Cheshire country dialect, and the children in contemporary idiom, modes that lend a good deal of interest as well as conviction to the narrative. The conclusion borrows from various sources, most notably from the tale of Cuchullin, and is melodramatic and sentimental but nonetheless appropriate, satisfying, and interesting. Events in the fantasy portions seem to be too numerous and lengthy for the amount of elapsed time in the realistic sections, but this may be bothersome to the reader only upon reflection. The borrowings from folklore and mythology provide ballast, support the themes of the unending battle between good and evil and the need for heroism, and keep this book from being just another fantasy where the "good guys" win after an intense struggle and some luck. The sequel is *The Moon of Gomrath*. Choice; Lewis Carroll.

WELCH, RONALD (RONALD OLIVER FELTON) (1909–1982), born in Aberavon, Glamorganshire, Wales; educator, historical novelist. He attended Berkhamsted School, Herfordshire, and Clare College, Cambridge, where he received his M.A. degree in history in 1931. He served in the Territorial Army from 1933 to 1939 and, during World War II, in the Welsh Regiment in Normandy and Germany. For several years he was assistant history master at Berkhamsted School, then senior teacher at Bedford Modern School, and for sixteen years served as headmaster of Okehampton Grammar School, Devon. He published nineteen books of fiction for young people, most of them historical novels, and a biography of Ferdinand Magellan. *The Gauntlet* (Oxford, 1951) is a time fantasy in which a modern boy experiences his ancestors' adventures in a fourteenth-century Welsh castle. His *Knight Crusader** (Oxford, 1954; Oxford, 1979), a highly adventurous story set in the Middle East at the end of the twelfth century, won the Carnegie Medal. A

number of his other books follow the Carey
family, founded by Philip* d'Aubigny of *Knight
Crusader*: *Captain of Dragoons* (Oxford, 1956;
Oxford, 1957), with Marlborough's army; *Mohawk
Valley* (Oxford, 1958; Criterion, 1958), with
Wolfe at Quebec; *Escape from France* (Oxford,
1960; Criterion, 1961), a story of the French
Revolution; *For the King* (Oxford, 1961; Criteri-
on, 1962), whose hero is a Royalist in the Eng-
lish Civil War; *Nicholas Carey* (Oxford, 1963;
Criterion, 1963), set during the Crimean War;
The Hawk (Oxford, 1967; Criterion, 1969), an
Elizabethan sea story; *Tank Commander* (Oxford
1972; Nelson, 1974), set in World War I; and
Captain of Foot (Oxford, 1959), whose protagonist is under Wellington in the Peninsular War.
His novels have been commended as "extremely
well researched, full of authentic detail, and
always excitingly plotted." Many of them have
been translated into Dutch, Swedish, German, and
Afrikaans.

WEMMICK, JOHN (*Great Expectations**), clerk to
the lawyer Jaggers*. Wemmick has two distinct
personalities. The first is a tight, humorless
one, almost as uncompromising and grasping as
that of his employer, which he exhibits at the
office. In this role he advises Pip* to get hold
of "portable property," bribes in the form of
rings, pins, watches, and so on, which those
desperate for the services of Jaggers give him
in hope of getting the ear of the lawyer. At his
home in Walworth, however, he is a different
person: playful, friendly, devoted to his father
whom he refers to as his Aged Parent and
addresses as Aged. Here he has constructed a
moat around his house, complete with a drawbridge and with many ingenious if impractical
devices. Here, also, a young lady named Miss
Skiffins keeps him company, and it is through
connections of hers that he helps Pip secretly
arrange a position for Herbert Pocket with a
business. In his Walworth personality, he also
helps Pip during the time the boy is trying to
hide the fugitive Magwitch*, and arranges to
get Magwitch out of the country. As he moves
from one place to the other, he changes
perceptibly in character.

WENDY DARLING (*Peter and Wendy**), little girl who flies off to the Neverland with Peter* Pan and becomes mother to the group of Lost Boys. Wendy is maternal feeling personified, and the author uses her as a vehicle to make many digs at the almost worshipful attitude toward mother-hood in the early years of the twentieth centu-ry. Although much of it is make-believe, she insists on half an hour rest after meals before swimming, regular bedtimes, and no rich food, thereby saving the boys from the pirate's poisoned cake. In the house underground, she is usually pictured with a basketful of darning, telling stories to the boys after they are in bed. Even the pirates want her as their mother, a prospect she scorns, though she does have a soft spot in her heart for Smee. When Peter returns to take her back to the Neverland for spring cleaning and finds her grown up, she is ashamed of her adult body and apologetic and does not try to stop her daughter, Jane, from going off with him.

WESTALL, ROBERT (ATKINSON) (1929-   ), born in Tynemouth, Northumberland; writer, artist, and educator. He attended Tynemouth High School, Durham University, where he received a B.A. in fine art, and Slade School, University of London. From 1953 to 1955, he served as a Lance Corporal in the Royal Signals and since 1957 has taught in various schools: at Erdington Hall Secondary Modern School in Birmingham, at Keighley Boys' Grammar School in Yorkshire, and at John Deane's College, Northwich, Cheshire. His best known book, *The Machine Gunners** (Macmillan, 1975; Greenwillow, 1976), which won the Carnegie Medal, was a *Boston Globe-Horn Book* honor book, and was named to the Junior High Contemporary Classics list, draws heavily from his memories of his young adolescence during World War II in Tynemouth. The same characters return, a few years older, in *Fathom Five** (Macmillan, 1975; Greenwillow, 1980), a mystery adventure, and Chas* McGill, the protagonist, also appears in the title story of *The Haunting of Chas McGill and Other Stories* (Macmillan, 1983; Greenwillow, 1983), set at the beginning of World War II, and as a grown man and a rather unconventional solicitor in *The Watch House**

(Macmillan, 1977; Greenwillow, 1978), set in the
1970s. *The Watch House* and most of his more
recent novels depart from realistic fiction and
delve into the supernatural: *The Wind Eye**
(Macmillan, 1976; Greenwillow, 1977) dealing
with time travel, *The Devil on the Road** (Macmillan, 1978; Greenwillow, 1979) with witchcraft, and *The Watch House* with ghosts, all with
unusual twists. *Break of Dark* (Chatto, 1982;
Greenwillow, 1982) is a book of four stories,
strong in fantasy elements. *The Scarecrows**
(Chatto, 1981; Greenwillow, 1981), probably his
psychologically most difficult and subtle novel,
was his second Carnegie winner, as well as a
Boston Globe-Horn Book honor book and a Contemporary Classic. Six of his novels have been included in the *Horn Book* Fanfare lists. Westall
has also written for the Whitehorn Press, Manchester, and has served as an art critic for the
Guardian and for the Chester *Chronicle.*

WHEN HITLER STOLE PINK RABBIT (Kerr*, Judith,
ill. author, Collins, 1971; Coward, 1972),
realistic novel of a refugee family in the years
1933 through 1936 in Germany, Switzerland, and
France. Anna*, at nine, and even her brother
Max*, 12, realize little of the importance of
the elections coming up in Germany, but Papa*,
their distinguished Jewish anti-Nazi writer
father, though ill with flu, has left for
Prague, having been warned that his passport may
be consficated if Hitler wins. It soon becomes
apparent that the family, which has concealed
his departure, will have to follow him, to meet
him in Zurich, and, if the Nazis win, stay in
Switzerland at least six months. Although Mama*
is tense and Anna is beginning to feel ill, they
safely join Papa, expecting their old nurse and
housekeeper, Heimpi (Fraulein Heimpel) to forward their belongings and come to live with them
if the election should go the wrong way. Anna
comes down with an extremely serious flu and
after four weeks of high fever and delirium
recovers to find that they escaped only days
before police came to seize their passports,
that all their property has been confiscated,
and that they have very little to live on. They
move to the Gasthol Zwirn, an inexpensive inn in
one of the villages on Lake Zurich. Max goes to

high school in Zurich, and Anna goes to the village school along with Franz and Vreneli Zwirn, the hotel-keeper's children. Since after some months it becomes apparent that the Swiss neutrality prevents the publication of most of Papa's writing, they move to Paris, narrowly escaping being put on the wrong train and heading back to Germany, a suspicious mistake by the porter since a price has been set on Papa's head. In Paris they live in a cramped apartment with a hostile concierge and a glum Austrian girl student named Grete to help out. Mama, whose whole training is in music, gradually learns to cook but is hopeless in other household tasks. Papa, always impractical, writes but can sell little of his work. Max and Anna adjust after an initial period of difficulty, Anna discovering in a sudden burst of inspiration that she can really speak French and Max working with fierce determination to fit in. They are aided by the Fernands, a French journalist and his family. An actor from Berlin brings the sad news that their family friend, Onkel Julius, a gentle naturalist, dismissed from his museum job and barred from the zoo because he has a Jewish grandmother, has committed suicide. Financially, in Paris the family is worse off than ever, and when a Hungarian producer in London sends 1,000 pounds for a script Papa has written about Napoleon's mother, they set off for England to start again there. Based on the author's own childhood, the story moves more like autobiography than fiction. Through Anna's eager and naive eyes, their life is full of interesting detail and, as long as the family is together, is not one of hardship. Despite the silly title, the book gives a perceptive picture of the times and of how with their remarkable adaptability children can flourish under traumatic conditions. Fanfare.

WHEN JAYS FLY TO BARBMO (Balderson*, Margaret, ill. Victor Ambrus, Oxford, 1968; World, 1969), realistic novel set on the island of Draugoy near Tromso, Norway, north of the Arctic Circle, starting shortly before World War II. Through the long, dark winters and the brief, glorious summers, Ingeborg* Nygaard, 14, lives a strange, isolated life with her conventional housekeeper

aunt, Anne-Sigri* Nygaard; her fisherman father,
Arne, who speaks to his sister only when absolutely necessary; and Per, the "Wood* Troll," a
worker of uncertain background who toils all
summer, drinks all winter, and carries on an
unspoken feud with disapproving Anne-Sigri.
Summer brings another worker, Veikko Kapanen,
16, who is helping Arne build a larger boat; he
is an optimistic, cheerful boy treated like a
son by Arne and doted on by Anne-Sigri. When
Ingeborg finds a complete Lappish outfit at the
bottom of a trunk in the storage shed and tries
it on, her father is infuriated, and they have
still not made up when he leaves for the fishing
grounds at Svolvaer. While he is gone, the
Germans take over Norway, and not long after
this, word comes that, as he tried to help
Norwegian soldiers escape to England, his boat
was sunk by the Germans leaving no survivors.
The Wood Troll, now under suspicion by Anne-
Sigri because he was born in Germany, reluctantly agrees to take Ingeborg to see the Lapps
arrive and drive their reindeer across from the
mainland to summer pasture on the island, and
she soon discovers what she had begun to suspect, that her mother was a Lapp, daughter of
old Mikkel, the leader of this particular Lapp
extended family. Trapped with her unsympathetic
sister-in-law when her husband was out fishing
through the long winter, the young wife missed
her own wandering family, and, the two women
having quarreled, she set out to find them and
died in the storm after giving birth to Ingeborg. For fourteen years Arne has blamed Anne-
Sigri. At first the German presence is not oppressive, but soon Veikko makes a plan to take
Per and several other youths in the nearly
finished boat and to try to escape and join a
fighting group. That very night soldiers come.
They arrest Per as a Jew, and then kill the
stock and burn the boat and outbuildings as
punishment for not reporting him. Veikko and his
friends hide out in the mountains. Ingeborg and
her aunt survive the winter, but in the early
spring Anne-Sigri dies. Alone, Ingeborg manages
until early in the winter she is eighteen, when
Veikko appears to warn her that, with the
Russians invading from the north, the Germans
are destroying everything before they leave.

Rather than let the Germans burn her house, she sets it afire herself and leaves with Veikko and his friends who intend to join the Russians while she travels with Veikko's sister to the south. Instead, Ingeborg starts off to find her Lapp grandfather and nearly dies as her mother did. She spends the winter with her Lapp family and intends to stay with them permanently, but after she gets back to Draugoy, she discovers that Veikko has returned and is rebuilding the farm, and she knows that her future is there with him. A rather slow-starting but well-constructed novel, it evokes the beauty as well as the harsh conditions of the far north. In this setting, the fourteen-year quarrel of Arne with his sister is credible. The hardships of war and the difficulties, as well as the pleasures, of life in the Lapp camp are essential and convincing parts of the story. Most of the characters are well delineated, though Veikko is perhaps not sufficiently drawn for the major role he plays. The end is predictable but does not seem contrived. The title comes from a Lapp proverb meaning something like "when Hell freezes over," jays being nonmigrating birds and Barbmo the unknown region beyond the horizon where other birds go in the winter. Carnegie Com.; Choice.

WHEN SHAKESPEARE LIVED IN SOUTHWARK (Seth-Smith*, E. K., ill. Ann Vaughn, Harrap, 1944; *VAGABONDS ALL*, Houghton, 1946), historical novel set in 1608 in London and the English country-side. In disgrace with his clergyman father, Sir Stephen Francis, who has threatened to take him from St. Paul's school and apprentice him to a draper, Miles Francis, 12, climbs rebelliously from his bedroom window and meets a boy entertaining a crowd by tumbling and singing. This proves to be Nat* (Fortunatus) Marlowe, son of the playwright Christopher Marlowe, who has been befriended since the death of his father in his infancy by Thomas* Heywood and other players of Lord Strange's Servants led by Master Alleyn. Nat takes Miles to a play and, when Miles finds himself locked out on his return, to the tavern, where Alleyn employs him since Miles, who gives his name as Frank, can sing and play the lute, and the lead boy has

just broken his leg. William Shakespeare, of
another company of players, tries to dissuade
Miles, but the boy is sure his father has cast
him off, and he eagerly joins the actors about
to go on the road. At first all goes well, but
at Frensham Nat and Miles take advantage of a
partial holiday to visit gypsies in the woods.
The gypsy queen who tells their fortune also
drugs them, so that when they wake at night and
escape, they lose their way until the gypsies'
dog leads them to an inn known as the Hen Roost,
run by Master Cock* Lorel. They soon discover
that it is a den of thieves and beggars, and
they are forced to become their apprentices.
After a beggars' annual feast, at which the
gypsy queen appears as one of the initiated, the
boys attempt an escape but are caught by the
brutal Numps, a senior boy, and returned to
Cock, who, in a drunken rage, seems about to
beat them to death until distracted by his
assistant, Hurly* Burly, who whips them soundly
but fairly. The first time Cock takes Miles out
alone at night, the boy is sent up a ladder and
through a window of a farmhouse to steal, but he
recognizes the child sleeping in the room as an
old playmate, Bettris, who is staying with
Mistress Susan Adams, a cousin of Miles's
father. The boy returns empty-handed and is
beaten unconscious by Cock. Mistress Adams, a
spinster in love with her widowed cousin, has
learned of his search for his son and, hearing
Bettris tell of her "dream" that Miles in rags
had appeared in her room, sets out with a
servant to try to find him. Miles and Nat
despair of escaping until a prosperous-looking
traveller, having lost his way, stops at the Hen
Roost and they realize that Cock will murder him
for his horse and money. They work out a plan to
warn him and escape with him, a plan that Hurly
discovers but does not prevent. After a harrowing series of near-captures, they part from the
gentleman, who gives them a gold piece and tells
them he is Lord Lumley of Nonsuch. Thereafter
they make their way toward Southwark with
various adventures: they are nearly caught by
Numps, who has been sent out to find and
silence them for good; they are put in the
stocks during a village sports afternoon when
their gold coin seems to prove them thieves;

Squire Grantley considers branding them but instead gives them a license to beg for a long enough period to get them to London; they are singing in a village near the Palace of Nonsuch when Lord Lumley hears them and at once engages their services for a masque he is giving for his guests, King James and Queen Anne; Nat so pleases the queen that she wants him for one of the Children of the Royal Chapel, but the jealous servants force them out, and they see Numps still hunting them; they run off and get a ride to London with a carter who tells them of a murder he has seen the previous evening, and they recognize that it was Numps who, having set upon Mistress Adams and been prevented from killing her by Hurly Burly, has killed Hurly. In London, Miles finds his home locked and learns that his father is out of town, so they go to the prison, Wood Street Counter, where Heywood is held for debt. He directs them to a lodging in a poor neighborhood, where first Nat, then Miles falls ill of prison fever, and where Miles discovers that the other roomer is Numps. The watchmen arrest Numps and leave the boys only because they fear they have plague, and there Miles's father finds them, having learned of their whereabouts from Mistress Adams, who visits Heywood. Miles, very ill, is forgiven by his father and gradually recovers but assumes that Nat has died until the boy visits him, splendidly dressed as one of the Children of the Chapel. Mistress Adams and Sir Stephen plan to marry and send Miles to Oxford. The story is full of fast-moving events and suspense, with interesting color from the period. The characters are types, but lively and mostly convincing. The plot, however, leans heavily upon unlikely coincidence at several crucial points. The introduction of Shakespeare is gratuitous and serves no real purpose, and that of the King and Queen implausible. Fanfare.

WHICH WITCH? (Ibbotson*, Eva, ill. Annabel Large, Macmillan, 1979), comic, tongue-in-cheek fantasy set recently about a wizard's efforts to find a bride. Arriman Frederick Canker, the Awful, the Loather of Light, the Blighter of the Beautiful, the famous black wizard of gray and gloomy Darkington Hall near Todcaster in the

north of England, awakens one morning so bored
with life that he feels he simply can't go on
"blighting and smiting, blasting and wuthering
and doing everything he could to keep darkness
and sorcery alive in the land." He is advised by
Lester*, his trusty ogre, to consult Esmerelda,
the gypsy fortune-teller of Todcaster Fair. She
informs him that he will be replaced by a "new
bloke" before long: "Soon there cometh a great
new wizard whose power shall be mightier and
darker even than your own...[and you] will be
able to lay down the burden of Darkness and Evil
which you have carried for so long...Got it?"
When, after 989 days, no replacement wizard
appears, Mr.* Leadbetter, Arriman's efficient,
resourceful secretary, suggests he get married
and father one. Since wizards can only marry
witches and a local bride seems best, Arriman
attends a grand meeting of the local coven on
Windylow Heath to declare a contest: the
Todcaster witch who perpetrates the magic of the
deepest black will have the honor of becoming
his bride. He makes this announcement in good
style but with misgivings, because the Todcaster
witches are all perfect hags in appearance save
one, the pretty, young, blue-eyed, soft-spoken,
warm-hearted Belladonna, who, unfortunately, is
widely known to be a white witch and completely
unable to do black magic. Mr. Leadbetter makes
the arrangements, like those for a beauty
contest, reserving accommodations for the
witches at the Grand Spa Hotel, and engaging the
judges: kind Mr. Chatterjee, the Indian genie
who lives in a bottle, and Mr. Sniveller, a
dark-faced, silent ghoul. The witches are in a
dither of preparation, planning their finest
spells and checking their familiars: the
ex-mermaid sea witch, Miss* Wrack, and her
octopus, Doris; the country witch, Ethel*
Feedbag, whose Wellingtons smell of manure, and
her pig; Nancy* and Nora Shouter, twin witches
who bicker constantly and use chickens;
forgetful old Mother* Bloodwort, who keeps
turning into a coffee table; Gwendolyn* Swamp,
whose sheep gets measles; her sudden
replacement, Madame* Olympia, an enchantress
whose necklace is made of the teeth of her five
dead husbands; and Belladonna, who loses her
heart immediately upon seeing Arriman ("dear

Arry") but despairs of winning him. They draw lots for the order of performance, and it is decided that Belladonna will go last on Halloween night. What proves to be the turning point of the story occurs when Belladonna, who has a gift of healing, cures Rover, the injured pet earthworm that belongs to little Terence* Mugg, the orphan whose Matron has abused him all his short life, and, when Matron grows roots, is elated to think she's performed black magic with Rover's help as familiar. She brings Rover and Terence back with her to Darkington, on whose park the witches have now encamped in preparation for the grand show. During the contest, each witch's try goes somewhat awry, with considerable comic effect, except for Madame Olympia's particularly horrible one. She creates a cellar full of rats that cannibalize one another, and Arriman and crew fear she will be the new mistress of Darkington. When Belladonna's turn comes, she announces she will conjure up Sir* Simon Montpelier, the sixteenth-century ghost who haunts the hall and whom Arriman has been trying for years to summon. Terence, however, discovers Rover is missing--stolen actually--and, fearful that Belladonna will fail without him, Lester, Mr. Leadbetter, and Terence secure an actor to impersonate the ghost. Unaware of Rover's absence, Belladonna puts her all into her act, Sir Simon dramatically appears, she is declared the winner, and she and Arriman commence billing and cooing. All seems rosy until Belladonna discovers Rover is gone and wails that her whiteness will now surely return. Lest the whole impersonation scheme come out and the jig be up, Lester insists they search for Rover, who is discovered shortly in Madame Olympia's possession. Entanglements pack the book's last twenty pages, and the hilarity culminates with the discovery that young Terence is the long-awaited, very powerful wizard. Reclaimed and about to be abused again by his terrible Matron, he accidentally enspells her as a spider, and then realizes it was his power and not Belladonna's that enabled her to succeed. The "good guys" realize that Sir Simon was real and not an actor, called up without the benefit of familiar, so strong is the lad's ability with black magic. As a wedding gift in reverse, Terence gives the witches what each most wishes, and Arriman and Belladonna then live happily in a little bungalow on the other side of the hall park. Terence sets up shop in Darkington Hall, grows up under Arriman's tutelage, and becomes famous in his own right as Mugg the Magnificent, Flayer of the Foolish, and Master of the Shades. Although the conclusion seems hasty and overfilled with unravelings and the whole seems dated, the characters are given personality touches that make them both horrible and endearing, and the ending--that Terence is the promised wizard--is cleverly foreshadowed. There is a waggish tone: in response to Belladonna's inquiry of Mr. Leadbetter about whether Arriman is as marvellous as he looks, Mr. Leadbetter thinks of Arriman's rage when he loses his suspenders and other typical situations, but then realizes Arriman is never mean-spirited or small and replies that he is "a gentleman. Most truly a gentleman." The sprightly style with plenty of wordplay and humor, some of it adult; the funny names; the meticulous attention to detail in the description of situations and, in particular, of the witches; and the carefully worked-out plot with its steady succession of complications that keep the pot boiling make for top-notch, lightweight, consistently interesting entertainment. (Wizard* Watcher) Carnegie Com.

THE WHISPERING MOUNTAIN (Aiken*, Joan, ill. Frank Bozzo, Cape, 1968; Doubleday, 1969), action-filled, lustily told adventure novel, which plays with the conventions of the adventure and Gothic forms, set in Wales in 1805 during the reign of nonhistorical old King James III. Half-orphaned Owen Hughes, twelve to fourteen, has been living with his dour grandfather, ex-sea captain Mr. Owen Hughes, curator of the museum in the little town of Pennygaff in the forested Black Mountains. Late one afternoon while he flees from school bullies, Owen receives unexpected and very welcome assistance from two old friends: resourceful, dark-haired, Arabis* Dando, an herbal curer about his age, and absent-minded poet and barber, Tom* Dando. Father and daughter

are on their way in their covered wagon to the
fair in the nearby village of Nant Agerddau
(Devil's Leap). When crotchety Mr. Hughes
refuses hospitality to the Dandos, Owen, who has
become increasingly unhappy living with his
Granda, decides to run away to sea, but before
he can, two London cutpurses, Toby Bilk and
Elijah Prigman, a Laurel-and-Hardy pair who are
in the hire of evil-hearted Lord* Malyn, kidnap
him and steal a valuable gold harp that Mr.
Hughes has recently found while investigating
monastery ruins and which turns out to be the
ancient Harp* of Teirtu of Arthurian vintage.
Lord Malyn wishes to add the harp to his already
extensive collection of gold valuables. Bilk and
Prigman cook up a scam: they force Owen to write
over his name notes to Mr. Hughes, Lord Malyn,
and two other nobles demanding money for the
return of the harp. Then they hide the harp in a
cave inside Fig-hat Ben, or Whispering Mountain,
the peak that dominates the region. When each
tries to cheat the other and moves the harp from
its original hiding-place, their scheme goes
awry and the harp is lost, not to appear again
till the end of the novel. In between transpires
a lengthy series of entertaining hijinks and
unlikely occurrences involving a large number of
assorted villains and good hearts who get
tangled up with one another both above and below
ground, in village, castle, river, and forest.
In addition to Lord Malyn, Bilk and Prigman, Mr.
Hughes, the Dandos, and Owen, these include the
Seljuk* of Rum, a fat, flamboyant, talkative
Ottoman who says he is hunting for a local
wonder, called the Devil's Leap, a drop-off
inside a cavern; David, Prince* of Wales, whom
Owen and the bullies-turned-cohorts discover
marooned and ill on an island where he has been
gored by a boar and who is subsequently nursed
to health by Arabis; Brother* Ianto, a thin, old
monk who lives in a cave and makes lenses for
eyeglasses; and old Yehimelek*, leader of the
Children of the Pit, the small, dark, hairy
people who live inside the mountain and mine
gold and who are also ill and nursed by Arabis.
Floods, landslides, fogs, druggings, impersonations, imprisonment in Lord Malyn's dismal
dungeon, schemes, counterschemes, threats,
chases--enough action and intrigue for several

books transpire before the truth about the
principals and the harp comes out in a series
of dramatic scenes that make up a grand climax
in an underground cavern. The Seljuk has really
been searching for the Children of the Pit, to
whose whereabouts the harp has been a clue since
they originally crafted it. He wishes to carry
them back to their long-lost Middle Eastern
homeland. Tom Dando deduces that he himself is
the hereditary owner of the harp, which has
been found by Abipaal, one of the Children of
the Pit, but he takes a shot intended for the
prince and dies. Bilk and Prigman plunge to
their deaths in the Devil's Leap pit. The prince
vows that the devious Lord Malyn shall be
punished for his many crimes against society
and offers to publish Tom Dando's just-
completed epic on King Arthur. An edge of a
cliff breaks off, Lord Malyn is gulped up by
the resulting pit, and steam caused by underground displacements blows up his castle. Arabis
inherits the harp from her father, Mr. Hughes
apologizes for his churlishness, asks Owen to
come home, and invites Arabis to live with them,
and Brother Ianto decides to stop living in
caves and to rebuild his order's ruined
monastery. The Seljuk offers him financial
assistance to repay Ianto for having saved his
life years before. The generously complicated
plot comes together with jigsaw puzzle
precision. Providing tenuous unity for the
elaborate set of circumstances is an obscure
verse prophecy about the harp made up by an
ancient bard, in which, among other events, the
Whispering Mountain shall scream and the
children from darkness shall creep, all of which
come true. The large cast consists of well-known
types which are interestingly distinguished by
cleverly exaggerated eccentric traits. Adding to
the hilarity is a great deal of snappy, witty
dialogue, much of it consisting of approxi-
mations of various dialects. Guardian.

WHITE KNIGHT (*Through the Looking-Glass**), kind,
befuddled, gentle figure who ushers Alice* to
the last brook before her arrival at the eighth
square where she becomes a queen. They meet when
the White Knight rescues Alice from the Red
Knight, who has taken her prisoner. A comic

figure, he often falls off his horse, wears ill-fitting armor, and carries affixed to his armor, saddle, and horse several objects, none of which works, but which he proudly claims as his own inventions. His conversation with Alice is a humorous comment on the difference between the names of things and the things themselves. Some think he is Carroll's humorous representation of himself.

THE WHITE MOUNTAINS (Christopher*, John, Hamilton, 1967; Macmillan, 1967), action-filled science fiction novel set 100 years in the future in England and the continent of Europe, both of which have reverted to a preindustrial age. Invading extraterrestrials called Tripods have conquered the earth, killing millions of people and devastating cities. They have imposed their rule upon the survivors, most of whom are feudalistic farmers. The Tripods appear as faceless machines, several times as high as a church, powerful hemispheres of gleaming metal that rock through the air on three spidery legs. They have long, grasping tentacles and make booming sounds as they walk. Customarily youths are initiated into adulthood at fourteen in a public ceremony. They are then taken inside a Tripod, where their heads are shaved and banded with a metal Cap by which the Tripods henceforth control their thoughts and behavior. Not long after Will Parker, thirteen-year-old miller's son of Wherton, England, who tells the story, witnesses his cousin's Capping ceremony, he has doubts about becoming Capped himself. Will becomes interested in the Vagrants, those people, mostly men, for whom Capping has not been successful and who mindlessly wander the countryside as outcasts from society, without homes or families. He becomes friends with a nonsense-speaking Vagrant named Ozymandias, who privately sheds his clownishness and speaks and behaves lucidly. He says he has come from the White Mountains, a place on the continent beyond the reach of the Tripods, where life is hard but people are free to do and think as they choose. He encourages Will to go there and gives him a map. Will decides to act on Ozymandias's advice, runs away, and is soon joined by his often surly cousin, Henry Parker, who is Will's age and also

resists Capping. The two make their way to the
Channel, cross by fishing boat to what is now
France, and are soon captured by ruffians from
whom they are helped to escape by a tall, thin,
bespectacled lad named Jean-Paul Deliet, whom
they call Beanpole and who joins their quest.
There follows a long and eventful journey as the
three boys tramp southeastward, living off the
land, constantly on guard. Their leader is
intelligent and resourceful Beanpole, who has
taught himself English and is somewhat of an
inventor. They hop the Shmand-Fair, the relic of
a train, at his suggestion, and in a chillingly
detailed passage, they explore the ruins of the
once great city of Paris. In the remains of a
subway, they find egg-like objects that they
discover explode when thrown in a certain way
and take a supply of these grenades with them
when they leave. Back in the countryside, Will
falls ill of a fever. Beanpole and Henry realize
he needs more help than they can give him, and,
even though they endanger themselves by doing
it, they contact a nearby farmer. He informs the
noble lady of the region, the Comtessa de la
Tour Rouge, who takes him to her castle to
recover and treats him like her own son. He
enjoys the attention and the luxurious life in
the castle and becomes romantically attracted to
her daughter, Eloise, who has been Capped. He is
soon faced with a dilemma: he can continue on
the dangerous and possibly unsuccessful quest
for freedom with his friends, or he can remain
at the court where his every wish will be
gratified and he will eventually become a
knight. After the other boys leave, he discovers
to his horror that Eloise, who has been chosen
Queen of the Tournament, an annual celebration,
must go to serve the Tripods and will no longer
be living in the castle. Horror-stricken by her
willing subservience to the Tripods and
tradition, he flees to join his friends, is
followed by and captured by a Tripod, then is
mysteriously released to continue on his way.
Shortly after he catches up with his friends,
they discover beneath Will's right arm a metal
button by which the Tripods are tracking them.
Beanpole operates to remove the button, a
painful but successful procedure. When a Tripod
attacks in furious retaliation, the boys lob

grenades at the machine without effect until Will manages to toss one inside what is apparently the creature's mouth, and it explodes there. Now pursued by a small army of Tripods, the boys take refuge in a valley, hiding in a cleft under a boulder for about two days, hungry, cold, and with Will in pain from his now festering wound. When the Tripods finally give up and depart, the weary and starving boys trudge on, sighting only one Tripod in the distance before arriving at the Mountains. There they join other refugees from the Tripods' totalitarian rule in a difficult but free existence in caves and tunnels high inside the range. As in most books of this genre, the focus is on ideas and action, and issues are clear-cut. Characterization is the minimum necessary for the plot, and the few figures are drawn in bold and stereotypical strokes. The Tripods are less monstrous than most sci-fi villains. Not much is made of the locale, except for ruined Paris. The plot is fast-paced, and, while readers will recognize some familiar cliches, there are enough twists and turns to keep the story interesting. Though Will is a likeable protagonist and candid enough about himself to give his character some depth, he is less interesting than Beanpole or the Vagrant. Completing the trilogy are *The City of Gold and Lead** and *The Pool of Fire**. Books Too Good; Choice; Stone.

WHITE QUEEN (*Through the Looking-Glass**), chess piece Alice* rescues from the cinders, when first she enters the Looking-Glass world. Alice reads to her and the White King the Looking-Glass poem, "Jabberwocky," whose strange words Humpty* Dumpty later explains to her. When Alice helps the frowsy Queen, grown person-sized, tidy her hair and garments, the Queen tries to explain to her how living backwards works and the necessity of believing in impossible things. A befuddled but benign caricature, the White Queen deals gently with Alice compared to some other figures. To her Alice gives her age as seven and a half.

WHITE RABBIT (*Alice's Adventures in Wonderland**; *Alice's Adventures under Ground**), the first

character Alice* meets and whom she follows into
Wonderland. Elderly, timid, evasive, and
nervous, he seems the antithesis of the
energetic, decisive, forthright little girl. He
is worried about the time, keeps checking his
watch and saying, "Oh, dear! Oh, dear! I shall
be too late!," and is very much afraid of
incurring the wrath of the Duchess*. Alice,
grown large, gets stuck in his house, and he and
his friends try to send in Bill, a lizard, to
get her out. He later appears at the trial of
the Knave of Hearts as the herald. He is the
best fleshed figure next to the well-drawn
Alice.

WHITLOCK, PAMELA (FRANCES) (1920-1982), born in
Penang, Malaysia; editor and author of books for
children. She attended St. Mary's Convent,
Ascot, Berkshire, from 1934 to 1939, where she
became friends with Katharine Hull*, with whom
she wrote adventure novels while they were
still in their teens. The first of these
achieved great popularity, was a Fanfare
selection of *Horn Book*, and is still read today
with enjoyment: *The Far-Distant Oxus** (Cape,
1937; Macmillan, 1938), about the exploits of
six children with ponies, camping, and a raft
on the Exmoor moors. Its sequels are *Escape to
Persia* (Cape, 1938; Macmillan, 1939) and *Oxus
in Summer* (Cape, 1939; Macmillan, 1940). Later
the two women coauthored *Crowns* (Cape, 1947),
which tells how four cousins create an imaginary
world where they can do anything they like, a
story that critics considered better crafted
than *Oxus* but that never caught on as well. By
herself, Whitlock published *All Day Long: An
Anthology of Poetry for Children* (Oxford, 1954)
and *The Open Book: A Collection of Stories,
Essays, Poems, Songs and Music* (Collins, 1956;
Kenedy, 1956). She was a publicity assistant for
Jonathan Cape, Publishers, from 1939 to 1940,
editor of children's books for Collins from 1946
to 1952, founding editor of *Collins Magazine*,
and children's book editor for Oxford Press in
the 1950s. During World War II she served in the
Women's Royal Air Force. She married John Bell
in 1954, and the couple had five daughters. She
illustrated the books she cowrote with Hull.

WHO LIES INSIDE (Ireland*, Timothy, Gay Men's Press, 1984), realistic novel set one school term in an urban community in present-day England, in which a youth describes his struggles to identify and come to terms with his sexual orientation. Schoolboy Martin Conway, 18, so tall, strong, and clumsy that he is good-naturedly called Jumbo by his friends, is fairly good at sports and his classes but is having increasing difficulty with what he calls the stranger inside him. He has trouble relating to his macho, emotionally inhibited father, Ron, a porter, and to his small, warm, but emotionally repressed mother, Sheila. Ron takes pride in Martin's athletic ability, supports him academically because education promises social advancement, doesn't want Sheila to demonstrate affection for Martin lest the boy become effeminate, and even provides Martin condoms and porn calendars to stimulate him toward what he thinks is proper male behavior. Martin, however, has been feeling more strongly attracted to his own sex, and, although he goes to the pub and plays squash with the macho types, their taunts about his virginity and boasts about their "scores" increase his self-doubts and sense of isolation. He studies hard to pass his college entrance exams but worries about what effect his homosexuality might have on his aspirations to become a physical education teacher. He feels both an affinity toward and revulsion for Charles, a good-looking, made-up, slight male prostitute who frequents the local pub. Martin feels honestly sorry for the man when two macho types work him over and fears the same thing might happen to him if he came out as homosexual. He goes to the house of the school rugby trainer, Tom, hoping to confide in the always affable older man, but leaves with mixed feelings and without communicating his problem when he finds Tom half-drunk and maudlin about his lonely life and old sexual conquests. Unable to talk to his parents or male friends, he finally confides in his best friend's girlfriend, Linda, telling her that he loves Richard, a nice-looking, physically smaller classmate, who is good at writing and whose essays Martin has been studying for organization. Linda's attempts to dissuade him

on social grounds only confuse him and increase
his pain. In an effort to prove himself heterosexual, he dates and beds beautiful, bright
Margaret Turner, whom his parents obviously
find highly acceptable and whom male rumor has
is "tight arsed," but then despises himself for
using her to establish his reputation as an
O.K. male. Finally he acknowledges his strong
romantic attraction for Richard, whom he has
repeatedly snubbed, and the two spend a
pleasant day at the seashore, where they declare
their love, assert that their love is just as
valid as that between heterosexuals, pledge
their mutual support, decide to be tolerant
toward a society that has branded their love
inferior, and opt to be happy if only just for
the day. Read on one level, Martin's story is
the rather pat account of a slowly developing
romance, the passions described being much like
those in any heterosexual love story. On another
level, the book predictably indicts heterosexual
society on charges of physical exploitation of
women and emotional abuse of women and
homosexual males. Except for the women, who are
mostly passively presented, the only characters
who seem capable of expressing their feelings
toward others on a human level are the
homosexuals. The book seems like a handbook
about the yearnings and pain of homosexuals and
the resentments and bitter antipathy they can
expect to meet from society. Characters and
situations seem stereotypical, the conclusion is
pat, and the theme is a strong plea for
understanding and acceptance. Other.

WIDDERSHINS CRESCENT (Townsend*, John Rowe,
Hutchinson, 1965; *GOOD-BYE TO THE JUNGLE*,
Lippincott, 1967), realistic novel of family and
neighborhood life set in Cobchester in northern
England probably in the late 1950s. The action
takes place two years after that in *Gumble's
Yard*. When the Jungle* is pulled down for slum
clearance, the Thompsons move to Widdowson
Crescent, commonly called Widdershins Crescent,
in the new, low-cost housing development of
Westwood Estates in another part of the city.
The family includes Uncle Walter*, Doris*, his
common-law wife, Kevin*, 15, who tells the
story, and Sandra*, 14, Walter's orphaned nephew

and niece, and Harold*, 10, and Jean*, 8, his
own children. In spite of Walter's irresponsibility and the usual bickering between him and
Doris, the children, from whose point of view
events are seen, approach their new life with
pleasant anticipation. After the move is
accomplished with the help of accommodating Mr.*
and Mrs. Hedley and their son, Dick*, who were
their Jungle neighbors, the children soon adjust
to their new surroundings and begin to make
friends. Kevin and Harold even have hopes of
attending better schools. Trouble is not long in
arriving, however, for with new surroundings
come new wants and expectations. "Sick of livin'
like a pig," Doris buys new furniture from
Widdowson's Store on time. Improvident Walter
sells the furniture for ready cash, squanders
the money on ale and horses, and then is unable
to make the payments because he has lost his
job. When Jean runs away because Walter angrily
threatens to "put down" her beloved tom, Pussy,
and Walter's problems close in, Kevin and
Sandra turn to Dick Hedley, who advises them to
consult Tony* Boyd, their curate friend from the
Jungle. Tony persuades Mr. Widdowson, the owner
of the furniture store and the wealthiest man in
the area, to hire Walter for manual work about
his warehouse to pay off the debt. Dick and
Sandra are skeptical about Mr. Widdowson's
motives, suspicions that eventually prove
accurate. Walter leaves one night on a
mysterious errand when he should have been
attending a parents' meeting at Cobchester
College, to which Harold has just won a
scholarship, a feat of which Walter has been
extremely proud. Kevin and Dick follow him to
the warehouse, where they discover him
apparently trying to put out a blaze. They pull
him out of the burning building and are hailed
as heroes. Shortly, however, Walter is arrested
for arson on circumstantial evidence. During the
trial he admits setting the fire but claims he
was told to do it so Mr. Widdowson could get the
insurance money. Mr. Widdowson denies complicity, of course, and the jury convicts
Walter. Even though Kevin sees no alternative
but to leave school and get a job to support the
family, he still feels a better future lies
ahead for all of them and is encouraged in this

attitude by Tony Boyd. Occasional humor lightens
the predominately serious tone, for example,
when Walter squanders money on a car and the
family takes a wild ride to the country, during
which the decrepit machine falls to pieces. A
keenly visualized setting, plentiful action, and
credible characters combine for top-notch
reading entertainment, marred only here and
there by narrative that does not seem to fit
Kevin's character as presented. Even though the
plot is conventional in the basics, the book has
more depth than its predecessor. Jean's love for
Pussy, Harold's success at school, Doris's
desire for a better life than that she has
known, Kevin's hopes for more schooling--all
these story strands contribute to the main plot
and give a view of city life not previously
reported in such a realistic way for young
readers. It is curious that Uncle Walter and
Doris speak the local dialect while the Hedleys
and the children do not. One of a series.
Choice.

THE WILD HORSE OF SANTANDER (Griffiths*, Helen,
ill. Victor G. Ambrus, Hutchinson, 1966;
Doubleday, 1967), horse story set in the
contemporary period on a farm just outside the
village of Bonifaz in the Spanish highlands of
Santander. Farmer Luis Murjica buys from his
neighbor Jose, who raises race horses, a
thoroughbred bay mare of unstable temperament
but great beauty, who is not suitable for racing
since she injured her hoof in a fractious
moment. He intends to use her to pull his milk
delivery cart. Although she is an extravagance,
Luis justifies her purchase because she is with
foal. Luis promises the foal to his son,
Joaquin, who is blind from a recent illness of
an undisclosed nature. Advised by Jose not to
baby the boy, Luis and Isabel, his wife, resist
their natural tendency to overprotect Joaquin
and allow him to roam the farm and adjust to his
disability. He gradually gains confidence in his
ability to get around, learns to compensate for
his blindness by using his other senses, eagerly
awaits the birth of the foal, and thrills to the
stories his grandmother, Abuelita, tells him
about the marvelous Arabian steed ridden by the
great Spanish hero of old, El Cid. The foal

turns out to be a filly, and, though he is told, especially by his jealous older sister, Mari-Bel, that the colt is ugly and chunky, the boy imagines her to be very beautiful and names her Linda, the pretty one. Months pass, and, in spite of the warnings of Joaquin's easily upset aunts, the parents continue to encourage the boy to be independent with the colt. One night he sneaks out and takes the colt to the mountains, hoping to expose her to the dawn mist which in Abuelita's stories is magical. He gets lost and is brought home safely by the colt. Two years pass, and Luis sells the mother horse to finance an operation on Joaquin's eyes. By now, Linda has grown into a large and powerful mare with a little of her mother's instability of temperament and is unfriendly to all but the boy. In an attempt to make her tractable, Jose takes her to his farm where she makes friends with a valuable chestnut colt of about her age. While Joaquin is in the hospital, the two horses break out and steadily resist all efforts to capture them. Joaquin's operation is successful, and he returns eager to see his colt with his own eyes for the first time. The men spot the horses not far from the farm, the home to which Linda has ironically returned, and, since they have given up hope of capturing the animals, Luis shoots Linda, just as Joaquin, who has learned from Mari-Bell that Linda has broken out, runs down the track toward his horse. The chestnut turns mean at the death of his mate and is also shot. A few days later Jose gives Joaquin a black pony named Talgo, which the boy sensibly accepts. He realizes that the Linda he loved belonged mostly to the world of imagination and dreams and that he must come to terms with reality. The plot summary makes the story, the conclusion in particular, seem more sentimental than it is. Some events are seen from the point of view of the animals, which are only slightly anthropomorphized. Their thoughts and motives are presented as though seen by a careful, sensitive, knowledgeable observer. Killing the horses at the end is in keeping with what would probably happen in real life, but the timing of events seems contrived for dramatic effect. It also seems unrealistic to state that no one else can approach Linda since the boy has

been unable to care for her and someone else has
had to do so. Moreover, it is not clear why,
once Joaquin is on the scene, the men give him
no opportunity to try to gentle Linda, since, at
that point, their main concern is the safety of
the valuable chestnut. Characters are types, and
the style, richly descriptive with words of
smell, touch, and taste, helps the reader
experience the farm world from Joaquin's
sightless perspective. The story is based on an
event reported in a Madrid newspaper. Carnegie
Com.

A WILD THING (Renvoize*, Jean, Macmillan, 1970;
Atlantic/Little, 1971), survival novel of a
runaway foster child, set in Scotland in the
last third of the twentieth century. Morag, 15,
an unhappy girl, has stolen a little money and
in early spring has run away from her puritanical foster mother, heading for the mountains
she has seen in a newspaper photograph. Although
not retarded, as her social workers thought when
they sent her to a special school, Morag has
never been able to organize her thoughts and
emotions, and she has not planned rationally
for the trip. When her money is gone, she
steals food and a blanket from an occupied
house, wanders on into less inhabited country,
and eventually finds a cave which she can make
habitable. On the way she comes upon an injured
nanny goat and its kid, and with great labor she
carries the goat along. With goat's milk, the
rabbits she is able to kill, and food she
steals from neighboring crofts, she manages
fairly well during the warm months, and she
becomes better able to control her thoughts and
to face the repressed memories of her mother,
from whom she was taken at four, her little
sister, who died of pneumonia through their
mother's neglect, and her baby brother, whose
fate she does not know. These memories make her
long for a child, and she plans to intercept a
hiker and offer herself to him so she can
conceive a baby. When the hiker she follows
screams at the sight of her, she is abashed, but
she later rescues a different hiker, Arthur
Figgs, who has been injured in a fall that
killed his companion. Morag and Arthur spend a
few idyllic weeks together, but he grows

increasingly uneasy about the situation and finally leaves in horror when she shows him the Mossman, a skeleton she has fantasized as being a man to love. Knowing she is pregnant, Morag lets him go without great trauma, and she makes some efforts to prepare for winter, but when cold weather finally arrives, she realizes she hasn't nearly enough supplies and for the baby's sake decides to return to civilization. As she approaches a village, she finds a crowd coming out to drive her away. She runs from their shots and eventually reaches the beach, where she has a miscarriage and dies. While her Robinson Crusoe existence is not always convincing, Morag's psychology is sensitively and believably portrayed, and her dependence on her fantasy life is skillfully incorporated. Arthur is a shallow character, but plausible in the context. Morag's need for love and for something to love and her frank acceptance of sex make the book poignant and yet earthy. Fanfare.

WILKINS, (WILLIAM) VAUGHAN (1890-1959), born in London; journalist, author of historical romances. At twenty-four he was named editor of the London *Daily Call*, a newspaper that became defunct during World War I while Wilkins was serving in Egypt, Palestine, and France. He returned to London to become assistant editor of the *Daily Express*, but gave up journalism after 1936 to become a full-time novelist. During World War II he did military duty with the Home Guard and was a billeting officer for refugees. Of his dozen novels, only one was set in the twentieth century, a picaresque novel titled *Once Upon a Time* (Cape, 1949; Macmillan, 1949), with smugglers, ex-Gestapo members, a protagonist with amnesia, an Irish monastery, and many other exciting but highly unlikely elements. His first novel remains his best known, *And So-- Victoria* (Cape, 1937; Macmillan, 1937), a story of intrigue and melodrama leading up to Victoria's ascension to the throne, which became a best seller, was translated into German, Danish, Dutch, Norwegian, and Swedish, with film rights sold to Metro-Goldwyn-Mayer. This was followed by two other novels about Victoria, *Seven Tempest* (Cape, 1941; Macmillan, 1942) and *Husband for Victoria* (Cape, 1958; as *Consort*

for Victoria, Doubleday, 1959), to make a trilogy of sorts. His one book considered to be primarily for young adults is *The City of Frozen
Fire** (Cape, 1950; Macmillan, 1951), an adventure novel set mostly in an imaginary South A-
merican country in the early nineteenth century.
Among his others works are *Crown Without Sceptre*
(Cape, 1952; Macmillan, 1952), about a Jacobite
earl and his adopted niece in Italy and England
in the 1770s; *A King Reluctant* (Cape, 1952; Macmillan, 1952), an imaginative projection of what
might have happened to Louis XVII, the "lost
dauphin" of France, had he been rescued via
balloon, brought to Wales, and become involved
with a spirited American girl; and *Fanfare for a
Witch* (Cape, 1954; Macmillan, 1954), about a son
of King George II who becomes involved with a
Moroccan Empress and her retinue.

WILL ANDREWS (*Ask Me No Questions**), protective
older brother of six-year-old Jamie* at the
Drouet school for workhouse children. When his
father, a coster, became sick and his mother
became pregnant, the family all went to the
workhouse, a move that Will bitterly regrets,
wishing he had taken Jamie and gone off on his
own. Of the three children that Laura* tries to
feed, he is the only one who may survive,
though even that is unsure since he is last seen
in the hospital, separated from Jamie.

WILLARD, BARBARA (MARY) (1909-   ), born in
Sussex, the area in which she now lives and that
has provided the subject matter and locale for
her most highly acclaimed books, the historical
novels that make up the Mantlemass*, or Forest,
series. Focused on an imposing manor in the
Ashdown Forest, or Wealdon, that once covered
much of southeastern England, the eight interlocking books trace the fortunes of the Medleys
and the Mallorys beginning with the War of the
Roses in the fifteenth century until the house
burns down in *Harrow and Harvest* (Kestrel, 1974;
Dutton, 1975) in the seventeenth century. *The
Lark and the Laurel** (Longman, 1970; Harcourt,
1970) introduces the series, paints a rich
picture of the political turmoil in England and
of the economic and social life of the forest,
and is listed in *Choice*. Winner of the

Guardian Award is *The Iron Lily** (Longman,
1973; Dutton, 1974), which deals with the
development of the iron industry and features an
unusually able and memorable woman protagonist.
Fleshing out the engrossing story of the manor
family are *The Sprig of Broom* (Longman, 1971;
Dutton, 1972); *A Cold Wind Blowing* (Longman,
1972; Dutton, 1973); *The Miller's Boy* (Kestrel, 1976; Dutton, 1976); *The Eldest Son*
(Kestrel, 1977); and *A Flight of Swans* (Kestrel,
1980). More recently, she won the Whitbread
Award for *The Queen of the Pharisees' Children**
(MacRae, 1983), a stark and poignant historical
novel about an unfortunate family of gypsies in
the years following the execution of Charles I.
She is also respected for her ability to create
contemporary family situations convincingly,
like those involving two English and American
families merged by marriage who gradually come
to terms in *The Battle of Wednesday Week**
(Constable, 1963; as *Storm from the West*,
Harcourt, 1964), a Fanfare book. The lone child
in a theatrical family until she was twelve, at
eleven she played a boy in *Macbeth* when her
father was acting at Stratford. She received a
convent education, wanted to write at any early
age, joined her immediate and extended family in
the theater instead, but then returned to her
first ambition. She wrote adult novels,
publishing the first of a dozen, *Love in Ambush*
(Howe), in 1930 when she was twenty-one; scripts
for films; articles; and short stories for
almost twenty years before attempting novels for
young readers at the end of the 1950s. Since
then she has written mainly for children, with a
few picture-book stories like *The Pocket Mouse*
(Hamilton, 1969; Knopf, 1969), but mainly
family, growing up, and historical books, over
fifty altogether. Her list includes *The Grove of
Green Holly* (Constable, 1967; as *Flight to the
Forest*, Doubleday, 1967), set during the time
the Puritans closed theaters; *A Dog and a Half*
(Hamilton, 1964; Nelson, 1971), an animal story,
and *Spell Me a Witch* (Hamilton, 1979; Harcourt,
1981), a fantasy of magic gone awry, both for
younger readers; *The Country Maid* (Hamilton,
1978; Greenwillow, 1980), in which an English
country girl gone into service in the city sorts
herself out; and *The Gardener's Grandchildren*

(Kestrel, 1978; McGraw, 1979), an intergenera-
tional story set on a Scottish island. A
versatile and daring writer, she has won praise
for her skill at capturing the sense of a
period, her ability with dialogue and dialect,
her keen depiction of the tensions, rewards, and
compensations of family life, and her gentle
humor.

WILLIAM (*Danny, The Champion of the World**),
Danny's father, who raises Danny after Danny's
mother dies at his birth and who has vowed to
give up his favorite sport of poaching until
Danny is old enough to be left alone at night.
In one of the book's funniest scenes, Danny
repeats William's story about how his father
invented ingenious methods of poaching pheasants
by experimenting on roosters. Danny's grandfather developed two secret, foolproof methods:
The Horsehair Stopper, whereby short pieces of
horse hair are inserted into raisins, causing
the raisins to stick in the pheasants' throats
and rendering them unable to make a sound; and
The Sticky Hat, whereby the pheasants' heads
become stuck inside paper cones in which
raisins have been glued. William is a hardworking, optimistic man, respected and well-
liked by his neighbors, all of whom also look
upon poaching as a grand old sport that has come
down to them from their ancestors. Danny thinks
his father "without the slightest doubt, was
the most marvelous and exciting father any boy
ever had." He sees William as always ready for
fun and as a loving, caring man.

WILLIAM BAGTHORPE (*Ordinary Jack**), Jack's older
brother of about sixteen, who, like all the
Bagthorpes except Jack has "several strings to
his bow," among them talents in tennis and
electronics. He contributes little to the plot,
just putting Jack down whenever he can and
exemplifying the Bagthorpes' low opinion of the
boy. He develops a crush on Atlanta, the Danish
maid, who mostly ignores him because he's such a
puppy.

WILLIAM BEECH (*Good Night, Mr. Tom**), abused
child evacuated from a London slum and billeted
with reclusive older Tom* Oakley in an English

village during World War II. Willie has been viciously beaten, cowed, and neglected by his fanatically religious mother, and only gradually adjusts to the kindness and decent living offered in Tom's cottage. A sensitive and intelligent boy, he works hard to learn to read so that he can be with his friends in school. His genuine artistic talent is encouraged, and his acting ability is discovered in the practice for the village Christmas play. Very small for his age, he is quickly beaten and terrorized into an almost vegetable state when he returns to London at his mother's summons, and even back in Little Weirwold he retains his sense of guilt at not having saved his baby half-sister when his mother tied him in a closet and abandoned them. In Tom's kindly company, he finally comes to terms with his guilt and even with his loss when his friend Zach* Wrench is killed. As Tom's adopted son he seems to have prospects for a stable and happy future.

WILLIAM JONAS (*The Islanders**), hard-headed, tough, old leader, propounder of the Halcyon* islanders' Teaching, and protector of tradition. He holds the office of Reader because he passes on the received Law, even though, like the other islanders, he is illiterate. He is easily offended, jealous of his prerogatives, and not above tipping the scales in the direction he wishes things to go. He often bickers with his neighbors, especially with those of his generation. When things begin to go badly on Halcyon after the Rikofians are exiled to Kingfisher* Island, he abdicates in favor of Adam* Goodall.

WILLIAM MCSHANE (*A Sound of Chariots**), Bridie's younger brother. When he is born she fears he will replace her in her father's affections, since she knows that Patrick* has longed for a son, but Patrick wisely helps Bridie from lapsing into jealousy. After Patrick dies, Bridie is for a time almost obsessed with the need to teach William what "dead" means. She helps with the funeral of Nell's (one of The Others*) rabbit, Bluey. In the process, she becomes aware that she, too, is mortal and feels afraid of what the future may bring. This fear of time running out plagues her for years to come.

WILLIAM RUSSELL (*Flambards**; *The Edge of the Cloud**; *Flambards in Summer**), quiet younger son of Uncle* Russell, thirteen when Christina* Parsons first comes to Flambards. The very day she arrives he is thrown from his horse and badly injured in a fox hunt, and she alone discovers that he later deliberately walks on his unhealed leg so that it will stiffen and he will be unable to ride, a sport he hates and fears. He survives his father's scorn and contempt by leading a secret life, learning mathematics from Mr. Dermot and helping him build and test the airplane *Emma*. In his own way, Will is just as obsessive and as willing to risk danger as his father and brother, though he is more intelligent and his interest turns to flying, not to hunting. He is clearly always more concerned with flying than with Christina, even after they are engaged, but he differs from his brother Mark* by being willing to put in long hours of work to pursue his interest. He has a promising future as an airplane designer when World War I breaks out and he enlists in the Royal Flying Corps. At the beginning of the third book, he has just been killed in action.

WILLIAM SEAGRAVE (*Masterman Ready**), youth of twelve, who with his parents, Mr*. and Mrs*. Seagrave; an elderly seaman, Masterman Ready*; a black nanny, Juno*; and two younger siblings is cast away on a desert isle and survives through hard work and perseverance. Manly, responsible, and willing, William assists Ready in many ways to make life as comfortable as possible for the family. In particular, he accompanies Ready on exploratory excursions, helps in constructing whatever needs to be built, and serves the family as fisherman. He falters just enough to avoid becoming a paragon of all virtues. His inquiries provide the opportunity for Mr. Seagrave and Ready to convey information on various subjects and instruction in manners and morals (and for the author to so educate his readers).

WILLIAMS, URSULA. See Moray Williams, Ursula.

WILL STANTON (*The Dark Is Rising**; *The Grey King**), bright, serious-minded, persevering boy, son of a Buckinghamshire jeweler. The seventh son of a seventh son, he learns from Merriman* Lyon on his eleventh birthday that he is an Old One, one of those immortals who have the responsibility of saving the world from the evil powers of the Dark. Among other deeds, he helps to save his village from the extreme cold sent by the Dark, assists Merriman in recovering the stolen Grail of King Arthur, wins a golden harp, awakens the Six Sleepers, and with Bran's* help acquires the sword by which the silvery mistletoe is cut from the Midsummer Tree and the Dark is finally defeated (in *Silver on the Tree*, the last book in The Dark Is Rising series). Will is not a memorable protagonist, serving more as a plot functionary or pivot than a flesh-and-blood heroic character, in spite of the many, often dangerous adventures he goes through.

WILLY OVERS (*A Likely Lad**), quiet, bookish boy, small for his age, who suffers from his father's ambitions for him and his mother's desire to keep him above the rougher boys on their street. A nervous, worrying type, Willy feels guilty that he can't share his father's pleasure in the prospect of getting a job for him in the Northern Star insurance company, but he views the great dark building as a prison, and the idea of working up the ladder of success there puts him into a cold sweat. When Willy does strike out on his own, it is not from a desire for success but in desperation to get away from a situation at home. His sympathy is caught by the confused old woman in the village shop, Nance* Price, and he feels an obligation to help her out and, after he is home again, to see that she is cared for. He often feels that a wheel of events takes over and carries him around with it, quite beyond his own control.

WILLY WONKA'S CHOCOLATE FACTORY (*Charlie and the Chocolate Factory**), a large and exotic place, much of it underground, from which drift luscious aromas of chocolate and other confections and in which Mr.* Wonka manufactures the candy bars and sweet concoctions for which

he has become famous around the world. The
factory produces such extraordinary products as
Eatable Marshmallow Pillows, Lickable Wallpaper,
Fizzy Lifting Drinks, and Square Candies That
Look Round. Through the plant winds a savory
river of rich, melted chocolate, on which Mr.
Wonka takes his guests for a ride in a great,
gleaming, pink, boiled-sweet boat with a
magnificent prow. He also takes them for rides
in a great glass elevator that can go in any
direction. Willy Wonka's Chocolate Factory is
such a wonderful place that all children long to
visit it.

THE WIND EYE (Westall*, Robert, Macmillan, 1976;
Greenwillow, 1977), fantasy that explores
relationships in a discordant family on their
two-week holiday in 1976 to the coast of
Northumberland where St. Cuthbert was a hermit
in the seventh century. Even when they start, it
is apparent that the three-year-old marriage of
Madeleine* and Bertrand* Studdard, a professor
at Cambridge, was a mistake and has deteriorated
to constant quarrelling. Madeleine, who drives
with combative recklessness, insists on burning
up the road in her red Triumph Spitfire, while
Bertrand prudently drives his Volvo with his
daughters, Beth*, a teenager, and Sally*, 6, and
Madeleine's son, Mike* (Michael) Hendrey, about
Beth's age. When they stop in Durham,
Madeleine*, who is assertive and given to
posturing, corners a workman to show them the
cathedral, all the time goading Bertrand, who is
an atheist, by exclaiming about miracles and
faith, and when they come to the tomb of St.
Cuthbert (Cuddy, the locals call him) where the
workman warns her sharply to step back, she
deliberately puts her foot on the marble slab.
Beth feels she has awakened some force by her
action. They are headed for Monk's Heugh, a
house left to Bertrand by his Uncle Henry,
recently drowned, which turns out to be crammed
with miscellanea in glass cases, all carefully
labeled. Sally, who has one hand crippled from a
bad burn which was Bertrand's fault, starts what
appears to be a series of sleepwalking episodes,
though she says she gets up to hear the angels
sing and to go out to a bald man who is waving
at her. Mike is bored and resentful of his

mother's theatrics and of Bertrand's constant,
niggling corrections, until they find a boat of
ancient Viking design in one of the sheds, with
some of the name worn off but the letters,
Resurre and Sum still legible. Told by Madeleine
that even an expert couldn't sail it, Bertrand
is determined to do so, but his efforts to put
in a mast only break his drill. A warning by a
local that he'll never manage the "Wind Eye's"
boat infuriates him. Mike finds the sail in the
shed and rigs her. When they sail they get into
a strange mist, and the next time, with only the
three youngsters aboard, they go from a hot
afternoon immediately into a moonlit night. It
is Mike who figures out that the *Resurre* works
like a time machine, sometimes moving of its own
volition, a theory they are careful not to
share with their parents. Another time the three
of them come upon what seems to be St.
Cuthbert's funeral, and later upon a Viking
raid, in which Mike gets a cut arm and a Viking
spear for souvenirs. A delegation of local
fishermen come to warn Bertrand that the
children should not use the *Resurre*, only irri-
tating him further. The next morning Sally runs
out to the boat, which is being lifted free by
the high tide, and climbs aboard, and only with
the greatest effort do both Beth and Mike
clamber on before it is too far out. They are
unable to control *Resurre* and just as it is
about to go aground on Inner Farne Island, they
are jerked back into the twentieth century, but
Sally is gone. Bertrand is sure she has drowned
and belatedly locks *Resurre* in the shed, but
some nights later Beth and Mike tear out the
rotten boards in the back and pull it out. At
first they are unable to return to the past, but
when Mike wishes to be at the time when St.
Cuthbert is through with Sally, they immediately
are at Inner Farne, and Sally is jumping up and
down on the beach waving. She babbles at length
about her time with the saint and shows them her
crippled hand, which is perfectly good again.
Bertrand takes her to the same doctor who saw
the hand earlier in the week and demands an
explanation. With his usual obsessive energy, he
decides that he must prove the supernatural
power of Cuthbert, and starts by renting skin-
diving equipment to see whether there are

remains of Viking longships off Holy Island,
where the saint is said to have sunk a raiding
party. A crowd of fishermen gathers, warns
Bertrand not to continue, and sets their biggest
man on him, but, when Bertrand displays his
skill with judo, they call their man off and
throw trophies of Viking ships at Bertrand's
feet. Still unconvinced, he takes *Resurre* and
leaves. Beth and Mike swim with the *Resurre*
steering oar, and it takes them out to the
island. Beth grasps a hold at the base of a
cliff, and Mike is washed back out. Thinking he
has failed, he wishes he were nowhere and is
washed up on a barren beach. To his intense
relief he finds a piece of twentieth-century
litter and then Madeleine and Sally. Beth climbs
with great difficulty and gets to the hut of
Saint Cuthbert. He shouts Latin at her and at
the little black devils who appear riding goats
and start his hut afire. Beth puts out the
flames, then has a conversation by mental
communication with the saint, who is dying. She
finds the steering oar, swims out, and sees the
boat coming for the body of the saint. It is
Resurre when it was new, with the lettering all
there: *Resurrectio Vitaque Sum*--I am the
Resurrection and the Life. In the meantime,
Bertrand, still in the boat, wills himself back
into St. Cuthbert's time thinking he will save
the Vikings against whom Cuthbert raised a storm
to wreck their boats. He meets them on the
beach, tries to communicate with them, and ends
up fighting one after the other with judo. Just
before he gives up exhausted, the storm raised
by the saint appears and the Vikings rush back
to their boats, which are wrecked just off
shore. The monks thank Bertrand, and he leaves,
taking with him a woman captive of the Vikings,
but he cannnot stay in the seventh century and
finds himself alone drifting back to the
twentieth century beach at Monks Heugh, feeling
that his rational life has been destroyed. Then
he realizes that Uncle Henry must have had the
same experience and finally found a way to
escape into the past. The title is an early word
for window, but obviously refers to a window in
time rather than space. In considering the
difference between rational thought and faith,
the book becomes somewhat programmatic, coming

down heavily on the side of the supernatural and calling Bertrand's world dry and boring. The fantasy scenes are believable and interesting, but the characterization is far more important, with each of the five family members, while not entirely likeable, clearly developed and the conflicts well evoked. An author's note at the end gives some information about the history of the area and the legends of St. Cuthbert. Fanfare.

WINDFALL (Peyton*, K. M., ill. Victor Ambrus, Oxford, 1962; *SEA FEVER*, World, 1963), novel of fishing boats and sailing competitions in the coastal waters off Essex in the late nineteenth century. Young Matt* Pullen, 15, has worked on his father's fishing smack, the aged *Fathom*, for nearly four years, a rough and demanding life but one he loves, when they hear distress signals from a ship one stormy night and sail out seeking any survivors and also salvage, since they badly need a new boat before the *Fathom* goes to pieces. As they approach the breaking vessel, Matt glimpses a man lashed to the mast. The only other smack to answer the signals, the *Charity* which is owned by arrogant, unpopular Beckett*, a suspected smuggler, turns back, when it is apparent that the ship is beyond salvage, rather than helping save the survivor. In a dangerous, difficult battle against the driving storm, Matt boards the vessel, cuts the man loose, and regains the *Fathom* with him only seconds before the other ship is swallowed by the sea. The stricken man, who has lost his wife and property but saved his money bag, gives Tom Pullen 100 pounds, the price of a new smack. Matt sails with his father from their home at Marshfield to Marchester to order the new boat (to be called the *Reward*), from Melville, the prime builder in the area. Tom pays one fourth down and keeps the remaining 75 pounds in his money belt. There Matt again sees the *Good Fortune*, an expensive racing yacht newly built for Peregrine Shelley, a wealthy diamond merchant. On an earlier trip to Marchester with his friend, George Firman, 20, Matt had managed to pull out a painter who had fallen from the *Good Fortune*, as well as the son of the owner, Francis* Shelley, who had dived

in to save the man. A few weeks later, in a
freak accident, Tom is knocked overboard by the
boom when the sail jibes, and Beckett, who is
bringing the *Charity* in just behind the *Fathom*,
makes no attempt to pick him up. Weighted down
by the money which he always wears, Tom sinks
almost immediately. When the body is finally
found, several days later, the money belt is
missing. Matt's Uncle Albert, a cheese merchant
in Marchester whom the boy despises, tries to
persuade Matt's mother to come live with him so
that he can have a free housekeeper and the
children's help in the store, but Matt refuses
to go, and his mother, though doubtful, agrees
to keep the family in Marshfield with Matt
supporting them by fishing. Though it is
terribly hard for the boy with only old,
demented Aaron to help, Matt struggles on, with
some good luck and much nerve. In a fog he is
almost hit by a Dutch schooner, to which he
shouts a warning that they will go aground. The
captain orders him on board to determine their
position and, when pressed by some passengers
who are diamond merchants, gets him to guide
them through the Spitway, a shortcut used by
smack fishermen but very risky for a ship this
size. On board are Francis Shelley and his
father, who is impressed by Matt's skill and
coolness, offers him an occasional job on the
Good Fortune, and pressures the captain to pay
him 25 pounds for his services. When the
season for racing starts, Matt is thrilled to go
aboard the beautiful yacht as one of the crew
until he discovers that Beckett has been hired
as the skipper. On the eve of the big regatta,
when the *Good Fortune* is to race Lord
Wickford's *Juno*, Matt is sent by Mr. Shelley's
steward Henry to a local tavern to pick up some
brandy. He overhears Beckett assuring two men
that *Juno* will win and realizes that he means
to lose the race deliberately. Beckett sees
him, knows Matt is on to his game, and pays
three youths to waylay and kill him. Matt
escapes with bruises and a serious cut on one
arm, hides in the unfinished hull of *Reward* until daylight, then bravely boards the *Good
Fortune*, knowing that his presence will change
Beckett's plan. Mr. Shelley, thinking from his
disheveled appearance that he has been in a

tavern fight, is disgusted, but it is too late to replace him, and in a thrilling race *Good Fortune* beats *Juno*. The same day, with Francis and Matt's twin brothers, Jack and Joe, 11, *Fathom* beats *Charity* in the smack race, though she is wrecked by the hard sailing over the hard sailing over the spit. The prize of 25 pounds goes partly toward *Reward* and partly to keep the family of six eating through the winter. Early in the fall *Reward* is ready, but Matt is still worried and exhausted, exhausted because Aaron is weakening, so the labor that used to take three strong men no longer has even two to do it, and worried because he still owes Melville nearly 40 pounds and because he knows he has an implacable enemy in Beckett. In November he gets a big lift of spirit when Francis comes to visit and crew for him. Two weeks before Christmas, the *Reward*, having ridden out a sudden gale, is coming in shortly before dawn when Matt sees an abandoned boat, the *Rose in June*, with an illegal cargo of French brandy. He sends Francis in *Reward* to fetch George Firmin while he stays aboard so he can claim the boat as salvage. Before the *Reward* can return with George and Francis, Beckett, who has been in on the smuggling, arrives in the *Charity* crewed by his brothers. As he tries to kill Matt, he falls into the water and is dragged down by Matt's father's money belt, which the boy glimpses as Beckett attacks him. At the book's end, Matt, now seventeen, can pay for the *Reward*, has escaped the threat of life with Uncle Albert, is no longer pursued by an implacable enemy, and has developed skill and confidence to support his family. Though too many fortuitous events occur to be fully credible, the story is exciting and holds interest with good pacing. Beckett is a stereotyped, blackhearted villain; the other characters are mostly stock figures, but still likeable. The strongest element in the novel is the description of sailing, both the day-to-day effort against heavy seas in the old, smelly smacks and the wild excitement of the competitions. The beauty and the hardship of the life are evoked convincingly. Carnegie Com.

THE WIND IN THE WILLOWS (Grahame*, Kenneth, ill.

Graham   Robertson,   Methuen,   1908;   Scribner,
1908),   gentle,   affectionate fantasy   featuring
several   small animals   of field   and riverside,
extolling   the   quiet   beauties of   nature,   and
exploring the obligations and rewards of friendship.   In the middle   of spring   house-cleaning,
Mole* throws down   his whitewash brush,   scurries
up his little   tunnel   into   the sunlight,   and
answers the call of the season. He comes to the
river,   the first   he has   ever seen,   and there
makes the acquaintance of Water Rat*,   a genial,
poetry-writing   bachelor   who   lives   in   a
comfortable hole in the riverbank, complete with
a   fireplace, a   teakettle, and   a   well-stocked
cupboard. Rat takes him   on a picnic and assures
him that "there is nothing--absolutely nothing--
half so much worth doing as simply messing about
in   boats."   After Mole   impulsively seizes   the
oars   and   capsizes   the   boat,   Rat   cheerfully
rescues him,   dives for   the picnic   basket, and
suggests that Mole   come to live with   him for a
while   and   learn   to row and   to   swim.   Their
further   adventures   are   of two   sorts: highly
amusing ones   that deal   with the antics   of Mr.
Toad* of Toad Hall,   which are interspersed with
quieter, more thoughtful episodes that underline
the deeper   themes of   the book.   Toad, to whose
palatial   home Rat   takes Mole,   is a   loveable,
exasperating, generous,   and boastful character,
given to sudden enthusiasms   to which he devotes
a great deal   of energy and money,   only to drop
each   in favor   of something   new.   When Rat and
Mole call,   he has   just given up   various types
of   boating   and   bought a   canary-yellow   gypsy
caravan   with red   wheels.   He insists that   his
friends come with him to sample the pleasures of
the open road.   Although Rat is   cautious, Mole
loses his   heart immediately to the   neat little
wagon,   and soon   they   are   strolling down   the
dusty lanes   and camping on the common.   After a
couple of days during which Rat and Mole do most
of the work, they come to a high road. Disaster,
in the   form of a motor   car, approaches, forces
them to   the verge,   terrifies the old   horse so
that   he   backs the   caravan   into a ditch   and
wrecks   it, and   zooms off   down the   road. They
comfort the   horse, try to right   the wagon, and
then   find Toad   sitting   in the   middle of   the
road gazing ecstatically   after the disappearing

automobile. From that time on, Toad is obsessed with motor cars. He buys and wrecks at least seven, since he is a terrible driver, before Badger*, the most respected senior citizen of the area, enlists Rat and Mole to help rescue Toad from his latest fascination. When he proves immune to reason, they lock him up, taking turns as guard and hoping the craze will pass, but he tricks kindhearted Ratty by pretending to be mortally ill and escapes while his friend runs for the doctor. Before the day is out, Toad has stolen a motor car, been apprehended, and, sentenced to twenty years, thrown into prison. For several weeks he languishes there, until the gaoler's daughter takes pity on him and helps him escape, dressed as her aunt, a washerwoman. By artifice and a sob story, he gets a ride in the engine of a train, which soon is being pursued by the police in another engine. After Toad has confessed the true story, the engineer tries to outrun the pursuers and failing that works out a scheme whereby Toad can jump off without being seen and hide in a wood. From there he hitches a ride on a barge until the woman insists that he do her washing and, discovering that he is an imposter, throws him into the canal. Furious, he gets to the bank and steals her horse, riding it off in triumph, until he meets a gypsy with whom he trades the animal for a few shillings and a plate of stew. Feeling very pleased with himself, he walks along singing conceited songs until he reaches the high road, where he sees approaching the very car he previously stole. In panic he faints and soon finds himself being solicitiously lifted into the car by the passengers who think he is a poor, overworked washerwoman. With the car's motion, his obsession again surfaces, and after begging for a chance to try his hand at driving, he takes control, speeds recklessly down the road, and drives the vehicle into a duck pond, being thrown clear across to the meadow on the other side. From there he strolls happily toward the river until he discovers that he is being pursued by the chauffeur and a couple of policemen. He rushes on with them gaining on him until he pitches forward into the river, is carried by the rushing water downstream, and finally is able to catch at the edge

of a hole in the bank that proves to be Ratty's
home. In the meantime, Mole and Rat have had a
series of quieter adventures, the only threatening one being the night Mole goes alone into the
Wild Wood, loses his way, and crouches in terror
in a hole under the roots of a fallen tree until
Rat rescues him. By the time they set out
again, however, snow has changed the look of
the wood, and they blunder along desperately
until Mole falls and cuts his shin on the
door-scraper of Badger's home. The good Badger
takes them in, gives them food and shelter, and
sets them on their way in the morning guided by
Otter, who has dropped by. Just before Christmas, as Mole and Rat are returning from an outing, they pass near Mole's old hole, and he is
overcome by homesickness. Rat understandingly
agrees to hunt for the entrance, helps brush
dust off the furniture, builds up the fire,
sends caroling field mice out for more provi-
sions, and they have a happy holiday party. In
an unusual, haunting episode, the two have been
out all night hunting for Otter's lost baby when
they hear beautiful music and on an island in
the river, just at dawn, come upon the god Pan
playing his pipes and protecting the little
otter. In the fall, Mole saves Rat from falling
under the charm of a wayfaring sea rat who
almost entices him away from the river. The two
stories come together again when Toad appears
dripping and bedraggled in his washerwoman
clothes at Rat's door. There Rat interrupts his
boastful recounting of his adventures to tell
him that Toad Hall has been taken over by
Stoats and Weasels. His loyal friends, Rat,
Mole, and Badger, work out a scheme to enter
Toad Hall through a tunnel known only to Badger
and surprise the weasels at their banquet. The
sudden attack routs the much more numerous Wild
Wooders, and Toad Hall is regained. The book is
often cited as the last of the Golden Age of
Children's Literature, and has been much loved
for many decades. Although the characters retain
some of their animal eccentricities, they are
much more like humans, with the independence
and companionship of an old-style men's club.
The language, both in vocabulary and syntax, is
difficult, but despite this the style is lucid
and can be understood by even young children.

Books Too Good; Children's Classics; ChLA Touchstones; Choice; Lewis Carroll.

THE WIND ON THE MOON: A STORY FOR CHILDREN (Linklater*, Eric, ill. Nicholas Bentley, Macmillan, 1944; Macmillan, 1944), fantasy set in the English village of Midmeddlecum in the mid-twentieth century. While their father, Major Palfrey, is packing for a year's absence, Dinah and Dorinda talk about trying to be good while he is gone, but they decide that, since their good intentions are so often misunderstood, they might just as well set out to be naughty and enjoy it. Besides, their father has noticed a wind on the moon, which will blow into their hearts and make them behave badly for a long time. They start out overeating until they resemble balloons, to the despair of their ineffectual mother, who is easily upset, and their humorless governess, Miss Serendip, who is a storehouse of irrelevant facts. When the village children stick pins in them, they start to cry and refuse to eat until they become thin as sticks and, with their red noses, are mistaken for matches. Dinah consults Mrs. Grimble, a witch who lives in the nearby Forest of Weal, about how to get revenge. She gives them a magic draught that will turn them into whatever they wish. Because they realize that they will need pockets, they choose to be kangaroos. They briefly terrorize the village but by accident end up in Sir Lankester Lemon's zoo. There they help the giraffe, who used to be a detective named Mr. Parker, solve the mystery of the disappearing egg of Lady Lil and Sir Bobadil, the ostrich couple. Then, with the help of a Silver Falcon who searches and finds the rest of the magic draught that makes them into children again, they rescue the Golden Puma from captivity and return home to find their mother has been too preoccupied with worry over Major Palfrey to miss them. Then they turn their attention to rescuing their dancing teacher, Mr. Casimir Corvo, from prison where, as one of a jury that has refused to bring the guilty verdict the judge wishes, has been incarcerated for an indefinite time. By hiding dead rats and other smelly objects in his house, they persuade Mr. Justice Rumple that his mind is giving off an unpleasant odor because it has not been changed recently, and he decides to let the jury go. When the girls intercept a letter from their father saying he is in a dungeon in the Castle of Gliedermannheim in Bombardy, they decide that with their experience in engineering escapes they must go to save him. Mr. Corvo arranges that a friend who is selling furniture to the tyrant of Bombardy, Count Hulagu Bloot, will smuggle them into the country in his furniture van. The Golden Puma and Mr. Corvo accompany them, and the falcon flies over the van. In a complicated set of adventures they rescue their father and destroy Count Bloot, but the puma is unfortunately killed in the operation. In their escape they are aided by Mr. Stevens and Notchy Knight, sappers from the Royal Engineers, who are still tunnelling from the Crimean War. When they get home, they discover that Mrs. Grimble has moved from the Forest of Weal but has left them a cuckoo clock. The two girls are almost indistinguishable, although Dinah is two years older than Dorinda, and other characters are caricatures. The whole story has a feel of having been made up as it goes along, with only a tenuous connection between the various adventures and no principle controlling the fantasy. There are many surprising and clever bits of nonsense and a sort of free imaginative charm, but no consistency. Carnegie Winner.

WINDRUFF OF LINKS TOR (Chipperfield*, Joseph E., ill. Helen Torrey, Hutchinson, 1954; Longman, 1951), realistic animal novel set among the tors (mountains) and moors of Dartmoor at an unspecified time but probably in the early twentieth century. When Dartymore Jack, an aged peddler of the moors, remarks to a gypsy that he has seen a fox family on Great Links Tor, he sets in motion a chain of events that affect the human and animal life of the entire region. The gypsy and his friend find and steal the five cubs of the vixen, Redbrush, hoping to sell them at Tavistock Fair. After the loss of her young, Redbrush's frustrated maternal instincts move her to lure a sandy-colored Alsatian puppy away from the Newsome farm nearby. Under her care and instruction, Windruff grows big, strong, and forceful, a match for any wild creature in the

area and a very canny hunter. When a crossbred,
gone-wild mastiff attacks Tawny, one of the wild
Dartmoor ponies, Windruff drives the creature
away. The conflict is observed by Dartymoor
Jack, who carries the information about Windruff
to the Newsomes, and by the gypsies, who plan to
capture the animals. They catch the mastiff,
abusing him cruelly, but, while they are
attempting to use him as bait to capture
Windruff, too, the animal turns on them and
escapes, crippling one of the gypsies. The other
gypsy vows to shoot both dogs in revenge. Young
Tom Newsome, a student at an Agricultural
College who is a naturalist and the nephew of
Windruff's former owner, and Dartymore Jack set
out to capture Windruff before the gypsy harms
him. Most of the rest of the book describes
their efforts to locate the dog and win his
confidence. The vixen acquires a new mate,
Greymask, after Windruff matures, and drops out
of the story. Her departure from their lair and
his recognition that the mastiff has been
cruelly used and needs companionship cause
Windruff to accept the dog, and the two become a
hunting pair. Tom and Dartymore Jack camp on the
moor by Rattle Creek to observe the dogs and
attempt to win over Windruff. After the mastiff
dies of some mysterious animal malady, Windruff
appears to sense that he must ease his
loneliness with human companionship. After Tom
fights off the gypsy, Tom and Jack know it is
only a matter of time before the dog accepts
Tom. It is the friendly advances of Willum,
Dartymore Jack's dog, however, that bring the
wild dog back to civilization. The two animals
soon gambol about the moor, and, when Tom and
Jack break camp to return to the farm, Windruff
follows them and before long becomes Tom's
special friend and loving companion. The author
early invokes the reader's sympathy for Windruff
and his fellow creatures of moor and tor by the
very detailed descriptions of life among the
birds and animals there; this is the book's
strongest quality. Life in the wild is presented
as rational and good compared with the behavior
of the gypsies, whose motives are presented as
utterly irrational--as almost a mindless evil.
The animals are anthropomorphized only to the
extent that the author attributes to them

thoughts, feelings, motives, and logical reasoning processes. The diction is rich with images and striking turns of phrase and is demanding, but is made accssible by the suspense of the carefully crafted plot, which only occasionally lapses into melodrama and didacticism. Fanfare.

WINNIE-THE-POOH (Milne*, A. A., ill. Ernest Shepard, Methuen, 1926; Dutton, 1926), whimsical episodic fantasy of Christopher* Robin and his friends based on stuffed toys, all living in the forest which surrounds the Hundred Acre Wood. Framed by conversations between the author and Christopher Robin, the ten episodes are presumably stories told by the father to his young son and his son's teddy bear. Pooh* (also called Winnie-the-Pooh), a Bear of Very Little Brain, has gentle adventures with his friend Piglet* and their neighbors, pedantic Owl, officious Rabbit, maternal Kanga and her baby Roo, and gloomy Eeyore*, the old grey donkey. In the first story, Pooh tries to get honey from a bee tree by hanging onto a balloon, pretending to be a cloud, and is rescued by Christopher Robin who shoots the balloon with his pop-gun. In others, Pooh goes visiting Rabbit, eats too much, and gets stuck in the hole where he has to wait for a week (with Christopher Robin reading a Sustaining Book at his North end, while Rabbit hangs his washing on his South end) until he is thin enough to be pulled out; he and Piglet hunt a Woozle, following the ever increasing number of tracks around and around a spinney and getting more and more worried until Christopher Robin points out their mistake; they dig a trap for a Heffalump, bait it with a jar of honey, and Pooh, remembering the honey in the night, gets his head stuck in the jar and terrifies Piglet; they suffer a flood, in which Piglet is cut off from the others by rising water and is rescued by Pooh and Christopher Robin riding in an upturned umbrella. Two episodes feature pessimistic Eeyore: in one, he loses his tail, and Pooh finds it being used as a bell pull by Owl; in the other, Eeyore has a birthday, for which Pooh gives him a jar, at first holding honey but empty by the time it is presented, and Piglet gives him a balloon, which he falls on and bursts before he reaches Eeyore, but the donkey is perfectly happy with a Useful Pot and Something to put in it. In one adventure, Rabbit has a plan to drive the newcomers, Kanga and Roo, from the forest by kidnapping Roo and substituting Piglet, who is about the same size, a plan that backfires when Kanga pretends she does not notice the deception and gives Piglet a bath and Roo's medicine and that ends happily when Rabbit becomes fond of little Roo. All the animals, including Rabbit's many friends-and-relations, are led by Christopher Robin on an "Expotition" to discover the North Pole, and Roo falls into the stream and is rescued when Pooh holds a pole across the water below him, on which he crawls out. Christopher Robin pronounces Pooh's find as the North Pole. In the last chapter Christopher Robin gives a party in honor of Pooh for rescuing Piglet from the flood and presents him with a pencil box just like his own. The mild adventures are made interesting by the clever style, which is understandable to toddlers just past the picture-book stage but has subtle, tongue-in-cheek humor to appeal to adults. The well-defined characters and the Shepard illustrations have helped make these stories twentieth-century classics for children. The sequel is *The House at Pooh Corner**. Books Too Good; Children's Classics; ChLA Touchstones; Choice; Lewis Carroll.

WINTER CARLISLE (*The Changeover: A Supernatural Romance**), grandmother of Sorry* and mother of Miryam*, she helps with the ritual that makes Laura* Chant a witch. She, Sorry, and Miryam constitute the trio of witches that live in a old mansion now surrounded by shopping centers and housing developments. The three contribute most of the novel's Gothic elements. Winter and Miryam are not well developed as individuals.

THE WINTER OF THE BIRDS (Cresswell*, Helen, Faber, 1975; Macmillan, 1976), realistic novel of family and community life with suspense-story aspects set recently in England from the beginning of November to New Year's. Young Edward Flack, age unspecified, aspires to be a hero. As the story unfolds, Edward learns something about what heroism really means, gains

some friends, and loses some enemies. He lives
in the town of Haunton on St. Savior's Street
with his foster parents, Lily*, who keeps a
grocery and complains a lot, and Denis, who
drives a bus and tries to keep peace in the
household and shop. Edward forces himself to
attempt brave deeds, among them waving one
night at Mr.* Rudge, a recluse who is viewed
with suspicion and shunned by everyone on the
street and whose house overlooks the street and
the old church, which is to be razed to make way
for a supermarket. Edward becomes acquainted
with Mr. Rudge, who shares with Edward his
intense misgivings about terrible steel birds he
says flit across the electric cables, kill the
real birds, and threaten the area. Then Patrick
Finn*, a big, articulate, managing Irishman,
arrives in St. Savior's with middle-aged
Alfred* Graves, Lily's accountant brother, whom
Finn has rescued from attempted suicide in
Liverpool harbor. Dressed flamboyantly, the two
drive up in an old taxi, shocking Lily and
setting tongues wagging. When Finn boldly
prevents the local bullies, the McKay brothers,
from setting Mr. Rudge's house afire on Guy
Fawkes Bonfire Night, Edward accepts Finn as the
embodiment of the heroes he's read about. Finn
takes on Mr. Rudge's cause and gradually enlists
the aid of the entire street in combatting the
steel birds. He, Alfie, and Edward raise pigeons
to replace the birds that are dying, ostensibly
because of the steel birds but probably because
the McKays are killing them, inspire Lily to
raise pigeons, and then even Mrs. Mckay, who
also begins to keep tabs on her hoodlum sons.
The story culminates with Finn staging a grand
New Year's Eve party to which the entire street
contributes. Although Mr. Rudge dies as the New
Year dawns, his vision of terror and hope for
salvation has resulted in uniting the residents
in a common cause and has forged new bonds of
friendship. Edward has gained greater respect
and affection for his mother, has come to
appreciate his father's great reservoir of
fortitude and to accept his lack of imagination,
and concludes that true heroism lies in doing
what one has to do even if everyone is against
it, as Mr. Rudge and Finn have done. After a
gripping beginning, the book loses focus and

intensity. The reader doubts the reality of the birds as interest shifts to the examination of heroism and the question of Finn's identity, which is never answered. Edward engages the attention, if not always the sympathy of the reader, and the youth's melodramatic reactions seem appropriate for a bookish adolescent. The book's unusual structure contributes to its diffuse effect. Part of it is in third-person omniscient, part in first person related by Mr. Rudge, and part in a "chronicle" written by Edward and commencing with "I lift up my hand...." Tone and style change with point of view. Fanfare.

WISEMAN, DAVID (1916-   ), born in Manchester; teacher, novelist. He attended Manchester Grammar School and received his B.A. in history from Victoria University of Manchester. During World War II, he served in Basutoland, Bechuanal, Egypt, and Germany; he then worked in adult education and edited *The Journal of Adult Education*. From 1952 to 1975 he was teacher and principal of high schools in Worcestershire, Yorkshire, and Cornwall, and in 1978 he became a full-time writer. Several of his novels for young people, while highly individual, follow the fantasy pattern of a child from this time coming into contact with a person or people from a past era. In *The Fate of Jeremy Visick** (Kestrel, 1982; as *Jeremy Visick*, Houghton, 1981), set in Cornwall, a present-day boy follows a miner boy from the past into the mine and stays with him during the cave-in, only to realize when he returns to this period that he has discovered the bones of long-dead Jeremy Visick. *Thimbles* (Kestrel, 1983; Houghton, 1982), which concerns a 1819 demonstration of Manchester mill-workers, has something of the same pattern of action switching from present to past. In *Blodwen and the Guardians* (Houghton, 1983), humans interested in protecting the environment from highway builders become allied with the Guardians of tombs of ancient chieftains. *Adam's Common* (Blackie, 1987; Houghton, 1984) also has an environmental theme, with an American girl who is attempting to preserve a piece of land getting vital information from a boy of the nineteenth century. Wiseman makes his home in Yorkshire.

THE WITCHES (Dahl*, Roald, ill. Quentin Blake, Cape, 1983; Farrar, 1983), humorous fantasy about witches and witchcraft set about the time the book was written. After his parents are killed in an auto accident, the narrator, a little boy, lives with his mother's mother in her native Norway and then in his native England. "Tremendously old and wrinkled, with a massive wide body which was smothered in gray lace," she smokes big, smelly cigars, lacks one thumb, and thumps about the house with a gold-topped cane. She tells wonderful stories, especially about witches, which the boy says are "*gospel* truth." Grandmamma informs the boy that witches exist all over the world, that they devote themselves primarily to causing children to disappear, and that, though they try to look like ordinary women, they can be recognized by certain signs. They wear gloves and wigs, because they are bald, and have large nose holes, queer eyes, bluish teeth, and no toes. She says every country has a Secret Society of Witches, and the ruler of them all is an all-powerful, unmerciful, extremely wealthy Grand High Witch, who travels from country to country lecturing to and organizing the local societies in their awful work. The boy meets his first witch shortly after they return to England, an ugly, raspy-voiced woman who offers him a snake while he's up in a tree building a tree house. Far more fateful is his next encounter, which occurs while he and Grandmamma are vacationing for her health at the luxurious seaside Hotel Magnificent at Bournemouth. Needing a secluded spot in which to train his two white mice, William and Mary, the boy thinks himself lucky to find a screened corner in a lecture hall reserved for the Royal Society for the Prevention of Cruelty to Children, only to discover soon to his horror that he has blundered upon a meeting of the English branch of witches. The Grand High Witch, whose face looks like it has been pickled in vinegar and who speaks with a heavy Russian accent, harangues the witches and orders them to get "rrrid of every single child in the whole of Inkland" in one year's time. They will do this by buying up all the sweet shops in the country and filling every sweet with her special Formula* 86 Delayed-Action Mouse-Maker. It will turn all the children who eat sweets to mice the day after ingestion, whereupon their school-teachers will trap and kill them. She demonstrates the formula's potency on an obnoxious brat called Bruno Jenkins, changing him into a small brown mouse. Then one of the witches, Mildred, scents the boy (boys smell like dog-droppings to witches). He is discovered and dragged out from behind the screen, and a whole bottle of elixir poured down his throat. Though now shrunken to mouse size, four-legged, and furry-coated, the boy still has his own mind and voice. A sort of mouse-person now, he musters his resources, collects Bruno, and makes his precarious way to Grandmamma's room, where he gets the idea of stealing a bottle of elixir and mixing it with the witches' food at their banquet that night. With considerable difficulty and danger, he manages to get the stuff from the Grand High Witch's room, and during dinner he bravely scurries from Grandmamma's table across the dining room to the kitchen, swings by his tail to a shelf above the tureen containing the witches' soup, dumps the mixture in, but then is spotted practicing trapeze stunts. He gets part of his tail chopped off, jumps down to the floor, runs up one of the cook's trouser legs and down the other, and thus makes his escape, leaving the kitchen in pandemonium. Back in the dining room with Grandmamma, the boy watches as the witches, who have received massive overdoses of their mouse-making formula, shriek and scream as they shrink rapidly to mouse size and are mashed and bashed to death. Grandmamma and the boy return to Norway and settle into her house, which is remodeled for his convenience. The boy remains pleased with his new existence because it "doesn't matter who you are or what you look like so long as somebody loves you." He is also pleased because now he and Grandmamma have about the same life expectancy. The two decide to spend the rest of their lives rooting out and exterminating witches with elixir and cats, starting with those in the Grand High Witch's castle, which Grandmamma has discovered stands on a mountain in Norway. Though it starts slowly

and the author's efforts to be funny sometimes
become tedious, the book is filled with action,
grotesquerie, and humor. Its strength lies in
its clear depiction of the witches' ways and
intentions and in its carefully controlled
hyperbolic silliness. Situations and characters
are effectively distorted, and the whole is
supported by many imaginative details. The
result is the slapstick, occasionally coarse
brand of humor that appeals in particular to the
upper elementary grades. For example, children
shouldn't take baths because, if they don't, the
stink will mask their normal dog-droppings'
smell, the extermination of the witches is
called "getting fried," and Bruno often suffers
"wind" from overeating to the extent that he
sounds like a "brass band." Grandmamma is
lively, resourceful, and consistently interesting and understanding, just the kind of
grandparent any child would appreciate, and
Bruno Jenkins remains greedy and disagreeable to
the end, no better as a mouse than he was as a
boy. The boy is sturdy, philosophical, and
likeable, and having him remain a mouse and
utilize his enchantment to make the world better
is an inventive twist. Whitbread.

THE WITCH'S BRAT (Sutcliff*, Rosemary, ill.
Robert Micklewright, Oxford, 1970; ill. Richard
Lebenson, Walck, 1970), historical novel of the
starting of the hospital at the Church of Saint
Bartholomew the Great in Smithfield, London, in
the early twelfth century. Orphan Lovel, 11,
whose mother died at his birth, lives in a West
Sussex village with his grandmother, an old
woman much skilled in herb-lore and healing.
After the grandmother's death, however, the
village people turn on Lovel, taking out on him
the fear they had of her "witchcraft," which is
intensified because he is deformed, with a
hunched shoulder and a twisted leg. Driven out,
he wanders along the Downs until he collapses at
the door of a swineherd's hut. The man gives him
food and, when he is feverish the next morning,
carries him to the monastery known as the New
Minster, outside the walls of the royal city of
Winchester. There he is cared for by kindly
Brother Peter and the infirmarer, cynical Brother Eustace, and overhears the latter saying that

he is not to be sent back to his overlord's
manor, as the law requires, because he is "as
good as useless, after all," and the lord
doesn't want him back. He stays on at the
minster as a sort of general servant for two
years, the only important event during that time
being that he meets Rahere*, the King's
Jongleur, who has stopped for a night. Rahere is
kind to the boy and hints that someday he might
come back and "whistle for him" to come away.
Then one day, seeing a book of physic herbs open
in the monastery library, he starts telling
Brother Anselm the Precentor what he knows of
the plants pictured there and their uses. The
old man realizes how much knowledge the boy has,
teaches him to read, and insists that Brother
Eustace place him with Brother John in the
physic garden. Gradually he is given the lesser
jobs in the infirmary. When a haycart runs over
the stable dog, Valiant, Lovel sets its leg
successfully and is accepted as a regular helper
by Brother Eustace. When he is eighteen, at the
suggestion of the Abbot, he becomes a Benedictine novice. Later that year old Brother Anselm
becomes ill, and Lovel tends him devotedly. It
is then that Rahere returns, now an Austin
canon, and tells Lovel of his plan to start a
hospital for the poor. He also confides in the
boy the vision he has had of Saint Bartholomew
telling him to build the hospital at Smithfield,
just outside the London Walls, and to get the
land from King Henry by building a priory,
because "the king is mean, but devout." Rahere
asks Lovel to go with him, but he reluctantly
refuses, since Brother Anselm is not happy with
any other person tending him. Before the time
for Lovel to take his final vows, the Abbot
tells him that Rahere has sent word, again
requesting to have the boy join him, and this
time Lovel is free to go, Brother Anselm having
died a few days after Rahere's last visit. With
some terror, Lovel again faces the world outside
the monastery and makes his way to London, where
he finds the church started and the hospital
already well along. He immediately starts work
on the herb garden and soon has patients from
among the old and the poor of the area. He takes
his vows as an Austin canon and is very busy in
the infirmary, but when a laborer with an

injured shoulder refuses his services because of
his own hunched shoulder, he begins to doubt his
skill. Not long after that he meets a boy named
Nick Redpoll acting as scullion for the stoneworkers. Nick walks with a crutch, and in talking with him Lovel discovers that he was a
stonemason's apprentice but was injured in a
fall. After examining his leg, Lovel believes he
can make it straight again, and the treatment,
though long and painful, works. During his
recovery, Nick carves a beautiful pair of
candlesticks in the shape of angels. Taking one
to prove that the boy has skill, Lovel persuades
the master mason to give him a chance to learn
the trade. On the day the church is consecrated,
Nick confesses to Lovel that he could not have
stood the pain of his treatment if he had not
had Lovel, with his own twisted leg and hump
back, as an example of courage. An author's note
at the end says that one of the miracles
credited to Saint Bartholomew's Priory is the
instant healing of the stiff leg of a boy named
Nicholas. The novel gives a good picture for
middle-grade readers of life in the monasteries
of the period and keeps a quiet interest alive
in Lovel and his connection with Rahere. The
plot, however, lacks the tension of Sutcliff's
stronger historical novels and the setting does
not have the compelling immediacy of her works
for an older audience. Lewis Carroll.

THE WITCH'S DAUGHTER (Bawden*, Nina, ill.
Shirley Hughes, Gollancz, 1966; Lippincott,
1966), mystery novel set on the Scottish island
of Skua in contemporary times. Perdita*, ten and
a half, the orphan daughter of a foreign woman
believed to be a witch, has been raised by Annie
MacLaren at isolated Luinpool, a dilapidated
house rented by a reclusive character named Mr.
Smith. Shunned by the village children, Perdita
approaches Janey* Hoggart, 9, blind daughter of
a visiting botanist, and later makes friends
with Janey's brother, Tim, 12. Also at the hotel
where the Hoggarts stay is a Mr. Jones, who has
suspiciously arrived with a golf bag to vacation
on the island which has no golf course. When
Tim, exploring Carlin's Cave, finds a stone he
thinks is a ruby, Mr. Smith expresses a strong
interest, and that evening their father is

injured in a fall in Janey's room and must be taken to the mainland hospital. Left in the care of the hotel-keeper's wife, Mrs. Tarbutt, Janey insists there was a man in her room, but the adults do not believe her. When Perdita, who cannot read, shows the children a newspaper picture of Mr. Smith connecting him with a jewel theft and shows them a diamond Mr. Jones has given her, they decide to explore Carlin's Cave for evidence. There Mr. Jones and a local, Will Campbell, lead them far into the cave, then abandon them, taking the lights with them. Janey, confident in the dark, leads them out, and while she and Tim go back to the inn to give the alarm, Perdita goes to Luinpool to warn Mr. Smith. In the storm that follows, Smith's boat is wrecked in sight of the town. Picnicking in Carlin's Cave a little later, Janey discovers a bag of jewels in an old sheep's skull. Perdita, too desperately shy to picnic with them or to say goodbye, comes at the last minute to the boat and thrusts flowers she has picked into Tim's hands. The interest in the story lies in its strong characterization rather than in its rather implausible plot. Perdita and Janey, particularly, are memorable, and the setting, with its bare crags and sudden storms, is more than a backdrop. Choice.

WIZARD WATCHER (*Which Witch?**), the big, lumbering monster created by the wizard Arriman to wait by the main gate of Darkington Hall, watch for the new wizard, and announce his arrival. The Wizard Watcher has a sea lion's shape, four feet, and a tail. It has three heads with keen, expressive eyes set on short stalks. It is a gentle, useful monster, whose three heads converse with one another or other characters in an amusing combination of high diction and contemporary slang. It is the first to recognize that Terence* Mugg is the promised wizard. This happens late in the story, when, although he has been around the place for a while, Terence ironically comes up the front drive for the first time. If Terence had entered by the front way earlier, most of the plot complications would never have occurred. The Wizard Watcher is an interesting concept that adds humor as well as contributing to plot.

WOLFF, KURT (*The Silver Sword**), Bavarian farmer
who, with his wife, gives refuge to the Balicki
children, Ruth*, Edek*, and Bronia*, and their
companion, Jan*, while the children are on their
way to Switzerland to seek the Balicki parents
at the end of World War II. He finds they have
spent the night in his haybarn and routs them
out with a pitchfork, and then listens sympathetically to their story. A kind and decent
man, he good-naturedly but firmly says they must
work for their board and room. He is mainly
instrumental in keeping the Burgomaster of the
area from sending the children back to Poland
by providing them with canoes and food and
sending them down the Falken River toward Lake
Constance. One of the book's most memorable
characters, he shows that good people can be
found even among the enemy.

WOLF OF BADENOCH: DOG OF THE GRAMPIAN HILLS
(Chipperfield*, Joseph E., ill. C. Gifford
Ambler, Hutchinson, 1958; Longman, 1959),
realistic animal novel set among the hills,
lochs, and forests of the Scottish Highlands at
an indefinite time but probably in the 1920s or
1930s. Wise, reclusive, aging John Mackenzie, a
Badenoch shepherd, realizes sadly that Laddie,
his faithful companion and herd dog of many
years, is getting too old for his tasks. Ernest
Robbie Craig, 16, who often visits John in his
lonely cottage on the mountain to listen to his
stories and to learn about herding sheep,
encourages John to add a younger dog to his
household before Laddie dies. At the Perth Sheep
Sale, John buys a nondescript, powerfully built
Alsatian puppy to which Robbie has called his
attention. Both John and Robbie soon love lively
and promising little Wolf, and before long, with
Laddie's help, John has trained him into a fine
sheep dog. A neighboring shepherd, dour,
sharp-tongued, pugnacious Duncan MacQueen, takes
a dislike to Wolf. He recognizes that Wolf is
much more skillful at herding than his own dog,
Bruce, whom he has not taken the pains to train
properly. MacQueen grows jealous of John and
often ridicules Wolf, disparaging his appearance
and breeding. When Wolf is about a year old,
Bruce initiaties a hostile encounter which the
two men break up and which leaves MacQueen even

more angry and resentful. Hostility builds between the two men and between their dogs as well. Once Bruce incites a pack of dogs to attack Wolf. Although Robbie's father witnesses the attack and refutes the allegation, MacQueen insists the fault was Wolf's. After Laddie dies, John relies even more heavily on Wolf, now full-grown, steady, and smart. When it is discovered that sheep are being mysteriously harried, savaged, and even slain, John and Robbie suspect that Bruce has gone bad, and even MacQueen has such suspicions. Adamantly refusing to admit the possibility, however, he calls a meeting of shepherds in which he viciously puts the blame for the maraudings on Mackenzie and Wolf. During a heavy, late-winter snowstorm, John suffers a heart attack while on the mountain. Wolf guards his master's body, howling the while to summon help. During the search for John, Bruce slips away from MacQueen and attacks the Mackenzie sheep. First on the scene, MacQueen distorts the facts, claiming Bruce attacked Wolf to keep Wolf from savaging his own flocks. MacQueen persists in defending Bruce, even though he knows now his dog is guilty, until Robbie, fearing for Wolf's life and with his father's encouragement, flees with Wolf, intending to hide in a cave on the mountainside until Wolf can be proved innocent. During a fierce blizzard, Robbie sustains a head injury, and once again Wolf summons help. By the time Robbie recovers, Wolf has been exonerated of guilt and proclaimed a hero. While the clear and detailed descriptions of terrain, weather, and animal life contribute to conflict, setting, and characterizations, they tend to slow up the story. Characters are one-dimensional, the plot is clumsy, cliched, and repetitive, and there are lapses into sentimentality. Details about training the dogs and herding the sheep and Scots dialect and terms create a sense of history, tradition, locale, and the passage of time. Fanfare.

THE WOLVES OF WILLOUGHBY CHASE (Aiken*, Joan, ill. Pat Marriott, Cape, 1962; Doubleday, 1963), humorous melodrama with fantasy aspects that pretends to be a historical fiction set in England during the reign of "Good King James III

in 1832," that is, "in a period of English
history that never happened." Ravenous wolves,
driven from the continent of Europe by hunger,
roam the landscape around the large and
comfortable country estate known as Willoughby
Chase. Unknown to its residents, the mansion is
soon to fall prey to human wolves who scheme to
devour its resources. Before he and his wife
leave for a trip abroad for her health, Sir
Willoughy Green, master of the house, engages a
relative from London to serve as administrator
of the estate and governess for his daughter,
lively Bonnie, about ten, and her cousin of the
same age, timid orphan Sylvia, little suspecting
that his trust is sorely misplaced. The two
girls find Miss Letitia Slighcarp cold and
forbidding from the start. As soon as the
parents leave, Miss Slighcarp discharges
servants, keeping on only a handful, among whom
are James the footman and Pattern the maid, who
pretend to be her lackeys in order to protect
the girls. Miss Slighcarp helps herself to Mrs.
Green's clothes, sells the children's toys and
other estate property, and otherwise assumes the
prerogatives of proprietorship. She is aided in
this by her accomplice, Mr. Josiah Grimshaw, who
ironically arrived on the same train as Sylvia,
stabbed to death a wolf who had leaped into
their compartment, thus saving her life, and was
subsequently brought to Willougby Chase to
recover his health. When Bonnie protests about
Miss Slighcarp's actions, she is locked in a
closet but then released secretly and cared for
by Sylvia, James, and Pattern. For weeks the
four communicate through a secret passage the
children discover. Bonnie writes a note to the
local physician asking for help, but Miss
Slighcarp intercepts it, informs the children
that Sir Willoughby's ship went down, announces
that she is now mistress of Willoughby Chase and
their guardian, and bundles them off to
Blastburn, a smoky, noisy factory city, where
she enrolls them in the dismal charity school
run by cruel Mrs. Brisket. The place is so
overcrowded with orphan girls that one half must
sleep by day and the other half by night. The
girls are fed on thin, gray porridge, are known
only by number, and are dressed in coarse
overalls. Bonnie and Sylvia are bullied by older

girls and must slave in the school laundry, which washes garments for half of Blastburn. After some weeks, the girls are discovered and helped to escape by Simon*, the gooseherd who lives in a cave near Willoughby Chase. Simon takes them in a donkey cart to a friendly blacksmith who lives near by, since Sylvia has fallen ill of overwork and malnutrition. When Sylvia is well enough to travel, he takes them by cart to London, an idyllic journey of two months, during which Simon sketches scenes that catch his eye, the girls teach him to read, and they all enjoy various pleasures the countryside offers. When they arrive in late April at Sylvia's Aunt Jane's boarding house, they discover her close to death from poor food and neglect. They confide in her physician, Dr. Field, and when Mr. Grimshaw is caught breaking into the boarding house, haul him off to the Willoughy lawyer, Mr. Gripe. The lawyer denounces him as a forger, and the nefarious scheme comes out. Grimshaw had provided Miss Slighcarp with the fake credentials with which she could convince Sir Willoughby that she was a relative. On the return to Willoughby Chase, they discover that Miss Slighcarp has joined with Mrs. Brisket to turn the place into a charity school. Then Sir Willoughby and his wife appear, having been carried after their shipwreck to the Canaries, during which adventure Mrs. Green's health is restored. Aunt Jane is summoned to come and open a school for the orphans on the other side of the estate park, and Sir Willoughby rewards Simon for his help by sending him to art school. The author sports merrily and adroitly with the conventions of the Victorian melodrama to produce a delightful romp that offers plenty of excitement and chuckles to sustain the interest from beginning to end. To have wolves so ravenous that they actually attack trains is a beautifully outrageous touch, the scenes in the charity school parody Dickens, and the name Blastburn is appropriate and memorable. The sequel is *Black Hearts in Battersea**. Others in the series. Choice; Contemporary Classics; Lewis Carroll.

THE WOOD TROLL (*When Jays Fly to Barbmo**), nickname for Per Knudsen, who was born Jacob Isaacs

and has lived in many places, finally ending as
a sort of hired man on the farm of Arne Nygaard
north of the Arctic Circle in Norway. A complex
man, he is alternately morose, drinking heavily
through the dark winters, and lively and interesting, revealing his wide knowledge of the languages and customs of many people. It is the
Wood Troll who finally tells Ingeborg* the story
of her mother after her father is killed and who
teaches her the language of her mother's people,
the Lapps. Among his other skills he is an
expert wood-carver, and a jay he has made
becomes a talisman for Ingeborg, one of the few
things she saves when she has to leave her home.

THE WOOL-PACK (Harnett*, Cynthia, ill. author,
Methuen, 1951; *NICHOLAS AND THE WOOLPACK*, Putnam, 1953), historical novel dealing with the
wool trade in the English Cotswolds in 1493.
Master* Thomas Fetterlock of Burford is a respected wool grower and merchant, whose large
and flourishing establishment markets through
the Staple*, the influential alliance of English
wool merchants. In need of cash, he borrows from
a Lombard banker, Master Antonio Bari, and later
at the Lombard's request, even though he knows
the Lombards are reputed to be unscrupulous
businessmen, goes surety for him with the Staple
that the Lombard will not export wool except as
specified by the Staple. At about the same time,
he betrothes his only son, Nicholas*, perhaps
fourteen, to Cicely* Bradshaw, 11, daughter of a
successful clothier, a match financially
advantageous to both houses. Cicely agrees with
Nicholas about the Lombards, that they are
untrustworthy and ruthless. Nicholas has
discovered that the Lombard and his secretary,
whom Nicholas has dubbed Toad Face, have been
seen in secret contact with Simon Leach, Master
Fetterlock's wool-packer. Then Giles*, the
Fetterlock chief shepherd, reports that
Fetterlock wool has been stolen and wool packs
bearded, that is, filled with refuse and covered
over with prime wool. Master Fetterlock and
Nicholas travel unsuccessfully to Southampton to
try to get to the bottom of things. While Cicely
and her mother are visiting the Fetterlocks, the
children and Hal*, Nicholas's loyal foster
brother and Giles's son, discover that Leach has

bales of Fetterlock wool stored in his own barn. At Cicely's suggestion, the three plant hen feathers in each·bale as identification. A map dropped by Master Antonio and found by Cicely bearing strange markings supports the children's conviction that Leach and the Lombards are smuggling prime Fetterlock wool out of England through the Isle of Wight, bypassing the Staple. Nicholas gets a message to his father, who is at Staple headquarters, and the culprits are apprehended making a shipment. The Fetterlock wool is identified by the feathers. Although most characters are stock, Nicholas, Cicely, and Nicholas's Uncle John (an adventurer who seeks the Indies, appears occasionally, and conveys information about the Lombards) are well-drawn, interesting figures. The overforeshadowed, uninspired plot moves unevenly to an abrupt conclusion that leaves the reader dangling. Even so, this is a rich, substantial novel, whose impact comes from the vivid picture it gives of the times, not only in the details of the wool trade, which are ample and engaging, but also in its colorful evocation of the daily life and thinking of the merchant class. Columbus's voyage is mentioned. (Mistress* Fetterlock) Carnegie Winner; Fanfare.

WRIGHTSON, PATRICIA (1921-   ), born in Lismore, New South Wales; hospital administrator, editor, leading novelist for preteen and teenaged readers. The daughter of a country solicitor, she attended state schools, the State Correspondence School for children in isolated areas, and St. Catherine's College in Queensland. For almost twenty years she held supervisory and management positions in hospitals (1946-1964) and for ten years she edited the Sydney *School Magazine* (1964-1975). She did not begin to write until after her two children were born, publishing her first novel, *The Crooked Snake* (Angus) in 1955. Twenty years and half a dozen novels later, she retired to give full time to her writing. Her books demand the involvement of the intellect as well as of the emotions. She has said that she deliberately chooses themes that lead to "mental exploration and a stretching of understanding." She has been preoccupied with the nature of reality and of ownership, employs and experiments with ideas and beings from indigenous folklore, and has a deep affinity for the land, subjects that recur and interlock in her books and are skillfully set in relief by humor and poignancy. Her ability to establish mood seemingly without artifice is outstanding. Her earlier books, like *The Crooked Snake* and *The Feather Star* (Hutchinson, 1962; Harcourt, 1963), are realistic novels of mild adventures and family and neighborhood life. *I Own the Racecourse!* (Hutchinson, 1968; as *A Racecourse for Andy*, Harcourt, 1968) is built around a retarded child's belief that he actually has bought the local race track. Her later books are fantasy, and of these the most compelling constitute a trilogy founded on Aborigine beliefs: *The Ice Is Coming* (Hutchinson, 1977; Atheneum, 1977), *The Dark Bright Water* (Hutchinson, 1979; Atheneum, 1979), and *Behind the Wind* (Hutchinson, 1981; as *Journey Behind the Wind*, Atheneum, 1981), and a separate novel, *A Little Fear**** (Hutchinson, 1983; Atheneum, 1983), her most honored book. About a stubborn old woman's struggles with an ancient, indigenous spirit for the right to live in her own small cottage, it received the Young Observer Teenage Fiction Award, won the *Boston Globe-Horn Book* Award, was commended for the Carnegie Medal, and was named to Fanfare by the editors of *Horn Book*. Almost all of her some dozen books have won or been nominated for awards of some kind, both in Australia and abroad, and in 1986 she received the international Hans Christian Andersen Award for the body of her work. Some of her other books are *An Older Kind of Magic* (Hutchinson, 1972; Harcourt, 1972) and *The Nargun and the Stars* (Hutchinson, 1973; Atheneum, 1974).

THE WRITING ON THE HEARTH (Harnett*, Cynthia, ill. Gareth Floyd, Metheun, 1971; Viking, 1973), historical novel in which almost all the figures except the protagonist and his family and friends were real, set mostly in and near the English village of Ewelme not far from London from 1439 to 1441, during the reign of Henry VI. For many weeks, Stephen Rudd, perhaps fifteen, has been living in suspense, after Dame* Alice, wife of the Earl* of Suffolk, whose hall distinguishes the village, asks him, a budding clerk, to copy out some papers for her and he erroneously also copies a politically compromising letter. The copy, which contains uncomplimentary remarks about Duchess Eleanor of Gloucester, wife of Duke Humphrey, the king's brother and the earl's political rival, mysteriously disappears, and Stephen is sure it has fallen into the hands of Roger Bolingbroke*, master of Oxford in service to Duchess Eleanor. His parents dead (his father died long ago in service to the earl in France) and no longer wanted in the house of his dead mother's second husband, Odo*, Stephen lodges for a while with a surly miller, Red* Jak, then is invited by Dame Alice to live at her hall, there to serve her chaplain, Master* Simon Brayles, who will also prepare the boy for possible entry into Oxford. Although conscience-stricken over the loss of the letter, which he keeps secret from his lady, Stephen diligently addresses himself to tasks about the hall and wins the respect of the earl for his virtuous attention to duty and his quick mind. State matters greatly affect Stephen's life. Since the earl has been advocating a scheme to make peace with France through using the captured Duc d'Orleans as intermediary, the family moves to their London house, taking Stephen and other intimate retainers with them. There Stephen enjoys the sights, mostly in the company of the rising young book-lover, William Caxton*, and further enhances himself in the eyes of his lord by circumspect behavior before the Lord Mayor. When plague threatens London and strikes the earl's household, the earl sends the family back to the country, where Stephen devotes himself zealously to his books for many weeks, and little of importance transpires. In late 1441, the earl's political star has risen and Duke Humphrey's has waned, peace with France seems imminent, and Duchess Eleanor and Roger Bolingbroke have been found guilty of treason and witchcraft. Stephen is summoned by the earl to London to be questioned about Meg*, an old woman rumored to be a witch, and her possible connection with Bolingbroke. Certain that Meg is not evil and grateful to her for many past favors, Stephen steals away to warn her, only to discover that she and her tiny cottage have been swallowed up by the pool beside her hovel (an incident based upon an actual, modern happening). Stephen learns shortly thereafter from his sister, Lys*, a nun once befriended by Meg, that Lys has been using the compromising letter as an innersole for her shoe, after she found it among the rushes in Meg's cottage, where Stephen evidently dropped it. The year 1441, a palindrome Stephen had seen Bolingbroke trace in the ashes of Meg's hearth two years earlier, has ironically proved crucial for them both. The book's end sees Stephen on his way to Oxford to study as a ward of the earl, while Bolingbroke has been sentenced to be hanged, drawn, and quartered. The cast of characters is large and too patly assembled for easy credibility. Though shallow, often cardboard, and mostly stock, they are clearly enough sketched so that there is no difficulty in keeping them straight. Stephen, if sympathetically drawn, serves mainly as a window to the times. Some characters seem appropriate to the plot, while others seem enlisted for the purpose of showing another facet of the period, for example, Gilles* the Outlaw and Doggett* the bedesman, though each has a part to play. The strength of this substantial, often exciting, ambitious novel lies in its generously detailed and clear picture of the times--views of life in hovel, hall, mill, nunnery, city, country, and Oxford, the superstitions, punishments, passages from hall to hall, stories of battles in France and, in particular, of Joan of Arc, the sense of the political complexities and intrigues, and cameo appearances of such important figures as the Duc d'Orleans and King Henry. The plot problem of the letter is slight but still strong enough to sustain interest, and the reader never doubts that Stephen will achieve his dream of attending Oxford, though that ambition is less on his mind most of the time than the letter. Political affairs are tangled and might be confusing to an American audience, but diagrams help somewhat in keeping the complex royal connections straight, and certainly politics must have seemed a mysterious and ticklish business to country lads in those days, so that part seems appropriate, too. A postscript adds much information of value for understanding the plot and times. (Barnabas*) Fanfare.

Y

YARL CORBIE (*A Stranger Came Ashore**), dour, inscrutable, reserved, almost sullen old Scottish schoolmaster, whom Robbie fears but consults for help in foiling Finn Learson. The schoolmaster is called Yarl Corbie, a nickname, by the people of the village, because he looks like a huge raven. He has a big, beaky nose, swarthy skin, and glittering black eyes, is thin and stooped, and always wears a black, tattered gown that flaps out from his shoulders like a raven's wings. He is reputed to have the powers of a wizard. After Robbie informs Yarl Corbie of his suspicions about Finn, the schoolmaster tells Robbie his life story. He says that years ago he lost his sweetheart to the Selkie man. By helping Robbie defeat Finn, he gains revenge for his lost love.

A YEAR AND A DAY (Mayne*, William, ill. Krystyna Turska, Hamilton, 1976; Dutton, 1976), short folkloric fantasy set on the Cornish coast. While their mother tends the grave of an older child in a cemetery near the sea, two little sisters, Becca (Rebecca) and Sara Polwarne, about four and five, explore. Sara discovers a strange, little, lost boy, about two years younger than they, sitting in a "grassy tangle like a nest." He has "dark hair and dark eyes and skin like milk." Since he is naked, the girls call him Adam after the Adam of Biblical story, and take him home, to "keep him like a finding." Adam seems sickly, pale and unused to

sun. He can barely walk, seems not to know how
to eat, and neither smiles nor frowns. When the
Rector coldly refuses to   accept him as a
foundling of St. Kirren's parish, Mother, Dad,
and the girls take him in. That night, the
shortest of the year, right in the middle of the
summer, the boy seems unusually restless and
cries like a sea gull. In the morning, Janey
Tregose, who is reputed to be a witch, tells the
Polwarnes that Adam is a fairy child, who will
be with them for a year and a day. Hoping to
find a home for him, since they are poor, Mother
carries the boy five miles to St. Cregan's
Foundling Hospital, where she and the girls have
misgivings about leaving him but do so anyway,
to recover him shortly on the return trip when
an orphan catches them up and informs them that
there is no room at St. Cregan's for one who
cries like a gull, is neither "Jew, nor Saracen,
nor Danish," and must be a bird- or elf-child.
When no one claims him, the boy is baptized Adam
and becomes an object of suspicion and curiosity
in the village. He eats little, and clothes slip
right off his body, but with the coming of fall,
he does grow stronger and learns some words. He
enjoys being with creatures in nature, can talk
to them and to the wind, hears sounds not
audible to others, and once gets spanked in
church because he imitates the bats. When a
Saracen boat puts in, Mother contacts the owner,
thinking he and his fat wife might have lost a
child, but they don't claim him either, and the
fat wife offers to buy Becca as a slave. During
the winter, Adam is quiet and inactive for the
most part. Janey says he is not "goodying," that
is, not thriving. She says that fairy folk
cannot "fatten this side of the ground" and that
only a milpreve (a magic stone made of knotted
snakes) can keep him from returning to his own
kind. The girls search in the cold sea, so cold
it makes them weep, and find one, which the
squire kindly helps them recover. Adam takes
immediately to the stone, which is warmed at the
fender, but not even that can keep him with the
Polwarnes. With the coming of spring, the hearth
fire is no longer kept, and Adam misses his warm
milpreve and even weeps for it. The girls take
him to bed at night to keep him warm, but he
grows steadily weaker and more disinterested in

life. Community attitudes have changed, however, and now neighbors bring gifts of tempting foods or curing herbs for him. The Saracens return to the village; they bring oranges and a large silver coin for the "holy child," and again offer to buy Becca. In summer, Adam prefers to sit in the garden, where he calls quietly like a gull or blackbird. The girls spend Midsummer Day with him, and the next morning he does not waken. They find him lying cold and still. Mother says he's dead, the girls say he's gone back to the fairies, and the family buries him with his milpreve. The girls feel the loss keenly, and they playact finding Adam and episodes of their life with him. Later, they return to the house one day to discover that they have a new baby brother, who in due time is christened Adam. This story of the power of unselfish love moves more like a literary tale than short story or novel. The visually descriptive style is rich with color and sensory words, figures of speech, and arresting language; the birth of the baby adds a sentimental note; the seaside setting is well depicted with wind, rocks, and birds; and there is some humor. The many folkloric elements, lack of a specific time, and the minimal characteri- zation necessary to depict the girls and parents as persevering and loving give the book the dreamy quality of legend. Fanfare.

YEHIMELEK (*The Whispering Mountain**), Tabut Elulaios Yehimelek, Architect, Engineer, and Hereditary Foreman of the Children of the Pit. He is · the very old leader of the small, dark, hairy, pale-skinned people who live inside Whispering Mountain and mine and work the gold there. His people were brought by force by the Romans 102 generations earlier as slaves because they were very skilled at their craft. The Children of the Pit long to return to their ancient homeland of Sa'ir and Taidon. They are dwindling and pining away, as are their camels, and they have become very small and thin. They are undernourished and ill, and Arabis* Dando nurses them. The Seljuk* of Rum has been searching for them, because they are his lost people, and makes arrangements to take them all home to the Kingdom of Rum, as their ancient homeland is now called.

YEMM, CHARLIE (*The City of Frozen Fire**), gro-
tesquely ugly, complex villain. Yemm, formerly a
schoolmaster, has joined his onetime pupil,
Captain* Vansittart Darkness, in a piratical sea
life aboard the *Ursula Howell*, which runs guns
for either or both sides in South American
revolutions. In league with Darkness, Yemm
pretends to be marooned on the island of
Natividad so that he will be picked up by the
Volcano and can ingratiate himself with the
treasure seekers. He genuinely admires Aunt
Tuppenny*, who pictures him in one of her
needlepoint chair covers. He knits a long red
and green scarf and teaches Latin to Tops and
the Quiveran princess Olwen*. When they are
captured, he saves them from the uncontrollable
temper of Darkness by thrashing them both,
schoolboy fashion. He lacks a moral sense but
follows a code of sorts and dies preventing
Darkness from molesting Tuppenny.

YOU NEVER KNEW HER AS I DID! (Hunter*, Mollie,
Hamilton, 1981; Harper, 1981), historical novel
set in 1567-1568, the year Mary, Queen of
Scots, is imprisoned in the island Castle of
Lochleven by rebellious nobles. Will Douglas,
bastard son of Sir William Douglas, receives
with deep sadness the news of Mary's beheading
in England. He looks back twenty years to his
sixteenth year and describes the royal intrigues
that surrounded the beautiful young queen. On
June 17, 1567, Mary is brought to the castle,
whose hereditary keeper is Sir William, to whom
Will is page. The large and powerful Douglas
family wishes Mary safely confined for reasons
of political expediency. They hope to force her
to abdicate in favor of her infant son, James
(later to become James VI of Scotland and James
I of England), whose regent will be Sir
William's half brother, James, Earl of Moray,
also half brother to Mary. Selfish, gossipy, and
ambitious for glory and money, Will agrees to
assist the scheme to free Mary which is promoted
by his half brother, George Douglas, captain of
the guard, who is in love with Mary. Will
sincerely likes the queen, who called him orphan
when others called him bastard, and he very much

longs for excitement. When Mary miscarries her
child by Bothwell, the nobles Ruthven and
Lindsay force her to sign a deed of abdication,
which her partisans assure her she has a moral
and legal right to reject since the signature
was gained under duress. When Moray, now the
regent and highly ambitious, refuses to support
Mary's request for release, George sets in
motion his plan to free her, with Will acting as
courier and spy. The plan fails, and George is
temporarily banished from the castle. Will
anticipates a dull winter but soon observes how
skillfully Mary creates a royal court in exile,
which provides diversion for all the Douglases.
She wins the affection and admiration, but not
the political loyalty, of the various Douglases:
Sir William, his mother, Lady* Margaret (the Old
Lady), and Ellen, Will's half sister about his
age, who becomes her lady-in-waiting, among
others. In addition to beauty, the tall,
red-golden-haired queen has a warm and winning
personality, is a good conversationalist, enjoys
having people about her, and has a knack for
inspiring good fellowship. Will says she creates
a Court of Dreams in her prisoner's quarters
where she spins a Web of Dreams that entices all
and that all enjoy. When the conspirators
realize that Moray plans to accuse the queen of
complicity in the murder of her previous
husband, Darnley, a second escape is planned,
one which Will plays a greater role in planning.
He arranges for Mary to impersonate the
laundress who comes regularly from the mainland.
This scheme fails, too, with the boatman
recognizing Mary, and Will is whipped and
banished from the castle. Alone and in despair
on Scart Island, he realizes that he, too, has
lost his heart to the queen. For a time he
lapses into drinking and gambling but then is
approached by George to help once again to free
the queen, for whom a promise of help has been
received from the powerful Earl of Argyll. Will
returns to the castle, ironically welcomed back
by Sir William, whose favorite he has always
been, and by William's seven sisters, called the
Porches from their tall and slender builds, and
quickly resumes his position as live wire of the
court, which this time is really playacting his
former role. This escape attempt hinges upon

Will's stealing the gate key, which he does when he serves Sir William's meal at Will's birthday celebration on May 2. Being Lord of Misrule for May Day gives Will the opportunity to make the necessary arrangements, and Mary and a lady-in-waiting in costumes prepared by Minny*, the castle laundress, walk out of the castle and are rowed to freedom by Will. Will's triumph is short-lived, however, since Argyll goes back on his support, the queen's forces are defeated by the rebellious nobles, and the queen flees for refuge to Elizabeth of England, who eventually has her beheaded as a political liability. The book concludes with Will weeping for the queen whom he has served as spymaster for twenty years, the queen whose sad lot and ironic fortunes he has devoted his life to elevating, the queen and woman about whom he asserts to the messenger of the bad news, "You never knew her as I did!" The author integrates smoothly the historical events and figures with Will's maturation from a conceited, posturing, dissembling, impudent adolescent with a passion for gambling to a young noble with a cause to which he is utterly devoted and thus makes likeable an earlier unsympathetic protagonist. The parade of characters is long, but most are drawn with bold strokes so the reader has no trouble recognizing them: Sir William, politically aware and ambitious, capable, generous and indulgent to his family; handsome George, called "pretty Geordie," astute, loyal, doggedly devoted to the queen he loves and believes wronged; Arnault, the pot-bellied, swarthy, merry-eyed French physician, thoroughly devoted to Mary, who informs Will of the political maneuverings that landed Mary in her predicament and who also serves as courier, among others. The female characters are particularly memorable: Lady Margaret Douglas (the Old Lady), the real power behind the Douglases; Minny, the laundress who seems unusually politically aware for her station in life and who appears to voice the author's feminist leanings in her statement that when a woman achieves high position, like Mary, men set out to bring her down by first casting aspersions on her morals, the method employed by Mary's antagonists; Ellen, who enjoys gossip as much as

Will and who grows to like the queen, but who carefully separates affection from family loyalty; and the book's centerpiece, the controversial Mary, presented as lovely and courageous, intelligent and witty, resourceful and kind, seen as a tragic and romantic heroine, not only by Will. The book shows much about castle life and the swirling tides of the politics of the day, with ambitious nobles readily cutting one another down for power and prestige. Especially vivid are the scenes in which Ruthven and Lindsay force the abdication and the May Day celebration with the nobles enjoying such games as Follow the Leader and Blind Man's Bluff. Not only is this a rich and substantial picture of a turbulent period but it is also a top-notch adventure story with never a dull moment. A genealogical table helps to keep the people straight. Fanfare.

YOUNG MARK: THE STORY OF A VENTURE (Almedingen*, E. M., ill. Victor G. Ambrus, Oxford, 1967; Farrar, 1968), biographical novel based upon the life of the author's great-great-grandfather, Mark Poltoratzky, who was born the son of a small landowner in the Ukraine in 1726, ran away from home, and rose, because of his beautiful singing voice, to be a favorite of the Empress Elizabeth, a member of the nobility and the founder of an important aristocratic family of Czarist Russia. The book tells of his two-year journey to St. Petersburg, a trip beset by dangers and hardships and ending in almost unbelievable good fortune. At about fifteen, Mark leaves Bielogorka, his father's manor, where he has been treated as inferior to the servants because he fears the horses, which are the main product of the steading. His immediate reason for flight is his impending betrothal to his godfather's niece, Nastia, whom he detests, but his decision has really been made earlier when he discovers he has a gorgeous voice, a gift that his father scorns and that could be developed locally only if he became a priest or monk, like his oldest brother, Mikhail. A boy he meets at a fair, a juggler and mime, encourages him and tells him that the man the Empress Elizabeth plans to marry, known as the Hetman, is from the Ukraine and is said to be helpful to his countrymen. He starts out with high hopes. At his first town, Mirgorod, he sings for a hawker at the fair, is cheated out of his share of the collection, fights, and is rescued by a cossack named Ilyich, who recognizes him and sends him on his way with directions to stop with a friend, the smith at Korenevo. He finds that town suffering from a plague that kills its horses and cattle, and the population turning to witchcraft, but the name of the smith, though he has died, paves his way with the priest, who takes him in. Trying to help by cleaning the pigsty, he drives a pitchfork into his foot and must stay on for more than a month. The long wait has eaten up much of the summer, and as he journeys north he is caught in a storm and nearly killed by a falling tree. Monks from Surazhy Abbey rescue him, then hold him virtually a prisoner, having investigated and discovered something of his background and knowing that by law his father will have to give a generous sum to the abbey if Mark becomes a novice. Father Hyacinth teaches him his letters and Father Iona the treasurer grills him and sets guards to watch him as he works. His rescuer is a jolly merchant named Kondraty Kolubin, who has been cheated by the monks and who helps Mark escape to get even with them. He travels happily with Kolubin's wagons for some time, but parts when they turn south and goes on to Moscow. There, by chance, he runs into Aunt Lusha, a market woman from the Ukraine, who takes him in for the rest of the winter, gets him jobs singing at weddings, and sees that he has good clothes and supplies as he starts toward St. Petersburg. His good luck is short-lived, however, as he is set upon by three bandits, stripped and given rags to wear, and is being held for ransom when his three captors attack a coach and are killed by the young nobles within. The nobles take Mark on to Tver, where the husband of Aunt Lusha's cousin arranges to send him on to St. Petersburg. There he gets a job cooking for a man with an erratic temper and saves enough to get some decent clothes. When he calls at the Hetman's house, however, a servant slams the door in his face. He still hopes to somehow meet the Hetman, but when his employer, annoyed by a burned dinner, rips up his clothes and throws him out penniless, he is completely discouraged. Nearly starving, he commits his first theft, three pasties, which in turn are stolen from him as he sleeps in the Summer Gardens. A roughly dressed man sees the theft, gives his breakfast to Mark, and listens to the exhausted boy's story. By remarkable coincidence, it turns out to be the Hetman on his morning walk. He takes Mark home and has him sing for a music master, and eventually for the Empress Elizabeth herself. A brief postscript, translated from Mark Poltoratzky's own record of his journey, tells of his subsequent rise in wealth and station. A biographical note preceding the novel tells how the manuscript came into the author's possession and gives some idea of how much is the author's invention. Without this, a reader might find the end too sudden and incredible. The best parts of the book seem to come from the original record, describing the variety of people and places the boy encounters and the customs and social stratification of the period. Boston Globe Honor; Choice; Fanfare.

Z

ZACH WRENCH (*Good Night, Mr. Tom**), Zacharias, talkative, theatrical evacuee boy who becomes a close friend of William* Beech in the village of Little Weirwold. Having been raised in the theater by his entertainer parents, Zach has an adult and literary vocabulary and an uninhibited personality, and serves as an exact contrast and foil for timid, almost silent Willie. Zach's relationship with his parents is also a contrast, having been close and loving, and while he seems to the villagers cheeky and brash, he is shown to be vulnerable when he worries about his parents' safety. A natural leader, he organizes George Fletcher and the Thatcher twins, all older than he is, as well as William, who is slightly younger, into a group for adventures. After he is killed, William seems to feel Zach talking to him, encouraging him to ride the bike and to assert himself.

ZERO (*Ordinary Jack**), Jack Bagthorpe's hound dog, described by Mr.* Bagthorpe as "a great pudding-footed thing covered in fur." Convinced that his dog has an inferiority complex from the derogatory remarks constantly flung at him by the family, Jack sets out to teach Zero to fetch. He is sure that the ability will earn the dog praise and hence lift his spirits. In a hilarious scene, which Mr. Bagthorpe interprets as another Manifestation of Mysterious Behavior on Jack's part, Jack gets down on all fours to demonstrate retrieving for the dog. Zero

eventually catches on and several times carries
off Mr. Bagthorpe's recording equipment.

ZOE VARDOE (*The Watcher Bee**), daughter of Lucy*
Denham-Lucie and some mysterious stranger, whom
Lucy has hinted is of noble birth and whom she
met while bicycling alone through Sherwood
Forest on a moonlit night. Nineteen when they
return to the village, Zoe is beautiful and
sophisticated and is suffering from some
unexplained malady, rumored to be the result of
something she took to end an unwanted pregnancy.
She easily charms Kate* and Charlie*, who find
her a rare and exotic creature and far more
interesting than anyone from school or the
village. She tolerates Kate and toys with
Charlie, letting him think she returns some of
his passion, but the only time her aloofness
really disappears is when Charlie, not yet
fifteen and with no driver's license, takes his
father's car at night and they speed through
Sherwood with Zoe screaming to go faster. When
her engagement is announced to an older man from
Sheffield, whom everyone has assumed is her
mother's beau, they all feel sorry for the girl
being pressured into an unsuitable marriage
until Charlie's mother thinks over the arguments
she has overheard between Zoe and Lucy and
decides that the girl has deliberately stolen
her mother's lover to get control of his money.
Beneath her cool and almost distant manner, one
gets a picture of a young woman as hard as
nails.

INDEX

Names and titles in ALL CAPITAL LETTERS refer to the actual entries of the dictionary, and page numbers in *italics* refer to the location of the actual entries in the dictionary.

aardvark, 973
Aaron, 1381
abbesses, treacherous, 1018
Abbey Lubbers, Banshees, and Boggarts: A Who's Who of Fairies, 151
Abbey of Athenmore, 215-16
abbeys: Athenmore, 408; Benedictine, 155, 915-17
abbots, robbed by outlaws, 146
abdication, forced, 1412
Abel, 626
Abel Magwitch, 494
ABEL OAKES, *1*, 587
Abel the gardener, 1241
aborigines, Baffin Land, 733
abortions: 1135; self-induced, 1323
About the Sleeping Beauty, 1250
Abraham Dinsdale, 125, 477
Abuelita, 1366-67
Abyss of Ragnarok, 167, 1343
academies, mathematics, 1204. *See also* boarding schools
Academy for Young Ladies, 1160
Academy of Projectors, 512
accidents: airplane crash, 355; auto, 354, 696, 728, 889, 1034-35; bear carried off by tide, 85; bicycle, 202, 565; broken ankle, 286; broken arm, 838; broken collar bone, 964, 1192; broken hand, 75, 1004; broken knee, 409; broken leg, 258, 764, 1153, 1068, 1105, 1298, caused by wizard, 1338, in riding fall, 419; broken pelvis, 436; burial in collapsed house, 415-16; burned hand, 451; car-caravan, 1382; car into pond, 1383; caused by child, 124-25; caused by racketeer, 119; causes paralysis from fall during escape, 1063; chest crushed, 459; child dropped, 720; death of brother, 931; deliberately set up, 649; dog breaks leg, 1395; dog causes auto, 1219; drowning, 684; fall, 430, 1186, 1397, down cliff, 890, down precipice, 244, down rabbit hole, 19, 22, during fox hunt, 354, during horse jump, 1191-92, from bridge, 732, 789, 883, from cliff, 384, from high wire, 88, 205, 1248, from pony, 698, from school roof, 1270, from tree, 370, 1241, from window, 558-59, into chasm, 80, into estuary, 559, into fire, 198, into mountain fissure, 741, into orchestra, 1267-68; near fatal, 832, onto rocks, 584, over cliff, 624, through henhouse roof, 842, under barrow, 264; foot cut, 311; freak aboard ship, 1379; gored by bull, 1357; gun explodes, 717; hand severed, 236; horse riding, 226, 296; knotting, 262; mine, 34-36, 30, 624; motorcycle, 873; nearly hit by car, 645; pitchfork into foot, 1416; planned, 195; poaching, 604; raft run down by tanker, 401; resulting in paralysis, 1063; routine air take-off, 355; runaway team, 171; seven with cars, 1283; sprained

ankle, 243, 1018; squashed by elephant, 830; stagecoach, 1200; struck by bus, 249; struck by car, 329; struck by truck, 1342; swept away by river, 125; three car, 597; thrown from horse, 404, 1374, child, 423; traffic, 1218-19; toboggan, 907; truck, 205; truck chassis dropping on boy, 183; washed overboard, 649; wheelchair rolling into lake, 19; wound in native uprising, 347. *See also* disasters.
accomplices, unwilling, in crime, 728
According to Mark, 728
accountants, 16, 1390
Accra, 249-52, 698
accusations: false, 14, 622, 829; impassioned, 554; mistaken, 81; of arson, 615; of attempted murder, 1050, 1058; of betrayal, 1104; of fratricide, 1121; of father's murder, 1245; of kidnapping, 1142; of murder, 102, 615, disproved, 726, false, 289, 650, 839; of sabotaging road construction, 404-5; of sheep killing, proved false, 1399; of theft, 53-54, 850, 901, of watch, 610, 1270, 1284; of witchcraft, 351; pig of killing sheep, 1083; proved false, 1082-84, 1133; unfounded, 171, 614
Achilles, the donkey, 913, 1003
Acre, 670
acrobats: circus, 88-89, 1057, girl, 728, traveling, 832; tumbler, 876. *See also* actors; actresses; players; tumblers.
acrophobia, 689-90, 1047, 1144, 1202
activists, ex-student, 1077
actors: 174-75, 909; children, 68-71, 777; down on luck, 1127-28; Elizabethan, 1202; formerly church clerk, 495; girl, 1076; impersonates ghost, 1355; Jewish, 478; natural, 1223; repertory, 40-41; Shakespearean, 165; stage, 1351-52; traveling, 30, 153-55, 169-71, 174-75, 304-6, 826-27, 832, 1127-28, 1222-23, 1351-52. *See also* acrobats; actresses; players; tumblers.
actresses: 811, 853; aging former, 728; child, 769, 1073; famous, 170; eighteenth-century, 169-71. *See also* acrobats; actors; players; tumblers.

Ada Bell, 60
Adam, 1409-11
Adam Carson, 243-44
ADAM CODLING, *1-2*, 94, 291, 615, 812-14, 817, 841, 858, 862, 1058
ADAM FORREST, *2*, 486-87, 779, 875, 960
ADAM GOODALL, *2*, 204, 586-87, 1202, 1373
Adam Henry, 404-5
ADAM SEYMOUR, *3-4*, 364, 763-64, 1229
Adams, Adrienne, 381
Adam's Common, 1391
Adamson, George, 583
ADAMS, RICHARD (GEORGE), *2-3*, 717, 1330
adders, 1038
addicts: drug, 1338; TV, 203
Addie, 47
ADDIE JONES, *4*, 286, 845, 968, 1039-41
Adela Cathcart, 701
Adelaide Harris, 855-56, 1149-50
Aderbaijan, 390
Admiral Boom, 783, 784
Admiral Benbow Inn, 100, 338, 965, 1253-54
Admirals, by courtesy appointment, 578-80
admirals, retired, 480-81
ADMIRAL SIR ARCHIBALD CUNNINGHAM TWISS, *4-5*, 318-20, 669
ADMIRAL SIR JOHN BEAUCHAMP-TROU-BRIDGE, *4*, 480-81, 51, 817, 959
admiration for Emperor, growing, 371-73
adoptions: of boys from Neverland, 958; of illegitimate boy, 422; of street boy, 611; plans for, 469; proposed, 671
Adventure (ship), 510
Adventure in Prague, 410
adventure novels: based on legend, 145-47, 1258-61; detective-investigation, 182-84, 184-85, 543-46, 786-89, 812-14; domestic, 119-21, 385-86, 606-8, 920-22, 1146-48; eighteenth century, 110-13, 339-42, 1108-11; escape, 425-27, 1247-50, 1415-17; fantasy, 351-53, 365-66, 593-95, 847-49, 974-80, 1035-36, 1091-94, 1111-13, 1119-21, 1208-11, 1274-76, 1327-30, 1330-34, 1342-45, 1385-86, 1388-89; farce, 143-44, 797-99, 1149-51; flying children, 1168; historical, 91-92, 102-5, 153-55, 215-17, 347-50,

601-2, 624-27, 648-51, 670-72,
672-75, 679-83, 738-40, 771-74,
926-27, 1017-20, 1068-71, 1085-
87, 1088-91, 1265-67, 1351-53,
1412-15; holiday, 193-94, 368-70,
614, 903-4, 963-65, 972-74, 1151-
54, 1177-79, 1340-42; kidnapping,
1004-7; melodrama, with fantasy
aspects, 236-37, 1141-43, 1356-
58; mystery, 403-5, 434-36, 662-
63, 729-30, 1151-54; otherworld,
710-13, 755-57; parody, 887-89;
science fiction, 39-41, 236-37,
989-92, 1359-61; sea, 1064-65,
1068-71, 1213-15, 1253-56, 1379-
81; Slavonic area, 1300-2; spy,
400-3, 651-54; strongly feminist,
1300-2; survival, 255-57, 586-88,
786-89, 1043-46; suspense, 1187-
89; terrorist, 33-36, 1076-78;
Viking, 116-19, 1298-1300; World
War II, 1096-99, 1339-40
adventure playgrounds, 520
adventurers: Canadian, 733; Scottish, 765-67; sea, 763-64; to
Indies, 1403
adventures: bizarre, 1238; comic, 996-99; domestic, 119-21,
186-88, 266-69, 385-86, 606-8,
801-4, 1146-48, 1186-87, 1204-
6, 1267-68; harrowing, 1352-53;
holiday, 119-21, 193-94, 382-85,
389-92, 1228; humorous, 920-22,
1007; imaginary, 570; midnight,
1240-42; numerous, of guinea
pig, 1186-87; suspicions of, 554;
underwater, 1328-30
THE ADVENTURES OF A BROWNIE, 5-6, 263
The Adventures of a Brownie, As Told
to My Child, 263
The Adventures of the Little Wooden
Horse, 831
The Adventures of Tom Leigh, 90
advice: based on animal courtship,
144; enigmatic, 189; from mother
horse, 105
advisors: housekeeper, 856; in love
affair, 529; to boy, 324
A. E., 1137
Aedgar Aetheling, 768
Aedigius de Hammo, 395
aeranth, 462
Aethelbert, King of Kent, 295-96,
358
affairs: extra-marital, 887; illicit love, 810; with married man,
597
afreets, 712

Africa: ancient times, Egypt, 121-
24; early nineteenth century,
1145-46, Kano valley, 113-15; mid-
nineteenth century, Sierra Leone,
1068-71; late twentieth century,
Ghana, 248-52, South Africa, 627-
28; slave patrol, 866; west coast,
839-41
AFRICAN SAMSON, 6, 113, 526. See
BLACK SAMSON, 113-15.
Africans: 160-61, 477-78; at Oxford,
160; in England, 613-14, 919;
stereotyped, 919-20
Aged Parent, 1346
ageism, 714-16
agents: double, World War II, 1339;
narcotics, 1063; Secret Service,
757-58
Age of Chivalry. See Medieval Period.
age of protagonists:
--five: girl, 717-20
--six: girl, 486-87
--seven: girl, 19-22, 381
--seven-and-a-half: 1208-11
--eight: boy, 217-19, 533-34, 1274;
girl, 818-20, 887, 1002-3, 1158-60
--nine: boy, 284, 667-68, 672-75,
1035, 1039, 1319-22, 1309-11;
girl, 215-17, 387, 722-24, 953-55,
999-1002, 1123, 1348-49
--ten: boy, 30-31, 113, 153-55, 281,
328-30, 359-60, 656-58, 870, 891,
912, 1154-55, 1204-6, 1234-36,
1262, 1327-30; girl, 173, 411,
900, 970-71, 1017, 1290, 1334-36,
1399-1401, 1396-97
--eleven: boy, 276, 287, 370-73,
427, 539-42, 703-6, 765-67, 801-
4, 812-14, 920, 1035, 1394-96;
girl, 176, 248-52, 361-62, 473-75,
523-25, 906, 1012, 1035, 1140-41,
1316-19
--twelve: boy, 33-36, 129, 188, 252-
54, 328-30, 397, 425, 560-62,
601, 610, 659-62, 729-30, 786-
89, 797-99, 912, 1010, 1108, 1114,
1149-51, 1155-57, 1180-82, 1240,
1211-13, 1215-18, 1248, 1267,
1351-53, 1356; girl, 127, 169,
309-313, 419, 434, 734-37, 897,
903, 1105, 1248, 1269
--junior high age, unspecified:
boy, 480-82; children, 689-
92
--thirteen: boy, 43-47, 77-78, 121,
290, 514-16, 651-54, 807-9, 917,
926, 1049, 1058, 1265, 1284, 1359;

girl, 132-34, 134-36, 136-38, 163-
66, 206, 382, 403, 495-98, 627,
724-27, 923, 1071, 1244, 1313-15
--fourteen: boy, 111-13, 279, 294,
377-79, 463-64, 505-8, 620, 624,
738-40, 747-50, 876, 963-65,
999-1002, 1402-3; girl, 138-40,
140-42, 200, 368-70, 1133, 1190-
92, 1196-99, 1300-2, 1349-51
--fifteen: boy, 255-57, 543-46, 662-
63, 1021, 1062, 1068, 1151-54,
1213-15, 1364, 1379-81, 1404-7,
1415; girl, 430, 447-49, 455-56,
536-38, 763-65, 1368
--mid-teenaged, unspecified: boy,
156-58, 193, 519-21, 732-34, 465-
67, 1298-1300; girl, 459-62,
1325-27
--sixteen: boy, 145-47, 258-61,
400, 558-59, 578, 763-65, 789-91,
809-10, 895, 944-45, 949-52, 1004-
7, 1064, 1187-89, 1259, 1294-95,
1412; girl, 683-84, 938-39, 1165-
67
--seventeen: boy, 102, 648-51, 833-
35, 1169-71; girl, 96-99, 213-15,
456-58, 685-87, 1076, 1169-71,
1223-25, 1287
--eighteen: boy, 499-501, 1161-64,
1276, 1363; girl, 1094
--nineteen: girl, 889
--adult: young man, 679-83, 771-74,
829-30; young woman, 421; older
man, 786-89; older woman, 642-43,
1287
ages, disparity between husband and
wife, 267
Agincourt, veterans of, 102
AGNES CHISEL-BROWN, 6-7, 207
AGNES MCSHANE, 7, 942, 1084, 1123-25
agreements: Arkenstone for treasure, 553; Aslan's life for boy's,
711; becoming slave for care of
girl, 294-95; between Noah's son
and animal trainer, 829; between
sister witches over familiars,
874; between wizard and fire demon, 168; broken, 1120; bull for
right in wolfpack, 65; chalk horse
for freedom, 1172-73; chance to
shine traded for money, 647; complex, 726; for guns, 313; for
release of friends, 1266; freedom in exchange for brother,
694; girl and baby for spinning
flax into yarn, 872; gold to prevent invasion, 871; housework
for right to keep puppy, 325, 343,
639; involving Arkenstone, 1204;
junk eaten instead of useful metal, 584; last wishes granted in
exchange for promise to stop wishing, 418;
loan of doll for new dollhouse
furniture, 331; mice to assist
snake in recovering home, 1120;
not to escape, 408-9; part of
treasure for lifelong friendship,
397; rash, 1095; safe conduct
for friends, 853; scrivener with
shady pedlar, 729; silence for
help to find spies, 402; spinning
flax into yarn, 1130; spinning for
queenship, 1094-95; to break spell
and free spirit, 568-69; to bring
siblings to witch, 356-57; to find
homes, 953; to find spy, 881; to go
on submarine if brothers discontinue quarrel, 369; to guess name,
1095-96; to recover pool, 1114;
to substitute gladiator for king,
772; dragon's treasure for his
freedom, 396-97; winter of slavery
for sword, 295; with Roman noble,
280. See also bargains; pledges;
treaties; truces.
Agricola, Gaius Julius, 1119
Agricultural College, 1387
Ahab, 1076
Ahura Mazda, 151
Aidan and the Strolling Players, 503
Aidan and the Strollers, 503
Aiken, Conrad, 7
AIKEN, JOAN (DELANO), 7-9, 41-42,
107, 807, 887, 889, 1141, 1356,
1399
THE AIMER GATE, 9-10, 399, 444, 1235
aircraft: balloons, 921, 991; early
planes, 410-21; fascination with,
202; gliders, 253; helicopter,
1338; planes considered obsolete,
28-29
airfields, early, 354-56
air-fish, 462
air force, World War II, 202
airline hostesses, Ghanan, 249
airmen: American, 496, 1046; early, 354-56; German, 1051; silver,
1271
airplanes: boy expert on, 1297;
crashed, 422, 435; early, 227,
354-56, 1374; interrupting
horserace, 420; Lancaster Avro,
253
air raid shelters. See bomb shelters.

air raids, World War II: of England, 377-79, 414-16, 735-36, 747-49, 887, 1235; of London, 925; of Nuremberg, 253; wardens, 468-69. *See also* bombings.

AJEET, *10*, 310-12, 648

AKELA, the wolf, *11*, 65, 630

AL, *11*, 1077-78

ALAIN DE FARRAR, *11-12*, 611, 739-40, 1104

ALAIN, DUC DE SAINT SERVAN-REZE, *12*, 1208

Alan A. B. Farquhar, 427-28

ALAN-A-DALE, *12*, 146

ALAN BRECK STEWART, *12-13*, 289, 649-51, 1139

Alan Graham, 79-81, 741

ALAN HOBBS, *13*, 193-94, 451, 799

Alan Kenton, 1284-87

Alaric, 928-30

ALASDAIR, *13*, 642-43

Alasdair Balfour, 428

ALASDAIR MACASKILL, *13-14*, 605, 1049-50

Alba, 299

Albert Finch, 127-28

Albert-next-door, 1147

ALBERT SANDWICH, *14-15*, 177-79, 179, 543, 826

alchemists, 120-21, 373

ALCOCK, VIVIEN (DELORES), *15*, 441, 1247

alcohol: manufactured, 990; mixed with water supply, 990; tool for overcoming tyrants, 990

alcoholics: barge captain, 1213; father, 495, 516, 526, 656, 1303-4; guardian, 807, 1104; hired man, 1402; horse groom, 106; mother, 748, 887; mother's lover, 277; pirate, 100, 1253; uncle, 419, 474. *See also* drunks.

Alderley Edge, Cheshire, 1342-43

ALDO GAMBADELLO, *15*, 662-63, 913

ALESHA HAMILTON, *15-16*, 1207-8

Alexander family, 1149-50

Alexander Hamilton, 15-16

ALEXANDER OLDKNOW, *16*, 211-12

Alexander the Great, 512

Alexia, 118-19

Alf Eckersley, 449, 1268

ALFRED DANE-LEG, *16*, 375, 870-72, 1243

Alfred Diamond, 610

ALFRED GRAVES, *16-17*, 410-11, 1390

Alfred of Wessex, 16, 18

ALFRED OVERS, *17*, 60, 703-6

ALFRED SMIRK, *17-18*

ALFRED THE GREAT, king of West Saxons, 16, *18*, 517, 870-72

Alfred the One-Legged, 870-72

aliases, 609, 615, 620

ALICE, *18-19*, 22-23, 69, 12-93, 211, 324, 334-35, 342-43, 343, 505, 572, 753, 767, 827, 836, 1024-25, 1208-11, 1274, 1358-59, 1361, 1361-62

ALICE BASTABLE, *19*, 899, 1146-47

Alice B. Toklas Cookbook, 82

Alice, Countess of Suffolk, 275-76

Alice Liddell, 22, 335

ALICE'S ADVENTURES IN WONDERLAND, *19-22*, 22-23, 180, 1208

ALICE'S ADVENTURES UNDER GROUND, *22-23*, 180

alienation: from animals and humans, 836-37; from parents, 75, 86

Aliens in the Family, 759

aliens, smuggled into England, 657

Ali Sayyid, 1303-5

Alison in Provence, 410

Alison Martin, 945, 1169

ALISON JOHNSTONE, *23-24*, 80, 206, 865

ALIX HAMILTON, 12, 16, *24*, 63, 1020, 1207-8

Allalonestone, 1329

ALLAN, MABEL ESTHER, *24-25*, 242, 588

All Day Long: An Anthology of Poetry for Children, 1362

Allectus, 271, 633, 1089-91

allegory: Christian, 712, 755-57, 974-80; for religious life, 462-63

ALLEN, ERIC (ERIC ALLEN BALLARD), *25*, 689

Allen, James, 999

Allen, Mr., 837

allergies, thought caused by witch, 452

Alleyn, Master, 1351

allies, Sirius and Sol, 325

ALLISON, *25-26*, 245, 518, 768, 873-74, 933-35, 1047

Allman family, 9-10, 484, 619, 1144, 1235, 1281

All Saints Church, 480

allusions: Biblical, 712, 755-57, 1180-82, 1276, 1409; Christian, 688; classical, 1180-82; literary, 1048; to Beatrix Potter, 696

Almedingen, Catherine A., 717

ALMEDINGEN, E. M. (MARTHA EDITH VON ALMEDINGEN), *26-27*, 717, 1415

alphabets, witches', 374

Alsatians, dogs, 1398-99

Altendorf, George, 1271
alternative endings, 495
alumni, satirized, 827
Al van Stratten, 15, 662-63
Alys de Renneville, 1017-20
Ama, 250, 252, 698, 762
Amabel Lee, 164-65
Amaryllis Terry, 536-38
Amazon (sailboat), 874, 949, 1178-79, 1228
Amazons, 874, 949, 1047
ambassadors, Mattean, son of, 219, 855, 1076
Amberhurst House, 4-5, 318-20, 670
ambiguities, marring novel, 337
ambitions: for daughters, 582-83, 799; for further education, 861, 1366; for son, 17, 703-6; insatiable, 43; musical, 668; political, 213-15, 350; realized, 1162; social, pretentious, 757; to attend art college, 835; to attend art school, 1401; to attend college, 1068, 1073; to attend medical school, 261; to attend Oxford, 1406; to attend secondary school, 473; to attend university, 904; to become actress, 62, 169-71; to become astronomer, 530; to become author, 339; to become chemist, 841; to become commercial artist, 1173; to become commerical travel-er, 1132; to become crack rider, 1190-92; to become designer in iron, 1225; to become doctor, 356, 988-89; to become famous, 489; to become famous scientist, 528; to become farmer, 385; to become gentleman, 981; to become hero, 1389; to become knight, 1137; to become officers on ship, 1064; to become physical education teach-er, 1363; to become priest, 101, 499; to become probation offic-er, 1024; to become a professional jockey, 961; to become profes-sor at Oxford, 1316; to become queen, 1024; to become singer, 685-86; to become soldier, 499; to become teacher, 473; to become veterinarian, 901; to become writ-er, 1123-25; to be different from sister, 517; to be made Fellow of Royal Society, 574; to construct a stronghold, 1161-63; to control Celtic tribes, 1190; to control own life, 433; to control portion

of world, 321; to control whole world, 1014; to develop independ-ence in neighbors, 490; to establish foundry, 581; to fly, 227; to get far in world, 698; to get revenge on men, 376; to have plastic surgery, 1248; to have ten children, 777; to join caravan, 1204; to join Navy, 290; to kill a king, 1012; to lead tribe, 245; to learn Latin and Greek, 1316, 1318; to learn to read, 1144; to learn to read and paint, 273; to learn use-ful profession, 1068; to live up to great name, 489; to make electric chair, 253; to make home for self and brother, 364; to marry foster-ling to king, 299-300; to marry princess, 1147; to marry wealth, 195; to raise pig, 619; to rebuild stud line, 972; to restore estate, 421; to restore fallen fortunes of family, 1146; to rise above birth, 492-95; to rise through education, 518; to "set up for a gentleman," 732; to turn area into resort, 579. *See also* desires.
Ambler, C. Gifford, 1398
Ambrosius, Prince of Britain, 681-83
Ambrus, Victor G., 190, 290, 354, 418, 421, 624, 717, 763, 897, 982, 1199, 1204, 1213, 1223, 1258, 1349, 1366, 1379, 1415
ambushes, 339, 341, 409, 738, 1086, 1103; by street gang, 662; in moun-tains, 1266; of Romans, 1245; prepared, 102
Amend-All, Jon, 615
America, Roman, early nineteenth century, 1141-43
Americans: in Chile, 585, 1188-89; in England, 404-5, 645, 754, 874, 885, 1046, 1325, 456; in Italy, 662-63; in Europe, post-World War II, 1098; in Scotland, 79-81, 741-42; in Venice, 15; in Wales, 177-78; resented, 842-43; stereo-typed villain, 1071
Amile, the dog, 915
amnesia, 449, 918, 1065
Amnesty International, 1077
Amos, 464
Amsterdam, late twentieth century, 1061-64
amulets, holding papers, 651-52
Amy Bowen, 74, 323, 906-7
Amy Gresham, 489-92
Amy Parker, 76-77, 100, 1088

ANADYOMENE (submarine), *27-28*, 29, 369-70

ancestors: 1, 1144; rebel, 536; revered, 522; royal hunchback, 582; Viking, 725

ancient times: British Isles, 679-83, 1035-36, 1171-73, 1319-22; Brittany, 1258-61; Cornwall, 1258-61; Europe, 335-37; Ireland, 298-99, 1258-61, Ulster, 299-301; Israel and Egypt, 829-30; Middle East, 624-27; Roman Britain, 347-50, 771-74, 1088-91, 1117-19, 1161-64; Ur, 1204-6

Ancret, 673-74

And Another Thing..., 1131

Anders Herulfson, 117-19

Andersen, Hans Christian, 488

Anderson, Nicol, 1156

Andes Mountains, 1142

Andito, 114

Andrayson family, 361

ANDREI HAMILTON, 12, 16, 24, *28*, 63, 1020, 1207-8

ANDRES LARRETA, *28*, 94, 585, 1187-89

Andret, 1260

Andrew Lindway, 505, 636-37

ANDREW MITCHELL, *28-29*, 1211-13, 1297-98

Andrews family, 53-54, 596-97, 1370

Androhan, 216

And So--Victoria, 1369

ANDY, *29*, 169, 1052, 1064-65

ANDY MCANDREW, *29*, 368-69, 1046-47

ANGEL, 11, *20-30*, 1077-78

Angelo, 30-31

ANGELO GOES TO THE CARNIVAL, 30-31, 425

Angels, 798

angels: 977; space, 584; visit children's kids, 1112

Angharad Goldenhand, 1344

Anglican Community for Men, 1165

Anglo-Saxon attitudes, 767

Angora, 964

Angus MacAngus, 1017-20

Ania, 1301

animal novels, fantasy: bird, raven, 41-42; cat, 893-94; dog, 325-28; donkey, 1232-34, 1270-73; dragon, 1029-31; fox, 388-89; guinea pig, 365-66, 1186-87; hen, 713-14; horse, 105-7; monkey, 839-41; mouse, 815-16, 1031-32; pig, 1082-84; rabbits, 1330-34; unicorn, 724-27; various, 829-30, 913, 1111-13, 1145-46, 1309-11; various field and river, 1381-85;

various jungle, 630-32; various small, 931-32

animal novels, realistic: dog, 328-30, 903-4, 911-12, 1386-88, 1398-99; elephant, 1247-50; gorilla, 1154-55; horse, 1190-92, 1339-40, 1366-68; pig, 953-55. *See also* cat stories; dog stories; horse stories.

animals: abused, 105-7, 454-55, 1112, 1387; cruelty toward, 279; domestic, mysteriously disappear, 1151, savaged by unknown beast, 877; for ark, 522; fostering children, 630-32, 1149; gorilla, 525; kindness toward, 1247-50; languages of, 988; love of, 946, 1174; miniature, exhibited, 510; pushmi-pullyu, 1145-46; rarest, 1145; responsible for household, 1145, 1309-11; sleepy dormouse, 335; small field, 1119-21; stuffed, 84-85, 232, 562-64; taking care of human, 1145; talking, cats, 173-75, 893-94, dog, 780, dormouse, 334-35, farm 1082-84, guinea pig, 1186-87, hen, 713-14, horses, 43, 560-62, 1081, lion, 43, 54-55, 321, mice, 815-16, 1031-32, 1119-21, mole, 827-28, monkey, 839-41, rabbit, 19-21, 1330-34, stuffed, 84-85, 1388-89, various, 19-20, 365-66, 388-89, 687-89, 710-12, 716-17, 756, 829-30, 931-32, 992, 995-96, 1026-27, 1145-46, 1208-11, 1270-73, 1306-9, 1309-11, 1382-85, various domestic, 675, 913-14, 1112, various jungle, 630-32, various water, 1327-30; turned to stone, 357; two-headed, 1145, various, 894

animal tamers, 829

ankus, jeweled, 631

Anlaf, 91

Anna (*Castle of Bone*), 189-90

ANNA (*The Other Way Round; When Hitler Stole Pink Rabbit*), 31, 562, 761, 793, 924-26, 937, 1348-49

Anna, 27

Annabel Banks, 782-83, 783, 785

Annabel Fairfax, 586

ANNA CLARE, *31*, 1105-6

Anna Johnson, 639

ANNA-MARIE MURGATROYD, *31-32*, 119, 302-3, 508, 677, 740, 807-8, 845

Anna, Princess of Constantinople, 117

Anna Sewell and Black Beauty, 67

ANNA TATE, *32*, 647, 862, 1314-15

ANNA VOGEL, *32-33*, 214, 546

Anne Fell, 722, 818

ANNE MELTON, *33*, 50-51, 942, 1225, 1325-27

Anne, Queen of England, 1353

ANNE ROSLEY, *33*, 802-3

Annerton Dike Disaster, 34-36

ANNERTON PIT, *33-36*, 315

ANNE SEKAR, *36-37*, 450, 547, 548-50, 608, 778, 864

ANNE-SIGRI NYGAARD, *37*, 1350

Anne Teesdale, 477, 556-57

Anne Woodall, 1015

Annie Corry, 778

Annie Dowsett, 365

Annie Dunham, 472-73, 473

Annie Leah, 1144

anniversaries: of battle, 350-51; wedding, 267; Twelfth of July, 1286

Ann Marlow, 382-84, 965

Ann O'Connor, 1134-36

announcers, radio, youthful, 1314

ANN RIDLEY, *37*, 777, 286-87, 591, 843

ANN TARRANT, *37-38*, 968-69, 1170

Ansel family, 1015, 1277

antagonisms: between tribal leaders, 1161-62; English-Welsh, 768; to aristocracy, 17; neighbor girls, 722-24; lower class toward upper, 732. *See also* conflcts.

Antelope (ship), 509

antelopes, nurses, 1145

ANTHEA, *38*, 416-18, 1007

Anthea Sykes, 63

Anthony Heritage, 153-55

ANTHONY HUNTERLY, *38*, 389-92, 960

anthropologists: great-grandfather, 564-65, 613; New Guinean, 613

antique dealers, 101, 200-1, 844

antique shops, 150, 189, 428

antiques, 1040

anti-Semitism, 278. *See also* apartheid; discrimination; prejudice; social classes, distinctions between.

anti-war stories, 585

ANTONIUS, *38-39*, 48, 159, 280-81, 1099

Anvard, 575

Anvil, 39

apartheid, 628

apartment houses, 606-7, 1240-41

apes: 525, 712; evil, 377, 603, 1227; scheming, ambitious, 687-88

aphoristic speaking, 844

apocalypse, 110, 112

apologies: after change of heart, 229; awkward, 202; to audience for bad performance, 170; to inferiors, 254; to old gentleman, 1147; to princess, 247

apothecaries, 824-26

apparitions, 208

appetite, voracious, 41-42

Appin, 649-50

applause, saves life, 958

apple barrels, 1254

Apple Plantaganet, 102, 330-31

apples: love for, 1037; of everlasting youth, 756; poisoned, 1037; silver, 756, 1090

The Apple-Stone, 489

Appleyard, Nick, 615

Appolyon, Prince, 976

apprentices: apothecary, 824-26; blacksmith, 484-85, 493, 981; chemist, 131, 841, 861; clerk, 1404-5; doctor, unofficial, 259; draper, 111, 1232; Druid, 148; garage mechanic, 516; girl to cake shop, 568, 698; merchant, 228, 409; miner, 197, 1238-39; overworked, 824-26; physician, 1200-1; printer, 195, 314, 729; runaway, 146; seaman, 168-69, 1052, 1064-65; surgeon, 191; thieves and beggars, 1352; to quack doctor, 112; unwilling, 824-26; wheelwright, 595; witch, 568; wizard, 568-69

The Apprentices, 442

Aquae Sulis, 294, 930, 1293

AQUARIUS, *39-41*, 771

Aquila, 679-83

Arabel and Mortimer, 42

Arabel Jones, 41-42

ARABEL'S RAVEN, 9, *41-42*

ARABIS DANDO, *42-43*, 737, 996, 1234, 1356-58, 1411

Aragorn, son of Arathorn, 407, 1158

Aral Sea, 390

Arathorn, 407

ARAVIS, *43*, 561, 575, 1082

Arawn, 326-27; hounds of, 326-28

arcade, clerestory, 480

Archenland, 561, 575, 1081-82

archeological digs, 452

archeologists, 130, 841

archeology, 1011

ARCHER, *43*, 44-46, 321, 470, 1014,
   1087
archers, 552; girl, 603, 1174;
   prince's, 248, 675
ARCHER'S GOON, *43-47*, 618
ARCHIE MEIKLE, *47*, 799-800, 1196-98
architects, 612-13, 613, 667, 738,
   1115, eighteenth-century, 480-
   82; Georgian, 613
architecture, unusual, 613
archives, 532
Arctic Circle, 578, 1349-51, 1402
Ardent, Mr., 224
Ardizzone, Edward, 812, 893
Ardwick, Manchester, 362
Are All the Giants Dead?, 905
Argentinans, in Ireland, 543
Argonne, 1215, 1217
Argos, the dog, 153-54
arguments: father-grandfather, 876;
   over cat, 697; violent husband-
   wife, 842. *See also* antagonisms;
   conflicts; fights.
Argyll, Earl of, 1413-14
ARIADNE, *47-48*, 158-59, 279-81, 1099
Arianrod, 1142
Ari Knudson, 1085
Arkenstone of Thrain, 95, 553, 1204
arks: building of, 829; instructions
   for, 77; Noah's, 196, 782, 895
Arlette, 558
Armand, Monsieur, 191, 828-29
armies: British, 595; British in
   India, 651-52; consultant to
   Russian, 1020; phantom, outside
   window, 352; Turkish, 1295-96;
   West Saxon, 375
Armistice, 207
armor: bearers, 358; diamond, 552;
   mail corselet, 96
arms, broken sword, 1374
ARMSTRONG, RICHARD, *48*, 1064
Arne Nygaard, 37, 1350, 1401-2
Arnie Lambert, 607
Arno (ship), 169, 1064-65
Arnold Haithwaite, 578-80
ARNOLD LUCKETT, *48-49*, 452, 1100
Arnold West, 639, 875, 1335
arrests, 205; as vagrant, 278; Boca
   del Sol, 1052; boy in school office, 646; for attempted murder,
   474; for driving get-away car,
   656; for dynamiting pool, 643; for
   fighting, 661; for poaching, 137;
   for receiving stolen goods, 101,
   426; of revolutionary leaders,
   499; of smugglers, 764; of soldier, 247

ARRIETTY CLOCK, *49-50*, 132-34, 135,
   136-37, 138-40, 140-42, 147-48,
   489, 559-60, 822, 854, 856, 948,
   985, 1130, 1236, 1282
Arriman Canker, 518, 697-98, 752,
   845, 1104, 1192-93, 1353-56, 1397
Arriman the wizard, 376, 824, 835,
   874
Arrow (ship), 255
Arrow Bowen, 524
arrows: black, 102-4, 316, 615;
   blood-soaked, 375, 870; magic,
   711; poisoned, 714
Arry, 1354-55
Arsheesh, 1081
arson: attempted, 1087; by child,
   1048; bakehouse, 51, 970; dome,
   1295; fowlhouse, 715, 861, 894;
   house, 609-10; mansion, 845, 807,
   809, 1104; prevented, 1390; sports
   complex, 1294; warehouse, 1365
arsonists, 599; poltergeist, 452;
   youthful, 275, 423, 477
Artaius, 1142-43
art collectors, 913; of fine glass,
   662-63
Arthur, the guinea pig, 365-66
ARTHUR BARNARD, *50*, 311, 648
Arthur Chisel-Brown, 6, 207
Arthur Figgs, 1368-69
Arthurian period, pre-, England,
   Thames Valley, 395-97
Arthur, King of Britain: 148-49,
   195, 502, 528, 682-83, 844, 1015,
   1037-39; epic on, 1358; Grail of,
   1375; legends of, 1342-45; story
   retold, 1141-43
ARTHUR PRUDIE, *50-51*, 1325, 1327
ARTHUR RAMSGILLL, *51*, 480-81
ARTHY ROLLER, *51*, 488, 600, 970-
   71
artifacts: hunting for, 74; in
   Yorkshire mounds, 802-3; Jael's
   nail, 976; literary, 22-23, 1113;
   Moses's rod, 976; New Guinean,
   564-66; religious, 798; verify
   tale, 971; Viking, 838; wood-
   en slab, 564-66
artists: 609, 1137, 1166; amputee veteran, 469; boy, 821, 1237,
   1401; charcoal, 1171-72; girl,
   411; medieval, 916-17; monk, 155,
   916-17; of Christmas cards, 822;
   painter, 1115; pavement, 780;
   pen and pencil, 1225; portrait,
   1215-17; potter, 1205; prehistoric youth, 336-37; ragamuffin,
   1215; stepfather, 1059; student,

108-9, at Poly, 540-42; wood carv-
er, 1402; youthful, 152, 155, 368,
468, 921, 944-45, 1048, 1373. *See
also* painters.
Artos, 682-83
Arundel, 672
Ascension Day, 1180-81
ascetics, unwashed, 279, 557
Ashdale Great Edge, 918-19
Ashdown, battle of, 18, 870
Ashdown forest, 581-83, 683, 762
ashes, revivified, 998
ASHLEY, BERNARD, *51-52*, 656, 1262
Ash Road, 1129
Ashton, Ralph, 460-61
Ashworth, 809
Ashworthy family, 1058
Ashworthy-Smith family, 813-14
Ashworthy-Smith, Andrew, 858
Asia: late nineteenth century, India, 630-32, 651-54; early
twentieth century, China, 1265-
67, Tibet, 1265-67; late twentieth
century, India, 1302-5
Ask for King Billy, 1257
ASLAN, the lion, 43, *54-55*, 167,
185, 321, 562, 603, 687-88, 699,
711-12, 742, 755-56, 864, 875-76,
961-62, 995-96, 987, 1009, 1026-
27, 1082, 1091-93, 1174, 1227,
1279, 1306-9
Aslan's How, 323, 995, 1264
assassinations: attempted, 1207;
foiled, 1013; of King of England,
planned, 888; of Russian nobles,
16, 64; of Scottish queen, foiled,
774; of wrong victim, 24; political, 1187
assassins, 601
Assassins, 671
associations, of wool growers and
merchants, 1132-33
Ass, Tom, 1232-34
Astercote, 727
astrology, 1168
Astronomer's Cave, 512
asylum, requested, 248
atavism, 746, 886, 1055, 1294-95
atheists, 93, 1376
Athena Price, 1165-67
athletes, 950-51, 1363; female,
151
Atlanta, 477, 1048, 1372
Atlantis, 1329
atmosphere: green, 238; heavy, un-
healthy, 238
attacks: by barbarians, 281; by
cricket teams, 622; by gang of

street boys, 609, 610; by intruder, 493; by Maltese toughs, 58;
by owl, 135; by terrorists, 10;
by toughs, 515; by wolves, 1046;
by young hoods, 45; Indian, 733;
on foundry, 582; on man who starts
motor, 310; on roundhouse, 13;
on Vienna, 214-15; planned, 312,
1086; Roman, 884, 1161-63; with
pitchfork, 826
attentions, unwanted romantic, 830
AT THE BACK OF THE NORTH WIND, *55-57*,
746, 1003
At the Sign of the Gilded Shoe, 1076
attics: Amsterdam house, 1063; contains dishes, 933; contains money,
1335; explored, 755; fairy gifts
discovered in, 997; of farmhouse,
1274-75; toy soldiers discovered
in, 1164
attorneys, 426, 610, 1109-10, 839.
See also lawyers; solicitors.
Attribates, 1172
Auchenskeoch, seventeenth century,
636-38
auctions: horse, 1190; personal pos-
sessions, 553; planned, 1132
auditioning, for stage job, 69-70
audit, mine, 398
AUDREY PARTON, *57-58*, 210, 401-2,
747, 1084
augustes, 516
Augustine, Saint, 297
AUGUSTUS GLOOP, *58*, 203
Aun Doorback, 1298, 1300
Aunt Alberta Scrubb, 377
Aunt Alison, 153
AUNT ANNE MAYFIELD, *62*, 564, 613,
792, 856
Aunt Ata, 249
Aunt B, 492
AUNT BETH, *58*, 741, 1280, 1322-24
AUNT BOLINGER, 52-54, *58-59*, 74
Aunt Boo, 1166-67
Aunt Celia Parker, 275, 1282-83
Aunt Clara Plowman, 620-23
Aunt Dinah, 813
Aunt Edna, 1071-73
Aunt Emmeline, 1114-16
Aunt Essie Roller, 488
Aunt Ester, 175
Aunt Grace Russell, 354, 421, 422
AUNT GWEN KITSON, *59*, 532-33, 1237,
1240-41
AUNT HARRIET GREENGRASS, *59*, 954-55
Aunt Hilda, 279
Aunt Honoria, 1089
Auntie Annie Marriot, 1247-48

Auntie Brenda, 41

Auntie Flora Bell, 900, 1192

AUNTIE JOAN MYHILL, *59-60*, 364, 523-24, 1042, 1283

Auntie Kitty Sowter, 362, 703, 706, 1282

AUNTIE LOU, *60*, 176-79, 179, 842-43, 886

AUNTIE MAGGIE CHAFFEY, *60*, 703-6, 1132, 1282

AUNTIE MOLLY BELL, *60-61*, 900

Auntie Posie Dixon, 1166-67

Aunt Jane, 1401

Aunt Julia Henchman, 94, 342, 828, 880

Aunt Lucy Tennant, 1151

AUNT LUPY, 50, *61*, 133, 135, 136, 141-42, 560, 811, 1130, 1282

Aunt Marie Mirkov, 718-19

Aunt Pesty, 176

AUNT POLLY DUNHAM, *61-62*, 473, 473-75

Aunt Poppy, 638, 753-54, 923

Aunt Rebecca, 234-35

Aunt Rose Andrayson, 361

aunts: abusive, 1241; acid-tongued, 523; bed-ridden, 703-4, 854; beer loving, 245; Borrower, 136; censorious, 620; cold, domineering, 888; conventional, 1349-50; critical, 1271; cruel, 533, 593; death of, 1316; disparaging of niece, 900; elderly, 817; exhibitionist, 1192; foster mother, 1, 37, 635; fussy, 880; great, 620-23, 717, 792; grudging foster parent, 415; guardian, 683, 692, 897-99; hard-driving, 523; hearty, 492; holder of freehold manor, 683-84; incompetent homemaker, 718-19; imperious, 683; impractical, 62; intellectual, 62; judgmental, 1116; keeper of boarding house, 1401; mean spirited, 58-59; near death, 1401; over-attentive, 59; preoccupied with writing, 339; resentful, 325, 327-28; rigid, imperious, 342; Romanized Briton, 348; scandalous, 473-75; scholar, 1035; schoolteacher, 59, 987; seamstress, 354; shrewish, 59-60, 153; snobbish, 516; story based on life of author, 1158-60; straitlaced, 741; strong-willed, 276; supportive, 889-90; unconventional, 683-84; unkind, 343, 639; youthful, 236

Aunt Sanders, 897-99

AUNT SARAH GREENGRASS, *62*, 954-55, 1195

Aunt Spike, 593

Aunt Sponge, 593

AUNT SUSAN AND AUNT ANNE MAYFIELD, *62*

Aunt Susan Henchman, 190-91, 342, 828

Aunt Susan Mayfield, 564, 613, 792, 856

Aunt Topsy, 889

Aunt Trib, 345

Aunt Tribulation, 888-89

Aunt Valaria, 261

Aunt Verity, 277

Austins, 1395

Australia: convict returned from, 757; emigrants to, 362, 604-5, 873, 1170, 1336; late twentieth century, 584-85, New South Wales, 620-23, swampy area, 714-16

Austria: tale set in, 659-62; seventeenth century Vienna, 213-15

authors: appearing as character in story, 55-57; avuncular commentator, 710-13, 755-57; judgments expressed, 131

The Autobiography of Howard Spring, 1131

automobiles: as hero, 221-23; Rolls Royce, 532, 1337

Autumn Festival, 1092

Autumn Term, 382, 428

auxiliaries, ladies, 815

avalanches, coastal, 1327

Avalon, 1038

Avatea, 256-57

AVERY, GILLIAN (ELISE), *63*, 489, 703, 1296, 1316, 1319

aviary, home for Borrower, 141, 947

Aviary Hall, 206, 367

aviation, development of, 354-56

AVOYE HAMILTON, *63-64*, 1207-8

award books:

--Books Too Good: *ALICE'S ADVENTURES IN WONDERLAND*, *19-22*; *THE BORROWERS*, *132-34*; *THE CHILDREN OF GREEN KNOWE*, *211-13*; *A CHRISTMAS CAROL*, *227-30*; *DAWN WIND*, *293-97*; *THE HOBBIT*, *550-53*; *THE JUNGLE BOOKS*, *630-32*; *THE LION, THE WITCH*

AND THE WARDROBE, 710-13; MARY
POPPINS, 779-81; PETER AND WENDY,
956-58; ROBINSON CRUSOE, 1043-46;
A STRANGER CAME ASHORE, 1155-57;
THROUGH THE LOOKING-GLASS, AND
WHAT ALICE FOUND THERE, 1208-11;
TOM'S MIDNIGHT GARDEN, 1240-42;
TREASURE ISLAND, 1253-56; THE
WHITE MOUNTAINS, 1359-61; THE WIND
IN THE WILLOWS, 1382-85; WINNIE-
THE-POOH, 1388-89
--Boston Globe Honor: ARCHER'S GOON,
43-47; ASK ME NO QUESTIONS, 52-54;
BLOOD FEUD, 116-19; THE CHANGE-
OVER: A SUPERNATURAL ROMANCE,
200-1; FLAMBARDS, 418-21; HOWL'S
MOVING CASTLE, 567-69; AN ISLAND
IN THE GREEN SEA, 588-89; JOHN
DIAMOND, 610-11; THE MACHINE GUN-
NERS, 747-50; ME AND MY MILLION,
797-99; NO WAY OF TELLING, 906-7;
THE ROAD TO CAMLANN, 1036-39; THE
SCARECROWS, 1058-60; THE SHEEP-
PIG, 1082-84; SMITH, 1108-10; A
STRANGER CAME ASHORE, 1155-57; THE
SUMMER AFTER THE FUNERAL, 1165-67;
THOMAS, 1199-1202; YOUNG MARK: THE
STORY OF A VENTURE, 1417
--Boston Globe Winner: CONRAD'S WAR,
252-54; THE DARK IS RISING, 287-
88; THE INTRUDER, 578-81; A LITTLE
FEAR, 714-16; TRISTAN AND ISEULT,
1258-61; UNLEAVING, 1287-90
--Carnegie Com.: THE BATTLE OF BUB-
BLE AND SQUEAK, 75-77; BLACK JACK,
110-13; THE BLUE BOAT, 119-21; THE
BLUE HAWK, 121-24; THE BONGLEWEED,
127-29; THE BONNIE PIT LADDIE,
129-31; THE BUS GIRLS, 163-
66; CANDIDATE FOR FAME, 169-71;
CARRIE'S WAR, 176-79;
CASTAWAY CHRISTMAS, 186-88;
CASTORS AWAY!, 190-91; CHARMED
LIFE, 208-9; THE CHILDREN OF GREEN
KNOWE, 211-13; THE CHIMNEYS OF
GREEN KNOWE, 217-19; CHORISTERS'
CAKE, 223-25; THE DANCING BEAR,
279-81; THE DARK IS RISING, 287-
88; THE DEVIL'S CHILDREN, 309-13;
THE DEVIL ON THE ROAD, 306-9;
DOGSBODY, 325-28;
THE DRUMMER BOY, 339-42; THE EAGLE
OF THE NINTH, 347-50; ELIDOR, 359-
60; THE EMPEROR'S WINDING SHEET,
370-73; THE FAIRY DOLL, 381-82;
FALCONER'S LURE: THE STORY OF A
SUMMER HOLIDAY, 382-85; FEBRUA-
RY'S ROAD, 403-5; FLAMBARDS,

418-21; THE FOX IN WINTER, 429-
32; FRIDAY'S TUNNEL, 434-36; GOOD
NIGHT, MR. TOM, 467-69; GRAN AT
COALGATE, 474-75; THE GREATEST
GRESHAM, 489-92; THE GREAT GALE,
495-98;
THE GREY KING, 501-2; HELL'S EDGE,
536-38; THE HORSE AND HIS BOY,
560-62; THE INTRUDER, 578-81; THE
JOURNEY OF THE ELDEST SON, 624-
27; A KIND OF WILD JUSTICE, 656-58;
THE LATCHKEY CHILDREN, 689-92; A
LITTLE FEAR, 714-16;
THE LOAD OF UNICORN, 729-30;
MARASSA AND MIDNIGHT, 765-67;
THE MEMBER FOR THE MARSH, 801-4;
"MINNOW" ON THE SAY, 812-14; MISS
HAPPINESS AND MISS FLOWER, 818-20;
THE NAMESAKE, 870-72; THE NIGHT
WATCHMEN, 891-92; NO WAY OF TEL-
LING, 906-7; ONE IS ONE, 915-17;
OVER THE HILLS TO FABYLON, 927-30;
PETER'S ROOM, 963-65;
RANSOM FOR A KNIGHT, 1017-20; THE
RESCUERS, 1031-32; SERAPHINA,
1071-74; THE SHIELD RING, 1085-
87; THE SILVER BRANCH, 1088-91;
THE SILVER SWORD, 1096-99; SMITH,
1108-10; SONGBERD'S GROVE, 1114-
17; THE STRONGHOLD, 1161-64;
THE SUMMER BIRDS, 1167-69; THE
THREE BROTHERS OF UR, 1204-6;
THUNDER IN THE SKY, 1213-15; THE
THURSDAY KIDNAPPING, 1218-20;
TRISTAN AND ISEULT, 1258-61; UNDER
GOLIATH, 1284-87; UP THE PIER,
1290-91; THE VANDAL, 1294-95; WALL
OF WORDS, 1313-15;
THE WARDEN'S NIECE, 1316-19;
WARRIOR SCARLET, 1319-22; THE WAY
TO SATTIN SHORE, 1334-36; WHEN
JAYS FLY TO BARBMO, 1349-51; WHICH
WITCH?, 1353-56; THE WILD HORSE
OF SANTANDER, 1366-68; WINDFALL,
1379-81
--Carnegie Highly Com.: BROTH-
ER IN THE LAND, 156-58; THE DARK
BEHIND THE CURTAIN, 287-88; THE
DREAM TIME, 335-37; THE HOLLOW
LAND, 555-57; A LIKELY LAD, 703-
6; THE NATURE OF THE BEAST, 876-78;
TALKING IN WHISPERS, 1187-89
--Carnegie Winner: THE BORROW-
ERS, 132-34; THE CHANGEOVER: A
SUPERNATURAL ROMANCE, 200-1; THE
CIRCUS IS COMING, 234-36; THE EDGE
OF THE CLOUD, 354-56; THE EXETER
BLITZ, 377-79; THE FAMILY FROM ONE

END STREET AND SOME OF THEIR ADVEN-
TURES, 385-86; THE GHOST OF THOMAS
KEMPE, 451-53; THE GRANGE AT HIGH
FORCE, 480-82; A GRASS ROPE, 486-
87; HANDLES, 523-25; THE HAUNTING,
533-34; JOSH, 620-23;
KNIGHT CRUSADER, 670-72; THE LAN-
TERN BEARERS, 679-83; THE LARK ON
THE WING, 685-87; THE LAST BAT-
TLE, 687-89; THE LITTLE GREY MEN,
716-17; THE LITTLE WHITE HORSE,
724-27; THE MACHINE GUNNERS, 747-
50; THE MOON IN THE CLOUD, 829-30;
NORDY BANK, 903-4; THE OWL SER-
VICE, 932-35; PIGEON POST, 972-74;
THE SCARECROWS, 1058-60; SEA
CHANGE, 1064-65; A STRANGER AT
GREEN KNOWE, 1154-55; THUNDER
AND LIGHTNINGS, 1211-13; TIME OF
TRIAL, 1223-25; TOM'S MIDNIGHT
GARDEN, 1240-42; TULKU, 1265-67;
THE TURBULENT TERM OF TYKE TILER,
1269-70; THE TWELVE AND THE GENII,
1274-76; WATERSHIP DOWN, 1330-34;
WE COULDN'T LEAVE DINAH, 1339-40;
THE WIND ON THE MOON, 1385-86; THE
WOOL-PACK, 1402-3
--Children's Classics: THE ADVEN-
TURES OF A BROWNIE, 5-6; ALICE'S
ADVENTURES IN WONDERLAND, 19-22;
ALICE'S ADVENTURES UNDER GROUND,
22-23; AT THE BACK OF THE NORTH
WIND, 55-57; THE BLACK ARROW, 102-
5; BLACK BEAUTY, 105-7; A CHRIST-
MAS CAROL, 227-30; THE CRICKET
ON THE HEARTH, 266-69; FIVE CHIL-
DREN AND IT, 416-18; GULLIVER'S
TRAVELS, 508-14; THE HOBBIT, 550-
53; THE HOUSE AT POOH CORNER,
562-64; THE JUNGLE BOOKS, 630-32;
KIDNAPPED, 648-51; THE KING OF THE
GOLDEN RIVER; OR, THE BLACK BROTH-
ERS: A LEGEND OF STIRIA, 659-62;
THE LION, THE WITCH AND THE WARD-
ROBE, 710-13; THE LITTLE LAME
PRINCE, 720-22;
MARY POPPINS, 779-81;
PETER AND WENDY, 956-58; PILGRIM'S
PROGRESS, 974-80; THE PRINCESS
AND CURDIE, 999-1002; THE PRINCESS
AND THE GOBLIN, 1002-4; ROBINSON
CRUSOE, 1043-46; THE STORY OF
THE TREASURE SEEKERS, 1146-48;
THROUGH THE LOOKING-GLASS, AND
WHAT ALICE FOUND THERE, 1208-11;
TREASURE ISLAND, 1253-56; THE VOY-
AGES OF DOCTOR DOLITTLE, 1309-11;
THE WATERBABIES: A FAIRY-TALE FOR

A LAND-BABY, 1327-30; THE WIND
IN THE WILLOWS, 1382-85; WINNIE-
THE-POOH, 1388-89
--Child Study: A SOUND OF CHARIOTS,
1123-25
--ChLA Touchstones: ALICE'S ADVEN-
TURES IN WONDERLAND, 19-22; THE
BORROWERS, 132-34; THE HOBBIT,
550-53; THE HORSE AND HIS BOY,
560-62; THE HOUSE AT POOH CORNER,
562-64; THE JUNGLE BOOKS, 630-
32; THE LAST BATTLE, 687-89; THE
LION, THE WITCH AND THE WARDROBE,
710-13; THE MAGICIAN'S NEPHEW,
755-57; THE PRINCESS AND CURDIE,
999-1002; THE PRINCESS AND THE
GOBLIN, 1002-3; THE SILVER CHAIR,
1091-94; THE STORY OF THE TREAS-
URE SEEKERS, 1146-48; SWALLOWS
AND AMAZONS, 1177-79; THROUGH
THE LOOKING-GLASS, AND WHAT ALICE
FOUND THERE, 1208-11; TOM'S MID-
NIGHT GARDEN, 1240-42; TREASURE
ISLAND, 1253-56; THE VOYAGE OF THE
"DAWN TREADER," 1306-9; THE WIND
IN THE WILLOWS, 1382-85; WINNIE-
THE-POOH, 1388-89
--Choice: THE AIMER GATE, 9-10;
ALICE'S ADVENTURES IN WONDER-
LAND, 19-22; ANNERTON PIT, 33-36;
ARABEL'S RAVEN, 41-42; AT THE BACK
OF THE NORTH WIND, 55-57; BALLET
SHOES, 68-71; THE BATTLE OF BUB-
BLE AND SQUEAK, 75-77; THE BATTLE
OF ST. GEORGE WITHOUT, 77-78; A
BEAR CALLED PADDINGTON, 84-85;
BILGEWATER, 96-99; BLACK HEARTS IN
BATTERSEA, 107-9; THE BORROWERS,
132-34; THE BORROWERS
AFIELD, 36;
THE BORROWERS AFLOAT, 136-38;
THE BORROWERS ALOFT, 138-40;
BOWS AGAINST THE BARONS, 145-47;
CARBONEL, THE KING OF THE CATS,
173-75; CARRIE'S WAR, 176-79; A
CHANCE CHILD, 197-200; CHARLIE AND
THE CHOCOLATE FACTORY, 203-4; THE
CHILDREN OF GREEN KNOWE, 211-13;
THE CHIMNEYS OF GREEN KNOWE, 217-
19; CHITTY-CHITTY-BANG-BANG, THE
MAGICAL CAR, 221-23; THE CITY OF
GOLD AND LEAD, 237-40; CONRAD'S
WAR, 252-54; THE CORAL ISLAND: A
TALE OF THE PACIFIC OCEAN, 255-57;
DANNY, THE CHAMPION OF THE WORLD,
283-85; THE DARK IS RISING, 287-
88; DAVID IN SILENCE, 290-91;
DAWN WIND, 293-97; THE DOLLS'

HOUSE, 330-32; THE EAGLE OF THE
NINTH, 347-50; EARTHFASTS, 351-
53; THE EDGE OF THE CLOUD, 354-56;
EMMA IN WINTER, 365-68; AN ENEMY
AT GREEN KNOWE, 373-75; FANTAS-
TIC MR. FOX, 388-89; FARMER GILES
OF HAM, 395-97; THE FATE OF JEREMY
VISICK, 397-99; THE FELLOWSHIP
OF THE RING, 405-8; FIREWEED,
414-16; FIVE CHILDREN AND IT,
416-18; FLAMBARDS, 418-21; THE
GHOST OF THOMAS KEMPE, 451-53;
GOLDENGROVE, 459-62; THE GOLDEN
KEY, 462-63; GOODBYE, DOVE SQUARE,
465-67; GRANNY REARDUN, 484-85; A
GRASS ROPE, 468-87;
GREAT EXPECTATIONS, 492-95; THE
GREY KING, 501-2; GULMBLE'S YARD,
514-16; HOBBERDY DICK, 548-50; THE
HOBBIT, 550-53; THE HOLLOW LAND,
555-57; THE HORSE AND HIS BOY,
560-62; THE HOUSE AT POOH CORNER,
562-64; THE INTRUDER, 578-81; THE
IRON MAN: A STORY IN FIVE NIGHTS,
583-85; JAMES AND THE GIANT PEACH,
593-95; KATE CRACKERNUTS, 636-
38; THE KELPIE'S PEARLS, 642-43;
KIM, 651-54; THE LANTERN BEARERS,
679-83; THE LARK AND THE LAUREL,
683-84; THE LAST BATTLE, 687-89;
THE LIGHT PRINCESS, 701-2; THE
LION, THE WITCH AND THE WARDROBE,
710-13;
THE MACHINE GUNNERS, 747-50; THE
MAGICIAN'S NEPHEW, 755-57; MARY
POPPINS, 779-81; MARY POPPINS
COMES BACK, 781-83; MARY POPPINS
IN THE PARK, 783-84; MARY POPPINS
OPENS THE DOOR, 784-86; MASTERMAN
READY, 786-89; MISS BIANCA, 815-
16; MISTER CORBETT'S GHOST, 824-
26; THE MOON IN THE CLOUD, 829-30;
THE PIEMAKERS, 970-71; THE POOL
OF FIRE, 989-92; PRINCE CASPIAN:
THE RETURN TO NARNIA, 994-96; THE
PRINCESS AND CURDIE, 999-1002; THE
PRINCESS AND THE GOBLIN, 1002-3;
NIGHTBIRDS ON NANTUCKET, 887-
89; ONE IS ONE, 915-17; ORDINARY
JACK: BEING THE FIRST PART OF THE
BAGTHROPE SAGA, 920-22; THE OWL
SERVICE, 932-35;
THE PEPPERMINT PIG, 953-55; PETER
AND WENDY, 956-58; RED SHIFT,
1025-26; THE RIVER AT GREEN KNOWE,
1035-36; ROBINSON CRUSOE, 1043-
46; THE SILVER BRANCH, 1088-91;
THE SILVER CHAIR, 1091-94; SMITH,

1108-10; A SOUND OF CHARIOTS,
1123-25; THE SOUND OF COACHES,
1125-28; A STITCH IN TIME, 1140-
41; THE STONE BOOK, 1143-44;
THE STORY OF THE TREASURE SEEK-
ERS, 1146-48; A STRANGER AT GREEN
KNOWE, 1154-55; A STRANGER CAME
ASHORE, 1155-57; THE STRONGHOLD,
1161-64;
THE SUMMER AFTER THE FUNERAL,
1165-67; THE SUMMER BIRDS, 1167-
69; SWALLOWS AND AMAZONS, 1177-79;
THE TALES OF OLGA DA POLGA, 1186-
87; THROUGH THE LOOKING-GLASS, AND
WHAT ALICE FOUND THERE, 1208-11;
THURSDAY'S CHILD, 1220-23; TIME OF
TRIAL, 1223-25; TOM FOBBLE'S DAY,
1234-36; TOM'S MIDNIGHT GARDEN,
1240-42; TO TELL MY PEOPLE, 1244-
45; TREASURE ISLAND, 1253-56;
THE TWELVE AND THE GENII, 1274-
76; UNLEAVING, 1287-90; VIKING'S
DAWN, 1298-1300; THE VOYAGE OF THE
"DAWN TREADER," 1306-9; WARRIOR
SCARLET, 1319-22; WATERSHIP DOWN,
1330-34;
THE WEATHERMONGER, 1336-38; THE
WEIRDSTONE OF BRISINGAMEN, 1342-
45; WHEN JAYS FLY TO BARBMO, 1349-
51; THE WHITE MOUNTAINS,
1359-61; WIDDERSHINS CRESCENT,
1364-66; THE WIND IN THE WILLOWS,
1382-85; WINNIE-THE-POOH, 1388-
89; THE WITCH'S DAUGHTER, 1396-97;
THE WOLVES OF WILLOUGHBY CHASE,
1399-1401; YOUNG MARK: THE STORY
OF A VENTURE, 1415-17
--Christopher: THE GUARDIANS, 505-
8; THE ISLANDERS, 586-88
--Contemporary Classics: CARRIE'S
WAR, 176-79; THE DANCING BEAR,
279-81; THE DARK IS RISING, 287-
88; ELIDOR, 359-60; FIREWEED,
414-16; THE GHOST OF THOMAS KEMPE,
451-53; THE INTRUDER, 578-81;
JOSH, 620-23; A PATTERN OF ROSES,
943-45; THE SCARECROWS, 1058-60;
A SOUND OF CHARIOTS, 1123-25; A
STRANGER AT GREEN KNOWE, 1154-55;
TOM'S MIDNIGHT GARDEN, 1240-42;
THE WOLVES OF WILLOUGHBY CHASE,
1399-1401
--Fanfare: THE AIMER GATE, 9-10;
ALICE'S ADVENTURES IN WONDERLAND,
19-22; ANGELO GOES TO THE CARNI-
VAL, 30-31; ANNERTON PIT, 33-36;
ASK ME NO QUESTIONS, 52-54; THE
BATTLE OF WEDNESDAY WEEK, 79-81;

THE BEETHOVEN MEDAL, 85-87; BEORN THE PROUD, 91-92; BILGEWATER, 96-99; BLACK JACK, 110-13; BLACK SAMSON, 113-15; BLOOD FEUD, 116-19; THE BLUE HAWK, 121-24; THE BONNIE PIT LADDIE, 129-31; THE BORROWERS, 132-34; THE BORROWERS AFIELD, 134-36; THE BORROWERS AFLOAT, 136-38; THE BORROWERS ALOFT, 138-40; THE BORROWERS AVENGED, 140-42; BOSTOCK AND HARRIS;
OR, THE NIGHT OF THE COMET, 143-44; BROTHER DUSTY-FEET, 153-55; CARRIE'S WAR, 176-79; A CASTLE OF BONE, 188-90; CASTORS AWAY!, 190-91; THE CAVE, 193-94; A CHANCE CHILD, 197-200; THE CHANGEOVER: A SUPERNATURAL ROMANCE, 200-1; CHARLOTTE SOMETIMES, 206-8; THE CHILDREN OF GREEN KNOWE, 211-13; CHILDREN OF THE RED KING, 215-17; THE CHIMNEYS OF GREEN KNOWE, 217-19; A CHRISTMAS CAROL; 227-30; THE CIRCUS IS COMING, 234-36; THE CITY OF FROZEN FIRE, 236-37; THE COLD FLAME, 246-48; CONRAD'S WAR, 252-54; THE CORIANDER, 258-61; DAN ALONE, 276-79; THE DANCING BEAR, 279-81; THE DARK IS RISING, 287-88; DAWN WIND, 293-97; DEIRDRE (Polland), 298-99; DEIRDRE (Stephens), 299-301;
THE DEVIL ON THE ROAD, 306-9; A DOG SO SMALL, 328-30; THE DOLLS' HOUSE, 330-32; THE DOLL WHO CAME ALIVE, 332-33; THE DREAM TIME, 335-37; THE DRUMMER BOY, 339-42; ELIDOR, 359-60; EMILY'S VOYAGE, 365-66; EMMA TUPPER'S DIARY, 368-70; THE EMPEROR'S WINDING SHEET, 370-73; FANNY'S SISTER, 387-88; THE FAR-DISTANT OXUS, 389-92; THE FATE OF JEREMY VISICK, 397-99; FATHOM FIVE, 400-3; FIRE AND HEM-LOCK, 411-14; FIREWEED, 414-16; FLAMBARDS, 418-21; FLAMBARDS IN SUMMER, 421-24;
THE FLIGHT OF THE DOVES, 425-27; THE GENTLE FALCON, 447-49; THE GHOST OF THOMAS KEMPE, 451-53; GIRL WITH A LANTERN, 456-58; GOLDENGROVE, 459-62; GOOD NIGHT, MR. TOM, 467-69; GRANNY REARDUN, 484-85; THE GREY KING, 501-2; GUMBLE'S YARD, 514-16; THE HOBBIT, 550-53; HOME IS THE SAILOR, 558-59;

THE HOUSE IN NORHAM GARDENS, 564-66; THE INTRUDER, 578-81; THE ISLANDERS, 586-88; JEREMY CRAVEN, 601-2; JOHN DIAMOND, 610-11; JOSH, 620-23; THE JUNGLE BOOKS, 630-32; THE KELPIE'S PEARLS, 642-43; THE KING'S GOBLET, 662-63; THE KITCH-EN MADONNA, 667-68; KNIGHT'S FEE, 672-75; THE LANTERN BEAR-ERS, 679-83; THE LARK ON THE WING, 685-87; THE LITTLE BLACK HEN: AN IRISH FAIRY STORY, 713-14; A LITTLE FEAR, 714-16; LITTLE KATIA, 717-20; LITTLE PLUM, 722-24; THE LITTLE WHITE HORSE, 724-27; THE LOAD OF UNICORN, 729-30; THE LONG TRAVERSE, 732-34; A LONG WAY FROM VERONA, 734-37; LOST JOHN, A YOUNG OUTLAW IN THE FOREST OF ARDEN, 738-40; THE MACHINE GUNNERS, 747-50; THE MAGICIAN'S NEPHEW, 755-57; THE MAPLIN BIRD, 763-65; THE MARK OF THE HORSE LORD, 771-74; MARY POPPINS OPENS THE DOOR, 784-86; MASTER OF MORGANA, 789-91; A MIDSUMMER NIGHT'S DEATH, 809-10; MIDNIGHT IS A PLACE, 807-9; "MINNOW" ON THE SAY, 812-14; MISS BIANCA, 815-16; MISS HAPPINESS AND MISS FLOWER, 818-20; THE MOON IN THE CLOUD, 829-30; MR. BUMPS AND HIS MONKEY, 839-41; THE NAMESAKE, 870-72; THE NATURE OF THE BEAST, 876-78; THE NINE LIVES OF ISLAND MACKENZIE, 893-94; NOAH'S CASTLE, 895-96; NOBODY'S GARDEN, 897-99; OLD JOHN, 913-14; ONE IS ONE, 915-17; ORDINARY JACK: BEING THE FIRST PART OF THE BAGTHORPE SAGA, 920-22; THE OTHER PEOPLE, 923-24; THE OTHER WAY ROUND, 924-26;
THE OVERLAND LAUNCH, 926-27; OWLGLASS, 931-32; THE OWL SERVICE, 932-35; A PARCEL OF PATTERNS, 938-39; A PATTERN OF ROSES, 943-45; PENNINGTON'S SEVENTEENTH SUMMER, 949-52; THE PEPPERMINT PIG, 953-55; THE PLAN FOR BIRDSMARSH, 982-84; PRINCE CASPIAN: THE RE-TURN TO NARNIA, 994-96; PRINCE PRIGIO, 996-99; PROVE YOURSELF A HERO, 1004-7; THE QUEEN'S BLESS-ING, 1012-13; RANSOM FOR A KNIGHT, 1017-20; RAVENSGILL, 1021-23; THE RESCUERS, 1031-32; THE ROB-BERS, 1039-41; THE ROUGH ROAD, 1049-50; THE SCARECROWS, 1058-60; THE SEVENTH RAVEN, 1076-78;

THE SHEEP-PIG, 1082-84; THE SIL-
VER BRANCH, 1088-91; THE SILVER
CURLEW, 1094-96; THE SINGING
CAVE, 1101-03; SISTERS AND BROTH-
ERS, 1105-6; SMOKY HOUSE, 1111-13;
A SOUND OF CHARIOTS, 1123-25; A
STITCH IN TIME, 1140-41; THE STOL-
EN LAKE, 1141-43;
THE STONE BOOK, 1143-44; THE
STRANGE AFFAIR OF ADELAIDE HARRIS,
1149-51; THE STRANGER, 1151-54;
A STRANGER AT GREEN KNOWE, 1154-
55; THE STRONGHOLD, 1161-64; THE
SUMMER BIRDS, 1167-69; THE SUMMER
PEOPLE, 1169-71; SUN HORSE, MOON
HORSE, 1171-73; A SWARM IN MAY,
1180-82; THE TEAM, 1190-92; THE
THIRD EYE, 1196-99; THREE LIVES
FOR THE CZAR, 1206-8; THROUGH THE
LOOKING-GLASS, AND WHAT ALICE
FOUND THERE, 1208-11; THUNDER OF
VALMY, 1215-18; TIME OF TRIAL,
1223-25; TOM ASS; OR, THE SECOND
GIFT, 1232-34; TOM FOBBLE'S DAY,
1234-36; TOM'S MIDNIGHT GARDEN,
1240-42; TRAVELERS BY NIGHT, 1247-
50; TRISTAN AND ISEULT, 1258-61;
TULKU, 1265-67; TUMBLEDOWN DICK,
1267-68; THE TURF-CUTTER'S DONKEY
GOES VISITING, 1270-72; THE TWELVE
AND THE GENII, 1274-76; UNLEAVING,
1287-90; UP THE PIER, 1290-91;
WARRIOR SCARLET, 1319-22; THE
WATCH HOUSE, 1325-27; WATERSHIP
DOWN, 1330-34; WE DIDN'T MEAN TO GO
TO SEA, 1340-42;
WHEN HITLER STOLE PINK RABBIT,
1348-49; WHEN SHAKESPEARE LIVED IN
SOUTHWARK, 1351-53;
A WILD THING, 1368-69; THE WIND
EYE, 1376-79; WINDRUFF OF LINKS
TOR, 1386-88; THE WINTER OF THE
BIRDS, 1389-91; WOLF OF BADENOCH;
DOG OF THE GRAMPIAN HILLS, 1398-
99; THE WOOL-PACK, 1402-3; THE
WRITING ON THE HEARTH, 1404-7; A
YEAR AND A DAY, 1409-11; YOU NEVER
KNEW HER AS I DID!, 1412-15; YOUNG
MARK: THE STORY OF A VENTURE, 1415-
17
--Guardian: THE BLUE HAWK, 121-24;
CHARMED LIFE, 208-9; CONRAD'S WAR,
252-54; DEVIL-IN-THE-FOG, 304-
6; FLAMBARDS, 418-21; FLAMBARDS
IN SUMMER, 421-24; GOOD NIGHT,
MR. TOM, 467-69; GRAN AT COALGATE,
474-75; THE GUARDIANS, 505-8; HEN-
RY'S LEG, 539-42; THE IRON LILY,
581-83; A LIKELY LAD, 703-6; THE
OWL SERVICE, 932-35; THE PEPPER-
MINT PIG, 953-55; THE SENTINELS,
1068-71; THE SHEEP-PIG, 1082-84;
THE VANDAL, 1094-95; THE VILLAGE
BY THE SEA: AN INDIAN FAMILY STORY,
1302-5; WATERSHIP DOWN, 1330-34;
THE WHISPERING MOUNTAIN, 1356-58
--IRA Honor: A FLUTE IN MAYFERRY
STREET, 427-28
--IRA Winner: GOOD NIGHT, MR. TOM,
467-69
--Jr. High Contemporary Classics:
GOOD NIGHT, MR. TOM, 467-69; THE
MACHINE GUNNERS, 747-50; PROVE
YOURSELF A HERO, 1004-7; THE ROAD
TO CAMLANN, 1036-39
--Lewis Carroll: THE BORROWERS, 132-
34; THE CHILDREN OF GREEN KNOWE,
211-13; EARTHFASTS, 351-53; A HERD
OF DEER, 543-46; THE HOUSE AT POOH
CORNER, 562-64; THE JUNGLE BOOKS,
630-32; THE LION, THE WITCH AND THE
WARDROBE, 710-13; "MINNOW" ON THE
SAY, 812-14; THE RELUCTANT DRA-
GON, 1029-31; THE STORY OF DOCTOR
DOLITTLE, 1145-46; TOM'S MID-
NIGHT GARDEN, 1240-42; THE TWELVE
AND THE GENII, 1274-76; THE WATER-
BABIES: A FAIRY-TALE FOR A LAND-
BABY, 1327-30; THE WEIRDSTONE OF
BRISINGA-MEN, 1342-45; THE WIND IN
THE WILLOWS, 1382-85; WINNIE-THE-
POOH, 1388-89; THE WITCH'S BRAT,
1394-96; THE WOLVES OF WILLOUGHBY
CHASE, 1399-1401
--Maxi: WATERSHIP DOWN, 1330-
34
--Other: THE BONNIE PIT LADDIE, 129-
31; BROTHER IN THE LAND, 156-58;
COMFORT HERSELF, 248-52; THE GREEN
BOUGH OF LIBERTY, 499-501; HAL,
519-21; JOE AND TIMOTHY TOGETHER,
606-8; JOURNEY TO JO'BURG: A SOUTH
AFRICAN STORY, 627-28; OLD DOG,
NEW TRICKS, 911-912; SONG FOR A
DARK QUEEN, 1117-19; STARRY NIGHT,
1133-36; A STRONG AND WILLING
GIRL, 1158-60; TALKING IN WHIS-
PERS, 1187-89; THE TROUBLE WITH
DONOVAN CROFT, 1262-64; THE TURBU-
LENT TERM OF TYKE TYLER, 1269-70;
TWOPENCE A TUB, 1276-78; VILA: AN
ADVENTURE STORY, 1300-2; WHO LIES
INSIDE, 1363-64
--Phoenix: THE MARK OF THE HORSE
LORD, 771-74; THE NIGHT WATCHMEN,
891-92; SMITH, 1108-10

--Poe Nominee: *THE CASE OF THE COP CATCHERS*, 182-84; *THE CASE OF THE SECRET SCRIBBLER*, 184-85; *CLIMBING TO DANGER*, 242-44; *ELIZABETH'S TOWER*, 361-62; *THE GIRL IN THE GROVE*, 455-56; *GOLD PIECES*, 463-64; *KEPT IN THE DARK*, 645-46; *MR. MOON'S LAST CASE*, 847-49; *ON THE EDGE*, 917-19; *SCREAMING HIGH*, 1061-63

--Poe Winner: *DANGER AT BLACK DYKE*, 281-83; *THE INTRUDER*, 578-81; *NIGHTFALL*, 889-91

--Stone: *THE CITY OF GOLD AND LEAD*, 237-40; *THE POOL OF FIRE*, 989-92; *THE WHITE MOUNTAINS*, 1359-61

--Whitbread: *THE BATTLE OF BUBBLE AND SQUEAK*, 75-77; *THE DIDDAKOI*, 318-21; *THE EMPEROR'S WINDING SHEET*, 370-73; *THE HOLLOW LAND*, 555-57; *JOHN DIAMOND*, 610-11; *NO END TO YESTERDAY*, 899-902; *THE QUEEN OF THE PHARISEE'S CHILDREN*, 1009-12; *SONG OF PENTECOST*, 1119-21; *A STITCH IN TIME*, 1140-41; *TULKU*, 1265-67; *THE WITCHES*, 1392-94

--Young Observer: *AQUARIUS*, 39-41; *CHILDREN OF THE BOOK*, 213-15; *A LITTLE FEAR*, 714-16; *MOSES BEECH*, 833-35; *THE WATCHER BEE*, 1322-25

awards. *See* prizes; rewards.
Away from Home, 395
Away from the Vicarage, 1157
AWFUL SYKES, 43-46, *63*, 470, 532, 1013-14, 1087
axes, stone, 1025, 1203
Ayrton family, 1072-74

Babe, the pig, 1082-83
BABE, THE GALLANT PIG, *65*, 665, 1082. See *THE SHEEP-PIG*, 1082-84
babies: birth of, 782, 1095, 1113, 1125, 1128, 1411; born deformed, 655-56; converse with nature, 782-83; dead, 468; demanded in payment, 1130; deposited at church door, 1150; exposed, 1149; illegitimate, 1323; kept secret, 468; kidnapped, 1219; lost in jungle, 630; lost otter, 1384; male gypsy, 1150; sister's, 655-56; sold, 306; suckled by wolf, 630; taken to poorhouse, 1150; water, 853
Baby, 236
baby carriages, to transport doped pheasants, 285, 852

baby sitters: authoritarian, 119-21; boy, 1087; guitar-playing, 42; unpaid aunt, 1133; wishing to be free from duty, 417; woman, 230; youthful, 363, 1218-20. *See also* governesses; nannies; nurses.
Bacchus, 995-96
bachelors: admiral and servants, 318-19; guinea pig, 365-66; old, 50-51
Back Home, 757
The Back House Ghost, 1066
Bacon, Francis, 657
Badenoch, 1398-99
BADGER, *65*, 828, 1229, 1383-84
Badger on the Barge, 567
Badgers, 156
badgers, 432, 893, 995, 1264; gentlemanly, 152, 388-89, 911, 931-32
badger's sets, 61, 133, 135
baggin, 1143
Baggins family, 95-96, 131-32, 405-8, 436-37, 439-40, 464-65, 551-53, 804, 981-82, 1056, 1107, 1204
BAGHEERA, the panther, *65-66*, 71, 630-31, 635, 836
Bag-jagderags, 988, 1310
bagpipers, 650, 1285
Bagthorpe Saga, 266
Bagthorpe family, 275, 477, 479, 838-39, 920-22, 1047-48, 1195, 1282-83, 1372, 1419-20
Bailey family, 833, 834-35, 963, 1173
Baillie, George, 457
Bainen, 1003
Bainen, the cat, 248, 675, 913
bakehouses, barn, 971
Baker, Alan, 75
BAKER, M(ARGARET) J(OYCE), *66-67*, 186
bakers: delivery boy, 85-87; pie-makers, 600; Viennese, 32, 214, 546; woman in play, 286-87
Baker Street Irregulars, 182
The Baker Street Irregulars in the Case of the Missing Masterpiece, 316
Balanter, the hound, 487
Balder, leader likened to, 1298
BALDERSON, MARGARET, *67*, 1349
BALDMONEY, *67*, 324, 716, 1114
bald persons: German, 888; man, 790
Balfour, Alasdair, 428
Balfour family, 13, 298, 648-51, 1281

Balicki family, 152, 353-54, 597-98, 619-20, 1052-53, 1097-99, 1398
Balin, 407, 553
The Ballad of Kon-Tiki and Other Verses, 1071
ballads, 411, 414
BALLANTYNE, ROBERT MICHAEL, *67-68*, 255
ballerinas: circus girl, 205, 1248; tumbling act, 88-89; with inherited ability, 68-71
BALLET SHOES, *68-71*, 1157
Ballinford doom, 47
Ballinford family, 1196-98
Ballinford Hall, 708
ballistas, 481-82, 959
balloons: burst, as birthday present, 358, 1388-89; girls overeat and become, 13
balloon woman, 782
balls: hunt, 420-21; of thread, invisible, 1002; small, white aromatic, 1181; soccer, 359; witch, 374
Ballyhoggin, 138, 837, 856
Ballymanus, 101, 445, 499-501, 879
Ballymurry, 1151-54
Balnibarbi, 512
BALOO, the bear, 65, 71, 630-31, 635, 836
Balrogs, 407, 439, 982
bamboche, 765
bamboo, thickets of, 1154-55
Bander-log, the monkeys, 65, 631, 635
bandits: Chinese, 1266; in forest of Arden, 739; Russian, 1416; children play, 1147. *See also* burglars; robbers; thieves.
bands: Irish walking, 1285-87; school, 542, 1062-63
Bang, You're Dead!, 1257
banishments, 1413; from tribe, 337
bankers, Lombard, 791, 1402-3
banknotes, stored in loft, 484
Banks family, 779-81, 781-83, 783-84, 785-86
Bannockburn, battle of, 1017
banquets, 65, 828, 1229, 1308
banshees, 518
baptisms, Christian, of captive, 871
Barbados, 172, 217, 591, 616
Barbara, 1000-1
Barbara Banks, 779-80, 781, 783, 785
Barbecue, 172, 732
barbers, 519; role in play, 286-87; traveling, 1234, 1356
Barbmo, 1351

Bard, 552-53, 1107, 1204
bards, 1142. *See also* minstrels; musicians; singers.
bare feet, with elaborate dress, 160
bargains: blanket for gold nugget, 1205; king's life for kingdom, 247; nonprosecution for participation in play, 286; nuts for pebbles to lift spell, 637; tools for food, 311. *See also* agreements; pledges; treaties; truces.
bargemen, 238
barges, 325; bear away dead husband, 1142; duchess's threatened, 1024; funeral, 123; Toad rides on, 1383; with three women, 1038
Bari, Master Antonio, 1402-3
Barker, Carol, 667
Barker family, 106, 171, 602
Barkridge's, 84
Barley family, 495
barmaids, 1126
Barnaby Palmer, 533-34
Barnaby Scholar, 498, 533-34
BARNABAS, 71, 1407
Barnabas Walks, 795
Barnard, Arthur, 50, 311, 648
Barnard family, 889
Barnes, 506
Barnet family, 360-61, 361-62, 696
Barney Drew, 804
Barney Palmer, 498, 498-99, 533-34, 1185, 1264
barns: children sleep in, 1398; collapsing, 340; holding hostage children, 312; Leaches, 519; once a seventeenth-century house, 303, 307-9, 609, 1174
barons: fourteenth-century, 145-47; Norman, 674; oppressive, 717
The Barons' Hostage, 1253
Baron Walter FitzGilbert, 1017-20
BARRETT, ANN (MAINWARING), *71-72*, 1114
BARRIE, JAMES M(ATTHEW), *72*, 956, 961
Barrier, between Conurb and County, 506
Barrinish, Ireland, early twentieth century, 737, 1101-3
barristers, woman, 822
barrow wights, 406
BARRY MORTIMER, *73*, 242, 399, 836, 895-96
BARRY PADGITT, *73-74*, 519-21, 522
bartering, 150
Bartholomew Boncourt, 916

Bartholomew family, 533, 1238, 1241-42, 1238, 1241-42
Barthomley church, 611, 1025-26, 1203
Bart Kodaly, 124, 597, 640, 880, 1218-20
Bartley MacDonagh, 259
BARTOLOMEO CORDOBA, *74*, 907
Barton family, 249, 251, 476, 482-83, 698
BARTY, *52-54*, 59, *74*, 694
Basher Byre, 696, 1116
BASIL DUFFIELD, *74-75*, 325, 327-28, 343, 639, 1042
Basil II, Emperor of Constantinople, 117
Bastable family, 19, 318, 334, 418, 547, 881-82, 899, 922, 1146-48
bassinet, 9
Bastille Day, 1216-17
Batchford, George, 450, 548-49
Bateman family, 89, 476-77, 531-32, 555-57
BATES, John, *75*, 86, 950-52
Bates Roller, 488
Bath, 169, 294
Bath Regis, 1142
baths, Piglet gets, 1389
bats, space, 584
Battersea, 354, 689
Battersea, Duchess of, 1121-22
Battersea family, 108-9, 1121-22
THE BATTLE OF BUBBLE AND SQUEAK, *75-77*, 949
THE BATTLE OF ST. GEORGE WITHOUT, *77-78*, 465, 797
The Battle of the Books, 1182-83
The Battle of the Braes, 751
Battle of the Five Armies, 439, 1204
THE BATTLE OF WEDNESDAY WEEK, *79-81*, 1371
Battle of Worcester, 1199
battles: against barons, 12; against giant, 120; between cannibals, 256; of Ashdown, 18; of Tenchebrai, 674; mock, 307; psychological, 413-14; reenacted, 307; single combat, 995, 1168, 1259, 1274; terrible, good vs. evil, 876. *See also* battle scenes; conflicts; fights; war novels; wars.
battle scenes: 12, 65, 113-15, 120, 402, 407, 562, 680-82, 766, 788, 865, 913, 995, 1085-86, 1091, 1114, 1120, 1162-63, 1172, 1209-10, 1226, 1237, 1255, 1296, 1299, 1310, 1343-44; against weasels,
828; attack by resistance group, 157; eighteenth-century France, 339, 342; English-Danes in Wessex, 870-72; in stable, 687-88; Irish rebellion, 500; jungle combat, 117; mock, 1047, 1228; Narnia, 712; on high seas, 1069-70; rabbit war, 1332-33; raids, 739; Roman Britain, 1119; Scottish tribal wars, 773; sham, 1030; Sikhs against robbers, 470; Toad Hall, 1384; Viennese-Turkish War, 213-15; Vikings in Byzantium, 117-18; War of Roses, 105; World War I, 1214; witchcraft, 569. *See also* battles; conflicts; fights; war novels; wars.
BATTY, *81*, 645
Baumer, Lewis, 1146
Bavaria, 354
BAWDEN, NINA (MABEY), *81-82*, 176, 645, 953, 1039, 1396
BAYLIS, SARAH, *82*, 1300
Baynes, Pauline, 140, 395, 560, 687, 710, 755, 994, 1091, 1306
Bay View Private Hotel, 579
BB (D(ENYS) J(AMES) WATKINS-PITCH-FORD), *82-84*, 716
beach-plumb jelly, diet of, 344
beacons, 391, 1178
Beadbonny Ash, 410
Beamish family, 496, 866-67
"beam of darkness," 1336
Beams Price, 1165, 1167
Bean, 388-89
Beanpole, 237-8, 240, 989-91, 1360-61
A BEAR CALLED PADDINGTON, *84-85*, 126
"bearding" of wool packs, 1402
Bear of Very Little Brain, 1388-89
bears: 552, 630-31, 996; cub, 159; dancing, 279-81, 1099; fat, stuffed, 989, 1388-89; gets stuck in rabbit hole, 1388; head stuck in honey jar, 1388; sleepy brown, 71, 836; stuffed, 84-85, 232, 844; tame, 929; talking, 71, 84-85; teacher of wolf cubs, 630-31; teddy, 1388-89; trained, 120, 158-59; two brown appear in flying balloon, 921
Bears Back in Business, 66
bear wardens, slave boy, 279-81
beasts, wierdly shaped, 1000-2
beatings: by brothers, 661; faked, 616; for getting sister pregnant, 317; in school, 818; of apprentice, 197; of bullies, 1093; of

crippled boy, 420; of illegitimate
son, 423; of overseer by boy's
mother, 198-99; of pianist on
hand, 951; of sister's seduc-
er, 420; of wife, 1243; of working
children, 198; reasonless, 525;
with belt, 176. *See also* floggings; whippings.
Beatrix Potter, allusion to, 696
Beauchamp-Troubridge, Admiral Sir
John, 4, 480-81, 516
Beaulieu Abbey, 1337
Beaumarchais family, 806, 959, 1339
Beauregarde family, 203, 1305
Beauty and the Beast, 570
beauty: love of, 15; of rural
countryside, 674-75; wished for,
417
beavers, talking, 711, 1009
Becca Polwarne, 1409-10
BECKETT, *85*, 792, 1379-81
Beckford family, 480, 959, 972, 974,
980
Becky Finch, 127-29
bed and breakfasts, 578
bedesmen, elderly, 324, 1406
Bedford, F. D., 956
Bedfordshire, early twentieth
century, 132-34, 134-36, 136-38,
140-42
Bedivere, Sir, 1038
Bedknob and Broomstick, 905-6
Bedonebyasyoudid, Mrs., 851, 853,
1329
beds: bitterly cold stable, 1160;
magic, 206-7, 365; misunderstood,
467; on wheels, 206-7; shared by
four grandparents, 203-4; wetted,
468
Beech family, 179, 467-69, 851-52,
1240, 1372-73, 1419
Beech, Moses, 833-35, 1173
beehives, remnants of, 1181
Beehive Secondary Modern, 950
Beekeeper, 1180-82
beer, fortifies singer's confidence, 75
bees: attracted by white ball, 1181;
respond to singing, 1181; swarming, 1181; watcher, 1322-24; wild,
631-32
THE BEETHOVEN MEDAL, *85-87*, 966
beetles, very rare Jabizri, 1310
beggars: girl in Roman Britain,
294-97, 930, 1029; girl,
unsuccessful, 1018; in
India, 651; in Manchester,
449, 1268; in Shakespearean

England, 246, 1352-53;
London, 1160; professional,
278; tinker's family, 1009-
12
beginning of world, 367
*Beginnings: Creation Myths of the
World*, 395
beheadings, ordered, 211
Behind the Wind, 1404
Beke, 765-67
Belaney, Roger, 47
Belanos, 1162
Belfast, late twentieth century,
1284-87
BELINDA FELL, *87-88*, 722-24, 818-19
Bellabelinda and the No-Good Angel,
831
Belladonna, the white witch, 698,
752, 845, 1104, 1192, 1354-56
Bella Slattery, 605
Belle, 228
BELLE CARTER, *88*, 110, 111-13, 1232
BELLE MARRIOT, *88-89*, 205, 425,
1247-50
Bell family, 60-61, 475-76, 538,
899-902, 1192, 1283-84
Bell House, 463
Bellinger family, 821, 883, 1024,
1237
Bell, Lucas, 31-32, 508, 807-9, 845,
1104
Bell-Pull family, 560
bells: golden, 755; in Charn, 987
BELL TEESDALE, *89*, 476-77, 531, 555-
57
Beltane, 387, 1162, 1321
Bemmerton family, 1199-1201
Ben Blewitt, 328-30, 479, 483, 852
Ben Clare, 1105-6
Bendy Goodrich, 195, 612, 729-30
Benedictine Abbey, 915-17
Benedictines, 1395
benefactors: Borrower, 1130; con-
vict, 376, 494-95; of acting fami-
ly, 306; restaurant owner, 1304-5;
secret, 592, 757, 981; supposed,
820; thought generous, 1147; night
watchman, 1304; wealthy family of
poor, 1303-4; woman, 763
Bengalis, obese, 574, 653
BEN GUNN, *89*, 1255-56
Benjamin Bussell, 153
Benjamin Partridge, 824-26
Benjamin Sullivan, 569
Ben Lodge, 150, 156-58, 283, 656
Bennet Hatch, 102-3, 615
Bennett, Jill, 283
Bennett, Mr., 652

Bentley automobile, 645, 728
Bentley, Nicholas, 1385
BENTLEY, PHYLLIS (ELEANOR), *89-91*,
   463
Bently Drummle, 495
Ben Willis, 235
Beorn (*Beorn the Proud*), 91-92
Beorn (*The Hobbit*), 552
Beornstead, 930
BEORN THE PROUD, 91-92, 986
Beornwulf, 295-96, 1293
Beowulf, 1230
Beowulf the Warrior, 1075
Bereford family, 560, 694-95, 959,
   1221-23
Bergen (ship), 1155-56
Berkshire Downs, 1171-73, 1330-34
Bern, 1307, 1309
Bernard, the mouse, 816, 1031-32
BERNARD HUNTER, *92*, 455, 618
Bernard into Battle, 1081
Bernard the Brave, 1081
Bernie, 164-66
Bernie Bradshaw, 205, 656-57
berry pickers, 606
berserkers, 117, 375-76, 746, 870,
   1299
BERT ELLISON, *92-93*, 452, 862
Bertha Plummer, 267-68
Bertold family, 33-36, 485-86, 592-
   93, 778
Bertoni family, 30
Bertram, 26, 245, 873, 934
Bertrand Lesseps, 558-59
BERTRAND STUDDARD, *93*, 752, 810,
   1055, 1376-78
Bert the Match-Man, 780, 783, 784
Besingtree, 307
Bess Mossock, 168, 1067, 1342-43
Beth Reeves, 2, 586
BETH STUDDARD, 93, *93-94*, 752, 810,
   1055, 1376-78
BETO, *94*, 585, 1187-88
betrayals: 738, 916, 1107, 1108-10,
   1202; assumed, 260; by bird-
   catcher, 681; by friend, 14; of
   people by government, 156-58; by
   king, 299, 300; by mill company,
   604; by mother, 656
betrothals: among Boar people, 245;
   announced, 1420; Byzantine, 47;
   child, 276, 827, 885, 1402; expected to princess, 248; feasts,
   279-81; princess to count, 247-48;
   resisted, 744, 909; unwanted, 1415
bets: cheating at, 1104; ill-fated,
   303; lost, 845; over treasure, 2,
   487

Betsey Smeaton, 474
BETSY ASHWORTHY-SMITH, *94*, 814, 858,
   1058
BETSY FARR, *94*, 190-91, 595, 880
Betsy O'Connor, 621-23
Betsy Smith, 1
Between the Forest and the Hills, 695
Beulah Land, 977, 979
Bevis d'Aquillon, 673-75
Beyond the Burning Lands, 232
Beyond the Vicarage, 1157
BEYOND THE WEIR BRIDGE, *94*, 162,
   1199. See THOMAS, 1199-1202
Bible: characters, 522-23, 894-95;
   Gospel of John, 155; quoters of,
   399, 508, 549, 1023; source of sto-
   ry, 829-30, 1076
Bickerson, Geordie, 160, 281-83,
   449-50, 486, 523, 1223
bicycles, 381, 469, 480, 697; bas-
   ket, as doll's home, 381-82;
   confiscated, 156; decrepit, 540;
   lamps, 351-52; ridden by blind
   boy, 592; ride, lengthy, 1335;
   tandem, 17, 704; willful, 523-25;
   Yellow Peril, 959
Biddums, Ursula, 450, 548
BIDDY, *94-95*, 493-94, 608
Biddy Murphy, 271, 713-14
Biddy of Craigengill, 1140
Big-Endians, 509
Big Friendly Giant, 284
Biggin family, 339, 577-78, 1035-
   36, 1154, 1183
Bight of Benin, 866, 1069
Big John Moran, 259-60
bigotry, 623, 1336-38
The Big Pink, 980
BIGWIG, the rabbit, *95*, 1331-32
BILBO BAGGINS, *95-96*, 406, 436-37,
   439-40, 464, 551-53, 804, 1056,
   1107, 1204, 1231
Bilgewater, 96-99, 532, 946, 1193-94
BILGEWATER, 96-99, 440
Bilgie, 96-99
Bilk, Toby, 737, 1357-58
Bill (*Fireweed*), 414-16
Bill (*Elizabeth's Tower*), 696
Bill, the lizard, 1362
Billandben, 689-91
BILL COWARD, *99-100*, 233, 603, 805-
   6, 876-78, 879-80, 910
Billeting Officers, 467
Billing, Mr., 821, 839, 1109-10
Bill O'Connor, 621-23
Bill Sparrow, 76-77, 100, 860, 1088
Billy (*Travelers by Night*), 425
Billy (*Old Dog, New Tricks*), 911-12

BILLY BONES, *100-1*, 338, 965, 1253-54
Billy-Boy, 641
BILLY BYRNE, *101*, 499-501, 879
Billy Kenton, 1285-86
Billy Pritchard, 926
BING JONES, 4, *101*, 285-86, 845, 968, 1039-40
Binks Marlow, 963
Binns family, 689-92
Binns, Miss Valerie, 579
biographical novels: 215-17, 447-49, 456-58, 499-501, 717-20, 870-72, 1012-13, 1117-19, 1412-15, 1415-17. *See also* didactic novels; historical novels; period novels.
bird-catchers, betrayers, 681
Bird Cottage, 480
BIRDIE PLANTAGANET, *101-2*, 303-31
birdlords, fiery Phoenix, 1168
bird lovers, 480-82, 817
Bird-of-Paradise, purple, 1309
birds: dead in cupboard, 74; dying, 707; helpful thrush, 552; instruments of evil, 1344; killed by cats, 525; magic, 1094-96; Molly, 1329; seagull, 1332-33; species almost extinct, 1168; steel, 17, 411, 707, 851, 1390; talking, 887-88; talking raven, 41-42; talking swallow, 1145; talking thrush, 1107; vicious, 1344
bird sanctuaries, 1154
Birdsmarsh, 225, 516-17, 946, 982-84, 1088
Bird Woman, sells crumbs for birds, 780, 784
Birkinshaw family, 539, 922, 1067-68
Birmingham, mid-twentieth century, 290-91
birth certificates, 708
birthday parties, 235, 251, 367, 386
birthday presents: burst balloon, 1388-89; empty honey jar, 1388-89
birthdays: 1072, 1166; disappointing, 328; Eeyore's, 358, 1388-89; eleventh, 1375; eleventy-first, 96, 406; ignored, 277; ninth, 921; ninetieth, 431; on Midwinter Day, 287; of older sister, 382; same shared, 406, 1169; seventy-fifth, 477; thirty-third, 406, twenty-first, 1198
births: of baby, 1201; of brother, 56; of daughter, 422; of deformed baby, 158; of girl, 1171; of lambs,

188; of longed-for prince, 997; of princess, 40; of seventh sibling, 387; of Sikh baby, 310; of son, 682, 879; of usurper's son, 323
Birtwick horseballs, 612
Birtwick Park, 105, 454
bishops, 78, 1180; boots drenched by accident, 1159
Bistro, the chimpanzee, 598, 1098
bitterness, self-destructive, 679-83
Bjorn, 1085-87
Black and Tan, 544
THE BLACK ARROW: A TALE OF THE TWO ROSES, 102-5, 1139
Black Beauty, the horse, 17-18, 171, 454-55, 596, 602, 612
BLACK BEAUTY: HIS GROOMS AND COMPANIONS, 105, 1079
BLACK BEAUTY: THE AUTOBIOGRAPHY OF A HORSE, 105-7, 1079-80
Blackberry, 1332-33
Blackbird, 336-37
The Blackbird in the Lilac, 1028
Black Castle, 1031-32
Black Clough Dale, 918
Black Dog, 1254
Black Dyke, 160, 282-83, 486, 1223
Blackett family, 171-72, 874, 949, 972-74, 1178-79
Black Faces, White Faces, 440
Blackfeet, 733
Black Ferdie, 212, 409
BLACK HEARTS IN BATTERSEA, 8, *107-9*, 887, 1401
BLACKIE, *109-10*, 198-200, 246, 1239
BLACK JACK, *110-11*, 111-13, 1232
BLACK JACK, 111-13, 442
Black Knight, 1092-93
Black Lake, 505
The Black Lamp, 182
blacklegs, 1276
Blackley, 291
blacklisting of miners, 130, 841
blackmail: 112, 184-85, 282, 525, 537, 545, 646, 825, 843, 954, 1162, 1196; attempted, 400; by fear of harm to grandchildren, 478; by servant, 195
blackmailers, 222, 242
blackmarketers, 242, 400, 896
blackmarket, World War II, 749
Black Men, wicked, 725-26
Black Mountains, 737, 1356
Black Narcissus, 458
Black Panther, 38, 65-66
Black Parrots, 988, 1310

Black Rider, 287-88

blacks: boy companion for blind
girl, 1173-74; cannibals, 256-
57; courageous, 743; enduring,
743; huge man, 236; in Africa,
743; in England, 248-49, 251-
52, 591-92, 616, 1067, 1173-74;
in Ghana, 249-52, 762; in Haiti,
937-38; Jamaican in London, 842;
in London, 689-92, 968, 1039,
1262-64; nanny, 632, 787-88,
1239, 1374; pictured as inferi-
or, 632; trumpeter, 1062-63;
slave boy, 172, 195, 217-19, 616,
765-67; South African, 627-28;
stereotyped, 919-20, 1145-46,
1311; treated comically, 1145-
46; well-educated, 249-51; wife
of Welshman, 4

BLACK SAMSON, 113-15, 526

blacksheep relatives, 533-34, 953-
55

blacksmiths: 9, 47, 94-95, 396, 463,
484-85, 492-93, 608, 619, 945,
981, 1225, 1235; friendly, 1401;
gnome-like, 1196-98; Sikh, 311

black spot, 100, 965, 1254-55

Black, Tim, 520-21, 522

The Blacktower, 1076

The Black Tower, 1076

Black William, 726

BLAI, *115*, 338, 1320-21

Blake, Quentin, 41-42, 1392

Blanche, the horse, 1017-19

Blanche Garde, 453, 670-72, 729

Bland, E., 882

Bland, Fabian, 882

Blastburn, 302, 677, 807-9, 1099,
1104, 1400-1

bleeding, as cure, 717

Blefuscu, 509-10

Bleriot plane, 355

Blewitt family, 328-30, 479, 483,
852

blindfolds, yellow horse leg bandage, 1005

blindness: metaphorical and physical, 846; simulated, 461

blind persons: as leaders in the
dark, 35-36, 1396-97; capable boy,
33-36, fiddler, 359; girl, 173,
195, 217-19, 1396-97; professor,
460-61

blitz, World War II, 414-16, 747-
50

blizzards, 1399

The Blob, 540-42

BLODEUWEDD, *26*, *116*, 574, 932

Blodwen and the Guardians, 1391

Blodwen Owen, 558

Blodwen Rowlands, 1050

blood brothers, 117

blood feud: averted, 296; pursued,
116-19

BLOOD FEUD, 116-19, 1176

bloodhounds, 765-66

Blood-Money Banks, 222

Bloody Bill, 256-57

Bloody Mary, 700

Bloodwort, Mother, 1354

blouses, red, for stepsister, 874

Blow, Peter, 404-5

BLUDWARD, BOB, *119*, 808-9

blue: girl turns, 1305; wall of,
1308

Blue and Gold Day, 67

Bluebell, 557, 1332

blueberry, giant, 1305

The Blue Bird, 69

THE BLUE BOAT, 119-21, 794

The Blue Fairy Book, 679

THE BLUE HAWK, 121-24, 315

"The Blue Light," 246, 1028

Blue Mountain, 248

*Blue Remembered Hills: A Recollec-
tion*, 1175

Bluey, the rabbit, 1373

Blunt family, 923-24, 1033

Boadicea, Queen. *See* Boudicca, Queen
of the Iceni, 1117-19.

Boakes, 98-99

boarders, 62, 68, 1224; at resort,
eccentric, 923-24; bizarre, 923-
24; mysterious, 753

boarding schools: boys', 228, 230,
532; boys', girl lives in, 96-99;
boys', girl stays in, 1166; boys',
posh, 413, 616; children on holiday from, 211-13, 221-23, 366-68,
382-85, 404-5, 434-36, 455, 497,
963-64, 972-74, 994-96, 1004-7,
1165-67, 1177-80, 1340-42; choir,
223-25, 1180-82; girls' 206, 206-
8, 1071-74, 1084; in prospect,
251; home for falcon, 384; murder
in, 809-10; proposed, 362; state-
run, 506; threatened, 166, 478,
520-21, 539, 640; undesirable,
1091-94, 1316-19

boar hunts, 296

Boar people, 245, 333, 387, 878,
884, 1161-64, 1190

boars, wild, attack, 996

boating, fad, 1382

A Boat in the Reeds, 1140

boat ride, rabbits take, 1332-33

boats: antique, 1088; as home, 198;
   blue row, 120-21, 230, 570; burned
   by Germans, 1350; coal and munitions, 1213-15; borrowed for
   voyage to Africa, 1145; canal,
   197-99, 560, 798, 1222; canoe,
   291, 1035; capsized by Mole, 1382;
   chasing and sinking, 637; coracle of frog skins, 717; currachs,
   258, 260, 544, 737, 1101-2, 1271;
   cut adrift, 402; cutlery-box, 137,
   141; cutter, 1340-42; derelict,
   197, 869; dinghy, 1178-79; elven,
   407; escapes in, 1337; fishing
   smack, 85, 312, 433-34, 763-65,
   792, 1379-81; gondola, 913; hauled
   overland, 926-27;
   homemade canoe, 513; house, 508,
   614, 1228; life, 926-27; lobster,
   740, 1102; made from knife box,
   1130; mail, 426; motor, 253; oak,
   bridge between wrecks, 969; old
   sail, 460-61; old smack, 517;
   outrigger canoe, 586; paddle, 716;
   pilot, 260; pink boiled-sweet,
   1376; row, 496, 535, 775; rubber dinghy, 496, 1046; run down by
   ship, 649; sail, 614, 874, 1178-
   79; salmon, 731; sardine, 740;
   soap-box punt, 141; smack, 946,
   982-84; small sail, 1044; toy
   steamboat, 717; sunk by Germans,
   1350; tin soapbox, 1130; trawler,
   1213-14; tug, 366, 401-3, 1177;
   Viking, 1101-2; Viking design,
   1377;
   Viking, wrecked, 1378; wrecked,
   1397; yacht, 3-4, 763-64, 1379-81.
   See also canoes; ships; yachts.
BOBBIN RAMSAY, 124-25, 1218-20
Bobby Fumpkins, 367-68
Bob Cratchit, 227-29, 353, 409
Bob Hardcastle, 988
Bob Randall, 506-8
Bob Tranter, 639, 669, 875
BOB WHITE, 125, 477, 1021-23
Boca del Sol, 1052, 1064
Boddser Brown, 245, 747-48, 886
Bodecker, N. M., 1114
bodies: disappearing, 243; found
   on shore, 190; iron, reassembled,
   584; of pirate, used as pointer,
   172; reassembled, 584; of tramp,
   243; transported to New World in
   ice, 1142
Bodleian Library, 1318-19
bodyguards, 1076-77
"bogey-man" rabbit, 446

boggarts, 351-53
Boggis, 211-13, 388-89
Boggis family, 616
bogs: 482; pursuit through, 684. See
   also marshes; swamps.
"Boheemyum," 1160
Boland, Michael, 145
Bolgolam, 509
Bolingbroke, Henry, 448, 453
BOLINGBROKE, ROGER, 125-26, 324,
   350, 799, 1405-6
Bolinger family, 52-54, 58-59, 74,
   262, 692, 821
Bombadil, Tom, 406
Bombay, late twentieth century,
   526, 706, 1302-5
bombed-out house, as home, 415-
   16
bombers, German, downed, 747, 749
bombings: destroys house, 887; of
   post office, 1286; of school, 427;
   of water reservoir, 1286; sectarian, 1286; World War I, 1214-15;
   World War II, 210, 226, 377-79,
   414-16, 562, 603, 735-36, 1235.
   See also air raids.
bombs, protestors', 798
bomb shelters: 415, 748, 1240; in
   medieval passages, 378; in village, 468.
Bombur, 553
BOND, (THOMAS) MICHAEL, 84, 126-27,
   1186
Bone, Florence, 427
bones: dog swipes from museum, 1316;
   of infant, discovered, 305; of
   long-dead boy found in mine, 398
Bones, Billy, 1253-54
bonfires: Guy Fawkes, 607; village,
   320
Bonfires and Broomsticks, 905
THE BONGLEWEED, 127-29, 266
Bonnie Green, 1099, 1400-1
THE BONNIE PIT LADDIE, 129-31, 503
Bonnie Prince Charlie, 648
Bonnie Prince Georgie, 837, 888,
   1048, 1100
bonsai trees, 506
booby-traps: for formmaster, 951; in
   cave, 222
Book, exhorting, 975
A Book for Boys and Girls, or Country
   Rhymes for Children, 161-62
Book of Gospels, 216
Book of Gramarye, 288
Book of Teaching, 204, 522, 586-
   87
A Book of the Seasons, 445

books: ancient, of magic, 800; herbal, 1395; library, 184; made of
dead bat, 374; of magic, 373, 1307;
on hawking, valuable, 385; rude,
705; scholarly, 339; smuggled
to sister, 491
booksellers, helpful; 723, 819;
idealistic, London, 338, 849,
858-59, 1224-25
bookshops: gathering place for
intellectuals, 1224; managers,
mother, 200, 636
"boomerang chuck," 262, 1114
Booth, Alec, 157
boots: as home, 135; go only in opposite directions, 913-14; magic red
and blue, 913-14; manure-smelling
Wellingtons, 376, 1354; seven
league, 569, 997-98
Borach, 300
borders, of North Ireland, 1133-
36
Born of the Sun, 270
BOROMIR, *131-32*, 407
Borrowers, 49-50, 61, 132-34, 136-
38, 138-40, 140-42, 489, 559-60,
811, 822, 837, 854, 857, 947-48,
985, 1129-30, 1236, 1282
THE BORROWERS, 134, *132-34*, 904-
6
THE BORROWERS AFIELD, 134-36, 136,
905
THE BORROWERS AFLOAT, 136-38, 138,
905
THE BORROWERS ALOFT, 138-40, 905
THE BORROWERS AVENGED, 140-42,
905
Bors, Sir, 1037-38
BOSIE, *142-43*, 478, 645-46
bosses: mine, 129-31; oppressive,
129-31
bossy characters: cat, 173; boy,
193; girl, 205
BOSTOCK, *143*, 143-44, 186, 529, 856,
1149-50
*BOSTOCK AND HARRIS; OR, THE NIGHT OF
THE COMET*, 143-44, 442
BOSTON, L(UCY) M(ARIA WOOD), *144-45*,
211, 217, 373, 1035, 1154
Boston, Peter, 144, 211, 217, 373,
1035, 1154
botanists: 1396; eccentric woman,
853, 1195, 1266-67
Boteler, Dr., 1200-1
Bothwell, 1413
bottles: discarded in attic, 1289;
genie in, 1354; washed up from sea,
1288

Boudicca, Queen of the Iceni, 1117-
19
boulders, with hole, 933
boundary line, marked by chalk
horse, 1172-73
bounty: of nature, lavish, 256;
on prince, 998
Bourke, Tot, 61, 474-75
Bournemouth, 1392-93
bow and arrow: discovered, 124;
stolen, 1218
Bowbridge, 208
Bowen, Arrow, 524
Bowen family, 74, 323, 906-7
Bowles, Sybil, 1166-67
Bowling, Mr. Gerald, 400, 836, 843-
44
BOWS AGAINST THE BARONS, 145-47,
1252
bows, magic, 711, 994
Boxer, the dog, 266-67
Boxer Rebellion, 1195, 1265
boxers, 238, 696, 1116
boxes: containing pistol and ring,
1125-28; false-bottomed, 183;
pencil, 1389
THE BOY (*The Borrowers*), 49, 132-34,
147-48, 489, 560, 854
Boy (*The Reluctant Dragon*), 1030
Boy (*The Rescuers*), 1031-32
Boyd family, 314, 515, 599, 1242-43,
1365-66
Boy in a Barn, 831
Boy: Tales of Childhood, 275
boys: abandoned, 293, 415-16, 1199;
absorbed into crack in sky, 352;
abused, at boarding school, 506,
because illegitimate, 264, by
brothers, 660, by foster parents, 605, 815, 1049-50, 1057-58,
by miner, 1238-39, by psychotic
mother, 467-69, 851-52, 1372-73,
by teacher, 844, by Turkish pirates, 371, by tyrannic father,
1284, emotionally, 277, in Norman
castle, 672; adopted, 31, 281,
360, 532, 958, 1373; adventurous,
604; affected, 1122-23; afraid
of heights, 1202; afraid of sea,
1202; always eating sweets, 539;
amoral, 597-98, 1099; angelic
looking, 560; angry at grandparents, 328; arrogant, 592;
artistic, 899, 1373; ashamed of
mother's drinking and affairs,
887; assertive, 1225; assumed dead
in air raid, 887; assumes role of
father during flood, 707; avid

reader, 880; banished from tribe, 115, 1319-22; big, clumsy, 1363; birdlike, 1168-69; bluntly honest, 316-17; bookish, 290, 367, 501, 667-68, 885, 899, 1391; book-loving, 129-31; bossy, 193; bought from mother, 422; bratty, 203; bratty, changed to mouse, 1393; businessman, 318; calm, methodical, 707; capable leader, 792-93; captured by goblins, 1002; cast out of village, 1394; casual student, 740; clever, 244; clever with hands, 697; clowning, 1258; confined to closet, 852; conscientious, 203-4; considered coward, 1137; considered hopeless by teachers, 656; consigned to monastery, 1137; cosmopolitan, 28; cries like seagull, 1410; cynical, 148; deceptive, 356-57; deeply resentful, 1100-1; definite, careful, 318; deserted at Christmas, 228; deserted by mother, 852; determined to fit in, 793; delicate chest, 899; directive, 314; disagreeable, 74-75; disliked, 558; disobedient, 291, 1064; displaced persons, 339; dominated by sister, 191; dreamy, 188, 273, 526, 528; dutiful, 1405; eager to go to war, 879; earnest, 230, 904; eccentric, 1225-26, 1326-27; efficient and sensible, 232-33; eighteenth-century in modern Yorkshire, 351-52; emaciated, representing Ignorance, 228; embarrassed by parents, 595; emotionally disturbed, 1262-64; emotionally reserved, 616; emotionally unstable, 1232; energetic, 252-54; enterprising, 884-85; especially interested in engines, 1047; especially understanding, 793-94; excellent horseman, 701; exceptionally handsome, 739; exceptionally responsible, 1374; exiled for political reasons, 701; expert on planes, 1297; extremely angry, 1288; extremely disagreeable, 1058-60; fat, 203, 367; fearful, 1262-64; feels abandoned by mother, 1263; fiercely protective of mongoloid sister, 1288; flying, 961; foster, 148, 304, 707, 1049-50, 1126-28; foundling, 1409;

full of ideas, 292; given lessons in boxing, 696; greedy, 176, 203; group carpenter, 960; handsome, manipulative, 886; handsome, self-centered, 1065; harebrained, 197; heir to industrial fortune, 807, 809; helpful, 314; highly imaginative, 880, 1046-47; high principled, 608; homeless, 277-78; idle dreamer, 1233; illegitimate, 197, 264, 317, 422, 677, 682, 814, 1228, 1412; illiterate, 821, 1395; imaginary, 740; imaginative, 147-48, 252-54, 290, 538, 570, 740, 801, 891-92, 1240; impossibly good, 57; imprisoned falsely for murder, 1109; impulsive, 729, 1041; insolent, 421-22; instructor in flying, 1168; intense, 225-26; in trouble with law, 285-86; inventive, 792-93; invisible to adults, 198-99, 398; invisible to other children, 1168; irresponsible, 451; jilted, 202; junk-loving, 539-42; kidnapped, 616, 846, 1004-7, 1357; kidnapped at uncle's request, 1281; kidnapped by Romans, 1161; kidnapped by terrorists, 917-19, 1265; knighted, 674, 916; lazy, 1042; level headed, 451; lonely, 147-48, 740, 1154, 1212, 1240-42; loner, 1062; lone survivor of battle, 294; long-haired genius, 1326-27; looks like ape, 696; lost, 961, in mine, 398; low self-esteem, 1033; macho Latin, 1076; maladjusted, 367-68; malnourished, 959; manipulative, 37, 518; manly, 272; mechanically inclined, 480, 959; mischievous, 129, 718, 885; misfit, 915; moral, 321; musical, flutist, 212, singer, 285-86; mute, 1262-64; mysterious, 793; naively trusting, 884; natural horseman, 962; natural leader, 1419; naughty, 1204, 1239; near-psychotic, 1058-60; neglected, 353; next door, 202, 596, 1203; obnoxious, 376-77, 810-11; obsessive, 1374; old for age, 968; on their own, 1380, 1405; opportunistic, 1065; over-attached to father's memory, 1060; overbearing, 453; overly polite, 516; over-protected, 73-74; overweight, 193; overworked, 660, 1049-50;

passive, 516; passive-resistant, 858, 1007; pathetic, 516; pick-pocket, 816, 1007-8, 1008-10; poorhouse, 197; possessed, 1100-1; practical, 461; psychotic, 1258; pusillanimous, 1147; quick minded, 519; quick tempered, 611; quick thinking, 529; quiet, thoughtful, 1171; raised by wolves, 836-37; rationalist, 1225-26; ready for fight, 614; rebellious, 286, 591; reckless, 193, 701; reclusive, 519-20, 522; refuses to cry, 1192-93; refuses to grow up, 956, 958, 961; requests foster home, 846; resourceful, 30-31; respectful, 203; responsible, 230, 899, 1375; responsible for home, 1380;

responsible for household and ill old man, 834; responsible for housekeeping, 99-100; retarded, 422; rude and hostile, 618; scholarly, 1199; scientific, 193, 292; scorned by father, 1374; selected for sacrifice, 625; self-congratulatory, 922; self-contained, 74, 615-16; self-deluding, 1122-23; self-effacing, 799; self-reliant, 353-54; semi-literate, 797-98; sensitive, 193, 337-38, 623; seventh son of a seventh son, 1375; severely emotionally disturbed, 846; ship pilot, 1380; ship's, 887-89; showoff, 539; shrinks to mouse size, 922, 1035; shy, 450; small and frightened, 467; small, bookish, 1375; snobbish, 1100-1, 1203; socially maladjusted, 941-42, 949-52, 962; sold as infant, 306, 826, to priests, 1261-62; sophisticated, 1419; spoiled, 916, 1042, 1067, 1076, 1306-7, by permissive parents, 376-77; spoiled younger brother, 719; stage-struck, 1127-28; stands up to father, 705; starving, 370; steady, 356, 787-88; stepson, 93, 968, 1059-60, 1065; streetwise, 651, 656-58, 797-99, 816-17, 845-46, 847, 1087-88, 1115-17, 1215; stubborn, 224; stubbornly courageous, 337-38; takes responsibility for crippled father, 286; takes responsibility for household, 817; takes up father's cause,

28; talks to animals, 1410; tall, bespectacled, 1360; teasing, 147-48; teasing brothers, 330; terrified, undernourished, 852; theatrical, 1419; thought retarded, 28-29, 1212; thought sickly, 1195-96; thought to have prophetic powers, 920-21; thrown out by guardian, 1126; tied in closet, 468; timid, 245, 703-6, 748-50, 886-87; tough, 245; trained as pickpocket, 246; troublemaking, 1058-60, 1204; truculent, 408, 1229;

turned out as useless when ill, 1160; TV addict, 203, 810; uncowed, 74; underachiever, 224, 920; undisciplined, 1202; unfriendly, 455; uninhibited, 468, 596; unstable, 612; unusually attached to father's memory, 1100-1; unusually resilient, 1297; venturesome, 291; village, with cut foot, 311; visible only to children, 264; waif, 273, 293, 360; well informed, 256-57; Welsh, 518; white-haired, 148-49, 502; wild, 1130; wildly drunk, 1126; willful, 356-57, 570; witch, 1122-23, 1389; withdrawn, 667-68; withdrawn after illness, 73-74; with ferret, 1236; with nine lives, 191; worried about sin, 1165, *See also* children; girls.
Boys' House, 1171, 1320
The Boy with the Erpingham Hood, 242
Bozzo, Frank, 1356
bracelets: jewel emits light, 414, 1343; military, 261; protective, 1344
Brackley, Sir Daniel, 316-17, 606, 615, 695, 1103
Bradley, Jim, 1340, 1342
Bradley family, 25-26, 244-45, 873-74, 933-34, 1047
Bradshaw, Cicely, 827
Bradshaw family, 205, 234, 656-57, 885, 1402-3
Bradwell, Mr., 130
Braes of Balquidden, 650
Braille postcards, 34
Brains Bellingham, 184-85
brakes, tampered with, 873
Bramber, 673-74
Bramble Hill, 673
Bran (*The Stolen Lake*), 1142
BRAN (*The Stronghold*), 148, 333, 387, 1161-62, 1190

BRAN DAVIES, *148-49*, 502, 1050, 1375

brands: of slave on left shoulder, 765-66; V for vagabond, 574

Brandybuck family, 132, 406-8, 437, 804-5, 982

brandy, illegal cargo, 1381

Brandywine River, 804

BRANFIELD, JOHN (CHARLES), *149*, 429

Branford, 156

Branton Colliery, 129-31

Branwell Bronte, 1275

BRANWELL, SAM, *149-50*, 157-58, 283, 1033

BRAQUE, CARMODY, *150*, 200-1, 692-93, 1123

Brass Button, 1180

bravery: of miniature people, 135-36; exceptional, 1069-70; of king's children, 217

Brayles, Master Simon, 791, 1405

Bread and Honey, 1129

breaking and entering, boys, 1040

break-ins: church, 78; on a dare, 1317; to mansion, 537; to spice shop, 402

Break in the Sun, 52

Break of Dark, 1348

Bree, 406, 1158

BREE, the horse, *150*, 561, 1081

Bree-hinny-brinny-hoohy-hah, 150

Bretons, in Ireland, 740, 1102

Brett, James, 1149-50

breweries, London, 422

Brian, 697

bribes: 713, 1109, 1260; by Sikh matriarch, 312; by sister, 70; for good behavior, 1317; from sister's boy friend, 197; of Syrian slave, 671; planned, 142-43; refused, 1096; suspected, 182; to control pupil, 596; to raft captain, 280; to sailor, 297; Turkish Delight, 710-11; urged, 1346

bride hunt, 773, 865

briderace, 1293

bride-prices, 114

brides: child, 447, 585, 586; kidnapped by her family, 114; made of flowers, 116; retrieved, 114; sought by black wizard, 1353-56

Bridestone, 1343

Bridge of Apes, 1145

bridges: collapsing, 40, 409; hiding place for jewels, 94; ladder, 723; leaps from, 621; over fiery chasm, 407; rope, 1266, 1302

Bridget and William, 441

BRIDGET HUNTERLY, *150-51*, 389-92

Bridget, Miss, 1108

Bridget Sanders, 897-99

Bridie McShane, 7, 339, 818, 850, 924, 942, 1084, 1123-25, 1373-74

Bridlington, 234

Brigantes, 348, 375

BRIGGS, K(ATHERINE) M(ARY), *151-52*, 548, 636

The Bright and Morning Star, 531

Brighton, 143-44, 186, 1149

Brightplace, 535

Brimstone Bellinger, 883, 944

Brisingamen, Weirdstone of, 414, 1343

Brisket, Mrs., 1099, 1400-1

Bristol, 170, 413, 509

Britannia Mews, 1081

British Isles:

--prehistoric period: 335-37

--ancient times: Cornwall, 1258-61; Ireland, 298-99, 299-301, 1258-61

--tenth century, B.C.: England, 1319-22

--first century, B.C.: England, 1171-73, 1244-45; Scotland, 1161-64

--first century, A.D.: England, 771-74, 1117-19; Scotland, 771-74

--second century: England, 347-50, 1025-26; Scotland, 347-50

--third century: England, 1088-91

--fifth century: England, 679-83

--pre-Arthurian period: England, 395-97

--sixth century: England, 294-97

--late eighth century: Ireland, 1298-1300; North Sea, 1298-1300; Scotland, 1298-1300

--ninth century: England, 870-72; Ireland, 91-92

--tenth century: England, 116-19; Ireland, 116-19

--late eleventh century: England, 672-75, 1012-13, 1085-87; Scotland, 1012-13

--early twelfth century: England, 1394-96

--late twelfth century: England, 671-72, 738-40

--thirteenth century: Ireland, 215-17

--late Middle Ages: England, 1232-34

--early fourteenth century: England, 915-17, 1017-20

--fourteenth century: England, 145-47

--late fourteenth century: England,
447-49
--fifteenth century: England, 102-
5
--mid-fifteenth century: England,
1404-7
--late fifteenth century: England,
683-84, 729-30, 1402-3
--sixteenth century: England, 581-
83
--mid-sixteenth century: Scotland,
1412-15
--Elizabethan era: England, 153-55,
581-83
--early seventeenth century: England, 1351-53
--seventeenth century: England,
306-9, 636-38; Scotland, 636-38
--mid-seventeenth century: England,
548-50, 938-39, 1009-12, 1025-26,
1199-1202
--late seventeenth century: Scotland, 456-58
--eighteenth century: England, 111-
13, 143-44, 169-71, 304-6, 339-42,
610-11, 824-26, 1108-10, 1125-28,
1253-56
--mid-eighteenth century: Scotland,
648-51
--late eighteenth century: England,
197-200, 463-64; Ireland, 499-501
--early nineteenth century: England, 107-9, 190-91, 236-37, 1111-
13, 1145-46, 1223-25; Scotland,
1155-57; Wales, 1356-58
--nineteenth century: England, 839-
41, 1149-51, 1327-30
--mid-nineteenth century: England,
5-6, 52-54, 227-30, 266-69, 397-
99, 492-95, 724-27, 763-65, 807-9,
1068-71, 1276-78, 1309-11, 1399-
1401
--late nineteenth century: England,
55-57, 105-7, 129-31, 387-88,
484-85, 489-92, 755-57, 926-27,
1143-44, 1146-48, 1158-60,
1316-19, 1379-81
--unspecified early period: England, 332-33, 970-71, 1094-96,
1409-11; Ireland, 913-14
--early twentieth century, England,
9-10, 132-34, 134-36, 136-38,
140-42, 206-8, 276-79, 354-56,
416-18, 418-21, 421-24, 459-62,
473-75, 703-6, 899-902, 943-45,
953-55, 1213-15, 1220-23, 1267-
68, 1287-90, 1322-25, 1386-88;
Ireland, 258-61, 1101-3, 1270-73;

Scotland, 588-89, 1123-25, 1398-
99
--World War I period: England, 9-10,
206-8, 421-24, 1212-15
--mid-twentieth century: England,
68-71, 77-78, 84-85, 96-99, 119-
21, 163-66, 173-75, 182-84,
186-88, 193-94, 203-4, 206-8,
211-13, 221-23, 223-25, 234-36,
281-83, 290-91, 328-30, 330-32,
351-53, 359-60, 361-62, 366-68,
377-79, 381-82, 382-85, 385-86,
389-92, 400-3, 403-5, 414-16,
434-36, 467-69, 480-82, 486-87,
495-98, 514-16, 536-38, 593-95,
667-68, 685-87, 689-92, 710-13,
716-17, 722-24, 734-37, 747-50,
779-81, 781-83, 783-84, 784-86,
801-4, 812-14,
815-16, 818-20, 889-91, 897-99,
903-4, 923-24, 924-26, 963-65,
972-74, 982-84, 1021-23, 1064-65,
1071-74, 1105-6, 1114-17, 1154-
55, 1167-69, 1169-71, 1177-79,
1180-82, 1218-20, 1234-36, 1240-
42, 1274-76, 1340-42, 1342-45,
1364-66, 1385-86; English Channel, 1339-40; Ireland, 425-27,
543-46, 713-14, 1151-54; Isle of
Skye, 1049-50; Scotland, 79-81,
368-70, 642-43, 789-91, 1196-99,
1396-97; Wales, 176-79, 558-59,
932-35
--World War II period: England, 377-
79, 400-3, 467-69, 414-16, 734-37,
747-50, 924-26, 1234-36; English
Channel, 1339-40; Wales, 176-79
--late twentieth century: England,
33-36, 41-42, 45-47, 85-87, 127-
29, 188-90, 248-52, 252-54, 283-
85, 286-87, 287-88, 306-9, 318-21,
325-28, 388-89, 397-99, 411-14,
429-32, 451-53, 455-56, 465-67,
519-21, 523-25, 539-42, 555-57,
564-66, 578-81, 583-85, 645-46,
656-58, 797-99, 833-35, 876-78,
891-92, 911-12, 917-19, 920-22,
943-45, 949-52, 1004-7, 1025-26,
1039-41, 1058-60, 1061-64, 1076-
78, 1082-84, 1119-21, 1140-41,
1165-67, 1186-87, 1190-92, 1211-
13, 1247-50, 1262-64, 1269-70,
1287-90, 1290-91, 1313-15, 1325-
27, 1330-34, 1334-36, 1353-56,
1363-64, 1376-79, 1389-91, 1392-
94; Ireland, 1284-87; Northern
Ireland, 1133-36; Scotland, 427-
28, 1368-69; Wales, 242-44, 501-2,

567-69, 847-49, 906-7
--modern times, unspecified: England, 931-32
--twenty-first century: England, 505-8, 989-92, 1359-61
--future, unspecified: 156-58, 309-13, 895-97, 1336-38
British Museum, 667
British Navy, 1068-70
Britons, Romanized, 261-62; tattooed, 347
Brittany: ancient times, 1258-61
Brixton, 86
Broad River, 535, 715
Broad Street Children's Home, 277
Brobdingnag, 509-11
"brochs," 1161
BROCK, the badger, *152*, 432, 911, 931-32
Brom, 713
BRONIA BALICKI, *152*, 353, 597, 619, 1052, 1097-99, 1398
Bronte, Emily, identification with, 1166
Bronte family, 90, 241, 793, 963-65, 1164, 1274-76
Bronte fans, 1275
The Brontes of Haworth, 471
Bronwen Owen, 903-4
Bronwen Parry, 243-44
Bronze Age: England, 1319-22
Bronze Age tribes, 336-37, 337-38, 1319-22
The Bronze Chrysanthemum, 993
brooches: dowry, 115; dropped from cloak, 349; elven, 982
BROOKE, *152-53*, 866, 1069-71
Brooke, Rupert, 226
Brook, Judith, 1031
Brook, Miss Olivia, 319-20, 822
broomsticks: enables cat to talk, 174-75; witch's, 174-75
brothels, 402, 881, 1084
Brother Anselm the Precentor, 1395
Brother Colman, 216, 408
BROTHER DUSTY-FEET, *153-55*, 1176
BROTHER ERNULF, *155*, 916-17
Brother Eustace, 1394-95
brotherhood: of thieves, 574; sworn, 116-19, 1298-99, 1320
Brotherhood of Free Traders, 1112
Brotherhood of St. Francis, 4
Brotherhood of the Road, 154
BROTHER IANTO, *155-56*, 1357-58
BROTHER IN THE LAND, 156-58, 1183
Brother John the gardener, 1395
Brother Ninnias, 681-82
Brother Peter, 1394

brothers: blood, 1298-99, 1320, 1344; foster, 1262, 1402; half, 729, 797, 1281; ill with measles, 1240; precocious, 1372; protective, 1370; rivals for girl, 1281, 1335; separated twins, 765-67; supportive, 230; sworn, 876; thought murdered, 931; thought to be cousin, 460; threatened by demon, 692-93
Brown, the dog, 329, 479, 483
Browne, Gordon, 1146
Brown family, (*A Bear Called Paddington*), 84-85, 844
Brown family, (*Carbonel, the King of the Cats*), 173, 173-75
brownies, 5-6
Brown, Lizzie, 53-54, 262
Brown, Serephina, 1071-74
brown, two men in, 1108-10
Bruce, the dog (*Dogsbody*), 326-27
Bruce, the dog (*Wolf of Badenoch*), 1398-99
Bruce family, 14, 605, 1049-50, 1057-58
Bruno Caraboose, 183
Bruno Jenkins, 1393-94
brutality: 3-4, 738-40, 1277, 1298-1300, 1352; by convict, 110; by leader of thieves, 246; by pirate, 100; by Saxon neighbor, 1293; by South Pacific blacks, 256-57; in Irish rebellion, 500-1; of war, 213-15; schoolgirls to gypsy girl, 319-20; towards African blacks, 743
Bruton Street, London, 340-41
Bryni, 295-96, 1293
Bryson, Bernarda, 1274
Bubba, the bear, 158-59, 279-81, 557
Bubb, James, 94, 190-91, 342, 356, 595, 1237
BUBBLE AND SQUEAK, the gerbils, 76-77, 100, 159, 293, 604-5, 860
buccaneers, 100-1, 338
BUCHAN, JOHN, *159-60*, 732
Bucket family, 203-4, 479-80, 864-65
Buckland, 406
Buckingham Palace, 529
Buckinghamshire, 287-88
Buckle, 108, 1122
Buddhism, 1266-67
Buddhists, 1194, 1195
BUD RILEY, *160*, 282-83, 523
buffalo, water, 631, 1085
Bugg family, 1196
bugs: cockle-snorkle, 432; conniving, 1121

Bulgars, in Thrace, 118
Bulgy Bears, 996
bulldozers: cover iron giant, 584;
   in quarry, 404-5; wrecking playground, 520-21
bullfights, 324, 1309-10
bullies: attack girl, 74; councillor, 176, 179; cousin, 703,
   1132; cousin and siblings, 915;
   ex-schoolmate, 157; girls, 319-
   20, 1401; McKay brothers, 1390;
   neighborhood, 446-47, 696, 738,
   778-79, 1115-17; older boy, 218;
   older brother, 1042; one locked
   in cellar, 1160; schoolmates,
   164-66, 319-20, 603, 747-48, 886,
   954-55, 1040, 1058-59, 1091, 1356;
   sea captain, 173; storekeeper,
   842-43; torment old spinster,
   1160; uncle, 1282, 1284; uncle
   crippled, 1284
The Bull Leapers, 1334
bulls: bad-tempered, 282; drawing
   of on cave wall, 1144; mad, 842,
   1318; price for pack acceptance,
   630; white, 1163
BUMPO KAHBOOBOO, Prince of Jolliginki, 160-61, 988, 1309-11,
   1145-46
Bumps family, 840
Bunce, 388-89
The Bunch of Grapes, 354, 1126-27
Bundle Raleigh, 558
bunkers: machine gun, 210; underground, 886, 1051; World War II,
   748-49
Bun, Miss Sybilla, 922, 1035
Bunnion family, 1149-50
Bunny, 524
Bunty, 161, 208
BUNYAN, JOHN, 161, 974
Bunyard, 1213-15
burdens, of sin, 975-76
burglar alarms: accidental, 542;
   diagram of, 184
burglars: advertise for job, 439;
   apprehended, 1401; hobbit, 551-
   52, 1204; leader of thieves' gang,
   246. See also bandits; robbers;
   thieves.
Burgomaster, Bavarian, 354
burials: of iron man, 584; of Roman eagle under house, 350; sea,
   1102; ship, 288
Burke family, 543, 545
Burkert, Nancy Ekholm, 593
Burley, Dick, 401-3
burnings, at stake, 1036-39, 1302

burns: cripple hand, 1055; deform
   face, 109
BURTON, HESTER (WOOD-HILL), 162-63,
   190, 495, 1199, 1223
bus: companies, small, 657; drivers,
   205, 656-57, 1390
buses: attempt to start, 310;
   boarded without sufficient fare,
   98; school, 669; stranded, 874
THE BUS GIRLS, 163-66, 530
businesses: failing, 1146; highly successful, 1233-34; rescued,
   1148
businessmen: jolly, 409;
   stereotypical, 245
Buster, the pony, 963
busybodies, village, 318, 452
Bute Street Site, 519-21
Butharsdale, 1085-86
Butter Crashey, 1274-75
butter, used to repair watch, 753,
   767
buttons: metal tracking, 1360; silver, 650
Bye-bye, Blackbird, 303
Byre family, 446-47, 612, 613, 678,
   696-97, 738, 778-79, 854, 863,
   1115-17
Byrne family, 101, 445-46, 499-501,
   879
Byron's poetry, 490
Byzantines, 557
Byzantium: sixth century, 47, 279-
   81; tenth century, 116-19

cabbies, London, 106, 602
CABBY, 167, 755-56
cab drivers, 56, 1066
cabin boys: on treasure ship, 1254;
   on wrecked ship, 371; water rat,
   366
cabins, log, 787
Cabinteely, 499-500
cabs, horsedrawn, 167
CADELLIN, 167-68, 344, 408, 414,
   504, 1342-45
Cadell-Twitten, Miss, 4, 290, 480-82
Cadfan's Way, 502
Cadwan, 1117-19
Caesar, 512
Caewlin, 295
Cafall, the dog, 148, 502
Caffa, 298-99. See also Cathfa, 299-
   300.
caftan, boy wears black, 1122
cages, bear, 1099
Cain, 625

Cair Paravel, 560, 687, 710, 994, 1092-93

cakes: decorated with a night train, 892; poisoned, 1347; wedding, 267; wedding, crumbling to dust, 493

cake shops, 698

Calais, 1133, 1213-14

CALCIFER, *168*, 567, 568-69, 1122

caldrons, glue, 809

CALEB, *168*, 538, 620, 891-92

Caleb Plummer, 267-68

Caledones, 967

Callendar family, 403-5, 434-36, 1296

Calleva, 271, 347

calliope, used as target, 481

The Call of the Valley, 63

The Call of the Wild Wood, 641

Callum family, 171-72, 972-74

Calormen, 43, 150, 377, 560-62, 575, 687, 689, 1081, 1174

Calstead, 523

Calvinists, staunch, 1123

Cambridge, 870, 1308

The Cambridge Book of Poetry for Children, 472

camels: crotchety, talking, 829; ghostly, 215; in Wales, 1411

cameraman, American, 1188-89

cameras, stolen, 806, 877, 910

Camilla, 261

Camlann, 1038

campaigns: clean-up, fix-up, 1115; to raise pigeons, 707; to save church, 707, 791; to save tree, 689-92

Campbell family, 650-51

Campden Hill, 897

Camperdown, Miss, 520-21

camping: during strike, 130; holiday adventure, 1047; in yard, 972; on expedition to sea, 390-91; on island, 1178-79; with caravan, 1382

camps: German prison, 1097; on desert island, 787; Red Cross refugee, 1098; refugee, World War II, 1098; secret, 482; slave labor, 1295

CAM RENTON, 29, *168-69*, 1052, 1064-65

Camulodunum, 1119

Canaan, 626

Canada: mid twentieth century, 732-34; various historical periods, 732-34

Canadians, in New Zealand, 200

canal builders, 199, 264

canals: 197-99, 446, 514, 542, 560, 1039, 1115; old, 435; through city, 629; Toad dunked in, 1383

Canal Street, 277-78

"canary," to warn of danger, 310

CANDIDATE FOR FAME, 169-71, 629

candies: clove, 244; square, look round, 1376; Turkish Delight, 710-11; whistling, 221

A Candle at Dusk, 27

A Candle in the Night, 1183

candles: from within hill, 641; carried by drummer boy, 351-52; lit in church, 124; palace, 529; with cold flame, 351-52

candlesticks, angel-shaped, 1396

Candlin, Mr., 130-31, 861

candy factories, 58

candy makers, 203-4, 669, 761

candymen, 130

candy shops, 174, 223

Canker, Arriman, 697-98, 845, 1353-56, 1397

cannibalism, 1092

cannibals: after nuclear holocaust, 157; on Pacific island, 256; on Caribbean island, 1045; rats, 1355

cannons: eighteenth-century, 4, 481-82; pulled to sea by whale, 889

canoes: for refugee children, 1398; found, 812. *See also* boats; ships; yachts.

Canon Crowfoot, 496

canons: Augustinian, 1015; Austin, 1395

Canterbury, mid-twentieth century, 223-25

Canterbury Choir, 223-25

Canterbury Choir School, 794, 1080-82

Canterbury College, Oxford, 1281, 1316

Cantisburg, 296

Cantoris, 224

Cantrip, Mrs., 174

Capping, 1359, unsuccessful, 1359

Capria Island, 434-35

caps: fairy mob, 714; invisible, 997-98; pitch, 501

Captain, 1227

CAPTAIN, the horse, 106, *171*

Captain Arblaster, 317

Captain Bostock, 186, 530

CAPTAIN FLINT (*Pigeon Post; Swallows and Amazons*), 71-72, 614, 972-74, 1047, 1178-79, 1228

CAPTAIN FLINT (*Treasure Island*) 89, 100, *172*, 732, 1254-55

Captain Gresham, 489-92
Captain Gumble, 404-5
CAPTAIN HOOK, *172*, 957-58
Captain Hoseason, 13, 649
Captain Hughes, 844, 1141-43
Captain Jabez Casket, 1048
Captain Jupiter Foster, 893-94
Captain Nathaniel Dark, 108
Captain of Dragoons, 1346
Captain of Foot, 1346
CAPTAIN OLDKNOW, *172-73*, 195, 217-
    18, 591-92, 616, 1173
Captain Raleigh, 558-59
Captain Richard Dexter, 304-6
captains: dishonest, scheming, 740;
    of beggars and thieves, 246; of
    fishing smack, 85; of Owsla, 557;
    of tugboat, 401-3; of turf barge,
    1272; sea, 591-92, 770; talking
    hare, 366
*Captains Courageous: A Story of the
    Grand Banks*, 666
The Captain's House, 675
Captain Simon Henchman, 190-91, 595
Captain Smollett, 732, 1254-56
CAPTAIN VANSITTART DARKNESS, *173*,
    236-37, 1412
The Captive Isle, 1043
captives: at Vanity Fair, 976; be-
    friended, 829; bound by spider
    webs, 551, 1095; boy held for ran-
    som, 1416; boy of goblins, 1002;
    boy of thieves, 730; boy ransomed
    by uncle for eight-pence, 1147;
    British girl of Romans, 1245; con-
    soled by flute music, 829; Danish
    soldier, 1243; entire enemy navy,
    509; fugitive convict, 494; girl
    and grandmother in isolated house,
    907; girl of cattle raiders, 294;
    held in lighthouse, 889; hen of
    fairies, 713-14; hermit, 91; in
    Anglo-French wars, 1405; in at-
    tic, 139, 140; in cellar passage,
    282; in dump, 45; in Egypt, 196;
    in fireplace grate, 168; in pit
    for poachers, 284; in mine tun-
    nel, 778; in Tower of London, 600;
    in underground stronghold, 1299-
    1300; mysteriously released,
    1360; of bird, 511;
    of caravan to Egypt, 829; of cut-
    throats, 39; of Danes, 871-72; of
    English soldiers, 500; of elves,
    551-52; of family friends, 243-44;
    of Germans, 253, 1097, 1339; of In-
    dians, 418; of King of Jolliginki,
    1145; of king's forester, 146; of

miniature people, 509; of Normans,
    1086; of outlaw leader, 739; of pi-
    rates, 256, 957-58; of reaper,
    510; of secret police, 1187-89;
    of slaver, 1307; of terrorists,
    34-36, 335, 592, 606, 918-19,
    1077-78; of Turks, 453, 671, 968;
    of turncoat noble, 104; of Vi-
    kings, 91-92; of willow tree, 406;
    of witch, 549; of young hoodlums,
    425;
    political, 28; released, 256-57;
    Saxon, 1089; sons of Uisneac, 300;
    Stone-Age girl, 336; storekeeper,
    157; woman Viking, 1378. *See also*
    prisoners.
captures: foiled, 811; of Ger-
    man submarine, 403; of slave ship
    by navy, 1069; of jewel thieves,
    41; of thief, 30
Caradhras, 407
Caradoc Clough, 196, 536
Caradog Prichard, 148, 502
Carausius, 270-71, 633, 1088-91
Carausius's Fool, 1090
Carausius's "hound," 1090
caravans: as home, 516, 1025; as
    prison, 34, 485; circus, 234, 516;
    gypsy, 284, 318, 320, 1021, 1382;
    house trailers, 1025, 1232; Middle
    Eastern, 624-26; to ancient Egypt,
    829; to White Mountains, 1204. *See
    also* gypsy wagons.
CARBONEL, the cat, *173*, 174-75, 909
Carbonel and Calidor, 1107
CARBONEL, THE KING OF THE CATS, 73-
    75, 1107
Cardiff Castle, 672
card sharps, 278
career novels, 68-71, 169-71, 234-
    36, 354-56, 685-87
careers, recovered, 678
caretakers: church, 467, 1240;
    graveyard, 197; manor house, 455;
    retarded man, 1151, 1153; stables,
    235; Watch House, 50-51, 1325
Carey, Mother, 851, 853, 1329-
    30
Caribbean Sea, mid-twentieth centu-
    ry, 1064-65
caricatures: 593-95, 753, 767, 827,
    829-30, 836, 851, 853, 970-71,
    1068, 1121; candy maker, 864-65;
    of English royalty, 902; of royal-
    ty, 996; of Victorian mother, 343;
    of woman in academe, 339, 1036
caricaturists, 608-9
Carlin's Cave, 1397

Carlisle family, 200-1, 636, 692, 815, 1122-23, 1389
Carmel Fay, 1133-36
Carmody Braque, 150, 692-93
Carmody, Dr., 1232
carnelians, smashed token, 1190
carnivals, Sicilian, 30-31
Carolina House, 676
Caroline House, 676
CAROLINE TEMPLETON, *175*, 806, 959, 1339
caroling, 1040, 1268
carpenters: choir school, 224; father, 290; ship's, 190; Viennese, 214; village, 92-93, 452
carpet mills, 807-809
The Carpet-Slipper Murder, 796
carpets, magic, 997
Carr, 90
Carraigmore village, 426
CARRIE, *175-76*, 362, 472, 667, 1056, 1208, 1290-91
CARRIE'S WAR, 81, *176-79*
CARRIE THATCHER, *179*, 468-69
CARRIE WILLOW, 14-15, 60, 176-79, *179-80*, 543, 826, 842-43, 886
Carrington, Nina, 411-12, 893
CARROLL, LEWIS (CHARLES LUTWIDGE DODGSON), 19, 22, *180-81*, 324, 343, 745, 1208, 1359
Carroll, Patsy, 544-46
Carrot-juice Carstairs, 748
cars: anthropomorphized, 221-23; almost strikes boy, 1263; as motorboat, 222; Bentley, 645; derelict, 221-23; falls to pieces, 1366; flying, 221-23; magic, 221-23; obsessions with, 1383-84; red Jaguar, 537; Rolls Royce, 421, 537, 1337; white Jaguar, damaged, 950; wrecked, 354
Carson family, 243-44
Cart and Cwidder, 617
Carter family, 88, 110, 1232
Carter, Helene, 1177
CARTER, PETER, *181-82*, 213, 1068, 1284
carters, 266-67, 484
Cartier, Jacques, 733
carts: donkey, escapes in, 1401; stolen, 1010
carvers, wood, 1402
Carver, Uncle Titus, 313, 601-2, 629, 1228
carvings: leopard, 1072-73; on stone wall, 1317, 1319
car watchers, 386
casanovas, 568-69

THE CASE OF THE COP CATCHERS, *182-84*, 316
THE CASE OF THE SECRET SCRIBBLER, *184-85*, 547
cases, trumpet, switched, 1062-63
Casino Royale, 424
Casket family, 344-45, 887-89, 1048
CASPIAN, Prince and King of Narnia, *185*, 323, 376, 893, 995-96, 1007, 1034, 1092-93, 1174, 1264-65, 1306-8
CASSIDY, MICHAEL, 143-44, *185-86*
Cassilus, 1244-45
CASTAWAY CHRISTMAS, 66-67, *186-88*
castaways: desert isle, 787-89, 855, 859, 1023, 1044-46, 1239, 1374; South Pacific, 255-57; teenagers, 1, 2, 586; tropical island, 893-94. *See also* maroons.
Castle Malyn, 737
Castle Merlin, 831
A CASTLE OF BONE, *188-90*, 394
Castle of Gleidermannheim in Bombardy, 1386
Castle of Lochleven, 677, 814, 1412-14
The Castle of Yew, 145
castles: 208, 739, 997, 1003, 999-1001; abandoned, 361; Arthurian, 1037-38; Arundel, 672; besieged, 417, 670, 1041; blown up, 109; burning, 146; Colditz, 253; demolished by explosion, 1358; dream, 189; dwarf's, 248; home in, 478, 1039-41; Hospitallers', 671; life in, 216, 1360, bizarre, 568-69; magnificent Middle Eastern, 670-71; medieval, 1360; medieval wasteland, 359-60; moving, 168, 567, 568-69, 777, 928-30, 1123; Necromancer's, 1338; Norman held, 216, 1103; of Black Men, 725; on mountain, 1002-3; ruins of, 994; stormed, 672; wrecked, 1338. *See also* manors; mansions; palaces.
Castle Wynd, 351-52
Castor luminary, 326-27
castor-oil beans, 1239
CASTORS AWAY!, 162-63, *190-91*
The Catalogue of the Universe, 759
catastrophes. *See* accidents; disasters.
A Cat Called Camouflage, 617
CAT CHANT, *191*, 208-9, 225, 517, 598
CATE, DICK (RICHARD EDWARD NELSON CATE), *191-92*, 911
CATERPILLAR, blue, 20, 22, 192, *192-93*

Caterpillar Hall, 72

catharsis, writing of story, 760

Cathedral, Canterbury, 1180-82

Cathedral Choir School in Canterbury, 794

cathedrals: Exeter, 377-78; visits to, 98

Catherine Loves, 581

Catherine Medley, 583, 972

CATHERINE MOMPHESSON, *193*, 938-39

Catherine Nobility Institute, Moscow, 719

Cat, Herself, 573

Cathfa, 299-300. *See also* Caffa, 289-99.

Cathlan, Old, 1319-20

Catholics, Irish, 1135, 1284-87

Cat in the Manger, 90

Cat on a Houseboat, 303

Catriona, 651, 1139

Catriona Sykes, 44-46, 470, 532, 1243

cats: aristocratic, 196; big, black, 173, 174-75; black, 724; carries message, 1271; Cheshire, 20-21, 211; china, visits king and queen, 785; Dinah, 836; fairy, 675; family black, 1186; ginger tom, 173, 175; grinning, 342; haughty black female, 196, 829; heartless, 1032; Hodge, 889-90; house, 328; independent, self-assured, 893-94; injures rabbit, 1333; kidnapped by dwarf, 913; kingdom of, 784; kitten, 1097; lives in seventeenth-century barn, 1175; lost, 714; mauls gerbil, 76; needed for ark, 829-30; on deserted island, 256; only confidant, 667; old tom, 599; plague of, 525; rescued from flood, 866-67; rescue princess, 929; resourceful, 893-94; run over, 477; sacred, 196, 829; shut in attic, 484, 697; Siamese, 186; small, white, 248; stolen, 173; talking, 173, 173-75, 893-94; 913; threatened with put down, 1365; threatening toy soldiers, 794; undernourished kitten, 614; vagabond tom, 639, 1335; with infected eyes, 1059

Catskin, 39

Cats'-Meat-Man, 1145

cat stories, 173-75, 893-94. *See* animal novels; dog stories; horse stories.

cattle: driven over cliff, 1102; endangered, 737; stolen, 113

cattle herders, 116

cattlemen: for Puritan family, 450, 548-49; Isle of Skye, 13-14, 605

Catty, the cat, 866-67

Catuvellauni, 1119

caucus-races, 20, 23, 324

Caudimordax, 396

cauldrons: magic, 359, 909; witch's, 173, 174

causes: dedication to Quaker, 685-86; devotion to, 681, 1390; exterminating witches, 1393; human rights, 1015; loyalty to father's, 28

A Cavalcade of Kings, 393

A Cavalcade of Queens, 393

Cavaliers, 307

THE CAVE, *193-94*, 233

cave-ins: mine, 130, 398, 431; of coal tip, 1277; tunnel in garden, 1147

caverns, underwater, 369

caves: 1, 123, 167, 766, 1142, 1339, 1399; ancestral footprints in, 1144; beavers' home, 711; beneath castle, 352, 1000; children abandoned in, 1397; closed by landslide, 1310; coastal, 1272; containing skeleton, 1101; dragon's, 1030; explored, 13, 431, 799, 1397; Fundindelve, 414; gooseherd lives in, 1401; harp hidden in, 1357; hiding place of gold, 1255; hideout, 260, 506; home for leprechan, 1271; home for monk, 155; home in, 308-9, 336, 1361, 1368; in French cliffs, 222; inside Alderley Edge, 1343; on desert isle, 1044; prehistoric drawings in, 1144; reputed haunted, 1153; roof collapsing, 1101; scene of wild revel, 637, 638; secret, for hoarding salvage, 259-60; underground glowworm, 929; underwater, 256, 1047; unexplored, 193-94; with seals, 430-31; with Viking relics, 838; wolves', 630

CAWLEY, WINIFRED (COZENS), *194-95*, 473

CAXTON, *195*, 218-19, 1067

CAXTON'S CHALLENGE, 195, 527. *See* THE LOAD OF UNICORN, 729-30

CAXTON, WILLIAM, *195-96*, 729-30, 1405

Ceawlin, 358

Cecily Gifford, 506
Cecily Jolland, 276, 293, 683-84
Cedricson, Vadir, 1293-94
CEFALU, *196*, 829
Ceiridwen Owen, 243-44
Celebration of Dolls, 723
celebrations: Beltane, 1321; July
    Twelfth, 1286; neighborhood, 863;
    of survival of flood, 497; Queen
    Victoria's Golden Jubilee, 1159-
    60; school centennial, 452
Celestial City of Zion, 975, 977-80
CELIA WITHENS, *196*, 537, 904, 1034
cellarmen, fosters boy, 1126
cellars: clubhouse, 1285-86; cider,
    389; king's wine, 1000
Cellini, Joseph, 642
cellists, 412-14, 857, 1076, 1238
Celts: ancient, 806; in Britain,
    679-83; in New World, 844
cemeteries, 278, 397-98, 1110
CEM JONES, *196-97*, 210, 400-2, 748,
    1177
Censoring Reality, 869
centaurs, 711, 1026
centenarians, 536, 1151-52
Centipede, 593-95
Central Park, 594
centurions: of boy's Mithraic club,
    450; Roman in Britain, 347, 767-
    68, 1089-91
ceremonies: Capping, resisted,
    1359-60; elaborate, 371-72;
    knighting, 674; of Renewal, 121;
    of Seisin, 154; of Showing of the
    New King, 122; primitive, 1036;
    survival of, 1294-95
Chaffey, Auntie Maggie, 1132,
    1282
chaffinches, 211
Chaffin, Donald, 388
chainmakers, 264
chairs, silver, 1034, 1093
chalk, hills of, 1172-73
champions: Irish, 1259; national
    band, 1062
chance, importance of, 309
A CHANCE CHILD, 941, *197-200*
Chance, Luck and Destiny, 316
Chance, Stephen, 1273
changelings, 1272
*THE CHANGEOVER: A SUPERNATURAL RO-
    MANCE, 200-1*, 759
Changes, 309-11, 449, 648, 886,
    1055, 1280, 1337
changes: inevitability of, 589;
    slowness of, 1161-64; technolo-
    gical, 1325

channel: cliffs, France, 221-23;
    river, altered, 862
Channel, English, 1213-14, 1359-60
Chant family (*The Changeover*), 150,
    200-1, 636, 692-93, 815, 1122-23,
    1389
Chant family (*Charmed Life*), 191,
    208-9, 225, 517-18, 598
Chapel, religion of, 176, 474, 624,
    1144
chaplains: British army, 652; of no-
    bles, 1405
Chapman family (*Ravensgill*), 125,
    1021-23
Chapman family (*The Trouble with
    Donovan Croft*), 844, 850, 1262-64
Chapultepec Park, 601
characters: ambiguous, 645-46;
    approach caricature, 857; carica-
    tures, 19-22, 67, 753, 767,
    810-11, 827, 829-30, 836, 851,
    853, 970-71, 1025, 1036, 1096,
    1117, 1121, 1208-11, 1239, 1297,
    1305, 1358-59, 1361, 1385-86;
    conniving son, 829; deliberately
    didactic caricature, 851; didac-
    tic types, 855; distorted for
    comic effect, 865; eccentric, 920-
    22, 1117, 1358; eccentrically
    treated, 863; enigmatic, 13, 289,
    575, 602, 649-51, 1228; important
    but never appearing, 172, 768;
    monkey, sensitively drawn, 839-
    41; nursery rhyme, 1209-11, 1274;
    obvious social mix, 606-8, 689-92;
    old women, unusually well drawn,
    211-13, 217-19, 258-61, 373-75,
    1035-36, 1151-52, 1287-90; parody
    of self, 753;
    particularly well drawn, 801-4,
    1087; pleasingly eccentricized,
    887-89; stereotypical heroic,
    344; stereotyped white masters,
    765-67; stock, many, 779-81,
    789-91; stock villain, 832-33;
    storybook, come alive, 783-84,
    785; strongly typed, 786-89, 855,
    859-60; symbolic, 742; unlikeable
    becomes sympathetic, 771-74, 896;
    unusually memorable, 732; zany,
    343, 753, 767, 1208-11, 1274,
    1385-86
charges, dropped, 515
Charity (*The Drummer Boy*), 341-42
Charity (*Hobberdy Dick*), 450
Charity (*Pilgrim's Progress*), 976
Charity (boat), 85, 1379-81
charity: 1121; instinctive, 659-62

charlatans, 827
CHARLEE LOON, *201-2*, 1094-96
Charles II, King of England, 456,
  1199
Charles Lynn, 1238
Charles of Orleans, 586
Charles Ramsay, 427-28
Charles Seccombe, 456
Charles the prostitute, 1363
the Charleston, 474
Charley, 2, 779
Charlie, 58, 202-3, 1322-24, 1420
CHARLIE AND THE CHOCOLATE FACTORY,
  203-4, 274
Charlie and the Great Glass Eleva-
  tor, 274
Charlie Bailey, 833, 834-35
Charlie Bucket, 203-4, 479-80, 864-
  65
Charlie Chumbles, 1106
Charlie Frick, 1080
CHARLIE HERRICK, 1, 2, *204*, 522,
  587, 659, 1203
CHARLIE MARRIOT, 88-89, *204-5*, 425,
  1247-50
Charlie Sampson, 339-42
CHARLIE WHITELAW, *205*, 656-57
Charlotte Dane, 330-32
CHARLOTTE LATTIMER, 24, 79-81, *205-*
  6, 450, 874, 885
CHARLOTTE MAKEPEACE, 6-7, 161, *206*,
  206-8, 365, 366, 393, 1168-69
CHARLOTTE SOMETIMES, 206-8, 366, 394
Charlotte's Web, 1084
Charlton, Tim, 160, 281-83, 523,
  1223
CHARMED LIFE, 208-9, 617
charms: good luck, 87; inherited,
  600, to quiet memories, 939
Charn, 755, 987
Chartists, 264
The Charwoman's Daughter, 1137
chases: 773, 816, 1090, 1108, 1115;
  after dwarf across Wales, 847-49,
  850, 869; along canal, 542; across
  Irish island, 260; across sands,
  579; across Scotland, 349-50,
  648-51; bride chases, 773; by police, 86; by rubbish trucks, 45;
  for pink whale, 888-89; gondola,
  663; Greeneyes of tramps, 891-92;
  harrowing, 537; into fox's hole,
  326; into funeral crowd, 77-78;
  London, 797-98; men in brown after pickpocket, 845; seaman by
  terrorists, 74; selkie after boy,
  1156; smugglers by customs men,
  764; through forest, 341; through

forest and bog, 684; through mine
  tunnel, 36; through mountains,
  244, 1357; through old mill, 542;
  through ruined city, 294; thugs
  of sailor, 906-7; Toad by police,
  1383; to escape Tripod, 1360-61
CHAS MCGILL, 57-58, 197, *210*, 245,
  262-63, 400-3, 747-50, 881, 887,
  1084, 1177, 1347
Chateaubriand, 829
chateaux, besieged by French peasants, 1217
Chatterjee, 1354
Chaucer, 275
Chauntesinger, Terry, 668, 685-86,
  1194
chauvinism: male, 400, 1042; religious, 257
cheating, on exam, 1270
check-reining, 106, 454
checks: bounced, 184-85; worthless,
  313
Checoba, Stallion of the Comanche,
  220
CHEE-CHEE, the monkey, *210-11*, 1145,
  1309
cheers, dislodge volcano rock, 1310
cheese, desire for toasted, 89
cheetahs, hunting, 118
chelas, 651, 653-54, 1194
chemists, 1216
cherries, freedom to pick, 5
cherry tart, prayed for, 387-88
Cheshire, 9-10, 399, 484-85, 609,
  1058-60, 1143-44, 1234-36, 1267-
  68, 1342-45
CHESHIRE-CAT, 20-21, 23, *211*, 342
chess: boards, as setting, 18, 1209;
  games, with boy to winner, 673;
  pattern for story, 1209; pieces,
  red queen, 1024-25; pieces, stol-
  en, 1040; pieces, white knight,
  1358; pieces, white queen, 1361;
  played with captive doctor, 259;
  played with eccentric duke, 108
chest protectors, pink wool,
  62
chests, sea, 1047, 1254
Chichester family, 1125-28
chickens: familiars, 874, 1354;
  growers, 388; harried by gnome,
  715; houses, home of gnome, 715;
  861; pet, 877; rescued from flood,
  187, 981; slaughtered by mysterious large animal, 877
Chief Rabbit, 446, 1332
chiefs: brutal, 336; Ghanian, 250;
  of Boar people, 245, 333, 878-79;

of British tribes, 349; of Scottish tribes, 387; of South Pacific tribe. 256-57; of wandering tribe, 625-26; outlawed Scottish, 650; prospective, 884

chieftainess, of wandering tribe, 625

chieftainship, goes through woman, 1171-72

child abuse: 593, 656-58, 815, 1212, 1355, 1368-69; by brothers, 660; by domineering father, 1284; by father's family, 900-2: by stepfather, 425; baby in Wonderland, 342-43; chimney sweep, 1328; evacuee boy, 467-69, 851-52, 1240, 1372-73; foster son, 605; illegitimate son, 230, 264; in Industrial Revolution, 109-10; medical help denied to child, 901; overwork and insensitive treatment by father, 846; thieves and pickpockets, 1352; workhouse children 596-97, 728, 1370

child abuse, novels of, 52-54, 197-200, 276-79, 467-69, 720-22, 899-902, 1012-13, 1049-50, 1220-23, 1399-1401

child abusers, former, 525

Childhood's Pattern: A Study of Heroes and Heroines of Children's Fiction 1770-1950, 63

child labor, 109-10, 197-200, 230, 264, 807-9, 1158-60, 1238-39, 1328

Child Life, 66

Child o' War: The True Story of a Boy Sailor in Nelson's Navy, 441

children: abandoned, 514, as babies, 1122; abused, 20, 37, 52-54, 59, 197-200, 262, 286-87, 596-97, 692, 728, 763, 821, 888, 1012, 1212, 1221-22, 1276, 1370, 1400-1; adopted, 31, 46, 768-69, 804; ambiguous in personality, 777; assist king against evil ape, 687; assume responsibility during flood, 775, for home, 1303-5, for household, 1124; band together to save tree, 689-92; captured by revolutionaries, 778; considered unsuitable as playmates, 748; conspiratorial, 747-50; contentious, 1269; converse with nature, 780; cosmopolitan, 24; crushed by carpet presses, 807, 809; disobedient, 203; displaced, 1035, 1154; dissembling, 318; dying of thirst, 661;

earnest, 1146-48; evacuated, World War II, 60, 1372-73; feel rejected by father, 842; children, foster, 1, 769, 842, 842-43, 1010-11, 1057, 1085; fostered by queen, 768-69, 1013; fostered, pig by dog, 1082-83; greedy, 58; half-starved, World War II, 1097-98; hostages of terrorists, 330; illegitimate, 616, 708, 761, 762, 858, 1197, 1266; imaginative, 963-65, 1178-79; independent, sturdy, 792; industrious, 1146-48; kidnapped, 1142-43; kings and queens of Narnia, 712; living with grandparents, 241; London beggar, 1160;

lost, advertised for, 1142; mean and manipulative, 777; mischievous, 776, 1269-70; musical, singers, 16; naughty, 781, 782, 784, 787-88; near-sighted, 778; neglected, 495; new in neighborhood, 778-79; on their own, 30-31, 31-32, 79-81, 206, 230, 294-96, 425-27, 514-16, 740, 763-64, 807-8, 885, 886, 1035-36, 1056-57, 1105-6, 1108-10, at sea, 1141, camping, 903, 1178-79, in flood, 186-88, 707, 786, 815, World War II, 210, 414-16, 747-50, 806, 887, 1097-99, 1339; pick berries, 1124; plucky, 1098-99; precocious, 1195; rescue fairy hen, 714; resourceful, 1340-42; responsible for family, 792; responsible for tutor, 740; runaway, 763; seventeenth-century in present, 859; Spartan upbringing, 718-19; spies, couriers, 758; spirits, 16; spoiled, 857, 1117; spunky, 385-86; starving, 53-54, 1370; step, 25, 76-77, 79-81, 93, 100, 694, 698, 719, 741, 744, 752, 754, 768, 810, 933-35, 1405; street ruffians, 808; streetwise, 748-50, 1107-8, 1108-10; thought gifted, 1270; three spirit, 710; tricked by uncle, 755; turned into mice, 429;

unselfish, 1148; waifs, 619, 1012-13, 1097-99, 1100, 1398; workhouse, 692, 1370; working-class, 689-92. See also boys; girls.

Children in Danger: The Causes and Prevention of Baby Battering, 1031

Children of Aries, 1164

THE CHILDREN OF GREEN KNOWE, 144-45, *211-13*, 219
CHILDREN OF THE BOOK, 182, *213-15*
The Children of the New Forest, 776
Children of the Pit, 528, 1068, 1357-58, 1411-12
CHILDREN OF THE RED KING, *215-17*, 986
Children of the Royal Chapel, 876, 1353
Children of the Salmon, and Other Irish Folktales, 910
Children of the Turnpike, 641
The Children's Academy of Dancing and Stage Training, 68
The Children's Bells: A Selection of Poems, 393
The Children's Crusade, 1257
The Children Who Changed, 425
A Child's Garden of Verses, 445, 1139
Chile, 28, 585, 1046, 1187-89; political terror in, 94, 1187-89
chimney sweeps, 363, 491, 556, 644, 783, 1328
chimneys: blocked by stuffed rabbit, 490-91; interlocking, 218-19; man stuck fast in, 1329; maze of, 1328
THE CHIMNEYS OF GREEN KNOWE, 145, *217-19*
chimpanzees, boy befriends, 1098; escaped from zoo, 598, 1098
china, from museum, 174
China: boys pretend marsh is, 801-2; early twentieth century, 1265-67
Chinese, in England, 373-75, 980-81, 1035, 1154-55
CHIP, *219-20*, 1077-78
CHIPPERFIELD, JOSEPH E (UGENE), *220-21*, 1386, 1398
Chippings, 109
Chiquitito, the dog, 329
Chisel-Brown family, 6-7. 207
Chittenden, Lady, 417-18, 598
CHITTY CHITTY BANG BANG, 424. See *CHITTY-CHITTY-BANG-BANG, THE MAGICAL CAR*.
CHITTY-CHITTY-BANG-BANG, THE MAGICAL CAR, *221-23*, 424
chocolate, factory, 479-80, 864-65, 919, 1375-76
choices, vocational: boys', 129-31, 153-55, 190-91, 200-1, 418-21, 484-85, 492-95, 662-63, 703-6, 729-30, 915-17, 943-45, 949-52, 1061-64, 1125-28, 1161-64, 1199-1202, 1379-81, 1404-7, 1415-17; girls', 68-71, 169-71, 200-1, 465-67, 588-89, 685-87, 1123-25, 1220-23, 1316-19; men's, 771-74,

911-12, 1145-46; women's, 581-83
choir master, 1181
choirs, boys', 51, 223-25, 1180-82
choir schools, 223-25, 1180-82
cholera, 52, 54
Choosing Feast, 1118
Chorasmia, 1133
CHORISTERS' CAKE, *223-25*, 794
Chorley, Cheshire, 9-10, 399, 484-85, 1143-44
CHRESTOMANCI, 208-9, *225*, 517, 617
Chris, 30
Chris Cross, 42
CHRIS FAIRFAX, *225*, 946, 983-84
Chris Holly, 200-1, 636, 692
christenings, 1096; of prince, 720; of princess, 701
Christian, 975-80
Christiana, 978-79
CHRISTIAN FANSHAWE-SMITHE, *225-26*, 735
Christian Hume, 458
Christianity: adopted, 1243; allegory, 974-80; allusions to, 688, 712, 755-57; conversions to, 257; pre-, sacred places, 673; rejected, 1243
Christians: children raised by Turks, 1296; fundamentalist, 1195; in Roman Britain, 294; in Saxon Britain, 358-59; Irish in Denmark, 91-92
CHRISTINA PARSONS (Russell), *226-27*, 317, 335, 354-56, 419-21, 421-24, 775, 1057, 1228-29, 1284, 1374
Christ-like figures, 54-55
Christmas: 212, 227-30, 409, 466-67, 922, 981, 1156, 1186-87, 1267, 1384; called humbug, 353; celebration forbidden, 450, 549; holidays, 186-88, 403-5, 963-65; in vision of past, 409; never comes, 710, 1009; tree ornaments, doll, 381-82; opera, 855; shopping for, 780; solicitations refused, 353; spirit of, 188; tree causes fire, 125; twelve days of, 287-88
A CHRISTMAS CAROL, *227-30*, 314, 269, 468
Christmas Eve, 329
Christobel the ballerina, 1248
CHRISTOPHER (*The Blue Boat*), 119-21, *230*, 570
CHRISTOPHER (*A Chance Child*), 198-99, *230-31*, 264, 947
CHRISTOPHER, JOHN (CHRISTOPHER SAMUEL YOUD), *231-32*, 237, 505, 989, 1359

CHRISTOPHER ROBIN, *232-33*, 358, 562-64, 974 989, 1388-89
Christopherson family, 607
Christopher Standish, 236-37
Christopher Uptake, 994
Christy Willard, 582-83
Chronicles of Narnia, 699, 710
Chronicles of Pantouflia, 679
Chrysophylax Dives, the dragon, 396-97
CHUNDER Coward, *233*, 876-78, 879-80, 910
churches: 387, 1076-78; abandoned, 77-78, 579; as home, 61; Barthomley, 611; campaign to save from razing, 707; deteriorating, 480, 482; endangered, 791; entrance to Elidor, 359; held by terrorists, 283, 330; old, 539; Saint Bartholomew the Great, 1015-16, shelter from flood, 496; shelter from rain, 667; to be razed for supermarket, 1390; torn down, 465; vacant, 1080; vandalized, 78; village, 1143-44
Church of Little St. Mary, 480, 817
Church of Saint Bartholomew the Great, hospital of, 1394-96
CHURCH, RICHARD (THOMAS), 193, *233-34*
church services: Christmas Eve, 154, innumerable, 372; Lenten evening, 165
church steeples, 484
church towers, children locked in, 417
churchyards, 229
Cibola, 236-37, 915
CICELY BRADSHAW, *234*, 827, 885, 1402-3
cigar sellers, girl, 808
cinema: girl falls asleep in, 386; leprechaun, dancing in, 970
Circin Rua, the red hen, 913
A Circle of Stones, 746
Circlet of Deirdre, 216
circuses: 339, 516, 962, 1036; bankrupt, 205; 1247; children run away to, 1057; in sky, 782; performers, 120-21, 204-5, 230, 570, 1248; retired performers, 607; Roman gladiators, 347; traveling, 234-35, 877; trapeze artists, 235; tumblers, 88-89, 235
THE CIRCUS IS COMING, *234-36*, 1157
CIRCUS SHOES, *234*, 1157. See *THE CIRCUS IS COMING*, 234-36.

cities: factory, 1400-1; in disrepair, 512; industrial, 400-3, 606-8; 747-50, 807-9; lost in jungle, 631; moving, 928; splendid but crumbling, 371. See also urban life.
Citroen automobiles, 69
City Hall, 594
The City of Destruction, 975
THE CITY OF FROZEN FIRE, 236-37, 1370
THE CITY OF GOLD AND LEAD, 231, *237-40*, 992, 989, 1361
City of Gold and Other Stories from the Old Testament, 316
City of Tripods, 238-40
Ciudad Juarez, 601
civilization, inroads of, 894
civil servants, Ghana, 249, 251
Civil War, English, 307, 611-12, 637, 1025-26, 1199, 1203
claims, of killing dragon, fraudulent, 1259-60
Claire Palmer, 533
clairvoyance, 1331-32. See also ESP; mental telepathy; second sight.
clans: family considers self as, 80; Scottish, 24, 650
CLARA, *240-41*, 645-46
Clara Barley, 495
Clare family, 31, 1105-6, 1193
Clare Mayfield, 62, 564-66, 613, 792, 856
Clare Moby, 6, 161, 206, 206-7, 365
Clarissa Cargill-Smith, 86
CLARKE, PAULINE, *241-42*, 1274
classmates, male, loved by boy, 1364
Claudius, Emperor of Rome, 1118
cleaning women, 7
cleanliness, Dutch, 332
cleanup, after flood, 496-97
Cleaver, 39-40
Clemens family, 397-99,
Clem Oliver, 319-20
clergymen: 515, 1351; eccentric, 842, 1317-18; immensely tall, 842; father, 734-37, 1165; teetotaler, 1148. See also curates; ministers; parsons; pastors; preachers; priests; rectors; vicars.
Clerinel Island, 175, 1339
Clerinel Pony Club, 1339
Clerk, N. W., 700
clerks: apprentice, 1404-5; jewelry store, 184, lawyer's, 495, 1346; lazy, 71; to attorney, 610; to miser, 227-29, 353
Cleverton family, 38, 389-90, 433, 600, 793, 959-60

Clifford Patrick White, 477
Clifford, Rowan, 539
CLIFF TRENT, 242, 843, 896
climaxes, grand spectacular, 798
CLIMBING TO DANGER, 24, *242-44*
climbs, to steeple, 1143-44
Clinton, Isabella, 447-49, 453-
    54, 585-86, 600
Cliona, queen of fairies, 713-14
CLIPPER, *244*, 801-3
clipping, of coins, 463-64
Clipstone family, 285, 852-53
CLIVE BRADLEY, 25, *244-45*, 768, 873,
    933, 1047
cloaks: eagle, 1344; elven, 407;
    magic, 1344; magic flying, 720-22
Clock family, 49-50, 61, 132-34,
    134-36, 136-38, 138-40, 140-42,
    147-48, 489, 559-60, 811, 822,
    854, 856, 857, 947-48, 985, 1130,
    1236, 1282
clocks: chapel, 9, 619; cuckoo,
    1386; heirloom, 860; home entrance
    under, 132; grandfather, erratic,
    1240; swallowed by crocodile, 172,
    957-58
clock towers, 9-10
CLODHA, *245*, 387, 878, 884, 1161-63,
    1190
CLOGGER DUNCAN, *245-46*, 748-50, 887,
    1051
clogs, identity marks burned on,
    1235
cloisters, 324
Clomper, Mrs., 1282, 1317
closets, boy kept in, 197, 230, 264
clothes: for gypsy girl, 319; for
    Japanese doll, rejected, 723
clothiers, father, 234
cloud, bear pretends to be, 1388
Cloudberry, 716-17
Cloud Farm, 389-91
Cloud-Men, 593
Clough family, 196, 536-37, 904,
    1035
clowns: 607, 1035-36; acrobatic,
    516; boy, 1248; circus, 205, 234-
    36, 962, 1057; of peach crew, 595;
    rabbit, 1332
clubfoot, 1150
club houses: cellar, 1285-86; in
    old tree, 689-91
clubs: adolescent boys', 193; ani-
    mal, 432, 529, 911, 931-32;
    boys', 33, 386, 523, 1223; school-
    boy's singing, 801-3, 1133;
    schoolchildren, 389-91; secret
    schoolboys', 281-82; men's, 152;

neighborhood, 490-92; pony, 1339
clues: about sampler, 1141; in li-
    brary book, 184; in notebook, 183;
    in rhyme, 615, 818, 841, 1058;
    inserted into sleeping mind, 450;
    in watch, 610; on Grail, 502; pur-
    sued, 184-85, 813-14; rose, 813;
    silver chain, 816; to spy, 401-3;
    to story of past generation, 427-
    28
Cluny Brown, 1081
Cluny Macpherson, 650
CNI, 1187-89
coaches: break down, 548-49; driven
    madly, 611; overturned, 111;
    thought to be ghost, 954
coachmen, 55-57, 111, 1125-28;
    former soldier, 595; for squire,
    596, 612; head, retired, 1160
Coalgate, 472, 473-75
coalmining, 129-31
coal, stealing, 1277
coats: inside out as protection,
    713; of arms, 324-25; servant's,
    428; thrown from window, 319
Cobalt, Martin, 795
cobblers, 605, 614
Cobchester, 276-69, 514-16, 579,
    629, 1364
Cobchester College, 528, 648, 1365
Cober, Alan E., 287, 824
Cobham family, 447-49, 453-54, 586
cobras, 631
Cob's Circus, 234-35, 1057
cockfights, 877
COCKLE-SNORKLE BUG, *246*, 432, 931,
    1120
COCK LOREL, *246*, 574, 1352
cockneys, 377-79, 1074
cocks: fairy, 271; feisty, 598;
    fighting, 233
codes, 1339; deciphered by boy, 806;
    leaf, 1; numbers in diary, 790;
    postcard in, 435
Codling family, 1-2, 94, 291, 615,
    812-14, 817-18, 841-42, 858, 862,
    985, 1058, 1094-96, 1130, 1131-32
Coel, King of Wessex, 358
coffee table, witch transformed
    into, 836, 1354
coffins: as hiding place, 122; ex-
    humed, 113
THE COLD FLAME, *246-48*, 1028
Cold Hazard, 48
Colditz Castle, 253
Cold Lairs, 631, 635
A Cold Wind Blowing, 1371
Colebridge area, 382-85

Colebridge and District Summer
    Festival, 383
Cole Scholar, Great-Uncle, 533-34,
    1264
coincidence: plot relies heavily on,
    679-83; unusual amount of, 1099,
    1351-53
coining, 463-64
coins: clipped, 463-64; foreign, 417
Colin, 344, 408, 504, 1067, 1342-45
Colin Forbes-Cowan, 590
Colin Jackus, 37, 777, 820
Colin Lockwood, 377-79
Colin Marshall, 37, 777
Colin Ramsay, 427-28
Colin Roy Campbell, 650
Coll, 148, 245, 333, 387, 879, 884,
    1161-64, 1190
collars, hounds', carrying treas-
    ure, 486
Collected Stories for Children, 302
collections: boxes, as hiding place,
    142; for orphan, 1126
college classes, literary criti-
    cism, 44
colleges, Cobchester, 528
collieries, 841, 861
colliers, 1276-78
COLLIN-SMITH, JOYCE, 248, 601
collisions, of boats, near, 1380
Colm, the pigeon, 248, 913
Colman Donnelly, 544-46
Colm Cooney, 260
Colonel Creighton, 652-53, 758
Colonel Sheperton's Clock, 480, 1273
Colonel Tedford, 500
colony, lost, 1068
"color fairy books," 679
Columbus Sails, 555
Columbus, voyage of, 1403
Colum Moriarity, 1153
Colum, Padriac, 514
comas, fairy queen in, 714
comedians, 753-54
Come Hither: A Collection of Rhymes
    and Poems for the Young of All
    Ages, 301
comfort, at price of freedom, 1331
COMFORT HERSELF, 248-52, 641
Comfort Kwatey-Jones, 248-52, 476,
    477-78, 482-83, 698, 762
comics: hide notebook, 920; secret
    passion for, 275; Wheazy-Fidgett
    strip, 435
Commander Caractacus Pott, 221-23
Commander Crackpott, 221-23
commanders: of convoy escort, 262-
    63; -in-chief, of British Indian

Army, 652
Commander Ted Walker, 1340, 1342
commendation, from king, 395
commercial travelers, 1132
Commons: fenced, 196, 536-37, 1034-
    35; reclaimed, 904
communists: boy, 226; in Chile,
    1187; woman, former, 855, 1077.
    See also radicals; terrorists.
community life: Ireland, 258-61;
    Russia, 717-20, Sicily, 30-31;
    World War II, during blitz, 747-50
Companion, of luminary, 325-28
Companions, 681
companions: black boy-blind girl,
    195; of woman scholar, 1183; to
    child queen, 585-86; to emperor,
    254; to noble lady, 170
companionship, need for, 1387
compasses, transport children
    around world, 781
competitions: focused on doll,
    87-88; scriveners and printer,
    729-30; with wife's family, 17.
    See also contests.
composers, musical, 428
compromises, between Irish and
    Norman, 261
computer specialist, 1212
Comtessa de la Tour Rouge, 1360
Conachur, King of Ulster, 299-300.
    See also Conor MacNessa, King of
    Ulster, 298-99.
concentration camps: post-nuclear
    war, 157; World War II, 620
concerto, Rachmaninov, 86-87
concerts: musical, 86; with Ger-
    man symphony, 86
conclusions: abrupt, 1206; fairy-
    tale, 684; frenzied, 46; ironic,
    715, 861, 894, 1338; lame, 1096;
    melodramatic, 1096; open-ended,
    134, 750; over-foreshadowed, 1169
condescension, humiliating, 183
condoms, provided son by father,
    1363
conferences, for world peace, 991.
    See also protests; rallies; riots;
    symposia.
confessions, 224; manuscript of,
    1036; of cheating partner, 610; of
    deception, 268
CONFETTI FOR CORTORELLI, 30, 252,
    425. See ANGELO GOES TO THE CARNI-
    VAL, 252.
confidence men: actually writ-
    er, 449; snake, 262, 1114,
    1120

conflicts: against Turks, 670–
71; among relatives, 533–34;
apprentice seaman vs. first mate,
169; between Borrower women, 136;
between boy and family pretensions, 226; between brothers, 29,
369; between brothers-in-law,
838–39; between clans, 650; between cousins over vocation,
685–86; between desire to fight
and advice to resign, 313; between
Greek and Roman church, 371; between High Heels and Low Heels,
509; between Irish islanders, 259–
60, 260; between living in jungle
and village, 632;
between oath and hero worship,
611; between obligations to feud
and as physician, 119; between
prehistoric women, 336; between priests and king, 122–24;
between rabbit warrens, 446; between schoolboys, 286–87; between
sheep dogs, 1398–99; between shepherds, 1398–99; between swimmers,
125; between two ghosts, 33; between two groups of singers, 224;
boy vs. uncle, 235; brother vs.
friend, 384; commoners vs. nobles
and church, 146–47; desire to
avoid, 179; Dog Folk vs. Fox Folk,
336; druid chief, for control of
tribe, 333; family, 226–27, 474–
75; father vs. aunt, 37; father
vs. daughter, 164–66; father vs.
grandfather, 233; for favor at
court, 350; girl vs. poshvoiced
new boy, 127–28; gnome vs. old woman, 861; good vs. evil, 148–49,
286–87, 287–88;
husband-wife, over old friend,
741, 1280; lady-in-waiting vs.
child queen's governess; 448;
manor house dame vs. brother,
276; matriarchal vs. patriarchal
groups, 772–73; miners vs. bosses,
129–31; of loyalties, 35–36,
408–9, 739, to mother vs. half-
brother, 230–31; of values,
305; old woman vs. gnome, 715;
otherworld wicked magicians vs.
good enchanter, 209; Protestant
vs. Catholic, 1284–87; over cat
in loft, 484; over cat's death,
477; over forms of worship, 456–
57; over gerbils, 76–77, 604–5,
860; over job offer, 205; over money, 334; over noise scaring birds,
480–81; over pets, 159; over pies,
970; over proposed marina, 982–84;
over treatment of granddaughter,
476; over tribal leadership, 879;
over which end of egg to crack
first, 509; over word in Creed,
371; racial, 627–28; rivalry between sisters, 362;
River Folk vs. Fish Folk, 336;
Russian agents vs. Tibetan
porters, 653; Saxon boy vs. cruel neighbor, 295–96; Scots vs.
Saxons, 804; sexual desire vs.
Catholic teaching, 879; step siblings, 79–81; to make biggest pie,
970–71; Turks vs. Christians, 213–
15; verbal, 474; visiting boy vs.
local youths, 620–23; with father,
611–12; young witch vs. enchanter's daughter, 517. See also
battles; battle scenes; fights;
war novels; wars.
Congregation of Christ Jesus, 1265–
66
The Conjuror's Box, 695
Connacht, 261, 299, 1103
Connacht, king of, 408, 482
Connemara, 543–46
Conner, Chris, 206
Connie, 282, 523
Conor MacNessa, King of Ulster, 298–
99. See also Conachur, King of
Ulster, 299–300.
CONORY, 252, 772, 806
Conrad, 928–30
Conrad Pike, 252–54
CONRAD'S WAR, 252–54, 292
conscience: 331, 457; active, 363,
778, 778–79; awakened, 864; struggle with, 879; troubling, 451, 692
Consort for Victoria, 1369–70
consorts, chosen through dream,
1171–72
conspiracies: defeated, 1100; Hanoverian, 888, 1048; land speculation, 404–5; to hi-jack oil rig,
35; to overthrow king, 108–9, 837;
to substitute look-alike for king,
806; with lover to kill husband,
116
Constable, Mr., 169
constables, 142, 822, 918; clever,
1074; cockney, 1074
CONSTANTINE, Emperor of Rome, 254,
370–73, 633, 1136, 1311–12
Constantinople: 254, 370–73, 633,
1311; fall of, 1136; fifteenth
century, 370–73; tenth century,

116-19. *See also* Istanbul.
Constantius, 271, 1090-91
constellations, 780, 782
The Consul's Daughter, 1061
contests: art, won by bear, 844;
  athletic, 238; baby, 386; band,
  1062; diving, 383-84; elocution,
  383-84; fancy dress, 1268; for
  hand of wizard, 376, 518, 752, 824,
  835, 845, 874, 1354-55; horseback
  riding, 383-85; musical, 950-
  52, 1061-64; of strength, 584-85;
  photography, 383-84; piano playing, 383-84; pie making, 51; poetry, 734-36, 736; point-to-point
  horse race, 420; Pony Club meet,
  615; radio, 1314; riddle, 551;
  sailing, 383-84; sheep herding,
  1083; singing, 383-84; St. George
  vs. dragon, 1030; storytelling,
  114; swimming, 383-84. *See also*
  competitions.
continuity of life, 453, 856
contraception, 1135, 1363
contracts, between wizard and fire
  demon, 168
contrition, for stealing ship, 104
Conurbs, 506-8
convention, of French States-
  General, 1216
convents, 147, 717, 1038
conversations: about imagining
  things, 412; circular, 192,
  1313-14; discourse on semantics, 1359; imaginary, 1140-41;
  natural gift for, 433; on garage
  roof, 289; overheard, 277, 282,
  732, 1071, 1086, 1190, 1380, by king,
  447, devastating, 1319, from apple barrel, 1254, incriminating,
  405, 673, planning war, 561, quarrel, 423; through interpreter,
  297; with deaf via signs and writing, 290; with dragon, 396-97;
  with queen, 543
conversions: changing characters,
  257; caused by drownings, 1015;
  from living in church, 61; religious, 141; to Christianity, 92,
  257
convictions: for arson, 1365; for
  endangering majesty, 247; for
  receiving stolen goods, 1040
convicts, 173, 376, 515; boy aids,
  757; becomes benefactor, 492-
  95; brutal, violent, 757; capture
  city, 915; fugitive, 981; returned
  from Australia, 757

convoy commanders, 403
convoys, World War II, 262-63
Conway family, 1363-64
cooks: angry, 20, 23; bad tempered,
  342, 1416; cook-housekeeper, 611;
  for large family, 383; for noble Scottish family, 901; Irish,
  1151; lazy, 5-6; on expedition,
  151; outlaw, 695; scolding, 1159;
  sea, 732; ship's, 1254; talkative
  dwarf, 725; tramp, 168; youthful, 1133. *See also* housekeepers;
  housemaids; maids; servants.
Cookson, Henry, 1326
Coolah Vrac, 271
Cooney, Colm, 260
Cooney family, 837, 1101-2
cooperation: 927, 1098-99, 1161-64,
  1330-34; emphasis on family, 786-
  89
Cooper, Maureen, 564-65, 792
Cooper, Rod, 496, 543
COOPER, SUSAN (MARY), *254-55*, 287,
  501
Copper Kettle, 174
coppersmiths, 625
copper, thought to be gold, 973
Copplestone family, 153-55
Copplestone, Rev. Mr., 596, 623,
  842, 1317-18
*THE CORAL ISLAND: A TALE OF THE
  PACIFIC OCEAN*, 68, *255-57*
Corbaci, 1296
Corbett, Mister, 824-26
CORBETT, W(ILLIAM) J(ESSE), *257-58*,
  1119
Corbie, Yarl, 1156, 1409
cordials, healing, 711-12, 1026
Cordoba, Bartolomeo, 74
Coriakin the magician, 1307
Coriander (ship), 258, 260
THE CORIANDER, 258-61, 322
Corin, Prince of Archenland, 561-62,
  1081
CORMAC, King of Connacht, 215-17,
  261, 408, 482, 986, 1103
Cornelius, Doctor, 185, 323
Cornelius Goodrich, 612,
  729
cornetists, 484, 619, 1281
Cornwall, 153; ancient times, 1258-
  61; unspecified early period,
  332-33; mid-nineteenth century,
  397-99; early twentieth century,
  459-62; mid-twentieth century,
  889-91; late twentieth century,
  397-99, 429-32; North, mid-
  twentieth century, 1105-6, 1193;

seacoast, 1287-89; seacoast village, 1409
coronations: of czar, 1207; of Doctor Dolittle, 1310; of Emperor Constantine, 371
coroners, 353
Corporal Finch, 339
Cor, Prince of Archenland, 43, 562, 575, 1081
corpses, 825; battlefield, 340; frozen in dairy, 644; revived, 111; sold, 110, 111, 113
corruption, pervasive societal, 39-41
Corry family, 778
Cortorelli, Signora, 30-31
Corvo, Mr. Casimir, 1385-86
Cosmo the Clown, 1248
cossacks, 1416
Cossey Dearg, 271, 713-14
costumes: aid in escape, 814; for Mary, Queen of Scots, 814; for parade, 30-31; handmaiden of Jezebel, 855; raven, 855
Cotswold Holiday, 410
Cotswolds, 548-50, 791, 1402-3
cottages: cleaned after flood, 775, 786; covered with bird droppings, 817; deserted, 981; Foulgers', 867; gamekeeper's, 136-37; gypsy, 341; haunted, 469; in forest, 462; inherited, 134, 163, 714, 857, 860-61, 894; isolated, 74, 323, 714-15, 860; isolated by flood, 707, made from chapel vaults, 373-74; on River Say, 328; on Visick land, 398; outside village, 455; owned by dead father, 455; remote, 906; rented for summer, 1141; rented for vacation, 476; rented to blind professor, 460; slips into sea, 1170; snug, 267, 713; swallowed up by pool, 1405-6; vacation, 186-88; village, 319-20. *See also* huts.
COTTIA, *261-62*, 348, 350, 768
Cottontree House, 578-79
Council Rock, 630
Councillor Evans, 60, 176, 842-43
councils: at Rivendell, 96, 406; of war, 372; ruling, 989, 1162; tribal, 1321
Count Bloot, 1386
Countess of Corkberry, 1221-23
Countess Tordis, 1085
The Country Maid, 1371
Count Starhemberg, 214
County, 506-8

County Wicklow, Ireland, 445, 499-501
coups, Mexico, 753
courage: 411, 738-40, 1096, 1120-21, 1342-45, 1298-1300; against witch's spells, 373-75; in besieged city, 372-73; of aged woman, 714-16; of blind boy, 33-36; of handicapped boy, 1319-22, 1394-96; of kidnapped boy, 1004-7; on long journey through Russia, 1415-17; to explore cave containing strange creatures, 368; to face future, 589; to follow humane instincts, 821
The Courage of Andy Robson, 503
couriers, Indian Secret Service, 758
courtesy, 1082-84
courtiers, 509-11; playing cards, 20-21
court-martials, sea captain, 866
Court of Dreams, 1413
Court of Honour, 1037
courts: celestial, 325; hearing at, 87; kangaroo, 247; Kentish, 296; life in, 447-48; royal in exile, 1413
COUSIN, the snake, 262, 437, 953, 1114, 1120
COUSIN HENRY BOLINGER, 53-54, *262*, 692, 821
Cousin Maudie, 77, 466-67, 753
Cousin Noreen, 540-42
COUSIN ROBERT MCGILL, *262-63*, 403
Cousin Rosa, 607
cousins: 599, 701, 722-24, 811, 1042, 1194, 1276; adopted, 1105, 1193; adopted as heir, 96, 436; antagonistic, 775; art student, 540-42; bogus, 1120; Borrower, 135; boys, 237-38, 1359-60; bullying, 451, 703, 915, 1132; charming but unfeeling, 419; circus performers, 88-89, 204-5, 1248; close, 459-60, 528; considered siblings, 250; disagreeable boy, 74-75, 325, 376-77, 488, 1306-7; disparaging, 818; distant, 1, 1089; dominating, 578-80; domineering, 685-86, 693; duke, 738; effeminate, 619; emigrate to Australia, 76-77; estranged, 1021-23; fifth of Queen Victoria, 1147; flapper, 902; foster mother, 668, 685-86, 693; girl considered bossy, 361; girl-young woman, 821; half, 142; half, threatening, 241, 288,

478, 645; hobbits, 406, 436-37, 804-5, 981-82; impertinent boy, 538; interested in lads, 473; irrepressible, 1192; Jamaican, 607; jealous girl, 482; Jimmy Dean's, 159; killed in plane crash, 383; lazy, 523; leader of expedition, 624; musical, 685; numerous, 718; of King Arthur, 528; of prince, 252; orphan, 31; patronizing boy, 1241; preoccupied, 692; really siblings, 460; recognized, 1352; rejected as housekeeper, 431; rivals, 1137; romance between, 499-500, 775; royal, married, 586; rude, 1042; scornful, 533; Scottish, 27, 368; Scottish tribe, 772; Sikhs, 10, 310-12;
sinister, 81, 645-46, 899; sniveling girls, 703; snotty, 278; stylish, 565; supportive boy, 900; supposed from Nepal, 506; tattle-tale girl, 900; teasing, 639; test pilot, 382;
usurping, 672; wealthy, 556; youthful arsonist, 275
Cousin Sophie Berquovist, 718-19
Covenant (ship), 13, 649, 651, 1281
Covenanters, 638
covens, of witches, 1354
Covent Garden, 170, 1127
Coventry, Daniel, 1127-28
Coward family, 99-100, 233, 603-4, 876-78, 879-80, 910-11
cowards: boy in cave, 193; Noah's son, 522; Genoese leader in Constantinople, 372, 633
cowmen, 50
cows: 496, 606; attacks boy, 1155; catches star and dances, 780; jumps over moon, 780; stomped on, 395
Cowslip, 1331
coxswains, resourceful, 926
Crackernuts, Kate, 505, 636-38, 638
Crack, Granny, 566
Cradoc, 1172
craftsmanship: appreciation for, 290; celebration of, 9-10; pride in, 15, 619, 863
craftsmen: blacksmith, 484-85; glass blower, 15; jewelry makers, 918; piemakers, 51, 600, 970-71; Pit People, 1068; stonemason, 399, 1143-44
Craig, John Eland, 221
Craig, Robbie, 1398-99

CRAIK, DINAH MARIA MULOCK, 5, *263-64*, 720
Crampfurl, 133, 137, 854
cranes, shipyard, 1285
Cranmere College, 520-21
crashes, auto, 537
Cratchit family, 227-29, 353, 409, 1226-27
craters, created by digging, 388-89
cravats, mistaken for belt, 572
Craven, Jeremy, 313, 399, 601-2, 629, 1228
crawfish, 1239
Cray family, 535, 685-86, 811, 988-89
crazies, 798
creations: of Narnia, 321, 756, 987; undone, 688; of worlds, 167
creators, 55
The Creatures, 1247
creatures: dangerous, 535; magical, 1328-30; mysterious, sighted, 877; prehistoric, 27-28, 369-70; summoned up by witch, 209; zany, 18
CREEP, 109-10, 197-200, 230-31, *264*, 947, 1239
creeper, used as ladder, 1164-65
CREGAN, MAIRIN, *264-65*, 913
Creighton, Colonel, 652-53
CRESSWELL, HELEN, 127, *265-66*, 891, 920, 970, 1290, 1389
Crewe station, 597
crew, ships, 1254-56
cricket matches, 506, 621-22
THE CRICKET ON THE HEARTH, *266-69*, 314
crickets, magic, 268
cricket whites, wrong size, 622
cries, wildcat-like, 369
crime: impossible examples of, 183: bosses, 656-57, 1087; farmed, 1087
Crimean War, 171, 1386
Crimp Watson, 520-21
crippled leg, deliberately caused, 419
Crispin Roller, 51, 600, 970
The Crock of Gold, 1137
crocodile, swallows clock, 172, 957-58
Croft family, 842, 844, 850-51, 1262-64
crofts, Scottish, 588-89, 590
Crompton, Danny, 540-42
Cromwell, Oliver, 1318
Crookback, 1034
The Crooked Snake, 1403-4
Crookleg, 336-37
croppies, 501

croquet, 20, 23, 343, 375
crosses: mother's, 91; with tomb, 975-76
CROSS, GILLIAN (CLARE), *269-70*, 286, 917
"Crossing the River," 374
Crossing to Salamis, 941
Crowds of Creatures, 241
Crow: From the Life and Songs of Crow, 571
Crowing Cock, 612, 729
crownings: four children in Narnia, 712; first king and queen of Narnia, 756; of brother, 16
crown prince of Jolliginki, 160-61
Crowns, 571, 1362
crowns, offer of Roman Empire's, 370
Crown Without Sceptre, 1370
crows, steal Firefrost, 1344
Croxley, 621
Crum, Giant, 324
Crusades, 1034, 1035
crushes: cat for cat, 196; disappeared, 226; embarrassing, 413; girl on smuggler, 364; girl on teacher, 73-74; Goon on college girl, 470; little girl on wizard, 63; on baker's boy, 942; on barmaid, 1126; on housemaid, 1372; on local noble, 635; on playground director, 522; on teacher, 616; schoolgirl, 777, 1322-23; teenage, 809; wizard on co-ed, 470; youth for "fast" young woman, 1323; youth for maid, 921. *See also* infatuations; romances.
crutches: pirates, 732; taunting, 870
A Cry of Players, 629
crypts, beneath church floor, 93, 452
C.25.1B, 757
Cub, the pet wolf, 261, 348
cubs, fox, stolen by gypsies, 1386
Cuchulain, descendants of, 217. *See also* Cuchullin.
Cuchullin, elements borrowed from story of, 344, 1342-45. *See also* Cuchulain.
cuckoo clocks, 1386
The Cuckoo Sister, 15
The Cuckoo Tree, 889
Cuddy, 1376
Cue for Treason, 1253
Cuernavaca, 601
Culibrum, 1142
CULLEN, *270-71*, 1090
Culloden, 648-49

Cully, the hen, 271, 713
cult novels, 408
cults, of Roman legionaries, 281-82
cultures: adjustment to, 613-14; in conflict, 1245; New Guinean, 613; primitive, 613-14. *See also* ethnic customs; rituals; understanding, intercultural.
Culver family, 450, 548, 550
Culver treasure, 37, 547
Cumbrian fells, 531-32, 555-57, 644, 1085
Cunning Murrell, 307, 614
cupboards, magic, 189
curates: bored, 1325; father, 734; helpful, 515, 1242-43, 1365-66. *See also* clergymen; ministers; parsons; pastors; preachers; priests; rectors; vicars.
curators, museum, 1356
Curdie, 57, 746, 999-1001, 1002-3
cures, astonishing, 428
curios, 1325
curio shops, 653
curiosity: aroused, 860; boy's about god, 1205-6; intense, 842; of raven, 41-42
Curly Raleigh, 558-59
curses: 43, 1019, 1190; ancient, 123-24; by slave boy, 177; family, 1196-98; gypsy, 737; haunting Welsh valley, 574-75; of Cain, 625-26; passed down, 933-35
Curtain Up, 1157
curtains: new, 206; used as rescue ropes, 193
customs officers, 612
customs, traditional, inherent, 1294-95
Cuthbert family, 319-20
Cuthbert, St., 93
Cut Off from Crumpets, 67
cynicism: in nuclear aftermath, 150, 283; worldly, 654
CYRIL, *271-72*, 416-18, 1007
Czar, 12
Czarina, 12, 64
czars, Russian, 24, 28

Dab-Dab, the duck, 1145, 1309
Dad Morrison, 47
Daedalus and Icarus, 395
DAG, *273*, 769, 804, 1012-13
daggers: magic, 711; thrown back in contempt, 633
d'Aguillon family, 673-74
DAHL, ROALD, 203, *273-75*, 388, 480, 593, 1392

dahlias, destroyed, 734
Daily News, the kitten, 307-9
Daily Recorder (newspaper), 1147
DAISY PARKER, *275*, 477, 921, 1048
Dalriadains, 865, 967
Dalriads, 1089-91
Dalton family, 603-4
Damascus, 453, 671, 968, 1291
DAME ALICE of Suffolk, 71, *275-76*,
    324, 350, 744, 791, 909, 1404-5
DAME ELIZABETH FITZEDMUND, *276*,
    683-84, 701, 762
Damper Latham, 484
dams, destroyed by storm, 643
DAN ALONE, 276-79, 1247
Dan-boy, 78
Danby Dale, 51, 600, 970-71
dancers: ballet, 378, 1115-16; child
    ballerina, 69; figures in church
    windows, 208; mother, Spanish,
    447, 678, 1115-17; traveling, 832,
    1019
Dancer Smith, 877
dances: Christmas, 228, 409; dread-
    ed, 404-5; forbidden, 474;
    guisers', 1156; harvest, 1196;
    juju, 591, 616; leprechaun in cin-
    ema, 970; Lobster-Quadrille, 21,
    23; mummers', 1156; of elephants,
    632; rainmaking, 832; slave,
    765; sun, 40; Twelfth Night, 964;
    victory, in pajamas, 479; village,
    1153; wild, 827, 1036; Youth Club,
    465
THE DANCING BEAR, 279-81, 315
dancing, forbidden, 177, 474
Dandelion, 1333
Dando family, 42-43, 529, 996, 1234,
    1356-58, 1411
Dane family, 330-32
Danes, in England, 16, 18, 376, 477,
    517, 920-21, 1048, 1243, 1372
Danes, in Norway, 1298
DANGER AT BLACK DYKE, 281-83, 410
Danger Rock, 48
Daniel Hunter, 277
Dan Lunn, 276-79
Danny (*Danny, the Champion of the
    World*), 283-85, 1074, 1372
DANNY (*The Seventh Raven*), 11, *283*,
    1077-78
Danny Crompton, 540-42
DANNY LODGE, 150, 156-58, *283*, 655-
    56, 1033
Danny Price, 1269-70
*DANNY, THE CHAMPION OF THE WORLD,
    274, 283-85*
Dan Robinson, 182-84

Danton, 1217
Danube River, 214, 280-81
Dan Wilde, 828
Dara, 1171-73
DARCY JONES, 4, 101, *285-86*, 478,
    539, 845, 968, 1039-41
daredevils, aviation, 355-56
dares, 1317
Daring family, 163-66
Dark, 149, 502, 1050, 1375
THE DARK BEHIND THE CURTAIN, 270,
    286-87
The Dark Bright Water, 1404
Dark Cloud, 40
Dark Dew (ship), 108, 887
Dark Dove, 1140
Darkie & Co., 1131
Darkington Hall, 845, 1104, 1193,
    1353-56, 1397
The Dark Island (Barrett), 72
The Dark Island (Treece), 1257
THE DARK IS RISING, 255, 287-88, 502
The Dark is Rising Series, 148, 501,
    1375
Dark Knight, 1034, 1092-93
Dark Riders, 406
Darkness, Captain Vansittart, 173,
    236-37, 1412
Darkness, prevailing, 688
Dark People, 1321
The Dark Swallows, 504
Darley family, 92, 455-56, 618, 947
Darling family, 956-58, 961, 1226,
    1347
Darner, the dog doll, 330
Darnley, 290, 480, 539-42, 1413
Darroch, Isobel, 588-89, 589-90,
    1048-49
Dartmoor, 1386-88
Dartymore Jack, 1386-87
Darwin's pimple, 369
da Souza, Father, 1226, 1325, 1327
d'Assailly, Gilbert, 453, 670-72
d'Aubigny family, 453, 619, 670-72,
    729, 968, 1034, 1291
daughters: companion to blind fa-
    ther, 820-21; dutiful, 6; foster,
    1320-21; illegitimate, 1197;
    leaving home, 896; thought dishon-
    ored, 1149
Daughters of Eve, 710
Dave Ferguson, 708, 799-800, 1197-98
Davey Ullathorne, 129-30
David (*Elidor*), 359
David (*Fire and Hemlock*), 590
DAVID (*Kept in the Dark*), 81, 142,
    288-89, 478, 645-46, 728, 899
DAVID BALFOUR, 13, *289*, 648-51, 1281

David Balfour, 651, 1139
David Hartley, 464
DAVID HOLDER, *289-90*, 1313
DAVID HUGHES, *290*, 480-81
DAVID IN SILENCE, 290-91, 1043
DAVID MOSS, 1-2, 94, *291*, 615, 812-
   14, 817, 858, 862, 1058
David, Prince of Wales, 996, 1234,
   1357-58
David Rosley, 33, 244, 669, 801-4,
   863, 1133
Davidson, Lionel. *See* LINE, DAVID,
   708-9.
David Williams, 290-91
DAVID WIX, *291-92*, 351-53, 641
Davie Dunham, 473
DAVIES, ANDREW, 252, *292-93*
Davies family (*The Grey King*), 148-
   49, 502, 1050
Davies family (*Twopence a Tub*),
   1015, 1276-78
Davie, Watt, 428
Davina Daring, 163-66
DAVY, *293*, 684
Davy Jones's Locker, 893-94
Dawn Gloria, 606
DAWN MUDD, 77, *293*
Dawn of Fear, 255
dawns, resurrection at, 711
Dawn Treader (ship), 185, 377, 1306
DAWN WIND, 293-97, 1176
Dawson, Farmer, 287-88
The Day after Yesterday, 641
DAYA WANTI, *297*, 310, 312, 1280
day-care centers, 522
The Day I Shot My Dad, 149
D.C., 1191
dead: land of, 830; taking over li-
   ving, 201
Deadly Honeymoon, 796
deaf and dumb. *See* handicapped per-
   sons.
deaf-mutes, German flyer impersonn-
   ates, 887
deafness: caused by wound, 190-91;
   selective, 479; threatened with,
   1120
Dealing with the Fairies, 462
Dean, 673-75
Dean, Jimmy, cousin of, 604-5
deans, rural, 225
Dear Brutus, 72
Dear Fred, 967
Dear Little Friend, 357
deaths: assumed, 624; before hanging, 494; beheadings, 299; bound
   to pillar, 1344; by black arrow,
   102, 104; by drowning, 792, 875,
1237, 1328; by trampling, 631;
causing no grief, 228-29; causing
relief, 229; demanded, 625;
foreseen calmly, 177; from broken
heart, 1261; from exploding gun,
717; from fall, 1196, 1329; from
fire, 820; from heart attack, 541;
from lack of medical care, 250;
from malnutrition and exposure,
1160; from neglect, 262; from
overwork, 455, 1066; from plague,
71, 193, 760, 938-39, 1201; from
radiation, 156-58;
from shock, 456, 841, of dogs
eating money, 60; from smallpox, 1202; from wind and tide,
579; from wound, 1; in air combat, 421; in airplane exhibition,
1057; in battle, 619, 1204, 1226,
1296; in childbirth, 37, 586,
1369; in collapsing barn, 340;
in fire, presumed, 195, 1067; in
flu epidemic, 207; in German air
raid, 735-36; in motorcycle crash,
873; in plane crash, 335, 354-55;
in railway accident, 688, 962; in
revolving palace, 1143;
in riding accident, 296; in
unsuccessful rescue, 244; in
World War II, 841, 1374; learning
about, 607; of abused child, 728;
of Aslan, 1174; of aunt, 234, 1316,
1350, squashed by peach, 593,
from tuberculosis, 719; of baby,
1010; of baby sister, 1373; of baby
waiting for doctor, 628; of blind
pirate, 965; of boy, 57; of brother, 246, 294, 931; of cab driver,
1066; of cousin, 383, 719; of crippled boy, 229; of customs officer,
612; of dog, 295, 1141; of dog nature, 75, 328; of early pilot, 355;
of elderly man, 431;
of elderly wife, 431; of elegant
pirate, 172; of emperor, 372;
of father, by drowning, 1380,
1335, elderly clergyman, 1165,
hatmaker, 698, in battle against
Saxons, 294, in plane crash, 618,
in World War II, 696, 1151, 1322,
killed by slave hunters, 1161,
liberal firebrand, 924, 942-43,
1123-25, leaving girl penniless, 685, 693, on daughter's
birthday, 1335, possibly suicide, 455, suspicious, 506, 1103,
the king, 720, welcomed, 355; of
fee-holder, 674; of fisherman in

attempt to rescue girl, 1288-89;
of friend, 179, 469, 674, 1137,
1390; of foundling, 1411; of Gold-
en Puma, 1386; of gondolier, 662,
913; of gorilla, 1155; of grandfather, 500, 1156;
of grandmother, 588, 1394; of
groom, 106; of guardian reported,
1400; of gypsy grandmother, 318;
of horse, 320; of husband, 1201; of
ironmaster, 581; of king, 16, 185,
1093, 1118; of leader, 789; of little girl, 363; of mastiff, 1387;
of monk, 1395; of mother, 116, 249,
356, 482, 720, 737, 889, at birth,
115, 1125, at sea, 344, by drowning, 638, in World War II, 898-99;
of naval captain, 191; of new husband, 939; of officer in war, 147;
of old woman, 830; of old sheep
dog, 1399; of outlaws, 738; of outlaw leader, 739;
of pet pig, 955, 987; of pirate
captain, 958; of prince announced
falsely, 720; of queen, 1414; of
rabbit leader, 535; of reformed
pirate, 257; of resistance leader, 158; of Robin Hood, 147, 717,
1043; of ruler of Slav village, 39;
of school friend, 1373; of servant boy, 1160; of sheep from heart
attack, 1083; of sister, 458; of
sister, prayed for, 387-88; of
snake father, 262; of son, 705,
in World War II, 1132; of squire,
917, 1137; of starving child, 54;
of sweetheart in plague, 1204; of
teacher, 603; of tiger, 1084-85;
of two children, 603; of unicorn, 360; of Viking leader, 91;
of village blind boy, 1197; of
White Witch, 864; of witch, 567,
by falling into bottomless hole,
874; of wizard, 407, 439; of workhouse boys, 596; on tampered with
motorcycle, 934; philosophical
question of, 1289; sacrificial,
1173; squashed by elephant, 523;
sympathetic, 300; undone by willing sacrifice, 711; various, 1358;
welcomed, 979
Deathwater, 1307
Debbie Llewellyn, 558
de Beauville family, 155, 915-17,
1103-4, 1202
Deborah, 583
Deborah Keate, 169-71
Debra, 1000-1

De Braose, 672, 673-74
De Brissac, Malcolm, 314
debtors, imprisoned, 305, 1202, 1353
debts: accumulated, 494; father's,
526; for furniture, 1365; for
operation, 354-55; gambling, 361;
paid, 1146; paid by friend, 494;
youth heavily in, 1067
Decani, 224
Decianus Catus, 1118
deceptions: concealing madness in
family, 88; of blind daughter,
267-68
de Chaworth family, 672
decisions, vocational. See choices,
vocational.
decorations, for jubilee, 1159-60
de Coucy, Lady, 447-48, 600
de Coucy, Sir Thiebaut, 673-74
de Courcy Rohan, Sir Jocelin, 261,
408-9, 1103
de Courville, Cadieux, 733
deductions: ex-policeman pursues
dwarf, 847, 850; gone awry, 856
Deep Magic, defeats witch, 711
deer: gored by buck, 545; king's,
slain, 145; pet, 211-12; raising
of, 543-46; shot, 350
de Farrar family, 738-40, 1104
DEFOE, DANIEL, *297-98*, 1043
Definite Article, 318
deformities, babies born after nuclear blast, 158
Deio, Prince of England, 996
Deirdre, 289-99, 299-300
DEIRDRE (Polland), *298-99*, 986
DEIRDRE (Stephens), *299-301*, 1137
Deirdre, Circlet of, 216
Deirdre, descendants of, 217
DE LA MARE, WALTER, *301-2*, 839
de la Pole, William, Earl of Suffolk,
275
de la Tour Rouge family, 1360
Deliet, Jean-Paul, 989, 1360-61
Delilah type, 1189-90
delirium tremens, 172
Deliverer, 522, 586-87
Delos, 1043
Delphi Swayne, 1010-11
demagogues, seventeenth century,
554
demented persons, 705, 888-89, 896,
1381
Demetriades, Alexius, 118-19
democracy: among rabbits,
1331; vs. totalitarianism,
1332
The Demon Headmaster, 270

demons: departing, 800; fire, 168, 567, 568-69, 1122; invasive of humans, 859
Denethor, 131, 982
Denham-Lucie, Lucy, 58, 636, 1280, 1323-24, 1420
Denis Flack, 1390
Denmark, ninth century, 91-2
dentist's offices, family home, 97
dentures, made of corpses' teeth, 340
DENZIL MURGATROYD, Sir, 31, *302-3*, 677, 809, 845, 1104
Departmental Ditties, Barrack-Room Ballads, and Other Verse, 666
Departmental Ditties and Other Verse, 666
department store scenes, 84
departures, ironic, 715, 861, 894
depressions: emotional, 970, 1132; psychological, 736, 743
Deptford, 468
deputations, to owl, 529
deputies, youthful, 185
Derbyshire, 335, 605, 917-19, 938-39
DEREK POOLEY, *303*, 307-9, 1174
de Renneville family, 1017-20
Dergdian, 349-50
Dermot, 216
Dermot (plane), 355
Dermot Byrne, 499
Dermot, Mr., 420-21
Derry Larkins, 926-27
Derval Dove, 425-27
DESAI, ANITA, *303*, 1302
deserters: from survival colony, 158; from Roman army, 680; sailor, 1255
desert isles, south sea, 855, 859, 1023
designers: airplane, 355, 1374; costume, 855; of military gun controls, 361
designs, for stronghold, 333
de Silva family, 1303-4
desires: dolls, for home, 330; for baby, 1368-69; for creature comforts, 559; for dog, 328-30; for father figure, 460; for glory, 612; for mother, 1239; for nice things, like new neighbors have, 334; for power, 505, 611; for prayer book, 1144; for security, 501; for world of peace, 336; to be part of a family, 598; to eat companion, 464; to get help from Pope, 371; to have doctor on island, 258-61; to have perfect family, 276-79; to have son, 1136; to inherit aunt's wealth, 620; to learn Danish, 1195; to sail, 516-17. *See also* ambitions.
desks, lap, 428
Desmond Treloar, 430-31
Desperate Dan, 540-42
Desperate Journey, 1257
de Staseley, Lord, 17
destiny, strong belief in, 1261-62
detectives: after dwarf, 847-49, 969; baldheaded, 790; becomes giraffe, 1385; boys, 812-14; Detective-Inspector Kingsland, 656-58; helpful, 426-27; methodical, 656; old man, 850; over-imaginative, 855-56; over-zealous, 855-56; theory incorrect, 1150; Victorian inquiry agent, 1150; youthful, 125, 182-84, 184-85, 314, 401-3, 427-28, 434-36, 480-82, 486-87, 515, 536-37, 615, 944-45, 1022, 1147, 1339
determination: of vicar's daughter, 821; to continue music, 87; to endure prison term, 87
de Vairmont, Madame, 1215-17
development, commercial, 225
DEVIL-IN-THE-FOG, 304-6, 441
DEVIL ON THE ROAD, 306-9, 1348
devils: boy feared to be, 554, 1241; daughter of, 374; in boy's head, 1058-60; little black, 1378; soul sold to, 824; thought in marsh, 801-2
THE DEVIL'S CHILDREN, 309-13, 315, 1338
Devil's Dyke, 143, 144
Devil's Fire, 304
Devil's Leap, 1357
Devil's Nob, 1273
The Devil's Piper, 994
Devil's Roustabouts, 302-3
Devonshire, 5-6, 389-92, 724-27, 926-27
devotion: forces renunciation, 988; housekeeper reveals, 859; to emperor, 1136; to music, 685-87; to preservation of empire, 254; thrall to Saxons, 930
Devshirme, 1296
Dexter family, 304-6, 827
diadems, ruby, 236
diagrams, of burglar alarm, 184
dialects: heavy, bogus Russian, 1392-93; Scots, 996. *See* style, dialect.
Diamond, 55-57, 746

Diamond Cave, 256
Diamond family, 609, 610-11
diamond merchants, 792
diamonds, 1397
diaries: as narrative device, 287, 366, 368-70; by aunt, 49; by Borrower girl, 135; by brother, 832; by guinea pig, 368; contains code, 790; from refuse heap, 452; of *Dawn Treader* journey, 377
DIAZ, PORFIRIO, *313*, 601-2, 753
Dick, 624
Dick Birkinshaw, 449, 922, 1267-68
Dick Burley, 401-3, 1177
Dick Callum, 972-74
DICKENS, CHARLES (JOHN HUFFAM), 227, 266, *313-14*, 442, 492
Dickensian characters: drawn by Dickens, 94-95, 227-30, 266-69, 353, 376, 409, 492-95, 592, 608, 757, 820, 981, 1226-27, 1346; drawn by other authors, boys, 143, 529-30, 740-41, 1087, 1099-1100, 1100, 1107-08, 1232, girls, 31-32, 88, 344-45, 1121-22, men, 110, 119, 185-86, 302-3, 508, 609-10, 738, 826-27, 837, 845, 845-46, 855-56, 1065-66, 1104, 1284, various, 107-9, 109, 111-13, 143-44, 304-6, 339-42, 610-11, 807-9, 824-26, 887-89, 1108-10, 1125-28, 1141-43, 1149-51, 1399-1401, women, 677, 816-17, 820-21
Dick Harvey, 763-64
DICK HEDLEY, *314*, 514-15, 599, 629, 647-48, 838, 1057, 1365
Dick, Hobberdy, 547-48, 548-50
Dickie, 415-16
DICKINSON, PETER, 33, 121, 279, 309, *314-16*, 368, 1076, 1265, 1336
Dick Mason, 1160
Dickon, 12, 145-47, 717, 1043
Dick Reeves, 586
DICK SHELTON, 102-5, *316-17*, 606, 695, 1103
DICKS, TERRANCE, 182, *316*
Dick Ullathorne, 129-31, 841, 861
Dick Wade, 463-64
Dick White, 125, 477
DICK WRIGHT, 226-27, *317*, 419-21, 422-24, 775, 1229
DICKY BASTABLE, *318*, 1146-47
dictators: Mexican, 601-2; rabbit, 418, 446, 535, 1332
A Dictionary of British Folk-tales in the English Language, 151
A Dictionary of Fairies: Hobgoblins, Brownies, Bogies, and Other

Supernatural Creatures, 151
didactic novels: about deafness, 290-91; anti-war, 585; deliberately excessive, 807-9; disguised by humor, 221-23; informational, 1204-6; informational and moralistic, 786-89; instructive of history, 732-34, 1020; moralistic, 105-7, 204, 659-62, 999-1002, 1002-3, 1327-30; religious, 974-80; sociological, 248-52, 628, 989-92, 1364; travelogue, 1020. *See also* biographical novels; historical novels; period novels.
THE DIDDAKOI, *318-21*, 459
Dido Twite, 8, 108, 344-45, 837, 844, 887-89, 1141-43
A Different Sort of Christmas, 641
digging, to get foxes, 388-89
dignity: despite slavery, 375; of animal, 839-41
DIGORY KIRKE, 167, *321*, 688, 710, 755-56, 987, 1279
dilemmas: endangering self to save friend, 1360; loyalty to father vs. social consciousness, 896; guilt at stealing vs. letting children starve, 692; religious, 1195
Diligence Widdison, 548
DILLIAN, 45-46, 63, *321*
DILLON, EILIS, 258, *321-23*, 543, 1101
Dilys Gotobed, 177-78, 542-43, 842
Dinah, 626, 1205
Dinah, the cat, 836
Dinah, the horse, 1339-40
Dinah Palfrey, 1385-86
Dinan, Carolyn, 1269
Dineo, 627-28
dinosaurs, 367
Dinsdale, Abraham, 125, 477
DINTIRION, *323*, 907
diplomats, South American, slain, 907
directions, for building Japanese doll house, 820
directors: of play, 286-87, 820; of playground, 522
disappearances: of artist, 108; of baby girl, mysterious, 855-56; of Borrowers, 822; of businessman, 183; of diamond necklace, 183; of hobbit, 96; of iron and steel machinery, 584; of man from tower, 361; of Ninth Roman Legion,

347, 349; of pigs, 351; of policeman, 182-84; of Ringbearer, 407-8;
of swimming competitor, 384; of
tutor, 373; of Yorkshire boy, 352-
53; sudden, 1130-31; with magic
ring, 132

disasters: ambush killing ten thou-
sand, 339; being seen, 132-33;
caused by young witch, 517-18;
flood, 186-88; march on Turks,
671; mine accident, 34-36, 486;
near, 193-94; nuclear, 149; sent
by witch, 800; series of, 1326-27.
See also accidents.

disciples, of Tibetan lama, 651,
653-54, 1194-95

discos, youth club, 1326

Discretion, 976

discrimination: against women,
1033; racial, 627-28. *See also*
anti-Semitism; apartheid; prejudice; social classes, distinctions between.

discussions: noisy family, 310, 312;
philosophical, 1287-90

disguises: boy as girl, 12, 739; boy
as maid, 1077; changed, 653; crea-
tor of, 12; detected, 1086; for
Mary, Queen of Scots, 814; girl as
black creature, 1095; girl as boy,
1086; grandmother as housemaid,
1001; handmaiden of Jezebel, 855;
mouse as knife grinder, 816; queen
as commoner, 1414; raven, 855. *See
also* impersonations.

dishes, with flower-owl decoration, 575, 933

dishwashers, stage magician, 922

disillusionment, 155, 1226

disintegrating families, novels of:
411-14; 418-21; 656-58; 895-97;
1009-12; 1313-15

Disney-type figures, 324

displaced children, 339

Disraeli, 99

dissension, over leadership, 1161-
62, 1168, 1253-56

*Divine Emblems, or Temporal Things
Spiritualized,* 162

diviners: for water, 92; for gold,
1148

diving, 383-84

divorces, 335, 1029; impending,
639; sought, 1314

D.L.F., 1265

Dnieper river, 117

do-as-you-pleasers, 168, 538, 620,
891

Doasyouwouldbedoneby, Mrs., 851,
853, 1329

Doc Spencer, 284-85, 1074

DOCTOR CORNELIUS, 185, *323*, 995-96

DOCTOR DOLITTLE, 160, 210-11, *323-
24*, 730-31, 988, 1145-46, 1309-11

Doctor Jakes, 69

Doctor Jasper, 840

Doctor Mayhew, 889

Doctor No, 424

doctors, 786, 982, 1200-1, 1224-25;
advising holiday, 473; animal,
1145-46; army surgeon, 340-42;
cares more for animals than humans, 1145; compassionate,
342; early nineteenth century, 356; efficient, dedicated,
352; fairy, 248; fairy, cat,
913; father, 880; genuinely good, 1145-46; helps rabbit,
1333; honorable, 338; impractical, 323-24; in Constantinople,
118-19; ineffective, 565; London,
1088; noble becomes, 457; of
slaves, 937-38; pediatrician,
498; poisons king, 1000-1; proud,
338; quack, 111-12, 154; Roman,
1089-91; ship's, 338; speaks language of animals, 1145, 1309-11;
student, 880-81; Swiss, 354;
sympathetic to poachers, 284-
85; uncle, 193-94. *See also* "harb
mothers"; healers; pediatricians;
physicians; psychiatrists;
psychologists.

Doctor Smith, 69

Doctor Who, 316

documents: as narrative device,
1206-8; important, found, 839; secret, 654; stolen, 1108; to add
authenticity, 309; unwitnessed,
537; valuable, 817

DODDER, 67, *324*, 716, 1114

Dodgson, Charles Lutwidge. *See*
CARROLL, LEWIS, 180

DODO, 20, 22, *324*, 836

Dodo Price, 1165-67

does: brave rabbit, 1332; quest for,
95, 418; rabbit, needed, 1332

Dog, the dog, 294-96, 1293

A Dog and a Half, 1371

The Dog at the Window, 504

dog boys, 672

A Dog Called George, 67

Dog Days and Cat Naps, 644

dog droppings, boys smell like,
1393-94

Dog Folk, 336

DOGGETT, the bedesman, 276, *324-25*, 1406

Doggie Dogfoot, 665

The Dog of Castle Crag, 221

dog pen, boy trapped in, 690

dogs, 212-13, 728, 823, 1309; active, 266-67; Alsatian, 253; Alsatian puppy, 1386, 1398, Alsatian sheep, 1398-99; Arawn's hounds, 326-28; army Alsatian stray, 903-4; army, retrained as family pet, 903-4; attacks old gentleman, 1147; Bavarian farmdog, 598; beagle, 535; bloodhounds, 765-66, 816; brown pup, 483; bull terrier, 186; buried in shifting sands, 1141; collie, 467-68; cowardly, 395-96; Dalmatians, 903; deer-hound, 153-54; derided, 75; destroy money, 1132; dislikes mysterious stranger, 1156; displays inferiority complex, 1419; doll made of darning needle, 330; dying of thirst, 661; eat banknotes, 706; English sheepdog, 647; English sheepdog pup, 463-64; exceptionally smart, 1398-99; faithful, feckless, 715, 861; faithful talking, 829; father to put down, 896; fear of, 915; gone wild, 1387; guards', 521; gypsy, 1352; half-drowned puppy, 639; herd, aging, 1398-99; heroic, 327; hounds, 454, 486-87, 921, 960, 1419-20; huge tawny, 724; incorrigible, 912; in heat, 326; inherited, 1080; imagined, 329, 490; Irish wolfhounds, 672; Kerry blue terrier, 675, 913; killed, 402; King Charles spaniel, 724; Labrador, 389; lonely, 1387; longed for and acquired, 852; lost, 464, 690, 714; lost puppy, 863; lost under ice, 945; lured away by vixen, 1386; magical, 1042; Mexican Chihuahua, 328-29; mongrel, 912, 1112; mother enchanted as, 929-30; Newfoundland nurse, 956; nondescript, 253, 848; old, Spaniellike, 328-29; overweight, 30; Pekinese, 78, 465, 467; performing poodles, 235; pet, 1320-21; poisoned, 1303; proclaimed hero, 1399; puppy, 955; put down, 915; released by rabbits, 1333; sheepdog, 1082-83, 1313; sheep killers, 1083; shot, 148; spaniel, 1219; stray mongrel, 1316; summons help for ill master, 1399; talking, 395, 780, 1145; taught to fetch, 1419-20; three wolf-like, 1067; to be put down, 75, 153, 327, 836; trapped, 154; tricked by gnome, 715; understanding human language, 639-40; used to track kidnappers, 1219; vicious guard, 60; war hound, 294-95; water-wary, 715; white with silver eyes, 502; wild mastiff, 1387; wild red, 631-32, 635; woolwork Chihuahua, 479, 483; wrapped in newspaper, 1316

DOGSBODY, *325-28*, 618

A DOG SO SMALL, *328-30*, 949

dog stories: fantasy, 325-28; realistic, 328-30, 903-4, 1386-88, 1398-99. *See also* animal novels; cat stories; horse stories.

dog walkers, 30

dole, shame of being on, 233

Doli, 1321

Dolittle, Doctor John, 160, 210-11, 323-24, 1145-46, 1309-11

Doll Codling, 872, 902-3, 985, 1094-96, 1130

dollhouse furniture, 135

dollhouses, 558, 723; directions for Japanese, 820; Japanese, 88, 819-20; left by great aunt, 330-31

DOLL JACOBS, 330, 857, 1076-78

dolls: believed bewitched, 332; celluloid, 101-2, 330-31; cradle, for bed, 510; dog made from darning needle, 330; Dutch, 850; elegant, of kid and china, 331; farthing, 330-31, 1245-46; from Christmas tree, 381-82; given to museum, 331; haughty, 101-2; highland, 850; Japanese, 87-88, 818-20; jointed at hip and shoulders, 1245-46; jointed wooden Dutch, 330-31; long for a home, 819; lost, 382; loved into life, 332; missing Japanese, 818; naval officer, 558-59; neglected, abused, 850; of good sense, 1246; plush, 330-31; proud, 331; rattle-brained, 331; sailor, 558-59; stolen, 723; talking, 330-32, 722-24; with china face, 330; wooden Dutch, 1245-46

THE DOLLS' HOUSE, *330-32*, 458

THE DOLL WHO CAME ALIVE, *332-33*, 1258

Dolly Barker, 602

Dolly Hawthorne, 538

Dolor, Prince of Nomansland, 720-22

Dolphin, 680
Dolphin (ship), 866, 1070
The Dolphin Crossing, 941
dolphins: engraved on emerald ring, 349-50; good-luck tattoo, 680
domes: blown up, 991; control weather, 1295; fired, 1295; green, 991; over city, 238
domestic bliss, 266-69
Domingues, 183
DOMNALL, 148, *333*, 879, 884, 1161-64, 1190
Donahue, Vic, 258
Donald, 732-34
Donald Bruce, 14, 1049-50
Donarink, 1151-53
donations: generous, for poor, 229; refused, for poor, 227
DONG PE, *333-34*, 1195, 1266
THE DONKEY GOES VISITING. See THE TURF-CUTTER'S DONKEY GOES VISITING, 1271.
donkeys, 149, 157-58, 391, 888, 1271-72; enchanted boy, 1233-34; gloomy, 1388, kidnapped, 675; lost white, 1003; naive dupe, 687-89; old grey stuffed, 358; recovered, 1152; stolen, 1151; stealing hay, 675; stuffed grey, 562-63; talking, 1112; white, rescued from dwarf, 913
Donnelly, Colman, 544-46
Donovan (boat), 496, 775
Donovan Croft, 842, 844, 851, 1262-64
doom, Ballinford, 1196, 1198
Doom window, 480-81
Doorback, Aun, 1298, 1300
Door, into eternal Narnia, 688
door knockers, showing Marley's face, 227
doors: front, painted and ruined, 1115; locked, 19; red front, 854; secret, 1217; to other dimension, 995-96; to other worlds, 209
door scraper, 1384
doorway, child-sized, 724
Doppler Effect, 1026
DORA BASTABLE, *334*, 1146-47
Dora Raleigh, 558
Dori, 551
Dorinda Palfrey, 1385-86
Doris, the octopus, 1354
DORIS Thompson, *334*, 514-15, 629, 1057, 1315, 1364-66
Dorking, 1125-28
Dorking family, 88, 110, 111-13, 1232

d'Orleans, Duc, 1405
dormice, sleepy, 20, 753, 767
DORMOUSE, 20, 23, *334-35*, 753, 767
Dorothea Callum, 972-73
Dorothy Harris, 143-44
DOROTHY SAUNDERS, *335*, 354-56, 423-24, 775, 1057
Dot, the dog, 912
Dot Perrybingle, 266-69
Dottie, 474-75
Dotty Crocker, 950-52
Dotty Dick, 775
doubles, from different worlds, 598
Douglas family, 677-78, 814-15, 1412-15
The Dove (boat), 340
Dove family, 425-27
Dove Square, 77-78, 465-67, 517, 539, 753, 791, 823, 1080
Down in the Cellar, 489
Down River, 194, 233
Downstream, 1247
Down's Syndrome, girl, 1288-91
downs, Watership, 418
Down the Bright Stream, 83, 717
Down the Long Stairs, 194
dowries, of trinket, 115
dowsers, 39-41, 973
Dowsett, Annie, 365
DOYLE, *335*, 525, 606, 918-19, 1265
Dragon Dance, 232
Dragonfly (boat), 716-17
Dragonfly, the pony, 389, 793
The Dragonfly Years, 573
The Dragon of an Ordinary Family, 759
dragons: boy transformed into, 377, 1307; in Middle-earth, 95, 439, 551-52, 1107, 1204; killed by cold monster, 997-98; nonaggressive, 1029-30; poet, 1030; pretend, 802; ravaging Ireland, 1259-60; space, 584; storyteller, 1030; tamed by farmer, 396-97; tongue of, 1259-60
dragon's blood, 209
Dragon's Hill, 1172
dragon slayers, reluctant, 396
Dragons Live Forever, 1183
Dragon Trouble, 728
drainage, of farm lands, 1133
Dr. and Mrs. Little, 468
drapers, 499
Drava River, 214
The Drawbridge Gate, 527
drawing lessons, 883
drawings: in chimney, 1237; of teacher, 367; pre-historic, 1144
Dr. Boteler, 1200-1
Dr. Bunion's Academy, 1149

Dr. Carmody, 111-12, 1232
Dr. Cray, 685
Dreaded Yellow Jelly Mould, 524
Dreadful Spiller, 1130
Dream Days, 472, 1029
Dream Gold, 1078
dreaming, nature of, 1211
dreams: 18, 19-22, 22-23, 1208-11,
    1344; about New Guinea tribesmen,
    564-65; as prophecy, 370; come
    true, 1308; going back in time,
    367: admonition, 870; of castle,
    188; of doom, 300; of flying, 367;
    of money, 864; of treasure, 550;
    psychologically upsetting, 564-
    65; Red King's, 1274; shared, 367,
    428, 533, 1241; sacred, 1171
Dreams, Court of, 1413
THE DREAM TIME, 335-37, 1257
DREM, 115, *337-38,* 1319-22
dressers, in London theatre, 678
dressmakers, 492
Drew family, 804
Dr. Gabriel Field, 108-9
Dr. Furnace, 108
Dr. Harper, 127
Drift, 795
The Driftway, 727
drink: causes change in size, 982;
    dangers of, 338; evils of, 602;
    fizzy lifting, 1376; magic,
    1385; produces amnesia, 1294-95;
    sacred, 1171; to erase memory,
    1294-95
Driver, Mrs., 559
driving: ability felicitous, 874;
    crazy, 921; illegal, 874; lessons,
    secret, 945; reckless, 1283
Dr. Jones, 110, 111-12
DR. KERRIDGE, *338,* 1224-25
DR. LIVESEY, *338,* 1254-56
DR. MAUD BIGGIN, *339,* 577, 1035-36,
    1183
DR. MCINTYRE, *339,* 1124
dropouts, school, 1124,
    1365
Drouet family, 728, 821
Drouet school, 53-54, 59, 262, 821,
    1370
droughts, 40, 660; jungle, 631; mag-
    ic, 1385
Drowned Ammet, 617
drownings: accidental, 669, 810,
    875; attempted, 402-3, 1177; in
    lake, 684; in sea, 1288-89, 1380;
    near, 225, 245, 263, 408, 461, 542,
    622, 1033, 1325; near, in bath-
    tub, 84; of cat, attempted, 893;

of chimney sweep, 1328; of daugh-
    ter, 923-24; of father, 85, 792,
    1335; of fishing smack captain,
    85; of panther in muck, 877-78;
    of poacher, 1328; of puppies, at-
    tempted, 325; of uncle, 1335,
    1376; of witches, 449, 1337; pre-
    tended, 78; prevented, 654;
    rescues from, 1264-65; suspected,
    1377; threatened, 36; thought sui-
    cide, 809-10; under ice, 945, 1237
Dr. Palmer, 1294-95
Dr. Sunderland, 224, 1181
drug addicts, father, 1062
druggings, 1357, 1393; by gypsies,
    1352; of pheasants, 284-85
drugs: heroin, 1062-63; Merlin ad-
    dicted to, 1056; smuggling, 1061-
    64; used in kidnapping, 1005
drug traffic, novels of, 1061-64
Druid stones, 373
Druids, 148, 298-99, 333, 491, 879,
    1161
Druid's Bottom, 14, 177-78, 542
Druid's Grove, 178
Drumbeats, 1078-79
THE DRUMMER BOY, 339-42, 442
drummer boys: eighteenth century ar-
    my, 292, 641; idealistic, 339-42;
    materializing from hillside, 351-
    52
Drummle, Bently, 495
Drummond, V. H., 173
drums: African, 592; army, 340, 342;
    Irish, 1285
drunkenness, soldier punished for,
    190
drunks: brothers, 660; buccaneer,
    1253; Earl, 1198; ex-gladiator,
    772; father, 706; handyman, 1131-
    32; leader of thieves, 1352; naval
    commander, 263; poorhouse keep-
    er's wife, 1150; ruins enterprize,
    695; seaman, 100; washed over-
    board, 595. *See also* alcoholics.
Drury Lane, 170
Dr. Vogel, 373, 800
Dr. Wallace, 457
DR. WILLIAM HENCHMAN, 190, *342,* 356,
    595, 880, 1236-37
Dr. Wix, 352
dryads, 711, 687, 875, 1093
Drynwyn, 344, 1343
dual natures, dog and luminary, 325-
    28
Duatha, 1118
Dublin, 116-19
Dubnet, 1180

ducal agents, 579
Duc d'Orleans, 1405
DUCHESS, 20, 22, 23, 211, *342-43*, 1362
Duchess, the dog, 1080
Duchess Eleanor of Gloucester, 125, 276, 325, 1024
Duchess of Battersea, 109, 1121-22
Duchy of Furness, 578
DUCK, 20, *343*, 836
duck growers, 388
ducklings, lured away, 5
duckpond, oblong, once pie-dish, 971
ducks: housekeeper, 1309; talking, 1145
Ducks and Dragons: Poems for Children, 644
Duckworth, Ellis, 615
Duckworth, the Rev. Mr. Robinson, 343
duels: between brothers, 304; by legless man, 119; father over daughter's honor, 1149-50; in Outremer, 670; with bagpipes, 650
DUFFIE Duffield, 325, 327-28, *343*, 639, 823
Duffield family, 74-75, 325-28, 343, 639, 823, 1042
Dufflepods, 1307
Duke, the dog, 1080
Duke Ellington Binns, 689-92
Duke Humphrey of Gloucester, 125
Duke of Battersea, 108-9
Duke of Gloucester, 448
Duke of York, 1164
dummies, Guy Fawkes, 197, 747-48
dummlings, 929
dumplings, entire batch consumed, 1094-96
dumps, 197; runaway destination, 76
The Dunadan, 1158
Duncan, Clogger, 245-46
Duncan dhu Maclaren, 650
Duncormac, 216, 408
Dunedin Street, 226, 603, 735-36
dunes, North Sea, 496
Dunfermline, 273, 1012-13
dungeons, 500, 712, 879, 977, 1000; elven, 551-52; escape from, 1204; father imprisoned in, 1386; poet in, 1031-32; royal, 1142, 1357
Dunham family, 61-62, 472-73, 473-75
DUNLOP, EILEEN (RHONA), *343-44*
Dunnitt, Mrs., 855, 1077-78
Dunya, 1301-2
duplicity: of bug, 432; of scholar, 838
DURATHROR, *344*, 1343-44

Durham County, England, 129-31
Durus Velanius, 1244-45
dustmen: father, 385-86, 618-19; refuse to take animals, 76
Dusty-Feet, 153
DUTIFUL PENITENCE CASKET, *344-45*, 887-89
Dvina River, 117
Dwali, 1305
dwarfs: chased by detective, 850, 1316; circus performers, 120, 570; created in Narnia, 756; duped by enemy, 687-88; envious, 1065-66; evil, 248, 675, 913-14; feisty, 1264; from another world, 847; golden, 660; good, 1343-45; half-dwarf tutor, 185, 323; helpful, 344, 408; in Narnia, 875, 892-93; in witch's army, 712; malicious, 511, 610; member of fellowship, 407; in expedition to regain ancestral treasure, 95-96, 551-53, 1107; patronized by boy, 357; pot-bellied, 388; red-faced, 660; regent, 1092; rescued, 994-95; resourceful, 869-70; Sikhs mistaken for, 311; street boy escapes from, 1087; talkative, 725; thirteen, 439, 1204; wicked, 1003
dying requests, by mother, 334
dynamite, 837; used on pool, 643
dyslexia, 1314-15
dyslexic persons, 655
Dyson family, 2, 486-87, 960

eagle of legion, symbol for rally, 348-50
THE EAGLE OF THE NINTH, *347-50*, 1089, 1176
eagles, 1271; rescuers from wolves, 439, 552; Roman legion, 271, 347-50, 1091
The Eagle's Nest, 671
Earl de Staseley, 705-6, 873
Earl of Arundel, 672
Earl of Ballinford, 760-61, 799, 1196-98
EARL OF SUFFOLK, 275, 324-25, *350-51*, 454, 1024, 1404
The Earl's Falconer, 831
early readers, books for, 606-8, 912
earrings, skull-shaped, 697
ears: magic silver, 721; misshapen from sawdust, 953
Earth, conquered by extra-terrestrial invaders, 1359; voice of, 326

earth, splits open, 584
EARTHFASTS, 351-53, 794
Earthmen, 1093
Earth Mother, 772-73, 806, 865
earthquakes, 112, 1044
earth-spirits, 406
Earthworm, 593-94
earthworms: pet, cured, 1355; stol-
   en, 1355; witch's familiar, 845,
   1192, 1355
East Anglia, 870-72, 1190-92
East Coast Smack Preservation Society, 1088
East End Cottage, 48, 451, 1100
Easter eggs, forbidden, 450, 549
East Wind, blows in nanny, 779
Ebenezer Jones, 41-42
EBENEZER SCROOGE, 227-30, *353*, 409,
   1227
eccentric persons: adults in Little
   Barley, 812-14; architect, 613;
   artist, 613; bird lover, 480-82,
   817; botanist, woman, 853, 1195,
   1266-67; clergyman, 1317-18;
   duchess, 342-43; early aircraft
   designer, 420-21; eighteenth-
   century London, 610-11; elderly
   couple, 6; family, 477, 920-22;
   father, 838; grandfather, 479;
   grandmother, 477, 1021; great-
   aunt, 60; mother figure, 77;
   parents of son killed in World War
   I, 207; seaside resort patrons,
   923-24; teenaged boy, 1325-27;
   tramps, 538, 891-92; tutor, 596,
   623; woman in tea shop, 736; woman scientist, 339; various, 18,
   19-22, 22-23, 108, 108-9, 111-13,
   807-9, 1208-11, 1128
*The Echoing Green: Memories of
   Victorian and Regency Youth*, 63
Eckersley, Alf, 449, 1268
eclipses, of sun, 476, 557
ecological novels, 403-5, 982-84,
   1330-34
Eddie Flint, 77-78
EDEK BALICKI, 152, *353-54*, 597, 619,
   1052, 1097-99, 1398
The Edge of Evening, 489
THE EDGE OF THE CLOUD, 354-56, 966,
   1284
Edgington, Helen, 535-36, 685-86
Edinburgh, 427-28
editors: newspaper, 404, 435, 1147;
   Yates, Elizabeth, 332
Edmund, King of Narnia, 561-62
Edmund, King of Saxons, 375, 870
Edmund de Beauville, 1137

EDMUND HENCHMAN, 190-91, *356*, 881
EDMUND PEVENSIE, 185, 323, *356-57*,
   376, 560-62, 688, 710-12, 742,
   893, 961-62, 994-95, 1009, 1027,
   1093, 1174, 1265, 1306, 1308
Edmund Tennant, 1151-54
education: advanced, father
   scorns, 704; sly comments on, 827;
   opportunity for, 1011; to become
   gentleman, 492-95, 608; value of,
   17. *See also* learning.
Edward II, King of England, 916,
   1018, 1104
Edward Bear, 989
Edward Flack, 16, 411, 707, 851,
   1389-91
Edward Plummer, 268
EDWARDS, DOROTHY (BROWN), *357-58*,
   606, 1158
EEYORE, the donkey, *358*, 562-63,
   1388-89
Efrafa, 95, 418, 446, 535, 557,
   1332
Efua Kwatey-Jones, 249
Egerton family, 1199-1201
Eggletina, 135, 560
egg rolls, Easter, 549
eggs: broken, 931; humanized, 572;
   ostrich, lost, 1385
Egypt, ancient, 121-24, 196, 658,
   829-30
Egypt Street, 541
eighteenth century: England,
   Brighton, 143-44, Bristol, 1253-
   56, Islington, 111-13, London,
   111-13, 339-42, 610-11, 824-26,
   1108-10, southeastern, 1125-28,
   Sussex, 304-6, various parts, 169-
   71; France, 339-42; high seas,
   1253-56; Treasure Island, 1253-
   56; early, various remote nations,
   508-14; mid-, Russia, St. Petersburg, 1415-17, Ukraine, 1415-17;
   mid-, Scotland, 648-51; late,
   England, 197-200, Yorkshire, 463-
   64; late, France, Paris, 765-67,
   1215-18; late, Haiti, 765-67;
   late, Ireland, 499-501, 1298-
   1300; late, North Sea, 1298-1300;
   late, Norway, 1298-1300; late,
   Scotland, Orkneys, 1298-1300
Eileen, 1271-72
Eileen Guest, 290-91
Eileen Teesdale, 555-56
Einon Hen, 295, 358-59
Einzig, Susan, 1240
El Cid, 1366
The Eldest Son, 137

Eleanor, Duchess of Gloucester, 325, 1405
elections, 1269; German, 1348
electrical disturbances, 359
electricars, 506
Elegant Patty, 1252
Elen, Princes of Lyonesse, 844, 1142-43
The Elephant and the Flower: Almost Fables, 943
elephant goads, jeweled, 631
elephants: aging circus, 89, 205, 425, 1247-49; for ark, 830; rogue, 235; trainers of, 235; wild, 631; with scarred ears, 1248
The Elephant War, 63
Elessar, Isildur's heir, 1158
elevators: great glass, 204, 1376; primitive, 1065-66; stuck in air raid, 378
eleventh century, late: England, 672-75, Cumberland Fells, 1085-87, Northumbria, 1012-13; Scotland, 1012-13
elfmen, 5-6
elf-woman, 1233-34
ELIDOR, 359-60, 443
Elijah (*The Seventh Raven*), 1076
ELIJAH (*Time of Trial*), *360*, 859, 1224
Elijah, Grandfather, 367
elixir, boy steals from witch, 1393
Elixir of Youth, 111, 1232
Eliza, 1146
Elizabeth, 381-82
Elizabeth, 530
Elizabeth, Empress of Russia, 1417
Elizabeth II, Queen of England, 497, 543, 604
Elizabethan era, England, 153-55; Sussex, 581-83
ELIZABETH BARNET, *360-61*, 361-62, 696
Elizabeth Elizabeth, 344
Elizabeth Keate, 169, 171
Elizabeth Oliver, 320
ELIZABETH'S TOWER, 361-62, 1140
Ellen, 779, 783
Ellen, 27
ELLEN CHAFFEY OVERS, 60, *362*, 703-4
Ellen Douglas, 677
Ellen Kennedy, 499-500, 879
Ellen Mortimer, 399, 836, 895-96
ELLEN PONTIFEX, *362-63*, 451, 667, 1290
ELLEN RAMSAY, *363*, 597, 640, 1218-20
ELLIE HARTHOVER, *363*, 1328-30
Ellie Willmay, 1294-95

Ellis Duckworth, 102, 615
Ellis, Grandpa, 1276-78
Ellison, Bert, 452
Ellison family, 579-80
Ellita, the dog, 389
Elm Park, 354
elocution, 383-84
Eloise de la Tour Rouge, 239, 1360
elopements, 60, 98, 178, 354, 694, 886, 1150, 1194
Eloquent Gentlewoman, 304
Elrond, 96, 131, 406, 436
Else Finch, 127-28
ELSIE WAINWRIGHT, *363-64*, 523-24, 1283
Elsie Whitelaw, 657
Elspeth Henderson, 911, 1155-56
elves: half, 96, 406; in Middle-earth, 406-7, 437, 440, 1056; wood, 95, 465, 551-53, 1204
Elvis, 797-98
Elvish language, 437
Em, the cat, 894
Emain Macha, 299, 299-300
emblems, protective, 287-88
embroideries: heirloom sampler, 860; needlepoint, 1412; picture of dog, 852; picture made of human hair, 217, 219, 770; supposedly by bride-to-be, 1018. *See also* needlepoint; samplers; tapestries.
emigrants: away from humans, 49; English to Mexico, 399; from South Africa, 627-28; from Wales, twelfth century, 236; Irish to Germany, 500-1; to Australia, 76-77, 323, 604-5, 669, 841, 873, 1286, planned, 305, supposed, 243; to badger set, 133; to Canada, 588-89; to Haiti, 765; to London from Jamaica, 842; to New England, 110-11, 113; to New World, 763, 881; to South America, 556; to West, 437, 440. *See also* particular nationalities.
emigration, resisted, 559-60
Emiliano Zapata, 601
Emily, the guinea pig, 365-66
Emily Dane, 330-32
Emily Fielding, 1289
EMILY GARLAND, 4, *364*, 763-64, 1068, 1229
EMILY GREENGRASS, 62, *364-65*, 953-54
EMILY MOBY, 6-7, 161, 206, 206-7, *365*
Emily Tennant, 1151-5,
Emily: The Story of a Traveller, 365, 1111

Emily, the Travelling Guinea Pig,
1111
EMILY'S VOYAGE, 365–66, 1111
Emir, aging, 1291
Emir Saladin, 670–71
Emir Usanah Ibn-Menquidh, 671
emissaries, from France to Russia,
1020
Emma (airplane), 354–55, 420, 1374
The Emma Dilemma, 1066
EMMA IN WINTER, 366–68, 394
Emma Makepeace, 206, 206–7, 365,
366–68, 393, 1168–69
Emma's Doll, 943
EMMA TUPPER, 27, 29, *368,* 368–70,
411, 992, 1046–47
EMMA TUPPER'S DIARY, 315, *368–70*
Emperor of Britain, 1088–91
emperors: Basil II, of Constantinople, 117; Carausius, of Britain,
270–71, 633, 1088–91; Claudius, of
Rome, 1118; Constantine, of Rome,
254, 370–73, 633, 1136, 1311–12;
last, 370–73; Roman, 254, 1136;
self-proclaimed, 270
THE EMPEROR'S WINDING SHEET, 370–73,
941
Empire State Building, 594
emplacements, machine gun, 197
employers: former, adulated, 896;
heartless, 627–28
empresses: Elizabeth, of Russia,
1417
Empty World, 232
Enborne River, 1331, 1333
Enchanted Place, at top of forest,
564
enchanters: 191, 225, 517. *See
also* enchantresses; magicians;
necromancers; warlocks; witches;
wizards.
enchantments: as old woman, 168;
broken, 202, 660; produces frenzy,
1093; various, 208–9
enchantresses: black, 518; evil,
752. *See also* enchanters; magicians; necromancers; warlocks;
witches; wizards.
*Encyclopaedia of Myths and Legends
of All Nations,* 969
An Encyclopedia of Fairies, 151
The End of the Tale, 258
AN ENEMY AT GREEN KNOWE, 145, *373–75*
engagements: announced, 1323; broken, 202, 228
engineers: idealistic, 890; mining, retired, 485
England:

--tenth century, B.C.: South Downs,
1319–22
--first century, B.C.: 1244–45;
Berkshire Downs, 1171–73
--first century, A.D.: 771–74, 1117–
19
--early second century: 347–50;
Cheshire, 1025–26
--third century: 1088–91
--fifth century: 679–83
--pre-Arthurian period: Thames valley, 395–97
--sixth century: southern area, 294–
97
--ninth century: East Anglia, 970–72
--tenth century: 116–19
--late eleventh century: 672–75;
Northumbria, 1012–13; Cumberland
Fells, 1085–87
--early twelfth century: London,
1394–96; Winchester, 1394–96
--late twelfth century: 670–72;
Warwickshire, 738–40
--late middle ages: 1232–34
--early fourteenth century: Sussex,
1017–20; Yorkshire, 915–17
--fourteenth century: Sherwood Forest, 145–47
--late fourteenth century: London,
447–49
--fifteenth century: 102–5, 153–55
--mid-fifteenth century: Ewelme,
1404–7; London, 1405
--late fifteenth century: Cotswolds, 1402–3; London, 729–30;
Sussex, 683–84; Warwickshire,
729–30
--sixteenth century: Sussex, 581–83
--Elizabethan era: 153–55; Sussex,
581–83
--early seventeenth century: countryside, 1351–53; London, 1351–53
--mid-seventeenth century: Cheshire, 1025–26; Cotswolds, 548–
50; countryside, 1009–12; Derbyshire, 938–39; London, 1199–1202;
southeast, 1199–1202; Suffolk,
306–9; Yorkshire, 636–38
--pre-Industrial Revolution: Danby
Dale, 970–71; Norfolk, 1094–96
--eighteenth century, 169–71;
Brighton, 143–44; Bristol, 1253–
56; Islington, 111–13; London,
111–13, 339–42, 610–11, 824–26,
1108–10; southeast, 1125–28;
Sussex, 304–6
--late eighteenth century: industrial area, 197–200; Yorkshire,

463-64
--unspecified early period: Cornwall, 332-33
--nineteenth century: 839-41; Brighton, 1149-50; "north country" town, 1327-30
--early nineteenth century: London, 107-9, 1223-25; Penbrokeshire, 236-37; Puddleby-on-the-Marsh, 1145-46, 1309-11; seacoast village, 1223-25; Suffolk, 190-91; West Country, 1111-13
--mid-nineteenth century: 1068-71; Blastburn, 807-9; coal town, 1276-78; Cornwall, 397-99; countryside, 492-95; Devonshire, 5-6, 724-27; London, 227-30, 1399-1401; Sussex, 763-65; Tooting, 52-54; village, 266-69; Willoughby Chase, 1399-1401
--late nineteenth century: 105-7, 387-88; Cheshire, 484-85, 1143-44; Devonshire, 926-27; Durham County, 129-31; Essex coast, 1379-81; London, 55-57, 489-92, 755-57, 1146-48; Teddington, 1158-60; Oxford, 1316-19
--early twentieth century: 206-8; Bedfordshire, 132-34, 134-36, 136-38, 140-42; Coalgate, 473-75; Cobchester, 276-79; Cheshire, 9-10, 1267-68; Cornwall, 459-62, 1287-90; Dartmoor, 1386-88; Essex, 418-21, 421-24; Kent, 416-18; Lancashire, 703-6; London, 354-56, 899-902, 1267-68; Midlands village, 1322-25; Norfolk, 953-55; Staffordshire, 1220-23; village, 943-45
--World War I period: 206-8, 1213-15; Essex, 421-24
--mid-twentieth century: 206-8, 221-23, 234-36, 381-82, 779-81, 781-83, 783-84, 784-86, 818-20, 1154-55, 1240-42; Birmingham, 290-91; Canterbury, 223-25, 1180-82; Cheshire, 1234-36, 1342-45; city, 182-84, 203-4; Cobchester, 514-16, 1364-66; Colebridge area, 382-85, 963-65; Cornwall, 889-91; countryside, 193-94, 361-62, 593-95, 710-13, 815-16; Devonshire, Exmoor, 389-92; Exeter, 377-79; Garmouth, 400-3, 747-50; Green Knowe, 211-13, 217-19, 373-75, 1035-36, 1154-55; Harwich Harbor, 1340-42; lake district, 972-74, 1177-79;

Little Barley, 328-30, 812-14; Little Weirwold, 467-69; Liverpool, 1064-65; London, 68-71, 84-85, 173-75, 330-32, 328-30, 414-16, 667-68, 685-87, 689-92, 722-24, 889-91, 897-99, 924-26, 1114-17, 1218-20; Manchester, 359-60; Midlands, 480-82, 1071-74; Midmeddlecum, 1385-86; northeast seacoast, 734-37; North Cornwall, 1105-6; northern marshes, 281-83; Otwell, 385-86; Redesmere, 495-98; seacoast, 982-84, 1169-71; Shropshire, 903-4; Somerset, 186-88; Suffolk, Pebblecomb, 163-66; Sunny Bay, 923-24; Sussex, 403-5, 434-36; unspecified urban setting, 77-78; village, 366-68, 1167-69; Warwickshire, rural, 716-17; Withern, 119-21; Yorkshire, 96-99, 351-53, 486-87, 536-38, 801-4, 1021-23, 1274-76
--World War II period: 710-13, 734-37; Exeter, 377-79, Garmouth, 400-3, 747-50; Little Weirwold, 467-69
--modern times: Sussex, 931-32
--late twentieth century: 127-29, 252-54, 325-28, 949-52, 1004-7, 1165-67; Berkshire Downs, 1330-34; Bournemouth, 1392-94; Buckinghamshire, 287-88; Cheshire, 1025-26, 1058-60; Cornwall, 397-99, 429-32, 1287-90; countryside, 283-85, 388-89, 583-85, 920-22; Cumbrian Fells, 555-57; Darnley, 539-42; Derbyshire, 917-19; East Anglia village, 1190-92; farm, 1082-84; Garmouth, 1325-27; Haunton, 1389-91; Ipston, 1334-36; Kensington, 1076-78; Kent, 248-52; Lancashire, 876-78; London, 41-42, 519-21, 656-58, 797-99, 1025-26, 1039-41, 1061-64, 1262-64, 1313-15; Mandover, 891-92; Middleton, 411-14; Midlands, 833-35, 1119-21; mining town in north, 911-12; Norfolk, 1211-13; Northend, 85-87; north of Newcastle, 33-36; North Oxford, 564-66; Northumberland, 1376-79; Oxfordshire, Ledsham, 451-53; rural area, 523-25, 645-46; seacoast, 1140-41; school, 286-87; Skirlston, 578-81; suburbs, 75-77, 1186-87; Suffolk, 306-9; Todcaster, 1353-56; town,

1269-70; urban area, 188-90, 465-
67, 1363-64; village, 318-21,
943-45; Wethershaf, 455-56; Yald
Forest, 1247-50
--twenty-first century: 989-92;
London, 505-8; Wherton, 1359-61
--future: 309-13; Midlands city,
895-97; non-industrial future
era, 1336-38; Skipley, 156-58
English: in Constantinople, 370-
73, 1136, 1311-12; in India, 651,
655; in Ireland, 1151-54, 1285; in
Mexico, 601; in Pantouflia, 998-
99; in Scotland, 588-89, 589-90;
in Wales, 176-79, 179, 244-45,
873-74, 933-35, 1047
Englishmen, exemplary, 1046
English Channel, 175, 1339-40, 1359-
60
Enlightenment, 1195
The Ennead, 771
Enoch, 625-26
Eowyn, 805
entertainers: on Pier, 667; Queens,
876; vaudeville, 754
entertainments, 509; about slave
trade, 520; masques, for king, 16
entrepreneurs, 865
Ents, 805, 982
Environment, 90
environmental concerns, 370
environmentalists: activist, 778;
terrorist, 34-36
envoys, British from Wales, 295, 358
Envy, 976
epics, on King Arthur, 1358
Epidaii tribe, 349-50
epidemics: flu, 1322; plague, 1405
epigraphs, 22, 99
epilogues, 115, 475, 880, 927, 992,
1070
Episode of Sparrows, 458
episodes, repetitive, 782-83, 783-
84, 785
episodic novels, 5-6, 19-22, 41-42,
79-81, 84-85, 385-86, 389-92, 416-
18, 555-57, 562-64, 606-8, 624-27,
630-32, 732-34, 779-81, 781-83,
783-84, 784-86, 927-30, 974-80,
1035-36, 1146-48, 1158-60, 1186-
87, 1204-6, 1208-11, 1269-70,
1306-9, 1313-15, 1322-25, 1327-
30, 1388-89, 1415-17
Epona, 1173
Erica Timperley, 59-60, 364, 523-
25, 1042, 1283
Ericson, Harold, 1170
Ernest Haithwaite, 578-80

Ernie Runacre, 137, 811
Eroica Symphony, 524
errands, taking father lunch, 1143
Erringden Moor, 463
errors, comedy of, 797-99, 996-99
Erskine, 45-46, 470
ESCA, 348-50, *375*, 768
Escape from France, 1346
Escape to Persia, 392, 571, 1362
escapes: aided by girl, 336; aided
by waif, 293; arranged for child
queen, 454; attempted, 283, from
robber den, 574; blind boy from
house trailer, 34; Borrowers,
aided by boy, 148; by balloon, 139,
140; by bribe, 170; by canoe, 1098;
by faking mental illness, 157; by
swimming to ship, 372, 633; clever, 830; close, 1092; daring,
by block and tackle, 1063; down
chimney, 432; down drain, 137;
down rope into moat, 103; escapees slaughtered, 1299; fox from
farmers, 388-89; frequent, 257;
girl from Maltese, 402; from abbess, 1018; from attic on creeper,
1275; from bag in stream, 325; from
burning monastery, 870; from closet, 264; from customs officers,
764; from Damascus, 671;
from Danes, 871-72; from death by
poison, 1026; from den of thieves,
246; from dungeon, 1000, 1032,
1204; from elven prison, 95; from
fallen city, 372; from flood on
roof of house, 866-67; from German
prison camps, 1097; from Germans
prevented, 1350; from giants, 603;
from Greeneyes, 168; from gypsies,
135, 1352; from hanging, 609; from
human sacrifice, 1238; from Huns,
281; from Jutish captors with sister's help, 681; from Lilliput,
510; from mad bull, 1318; from
mine, 485-86; from mine cave-in,
130; from military authorities,
94; from Normans, 1086; from old
Caribbean fort, 1064; from orcs,
407, 982; from orphanage, 560,
769; from palace, 185; from pirates, 1311;
from police, 1237; from prison,
977; from prison camp, 619; from
Romans, 1161, 1190; from ruffians,
1360; from school bullies, 1091-
92; from secret police, 1187-89;
from sharks, 893; from slave camp,
1295; from slavery, 1012; from

spies, 361; from thugs, 446; from
Turkish pirates, 371; from Turks,
453, 1044; from underwater cavern,
369; from usurper, 995; from water
falls, 123; from witches, 1393;
from zoo, 525; girls from school,
1401; gorilla from zoo, 1154;
hairbreadth, 362; half-hearted
attempt, 1051; harrowing, 240;
in barrels, 552; in fog, 1337; in
glider, 253; mastiff from gypsies,
1387; narrow, 805; near, 717,
1120-21, 1166, 1302, 1332, 1352,
1380; of arrested soldier, 595;
of caged panther, 65-66; of German
flyer, failed, 749;
of Italian war prisoner, 734-35;
of mad girl, 111; of Mary, Queen
of Scots, 814; of pirate leader,
1256; of soldier, 356; of usurper
queen, 772-73; on friendly leopard, 1142-43; on funeral barge,
122; perilous, 146; planned, 281;
repeated, near, 797-98; through
mine tunnel, 35-36; through river outlet, 240; through trap door,
103; through ventilator shaft,
817, 1109; thwarted, 244; timely,
837, 1260, 1307; Toad from prison,
1383; to Alba, 299;
to Conurb, 507; to England from
France, 832; to France, 448,
454, 1337; to France from customs
men, 764; to France of Royalists,
1318-19; to freedom, 40; to Gaul,
attempted, 294; to Germany, 446;
to Hadrian's Wall, 350; to hermit's hut, 216; to mine workings,
244; to Netherlands, 457; to other dimension, 359-60; to Overland,
1093; to warn king, 91-92; under
hoop skirt, 817, 1109; using ring,
552-53; various, 1018-19, 1229;
via church bell rope, 146. See also
liberation; rescues.
ESDRAS, 375-76, 870
Eskimos, 733
Esk (ship), 866, 1070
Esmerelda the gypsy, 1354
ESP, 418, 592, 1196, 1331. See also
clairvoyance; mental telepathy; second sight.
Essex, 418-21, 421-24, 1379-81
Essie Roller, 51, 600
Essylt, 1118
Estate (housing complex), 1294
estates: belonging to duke, 738;
bombed out, 898; confiscated by

crown, 457; decaying, 419-21;
dilapidated, 421-24; entailed,
383, 1151; forfeit to crown, 454;
freehold from crown, 762-63; in
debt, 383; inherited, 1151-53;
neglected, 226, 748-49; rambling,
920; recovered through marriage,
448; restored, 457; rundown,
775; Russian country, 718-20;
Scottish, 765, 1227; usurped, 738
ESTELLA, 95, 376, 493-95, 592, 757,
820, 981
Estoril, Jean, 25
estrangements: brothers, 834-35;
daughters from mother, 1197-
98; father-daughter, 538, 896,
883; father from family, 862;
father-sons, 846, 923-24, 997-98;
grandmother from family, 874-
75; healed, 726; husband-wife,
842; mother-daughter, 708; sisters, 703-4, 706
Etain, Queen of Fairies, 713-14
Ethel, 388
Ethel Feedbag, 376, 1354
Ethelred, King of Wessex, 16, 18,
376, 870-71
Ethelwulf, King of West Saxons, 18
ethnic customs: ancient, 1204-6;
ancient British, 1117-19; Asian
Indian, 651-54, 1302-5; British
tribal, 1171-73, 1319-22; Celtic,
1155-57; Ghanan, 249-52; Irish,
543-46; Japanese, 819; Russian,
1417; Scottish, 589, 642-43, 1196-
99; Scottish tribal, 771-74, 1161-
64; Viking, 1298-1300. See also
cultures; rituals; understanding,
intercultural.
ethnic dances, 520
ethnic groups, stereotyped, 781,
919-20, 1145-46, 1147
ethnic songs, 520
ethnology, 574
Etty, 689-90
Etty, Peter, 169-71
eunuchs: Byzantine official, 280;
emperor's loyal servant, 371-72,
1136
Euphemia, 208-9
Euphrates River, 1204
Eurasians, black-bearded, 742-43
"Eureka," 932
Europe:
--ancient times: Brittany, 1258-61
--first century, B.C.: Rome, 1244-45
--fifth century, A.D.: Juteland, 680
--sixth century: Romania, 279-81

--late eighth century: Norway, 1298-1300
--ninth century: Denmark, 91-92
--late fourteenth century: France, 447-49
--seventeenth century: Austria, 213-15; Netherlands, 456-58; Poland, 213-15; Turkey, 213-15
--eighteenth century: France, 339-42, 765-67, 1215-18; Russia, 1415-17
--nineteenth century: Russia, 717-20, 1206-8
--early twentieth century: France, 1213-15; Russia, 1206-8
--mid-twentieth century: France, 221-23, 1348-49; Germany, 1096-99, 1348-49; Italy, 662-63; Norway, 1349-51; Poland, 1096-99; Sicily, 30-31; Spain, 1366-68; Switzerland, 1096-99, 1348-49
--late twentieth century: Netherlands, 1061-64; Norway, 1392-94
--twenty-first century: France, 989-92, 1359-61; Switzerland, 989-92, 1359-61
--future: France, 237-40, 1337
EUSTACE SCRUBB, *376-77*, 603, 687-89, 1007, 1027, 1034, 1091-93, 1306-9
evacuations: after air raid, 736; from London, 842; of Channel island, 806, 1339
evacuees, children, World War II, 14, 60, 176, 179, 377-79, 415, 467, 710, 851, 1240, 1372-73, 1419
Evangelist, 975
Evans family, 60, 176-79, 179, 543, 826, 842-43, 886
Eve: Her Story, 395
Evicatus, 1089-91
evictions: by king's factor, 650; from company houses, 1276; from farm home, 500-1; from home, 130, 1114; from stone house, 484, 619
evidence: film, 1188-89; of witchcraft, fragments of helmet, 308
evil, 359-60, 373-75, 504-5, 710-13, 985, 1009; afflicts Narnia, 687-88; corrupting power of, 864; imp, 1095-96; in Narnia, 987; machines considered, 1337; personified, 974-80; power, 1130-31; queen completely, 694; spreading from character to actor, 286-87
Ewelme, 324, 454, 1404-7
examinations: for chorister, 224-25; for scholarship, 491-92
Excalibur, 352, 1038

excavations, archeological, 802-3
exchanges: bargains with witch, 694; gypsy baby boy for baby girl, 855-56; horse for gold, silver, and jewels, 167; of appearance, 698
executions: beheading of Mary, Queen of Scots, 1412-14; burning at stake, 1038, 1302; escaped, 1185; exemplary, 214-15; foiled, 830; for treason, 1405; for witchcraft, 126, 1405; hanging, 101, 879; Irish rebellion, 500; mass, 1188; of general, 215; of rebel, 101; of Russian Imperial Family, 28; of self-appointed village headman, 50; ordered, 20-22; ordered for lovers, 1260; sons of Uisneac, 300; threatened, 256; unsuccessful, 29
Exeter, 154, 377-79, 517
THE EXETER BLITZ, *377-79*, 1027
Exeter cathedral, 377-78
exhibitionists, Toad, 1382-84
exhibitions: art, 1059; Dolls through the Ages, 331; early flights, 355; of miniature people, foiled, 856; of pushmi-pullyu, 1146
exiles: dwarf, 344; from island community, 1; in Wars of Roses, 683; Rikofian, 659; to France, 1038; to Kingfisher Island, 1373; youth to country, 701
Exmoor, 389-92
exorcisms: attempted, 452; attempted by black boy, 591; ghost lured into bottle, 49, interrupted by busybody, 452; of demon from woman, 800; of Watch House ghosts, 1226, 1327; with firecrackers, 669
exorcists, 92
expectations: dashed, of wealth and position, 981; false, 981; of wealth, 1132; undeserved, evils of, 492-95
"expeditionary force," 38, 150-51, 433, 600, 960
expeditions: by raft and pony, 390-91; for gold, 874; to explore cave, 13; to mine gold, 172
Experiment House, 1091-92
experiments: on guinea pigs, 1279; scientific, 529, 755, 1149
experts: handwriting analysts, 184; in firearms and explosives, 888
exploitation: of women, 1364; of workers, 807-9

explorations: of cave, 193-94; of empty buildings, 466; of mine pit, 129

explosions: credited to devil, 554; in kitchen, 669; in mine, 398; of domed cities, 991; of gangster's munitions, 222; of imp, 1096; of munitions barge, 1215; of pistol, 306; seals off country, 237; threatened, 34-36; with plastic explosives, 308

Expositions of Musical Theory, 224

Expotition to North Pole, 1389

expulsion, from Denmark, 92

exterminations, attempted, 857

exterminators, 133, 135-36

extortionists, 808

Extract of Malt, 563

Eyam village, 193, 760, 938-39, 940, 1203

eyeglasses: for owl, 911; made by monk, 1357; making learned in China, 155; smashed, 932

eye patches, black, 698

eyes: one black, one blue, 953; one dark, one pale and drooping, 811; on horns, 1007; third, 1198

eyesight: miraculously restored, 1300; owl's, failing, 529, 931

Eyvind the Ancient, 912

Fabylon, 927-30

facsimiles, 22-23

factories: carpet, 302, 807-9; chemical, proposed, 1303, 1305; chocolate, 203-4, 479-80, 810, 864-65, 919, 1297, 1305, 1375-76; clothing, 1170; fertilizer, 526; partly underground, 1375; sweatshop, 1104; textile, 197-200. *See also* manufacturers; mills.

factors, king's, hated, 650

factory tours, 480

Faddock Allman, 9-10, 1281

Fagin-like persons, 278, 1352-53

failures: faced, 1319-22; overcome, 338; psychological effects of, 1319-22; to kill wolf, 337; to love enough, 309

Fairfax family, 225, 516-17, 946, 982-84

Fairfax Market, 173

Fairfax, Mrs., 777

Fairfax Museum, 174

Fairhair, Torkell, 1298-1300

fairies, 363, 462, 637, 713-14, 779, 822, 956, 958, 961, 1328-30, 1410-11; belief in, 486; Borrower mistaken for, 148; cat doctor, 913; claim hen, 713; cross, 1007; dislikes water, 1007; doctor, 248; godmother, 720, 1096; good, 381; helpful housekeeping, 1112; knights, 332-33; little sister believes in, 875; not believed in, 997; not invited to christening, 997; one hundred at christening, 997; one old angry, 997; pretty, tall, 853; queen of, 1010-11; rule water-babies, 851, 853; sand, 416-18, 1007; sexy, 1226; spiteful, 1226; ugliest, 851

Fairlight, 1010-11

fairs, 154, 417, 955, 1082, 1386; giant at, 1041; Russian, 1415-16; Todcaster, 1354; traveling, 110, 111, 1232; Vanity, 976; Welsh, 1357

THE FAIRY DOLL, 381-82, 458

fairy food, grants wish, 333

Fairyland, 271, 462-63; experiences in, 333

fairy tales, pastoral 724-27

faith: crisis of, 1124; exploration of, 1378-79

FALCONER'S LURE: THE STORY OF A SUMMER HOLIDAY, 382-85, 429, 963

falconing, 383-85

falcons, 42, 383-85; freed, 384; lost, 384; silver, 1385

Falcon's Crag, 1140

falling stars, 569

falls: chimney sweep into girl's room, 363; down rabbit hole, 22; during horse meets, 1191-92; from cliff into sea, 1288-89; from school roof, 1270, into fiery chasm, 439; into river, 1383; into stream, 1389

familiars: chickens, 874, 1354; Cloud of Flies, 836; comic "thing," 928; drinks ink, 928; earthworm, 845, 1355; octopus, 824, 1354; pig, 1354; sheep, 1354; witches', 376, 518, 752, 1354-55

families: anti, 917-19; bi-racial, 968; discordant, 226-27, 1376-79; disintegrating, 411-14, 639, 843, 895-97, 1010, 1314, 1365, 1376-79; dysfunctional, 895-97, 900-2, 1232; exceptionally close, 1009-12; ideal, 602; merged by marriage, 23-24, 79-81, 93, 100, 206, 455, 605, 741-42, 768, 860, 874,

885, 933, 1047, 1088, 1376-79; of
dean, snobbish, 734-36; poverty
stricken, 479, 1010; Russian upper
class life, 717-20; single parent,
96-97, 190-91, 429-32, 467-69,
578-81, 601-2, 627-28, 689-92,
873-74, 879-80, 889-90, 1262-64,
1313-15; troubled, 1276-78, 1334-
36
"the family," 278
A Family Affair, 986
THE FAMILY FROM ONE END STREET AND
SOME OF THEIR ADVENTURES, *385-86*,
445
family life, 200-201, 276-79, 328-
30, 361-62, 385-86, 451-53,
514-16, 533-34, 903-4, 911-12,
1010-12, 1021-23, 1114-17, 1123-
25, 1143-44, 1196-99, 1211-13,
1262-64, 1284-87, 1290-91, 1313-
15, 1334-36, 1364-66, 1376-79,
1389-91; Asian Indian, 1302-
5; at aunt's home, 523-25; at
grandmother's home, 459-62; at
seaside hotel, 923-24; children
mostly on their own, 1146-48;
competitive, 17;
contrasted, 1039-41; discordant,
418-21; disrupted by addition of
adopted cousin, 1105-6; dominated
by grandmother, 475-76; eccentric, 920-22; English suburban,
75-77; English village, 248-52;
Ghanan, 248-52; group dedicated to
abolish, 525; in father's absence,
953-55; in thieves' group, 278;
in Welsh valley, 932-35; Ireland,
1133-36; Jewish refugee, 924-26;
managed by competent oldest sibling, 1218-20; miners', 473-75;
Norway, 1349-51; of traveling
actors, 304-6; on Scottish island, 588-89; rural Yorkshire,
801-4; Scotland, 79-81; Sikh, 310-
12; spoofs on, 252-54; stability
brought by Ukranian maid, 667-68;
turn-of-century Lancaster shopkeeper's, 703-6;
unconventional for period, 421-
24; unusual, 14; Victorian,
387-88, 489-92; Viennese, 214-15;
Wales, 176-79; with obsessive father, 895-97; wolves', 630-32;
working class, 9-10; World War II,
747-50
family life, novels of: African,
248-52; 627-28; children on
their own, 79-81, 276-79, 514-16,

1105-6, 1218-20; domestic adventures, 486-87, 667-68, 1114-17,
1364-66; farcical, 920-22; in
conflict, 1021-23, 1262-64, 1313-
15; Irish, 1133-36; neighborhood
life, 1211-12, 1364-66, 1389-91;
pets, problems of, 75-77, 328-30,
903-4; Scottish, 588-89, 1123-25,
1196-99; unemployment, 911-12;
Victorian, 387-88, 484-85, 489-
92, 703-6, 1143-44, 1146-48; while
visiting, 523-25, 923-24, 953-55,
1039-41, 1165-67, 1169-71; World
War II period, 1234-36
family love, 186-88, 328-30, 385-86,
903-4; despite poverty, 228-29;
especially strong, 1158-60; in
mining community, 473-75
family novels: fantasy, 416-18,
970-71, 1111-13, 1270-73, 1342-
45, 1376-79, 1385-86, 1409-11;
realistic, pre-twentieth century
setting, 190-91, 489-92, 1146-48,
1204-6; realistic, twentieth-
century setting, 68-71, 75-77,
79-81, 119-21, 186-88, 234-36,
382-85, 385-86, 389-92, 425-27,
486-87, 495-98, 514-16, 645-46,
963-64, 972-74, 995-97, 1105-6,
1151-54, 1167-69, 1169-71, 1177-
79, 1218-20, 1247-50, 1302-5,
1313-15, 1339-40, 1340-42, 1364-
66
family structure, examined, 919
FAND, 148, 245, *386-87*, 879, 884,
1161-63, 1190
Fand, the dog, 1320
Fanfare for a Witch, 1370
Fangorn, 440
Fannie Corry, 778
Fanny, 387-88
Fanny, 27
Fanny Byrne, 499-501
Fanny Hatter, 568, 777
Fanny, Miss, 1108-10
FANNY'S SISTER, 387-88, 727
fans, Bronte, 1275
Fanshawe, Lady, 170-71
Fanshawe-Smithe family, 225-26,
734-36
The Fantastic Feats of Doctor Boox,
292
FANTASTIC MR. FOX, 274, *388-89*
fantasy life, dependence on, 1369
fantasy novels: adventure, 39-41,
134-36, 136-38, 138-40, 221-23,
351-53, 359-60, 560-62, 593-95,
710-13, 716-17, 755-57, 847-49,

956-58, 974-80, 989-92, 994-96, 1091-96, 1111-13, 1141-43, 1306-9, 1342-45, 1359-61, 1385-86; animal, 41-42, 84-85, 105-7, 173-75, 325-28, 365-66, 388-89, 560-62, 593-95, 630-32, 713-14, 716-17, 829-30, 839-41, 893-94, 913, 931-32, 1031-32, 1082-84, 1111-13, 1119-21, 1145-46, 1186-87, 1270-73, 1309-11, 1327-30, 1330-34, 1382-85; anthropomorphized machines, 583-85; Arthurian elements, 351-53, 359-60, 501-2, 1036-39, 1141-43, 1258-61; astronomical, 325-28; based on folk tale, 246-48, 636-38, 1094-96; based on legend, 289-99, 299-301, 351-53, 932-35, 1036-37, 1258-61; based on Noah story, 829-30; Christian allegory, 974-80; Christmas, 227-30; comic, 203-4, 221-23, 593-95, 1353-56; doll, 330-32, 332-33, 381-82, 558-59, 722-24, 818-20; domestic adventures, 266-69; dream, 19-22, 22-23, 188-90, 252-54, 366-68, 974-80, 1208-11; eccentric central character, 779-81, 781-83, 783-84, 784-86; family, 416-18; folklore elements, 5-6, 351-53, 359-60, 395-97, 411-14, 501-2, 548-50, 550-53, 567-69, 642-43, 701-2, 713-14, 714-16, 927-30, 1029-31, 1232-34, 1270-73, 1409-11; futuristic, 237-40, 309-13, 505-8, 895-97, 989-92, 1294-95, 1336-38, 1359-61; ghost, 211-13, 217-19, 227-30, 286-87, 451-53, 455-56, 533-34, 824-26, 1325-27; gnomes, 714-16, 716-17; good vs. evil, 287-88, 405-8, 501-2; historical aspects, 732-34; horror, 1058-60; humorous, 19-22, 22-23, 41-42, 107-9, 127-29, 132-34, 134-36, 325-28, 388-89, 416-18, 562- 64, 779-81, 781-83, 783-84, 784-86, 847-49, 927-30, 970-71, 996-99, 1094-96, 1232-34, 1388-89, 1392-94; literary tale, 395-97, 659-62, 701-2, 1029-31; magic, 43-47, 55-57, 127-29, 173-75, 188-90, 208-9, 221-23, 227-30, 246-48, 287-88, 298-99, 299-301, 373-75, 416-18, 501-2, 533-34, 548-50, 567-69, 593-95, 659-62, 710-13, 755-57, 779-81, 781-83, 783-84, 784-86, 927-30, 932-35, 994-96, 996-99, 999-1002, 1002-3,

1035-36, 1091-94, 1094-96, 1111-13, 1167-69, 1232-34, 1290-91, 1306-9, 1327-30, 1336-38, 1342-45, 1353-56, 1385-86, 1392-94; marchen type, 701-2, 720-22, 927-30, 996-99, 999-1002, 1002-3; miniature people, 132-34, 134-36, 136-38, 138-40, 140-42, 508-14; mystical, 55-57, 462-63; mythological, 39-41, 287-88, 405-8, 560-62, 687-89, 710-13, 755-57, 1091-94, 1306-9, 1342-45; otherworld, 19-22, 22-23, 39-41, 208-9, 359-60, 405-8, 462-63, 501-2, 508-14, 550-53, 560-62, 567-69, 687-89, 710-13, 755-57, 994-96, 1091-94, 1306-9; pastoral fairy-tale, 724-27; science, 237-40, 309-13, 368-70, 505-8, 989-92, 1294-95, 1336-38, 1359-61; size differences, 19-22, 22-23, 132-34, 134-36, 136-38, 138-40, 140-42, 508-14, 1035-36, 1274-76; surrealism, 583-85; suspense, 132-34, 134-36, 138-40, 140-42, 200-1, 373-75, 405-8, 455-56, 550-53, 714-16, 891-92, 1155-57; talking toy, 84-85, 330-32, 332-33, 562-64, 722-24, 818-20, 1274-76, 1388-89; telepathic, 252-54; time, 188-90, 197-200, 206-8, 211-13, 217-19, 227-30, 252-54, 287-88, 306-9, 366-68, 397-99, 903-4, 943-45, 1025-26, 1240-42, 1290-91, 1376-79; witchcraft, 200-1, 208-9, 306-9, 373-75, 533-34, 1353-56
Faramir, 982
Faraway, 1111
farces, 143-44, 593-95, 797-99, 1149-51, 1392-94
The Far Cry, 1111
THE FAR-DISTANT OXUS, 389-92, 571, 1362
Far East, early twentieth century: China and Tibet, 1265-67
FARJEON, ELEANOR, 333, *392-93,* 795, 1094
Farjeon, Herbert, 392-93
Farmer Dawson, 287-88
FARMER GILES OF HAM, 395-97, 1231
FARMER, PENELOPE, 188, 206, 365, *393-95,* 1167
farmers: African black, 743; Bavarian, 1098, 1398; bookish, 445; Cheshire, 1342; Cornish, 1242; disturbed by machinery disappearing, 584; English, 1224; giant,

510; grasping, 388; helpful
Chilian, 1189; helpful French,
1360; home-and-comfort-loving,
395; old, 863; owner of white
horse, 167; resistance leader,
157-58; sheep, 480-81, 1082-
84; smallholder, 149; Spanish,
1366-68; well-off, 742, 1133;
Yorkshire, 802-4; Yoruba, 1068
farmhouses: as clubhouse, 1223; old,
486; Yorkshire, 1274-75
farming, euphemism for control, 470,
532, 1014, 1087
farm life, 250, 481-82, 543-46, 548-
50, 555-57, 742, 834-35, 1049-50,
1082-83, 1366-68, 1386, 1402
farm managers, successful, 317
farms, 963-65, 1021-23, 1233, 1386;
Cheshire, 1342; Cumbrian, 531,
555-57; Derbyshire, 605; deserted, 310-11; destroyed, 578;
fruit, 1335; goat and chicken,
157; Ireland, 1133-36; isolated
coastal, 430-31; lakeside, 1178;
marginal, 833; Massachusetts,
888; Nuthanger, 535; north of Arctic Circle, 578; rebuilt, 1351;
seacoast, 982-84; Welsh, 323
farmworkers, German prisoners, 422
Farquhar, Alan A. B., 427-28
Farrar family, 73, 242, 896
Farr, Betsy, 94, 595, 880
farthing doll, 330-31
fascists, 149-50, 157-58
fashion shows: hilarious, 378;
in hospital, 379
fate: attempts to avert, 298, 299; of
terrorist, uncertain, 335; power
of, 767; reconciled to, 825-26
THE FATE OF JEREMY VISICK, 397-99,
1391
Father, 10, 399, 484, 619, 914, 1143-
44, 1235
Father Christmas, 711, 994, 1186
Father de Souza, 1226, 1325, 1327
Father Donald, 588
father-figures, 154
Father Fletcher, 1325-27
FATHER GONZALEZ, 399, 601-2, 753
Father Laflamme, 733
FATHER MORTIMER, 73, 242, 399-400,
836, 843, 883, 895-97
fathers: absent from home, 175-
76, 368-70, 697, 862, 875, 987,
1020, 1313-15, 1335, 1340, 1385-
86, 1400-1; abstracted, 96-99;
abusive, 335, 806, 1062; addicted to comics, 838; adoptive,

1240; alcoholic, 495, 526, 1303-
4; aloof, 718-19; ambitious for
son, 1363, 1375; ambitious politically and socially, 683-84; army
sergeant, 1025; arrival timely, 1342; arthritic, 845; artist,
336; assassinated, 16; atheist,
1376; authoritarian, 546, 883,
895-97; bigoted, 473; blind, 820-
21; bombardier, 253; bookseller,
1224-25; Borrower, 985; boxer,
1116; Breton man-at-arms, 672;
brilliant but impractical, 937; bus
driver, 606, 1390; businessman,
186; cabinet maker, 480; called
"bloody Red," 850; Cambridge
professor, 93, 1376; Cardiff
sailor, 579; cautious, 1298;
Chancellor of Scotland, 457;
clergyman, 1165, 1351; coachman,
55-57; cobbler, 985; cold, distant, 889, 968; cold, selfish,
1040-41; college teacher, 44-46;
coming from Burma, 375; commercial
traveler, 1132; computer specialist, 1212; curate, 734; death of,
355, 720, 792, 924, 1123-25, 1161,
1165; departed, 99; deported to
India, 657; deserting family,
200, 289, 880; detested by son,
1165;
devoted, 267-68; diamond merchant, 433; disappeared, 639;
disapproving, 473-75, 538;
disapproving of marriage, 478;
discovered, 376, 466-67, 518,
753, 757, 1127-28, 1335; distant,
1212; distant patriarch, 387; doctor, 118-19, 190, 291-92, 352,
356, 496, 880, 889, 1041-42, 1224-
25; doll, lost in sand, 558-59;
dominating, 399-400; domineering,
923;
double-agent, World War II, 959;
dour, 459; drowned, 1380; drug addict, 1062; drunken, 706; dustman,
618-19; dying, 610; elderly, 1165;
electrician, 506; emotionally
inhibited, 1363; ever optimistic,
304; ex-convict, 753, 941;
executed neighbor, 457;
exhibitionist, 838; ex-race car
driver, 656; ex-World War II soldier, dons uniform, 896; farmer,
584; feared by daughter, 640;
feared by son, 1132; figure, 865;
film writer, 924; finally proud,
633; financier, 618; fisherman,

792, 1349-50, 1379-80; forgiven
by son for misdeeds, 827; foster,
1, 148, 879, 972, 1402; foster,
chief, 1161; foster, cruel, 1081;
foster, grandfather, 1101; foster, shepherd, 453; foster, wolf,
1084; free-loading, 833; gardener, 1267; gambler, 1365-66;
glassblower, 15, 662-63; gone to
America, 365; greedy, 94; grim,
1204;
gypsy, 669; hard-drinking, 516,
879-80; hard-driving, 846; hard
working, 284, 970-71, 985; head
verger, 378; historian, 236, 685;
history professor, 685, 693; hotel owner, 335, 354; hot-tempered,
693; housemaster, 96-
99; idealistic, 942-43, 1123-25,
1224-25; identity discov-
ered, 934; ill, 81; immigrant to
America, 953; impatient, 398-99;
imperious but base, 338; impractical, 1349; improvident, 304;
imprisoned, 233, 325, 327, 338,
466, 880, 1133; in army, 415; in
Burma, 211; ineffectual, 536;
in hiding, 457; injured in bombing, 469; insensitive, 538-39;
interested in local history, 397;
intimidated by employer-house
guest, 896; Irish, 1123; Irish
activist, 343, 639;
Irish soldier, 651;
irresponsible, 289, 514-15, 728,
862, 1314, 1315, 1365-66; irritable, 912; jailed, 1011; jailed
for assaulting policeman, 878;
jewelry maker, 918; killed by Germans, 1350; killed by Romans,
1244-45; killed by spies, 362;
killed in prison break, 327, 343,
639; killed in World War I, 161,
1322; killed in World War II, 696,
841, 887, 1059, 1151; leaves home,
877; level-headed, generous, 761;
loving, 1010; loving but busy,
1263; macho, 609, 1342, 1363;
male chauvinist, 968; marrying
again, 201, 478, 505, 539, 636,
915-17, 960, 1039, 1047, 1289;
martinet, 489-92; materialistic,
251-52, 762; mean-tempered, 502;
member of Parliament, 383; mentally unbalanced, 806; mild, scholarly, 491; miller, 237; mill worker,
876-78, 879-80; minister, 52, 54,
692; morally weak, 413; murdered,

738; musician, 1187; naval captain, 383; naval commander, 614;
near-psychotic, 896; newscaster,
539; newspaperman, 404-5, 434-36;
Norwegian, 578; noted boxer, 696;
obsequious, 843; obsessed, 896;
officious, 17; outlaw, 11; out of
work, 912, 1159;
overambitious for son, 703-6;
overbearing, 821; overly daugh-
oritarian, 843; overly fearful
because of abuse, 850; overworked, 203; parasite, 962;
paratrooper, deceased, 1100; parson, 616; parvenu, 92; patient,
1146; peacemaker, 76; pedantic,
93; philosophical, 451, 985; piemaker, 51, 488; pierrot, 1194;
playwright, 876; poacher, 1372;
possibly suicide, 455; practical, 132-33; pretentious, 837;
professor, 668, 1287-88; profligate, 706; protective, 928-29;
protective of son, 1196; race-
horse trainer, 822;
reappearing, 375, 483, 669, 981;
rector, 480; rejecting daughter, 460, 1319-22; rescued, 1045;
returning, 542, 697, 955; road
worker, 606; runaway, 539, 541-42;
runs for Council, 1269; schoolmaster, 650; schoolteacher,
1097; scientist, 1218; scornful
of boy's singing, 1415; scribe,
612, 729; sea captain, 172-73,
217-18, 1173, 1340, 1342; second
in command of Ninth Legion, 347;
self-deluding, 862; self-made,
703; self-righteous, 473; sheep
farmer, 480-81; shoe-store manager, 895; shoots daughter's dog and
pony, 693; shopkeeper, 17, 703;
smuggler of military technology,
361; social reformer, 7, 1123-25,
1224-25; soldier, 361; soldier
in World War I, 206; solicitous,
1372; sparky, 284; spy, 1339;
step, 25, 76, 79-81, 92, 93, 738,
810, 933, 1065, 1405; step, artist, 599, 608-9, 1059;
step, brutal, 425; step, cold,
744; step, despised by stepson, 1059-60, 1100-1; step,
dour Presbyterian, 1200;
step, sympathetic, 100; step,
understanding, 860, 1088; step,
unsympathetic, 909; step, usurping, 611; storekeeper, 156-57,

473; straitlaced, 623-24; subway worker, 328; thought to be thief, 953, 955; thought to be traitor in World War II, 959; tinker, 1009-11; toothpaste maker, 203; town councillor, 881; traitor, 696; TV addict, 1212; TV news correspondent, 1039; TV writer, 921; unable to cope, 842; underpaid, 203; uninterested in daughter, 900; uninterested in family, 655; uninterested in son, 539; unloving, 754; unreasonable in expectations, 1033; unsentimental, 846; untrustworthy, 827; vague, 506; vicar, 1024; vocal liberal, 942-43; weak in character, 762, 1029; wealthy, 722-23; wealthy businessman, 615; wealthy trader, 624-26; weaver, 463; widowed laird, 636; widower, 342, 536, 946; wise, well-informed, 855; wool merchant, 791, 1402; writer, 252-54, 555, 762, 838, 937, 1313-15, 1348-49; Yorkist, 701. *See also* mothers; parents.

fathers-in-law, crippled, 4

father-son relationships, novels of: 252-54, 276-79, 283-85, 304-6, 578-81, 656-58, 703-6, 729-30, 895-97, 911-12, 996-99, 1039-41, 1058-60, 1262-64, 1363-64, 1402-3

Father Victor, 652

"Father William," 20, 22, 192

Father Wolf, 1084

Fathom (boat), 85, 1379-81

FATHOM FIVE, 400-3, 1347

fat persons: artist, 609; Bengali, 574, 653-54; boy, 58, 193, 367, 689; chicken grower, 388; Choir Master, 1181; common-law wife, 334; ex-dancer, 678, 1116; girl, 411, 942; jailer, 1031-32; man, 1228; man next door, 1040; Ottoman, 1068, 1357; plump cousin, 289; policeman, 749; portraits of, 613; schoolgirl, 286; slovenly woman, 514; talkative, 1068; tomb robber, 1185; wizard, 1087; woman artist, 1215; woman companion to scholar, 1183; woman met on bus, 98

Fatty Hardy, 749

The Faun and the Woodcutter's Daughter, 969

fauns, 688, 710, 742, 864, 875, 995, 1093

Fawcett family, 434-35

Fay family, 133-36

fears, of: being abandoned, 450; being branded, 467; being "seen," 985; children's anger, 290; crocodile, 172; developing sexuality, 200-1; diving, 256; dog, 467; end of world, 110; fairies, 259-60; father not returning, 987; flying, 355; going to orphan home, 277; heights, 383-84, 828; looking ahead, 955; losing identity, 207; madness, 110, 112; opposing mother, 262; prayer being answered, 387; torture, 1085-87

Feast of Corn God, 625

Feast of the Serpent, 195

Feast of the New Spears, 349

feasts, 300; beggars' annual, 1352; chicken dinner, 803; for displaced animals, 389; of Guenever for knights, 1037

feathers: hen, as identification, 1402-3; in wool bales, 234

The Feather Star, 1404

February Callendar, 403-5, 434-36

FEBRUARY'S ROAD, 403-5, 436, 1296

Federales, 601-2

Feedbag, Ethel, 376, 1354

feeding homeless, after air raid, 379

fee-holders, Norman England, 672-75

feet: enormous, 470; hair-covered, 553

Feet and Other Stories, 771

Felim, 215-16, 408

Felim the Harper, 298

Felix Hardcastle, 1194

Fell family, 87-88, 722-24, 818-20

Fell, Margaret, 1200

fellowship, 465

THE FELLOWSHIP OF THE RING, 405-8, 1230

Felpham, 50, 310

Felts, Shirley, 1036-37, 1171

female characters, especially: assertive, 43-46; big, birdlike, 1067; dramatic, 61-62; sturdy older woman, 714-16; independent old woman, 714-16; intellectual, 62, 751-52; shrewish, 59-60; spunky, 815-16; strong-willed, 57-58, 276, 751-52; timid, 60; very sensible, 822

femme fatale, 340-42, 1323, 1420

fences, for stolen goods, 101, 278

fencing, of common, 196

Fenians, 1285

Fenny Brown, 1071

FENODYREE, 344, *408,* 1343-44

Feraille, 938
Ferdie, Black, 409
Ferdy, 1077
FERGUS (*Children of the Red King*),
  215-17, *408-9*, 482, 1103
Fergus (*Under Goliath*), 1286-87
Fergus mac Roy, 300. *See also* Fergus
  MacRoy, 299.
Fergus MacRoy, 299. *See also Fergus
  mac Roy, 300.*
Ferguson, Dave, 799-800, 1197-98
Fernand family, 1349
ferrets, 133, 134, 137, 777, 1236
ferry, snake acts as, 1120
fertilizer factories, proposed,
  1303, 1305
FESTE, the horse, 212-13, *409*, 1230
festival competition, 383-85
Festival Hall, 86
Festival of Our Lady, 601
festivals, 658; fairies', 713; moonlight, 1093; regarded as pagan,
  778
Fetterlock family, 234, 453, 519,
  791, 827, 884-85, 1132-33, 1402-
  3
feudal societies: set up in village,
  311; reversion to, 1359
feuds: among tribes, 811; blood,
  1037; family, 37; father and aunt,
  1350; Irish, 543-46; Viking, 116-
  19; worker, housewife, 1350;
  Yorkshire families, 1021-23
A Few Fair Days, 440
Fezziwig, Old, 228, 409
Fiddler, 1111-13
fiddlers, 725; blind, 359
Fiddler's Quest, 744
Field, Dr. Gabriel, 108-9
Field family, 839, 1109-10
Fielding family (*The Cricket on the
  Hearth*), 267-68
Fielding family (*Goldengrove; Unleaving*), 459-61, 1287-90
fields, drained, 802-3
Fields, W. C., 262
field trips, to zoo, 1154
fifes, 1285
Fifi, 43, 45-46, 321, 470
Fifi Moulin, 235
fifteenth century: Constantinople,
  370-73; England, Cotswolds, 1402-
  3, Ewelme, 1404-7, London, 729-30,
  Sussex, 683-84, various, 102-5,
  153-55, Warwickshire, 729-30
fifth century: England, 679-83;
  Juteland, 680
Figgs, Arthur, 1368-69

fighters: big strong, 717; figures
  in church windows, 208
The Fighting Cocks, 67
fights: against devil, 309; brutal,
  245; dog, 1399; dog, encouraged,
  295; fist, 582-83, 622, 1134-
  35, 1156, 1285, 1320; ironman vs.
  space monster, 584-85; man vs.
  boar, 1162; mounted robbers vs.
  Sikh uncles, 312; schoolgirl,
  319; single combat, 1320; street,
  1115-16. *See also* battles; battle scenes; conflicts; war novels;
  wars.
figs, dropped on horse, 672
Fili, 553
films, of monster, faked, 369
fimbulwinter, terribly cold, 1344
financier, formerly gypsy, 435-36
Finch family, 127-29
Finchley Common, 738
finders, of missing things, 141,
  856, 857
Findhorn, the unicorn, 359-60
The Finding, 81
fingerprints, 405
fingers, bitten off, 465
Finlay Bruce, 605, 1049-50
FINLAY, WINIFRED, 281, *409-10*
Finn, 1271
Finn Dove, 425-27
Finn Learson, 911, 1155-56, 1409
FINN MCANDREW, 368-69, *411*
FINN, PATRICK, 17, *410-11*, 707,
  1309-91
Fionuala, Princess of Gleann na
  Nean, 913, 1003
Firbank Hall, 61, 132, 134-35, 137,
  854, 857, 1236
FIRE AND HEMLOCK, 411-14, 618
Fireball, 232
*The Firebrand of the Indies, a Ro-
  mance of Francis Xavier*, 1076
firecrackers: homemade, 669;
  thought to exorcise devils, 802.
  See also fireworks.
fire demons, 168
Firedrake, 997-98
fire escapes, used to get to garden,
  446
fireflies, thought soldiers, 929
FIREFROST, 168, 344, 408, *414*, 1343-
  44; recovered, 1344
Fire on the Mountain, 303
fireplaces, discovered in barn,
  307
fires: arson, 807, 809, 845, 1104,
  1365; as weapon, 11, 65, 773;

at birthday party, 1048; bakehouse, 970; brush, 773, 973-74;
burning castle, 146; burning spider webs, 1095; called Red Flower,
630; chateau, 1217; cottage, 320;
destroying doll mother, 102; dome,
1295; fowlhouse, 715, 861, 894;
from lightning, 788; grass, 1228;
house, 14, 178, 180, 218-19, 452,
467, 500, 609-10, 611, 616; hut,
1378; in air raid, 378; in theater,
1122; jungle, 894; manor house,
763; mansion, 32, 740, 1067;
neighborhood, 1080; of basilica,
271; of dead gypsy in her wagon,
318; of hostel, 300; old theater, 1090; on mountain, 502; set by
child, 423, 477; shipboard, 108,
887, 1065, 1215; signal, 788; stables, 235, 596, 972; under dining
table, 275; use of taught, 1310
FIREWEED, 414-16, 940
fireworks, 237; Guy Fawkes, 607;
ship's cargo, 366; to combat
Greeneyes, 892. *See also* firecrackers.
Fir Grove, 539
Firman, George, 1379
The Firs, 374
First Affections, 445
The First Book of Ballet, 1157
The First Book of England, 1157
first century, B.C.: England, Berkshire Downs, 1171-73, 1244-45;
Rome, 1244-45; Scotland, Orkney
Islands, 1161-64
first century, A.D.: England, 771-7,
1117-19; Scotland, 771-74
First Duma, 1207
*The First Margaret Mahy Story Book:
Stories and Poems,* 760
first person narrators: author, 974-
80; boy, 156-58, 184, 237-40, 255-
57, 258-61, 304, 306, 414, 463-64,
492-95, 514-16, 556, 647-48, 648-
51, 662-63, 789-91, 797-99, 876,
895, 922, 989-92, 1062, 1102,
1146-47, 1169-71, 1206-8, 1215-
18, 1256, 1284, 1309-11, 1364,
1389-91, 1392-94; girl, 96-99,
132-34, 243-44, 403, 434, 447-49,
635-36, 734-37, 891, 938-39, 1074,
1076-78, 1269, 1322-25; horse,
105; man, 338, 508-14, 1046; old
man, 116, 870-72
Firth of Forth, 13, 650
Fiscal, 800
Fisher family, 363, 640

fisherfolk, Scottish, 1155-57
fishermen, 201, 461, 516, 982, 1170,
1379-81; boy, 1374; Breton, 740;
cruel, 1081; dour, 1094; elderly, 1288; Irish, 544; Norwegian,
1349-50; pretends to be poet, 829;
salmon, 731-32; Skye, 789-90;
storyteller, 740; superstitious,
740; Sussex, 763, 792, 1229
Fisher, Michael, 568-69, 777
fishes: evil dwarf, 913; talking,
1310; tropical, 539
Fish Folk, 336
fishing: shark, 545; trip in rain,
556
Fitch family, 328-29, 479, 483, 852
fits, berserk, 746
Fittiplace family, 549-50
Fitzackerley family, 769, 1317-19
FitzAmory family, 916-17, 1202
FitzEdmund family, 276, 683-84, 701
Fitzwilliam, John, 12, 611, 738-40,
1104
FIVE BOYS IN A CAVE, 193, 233. *See
THE CAVE, 193-94.*
FIVE CHILDREN AND IT, 416-18, 881
Five From Me, Five From You, 746
Five Minutes to Morning, 801
The Five Hundred, 322
FIVER, the rabbit, 418, 557, 1331-32
Flack family, 16-17, 411, 707, 851,
1389-91
flags: regimental, 651-52; ship's,
1341; skull-and-crossbones, 1178
Flambards, 226-27, 354, 419-21, 421-
24, 775, 1228, 1284, 1374
FLAMBARDS, 354, 418-21, 966
Flambards Divided, 227, 335, 424,
775, 966
FLAMBARDS IN SUMMER, 356, *421-24,*
966, 1284
flamingoes, as croquet mallets, 20
flappers, 511-12
flashbacks, 847, 870-72, 1123, 1169-
71, 1196-99; as dreams, 1163. *See
also* frame stories; stories within
a story.
flashlights, thrown away, 194
Flats, 465-66
flattery: of dragon, 1107;
man's undoing, 114-15, 754;
susceptibility to, 196
Flavia, 680-83
Flavius, 271, 633, 1089-91
flax, must be spun into yarn, 872,
1094-95, 1130
Fledge, the horse, 167, 688, 756
FLEMING, IAN (LANCASTER), 221, *424*

FLETCHER, DAVID (LESLIE), 30, *424-25*, 662
Fletcher family, 468
Fletcher, Father, 1325-27
Finch, Harry, 1213-15
FLICK, *425*, 1249
Flick Williams, 515
THE FLIGHT OF THE DOVES, 425-27, 750
A Flight of Swans, 1371
Flight to Adventure, 1075
Flight to the Forest, 1371
flights: across channel in early airplane, 355; dwarf to own dimension, 847-49; from cruel duchess and bloodhounds, 816; from lecherous artist, 1166; from volcanic eruption, 1143; magical power of, 417; on magic cloak, 721; on Silver Curlew, 1095; overland, 1089; over moors, 1328; pickpocket from two men in brown, 845; queen of Scots to England, 1414; rabbits from dog, 1333; through copper mines, 1343-44; through forest and bog, 684; to Neverland, 1347
Flimnap, 509
Flint, Captain (Swallows and Amazons series), 171-72, 614, 1047, 1178-79, 1228
Flint, Captain, (*Treasure Island*), 89, 100, 172, 1253-55
Flint family, 77-78, 465-67, 823
flints, bored, protect against witches, 450
flirts, 474, 693, 883, 1323; boy, 697; Irishman, 186
flits, 514-15, 528
Floethe, Richard, 1111
floggings: at sea, 153; ordered for drunkenness, 190. *See also* beatings; whippings.
THE FLOOD AT REEDSMERE, 162, 427. *See THE GREAT GALE, 495-98*.
floods, 105, 186-88, 211, 288, 291, 409, 566, 604, 658, 775, 786, 829-30, 866-67, 1230, 1357, 1388; cottage marooned, 815; English coast, 495-98; impending, 523; in Underland, 1093; Noah's, 1185; river, 812, 1035
flophouses, Manchester, 449, 1268
FLORENCE BONE, *427*, 736
Florestan, the horse, 1005
Florrie Clough, 536
Flowering Spring, 1306
Flower of Ipswich (barge), 1213-15
flower pots, thrown as warning, 520

flowers: maiden of, 932; talking, 1209
Floyd, Gareth, 683, 891, 1290, 1404
Fluff, the guinea pig, 1263
Fluffy Tail, the squirrel, 1271
A FLUTE IN MAYFERRY STREET, 344, *427-28*
flute music, mysterious, 428
flutes, 16, 211-12, 1185
flutists, 16, 428, 694, 697, 829-30
Fly, the dog, 1082-83
Fly-by-Night, the horse, 1190-92
Fly-by-Night, 85, 960, 966, 1053, 1190-92
flyers, German, captured by children, 749
flying, 367; boy teaches children, 956, 1168; fear of, 227; learning to, 70, 335
The Flying Cradle (stagecoach), 1125
Flying Free, 192
The Flying Ship, 531
flying shuttle, 464
foals: white colt, 295-96; wild, 390
fogs, 154, 983, 1357; at sea, 1340-41, 1380; created, 1337; fairy mist, 713; sudden, 222, 888, 1343. *See also* mists.
foil characters, obvious: Borrower boys, 948, 1130; Borrower wives, 61, 560; bratty girl--worthy boy, 1305; bully--neighboring youngsters, 697; careful, exact boy--talkative brother, 318; carefully arranged within family, 1336; caring helper at model village--greedy tourist trap owner, 822; casual boy--tense boy, 961; clowning schoolboy--overwrought schoolmate, 1258; confident brother--self-flagellating boyfriend, 1290; conscientious girl--stylish cousin, 565; democratic rabbit leader--rabbit dictator, 446, 535; dissatisfied wealthy girl--hardworking servant girl, 1068; domineering grandmother--kindly grandmother, 484, 875; dreamy, bookish boy--outdoor-games-loving boy, 190; dull uncle--clever motorcycle repairman, 1283; dwarfs, 893, 1265; English grandmother--Ghanan grandmother, 251, 483; English mother--Welsh mother, 768, 873-74; English seamen stopping slave ships--cruel

American slavers, 1071; English
village girl--black girl, 698;
farm girl--London bookseller's
daughter, 742; father--fos-
ter father, 916; fathers, 1224;
fine craftsman of miniature
village--unscrupulous promotor
of tourist trap, 139, 837, 856-57,
857; gentle boy--aggressive
roughneck, 75; good-natured artist step-father--deceased macho
father, 609; good village girl---
heartless worldly girl, 95;
gypsy child--captive boy, 606,
1265; happy younger brother--in-
tense siblings, 547; haughty
heiress--earnest girl, 196;
independent old man--free-loading
father, 833; lazy boy--hard-
working girl cousin, 1042; lazy
clerk--conscientious boy, 71;
lively, confident girl--in-
secure cousin, 87, 722-24; modest
nephew--boastful uncle, 920;
neighboring mothers, 678, 854,
1117; outgoing actor's son--tim-
id evacuee boy, 1419; outgoing,
thoughtless boy--timid, worried brother, 451; overachieving
boy--ordinary brother, 1372;
possessive mother--self-
indulgent earl,
1198; poverty-stricken miners--
greedy owners, 1277; pseudo-
family--real families, 919;
rabbit--girl, 1362; retarded boy--malicious intruder,
580; schoolboys, 1100; Selkie
man--honest beau, 1156; sensitive
boy--siblings, 899; sensitive refugee girl--bumbling,
good-hearted schoolmate, 897-
99; sharp-witted resourceful
girl--shy, fearful girl, 887-89;
shopgirl lodger--serious younger
girl, 792; sisters, 708; spoiled
boy--Pevensie cousins, 377;
spoiled daughter--sweet niece,
1217; steady mathematical girl--
emotional girl, 427; take-charge
girl--neighboring boys, 447;
three suitors, 456-58; unstable brother--steady boyfriend,
612; warm, caring Viennese--brut-
ish Poles, 215; warm, sensitive
boy--eccentric schoolmate,
28-29, 1212, 1297-98; willful
girl--worthy boy, 1297; worldly,

flirtatious girl--steady devoted girl, 335; worldly, free-living
neighbor--strait-laced aunt, 741
foils, wooden, symbol of freedom,
772, 967
Folan, Lord, 258-61, 1102
folklore: basis for story, 246-48,
298-99, 299-301, 659-62, 824-26,
996-99, 1037-39, 1043, 1094-96,
1376-79; Celtic, 287-88, 501-2;
elements of, 120, 486-87, 548-50,
550-53, 567-69, 636-38, 659-62,
1067, 1094, 1155-57, 1342-45,
1409-11; folktale pattern, 927-
30, 1232-34; Irish, 216, 713-14,
913, 1270-73; legend basis for
novel, 113-15, 1258-61; legends
of King Arthur, 1037-39; legends
of Robin Hood, 1043; Scottish,
911; Slavonic, 1302; student of,
567. See also legends; literature,
oral; oral tradition.
Folk Tales of the North, 410
Follow the Footprints, 795
Folly Grange, 4, 480, 516
Folly Mill, 862
Folly River, 716-17
food, frequently mentioned, 712,
799; hoarding, 73; molasses and
whale oil, 887; smuggled to ill
boy, 1160; strong interest in,
1183; thefts of, 7
Fools, 270-71
football matches, 1263
footprints: ancestral, in cave,
1144; on shore, 1045; unexplained,
37, 286
footsteps: at night, 362; of dying father, 610
FOOTSTEPS, 428, 442. See JOHN DIA-
MOND, 610.
Forbes-Cowan, Colin, 590
Ford, Hilary, 231
foreign agents, villainous, 282-
83
"Foreign Lands," 384
Foreman, Michael, 9, 484, 1143,
1234
foremen, mine, 1411
FOREST, ANTONIA, 382, 428-29, 963,
1218
Forest Hall (ship), 926
Forest of Arden, 11
Forest of Weal, 1385-86
forests: Ashdown, 581-83; Sherwood,
1420; Sussex, 581-83; symbol of
security, 684; Yald, 425
Forest series, 1370

forgers, 464, 1401
FORGERY!, 90, *429*. See *GOLD PIECES*, 463-64.
forgiveness, 287, 693-94, 800, 827, 902-3, 1123; importance of, 248; promised, 299
Form Lower IVA, 164-65
formmasters, tyrant, 950-51
FORMULA 8 DELAYED-ACTION MOUSE-MAKER, *429*, 1393
Forrest, Adam, 2, 486-87, 779, 875, 960
For the King, 1346
Fortnum, Peggy, 84, 169, 1220
Fortress Caparetto, 210, 748-50
fortresses: for machine gun, 245; mountain of Assassins, 671
forts: deserted, 348; fairies, 713; iron age, 903
The Fortunate Few, 644
The Fortune of Virginia, 1076
fortunes: bestowed on boy, 757; fallen, 419-21, 922, 1146; favorable turn, 95; restored, 547, 812-14; sought, 1233
fortune tellers, gypsy, 770, 1193, 1352, 1354
Fortune Theater, 840
Fossil family, 68-71
The Fossil Snake, 145
fossils, 1141, 1144
Foster, Captain Jupiter, 893-94
Foster family, 860, 1140-41
foster parents. See parents, foster; mothers, foster; fathers, foster; grandparents, foster.
Foulds, E. V., 1306
Foulger family, 496-97, 543, 604, 775-76, 786, 867
founders: of Life Brigade, 1326; iron, 1277
foundlings: boy, 30-31, 1100, 1125-28, 1149-50, 1192, 1409; girl, on church steps, 769, 1221; rejected in parish, 1409-10
foundries, 198; iron, 459, 581-83, 1033
Fountain of Lions, 998
fourteenth century: England, 145-47, 447-49, Yorkshire, 915-17, 1017-20; France, 447-49; Scotland, 1017-20
Fowler, 420, 421-22
Fowler family, 611-12, 1026
fowlhouses: home of gnome, 715, 861, 894; "maggoty old," 715
Fox, 953
The Fox Busters, 665

foxes: 152, 324, 388-89, 502; aristocratic, 432; cub, 2, 487; obliterate tracks, 1344; on moor, 1386-87; poet, 432
Foxes Court, 1065-66
Fox family (*Fantastic Mr. Fox*), 388-89
Fox family (*The Summer People*), 1169-70
Fox Farm, 344
Foxfire, 255
Foxham, Lord, 606
fox hunts, 2, 226-27, 388-89, 404, 419-21, 432, 506, 945, 964
The Fox in the Manger, 1250
THE FOX IN WINTER, 149, *429-32*
FOX OF FURROWFIELD, *432*, 1120-21
Foxy-Boy, 1079
FOXY WILLIAMS, the fox, 152, *432*, 932
Fradd family, 389-91
frame stories, 14, 99, 132-34, 134-36, 136, 178, 732-34, 1196-98, 1284-87, 1412; conversations, 1388; in form of letters, 1169-71; unusual pattern, 902. See also flashbacks; stories within a story.
Fran, 430-32
France: late fourteenth century, 447-49; eighteenth century; 339-42, 765-67, 1215-18; early twentieth century, Calais, 1213-15; mid-twentieth century, Channel cliffs, 221-23, Paris, 1348-49; twenty-first century, 989-92, 1359-61; future, 1337
France: fall of, 1339; German refugees in, 31
Frances, 430-32, 433, 873, 1242
FRANCES HUNTERLY, 389-92, *433*, 600
Frances Kemble, 170
Frances Tate, 862, 1314
Francis, King of Fabylon, 928-29
Francis Archdale, 939
Francis family, 574, 876, 1351-53
FRANCIS SHELLEY, 85, *433-34*, 1379-81
Frangio, the hedgehog, 1186
Frank, 1351
Frank, King of Narnia, 167, 688, 756
Frank Fay, 1133-36
Frankland family, 637, 638
Frank Watson, 351-53
Fraser, Simon, 733
fratricide, 890; accusation of, 1121
frauds, 809; attempted, 373-74; by bankers, 791; girl pretending illness, 341-42; gold mixed with copper, 660; investigation for, 618;

unemployment compensation, 1134
Frau Gruber, 562
Frazer family, 889-91
Frazer, Sir James George, 411, 437
Fred, 228
Fred Boggis, 218, 616
Fred Clough, 536
Freddy, 880
Frederick Evans, 826, 843
Frederick Guelph, Duke of York, 1164
Fred Holt, 540, 542
Fred Tranter, 483, 669, 697, 1335-
   36
Fred Vye, 226
freedmen, 1099
freedom: earned by three good deeds,
   675; fight for, 507-8; from slav-
   ery, 281; gained by sacrifice,
   1173; granted to slave, 117, 348;
   in White Mountains, 1359; tokens
   of, 658; won, 117
The Freedom Tree, 1334
Free Love, advocated but not prac-
   ticed, 93
Free People, 335, 525, 917, 1265
Free Rein, 858, 961, 967
Free Traders, 1112-13
Freetown, Sierra Leone, 1069-70
freezers, for dead hedgehogs, 541-
   42
French language, 1018
French persons: in England, 31-32,
   454, 600; in Russia, 12, 1020; in
   Wales, 558-59; joining English ar-
   my survivors, 340
frenzies, 1093
Frey, 195
Friar Tuck, 12, 146
friars: fake, 673-74; impersona-
   tions of, 103. *See also* monks.
Frick, Shaky, 78, 465-67, 823, 1080
Friday, 1045
Friday Callendar, 403-4, 434-36
The Friday Parcel, 980
FRIDAY'S TUNNEL, 403, *434-36*, 1296
Friend family, 61, 473, 473-75, 623-
   24
Friendly Association, 119
Friendly Boys, 808
Friend Monkey, 1250
friends: abused boy-boy killed in
   airraid, 469; Alsatian-mastiff,
   1387; betrothed children, 276;
   black girl-black servant, 762;
   black girl-village girl, 249,
   698; black slave boy-blind white
   girl, 172-73, 218-19, 591-92,
   1173-74; boarding school girls,
1071-74; Borrower girl-human boy,
   49, 132-34, 489; boy-abused foster boy, 1049-50; boy-Afghan spy
   in India, 758; boy-boat owning
   boy, 291; boy-boy, 292, 697, 729,
   1100, 1402, through mothers, 777;
   boy-chieftain's son, 1320-21;
   boy-dog, 915, 1320-21; boy-
   dragon, 1030; boy-eccentric boy
   schoolmate, 28-29, 1211-13; boy-
   French Canadians, 733; boy-French
   girl, 740; boy-girl, 289-90, 755-
   56, 896, 904, 987, 1065, 1092-93,
   1363-64, 1402-3; boy-girl, classmates, 323; boy-girl upstairs,
   446-47, 779; boy-gorilla, 525,
   1154-55;
boy-grandfather, 911; boy-horse,
   1367-68; boy-Jacobite courier,
   13; boy-Mexican boy, 629; boy
   of Ur-contemptuous Hiberu boy,
   625; boy-old recluse, 962-63;
   boy-old schoolmaster, 1156; boy-
   outlaw, 717; boy-recluse, 1390;
   boy-spirit children, 212-13;
   boy-stuffed animals, 232; boy-
   talking toy soldiers, 1274-76;
   boy-tramps, 538, 891-92; boy-
   Vagrant, 1359; boy-waitress,
   523; boy-Welsh boy, 968, 1039-41;
   boy-wolves and jungle animals,
   836-37; bright boy-slower classmate, 529, 1149-50; British tribal
   boys, 1171-72; Bronze age boy-
   orphan girl, 338;
castaway boys-cannibals, 256-
   57; children-old
gentleman, 1147; Chinese boy-old
   English woman, 1154-55; city boy-
   country gentry boy, 506-7; city
   girl-farm girl, 742; clergyman's
   communist son-curate's daughter,
   735; competent girl-disagreeable
   neighbor girl, 363; cousin-
   cousin, 900; created
through Japanese dolls, 819;
   dreamy boy-practical boy, 516-17;
   dubious, 1298; Earl and blacksmith, 47; eccentric boy-plump
   girl, 942, 1136; English boy-
   Emperor Constantine, 370-73;
   English boy-Quivera princess,
   915; English children-German airman, 1051; evacuee girl-older boy,
   14, 177-79; ex-chimney sweep-ex-
   rich girl, 363; family, suddenly
   inhospitable, 243; gamekeeper's
   grandson-Borrower girl, 136-37;

girl-boy, 1141, 1313; girl-boy-boy, 1199; girl-boy, later developing into romance, 684; girl-boy next door, 202, 1322-24; girl-boys, three, next door, 1203; girl-daughter of Czar, 24; girl-English teacher, 823; girl-fractious refugee boy, 1052-53; girl-girl, 893, 903-4, aboard ship, 887-89, developing, 723, distant cousins, 718-19; girl-intense, unusual boy, 1288-91; girl, Christian-Jewish girl, 900; girl-local Earl, 1197-98; girl-lower class girl, 954; girl-musicians, 685-86; girl-old Sikh woman, 297; girl-orphan girl, 1159; girl-refugee girl, 897-99; girl-saint, 1055; girl-servant girl, 94; girl-shepherd boy, 725-26; girl-ship's boy, 887-89; girl-ship's steward, 844; girl-Sikh boy, 10; girl-storekeeper, 850; girl-stranger, 696; girl-stray dog, 903-4; girl-time transported family, 1290-91; girl-wealthy girl, 354-56; good boy-saucy youth, 464; hearing boy-deaf boy, 290-91; horse-loving girl-boy, 1191; horse-loving girl-experienced girl rider, 1191; Irish farm girl-Irish city girl, 1134; London boy-older Cumbrian boy, 531, 556-57; magician-girl magician, 534; maladjusted girl-crippled man, 360-61; man-monkey, 839-41; man-wild creatures, 201; millworker's son-union organizer's son, 805-6, 876; mole-rat, 1020-21; mole-water rat-toad-badger, 1382-84; neighbor boy-abandoned children, 314; neighborhood group, 689-92; noble boy-former dog boy, 673-74; noble girl-boy waif, 293; novice priest-king, 122; old teacher-kidnapped doctor, 258-61; old woman-dog, 568; old woman-kelpie, 830; old woman-scarecrow, 568; one armed boy-one armed man, 1319-20; orphaned English boy-captured German flyer, 887; pickpocket-blind magistrate, 845-46; poodle-elephant, 235; Protestant boy-Catholic boy, 1285-87; python-jungle boy, 635; Quaker girls, 988; rich boy-fisherman boy, 433-34; riverbankers, 1229; royal cousin-imposter, 252; runaway boy-farm girl, 834-35; runaway boy-knight, 916; runaway boy-old man, 834-35; schoolboys, 143, 244, 282-83, 641, 801-3, 1059-60; schoolgirl-schoolboy, 73; schoolgirls, 293; schoolgirl-Ugandan student, 613; Scottish boy-girl, 387; scribe-printer, 195; stablemates, 454; steady girl-emotional girl, 736; stuffed animals, 989, 1388-89; surgeon-centurion, 1089; talking animals, 931-32; talking dog-fairy cat, 675; teacher-teacher, 1166-67; teasing girl-fat boy, 367; teenaged girl-old man, 429-32; teenaged girl bus riders, 163-66; toy bear-antique dealer, 844; truculent pianist-self effacing folk singer, 75; twentieth century boy-nineteenth century miner boy, 398; uncle-Irishman, 17; uninhibited boy-timid boy, 1419; Venetian boy-American boy, 662-63; Victorian girl-modern boy, 532-33; villagers-Sikhs, 312; village girl-doctor's daughter, 866-67; waif-village children, 360; wealthy girl-chimney sweep, 363; wealthy girl-working girl, 335; Welsh boy-English girl, 768; white boy-black boy musician, 1062-63; white boy-mute black boy, 1263; wild dog-tame dog, 1387; woman-cat, 894; working class boy-upper crust girl, 400-3; writer-Borrower girl, 138-39; young knights, 453; youth-old shepherd, 1398-99
friendship, novels of: fantasy, 200-1, 560-62, 891-92, 1031-32, 1082-84, 1240-42, 1290-91, 1381-85; realistic, 389-92, 429-32, 467-69, 606-8, 801-4, 833-35, 1039-41, 1114-17, 1154-55, 1211-12, 1268-70, 1284-87
friendships: exploitive, 843-44; fractured, 843-44; long-suffering, 65, 1382-85; pretense of, 864; renewed, 863, 1116
Friends International Service Center, 685
Frith, Lord, 535
Fritz, 238-40, 990-91
frivolity, frowned upon, 177

FRODO BAGGINS, 96, 131-32, 406-8,
    436-37, 439, 465, 804, 981-82,
    1056, 1231
FROG, 262, *437*, 1114, 1120
Froggy, 689-90
frog-man, 1007, 1092
From Russia, With Love, 424
From Where I Stand, 994
Frontier Wolf, 1176
Froreden foundry, 459, 581
Frumpkins family, 367-68
Frytha, 1085-87
fugitives, 492, 494, 1346; from
    French Revolution, 832-33, 828;
    from murder charge, 650
Fulbrook Hill, 549
Fulford High School, 635-36
Fundindelve, 167, 414, 1343-44
funeral directors, 1315
funeral pyres, gypsy wagon, 318
funerals: attended by accident,
    412, 694, 987, 1065; encountered
    by accident, 278; father's, 1165;
    grandmother's, 1287; interrupt-
    ed, 77-78; of great aunt, 706; of
    king, 1320; of rabbit, 1373; of St.
    Cuthbert, 1377; pretended, 720
Funny Sort of Christmas, 192
Fur, 771
Furbelow, Willoughby, 1338
furnaces, blast, 973
Furness family, 903-4
furniture: bought on time, 1365;
    dollhouse, 133, 135, refinished,
    331; makers, 595; sold for cash,
    1365
Furrowfield, Fox of, 432
*Further Adventures of the Family
    from One End Street*, 445
future: England, 309-13, 1294-95,
    1336-38, 1359-61, countryside,
    505-8, London, 505-8, Midlands
    city, 895-97; Skipley, 156-58;
    Europe, 1359-61, France, Morlaix,
    1337; telescoped into present, 46
futuristic novels, 156-58, 237-40,
    309-13, 505-8, 555-57, 895-97,
    989-92, 1294-95, 1336-38, 1359-61
FYSON J(ENNY) G(RACE), *437-38*, 624,
    1204

Gaberlunzie, 1344
The Gables, 427
Gaelic language, 590; learning of,
    588
Gaffer, cruel, 1276-78
Gail Callendar, 404-5

Gairfowl, 1329
Galadriel, 407
Galahad, 1270
Galahad, the horse, 1234
Galapagos Islands, 888
gallows, 110, 111, 308
Galway: thirteenth century, 215-17;
    mid-twentieth century, 543
Gambadello family, 15, 662-63
gamblers, 195, 673, 730, 1104; fa-
    ther, 361, 1365
gamekeepers, 134-35, 136, 464, 705,
    1236, 1254
games: annual athletic, 238; card,
    493; chess, 108, 673, 1209; cro-
    quet, 20, 23, 343; flags, 519; fox
    and geese, 431, 433; imaginary,
    172; imaginative, 119-230; High
    Priestess, 411; parlor, 228; play-
    ing house, 38; Pooh-sticks, 563;
    pretend, 535, 801-3; riddle, 464;
    rural Cornish, 332-33; war, 519-
    20; watched from window, 73
Gamgee family, 96, 406-8, 437, 465,
    1056
GANDALF, 96, 131, 406-7, *439-40*,
    465, 551, 553, 1158; the Grey, 439;
    the White, 440
Gang of the Black Hand, 386
gangrene, leg wound, 764
gangs: attacks by, 125; fac-
    tory, 808-9; Friendly Boys, 808;
    hoodlums, 157; London, 798; motor-
    cycle, 1033; Robin Hood tradition,
    425; schoolboy, 245; shoplifters,
    992; street, 748-50, 808-9, 1115-
    17; thieves', 542; Venetian
    street, 15, 662
gangsters, 222; admired by boy, 811
garage roofs, site of confidences,
    289
garbage, girl thrown into, 1297
GARDAM, JANE (PEARSON), 96, *440-41*,
    555, 734, 1165
gardeners, 127-28, 133, 137, 211-
    13, 854, 1241; cross, 5-6; hobbit,
    406, 1056; kind monk, 1395; re-
    tired, 78, 1080
The Gardener's Grandchildren, 1371
gardens, 446, 476; down rabbit hole,
    19-20, 23, 211; eternal Narnia,
    688; herb, 1395; large, neglected,
    site of gun emplacement, 886-87;
    midnight, 1237; near idyllic,
    532-33; physic, 1395; play area
    in slum, 1115; secret, 897-99;
    vandalized, 1115; Victorian mid-
    night, 1240-41; walled, 1115

Garebridge, 292, 351-52, 641
GARFIELD, LEON, 15, 111, 143, 304,
    339, *441-42*, 610, 824, 1108, 1125,
    1149
Gargery family, 94-95, 492-95, 608
gargoyles, 930
Garland family, 4, 364, 1068, 1229
Garm, the dog, 395-96
garments, mysteriously provided,
    724
Garmouth, 210, 245, 262-63, 400-403,
    747-50, 881, 1325-27
Garmouth Volunteer Life Brigade, 33,
    50
Garmouth Watch House, 33
GARNER, ALAN, 9, 359, *442-44*, 484,
    932, 1025, 1143, 1234, 1342
Garner, Mr. 37, 286, 591, 820, 843
GARNETT, EVE, 385, *444-45*
Garnie, 68
Garret, 713-14
GARRET BYRNE, *445-46*, 499-501
Garrick, David, 169
Gar River, 1325
gate keepers, 975; of pier, 1056,
    1290-91
Gate of Vapour, 236
The Gates of Eden, 796
The Gates of Paradise, 182
gates, water, escape route, 1032
Gathering family, 1194
Gathering, to choose heir, 215-16
The Gauntlet, 1345
Gawain, Sir, 1037-38
Gayner, Sir Richard, 237
G. B. (Generous Benefactor), 1147
Gdu, Egyptian hawk god, 122-123,
    1261
geasas, 300
geese, Christmas, 177, 229
Gemefer Trequddick, 1111-13
Gem Tiffany Jones, 87, 722-24
General Dundas, 500, 879
General Lawrence, 341-42
General Turnville, 1337
GENERAL WOUNDWORT, the rabbit, 418,
    446, 535, 1332-33
General Zuckerman, 1187
General Zuckeroo, 585
generations: bound together, 399;
    unity of, 914
Genesis, story of Joseph, 830
GENEVA, *446-47*, 612, 613, 678, 697,
    779, 1115-17
genies: of light, 247; Indian in bot-
    tle, 1354
Genii Maxii, 794, 1274-75
geniuses, four-year-old, 275

Genoese, in Constantinople, 371-72,
    633
THE GENTLE FALCON, 447-49, 701
GENTLEMAN GEORGE, *449*, 1268
gentry, country, 419-21, 421-24,
    548-50, 506, 609
Geoff Mortimer, 399, 836, 895-96
Geoffrey Sanderton, 469
GEOFFREY TINKER, *449*, 1055, 1336-38
geographers, Roman, 1244
GEORDIE BICKERSON, 160, 281-83, *449-
    50*, 486, 523, 1223
GEORDIE MONROE, 81, *450*, 741-42
George Baillie, 457
George Barnard, 889
GEORGE BATCHFORD, *450*, 548-49
George Dexter, 304-6
George Douglas, 677-78, 1412-15
George Dunham, 474
George Firman, 1379
George Greengrass, 62
GEORGE OVERS, 17, *450-51*, 703-4,
    1132
GEORGE PONTIFEX, *451*, 667, 1056,
    1290
GEORGE REYNOLD, 193-94, *451*
George Treet, 304-6, 826-27
George Williams, 397
Georgie-Porgie, 697
Georgiou family, 74, 520-21
Gerald Trevelyan, 890
gerbils, 76-77, 100, 159, 293, 604-
    5, 860, 1088
Gerlath, Rudi, 1051
German: language, 401; occupation
    forces, 175; occupation of Norway,
    578
Germans: in England, 422, 924-26,
    937, 1051; in Norway, 578; pidgin-
    English-speaking, 888; World War
    II, 1339-40
Germany, mid-twentieth century,
    1096-99; 1348-49
Gervis, Ruth, 68
Ghana: late twentieth century,
    Accra, 248-52; village, 248-52
ghettoes, 1315, 1364
The Ghost and Bertie Boggin, 1066
The Ghost Downstairs, 442
The Ghost Drum, 994
*Ghost Horse: Stallion of the Oregon
    Trail*, 220
Ghostly Companions, 15
Ghostly Tales, 994
Ghost of Christmas Future, 353
Ghost of Christmas Past, 228, 353,
    409
Ghost of Christmas Present, 228, 353

Ghost of Christmas Yet to Come, 228–29
The Ghost of Riddle Me Heights, 943
THE GHOST OF THOMAS KEMPE, *451–53*, 727
ghosts: 286–87, 353, 398, 450, 533–34, 548, 591, 595–96, 743, 790, 825–26, 1100, 1225–26, 1241; brought to life, 1104–5; called up, 1355; called up as servants, 512; climbing into window, 341; contained in bottle, 49; debunkers of, 33–36; disappearing into grave, 452; doomed to wander, 227; fear of, 249; in watchhouse, 33, 51; laid, 1327; local, 556; of business partner, 227; of drunk grandfather, 212; of girl, 455–56, 618; of gorilla, 374, 525; of grove, 693–94; of long-dead horse, 409; of miser, 864; of murdered mill family, 1059–60; of sailor boy, 591; of seventeenth-century children, 710, 1230; of Victorian children, 37; sixteenth century of Darkington Hall, 1355; stories of, 644; transparent, 825; walking, 1104–5. *See also* spirits.
Ghosts at Large, 994
Ghosts' High Noon, 1306
A Ghost Ship to Ganymede, 1183
ghost stories: 211–13, 217–19, 227–0, 286–87, 306–9, 339–42, 351–53, 359–60, 397–99, 451–53, 455–56, 485, 533–34, 824–26, 1058–60, 1240–42, 1325–27, 1353–56, 1376–79
ghouls, dark, silent, 1354
Ghylls Hatch, 683, 701, 972
Giant Crum, 324, 716
Giant Despair, 977, 979
Giant Grim, 978
giants, 292, 351–52, 417, 510–11, 603, 875, 1009, 1035–36, 1092; arouses dragon, 395–96; at fair, 1041; believed to exist in past, 339; circus performer, 120–21; girls, 780; ice, 1344; in circus, 339; in supermarket, 412; Irish, 410–11; iron, 583–85; jolly, 228; plants, 128; revived from gallows, 110, 111; smelly, 470
Gideon Ahoy!, 795
Gideon Ibbotson, 637
Gifford family, 506–7
The Gift, 315
gifts: bag of coins, 450; Beethoven medal, 87; birthday, silver

sword, 1097–99; black pearls, 671; christening, 1096; crocodile tongues, 593; dead rabbits, 307; desk from manor, 455–56; dropped and smashed, 381; Dutch doll, 332; father's watch, 610–11; flute, 428; for hobgoblin, 550; heart, 168, 567, 569; heirloom locket, 543; holy water, 661; iron emblem, 287; Italian dagger, 633; magic, 994–95, 997–98, 1233–34; metal "F" from wrecked ship, 433; meteorite, 327; money, 649; naval officer doll, 558–59; old sword, 396; oranges, 627; pets, returned, 76; powerful magic, 711; puppy, 327; rejected, 319, 1050; requests fulfilled, 327; shield to museum, 565; slice of mutton, 660; sliding tray, 484; stone from Wheal Maid mine, 398; suspected, 590; to King Henry III of Navarre, 662; to placate servant, 245; trait of character, 997–99; un-birthday, 572
GILBERT D'ASSAILLY, *453*, 670–72
Gilbert Makepeace Lives!, 1334
Gilbride family, 588–89, 589–90, 1048–49
GILES, *453*, 519, 1402
Giles Fanshawe-Smithe, 226
Giles Marlow, 382
Giles of Ham, 395–97
Gil Goodchild, 1213–15
GILLES COBHAM, 447–49, *453–54*, 586
GILLES THE OUTLAW, *454*, 744, 1406
Gimli, 407
Ginevra, Queen of New Cumbria, 844, 1142–43. *See also* Guenever, Queen of Britain, 1037–38; Guinevere, Queen of Britain, 148.
GINGER, the horse, 105, *454–55*, 596
ginger bread, with stars, 780
Ginger Hind, 45
Ginnie Thatcher, 179, 468
Gino the Fox, 15, 662–63
Ginty Marlow, 382–84, 96–65
The Giraffe and the Pelly and Me, 275
giraffe, former detective, 1385
Girl Guides, 361, 386
The Girl in a Swing, 3
THE GIRL IN THE GROVE, *455–56*, 1079
girls: abandoned as infant, 1071; abandoned by father, 115; abandoned by parents, 57; abandoned to workhouse, 728; abused, 109–10, 277–78, 586, 728, 815, 900–2,

1368-69; abused psychologically, 538, 1368-69; adaptable, 248-52; adopted, 320, 376, 404, 493-95, 592, 820; adventurous, 778, 874; afraid of traffic, 818; aloof, 533, 1264; ambitious, 386, 707-8; archer, 1174; arsonist, 921; artistic, 152, 1301; ashamed of farm life, 742; assertive, 43, 63, 281, 747-48, 769, 880-81, 986, 1052-53, 1167, 1168, 1221-23, 1327; athletic, 151; avid reader, 819, awkward, 647; becomes witch, 692;

beggar, 294-97, 1029; black of "modest demeanor," 256; bookish, 179; bored, lonely, 1325; bossy, 205, 286, 988, 1185; brassy, 203; bright, takes lead in research, 1024; budding writer, 818; can't learn to read, 1313-14; capable, 360-61, 1034-35; captain of boat, 874; chatterer, 949; cleverer than thought, 32; clumsy, 381; companion-servant, 37; competent, 361-62, 786, 1158; confident, 163-66; conscience-laden, 1175; conscientious, 176; considered ideal daughter, 1165; considered prig, 1168-69; considered ugly, 97;

cool-headed, 330; courageous, 742; curious, 1094; cynical, 156-58, 655; decide to be naughty, 1385; declared dog, 803; deformed, 109-10; depressed by loss of dog, 896; determined, 1316-19; dies of illness and abuse, 728; directive, 38; disbelieved by siblings, 742; disruptive in school, 70; domestic, 1314, 1175; dutiful, 1197; easily bullied, 37-38; easily swayed by parents, 518; eaten by cat, 560; emaciated, representing Want, 228; emotionally repressed, 770; enterprising, 769-70; erroneously thought retarded, 1165; excellent student, 1072-73; excluded, 1168-69; expert with weapons, 915; fearful and whiney, 345; feels overworked, 606; first to enter Narnia, 742; flirtatious, 335, 354-55; forthright, 18, 19; foster, 115, 827, 1280, 1322, 1368, 1396; foster of cousin, 685, 693; foundling, 769; found unconscious in North Sea, 887; frail, 1170;

French-speaking, 31-32; full of vitality, 164-66; gifted, 655; guilt-ridden for death of mother, 898-99; gullible, 282; gum-chewing, 203, 1305; hard-working, 1158-60; has locked herself in ship's cabin, 344; headstrong, 80; heartless, 820; helpful, 386; highly intelligent, 368; high-spirited, 234, 710; homeless, 744; husky and assertive, 828; illegitimate, 47, 1135-36; illiterate, 744, 1397; imaginative, 489-90, 598, 987, 1290-91; independent, 763-65; independent minded, 597; independent, quick-witted, 887-89; indomitable, 770; insane, 111-13; insubordinate prisoner, 91-92; irrepressible, 1270; intelligent, 37, 200; isolated, 289, 1168-69; kidnapped, 279; lazy, 1094; leader of group, 874; literary, 1228; little German, 1339-40; lively, 31-32, 87-88, 208, 722-24, 741-42; lonely, 367, 818-19, 889-90, 1140-41, 1240-42; loyal to absent father, 728; madcap, 893; maladjusted, 360-61, 361-62, 367; man-hating, 1169-71; manipulative, 88-89, 478; maternal, 334, 815, 1347; mechanically adept, 69; mischievous, 161; museum specimens, 239; naive, 668; natural actor, 1223; neglected, 462, 1168; neurotic, 616; new in neighborhood, 722-24, 1191; new in school, 897; newly self-destructive, 1135-36; noble, country-bred, 447; noble, mistaken for servant, 453; obnoxious, 1297, 1305; obsessed with motorcycles, 523; of stone-age Fox tribe, 336-37; old beyond years, 1056-57; on her own, 309-11; only child, 1140; outcast, 956; outspoken, 602-3, 636, 698, 734; over-achiever, 1048; pampered daughter, marriage pawn, 683; peacemaker, 19, 1168-69; possessed, 903; practical, 515-16, 1055-56; precocious, 32, 41-42, 275; pretentious, 404; pricked with pins, 1385; prim and proper Victorian, 769-70; prissy, 364, 451, 524; prodigy, 719; protective of brother, 1012-13; psychic, 692; quick-tempered, 482; quick-witted, 585; reader, 491; reared

by grandmother, 770; rebellious, 191, 365, 895-96; reclusive, 344; refined orphan, 1222; religious, 93; repeatedly disparaged, 900-2; rescued from sinking ship, 69; rescues rabbit, 1333; resented by aunt, 343; resentful, 208-9; resents brother's romance, 693; resourceful, 31-32, 42-43, 446, 740, 1121-22, 1233-34, 1402-3; responsible, 523-25, 815; responsible for boy, 735; responsible for family, 1056-57, 1356-58; responsible for home, 1034, 1072-73, 924, 457, 1117, 1218-20; responsible for housework, 361; responsible for mother, 447, 866-67; responsible for neighbors, 466; responsible for parents, 31; responsible for refugee children, 1097-98; responsible for siblings, 363, 522, 1052-53; ridiculed by schoolmates, 897; romantic, 516, 599; sassy, 203; scarred face from fall, 1248-50; scorned as dreamer, 1244; seasick, 1175; self-assured, 533; self-congratulatory, 599; self-dramatizing, 517, 769; self-important, 70; self-reliant, 1056-57; sensible, 427, 535-36, 1158-60; sensitive, 180, 332, 461; separated from parents, 309; serene, 1015; shallow, 26; shoplifter, 1105; short and fat, 381; shot at by villagers, 1369; shy, 769-70, 887-89; simple-minded, 620; small but self-reliant, 577; sold by mother, 109; spineless, 1342; spirited, 19, 19-22, 22-23, 49-50, 91-92, 115, 132-34, 330, 482, 603, 883, 1017-20, 1115-17, 1121-22, 1199, 1205; spiteful, rude, 719; spoiled, 32, 43-46, 63, 203, 566, 599, 693, 1018, 1206, 1297; spunky, 175, 536-38, 779, 807-8, 985, 1094-96, 1206, 1220-23, 1402-3; stage-struck, 383, 1314-15; staunch, 532-33; steals food for starving children, 692; stepdaughter, 1185; stoic, 706-7; stout-hearted, 332-33; strongly emotional, 240-41; strong-willed, 753; stubborn, 319; stuck fast in house, 20, 22; swearing, 987; tactless, 897; tall and thin, 202-3; tart-tongued, 108; teasing, 367; teenager, reverts to babyhood, 1053; theatrical, 32; thin as matches, 1385; thought drowned, 1377; thought illegitimate, 476; thought mad, 1232; thought retarded, 946, 1368; thought to be designing, 338; tomboy, 598; trained to break men's hearts, 820; truant from school, 897-99; ugly, disagreeable, 1165; unfavorably compared to cousin, 770; unpopular because of outspokenness, 734; unprincipled, 517-18; unscrupulous witch, 208-9; unusually clumsy, 1313-14; unusually imaginative, 779; unusually independent, 886; unusually perceptive, 734-37; upper crust, 400-3; very loyal to mother, 678; Victorian, 532-33; waif, 55-57, 294-97, 670, 1029; wealthy indulged, 722-24; wealthy neglected, 1084; wild but steadfast, 638; willful, 127-28, 335; willing, strong at eight, 1158; with crippled hand, 1055; witness at trial, 21; young, holds many domestic jobs, 1158-60. See also boys; children.
Girls of Paris, 747
Girls' Own Paper, 882
GIRL WITH A LANTERN, 456-58, 676
Gisela, 674
Giselli, Teresa, 31, 1105-6
gladiator fights, to the death, 347
gladiators: ex-, 806; freed, 1090; Roman slave, 347, 375, 771-72, 967
Glasgow, 245
glass blowers, Venetian, 15, 662-63, 913
glass burners, 109
The Glass Slipper, 393
Glastonbury, 1038-39
glaziers, Jewish, 278
gleaning, 1233
Glegg, Creina, 318
Glennashee, 713
Glen of the Fairies, 713
Glimfeather, 1092
Gloin, 407
Gloop, Augustus, 58, 203
Glorious Revolution, 456
Glory Piercy, 522
Gloucester, Duke of, 448
Gloucester family, 125-26, 350, 1405
Gloucester, Richard of, 606
gloves, to conceal burn, 1055
Glow-Worm, 593-94

Glubbduddrib, 512

Gluck, 659-62

Glumdalclitch, 510-11

Glyn Owen, 243-44

gnat, talking, 1209

gnomes, 67, 324, 875, 1092, 1114; angry, 715, 861, 894; grey, last in
   Britain, 716-17; hairy, 716-17;
   living in fowlhouse, 715; sly,
   cunning, ancient, 715, 860-61, 894

goats: herd started, 1044; injured
   nanny, 1368; talking, 913; wild,
   659

goat-stone, 122

goblets: from dragon's hoard, 552;
   missing, 662-63; ruby glass, 662-
   63; shattered, 663; sixteenth-
   century, 913

Goblin (boat), 614, 1340-42

goblins, 120-21, 439, 464, 551, 570,
   1002-3, 1343

gob-stoppers: pictures of, 607;
   substituted for explosive, 436

The God Beneath the Sea, 441

"God Bless us, every one," 1227

GODDEN, (MARGARET) RUMER, 318, 330,
   381, 458-59, 558, 667, 722, 818

goddesses: Earth Mother, 772-73;
   horse, 1173; moon, 123-24

Goddess on Earth, 1117

goddess-queens, 252, 865, 1117-19

Godfrey, William, 231

God-horses, 295-96

god-like figures, 55

Godman family, 459, 581-83, 971-72,
   1033,

godmothers, fairy, 720-21, 1096

Godolphin, Mary, 161, 975

Godrevy, Cornwall, 459-62

gods: appearing as still, small
   voice, 737; Celtic, 387, 1162;
   Egyptian, 829; family, 624-26;
   Greek, 828, 1384; Haitian, 765-
   66, 938, 1227; hawk, 122-23, 1261;
   household, 1205-6; rabbit, 535;
   sun, 772, 1321; wraithlike, of
   Calormemes, 687

*God So Loved the World: A Life of
   Christ*, 471

Goggles, 689-91

gold: discovered, 1001; pirate,
   1253-56; produced by water, 1307;
   quests for, 172, 972-73; really
   copper, 973; sought with divining
   rod, 1148; thought discovered,
   733; witch's ill-gotten, 247

The Golden Age, 472

Golden Apple, 213

The Golden Bough, 411, 437, 618

Golden Galleon (ship), 558

Goldengrove, 459-62, 1287

GOLDENGROVE, 459-62, 941, 1287, 1290

Goldenhand, Angharad, 1344

Golden Horn, 372

Golden Jubilee of Queen Victoria,
   1159-60

THE GOLDEN KEY, 462-63, 745

Golden Puma, rescued, 1385

The Golden Shadow, 441

*The Golden Sovereign: A Conclusion
   to "Over the Bridge,"* 233

Golden Tickets, 203

The Goldfinch Garden: Seven Tales,
   969

Goldfinger, 424

The Gold of Fairnilee, 679

gold pieces, 1205

GOLD PIECES, 90, *463-64*

gold plates, buried, 237

goldsmiths, 660

Goliath, a crane, 1285

GOLLUM, 96, *464-65*, 551

Gondal, 963-64

gondolas, willed to boy, 913

gondoliers: aging, 912-13; Venetian, 662

Gondor, 131, 407, 440, 805, 982, 1158

Gondor, king of, 1158

Gonzales, Father, 399, 601-2

Goodall family, 204, 586-87, 1202,
   1373

GOODBYE, DOVE SQUARE, 465-67, 797

GOOD-BYE TO THE JUNGLE, 467, 1246.
   See WIDDERSHINS CRESCENT, 1364-
   66.

Goodchild family, 1213-15

Goodenough family, 61, 1236

Goodenough, Tom, 811, 857

Good Fortune (yacht), 85, 433, 1379-
   81

Good Hope (ship), 103-4, 317, 695

The Good Little Devil, 696

goodness: power of, 720-22, 724-27;
   triumph of, 1113; vs. selfishness,
   642-43

GOOD NIGHT, MR. TOM, 467-69, 757

Good People, 1112

Goodrich family, 195, 612, 729-30

goods, stolen, receivers of, 1040

good vs. evil, 131-32, 167-68,
   287-88, 356-57, 359-60, 373-75,
   376-77, 405-8, 408, 436-37, 439-
   40, 501-2, 504-5, 517-18, 550-53,
   636-38, 638, 710-13, 755-57, 804,
   864, 913-14, 994-96, 1050, 1067,
   1091-94, 1095-96, 1227, 1272,

1342-45, 1375, 1386-88
Good-will, 975
Goodwin Sands, 221-23
Good Words for the Young, 745
Goody Hooper, 308-9
THE GOON, 43-46, *470*, 1087
Goosefeather, the pony, 389
Goose-girl, 783
goose growers, 388
gooseherds, 1099-1100, 1401
GOPAL, 10, 297, 310-11, *470*, 648,
    1280
Gorby, 600
Gordon family, 596, 612
Gordon, Margaret, 365
Gordon, Squire, 454
Gore, Nicky, 10, 297, 309-13, 470,
    648, 886, 1280
gorillas, 525, 980, 1154-55; escaped
    from London zoo, 859, 1154; pro-
    tects boy from cow, 1155; shot by
    police hunter, 1155
Gorvenal, 1259-61
goshawks, 383-84
Gospel of John, 155
Gospels, Book of, 216
gossips, 318, 600, 862; malicious,
    246
Gothic Adams, 480-82
Gothic elements, 304-6, 806-7, 807-
    9, 824-26, 887-89, 889, 889-91,
    935, 1108-9, 1135, 1356-58, 1389,
    1399-1401
Gothic novels, 304-6, 806-9, 887-89.
    See also melodramas.
Goths, 157
Gotobed family, 14, 177-79, 542-43,
    826, 886
GOUDGE, ELIZABETH, *470-71*, 724, 1111
Govannon, 504
governesses: abusive, 1400-1; doll,
    558; grasping, 1400-1; humorless,
    1385; imposter, 1400-1; sweet,
    elderly, 724-26; to child queen,
    447-48. *See also* babysitters;
    nannies; nurses.
governors, Roman, 1118-19
Gov'nor's Kip, 449
Gowan, Uncle Jack, 1285-86
Gowie Corby Plays Chicken, 644
Gowther Mossock, 1067, 1342, 1344-45
Gozzling, Miss, 367
Graaf, Peter, 231
Grace Gathering, 97-98,
    1194
Grace Nbatha, 627-28
graffiti, 647, 1315
Graham, the turtle, 1186

GRAHAME, KENNETH, *472*, 717, 812,
    885, 1029, 1106, 1382
Graham family, 24, 79-81, 206, 450,
    741-42, 865, 874, 885
Graham, Miss, 1071-73
Graham Snell, 541-42
Grail of King Arthur, 502, 1375
Gramercie, 1194
GRAMPER PONTIFEX, 176, 363, *472*,
    667, 1056, 1290-91
Gran, 282
Gran-at-Barton, 473
GRAN-AT-COALGATE, 62, *472-73*, 473-
    75
GRAN-AT-COALGATE, 194, *473-75*
GRAN BELL, 60, *475-76*, 538, 770, 900-
    2, 1192, 1283-84
Gran Chapman, 125, 1021-22
Granda, crotchety, 1357
Grandad, 1235
GRANDAD BARTON, 249, *476*, 482, 698
Grandad Bell, 900, 1192
GRANDAD HEWITSON, *476-77*, 555-57
Grand Challenge Trials, 1083
granddaughters, of German comman-
    dant, 1339
Grand Duchess of the Diamond Palace,
    815
Grand Duchess Olga, 24, 28
Grand Duc Serge, 16
Grandfather, 484-85
Grandfather Byrne, 499-500
Grandfather Elijah, 367, 1168
grandfathers: 399, 528, 910, 1156,
    1235; abstracted, 366-67; accepts
    children, 694; accused of murder,
    1022; addled, 813-14, 817, 841;
    blacksmith, 1235; commanding,
    81, 478; congenial, 1101-2; dour,
    1356-58; ex-sea captain, 1356;
    fiery, 499-500; French noble-
    man, 12; gamekeeper, 135, 1236;
    gentle, 900; great, 399; great,
    anthropologist, 613; great-
    great, 399; great, stonemason, 9-
    10; gregarious, 805; guardian,
    1168; honest, 838; independent,
    476-77; irascible, 156, 233; Lapp,
    578, 1351; loving, 479; marti-
    net, 645; mentally ill, 210; mill
    worker, hot-tempered, 876-78;
    patient, 476; patient, accepting,
    249; poacher, 1372; raises roses,
    900; rationalist, 485, 592-93;
    religious, 276, 1276-78; scornful
    of grandson, 1319; searching for
    treasure, 862; skeptic, 33-36;
    smith, 9-10; stonemason, 484,

619; storyteller, 911; supportive, 479-80, 805; trusting, 805;
youthful in spirit, 805. *See also*
grandmothers; grandparents; old
persons.
Grand High Witch, 429, 1392
Grandma, 912
GRANDMA BAGTHORPE, 275, *477*, 912,
  1048, 1283
GRANDMA LIZZIE WHITE, 125, *477*,
  1021-23
Grandmamma, 1392-94
GRANDMOTHER, 250, *477-78*, 483, 762
GRANDMOTHER HOLBEIN, *478*, 1039-41
grandmothers: admiral's, 5; African
  matriarch, 477-78, 762; assuming
  role of, 823; becoming frail,
  460; caring, 677; death of, 588;
  discovered, 1335; domineering,
  483-84, 900-2, 1335-36; eccentric, 477; enigmatic but warm,
  874-75; estranged from family,
  874-75; fearful, 728; fond, 858;
  former actress, 728; foster mother, 323, 486, 968; gentle, 548-49;
  great-, 211-13, 217-19, 373,
  498, 1231; great-, autocratic,
  498; great-, independent, 859;
  great-great-, 999-1001, 1002-3;
  great-great-, gypsy, 5, 318, 669-
  70; great-great-, senile, 1294;
  great-, understanding, 381-82;
  great-, witch, 600; harridan, 900-
  2; healer, 1394; helpful, 131;
  hunched, 861; imaginative, 478;
  imperious, 125, 250; influential,
  841; inherited with house, 202;
  judgmental, 249; lacks one thumb,
  1392; magician, 534; manipulative, 250; matriarchal, 297, 770;
  music teacher, 677; no-nonsense,
  485; nursemaid in youth, 455-56;
  perceptive, 486, 898; pious, 592;
  practical, 328; presumed dead,
  reappearing, 808; pretentious,
  81; puritanical, 473; purpose-
  ly charming, 728; reconciled to
  daughter through grandchild,
  800; rescued from terrorists, 74;
  scuttling, 728; self-righteous,
  475-76, 482; sharp-tongued, 1335-
  6; shy, quiet, 1335; Sikh, 297,
  310, 312; small, independent,
  861; smokes cigars, 1392; strict,
  religious, 217; strong-minded,
  483; supportive, 861; tells stories re witches, 1392; thought
  witch, 1394; tyrannical, 475-76;

understanding, 473-75, 539, 1039-
  41, 1289;
warm-hearted, 472-73; warm,
  workworn, 677; white witch, 642;
  witch, 200-1, 1389. *See also*
  grandfathers; grandparents; old
  persons.
Grand National, 616
GRANDPA, 241, 288-89, *478-79*, 728
GRANDPA BAGTHORPE, *479*, 922
Grandpa Ellis, 1276-78
GRANDPA FITCH, 328-30, *479*, 483, 852
Grandpa Greengrass, 955
GRANDPA JOE, 203-4, *479-80*
Grandpa Percy Purvis, 276-78
grandparents, 1124-25; foster parents, 277-78; four in one bed, 203-
  4, 479; guardians, 900; previously
  unknown, 645-46; terrorized by
  grandson, 899; unconventional,
  899. *See also* grandfathers; grand-
  mothers; old persons.
*Grandpa's Folly and the Woodworn-
  Bookworm*, 831
grandsons, 1; great, 1154; greedy,
  430; of composer, 428
Grand Viziers, Turkish, 213
Gran Fielding, 1287-90
THE GRANGE AT HIGH FORCE, *480-82*,
  1273
granges, 480-82, 516
GRANIA, 216-17, 408, *482*, 1103
Grania of Castle O'Hara, 744
Gran Lovell, 318-21
GRANNY BARTON, 249, 476, 478, *482-
  83*, 698
Granny Bowen, 906-7
Granny Crack, 566
GRANNY FITCH, 328, 479, *483*, 852
Granny O'Flaherty, 425-27
GRANNY RANDALL, *483-84*, 669, 697,
  875, 1335-36
GRANNY REARDUN, 9, 444, *484-85*, 1234
GRANNY WHITTACKER, 411-13, *485*, 1065
GRANPA UTTERY, 33-36, *485-86*, 592-
  93, 778
GRAN RIDLEY, 449, *486*
Grant, Elisabeth, 1339
A GRASS ROPE, *486-87*, 794
grass ropes, to catch unicorns, 487
GRAVELLA ROLLER, 51, *488*, 600, 970-
  71
gravel pits, digging for Australia,
  416
graves: dug in front yard, 645-46; of
  mother, 150, 157; purple rose on,
  821; search for, 92-93; unmarked,
  147

Graves, Alfred, 16-17, 410-11, 1390
gravestones, 944, 1126; disappear-
    ing, 1335
graveyard caretaker, 197
graveyards, 397-98, 825, 1319, 1325-
    26
gravity: princess has in water, 702;
    princess lacks, 702
GRAY, NICHOLAS STUART, *488-89*, 927-
    28
Gray Owl, the pony, 389
Grazing Island, 259-60
Great-Aunt Martha, 536
great aunts, scholarly, 564
GREAT AUNT SOPHY, 132, 147, *489*, 560,
    854
Greatchurch, 212
THE GREATEST GRESHAM, 63, *489-92*
GREAT EXPECTATIONS, 313, *492-95*
THE GREAT GALE, 162-63, *495-98*
Great Game, 653
The Great Ghost Rescue, 577
Great Glass Sea Snail, 1310
GREAT-GRANDMOTHER SCHOLAR, *498*,
    534, 1264
Great Green River, 1120
Great-heart, 978
The Great House, 527
Great Links Tor, 1386
Great One, 765-66
Great Orb, 1322
Great Plague of 1665, 212, 710
Great Ring of Power, 406-8
Great Selkie, 911, 1155-56
Great Serpent (ship), 91
Great Snow Dance, 1093
Great-Uncle Barnaby Scholar, 533-34
GREAT-UNCLE COLE SCHOLAR, *498*, 533-
    34, 1264
GREAT-UNCLE GUY SCHOLAR, *498-99*, 534
Great-Uncle Matthew, 68-70
Great-Uncle Merry, 804
Great Wall, 1089
greed, 95, 552, 650-51, 807-9, 1011,
    1204, 1277; destructive, 631; for
    gold, 1204, 1307
Greeka, Eagle of the Hebrides, 220
Greeks, in England, 402, 520-21
The Green Book, 941
THE GREEN BOUGH OF LIBERTY, *499-501*,
    1027
Green Branches, 1138
The Green Dragon, 743
Green Dolphin Street, 471
Green, Eileen, 163
Greeneyes, 168, 538, 620, 891-92
Green family, 1400-1
Green Finger House, 531

Greengage Summer, 458
Greengrass family, 59, 62, 364-65,
    953-55, 986-87, 1195-96
Green, Hepzibah, 14, 177-79, 179,
    542-43, 826
greenhouses, 127-28; wrecked, 521
Green Knowe, 172, 211-13, 217-19,
    339, 373-75, 525, 577, 710, 800,
    859, 922, 980, 1035-36, 1154-
    55, 1183, 1230
Green Noah, 211-12, 710
Green Revolution, 35-36, 778
Greenwich Park, 1147
Greenwitch, 255
greenwood, 12, 717
Greenwood, Bill, 1238
Gregory, Sir Percy, 507
GREGORY THOMAS, *501*, 599, 667-68
Gremlin, 524
The Gremlins, 274
grenades, 1360
Grendel, 505
Gresham family, 489-92
Gretel at St. Bride's, 530
Grey Brother, 836
Grey Chieftain, 220
Grey family, 163-66
Grey King, 148, 502
THE GREY KING, 255, 287, *501-2*
GRICE, FREDERICK, 129, *502-3*
A Grief Observed, 700
Griff, the dog, 903-4
GRIFFITHS, HELEN, *503-4*, 1366
Grildrig, 510
Grim (*Hobberdy Dick*), 549
Grim (*The Shield Ring*), 1085
Grimblegraw and the Wuthering Witch,
    1106
Grimble, Mrs., 1385-86
Grimbold's Other World, 489
Grimes, Mr., 1328-30
Grimm brothers, 246
GRIMNIR, 344, 408, *504-5*, 1067,
    1343-44
Grimsby, Sir Randolph, 31, 302-3,
    807, 809, 1104
Grimshaw, Mr. Josiah, 1400-1
Grimstone, 615
grins, of Cheshire-Cat, 211, 342
Gripe, Mr., 1401
Grizel Hume, 457-58
GRIZEL MAXWELL, *505*, 636-37
grocers, 376; mother, 1390
Grognio, King of Pantouflia, 997-98
Gronw Pebyr, 116, 933
Gronw's Stone, 116
grooms, 17-18, 105-7, 318, 420, 421-
    22, 596, 1107; assistant, 1108-9;

faithful, 457; bashful, 583; youthful, 1222

Groot, 1063

ground swelling, mysterious, 351

Grouser, the owl, 713

grove, haunted, 947

Grover Godman, 581, 1033

The Grove of Green Holly, 1371

growing up, nature of, 1211

growing up novels: boys': 113-15, 213-15, 278-81, 304-6, 484-85, 492-95, 555-57, 558-59, 601-2, 620-23, 651-54, 656-58, 672-75, 703-6, 720-22, 738-40, 1125-28, 1284-87, 1298-1300, 1319-22, 1379-81, 1412-15; girls', 19-22, 96-99, 169-70, 200-1, 248-52, 318-21, 411-14, 418-21, 421-24, 459-62, 473-75, 523-25, 564-66, 588-89, 627-28, 717-20, 734-37, 899-902, 903-4, 923-24, 924-26, 1012-13, 1123-25, 1133-36, 1158-60, 1165-67, 1196-99, 1313-15, 1316-19, 1322-25, 1349-51

Gruaga, 675, 913-14, 1003

Gruber, Frau, 562

Gruber, Mr., 84, 844

Gruff and Tackleton, 267

GRYPHON, 20-21, 23, *505*, 827

guardians: actor, 1202; aunt, 692, 897-99, 683; churlish, irresponsible, 807, 1104; cousin, 718; girl's, 724-26; grandparents, 900; grandfather, 1168; hard-drinking, 740; imperious, 592; irresponsible uncle, 1315; knight, 1104; rightful, 103; uncle, 1056-57, 1364-65; unsympathetic, 914-15; usurping, 102-4, 316, 738, 809, 1103

THE GUARDIANS, 231, *505-8*

The Guardians of the House, 145

guards: drunk, 552; Galway, 260; of Sleeping Knights, 167-68; prison, bribed, 1109; whip-wielding, 520; wife, 1126

Gub-Gub, the pig, 1145

GUDGEON, TOM, *508*, 808

Guenever, Queen of Britain, 1037-38. *See also* Guinevere, Queen of Britain, 148; Ginevra, Queen of New Cumbria, 844, 1142-43.

Guern, 348-50

guerrilla fighters, 615, 1032-33

guerrilla warfare, 149-50, 157-58

guesses, of imp's name, 1095-96

Guest family, 290-91

guests, tyrannizing, 259

guidebooks, to Watch House collection, 1326

guides: across tidal flats, 578; Chinese poet, 853, 1195, 1266; false, 975; forest, 805; Indian, 733; Middle-earth, 406-7; of schooner, 792; to American boy, 662; treacherous, 465; Venetian, 15

guilt: at losing baby, 363; for bombing, 226; for broken promise, 479; for brother's death, 246; for causing fire, 178-79, 179-80; for death of baby sister, 469, 1373; for not escaping kidnappers, 616, 1006; for overeating, 277; lifetime of, 931; short-lived, 517; unnecessary, 692

guinea pigs, 29, 1262-63; adventurous, 1186-87; in experiments, 755; maiden lady, 365-66; proud, white and brown, 1186-87

Guinevere, Queen of Britain, 148. *See also* Guenever, Queen of Britain, 1037-38; Ginevra, Queen of New Cumbria, 844, 1142-43.

GULLIVER'S TRAVELS, *508-14*, 1182

GUM, 70

Gumble's Yard, 314, 514, 579, 599

GUMBLE'S YARD, *514-16*, 1246, 1364

Gummery, 804

gum, turns girl into blueberry, 1305

guisers, dances of, 1156

The Guizer: A Book of Fools, 444

gun emplacements, 748-49

Gunn, Ben, 1255-56

gunners: machine, dead, 747-48; pirate, 1255; World War II destroyer, 516

gunpowder, mention prohibited, 511

gun runners, 173, 313, 601-2, 629, 1412

guns, discovered in cellar, 1285-86

GUNS KELLY, 4, 290, 480-81, *516*, 959

The Guns of Darkness, 1061

Gurnsey, World War II, 898-99

Gus Callendar, 404-5, 434-36

GUS POSSIT, 234-36, *516*, 962, 1057

GUS ROPER, *516-17*, 946, 982-84

GUTHORM, *517*, 871-72, 1243

Guthrum, 517

Guy Fawkes Bonfire Night, 1390

Guy Fawkes Day, 224-25, 607, 785, 1147; dim memory of, 1294; dummy, 197, 747-48

Guy of Lusignan, 670

"guys," 1294

Guy Scholar, 534

GWEN, 77-78, *517*, 465-66, 539
Gwenap, 397
GWENDOLEN CHANT, 191, 225, 208-
    9, *517-18*, 598
GWENDOLYN SWAMP, *518*, 752, 1354
Gwydion, 116, 932
GWYN, 25-26, *518*, 574-75, 768, 873,
    933-35, 1047
Gwyntfa, 74, 323, 906
Gwyntystorm, 999-1001
gypsies, 43, 417, 426, 435-36,
    549, 1009-12, 1236, 1386-87;
    ambushing, 637; capturing Borrow-
    ers, 135; caravan, 1383; curse,
    212; disliked, 737; fortune tell-
    er, 219, 770, 1352, 1354; grand-
    mother, 233; half-gypsy girl,
    318-21, 669, 822; living in admi-
    ral's orchard, 4-5; queen drugs
    boys, 1352; steal boy's tent while
    he's sleeping, 543-46; steal ta-
    ble, 556; stereotyped as villains,
    1387; threat to Borrowers, 136-37,
    811
Gypsy Joe Slattery, 605, 918
gypsy wagons: child sized, 320; re-
    stored, 320. *See also* caravans.

haciendas, 601
Hacketstown, 500
Hadden, Uncle, 596
Hadden family, 1316-19
Hadrian's Wall, 348, 350
Haegel the King, 295-96
Haethcyn, 1085
"The Haggard Mountains," 58
Hagon, Priscilla, 25
hags, 712, 875, 893, 1354
Hague, Major Scobie, 1326-27
Hague, Michael, 22
Haigha, 753, 767, 1210
hairdressers: aunt, 1071-73; in
    Irontown, 579
hair, human: long, becomes issue,
    950-51; used for picture, 217, 219
Hairy Man, 715
Haiti, late 18th century, 765-67
Haithwaite family, 578-80
Hal (*Hal*), 73-74
HAL (*The Wool-Pack*), *519*, 1402
HAL, *519-21*, 747
HALCYON ISLAND, 1, 2, *521-22*, 659,
    586-87, 1202, 1373
Hal Fawcett, 434-35
Halfbacon, Huw, 518, *574-75*
The Half-Brothers, 695
Halfdan, 871

Halflings, 553
Half-People, 1321
Hall, Douglas, 79, 1049
Haller, Kaspar, 32, 214
Hallersage, Yorkshire, mid-20th
    century, 536, 1034
Hallersage Common, 196
Hall Farm Cottage, 364, 523
Hallibutt, Miss, 367
Halloween, 411, 413, 717, 784, 1355
hallucinations, 36, 1060, 1258
Hallward, 733
HAL PIERCY, 520-21, *522*
HAM, 196, *522-23*, 737, 829-30, 895
Ham, village, 395-97
Hamid of Aleppo, 659
Hamilton, Clive, 700
Hamilton family, 12, 15-16, 24, 28,
    63-64, 1020, 1207-8
The Hamish Hamilton Book of Queens,
    393
HAMISH MACLEISH, 160, 281-83, *523*,
    1223
Hampstead, mid-20th century, 1218-
    20
Hampstead Heath, 329
Hampton, Professor, 1003-
    4
handicapped children, novels of,
    33-36, 217-19, 290-91, 720-22,
    1262-64, 1313-15
handicapped persons: amputees, 469
    arthritic, 4, 285, 845, 1039-40;
    blind boy, 33-36, 485, 592-93,
    778, 1197-98, 1366-68; blind fa-
    ther, 680; blind girl, 172, 195,
    217-19, 267-68, 591-92, 599, 770,
    859, 956, 1067, 1173-74, 1231,
    1396-97; blind heir to throne,
    806; blind king, 772-74; blind
    leader, 1299-1300; blind magis-
    trate, 845-46, 820-21, 1107-8,
    1108-10; blind man, 359; blind
    monk, partially, 155; blind pi-
    rate, 965, 1254; blind professor,
    460-61; blind singer, 1272; boy,
    speech defect, 1269; cripple,
    Borrower, 141-42, 948; crip-
    ples, boys, 57, 109, 199, 228-29,
    290, 336-37, 1161-63, 1226-27;
    cripple, boy, polio, 15, 662, 947;
    cripples, hunchback boy, 1394-
    96; cripples, daughter of vicar,
    821, 944; cripples, girls, 427-
    28, 1377; cripples, men, 16, 118,
    226, 264, 347-50, 361-62, 419,
    556, 696, 1108-10, 1126, 1284;
    cripples, clubfooted men, 295,

855, 1150, 1293; cripples, priest, 123; cripples, leader, 238; cripples, prince, 720-22; cripples, stiff knee, 118; cripples, stiff leg, 354, 1374; cripples, war, 1106;

cripples, woman, 746; cripples, wooden leg, 324, 540-42; crooked shouldered, 581-82; deaf boy, 290-91; deaf men, 267, 595; deaf-mute man, 720-21; deaf, nearsighted giant, 395; deaf man, selectively, 479; deaf woman, 798; deformed babies, 158; doll with foot half bitten off, 330; dumb servant, pretense, 308; dyslexic, 647, 655; fraudulent invalid, 341-42; girl, extremely farsighted, 1173; girls, facially disfigured, 109, 198, 205, 425; girl thought to be retarded, 97; girl walking for first time, 428;

girls with crippled hand, 1015, 1055; legless woman, 735; mentally ill, 110, 111-13, 375-76, 554, 604, 1011, 1025; mentally ill, boy thought, 468; mentally ill, half-mad tosher, 508; mentally retarded, 177, 293, 422, 466-67, 543, 578-80, 748, 826; mentally retarded, seemingly, 470, 1368; minus two fingers, tutor, 807, 845; mute boy, 1262-64; one-armed man, 1019; one-eyed man, 358-59; one-eyed ogre, 698; one-eyed Selkie man, 1156; one-handed boy, 1086; one-handed girl, 1376; one-handed pirate, 172, 957; one-handed warrior, 1319-20; one-legged man, 16, 870-72; one-legged pirate, 732, 1253-56; one-legged sea captain, 731, 884;

palsied man, 1080; paralytic woman, 379; paraplegic ex-soldier, 9-10, 1281; rattling head, 101-2; small tail, 845; stammerer, 633; weightless, 701-2; wheelchair-ridden, 119; withered arm, 337-38, 1319-22; woman with partial sight, 483; wooden leg, 837. See also mutes.

handles, nicknames, 364
HANDLES, 523-25, 771
Hands, Israel, 1255
handwriting: analysts, 184; clue, 184
handyboys: old woman's, 715; waterman's, 729

handymen: demented, 1381; former World War II gunner, 516; hotel, 30; lazy, 779, 781, 782; old man, 833, 834-35; retarded man, 826; seemingly slow-witted, 933-34; steals treasure, 814, 1131-32. See also hired men; men-of-all-work.
hangars, as home, 354
hangings: escapes from, 609; for gun-running, 237; of brother, 879; of coiner, 464; of grandfather, 233; of Irish rebel, 101, 500; of knight, 916, 1104; of witches, 308; of witches, 554; rescues from, 614; revived, 110, 111, 1232
Hank Shakespeare, 1265
Hannibal, 512
HANNO, the gorilla, 374, 525, 859, 980, 1154-55
Hanoverians, conspiracy of, 887-89, 1100
Hanrahan, Mrs., 289, 647, 1313-15
Hans, 660-61
Hanseatic League, 1234
Hapiypacha, 1143
Happily Ever After, 1075
Happy Day, 182-84
Happy Land, 465
Harald Sigurdson, 1298-1300
Haran, 626, 1204-6
"harb mother": 303, 609. See also doctors; healers.
Hardcastle, Felix, 1194
Hardcastle, Sandy, 335, 354-56, 1057
Hardy, Thomas, 736
hares: 212; March, 20, 22, 23, 753, 767
HARE-WOMAN, 335, 525, 606, 918-19, 1265
HARI, 526, 706, 1303-5
HARMAN, HUMPHREY, 113, 526
Harmonious Mud Stickers, 33, 244, 669, 801, 1133
harness makers, disguise, 806
HARNETT, CYNTHIA (MARY), 526-28, 729, 1402, 1404
Harold Ericson, 1170
HAROLD THOMPSON, 334, 514, 516, 528, 599, 629, 648, 1057, 1315, 1365-66
Harold Was My King, 700
Harper, Major Cass, 177-78
Harper family, 127-28
harpers, 298, 518, 1085-86, 1117
HARP OF TEIRTU, 528-29, 1068, 1357-58
harps: golden, 148, 502, 528, 1375; stolen, 737, 1357
Harpsichord family, 560

Harriet, 860, 1141
Harriet Bartholomew, 533, 917-19
HARRIS, 143-44, 186, *529-30*, 856, 1149-50
HARRIS, MARY K (ATHLEEN), 163, *530*, 1071
HARRIS, ROSEMARY (JEANNE), *530-31*, 829
HARRIS, the rat, *529*, 931-32
Harris family, 143, 855-56, 1149-50
Harrison, Edwin, 25
Harrison, Miss Queenie, 823, 1080
Harrison family (*The Battle of St. George Without*), 77-78
Harrison family (*The Ghost of Thomas Kempe*), 49, 92-93, 451-53, 595-96, 862, 1100
Harrow and Harvest, 763, 1370
Harry, 422
Harry Barker, 602
HARRY BATEMAN, 89, 476-77, *531-32*, 555-57
Harry Jones, 621-23
Hart, Dick, 1316
Harthover family, 363, 1328-30
Harthover Place, 363, 1328
Hartley family, 463-64
Harvest Mice, 246, 437, 914, 931, 952, 1114, 1120-21
harvests: wheat, 390; with scythes, 9
Harwich Harbor, 1340
HASTINGS-BENSON, 97, *532*
Hatch, 112
Hatch, Bennet, 615
Hategood, Lord, 976
HATHAWAY, 45-46, 63, *532*
Hathi, the elephant, 631
hatred: destructiveness of, 1013; nursed, 804; of father, 1127; of machines, 309-11, 886; perpetuated, 1287
hats: magical, 1122; witch's steeple, 909
Hatta, 753, 767, 1210
Hatter family, 168, 567, 568-69, 698, 777, 1122
hatters: 30-31, 568; mad, 20, 22, 23, 753
HATTY MELBOURNE, *532-33*, 1238, 1240-42
The Haunted Valley and Other Poems, 25
THE HAUNTING, *533-34*, 759
The Haunting of Cassie Palmer, 15
The Haunting of Chas McGill and Other Stories, 210, 1347

The Haunting of Ellen: A Story of Suspense, 1066
The Haunting of Hiram C. Hapgood, 577
Haunton, late 20th century, 17, 411, 1389-91
havens, of elves, 407
Haverard family, 535-36, 668, 685-87, 693, 811, 937, 988, 1194, 1306
Haverston Beast, 99, 806, 877-78
Havisham, Miss, 820, 981
Havisham family, 376, 592
Haw Bank, 292, 351, 641
Hawc, 42
The Hawk, 1346
Hawkins family, 338, 604, 965, 1253-56
hawks: 673; blue, 121-24, 382-85; diverted from sacrifice, 1261
Haworth, Bronte home, 793, 1165, 1166, 1274-75
Hawthorne, Dolly, 538
haycorns, 563
HAZEL, the rabbit, 95, 418, 535, 557, 1331-34
Hazell, Victor, 284-85, 853, 1010-12, 1074
head boys, 2, 97-98, 200, 223-25, 224, 367, 404, 486, 875, 960, 1180-82
headdresses, antler, 1036
head girls, 367
headmasters: 131, 224, 286, 352, 487, 591, 843, 850-51, 1180-82, 1269-70. *See also* headmistresses; schoolteachers; teachers; tutors.
headmen, African village, 250
headmistresses: 635-36, 818, 897, 954, 1071-73, 1123, 1322. *See also* headmasters; schoolteachers; teachers; tutors.
heads: standing on, 782; shaved, capped, 1359; sideways, 271
Healer of Sick Pearls, 743
healers: chieftainess of wandering tribe, 625; dedicated, 338; elves, 407; eye, 348-49; fairy cat, 675; girl, 42-43, 581; grandmother, 1394; herbal, 1356-57; in folk medicine, 543; King of Ireland's daughter, 1259-61; monk, 681-82; non-Christian, 11; of horses, 612; of slaves, 937; old British, 673-74; Sikh with medical training, 311; squire, 1112; witch, 1355. *See also* doctors; "harb mother"; pediatricians; physicians; psychologists; psychiatrists.

healings, 93, 714, 978-79, 1001, 1055
hearings, court, 319, 1050, 1058, 1196-99
heart attacks, 813, 890
Hearts, Knave of, 21, 23, 1362
Hearts, King of, 20, 211
Hearts, Queen of, 20-22, 23, 211, 343
hearts: gift of, 168; retrieved for wizard, 567, 569
Heartsease, 309, 315, 1338
heat, as test of strength, 584
Heaven Hounds, 717
Heaven Lies About Us: A Fragment of Infancy, 1131
Hebrides, early 20th century, 588-89, 589, 1048
HECTOR, the dog, *535*, 715, 861
hedgehogs: 540-42, 931, 1186; as croquet balls, 20
Hedges, Mrs., 565, 856
Hedley family, 314, 514-16, 599, 629, 647-48, 838, 1057, 1365
Heffalump, 563, 974, 1388
Heffernan, Matt, 1151, 1153
Heidi, 531
Heimpi, 1348
heiresses: beautiful, haughty, 196, 537; potential, 226; young widow, 421
heirlooms: Circlet of Deirdre, 216; clock, 860; jewels, lost, 291, 841-42, 858, 862, 1058, 1314, 1131-32, 1343; locket, 543; ruby glass goblet, 662-63; signet ring, 294, 296, 681; sword and ring, 1085-86; Victorian sampler, 860, 1141
heirs: Battersea dukedom, 108-9; choice of, 215-16; elected, 408; girl, 419; of hobbit, 436; to chocolate factory, 204, 865; to estate, 289; to iron fortune, 582-83; to industrial fortune, 807, 809; to mansion and factory, 740; to treasure, 550; to tribal leadership, 245
Helen, 359-60
Helen, Queen of Narnia, 167, 688, 756
Helena, 530
HELEN EDGINGTON, *535-36*, 685-86
Helen Harrison, 451, 596
Helen Ponton, 404
Helge, 91-92, 296, 1293
helicopters, Swiss army, 158
Hell, cold, 825
Hell's Edge, 1034
HELL'S EDGE, *536-38*, 1246

helmets: air, 239; German war souvenir, 210; motorcycle, blown up, 307
Help, 975
Helweg, Hans, 1186
hemispheres, 3-legged, called Tripods, 1359
Henchman family, 94, 190-91, 342, 356, 595, 828-29, 880-81, 1236-37
Henderson family, 911, 1155-56
Hendon (boat), 401-3, 1177
Hendreary, Uncle, 132-33, 135, 136, 140-41, 1282
Hendrick Hudson, the molly bird, 1329
Hendry, Mike, 93, 810, 1055, 1376-78
Hendry, Miss Katherine, 579
Hengest's Tale, 940
hen houses, home of gnome, 894
Henniker-Hadden, Maria, 596, 623, 842, 1203, 1316-19
Hen Roost, 246, 1352
HENRY, 168, *538*, 620, 891-92, 991
Henry I, King of England, 674, 1016
Henry IV, King of England, 448, 453, 586
Henry V, King of England, 586
Henry VI, King of England, 1404, 1406
Henry VII, King of England, 683
Henry VIII, King of England, legend from days of, 1181
Henry, Mr., 1262
HENRY BELL (*No End to Yesterday*), 476, *538-39*, 900-2
Henry Bell (*The Summer After the Funeral*), 1166
HENRY BIRKINSHAW, *539*, 922, 1267-68
Henry family, 404-5
Henry Gresham, 489-92
HENRY HOLBEIN, 101, *539*, 1039-41
Henry Hooper, 539-42
HENRY MICKLE, 77-78, 465-66, *539*
Henry Parker, 237-38, 1359-61
HENRY'S LEG, *539-42*, 980
Henry Tudor, pretender, 730
hens: fairy, 271, 713-14; talking red, 913; three, 713-14
HEPZIE FOULGER, 496, *543*, 604, 786
HEPZIBAH GREEN, 14, 177-79, 179, *542-43*, 826
Herald, Kathleen, 966
heralds, rabbit, 1362
herbalists, 600
Herbert, Mrs, 383
Herbert Pocket, 494, 820, 981, 1346

herders, 48, 281, 544-45, 631
A HERD OF DEER, 322, *543-46*
Here, 891
Here Comes Harry, 700
Here Comes Thursday, 126
Here Lies Price: Tall Tales and Ghost Stories, 994
Hereward the Wake, 664
Heritage family, 153-55
Herluin, 673-74
hermits: 91, 216, 238, 408, 561, 1035, 1038; St. Cuthbert, 1376-79. *See also* recluses.
Hern, 39-40
Hernon, Rooster, 1102
Hernon family, 258-61, 544-45
Hero, 988
heroes: admired, 205; based on oral tradition type, 1158; dashing young, 364; disguised as iron-monger, 412; disillusioning, 372; dog, 1399; genuine, 372-73; motorcycle repairmen, 364; of great flood, 1046; of legend, at-tacks dragon, 1030; shepherd, 929; unlikely, 411; youthful, 184
The Heroes, 664
Heroes and Heroines, 393
heroin, 1062-63
heroines, from oral tradition, 298-99, 299-301
heroism, nature of explored, 1389-91
Heron, the heron, 716
The Heron Ride, 1252
hero tales, basis for novel, 298-99, 299-301, 729-30, 1036-39, 1258-61
Hero-Tales from the British Isles, 969
Herrick, Charlie, 1, 2, *204*, 522, 587, 659, 1203
Herringsby, early 19th century, 338, 360, 612, 742, 1224-25
HERR JAKOB VOGEL, 32, 214, *546*
Hertford, 609, 611
Herulf Herulfson, 117
Heseltine, Keith, 292, 351-52, 641
Heslop, Michael, 501
Hester Reeves, 586
the Hetman, 1415-17
Hetty Grey, 163-66
Hetty Ullathorne, 129
Hewitson, Grandad, 476-77, 555-57
Hewlin, the hound, 487, 960

Heywood, Thomas, 1202, 1351, 1353
Hiberu tribe, 624-26
hiccups: frequent, 1114; from pars-nip wine, 376
hidingplaces: abandoned house, 282-83, 1080; apple barrel, 1254; behind Christmas ornament chest, 381; behind fireplace, 1112; blub-ber room, 887; bunker, 887; cave, 260, 506, 1339, 1399; cemetery, 1110; chair, 817; church tow-er, 1167; coffin, 122; collection box, 142; culvert, 327; dovecote, 816; dry well, 372; Earth, of Zoi, 326; for machine gun, 197; friend's empty house, 605; for-est, 695; garden, 899; glass factory, 663; hypocaust, 1090; in derelict mansion, 616; in moun-tains, 766; jewels in mannequin's leg, 542; jewels in wine jar, 1131-32; jewels under roof, 841; letter in shoe, 744; load of wool, 585; Norwegian mountains, 1350; old paper mill, 1270; old Roman sig-nal tower, 350; old theatre, 1090; overhanging bank of lake, 349; playground tower, 521; pool, 1113; pyramids, 1185; room over shed, 963-64; seminary, 1188-89; shack made of old clothes on roof, 1087; stable, 1160; thieves', 541-42; tunnel, 290-91, 1022; tunnel under chapel, 218; under boulder, 1361; un-der floor boards, 466; under hoop skirt, 817; under tree roots, 103; wheatfield, 190; woods, 1383; yacht, 184
High Admiral, 509
High Force, 480
High King, returned, 844
Highlanders, Scottish, 12-13, 650-51
Highmost Redmanhey farm, 1342
High Sang the Sword, 910
High Topps, 972
highwaymen, swashbuckling, 738, 818, 1108
hijackings: of oil rig, planned, 35; truck, 183
Hi-Jinks Joins the Bears, 66
Hilary Toft, 897-99
Hilda Woodward, 536-37
HILDICK, E(DMUND) W(ALLACE), 184, *546-47*
The Hill of the Red Fox, 796

The Hill of Vision, 1138
hills, fairy, 713-14
Hills End, 1129
The Hills of Varna, 1253
Hindus, 651, 1305
hippies, 17, 798
hired men, 2, 779, 1021-23, 1401-2.
   See also handyboys; handymen.
Hiroshima, 158
Hispaniola (ship), 89, 338, 732,
   1132, 1254-56
historians, 130, 236, 685, 841
historical figures, actual: Aedgar
   Aetheling, 768; Aethelbert, King
   of Kent, 295-96, 358; Alexander
   the Great, 512; Alfred the Great,
   16, 18, 517, 870-72; Alice,
   Countess of Suffolk, 275-76;
   Almedingen, Catherine A., 717;
   Anna, Princess of Constantinople,
   117; Anne, Queen of England, 1353;
   Athelred, King of Wessex, 870-
   71; Augustine, Saint, 297; Basil
   II, Emperor of Constantinople,
   117; Bolingbroke, Roger, 125-26;
   Boudicca, 1117-19; British-Roman
   period, various, 271; Bubb, James,
   595; Byrne, Billy, 101, 499-501,
   879;
   Caesar, 512; Caewlin, 295, 358;
   Campbell, Colin Roy, the Red Fox,
   650-51; Canadian, various peri-
   ods, 733; Carausius, 270-71;
   Cartier, Jacques, 733; Caxton,
   William, 195-96, 729-30, 1405;
   Charles of Orleans, 586; Charles
   II, King of England, 456; Chilean,
   various 20th century, 1187-
   89; Coel, King of Wessex, 358;
   Constantine, Emperor, 370-73,
   633; Constantius, 271; Cormac,
   Red King of Connacht, 215-17;
   de Courville, Cadieux, 733;
   Diaz, Porfirio, 313, 601-2, 753;
   d'Orleans, Duc, 1405; Douglas,
   George, 677-78; Douglas, Will,
   677-78; Douglas, Sir William, 677-
   78; Douglas family of Scotland,
   1412-15;
   Dundee, General, 500; Earl of
   Suffolk, 350-51, 454, 1024;
   Edmund, King of Saxons, 375, 870;
   Edward II, King of England, 916,
   1018; 18th century highland-
   er Scots, various, 650-51; 18th
   century Irish, various, 879;
   18th century theatre, 169-71;
   Eleanor, Duchess of Suffolk,
   1024; Elizabeth, Empress of
   Russia, various 17th century figures associated with, 1415-17;
   Ethelred, King of Saxons, 16, 18,
   376; Ethelwulf, King of Wessex,
   18; Fell, Margaret, 1200; fifth
   century Saxon and Roman leaders, various, 679-83; fifteenth
   century, Constantinople, 370-
   73; fifteenth century, England,
   various, 125-26, 324-25, 350-51,
   1404-7; first century, British,
   1117-19; first century Romans,
   1117-19; fourteenth century English court, 447-49; French
   Revolution, various, 1215-18;
   Garrick, David, 169; Gloucester,
   Duke of, late 14th century, 448;
   Guthorm, 517; Guy of Lusignan,
   King of Outremer, 670; Halfdan,
   871; Hallward, 733; Hannibal,
   512; Henry I, King of England,
   1016; Henry IV, King of England,
   448, 453, 586; Henry V, King of
   England, 586; Henry VI, King of
   England, 1404, 1406; the Hetman,
   1415-17; Heywood, Thomas, 1202;
   Hobekinus, 308, 554; Hopkins,
   Matthew, 554; Hubba, 517; Hume
   family of Redbraes, 456-58; Ibn-
   Menquidh, Usamah, 671, 1291;
   Irish rebellion, various, 499-
   501; Isabella of France, child
   queen of England, 447-49, 454,
   586, 585-86; Isabella, Queen
   of England, 1018; James, King
   of England, 1353; John, King of
   England, 215-17; John Sobieski,
   King of Poland, 214; Johnson, Dr.
   Samuel, 171; Justiniani Longo,
   372, 633; Kemble, Frances, 170;
   Khan Vladimir of Kiev, 117;
   Leming, Reis, 1046; Leopold of
   Austria, 214; Macdonnell, Alan,
   733; Madero, Francisco, 601, 752-
   53; Malcolm, King of Scots, 273,
   760, 768, 1012-13; Margaret, Queen
   of Scotland, 760, 768-69, 1012-13;
   Marlowe, Christopher, 876, 1202;
   Mary, Queen of England, 457; Mary,
   Queen of Scots, 677-78, 1412-
   15; Mehmed IV, Sultan of Turkey,
   213-15; Moorhouse, Tom, 1238-39;
   Mr. Drouet, 53-54; Mrs. Siddons,
   169-70; Mustafa, Kara, 213-15;
   Nicholas II, Czar of Russia, 28;
   19th century British colonial,
   various minor, 1070; 19th century

English, various, 190-91; 19th and early 20th century Russian, various, 1207-8; Olga, Grand Duchess of Russia, 24, 28; Poltoratzky, Mark, 1415-17; Pompey, 512; Rahere, 1015-16; Raleigh, Sir Walter, 154; Rasputin, 1207; Richard I, King of England, 671, 729, 968, 1034; Richard II, King of England, 447-48, 453-54, 585, 586, 600; Richard III, King of England, 103-4, 1034; Richard of Gloucester, 317, 606; Rowena, daughter of Hengest, 681; Russian Royal Family, 1207-8; Saladin, 670-71; Selkirk, Alexander, 1046 17th century European and Turkish, 213-15; Shakespeare, William, 1352-53; Sheridan, Richard, 169-70; Shirras, 733; Sir Jocelin de Courcy Rohan, 216-17; 16th century Scottish, various, 677-78; 16th century associated with Mary, Queen of Scots, 1412-15; Starhemberg, Count of Austria, 214; Tate, Robert, 195; 12th century English and French, various, 672-75; 12th century, Middle Eastern 670-71; Villa, Pancho, 601-2; Wesley, John, 464; Ysabeau, Queen of France, 448, 586; Zapata, Emiliano, 601

historical novels: Bronze Age, Britain, 1319-22; ancient times, Ur, 624-27, 1204-6; 1st century, B.C., England, 1171-73; 1st century, B.C., Britain and Rome, 1244-45; 1st century, B.C., Scotland, 1161-64; 1st century, A.D., Roman Britain, 771-74, 1117-19; 2nd century, A.D., 347-50; 3rd century A.D., England, 1088-91; 5th century, A.D., Britain, 679-83; 6th century, Byzantium, 279-81; 6th century, southern England, 293-97; 8th century, Norway, 1298-1300; 8th century, North Sea, 1298-1300; 9th century, England, 870-72; 9th century, Ireland and Denmark, 91-92; 10th century, England and Constantinople, 116-19; 11th century England, 672-75, 1085-87; 11th century, Northumbria and Scotland, 1012-13; 12th century, Jerusalem, 670-72; 12th century, 1394-96;

12th century, Warwickshire, 738-40; 13th century, Ireland, 215-17; 14th century, England, 145-47; 14th century, 915-17; 14th century, England and France, 447-49; 14th century, England and Scotland, 1017-20; 15th century, Constantinople, 370-73; 15th century, England, 102-5; 15th, England, 683-84; 15th century, England, Cotswolds, 1402-3; 15th century, English village, 1404-7; 15th century, London and Warwickshire, 729-30; 16th century, Scotland, 1412-15; 17th century, England, 938-39, 1199-202; 17th century, London and countryside, 1351-53; Europe and Turkey, 213-15; 17th century, Scotland and Netherlands, 456-58; 17th century, Scotland and Yorkshire, 636-38; 17th century, Vienna, 213-15; 18th century, England, 169-71; 18th century, France, 1215-18; 18th century, Haiti, 765-67; 18th century, Ireland, 499-501; 18th century, Paris, 765-67; 18th century, Scotland, 648-51; 18th century, Yorkshire, 463-64; 19th century, England, 52-54;

19th century, English seacoast village, 1223-25; 19th century, English coal town, 1276-78; 19th century, Devonshire coast, 926-27; 19th century, England, Durham County, 129-31; 19th century, England, Africa, and high seas, 1068-71; 19th century, London, 1223-25; 19th century, Russia, 717-20; 19th century, Russia, 1206-8; 20th century, England, 354-56, 495-98; 20th century, Mexico, 601-2; 20th century, Russia, 1206-8; 20th century, England, 1213-15; 20th century, China and Tibet, 1265-67; 20th century, Ireland, 1284-87; 20th century, Norway, 1349-51; Elizabethan England, 153-55, 581-83; various periods, 732-34; World War I, England, Essex, 421-24; World War I, England, 1213-15; World War II, England, 377-79, 414-16; World War II, Garmouth, 747-50; World War II, 924-26; World War II, pre, Germany, Switzerland, France,

1096-99, 1348-49; World War II,
Norway, 1349-51; fantasy aspects,
732-34; pretense of, England,
19th century, 107-9; 1399-1401;
pretense of, 19th century high
seas and Nantucket, 887-89;
single incident, 926-27. *See also*
biographical novels; period novels.
history: Canadian, 732-34; considered rubbish, 397; English,
dry, 836; forgotten, 311-12, 1359-
61
The History of the Young Men, 241,
1275
Hitler, 31, 1348
hoarders: food, supplies, threatened with prosecution, 73, 242,
400, 843-44, 895-97; laws against,
896
hoaxes: attempted, 368-69, 411; fake
poltergeist, 1052, 1064. *See also*
mischief; pranks; scams; schemes;
tricks.
H. O. BASTABLE, *547,* 1146-47
HOBBERDY DICK, 450, *547-48,* 548-50,
778
HOBBERDY DICK, 151, *548-50*
hobbies: miniature ships, 5; model village, 837
THE HOBBIT, 405, 408, 436-37, *550-
53,* 1230
HOBBITS, 95-96, 131-2, 405-8, 436-
37, 464-65, 551-53, *553-54,* 805,
981-82, 1056, 1107, 1158, 1231
Hobbs, Alan, 13, 799
Hobbs family, 451
HOBEKINUS, 308, 554
hobgoblins: guard manor, 450,
547-48, 548-50, 778, 864; Sikhs
mistaken for, 311
hoboy, 837
"Hockey School," 1322
Hodge, the cat, 889-90
HODGES, C(YRIL) WALTER, 153, 223,
347, *554-55,* 724, 870, 926, 1017,
1085, 1096-97, 1111, 1180
Hogarth, 584
Hoggart family, 599, 956, 1396-97
Hogget, Farmer, 1082-83
Hogget family, 1082-83
Hogrogian, Nonny, 301
hogs, wild, in sewers, 808
Holbein family, 4, 101, 285-86, 478,
539, 968, 1039-41
Holder, David, *289-90,* 1313
Holder, John, 1244
Holder family, 1199-201

Hold on to Love, 573
holes: bottomless, 874; Bear gets
stuck in Rabbit's, 1388
*Holiday at the Dew Drop Inn: A One End
Street Story,* 445
holidays: Christmas, 186-88, 963-
65; Easter, 1039; in Scotland,
368; in Ukraine, 719; motorcycle,
614; mountain climbing, 243-44; on
farm, 523-24; prescribed by doctor, 704; seaside, 469; school, in
country, 898; Shropshire Hills,
903; spring, 898; summer, 119-21,
193-94, 328, 523-24, 577-78, 968-
69, 980, 1035, 1040, 1141, 1154,
1168, 1169-71, 1240, 1313, 1318-
19, 1376-79; too poor for, 1147;
Yarmouth, 901; Yule, 1156
Hollis, Ruth, 75
Hollis family, 85-87, 846, 960,
1003-4, 1053, 1190-92
Hollins family, 918-19
THE HOLLOW LAND, 440, *555-57*
Holly, Chris, 636
HOLLY, the rabbit, *557,* 1332
Holly Hotel, 675
Holly Howe, 1178
Holmes, Sherlock, 182
Holm Ganging, 117
holovision, 506
Holt, Fred, 540, 542
Holt, Ivy, 1323
Holt family, 489-92
Holy Island, 158
HOLY JOHN, 279-81, *557-58*
Holy Land, 968, 1034
Holy Places, of Epidaii tribe, 349
Holystone, Mr., *844*
Holy Terror, nanny, 782
Holy War, 213-15
holy water, three drops, 660-61
Home from Home, 994
Home Guard, World War II, 750
HOME IS THE SAILOR, 458, *558-59*
Homer Goes West, 66
Homer the Tortoise, 66
homes: ancestral, retained, 291;
behind shop, 176; blown down,
563; choice of, with father, 33;
collapsed, 415-16; community,
proposed, 525; destroyed in air
raid, 378; dilapidated, 539;
disintegrating, 833, 835; entrance under clock, 132; for doll,
in bicycle basket, 381-82; group,
249; in abandoned church, 17; in
attic of abandoned cottage, 515;
in aviary, 141, 947; in badger's

set, 133, 135; in bombed cellar, 1097; in bombed-out house, 415-16; in boot, 135, 811; in castle, 208; in coal cellar, 1062; in condemned building, 465-66; in conservatory stove, 141; in cottage wall, 135, 136; in deserted farm, 310-14; in fowlhouse, 894; in giant peach, 593-94; in grimy attic, 807; in half-ruined mill, 1187-88; in hangar, 354; in hollow tree, 1097; in hut in woods, 454; in ice-house, 677, 808; in model village, 138-39; in past, 532; in riverbank, 1382-84; in tea kettle, 137; in windowseat, 141, 947; lost, 437; moves to new, 629, 903, 1290; now for a shed, 398; offered to orphan, 294; on canal boat, 198; rediscovered, 1021; returning to African, 840; taken by Germans for headquarters, 1339; turned into fortress, 400; underground, 957-58, 1331, 1347; washed away, 137. *See also* houses; mansions.

homesickness, 1304-5, 1384
HOMILY CLOCK, 49, 61, 132-33, 135, 136-37, 138-39, 140-41, 147, 489, *559-60*, 854, 856, 857, 948, 985, 1130, 1236, 1282
homosexuality, acknowledged, 1363-64
honey: bait for Heffalump, 1388; bear likes, 989; empty jar as birthday present, 1388-89; sought, 1388
Honeycomb, 1331
honor, redeemed, 350
Hooded One, 504, 1343
hoodlums: attacks by, 515; dressed in armor, 312; Maltese, 58; terrorists, 50; young, 45, 609, 610-11, 612, 613, 425, 446, 863, 950, 1115-17, 1249. *See also* Teddy boys; thugs; vandals.
hookahs, 20, 192
hooks, for missing hand, 172, 957
Hooper family, 539-42
Hope family, 900
Hopewell (ship), 511
Hopkins, Matthew, 554
Hoplike (ship), 1326
Horace Octavius Bastable, 547
HORATIO BERESFORD, *560*, 769, 1221-23
Horned Helmet, 1257
horns: hunting, 487, 960; magic ivory, 711, 995; of help, 893; Robin Hood's, 146-47, 717

The Horrible Story and Others, 760
horror novels, 286-87, 311-12, 373-75, 610-11, 645-46, 714-16, 824-26, 889-91, 906-7, 917-19, 1058-60, 1076-78, 1187-89
Horse, 441
THE HORSE AND HIS BOY, *560-62*, 699
The Horsehair Stopper, 1372
Horse in the Clouds, 504
horses: abused, 18, 106, 612; arrogant, 150; at Cloud Farm, 389-92; breeders of, 762, 1171-73; cab, 171, 455, 602, 756; canal boat, 560; carved into mountainside, 1172-73; chestnut, 409, 454, 1367-68; coach, 55-56; condemned to be dog food, 419-20; dapple gray, 513; dealers in, 757, 772, 846, 1004; dealers in, Afghan, 651-52, 654; difficult to control, 1191; dray, 422; erratic, 423; farms, Sussex, 683, 701; first among Blackfeet, 733; flying, 688, 756, 928, 1035; fox hunting, 354; gambling on, 1365; gypsy, 318, 320; harness, with Christian symbols, 870-71; huge, 1272, 642-43; like humans, 513; little white, 724, 726; love of, 1229; marvelous, 1230; moon, 1173; Narnian, 150; of traveling actors, 153; painted green, 990; peppermint stick ridden, 785; performing circus, 235; pet of blind boy, 1367-68; protects boy, 1367; pure white steeds, 167; race, 1366-68; renowned stud line, 972; riders, boy, 962; riders, children, adept, 793; riders, deaf and dumb, 720-21; riders, expert, 226; riding, 383-85, 419-21, 422-23, 960-61, 963-64, 1053, 1190-92; riding and carriage, 105-7; riding of, boy hates, 1374; rocking, 212; runaway, 1382; running, 1172-73; sacred, 1293; saved from slaughter, 317, 318; servants ride, 4; shot, 1367; spirit of, 212-13; stolen, 1005, 1383; sun, 1173; switched, 1191; talking, 43, 150, 561-62, 575, 596, 1081; temperamental, 1367; thieves, 409; thoroughbred bay, 1366-67; trainers of, 822; turned wild, 1367; unmanageable, 846; very intelligent, 1234; war, 150, 171; white, 295-96, 1293; wild, 390;

winged, 167; with foal, 1366.
horse stories: 105-7, 389-92, 419-21, 421-24, 560-62, 724-27, 1171-73, 1190-92, 1339-40, 1366-68. *See also* animal novels; cat stories; dog stories.
Hoseason, Captain, 13, 649
The Hospital, 993
hospitality: Badger's, 1384; refused, 1357
Hospitallers, 670-71
hospitals, founding of, for poor, 1015-16, 1394-94
hospital scenes: 42, 56, 201, 329, 378-79, 416, 430-31, 468, 537, 565, 807, 1295, 1304-5, 1370; South Africa, 628
hostages: boy of pirates, 1255; children, 1103; children's opera cast by terrorists, 11, 29, 219-20, 283, 330, 525, 855, 857, 1077-78; by murderer, 243; of Danes, 871; of Saxons, 358; ship's captain of queen, 1142; village children, 10, 311-12; youths of ship's captain, 237
hostels, Irish, burned, 300
HOTEL CONTINENTAL, London, *562*, 925
Hotel Magnificent, 1392
hotels: girl's mother works at, 37; hydropathic, 1166; in Kingston, 354; owners, 30
Hotel Splendide, 923, 1033
Hot News, 25
Hotspur, 171
Hotspur Treet, 304
Hounds, of king, 1320
hounds: 960; of Carausius, 271; vile, of Morrigan, 1344
THE HOUSE AT POOH CORNER, *562-64*, 812, 1389
houseboats, 171, 1179
houseguests, source of dissension in family, 896
Household Word, 89, 566
housing projects, 465-66, 517, 689-92, 689-91, 753, 792, 1364-66
THE HOUSE IN NORHAM GARDENS, *564-66*, 727
A House in Town, 795
housekeepers: abused, 592; bad tempered, 1282; crotchety Welsh, 873; daily, 81; demanding, 763; disabled, 1105; dreamy, nostalgic, 856; faithful, 1224; fired, 81; fond of stuffed Bear, 84; former, 923; German, 1348; gossip, 921; healer, with second sight,

542-43; imperious, 872; king's practical, very old nurse, 902, 1094; lazy, 367, 1168; leaving in a huff, 431; loyal, 858-59; mother, 127-28, 933-34; of attorney, 376; of enchanter, 208; overworked, 419, 421; practical and kind, 856; protective, 1317; silvery old woman, 725; sharp-eyed, 854; slovenly, 81, 142, 1146; suspicious, 133-34, 137, 148; troublemaking, 81, "very, very, very old," 872; Welsh mother, 245, 518, 768, 933-34. *See also* cooks; housemaids; maids; servants.
housemaids: 364, 581, 920-22, 1196-99. *See also* cooks; housekeepers; maids; servants.
House Next Door, 87, 722-24
The House of Cards, 442
The House of Hanover: England in the Eighteenth Century, 441
House of Laughter, 1189
The House of the Pelican, 675
The House of the Sleeping Winds and Other Stories, Some Based on Cornish Folklore, 1258
THE HOUSE ON MAYFERRY STREET, 344, 427, 566. *See A FLUTE IN MAYFERRY STREET*, *427-28*.
houses: ancestral medieval, 859; "ancient," of Bastable, 547, 1146; apartment, 532-33; big old countryside, 933; big old Victorian, 895; blinds drawn, 923; blown down, 974; boarding, 1401; bombed, 619; built by Pooh and Piglet, 563; burned by girl, 1351; burned, rebuilt, 178-79; company-owned, 1276-78; dark, mysterious, 824; decorated for queen's jubilee, 1159-60; demolished, 197; deserted manor, 455-56; doll, 558; for sale, 70; fortress-like, 895; Georgian country house, 132, 147, 854; girl stuck in, 1362; inherited, 26, 1376; marvelous big old, 373-75, 339, 710; old country, 710-712; old haunted, 947; old Welsh countryside, 873; old with hobgoblin, 450; owner mistaken, 358; rambling, 427-28; rent free, 622; tree, 390; underground, 1226; Victorian, 564-65, 1141. *See also* homes; mansions.
The Houses in Between: A Novel, 1131
house trailers. *See* caravans.
Houyhnhnms, 513-14

Howard, James, 105, 596
HOWARD SYKES, 43-47, 63, 470, 532, *566*, 1013-14, 1087
Howell Jenkins, 567
"How Fear Came," 631
HOWKER, JANNI, *566-67*, 876
HOWL, 168, *567*, 568-69, 698, 777, 1122
HOWL'S MOVING CASTLE, *567-69*, 617
How the Whale Became and Other Stories, 570
hrududu, 1333
Hsu, 1035
Hubba, 517
HUGH (*The Blue Boat*), 119-21, 230, *570*
Hugh (*A Castle of Bone*), 188-90
Hugh (*Ransom for a Knight*), 1017-20
Hugh Copplestone, 153-55
Hughes, Arthur, 55, 701, 1002
Hughes, Captain, 1141-43
Hughes, David, 290
Hughes, Owen, 42
Hughes, Shirley, 1396
HUGHES, TED (EDWARD JAMES HUGHES), 570-71, 583
Hughes family (*The Grange at High Force*), 480-81
Hughes family (*The Whispering Mountain*), 156, 528, 1356-58
Hugh Goch, 672-73
Hugh the Red, 672-73
Hugo, Charles, 809-10
HULL, KATHARINE, 389, *571-72*, 1362
human beans, exist for Borrowers, 133
humankind, destruction for wickedness planned, 829
humanoids: beasts of burden, 513; extraterrestrials, 1359
humbug, Christmas called, 227, 353
Hume family, 456-58
humor: adult, 799; character, 1313-15; coarse, 1392-94; comic, 19-22, 221-23, 388-89, 593-95, 930, 970-71, 996-99; comic relief, 71, 755-57; comic satire, 203-4; domestic adventures, 920-22, 1269-70; droll, 970-71; exaggeration, 43-47, 203-4, 221-23, 283-85, 807-9, 1399-1401; family, 405; farcical, 41-42, 797-99; gentle, 839-41, 1211-13; Gothic, 1399-1401; grim, 306; insult, 19-22, 252-54; intellectual, 19-22; ironic, 252-54, 306, 453, 533-34, 707, 749, 849, 1030, 1083-84, 1128, 1270, 1313-15; malapropisms, 160;

melodramatic, 887-89, 1399-1401; point of view, 1270; rollicking, 1125-28; satiric, 19-22, 508-14, 1208-11, 1313-15; schoolboy, 669; situation, 252-54, 1146-48, 1186-87, 1313-15, 1388-89; slapstick, 342-43, 389, 849, 922, 1186-87, 1392-94; subtle, 523-25, 734-37; tall tale, 389; tongue-in-cheek, 109, 143-44; various kinds, 19-22, 829-30, 1208-11; whimsical, 710-13 (others in series), 932, 1082-84, 1382-85; wordplay, 19-22, 849, 1186-87, 1208-11, 1388-89
humorous novels: fantasy, 19-22, 41-42, 43-46, 84-85, 127-29, 203-4, 208-9, 221-23, 252-54, 365-66, 388-89, 395-97, 416-18, 451-53, 562-64, 568-70, 593-95, 701-3, 716-18, 779-81, 781-83, 783-84, 784-86, 815-16, 829-30, 887-89, 893-94, 927-30, 956-58, 970-71, 996-99, 1029-32, 1082-84, 1094-96, 1119-21, 1142-43, 1145-46, 1186-87, 1208-11, 1232-34, 1309-11, 1353-56, 1388-89, 1392-94; realistic, 96-99, 107-9, 143-44, 283-85, 385-86, 489-92, 539-42, 734-37, 797-99, 911-12, 920-22, 1146-48, 1149-51, 1267-68, 1269-70, 1316-19, 1399-1401
humpbacks, 582, 1033, 1034, 1394-96
Humphrey, Duke of Gloucester, 350, 1405
Humphreys, Graham, 578
HUMPTY DUMPTY, *572*, 1210, 1361
hums, by Pooh, 974, 989
Hundred Acre Wood, 562, 1388
Hunger-Strike: A Play in Two Acts, 265
Huns, Kurtrigur, 47-48, 279-81, 557, 1099
Hunsdon House, 412-13, 485, 987, 1065, 1238
Hunt Ball, 227
HUNTER, MOLLIE (MAUREEN MOLLIE HUNTER MCVEIGH MCILWRAITH), *572-74*, 642, 1123, 1155, 1161, 1196, 1412
Hunter family (*Castaway Christmas*), 187-88, 981
Hunter family (*Dan Alone*), 279
Hunter family (*The Girl in the Grove*), 92, 455-56, 618, 694, 946-47
Hunterly family, 38, 150-51, 389-92, 433, 600, 960

hunters: big game, 1155; Borrower boy, 1130; boy of mysterious
beast, 877-78; one-handed, 1319-
20; villain, 716
hunting, organizations against, 806
*The Hunting of the Snark: An Agony in
Eight Fits*, 181
hunts: fairies, 714; for Woozle,
1388; fox, 388-89, 404, 419-21,
432, 506, 963-65; 1374; man, 305-
6; Wild, 1042
HURLY BURLY, *574*, 1352-53
HURREE BABU, *574*, 653-54
Hurree Chunder Mookerjee, 574
hurricanes, 786
Husband for Victoria, 1369
husbands: domineering, 728;
doting, 114-15; five dead, 752,
1105, 1354; henpecked, 1282;
irresponsible, 775; wronged but
compassionate, 268
huts: built by children, 390; disappears into pool, 1405-6; of
bamboo, 1154; of Saint Cuthbert,
1378; of ship's timbers, 204; of
wise woman, 246. *See also* cottages.
Hutton, Clarke, 234
HUW HALFBACON, 518, *574-75*, 873,
933-34
HWIN, the horse, 43, 150, 561, 575
hypnotism, 635, 637, 641, 743, 942,
1326-27
hypocausts, 294, 1090
hypochondriacs, 556
hypocrisy, 53-54, 59, 61, 538, 970-
71
Hyzenthlay, 1332

I Am Mary Tudor, 700
Ianto, Brother, 155, 1357-58
Ibald, Isa, 1322
IBBOTSON, EVA, *577*, 1353
Ibbotson, Gideon, 637
Ibn-Menquidh, Usamah, *1291*
I Can't Stand Losing, 644
ice: falling through, 6; skating,
449, 1238, 1241, 1267
Ice Age, 367, 369-70
ice-giant, 1344
icehouse, home in, 808
The Ice Is Coming, 1404
Iceni, 261, 1117-19, 1171-73
The Ice-Palace, 1183
icons, 667
IDA BIGGIN, 339, *577-78*, 980, 1035-
36, 1154

Iddlingley, 1180
ideas, planted in sleeping minds,
548-50
idealists, bookseller, imprisoned
for beliefs, 849
identity: clues to, 581-83; discovered, 46, 109, 209, 460,
466-67, 507, 534, 562, 579, 611,
739, 844, 1081, 1099, 1100, 1112,
1121-22, 1127-28, 1143, 1222-23;
exchanged, 777; exchanged, twins,
384; mistaken, boy for dead son,
841, 872; pondered, 19-22, 192-93;
problem with, 1208-11; revealed
by feet, 938; revealed by miniature, 341; revealed by silver
sword paper knife, 1099; revealed
by transparency, 825; revealed by
yellow horse bandage, 1006; revealed, of Great Selkie by grandfather, 911; shared, 207, 944-45;
sought, 581-83; tests of, 20, 22-
23; contrasted, 1332
Ignorance, 228
I Go by Sea, I Go by Land, 1250
The Iliad, 969
illegitimate children: boys, 197,
264, 317, 422, 456, 484, 579, 582-
83, 677, 682, 1228, 1412; girls,
47, 433, 581, 1135
I'll Go My Own Way, 573
Illi Silli the Image Maker,
1205
illiterates: boys, 817, 818, 821,
1107, 1108-9, 1277-78; community,
586-87, 1203; girls, 1397, 1406;
man, leader, 1373; old man, 833,
834-35
illnesses: acrophobia, 1047; affec-
ting school, 98-99; aftermath
of near drowning, 461; allergies, 452; amnesia, 449, 918,
1065; among African monkeys, 210;
apparently psychosomatic, 1313;
arthritis, 285, 483, 543, 845;
bedridden after hunting accident,
489; bronchitis, 163, 602; broken
back, 205; broken bones, concussion, 1270; cancer, assumed, 413,
988; caused by heavy atmosphere,
238; caused by wound, 304, 653-54;
chicken pox, 491;
chill, 559; cholera, 52, 54, 59,
692; cold, 34-36; collapse from
hunger and exposure, 294; concussion, 1191; conjunctivitis, 636;
cough, 425; Curse of the Skloodzi,
239; diabetes, 604; diphtheria,

342, 901; dyslexia, 647, 1314-15; epileptic seizures, 557; eye infection, 596; failing eyesight, 155; fever, 123, 458, 627, 654, 1016, 1230, 1300, 1328, 1360; fits, 1025; flu, 98, 207, 236, 365, 1072, 1322, 1348; from cold and undernourishment, 170; from drinking libation, 492; from exposure, 198; gangrene in leg, 764; gout, 144; headache, 1228, 1341; heart attack, 241, 277, 456, 649, 833, 951-52, 1399; heart condition, 478, 662, 834-35; hepatitis, 502; horse, pneumonia, 106; imaginary, 566; indigestion, 724, 726; invalid after intruder's attack, 493; keeping boy from school, 519; kills African animals, 1145; lung fever, 119; lung injury, 317; making boy withdrawn, 73-74; malaria, 338, 1044; malaria, pretended, 349; malnutrition, 353, 852, 1401; measles, 59, 98, 491, 518, 1237, 1240, 1279; measles, sheep gets, 1354; mental, 88, 604, 970; mental, war-induced, 210; mental and physical, 637; miner's coughing sickness, 627; monk's, 1395;

mysterious, 18, 114, 1142; mysterious dog, 1387; of abandoned child, 415-16; of debtor, 494; of father, 478; of old teacher, 259; overbleeding as treatment, 147; overwork, 923, 1401; palsy, 1080; plague, 71, 193, 212, 581, 760, 938-39, 940, 1019, 1199, 1201-202, 1203; plague, suspected, 448; pleurisy, 38, 1170; pneumonia, 318-19, 485, 543, 604, 775, 876, 1019, 1118; polio, 15, 662, 722, 947; poodle, 235; pretense, 650, 1383; prison fever, 1353; probably poisoning, 579; psychological, 60, 960, 955; psychosomatic, 703-4; radiation sickness, 156-58; rheumatic fever, 130, 132, 147; rheumatism, 7; rheumatism, supposed, 888; scarlet fever, 596, 954;

seasickness, 366, 1341; seizure, 430, 1203; sick at school, 647; smallpox, 581, 917, 1199-200, 1202; smoke inhalation, 423; strange, 1093; stress and torture, 1086; stroke, 100, 619, 926, 937, 1248, 1254; stroke or heart attack, 1235; sudden, 834, 1191; sunstroke, 788; swamp opthalmia, 349; toothache, 313; tuberculosis, 38, 193, 263, 353, 719, 735, 1098, 1213; tuberculosis, feared, 1170;

undernourishment and exposure, 294; unspecified, 56-57, 341-42, 538; various, 1357; vomiting, 473, 521, 624. *See also* injuries.
Illustrated London News, 139
illustrators: Adams, Adrienne, 381; Adamson, George, 583; Allen, James, 999; Altendorf, George, 1271; Ambler, C. Gifford, 1398; Ambrus, Victor, G., 190, 290, 354, 418, 421, 717, 763, 897, 982, 1204, 1213, 1223, 1258, 1349, 1366, 1379, 1415; Ardizzone, Edward, 812, 893; Baker, Alan, 75; Ballantyne, R. M., 255; Barker, Carol, 667; Baumer, Lewis, 1146; Baynes, Pauline, 140, 395, 560, 687, 710, 755, 994, 1091, 1306; Bedford, F. D., 956; Bennett, Jill, 283; Bentley, Nicholas, 1385; Blake, Quentin, 41-42, 1392; Bodecker, N. M., 1114; Boland, Michael, 145; Boston, Peter, 211, 217, 373, 1035, 1154; Bozzo, Frank, 1356; Brook, Judith, 1031; Browne, Gordon, 1146; Bryson, Bernarda, 1274;

Burkert, Nancy Ekholm, 593; Carroll, Lewis, 22; Carter, Helene, 1177; Cellini, Joseph, 642; Chaffin, Donald, 388; Clifford, Rowan, 539; Cober, Alan E., 287, 824; Conner, Chris, 206; Dinan, Carolyn, 1269; Donahue, Vic, 258; Drummond, V. H., 173; Einzig, Susan, 1240; Felts, Shirley, 1171, 1036-37; Floethe, Richard, 1111; Floyd, Gareth, 683, 891, 1290-91, 1404; Foreman, Michael, 9, 484, 1143, 1234; Fortnum, Peggy, 84, 169; Garnett, Eve, 385; Gervis, Ruth, 68; Glegg, Creina, 318; Gordon, Margaret, 365; Grant, Elizabeth, 1339; Green, Eileen, 163; Hague, Michael, 22; Hall, Douglas, 79, 1049;

Harnett, Cynthia, 729, 1402; Hart, Dick, 1316; Helweg, Hans, 1186; Heslop, Michael, 501; Hodges, C. Walter, 153, 223, 347, 724,

870, 926, 1017, 1085, 1096-97,
1180, 1111; Hogrogian, Nonny,
301; Holder, John, 1244; Hughes,
Arthur, 55, 701, 1002; Hughes,
Shirley, 1396; Humphreys, Graham,
578; Hutton, Clarke, 234; Ionicus,
1232; Jacques, Robin, 495; Jaques,
Faith, 176, 703; Kallin, Tasha,
384; Keeping, Charles, 116,
246, 293, 335-36, 642, 656, 672,
679, 689, 738, 771, 1088, 1319;
Kennedy, Richard, 186, 543, 1101;
Kerr, Judith, 1348;
Kettlewell, Doritie, 30; Kipling,
J. Lockwood, 630, 651; Krush,
Beth, 132, 134, 136, 138, 140;
Krush, Joe, 132, 134, 136, 138,
140; Lamb, Lynton, 486; Large,
Annabel, 1353; Lathrop, Dorothy,
839; Laurence, John, 387; Lawson,
Robert, 161, 975, 980, 996;
Leech, John, 227; Leslie, Cecil,
1274; Leczczynski, M., 1064;
Levenson, S., 732; Lobel, Anita,
387; Lofting, Hugh, 1145, 1309;
Macarthur-Onslow, Annette, 215,
903; Maitland, Antony, 111, 304,
328, 339, 451, 1108; Marriott,
Pat, 1399; Mars, W. T., 480, 970;
Micklewright, Robert, 1158, 1169,
1394;
Millar, H. R., 416; Moore,
Mary, 847; Nadler, Robert, 583;
Northway, Jennifer, 248; Parkins,
David, 286; Peyton, K. M., 85, 943,
949, 1190; Pogany, Willy, 514;
Price, Christine, 1298; Primrose,
Jean, 558, 722, 818; Rackham,
Arthur, 22, 514; Ransome, Arthur,
972, 1340; Rawlins, Janet, 555;
Rayner, Mary, 1082; Russell, Jim,
1211; Relf, Douglas, 456; Robbins,
Ian, 1284; Robertson, Graham,
1382; Robinson, Charles, 588;
Rocker, Fermin, 473, 1262; Russon,
Mary, 77, 465; Saintsbury, Joseph,
330; Sale, Morton, 732;
Schindelman, Joseph, 203; Sewell,
Helen, 913; Shepard, Ernest H.,
562, 1029, 1031, 1094, 1388;
Shepard, Mary, 779, 781, 783, 784;
Sims, Agnes, 784; Smee, David,
121, 279; Smith, Alvin, 765;
Spanfeller, James J., 365, 1167;
Spence, Geraldine, 119; Spurrier,
Steven, 1267; Stanley, Diana, 132,
134, 136, 138; Stobbs, William,
91, 670, 1012; Stubley, Trevor,

911; Tenniel, Sir John, 19, 22-23,
1208; Torrey, Helen, 1386; Tudor,
Tasha, 22; Turska,
Krystyna, 1409; Unwin, Nora S.,
332; Ursell, Martin, 1119; Vaughn,
Ann, 1351; Vaughan-Jackson,
Genevieve, 1151; Velasquez, Eric,
627; Venema, Reintje, 606; Verney,
John, 403, 434, 489; Voake, Char-
lotte, 1334; Wegner, Fritz, 1149;
Weil, Lisl, 184; White, David
Omar, 368; Whitlock, Pamela, 389;
Wildsmith, Brian, 129; Williams,
Garth, 815

images, of god, broken, 1205
imaginary play: adventures becom-
    ing real, 412-14; cult of Mithra,
    282-83; with Chihuahua dog, 329;
    realm, boys play in, 120-21
Imelda Fay, 1133-36
immigrants. See emigrants; particu-
    lar nationalities.
immortality, by placing in fire,
    189
Immortals, 512-13
immortals, Old Ones, 288, 804,
    1375
Imp, 673
imperialism, Roman, 1117-19
Imperial Family, Russian, 12
impersonations: as camper, 544-
    46; as cleaning woman, 568-69; as
    cousin from Nepal, 506; as devil,
    554; as down-and-outer, 1268; as
    friars, 695; as grandmother, 823;
    as Greek eye-healer, 348-49; as
    half-wit, 574-75; as ironmonger,
    414; as leather worker, 773; as
    leper, 1260; as members of large
    family, 426; as mentally ill, 157;
    as monk, 110; as plague victim,
    154; as porter, 1188; as security
    guard, 541; as uncle, 845; as Va-
    grant, 1359; aunt, 888-889; bear
    as cloud, 1388; Bengali as Dacca
    physician, 653-54; Bengali as
    representative of local rajah,
    653-54; boy as Druid, 491;
    boy as duke's son, 1122; boy as
    girl, 739; boy as older brother,
    1215; boy as priest, 1216; boys as
    ship's greasers, 402; business-
    man as watchman, 183; celestial
    companion as human, 326-27;
    cleaning woman, 1122; Diamond
    as Robinson, 610; discovered,
    1383; donkey as Aslan, 687; dwarf
    as leprechaun, 969-70; drowning

person, 78; escaped prisoner
as beggar, 658; escaped prisoner as madman, 658; ex-gladiator
as prince, 252, 771-74, 806, 865-
66, 967-68; fairy doctor as cat,
248; former legionaire as British
native, 348; German flyer as deaf-
mute, 887; girl as boy, 102-4, 448,
585, 606, 1086, 1245; girl as dog,
33; girl as gun-slinger, 597; girl
as her sister, 568;
girl as page, 447; girl as princess, 532-33; girl from other
world as her double, 598; girls
as tarts, 402; governess, 1400-1;
grandmother as housemaid, 1001;
gun runner as sugar grower, 601;
healthy girl as invalid, 341-42;
hobgoblin as mare, 549; innocent,
306; ironmonger, 1238; kidnappers as plumbers, 1004; knight
of Hospitallers as beggar, 671;
knight as friar, 673-74; leper,
1103; lover as old, deaf man, 267-
68; married man as bachelor boy
friend, 61; merchants, 1259; monkey as woman, 210;
mother as cousin, 466-67; mouse
of knife grinder, 816; of capped
slaves, 239; of deaf-and-dumb
servant, 308; of devil, 309; of
dog, 1419; of friars, 103; of German soldiers, 253; of ghost, 1355;
of hikers, 1344; of marooner,
237, 1412; of princess, 1142;
of Scotland Yard police, 906-
7; ornithologists, 888; outlaw
as page, 146; outlaw as weaver's apprentice, 146; panther for
villagers, 66; penetrated, 865-
66; piglet as kangaroo baby, 974;
pilgrim, 1103; pirates as traders, 256; possible, 289; poverty
stricken man as well off, 267-68;
queen as laundress, 1413; rabbit
as renegade, 1332; Romans as gods,
1244-45; runaways as peasants,
561;
Russian agents as hunters, 653-54;
slave as Roman noble, 281; spinster neighbor as grandmother,
466; spy as court minstrel, 600;
spy as harper, 1086; spy as minstrel girl, 600; spy as page boy,
600; as stableboy, 1339; tart,
881; terrorists as archeologists,
34; thieves as vacationers, 1397;
Mole as washerwoman, 828; Toad as
washerwoman, 1383; tramps of workmen, 891; Wise Woman as toffee shop
keeper, 1271; writer as confidence
man, 449. See also disguises.
impressments, into British navy,
1067, 1118
imps: called by lighting pipe with
blue flame, 247; demands baby and
mother, 872, 902-3, 1094-96
I'm Trying to Tell You, 52
In a Blue Velvet Dress: Almost a
Ghost Story, 1066
In a Nutshell, 994
incarnations, of Tulku of Siddha
Asara, 334, 1266
The Incredible Adventures of Don
Quixote: A Retelling, 25
independence: developing, 73-74;
extreme, 833; gained, 833-35;
importance of, 138-40, 140-
42; mental, 281; of blind child
encouraged, 217-19, 1366; old woman seeks, 714-16. See also initiative.
India: girl from, 722; late 19th
century, Seonee hills, 630-32,
651-54; late 20th century, Bombay,
1302-5; late 20th century, Thul,
1302-5
The Indian Queen, 73, 519, 522
Indians: Asian, in England, 297;
Blackfeet, 733; Canadian, 733;
Iroquois, 733; one-quarter Chero-
kee, 754; Piegan, 733; Red, 38,
418; Snake, 733; South American, 1310; South Sea, attacking,
788; Toonits, 733
Indians, novels of. See ethnic
groups, novels of.
Indian Secret Service, 574, 651-54,
655, 743, 757-58
Indies, sought, 1403
indigestion, cured, 726
industrialization: affects of,
197-99, 390-91, 806-9, 1302-5,
1399-1401; anti-, 505-6, 1336-38,
1359-61
Industrial Revolution: 199; pre,
England, 970-71, 1359, 1094-96
industrial towns, dirty, 390, 536-
38, 806-9, 1399-1401
Infants School, 522
infatuations: drummer boy for General's daughter, 341; page for
queen, 1413-14; with gentleman
smuggler, 364; with silly wife,
583. See also crushes; romances.
infirmarers, cynical monks, 1394-95

inflation, runaway, 895
Ingary, 568
INGEBORG NYGAARD, 37, *578*, 1349-51, 1402
Ingram, Tim, 883
Ingram family, 821, 944-45, 1024, 1225, 1237
Inheritance, 90
inheritances: cottage, 857; coveted, 606; house, 26; isolated Australian cottage, 714, 860, 894; Pekinese dogs, 1080; rejected, 48, 281; refused, 706; shared, 693; substantial, 809; usurped, 650-51, 738. *See also* legacies.
Inishgillan, early 20th century, 258-61
Inish Goill, 544-45
Inishthorav, 259-60
initials, shared, 944
initiations: at Beltane, 1321; boys in Epidaii tribe, 349; Iceni, 1171; into adulthood, 1359; into club, 490-91; into Pony Club, 1339; stories, 623; wolf kill, 337, 1320-21
initiative: necessary for survival, 49-50, 134. *See also* independence.
injuries: broken elbow, 602; broken hip, back, 264; broken leg, 625, 1396; broken sword arm, 1344; burned hand, 93; burns, 807; by Ringwraiths, 436-37; cut arm in Viking raid, 1377; deliberately aggravated, 1374; dog bites leg, 343; facial, 88-89; Frodo, 407; from wild boars, 996; gerbil by cat, 76; hand, 604; head, 397, 402, 1399; in raid, 279; of cellist's hand, 857; pigeon in storm, 248; paralysis from waist down, 379; paralyzed arm injuries, 805; smashed knee, 118; spear wound, 271; sprained ankle, 671; tongue cut out, 376; war, blindness, 460; wounds, 513. *See also* illnesses.
injustice, extreme social, 52-55, 155-58, 197-99, 627-28, 1011-12, 1187-89, 1276-78, 1368-69, 1394-96
innkeepers, wicked, 1018
innocence: aiding healing, 1001; proved, 1037
innovation, difficulty of, 1161-64
inns: Admiral Benbow, 338, 965, 1253-54; at Bree, 406, 1158; country, 2, 1352; den of thieves and beggars, 246, 1352; on French

coast, 340; stagecoach, 1125-28; Swiss, 1348; village, 1111-12, 1396-97; Wanton Child, 247
inquests, 353, 1196-99, 1289
Inquisition, 1045
insane persons. *See* mad people.
inscriptions, tombstone, 397
insects: talking, 246, 593-95, 1209
Inskip, Tom, 883
Inskip family, 821, 944-45, 1024, 1225, 1237
In Spite of All Terror, 162
insurance agencies, 703-6
insurance money, fire for, 1365
insurrections. *See* rebellions.
Insurrections, 1137
intellectuals: French, 18th century, 751-52; French, 19th century, 828-29
internments, German Jews in England as enemy aliens, 793, 925
interpreters, English boy, 1266
interrogations: by Nazis, 253; by Earl, 351; by Fiscal, 1196-99; into possible treason, 1405
interviews: with college principal, 99; with old man, 430-32, 433
In the Meantime, 1131
intrigues: Britain, 5th century, 683; British-Saxon, 359; Byzantium and Romania, 279-81; caused by evil Ape, 687-89; Chile, 1187-89; China and Tibet, 334; Constantinople, 15th century, 370-73; court, 39-41, 447-48, 670, 672, 832; crusades, 12th century, 670-71; during French Revolution, 832; English, mid-15th century, 125-26, 1404-6; English-French, late 14th century, 454; family, 304-6; Haiti, 765-67; Hanoverian, 887-89, 1100; in ancient Egypt, 829; in Lahore, 651; international, 74, 282-83, 434-46, 454, 907, 1061-64, 1076-78, 1213-15; Mexico, 601-2; political, various, 509-10; political and military, Danish invasion, 871-72; political in India, 651-54, 655; political during early Norman period, 673-74; political, pro-Henry Tudor, 730; religious, 279-81, 370-71; Roman America, 1142-43; Royalists-Covenanters, 638; Russia, 1206-8; Scottish court, 677-78, 814-15, 1412-15; Scottish tribal, 772-74, 806, 1161-62;

sinister, 610-11, 1107, 1108-10;
surrounding Arthur, 1037-39; surrounding Carausius of Britain,
3rd century, 1088-91; tangled 14th
century English political, 916-
17; usurping regent, 720; Wars of
Roses, 102-5, 276, 316-17, 683,
701, 762-63; World War II, 175,
1339-40
Introit, Beekeeper's, 1180-81
THE INTRUDER, *578-81*, 1246
invalids: former trick rider, 607;
fraudulent, 341-42; boy, teenaged, 519-21, 522; murdered
man, 890; old woman, 177, 703-6;
supposed, 888-89
invasions: Danish, 18; false alarm,
57; German of English Channel, 1339; Irish of England, 611;
Norman, 1085; of minds, 1087; of
Narnia, 1093; Saxons, 358, 679-83;
supposed German of England, 749,
887; Toad Hall, 1384
inventiveness: in evading hanging,
110-13; in poaching, 284-85; in
taking advantage of fairy's gift,
1232-34
inventors: boy, 1360; chocolate maker, 811; impractical, 1359; of
lighter than air machine, 1143; of
steam wheelchair, 119; of survival suit, 225, 983-84; of tongs for
carding wool, 808; of tower, 1161-
63; White Knight, 1210, 1359
Inverness, mid-20th century, 642-43
invitations: forgotten by host, 97-
98; to Hunt Ball, 420; to sister
for christening, omitted, 701; to
boy's home, 97; to Christmas dinner, refused, 353; to execution,
374; to tea, 412
invulnerability: reputation for,
113-15; secret of, 116. *See also*
life.
Iona, 1013
Ionicus, 1232
I Own the Racecourse!, 1404
Ipston, 669, 1334-36
Ipswich, 1224
Ipswich Gaol, 1224
Irad, 625-26
IRELAND, TIMOTHY, *581*, 1363
Ireland: 913-14; ancient times,
298-99, 299-301, 1258-61; late
8th century, coast, 1298-1300;
9th century, 91-92; 10th century,
Dublin, 116-19; 13th century,
Galway, 215-17, 261; late 18th

century, County Wicklow, 499-501;
early 20th century, 1270-73; early
20th century, Barrinish, 1101-3;
early 20th century, Inishgillan,
258-61; mid-20th century, 425-
27; mid-20th century, Ballymurry,
1151-54; mid-20th century,
Connemara, 543-46; mid-20th
century, Glennashee, 713-14; late
20th century, Belfast, 1284-87;
late 20th century, Northern, 1133-
36
Ireland, novels of, 215-17, 258-61,
298-99, 299-301, 425-27, 499-501,
543-46, 713-14, 913-14, 1101-3,
1133-36, 1151-54, 1270-73, 1284-
87
Irene, Princess, 999-1001, 1002-3
Irish activists, 325, 499-501
Irish Fairy Tales, 1138
Irish Sagas and Folktales, 910
Irish persons: huge, 17; in England,
186, 343, 410-11, 639-40, 900,
1004, 1390-91; in Scotland, 942,
1123, 1196; in Wales, 42-43; jokes
about, 74
Irishwoman, mysterious, 851, 853,
1328, 1330
Iris Webster, 810, 616
iron, red hot bar, 739
Iron Age: advent of, 1319-22; tumps,
802-3
Iron Age Fort, 903
Iron Cow, 524
iron founders, 762, 1015, 1277
THE IRON GIANT, 570, 581, 583. *See*
THE IRON MAN, *583-85.*
Iron Hills, 552
ironic conclusions, 39-41, 55-57,
127-29, 143-44, 252-54, 304-6,
388-89, 395-97, 492-95, 714-16,
771-74, 824-26, 829-30, 846-49,
1029-31, 1149-51, 1353-56
THE IRON LILY, *581-83*, 684, 1371
THE IRON MAN: A STORY IN FIVE NIGHTS,
570, *583-85*
ironmasters, 459, 581-83
ironmongers, 412-14
Irontown, 579
The Iron Way, 269
Iroquois, 733
ISA, 28, 94, *585*, 1187-88
Isaac Campion, 567
Isaac Gulliver, 340
Isabel, 585
Isabella, child queen of England,
447-49, 454
Isabella, Queen of England, 1017-20

ISABELLA CLINTON, 447-49, 453-54,
    585-86, 600
ISABELLA OF FRANCE, 585-86, *586*
Isa Ibald, 1322
Isca Dumnoniorum, 347-50
Isengard, 440, 805, 982
Iseult, 1259-61
Iseult of the White Hands, 1261
Ishakeen, 625
Ishak Enoch, 625-26
Isis River, 343
"Is It Well with the Child?" 445
The Islander, 796
THE ISLANDERS, *586-88*, 1247
AN ISLAND IN A GREEN SEA, 25, *588-89*
ISLAND MACKENZIE, 589, 831, 893.
    See *THE NINE LIVES OF ISLAND
    MACKENZIE, 893-94*.
Island Magic, 471
Island of Dreams, 1308
The Island of Horses, 322
Island of the Great Yellow Ox, 750
Island of the Strangers, 1067
islands: Arctic, 1349-51; barren,
    659; destroyed by volcano, 586;
    eastern Mediterranean, 434; Eng-
    lish Channel, 108, 175, 1339;
    floating, 1310, 1344; flying,
    511-12; Halcyon, 1373; inhospi-
    table, 521-22; in lake, 120, 545;
    in river, 1384; Inner Farne, 1377;
    Iona, 1013; Irish, 737, 1101-2,
    1272; Kingfisher, 204; Lake Dis-
    trict, 1178-79; Lilliput, 509-10;
    maroons on, 89; Natividad, 1412;
    Norwegian, 578; of birds, 1168; of
    sorcerers, 512; off Galway coast,
    258-61; off South America, 237;
    Orkneys, 1161-64; Pacific, 1, 2,
    256-57, 586-87, 659, 828; river,
    1036; Scottish, 588-89, 1396-97;
    sea, 1307-8; Shetland, 1155-57;
    South Seas desert, 632, 787, 855,
    859-60, 1023, 1239, 1373, 1374;
    Spidermonkey, 211; tropical, 366,
    893-94
Isle of Skye, 605
Isle of Mull, 650
Isle of Wight, 1403
Islington, 18th century, 88, 111-13
Isobel Darley, 455
ISOBEL DARROCH, *589-90*, 1048-
    49
Isobel Russell, 422
Israel: ancient, 829-30, 895, 1185;
    12th century, 670-72
Istanbul: 17th century, 213-15. *See
    also* Constantinople.

Italians: in Constantinople, 633;
    in England, 840; mid-20th century,
    Venice, 662-63
Ivor Protheroe, 323, 907
Ivy Holt, 202, 1323
Ivy Hooper, 539-40, 542
IVY WHITTACKER, 411-14, *590*, 1029

Jabberwocky, 572, 1210, 1361
Jabez Casket, 344, 887-89
Jabizri beetle, 1310
Jack Bagthorpe, 275, 477, 838, 920-
    21, 1048, 1195, 1282-83, 1372,
    1419
jackdaws, helpful, 931-32, 992
Jack Field, 738, 839, 1110
Jackie the Lantern, 713
Jack Lunn, 277-78
Jack Martin, 255-57
Jack Matcham, 102-4, 606
Jacko Chant, 150, 200-1, 636, 692-93
Jack P. McGurk, 184-85
Jack Rose, 97-98
Jack Straw's Castle, 824
JACKUS, COLIN, 37, 286-87, *591*, 777,
    820, 843
JACOB, 172-73, 195, 218-19, *591-92*,
    616, 1067, 1173-74, 1231
Jacobites, 12, 289, 648-49, 651
Jacob Marley, 227
Jacobs family, 29, 219, 330, 857,
    1076-78
Jacques, Robin, 495
Jadis, the witch, Queen of Narnia,
    167, 321, 356-57, 710, 742, 755,
    864, 961-62, 987, 1009, 1279
Jael, nail of, 976
Jael, the goshawk, 383-84
Jaffa, 670
JAGGERS, 376, 493-95, *592*, 1346
jailers: cruel, fat, 1031-32;
    daughter helps Toad escape, 1383
jails: dancing teacher in, 1385-86;
    debtors', 1353; father in, 233,
    1224; Newgate, 1107, 1109; sen-
    tence of 3 months for grievous
    bodily harm, 86; Toad in, 1383; un-
    cle in, 1242, 1315
Jack, Red, 325, 1405
JAKE BERTOLD, 33-36, 485-86, *592-93*,
    778
Jamaicans: black, in England, 606;
    black, in London, 842, 1262-64
James, Dynley, 795
James, Earl of Moray, 677-78
James I, King of England, 1353, 1412
James III, King of England (ficti-
    tious), 108-9, 837, 887-88, 1048,

1356, 1399-1400
James and the Black Van, 241
JAMES AND THE GIANT PEACH, 274, *593-95*
James and the Robbers, 241
James and the Smugglers, 241
JAMES BUBB, 94, 190, 342, 356, *595*, 1237
James Digby, 340-41
JAMES HARRISON, 49, 92-93, 451-53, *595-96*, 862, 1100
James Henry Trotter, 593-95
JAMES HOWARD, *596*
Jamesie Dunham, 473-75
Jamesina Ramsay, 597
James Murray, 152-53
JAMES SMITH, *596*, 1203, 1317
James the Policeman, 241
Jamie, 1004-6
JAMIE ANDREWS, 53-54, *596-97*, 1370
Jamie Hartley, 463-64
JAMIE RAMSAY, *597*, 640, 1218-20
JAN (*Red Shift*), *597*, 1025, 1232
JAN (*The Silver Sword*), 152, 353-54, *597-98*, 619-20, 1052-53, 1097-99, 1398
Jane (*The Doll Who Came Alive*), 332-33, 1347
JANE (*Five Children and It*), 416-18, *598*, 1007
Jane Banks, 779-81, 781-82, 783-84, 785-86
Jane Ellison, 579-80
Jane Eyre, 1275
Jane Kitson Haverard, 668
Jane Morley, 1275
JANET CHANT, 191, 209, *598*
Janet Clemens, 397
JANET THOMAS, *598-99*, 667-68
Janet Treet, 304
Jane Treguddick, 1112-13
JANE WOOD, *599*, 1059-60
JANEY HOGGART, *599*, 956, 1396-97
Janey Tregose, 1410
Janissaries, Turkish, 214-15, 1226, 1295-96
Japan, 513
Jaques, Faith, 176, 703, 831
jar, Bear's head gets stuck in honey, 1388
Jarl Buthar, 1085-86
Jason Harper, 127-28
Jason Bodger and the Priory Ghost, 644
Jasper, the monkey, 839-41
Jasper Nye, 153
jazz, Dixieland, 1062

jealousy: between brothers, 305-6; brother of sister, 842-43; girl for mother's lover, 692; of cousin, 87-88; of mother's man friend, 200-1; of singer over girl, 1194; of sister's boyfriend, 94; over borrowing abilities, 136; over entailed property, 305; sister of baby brother, 1373
Jean, 189-90
Jean Gilbride, 588-89, 1048-49
Jeanie Deans (boat), 717
Jean-Paul Deliet, 989, 1360-61
Jean Morrison, 760, 1196
JEAN THOMPSON, 334, 514, 516, 528, *599-600*, 629, 1057, 1315, 1365-66
Jeff Dickson: Cowhand, 1079
Jefferson School, 520
Jeff Webster, 183-84
Jeffy, the Burglar's Cat, 831
JEHANNE, 447-48, *600*
Jek Davies, 1015, 1276-78
Jemima Potts, 221-23
Jemmy Kane, 587
JEM ROLLER, 51, 488, *600*, 970-71
Jem Smith, 1222
Jenkins, 610
Jenkins, Bruno, 1393-94
Jenkins, Howell, 567
Jennifer, 1233-34
JENNIFER CLEVERTON, 389-92, 433, *600*
Jenny, 1127-28
Jeremiah Barker, 602
Jeremy, 461
Jeremy Craven, 313, 399, 601-2, 629, 752, 1228
JEREMY CRAVEN, 248, *601-2*
Jeremy Fisher, 696
Jeremy Potts, 221-23
Jeremy Stevens, 1288-89
Jeremy Visick, 397-98
JEREMY VISICK, 397, 602, 1391. *See THE FATE OF JEREMY VISICK, 397-99.*
JERRY BARKER, 106, 171, *602*
Jerusalem, late 12th century, 670-72, 968
Jerusalem House, 1281, 1317-19
Jessamine Treguddick, 1111-13
Jessamy, 1107
Jessica Meredith, 858, 1006
Jessica on Her Own, 530
JESSICA VYE, 226, 427, *602-3*, 734-37, 823
Jessie, 606-8
jesters: 782, 1015; rabbit, 557
Jestyn the Englishman, 116-19
jewelers, 541-42, 667
jewelry: makers, 605; stores, 183

jewels: Arkenstone of Thrain, 553;
  family treasure lost, 94, 858,
  862; family, sold, 1314; hidden,
  291, 615, 841; mother's, 1017-19;
  on dragon, 1107; recovered, 542;
  spy deals in, 743; stolen, 218-19,
  418, 598, 1397; tear-shaped magic,
  lost, 414, 1343
Jews: actors, 468, 478; arrested by
  Nazis, 37; German refugees, World
  War II, 31, 761, 793, 924-26, 937;
  glazier, 278; in Germany, 31,
  1348-49; in Norway, 1350; mother
  dies in concentration camp, 1106,
  1193; school friend, 900
Jews, novels of. See ethnic groups,
  novels of.
Jezebel, 1076-77
JILL POLE, 377, *603*, 687-89, 1034,
  1007, 1091-93, 1174
Jim Brading, 1340, 1342
JIM DALTON, *603-4*, 876
JIM FOULGER, 496, 543, *604*, 775, 786
JIM HAWKINS, 338, *604*, 732, 965,
  1253-56
Jimmie Meccer, 556
JIMMY DEAN'S COUSIN, 76-77, 159,
  604-5
Jimpy, the cock, 598
Jim Ruggles, 386
JIM SMITH, 14, *605*, 1049-50, 1057-58
Jim Starling, 547
Jim Turner, 972
Jim Woodall, 1015, 1276-77
Jingle Stones, 351
jinn, 1009
Jinnie Friend, 61, 473-75, 623-24
JINNY SLATTERY, 335, 525, *605-
  6*, 918-19, 1265
Jinty Morrison, 47, 707-8, 760-61,
  799-800, 1196-99
Jip, the dog, 1145, 1309
Joan, 1130
JOANNA SEDLEY, 102-4, *606*, 615, 695,
  1103
Joanna Whittacker, 1029
Joan of Arc, 1406
Joaquin Murjica, 1366-68
jobs: applicant as vicar's maid,
  387; father secures, 912; live-in,
  1159-60; lost, 317, 1363-64; odd,
  1303, 1313, 1416; secured to pay
  off debt, 1365
Joe, 606-8
Joe, the cellarman, 1126
Joe, the horse, 318, 320
Joe, the Monster, 222
JOE AND TIMOTHY TOGETHER, 357, *606-8*

JOE GARGERY, 94-95, 492-95, *608*, 981
Joe Green, 105, 107
Joe Hardwick, 578-80
Joe Wade, 463
JOE WIDDISON, 547, 548-50, *608*, 778,
  864
JOE MORETON, 599, *608-9*, 1058-60,
  1100-1
Joey Rockaway, 184-85
JOHANNA VAVASOUR, 303, 308-9, 554,
  609, 614
Johannesburg, late 20th century,
  627-28
John (*Carbonel, the King of the
  Cats*), 173
John (*The Cave*), 701
John (*Prove Yourself a Hero*), 1004
John, King of England, 215-17, 261,
  1103
John Banks, 779-80, 781, 783, 785
John Bumps, 839-41
John Codling, 1132
John Darling, 956-57
JOHN DIAMOND, *610*, 610-11
JOHN DIAMOND, 442, *610-11*
John Dolittle, M.D., 323-24
John Edmunds, 169
JOHN FITZWILLIAM, 12, 738-40, *611*,
  1104
JOHN FOWLER, *611-12*, 1026
JOHN GOODRICH, 195, *612*, 729-30
John Halifax, Gentleman, 263
John Hernon, 544-45
John Mackenzie, 1398-99
JOHN MANLY, 596, *612*
John Meneot, 1193
Johnnie, the pig, 59, 954-55
Johnny Golightly and His Crocodile,
  831
Johnny-Head-in-Air, 503
Johnny Plackham, 847-48
John Palmer, 533
John Paston, 880-81
JOHN PARGETER, *612*, 742, 849, 1224-
  25
John Parker, 174-75
John Perrybingle, 266-69
JOHN PIM, 446, *612-13*, 613, 738, 863,
  1115
JOHN POLLARD, 446, *613*, 1115
John Rowlands, 502
John Ruggles, 386
JOHN SEMPEBWA, 564-65, *613-14*
John Sobieski, King of Poland, 214
Johnson, Dr. Samuel, 171
John Spencer, 1068-71
Johnstone family, 23-24, 80, 206,
  865

John Treguddick, 1111
JOHN WALKER, 171, *614*, 972, 974,
    1177-79, 1340-42
John Walters, 193-94
JOHN WEBSTER, 303, 306-9, 554, 609,
    614, 1174-75
Jolland family, 276, 293, 683-84,
    701
Jolliginki, 160, 988, 1145-46, 1309
Jolly Roger (ship), 172
Joluo tribe, 113-15, 754, 1189
Jonah and the Cat, 1076
JON AMEND-ALL, 102, 316, *615*, 695,
    1103
Jonas, William, 586-87, 1373
Jonathan Brown, 84-85
JONATHAN CODLING, 1, 94, *615*, 813,
    817, 841, 1058
JONATHAN MEREDITH, *615-16*, 809-10,
    846, 857-58, 960-61, 967, 1004-7,
    1191-92
Jonathan Marlow, 382-83
JONATHAN MORLEY, 173, 218-19, *616*,
    1067, 1174
Jonathan Whiteleafe, 153
Jones, Cem, 400-2, 1177
JONES, CORDELIA, *617*, 897
JONES, DIANA WYNNE, 43, 208, 325,
    411, 567, *617-18*
Jones family (*Arabel's Raven*), 41-42
Jones family (*Fathom Five; The Ma-
    chine Gunners*), 196-97, 210
Jones family (*John Diamond*), 609-10,
    610-11, 1087, 1284
Jones family (*Josh*), 620-23
Jones family (*The Robbers*), 4, 101,
    285-6, 478, 539, 845, 968, 1039-41
Jones, Mr., 1396-97
Jones, Mrs. Daisy, 333-34, 853,
    1195, 1266
Jones, Timmo, 50-51, 942, 1225-26,
    1326-27
Jonesy, 657
Jongleur, King's, 1015, 1395
JONQUIL DARLEY, 92, 455-56, *618*, 947
JO RUGGLES, 385-86, *618-19*
JOSCELIN D'AUBIGNY, *619*, 670
Jose, 1366-67
JOSEPH, 9-10, 399, 484-85, *619*,
    1235, 1281
JOSEPH BALICKI, 597, *619-20*, 1097-98
Joseph Kane, 522, 586-87
JOSH, 168, 538, *620*, 891-92
JOSH, *620-23*, 1129
Josh Plowman, 620-23
Joshua M. Smith, 620
JOSHUA SMITH, *623*, 1317, 1203
JOSIAH FRIEND, 473, *623-24*

JOSSIE MILBURN, 131, *624*
journalists: French, 1349. *See also*
    newsmen; reporters.
A Journal of the Plague Year, 298
Journey Behind the Wind, 1404
Journey from the Heron, 1252
The Journey of Johnny Rew, 72
THE JOURNEY OF THE ELDEST SON, 438,
    624-27, 1206
journeys: across Europe, 619-20;
    across Europe in World War II,
    1097-99; by foot, 585, 995; by
    pony, 150; by gull-drawn peach,
    594; by horseback, 561; by lit-
    ter, 654; by raft, 150; China
    to Tibet, 1266; down Oxus, 38,
    600; eventful, 1120-21; girl and
    enchanted ass, 1233-34; harrow-
    ing, 1092-93, 1275, 1331-32, 1344;
    households undertake, 719-20;
    Israel to Egypt by camel, 829;
    north to Wales, 1337-38; of
    Christian to Celestial City, 974-
    80; of mice for home, 437; over-
    land, 1275; Poland to Switzerland,
    post World War II, 353, 1098, 1398;
    through bog, 482; through dark
    mine, 398; through strange land-
    scape, 462; to freedom in Narnia,
    1081-82; to freedom in White Mts.,
    1359-61; to Lapps, 578, 1351; to
    London, 1401; to Mordor, 407-8,
    1056; to other worlds, 755-56;
    to ransom father, 1017-20; to
    save elephant, 1248-49; to South
    America, 172; to Southampton,
    1402; up Folly River, 67, 716-17.
    See also quests; searches; trips;
    voyages.
*JOURNEY TO JO'BURG; A SOUTH AFRICAN
    STORY*, *627-28*, 869
jousts, 672
JOWETT, MARGARET, 169, *628-29*
Joyce, James, 1138
Joyce, Michael, 543-46
Juan Larreta, 28, 1187-88
Juan O'Grady, 1076-78
Jude the Obscure, 736
judges: at mock trial, 29; for
    witches' contest, 1354; in elocu-
    tion contest, 384; Irish village,
    426; mind so fixed it is odorous,
    1385-86; Scottish village, 1196,
    1198. *See also* magistrates.
Judith Chapman, 1022
Judith in Hanover, 410
judo, 93, 1378
Judy Brown, 84-85

jugglers, 1019, 1415
Julia, 208, 517
Julia Gresham, 489-92
Julie, 713-14
Juliets, four little English, 736
Julie Vernon-Greene, 415-16
JULIO, 601, *629*
Julius, 238, 989-91
Julius van Bergh, 1062
Jumbo, 1363
jumping rope, 728
Jump James, 484
June Lockwood, 378
THE JUNGLE, 277-78, 334, 514, 599,
    629-30, 648, 1242, 1315, 1364
THE JUNGLE BOOKS, *630-32*, 666
jungles, Indian, 630-32, 836-37
The Jungle Trilogy, 1246
Juniper: A Mystery, 644
junk: 539-42; collectors of, sinis-
    ter, 808; dealers, 229
JUNO, the black nanny, *632*, 787-88,
    859, 1239, 1374
Juno (yacht), 85, 1380-81
Junta, oppressive, 1187-89
jury, incarcerated, 1385-86
Justice: the horse, 105; blind, 846,
    1110; champion of, 1043; economic
    sought, 1123-25
Justice of the Peace, 1113
justices of the peace, woman, 822
Justin (*Black Hearts in Battersea*),
    108, 1122
JUSTIN (*The Silver Branch*), 271,
    632-33, 1089-91
Justin, Prince of Ingary, 569
JUSTINIANI LONGO, 372, *633*
Just So Stories for Little Children,
    666
Jusuf Al-Hafiz, 670-71
Juteland: 5th century, 680; 10th
    century, 117
Jutes, in England, 680-81
Jyd Trewerry, 332-33

KAA, the python, 71, 631-32, *635*
"Kaa's Hunting," 631
Kalavin, 122-23
Kallin, Tasha, 382
Kallonas, Xenophon, 402
Kane, Joseph, 522
Kane family, 586-87
Kanga, the kangaroo, 562-63, 1388-89
kangaroos, girls become, 1385;
    maternal, 1388
Kano, valley, 19th century, 113-15
Kapenen, Veikko, 1350-51

Kara Mustafa, 213-15
Karen Marlow, 382-84, 965
Karen Sawdust, 1186
Karherdin, 1261
Kaspar Haller, 32, 214
Kate (The Borrowers Books), 132-33,
    134-35, 136, 147-48, 857, 1236
KATE (*The Watcher Bee*), 58, 202-3,
    635-36, 741, 1280, 1322-25, 1420
KATE CHANT, 200-1, *636*, 692
Kate Crackernuts, 505, 638
KATE CRACKERNUTS, 151, *636-38*
Kate Friend, 473
Kate Holt, 489-92
KATE LUCAS, *638*, 753-54, 923-24,
    1033
KATE MAXWELL, 505, 636-38, *638*
Kate Rider, 163
Kate Ruggles, 386
Kate Ryder, 163
KATE TRANTER, 483-84, *638-39*, 669,
    697, 874-75, 1020, 1334-36
Katherine Lindsay, 505, 636-38
Kathleen Fay, 1133-36
KATHLEEN O'BRIEN, 74-75, 325-28,
    343, *639-40*, 823, 1042
KATHY FISHER, 124, 363, *640*, 1218-20
Katia, 717-20
KATIA, 640. *See LITTLE KATIA*, 717-
    20.
KAYE, GERALDINE, 248, *640-41*
Keate family, 169-71
keepers, of castle prison, 1412
Keeping, Charles, 116, 246, 293,
    335-36, 642, 656, 672, 679, 689,
    738, 771, 1088, 1319
Keep the Pot Boiling, 241
Kehaar, 1332
Keith Chapman, 844, 850, 1262-64
KEITH HESELTINE, 292, 351-52, *641*
Keith Hollins, 918
Kelly, Guns, 290
KELPIE, *641-42*
kelpies, 13, 642-43, 830
THE KELPIE'S PEARLS, 573, *642-43*
Kelyddon, Prince, legendary, 528
Kemble, Frances, 170
Kemi, 196, 658, 829, 1185
KEMP, GENE, *643-44*, 1269
Kempe, Thomas, 451-52, 595-96, 862
Kenan, 625-26
Kendal, 556, *644*
Kenet, Ted, 235
Kennealy family, 506
Kennedy, Richard, 186, 543, 1101
Kennedy family, 499-500
KENNEMORE, TIM, *644-45*, 1313
Kenneth Llewellyn, 558

Kensington: church, 11; late 20th
century, 283, 330, 1076
Kent: early 20th century, country-
side, 416-18; late 20th century,
Penfield, 248-52, 476, 482-83, 698
Kentish Historical Association,
1319
Kenton family, 1284-87
KEPT IN THE DARK, 81, *645-46*
Kermit, 524
KERR, (ANNE) JUDITH, *646-47*, 924,
1348
Kerridge family, 338, 612, 849, 859,
1041-42, 1224-25
KERRY TATE, 289, *647*, 655, 862, 1313-
14
Kershaw Farm, 149, 156-57
Ketterley, Uncle Andrew, 321, 1279-
80
Kettlewell, Doritie, 30
KEVIN THOMPSON, 314, 334, 514-16,
528, 599, 629, *647-48*, 1056-57,
1242, 1315, 1364-66
KEWAL, 310, *648*, 1280
keyholes, in cliff, 463
keys: golden, 462-63; old one on
chain, 1181; to castle, stolen,
1414; to dungeon, 552
Kezia, 5, 320
Keziah Hope, 900
Khan Vladimir, 117
Khan Zabergan, 280
KIDNAPPED, *648-51*, 1139
kidnappings: abused boy, 1240; assumed, 78, 124; attempted, 299;
baby, supposed, 363, 640, 597;
baby, political ends, 880, 1219;
baby boy, 304-5, 826; baby sister,
143, 529, 1149; baby prince, 562;
blacks for slavery, 743, 1068;
black slave, 766; Borrower family,
139-40, 822, 856, 857; boy aboard
ship, 108; boy by black rider, 292;
boy by London cutpurses, 1357; boy
by monkeys, 71, 631; boy by terrorists, 335, 525, 917-19, 1265; boy
from hospital, 468; boys for press
gang, 195, 218, 1067; bride, 1293;
bungled attempt, 219, 1077; by
monkey, attempted, 511; Byzantine
girl, 1099;
cat, 913; cat attempted, 893-
94; children, 888; daughter of
town councilor, 402; donkey, 675,
1003; elephant, 205, 1248; girl by
conspirators, 345; girl by cruel
duchess, 815-16; girl by drunk-
en thugs, 170; girl by evil queen,

1142-43; girl for brothel, 881;
girl for fortune, 1103; girl heiress, 606; in bedsheets, 223;
mother, 1161; nephew, 13, 289,
649, 651, 1281; planned, 1389;
policeman, 184; prince, 1007,
1034, 1092-94; of princess attempted, 1002-3; Queen Guenever,
1037; shipwrecked doctor, 258-
61; sister by Saxon, 680; teenaged
boy, 616, 846, 858, 960, 1004-6
Kidsline, radio, 647, 1314
Kiev, 117
Kilhwch, 528
Kili, 553
Killer in Dark Glasses, 1257
Killer's Notebook, 489
killings: accidental, 1121; attempted on stage, 286; by orcs,
132; chance rejected, 253; first,
1299; hoodlum with sword, 470;
king of assassin, 1013; of chief
goblin, 439; of deserter from
survival colony, 158; of dog in
dog fight, 1293; of dog luminary
attempted, 326; of dragon, 552,
1107; of friend, 967; of goshawk,
384; of Hun by bear, 280; of king,
ritual, 252;
of king's deer, 145; of kitten, attempted, 307; of mouse, 432; of
old woman, 1302; of pirates, 257;
of reptilian Master, 239; of revenue agent, 464; of robber, 1280;
of Scots queen, 774; of terrorists, 656, 1033; of traitor, 245;
of usurper, 672; of wolf as test of
manhood, 1320-21; of wolf, failed,
1320-21; poison, 1025; prevented,
286; suggested, 893; wartime, 879;
witch of boy, 711; with black arrow, 615; with sword, 504. *See also*
murders.
Kilmorah, mid-20th century, 79-81
kilns, pottery, 198, 1204-6
Kilta, red-topped, 654
Kiltarragh, 1133-36
KIM, *651-54*, 666
Kimball O'Hara. *See* KIM O'HARA.
Kimber, 1068-71
KIM O'HARA, 651-54, *654-55*, 743,
758, 1194-95
KIM TATE, 289, 647, *655*, 862, 1313-15
KIM TYSON, 150, 156-58, 283, *655-56*,
1033
kindness, to animals, 328-29, 454-
44, 487, 497, 614, 903, 912, 913,
921, 954, 1082-83, 1112, 1309,

1145-46, 1248, 1366, 1398
A KIND OF WILD JUSTICE, 52, *656-58*
King *(Aquarius)*, 832
KING *(The Moon in the Cloud)*, *658*,
    829, 1185
KING, (DAVID) CLIVE, *658-59*, 797
King Arthur. *See* kings, Arthur.
King Arthur, the bull, 282
King Creature, Come, 1247
The Kingdom and the Cave, 8
The Kingdom of Carbonel, 1107
kingdoms: at bottom of lake, 930;
    fairy-tale, 567-69, 701-2;
    imaginary, 996-99; marchen, 927-
    30; mythical, 687-89, 1306-8;
    undersea, 1155
Kingfisher (boat), 731
KINGFISHER ISLAND, 1, 2, 204, 586-
    87, *659*, 828, 1373
King Nimrod's Tower, 442
King of Hearts, 20, 211
King of the Cats, 910
THE KING OF THE GOLDEN RIVER; OR,
    THE BLACK BROTHERS: A LEGEND OF
    STIRIA, *659-62*, 1052
A King Reluctant, 1370
kings: Aethelbert of Kent, 295-96,
    358; Alexander the Great, 512;
    Alfred the Great, 16, 18, 517,
    870-72; Arthur, 148-49, 195, 502,
    682-83, 729-30, 844, 1015, class
    play on, 1270, epic on, 528, 1234,
    1358, grail of, 1375, legends
    of, 351-53, 1342-45, manuscript
    about, 195, 729-30, story retold,
    844, 1037-39, 1141-43; Athelred
    of Wessex, 870-71; Basil II of
    Constantinople, 117; Caesar,
    512; Carausius, 270-71; Caspian,
    King and Prince of Narnia, 185,
    323, 376, 893, 995-96, 1007, 1034,
    1092-93, 1174, 1264-65, 1306-8;
    Charles II of England, 456, 1199;
    Coel of Wessex, 358; Conachur of
    Ulster, 299-300; Conor MacNessa
    of Ulster, 298-99; conscientious,
    185; Constantine, 370-73; Con-
    stantius, 271;
    Cormac of Connacht, 215-217, 261,
    408, 482, 986, 1103; crowned, 995;
    deposed, 585; double-natured,
    902-3; Edmund of Saxons, 375, 870;
    Edward II of England, 916, 1018,
    1104; English, 585, 586, 600,
    837, 870, 887-88, 916, 1018, 1103,
    1104; Ethelred of Wessex, 16, 18,
    376, 870-71; Ethelwulf of Wessex,
    18; figurehead, 39-41; Francis of

Fabylon, 928-29; Frank of Narnia,
    167, 688, 756; giant, 511; greedy
    for treasure, 396; Grognio
    of Pantouflia, 997-98; Guy of
    Outremer, 670; Halfdan, 871;
    Hearts, 19-22; Henry I of England,
    674, 1016; Henry IV of England,
    448, 453, 586; Henry V of England,
    586;
Henry VI of England, 1404, 1406;
    Henry VII of England, 683; ill,
    1000-1; insists girl baby is boy,
    902; Irish, 298-99, 299-300;
    James I of England, 1353, 1412;
    James III (non-historical) of
    England, 108-9, 887-89, 1356-58,
    1399-1400; John of England, 215-
    7; John Sobieski of Poland, 214;
    Leopold of Austria, 214; Lou-
    is XVI of France, 1216-17; Lune
    of Archenland, 1081; Mabon of
    Lyonesse, 1142; Malcolm of Scots,
    273, 760, 768, 1012-13; Marc of
    Cornwall, 1259-61; Mehmed of Tur-
    key, 213-15; Morning Light, 39-41;
    murdered ritually, 697, 772, 832,
    833; Narnia, 167, 357, 561-62,
    603, 687-89, 712, 742, 961-62,
    1027, 1227; nature depends on
    which foot out of bed first, 902;
    Nicholas of Russia, 28, 1207-8;
    noble, 1227; Nollekens of Norfolk,
    872, 902-3, 985, 1130; of Norfolk,
    985, 1130; of cats, 173, 175; of
    Connacht, 261, 408, 482; of Golden
    River, 660-61; of Gondor, 1158; of
    Jolliginki, 1145-46; of Navarre,
    913;
    of Pantouflia, 997-98; of Scotia,
    273; of seal people, 1155-56;
    of Wessex, 18; pious, 870-71;
    rainbringer, 832; red, 1274; re-
    vived from death, 185; Richard I of
    England, 729, 968, 1034; Richard
    II of England, 447-48, 453-54;
    Richard III of England, 103-4,
    582, 683, 762, 1034; sacrificed,
    694; scapegoat, 39-41, 832;
    spoiled, willful, 902-3, 1094;
    Sultan of Turkey, 213-15; terrible
    tempered, 902; Theoden of Rohan,
    805; toy, 1234; Vladimir of Kiev,
    117; white, 1361
Kings and Queens, 393
Kingsbury, 567, 569
THE KING'S GOBLET, 425, *662-63*
Kingsland, Detective-Inspector,
    656-58

KINGSLEY, CHARLES, *663-64*, 745, 1327
KING-SMITH, DICK, *664-65*, 1082
King's Renewal, 1261
kiosks: as home, 362; on pier, 1290
kip, 1268
Kipling, J. Lockwood, 630, 651
KIPLING, (JOSEPH) RUDYARD, 630,
    651, *665-67*, 733
Kirke, Digory, 167, 987, 1279
Kirke family, 321
Kirklees, Prioress at, 147, 717
kirn, 1196
Kitchen, Mr., 378
KITCHENER PONTIFEX, 451, *667*, 1208,
    1290
THE KITCHEN MADONNA, 458, *667-68*
kitchens, filled with pepper, 342
kites, bring nanny, 781
KIT HAVERARD, 535-36, *668*, 685-87,
    693, 811, 937, 988, 1194
KITSON, 244, *669*, 801-3, 1133
Kitson family (*The Lark on the Wing*),
    536, 668, 685-86, 811, 1194
Kitson family (*Tom's Midnight Gar-
    den*), 59, 532-33, 1237-38,
    1240-41, 1279
Kit Standish, 236
kittens: guide to time travel,
    308; leaps at pistol, 309; little
    black, 1210; rescued from storm,
    1341; undernourished, 307
KITTY TRANTER, 483-84, 639, *669*,
    875, 1020, 1335
Kit Ullathorne, 129-30, 624
KIZZY LOVELL, 4-5, 318-21, *669-70*,
    822
Knave of Hearts, 21, 23, 1362
knees, horses' broken, 106
Kneeshaw, Martin, 1269
Kneeshaw family, 1269
knife box, boat made of, 1130
knife throwers, circus, 205
knifings, 117-18, 648, 1018, 1118,
    1280
KNIGHT CRUSADER, *670-72*, 1345
knightings, 564, 670
knights: Arthur's, 1037-39; coura-
    geous, 978; dark, 1034, 1092-93;
    early Norman England, 672-75;
    English, 915-17; falls off horse,
    1210, 1359; fantasy, 1041; French
    castle, 1360; gentle, befuddled,
    1210, 1358-59; good-natured,
    1103-4; in Middle East, 670-72;
    Polish, 215; red, 1358; sleeping,
    167, 414, 1343; various national-
    ities, 670-72; white, 1358-59;
    wounded, 1017

KNIGHT'S FEE, 1176, *672-75*
The Knights of the Golden Table, 27
knives: ivory-handled, lost, 143;
    weapons, 173
knucklebones, of service, 1298
Knudsen, Per, 1401
Kodaly family, 363, 1218-20
Kolia Mirkov, 718
Kooky Kapers, 754
Krak des Chevaliers, 671
Kraken, 824
KRUGER, the dog, *675*, 913
Krush, Beth, 132, 134, 136, 138, 140
Krush, Joe, 132, 134, 136, 138, 140
Kulu, woman from, 654
Kurtrigur Huns, 47-48, 159, 279-81,
    280, 557
Kwatey-Jones family, 248-52, 698
KYLE, ELISABETH (AGNES MARY
    ROBERTSON DUNLOP), 456, *675-76*

laboratories, 127-28, 765, 824, 990,
    1338, 1343. *See also* workrooms.
labor, strife, 129-30, 473, 807,
    876, 910, 1033, 1276-78
labyrinths: in chocolate factory,
    203. *See also* mazes.
la Chard, Tris, 1059-60, 1258
ladders: boy stuck on, 690; creeper
    used as, 1164-65
Laddie, the dog, 1398-99
Ladies' Guild, 815
Ladies in Waiting, 447-48
ladies in waiting: 585-86; mechan-
    ical, 815-16; position declined,
    457
Ladies of the Putney Bright Hour, 490
Ladislau Zabruski, 214
The Lad of the Gad, 444
Lady Blanche de Courcy Rohan, 216,
    408
Ladybug, 593-94
Lady Chittenden, 417-18, 598
Lady Corkberry, 560
Lady de Coucy, 447-48
Lady Dexter, 304-6, 827
Lady Ermengarde, 1017-1020
LADY EULALIA MURGATROYD, 302, 508,
    677, 741, 808-9, 845
Lady Fanshaw, 170-71
Lady Galadriel, 407
Lady in the Moon, 202, 1096
Lady Lil, 1385
Lady March, 365
LADY MARGARET DOUGLAS, *677-78*, 1412-
    15
Lady Mary Sydney, 581-83

Lady Mayoress of Manchester, 922, 1267-68
Lady Mullings, 141-42, 856, 857
Lady of the Green Kirtle, 377, 1034, 1092-93
The Lady of the Linden Tree, 969
Lady of the Lake (*The Road to Camlann*), 1038
Lady of the Lake (*The Weirdstone of Brisingamen*), 1344
Lady Rosalind, 998-99
Lady Spekes, 496
Lady Standwich, 447
Lady's Well, 637
Lagado, 512
LA GOLONDRINA, 446, 613, *678*, 854, 1115-17
Lahore, India, 651
Lahore Museum, 651
the Laird, 80
Laird of Auchenskeoch, 636-37
Lake Constance, 620
Lake District, England, 972-74, 1177-79
Lake Hernon, 258-59
LAKE OF GOLD, 160, 678. *See THE LONG TRAVERSE, 732.*
lakes: dry up, 702; kingdom at bottom of, 930; loch, 368-70; Loch Ness, 642-43; reservoir, 1021-22; shallow, 230; stolen, 1142; with island in center, 120
Laketown, 95, 552, 1107, 1204
Lake Zurich, 1348
"la Longue Traverse," 733
Lama Anchi, 334, 1266
lamas, Tibetan, 334, 651-54, 655, 758, 853, 1194-95
Lamb, 38, 417-18
Lamb, Lynton, 486
Lamb, White, 1308
lambeg, 1285
Lampeter, Miss, 286, 820, 843
lamp-posts, in Narnia, 710, 712
lamps, vigil, 667
Lancashire: early 20th century, 703-6; late 20th century, 876-78
Lancaster Avro, 253
Lancastrians, in War of Roses, 102-4, 317, 683, 701
Lancelot, Sir, 1037-38
Land Between the Two Rivers, 624-27
landladies: old, 1241; old fashioned, 860, 1141; untrustworthy, 108
landlords, disagreeable, 267-68

landmark books: *ALICE'S ADVENTURES IN WONDERLAND, 19-22; BLACK BEAUTY, 105-7; THE BORROWERS, 132-34; FIVE CHILDREN AND IT, 416-18; GULLIVER'S TRAVELS, 508-14; THE HOBBIT, 550-53; THE HOUSE AT POOH CORNER, 562-64; THE JUNGLE BOOKS, 630-632; MARY POPPINS, 779-81; MASTERMAN READY, 786-89;* Narnia series: *THE HORSE AND HIS BOY, 560-62, THE LAST BATTLE, 687-89, THE LION, THE WITCH AND THE WARDROBE, 710-13, THE MAGICIAN'S NEPHEW, 755-57, PRINCE CASPIAN, 994-96, THE SILVER CHAIR, 1091-94, THE VOYAGE OF THE "DAWN TREADER," 1306-09; PETER AND WENDY, 956-58; ROBINSON CRUSOE, 1043-46; THE STORY OF DOCTOR DOLITTLE, 1145-46; THE STORY OF THE TREASURE SEEKERS, 1146-48; THROUGH THE LOOKING-GLASS, 1208-11; TREASURE ISLAND, 1253-56; THE WATER-BABIES, 1327-30; WATERSHIP DOWN, 1330-34; THE WIND IN THE WILLOWS, 1382-85; WINNIE-THE-POOH, 1388-89*
Land of Beulah, 977, 979
Land of Heart's Desire, Celtic, 643, 1227
Land of Youth, 1271
landowners: of city common, 536-37; wealthy, 890; insurrections against, 145, 1216-17
landslides, 1153, 1357
LANG, ANDREW, 83, *678-79*, 996
Lang, Leonora, 679
Langdale (ship), 29, 168, 1064-65
languages: ability in emergency, 450; discussion about meaning of words, 572; reflecting school social class, 427; barrier, prisoner knows no English, 422; Elvish, 437; foreign, misused, 340; French, 1018; Gaelic, 588, 590; German, 1051, 1136, 1316, 1318; Latin, 371, 1136, 1180-81, 1199, 1316, 1318; learning of, 325, 509, 513; of animals, 988, 1145; reforms, impractical, 512; Tibetan, 1266; Welsh, 1180
La Notre Dame de Calais (boat), 1214
THE LANTERN BEARERS, 350, *679-83*, 1091, 1176
lanterns, kerosene, 194
Lapps, 37, 578, 1350-51, 1402
Laputa, 511
Large, Annabel, 1353

THE LARK AND THE LAUREL, 581, *683-84*,
　1370
Larkins family, 926-27
The Lark in the Morn, 668, 685, 1306
THE LARK ON THE WING, *685-87*, 1306
larks: 721; ring with lark insig-
　nia, 581, 683-84
Larreta, Andres, 94
Larreta family, 28, 585, 1187-89
Lars, 378
Lasaraleen, 561
THE LAST BATTLE, 167, 321, *687-89*,
　699, 864, 987, 1027, 1174
last judgment, 688
Last of the Magicians, 472
The Last of the Mohicans, 418
The Last of the Vikings, 1257
The Last Viking, 1257
THE LATCHKEY CHILDREN, 25, *689-92*
Lathrop, Dorothy, 839
Latin Americans: in Chile, 1187-89;
　in England, 1076-78; in Mexico,
　601-2
Latin language: bane of student,
　164; church music, 1180-81;
　communication in, 236-37, 261,
　371, 915, 1056, 1311, 1412;
　importance of knowing, 38; learn-
　ing in, 1199; manuscript in, 1036;
　saint speaks in, 1378; study of,
　1200
Latin Master, 1180
Lattimer family, 23-24, 79-81, 205-
　6, 450, 741-42, 865, 874, 885
laughing gas, 780-81
laughs, causing boy's appearance,
　199
launches, of lifeboat, 927
launderettes, 607, 797-98
laundresses: 385-86, 814, 1048,
　1124, 1414; schoolgirls, 1401
LAURA, 52-54, 59, 74, 262, *692*, 728,
　821, 1370
LAURA CHANT, 150, 200-1, 636, *692-
　93*, 815, 1122-23, 1389
LAURA HAVERARD, 668, 685-86, *693*,
　1194
Laura Jones, 620-23
LAURA SECCOMBE, 455-56, 618, *693-94*,
　947
laurel, ring with symbol, 581, 683-
　84
LAUREL LYNN LEROY, *694*, 697, 412-14,
　485, 833, 988, 1065, 1238
Laurence, John, 387
Laurence Clare, 1105-6
Lavarcham, 299-300. *See also*
　Lavercam, 298-99.

Lavercam, 298-99. *See also*
　Lavarcham, 299-300.
LAVINIA BERESFORD, 560, *694-95*, 769,
　1221-23
law: scrapes with by Toad, 1229;
　scrapes with by talented pianist,
　86-87, 949-52
Law, of Islanders, 2, 1373
Lawgiving, cat's, 175
LAWLESS, WILL, 102-4, *695*, 1103
Law of the Jungle, 71, 630-32, 836
LAWRENCE, ANN, *695-96*, 1232
Lawrence family, 340-42
LAWRENCE WILLOUGHBY, 360-61, 361-
　62, *696*
Lawrie Marlow, 383-84, 963-65
Lawson, Robert, 161, 974-75, 980,
　996
lawyers: clerk of, 1346; family,
　649-51, 1401; gives girl advice
　about rights in family dispute,
　1326; shyster, 807; sinister,
　592, 493-95. *See also* attorneys;
　solicitors.
The Lay of the Starved Fool, 359
L. C. Wainwright, 363, 524
Leach, Simon, 453, 519, 791, 827,
　1133, 1402-3
Leadbetter, Mr., 845, 1354-55
leaders: abdicating in favor of
　younger man, 879; charismat-
　ic, 1104, 1298-1300; dedicated,
　254; deposed, 11; legendary, 754;
　legendary outlaw, Robin Hood, 145-
　47; natural, schoolboy, 449-50;
　of cave expedition, 13; of fellow-
　ship, 1158; of siblings, 614; old
　Sikh woman, 297; second mate, 787;
　self-proclaimed, 193; steady and
　sensible, 535; sturdy, wise, 787-
　89; unsure of self, 1158; wise, 238
leaflets, campaign, 1269
Leah family, 1144
Leah's Hill, 9
The Leaping Song, 984
leaps, daring from sail loft,
　951
learning: about Arthur, 1357-58; boy
　sees as social advancement, 933;
　boys seek, 1365-66; dedication
　to 565, 588-89, 1199; desire
　for, 179; girl seeks, 191, 386;
　love of, 185; love of Irish lore,
　216; mother eager that daughters
　pursue, 1196-97; Owl displays
　pretentiously, 1388; pretentious
　display, 1288; scholar dabbles in
　occult, 373; to read, 56; to read

and write, 16, 218. *See also* education.
Learson, Finn, 1155-56, 1409
lechers: elderly, 883, 896; uncle,
900
lectures: moralistic, 865; on Rome,
1149
ledges, narrow, 194
Ledsham, mid-20th century, 92-3,
451, 1100
Ledyard, 515
Leech, John, 227
Leek, Lillah, 1072-73
LEFT TILL CALLED FOR, 696, 1251,
1339. *See WE COULDN'T LEAVE DINAH*,
1339.
legacies: ability with witchcraft,
534; artifact, stone ax, 1025;
clouded reputation, 348; cottage,
477, 714; curse of reenacting
tragic legend, 923; debt-ridden
estate, 423; early airplane, 354;
entailed estate, 383; fear and
hatred, 286-87; grandfather's
anthropological discoveries, 564;
house and farm, 557; ill feeling
between families, 1021; kelpie
comes with land, 642; left to orphans, 426; local legend, 486;
lost, 813; poltergeist comes with
cottage, 451-53; pride in craft,
10, 484, 970, 1144, 1235; prophecy, 725; ring and humpback, 581;
ring of power and other property,
96, 406-8; skill at poaching, 284;
stone of power, 1343; to nurse and
nurse's daughter, 431. *See also*
inheritances.
Legalos, 407
Legates, of 6th Roman Legion, 348
The Legend of Maiden-Hair, 151
legends: Arthurian, 730, 1037-
39, 1141-43, 1258-59, 1342-45;
basis for novel, 113, 116, 145-47,
824-26, 1037-39, 1043, 1141-43,
1156-57; "bogey-man" rabbit, 446;
local, 1153; of lost Beekeeper,
1181; of St. Cuthbert, 1376-79;
of Robin Hood, 1043; parallels to
Robin Hood, 740; Scottish, basis
for novel, 1155-57; Welsh, basis
for novel, 932. *See also* folklore;
literature, oral; oral tradition.
leggers, on canal, 560, 959
Legions: Roman in Britain, 347-50,
633, 767-68; lost Roman, 375
legs: dog breaks, 1395; broken, set,
258; healed, 1396; mannequin's,

540-42; wooden, from Danish spear,
16, 871
Leif the Giant, 91-2
Leighton Buzzard, Bedfordshire,
early 20th century, 134-36, 137
Leire, the pirate, 1299-1300
lembas, 407
Lemuel Gulliver, 508-14
lemures, 200-1
LENNIE BYRE, 446-47, 612, 613, *696-
97*, 738, 778-79, 863, 1115-17
LENNY TRANTER, 483-84, 669, *697*,
874, 1020, 1335-36
Leo, the dog, 325, 639-40
Leon, 504
leopards, friendly, 1142-43
Leopold, King of Austria, 214
lepers, 1260
leprechauns, 713, 847, 850, 970,
1271, 1316
Leroy family, 412-14, 485, 694, 697,
833, 1065, 1238
lesbians, 1167
Leslie, Cecil, 1274
LESLIE PIPER, 414, 694, *697*, 1238
Lesseps, Bertrand, 558-59
lessons: dog in fetching, 921; drawing, 821; driving, 912; fife in
walking band, 1285; flying, 956;
Latin and other school subjects,
1200; musical theory, 224; piano,
86, 950; school drama, 286; singing, 1041; 1180-81; trumpet, 1062
Lessor, Miss, 656
LESTER, the ogre, *697-98*, 1354-55
Leszczynski, M. 1064
lettering, ancient, 1377
letters: can prevent a war, 907;
complaining, 524; compromising, 744, 1405; copied by mistake,
1404-5; delivered to badger set,
133; exonerating father, 1133;
folded into book, 427; found in old
desk, 456; fragment of, 1022; from
judge, 236; hidden, 693; hints at
past, 125; incriminating, 104,
276, 324; innersole, 744, 1406;
in violet ink, 1335; man's last
words, 662; lost, 909;
narrative device, 1165-67, 1169-
71, 1206-8, 1389-91; of imaginary
adventure, 412; of introduction, 620; of reference, 1197; of
reference from Earl, 708; sent by
hobgoblin, 549; 17th century, 963;
stolen, 404-5, 1318; threatening, 545; to art collector, 913;
to brother, 1238; to editor to save

church, 707; to grandmother, 1021–22; to influential people, 823; torn, pieced together, 428; urging invitation, 578. *See also* mail; messages; notes.

A Letter to the World: Poems for Young Readers, by Emily Dickinson, 459

Let the Balloon Go, 1129

LETTIE HATTER, 568–69, *698*, 777

LETTIE STAMP, 249, *698*, 762

Lettie Treloar, 430–31, 1242

"Letting in the Jungle," 631

lettre de cachet, 1216

Levenson, S., 732

Lew Farm, 486–87, 875

Lewin, 674

LEWIS, C(LIVE) S(TAPLES), 163, 376–77, 560, 687, *699–700*, 710, 755, 962, 994, 1091, 1306

LEWIS, HILDA (WINIFRED), 447, *700–1*

Lewisham Road, 1146

LEWIS MALLORY, 276, 683–84, *701*

Lewsbury Cathedral, museum, at, 1316

Liadhan, 252, 772–74, 806, 865

Liam Shakespeare, 1271–72, 606

libel: charges of, 360; imprisonment for, 849

Liberal Studies in Further Education--An Informal Survey, 1334

"liberation," of animals from zoo, 798

liberation: from evil, 688; from evil queen, 1143; from Masters, 991; from oppressive nobles, 1217; of Poland, World War II, 1097–98; of Vienna, 215. *See also* escapes; rescues.

librarians: Canadian, 200; mother, 1212; mother's sweetheart, 636, 692

libraries: at Oxford Univ., 126; children go to, 597, 1218; girl frequents, 736; public, 184, 199, 230

license plates, GEN11, 221

licenses: to perform plays, 154; for theater performances, 169; driving, 885

Lickey Hills, 1120

Lickey Top, 437, 931, 953, 1114, 1120–21

lies: about complicity in father's death, 1103; about identity of father, 1205; about retarded girl's death, 1289; about thefts of food, 692; Ape's duplicity, 687; create guilt, 931; death of prince,

720; frequent, 437, 640; mother is explorer in Africa, 1072–73; mother tells son boxer father was florist, 696; of barn owner, 307; of beauty departed, 300; of frog, 1114, 1120; ordered, 279; possible, 1236; sister tells blind brother about horse, 1367; spoken by inveterate Irish rogue, 186; threatened, 176, 886; to police, 809; to protect gorilla, 1155; to protect Robin Hood, 717; to thwart rival, 1226; to save girl's life, 341; to save lover from plague, 760, 939; various, 621; 1120–21

Lieutenant John Neville, 457

life: bound in book of matches, 209; brigades, 33; continuity of, 856; prolonged by ring, 465; secret of invulnerability, 114–15, 116, 754, 1189–90

The Life and Strange Surprizing Adventures of Robinson Crusoe..., 1043–44

lifeboats: Aran, 258; gateway to otherworld, 847–49

Life Brigade, 1325–26

life expectancy, of miners, short, 1277

Light, 1050

The Light Beyond the Forest: The Quest for the Holy Grail, 1037, 1175

lighthouses: 461; Roman, 680–81

lightning, 661

Lightnings, fighter planes, 29, 1212

LIGHTNING SOAMES, 193–94, *701*

THE LIGHT PRINCESS, *701–3*, 745

lights: bluish-green, 246–47; dropped down well, 246–47; dropped in moat, 247; watch, for ships, 680–81

The Light That Failed, 666

Light Trees, 476–77, 531, 555–57

A LIKELY LAD, 63, *703–6*

LILA, 526, *706–7*, 1302–5

Lilias Godman, 459, 581–83, 971, 1033

Lilias Rowan, 581

lilies: exotic, 1266–67; iron, 459; sea of water, 1308; with three drops of water, 661

Lilith, 1009

Lilla, 296, 1293

Lillah Leek, 1072–73

Lilliput, 509–10, 514

LILY FLACK, 16–17, 411, 707, 1390

Lily Greengrass, 62

Lily Rose Ruggles, 385-86, 1048
Lina, 1000-1
LINCOLN RIDLEY, 186-88, *707*, 815,
    981
Linda, 1363
Linda, the horse, 1367
LINDA MORRISON, *707-8*, 760, 799-800,
    1196-97
Linda's Lie, 52
Lindsay, Scottish noble, 1413
Lindsay family, 505, 636-38, 638
The Line, 831
LINE, DAVID (LIONEL DAVIDSON), *708-*
    9, 1061
liners, in pottery, 198
linguists: 844; of animal languages,
    323
LINKLATER, ERIC (ROBERT RUSSELL),
    709-10, 1385
Linley Bottom: mid-20th century, 37,
    1169; pre-World War II, 1169
Linnet, 337
LINNET OLDKNOW, 16, 211-13, *710*,
    1230
Linnets and Valerians, 471
A Lion in the Meadow, 758-60
lions: fight with unicorn, 1210;
    figurine becomes complete with
    policeman, 784; for ark, 829-
    30; talking, 43, 54-55, 185, 321,
    561-62, 687-88, 711-12, 755-56,
    875-76, 1082, 1306-8; wooden, 1205
THE LION, THE WITCH AND THE WARDROBE,
    699, *710-13*, 944
Lisbon, 513
lists, of offenders against emperor,
    280
literature: oral, 114, 513. *See also*
    folklore; legends; oral tradi-
    tion.
Little, Dr. and Mrs., 468
Little Barley, mid-20th century,
    328-30, 812-14
THE LITTLE BLACK HEN: AN IRISH FAIRY
    STORY, *713-14*, 909
The Little Book-Room, 393
Little Brother, 1120
Little Dorrit, 313
Little-Endians, 509
little Fan Scrooge, 228
A LITTLE FEAR, *714-16*, 1404
Little Fordham, early 20th centu-
    ry, 137, 138-39, 140-41, 822, 837,
    854, 856, 857
Little Friend of All the World, 651
THE LITTLE GREY MEN, 83, *716-17*
LITTLE JOHN, 146-47, *717*
Little Johnny's Confession, 943

LITTLE KATIA, 27, *717-720*
Little Kingdom, 397
THE LITTLE LAME PRINCE, 263, *720-22*
The Little Lame Prince and His
    Travelling Cloak, 263
Little Lord Fauntleroy, 962
Little Lord Fauntleroy, 1223
Little Peach, 818-19
Little Plum, 723
LITTLE PLUM, 458, *722-24*, 820
Little Merton, 1017
The Little Minister, 72
The Little Savage, 776
Little St. Mary's Chapel, 4
Little Sunshine's Holiday, 263
Little Topsails, mid-20th century,
    186-88, 707, 815, 981
The Little White Bird, 72
The Little White Bird; or, Adven-
    tures in Kensington Gardens, 72
THE LITTLE WHITE HORSE, 471, *724-27*
Little Weirwold: World War II peri-
    od, 179, 467-69, 1240, 1373, 1419;
    mid-20th century, 467-69
Live Flowers, 1209
LIVELY, PENELOPE (MARGARET), 387,
    451, 564, *727-28*, 1140
Liverpool, mid-20th century, 1064-
    65
livery stables, 106
Livesey, Doctor, 338, 1254-56
LIZ, 81, 645-46, *728*
Liz, 747
"the Lizard," 728
lizards, 1362
Liz Spencer, 183
Lizzie, the maid, 1281-82
Lizzie Allman, 1144
LIZZIE BROWN, 53-54, 262, *728*
Lizzie Leah's Hill, 1234-35
Lizzie White, 1021-23
Llangolly, Wales, 1056, 1290
Llanstephan, 672
Lleu Llau Gyffes, 116
LLEWELLYN, 671-72, *729*
Llewellyn family, 558-59
THE LOAD OF UNICORN, 527, *729-30*
loads, of sins, 975-76
loadstones, 512
loans: high finance, 1402; to buy
    horse, 1190; to restore fall-
    en fortunes of house of Bastable,
    1146-48
Lobel, Anita, 387
Lobster-Quadrille, 21, 23, 505, 827
lobsters, 1328
lobster traps, 544
local young people, hostile, 620-23

Lochleven, Castle of, 677, 1412-14
Loch Ness monster, 368, 642
lochs: thought to contain monster,
    27-28, 29
lockets, broken, 782
locks, canal, 197
Lockwood family, 377-79
Lodge family, 150, 156-58, 283, 655-
    56, 1033
lodgers: dispossessed, 242; lov-
    ers, 413, 590; next door, 1323;
    shopgirl and student, 564-65, 856,
    792; student couple, 428; Ugandan,
    613
lodges, Loyal Order of United
    Orangemen, 1285-87
LOFTING, HUGH (JOHN), *730-31*, 1145,
    1309
logic: convoluted, 557; representa-
    tive of, 19-22, 1208-11
Lombards, bankers, 234, 519, 791,
    1133, 1402-3
Londinium, burned, 1119
London: early 12th century, 1015,
    1394-96; early 14th century,
    1018; late 14th century, 447-49;
    mid-15th century, 71, 1405; late
    15th century, 196, 729-30; early
    17th century, 1351-53; mid-17th
    century, 1199-202; 18th century,
    111-13, 169-71, 339-42, 610-11,
    824-26, 1065-66, 1108-10, 1125-
    28; 19th century, 839-41; early
    19th century, 107-9, 1223-25;
    mid-19th century, 227-30, 1399-
    1401; late 19th century, 55-57,
    489-92, 755-57, 1066, 1146-48;
    early 20th century, 354-56, 899-
    902; mid-20th century, 68-71,
    84-85, 173-75, 328-30, 330-32,
    386, 414-16, 501, 667-68, 685-
    87, 689-92, 722-24, 889, 897-99,
    1114-17, 1218; late 20th century,
    41-42, 519-21, 285, 597, 656-58,
    797-99, 917, 1025-26, 1039-41,
    1061-64, 1262-64, 1313-15; World
    War II period, 414-16, 468, 924-
    26; mid-21st century, 505-8. *See
    also* Londinium.
The London Child, 445
London Philharmonic, 412
London School of Economics, 536
Lone Islands, 1306
Lonely Mountain, 551-53, 1107, 1204
Lone Wolf, 11, 630
Long Arrow, 1309-10
Long Ears, the donkey, 1271-
    72

Long family, 59, 532-33, 1237-38,
    1240-42, 1279
LONG JOHN MACGREGOR, *731-32*, 790-91,
    832, 884
LONG JOHN SILVER, 172, 237, 338, 731,
    732, 796, 965, 1132, 1139, 1254-56
THE LONG TRAVERSE, 160, *732-34*
A LONG WAY FROM VERONA, 440, *734-37*
A Long Way to Shiloh, 708
look-alikes, 771-72, 967-68
Looking-Glass House, 1024, 1209
Looking-Glass Insects, 1209
Looking-Glass world, 1361
looking glasses: entrance to other
    world, 18; Persian, 374
looms, wood used for sled, 1235
Loon, Charlee, 1094-96
loot, robbers', recovered, 1179
Lootie, 1002
looting, 4, 91, 146, 214, 279, 372,
    870, 896, 1097-98, 1216-17, 1299
Lorbrulgrud, 510
Lord, slave-master, 1295
Lord Bakerloo, 108
Lord Brutus, 279-80
Lord Celsus, 47, 158, 279, 557
Lord de Staseley, 17
Lord Digory, 321
The Lord Fish and Other Tales, 302,
    839
LORD FOLAN, *737,* 1102
Lord Foxham, 103, 606
Lord Frith, 535
Lord Garvald, 1196, 1198
LORD GOD, *737,* 829, 895
lord-high treasurer, 509
Lord Lieutenant of the County, 507
Lord Lumley of Nonsuch, 574, 1352-53
LORD MALYN, 43, *37-38*, 996, 1234,
    1357-58
Lord Mayor of London, 1405
Lord Melbourne, 529
Lord of Evil, 406, 436
Lord of Misrule, 1414
Lord of the Flies, 48, 443
The Lord of the Rings, 405, 553, 1230
Lord of the Tame Worm, 397
Lord of the Whole Wood of Narnia, 54
Lord of the Wood, 711
lords, hereditary, of Welsh valley,
    575
Lord Shoreby, 103, 606, 615, 1103
LORD SIMON VIGO, 115-16, 613, 697,
    738, 863
Lord Skrumshus, 221
Lords of Ranelagh, 499
Lord Sprockett, 435-36
Lord Strange's Servants, 1351

LORD TOM, *738*, 818, 839, 1108-10
Lord Tottenham, 1147
Lorel, Master Cock, 1352
lore-masters, 505
Lorna Wimbleball, 378-79
lorry drivers, 426
Lory, 22
Los Obstinados, 1187
losses: of mill and mansion, 303; of
    pet pig, 59
Lost Boys, 956-58, 961, 1226, 1347
LOST JOHN, A YOUNG OUTLAW IN THE FOR-
    EST OF ARDEN, *738-40*, 969
The Lost Princess, 83
Lothlorien, 407
lots: drawn for contest, 1355; draw
    straws, 1293; for wolf killing,
    1320
love: chaste, 1170; confession of,
    87; domestic, 266-69; family,
    266-69; healing power of, 88;
    hopeless, 202-3; insufficient,
    309; need for, 1368-69; power of,
    150, 332-33, 609; power of to break
    spells, 569; redemptive force of,
    283; unrequited, 378; to establish
    communication, 1026; unselfish,
    1411; versus greed, 642-43
Loveday Minette, 725-26
Lovell, 1394-96
Lovell family, 4-5, 318-21, 669-70,
    822
Love in Ambush, 1371
lovers: adulterous, 810; botanist
    and guide, 1266; dies in plague,
    760, 939; estranged, reconciled,
    726; different social classes,
    25-26; illicit, 748; inconstant,
    186; killed in motorcycle crash,
    873; killed in World War I, 761;
    live-in, 590; male, 1364; mar-
    ried man, 277; mother's, 1326-27;
    mother's dead, 47; mother's stolen
    by daughter, 1323, 1420; occasion-
    al, of mother, 277; old, 1280; on
    kitchen floor, 98; rejected, 532;
    sentenced to be slain, 1260; World
    War I period, 761
LOUAN, *740*, 1102
Louisa (boat), 926
Louisa Evans, 60
Louis XVI, King of France, 1216-17
Low Street, 262, 401
loyalty: between cousins, 1248; de-
    spite misgivings, 73; despite
    rejection, 115; dilemma about,
    1012; epitomized, 845; misplaced,
    777, 791; of animals, 1382-85; of

family, 338; to cause, 1284-87,
    1414; to cause and group, 747-50;
    to city, 546; to companion on road,
    876; to emperor, 1091; to fami-
    ly, 457; to family as clan, 80;
    to father, 15, 896; to fellow re-
    bels, 101; to Iceni heritage, 261;
    to King Edward, 1104; to medical
    code, 119; to Viking master, 116-
    18
Lubrin Dhu, 1171-73
Lucas, Kate, 638, 1033
LUCAS BELL, 31-32, 508, 677, *740-41*,
    807-809, 845, 1104
Lucas family, 1141
Lucifer's Smoke, 304
luck, 812-14, 847, 1069
Luckett, Arnold, 48-49, 452, 1100
Lucknow, 652
lucky pieces. *See* talismans.
Lucy (*A Chance Child*), 110, 264
Lucy (*Watership Down*), 1333
LUCY DENHAM-LUCIE, 58, 636, *741*,
    1280, 1323-24, 1420
LUCY GRAHAM, 79-81, *741-42*, 865,
    874, 450
LUCY MOORE, *742*, 1225
LUCY PEVENSIE, 55, 185, 321, 356-57,
    376, 560, 603, 688, 710-12, *742-*
    43, 864, 961-62, 994-96, 1009,
    1026-27, 1093, 1174, 1306-8
Ludwig, the dog, 598
Luga, 1320
Luggnagg, 512-13
Luis Murjica, 1366-67
Lullaby Land: Songs of Childhood by
    Eugene Field, 472
Lumba, Sidney, 77-78, 465
luminaries, 75, 325-28, 640
Lumley, Lord, 574
Lumna, 1244-45
lunch counters, wrecked, 521
Lune, King of Archenland, 561, 1081
Lung, 333-34, 853, 1195, 1266
Lunn family, 276-79
Lupercal, 571
Lupy, Aunt, 1282
LURGAN SAHIB, 653, *742-43*
luxury, of Middle East, 670, 672
LYAPO, *743*, 1068-71
Lydia Dukes, 1071-73
LYNCH, PATRICIA (NORA), *743-44*,
    1270-71
Lynmouth lifeboat crew, 926-27
Lynn, Tom, 412-14, 485, 590, 694,
    697, 833, 893, 987-88, 1065
Lynn family, 1238
Lyon, Merriman, 148, 288, 502, 1375

Lyonesse, 1142–43
LYS Rudd, 454, *744*, 799, 909, 1406

Ma, the sheep, 1082–83
Maarten Van Mierevelt, 457
Mabinogion, 444
Mabon, King of Lyonesse, 1142
Macarthur-Onslow, Annette, 215, 903
MacAskill, Alasdair, 605, 1049–50
MacBride, Ros, 588–89, 1048–49
MACDONALD, GEORGE, 55, 57, 84, 180,
  462–63, 701, *745–46*, 999, 1002
MACDONALD, SHELAGH, *746*, 899
Macdonnell, Alan, 783
MACEY, *746–47*, 1025, 1203
MACGIBBON, JEAN (HOWARD), 519, *747*
Macha, 91
THE MACHINE GUNNERS, 400, *747–50*,
  1347
machine guns. *See* weapons.
machines: considered evil, 1055,
  1337–38; hated, 449, 886; light-
  er than air, 1143; shops, auto,
  904, motorcycle, 523–24; road-
  building, 404–5
MACKEN, WALTER, 425, *750*
Mackenzie, the cat, 893–94
Mackenzie, John, 1398–99
Mackenzie family, 1049–50, 1058
Mackie, Mrs., 1123
Mackracken, Mr., 1285–87
Maclaren family, 650
MacLeish, Hamish, 160, 281–83, 523,
  1223
MacLeod, Morag, 13, 641–42, 830,
  914–15
MACPHERSON, MARGARET, *750–51*, 1049
Macpherson family, 650
MacQueen, Duncan, 1398–99
MacVinish, Torquil, 642–43, 1243–44
madam, of brothel, 402, 881, 1084
Madam de Coucy, 600
MADAME DE VAIRMONT, *751–52*, 832,
  1215–17
Madame Fidolia, 69
Madame Ginette, 668
Madame How and Lady Why, 664
MADAME OLYMPIA, 518, *752*, 1105,
  1354–55
Madam Fettiplace, 549–50
Maddox, 340–41
MADELEINE STUDDARD, 93, *752*, 810,
  1376–78
Madely, Piers, 1036
Maderistas, 601–2, 753
MADERO, FRANCISCO, 601, *752–53*
MADGE, 77–78, 465–67, *753*, 792, 1080
Madge Fielding, 459–62, 1287–90

Madge Rowley, 1026, 1203
MAD HATTER, 20, 22, 23, 334–35, *753–
  54*, 767, 923–24, 1210
madhouses, private, 88, 110, 111
Madington, 224, 1180, 1182
madness: assumed inherited, 110;
  caused by Changes, 311–12;
  deviation from norm in mind controlled society, 1295; in family,
  concealed, 88; treated in slave
  labor camp, 1295
Madoc, Prince of Quivera, 236–37,
  915, 1268
The Mad O'Haras, 744
madonnas: 599, 668; painting stolen,
  797–98
mad people: assumed, 74; battle-mad
  monk, 375; harmless, 154; young
  girl, 88, 110, 111
Maenads, 996
Maeve, Queen of Connacht, 299
Mafia, Opera, 1076–77
Ma Flint, 466–67
Maggie Hemp, 144
MAGGIE HOLBEIN, 539, *754*, 1039
Maggot Hobbin, 1168
MAGERE the Stone, 113–15, *754*, 920,
  1189
magic: 55–57, 127–28, 150, 168,
  173–75, 188–90, 191, 201–2, 208–
  9, 221–23, 227–30, 246–48, 268,
  287–88, 298–99, 321, 359–60, 365,
  414, 429, 439–40, 462–63, 472,
  485, 517–18, 505, 568–69, 593–95,
  598, 636–38, 659–62, 675, 710–13,
  720–22, 743, 755–57, 777, 779–81,
  830, 928–30, 913–14, 932–35, 960,
  969, 994–96, 996–99, 1009, 1035–
  36, 1042, 1056, 1067, 1091–93,
  1094–96, 1111–13, 1122, 1155–
  57, 1232–34, 1261, 1271–72, 1279,
  1298, 1327–30, 1336–38, 1342–45,
  1375, 1376–79, 1385–86, 1392–94,
  1409–11; ability suppressed, 498,
  533–34; accusations of, 631; ancient book of, 800; black, 373–75,
  505, 874, 893, 1067, 1231; books
  of, 174; dawn mist, 1367; goes
  awry, 1355; inherited, 1264; lasting only one day, 416–18, 598,
  1041; silent, 173; of deepest
  black, 1354; tricks, 844; wishes,
  1377–78
magical objects. *See* talismans.
The Magic Bed-Knob, 905
magicians: ancient Ireland, 299;
  assistant to, bumbling, 777; devious uncle, 755–57; boy suspected,

498; elegant enchanter, 225; girl revealed as, 264; great-uncle, 498; has enspelled Monopods, 1307; has magical book, 1307; runaway, 498, unemployed stage, 922, 1267-68; with wayward spell, 1290. *See also* enchanters; necromancers; warlocks; witches; wizards.
THE MAGICIAN'S NEPHEW, 688, 699, 710, *755-57*
The Magicians of Caprona, 617
The Magic Stone, 394
The Magic Walking Stick, 160
magistrates: blind, 845-46, 820-21, 1107-8, 1108-10; doctor, 338, 1254; elderly, 1206; female, 319; kindly, 169; whimsical, 169. *See also* judges.
magneto: boat, 449; considered evil, 1337
MAGORIAN, MICHELLE, 467, 757
MAGWITCH, ABEL, 376, 494, 592, *757*, 981, 1346
MAHBUB ALI, 651-52, 654, *757-58*
MAHY, MARGARET, 200, 533, *758*
Maia, 780
maiden, of flowers, 932
Maiden's Trip, 1111
maids: Ballinford Hall, 1197; companion on journey to Celestial City, 978; Danish, 477, 920-21, 1048, 1195, 1372; dismissed for theft, 854; doll, 558; four, 976; farm girl, 94; fired, 645; Glasgow, 588-89; hen of royal cook, 713; house, 4, 763-64, 1068; in service at eight, 1158; kitchen, pregnant, 422; lady's, 234, 516, 1121; mean tricker, 645; mother, 1124; of enchanter, 208-9; practical, 190, 341-42, 880; scullery, 560, 694, 1221; tavern, 1127-28; 13-year-old Russian, 718; to Duchess, 108; Ukrainian, 501, 599, 667-68; Welsh, 558; wispy, 1241; youthful, 1115-60. *See also* housekeepers; housemaids.
Maids' Ribbons, 1252
mail: censored, 1084. *See also* letters; messages; notes.
Mainly in Moonlight, 488
Mairi, 216, 482
Mairi Gilbride, 588-89, 590, 1048-49
Maitland, Antony, 111, 304, 328, 339, 451, 1108
Major Alexander, 1149-50
Major Cass Harper, 60, 177-78
Major McAndrew, 368, 370, 992
Major Fitzwarren, 341
Major Hague, 33
Makemnoit, Princess, 701-2
Makepeace family, 6-7, 161, 206-8, 365, 366-68, 1168-69
malapropisms, 160
MALCOLM III, King of Scotia, 273, *760*, 768, 804, 986, 1012-13
Malebron, 359
Malise Marlow, 963-64
Malkin's Mountain, 831
Mallie Gross, 637
Mallory family, 276, 583, 683-84, 701, 762
MALL PERCIVAL, *760*, 938-39, 1203
Malone, Mary, 521
Malory, Sir Thomas, 195, 729-30, 1037
malnutrition, 852, 1098, 1276
Maltese, in England, 401-2, 881
Malyn, Lord, 43, 1234, 1357-58
MAMA, *761*, 924-26, 1348-49
Mamelouke, the cat, 1032
MAM Morrison, 47, 708, 800, *760-61*, 1196-98
Mammy Fay, 1133-36
Mamo, 258-59, 261
man, frog-like, 1007
managers, shoestore, 399
Manchester, England: early 20th century, 17, 449, 539, 703-6, 1267-68; mid-20th century, 359-60
Manchild, 943
man-cub, 65
Mandover, 891
Mandrake, 255
Mango Island, 257
Manhattan Is Missing, 547
Manifestation of Mysterious Behavior, 1419
manifestos, of social reform, 360, 1224
manikin: slave of light, 247. *See also* mannikin, 510.
Man in the Moon, 202, 1096
Manitou River, 733
Manjit Miram, 657-58
Manly, John, 105, 596, 612
Man-Mountain, 509
Man-Mountain Fink, 222
mannequins, 540-42
mannikin: 510. *See also* manikin, 247.
Manny Goodchild, 1213-15
The Man of the House, 796
Man of the West, 1158

manors: ancestral near Fulking, 304-
6; burned out, 1010: bustling forest freehold, 276, 582-83, 683-84,
762; decaying, 1281; in Cotswolds
with resident hobgoblin, 450, 547,
548-50; Jerusalem, 1317-19; late
11th century, 673-75; Marsh, 403-
5, 434-36; on coast of England's
West Country, 1112; on Devonshire
coast, 724-26; ramshackle, 243;
spirit of girl haunts, 455-56,
947. See also castles; mansions;
palaces.
Mansfield family, 820-21, 839, 845-
46, 1108-10
mansions: ancestral country, 1400;
big old, 4; burned, 32, 740, 845;
chimney sweep visits, 363, 1328;
Darkington Hall, 1397; dating from
Crusades, 211-13, 217-19, 373-
75, 525, 577-78, 1035-36, 1229-30;
decaying, 177-78, 419-21, 421-24,
542-43; derelict, 98, 226, 648-
49, 616, 813-14, 1115; dominates
town, 537; Georgian, 1236; large,
gloomy, 677, 807, 1104; Midnight
Court, 119; mysterious, 412-
13; old, 1389; refuge in flood,
496-97, 543; rock crystal, 815;
Toad's, 828; witches', 200; wizard's, 1353-56. See also castles;
homes; houses; manors; palaces.
manservant, wicked, 218-19
MANTE Kwatey-Jones, 249-52, 478,
482, 762
MANTLEMASS, 276, 581-83, 683-84,
762-63, 971-72, 1033, 1370
manufacturers: of candy, 203-4, 221;
of rugs, 806-9. See also factories; mills.
manuscripts: about Napoleon's mother, 1349; illuminated, 155; in
bottle, 1036; musical, 428; of
Arthurian legends, 730; of Sir
Thomas Malory, 730
The-Man-with-the-Red-Handkerchief,
1112
Mao, 182
Maplin Bird (yacht), 3, 763-64
THE MAPLIN BIRD, 763-65, 966
mapmakers, 67
maps: for rescue party, 193; to freedom, 1359; to mountain provided
by wizard, 552; to Tibet, 1266;
treasure, 100, 338, 1254; used by
wood smugglers, 1403; valuable,
lost, 165-66
Marassa, 765-67, 938, 1227

MARASSA AND MIDNIGHT, 765-67, 1164
The Marble in the Water: Essays on
Contemporary Writers for Children
and Young People, 1027-28
Marc, King, of Cornwall, 1259-61
marchen: basis for story, 996-99;
elements, 701-2, 927-30
MARCH HARE, 20, 23, 334-35, 753, 767,
1210
Marchioness, 23
Marchpane, 102, 331
MARCUS AQUILA, 261, 347-50, 375,
767-68, 1089, 1091
Margaret, 565
MARGARET, QUEEN OF SCOTIA, 760, 768-
69, 986, 1012-13
MARGARET BRADLEY, 25, 245, 768, 873-
74, 933, 1047
Margaret Rose, Princess of England,
1048
Margaret Kwatey-Jones, 249, 478, 762
MARGARET THURSDAY, 560, 694-95,
769, 959, 1220-23
Margaret Turner, 1364
Margery Furness, 903-4
Margery Rowley, 1026, 1203
Maria Foster, 860, 1140-41
MARIA HENNIKER-HADDEN, 596, 623,
769-70, 842, 1203, 1281-82, 1316-
19
Maria Merryweather, 724-27
MARIA OLDKNOW, 195, 217-19, 770
Mari-Bel Murjica, 1367
Marie Antoinette, 1217
Marigold (ship), 893
Marika Kodaly, 363
marinas, proposed, 517
Marionetas de los Gemelos, 1187
marionette shows, 28, 94, 585
Marion Ramsay, 427-28
Marion's Angels, 87, 942, 966, 1053
Mari Parry, 567
MARJORY BELL, 60-61, 475-76, 538-39,
770, 899-902, 1192, 1283-84
MARK, JAN (ET MARJORIE), 39, 523,
770-71, 1211
markets: cattle, 605; Chilean, 585;
Fairfax, 174; Manchester, 1267
Market Chipping, 568-69
THE MARK OF THE HORSE LORD, 171-74,
1176
Mark Poltoratzky, 1415-17
MARK RUSSELL, 226-27, 317, 335, 355-
56, 419-21, 421-24, 775, 1228,
1284, 1374
marks: of stonemason, 1144; on forehead, 772; protective, 976
marksman, crack, 1132

Mark Trevelyan, 890
MARK VAUGHAN, 495-98, 543, 604, 775-76, 786
Marley's ghost, 227
Marlowe, Christopher, 876, 1202, 1351
Marlowe, Nat, 876
Marlowe family, 574, 1202, 1351-53
Marlow family, 382-85, 428-29, 963-65
Marmaduke Scarlet, 724-25
marmalade: promise of, 84; sandwich dropped on bald head, 84
Marmalade and Rufus, 292
Marooners Rock, 957
Maroons, 766
maroons: 89, 108, 513, 579-80, 632, 659, 787-89, 855, 859, 1044-45, 1255-56. *See also* castaways.
marriages: anvil, 1197; arranged, 276, 459, 606, 827, 885, 117-181, 1200, 1266, 1402, unhappy, 276, unwelcome, 103, 550, 684; as political tool, 276; British Roman girl to Saxon, 681; broken, 227, 775; child, 276, 684, 701; contracts, 279; dissolved, 317; English horse dealer-Neapolitan opera singer, 846; ex-slave-Byzantine lady, 281; for ulterior purpose, 754; interracial, black woman-Welsh man, 4, 101, 286, 1039-41; interracial, black Ghanian-white Englishwoman, 249; made possible by father's death, 355-56; man to socially superior woman, 703-4; of convenience, 58; opposed by mother, 800; planned to avert prophecy, 298; political, 117-18, 681; to French noble, opposed by girl, 684; to missionary, 693; royal tribal, 773, 865; stormy, 752; unwanted, 256-57; wartime, 500
Marriot family, 88-89, 204-5, 425, 1247-50
Marriott, Pat, 1399
Marryat, Florence, 777
MARRYAT, FREDERICK, 776-77, 786
Mars, W. T., 480, 970
MARSHALL, COLIN, 37, 286-87, 591, 777, 843
marshes: convict found in, 492; demons thought in, 863; drained, 1133; flooded, 33, 802-3, 863; north of Hadrian's Wall, 350; pretended to be China, 801; Yorkshire, 801-4. *See also* bogs; swamps.
Marshfield, 433, 792
The Marsh King, 555, 872
Marsh Manor, 403-5, 434-36
Marsh-wiggles, 1092
Marston Hall, 98, 1193
Marta, 501, 599, 667-68
Martha, 38
MARTHA HATTER, 569-69, 698, 777
MARTHA WIDDISON, 450, 548-50, *778*
Martin, 146
MARTIN BERTOLD, 33-36, 592, *778*
Martin Conway, 1363-64
Martin family, 37-38, 945-46, 968-69, 1169-71
Martin Folan, 259-60
Martin Henchman, 190
Martin Heritage, 154-55
Martin Lucas, 1141
Martin Pippin in the Apple-Orchard, 393
Martin Pippin in the Daisy-Field, 393
MARTIN SINGER, 446-47, 612, 613, 697, 738, *778-79*, 853-54, 863, 1114-17
martyrs: grandmother, 476; King Edmund, 375; Quaker zealot, 686, 811; to political cause, 101
Marvell, Andrew, 1124, 1143-44
The Marvelous Story of Puss in Boots, 488
Mary (Stone Book Series), 399, 484, 619, 914, 1143-44
Mary, Queen of England, 457-58
Mary, Queen of Scots, 677-78, 814-15, 1412-15
Mary Arundel, 1126
Mary Byrne, 499
Mary Flatley, 143-44, 186
Mary Harris, 143
Mary Lockwood, 378
Mary Malone, 521
Mary, Mary, 1138
MARY OWLAND, 2, 486-87, *779*, 875
Mary Poppins, 779-81, 781-83, 783-84, 784-86
MARY POPPINS, 779-81, 782, 783, 784, 1250
MARY POPPINS COMES BACK, 781-83, 784, 1250
Mary Poppins from A to Z, 1250
Mary Poppins in Cherry Tree Lane, 1250
Mary Poppins in the Kitchen: A Cookery Book with a Story, 1250
MARY POPPINS IN THE PARK, 783, *783-84*, 1250

MARY POPPINS OPENS THE DOOR, 783, *784-86*, 1250
Mary the Queen, 700
Mary Thomas, 397-98
MARY VAUGHAN, 496-98, 543, 604, 775, *786*, 866-67
Masada, 150, 157-58, 283, 1033
mascots, sailor doll, 558-59
Masha, 1300-2
The Masker, 1031
masks, golden, 88
Mason, Dick, 1160
Masonic Orphanage, 652
masques, 1353
massacres: at Kilcullen, 500; English Civil War, 611-12; of captain and crew by natives, 256-57; of Barthomley church, 1026, 1203; of Irish stronghold, 216; of mentally ill, 157; of nuclear ill, 156-57; of Russian peasants, 16; of slaves, 1070; on high seas, 1069-70; revenge, 1070; revenge killings, 866
Master, of village, 50, 311, 648
Master Alleyn, 1351
Master Antonio Bari, 1402-3
Masterman Ready, 855, 859
MASTERMAN READY, 776, *786-89*
MASTER OF MORGANA, *789-91*, 796
Master of the Hunt, 1042
Master of Wild Hunt, 326-27
Masters: contemplative, 239-40; cruel, 239-40; destroyed, 989-91; reptilian, 239
masters: abusive, 1328; cruel miner, 1238-39; cruel to animals, 106, 1112; dapple-gray horse, 513; demanding, 824; female, of iron foundry, 582-83; worthy, 350-51
MASTER SIMON BRAYLES, *791*, 1405
MASTER THOMAS FETTERLOCK, 453, 519, *791*, 827, 884-85, 1133, 1402-3
Master Welford, 1233
mastiffs, captured by gypsies, 1387
Matadan, 182
Matcham, Jack, 606
matches: girls mistaken for, 1385; lives bound in, 209
matchmen, 780, 783
mates: brutal, 649; chosen, 1321; first, 29, 168-19, 887, 893, 1052, 1064-65, 1069; of boat, 949; second, sturdy, 787; superstitious ship's, 1064. *See also* marriages.
mathematics, boy learns secretly, 1374
Mathilda, the donkey, 1112

Mati, 1301-2
mating season, 632
matriarchal societies, 39-41, 772-73, 865-66
matriarchs: African, 477-78; domineering grandmother, 475-76; eccentric, 477; queen, 654; witch, 498
matrilineal societies, 1161, 1171-72
matrons: abusive, 1192, 1355; cruel, 769, 1400-1; dormitory, 946; evil, 1221-23; house, at boy's school, 96-9
Mattean ambassador's son, 219
Matteans: 30; terrorists, 330
Matteo, 11, 283, 1076-78
Matt Heffernan, 1151, 1153
Matthew Clemens, 397-99
Matthew Hopkins, 308
Matthew Goodrich, 612, 729-30
MATT MCGINLEY, 77-78, 465-67, 539, *791-92*; 1080
MATT PULLEN, 85, 433-34, 792, 1379-81
maturity, in younger brother, 33-36
Maudlyn, the witch, 1019
Maugrim, 711
MAUREEN COOPER, 564-65, *792*
MAURICE, 150, 389-92, *792-93*
MAX, 761, *793*, 924-26, 937, 1348-49
MAX MORLEY, *793-94*, 1164, 1274-75
Maxwell, 86
Maxwell family, 505, 636-38
May, Mrs., 713-14, 1236
May Day, 713-14, 1414
May Eve, 713
Mayfield family, 62, 564-66, 613, 792, 856
May Fielding, 267-68
Mayflower (ship), 747
May Mortimer, 399-400, 836
MAYNE, WILLIAM (JAMES CARTER), 84, 119, 223, 351, 393, 486, *794-95*, 801, 1021, 1180, 1409
mayors: helpful, 889; of London, 1405; of New York City, 594; woman, 922, 1267-68
The Maythorn Story, 1253
mazes: of chimneys, 1328; outdoor, 120; underground, 1343. *See also* labyrinths.
McAndrew family, 27, 29, 368-70, 411, 992, 1046-47
McAndrew's Infallible Linament, 368
McCluskey, the sheep dog, 1313
McGill, Mr., 1326

McGill family, 57-58, 197, 210, 245,
   262-63, 400-3, 747-50, 881, 887,
   1084, 1177
McGinley, Matt, 465-67, 539, 1080
McGinley family, 77-78, 791-92
McGurk Organization, 184-85
McIntyre, Dr., 339, 1124
McKay family, 1390
MCLEAN, ALLAN CAMPBELL, 789, *795-96*
McNair family, 616, 846, 960-61,
   1004-6, 1190-92
MCNEILL (ALEXANDER), JANET, 77,
   465, *796-97*, 923
McShane family, 7, 339, 818, 850,
   924, 942-43, 1084, 1123-25, 1337-
   74
ME AND MY MILLION, 659, *797-799*
measles, sheep gets, 1354
MEATY SANDERS, 13, 193-94, *799*
Meccer, Jimmie, 556
mechanical things: ambivalent attitude toward, 1338; forbidden,
   1337; ruins, of, 1359
mechanics: airplane, early, 354;
   auto, 284, 708, 904, 1197; motorcycle, 523-24
medals: for Greatness, 492; for val-
   or, 816, 1032
Medborough, 1071-74
Meddington, 809
media: focus on dwarf, 848; focus on
   painting, 797-99; focus on terrorists, 1078; focus on runaways,
   1249
medicines: folk, 233; for removing
   facial pigmentation, 1145; ordered mysteriously, 824; Piglet
   takes Roo's, 1389; strengthening,
   563
Medieval Period: British Isles, 102-
   5, 145-47, 153-55, 215-17, 672-75,
   738-40, 915-17, 1012-13, 1017-
   20, 1035-36, 1085-87, 1394-96;
   British Isles and Europe, 91-
   92, 116-19; Middle East, 670-72;
   Vikings, 91-92, 116-17, 1298-1300
medieval worlds: fantasy, 246-48,
   359-60, 560-62, 659-62, 687-89,
   710-13, 720-22, 755-57, 994-96,
   996-99, 999-1002, 1002-3, 1091-
   94, 1232-34, 1258-61, 1306-9;
   reversion to, 237-40, 309-13, 989-
   92, 1336-38, 1359-61
mediums, 305, 942
Medley family, 581-83, 762, 971-72,
   1033
meetings: family, 80, 132, 370, 970;
   in Fiscal's office about death,

1196; of animals, 389, 911; of
   cats, 175; of nations, future,
   991; of Prisoner's Aid Society,
   815, 1032; of Turkish leaders,
   213; of union, 1276; on school bus,
   801-3; philosophical discussions,
   1288; secret, of tribal leaders to
   enlist look-alike for king, 772;
   secret, in train, 1084; to rescue ship, 926; witches, 429, 1354;
   wolves, 630
Meet My Folks!, 570
Meet Simon Black, 1129
meets, horse, 382-85, 419-21, 1006,
   1190-92, 1339-44
MEG, 324, 350-51, 454, 744, *799*, 909,
   1405-6,
Megan Parry, 567
Meg Frazer, 889-91
MEG MORRISON, 47, 707-8, 760-61,
   799-800, 1196-98
Meg Pargeter, 338, 612, 742, 849,
   859, 1041-42, 1224-25
Mehmed the Fourth, Sultan of Turkey,
   213-15
Meikle, Archie, 799-800
Meikle family, 47, 799-800, 1196-98
MELANIE DELIA POWERS, 373-75, *800*,
   859
Melbourne, Hatty, 532-33
Melbourne family, 1238, 1240-42
Meles-Brock, 152, 931
Melligraunce, Sir, 1037
melodramas: fantasy, 887-89, 1142-
   43, 1356-58; realistic, 107-9,
   110-13, 806-9, 889-91, 1108-10,
   1125-28, 1149-51, 1399-1401. *See
   also* Gothic novels.
Meluseth, 196
Melusine Demogorgona Phospher, 800
Melton family, 33, 50-51, 942, 1225,
   1325-27
MELWOOD, MARY (EILEEN MARY HALL LEW-
   IS), *800-1*, 1322
Melynedd Valley, 143
THE MEMBER FOR THE MARSH, 794, *801-
   4*
memoirs: dictated to girl, 430-31;
   taped, 873, 1242; written down,
   508-14
Memoirs of a Midget, 302
memorable characters, 19-22, 105-
   7, 132-34, 227-30, 508-14, 550-53,
   562-64, 630-32, 710-13, 779-81,
   956-58, 1043-46, 1145-46, 1146-
   48, 1208-11, 1253-56, 1330-34,
   1382-85, 1388-89
Memoranda books, 134

memories: double, 411-14; erased, 413, 694, 893, 1294-95; repressed, 1368; restored, 1142; suppressed, 411

Memory, programmed, 1294

Memory Hold-the-Door, 159

men: big-bearded, green-eyed, 738; especially self-assured, 737; in lavender suit, 920; two in brown, 738, 1108-10

The Men and the Boats: Britain's Life-Boat Service, 52

men-of-all-work: 480. *See also* handymen; hired men.

Men of Masaba, 526

Meneot, John, 1193

The Menorah Men, 708

menstrual periods, first, 250, 252

mental telepathy: 1123, 1378. *See also* clairvoyance; ESP; second sight.

mentors: advising making boy friend jealous, 335; artistic, 108-9, 751; artist, 1215; death of, 354; encouraging girl to write, 339; immortal, 804; of man cub, 65-66, 71; sea captain of youth, 1069-70; seaman, 29

Menzies, Miss, 822, 837, 857

MERCA, 273, 768-69, *804*, 1012-13

Mercedes, windshield smashed in strife, 876, 910

mercenaries, soldiers, 117-18, 371

Merchant, Mr., 1270

merchants: ancient Ur, 1204; diamond, 1379-80; too trusting, 791; wealthy Dutch, 457; wool, 791, 884, 1018, 1233-34, 1402-3

Mercier, Pierre, 1215-18

Mercury Motor Sales, 363

Mercy, 978-79

the Mere, 120

Meredith family, 615-16, 809-10, 846, 857-58, 960-61, 1004-7, 1191-92

merged families, novels of, 79-81, 455-56, 514-16, 932-35, 1364-65, 1376-79

Merlin: 804; buried in ruined castle, 1056, 1338; drugged with morphine, 1338; imprisoned in Wales, 1338

merlins, 383-84

Mermaid, the dog, 944-45

The Mermaid and the Simpleton, 969

mermaids: 893-94, 1272; former, 824, 1354

Merrick, Patrick, 963-65

Merrick family, 383-85

MERRIMAN LYON, 148, 288, 502, *804*, 1375

MERRY BRANDYBUCK, 132, 406-8, 437, *804-5*, 981

merry-go-rounds, 782

Merrylegs, the pony, 105

Merryweather family, 724-27

The Mersey Sound, 943

Mesopotamia, ancient times, 624-27, 1204-6

Message to Hadrian, 1253

messages: cat carries, 1271; code, 1339; false, 637; from emperor, 271; from monkey's cousin, 210; from owl via sea gull, 366; from supposedly dead father, 1017; hidden in hair, 545; in alarm clock, 1020, 1335; in dust, 1325-26; in blood on beetle's leg, 1310; in rhyme, 615; left for children, 619-10; mysterious, 536, 1151-52; of sweetheart's death, erroneous, 1203; pigeon-post, 972-74; scatched into stone bridge, 198-99, 230; sent by mirror, 1245; signet ring, 682; to be delivered after death, 177; to German submarines, 262-63; to Staple, 1403; to warn of attack, 561-62; via swallow, 1145; written on cigarette packet, 401. *See also* letters; mail; notes.

Messenger, newspaper, 404, 434-36

messengers: for army, 358; Jacobite, 649; strange, 1210; to British forces, 295; waylaid, 1089; zany, 753, 767

Messua, 66, 631-32

metals, mythical 435

metaphysics, 702

meteorites, 75, 325-27

Methodists, Primitive, 264

Mexico: early 20th century, 399, 601-2

Mexico City, early 20th century, 601

mice: assist snake, 1120; bold, 688, 1026-27, 1031-32; carolling field, 1384; children turned into, 429; courageous, 1007; earnest pantry, 1031-32; elegant white lady, 815; feisty, 996; field, 135; gnaw ropes, 711; harvest, 246, 262, 437, 914, 931, 952-53, 1114, 1120-21; homeless, 1120-21; loses tail, 1026; crotchety patriarch of, 914; pretty white, 1031; refugees, 432; ruffians, 1120;

small brown, was boy, 1393-94;
warrior, 1307-8; witches seek to
turn boys into, 1393
Michael, 426-27
Michael Banks, 779-81, 783-84, 785-
86
Michael Darling, 956-57
Michael Fisher, 568-69, 777
Michael Guest, 290-91
Michael Joyce, 543-46
Michael Saunders, 208-9
Michael the Miner, 263
Michael Treguddick, 1112-13
Mick Chapman, 125
MICK COONEY, *805*, 1101-2
MICK DALTON, 603, *805-6*, 876, 880
Mickey Denning, 183-84
Mickle, Henry, 77-78, 465-66, 539
Micklewright, Robert, 1158, 1169,
1394
MICK TEMPLETON, *806*, 959, 1339
Middle Ages: future similar to, 309-
13. *See also* Medieval Period;
medieval worlds.
Middle America. *See* Latin Americans.
Middle-earth, 96, 437, 439, 550-53,
1158
Middle East: ancient times, Ur,
624-27, 1204-6; sixth century,
Byzantium, 279-81; 12th century,
Jerusalem, 670-72; 15th century,
Constantinople, 370-73
The Middle of the Sandwich, 644
Middleton, late 20th century, 411-14
Middle Way, 1194
midgets: 112; overstretched, 811
MIDIR, 252, 772-74, *806*, 865-66,
967
Midlands: early 20th century, 1322-
25; mid-20th century, 480-82,
1071-74; late 20th century, 1119-
20; future, 895-97
Midmeddlecum, 1385-86
Midnight, 765-67, 938, 1227
Midnight Court, 31-32, 119, 677,
740, 807-8, 845, 1104
Midnight Fairy, 1096
MIDNIGHT IS A PLACE, 9, *807-9*
Midnight Mass, 212
Midnight Mill, 302
Midsummer Day, 1411
Midsummer Eve, 716
A MIDSUMMER NIGHT'S DEATH, *809-10*,
967, 1007, 1192
A Midsummer Night's Dream, 70
Midsummer's Eve, 450, 549
midsummer's night, 1410
Midsummer Tree, 149, 1375

Midway, 72
Midwinter, Day, 287
migrations, instinctive lure of,
1021
migwn, 502
Mike and Me, 709
Mike Andrayson, 361
Mike Fay, 1133-36
Mike Gifford, 506-7
MIKE HENDREY, 93, 752, *810*, 1055,
1376-78
Mike Moriarity, 1151-53
Mike Sallow, 311
Mike Spillergun, 404-5
MIKE TEAVEE, 203, *810-11*
Mikkel, the Lapp, 1350
Miklagard, 117
Milburn, Jossie, 131
Mildendo, 509
MILD EYE, 135, 136-37, *811*, 1236
Mildred Blount, 318-19
Miles Cross, 413
Miles Francis, 574, 876, 1202, 1351-
53
militia, Viennese, 546
milking, to prove country back-
ground, 545
The Milkman's on His Way, 1027
Millar, H. R., 416
Miller, Mr., 1124
millers: father, 237; helpful, 813;
rival of farmer, 396; scarred,
ugly, 1024; surly, 1405; talkative
old, 862
The Miller's Boy, 1371
milliners, 668
mills: carpet, 740-41, 807-9;
closed, 99, 233, 604, 876-78, 880;
deserted, 541-42; half-ruined,
home in, 1187-88; Lancashire, 805;
old, 140, 862, 1059-60, 1258; old,
collapses, 1060; on the Say, 813;
striking, 910; textile, 198, 264.
See also factories; manufacturers.
MILNE, A(LAN) A(LEXANDER), 85, 472,
562, *811-12*, 1187, 1388
MILLY KITSON, 685-86, *811*
milpreve, 1410-11
mimics, of recitation style, 384
Mimsie Potts, 221-23
miners: 999, 1001, 1002-3; black-
listed, 841; children, 972-73;
coal, 129-31, 473, 623, 624, 861,
1276-78; father and sons, 397-99;
gold, 1068, 1357; pony boy, 129-
30; small, dark, 1411; trapped,
130, 193. *See also* mines.

mines: abandoned, 34-36, 487,
    556-57, 592, 624; ancient cop-
    per, 1343-44; boy lost in, 398;
    boys trapped in, 476; cave-in,
    398, 558; closed, 912; coal, 33-
    36, 129-31, 197, 1015; copper,
    397-98, 1343-44; Cornish, 398-
    99; explosion in, 398; floating,
    1106; gold, 236, 972-73, 1411;
    mysterious accident, 34-36; old,
    485-86; pithead collapses, 624;
    ruby, 236; silver, proposed, 556;
    tunnel collapses, 1047; Welsh, 179
Mines of Moria, 407, 439, 982, 1158
mineshafts, old, 2, 398
miniature animals, exhibited, 510
miniature people: 49-50, 132-34,
    134-36, 136-38, 138-40, 140-42,
    509-10, 551-53, 553-54, 559-60;
    coming from decanter of fine Old
    Pale Madeira, 489; man sold to
    Queen, 510-11; man exhibited, 511
ministers: prototype for character,
    343; during plague, 940; London,
    52-54, 692; studying to become,
    262. See also clergymen; curates;
    parsons; pastors; preachers;
    priests; rectors; vicars.
Mink, 931
Minnow, 682-83
Minnow (boat), 94, 291
THE "MINNOW" LEADS TO TREASURE, 812,
    948. See "MINNOW" ON THE SAY, 812-
    14.
"MINNOW" ON THE SAY, 812-14, 948
MINNY, 1414, 814-15
minstrels: 12, 146, 673-74; girl,
    447-48. See also bards; musicians.
The Mintyglow Kid, 270
Mirabeau, 1217
miracles: personal, 124; healed
    hand, 1055; healing boy's stiff
    leg, 1396; possibilities ex-
    plored, 849
Miranda, the bird, 1309
MIRANDA RIDLEY, 186-88, 707, 815,
    981
Miraz, 185, 323, 893, 995, 1026,
    1264, 1306
Mirkwood, 95, 407, 465, 552, 1204
mirrors: as weapon, 892; over man-
    tel, 18, 1209; reflecting future,
    374; used to send messages, 1245
mirror-worlds, 1208-11
MIRYAM CARLISLE, 200-1, 692, 815,
    1122, 1389
misanthropes: fiddler, 1113;
    kidnappers, 919; man well off,

353; old woman, 914
miscarriages, of baby, 1369
mischief: of brownie, 5-6; of ghost,
    451-53. See also pranks; tricks.
mischief night, 110
misconceptions: friend as wife's
    lover, 267-68; miser as benevo-
    lent man, 267-68. See also
    misunderstandings.
misers: deceitful uncle, 648-51;
    elderly toymaker, 267; kidnaps
    nephew, 1281; old Puritan tor-
    mented by dreams of money, 864;
    reformed, 227, 229, 353
misfits: joining together, 120-21;
    jungle boy, 632
misogynists, 725, 737
Misrule, Lord of, 1414
Miss Agnes Tiffany Jones, 722, 724
Miss Angorian, 569
Miss Bex, 98, 946
Miss Bianca, the mouse, 815-16,
    1031-32
MISS BIANCA, 815-16, 1080
Miss Bianca in the Antarctic, 1081
Miss Bianca in the Orient, 1081
Miss Bianca in the Salt Mines, 1081
MISS BRIDGET, 816-17, 818, 1108-10
MISS CADELL-TWITTEN, 4, 290, 480-82,
    817
Miss Calico, 785
Miss Camperdown, 520-21
Miss Charlotte, 558-59
MISS CODLING, 1, 615, 812-14, 817-
    18, 858, 1058, 1132
Miss Coleman, 55-56
Miss Dobbs, 734-35
MISS DUNSTAN, 818, 1125
Miss Ellum, 1160
MISS FANNY, 738, 816, 818, 1108-10
Miss Flower, 88, 723, 818-19
Miss Gozzling, 367, 1168
Miss Graham, 1071-73
Miss Hallibutt, 367, 1168
Miss Hanker, 249, 482
Miss Happiness, 723, 818-19
MISS HAPPINESS AND MISS FLOWER, 818-
    20, 458, 722
Miss Harry, 59
MISS HAVISHAM, 376, 493-95, 592,
    820, 981
Miss Heart, 179
missing persons: boy discovered,
    1353; brothers discovered, 766;
    discovered, child lost during
    war, 1106; reappearing, aunt,
    889, doll, 559, father, 697, 875,
    955, 981, 1020, 1335, gnome, 717,

grandpa, 34, great-uncle, 534, long-lost son, 268, parents, 1401, pretentious sophisticate, 741, prince, 562, 1092-93, prisoner of war of Turks, 422-23, sister, 680, wife of founder of factory, 677, wizard, 440; World War I near Gaza, 421
missionaries: Christian, 297, 358-59; South Pacific native, 257; to Kurtrigur Huns, 279, 557; Quaker, killed by feuding factions, 811; in China, 1195, 1265
The Mission, or, Scenes in Africa, 776
Miss Jane Heliotrope, 724-726
Miss Johnson, 1160
Miss Katherine Hendry, 579
MISS LAMPETER, 286, *820*, 843
Miss Lark, 780, 783, 784
Miss Lessor, 656
Miss Letitia Slighcarp, 888, 1100, 1400-1
Miss Louisa Evans, 176-79
MISS MANSFIELD, *820-21*, 839, 1108-10
MISS MARGARET ROYLANCE, 53-54, 262, *821*
Miss Mary Pettifer, 893-94
MISS MAY BELLINGER, *821*, 883, 944, 1237
MISS MENZIES, 49, 138-40, *822*, 837, 857
Miss Metcalfe's Boarding School for Girls, 31
Miss Moule, 490-92
MISS OLIVIA BROOK, 319-20, *822*
Miss Orange Nankelly, 332
MISS PHILEMON, 603, 734-36, *822-23*
Miss Pennyfeather and the Pooka, 910
Miss Pennyfeather in the Springtime, 910
Miss Primrose Clarke, 1166-67
MISS QUEENIE HARRISON, 78, 466-67, *823*, 1080
Miss Serendip, 1385
Miss Skiffins, 1346
MISS SMITH, 75, 326-28, 640, *823*, 1042
Miss Theo Dane, 68
Miss Valerie Binns, 579
MISS WRACK, 824, 1354
mistakes: multiple, 856; shot from blunderbuss for stinging fly, 395
Mister Corbett, 824-26
MISTER CORBETT'S GHOST, 442, *824-26*
Mister Corbett's Ghost and Other Stories, 824

MISTER JOHNNY GOTOBED, 14, 177-78, 543, *826*, 886
Mister Shaw, 340-42
MISTER TREET, 304-6, *826-27*
mistletoe, 148, 1267, 1375
Mistra, 370
Mistress Adams, 1202
MISTRESS FETTERLOCK, *827*, 1403
Mistress Susan, 574
mistresses, of James V, King of England, 677
mists: blind boy lost in, 1367; lost in, 563; mountain, 1272; sudden, 1377. *See also* fogs.
misunderstandings: of girl's ability, 1094; confusing grandson with son, 841; of deaf boy, 290-91. *See also* misconceptions.
Mitchell, the coachman, 111
Mitchell, the police constable, 950-51
Mitchell family, 28-29, 1211-13, 1297-98
Mithras, society of, 281-82, 348, 450, 523, 1223
mithril, mail of, 96
mixed marriages. *See* marriages, interracial.
Mma, 627-28
Moab, ancient times, 625
Moat House, 882
moats, around house, 1346
mobs: French, 1216-17; on witch hunt, 673-74
Moby Dick, 1048
Moby family, 6-7, 161, 206-7, 365
MOCK TURTLE, 20-22, 23, 505, *827*
model villages, 137, 138-39, 140-41, 290, 856
Modern Painters, 1051
Modern Poetry, 1247
A Modern Tragedy, 90
"A Modest Proposal," 1182
Mog, 831
Mog, the Forgetful Cat, 647
Mohawk Valley, 1346
Mohorrim, 123-24
molasses: as food, 887-88
MOLE, 65, *827-28*, 1020-21, 1382-84
molehills, 208
Molepie, 885
moles, 212, 827-28
molestations: sexual, 1326-27. *See also* rapes.
Molin, Charles, 795
Moll Flanders, 298
Moll Swayne, 1010-11
MOLLY REEVES, 1, 586-87, *828*, 1202

Molly Tregeagle, 1288-91
Momphesson family, 193, 938-39
monasteries: Bedford, 870; boy
   imprisoned in, 1416; boy runs
   from, 11; boy runs from, then returns to, 1137; Buddhist, 1165;
   closed by wars, 454; deformed boy
   given refuge, 1394-96; Irish,
   1298; raided by Vikings, 91;
   rebuilt, 1358; returned to order, 725; ruined, 155, 528-29;
   Thornham, burned, 870; Tibetan,
   333-34, 1195, 1266
money: affection for, 142; buried, 1327; burned, 467; eaten by
   dog, 60, 1132; dreams of, 864;
   dwarf holly and oak gold coins,
   848; found in trash, 386; lost,
   668; stolen, 466-67, 1368. See
   also treasure.
money bags, 1379
money belt: missing, 1380; stolen,
   85
moneylenders, 1147
mongoloids, 1288-91
mongooses, 632
monkeys: dying in Africa, 1145; Indian, 631, 635; kidnappers, 71;
   performing on stage, 840; recovered, 839-40; talking, 210-11,
   839-41, 1145, 1309; urinates on
   aunt's clothes, 1192; vaccinated
   and cured, 1145; wealthy, 840
monkey suits, for slave boy, 218
monks: battle-maddened, 375-76;
   Benedictine, 915-17; captured
   by Vikings, 1299; cave-dwelling,
   155-56, 528, 1357; former English officer, 1266; French, 454;
   grouchy, 155; helpful, 730; hospi-
   table, 681-82; impersonated, 110;
   imprison boy, 1416; literate,
   870; mad, 870; makes eyeglasses, 1357; old, 870; Scots, 273; St.
   Cuthbert, 1378; take in deformed
   boy, 1394-96. See also friars.
Monk's Heugh, 1376, 1378
Monophysites, 557
Monopods, 1307
monotheism, 625
Monroe, Geordie, 81
Monroe family, 450
MONSIEUR ARMAND, 191, 828-29, 880
Monsieur Bon-Bon, 223
Monsieur Cocq de Noir, 725-26
Monsieur Pallieu, 1337
Monsieur Pampelmousse, 127
monsoons, 1304-5

monsters: comic, 929; composite,
   584; created by wizard, 1397;
   fake, 29, 368-69, 411; gentle,
   useful, 1397; Hairy Man, 715;
   humorous, 1397; imagined in marsh,
   801; iron, buried, 584; Loch Ness,
   368, 642; three-headed, 1397; very
   cold, 998; winged, 976
monuments: national, 244; to Darwin,
   369
Montpelier, Sir Simon, 1104-5, 1355
Monty German, 853
moods, wildly changing, 88
Moon, Mr. Reginald, 847-49, 850,
   1316
Moonacre Manor, 724-26
Moon Bells and Other Moon Poems, 570
Mooney, 775
THE MOON IN THE CLOUD, 531, 829-30
The Moon of Gomrath, 443, 1345
moons: man and woman in, 202, 1096;
   wind from makes children naughty,
   1385
moon horse, 1173
Moore, Mary, 847
Moore family, 742, 1224-25
Moorhouse, Tom, 197-200, 264, 1238-
   39
moors: Dartmoor, 1386-88; night
   lights on, 707; Yorkshire, 1021
Morag, 1368-69
MORAG MACLEOD, 13, 641-42, 642-43,
   830, 914-15, 1243-44
morality: repressive in home, 902
Moray, Earl of, 1412-13
MORAY WILLIAMS, URSULA, 830-31, 893
Mordor, 96, 132, 406-8, 465, 1056
Mordred, Sir, 1037-38
Morello, 558
More Stories of the Wild, 83
More Tales Told Near a Crocodile, 526
Moreton, Joe, 599, 608-9, 1058-60,
   1100-1
MORGANA (boat), 731, 790, 832
Morholt, 1259-60
Moriarity, Mike, 1151-53
Moriarity family, 1151-53
Morlaix, France, 1337
Morley, Jonathan, 173, 218-19, 616,
   1067, 1174
Morley family, 793-94, 1164, 1274-76
Morning Fairy, 1096
MORNING LIGHT, King, 39-41, 832
Morocco, book on, 184
morphine, sedates Merlin, 1338
Morrigan, 1067, 1343
Morrison family, 47, 707-8, 799-800,
   1196-99

MORSAC, MARQUIS DE, 751, *832-33*, 1216-17
mortgages, sale to pay off, 404
morthbrood, evil, 1343-44
Mortimer, the raven, 41-42
Mortimer family, 73, 242, 399-400, 836, 843, 883, 895-97
MORTON LEROY, 412-14, 694, 697, *833*, 1065
Moses: gypsy boy, 426; rod of, 976
MOSES BEECH, *833*, 834-35, 962-63, 1173
MOSES BEECH, 833-35, 1148
Moshie Cat: The True Adventures of a Majorcan Kitten, 504
Moss, David, 1-2
Moss family, 94, 291, 615, 812-14, 817, 858, 862, 1058
Mossman, 1369
Mossock family, 168, 1067, 1342-45
Mossy, 462-63
MOTHER BLOODWORT, *835-36*, 1354
Mother Carey, 851, 853, 1329-30
Mother Codling, 985, 1094
mother-daughter relationships, novels of, 1071-74, 1123-26, 1134-36, 1196-99
Mother Drake, 549
MOTHER MORTIMER, 73, *836*, 399-400, 843, 883, 895-96
Mother o'Pearl, 425
mothers: abandoning family, 823; absent from home, 277-78, 836, 896, 900-2, 1071-73, 1263; abusive, 342-43, 851-52, 1212, 1373; actress, 889; adopted, 957; adoptive, 376, 768-69; ailing, 457; alcoholic, 748, 887; ambitious, 267; ambitious and overprotective, 799; ambitious for daughters, 708, 761, 1197-98; anti-pets, 860; appearance and status conscious, 761; assumed dead, 770; ballerina, 69; become more considerate, 707; bedridden, 420; bookshop manager, 200; break up daughter's marriage, 1335; Calvinist, 1123; captured, executed by Germans, World War II, 898-99; cellist, 1076; chronic cleaner, 1114; columnist, 921; commanding, 76-77; complainers, 132-33, 135; condemned in mock trial, 1078; controlling, 1133-36; coping, World War II, 761; dating, 200-1, 692; death at sea, 344; death by suicide, 1852; death in childbirth,

499, 1125; death in flu epidemic, 1322; death of, 334, 730, 737; delicate health, 788; desert family, 876, 879-80; descended from witch, 488; despised by grandparents, 900-2; destructive, 865; diplomatic, 328-30; discontented, 590; discovered, 92, 753, 814; disorganized, 542, 636; disreputable, 475-76; district nurse, 430-31, 432; divorced, 200, 249, 636; domineering, 262, 582-83, 615-16, 669, 1005-6, 1165-67; dreamy, irresponsible, 854; dressmaker, 954; dying, 321; dying of malnutrition, 73, 896; earth, 865; easily upset, 362, 1385; emotionally disturbed, 857; emotionally immature, 852; emotionally repressed, 1363; employed as housekeeper and cook, 127-28; enchanted as dog, 929-30; excessively fat, 678; exhibitionist, 1376; exploitive, 777; fanatically religious, 1373; feared, 638; foster, 37, 58, 673-74, 768-69, 827; foster, abusive, 1057-58; foster, aunt, 1; foster, cousin, 668, 685-86, 693; foster, cruel, 14; foster mother, dog of pig, 1082-83; foster, grandmother, 323; foster, grocer, 707; foster, housekeeper, 859; foster, Irish Christian, 91; foster, puritanical, 1368; foster, queen, 1013; foster, reclusive, 1396; foster, sister as, 492-93; foster, village woman, 631; foster, wolf of boy, 1084; frivolous, 770; full of gumption, 365; girl acts as, 957; greedy, 586; grief-stricken, 1124; grocer, 1390; has lovers, 748; housekeeper, 518, 933-34; house-proud, 29, 1332-33, 362, 362-63, 559, 703, 838, 1297; hated, 865; identity discovered, 1350; ill, 32, 526, 756, 1305-5; imperious, 533-34, 677-78, 846; impractical, 1349; in doll family, 101-2; invalid, 722, 724; intimidating mother-in-law, 1335; involved in triangle relationship, 873; Irish, 669; irresponsible, 1368; kidnapped, 1161; killed in air raid, 887; killed in auto accident, 762; killed in nuclear blast, 156;

kind-hearted, 506-7; Labrador dog, 325; Lapp, 578, 1350; laundress, 1048; leaving family, 466-67; librarian, 1212; lose job, 1313; losing mind, 1011; maid, 627-28; managerial, 768; manipulative, 857-58, 1165-67; marrying again, 638, 738, 923-24, 1047, 1058-60, 1116, 1199-200; mean and petty, 262; mean-minded, 1025; mentally ill, 851-52; misunderstanding, 645; moralistic, 20, 22; musician, 1349; music teacher, 44-46; neglectful, 656; never married, 432; newspaper woman, 540; nurse, 496; nursemaid, 651; obsessed with cleaning, 853-54; of eight, 483; of Lost Boys, 1347; opposes daughter's marriage, 708; over-directive, 25-26, 1197-98; overpossessive, 768, 1283-84, 1335; overprotective, 367, 696, 854, 1117, 1196, 1319, 1375; overworked, 1124; particularly persistent, 761; perceptive, 897-99; penny-pinching, 838; pianist, 186, 761; pretentious, 741, 1048; psychotic, 468-69; religious fanatic, 852; reporter, 917; ritually sacrificed, 694; romantic, 1048; runaway, 293; sacrificing, 203; Saxon lady, 672; seamstress, 173-75; secretary, 924, 1151; shallow, 656; shrewish, 941; sick, 706; slow to accept change, 293; socially ambitious, 536, 708; socially conscious, 806; Spanish dancer, 678, 1115-17; status-conscious, 827, 970; step, 79-81, 93, 332, 505, 533, 548, 568, 608, 636-37, 694, 698, 719, 741, 752, 754, 768, 846, 932-35, 968, 1039, 1047, 1185, 1376-79; stereotyped as weak, anxious, totally devoted, passive, 859-60; submissive, suddenly assertive, 895-97; substitute, 23-24; suicide, 469; suspicious, 413; undemonstrative, 583; unloving, 640; unsympathetic, 1005-6; visiting, 177; warm, caring, 852; wealthy, imperious, 857-58; widowed, 163, 428, 588-89; wild driver, 1376; witch, 200-1, 1389; witch leader, 637; works at confectioner's, 669; worrying,

87; wounded during flood, 866-67. *See also* parents.
Mother Wolf, 630, 1084
motifs: lark and laurel in tapestry, 581-83; recurring, 349, 399, 581-83, 1234-36. *See also* patterns; symbols.
motorcars, passion for, 1229
motorcycles: attackers ride, 656; BMW, 34, 36; brakes tampered, 873; gift from grandfather, 479; girl causes injury to rider, 597; girl obsessed with, 523, 1283; owned by beefy young man called The Blob, 540-42; purchased with college money, 778; ridden by woman scientist, 339; shopowner admired by girl, 364; Triumph Tiger-Cub, 306-9, 554, 614; youth escapes on, 616, 646; youth swipes father's, 951
motors, awaken fear, 310
mottos: family, 196; Girl Guide, 386
mounds: ancient, 359, 802, 841, 863, 995
mountain climbers, 194, 243-44, 809-10
mountains: 1002-3, 1368-88; city in, 928; door into, 1272; Middle-earth, 407, 464-65, 1107; Scotland, 1368-69, 1399; Tibetan, 333, 653-54, 1266; Wales, 502, 1411
Mount Doom, 406-7, 465
Mount Elbruz, 391
Mount Etna, 1330
Mountjoy family, 1062-63
Moupetit, Charles, 733
MOUSE, 20, 22, *836*
The Mouse Butcher, 665
mouse-persons, 1393-94
Mouse Prisoners' Aid Society, 815
The Mousewife, 458
moves: of family, 852; to London, 1405; to new home, 314, 895, 1364-66; to new neighborhood, 1114-15; to North London, 329
movies: contracts, 70; forbidden, 474; horror, 540
The Moving Finger, 503
moving vans, mysterious, 515
Mow Cop, 746, 1025-26, 1203
MOWGLI, 11, 65-66, 71, 630-32, 635, *836-37*, 1084-85
"Mowgli's Brothers," 630
MR. ABEDNEGO TWITE, 108-9, *837*, 1100
MR. ABEL POTT, 138-40, *837*
MR. ALLEN, 737, 805, *838*, 1101-2
MR. AND MRS. HEDLEY, *838*, 1365
Mr. and Mrs. Twite, 108-9

Mr. Andrew Ashworthy Smith, 1058
Mr. Ardent, 224, 1180
Mr. Badger, 388-89
MR. BAGTHORPE, 275, *838-39*, 921,
    1283, 1419-20
Mr. Bateman, 555-56
Mr. Bear's Picnic, 531
Mr. Beaver, 711, 1009
Mr. Bennett, 652
MR. BILLING, 821, *839*, 1109-10
Mr. Bradwell, 130
Mr. Brett, 529, 856, 1149-50
Mr. Brown, 84-85, 844
MR. BUMPS AND HIS MONKEY, 302, *839-41*
Mr. Button, 1160
MR. CANDLIN, 130, 861, *841*
Mr. Casimir Corvo, 1385-86
Mr. Chatterjee, 1354
Mr. Chisel-Brown, 207
Mr. Cob, 235, 108
MR. CODLING, 1, 615, 813-14, 817,
    841-42, 862, 1058, 1131-32
Mr. Constable, 169
MR. COPPLESTONE, 63, 596, 623, *842*,
    1317-18
MR. CROFT, *842*, 1263-64
Mr. Dermot, 354, 420-21
Mr. Dorman, 131
Mr. Drouet, 53-54
Mr. Evans (*At the Back of the North
    Wind*), 56
MR. EVANS (*Carrie's War*), 60, 176-
    79, 543, *842-43*, 886
Mr. Field, 839, 1109-10
Mr. Fox, 696
Mr. Fradd, 389-91
MR. GARNER, 37, 286, 591, 820, *843*
MR. GERALD BOWLING, 400, 836, *843-
    44*, 883, 896
Mr. Gifford, 506-7
Mr. Grimes, 1328-30
Mr. Gripe, 1401
MR. GRUBER, 84, *844*
Mr. Harold Tiffany Jones, 722-23
Mr. Hazell, 853
Mr. Hazelwood, 1010-12
Mr. Head, 179
Mr. Hedley, 516, 629
MR. HENRY, *844*, 851, 1262
Mr. Hollings, 453
Mr. Holt, 491
MR. HOLYSTONE, *844*, 1142-43
Mr. Hughes, 156, 737
Mr. Jenkins, 887
Mr. John Wemmick, 495
MR. JONES, *845*, 1396-97
Mr. Josiah Grimshaw, 1400-1
MR. JULIAN OAKAPPLE, 31-32, 807, *845*

Mr. Justice Rumple, 1385
Mr. Kay, 464
Mr. Kitchen, 378
Mr. K'Nee, 610
MR. LEADBETTER, *845*, 1354-55
Mr. Mackracken, 1285-87
Mr. Maitland Pope, 373-75
MR. MANSFIELD, 839, *845-46*, 1108-10
Mr. Matthew Pocket, 494
Mr. McFadden's Halloween, 458
Mr. McGill, 1326
MR. MCNAIR, *846*, 960, 1006, 1190-91
Mr. Merchant, 1270
Mr. Midshipman Easy, 777
Mr. Miller, 1124
Mr. Mnason, 979
MR. MOON'S LAST CASE, *847-49*, 943
Mr. Mountjoy, 44
Mr. Nobody, 5
Mr. Nostrum, 208
Mr. Oakapple, 740
Mr. Owen, 243-44
Mr. Panwallah, 526, 1304
MR. PARGETER, 338, 360, 612, *849*,
    858-59, 1041-42, 1224-25
MR. PLANTAGANET, 330-31, *849-50*
Mr. Pott, 822, 856-57
MR. PURVES, *850*, 1125
Mr. Rankeillor, 649-51
Mr. Raymond, 56-57
MR. REGINALD MOON, 847-49, *850*, 969,
    1316
Mr. Robertson's Hundred Pounds, 695
Mr. Robinson, 609, 610
Mr. Rochester, 460, 1275
MR. ROPER, *850-51*, 1264
MR. RUDGE, 17, 411, 707, *851*, 1390
Mrs. Abednego Twite, 1100
Mrs. Alice, 611
Mrs. Bagthorpe, 920-21, 1195
Mrs. Bartholomew, 1241
Mrs. Beaver, 711
MRS. BEDONEBYASYOUDID, *851*, 853,
    1329
MRS. BEECH, 468-69, *851-52*
Mrs. Bird, 84
MRS. BLEWITT, 328-30, 479, 483, *852*
Mrs. Bonney, 1150
Mrs. Bowen, 323
Mrs. Brill, 779, 783
Mrs. Brisket, 1099, 1400-1
Mrs. Brown, 84-85
Mrs. Buckle, 109
Mrs. Byre, 678, 854
Mrs. Cantrip, 173, 174
Mrs. Chisel-Brown, 207
Mr. Schneider, 205
Mr. Schofield, 541-42

MRS. CLIPSTONE, 285, *852-53*
Mrs. Clomper, 1282, 1317
Mrs. Corry, 778, 784
Mrs. Cuthbert, 318
MRS. DAISY JONES, 333-34, *853*, 1195, 1266
Mrs. Daring, 163, 165
Mrs. Dimbleby, 548-49
Mrs. Discombobulous, 759
MRS. DOASYOUWOULDBEDONEBY, 851, *853*, 1329
MRS. DORA SINGER, 678, *853-54*, 1114-17
MRS. DRIVER, 49, 133-34, 137, 148, 559, *854*
MRS. DUNNITT, *855*, 1077-78
MR. SEAGRAVE, 632, 787, *855*, 859, 1239, 1374
Mrs. Ella Twite, 837
MR. SELWYN RAVEN, *855-56*, 1150
Mrs. Fairfax, 698
Mrs. Fletcher, 468
Mrs. Fox, 388-89
Mrs. Fradd, 389-90
Mrs. Gifford, 506-7
Mrs. Gorgandy, 111-13
Mrs. Gresham, 489, 492
Mrs. Grimble, 1385-86
Mrs. Hanrahan, 289, 647, 1313-15
Mrs. Hartridge, 469
MRS. HEDGES, 62, 565, *856*
Mrs. Hedley, 516, 629, 838
Mr. Shelley, 1379-80
Mrs. Herbert, 383
Mrs. Hogget, 1082-83
Mrs. Hunter, 456, 694
MR. SIDNEY PLATTER, 138-39, 140-42, 822, 837, *856-57*, 947, 985
Mrs. Innisfree, 331
MRS. JACOBS, 29, 219, *857*, 1078
Mrs. Kerridge, 338
Mrs. Lemon, 606-7
Mrs. Lewis, 558
Mr. Slighcarp, 887-89
MRS. MABEL PLATTER, 138-39, 140-42, 822, 856, *857*, 947, 985
Mrs. Mackie, 1123
MRS. MAY, 132-34, 136, 147-48, *857*, 1236
Mrs. McKay, 1390
MRS. MEREDITH, 846, *857-58*, 1004, 1006, 1191-92
Mrs. Minetti, 677
MR. SMITH (*The "Minnow on the Say*), 94, 813, *858*
Mr. Smith (*The Witch's Daughter*), 1396-97
Mrs. Montague, 305

MRS. NEECH, *858-59*, 1224
Mrs. Sniveller, 1354
Mrs. Noah, 522, 895
MRS. OLDKNOW, 211-13, 217-19, 373-75, 525, 578, 800, *859*, 1154-55, 1230, 1231
Mrs. Owen, 243
Mrs. Padgitt, 519-21
Mrs. Pendlebury Parker, 174-75
Mrs. Pentstemmon, 567
Mrs. Pocket, 495
Mrs. Raleigh, 558
Mrs. Rees-Goring, 54
Mrs. Roggs, 1125-26
MRS. SEAGRAVE, 632, 787-88, *859-60*, 1239, 1374
Mrs. Seymour, 763-64
MRS. SHAND, *860*, 1141
Mrs. Sharp, 208
Mrs. Siddons, 169-70
MRS. SPARROW, 76-77, 100, 159, 293, 605, *860*, 1088
Mrs. Tarbutt, 1397
Mrs. Tate, 862
Mrs. Timorous, 978
Mrs. Toft, 897-99
Mr. Stringston, 927
MRS. TUCKER, 535, 714-16, *860-61*, 894
MRS. ULLATHORNE, 131, 841, *861*
Mr. Sutton, 1180-81
MRS. VERITY, 92, 452, *862*
Mrs. Vernon-Greene, 416
Mrs. Vonnister, the stuffed rabbit, 490-91
Mrs. Widdison, 36
Mrs. Wrigley, 119-21, 230, 570
Mr. Tackleton, 267-69
MR. TATE, 655, *862*, 1313-14
MR. TEY, 813, *862*
Mr. Thoroughgood, 107
Mr. Throgmorton, 741
MR. TRIPLETT, 738, *863*, 1116
MR. TUCKEE, 802-4, *863*, 1133
MR. TUMNUS, 688, 710, 742, *864*
Mr. Turvey, 782-83
Mr. Twilfit, 723, 819
MR. WIDDISON, 450, 548-50, *864*
Mr. Widdowson, 314, 599, 1242, 1365
Mr. Williams, 152
MR. WILLY WONKA, 58, 203-4, 811, *864-65*, 919, 1297, 1305, 1375-76
Mr. Wopsle, 495
Mr. Worldly Wiseman, 975
Mua, 1, 828
Mudd, Dawn, 293
Mudd family, 76-77
Mudface, 1115

mudfish, ridden by child, 920
Mugg, Terence, 845, 1104, 1355-56, 1397
Mugg, the Magnificent, 1356
Mullings, Lady, 856, 857
Mullugutherium, 1092
Mum, the dog, 1082-83
mummers, dances of, 1156
Mungo, the donkey, 888
munitions: makers, 237; stored in cave, 222
Munodi, 512
Murder at the Flood, 25
murders: accusations of, 1413; attempted, 61-62, 119, 260, 508, 792, 808, 833, 865, 1281, 1397; by police, 28; by poisoned stew, 157; by salvagers, 1326; by ship's mate, 649; compassionate, 1288-89; contemplated, 268; culprit hiding in cave, 243-44; culprit known but not identified, 464; desired, 341; disguised as suicide, 111, 112; drowning, 639; foreseen, 122; for jeweled ankus, 631; finally solved, 125; in church sanctuary, 1026; in feud, 117; in prison, 839; numerous, 105, 1103; of brothel madame, 402; of brother, proved false, 931; 1121; of contingent of priests, 124; of cousin, 464; of dog attempted, 464; of emperor, 271, 1089; of father, 611, 738-39; of father, accused, 477; of king, 122, 185; of king's factor, 289; of minor luminary, 325; of poet-teacher, suspected, 810; of revenue agent, 464; of robber, 574; of servant, 236; of six pirates, 172; of South American diplomat, 907; of thief by another thief, 1353; of wife, 1104; of old gentleman, 1107, 1108; of seven wives, 1104-5; old, 1059-60; orders to, 671; planned, 246, 1177; planned, observed by attorney, 839; planned for grandmother by grandchildren, 900; poison, 1089; political, 1207; potential, 289; prevented, 1352-53; reported, 474; revealed, 110, 113; ritual, 772, 832, 833; schemes for, 1192; suspected, 855-56; tales of, 522, 587; through deal with sinister old man, 825; trials for, 592; unsolved, 890, 1022-23. *See also* killings.

Murdo (*Master of Morgana*), 790, 832, 883-84
MURDO JOHNSTONE, 23, 80, *865*
Murdo MacKenzie, 1049-50
Murgatroyd family, 31-32, 302-3, 508, 677, 740-41, 807-9, 845, 1104
Murgatroyd's Carpet, Rug, and Matting Manufactury, 31, 119, 302, 677, 740, 807, 1104
Mulock, Dinah Marie. *See* CRAIK, DINAH MARIE MULOCK, *263*.
Murjica family, 1366-68
MURNA, 252, 772-73, 806, *865*, 968
Murphy, Biddy, 271
MURRAY, JAMES, 152-53, *866*, 1068-71
Murrell, E. K., 1076
museums: 45; antique car, 1337; art, London, 797; bone stolen from, 1316; British, 667; Bronte, 1275; of human world, 239; Pitt Rivers, 564, 613; Wales, 1356; Watch House, 50-51, 1325-27
Mushoo, 340
mushroom clouds, 156
mushrooms, for stool, 20, 192
music: beautiful on island, 1384; heard in Cathedral Tower, 1180-81; of spheres, 584-85; space, 584-85; string quartet, 1238; used for harassment, 1243
music, novels of, 85-87, 223-25, 685-87, 949-52, 1061-64, 1180-82, 1415-17
musical instrument: branch with silver apples, 1090. *See* other instruments by name.
musical performances, major: 85-87, 285-87, 382-85, 685-87, 949-52, 1061-64, 1076-78, 1415-17; boy choir, 211-13, 223-25, 1180-82
musical theory, 224
musicians: bagpipers, 650, 1285; boys' group, 669; British slave, "Carausius's Fool," 1090; cellist, 412-13, 857, 1076, 1238; Chilean, 28; composers, 96, 123, 302; cornet player, 10, 619, 484; court, 829-30; dance band, 465; fiddler, 1111-13; fiddling parson, 725; fifer, 1285; flutists, 16, 323, 428, 697, 829-30, 1185; folk singer, 75; god Pan, 1384; group, 1187; harper, 148, 518, 1085-86, 1117; hoboy, 837; jazz star, 1063; lute, 1351; natural, 1062; on silver branch, 271; ophicleide player, 399; penny whistle, 202; pianist, 4, 86, 186, 383-84,

761, 941-42, 950-52, 1053, 1288;
piano tuner and instrument maker,
785; practice secretly, 1062;
preference for, 694; singers, 51,
212, 223-25, 285-86, 302, 383-
84, 399, 484, 668, 801, 803, 937,
950-51, 1040-41, 1073, 1180-
82, 1194, 1415-17; singer, girl,
685-87; singers, mice, 1384;
singers, Neapolitan opera, 846;
singers, rat tenor, 529; singers, Welsh, 845; singers, boy, 16,
223-25, 1180-82, 1351, 1353; rock
star, 1063; spinet player, 511;
trumpeter, 1061-64; tutor, 807;
violinist, 485; violinist, girl,
786; violinist, left-handed, 845;
violinist, tutor, 807; ukelele
players, 667. *See also* bards; minstrels; pianists; singers; names
of particular instruments.
Muslims: in Europe, 1226, 1296; in
India, 651
Mustard-seed, 70
mutes, 720-21, 842. *See also* handicapped persons.
mutineers: English, 1045; from island, 522, 587; pirates, 1254-56
The Mutineers, 48
Mutiny, tales of, 587
mutiny, 513, 1299
My Alice (boat), 763-64
My Friend Specs McCann, 797
Myhill family, 59-60, 364, 523-
24, 1042, 1283
My Kingdom for a Grave, 28, 984, 1208
*My Naughty Little Sister: Stories
from "Listen With Mother",* 357
MYRTLE BEAMISH, 496, *866-67*
My Son, My Son!, 1131
mysteries: concerning mother, 770;
disappearing ostrich egg, 1385;
echo and legend explained, 486-
87; identity unresolved, 391;
local legend, 486-87; of boy's
death, 883; of missing statue, 4,
51; personal identity resolved,
581-83; smuggler leader, 1224-25
mystery novels: 1140-41, 1396-97,
1398-99, adventure, 434-36, 729-
30, 812-14, 1141-43, 1151-54;
amusing, 539-42; fantasy, 200-1,
533-34, 943-45; detective, 182-
85, 184-85, 281-83, 403-5, 427-28,
480-82, 486-87, 514-16, 536-38,
578-81, 656-58, 789-91, 812-14,
847-49, 917-19, 1021-23, 1334-
36; Gothic, 806-9; historical,

463-64, 683-84; horror, 1058-60;
international intrigue, 1061-64;
suspense, 242-44, 286-87, 304-6,
578-81, 610-11, 645-46, 656-58,
662-63, 809-10, 889-91, 906-7,
917-19, 1061-64, 1108-10, 1155-
57, 1220-23; spy, 400-403
Mystery in the Middle Marches, 410
MYSTERY IN WALES, 24, 243, 867. *See
CLIMBING TO DANGER,* 24.
The Mystery of Edwin Drood, 442
Mystery of the Good Adventure, 676
The Mystery of the "Polly Harris,"
1251
mythical kingdoms. *See* otherworlds.
mythological elements: Celtic
1342-45; Greek and Celtic, 189;
Greek and Norse, 710-13; Norse,
1342-45; various, 325-28
mythologies: Celtic, 932; Greek,
875, 927; Greek and Norse, 755-56;
Iceni, 1173; Norse, 875; rabbit,
1333
myths, Welsh, basis for novel, 116,
574-75

Nadler, Robert, 583
naiads, 711
NAIDOO, BEVERLEY, 627, *869*
nail and chain makers, 109, 198, 264
nailers, 1015, 1277
Naledi, 627-28
Nameless (ship), 1298-99
NAMEON, the dwarf, 847-49, 850, *869-
70,* 1316
names: at christening, 720; changed,
320; from "Sohrab and Rustum,"
389-90; guessing of, 1095-96,
1130-31; how acquired, 385, 432;
ironic, 678, 895; meaning little frog, 630; origin of Thames,
397; over cage door, 1186; power
of true, 374-75; secret, 201, 374,
800; significant, 832; Sikh, 470;
taken from environment, 132-33;
taken from cabbage and sausage,
159; taken from parent's profession, 488; true, 985, 1130-31;
wordplay on real names, 335
namesake, youth searches for, 870
THE NAMESAKE, 555, *870-72*
NAN (*The Silver Curlew*), *872,* 902,
1094
Nan (*A Strong and Willing Girl*),
1159-61
Nana, 68
Nana, the dog, 956

Nancekuke, 149
NANCE PRICE, 705, *872-73*, 1375
NANCY (*The Fox in Winter*), 430-31, *873*
NANCY (*The Owl Service*), 26, 245, 518, 768, *873-74*, 933-34
NANCY AND NORA SHOUTER, *874*, 1354
NANCY BLACKETT, 171-72, *874*, 972, 974, 1178-79
Nandi tribe, 113-15, 754, 1189
Nan Dunham, 473-74
NAN GRAHAM, 79-81, 206, 741, *874*, 885
Nannerl, 1339
nannies: acerbic, 779-81, 781-83, 783-84, 784-86; arrive on East wind, 779; arrive on kite, 781; black, 632, 786-89, 1239; caged, 782; dreadful, 784; eccentric, 779-81, 781-83, 783-84, 784-86; possess magic, 779-81, 781-83, 783-84, 784-86; retired, 1325-27; stern disciplinarian, 780, 781-83, 783-84, 784-86; very vain, 780, 781-83, 783-84, 784-86. *See also* babysitters; governesses; nurses.
Nanny, 56-57
Nanny, the goat, 913
NANNY TRANTER, 483-84, 639, *874-75*, 1335
NAN OWLAND, 2, 486-87, 779, *875*
Nantucket: mid-19th century, 887-89; threatened, 888-89
Naoise, 298-99, 300
Napoleonic Wars, 190-91, 342, 595, 1237
Nardac, 509
The Nargun and the Stars, 1404
NARNIA: 43, 54, 150, 167, 185, 321, 323, 356-57, 376-77, 560-62, 575, 603, 687-89, 699, 710-13, 742, 864, *875-76*, 893, 961-62, 987, 994-96, 1009, 1026-27, 1034, 1081-82, 1091-93, 1174, 1227, 1264, 1279, 1306-8; creation of, 755-57; queen of, 167, 279, 321, 356-57, 561-62, 603, 688, 710, 712, 742, 755, 756, 864, 961-62, 987, 1009, 1027, 1174; replaced by real Narnia, 876
Narnians, Old, 323, 1264
Narrative of the Travels and Adventures of Monsieur Violet in California, Sonora, and Western Texas, 776
Nat, 4, 318
Nate Pardon, 887-89
Nathaniel Creep, 199

National Stadium, Santiago, 1188
Natividad Island, 237, 1412
NAT MARLOWE, 574, *876*, 1202, 1351-53
Naturalist, 1244
naturalists: 363, 1159, 1387; able to talk to animals, 323
The Natural Need, 1028
nature: appreciation for, 337, 432, 451, 517, 706, 716-17, 717-20, 827-28, 946, 1029, 1327-30, 1386-88, 1398-99; babies converse with, 782-83; beauty of, 128; healing power of, 898; idealized, 827-28; love of, 1382-85; power of, 128; respect for, 659-62
THE NATURE OF THE BEAST, 567, *876-78*
The Naval Officer, or, Scenes and Adventures in the Life of Frank Mildmay, 777
naval officers, retired, 4
Navarre, King of, 913
navvies, 199
Navy, British, ships on anti-slave patrol, 1068-70
Naychor, 626, 1204-5
Nazis, World War II, 37, 761, 898-99, 959, 1348
necklaces: amber, 431; of dead husbands' teeth, 1354; opal, 4
Necromancer, 1338
necromancers: 208-9. *See also* enchanters; magicians; warlocks; witches; wizards.
NECTAN, 245, 333, 387, *878-79*, 884, 1161-63
Ned Brewster, 495
NED BYRNE, 101, 499-501, *879*
Ned Carver in Danger, 90
NED COWARD, 233, 604, 876-78, *879-80*, 910
Ned Hernon, 544
Neech, Mrs., *858-59*, 1224
needlepoint: 1269. *See also* embroideries; samplers; tapestries.
ne'er-do-wells, 544, 1110, 1132, 1315, 1365-66
Negog, 733
neighborhood life: Australia, 620-23; Belfast, 1284-87; city, 514-16, 606-8, 689-92, 1114-17, 1218-20, 1269-70, 1364-66, 1389-91; Ireland, 258-61, 543-46; polyglot, 519-21, 522; rural, 523-25, 801-4, 1021-23; Scotland, 642-43; village, 9-10, 484-85, 1196-99, 1211-13, 1234-36, 1410-11; World War II, 467-69

neighbors: angry foreign man, 434–
36; busybody, 92, 862; disagreeable girl, 640; fatherly, 865;
helpful, 79–81, 838, 912, 1365;
helpful tailor, 863; misanthrope,
914–15; next door, 261, 623; new,
wealthy, 722–24; presumed on holiday, 1147; pretentious, unfriendly, 722–24; scolding, 1263
Neil Parry, 567
NEIL RAMSAY, *880*, 1218–20
Neleus, 785
NELL HENCHMAN, 94, 190–91, 356, 828–
29, *880–81*, 1236
Nellie Jack John Cherry, 292, 351–
52, 641
Nell McShane, 1124, 1373
NELLY STAGG, 402, *881*, 1084
nephews: 1, 9–10, 16, 683; kidnapped, 13; low self-esteem, 920;
of Grand Master of Hospitallers,
670; of gun runner, 1228; of miser, 227–29; of iron monger, boy
brought up as, 697; of usurper,
995; of war leader, 920; successor
to enchanter, 209
Nero, Emperor of Rome, 1118
Nero, the dog, 728
NESBIT, E(DITH), 416, 418, *881–82*,
1146
Ness (*Beorn the Proud*), 91–92
Ness (*The Lantern Bearers*), 681–82
Nessan, 1118–19
NESSIE MORTIMER, 242, 399, 836, 843,
883, 895–96
nests: hen steals, 713; inside fairy
hill, 271; mouse-sized, 1035; of
wild peregrine falcon, 383–84
The Net, 1031
Netherlands: late 17th century,
Utrecht, 456–58; late 20th centu-
ry, Amsterdam, 1061–64
Nettlewood, 801
NETTY BELLINGER, 821, *883*, 1024,
938–39, 1237
Never Is a Long, Long Time, 192
Neverland, 172, 956–58, 961, 1226,
1347
"Nevermore!," 41
Nev Hodgkinson, 540
Neville, Lt. John, 457
Newcastle, mining country, late 20th
century, 33–36
New Clothes for the Emperor, 488
Newcombe, Poop, 368, 370, 992
New Cumbria, 844, 1142–43
New Forest, 341–42
New Found Land, 232

Newgate Gaol, 817, 839, 1107, 1109,
1201
New Guinea, 564–65, 613
New Holland, 513
"The New Jerusalem," 360
New Minster, 1015, 1394
News, Daily, the kitten, 307–9, 1174
New-Sirius, 326–27
newsmen: American in Chile, 585;
columnist, 404–5, 434–36; cover
neighborhood renovation, 1116;
cover phenomenon of Loch Ness mon-
ster, 642; television, 539; women,
57, 917–19. *See also* journalists;
reporters.
Newsome family, 1386–87
New South Wales, late 20th century,
Ryan Creek, 620–23
newspapers: files of, 1022; written
by children, 1147
New Spears, 1320
The New Tenants, 751
The New Treasure-Seekers, 881, 1148
The New Venturers, 90
New World: Celts in, 844, 1142; emi-
grants to, 763, 881, 939, 1150
New Year's Day, 360, 1032
New Year's Eve, 824–25, 1390
New York City, mid-20th century,
593–95
New Zealand, late 20th century, sub-
urb, 200–1
NIALL (*The Master of Morgana*), 731–
32, 796, 789–91, 832, *883–84*
NIALL (*The Stronghold*), 245, 878,
884, 1161–63, 1190
Niam of the Golden Hair, 1271
*Nibelungenlied: The Treasure of
Siegfried*, 27
A Nice Day Out?, 192
Nicola Marlow, 382–85, 963–65
Nicol Anderson, 1156
Nicholas, 359
NICHOLAS AND THE WOOLPACK, 527, 884,
1402. *See THE WOOL-PACK, 1402–3.*
Nicholas Bodkyn, 153
Nicholas Carey, 1346
NICHOLAS FETTERLOCK, 234, 453, 519,
791, 827, *884–85*, 1133, 1402–3
NICHOLAS LATTIMER, 79–81, 206, 741,
885
Nicholas II, Czar of Russia, 28,
1207–8
Nichol family, 57, 245
Nichols, Peter, 231
Nick Appleyard, 102, 316, 615
NICKLESS, WILL, 931, *885–
86*

nicknames: Great Orb, 1322; "han-
    dles," 364, 524; Wood Troll, 1401;
    Yarl Corbie, 1409
Nicko, 426
Nick Redpoll, 1396
Nick Sanders, 1062-63
Nickster, 426
NICK WILLOW, 14, 60, 176-79, 179,
    543, 826, 842-43, *886*
NICKY GORE, 10, 297, 309-13, 470,
    648, *886*, 1280
NICKY NICHOL, 57, 245, 748-50, *886-
    87*
nieces, 68-71, 339, 577, 683-84,
    792, 900, 1035, 1056, 1133-36,
    1316-19
Nigeria, slavery in, 743
NIGHTBIRDS ON NANTUCKET, 8, 109,
    887-89, 1141
NIGHT FALL, 9, *889-91*
nightmares: of hangings, 1126;
    recurring, 889-90, 900-2, 1006
THE NIGHT OF THE COMET, 143, 442,
    891. *See BOSTOCK AND HARRIS; OR,
    THE NIGHT OF THE COMET, 143-44*.
Night of the Drums, 765
The Night of Wenceslas, 708
Nightrider, 1164
night train, summoned by whistle,
    891-92
THE NIGHT WATCHMEN, 266, *891-92*
NIKABRIK, the dwarf, *892-93*, 995,
    1264-65
Nils, the mouse, 1031-32
Nina, 1300-2
NINA CARRINGTON, 411-12, *893*
Nina Mirkov, 718-19
Ninny's Boat, 659
Nine Lives: Cats in Folklore, 152
THE NINE LIVES OF ISLAND MACKENZIE,
    831, *893-94*
Nine Standards, 557
nineteenth century: Africa: 113-15
--British Isles: England, Brighton,
    1149-51; London, 839-411; north
    country, 1327-30
--*early*: Africa, 1145-46
--British Isles: England, London,
    107-9, 1223-25; Pembrokeshire,
    236-37; Puddleby-on-the-Marsh,
    1145-46; seacoast village, 1223-
    25; Suffolk, 190-91; West Country,
    1111-13; Scotland, Shetland Is-
    lands, 1155-57; Wales, Pennygaff,
    1356-58
--Europe: Russia, 717-20
--South America: Quivera, Cibola,
    236-37; Roman America, 1141-43

--*mid*: Africa and high seas off,
    1068-71
--British Isles: England, 492-
    95, 1068-71; coal town, 1276-78;
    Cornwall, 397-99; Devonshire, 5-
    6, 724-27; industrial city, 807-9;
    London, 227-30; Puddleby-on-the-
    Marsh, 1309-11; Sussex, 763-65;
    Tooting, 52-54; village, 266-69;
    Willoughby Chase, 1399-1401
--South America, Spidermonkey Is-
    land, 1309-11
--South Pacific, island, 255-57
--South Seas, island, 786-89
--Western Hemisphere: high seas and
    Nantucket, 887-89
--*late*: Asia: India, 651-54; Seonee
    Hills, 630-32
--British Isles: England, 105-
    7, 387-88; Cheshire, Chorley,
    9-10, 484-85, 1143-44, 1234-
    36; Devonshire, 926-27; Durham
    County, 129-31; Essex coast,
    1379-81; London, 55-57, 489-92,
    755-57, 1146-48; Oxford, 1316-19;
    Teddington, 1158-60
--Europe: Russia, 1206-8
*Nineteenth Century Children: Heroes
    and Heroines in English Children's
    Stories 1780-1900*, 63
ninth century: Denmark, 91-92;
    England, East Anglia and Wessex,
    870-72; Ireland, 91-92
Ninth Roman Legion, 347-50, 375,
    746, 768, 1025-26
The Nitehood, 885
NJIMBIN, 535, 715, 860-61, *894*
NOAH, 522-23, 737, 829, *894-
    95*
Noah Bugg, 954-55, 1196
Noah's Ark: 782; 829-30
NOAH'S CASTLE, *895-97*, 1247
No Beat of Drum, 163
The Noble Hawks, 831
nobles: benevolent, 47; Byzantine,
    47; Calormene, 43; cruel, 737;
    cutthroats, 39-40; English, 350-
    51, 915-17, 1137, 1404-6; English,
    eccentric, 108; English, oppres-
    sive, 1043; English, unscrupu-
    lous, 102-5, 606, 611, 615,
    738-40; English, untrustworthy,
    1103; English, zealous, 613, 738,
    863; exiled, 185; girl companion,
    36-37; greedy, grasping, 737-38;
    French, cruel, 832-33, 1215-
    17; European, 28; future, 1360;
    half-native, 670; lost, 246, 574;

Norman, 968; Outremer, 619; penny-
pinching, 1160; Russian, 12,
63-64, 1207-8; Scottish, 1196-98,
1412-15; various nationalities,
670-72
No Boats on Bannermere, 1253
NOBODY'S GARDEN, 617, *897-99*
NOEL, 142, *899*, 645-46
Noel, the cat, 1186
NOEL BASTABLE, 19, 318, *899*, 1146-47
NO END TO YESTERDAY, 746, *899-902*
No Guns, No Oranges, 980
NOLLEKENS, King of Norfolk, 872,
902-3, 985, 1094-96, 1130
Nolly, King of Norfolk. *See*
NOLLEKENS, King of Norfolk, 872,
902-3, 985, 1094-96, 1130.
Nomansland, 720
Nona Fell, 87, 722-24, 818-19
"Nonsense," Said the Tortoise, 66
Nonsuch, Lord Lumley of, 1352-53
non-violence, repudiated, 35
Noontide Fairy, 1096
No Place Like, 644
No Ponies, 1251
NORA SHOUTER, *874*, 1354
Nora Whitehead, 474
Nordy Bank, 903
NORDY BANK, *903-4*, 993
Noreen, 540-42
Norfolk, King of, 902-3
Norfolk: early 20th century, 953-55,
987; mid-20th century, 604; late
20th century, 1211-13, 1297-98
Norham Gardens, 564-65
NORMAN CLOUGH, 536-37, *904*, 1035
Norman Mortimer, 242, *399-400*
Normans: in England, 672-75, 1085-
87; in Ireland, 215-17, 261, 408-
9, 482, 1103; in Outremer, 670, 968
North Cornwall Fairies and Legends,
1258
Northend, late 20th century, 85-87
Northern Lights, 112
Northern Star, insurance company,
1375
North Oxford, late 20th century,
564-66
North Pole, Expotition to, 989, 1389
North Sea, 496, 614, 946, 1004-5,
1298-1300, 1341-42
Northumberland: mid-20th century,
486; late 20th century, seacoast,
1376-79
Northway, Jennifer, 248
North Wind, land at back of, 55-57
NORTON, MARY, 132, 134, 136, 138,
140, *904-6*

Norway: late 8th century, village,
1298-1300; mid-20th century, Arctic, 1349-51; late 20th century,
1392-94
Norwegians, in England, 401-3
Norwich, man in moon comes to, 202
No. 7 Songberd's Grove, 1114, 1116
noses, very hooked, 851
Nostrand, Great Spirit of Darkness,
167, 1343
notebooks: compromising discovered under comics, 275, 838, 920;
containing clues, 183; incriminating, 275
notes: in violet-colored ink, 483,
875; old-fashioned, 451-52;
scornful, 723; taken from corpse,
340. *See also* letters; mail; messages.
Notes to the Hurrying Man, 943
Nottingham, 146
novels, unfinished Russian, 655
novices: Benedictine, 916, 1395;
priest, 1261
NO WAY OF TELLING, *906-7*, 1111
Now We Are Six, 233, 812, 989
Nua, 586-87
nuclear war, aftermath, 149, 156-58,
283, 655
nuggets, gold, 1205-6
Numenorean, 1158
Numps, 574, 1352-53
nuns, 744, 799, 1406
nunneries, 1406
Nuremberg, World War II, 253
nurseries: Bronte, 1275; children's, 956, 958; plant,
183
The Nursery Alice, 180-81
nursery rhymes, characters, 202,
572, 1274
nurses: antelopes, 1145; condemned
woman, 720-21; district, 430-31,
433, 873; efficient, 764, 1068;
faithful, 299-300; foolish, 1002;
imperious, 872, 1094; king's very
old, 902, 1094; mother's, 1342;
Newfoundland dog, 956; of Irish
beauty, 298-99; of mentally injured woman, 95; practical, sensitive, 873; Quaker, 1200; Saxon
girl, 1086; student, 378, 465-66,
517, 597, 1025; to retarded boy,
543; "very, very, very old," 872;
World War I, 335, 423-24, 761,
883; wronged, 92, 693-94. *See also*
babysitters; governesses; nannies.

nursing homes: idea rejected, 835;
   inferior, 431. *See also* rest
   homes.
Nuthanger Farm, 535, 1332-33
The Nutmeg Tree, 1081
Nygaard family, 37, 578, 1349-51,
   1401-2

O Absalom!, 1131
The Oak and the Ash, 503
Oakapple, Mr. Julian, 31-32, 807,
   845
Oakenshield, Thorin, 552-53, 1204
Oakes, Abel, 1, 587
Oakley, Tom, 467-69, 851, 1239-40,
   1372-73
oaks: gateway to world of dwarves,
   847-49; magic wood, 969
Oates, Sir Oliver, 615, 1103
oaths: blood, 1299; foresworn, 102,
   396-97, 517, 1158, 1243; to care
   for friend's wife and child, 252;
   to be helpful, 361
Oblate Fathers, 733
obituaries, 1315
O'Brien, Kathleen, 74-75, 325-28,
   343, 639-40, 823, 1042
obsolescence, of planes, 1212
obsessions: boats, 1382; boy has
   various crazes, 942; detective
   to find dwarf, 847, 850; father
   to provide for family, 896; fear
   of crocodile, 172; flying, 1374;
   for dog, 329; for pink whale, 887;
   fox hunting, 775, 1284; good form,
   172; horses and hunting, 419-21;
   killing a peacock, 1283; mother
   with cleaning, 853-54; motor car,
   Toad, 1383-84; motorcycles, girl,
   523, 1283; series of, 942, 1229;
   with death, 1373-74; with fighter planes, 1212
Obstinate, 975
O'Conner, Ann, 1134-36
O'Connor family, 621-23
Occupation: German of France, World
   War II, 1339; German of Channel Islands, World War II, 806; German of
   Norway, World War II, 1350
OCCUPIER, 174-75, *909*
octopuses, witch's familiar, 824,
   1354
Odah, 123-24
odors, peppermint, 200
ODO THE PLOWMAN, 454, 744, 799, *909*,
   1405
The Odyssey, 680, 969

Oedipus complex, 1060
O'FAOLAIN, EILEEN (GOULD), 713, *909-
   10*
Officer Mitchell, 86
offices, school, trashed, 646
O'Flaherty family, 425-27
OGGY, 876-78, *910-11*
Ogoun, Haitian war god, 765-66, 938,
   1227
O'Grady, Juan, 1076-78
ogres: evil, 712; loyal to wizard,
   697; trusty, 1354-55
O'Hara, Kimball. *See* O'Hara, Kim.
O'Hara, Kim, 651-54, 654-55, 743,
   1194-95
oil reserves, depleted, 476
Oily Green Pool, 262, 437, 953, 1114,
   1120
Oisin, 1271
Olaf, 1299
old age, novels of, 429-32, 714-16,
   832-35
OLD BEAK AND CLAWS, 152, 529, *911*,
   931-32, 992
Old Brimstone Bellinger, 821
Oldbury, 19th century English coal
   town, 1276
Old Cathlan, 1319-20
OLD DA, *911*, 1156
Old Dame, 490-92
Old Diamond, 55, 56
OLD DOG, NEW TRICKS, 192, *911-12*
An Older Kind of Magic, 1404
Old Feller, 33, 51, 1325-27
Old Fordham church, 61
Old Forest, 406, 805
Old-Green-Grasshopper, 593-94
OLD GUIDO Falieri, 662, *912-13*
Old John, 248, 675, 913-14, 1003
OLD JOHN, 265, *913-14*
Oldknow family, 16, 172-73, 195,
   211-13, 217-19, 373-75, 409, 525,
   578, 591-92, 616, 710, 800, 859,
   1067, 1154-55, 1173-74, 1229-30,
   1231-32
Old Lady, 677
"The Old Lion," 839
The Old Lion (ship), 839-40
The Old Lion and Other Stories, 302
Old Man of the Earth, 462
Old Man of the Fire, 462
Old Man of the Mountains, 671
Old Man of the Sea, 462-63
Old Narnians, 323, 893, 995-96,
   1026, 1264
Old Ones, 288, 502, 804,
   1375
Old Parson, 725-26

Old People, 1171

old persons: aging Emir, 1291; antique dealer, 844; ascetic looking priest, 399; assertive, 1242; bachelor, 50; beautiful woman, 725; bedesman, 324; bedridden woman, 703-6; busy-body, 862; canny, spirited, woman, 860-61; caretaker, 857; confused old woman, 872-73, 1375; confused woman shopkeeper, 705; coping aunt, 813-14; crusty man, 467-69; deaf gentleman, 267; deaf woman, 798; dejected, 313; demented woman, 308-9, 705; domineering, 873; domineering, illiterate leader, 587; domineering grandmother, accommodating grandfather, 330; eccentric couple, 6; enchanted woman, 168; enigmatic shepherd, 1321; farmer, 863; fiercely independent man, 834-35; fisherman, 1288; formidable man, 433; frail, untidy tailor, 863; French woman portrait painter and revolutionist, 751-52; gentle ex-railway signalman, 837; gnome, 714-16, 716-17, 1114; gondolier, 912-13; great-great-grandmother, unusually well-drawn, 211-13, 217-19, 373-75, 1035-36, 1154-55; gun runner, 1228; half-blind woman, 1010; hobgoblin, 548-550; hypochondriac, 566; independent man, 429-432; independent woman, 642-43, 894, 714-16; intellectual aunts, 62; Irish, 258-61; king, 1092-93; king's nurse, 1094; king's practical housekeeper, 902; landlady, 1141; maker of model village, 837; man dying of thirst, 661; man in black, 824-26; manipulative man, 429-32, 433; man ridiculed, 894-95; man who loves literature, 1124; miller, 862; miner, 624; misanthropic man, 353; misanthropic woman, 642-43; miser, man, 353; monk, 870, 1357; nanny, 1325-27; nurse-housekeeper, king's, 872; old-fashioned landlady, 860; peddler, 1386-87; peppery dwarf, 1265; peppery woman, 282; plain Scottish woman, 830; professor, 321, 710, 712; retired policeman, 847; reclusive man, 587, 833, 834-35, 851, 962-63; righteous man, 894-95; schoolmaster, 1156; Scottish woman, 914-15; seaman, 1374; senile great-great-grandmother, 1294; senile woman, 1242; shepherd, 1398; Sikh matriarch, 297; sinister stranger, 824-26; speaks in aphorisms, 844; spinsters, 1160; sweet governess, 724-26; tailor, 1116; trusty gatekeeper, 1056; very tall, independent woman, 861; village woman, 543; waspish woman, 719; watchmaker, 1304; wise woman, 857; witch, 835; woman intellectual leader, 751-52; woman nurse in World War I, 883; woman of 106, 1151-52; woman said to have second sight, 799, 1151-52; woman skilled in healing, 799; woman spinner, 1002; woman storyteller, 713-14; woman tormented by boys, 1160; woman thought witch, 13, 351, 799, 1405-6; woman who lives in tree house, 1301-2. *See also* grandfathers; grandmothers; grandparents.

Old Peter's Russian Tales, 1017
Old Petronella, 212
Old Rectory, 140-41, 947
Old Sal, 55-56
Old Sam, 183
OLD WILLIAM, *914*, 1143, 1235
OLD WOMAN, 642-43, *914-15*, 1243-44
OLD UNCLE, *914*, 1121
Olga, Grand Duchess of Russia, 24, 28
Olga da Polga, the guinea pig, 1186-87
Olive, 277-78
Oliver Cromwell, the dog, 186-87
Oliver family, 319-20
Oliver Twist, or the Parish Boy's Progress, 313
OLWEN, 237, *915*, 1412
Olwen, Princess, of legend, 528
Olympia, Madame, 518, 1354-55
omens: evil, 1206; of death, 1156. *See also* prophecies; predictions; premonitions; warnings.
Once on a Time: A Fairy Tale for Grown Ups, 812
Once Upon a Time, 1369
ONE IS ONE, *915-17*, 969
One of Gdu, 122
One of Sinu, 123-24
On Lennox Moor, 675
ON THE EDGE, *917-19*, 270
On the Run, 192
On Tour, 1157

Ooly-Sees (Ulysses), 927
OOMPA-LOOMPAS, *919-20*, 203, 811
Opal Raleigh, 558
The Open Book: a Collection of Stories, Essays, Poems, Songs and Music, 1362
Opera Mafia, 1076-77
operas, children's Christmas, 219, 283, 855, 857, 1076
operations: for eyes, 1367; plastic surgery, 205; to clean leg wound, 348; to remove button, 1360; to repair stiff leg, 354; to stifle dissent, 507
Operation Sippacik, 458
ophicleide, 395, 914
OPIO the Fish, 113-15, 754, *920*
Opportunity of a Lifetime, 1111
oppression: by employers, 1277; political, 1043, 1187-89
oracles, of Lord God, 895
oral tradition: on remote Halcyon Island, 2, 522. *See also* folklore; legends; literature, oral.
Orangemen, 1285
Orchid Street, 514-15
orcs, 96, 132, 407, 439, 551, 805, 982
ordeals, trial by, 739
order marks, school, 734, 823
Order of St. Ennodawg, 528
orders, from King for pie, 970
ORDINARY JACK: BEING THE FIRST PART OF THE BAGTHORPE SAGA, 266, *920-22*
organ grinders, unkind, 210
organists, 224
orgies: sex, 505; sex, supposed, 1324
Oriel College, Oxford, 153-54
Orinoco River, 1044
Orkney Islands: 1st century B.C., 1161-64; late 8th century, 1298-1300
Orlando, the dog, 212-13
Orlebar, Roger, 701
ornaments, of bronze, 336
ornithologists, youthful, 38
Oronde, 114
O'Rourke, 143
Orphan Alice, 1159
orphanages: abusive, 821; cruel, 1192, 1221-22; refuse orphan, 1410; St. Luke's, 560, 769, 959
orphans: abused, 605, 821, 1192, 1355; baby Kraken, 824; bookish, 959; boy and girl, 234-36, 514, 763-65, 1029, 334; boys, 14, 108-9, 148, 360, 492-95, 560, 608, 642,
740-41, 807, 812, 876, 981, 1021, 1068, 1081, 1085, 1125-28, 1161-64, 1228, 1238, 1247, 1243-44, 1351, 1364-65, 1392-94, 1394-96, 1405; boy, American in England, 289; boy, circus performer, 204-5; boy, English in Mexico, 601-2; boy, grown-up half-cousin, sinister, 241, 645; boys, half Saxon, 672; boy, Northumberland, 449; boy, Roman Britain, 294-97, 930; boy, Sicilian, 30-31; boy, slow-witted, 579; boy, wild, 1130; brother and sister, 191, 208, 273, 804, 1057, 1315; brothers, 425; dog boy, 672; girl, 36-37, 58, 226-27, 364, 419-21, 548-50, 807-8, 955, 1085, 1105, 1159, 1168, 1220-23, 1240-42, 1320-21, 1322-25, 1364-65, 1396-97, 1400-1; girl, beggar, 294-97; girl, Cornish, 332-33; girl, French, 31-32; girls, half-gypsy, 318-21, 669, 822; girls, half orphans, 206; girl, kidnapped, 815-16; girls, penniless, 724; girl, raised in luxury, 724; girl, shy, 897-99; girl, taking place in family, 598; prince, 720-22; rabbit, 446; rejected at institution, 1410; runaway joins traveling players, 153; scullery maid, 694; self-dramatizing foundling, 769; siblings, 1056-57, 1146; sisters, 1168-69; stage children, 68-71; street urchin in India, 651; war orphan adopted by Cornish family, 1193; workhouse, 1238
Orpheus, 570
Orwell River, 1340
oscillators, 401
OSWALD BASTABLE, 320, 334, 547, 899, *922*, 1146-47
Oswald Bastable and Others, 881
OSKAR STANISLAWSKY, *922*, 980, 1035-36, 1183
OSWALD TUBBS, *922-23*, 1267-68
Ossian House, 1140
ostriches, egg disappears, 1385
Other-end-of-Nowhere, 1329
THE OTHER PEOPLE, 797, *923-24*
THE OTHERS, *924*, 1123-24, 1373
THE OTHER WAY ROUND, 647, *924-26*
Otherworld, 1162
otherworlds: Celtic, 1227; coexisting, 191, 209, 225; complex fantasy, 414; enchanted, 710-13,

755-57; land of dwarves, 847-49, 970; Narnia, 875-76; wasteland, 359-60; Wonderland, 19-22, 1208-11. *See also* medieval worlds.

Otipo, 1, 586-87, 828

Otley, 1066

Otter (*The Little Grey Men*), 716

Otter (*The Wind in the Willows*), 1384

otters, lost baby, 1384

Ottoman Turks, 213

ottomans: fat, overdressed, 1068; talkative, 1357

Otwell, mid-20th century, 385-86

Our Best Stories: A Collection of Stories Chosen by Children, 980

outcasts: girl, 1396; hunchback boy, 1394; social, 1359, 1368-69; tribal, 1321. *See also* rejections.

Outer Isles, Scotland, 588-89, 589-90, 1048

outlaws: after nuclear war, 157-58; father declared, 457; forest, 11-12, 246, 695; helpful, 744, 1406; lead revolt against barons, 146-47; mercurial leader of, 611, 739-40; Robin Hood's, 12, 1042-43; Robin Hood type, 1104; swashbuckling highwayman, 738; unprincipled, 739-40; wounded, 717

Out of Hand, 111

OUT OF THE MINES: THE STORY OF A PIT BOY, 129, 503, 926. *See THE BONNIE PIT LADDIE*, 129.

Out of the Oven, 771

Outremer, late 12th century, 619, 670-72, 729, 968, 1034

overachievers, family of, 920-22

overeaters, girls, 1385

overindulgence, causing son to go wrong, 244

THE OVERLAND LAUNCH, 555, *926-27*

Overmantel family, 141, 560, 947-48

overprotection: family of blind girl, 172; avoided by family of blind boy, 1366

Over Sea, Under Stone, 255, 502, 804

Overs family, 17, 60, 362, 450-51, 703-6, 872-73, 1132, 1282, 1375

Over the Bridge: An Autobiography, 233

Over the Bridge: An Essay in Autobiography, 233

OVER THE HILLS TO FABYLON, 488, *927-30*

OWAIN, 294-97, 358, *930*, 1029, 1293

Owen, John, 1180-82

Owen Davies, 148, 502

Owen family, 243-44, 903-4

Owen Hughes, 42, 156, 528, 996, 1234, 1356-58

Owl (*The House at Pooh Corner; Winnie-the-Pooh*), 358, 562-63, 974, 989, 1388

OWL (*The Song of Pentecost*), 246, *930-31*, 1120-21

Owland, Nan, 2

Owland family, 486-87, 779, 875

OWLGLASS, 885, *931-32*

owls: attacks Borrowers, 135; carries warning, 713; disappearing, 933; failing eyesight, 931; learned, 529, 911, 1388; maiden transformed to, 116, 932; paper, 575, 933-34; partially sighted, 152, 911, 992; pedantic, 1388; stuffed, 934; talking 1092, 562-63, 1388

THE OWL SERVICE, *932-35*, 444

Owsla, 95, 446, 557, 1332

Oxbridge exams, 98

Oxfordshire, late 20th century, Ledsham, 451-53

Oxford University, 126, 153-54, 160, 507, 549, 596, 769, 791, 1200, 1281, 1287, 1316-19, 1353, 1405-6

Oxus in Summer, 392, 571, 1362

Oxus River, 156, 389-91, 433, 600, 792-93, 960

Oz Slattery, 606

Ozymandias, 238, 1359

Pablo, 504

Pacific (ship), 632, 786-87, 855, 859

Pacific, discovery of, 733

pacifists, 93

packing cases, mysterious, 434

pack trains, waylaid, 216

Paddington, the bear, 84-85, 126-17, 844

Paddington railway station, bear found in, 84

Padgitt family, 73-74, 519-21, 522

page boys: black, in Paris, 765; Scotland, 677, 1412

pagoda, porcelain, 1031

painters: French portrait, 751-52, 832; house, 465; of coats of arms, 324; of copies, 798; portrait, 613, 889-90; signboard, 486, 960; talented young man, 590. *See also* artists.

paintings: containing clues, 615; destroyed, 84, 844; of niece, 1216; of woman of flowers, 575;

prize winning, by bear, 84; purchased with prize, 736; stolen
madonna, 797-98; thought to be a
master, 844. *See also* photographs;
pictures; portraits.
Palace Guard, Netherlands, 457
palaces: Mexico City, 313; moving,
569, 928-929; revolving, 1142-43;
run-down, 39. *See also* castles;
manors; mansions.
Palantir, 982
Palfrey family, 1385-86
palindrome, traced in ashes, 1406
Palmer, Dr., 1294-95
Palmer family, 498, 498-99, 533-34,
1264
palmers, 153-54
pamphlets, autobiographical, 199,
264
Pan (*The Little Grey Men*), 324, 716
Pan (*The Wind in the Willows*), 828,
1384
Pan, Peter, 956-58, 961, 1226, 1347
Pancho Villa, 601-2
Pandarus, 1090
Panther, 38, 416
panthers: black, 65-66, 630-31, 836;
black, drowned in muck, 877-78;
black circus, 877-78
Pantouflia, 997-99
pantries, huge basement, 895
Panwallah, Mr., 526, 1304
PAPA (*When Hitler Stole Pink Rabbit;
The Other Way Round*), 924-26, *397*,
1348-49
PAPA ANDREAS, 668, 685-86, *937*, 1194
PAPA DOCTOR, 765-67, *937-38*
Papa Gresham, 490-92
paper: routes, 314; routes, girl
has, 1124, 1218; unavailable for
press, 195; with unicorn watermark, 729-30; writing, special,
184
parachutes, from damaged plane, 253
parades: Children's Fancy Dress, 30-
31; dustmen's, 386; ticker tape,
594
Paragon Panther, 221
paranormal, debunked, 485
A PARCEL OF PATTERNS, *938-39*, 941
Pardon, Nate, 887-89
pardons: political, 454; refused,
615
parents: abusive, 1276; abusive foster, 605, 815, 1049-50; adoptive,
820, 958, 1373; architects, 667,
coachman and guard serve as foster, 1126-28; divorced, 413;

executed, 94; foster, 14, 605,
630, 815, 816, 842-43, 1010-11,
1049-50, 1057, 1085, 1126-28,
1262, 1280, 1322, 1390; feuding,
460; fled to France, 309; missing, 186-88; marrying again, 885;
obnoxious, 203; over-controlling,
498;
poverty-stricken, 203-4; professional, 501; psychiatrists,
597; queen, adoptive, 804; refuse to overprotect blind son,
1366; rejecting, 485; returned
from Africa, 121; separated from
children, World War II, 1097-99;
single, father, 842; styles in
parenting, 1117; unable to adjust
to change, 925-26; uninterested,
415; Welsh foster, 14; wolves
foster, 630. *See also* fathers;
mothers.
Pargeter family, 338, 360, 612, 742,
849, 858-59, 1041-42, 1224-25
Paris: future, in ruins, 1359-61;
late 18th century, 765-67, 1215-
18; late 20th century, 657; World
War II period, 1349
Parker, Thea, 1191
Parker family (*The Battle of Bubble and Squeak*), 75-77, 100, 159,
293, 604-5, 860
Parker family (*Carbonel...*), 174-75
Parker family (*Ordinary Jack*), 275,
477, 479, 1048, 1195, 1282-83
Parker family (The White Mountains
Trilogy), 237-40, 989-92, 1359-61
Park Keeper, 781, 784
parks, scene of adventures, 783-84,
785
Parker-Sparrow family, 1088
Parkins, David, 286
Parkin's Beck, 61, 133, 1236
Parktown sector, Johannesburg, 627
Parliament: member of, 1147; visit
to, 690-91
Parliamentary Papers, 199, 230, 1239
parlor games, at Christmas, 228
parodies, 19-22, 192-93, 343, 753,
767, 847, 887-89, 1209, 1274
parrots: black, 1310; destroyed,
1294-95; fight in battle, 1310;
freed, 1294; frighten children,
607; gift of, 1179; named after pirate leader, 172; talking, 732,
1145; wily old, 988, 1145, 1309-
10; writer uncle's, 171
Parry family (*Climbing to Danger*),
243-44

Parry family (*Howl's Moving Castle*), 567

parsnip wine, 376

Parson, 1113

Parson Hall, 111

Parsons, 340

Parsons, Christina, 226-27, 317, 335, 354-56, 419-21, 421, 1057, 1228-29, 1284, 1374

parsons: aging, 262; Bronte fan, 1275; eaten by dragon, 396; fiddler, 725; in conflict with son, 611; kindly, adopts boy, 1010-12; kind, senile, 821; new, 193; son of leads resistance to raiders from Ireland, 1026; wife of, 938-39. *See also* clergymen; curates; pastors; ministers; preachers; priests; rectors; vicars.

PARSON THOMAS STANLEY, 938-39, *940*

PARSON WILLIAM MOMPHESSON, 938, *940*

parties: anniversary, 85; apartment house, 607; birthday, 275, 320, 386, 1048, 1198; birthday at zoo, 780-81; birthday, bear's, 844; children's, 24; Christmas, 403-4, 1267, 1384; dollhouse warming, 723; end of term, 736; farewell, 303; for Pooh, 358; grandmother's birthday, 477; illicit, 549; in empty manor, 456; in honor of rescue, 1389; in park of shadows, 784; in the sea, 785; mad tea, 334; mince pie dinner, 109; neighborhood, 1390; New Year's Eve, 785; on frozen lake, 1198; proclivity for, 554; tea, 726; to celebrate achieving queenship, 1024; to celebrate neighborhood renovation, 863; to pour libation to gods, 491; university student, Amsterdam, 1062

partners, business, Scrooge and Marley, 227-28

Parton, Audrey, 210, 401-2

Parton family, 57-58, 1084

Partridge, Benjamin, 824-26

passages: secret, 1400; underground, 203

passengers: stagecoach, attacked by wolves, 1400; stagecoach, pregnant, 1125, 1128

passing, of King Arthur, 1038-39

Pass of Gebindrath, 123

passports, fake, 657

passwords: in spy network, 653; in verse, 1083

pastors: aging, 54. *See also* clergymen; curates; ministers; parsons; preachers; priests; rectors; vicars.

Paternoster Row, 729

Paterson, 224-25

Patchie, the dog, 326, 328, 640

patchwork quilts, 217

Pat Cooney, 805, 838, 1101-2

Pat Folan, 258-61

Pathan, horse dealer, 757

The Path of Gold, 1028

Paths of Dead, 1158

Patience, 815-16

PATON WALSH, JILL (GILLIAN BLISS PATON WALSH), 82, 197, 370, 414, 459, 938, *940-41*, 1287

PAT PENNINGTON, 75, 85-87, *941-42*, 949-52, 966, 1003-4, 1053

PAT PIERSON, *942*, 1225, 1326

patriarchs: mouse, 914; toy soldiers, 1274

Patrick Hume, 457

Patrick Kentigern Keenan, 572

PATRICK MCSHANE, 7, 818, 924, *942-43*, 1123-25, 1373

Patrick Merrick, 383-87, 963-65

Patrick Pennington, 941-42

Patrick Tregeagle, 1288-91

Patsy Carroll, 544-46

PATTEN, BRIAN, 847, *943*

A PATTERN OF ROSES, 967, *943-45*

patterns: cut in sackcloth, 938; dress, 193; rose, 944. *See also* motifs; symbols.

Paul, 1004

PAULA MARTIN, *945-46*, 968-69, 1169-71

PAULA RIGG, 97-99, *946*

Paul Dallas, 25

Paul Fielding, 459-61, 1287-91

PAUL FAIRFAX, 225, 516-17, *946*, 982-84

PAUL HUNTER, 92, 455-56, 618, *946-47*

Paulie Mountjoy, 1062

PAULINE, 199, *947*, 832, 1216-17

Pauline Fossil, 68-71

Paulinus, 1089-90

Paul Simonds, 1294-95

pawns, 1209

Pebblecomb, Suffolk, mid-20th century, 163-66

peace: elusive, 337; created by music, 585; negotiated by children, 217

Peacemaker, Doctor Sidney, 1088

peacemakers, sister, 411, 1174

Peace Rock, 631

Peachem's Circus, 1247

peaches, huge, 593

The Peacock Garden, 303

Peacock Pie: A Book of Rhymes, 302

peacocks, uncle strives to kill, 1283

PEAGREEN Overmantel, 141-42, *947-48*, 1130

Peak of Darien, 1178

PEARCE, (ANN) PHILIPPA, 75, 328, 812, *948-49*, 1240, 1334

Pearl Raleigh, 558

pearls: gift from kelpie, 830; kelpie's, 13; lost, discovered in well, 726; reward for help, 642

peasants: march of, 1207; Mattean, 1077; Russian, massacred, 16; uprising, 145-47, 1216-17

Pease-blossom, 70

peddlers: aged of moor, 1386-87; gypsy, 729; shady, 729

pediatricians: 498, 534. *See also* doctors; healers; physicians; psychiatrists; psychologists.

pedigrees, of white stallion, 652

Peg Ruggles, 1048

The Pekinese Princess, 242

Peggy, the dog, 836, 896

PEGGY BLACKETT, 171-72, *949*, 972, 974, 1178-79

Peggy Parker, 76-77, 100, 293, 605, 1088

Pembrokeshire, early 19th century, 236-37

Pen Casket, 345, 887-89

pencil box, reward, 1389

pendants, owl, 934

Pendragon, 502

Penfold, Kent, 249, 251-52, 476, 482

Penfold family, 506-7

Penhallow farm, 430-31

Penlelig, mid-20th century, 558-59

Penn (*A Castle of Bone*), 189-90

Penn (The Pennington Books), 941, 950

Pennington, Pat, 75, 1003-4, 1053

Pennington family, 75, 85-87, 1003-4, 1053

Pennington's Heir, 75, 87, 942, 966, 1003, 1053

PENNINGTON'S LAST TERM, 949, 966. *See PENNINGTON'S SEVENTEENTH SUMMER, 949-52.*

PENNINGTON'S SEVENTEENTH SUMMER, 85, *949-52*, 966

Penny Casket, 345

Pennygaff, Wales, 155, 1356

Pepe Moreno, 25

Penshurst, 581

PENTECOST, the mouse, 262, 432, 914, *952-53*, 1120-21

Pentecost and the Chosen One, 258

Pentecost Farm, 952, 1114, 1120

Pentecost of Lickey Top, 258

people: invisible, 1307; miniature, 822, 854, 856, 857; waxwork-like, 755

pepper, causes sneezing, 342

peppermint, odor of, 200

THE PEPPERMINT PIG, 81, *953-55*

Per, the "Wood Troll," 37, 1350

Peran-Wisa, 390

perceptiveness, blind boy has unusual, 33-36

Percival family, 938-39, 1203

Percy, the sheep, 518

Perdita, in *A Winter's Tale*, 171

PERDITA (*The Witch's Daughter*), *954-56*, 1396-97

Peregrine Shelley, 433

Peregrin Took, 981-82

performances: before king, 212; in inn yard, 1128, stellar, of pig, 1083

Pergale family, 224

Pericles (ship), 190, 342, 595, 1236-37

Perilous Pilgrimage, 1257

period novels: mid-17th century, England, 1009-12; 18th century, England, 111-13, 1125-28; France and England, 339-42; London, 610-11, 1108-10; Sussex, 304-6; mid-19th century, England, 492-95, 763-65; late 19th century, England, 387-88, 1143-44; London, 489-92; early 20th century, Essex, 418-21, Manchester, 1267-68; pre-World War I, England, 418-21; Cheshire, 9-10; Essex, 421-24; World War II, England, Cheshire, 1234-36. *See also* biographical novels; historical novels.

periwinkle, pot of, 153

perjury: about father's death, 1103; of frog, 262; to save girl's life, 341

Perkin's Beck, 135

Per Knudson, 1401

Perrott, Rob, 506

persecution, religious, against Quakers, 1199-202

perseverance: 135-36, 689-92, 786-89, 812-14, 927, 1088, 1098-99, 1125, 1158-60, 1190-92, 1262-64, 1320-34, 1342-45, 1415-17.

See also persistence; pluck; resource; tenacity.

Persian, names from, 389-90

Persian Gold, 941

Persian looking glass, 374

persistence: dogged, of aged detective, 847-49, 850. *See also* perseverance; pluck; resource; tenacity.

The Personal History of David Copperfield, 313

personalities, two distinct, 1346

personifications, 228, 974-80

Perverse and Foolish: A Memoir of Childhood and Youth, 144

Perrybingle family, 266-69

pessimists, donkey, 358

Pet, the horse, 105

Peter, the miner, 1001, 1002

PETER AND WENDY, 72, *956-58*

PETER BEAUMARCHAIS, 806, *959*, 1339

PETER BECKFORD, 480, *959*

PETER BERESFORD, 769, *959*, 1221-23

Peter Blow, 404-5

PETER CLEVERTON, 38, 389-92, 793, *959-60*

Peter de Chaworth, 672

PETER DYSON, 2, 486-87, *960*

Peter Ellison, 579-80

Peter Etty, 169-71

Peterkin, 729

Peterkin Gay, 256

Peter Long, 59, 1237-38, 1240, 1279

Peter Marlow (*Falconer's Lure*), 383-84

Peter Marlow (*Peter's Room*), 963-65

PETER MCNAIR, 616, 846, *960-61*, 1004-6, 1190-92

PETER PAN, 72, 172, 956-58, *961*, 1226, 1347

PETER PAN, 961. *See PETER AND WENDY*, *956-58*.

PETER PAN AND WENDY, 73, 956. *See PETER AND WENDY*, *956-58*.

Peter Pan in Kensington Gardens, 72

PETER PEVENSIE, 185, 321, 356, 376, 560, 688, 710-12, 742, 864, 893, *961-62*, 994-95, 1009, 1093, 1174

PETER POSSIT, 234-36, 516, *962*, 1057

Peter Regan, 543-46

Peters, 4, 318-19

Peter Sandwell, 223-25

PETER SIMPSON, 833-35, *962-63*, 1173

PETER'S ROOM, 429, *963-65*

Peter Winnington, 225

Petoff family, 235

Petrova Fossil, 68-71

pets: blood hound, 765-66; bony gray kitten, 1097; cat, 697, 724, 889-90, 1174, 1186, 1365; cat locked in attic, 1335; cat saved from flood, 866-67; destructive, 76; dogs, 715, 724, 728, 861, 903-4, 913, 915, 1112, 1320-21; dog, to be "put down," 896; earthworm, 1192, 1355; gerbils, 76-77, 100, 159, 860, 1088; goat, 913; guinea pig, 29, 1186-87, 1262-63; half-wolf dog, 1320-21; hens, 713-14; hen named Alice, 877; horses, 1339-40, 1367-68; hound dog, 921, 1419-20; lark of lame prince, 721; mice, 1392; mongrel dog, 912; Newfoundland dog, 956; numerous, 598; otter, slain cruelly, 865; overweight dog, 30; pigeons, 913; pigs, 1082-84, 987; puppy, 59, 955; rats, 1; red hen, 913; rooster, 725-26, 1097; runt pig, 954; sheepdog, 1313; shot by father, 693; statues of, 693; talking bird, 887-88; talking cat, 913; talking parrot, 732; talking raven, 41-42; turtle, 1186; white donkey, 913; white mouse, 1031; wolf cub, 348; wolf-like dogs, 1067

pet shops, 539

petticoats, burned, 386

Pettifer, Miss Mary, 893-94

Pevensie family, 55, 185, 321, 356-57, 376-77, 560-62, 603, 688, 710-12, 742-43, 756, 864, 893, 961-62, 994-96, 1009, 1026-27, 1093, 1174, 1264-65, 1306-8

PEW, *965*, 1254

Pew Gardens, 127-28

PEYTON, K. M. (KATHLEEN WENDY PEYTON), 85, 354, 418, 421, 763, 809, 943, 949, *965-67*, 982, 1004, 1190, 1213, 1379

Peyton, Michael, 966

PHAEDRUS, 252, 772-74, 806, 865, *967-68*

Pharisees, Queen of, 1010-11

pharmacists: boy studies to be, 131; unscrupulous, 1338

Phantom (ship), 866, 1068-70

Pheasant, the horse, 423

pheasants, poached and doped, 284-85, 852-53, 1074, 1372

Philemon, Miss, 603, 822-23

Philip, 918

PHILIP D'AUBIGNY, 453, 619, 670-72, 729, *968*, 1034, 1291, 1346

PHILIP HOLBEIN, 4, 285-86, 478, 539, 754, *968*, 1039-41
Philip Kitson, 536
PHILIP MARTIN, 37-38, 945, *968-69*, 1169-70
Philip Morley, 1275
Philip Pirrip, 492, 981
Philip Top-Morlion, 143
Philip Wilson, 1131-32
The Philosopher (ship), 113
philosophers, gathering of, 1287-90
Philosophical Society of Jerusalem, 373, 800
phobias, school, owing to dyslexia, 1313
Phoebe (boat), 982, 1088
Phoenix, fiery birdlord, 1168
The Phoenix and the Carpet, 418, 881
photographers, 383-84, 910, 1116, 1160
photographs: between floor boards, 427; framed, 412-13; incriminating, 585. *See also* paintings; pictures; portraits.
physicians: animal, 323-24; Dacca, 653-54; magistrate, 1254-56; medical student, 191, 1041-42, 1200. *See also* doctors; "harb mother"; healers; pediatricians; psychiatrists; psychologists.
pianists: 4, 86, 186, 761, 941-42, 950-52, 383-84. *See also* musicians; singers.
PICARD, BARBARA LEONIE, 738, 915, *969*, 1017
picaresque novels, 153-55, 797-99, 846-49, 1232-34, 1267-68, 1351-53, 1415-17
Piccaninnie tribe, 957
pickaxe, swiped, used to escape from collapsed mine, 624
pickpockets, 246, 278, 597-98, 610, 816, 1087, 1107, 1108, 1186
Pick-thank, 976
picnics: ending in quarrel, 79; on Goodwin Sands, 222; blackberrying, 468; on seacoast, 1288; on riverbank, 1382
A Picnic with the Aunts, 831
Picts, 1088-91, 1299
pictures: drawn by children, 607; dressed up, 668; embroidered, 582, 217, 219, 770; lost on train, 328; newspaper, 1397; of dog, embroidered, 328-29; of mysterious beast, 877; selected, 412; wool work, 852. *See also* paintings, photographs; portraits.

pieceners, textile mill, 198
pie dishes, floated down river, 971
Piegans, 733
piemakers, family of, 51, 488, 600, 970-71
THE PIEMAKERS, 266, *970-71*
pies: enormous meat, 51, 488, 970-71; king's, 488; for 2000, 970-71
Piercy family, 520-21, 522
Pierre Mercier, 751-52, 832, 1215-18
piers: amusement, 176, 362; antique wooden, 1208; entertainment, 667; fog-shrouded, abandoned, 1290; passage to other time, 1056; ruined, 1337
Piers Barber, 370, 1311
PIERS MEDLEY, 582-83, *971-72*, 1033, 1036
Pierson, Pat, 942, 1225, 1326
Piety, 976, 978
piety: hypocritical, 53-54. *See also* didactic novels, moralistic.
PIGEON POST, 972-74, 1016
pigeons: aid in battle, 1001; campaign to raise, 707; carrier, 972-74; old woman keeps, 1002; raising of, 1286, 1390; talking, 248, 913; white, shot, 999
PIGLET, 358, 562-63, *974*, 989, 1388-89
pigmentation, removed, 1145
The Pig Organ; or, Pork with Perfect Pitch, 570
Pigott's Comet, 144
pigs: baby turns into, 23; death of pet, 987; disappearing, 351; familiar of witch, 376, 1354; pet, 59; pet butchered, 955; runt, 954; suspected sheep killer, 1083; stuffed, 974, 1388-89; talking, 1145
Pigs Might Fly, 665
Pike family, 252-54
pikes, vicious, wrecks boat, 717
Pilgrim, Anne, 25
pilgrimages: to Holy Land, 916; to Rome, 1015-16
Pilgrims, 747
PILGRIM'S PROGRESS, 161, *974-80*
The Pilgrim's Progress from This World to That Which Is to Come..., 974
pilgrim trails, 502
Pilgrim's Way: An Essay in Recollection, 159
pillars, natural, moving, 351
PILLING, ANN, 539, *980*
Pilling family, 968, 1169-70

pillows, of marshmallow, 1376
Pillycock's Shop, 759
pilots: of early airplanes, 354–56; ship's, 1341–42, 1380; stunt, 1057; test, secret, 420, 1374
Pilot's Cottage, 163
PIM, JOHN, 446, *613*, 863, 1115
Pincher, the dog, 1147
PING, 373–75, 525, 578, 800, 859, *980–81*, 1035–36, 1154–55, 1183, 1231
PINKS RIDLEY, 186–88, 707, 815, *981*
Pinto, the dog, 1303
Piper at the Gates of Dawn, 828
Piper family, 412–14, 694, 697, 1238
pipes: buried and found, 399; great-great-grandfather's, 1235; Macclesfield, 399; of Pan, 1384
PIPKIN, the rabbit, 1332
PIPPIN TOOK, 132, 406–8, 437, 805, *981–82*, 1056
PIP PIRRIP, 94–95, 376, 492–95, 592, 608, 757, 820, *981*, 1346
pirates: 100–1, 172, 236, 256, 511, 1069, 1132, 1146, 1253–56, 1299, 1311, 1347, 1412; attack camp, 1178; blind, 965; Caribbean, 1045; demented, 89; elegant leader, 172; girl likes to play, 874; in Neverland, 957–58; one-legged, 732; ship of, 173; sisters play, 1178–79; Turkish, 371, 1044; wounded, 338
The Pirates in the Deep Green Sea, 709
Pirate's Island, 1246
Pirrip family, 492–94
Piskey Folk: A Book of Cornish Legends, 1258
The Piskey-purse: Legends and Tales of North Cornwall, 1258
pistols: antique, 307; dueling, 1125–28; means of identification, 1127; tampered with, 305. *See also* weapons.
Pit, Children of, 1357–58
pitch caps, 501
Pit People, 1068
Pitt Rivers Museum, 569, 613
the Place, 197
Place, Selina, 344, 408, 504, 1067, 1343–44
Place of Happy Release, 240
Place of the Tombs, 561
place of vulnerability, 114, 1107
Plague, Great, of 1665, 1230, 1231
The Plague Dogs, 3

plagues: cattle, 1416, England, Derbyshire, of 1665, 193, 760, 938–39, 940; midges and others, 715; of cats, 374, 525; of maggots, 374–75; of rats, 587; of snakes, 374–75; of 1665, children die in, 212, 710; of 1665, London, 1199, 1201–2; various, 715, 861, 894; warning of 310
Plain Tales from the Hills, 666
Plan, to annihilate life on earth, 239
planes: early aviation, 354–56; model, 1212; RAF Lightning, 1212
THE PLAN FOR BIRDSMARSH, 966, *982–84*
plank, walk the, in play, 1179
Plan of Campaign, 920
plans: go consistently awry, 690–91; to free Mary, Queen of Scots, 1413–14; to kidnap and expose baby sister, 1149; to unbounce Tigger, 563
Plantaganet family, 101–2, 330–31, 849–50, 1245–46
plantations: Brazil, 1046; coffee, in Haiti, 765
planters, Australian, 787
plants: destroyed, 1295; enormous tropical growing rampant, 128; killed by frost, 128
plastic surgery, 205
Plato, 1329
Platter family, 140–42, 138–39, 822, 837, 947, 856–57, 985
players: strolling, 153–55, 169–71; traveling, 1248, 1352; traveling puppet show, 1187–89. *See also* acrobats; actors; actresses; tumblers.
playgrounds: adventure, 522; converted to wealthy flats, 521
"play house," 1170
Playhouse Tales, 555
playing cards, as characters, 20–21, 23
playmates: conjured, 1264; imaginary, 49
plays: adapted, 1094; Christmas, 1373; Christmas musical, 1076; class, 591, 820, 1270; Coventry, 1018; dramatic, 286–87; London stage, 1126–28; produced at festival, 635–36; school, 37, 843, 1073
playwrights, 876, 1202
Pleiades, 780
pledges: of abstinence, 479. *See also* agreements; bargains; treaties; truces.

Plethon, 370

Pliable, 975

plots: foiled, 772; labyrinthine, 1110; to kill king, 1013; to steal treasure, 173

Plowman family, 620-23

PLOWMAN, STEPHANIE, *984-85*, 1206

pluck: 109-10, 563, 716-17, 1116, 1314-15. *See also* perseverance; persistence; resource; tenacity.

plumbers, 524

Plummer, Polly, 167, 321, 987, 1279

Plummer family, 267-68

poachers: 13, 137, 195, 218, 284-85, 353, 454, 616, 642-43, 732, 790, 873, 884, 918, 1276, 1328, 1372; supposed, 705; methods for, 1372

Pocket family, 494-95, 820, 981, 1346

The Pocket Mouse, 1371

POD CLOCK, 49, 811, 132-33, 135, 136-37, 138-40, 140-42, 147, 489, 559-60, 854, 856, 948, *985*, 1130, 1282, 1236

poems: by girl, 734-36; by boy, 620; destroyed, 622; for elocution contest, 384; framing stories, 632; in shape of mouse's tail, 836; "Jabberwocky," 1361; night thoughts, 536; nonsense, 572, 594; prize-winning, 823; published, 226; recited, 192-93; selling, 1147; shared with friends, 600; test of identity, 20, 22-23. *See also* rhymes; verses.

Poems for Children 393

poets: absentminded, 1356; ancient Ireland, 299; Andrew Marvell, 1124; boy, 899; Chinese, 853, 1195, 1266; drowned, 809-10; fox, 432; French, 829; hobbit, 96, 1056; imprisoned Norwegian, 1031-32; mouse, 953; rat, 1021, 1382; sea captain hare, 366; stuffed bear, 989; traveling, 1234; white lady mouse, 1032; youthful, 620-23, 734-36, 1034, 1124-25

Pogany, Willy, 514

point of view: alternating, 558-59, 1301-5; continually shifting, 459-62; especially effective, 132-34, 134-36, 136-38, 138-40, 140-42; of animals, 1368; sharply focused, 33-36, 703-6

Pointz, the hedgehog, 931

poison, 116, 122, 958, 1000-1, 1025, 1347

The Poison Factory, 149

poisonings: of mentally ill, 157; of town well, 157

Poland: 17th century, 213-15; mid-20th century, 1096-99; World War II period, 152, 619-20, 1096-99

Pole, Jill, 377, 603, 687-89, 1007, 1034, 1091-93, 1174

Poles: in England, 922, 1035; refugees, 1096-99

police: 34, 36, 86-87, 137, 182-84, 243-44, 326, 404-5, 426-27, 481, 514-15, 605, 749, 784, 798, 811, 950-52, 1003, 1005, 1022, 1134-35, 1155, 1173, 1219-20, 1337, 1383; brutality, 1187-89; dog caricatures of, 816; impersonated, 906-7; rabbit, 1332; raid gang, 278; retired superintendent, Welsh, 847, 850; river, 403; secret, 1187-89; vs. terrorists, 1077-78; wolf, 711; woman, 34

Polish Free Army, 749

politeness, especially effective tool, 1082-84

political repression, intense, 155-58, 237-40, 505-6, 989-92, 1187-89, 1294-95, 1330-34, 1359-61

POLLAND, MADELEINE A (NGELA CAHILL), 91, 215, 298, *985*, 1012, 1244

Pollard, John, 613, 446, 1115

POLL Codling, 201, *985*, 1094-96, 1130

POLL GREENGRASS, 59, 62, 364-65, 953-55, *986-87*, 1195-96

pollution: environmentalists protest, 33-36; industrial of river, 390; nuclear, 155-58

Polly Barker, 602

The "Polly Harris," 1251

POLLY PLUMMER, 167, 321, 688, 755-56, *987*, 1279

POLLY WHITTACKER, 411-14, 485, 590, 694, 697, 833, 893, *987-88*, 1029, 1065, 1238

poltergeist-like events, 286-87

poltergeists, 49, 92, 452, 595-96, 1052

Polthorpe, late 20th century, 364, 523

Poltoratzky family, 1415-17

Polwarne family, 1409-11

polygamy, 160, 1015

POLYNESIA, the parrot, 731, *988*, 1145, 1309-11

Polytecnic, 44, 46, 1014

Pompey, 512

ponies: black of blind boy, 1367; Dartmoor wild, 1387; fall from,

693; fat little gray, 105;
Galloway, 50-51; gypsy, 436;
killed, 1327; Shetland, 6
Ponies for Hire, 757
Pontifex family, 176, 362-63, 451,
472, 667, 1056, 1208, 1290-91
Ponton, Helen, 404
Ponty Pontifex, 472, 1290
pony boys, in mine, 129-30
Pony Club, 615, 858, 1004, 1053,
1191, 1339
PONY CRAY, 535, 685-86, *988-89*
poodles, trained, 235
Pooh, Winnie-the-, 1388-89
POOH BEAR, 85, 232, 358, 562-64, 974,
989
Poohsticks, 563, 989
Pooley family, 303, 307-9, 1174-75
Pool of Fire, 990
THE POOL OF FIRE, 231, 240, *989-92*,
1361
pools: between worlds, 755-56, 987;
containing kelpie, 642-43; of
tears, 20, 22, 324, 343, 836; oily
green, 953; produce visions, 733;
water changes things to gold, 1307
POOP NEWCOMBE, 368, 370, *992*
poor, advocates for, imprisoned, 849
Poor Farm, 1100
poorhouses, 197, 1150, 1370. *See
also* workhouses.
Poor Patty, 1252
Poor Stainless, 905
Pop, 278
Pope, Mr. Maitland, 373-75
popes, sending no aid, 633
Popeye, 1287
POPGHOSE, the weasel, 931-32, *992*
Poppet, 89, 556
A POPPY IN THE CORN, 992. *See SISTERS
AND BROTHERS*, *1105*, 1338.
Popsey Dinkums, 173, 175
Popsipetel, 1310
the Porches, 1413
Porlock Weir, 926
porn calendars, provided son by fa-
ther, 1363
porpoises, helpful, 1310
*Porridge Poetry: Cooked, Ornamented
and Served by Hugh Lofting*, 731
PORTER, SHEENA, 903, *992-93*
porteress, of manor gate, 725
Porthaven, 569
portraits: birthday, 477; containing clues, 813; family, 211; missing, 217; of fat women, 613. *See
also* paintings; pictures; photographs.

Portsmouth, 513
Posie Dixon, 1165-67
possession: by demons, 373-75; by
evil king, 502
Possit family, 234-36, 516, 962,
1057
postal papers, girl saves during flood, 866-67
postcards, as clue, 243
*The Posthumous Papers of the
Pickwick Club*, 313
postmasters: doll, 850; village,
258-59
postmistresses, village, 866
post office, bombed, 1286
Posy Fossil, 68-71
pots: smashed by girl, 327, 343; useful, 358
Pott, Mr. Abel, 138-40, 822, 837,
856-57
Pott family, 221-23
potters, 198, 250, 264, 343, 1205,
1239
pounds, dog, 535
poverty: among coal miners, 129-
31, 1276-78; genteel, 68; India,
1302-5; of World War II refugees in
England, 924-26; protested, 849
Powder, 426
Powder Quay, 1273
power: created by repelling metal,
435; failures, 1294; little black
evil, 1130-31; of flight, 344;
of going unseen, 344; struggles,
neighborhood, 1117; will, 176
Powers, Dr. Melanie Delia, 373-75,
800, 859
Pozzidon (Poseidon), 927
pranks: attributed to local louts,
452; boys' school, 224; by ghost,
49; of sorcerer, 451-52. *See also*
hoaxes; mischief; scams; schemes;
tricks.
Prasutagus, 1117-19
prayers: book of fossil stone,
1144; for cherry tart, 387-
88; for death of sister,
387
preachers: street, 112. *See also*
clergymen; curates; ministers;
parsons; pastors; priests; rectors; vicars.
precentors, 1395
Precious, 465
predicaments, imp claims queen and
baby, 902-3
predictions: about Brown Bear, 477;
fulfilled, 11, 1193; new wizard,

1354; of end of world, 112; of visit of three spirits, 227; that
foundling is fairy child, 1410.
See also premonitions; prophecies; warnings.
"Pre-Enlightenment," 1294
Prefabulous Animiles, 1028
prefects, 206, 224
pregnancies: extra-marital, 317,
420, 422, 521, 775, 799, 799-800,
942, 1004, 1197, 1369; feared,
835; mistaken, 1173; of raped
girl, 1025-26; premarital, 1053,
1134-36
prehistoric creatures, 367, 368,
369-70
prehistoric period, British Isles,
335-37
prejudice: against blacks, 251,
627-28, 1262-63; against foreign-
ers, 521; against hunchback,
1396; against Asian Indians,
1280; against Mexicans, 1228;
against Welsh, 1047. *See also*
anti-Semitism; apartheid;
discrimination; social classes,
distinctions between.
premonitions: of danger by rabbit,
1331; of seaman's death fulfilled,
1023; of disaster, 200. *See also*
omens; predictions; prophecies;
warnings.
Presbyterians, devout, 7
*The Presence of the Past: An
Introduction to Landscape History*, 728
preservation: of sailing smacks,
1088; society for, 982
presidents: of schoolboys' club,
244; of island nation, 434-36;
overly idealistic Mexican, 313,
752; shot, 753
press gangs: boys sold to, 195, 218;
kidnapings for, 1067; Scotland,
1156
Prester John, 160
pre-technological era, reversion
to, 237-40, 886, 989-92, 1336-38,
1359-61
pretence, of fight between dragon
and hero, 1030
pretenders: to throne, 730; to kingship of Scottish tribe, 772-74
pretending, obsessive, 964
Presumption, 976
Price, Christine, 1298
Price, Danny, 1269-70
Price, Nance, 1375

PRICE, SUSAN, *993-94*, 1276
Price family, 1165-67
price fixing, wool, 1133
Prichard, Caradog, 148, 502
pride: blinding, 92; excessive,
1210; in craftsmanship, 399, 1143-
44; in family and craft, 9-10,
970-71; sensitivity to, 51
Pride of the Universe, 510
priests: ancient British tribal, Iceni, 1171; arrogant, 333;
attached to noble's household,
615; carrying Roman Eagle, 349;
Catholic chaplain in India, 652;
crippled, 123; elderly Mexican,
399, 601-2; helpful, 1416; helps
escaped prisoners, 1188-89;
novice, 1261; political activist,
1216; power struggles, 121-24;
responsibility for father's
death, 1103; terrorist, 11, 1077-
78; tribal, 1161-64, 1321; tutor,
701; unconventional, 1226; village, 588. *See also* clergymen;
curates; ministers; parsons; pastors; preachers; rectors; vicars.
Prigio, Prince of Pantouflia, 996-99
Prigman, Elijah, 737, 1357-58
Primrose, Jean, 558, 722, 818
*PRINCE CASPIAN: THE RETURN TO
NARNIA*, 699, *994-96*, 1306
PRINCE DAVID, 996, 1234
The Prince in Waiting, 232
PRINCE PRIGIO, 83, 679, *996-99*
princes: Ambrosius of Britain, 681-
83; Appolyon, the winged monster,
976; black made white, 1145; Bumpo
Kahbooboo of Jolliginki, 160-61,
988, 1145-46, 1309-11; Caspian of
Narnia, 185, 323, 376, 893, 995-
96, 1007, 1034, 1092-93, 1174,
1264-65, 1306-8; caricatured,
996; Charlie, Bonnie Prince, 648;
Cor of Archenland, 43, 562, 575,
1081; Corin of Archenland, 561-62,
1081; crown, too serious, 928-
30; David of Wales (England?),
996, 1234, 1357-58; Deio of
Wales (England?), 996; Dolor of
Nomansland, 720-22; Georgie,
Bonnie Prince, 837, 888, 1048,
1100; handsome, 928; in Ghana,
762; in Narnia, 1227; Justin of
Ingary, 569; Kelyddon, legendary,
528; kidnapped, 185, 377, 1007,
1034; killed by dragon, 997; lame,
determined to become king, 720-22;
lost, 1092-93; Madoc of Quivera,

236-37; 1268; of Archenland, 43,
575; of Britain, 681; of Gleann
na Nean, 913; of Narnia, 185, 603;
of Wales, 996, 1357-58; Prigio of
Pantouflia, 996-99; Rabadash of
Calormen, 561-62; "rescues" princess, 702; restored to throne,
721, 994-96; Ricardo of Pantouflia, 670; Rilian of Narnia, 1034;
scapegraces, 561-62, 1081-82;
seeks to abdicate, 1308; spokesman for tribe, 1172-73; three from
The Silver Fairy Book, 783; throne
usurped, 995; very clever, 997-99
Princess Alice, 81
THE PRINCESS AND CURDIE, 746, *999-
1002*
THE PRINCESS AND THE GOBLIN, 746,
999, *1002-3*
PRINCESS FIONUALA, 913, *1003*
The Princess Nobody, 679
princesses: Anna of Constantinople,
117; affects numerous disguises, 928; always merry, 701-2;
baby enchanted to be light, 701;
beautiful, 928; cleaning soldiers' quarters, 247-48; Elen of
Lyonesse, 844, 1142-43; Fionuala
of Gleann na Nean, 1003; French,
600; ill, 1003; Indian captured,
957; met in Park, 1147; Irene, 999-
1001, 1002-3; Makemnoit, 701-2;
Margaret Rose of England, 1048;
Moonacre, 724-26; much wooed, 928-
29; of Quivera, 237, 915; Olwen of
legend, 528; promised in marriage
to dragon slayer, 1259; rejected
by betrothed, 248; Saxon, 768;
weightless, 701-2
The Prince, the Fox, and the Dragon,
151
Principal, 304-5
principals: art school, 108; conduct book altered, 142-43; woman,
of college, 99
printers: first in England, 195-96,
729; former "chance child," 199
printing press, dismantled,
1188
Prioress at Kirklees, treacherous,
147, 717
Priscilla, 294, 296
Priscus, 294, 296
prison camps, German, 619
prisoners: actor, 1353; aided by
mice, 1031-32; brutalized, 1187-
89; Calais, 1133; child queen,
585; dungeon, struggle for food,

879; during queen's jubilee, 1159-
60; escaped Italian, 734-35;
father, 233; father and brother,
1017-20; for sedition and libel, 338, 1224; German, 422, 1051;
girl of Red Knight, 1358; family in attic, 856; in caravan, 485;
in church tower, 272; in dungeon,
1000; in Egypt, 1185; in Hopeless
Tower, prince, 720-21; in magic
net, 1271; in old Caribbean fort,
1064; in prison of hardened paper, 1271; in royal dungeon, 1142,
1357; Irish rebels, 101; island
castle, 1412-15; Italian war, 603,
823; jurymen, 1385-86; king, 916;
minstrel, 674; of dictatorship,
219; of drug smugglers, 1063; of
Germans, World War I, 942; of religious persecution, 1201; of White
Witch, 864; poet in Black Castle, 1031-32; political, 849, 859;
queen, 677, 1413-14; smuggler,
4; Toad of friends, 1383. *See also*
captives.
Prisoners' Aid Society, 1031-32
prisons: Bastille, 1216-17; brother
in, 286; debtors', 305, 1202;
Egyptian, 829; elven, 95; fathers
in, 325, 327, 1223-25; for sedition, 612; in church tower, 1113;
Irish, 101; Mexican, 601; musician in, 941-42, 1003; scenes in,
601; ship's, 492
private eyes, gently parodied, 847
prizes: boat races, 1381; boy, 673;
comfits, 324; competitor as slave,
584; donkey and cart, 31; first,
in art contest, 844; for best costume, 31; for fattest guinea pig,
1186; for originality of painting,
84; own thimble, 324; scout knife,
386; twenty pounds for poem, 736.
See also rewards.
problem novels: domestic, 1105-
6; physical, 290-91, 1313-15;
psychological, 519-21, 679-
83, 833-35, 895-97, 897-99,
949-52, 1004-7, 1058-60, 1167-
69, 1262-64, 1363-64, 1368-69;
sociological, 33-36, 52-54, 105-
7, 465-67, 467-69, 514-16, 519-21,
536-38, 586-88, 656-58, 689-92,
714-16, 876-78, 895-97, 982-84,
1049-50, 1187-89, 1220-23, 1262-
64, 1284-87, 1302-5, 1363-64,
1368-69
processions, of Sikhs, 310

Procurator Fiscal, 1196, 1198
prodigies, child, girl, 1314-15
Professor Breadno, 888
PROFESSOR HAMPTON, 86-87, 952, *1003-4*
Professor Ptthmllnsprts, 363
professors: American, 1275; blind, of literature, 460-61; Cambridge, 93, 1376; ex, 1203; elderly, 321, 710, 712; of history, father, 685, 693; Oxford, 1287-88; retired, 69
Professor Tregeagle, 1288
promises: deathbed, to care for master's family, 296; of dog, 479; of secrecy, 708, 1198; unfulfilled, 328
prophecies: ancient, fulfilled, 360; arrival of two Sons of Adam and two Daughters of Eve in Narnia, 710; attempt to avert, 298, 299; return of Moon Princess, 725-26; revealed in dream, 1311; to keep city safe, 370; unbelieved, 254; verse, 529, 1358. *See also* omens; predictions; premonitions; warnings.
proposals: at Hunt Ball, 421; of marriage, 889; of marriage to prevent gossip, 320; rejected, 227, 460
The Proprietor, 1061
proscriptions, 280
prostitutes: 278, 450; male, beaten, 1363
protagonists, initially unsympathetic, 747-50, 1110
protection rackets, 119, 808
Protestants, Irish, 1135, 1284-87
protests: against working conditions, 807; against chemical factory, 526, 1303; against cutting old tree, 689-91; against marina, 982; ecological, 1303; political, 1187; social, 798. *See also* conferences; rallies; riots; symposia.
Protheroe family, 323, 906-7
proverbs, 572
PROVE YOURSELF A HERO, 967, *1004-7*, 1192
Prudence, 976, 978
Prudence Cuthbert, 319-20
Prudie, the nanny, 33, 1225, 1325-27
Prudie family, 1325-27
PSAMMEAD, 38, 271, 416-18, 598, 1041, *1007*
psychiatrists: 597, 960, 1165, 1294. *See also* doctors; healers; pediatricians; physicians; psychologists.
psychics: 141, 200, 692, 856, 857; rabbit, 418
psychologists: 597; baffled, 647, 1313-14; school, patronizes headmaster, 851. *See also* doctors; healers; pediatricians; physicians; psychiatrists.
Ptthmllnsprts, Professor, 363
publishing, early, 195-96
pubs: keepers of, 164; male prostitute frequents, 1363; Welsh, 177
Puck of Pook's Hill, 666, 733
Puddleby-on-the-Marsh, 211, 1145, 1309-11
PUDDLEGLUM, 1007, 1092
Puffy Coleman, 97
Pug, the slaver, 1307, 1309
Pullani, 670
Pullen family, 433-34, 792, 1379-81
pumas, golden, 1385-86
Pumblechook, 493, 495
Punch, the horse, 1339-40
Punch and Judy Show, 529
punishments: "amendment," 1294; being locked in guest room, 491; caning, 129; for saying "tractor," 311; labor camp, 1295; schoolgirls shamed by schoolboys, 320; shut in coal cellar, 660; to inhabit earthly creature, 325; 20 years in prison for theft of car and cheeking judge, 1383; work with sick woman, 1294
Punjabi language, spoken by Sikhs, 310, 648
punks, cousin, 540-42
puppeteer, Sicilian, 529
puppets: live, 529; satirical, 585; shows, 1187-89
puppies: 20; mongrels, 325; half-wolf, 1320; Tilly's, 329; saved from drowning, 343; to cushion shock of loss of pet pig, 59; wolf, 348
purchases, of slave, 347
Puritans, 450, 548-50, 554, 608, 778, 864, 938-39, 940
Purples, 157
pursuits. *See* chases.
Purvis family, 276-78
pushmi-pullyu, 1145-46
Pussy, the cat, 599, 1365
Putney, 562
Puzzle the Donkey, 687-89
pygmies, 203, 919
pylons, protection for Sikhs, 311
Pyramid of Beauty, 239

pyramids, robbers of, 1185
Pyrenees Mts., 1046
pyromaniacs, child, girl, 477
pythons, rock, 631, 635

Quakers: 668, 685-87, 693, 811, 988,
    1194; morose sea captain, 887-89;
    persecution of, 1199-202
quarantines: self-imposed, 939;
    village, 1203
quarrels: drunken, 296; father and
    daughter, 1350; mended, 723; over
    father's novel, 289; sibling, 1170
quarries: cannon set near, 481; sa-
    cred place, 1025; stone, 1144
The Quarry Line Mystery, 1140
quartermaster, pirate, 732
Quebec, mid-20th century, Mani-
    tou River, 732-34
Queen, wants to buy doll, 331
Queen Mary ship, 593
THE QUEEN OF THE PHARISEES' CHIL-
    DREN, 1009-12, 1371
queens: Anne of England, 1353; Alice
    becomes, 1210; beautiful old,
    1142-43; bossy, 1024-25; Boudicca
    of Iceni, 1117-19; child, 447-49,
    454, 585-86; Cliona of Fairies,
    713-14; considered goddess, 806;
    Christian in Saxon Britain, 358;
    cruel, 1009; disagreeable, 1024-
    25; Elain of Fairies, 713-14;
    Elizabeth II of England, 497, 543,
    604; Elizabeth of Russia, 1415-17;
    English, 585-86, 600, 604, 1018;
    1034; fairy, 713-14, 913, 1010-
    11, 1328-30; French, 586; frowsy,
    1361; giant, 510-511; Ginevra
    of New Cumberland, 844, 1142-43;
    greedy, of France, 448; Guenever
    of Britain, 1037-38; Guinevere of
    Britain, 148; gypsy, 1352;
    Helen of Narnia, 167, 688, 756;
    head of tribe, 772; Irish, 299-
    300; Isabella of England, 447-49,
    1017-20; Isabella of France, 585-
    86; Jadis of Narnia, 167, 279, 321,
    356-57, 710, 742, 755, 864, 961-
    62, 987, 1009; loved, 1095; Maeve
    of Connacht, 299; Margaret of Sco-
    tia, 768-69, 804, 1012-13; Mary
    of England, 457-58; Mary, Queen of
    Scots, 677-78, 1412-15; of Hearts,
    20-22, 23, 211, 343; of hill vil-
    lage, 654; of Narnia, 167, 356-57,
    561-62, 603, 688, 712, 742,
    1027, 1174; of the Tournament,
    1360; otherworld, 694; prisoner,

1413-14; termagent, 1024-25;
    unimaginative, 997; Underland,
    1034; untidy, 1210; very person-
    able, 1413; Victoria, Golden
    Jubilee of, 1159-60; white, 1361;
    wicked, 377, 844; witch, 321;
    Ysabeau of France, 448, 586
THE QUEEN'S BLESSING, 986, 1012-13
Queen Victoria, Golden Jubilee of,
    1159-60
Queer Things, 1095
QUENTIN SYKES, 44-46, 321, 470, 532,
    1013-14, 1087, 1243
Quern (boat), 1337
A Quest for Orion, 531
quests: for animals for ark, 829-30;
    for appleseed, 756; for Arthur's
    treasure, 351; to find brother,
    230; for best spinster, 1094; for
    cure for mother, 321; for dwarf,
    1316; for exiled nobles, 185, 376,
    1306-8; for freed parrot, 1294-95;
    for freedom, 1359-61; for gold,
    172, 972-73; for grandfather,
    778; for great pink whale, 887-89,
    1048; for half brother, 947; for
    information about Changes, 1337;
    for icon, 667; for knowledge of fa-
    ther, 1335; for legends of Arthur,
    730; for lost brother, 716-17;
    for lost family treasure, 1058;
    for lost prince, 1092-93; for milk
    during air raid, 415; for missing
    prince, 998; for mother, 627; for
    new home, 437, 1120-21, 1331; for
    new house for Owl, 563; for news
    of kidnapped son, 185; for objects
    of power, 501-2;
    for parents, 152, 1097-99; for
    place of safety, 310; for rab-
    bit does, 95, 418, 557, 1332; for
    real father, 277-78; for Red Bull
    on green field, 651-52; for sacred
    river, 651, 654; for Small, 563;
    for source of Folly, 716-17, 386;
    for stone of power, 408; for sweet-
    heart, 186; for treasure, 550-53,
    922, 1132, 1204; for zoi, 325-28;
    of dwarf for own dimension, 847-
    49; pattern of, 287-88; refugee
    children for parents, 1052-53; to
    bring light to Elidor, 359-60;
    to capture dog, 1387; to destroy
    ring, 405-8, 982, 1056; to find
    abused brother, 199; to kill dra-
    gon, unsuccessful, 997; to prove
    worthy of princess, 929; to regain
    home and treasure, 439; to rescue

poet, 1031-32; unwelcome, 1166; whale by sea captain, 1048; youth for namesake, 870. *See also* journeys; searches; trips; voyages.
Quinbus Festrin, 509
Quivera, early 19th century, Cibola, 173, 236-37, 915
quotations: from Coleridge and Dickens, 244; from Shakespeare, 845; misinterpreted, 1322

Rabadash, Prince of Calormen, 561-62, 1174
Rabbit, 562-63, 974, 989, 1388-89
rabbit holes, 18, 19, 22
rabbits: aristocratic, 1331; attack by, 1275; death of, 1373; democratic warren, 1331; fears Duchess, 1362; fighting, 1331; intuitive, 418, 1331; killed, 621; officious, 1388-89; rescued from cat by girl, 1333; seasick, 366; shining stranger, 535; shot in harvest, 10; strong, 95; stuffed, 490, 562-63, 989; strong leader, 535; survivor, 557; talking, 19-20, 22-23, 418, 1330-34, 1362; timid, 1362; tyrant, 446; white, 1361-62; yearling, 1331
race car drivers, ex, 656
A Racecourse for Andy, 1404
races: boat, 983, 1102; caucus, 20, 23, 324; currach, 737; early airplane, 355; fishing smacks, 85, 792; Grand National, 616; horse, 846, 1006; plans to throw, 1380; pony, 390-91; sailing, 1004; to stay in same place, 1209; yacht, 792; yacht, plans to throw, 85
RACHEL ANSEL, *1015*, 1277
Rachel Widdison, 548
Rachminov concertos, 86-87
racial mix of characters, studied, 248-52, 519-21, 606-8, 627-28, 689-92, 1262-64
racketeers: factory "protection," 119; London, 798
Rackham, Arthur, 22, 514
radiation, 149-50, 155-58, 283, 655-56, 1033
radicals: French, 18th century, 751-52, 1215-17; Marxist father, 942-43, 1124. *See also* communists; terrorists.
radios: contests on, 1314; disappearing, 243; forbidden, discovered, 898

RAF: bombs German invasion barges, 1339; Lightning planes, 1212
rafts: castaway's, 1044; down Oxus, 390-91; homemade, 291; in Garmouth harbor, 401-2; log, 280; makeshift, 238; on marsh, 802-3
rage, intense and uncontrollable, 1058
ragpickers, peg-legged, 540-42
Ragnar, 91-92
Ragnarok, Abyss of, 167, 1343
Ragnar Raven, 1298-99
RAHERE, *1015-15*, 1395-96
raids: against barons, 146; British cattle, 294; by Huns, 279-81, 557; by neighboring tribe, 113; by Roman slavers, 333; cattle, 754; Danish, 870-72; ill-fated, 114; of chicken house, 388; of cider cellar, 388-89; on "family" of thieves, 278; on monastery, 91; on Fox village, 336; on Normans, 261; police, 627; Viking, 91-92, 116, 1377-78
railroads: rackety-pack, 1142-43; stations, 994
The Railway Children, 882
rainbows, 462
Rainbow Spell, 174
rainbringers, 832
rain dances, 39-41
Rain-Pipe family, 560
raisins: glued to paper cones, 1372; horsehair in, 1372; spiked, as pheasant bait, 284
Raleigh, Sir Walter, 154
Raleigh family, 558-59
rallies: political, 1187, 1200. *See also* conferences; protests; riots; symposia.
Ralph Ashton, 460-61
Ralph Bunnion, 1149-50
Ralph Rover, 255-57
Ralston, Jan, 676
Ramora, 998
Ramsay family (*The Flute in Mayferry Street*), 427-28
Ramsay family (*The Thursday Kidnapping*), 124-25, 363, 597, 640, 1218-20
Ramsgill family, 51, 480-81
Randal, 672-75
Randall, Granny, 483-84, 669, 875, 1335-36
Randall family (*The Guardians*), 506-8
Randall family (*The Way to Sattin Shore*), 697

Rangers, 406-7, 1158
Rankeillor, Mr., 648-49
ransom: community homes, 918;
  for kidnapped son, 858; 500,000
  pounds, 1005; for father and
  brother, 1017; ruby, 280; uncle
  pays 8 pence, 1147
Ransome, ship's boy, 649
RANSOME, ARTHUR (MITCHELL), 80, 385,
  482, 571, 904, 972, *1016-17*, 1177,
  1340
RANSOM FOR A KNIGHT, 969, *1017-20*
RAN TRANTER, 483, 669, 697, 874,
  1020, 1335-36
Ranulf (*One Is One*), 916
Ranulf de Meschin (*The Shield Ring*),
  1086
RAOUL, *1020*, 1208
rape: attempted, 901; by soldiers,
  746; gang, 1025; of Royal Daughters, 1118; rumors of, 945. *See
  also* molestations, sexual.
rapport between generations,
  especially good, 282-83, 211-13,
  373-75
Rasputin, 1207
RAT, Water, 65, 828, *1020-21*, 1229,
  1382-84
Ratbag, 1062-63
rat catchers, 133
Rathina, 265
raths, fairy queen's, 675
rats: assists owl with failing eyesight, 931-32; black plague, 308;
  cannibalize one another, 1355;
  dangerous, 511; drunken, 389;
  gnome gives chicken mash to, 715-
  16; leave unseaworthy ship, 1146;
  locked in car, 890; nearly killed
  by owl friend, 529; pets, 1; plague
  of, 587; poets, 1382-84; sea,
  1021; self-cannibalizing, 752;
  tenors, 529; wayfaring sea, 1384;
  water, 366, 1020-21
The Rattle Bag: An Anthology, 570
rattles, broken, 1274
Ratty, 1021
Raven, Mr. Selwyn, 1150
Raven, Ragnar, 1298-99
ravens: disguise, 855; mischievous,
  41-42; pet, 120; schoolmaster
  resembles, 1409; seventh in play,
  1076-77
RAVENSGILL, 794, *1021-23*
Ravensgill farm, 125, 1021-22
Ravenshall Court, 1004
ravings, opium induced, 651
Rawlins, Janet, 555

Rayner, Mary, 1082
the Reader, 2, 586-87, 1373
readers, girl, avid, 819
reading: ability advantageous to
  slave, 680; aloud by girl to boy,
  133; inability to, 647, 656;
  inability to learn, 1313-14;
  inappropriate for girls, 1144;
  instruction in sought, 1108;
  learned by using dough, 218;
  learning to, 16, 199, 264, 468,
  871, 1203, 1373, 1401; remedial
  cards, 656; teaching of, 821, 948,
  1395; to blind professor, 460
READY, MASTERMAN, 787-89, 855, 859,
  1023-24, 1239, 1374
realistic novels. *See* particular
  types, e.g., adventure novels;
  problem novels.
realistic novels, with fantasy aspects, 266-69, 286-87, 368-70,
  427-28, 564-66, 1058-60, 1140-41,
  1399-1401
Reapers, 1295
reapers, 9-10, 510
REBECCA, 821, 883, 944-45, 1024,
  1225
Rebecca Possit, 516
rebellions: against Arthur, 1038;
  against authority, 204, 507, 941-
  42; against barons, 1043; against
  fencing common, 196; girl against
  aunt, 343; Irish of 1798, 101, 445,
  499-501, 879; mare at check-rein,
  454-55; native uprising, Roman
  Britain, 347, 1117-19; Scottish
  tribes, 252; schoolboy, 224;
  unsuccessful, 507, 536; violent,
  of black slaves, 766
The Rebels, 1256
rebirths, of Arthur as American noble, 844
recidivism: girl in World War II,
  1053; turncoat, 1120
recipes: for meat pie, 970; for
  mouse-maker, 429; pie, read for
  recreation, 51, 600
recitations: of poem, 192; of self-
  praising poem by Toad, 1229
recluses: badger, 65; jewel thief,
  1396; old man, 587, 754, 834-35,
  923, 962-63, 1173, 1239-40, 1372-
  73, 1390, 1398-99; owl, 930-31,
  1120; supposed, 1233-34; woman,
  1301; wealthy woman, 820. *See also*
  hermits.
reconciliations, 611, 248, 296, 329,
  674, 726, 1022, 1053, 1198

recorders, cassette, 286-87, 430-31
recording equipment, stolen by dog, 1420
records, parish baptismal, 581
rectories, Borrower home, 947-48
rectors: 49, 98, 449, 611, 959, 1221, 1410. *See also* clergymen; curates; ministers; parsons; pastors; preachers; priests; vicars.
Redbraes, 456-57
Red Branch heroes, 298-99, 300
Redbrush, the fox, 1386-87
Red-Coats, 1112-13
Red Cow, catches star and dances, 780
Red Cross, 620, 942
Red Dog, 11
"Red Dog," 631, 635
Redesmere Lake, 1344
Red Flower, fire, 630
Red Fox, 650-51
red-haired persons: apprentice seaman, 1064; bagpiper, 1285; bearded Afghan, 757; boys, 1-2, 304, 314, 748, 778, 876, 887, 1039, 1114, 1194; Captain, 1227; child dancer, 69; Cormac, King of Connacht, 261, 409; desired bride, 1259; dyslexic girl, 647; ex-gladiator, 771-72, 967; fisherman, 883; girls, 97, 261, 482, 674, 724, 753, 1024; Irish soldier, 1284-85; Malcolm, King of Scotland, 760; man, proud piemaker, 51; Mary, Queen of Scots, 1413; Roman centurion, 1089; Scottish army captain, 765; sons of Saxon leader, 681; spoiled boy, 1271; surly man, 790; tutor, 807, 845; vicar's daughter, 944; Viking, 1298; Welsh boy, 285; woman lacking spunk, 60; woman wed in anvil ceremony, 800; youth, romantically inclined, 928
RED JAK, 325, *1024*, 1405
Red King, 1209, 1211, 1274
Red King of Connacht, 215-17
Red Knight, 1358
Red Lion Inn, 1125-28
Red Lion Tavern, 1108
Red Men, 336-37
Red Mist, 253
Red Pale, 729
Red Phaedrus, 967-98
Redpoll, Nick, 1396
RED QUEEN, *1024-25*, 1209-11
Redruth, Tom, 1254
RED SHIFT, 443, *1025-26*
redskins, 957
Red Spear, 123

Red Witch (boat), 117
Reedsmere, mid-20th century, 495-98, 543, 604, 775, 786, 866, 1046
Reedsmere Broad, 496, 543
Reedsmere Gap, 604
Reedsmere Hall, 496-97, 543
REEPICHEEP, the mouse, 688, 996, 1007, *1026-27*, 1307-8
REES, DAVID (BARTLETT), 377, 499, *1027-28*
Reeves, Beth, 2
REEVES, JAMES (JOHN MORRIS REEVES), 246, *1028-29*,
Reeves, Molly, 1
Reeves family, 586-87, 828, 1202-3
reformed characters: abusive master, 1330; apprentice seamen, 1065; backsliding, 186; by Bible quotations, 257; by Christmas spirit, 229; convincing, 334, 824-26, 893-94, 1306-9; drunkard father, 1304; exhibitionist girl, 603; flirt becomes World War I nurse, 883; French boy, 559; miser, 353; outlaw to friar, 695; possibly, 827; predictable, 726; refugee boy, 598; reverting, 437; servants, 6; sham, 1120; spoiled boy, 377; sudden, 706; teacher, 844; temporary, 1120; townsman, 979; traitorous sibling, 357; unconvincing, 244, 269, 376, 1229; villain, 1113; wizard, 566
reformers: social, 849, 942-43, 1123-25, 1216-17, 1224-25; youthful, 226
refugees: animals, 388-89, 1119-21, 1330-34; camp, 620; Chinese, 373-75, 1154; Chinese and Polish boys, 339, 980-81, 1035; from Danish raids, 870; from flood, 496-97, 1046; from Normans, 1085; from pre-industrialized England, 1337; from restrictive villages, 1301; from Tripods, 238, 1361; from volcanic eruption, 828; German Jews in World War II, 31, 562, 761, 793, 924-26, 1348-49; Hungarian, 1218-19; of attack on mission, 1265-66; of nuclear war, 1033; Polish, in World War II, 152, 353-54, 597-98, 619-20, 922, 1052-53, 1097-99, 1398; Saxon children from Scots, 804
Regan, Peter, 543-46
regattas, 506, 1380
regents: dwarf, 1092, 1265, 1306; of James VI (James I), 677-78; of

Scotland, 1413; usurping throne,
720, 995
Regent Street, 667
REGINA, 294-97, 930, *1029*
Regina, the falcon, 383-
84
REG WHITTACKER, 413, 590,
1029
reincarnations, of Buddhist leader,
853, 1195
reindeer: Lapp, 1350; pull sleigh,
711
The Reiver's Road, 675
rejections: for social differences,
120-21; girl by sweetheart's parents, 859; girl for roughness, 87;
shared, 338. *See also* outcasts.
relationships: apprentices-
first mate,
hostile, 1064; aunt-
niece, increasingly respectful
and close, 683-84; aunt-niece,
strained, 880; aunts (great)-
niece, satisfying, 564-65;
black-white, very hostile, 765-
67; blind boy-grandfather, close,
485-86; boy-spirit children,
710; brother-brother, abrasive,
729; brother-brother, antagonism, 1335-36; brother-brother,
needling, 1046-47; brother-
brother, older dependent on
younger, 778; brother-brother,
protective, 33-36, 570; brother-
brother, quarrelsome, 29;
brother-abused half-brother,
close, 230;
brother-sister, accepting, 1185;
brother-sister, close, 775,
806, 953-55; brother-sister,
condescending, 806; brother-
sister, 885; brother-sisters,
protective, 707, 1156; brother-
sister, strained, 968-69, 1350;
brother-sister, very close, 1277;
brothers, tramp, protective,
620; cousin-cousin, abrasive,
818; cousin-cousin, close,
701; engaged couple, trustful,
335; family members, taut, 900-
2; father-children, strained,
400; father-daughter, close and
deeply trusting, 1143-44; father-
daughter, disillusioned, 1029;
father-daughter, estranged, 902,
883; father-daughter, strained,
945; father-daughter, unrealistic, 846;

father-daughter, undeveloped
relationship, 762; father-
daughter, unusually close, 1123-
25; father-family, very strained,
895-97; father-niece, Freudian
implications, 693; father-son,
abrasive, 252-54;
father-son, ambivalently loving,
826-27; father-son, antagonistic, 1033; father-son, close,
284-85, 1372, 1402; father-son,
contemptuous, 11; father-son,
despised, 1104; father-son, fractured, 960; father-son, improved,
683; father-son, reconciled, 754;
father-son, stormy and tense,
703-6, 842, 849, 880, 968, 1363;
grandfather-granddaughter,
close, 900; grandfather-grandson,
close, 9-10, 805, 1101-2;
grandmother-granddaughter,
close, 906;
grandmother (great-great)-
grandson, unusually strong
rapport, 211-13, 859; grownups-
boys, sympathetic, 812-14;
husband-wife, strained by husband's bitterness, 681-83;
king-prince, estranged, 997-98;
men and gods, 121-24; mother-
daughter, antagonistic, 799-800;
mother-daughter, close, 768;
mother-daughter, competitive,
1323; mother-daughter, cool, 770;
mother-daughter, improving, 708,
761, 1123-25; mother-daughter,
reconciled, 800; mother-daughter,
strained, 777, 1084, 1196-98;
mother-son, broken, 1059;
mother-son, solid, 1265; mother-
son, strained, 858, 1006-7,
1088; page-laundress, unusually close and comfortable, 814;
parents-son, very strained, 1025;
parents-son, warm and accepting,
1116; siblings, older, -younger
sister, scornful, 381-82;
sister-brother, close, 778;
sister-brother, protective, 804,
1196; sister-brother, improved,
1373; sister-sisters, close, 800,
1094, 96, 1313-15, 1165; sister,
older, -dyslexic sister, protective, 655; sister-sister, fond and
indulgent, 875; sister-sister,
protective, 779; sister-sister,
strained, 1314; sisters-in-law,
tense, 560;

son-parents, fractured, 945;
stepbrother and stepsister,
close, 810; stepmother-stepson,
understanding, 754; subtly
drawn, 801-4; thought inappropriate, 416; uncle-nephews, 4;
uncle-nephew, close, 683, 754;
uncle-nephew, strained, 703-4,
706, 755-56, 1057; uncle-nephew,
understanding, 1228; uncle-nephew
and niece, abusive, 763; uncle-
niece, understanding, 1316-19
relatives: black sheep, 533-34;
bogus, 1401; discovered, 813;
grasping, 1400-1
Reldresal, 509
Relf, Douglas, 456
religion: a comfort, 1044; adjustment to new, 938-39; as social
restraint, 1278; caught from
surroundings, 141-42; Islam, 213-
15; pre-Christian, 298-99, 299-
301, 335-37, 673, 771-74, 1161-64,
1171-73; prominent element in novel, 91-92; Quaker, 1199-1202;
source of strife, 456-58, 1199-
1202, 1284-87; strife between
Catholic and Protestant, 1284-87;
survival of old, 638; switched,
1194; traditional, 523
religious beliefs, contrasted, 334,
1267
religious customs. See cultures; ethnic customs; rituals;
understanding, intercultural.
religious fanatics, 279-80
THE RELUCTANT DRAGON, 472, 1029-31
Remarkable Instances of Early Piety,
491
remittance women, 1266
renegades: blacks, 766; British,
294; mice, 1120; rabbit impersonates, 1332
Renewal, ceremony of, 121
renovations, of neighborhood, 863
rent, bunch of violets yearly, 578
Renton, Cam, 29, 1052, 1064-65
RENVOIZE, JEAN, 1031, 1368
reporters: investigating sabotage,
404-5; investigative, woman, 917-
18, 1265; newspaper, 401, 1275; TV
news correspondent, 1039. See also
journalists; newsmen.
reptiles, slavemasters, 239
requests: last, for pipe, 247; of
King, for dragon-slayer, 396
researchers: on dwarfs, 850; youthful, about Chihuahuas, 329, into

the first decade of 20th century, 944-45, 1024, into New Guinea
artifacts, 564-65, into ownership
of common, 536, into Parliamentary Papers, 230, into 17th century
witchfinder, 308, leading to musical manuscript, 427-28, on murder,
1022, on 17th century boy, 769-70,
1317-19; wizard who "farms" records and archives, 532
THE RESCUERS, 815-16, 1031-32, 1080-
81
rescues: at sea, 517, 792, 1379;
at sea of unconscious girl, 887;
attempted, 133, 1045, 1413-14;
baby pink whale, 1048; bitterly
unappreciated, 340; black slave,
766; blind girl from fire, 219; boy
doll from flame, 331; boy from goblins, 1002; boy poacher, 616; boy
thrown from horse, 404; boys from
old mine, 476; brave, failed, 845;
brother, 482; by angel, 1112; by
balloon, 109; by blind girl, 599;
by bus, 45; by Coast Guard, 384;
by cobbler, 605; by Dane, 871; by
cousin, 88; by dog, 187, 929; by
eagles, 439, 552; by friend, 244;
by hole in roof, 543; by musical diversion, 46; by pink whale,
889; by police cars, 46; by Polish
army, 214-15; by quoting Bible,
549; by renunciation, 414; by
ship, 511; by shootout, 46; by St.
Christopher, 212;
by street boy, 610; by storekeeper, 203; by string quartet,
413; cat, 913; cat during flood,
866-67; cat from mermaids, 893-94;
cat from savages, 894; chickens, 187; children of father from
fire, 1365; condemned dog, 153;
condemned soldier, 190; crews,
historical incident, to save ship,
926-27; dancing teacher, 1385-
86; disturbed girl, 810; doctor
by parrot, 988; dog, 253; dog from
"put down," 896; dog of hurt boy,
1399; dog of master, 1399; donkey,
1003; dramatic overland, 926-27;
drifting boat, 30; drowning man
with drum, 340; drowning soldier,
94, 595; during flood, 981; dwarf
of prince, 892-93; dwarf by children, 994-95; eight-year-old boy
and uncle, 1146;
elderly couple, 496, 786;
eventually succeeds, 816; ewe in

snowdrift, 74; failed, 1104; fairy cat, 675; father and others, 436; father from castle, 1386; foiled, 1413; friend, 189; fawn from dead doe, 118; from abbey, 408; from being run down by carriage, 169; from blinding blizzard, 834; from blocked cave, 1310; from bloody lambs' tails, 1084; from burning house, 611; from canal, 542; from cannibals, 1045; from cats, 784; from cave by blind girl, 1397; from cheetah, 118; from collapsed house, 415-16; from desert isle, 788-89, 1045; from disastrous weekend, 532; from drowning, 370, 654, 983-84, 1033, 1040, 1264-65, 1325; from drug smugglers, 1063; from fire, 974; from flood, 39-40, 186-87, 495-97, 543; from gang, 1087; from garbage, 1297; from gypsy, 135; from hanging, 614; from illness and debt, 608; from lion, 1082; from lobster pot, 1328; from magician, 150; from mansion fire, 807; from mine, 398; from miserable weekend, 98; from monkeys, 631; from monks, 1416; from mountain fissure, 741; from North Sea, 984; from pirates, 958; from probable murder, 579; from river, 155-56; from roof top, 496; from slavery, 1307; from Spindle-Imp, 1096; from stocks, 154; from storm, 742; from stranded bus, 874; from stream, 1389; from sudden snow, 906-7; from suicide, 411, 1390; from terrorists, 1265; from thugs, 156, 655; from tide, 924; from torrent, 240; from tree, 563; from various evil beings, 1096; from water, 1301; from yacht, 184; gentleman from deadly peril, 1147; ghost, 33; girl of brother from demon, 692-93; girl from Red Knight, 1358; girl lost in mine, 197; girl on ladder bridge, 723; girl on toboggan, 74; Golden Puma, 1385; grandmother from terrorists, 74; Guenever from burning, 1038; guinea pig, 366; guinea pigs in flood, 497; gypsy girl, 320; hawk, 122; hens in flood, 497; horses, 420, 235, 596; infant by bear, 158; injured hiker, 1368; in snowstorm, 1109-10; in umbrella boat, 989, 1388; Irish

heir, 216; Irish rebel, 500; ironic of fugitive, 1217; king and queen chess pieces, 1209; king from usurpers, 1001; kitten, 690; magic bird, 1094; marooned brother, 187; Mole by Rat, 828, 1021, 1382, 1384; music teacher, 951-52; native maiden, 256-57; newspaper, 1249; off seacoast, 763; on high seas, 737; on snowshoes, 290; pigeon, 248; pigs from rustlers, 1082; planned, 216; poet from dungeon, 1032; prince, 377, 1264; princess, 1003, 702; princess of prince, 702; puppy, 915; Queen Guenever, 1037; rafters, 401; raven, 41; sailor, 1236-37; sailor doll, 559; school bus, 80; sheep, 187, 906, 1083; shepherd, 1321; shipwrecked doctor, 258; shipwrecked soldier, 342; siblings, 359; sister, 911; sister from Spindle-Imp, 1096; sister's son, 682; spirit girl of boy, 710; squire, 12; Stone-Age girl, 336; storekeeper's daughter, 1105; stranded family, 187-88; successful, 1104; summoning of doctor, 1050; survivors of wrecked ship, 1069-70; thwarted, 788; tight, 711; timely, 687-88, 738, 739, 888, 890, 1056, 1115-16, 1142, 1155, 1162, 1263, 1286, 1321, 1333, 1416, 1379; toad from obsession, 1383; toboggan accident, 907; toy soldiers from cat, 794; unicorn, 360; unsuccessful, 28, 103, 244; via chimney, 219; via letter box, 563; Viking master, 117; White Queen, 1361; white sailor by black slave, 1069; woman in snow storm, 481; woman from burning cottage, 320; woman from terrorists, 219; wounded hero, 1259-60, 1324; yacht owner's son, 1379. *See also* liberation; escapes.

resentment: of king's affection, 92; of stepfather, extreme, 1058-60; of step siblings, 79-81; toward Americans, 842-43; toward mother, 1196-98

reservoir, separates feuding families, 1021

resignation, of Mexican president, 313

Resistance, World War II, 253, 1106, 1193

resistance: fighters, 1089-91; to
evil, 436-37; workers in nuclear
aftermath, 149-50, 157-58, 283;
groups, 1033

resorts: proposed, 517, 579, 982-84;
rundown seaside, 923-24; shabby,
638

resource: 138-40, 812-14, 847, 893-
94, 1046. See also perseverance;
persistence; pluck.

respect: for animal's dignity, 839-
41; mutual, boy and toy soldiers,
1276

responsibility: boy assumes for
blind man, 1110; boy assumes for
cattle, 1049-50; boy assumes for
farm, 834-35; boy assumes for
housekeeping, 99-100; boy assumes
for siblings, 353-54; boys assume
for maintaining house, 812-14;
boys assume for ship, 1065; children assume during flood, 775;
children assume for family, 792;
children assume for household,
885, 1105; children assume for tutor, 740; children develop, 788;
extent of probed, 896; for disaster shited to dead man, 341; girl
assumes during flood, 866-67; girl
assumes for boy after air raid,
735; girl assumes for brothers,
694-95; girl assumes for family,
1356-58;
girl assumes for household, 706-7,
1056-57; girl assumes for orphan boys, 769; girl assumes for
self and brother, 763-65; girl
assumes for siblings, 1052-53;
importance of, 224; imposter for
adopted tribe, 774; learned, 168-
69; pampered girl assumes, 684;
personal, 49-50; refused, 1180;
sense of, 166, 191; toward old
woman, neglected, 873; younger
brother for older, 778

restaurants, 30

rest homes: 714. See also nursing
homes.

The Restless Ghost, 143, 442, 530

Restoration, 938, 940, 1199-1202

restorations, of historic area, 446,
1115-16

Resurre (boat), 93, 810

Resurre and Sum (boat), 1377-78

resurrections, of Aslan, 711, 1174

resuscitation, mouth to mouth, 1324

retarded persons: boy, 543; boy,
assumed, 918, 1297; boy, waif,

293; girl, assumed, 1368; man,
caretaker, 1152; man good with
animals, 177, 826; huge man, 748;
mongoloid girl, mocked, 1288-91

retribution: for wicked,
deliberately obvious, 807-9; for
wicked, 829-30, 839. See also revenge.

The Return of the King, 1230

THE RETURN OF THE TWELVES, 241, 1032,
1274. See THE TWELVE AND THE GE-
NII, 241, 1274-76.

returns: of Aslan anticipated, 711;
of Moon Princess, 726

Return to the Heron, 1252

Reuben, 196, 522, 658, 737, 829-30,
895, 1185

Reuben Smith, 106

reunions: family, 188, 680-81, 1019,
1053, 1098, 1223; in abandoned
city, 296; of lovers, 56; of separated twins, 766

revenge: feud, 117-19; against
usurping overlords, 146-47; backfires, 1159; boy on mother and
stepfather, 1059-60; desired by
apprentice, 824; for lost love,
1409; girls seek on village children, 1385; lake stolen in revenge
for accusation of kidnapping,
1142; massacre, 1070; on bullies, 1093; on men sought, 376,
493; sought against betrayer,
681; sought by king's sister,
701; sought by spirits, 286-87;
sought for blinding, 806; sought
for jilting, 820; sought for 20
years, 610; sought on enemies,
615; sought on father's murderer,
738-39; taking liquor and food,
843-44; threatened, 102. See also
retribution.

revenue men, 3-4, 259, 764, 965

Revolt at Ratcliffe's Rags, 270

revolutionaries: anti-family, 525,
917-19; environmental, 35-36;
French intelligentsia, 1215-17;
invade church, 1077; Irish, 499-
501; students, 506-8

revolutions: against Richard II,
448; French, 752, 765, 828, 832,
1215-18; Haitian, 765-67, 938;
Mexican, 752-53, 601-2; South
American, 1412

Reward (boat), 434, 792, 1379-
81

rewards: art school, 1401; being made heir, 204; bounties for

capturing slave ships, 1070; coveted for betraying children, 426; dollar for 25 years in army, 246; fairy gives for animals' help, 714; for apprehending Robin Hood, 717; for father's capture, 1349; for killing dragon, 998; for recovering jewels, 542; for saving life, 1379; for taking girl to madhouse, 112; for picture of mysterious beast, 877; for toy soldiers, 1275; for virtue, 204; gift of pearls, 830; life of sea captain, 317; marriage for faithful service, 459; of cauldron, 174; of battle, 1226; of flute, 212; of money, 1110; 100 marks, 1098; pearl necklace, 642; pencil box, 1389; refused, 1003; Roman citizenship, 375; to be slaves, 238; used for trip to London, 386. *See also* prizes.
Rewards and Fairies, 666
Rex O'Connor, 622
Rex of Larkbarrow, 220
Reynold, George, 451
Rhine Journey, 1061
RHODES, 150, 157-58, 656, *1032-33*
rhymes: clues to treasure, 615, 813, 818, 1058; nursery, 692, 1329; speech in, 203; threatening, 615. *See also* poems; verses.
Rhymes and Verses: Collected Poems for Children, 302
Ribbon of Fire, 796
Ricardo, Prince of Pantouflia, 679
rice, too much, 497
RICHARD I, KING OF ENGLAND, 671, 729, 968, *1034*
Richard II, King of England, 447-48, 453-54, 585, 586, 600
Richard III, King of England, 582, 683, 762, 1034
Richard, the lover, 1363-64
RICHARD BLUNT, 923-24, *1033*
Richard Dexter, 827
Richard Holder, 1199-201
Richard Holt, 490-92
RICHARD MEDLEY, 582, 971, *1033*
RICHARD OF GLOUCESTER, 103-4, 317, 606, *1034*
Richard the Third, 70
Richenda Bemmerton, 1199-201
riches, wished for, 417
Richley Abbey, 155
riddles, 96, 148, 464, 502, 551, 783-84, 1107, 1095

riders: horseback, helpful, 506; horse, skilled, 235, 419, 960-61, 962; strange dark, 1344; Toad in train engine, 1383
Ridley, Gran, 449
Ridley, Ann, *37*, 286-87, 591, 777, 843
Ridley family, 186-88, 707, 815, 981
Rigg, Paula, *946*
The Right-Hand Man, 967
right-hand men: Scottish tutor, 637; threatened with death, 615. *See also* servants.
"Rikki-tikki-tavi," 632
Rikofia, 1, 522, 586-87, 659, 828, 1373
Riley, Bud, *160*, 282-83, 523
RILIAN, Prince of Narnia, 185, 377, 603, 1007, *1034*, 1092-93, 1227
RIL TERRY, 196, 536-38, 904, *1034-35*
Rinaldo Gambadello, 15
Ringbearer, 407
Ringo, 797-99, 1004
Ring Out, Bow Bells!, 527
rings: buried, 294; causing invisibility, 551-53; corrupting, 406-8; dolphin emerald signet heirloom, 294, 96, 349-50, 681, 1085-86; gifts, 178; green and yellow magic, 755-56, 1279; lark and laurel crest, 581, 684; magical, 1261; many, worn by Sikh matriarch, 297; of power, 96, 131-32, 406-8, 436-37, 439, 464-65, 551-53, 1056; pewter with emerald, 1125-28; returned, 350; royal signet, 658; taking to other worlds, 321; token of identity, 1261
Ringwraiths, 406, 436, 805
riots: Catholic, 1286; French Revolution, 1216-17; mill workers, 878; over food, 896. *See also* protests; rallies.
Rissolutions, 564
rites of passage: 201; wolf-kill, 337
rituals: ancient, reenacted, 1181; Celtic, 1162; closing the pass, 123; curse-lifting, 124; endured by emperor, 254; initiation, 349; killing of king, 252; of fertility, 1321; of Mithras, 281-82; power of, 123-24, 1294-95; primitive, 1036; witch making, 201, 815, 1389; wolf killing, 1320-21. *See also* cultures; ethnic customs; understanding, intercultural.

rivals: currach race, 737; fairy
    queens, 713-14; for outlaw
    leader's affection, 739; intra-
    family, 1114-16; political, 1405;
    religious, 281
Rivendell, 96, 131, 406, 436, 551,
    1158
River Anduin, 407
THE RIVER AT GREEN KNOWE, 145, *1035-
    36*
riverbank: creatures of, 65, 1021,
    1229; life on, 1382-85
River Folk, 336
River of the Arrow, 1195
rivers: adventures, 1035, 1382-85;
    breaking through to Golden Valley,
    661; Broad, 715; Folly, 716-17;
    Manitou, 733; of chocolate, 1376;
    Oxus, 433, 792-93; produces vi-
    sions, 733; sacred, 651, 654;
    travel on, Russian, 117; turning
    to gold, 660-61; underground, 194
River Say, 291, 812, 858, 862
River Skirl, 578
River Test, 1332
Riviere Academy, 108
THE ROAD TO CAMLANN, *1036-39*, 1176
The Road to Miklagard, 1257, 1300
Road to Nowhere, 1086
The Road to Sardis, 984
robberies: planned, 184-85; for
    insurance, 185; of jewelry store,
    41, 541-42; of traveling abbot,
    146. *See also* thefts.
robbers: bank turned secretary, 845;
    gang, 574; of houseboat, 1179;
    terrorize village, 10, 311-12,
    470; tomb, 829, 1185-86. *See also*
    bandits; burglars; thieves.
THE ROBBERS, 81, *1039-41*
Robbie Craig, 1398-99
Robbie Friend, 473
Robbie Henderson, 911, 1156, 1409
Robbins, Ian, 1284
ROBERT (*Five Children and It*), 272,
    416-18, 1007, *1041*
Robert (The Stone Book Series), 9-
    10, 399, 619, 1281
Robert de Beauville, Earl of
    Greavesby, 915-17
Robert de Belleme, 673-74
Robert Graham, 24, 70-81, 206, 865
ROBERT KERRIDGE, 338, 612, 849, 859,
    1041-42, 1224-25
ROBERT MYHILL, 59, 523, 364, *1042*,
    1283
Robert of Normandy, 674
Robert Parry, 243-44

Roberts, Rusty, 1052, 1064-65
Robertson, Graham, 1382
Robertson Ay, 779, 781, 782
Robert Terry, 536
Robespierre, 1217
Robin, 582-83, 972
ROBIN DUFFIELD, 75, 325, 327-28,
    343, *1042*
Robin Fawcett, 434-35
Robin Hood: exploits, 285; inspira-
    tion for gang, 425; parallels to,
    740; prototype for, 1104; types,
    454, 1112, 1249
ROBIN HOOD, 12, 145-47, 717, *1042-
    43*, 1252
Robin Minette, 725-26
Robin Oig, 650
Robinsheugh 344
Robinson, 809-10
Robinson, Charles, 588
Robinson, Mr., 610
ROBINSON, (WANDA) VERONICA, 290,
    1043
Robinson Crusoe, 1043-46
ROBINSON CRUSOE, 298, *1043-46*
Robinsonnades. *See* survival novels.
robots: ladies-in-waiting, 815-16
Rob Perrott, 506
Rob Roy, 650
Rochester, Mr., of *Jane Eyre*, 1275
Rocker, Fermin, 473, 1262
rockets, bring nanny, 785
Rocking-horse-fly, 1209
"rocking-rule," coal mine, 129
Rock Python, 631, 635
rocks, sacred, girl scatters flowers
    on, 706
rock screen, chipped away, 194
ROD COOPER, 496, 543, *1046*
Roddy Hernon, 258-61
RODDY MCANDREW, 29, 368-69, *1046-47*
Roderick Graham, 79-81, 741
Rodney Fox, 1169-70
Roger, 208
Roger Belaney, 47
ROGER BRADLEY, 25, 768, 933-35, *1047*
Roger Orlebar, 683, 701
Roger Penfold, 507
ROGER WALKER, 972-73, *1047*, 1178-79,
    1340-42
Roggs family, 1125-26
Roland, 359-60
Roller family, 51, 488, 600, 970-71
Rolls-Royces: 61, 481, 532, 537;
    birds foul, 285, 853, 1074
Rolls Royce Silver Ghost, 1337
Roman America, early 19th centu-
    ry, 844, 1141-43

romance, novels of love and, 85-87, 298-99, 299-01, 335-37, 354-56, 419-21, 477-79, 683-85, 724-27, 1155-57, 1169-71, 1199-1202, 1258-61

romances: actress-mssionary, 811; advice in, 143; ambivalent courtship, 1065; American officer-Welsh woman, 60; artist-engineer, 890; begun while skating, 1241; Borrowers, unrequited, 140; boy-boy, 1364; boy-mad girl, 1232; boy's father opposes, 1224; broken, 186, 1170; broken up by mother, 476; brother and nursemaid, 456; by mail, 942, 1242; cast-away and sea captain, 894; chaste, 1170; child marriage develops into, 684; cousins, 421; crippled girl-composer's grandson, 428; curate-English teacher, 1243; dancer mother's, 1116; deformed girl-crippled youth, 109-110; destroyed by grandmother, 901; developing 1057; during French Revolution, 752, 1216-17; during plague, 938-39, 1200-1; during political violence, 28; elderly, 823; encouraged by mother, 314; ended by death, 901; English boy-French girl, 1360; estate owner-former stable boy, 423-24; failed, 262, faltering, 369; father-school matron, 946; first, 963; fractured, 873; frustrated, 25-26; girl-hardworker, 828; girl-king, 1096; girl-married teacher, 925-26, 1166; girl-musician, 942; girl-Selkie, 1156; girl-wizard, 698, 777; guilty, 1037-38; handsome youth-daughter of arithmetic master, 1149-50; heiress-car salesman, 196; hopeless, 944-45, 1237; housemaid-smuggler, 763-64; ill-fated, 1258-61; illicit, 116; incipient, opposed by parents, 933-34; lady-in-waiting-noble, 586; low key, 32, 1015, 1041-42; manor girl-shepherd boy, 726; mother-neighboring widower, 455; never blossom, 49-50, 821, 1130, 1173; of cats, 829-30; of childhood friends, 1200-1; of grandmother, 947; of the two Kates, 637; of young witches, 1122-23; opposed by mothers, 582-83, 799-800, 873; opposed by girl's father, 1022-23; opposed by parents, 1232; pretence of, 968-69, 1170; prince-lady, 998-99; prince-laundry maid, 928; prince-"light" princess, 702; puppeteer-musician, 585; Puritan boy-gentlewoman, 608; Puritan boy-orphan girl, 550; put on hold, 201; renewed, 678; retarded girl-hiker, 1368-69; sabotaged by sister, 947; seamstress-highwayman, 818; secret summer, 945-46, 968-69, 1170; several, 1412-14; several throughout time, 1025-26; shattered, 821; shipwrecked soldier-maid, 595; singers, 686; soldier-nurse, 423-24; stableboy-high-class girl, 317; student minister-schoolteacher, 53-54; students, 597; theater young people, 170-71; thwarted, 650; uncle-witch, 1279; unrequited, 45, 532, 1057, 1194; unwanted, 896; upper class girl-working class boy, 1084; various, 588-89; village girl-shepherd, 1203; visitor's, 1048-49; wartime, 414-16, 499-500; Welsh boy-English girl, 873; with American soldier, 886; with chauffer's son, 1197; with distant cousin, 499-500; with ice maiden, 929-30; with married man, 538, 902; wizard-college girl, 43-46. See also crushes; infatuations.

Romania, sixth century, 279-81

Roman Procurator, 1118-19

Romans: eagles of, 347-50; in Britain, 148, 261-62, 294-97, 333, 347-50, 375, 387, 632-33, 679-83, 746-47, 767-68, 773-74, 806, 1025-26, 1088-91, 1117-19, 1244-45; in Romania, 38-39; in Scotland, 245, 879, 884, 1161-63, 1190; in Slavic village, 280; slavers, 1411

Roman Wall, 281, 348

Rome: ancient, lectures on, 529, 1149; first century B.C., 1244-45

Romulus and Remus, 529, 1149

Ronnie Webster, 205, 656-58

Roo, the kangaroo baby, 562-63, 974, 989, 1388-89

roofers, Irish, 143, 186

roofs: conversing on, 289; playing on, 607; school, scaled, fall from, 1270

Rooloo, Stag of the Dark Water, 220

roommates, oafish, 809
rooms: filled with junk, 963; spare,
    wardrobe in serves as gateway
    to Narnia, 710
Rooster Hernon, 737, 1102
roosters, pet, 725-26, 1097
Rootles, the cat, 667
ropes, gnawed, 711, 1333
Rosa Pickhatchet, 854
rosaries, ridiculed, 165
Rose, the cat, 1271
Rose Darlington, 923
Rose family, 532
Rose Fay, 1133-36
Rose Grove, 895
Rose in June (ship), 434, 1381
Rosemary Brown, 173-75
Rosenbaum, Z., moneylender, 1147
Rosenberg family, 925
Roses, Wars of, 102-5
roses: clue, 813; pattern of, 944;
    purple, 944; purple, on grave, 821
Rosetta, 928-30
Rosie (boat), 498
ROSIE BAGTHORPE, 477, 921, 1047-48
ROSIE LEE, 887-89, 1048
ROSIE RUGGLES, 385-86, 1048
Rosley family, 33, 244, 669, 801-3,
    863, 1133
ROS MACBRIDE, 588-89, 1048-49
Rostov's, Court Jewelers, 667
"rough musicked," 1222-23
THE ROUGH ROAD, 751, 1049-50
Roundheads, 307, 1199
roundups, of horses, 390
Rover, Ralph, 255-57
Rover, the earthworm familiar, 752,
    845, 1192, 1355
Rowan, Lilias, 581
Rowan Marlow, 382-85, 965
Rowena, 681
ROWLANDS, JOHN, 502, 1050
Rowlands family, 1050
Rowley, Thomas, 611
Rowley family, 1203
Rowley Vye, 226, 736
Royal Aircraft Factory, 355
Royal Daughter, 1118
Royal Doulton Bowl, cracked, 782
Royal Engineers, 1386
royal family, at theater, 840
Royal Flying Corps, 1374
Royalists, 638, 1199
Royal Society for Prevention of
    Cruelty to Animals, 912
Royal Society for Prevention of
    Cruelty to Children, 1392
Royal Woman, 865, 1117-18

Roy Bradshaw, 656-57
Roylance, Margaret, 262
Roy Wentworth, 196, 537, 904
R.17, 574
Ruairidh, 489-90, 732, 832, 883
Ruby, 56
ruby, discovered, 1397
Rudd family, 71, 324-25, 350-51,
    1024, 1404-6
rudeness: caterpillar's, 192-93;
    deliberate, 164; to son's sweet-
    heart, 338
Rudge, Mr., 17, 411, 851, 1390
RUDI GERLATH, 749-50, 887, 1051
Ruffians, wild mice, 1120
ruffians: attack runaway, 1360;
    driven from village, 311-12; huge,
    1232
Rugby, 1203
rugby, trainers, 1363
Ruggles family, 385-86, 618-19, 1048
Ruined City of the Giants, 1092
Rukush, the foal, 390
rule of silence, boarding school,
    224
Rum, Kingdom of, 1411
Rum, Seljuk of, 1068, 1357-58
Rumbury Town, 41
rumors: about escaped gorilla, 1154;
    of rape, 945; sun and moon switch
    place, 1186
Rumple, Mr. Justice, 1386
Runacre, Ernie, 811
The Runaway, 269
runaways: at sight of police car,
    646; boy, 656, 706, 833-35, 849,
    962, 1011, 1049, 1081-82, 1173,
    1270, 1284, 1324, 1351-53, 1415-
    17; boy and dog, 153, 1399; boy and
    girl, 962; boy evacuee, 415; boy
    from abbey, 916; boy from insur-
    ance job, 704; boy from monastery,
    11, 739; boy from pier, 1056; boy
    from psychologically abusive fa-
    ther, 846; boy of jailed father,
    878; boy pickpocket, 1108-10; boy
    sorcerer, 533; boy to join play-
    ers, 169; boy to London, 610-11;
    boy to save dog, 75; boy who hates
    father, 521; boys, cousins, 1359-
    60; brother-sister, 234; chimney
    sweep, 1328; deaf boy, 290-91;
    discovered and sent home, 169;
    father, to Australia, 669; fisher-
    man's boy, 561-62; foster girl,
    1368-69; from abusive foster moth-
    er, 605; from boarding school,
    455, 506; from cruel orphanage,

1222; from cruel uncle, 763; from
domestic service, 581; from foundry, 198, from mine, 1239; from
police, 478-79; from school disgrace, 616; from stepfather, 611;
from uncle to priest, 602; from
unwanted marriage, 561, 575; from
visit, 622; from Webfeet, 39;
girl, 387-88, 828, 898-99, 1106,
1365; girl, evacuee, 415; girl
from African home, 250; girl
from boarding school, 769, 1316; girl
from undesirable marriage, 744,
799, 909; girl into forest to avoid
marriage, 684; girl sheltered
by witch woman, 799; girl with
cat, 599; group of children, 528;
handicapped boy, 1319; horses,
1382, 1367; in anger over pet
removal, 76; in horror from spell,
637; illegitimate girl, 581; Irish
beauty and sons of Usna, 298-99,
300;
Jamaican boy, 844; magician, 498;
mother, 277-78, 293; mother to
join lover, 656; mute black boy,
1262; neglected children, 514; noble girl, 43; old woman from rest
home, 714-15, 860; planned, 320,
469, 714-15; protesting getting
rid of pets, 100; siblings, to circus, 105-7; sister and brother,
425-27; slave boy and holy man,
279-81; slave in Haiti, 765; slave
of Saxons, 296; slum children,
314; to Bombay, 526; to escape marriage, 43; to save dog from being
put down, 153, 327; to save doll
from being burned, 332; two boys
and girl, 769; wife, 1175
runaways, novels of, 39-41, 110-13,
153-55, 276-79, 298-99, 299-01,
387-88, 425-27, 514-16, 560-62,
763-65, 833-35, 915-17, 956-58,
1017-20, 1220-23, 1247-50, 1302-
5, 1351-53, 1359-61, 1368-69,
1399-1401, 1415-17
running, to stay in place, 1024
The Running Child, 1252
Running Wild, 504
runs: boy, 917-19; boy through jungle, 632; boy along edge, 1265
Rusalka, 1300, 1302
RUSKIN, JOHN, 659, 745, 1051-52
Russell, Jim, 1211
Russell family, 226-27, 317, 335,
354-56, 419-21, 421-24, 775, 1057,
1228-29, 1284, 1374

Russia: mid-18th century, St.
Petersburg, 1415-17, Ukraine,
1415-17; early 19th century, Lit-
tle Russia, 717-20; late 19th
century, various, 1206-8; novel in
progress about, 862, 1313; travel
in, 117
Russian Imperial Family, 12, 1207-8
Russians: in England, 69; in Poland,
World War II, 1097-98; invade
Norway, World War II, 1351
Russon, Mary, 77, 465
rustlers, sheep, foiled by pig, 1082
Rusty, 1115
RUSTY ROBERTS, 1052, 1064-65
Ruth, 625
RUTH BALICKI, 152, 353, 597-98, 619,
1052-53, 1097-99, 1398
RUTH HOLLIS, 75, 85-87, 846, 942,
960, 966, 1003-4, 1053, 1190-92
Ruthven, Scottish noble, 1413
Ryan Creek, Australia, late 20th
century, 620-23
Rye, Anthony, 231

sabotages: sand in engines, 405; water in exhaust, 404-5
Sabotage at the Forge, 48
Sabre of Storm Valley, 220
sacking of Constantinople, 372
sacred places, old quarry, 1025
sacrifices: futile, 612; future,
697, 833; human, 387, 625, 1119,
1142; of child, planned, 209; of
king every 9 years, 694; of mani-
cure set, 151; of ship picture,
668; of virgin, 884, 1162; of white
horse, 295-96; of wife, 1050;
prince offers to save princess,
702; ritual 9-year, 485, 413-14;
self, 387; to renew king, 121-22
sacrileges: accusation of, 1162;
composing songs, 123; riding god-
horse, 296, 1294; various acts,
1118
safari park, 1248-49
safecrackers, London, 798
Saffronilla, 153
SAGBOHEICIM, 490, 492
sahibs, 652
sailing: contests, 383-84, 1379-
81; in magical boat, 1377-78; in
peach, 593-95; invitation to go,
1340; love of, 516-17, 982-83,
1088, 1299; to Europe, 1101-3
sailing novels, 255-57, 365-66,
558-59, 763-65, 887-89, 893-94,

982-84, 1068-71, 1177-79, 1253-
56, 1298-1300, 1306-9, 1309-11,
1340-42, 1379-81
sail loft, locked in, great leap
from, 950-51
sailors: apprentice, 29, 1068-70;
barge, 1213-15; brings Dutch doll,
332-33; exemplary, 1239; first
mate, 29; foreign, 401-3; girl,
1175; "gentleman volunteer,"
1068; huge, 74, 907; mouse, 1031-
32; Napoleonic wars, 595; naval,
743; Norwegian, 1177; one-legged,
1253-56; rich boy on working
smack, 433-34; Sentinels, 1068-
70; shipwrecked, 587, 1155-56;
toy, 1274; youthful, 255-57, 614.
See also sea captains; seamen.
sails, black instead of white, 1261
Saint Augustine, 297
Saint Bartholomew, 1016, 1395
Saint Ronan, 740
saints: Byzantine, 279; hosts of,
977; household, 557; missionary,
297; Scottish queen, 768; seventh
century, Cuthbert, 1376-79. See
also St. plus saint's name.
Saintsbury, Joseph, 330
Saladin, 670-71
Sale, Morton, 732
Sale of Work, 165
sales: cattle, 1050; clerks,
supercilious, 667; half the pad-
dock, 404-5; of baked goods, 165
Salesman, 466-67, 753
salesmen: dishonest car, 196, 904;
of Castilian Amaroso wine, 1148;
street, 449; traveling, 1132
Salleen, 544
Sallow family, 311
SALLY STUDDARD, 93, 1055, 1376-78
SALLY TINKER, 449, 1055-56, 1337-38
salmon: smuggled, 832; talking, 1272
Salt, Veruca, 203
Salt family, 1297
salvation, instructions for, 975
salvage: abandoned, ship, 434; from
shipwreck, 258-59, 1044; junk from
sewers, 808-9; sought, 1379; war,
619
Sam, 1125-28
Sam, the dog, 464
Sam Branwell, 149-50, 1033
SAM GAMGEE, 96, 406-8, 437, 465,
1056
Sam Goodchild, 1213-15
Sammy, the dog, 467-69
Sammy Flint, 466-67, 753

samplers: Victorian heirloom, 860,
1141; worked by great-
grandmother, 331. See also embroi-
deries; needlepoint; tapestries.
Sampson, Charlie, 339-42
Sampson's Circus, 1131
Samson: abusive horsebreaker, 454;
African, 114-15; Biblical, 115
Samson's Hoard, 1297
Sam Thwaite, 537
SAMUEL PONTIFEX, 176, 451, 362, 472,
1056, 1290-91
Samuel Widdison, 548
Samways, Sergeant, 285, 1074
San Andreas Fault, 364
sanctuaries: bird, 1154; church,
611, 1026
Sanders, Meaty, 13, 799
Sanders, Nick, 1062-63
Sanders family, 897-99
Sanderton, Geoffrey, 469
Sand-fairy, 1007
Sandleford Warren, 95, 418, 535,
557, 1331-32
San Domingo, late 18th century, 765-
67
Sand Pilot, 578
Sandra, 912
SANDRA THOMPSON, 314, 334, 514-15,
528, 599, 629, 647-48, 1056-57,
1315, 1364
Sandwich, 56
Sandwich, Albert, 177-79, 543, 826
SANDY HARDCASTLE, 335, 354-55, 1057
Sandy Sandwell, 223-25
San Felipe (ship), 1069
San Miguel, Chile, late 20th centu-
ry, 585
Santander, mid-20th century, 1366
SANTA POSSIT, 234-36, 516, 1057
Santiago, Chile, late 20th century,
1187-89
Santos, Marko, 183-84
sappers, 214, 1386
Sappho: Poems and Fragments, 82
Saracens, in England, 1410-11
Sarah, 626, 1206
SARAH BRUCE, 605, 1049-50, 1057-58
Sarah Casket (ship), 344, 887-
88
SARAH CODLING, 615, 814, 841-42,
1058
Sarah Graham, 741
Sarah Keate, 169, 171
Sarah Reynolds, 206-8
Sara Polwarne, 1409-10
Saruman, 805
Sasha Henry, 405

satires, or significant satirical elements, 19-22, 96-99, 143-44, 203-4, 227-30, 252-54, 508-14, 583-85, 593-95, 703-6, 797-99, 1149-51, 1313-14, 1353-56, 1392-94

Sattin Shore, 639, 697, 874-75, 1020, 1335

satyrs, 875

Saul and David, 438

Saunders, Dorothy, 335, 354-565, 423-24, 775, 1057

Saunders, Michael, 208-9

Sauron, 131, 406-8, 436, 982, 1158

Sausage, the dog, 1112

savages: attack castaways, 788; blue painted, 123; try to cook cat, 894

savings, for education used for lawyer, 474-75

saviors, lion gives life in a Christ scene, 55

Sawdust family, 1186

Saxons: in Britain, 271, 273, 293-97, 760, 930, 1029, 1085-87, 1089-90

Say River, 291, 812, 858, 862

Sayyid Ali, 1303-5

scabs, in coal strike, 1276

scams: bilk clergymen, 1268; money for harp, 1357; revising principal's conduct book, 646; steal pool, 1120-21; wool theft, 1402. *See also* hoaxes; mischief; pranks; schemes; tricks.

scandals, family, 473-75, 1021-23, 1134-36, 1334-36, 1196-99

The Scapegoat, 993

scapegoats, king as ritual, 39-41, 832

scapegraces, 143-44, 304-6, 533-34, 561-62, 797-99, 969-99, 1149-51, 1269-70, 1354-66

scarcity. *See* shortages.

scarecrows, 568-69, 599, 741, 1060, 1258

THE SCARECROWS, 1058-60, 1348

Scarlet, Will, 12

Scarlett, Susan, 1157

scars: facial, 88-89, 101, 205, 425, 772, 1248-50; girl and elephant, 1248

scarves, long red and green knitted, 1412

scavengers: from sewer, 508; of wrecked vessels, 85; on riverbank, 400-1; refugee boy, World War II, 1097

schemes: for animals for ark, 522-23; of king, 300; revitalize Cornish village, 890; to elevate boy's image, 920; to kill fox, 388-89; to overthrow South American government, 282-83. *See also* hoaxes; mischief; pranks; scams; tricks.

Schindelman, Joseph, 203

SCHLEE, ANN (CUMMING), 52, *1060-61*, 1294

Schmidt family, 235

schnapps, poured into food, 990

Schofield family, 541-42

Scholar family, 498-99, 533-34, 1264

scholars: boy, 730; Celtic, 804; girl, 769-70; of languages, was King Arthur in previous life, 844; of magic, 800; of 9th century manuscripts, 373-75; of Vikings, 838, 1101; presumed legitimate, 800; woman, pushy, 373-75

scholarships: art, 108, 889, 926, 1401; Cambridge, 924-25; college, 697; in economics, 536; lost because of grandmother, 901; music, 952, 1003, 1062-63; suggested, 704, 706; to Christ's Church College, Oxford, 490-92; to Cobchester college, 528, 1365; to domestic science college, 901; to secondary school, 386, 1322; won, 475

school assignments: interview old person, 430-32, 433; local history, 281

schoolboys, form singing club on bus, 801, 1133

school buses: meeting place for club, 801; stranded in storm, 80, 865

schoolchildren, assist dwarf, 848

school life. *See* schools; school scenes; school stories.

school programs, Open Day, 520

schools: art, 31, 108, 952; at Lucknow, 652-53; at bottom of sea, 21, 23, 827; boarding, 96-99, 161, 169, 206-8, 223-25, 228, 230, 365, 366, 404-5, 413, 455, 497, 532, 564, 616, 735-36, 809-10, 963, 988, 1006, 1058-59, 1084, 1180-82, 1193-94, in Russia, 719, state-run boarding, 506; bombed, 427, 735-36; boy to leave for insurance job, 704; choir, 1180-82; cloister, 324; cruel charity,

1099, 1400-1; Dr. Bunion's Academy, 1149; dropouts, 924, 962,
1242, 1303; Drouet's charity, 596;
expulsion, 1200, 1324; financed by
prominent woman, 622;
for dogs, 903-4; for gifted proposed, 1270; for orphans at
Willoughby Chase, 1401; for refugee children, 1097; for retarded,
1368; for workhouse children,
53-54, 59, 596, 1370; for young
monkeys, 366; girl leaves to care
for family, 706; girl's in Tver,
Russia, 719; grammar, 1200; hated,
670; "hockey," 636; impending,
232; improved, 1093; language in
Brussels, 1324; last day, 484;
newly co-ed, 809; of stage training, 68; oppressive boarding,
1316; outing, 742; overcrowded,
378, 736; phobias toward, 1313;
posh boarding, 736, 427; progressive, 1091, 1093; Quaker training,
685; reform, 1003; sailing, 558-
59; secretarial, 925; skipping,
129, 495, 697, 897-99, 1040, 1049-
50, 1191, 1205; snobbish, 31;
underachievers, 1313; working
class, 427; workhouse, 821; worry over, 624. See also academies;
boarding schools.
school scenes, 28-29, 44, 164-66,
206-8, 286-87, 367, 378, 520,
560, 591, 734-36, 801, 809-10,
819, 820, 897, 901, 1040, 1058-
59, 1062, 1149, 1168-69, 1180-82,
1200, 1262, 1269-70, 1316
school stories: 163-66, 223-25,
286-89, 801-4, 809-10, 949-52,
1071-74, 1168-69, 1180-82, 1262-
64, 1269-70. See also school life;
school scenes.
schoolteachers: ancient history, 529; band director, 1062-63;
beloved, 469; courageous, 53-
54; cruel, 1400; dour Scottish,
1156, 1409; dyslexic, 1313-15;
encouraging, 924, 1123-24; English and maths master, 532;
exuberant, 453; former, 173, 364,
619-20, 1323; fuzzy-headed form
master, 339; geography mistress,
1316; helps with ship's rescue,
927; history, 199, 230, 378, 397;
housemaster, 96-99; imprisoned
by Nazis, 1097; kind, 1328-29;
merry, 59, 954; musically gifted youth sore trial to, 950-52;

no nonsense, 367; object of ridicule, 339; Oxford, 1405; physical
education, 157-58; remedial reading, 656; retired, 258-59, 261,
326-28, 640, 823; Senior English
mistress, 822; strict, 791; umpire
for cricket, 622; unconventional, 520-21, 823; various, 1269-70;
village, 262, 635; village pupil-
teacher, 560; woman, concerned
about possible child abuse, 821;
woman, disheveled, 822. See also
headmasters; headmistresses;
teachers; tutors.
Schwartz, 669-61
science fiction novels, 155-58,
237-40, 505-8, 989-92, 1294-95,
1359-61
scientists: believe in giants, 339;
experimental, 127; impractical,
512; woman, 1035-36
The Scillies Trip, 149
scimitars, 377
Scotland: ancient, 299; first century, B.C., Orkneys, 1161-64;
first century, 771-74, 347-
50; late 8th century, Orkneys,
1298-1300; late 11th century, 1012-13; early 14th century,
1017-20; mid-16th century, Castle of Lochleven, 1412-15; 17th
century Auchenskeoch, 636-8;
late 17th century, 456-58; mid-
18th century, 289, 648-51; early
19th century, Shetlands, 1155-
57; early 20th century, Hebrides,
588-89, highlands, 1398-99, Outer
Isles, 588-89, village, 1123-
25; mid-20th century, Kilmorah,
79-81, near Inverness, 642-43,
Skua, 1396-97, Skye, 789-91, 1049-
50, West Highlands, 368-70, West
Lothian, 1196-99; late 20th century, Edinburgh, 427-28, mountains,
1368-69
Scotland, novels of, 79-80, 347-50,
368-70, 427-28, 588-89, 636-38,
642-43, 648-51, 771-74, 789-91,
1012-13, 1049-50, 1123-26, 1155-
57, 1161-64, 1196-99, 1368-69,
1396-97, 1398-99, 1412-15
Scotland Yard, 405
Scots: in Ireland, 544-45; in Wales,
996
Scratcherd, Davey, 119
SCREAMING HIGH, 709, 1061-64
Screeb, 545
The Screwtape Letters, 700

scribes: 195, 276, 612, 729. *See also* scriveners.

scriveners: 612, 729. *See also* scribes.

Scrooge, Ebenezer, 227-30, 353, 409, 468, 1227

SCRUBB, EUSTACE, 376-77, 603, 687-89, 1007, 1034, 1091-93

scullions, for stoneworkers, 1396

sculptors, 1205

sculptures: all white, 541-42; found art, 540-42; stone face, 1115-16

S.D., Selective Deafness, 479

Seabridge, 391

sea captains: barge, hard driving, 1213; capable gentleman, 1141-43; capable, of wrecked ship, 786, 788; cruel, 1068-71; father, 1340, 1342; father of blind girl, 172-73, 195, 217-18, 591-92, 616, 1173; gloomy Quaker, 344, 887-89; grandfather, former, 1356; kidnaps youth for slavery, 649; life of chosen by youth as reward, 317; marries castaway, 893-94; one-legged, 731, 790-91; religious, humane, 866, 1068-71; salmon-boat, 731; uncle, 112, 342, 1231, 1232, 1236-37. *See also* sailors; seamen.

SEA CHANGE, 48, *1064-65*

sea-chests, 100, 930, 1228, 1254

seacoasts: Cornwall, 459-62, 890, 1287-89, 1409-10; Devonshire, 724-27, 926-27; England, 119-21, 190-91, 495-98, 578-80, 604, 614, 734-37, 923-24, 982-84, 1140-41, 1169-71, 1213-15, 1223-25; eroding, 578-80, 1170; Essex, 1379-81; Exmoor, 389-92; Ireland, 1101-2; North Sea, 1325-27; Northumberland, 1376-79; Scotland, 79-81, 1161-64; Sussex, 763-65; Wales, 175-76

sea cooks, villain, 732

The Sea-Egg, 145

SEA FEVER, 966, 1064, 1379. *See WINDFALL, 1379.*

Seagrave family, 632, 786-89, 855, 859-60, 1023, 1239, 1374

seagulls: helpful, 1332-33; reassemble iron man, 584; talking, 1332-33

sea lions, trained, 235

seals, bull, 1155-56

The Seal-Singing, 531

Seals' Island, 294-95

seamanship, superior, 1069

seamen: apprentice, 168-69; commander of convoy, 262-63; filthy, 494; officer, 173; second mate, 839; staunch old master, 1023, 1374; wounded, 356. *See also* sailors; sea captains.

seamstresses, 354, 365, 421, 814, 816, 1142

Seamus, 1271-72

seances, 207, 286

sea otters, 1328

Sea People, 1308

Sea Rat, 1021

searches: for lost boys, 398; for lost Jamaican boy, 844; for lost treasure, 219; for lost tribe, 1357-58; for Mr. Grimes, 1329. *See also* journeys; quests; trips; voyages.

searchlights: creating fear, 369; dropped, 194

seas, raging, walking on, 463

Sea School, 558-59

Sea Serpents, 1307

sea shells, singing, 1096

seasickness, 1341

Season Songs, 570

sea stories, 255-57, 365-66, 763-65, 786-89, 887-89, 1043-46, 1064-65, 1068-71, 1253-56, 1298-1300, 1306-9, 1340-42, 1379-81

Sea Swallow (ship), 117

Sea View Guest House, 638, 753, 923, 1033

The Sea Wall, 322

Seaward, 255

Sebastian Price, 1165, 1167

SEB LEROY, 412-14, 485, 694, 697, 833, *1065*

Seccombe family, 92, 455-56, 618, 693-94, 947

second century: England, 347-50, 1025-26; Scotland, 347-50

Second Roman Legion, 768

second sight: 418, 543, 589, 956, 1151-52, 1196, 1331. *See also* clairvoyance; ESP; mental telepathy.

secretaries: 1151; father's, 668; Lombard, 1402; loyal, efficient to wizard, 845, 1355; Quaker, 685; youth of King Alfred, 871

Secretary of Private Affairs, 509

The Secret Garden, 897

secret meetings, at timber yard, 389

The Secret of the Libyan Caves, 503

secret passages, 65, 103, 122, 146, 216, 282, 350, 486

secret rooms, 122
secrets: disclosed, 1132; family,
841, 1134-36; industrial, stolen,
984; lost letter, 1405-6; midnight
garden, 1237; of elopements,
886; of escaped gorilla, 1154;
of invulnerability, 114-15, 116,
754, 1189-90 (See also life.); of
mad daughter, 111-13; of prehistoric creatures, 368, 370; plans
to elope, 60; presence of doctor,
258-60; shared, 1283
Secret Service, India, 651-54, 655
secret societies, boys', 281-83
Secret Society of Witches, 1392
secret trails, 216
sectarianism, Ireland, 1284-87
sects: Christian, 557; religious,
671
security blankets, 490
Sedley, Joanna, 103-4, 606, 615,
1103
Sedley family, 695
sedition: imprisonment for, 360,
849, 859, 1224
seductions: attempted, 1149. See
also molestations, sexual; rapes.
SEED, 610, *1065-66*, 1087
seeds: damaged by radiation, 157-58;
experimental, 127; exotic, 127,
1044
SEEDY SAM, *1066*, 107
SEFTON, CATHERINE (MARTIN WADDELL),
1066-67, 1133
SEFTON OLDKNOW, 195, 217-18, 592,
616, 770, *1067*
Seisin, 154
Sekar, Anne, 36-37, 547, 608, 778,
864
Sekar family, 450, 548-50
Sekhmet, goddess, 196, 829
self-confidence: enhanced, 32-33,
194, 472, 692-93, 1135-36, 1140-
41, 1381; of circus performer,
lost, 88. See also self-esteem;
self-image.
self-control, 968
self-determination: girl acquires,
250-51; old woman earns, 714-16
self-esteem: damaged, 686; developed, 39, 468-69, 345, 591, 703-6,
743, 833-35, 963, 1121, 1140-41,
1161-64, 1167-69, 1181-82; low,
75, 696; plan to enhance boy's,
920; plan to enhance dog's, 920;
regained, 355; reinforced, 9-10;
resilient, 770. See also self-
confidence; self-image.

self-image: enhanced, 205, 382, 656-
58, 683-84, 921, 1135-36. See also
self-confidence; self-
esteem.
self-importance, deflated, 70
self-reliance: enhanced, 345;
gained, 833-35
self-sacrifice: aunt for family, 62; drinks poisoned medicine,
1226; for emperor, 1136; for master's family, 296; for son, 1198;
for tribe, 771-74, 968, 1172-73;
for village, 260; in barge explosion, 1215; life for master's,
824-26; lion for boy, 711; monk for
Viking boy, 1300; of doll mother,
102, 331; of dwarf, 344; of fairy,
958; of highwayman, 738, 1110; of
old seaman, 786-89; outlaw's, 739-
40, 1104; to defeat Masters, 991;
to destroy ghosts, 1060; to save
friend from river, 1300; to save
girl's life, 148, 1162; to save
woman, 1412; various noble acts of
Piglet, 974; Viking for comrades,
1300
SELINA PLACE, 344, 408, 504, *1067*,
1343-44
SELINA SEYMOUR, 763-64, *1067-68*
SELJUK OF RUM, 155, *1068*, 1357-58,
1411
Selkie: blinded in one eye, 1156;
the great, 1409
The Selkie Girl, 255
selkies, 1155-56
Selkirk, Alexander, 1046
semantics, 1210, 1359
seminaries, 1188-89
Sempebwa, John, 564-65, 613-14
Sendak, Maurice, 463, 746
senior citizens' trip, 657
A Sense of Story, 1247
*Sentimental Tommy: The Story of His
Boyhood*, 72
Sentinel (ship), 152, 743, 866,
1068-70
Sentinels, 1068-70
THE SENTINELS, 182, *1068-71*
Seonee Hills, India, 630, 1084
Seonee Wolf Pack, 11, 630-32
Serag, 624, 1204, 1206
SERAPHINA, 530, *1071-74*
Seraphina Brown, 1071-74
Serendip, Miss, 1385
serfs, 145, 1017
Sergeant Abraham, 34-35
Sergeant James Bubb, 342
Sergeant Macintosh, 481

SERGEANT SAMWAYS, 285, *1074*
series novels:
--Bagthorpe, *ORDINARY JACK*, *920-22*
--Bastable, *THE STORY OF THE TREAS-
URE SEEKERS*, *1146-48*
--Billy, *OLD DOG, NEW TRICKS*, *911-12*
--Borrowers, *THE BORROWERS*, *132-
34*, *THE BORROWERS AFIELD*, *134-36*,
THE BORROWERS AFLOAT, *136-38*,
THE BORROWERS ALOFT, *138-40*, *THE
BORROWERS AVENGED*, *140-42*
--Canterbury Choir School, *CHORIS-
TERS' CAKE*, *223-25*, *A SWARM IN MAY*,
1180-82
--Career by Streatfeild, *BAL-
LET SHOES*, *69-71*
--Chas McGill, *THE MACHINE GUNNERS*,
747-50, *FATHOM FIVE*, *400-3*
--Chrestomanci, *CHARMED LIFE*, *208-
9*
--Dark Is Rising, *THE DARK IS RISING*,
287-88, *THE GREY KING*, *501-2*
--Dido Twite, *BLACK HEARTS IN
BATTERSEA*, *107-9*, *NIGHTBIRDS
ON NANTUCKET*, *887-89*, *THE STOL-
EN LAKE*, *1141-43*
--Doctor Dolittle, *THE STORY OF DOC-
TOR DOLITTLE*, *1145-46*, *THE VOYAGES
OF DOCTOR DOLITTLE*, *1309-11*
--Egyptian by Harris, *THE MOON IN
THE CLOUD*, *829-30*
--Flambards, *THE EDGE OF THE CLOUD*,
354-56, *FLAMBARDS*, *419-21*,
FLAMBARDS IN SUMMER, *421-24*
--Green Knowe, *THE CHILDREN OF GREEN
KNOWE*, *211-13*, *THE CHIMNEYS OF
GREEN KNOWE*, *217-19*, *THE RIVER AT
GREEN KNOWE*, *1035-36*, *A STRANGER
AT GREEN KNOWE*, *1154-56*
--Hobbit, *THE HOBBIT*, *550-53*, *THE
FELLOWSHIP OF THE RING*, *405-8*
--Jungle, *DAN ALONE*, *276-79*, *GUM-
BLE'S YARD*, *514-16*, *WIDDERSHINS
CRESCENT*, *1364-66*
--Magic by Nesbit, *FIVE CHILDREN
AND IT*, *416-18*
--Mantlemass, *THE LARK AND THE LAU-
REL*, *683-84*, *THE IRON LILY*, *581-83*
--Mary Poppins, *MARY POPPINS*, *779-
81*, *MARY POPPINS COMES BACK*,
781-83, *MARY POPPINS IN THE PARK*,
783-84, *MARY POPPINS OPENS THE
DOOR*, *784-86*
--Meredith, *A MIDSUMMER NIGHT'S
DEATH*, *809-10*, *PROVE YOURSELF A
HERO*, *1004-7*, *THE TEAM*, *1190-92*
--Narnia, *THE HORSE AND HIS BOY*,
560-62, *THE LAST BATTLE*, *687-89*,
*THE LION, THE WITCH AND THE WARD-
ROBE*, *710-13*, *THE MAGICIAN'S
NEPHEW*, *755-57*, *PRINCE CASPIAN*,
994-96, *THE SILVER CHAIR*, *1091-94*,
THE VOYAGE OF THE "DAWN TREADER",
1306-10
--One End Street, *THE FAMILY FROM ONE
END STREET*, *385-86*
--Oxus, *THE FAR-DISTANT OXUS*, *389-92*
--Pennington, *BEETHOVEN MEDAL*, *85-
87*, *PENNINGTON'S SEVENTEENTH
SUMMER*, *949-52*
--Pentecost, *THE SONG OF PENTECOST*,
1119-21
--Pony Club, *PROVE YOURSELF A HERO*,
1004-7, *THE TEAM*, *1190-92*
--Ring, *THE HOBBIT*, *550-53*, *THE
FELLOWSHIP OF THE RING*, *405-8*
--Roman, *THE EAGLE OF THE NINTH*, *347-
50*, *THE LANTERN BEARERS*, *679-83*,
THE SILVER BRANCH, *1088-91*
--Stone Book, *THE AIMER GATE*, *9-10*,
GRANNY REARDON, *484-85*, *THE STONE
BOOK*, *1143-44*, *TOM FOBBLE'S DAY*,
1234-36
--Swallows and Amazons, *PIGEON
POST*, *972-74*, *SWALLOWS AND AMA-
ZONS*, *1177-79*, *WE DIDN'T MEAN TO GO
TO SEA*, *1340-42*
--Tripods, *THE CITY OF GOLD AND LEAD*,
237-40, *THE POOL OF FIRE*, *989-92*,
THE WHITE MOUNTAINS, *1359-61*
seriousness, essential for good
life, 701-2
serpents, emerging from egg, 462-63
SERRAILLIER, IAN (LUCIEN), *1074-75*,
1096
servants: ambitious, 195;
cleaning woman, 567; companion-
gentlewoman, 37, 548; cook, 68;
corrupt, 195, 1067; day-lady, 565;
discharged, 1400; doll becomes,
331; domestic, 637; dumb, 308; ex-
gladiatior, 375; faithful, 4, 216,
406, 671-72, 751, 1056; faithful
ogre, 697; friend and companion, 516; girl, 450; housemaids,
4, 68; jealous, 1353; loyal, 4,
729; man Friday, 1045; man-of-all-
work, 318-19, 516; mysterious,
724; of Sauron, 406; of Tripods,
1360; reformed, 6; Russian, 718;
sharp-tongued, 548; thieving,
428; well-trained, 506; widow, 7;
young black mother, 627-28, 762;
youthful, 266. *See also* cooks;
housekeepers; housemaids; maids;
right-hand men.

servitor, at Oxford, 153-54
SETH-SMITH, E(LSIE) K(ATHLEEN),
   1075-76, 1351
The Seven Days, 1107
Seven Kings and Queens of Narnia,
   321, 357, 377, 603, 688, 742, 962,
   987, 1027, 1174
The Seven Lamps of Architecture,
   1051
seven league boots, 569
Seven Sunflower Seeds, 1296
17 Cherry Tree Lane, 779, 783
seventeenth century:
--British Isles: England, Suffolk,
   306-9; Yorkshire, 636-38; early,
   countryside, 1351-53, London,
   1351-53; mid, England and high
   seas, 1043-46; Cheshire, 1025-26,
   Cotswolds, 548-50; Derbyshire,
   938-39; countryside, 1009-12;
   London, 1199-202; southeastern,
   1199-202; Scotland, 456-58, 636-
   38
--Europe: Austria, Vienna, 213-15;
   Netherlands, 456-58; Poland, 213-
   15
--Middle East: Turkey, 213-15
--South America: Venezuela, 1043-46
Seven Tempest, 1369
THE SEVENTH RAVEN, 315, *1077-78*
seventh sons, of seventh son, 287
The Seventh Swan, 489
Seven Whistlers, 637
SEVERN, DAVID (DAVID STORR UNWIN),
   455, *1078-79*
SEWELL, ANNA, 105, *1079-80*
Sewell, Helen, 913
sewers, 45, 508, 808-9
sex: frank acceptance of, 1369; premarital, 202, 835
sex roles: strongly defined, 828,
   1301; undefined, 1301
sexual encounters: boasted of,
   1363; girl naive, 925-26; girl
   propositions older man, 459-62;
   observed, 1289, 1323; outcast
   girl and hiker, 1368-69; rejected,
   1118; to prove heterosexuality,
   1364; unconsummated, 969; woman
   propositions boy, 402, 654
sexual intercourse, averted, 98-
   99
sexuality: awakening, 603, 879;
   awareness of, 632; awareness of
   homosexuality, 1363-64; developing, 201; discovered, 1166-67;
   girl frightened of developing,
   692-93; of mother discovered,

1058-59; precocious, 599; recog-
   nized, 924
Seymour family, 3-4, 364, 1067-68,
   1229
Shadow of the Hawk, 1253
The Shadow on the Sun, 531
shadows: avoided, 1173; come from
   land, 463; have party, 784; lost
   and folded in drawer, 956; secret
   of strength, 1190; sewn on, 956;
   vulnerable, 115
Shakespeare, quotations from, 173,
   845
Shakespeare, Tug, 335
Shakespeare, William, 1352-53
Shakespeare family, 525, 606, 917-
   19, 1265
The Shakespeare's Head, 1127
Shakespeare's Theater, 555
SHAKY FRICK, 78, 465-67, 823, *1080*
Shamashazir, 624-26, 1204-6
Shambles, 277
Shamlegh-under-the-Snow, 653-54
Shamus Rat, 74
Shan, 252
Shannon family, 1276-78
Shanny Shannon, 1276-78
shape changers, 552, 642-43, 1343
Shardik, 3
Share Alike, 73, 242, 843-44, 896
shareholders' meetings, 368
Shark, 336
sharks: pursue cat, 893; two caught
   at once, 544
Sharon Willmay, 1294-95
SHARP, MARGERY, 815, 1031, *1080-81*
SHASTA, 43, 150, 561-62, 575, *1081-
   82*
Shaul, 625
Shaws, estate of, 648, 1281
Sheba, the cat, 186
sheep: bring girl and lover togeth-
   er, 938; brought to shelter in
   storm, 481-82; caught in snowdrift, 74; disappearing, 259;
   familiar gets measles, 1354; growers, 51, 1402-3; herded by dark
   people, 338; old ewe, 1082-83; pig
   herds, 1082-83; queen turns into,
   1210; ranch in Australia, 362;
   rescued from storm, 906; savaged
   and slain, 1399; shearing, 115;
   witch's familiar, 518
Sheep May Safely Graze, 90
THE SHEEP-PIG, 665, *1082-84*
Sheffield, 1322
Sheikh Rashid ed-Din of Basra, 671
Sheila Boyd, 515, 1243

Sheila Burton, Dental Assistant, 72
Sheila Howarth, 539, 541
SHEILA SMYTHSON, 58, 210, 400-3, 881, *1084*
Shelley family, 433-34, 1379-81
Shelley, Francis, 85
Shelton, Dick, *316-17*, 606, 1103
Shelton family, 102-5, 695, 1297-98
Shepard, Ernest H., 85, 562, 932, 1029-1031, 1094, 1187, 1388
Shepard, Mary, 779, 781, 783, 784
THE SHEPHERD, *1084*, 1125
shepherds: 453, 502, 519, 674, 725-26, 929, 977, 979, 1050, 1085, 1203, 1233-34, 1321, 1398, 1402; rescued by children in flood, 187-88
Sherborne, 154-55
SHERE KHAN, 11, 65, 630-31, *1084-85*
Sheridan, Richard, 169-70
sheriffs, 146, 195
Sherlock Holmes, 182
Sherwood Forest, 14th century, 145-47, 1343, 1420
Shetland Islands, 1155-57
THE SHIELD RING, *1085-87*, 1176
shields: ceremonial, 565-66, 613; magic, 711
Shift the Ape, 377, 603, 687-88, 1227
shillings, five for singing, 1180-81
SHINE, 44-46, 63, *1087*
The Shinty Boys, 751
ships: abandoned, 434, 1064-65; blown up, 401; Bristow vessel, 371; burials, 288; burned, 866, 887; captured, 237; carried overland, 372; crewed by rabbits, 366; holy, captured by Vikings, 1299; in distress, 1379; instruction, 558-59; launching, 1298; Narnian, 1306-9; pirate, 173; reported lost, 1400; sinking, 56; slave, 1044, 1069-70; steam, 237, 1064-65; stolen, 103; supply schooner, 587; torpedoed, 415; transport wrecked, 190, 595; uncle's, 88; whaler, 887; war, 1069-70. *See also* boats; canoes, yachts.
The Ship's Cat, 3
The Ship that Flew, 700
shipwrecks: 366, 371, 509, 763-64, 888, 893, 983, 1044, 1145, 1310, 1311, 1326; averted, 222; convict ship, 236; Danish fleet, 517; Devonshire, coast, 926; high seas, 786-87, 855, 859, 1023, 1069; of toy soldiers, 1275; off Galway, 258; off Scotland, 12-13, 289; off

Suffolk, 595; on rocks near home, 295; paddle boat, 716; parents lost, 1401; sinister survivor, 1155-56; South Pacific, 255; south seas, 4, 204; transport, 190; Viking, 1299
shipyards, Belfast, 1285
The Shire, 95, 406, 437, 551, 553, 804, 1056, 1158
Shirras, 733
Shmand-Fair, 1360
shoemakers: Borrower, 985; Irish, 913
shoes, magical dancing, 1272
The Shoe Shop Bears, 66
shootings: accidental, 953, 964; at car, 434; attempted, 321; by police, 525; highwayman, 738; in buttocks, 1006; of absentminded poet, 1358; of boy in revolution, 602; of coachman, 1126; of dog and pony by father, 693; of fox's tail, 388; of gorilla, 1155; of pirate, 1255; of rabbit, 1332; police shootout, 11, 1077; with bow and arrow, 957
shopkeepers: 17, 544-46, 623, 644, 703-5. *See also* storekeepers.
shoplifters, 640, 992, 1218
shops: antique, 200, 428; apothecary, 824-26; cake, 777; candy, 174; cluttered and dusty, 705, 872-73; curio, 743; hat, 568; pawn, 402; pet, 1267; pottery, 343; sheep in, 1210; spice, 402; sweets, proprietor sympathetic, 668; tea, 174; witches plan to buy all sweet shops in England, 1392-94. *See also* stores.
Shoreby, Lord, 606, 615, 1103
shortages: food, 337; food and fuel, 897-99, 1277; wartime, 208, 1340.
SHOT-IN-THE-HEAD, 610-11, *1087-88*
Shouter family, 874, 1354
showmen, kindhearted, small-time, 839-40
shrines, household, 501, 667-68
shrinkers, of children, 429
Shropshire, mid-20th century, 903-4
Sian Llewellyn, 558-59
siblings: half, 215-16, 264, 698, 915, 947, 1412; foster, 115, 338, 519; overly responsible sister, 334; rivalry, 1270; spirit children, 710; step, 25, 455, 810, 874, 933-35, 1047, 1055; three beautiful sisters, 698

Sicily, mid-20th century, Syracuse, 30-31
Siddha Asara, 1266
Siddons, Mrs., 169-70
sidekicks, 197, 657
Sidney Lumba, 77-78, 465
SIDNEY PEACEMAKER, 982-83, *1088*
SID PARKER, 76-77, 100, 159, 293, 604-5, 860, *1088*
sieges: in church, 219; of Constantinople by Turks, 371-72; of Danish force, 517, 871-72; of foxes, 388-89; of Sherwood Forest, 147; of shipwrecked family, 788; of Vienna, 214-15, 546, 1226, 1295-96
Sierra Leone, mid-19th century, 1068-71
signaling device, to submarines, 401
signalman, retired railway, 138, 837
signals: secret code, 1339; ship's distress, 1379; system with fishing rods, 959
signboards, inn, painted, 2
Signora Cortorelli, 30-31
Signor Dolcetto Antonio, 840
signs, of power to combat evil, 287-88
Sign-Seeker, 288
Sigurd Sigurdson, 1298
Sigurdson family, 1298-1300
Sikhs, in England, 10, 50, 297, 310-12, 470, 648, 656-57, 886, 1280
Silas and Con, 1140
Silent Magic spell, 173, 174, 909
Silkworm, 593-94
Sillo, 47
The Silmarillion, 1231
Silver, Long John, 172, 338, 1132, 1254-56
Silver Airman, 1271
Silver Bells and Cockle Shells, 241
THE SILVER BRANCH, 350, *1088-91*, 1176
THE SILVER CHAIR, 687, 699, *1091-94*, 1227
The Silver Cow, 255
Silver Curlew, 202, 985, 1094-96
THE SILVER CURLEW, 393, *1094-96*
Silver Everything and Many Mansions, 194
Silver Falcon, 1385
Silver Fidget, 1310
Silver on the Tree, 148, 255, 1375
silver sword, paper knife, 597
THE SILVER SWORD, 1074, *1096-99*
Silverydew, 724

SILVESTER, 38-39, 47-48, 158-59, 279-81, 557-58, *1099*
Simla, 653
Simon (*Lost John*), 11-12, 739
SIMON (*The Ghost of Thomas Kempe*), 453, *1100*
SIMON, the gooseherd, 108-9, 837, *1099-1100*, 1121-22, 1401
Simon Black in Peril, 1129
Simonds, Paul, 1294-95
Simon Henchman, 342, 1236-37
SIMON WOOD, 599, 608-9, 1058-60, *1100-1*, 1258
Simple, 976
Simpson, Mr. and Mrs. John, 69-70
Simpson family, 833-35, 962-63, 1173
Sims, Agnes, 784
Sim Swayne, 1009-11
Sinbad, the kitten, 1341
Sinclair, Magnus, 733
Singer family, 446-47, 612, 613, 678, 738, 778-79, 853-54, 863, 1114-17
singers: blind ballad, 1272; boys, 285-86, 1040-41, 1351, 1353, 1415-17; boys' choir, 51, 77-78, 223-25, 1180-82; creates Narnia, 756; folk, 75; girl, 685-87, 1073, 1194; inspired by beer, 950-52; mice, 1384; Neopolitan opera, 846; of life story, 202; of scurrilous songs, 832, 837; professional, 668; rat tenor, 529; schoolboys on bus, 801; traveling, 832; vocal teacher, 937; Welsh, 4, 845. *See also* bards; minstrels; musicians; pianists; other instruments.
Singh, meaning Lion, 470
singing contests, 383-84
Singing Cave, 737, 838, 1101-2
THE SINGING CAVE, 322, *1101-3*
Singing Stones, 410
The Singing Wreath and Other Stories, 1106
Sin Island, 659
Sink family, 560
sins: burden of, 975-76; ideas of, 475; illness as punishment for, 940; numerous, 623; reported weekly to father, 475
Sir Bartlett Spekes, 496
Sir Bedivere, 1038
Sir Benjamin Merryweather, 724-26
Sir Bobadil, 1385
Sir Bors, 1037-38
Sir Bronzebeard, 1001
SIR DANIEL BRACKLEY, 102-4, 316-17, 606, 615, 695, *1103*

Sir Everard d'Aguillon, 673-74
Sir Fulk d'Aubigny, 670
Sir Gawain, 1037-38
Sir Geoffrey Cobham, 447
Sir Geoffrey de Chaworth, 672
Sir George St. Orbin, 635, 1322-23
Sir George Withens, 196, 536-37, 904
Sir Henry Sydney, 459, 581-82
Sir Hugo d'Aubigny, 453, 670
Sirius, the dog-star, 74-75, 325-28,
    343, 639-40, 823, 1042
Sirius, the horse, 846, 960, 1005,
    1191
Sir James, 701
SIR JOCELIN DE COURCY ROHAN, 216-17,
    261, 408-9, *1103*
Sir John Dexter, 304-6, 827
Sir John Harthover, 363
Sir Joshua Cadell, 480-82
Sir Lancelot, 1037-38
Sir Meliagraunce, 1037
Sir Mordred, 1037-38
Sir Oliver, the horse, 105
SIR OLIVER OATES, 102-4, 615, *1103*
SIR PAGAN LATOURELLE, 916, *1103-4*,
    1137
Sir Patrick Hume, 456-57
Sir Percy Gregory, 507
Sir Quincy Murgatroyd, 302, 677
SIR RALF THE RED, 11, 611, 739-40,
    1104
SIR RANDOLPH GRIMSBY, 31, 302-3,
    740, 807, 809, 845, *1104*
Sir Raoul de Farrar, 738-39, 1104
Sir Richard Gayner, 237
Sir Rolf D'Eyncourt, 145-46
SIR SIMON MONTPELIER, 752, *1104-5*,
    1355
Sir Thiebaut de Coucy, 673-74
Sir Thomas Jolland, 276, 293, 683-
    84, 701
Sir William Douglas, 677-78, 1412
Sir Willoughby Green, 1400-1
Sir Wrolf the Viking, 725-26
sisters: baby, death of, 1373; bad
    tempered, as foster mother, 492;
    bossy, 924; close, 707-8, 1094-
    96, 1167-69; discovered, 1100;
    dressmakers, 738; encouraging,
    1195; endangered by Selkie, 1156;
    envied, 1134; estranged, 177; ex-
    posed, 1149; fairy, 851, 853; fos-
    ter, 245, 1161; instructs brother
    about "dead," 1373; intensely loy-
    al, 985; jealous, 1367; kidnapped,
    1149; older, 924; opportunistic,
    816-17, 818; prattling younger,
    1169; rebellious younger, 1169;

scornful, 1123-24; seamstresses,
    816-17; supportive, 1185;
    terrible-tempered, 981; young-
    est of three, 777
SISTERS AND BROTHERS, 1105-6, 1338
Six Sleepers, 148, 502, 1050, 1375
sixteenth century: England, Sussex,
    581-83; Scotland, Castle of
    Lochleven, 1412-15
sixth century: Byzantium, 279-
    81; Romania, 279-81; southern
    England, 294-97
size changes: frequent, 18, 19-21,
    22; caused by mushrooms, 193; un-
    usual changes, 982, 1035
skates, as carriage, 1275
skating: ice, 449, 1238, 1241, 1267;
    roller, 41
Skating Shoes, 1157
skeletons: Anglo-Saxon chief, 841;
    fantasized into man, 1369; hang-
    ing in cave, 222; in hypocaust,
    294; in river, 1269; of primi-
    tive man, 194; on deserted island,
    256; "skellinton" of murdered man,
    1269; Viking, 1101-2
Skelton family, 28-29, 1212
Sketches by Boz, 313
skiers, strange, sinister, 906
Skiffins, Miss, 1346
Skinhead, 1062-63
skins, Selkie, hidden, 1156
The Skin Spinners, 8
Skipley, future, 149, 156-58, 655
skipping school. *See* school, skip-
    ping.
Skipton Barrow, 549
Skirlston, late 20th century, 578-81
Skirlston Manor, 579
skirts, hoop, as means of escape,
    1109
Skrumshus, Lord, 221
Skua Island, 1396-97
skulls: of slave boy, 177-79;
    shatters glass case, 1325
Skullsplitter, 1298
Skye, Isle of, mid-20th century,
    789-91, 1049-50
Sky Gipsy: The Story of a Wild Goose,
    83
Slamecksan, 509
Slattery family, 335, 525, 605-
    6, 918-19, 1265
slavery, novels of, 765-67, 1068-71
slaves: abused boy, 1205; as ances-
    tors, 39; black companion to blind
    English girl, 172, 195, 591-92,
    616, 1067, 1173-74, 1231; black,

Haiti, 765-67; black, in Africa, 743; boy to be sold as, 649; British in Rome, 1245; British of Roman, 270-71, 1090, 1118; British of Saxons, 1293; Byzantine, 39, 47-48, 279-81, 1099, 1311; Calormen, 561; ex-Roman soldier of Jutes, 680-81; feel honored, 239; free Narnians enslaved, 687; girl sought by Saracen, 1410; Haitian, 937-38; in ancient Rome, 1136; Indians, 236-37; in futuristic society, 1295; in Welsh mountains, 1068; labor camp, future, 1295; in World War II, 353; noble girl, 48; of Constantine, 371-72; of Kutrigur Huns, 281; of light, 247; of ring, 465; of Romans in Britain, 347-48, 772, 1068, 1244-45, 1411; of Turks, 671, 1044; of Vikings, 91-92, 116-17; owners, acted, 520; petted like dogs, 239; raids, 148, 1161-63, 1307; Roman gladiator, 375; Saxons in Scotland, 273; Saxons of Scots, 804, 1012; Syrian, 671; thrall to Saxons, 930; thrown overboard, 1070; trained as clerk, 279; trained as doctor, 279-80; tribal, 1172-73; willing, 270-71; young boy, 217-19

slave trade: 1044; Africa, 743, 1068-71; American in Africa, 1068-71; anti-slave patrol off Africa, 866, 1068-71; Dahomeys, in Africa, 1068; international law against, 866; Mandingos, in Africa, 1068; Portuguese, in Africa, 1069

Slavonic area, 1300-2

Slavs, 38-39

Sleath, 129-31

sledding, 1235, 367

sleds: grandfather makes, 619, 1235; made of wood from loom, 914; makeshift, 1235

Sleepers: at table, 1308; of Knights of Arthur, 414, 1343; Six, awakened, 1375

Sleeping Beauty, 160, 1145

"Sleeping Beauty," retold, 996-99

Sleeping Knights, 167

sleepouts, in strawstack, 390

sleeps: two-day, 735; ten months', 887

sleepwalkers, 397, 1376

SLEIGH, BARBARA (DE RIEMER), 173, 1106-7

sleighs, reindeer-drawn, 711

Slighcarp, Miss Letitia, 1100, 1400-1

slippers, incriminating, 247

Sloth, 976

Slough of Despond, 975, 978

Slowboy, Tilly, 266

slums: Cobchester, 277-78, 314, 514-16, 629-30, 1364; English city, 465-67; London, 73-74, 113, 422, 468, 519-21, 522, 816-17, 1087, 1114-17, 1372; swamp, 262; visited, 735-36

The Sly Cormorant and the Fishes, 943

The Small Blue Hoping Stone, 801

A Small Person Far Away, 647

The Smartest Man in Ireland, 572

SMAUG, the dragon, 95, 439, 551-52, *1107*, 1204

Smeagol, 464

Smeaton, Betsey, 474

Smee, 1347

Smee, David, 121, 279

Smeeton, 950

The Smell of Privet, 1107

Smirk, Alfred, 107

SMITH, 738, 816-17, 818, 820-21, 839, 845-46, *1107-8*, 1108-10

SMITH, 441, *1108-10*

Smith, Alvin, 765

Smith, Betsy, 1

SMITH, EMMA, 365, 906, *1111*

Smith, Jim, 14, 605, 1049-50, 1057-58

Smith, J. L. S., 753

Smith, Joshua M., 620

Smith, Miss, 326-28, 823, 640, 1042

Smith, Mr., (*The Witch's Daughter*), 1396-97

Smith, Mr., (*Mr. Bumps and His Monkey*), 840

Smith family (*The "Minnow" on the Say*), 94, 858, 1058

Smith family (*Smith*), 1108-10

Smith family (*Thursday's Child*), 1222

Smith family (*The Warden's Niece*), 596, 623, 842, 1203, 1281, 1317-18

Smithfield, 12th century, 1394-96

Smithfield market, 1267

Smith of Wooton Major, 1231

Smith, Reuben, 106

smiths: blacksmith, 484-85; helpful, 1416; retiring, 1235; smithy setting for anvil wedding, 799-800; traveling, 115

Smithy Cottage, 249, 476, 482

Smoky House, 1111

SMOKY HOUSE, 471, *1111-13*

Smollett, Captain, 1254-56
smugglers: apprehended, 763-64,
  1229; captain of fishing smack,
  85; contraband, 515; dashing, romantic, 364; discovered,
  340-41; doctor suspected as leader, 338; east English coast,
  360, 1224-25; gentlemen, 3-4;
  guns, 629, 1228, 1412; drugs,
  international ring, 1061-64; of
  government secrets, 696; of military technology, 361; salmon, 832;
  shot by soldiers, 338; squire,
  1112-13; suspected,
  drowned, 1379, 1381; uncle of guns
  to Mexicans, 601-2; village, 1112-
  13; with France, 612; wool, 1133,
  1403
"Smut," 817
Smythson family, 58, 210, 400-3,
  881, 1084
Snap-dragon-fly, 1209
Snake (Dawn Wind), 931
SNAKE, the snake (The Song of
  Pentecost), 437, 953, 1114, 1120
Snake Indians, 733
snakes: adder, 1038; cobra, 631;
  composing skirt, 208; green with
  yellow ear muffs, 1114; huge rock
  python, 631-32, 635; huge, slain,
  979; in market basket, 539; naive,
  1114; suck up water from lake, 702
sneezes, from pepper, 342
SNEEZEWORT, 67, 324, 716, 1114
Snell family, 541-42
Sniveller, Mr., 1354
snobbishness: because of speech,
  179; resented, 210
snobs: social, 152, 169, 234, 516,
  896-97. See also social classes.
Snowden peaks, Wales, late 20th
  century, 242-44
Snowflakes and Sunbeams, 68
snowshoes, used in rescue, 290
Soames family, 701
soapbox, boat made of, 1130
Soapy Sam, 222
soccer matches, 290, 1189
social classes: as barrier to love,
  38; changed by war, 424; distinctions between, 7, 26, 38, 92, 94,
  127, 152, 179, 196, 210, 226-27,
  245-46, 262, 289, 304-6, 317, 338,
  362, 363, 364, 385-86, 399-400,
  400-3, 416, 421-24, 427, 433-
  34, 451, 456, 473, 492-95, 498,
  518, 536-38, 543-46, 548-50, 558-
  59, 561-62, 608, 608-9, 683-84,

694, 703-6, 708, 717-20, 725-26,
  732, 735-36, 748, 750, 757, 761,
  763-65, 768, 799-800, 843, 861,
  866-67, 876-78, 884, 933-35, 944-
  45, 968, 969, 981, 1047, 1058-59,
  1068, 1084, 1100-1, 1123-25, 1153-
  54, 1158-60, 1170, 1177, 1215-18,
  1221-23, 1224, 1258, 1276-78,
  1303-5, 1321, 1323, 1359, 1363,
  1402-3, 1417; distinctions between, animals, 931-32, 992, cats,
  196, English and Sikhs, 311-12,
  rabbits, 446; gentry, 506; gentry,
  in reduced circumstances, 499;
  need for understanding between,
  311-12; nobles, Byzantium, 279-
  81;
  working class, 9-10, 210, 245-46,
  385-86, 400-3, 427, 536-38, 558,
  689-92, 736, 750, 765, 911-12,
  1123, 1143-44; working together, 276. See also anti-Semitism;
  apartheid; discrimination; prejudice.
social climbers, 548
social comment, 19-22, 797-99, 849,
  1208-11, 1364
social mix, obvious, 248-52, 627-28,
  689-92, 1262-64
social outcasts, 1368-69
social reformers, 7, 1223-25, 1303-5
social unrest, rife, 895
social workers: 230, 249, 482, 835,
  910, 947, 1262. See also volunteers; welfare, workers.
societies: closed, 446; controlled,
  505-8; free-thinking, 1301-2;
  matriarchal, 772-73, 865-66;
  matrilineal, 1117, 1161, 1171; of
  witches, 1392; reversion to medieval, 449
The Society for the Achieving of
  Greatness, Broadening of Hori-
  zons, Enlarging of Ideas, and the
  Cultivating of Independent Minds,
  490
Society of United Irishmen, 499
"Soggy" Marsh, 950-51
"Sohrab and Rustum," 389
Sol, luminary of Sun, 325
Soldier and Me, 709
soldiers: American in flood, 495-96;
  American in Europe, 1098; American
  in Wales, 60, 177-78, 886; chasing
  smugglers, 338; Chilean, 1187-
  89; commissioned officer, 612;
  Danish, 1243; dregs of army, 339-
  42; English vs. smugglers, 1224;

English in Ireland, 499-50, 1135; English, World War I, 355, 1123-26, 1213-15; faithful, ill rewarded, 246; father, 361; former, 478, 557, 574; German, 1350; German flyer, downed, 749, 887; "go tribal," 1025; hated, 598; invalided out, World War I, 422; killed in World War I, 6, 1281; live toy, 1274-75; mercenary, 117-18, 916; mustered out, 768; of fortune, 633; playing cards, 20-21; pre-World War I, 420; professional, 1281; retired, 246; revived, 190; Roman, in Britain, 632-33, 679-83, 746, 767-68, 773-74, 1025-26, 1089-91; Russian, 1097; Saxon mercenaries, 1090; shot in street, 691; thugs, 156-58; toy Napoleonic of Brontes, 793, 1164-65, 1274-75; tricked into army, 595; tumble through forest, 1210; Turkish, 214-15, 1226, 1295-96; Verangian Guard, mercenary, 371; World War I, 9-10, 227. See also warriors; women, warriors.

solicitors: 210, 423, 1326. See also attorneys; lawyers.

Somerset, mid-20th century, 186-88, 707, 981

Song for a Dark Queen, 1117-19, 1176

Songberd's Grove, 612-13, 696, 738, 863

SONGBERD'S GROVE, 72, 1114-17

THE SONG OF PENTECOST, 258, 1119-21

songs: impromptu, 427; of Middle-earth, 437; scare away goblins, 1002; sea, 100, 887; sentimental school, 827; temperance, 399, 484; Toad's conceited, 1383

Sonny, 622

Sonny Smith, 578-80

A Son of Odin: A Tale of East Anglia, 1076

sons: adopted, 1240; castrated by father, 1136; devoted to father, 1346; foster, 879, 960, 972, 1262, 1390, 1402; foster, of chief, 1161; foster, of wolves, 1084; hated, 1104; in Buddhist monastery, 1165; killed in World War II, 841; long dead, 705; ne'er-do-well, 1110; of Uisneac, 300; of Usna, 299; rebellious, 1194; step, 738, 1039, 1047, 1088; resentful of stepfather, 1100-1; yokels, 1094; youngest, 1232

Sons of Adam, 710

Sophia Lawrence, 340-42

SOPHIE, 108-9, 1100, 1121-22

SOPHIE HATTER, 168, 567-69, 777, 1122

Sophie, Great Aunt, 489

sorcerers, 93, 451-52, 505, 694, 928

Sorensen Carlisle, 1122

SORRY CARLISLE, 200-1, 636, 692, 815, 1122-23, 1389

soul: discussion of, 1288; progress of, 974-80; sold to Devil, 824; wrenched back to life, 654

A Sounding of Storytellers, 1247

A SOUND OF CHARIOTS, 573, 1123-25

THE SOUND OF COACHES, 442, 1125-28

A Sound of Trumpets, 796

soup, witches', drugged, 1393

South Africa: girl from, 368; late 20th century, Johannesburg, 627-28

South America: mid-17th century, Venezuela, 1043-46; early 19th century, Quivera, 236-37; mid-19th century, Spidermonkey Island, 1309-11; late 20th century, Chile, 1187-89

South Downs, 403-5, 1319-22

Southend shark, looter, 4

Southampton, late 15th century, 1402

South Pacific: mid-19th century, island, 255-57; early 20th century, Halcyon Island, 586-87

South Seas, 509, 786-89

South West Wind Esquire, 660

souvenirs: sea cap, 263; war, 210, 747-48

Sowter family, 60, 362, 451, 703-6, 1132, 1282

space: craft, 46; creatures, 584-85; helmets, 528; ships, 239, 321, 566, 989, 991, 1014

Spacers, 156-57

spaghetti, goat eating, 30

Spain, mid-20th century, Santander, 1366-68

Spanfeller, James J., 366, 1167

The Spaniard, 73, 519

Spaniards: in England, 678, 1115-17; rescued from cannibals, 1045

Spanish Armada, 841, 1058

Spanish Civil War, 635

spankings, with shoe, 209

Spare Oom, land of, 864

sparklers, 607

Sparrow family, 75-77, 100, 159, 293, 605, 860, 1088

spears: magic, 359; man skilled
   with, 337; poisoned, 116; Viking,
   1377
A Special Providence, 747
spectacles: for owl, 152, 529, 931-
   32, 992; magic gold, 721; monk
   makes, 155
speedups, cause of coal strike, 129
Spekes family, 496
The Spellcoats, 617
Spell Me a Witch, 1371
spells: alter appearance, 698,
   777; as old woman, 567, 568-69;
   binding, 642; broken, 173, 175,
   189, 549; changing head to sheep's
   head, 637; evil, 505, 859, 1034;
   fairy, 271; forcing man to dance
   with fairies, 637; girl into old
   woman, 1122-23; girl uses without
   permission, 742, 1307; gone awry,
   472, 1056; helps to break, 485;
   mean tricks, 208-9; mind-control,
   1266; mixed up, 376; on sword hand,
   1190; protective, 928; put on
   princess, 701; Silent Magic, 909;
   tampered with, 363; things become
   true, 987-88; time, 1208; to call
   up storm, 642-43; to keep lover,
   309; various, 373-75, 1271, 1354-
   55; wayward, 667, 1290; written in
   snake's egg, 374
spelunking, 193-94
Spence, Geraldine, 119
Spence, John, 153, 743, 866, 1068-71
spendthrifts, father, 1315
Spenser, Edmund, 904
Spider, Miss, 593-94
Spidermonkey Island, 160, 211, 988,
   1309-10
Spider-Mother, 1095
spiders: huge, 95, 551-52; matron
   enchanted as, 1355; sent by leprechaun, 1271
spies: accusations of, 829, 1286;
   among Normans, 1086; boy, 543-46;
   chasing of, 57; discovered, 239;
   foreign in England, 361, 696; for
   revenue agents, 1112; for Robin
   Hood, 146; French girl, 448, 600;
   German, World War II, 881; Indian
   Secret Service, 574, 651-54, 655,
   743, 758; international industrial, 984; Irish nurse, 299-300;
   of Assassins, 671; on neighbors,
   127; on pier family, 362; Roman in
   Britain, 1089-90; Scottish, 1414;
   suspected, 37; unmasked, 1177;
   World War II, 210, 262-63, 401-3,

   1084, 1339; wounded, 653
SPILLER, 49, 135, 137, 138-40, 140-
   41, 811, 854, 948, 1129-30
Spillergun, Mike, 404-5
SPINDLE-IMP, 201, 872, 902, 985,
   1095-96, 1130-31
"spindle shanks," distinctive family trait, 704
spinners: evil Imp, 1130; flax into
   yarn, 872; girl, 1233-34; old woman in tower room, 1002
spinning machines, 198, 264
spinsters: aunts, 564; care for father, 823; childish, 817; devoted
   to family, 207; elderly, 817-18;
   frugal, 817; girl aided by imp,
   1094; girl works as maid for, 1159-
   60; hates men, 820; idolizes dead
   brother, 6-7; mistress of man-
   or, 583; two older sisters, 1133;
   vengeful, 820
The Spirit of Sicily, 31
spirits: finally at rest, 456; in
   conflict, 1326-27; indigenous,
   715, 860-61, 894; inhabit old
   house, 710; lured into bottle,
   452; of air fish, 462; of Christmas, 227-30; of girl long dead,
   455-56; of star, 325-28; of those
   killed in mine, 398; of Victorian children, 286-87, 591, 843;
   protective, 547-48, 548-50;
   released by workmen, 451; restless, 693-94; roused, 1158; star,
   584-85; wandering in grove, 946-
   47; water, 641-42, 642-43. See
   also ghosts.
Spitfires, 1212
Splintered Sword, 1257
SPLOT, 847-48, 970
sponsors, of man-cub, 65, 71
Spooky Cott, 469
sports: cricket, 621-22; poaching,
   284-85, 1372; state-run, 506-7
Sports Centre, opening, 647
Spot, the dog, 1112
spots, black, 100
The Sprig of Broom, 1371
SPRING, (ROBERT) HOWARD, 1267, 1131
spring: cleaning abandoned, 1382;
   nanny brings to park, 782; re-
   turns to manor, 725
Spring Mill, 541-42
The Spring of the Year, 1306
"The Spring Running," 632
The Sprog, the merlin, 383-
   84
Spurrier, Steven, 1267

spy novels, 237-40, 347-50, 361-62, 400-3, 651-54, 771-74, 989-92, 1088-91, 1213-15
Spyri, Johanna, 531
squares, eighth chess, 1024, 1358
Squashy Hat, 973-74
Squeak, the gerbil, 76-77, 100, 293, 604-5, 860
SQUEAK WILSON, 814, 817, *1131-32*
Squib, 81
Squire, kindly village, 1112-13, 1410
Squire Gordon, 105-6, 454, 596, 612
Squire Pooley, 303
Squire Roger Frankland, 637
squires, 673-74, 739, 917-17, 1104, 1132, 1153, 1202
SQUIRE TRELAWNEY, 338, 732, *1132,* 1254-56
Squirrel, 416
A Squirrel Called Rufus, 234
squirrels: Fluffy Tail, 1271; hair used for paint brushes, 324; in chocolate factory, 1297
Sri Krishna Eating House, 526, 1304
stable, site of battle, 687-88
stable boys, 5-6, 105-7, 226, 317, 420, 596, 926
Staffordshire, early 20th century, 1220-23
stage coaches: foundling grows up on, 1125-28; overturned, 88; wrecked, 1126
stage effects, spectacular, 304
Stagg, Nelly, 402, 1084
stags, talking, 562
stairs: devoured by raven, 41; ending in dropoff, 649; forbidden to use, 843
stake, burning at, 1260
Stalky & Co., 665
Stallion of the Sands, 504
stallions, white pedigreed, 758
Stamp, Lettie, 249
stampedes: cattle through ruined city, 294; of water buffalo, 631, 1085
Stamp family, 698
stamps, picture on hand, 200
Standing in the Shadow, 395
Standish family, 236-37, 1268-69
St. Andrew's Church, 219, 283, 1076-78
Standwich, Lady, 447
Stanhope, Michael, 224-25
Stanislawsky, Oskar, 922, 1035-36
Stanley, 421-22
Stanley, Diana, 132, 134, 136, 138

STAN SOWTER, 60, 451, 703-4, 706, *1132,* 1282
Stanton, Will, 1375
Stanton family, 148-49, 287-88, 501-2, 1050
STAPLE, 885, *1132-33,* 1402-3
STARR, 669, 801-3, *1133*
STARRY NIGHT, 1067, *1133-36*
stars: dog, 325-28; falling, 168, 569; jazz and rock, 1063; pasted to sky by giants, 780; retired, 1308
Star Spinner act, 88, 205
Star Swayne, 1010
starvation: death by, 53-54; imminent, 894
States-General, French, 1216
statues: marble, come alive, 785; missing, 4, 290, 480-81; of gold, underwater, 1307; of pets over graves, 693; rediscovered, 481-82; stone, revivified, 712; stone, of St. Christopher, 591, 710; transformed animals, 357
St. Boniface, A.D. 679-755, 1076
St. Brandan's Isle, 851, 853, 1329-30
St. Brendan's Church, 579
St. Christopher, statue, 212, 591, 710
St. Cregan's Foundling Hospital, 1410
St. Cuthbert, 93, 94, 752, 1055, 1376-79
Steam on the Line, 1273
steeples, church, 484, 1143-44; climbed, 1143-44
Stefan Zabruski, 214-15
stenches, of prehistoric creatures, 369
St. Ennodawg, order of, 155
stepfathers. *See* fathers, step.
Stephanie Ayrton, 1072-74
STEPHANOS BULGARICOS, 371-72, *1136,* 1311
STEPHEN DE BEAUVILLE, 155, 915-17, 1103-4, *1137,* 1202
Stephen Fitzackerly, 1318-19
Stephen Rudd, 71, 196, 276, 324-25, 350-51, 454, 744, 791, 799, 909, 1024, 1404-6
STEPHENS, JAMES, 299, 300, 1137-38
stepmothers. *See* mothers, step.
stereotypes: Americans, 663, 1068-71; girls' roles, 1179; gypsies, 543-46, 556, 1387
Steven, 912
Stevens, Jeremy, 1288-89

STEVENSON, ROBERT LOUIS (BALFOUR),
   68, 102, 384, 445, 648, *1138-39*,
   1253
Steve Webster, 205, 656-57
Steward of the Spent Candle, 529
stewards, ship's, 844, 1142
STEWART, AGNES C (HARLOTTE), 361,
   1139-40
Stewart, Alan Breck, 289, 649-51
Stewart Allman, 1235
St. George, 155, 1030
St. George's Church, 1080
St. George's Eve, celebration, 78
St. George Without, 77-78
St. Hugh of Lincoln, 1140-1200, 1076
Sticks and Stones, 994
The Sticky Hat, 1372
Stig of the Dump, 659
stills, Irish, 545
Sting, 96, 551
Stirabout Stories, 1106
A STITCH IN TIME, 727, *1140-41*
St. Joan, 1073
St. Justin's Estate, 689-91
St. Luke's orphanage, 560, 694, 769,
   1221-22
St. Nicholas, 630, 666
Stoats: take over Toad Hall, 1384;
   tricked, 828
Stobbs, William, 91, 670, 1012
stock, killed by Germans, 1350
stockades, 787-88, 1255
stockbrokers, 889
stocks, as punishment, 154, 304,
   1352
Stokes, G. Vernon, 527
stolen goods, buyers of, 101
THE STOLEN LAKE, 8, 889, *1141-43*
Stolen Summer, 71-72
Stolypin, "Uncle" Peter, 1207
Stone Age tribes, 336-37, 565
THE STONE BOOK, 444, 484, *1143-44*
The Stone Book Quartet, 443-44
The Stone Cage, 489
Stone Cross Mill, 604, 805, 876-78
stonemasons, 399, 484-85, 619, 1143-
   44, 1235
Stone of Gronw, 933
stones: black, once brothers, 661;
   black, once warrior, 754; mag-
   ic, 359, 1410-11; of power, 168;
   pierced by spear, 116
The Stones of Green Knowe, 145
The Stones of Venice, 1052
Stone Table, 711, 995
The Stonewalkers, 15
St. Orbin, Sir George, 1322-
   23

storehouses: of ham, bacon, and
   dressed fowl, 388-89; of hoarded
   supplies, 896-97
storekeepers: 176, 242, 473, 842-43,
   843-44, 850, 1390. *See also* shopkeepers.
stores: as home, 141; general, 578;
   grocery, 156-57, 1390; jewelry,
   41-42, 184-85; shoe, 399. *See also*
   shops.
stories: about World War II, 856;
   collaborative, 1147; ghost, 556;
   quieting frightened hostage children, 312; within story, 105-7,
   155, 171, 212, 217, 284, 335, 348,
   432, 453, 454, 529, 725, 788, 932,
   963-65, 992, 995, 1023, 1299,
   1409. *See also* flashbacks; frame
   stories.
Stories from the Bible, 301
Stories of the Wild, 83
STORM FROM THE WEST, 79, 1145, 1371.
   See BATTLE OF WEDNESDAY WEEK, 79.
Storm of Dancerwood, 220
Storm over Skye, 796
storms: at night, 1125; at sea, 366,
   510, 614, 695, 855, 859, 1044,
   1155, 1299, 1307, 1341, 1379;
   blizzards, 833, 834, 1399; buries
   Merlin's underground chamber,
   1338; caused by shudders of morphine withdrawal, 1338; caused by
   spell, 642-43; coastal, 190, 1101,
   1224; freak, 1337; heavy snow,
   1399; Helm Wind, 1085; hurricane,
   632, 786, 1210, 1044; in Scotland,
   80; in Wild Wood, 65; localized
   rain, 307; monsoon, 1304-5; on
   Lake Constance, 1098-99; rain,
   186-88, 211-12, 243, 340, 742;
   rain, causes great flood, 786;
   raised by saint, 1378; ruins valley, 660; snow, 51, 165-66, 288,
   407, 481, 549, 1109-10; sudden
   snow, 906-7; strand bus, 874;
   thunder, 156, 288, 1332; thunder
   and wind, 766; typhoon, 893; wind,
   235, 934, 1341; wind and rain, 587,
   865, 1416; wind and tide, 496; winter, 926, 1321; wreck boat, 1397;
   wreck car, 1337; wreck Danish
   fleet, 872, 517; wreck paddleboat,
   717
Storm Surge, 1027
*The Story of a Great Ship: The Birth
   and Death of the Steamship Titan-
   ic*, 220-21
The Story of a Little Girl, 717-18

THE STORY OF DOCTOR DOLITTLE, 731, *1145-46*, 1311
THE STORY OF GRIZEL, 456, 676, 1146. *See GIRL WITH A LANTERN*, 456.
The Story of Persephone, 395
The Story of the Amulet, 418, 881
THE STORY OF THE TREASURE SEEKERS, 881, *1146-48*
storytellers: about war, 595; African, 114, 920; always begins, "One starry night..," 1136; boy, 648; Breton fisherman, 740; dragon, 1030; girl, 956, 1124, 1347; grandmother, 1366-67; great-grandmother, 373; guinea pig, 1186; little old woman, 713-14; mother, 364; nanny, 780, 782, 783, 785; old man, 1242; old woman, 857; owl, 911; rabbit, 1333; Scottish grandfather, 911; Sikh girl, 10, 312; tells of skull, 177
A Story-Teller's Childhood, 744
storytelling contests, 114
Stourbridge Fair, 153
stowaways: aboard whaler, 887; Dido Twite, 108; girl, 237; in car, 386; in drain tile, 386; in lobster boat, 1102; monkey, 210; weasel, 366
Stow churchyard, 549
St Paul's, London, 612
St. Petersburg, Russia, 1415-17
STRACHAN, IAN, 833, *1148-49*
Strand Magazine, 882
THE STRANGE AFFAIR OF ADELAIDE HARRIS, 143, 442, *1149-51*
The Strange Case of Dr. Jekyll and Mr. Hyde, 1139
The Strange Light, 1028
Stranger (*Devil-in-the-Fog*), 304
Stranger (*The Stranger*), 1152-53
THE STRANGER, *1151-54*, 1338
A STRANGER AT GREEN KNOWE, 145, 373, *1154-55*
A STRANGER CAME ASHORE, 573, *1155-57*
The Strangers, 1061
strangers: handsome, sinister, 1155; huge, sinister, 906-7; lame, 696; men on skis, 906; old, sinister, 824-26; rude, overly inquisitive, 858; sinister, 289, 304, 373, 466-67, 523, 578-80, 790, 813, 1150, 1396
Strawberry, the horse, 167, 756
Strawberry, the rabbit, 1331
STREATFEILD, (MARY) NOEL, 68, 234, *1157-58*, 1220
streets, named for flowers, 629

STRIDER, 131, 406-7, 1158
strikes: breakers, 130; coal mine, 129-30, 473, 841, 1015, 1276-78; conflicting opinions about, 1276-78; in iron foundry, 1033; in sympathy of children, 691; mill, 876, 910; scabs, 1276; unsuccessful, 130
string quartets, 412-13
strings to the bow, 1195
Strives Minnis, 459, 582, 1033
A STRONG AND WILLING GIRL, 358, *1158-60*
THE STRONGHOLD, 573, *1161-64*
strongholds: against Romans, 333, 879, 1190; plans for, 884
Struldbrugs, 512
St. Savior's Church, 17, 707
St. Savior's Street, 411, 851, 1390
St. Stephen's Day, dim memory of, 1295
STUART, MORNA, 765, *1164*
Stubbins, Tommy, 988, 1309-11
stubbornness, 14, 44-46, 261, 1204
Stubley, Trevor, 911
Studdard family, 93, 810, 1055, 1376-79
Studdington estate, 134
students: activists, 219; agricultural, 1387; apt, 1199; art, 108, 1100; engineering, 614; exemplary, 1122; gifted in classics, 1194; medical, 356, 880-81, 1041-42, 1224-25; Oxford, 1406; Ugandan, 564-65
STUMPS, *1164-65*, 1274
stunts, to lure girl from ship's cabin, 345
stutterers, 47-48
St. Wilfrid's School, 96, 427, 532, 1193
style: action-packed, 789-91, 1099; adorned, 1327-30; adventure conventions, early, 786-89; allegorical, 710-13, 755-57; alternating time frames, 199, 1287; allusions, Biblical, 1180-82; allusions, Classical, 1180-82; allusions, literary, 903; allusions, various, 889; antiquated, 1046; author intrusions, 6, 55-57, 175, 221-23, 330-32, 687-89, 710-13, 720-22, 724-27, 755-57, 818-20, 956-58, 1002-3, 1113, 1327-30, 1306-9; Biblical rhythms, 974-80, 1204-6; Biblical quotations, 786-89;

bird imagery, 1167-69; bizarre elements, 1036; breezy, 797-99, 1146-48; breakneck pace, 797-99, 1110; British school-boy slang, 482;

chapters introduced by dramatic scene, 902; characterizations unusually subtle, 734-37; characterizations rich of an unusually large number of figures, 902; cinematic, 213-15, 932-35, 1026; circular conversations, 19-22; circular plot, 1128; coincidence, excessive use of, 1351-53; conscious hyperbole for comic effect, 737-38, 1141-43; conventional thriller aspects, 919; comic humor, 849, 1096; conversational, light, avuncular, 710-13 (and other books in Narnia series); cryptic, 1022; dense, 1206-8; deliberately arch, 956-58; deliberately flamboyant, 807-9; deliberately pretentious, 996-99; descriptive, 716-17, 771-74; *deus ex machina*, 1340, 1342; Dickensian, 107-9, 806-9, 887-89, 1108-10, 1126-29, 1141-43, 1399-401; didactic, 974-80, 1330-34; diffuse, 1389-91; dialect, Celtic, 1155-57;

dialect, Cheshire, 9-10, 484-85, 1143-44, 1342-45; dialect, Cockney, 167, 505, 1074; dialect, colloquial, 797-99, 807-9, 1158-60; dialect, Cornish, 332-33; dialect, Cumbrian, 555-57; dialect, 18th century, 351-53; dialect, Gaelic, 589, 642-43, 789-91, 914; dialect, German pidgin English, 888; dialect, Irish rhythms, 301, 713-14, 1102-3; dialect, miners' 19th century, 131, 1278; dialect, pirate speech, 1256; dialect, rural, 495-98, 938-39, 1096, 1130, 1366; dialect, Scots, 456-58, 1398-99; slang, modern, 51; dialect, southern American, 874; dialect, street, 656-58; dialect, various, 1330-34, 1358; dialect, Yorkshire, 351-53, 463-64, 486-87, 801-4; different points of view, 963-65;

easygoing, 486-87; 18th century conventions, 1110; especially effective point of view, 132-34, 134-36, 136-38, 138-40, 140-42, 953-55, 1330-34; especially

effective use of detail, 131, 132-34, 134-36, 136-38, 138-40, 140-42, 237-40, 872, 849, 927, 970-71, 989-92, 1046, 1199-202, 1241-42, 1249, 1275, 1277-78, 1330-34, 1392-94, 1402-3, 1404-7; excessively detailed, 1327-30; euphonious language, 585; exaggerated humor, 19-22, 22-23, 43-47, 1208-11; extensive dialogue, 19-22, 22-23, 385, 935, 1026, 1208-11; extremely convoluted plot, 209, 414, 567-69; fast-paced, 1187-89, 1218-20, 1356, 1366, 1379-81; first and third person narrators, 872; flamboyant pace, 41-42, 797-99;

flavor of legend, 115, 1409-11; florid, 662-63; folkloric, 1409-11; folk tale conventions, 930; formal speech, 1274; frequent coincidence, 153-55, 492-95; full canvas, 105, 370-73, 670-72, 1070-71, 1404-7; grandiloquent, 815-16; gentle humor, 1030; Gothic conventions, 889-91; highly detailed, 724-27, 786-89; high diction, 1227, 1342-45; high diction in dialogue, 687-89; highly ironic, 714-16; highly metaphorical, 128; highly understated, 9-10, 484-85, 1143-44, 1234-36, 1298-1300; homely imagery, 854; humorous, 687-89, 713-14, 815-16, 887-89, 894, 1276, 1399-1401; humorously adventurous, 1094; humorously suspenseful, 892; hyperbolic, 824-26; hyperbole of diction and incident, 887-89, 1354-1356, 1392-94; intentionally crowded canvas, 107-9; intricate plot, 1149-51; italicized Waves, 587-88; ironic humor, 734-37, 1204-6; labyrinthine, 1356-58; letters as narrative device, 1165-67, 1169-71; light, conversational, 755-57; lightly humorous, 710-13, 755-57; literary, 931-32; local color, 812-14, 1021-23; melodramatic, 824-26, 1091-94, 1126-29, 1149-51, 1342-45, 1389-91; metaphorical language, 351-53; mixed first and third person, 1206-8; moralizing, 999-1002, 1002-3, 1152-54, 1327-30; much irony, 110-13; much use of coincidence, 96-99; 710-13; mystical elements, 999-1002, 1002-3; narrative structure repetitive, 783-84; objective, 989-92; occasional letters, 1119; occasional present tense, 1070-71; old-fashioned, 6; oral storytelling, 266-69; overwritten, 1330-34; playful, 829-30; parallel stories, 565-66; parody, 753 (and elsewhere in the *Alice* books); point of view shifting, 1165-67; plodding, 1204-6; poetic, 484-85, 839-41, 1171-73, 1234-36; viewpoint tightly focused, 1196-99; present tense, 459-62, 1169-71, 1290; protagonist omniscient observer, 732-34; proverbial expressions, 248-52; proverbial language, 1298-1300; puns, 19-22, 1208-11; regional dialect, 283; reportorial, 237-40, 989-92, 1361; rich in atmosphere, 714-16; rich language, 227-30; richly descriptive, 812-14; robust imagery, 1211-13; satirical, 19-22, 143-44, 492-95, 701-2, 956-58, 1208-11; sea details, 1379-81; self-conscious, 1094-97; sensory, 217-19, 1036, 1110, 1154-55, 1180-82, 1334-36, 1366-68, 1386-88, 1409-11; sentimental, 55-57; sentimentality, 318-21, 1327-30; setting well evoked, 765-67, 786-89, 903-4; slang, 51; slapstick scenes, 342-43, 920-22; sly humor, 1316-19, 701-2; somewhat archaic, 729-30; songs and poems interjected, 19-22, 55-57, 1208-11; spare, 9-10, 318-21, 1143-44; stories told concurrently, 1025-26; stories within story, 912-14; storytelling, 227-30, 330-32, 593-95, 687-89, 710-13, 755-57, 1155-57; street jargon, 656-58; striking figures, 110-13, 143-44, 523-25; subplots, 1116; subtly humorous, 801-4; surrealistic, 189; survival story conventions, early, 786-89; suspenseful, 1021-23, 1253-56, 1274-76, 1290-91; tall tale, 283-85; tedious, 1111-13; understated, 335-37, 484-85, 765-67; unexpected figures of speech, 610-11; unusual structure, 1025-26; very dated, 105-7; Victorian melodrama, 1399-1401; vigorous and humorous, 829-30; without climax, 717-20; witty, 227-30, 734-37; wordplay, 41-42, 127-29, 19-22, 797-99, 887-89, 1094-97, 1119-21, 1208-11, 1211-13, 1313-15, 1354-56, 1388-89; zany characters, 19-22, 1208-11. *See also* tone.

submarines: German, World War II, 210, 262-63, 401-3; two-man, 27-28, 29, 368-70

subways, 84, 797-98, 1360

substitutions: dark gypsy male baby for blond girl baby, 1150; trumpets, 1062-63

succession, to throne through woman, 1117-19, 1161-64, 1171-72

Suffolk: 17th century, 306-9; early 19th century, 190-91; late 20th century, 306-9; shipwreck off, 595

Suffolk family, 275, 324, 350-51, 454, 1024, 1404-5

Sugar Mouse, 149

suicides: assumed, 1167; attempted, 340, 411, 461, 820, 1390; by fire, 845, 1104; by shooting, 835; contemplated, 16-17, 925; notes, spurious, 809-10; of foppish noble, 619; of guardian, 807; of Iceni queen, 1119; of tribal leader, 774; of Mohorrim, 124; of mother, 852; of serf, 718; of slaves, 240; of uncle, 1349; presumed, 809-10; thought imminent, 492; to stop family curse, 1198

suitcase: bear's, 84; contains banknotes, 1335

suitors, 237, 242, 262, 264, 267, 457-58, 686, 738, 821, 828, 839, 928-29, 1109, 1161-63, 1155-57

suits: blue serge, salvaged, 259; inflatable survival, 946; lavender, 920

Suliman, 569, 698

sultans, of Turkey, 213-15

THE SUMMER AFTER THE FUNERAL, 440, 1165-67

THE SUMMER BIRDS, 206, 366, 393-94, 1167-69

The Summer-House, 531

THE SUMMER PEOPLE, 1169-71, 1247

summons: by fairy cock, 271; to court, 447; to fiscal's, 1123-26

sun bringers, king, 40

Sundays: first, spent with mother's sister, 703; place, sought, 1329-30

Sunday School, 620-21

Sunday School Treat, 1160
Sunderland, Dr., 224
Sun God, 1321
SUN HORSE, MOON HORSE, *1171-73*, 1176
Sunny Bay, mid-20th century, 923-24, 638
Supernature, alternative to religion, 93
Superstition, 976
superstitions: about St. Cuthbert, 93; about witches and omens, 1405; African, 249; against ghosts, hobgoblins, 864; encouraged by leader, 50, 303; ghosts, hobgoblins, 450; Irish, 259-60, 543-46, 642-43; local, about foundling, 1410; local lore, 644; machine-hating, witch baiting, 449, 1336-38; of first mate, 1064; Scottish tribal, 1190; Slavonic, 1300-2; Tibetan, 334; to keep city safe, 370-72; various in India, 651-54; witches, 637
The Supreme Prize and Other Poems, 1253
surfboarders, South Pacific blacks, 256
surgeons: in English army, 340-42; junior, 632; ship's, 509. *See also* doctors; healers.
surgery, plastic, planned, 89
Surprised by Joy: The Shape of My Early Life, 700
surrenders: Irish to English, 445-46, 500; play battle, 120
survival novels, 134-36, 136-38, 186-88, 255-57, 335-37, 365-66, 414-16, 495-97, 586-88, 716-17, 786-89, 893-94, 1043-46, 1330-34, 1368-69
survivors: abused children, 200; against Romans, 1161-64; at sea, 743; battlefield, 339-42; by stealing from bars, 310; colonies, 157-58; colony, condemned as commune, 158; from 18th century war in France, 339-42; from wrecked boat, 649; in North Sea, 946; journey across Europe, 1098-99; of adversity, 377-79; of battle, 294; of bombing, 210; of destroyed warren, 535, 557; of extermination, 134; of mine accident, demented, 34-35; of various adversities, 1, 2; of volcanic eruption, 828; of wrecked ketch, 763; shipwreck, 204, 786-89, 1043-46; sole, of

mutineers, 522; through initiative, 49-50; tough kids, 521
survival suits, inflatable, 225, 983
Susan, 168, 344, 408, 414, 504, 1067, 1342-45
Susan, Queen of Narnia, 561-62
SUSAN BAILEY, 834-35, 963, *1173*
Susannah Mallory, 583
SUSAN OLDKNOW, 172-73, 195, 217-19, 591-92, 616, 770, 859, 1067, *1173-74*, 1231
SUSAN PEVENSIE, 185, 321, 356, 376, 560-62, 710-11, 742, 864, 893, 961, 994-95, 1009, 1093, *1174*
SUSAN POOLEY, 303, 307-8, *1174-75*
SUSAN WALKER, 614, 972, 974, 1047, *1175*, 1177-79, 1340-42
suspense novels, 33-36, 200-1, 237-40, 242-44, 281-83, 286-87, 287-88, 304-6, 373-75, 578-81, 645-46, 714-16, 824-26, 889-91, 896-97, 906-7, 917-19, 989-92, 1076-78, 1156-57, 1187-89, 1376-79
Sussex: late 6th century, 294-96; early 14th century, 1017-20; late 15th century, 683-84; 16th century, 581-83; 18th century, 304-6; mid-19th century, 763-65; mid-20th century, 403-5, 434-36; Elizabethan era, 581-83, 701; modern times, 931-32
SUTCLIFF, ROSEMARY, 116, 153, 155, 293, 337, 347, 672, 679, 771, 1036, 1085, 1088, 1117, 1171, *1175-77*, 1258, 1319, 1394
SVEN, 263, 401-3, 881, *1177*
Svendale, 117
Swallow (boat), 614, 1178-79
Swallows, 874, 949, 1047
swallows: pull ship, 1145-46; talking, 1145
SWALLOWS AND AMAZONS, 390, 1016-17, *1177-79*
Swamp, Gwendolyn, 1354
swamps: Australia, 535, 714; crossed by night, 217. *See also* bogs; marshes.
Swannie (boat), 517, 946, 982-84, 1088
swans, white, killed, 1320
A SWARM IN MAY, 225, 794, *1180-82*
swarms, of bees, 1181
swarts, 1343-44
Swayne family, 1009-12
sweatshops, 677, 807-9, 1104
Sweeney Todd, 777
Sweeney Todd, the Demon Barber of Fleet Street, 37, 270,

286, 591, 820
sweepers, crossing, 55-56
sweeps, chimney, 1328
Sweetbriar, the horse, 419-20
sweetheart, lost to Selkie, 1409
Sweet Singer, 1086
SWIFT, JONATHAN, 508, *1182-83*
swimmers, 125, 370, 383-84
swims, near-fatal, 1022
SWINDELLS, ROBERT E (DWARD), 156, *1183*
swindlers, international, 183-84
swineherds: helpful, 1394; story of Princess and, 783
swings, buried, 1141
Swiss Family Robinson, 707, 776
Swiss people, in England, future, 149
Switzerland: mid-20th century, 597-98, 619-20, 1096-99, 1348-49; 21st century, 989-92, 1359-61; German refugees in, 31; surgeon, 354; World War II, 1096-99, 1348-49
The Sword and the Circle: King Arthur and the Knights of the Round Table, 1037, 1175
Sword at Sunset, 1176
Sword of Islam, 214
The Sword of the Spirits, 232
swords: blue, 247; cast into water, 1038; dwarf's, 344; elven, 96; fragment of in skull, 1259-60; heirloom, 1085; magic, 359, 396, 711, 998, 1142, 1343, 1375; on marriage bed, 1118; silver paper knife, 619, 1097-99; swallowers, ex-fair, 698
Sword Trilogy, 232
Sybil Bowles, 1166-67
SYBILLA BUN, 922, 1035, *1183*
Sydney family, 459, 581-82
Sykes family, 43-47, 63, 321, 470, 532, 566, 1013-14, 1087, 1243
Sylvia, 1099, 1400-1
Sylvia Brown, 68-71
Sylvia Pilling, 945, 968, 1169-70
Sylvie and Bruno, 181
Sylvie and Bruno Concluded, 181
symbols: Christian, 870; iron lily, 459; lark, laurel, 683-84; need for cultural, 856; obvious, 1, 2, 124, 150, 725, 914, 930, 961, 1170, 1242, 1321, 1336; labored, 1227; obvious, dolphin tattoo and ring, 680-81; obvious, forest of security, 684; obvious, of hope, 952; obvious, silver paper knife, 1099;

obvious, stone head, 779; of freedom, wooden foil, 772; of treaty, Red Spear, 123; overused, 360. See *also* motifs; patterns.
symposia: on futurism, 1295. See *also* conferences; protests; rallies; riots.
Syrup, the cat, 484, 639, 697, 1335

TABITHA PALMER, 498, 533-34, *1185*
tables, stone, place of execution, meeting, 995
Tackleton, Mr., 267-69
Tadhg Hernon, 544
Tahiti, 257
TAHLEVI, 658, 829-30, *1185-86*
Tailbiter, 396-97
tailors, 193, 738, 1116
tails: bloody lambs', 1084; docking of horses', 106; donkey loses, 358, 1388; guinea pig nips, 1186; of mouse, restored, 996; shot away, 388
Taleel, 123
Talent Is Not Enough: Mollie Hunter on Writing for Children, 574
talents: need to develop, 1125; radio search, 1314
A Tale of a Tub, 1182
A Tale of Two Cities, 313
tales: in shape of tail, 20, 23; literary, 395-97, 462-63, 659-62
Tales from Shakespeare, 441
Tales from the Borders, 410
Tales of a Fairy Court, 679
Tales of Joe and Timothy, 357
Tales of Norse Gods and Heroes, 969
THE TALES OF OLGA DA POLGA, 126, *1186-87*
Tales of the British People, 969
Tales of Troy and Greece, 679
Tales Out of School: A Survey of Children's Fiction, 1253
Tales Told Near a Crocodile: Stories from Nyanza, 526
A Tale to Tell: Stories by Young People from Northern Ireland, 1066
Talgo, the pony, 1367
Talisman, the pony, 389
talismans: amber piece shaped like Thor's hammer, 116-17; carnelian stone, 1190; stone ax, 1025, 1203; stone of power, 414
Talking Animals, 687-89
TALKING IN WHISPERS, *1187-89*, 1334
Talking Trees, 687
tall tales, 41-42, 203-4, 283-85, 388-89, 489-92, 797-99,

1353-56, 1392-94

Talore, 1319-20

Tam, the dog, 1156

tamburans, 565-66, 613

Tam Lynn, 411

Tan Coul, 412, 1238

Tangle, 462-63

Tank Commander, 1346

tanks, fantasy, commandeered, 253

tantrums, king throws, 902

tapestries: 108, 582, 1122. *See also*
   embroideries; needlepoint; samplers.

TAPKESOS, 114-15, 754, *1189-90*

TARAN, 148, 245, 333, 884, 1161-63,
   1190

Tararo, 256-57

Tarbutt, Mrs., 1397

Tarnhelm, 344

Tarrant, Ann, *37-38*, 1170

Tarrant family, 968-69

tarts, stolen, 21

Tash, 687-88

Tashbaan, 561

Tate, Robert, 195

Tate family, 32, 289-90, 647, 656,
   862, 1313-15

Tate Wilkinson, 169

tattoos: Dane, of forehead and
   cheekbones, 1298; dolphin on
   shoulder, 680; facial, 270; Mark
   of Horse Lord, 772; of British
   slave, 347, 375; snake patterns,
   539

taverns, 1127, 1351, 1380

Tavistock Fair, 1386

Taxco, Mexico, early 20th century, 399, 601-2

taxes: back owing, 45-47; words
   in lieu of, 1014

taxi drivers, 41, 249, 285, 411

Tawny, the pony, 1387

tea: parties, mad, never-ending,
   20, 23, 334, 753, 767; pots, mouse
   stuffed in, 335; shops, party at,
   736; shops, village, 174, 1072-73;
   with famous actress, 384

teachers: acerbic, 1180; ballet,
   69; conservative, 818; dancing, rescued, 1385-86; disliked,
   863; doting bear, 71; drama,
   820; English, 44-46, 704, 734-
   36, 1013-14, 1234; ex-college,
   of Gaelic literature, 1048; ex-
   drama, 283, 1077; ex-phys. ed.,
   1032-33; French intellectual,
   828; funny old, 734-36; girl to
   live with, 1166; headmistress of

village school, 62; head of local
   Home Guard, 750; helper at village
   school, 95; helpful woman, 819;
   history, 876-78, 910;
   inspiring, 130; killed in air
   raid, 735-36; literature,
   drowned, 809-10; mathematics,
   809; medicine, 356; mentor, 734-
   36; music, 44-46, 86-87, 143,
   677, 1003-4, 1073; militaristic,
   844; of flying, 354-55, 1057;
   man, 1149-50; of mountain climbing, 809-10; of spies, 743; of
   wolf cubs, 71; on holiday, 119-21;
   physically and verbally abusive, 844; possessive of father,
   98; prejudiced against blacks,
   1262; reformed, 844; riding, 419;
   supportive, 880, 910; thought murdered, 810; too old to fly, 1168;
   unsupportive to young writer, 734-
   35; vocal, 668, 685-86, 937; well-
   meaning, tactless, 318-19. *See
   also* headmasters; headmistresses;
   schoolteachers; tutors.

Teaching, 1373

THE TEAM, 85, 966, 1007, *1190-92*

teams, Pony Club, 615

Tear, 1343

tears: give princess gravity, 702;
   pool of, 20, 22, 324, 343; release
   prisoner, 1330

Teavee, Mike, 203

technology: changing, 9-10; lost,
   990; pre-industrial, 1336-38

Teddington, 1158

Ted Kenet, 235

TEDDY BELL, 538, 900, *1192*

Teddy boys: 863, 1115-16. *See also*
   hoodlums; thugs; vandals.

Teesdale family, 89, 467-77, 531,
   555-57

teeth: collected from battlefield
   corpses, 340; false, ill-fitting,
   843; of giant, 339

teetotalers, clergyman, 1148

Teirtu, Harp of, 1357-58

Teitri, the horse, 295-96, 1293

telegrams, 186, 492, 705, 1178

telegraph, dead, 926

teleporting, by TV, 811

telescopes, stolen, 143-44, 186, 530

television: control through, 1987;
   interviewer, 690-91; people in,
   29, 411; personalities, 539, 566.
   See also TV.

Telmarines, 893, 995, 1264

Telyn Teirtu, 528

temperance songs, 399
temper: results in loss of flash-
light, 194; slow fuse, 99
Temple of Tan, 122
Temple Rock, 1196
temples, 122, 196
Templeton family, 175, 806, 959,
1339
tenacity: of abused children, 197-
200. *See also* perseverance;
persistence; pluck; resource.
Tenchebrai, battle of, 674
tenements: London, 519-21; London,
collapse, 1224
Tennant family, 1151-54
Tenniel, Sir John, 19, 22-23, 1208
Tennis Shoes, 1157
tenth century: B.C., England,
South Downs, 1319-22; A.D.,
England, southwest coast, 116-19;
Constantinople, 116-19; Ireland,
Dublin, 116-19
Tepoztlan, Mexico, early 20th centu-
ry, 601-2
Terak the Giant, 1036
Teraphim, 624-26, 1205-6
Terence, 159
TERENCE MUGG, 845, 1104, *1192-93*,
1355-56, 1397
Teresa Fay, 1133-36
TERESA GISELLI, 31, 1105-6, *1193*
Teresh the Stern, 624-26, 1204-6
Teri, 114-15
Terminals, 157
TERRAPIN, Tom, *1193-94*, 97-99
*Terror by Night: A Book of Strange
Stories*, 1306
terrorists: amateur, 283; anti-
family, 525, 606, 917-19, 1265;
Chile, 94; Free People, 335; Green
Revolution, environmentalists,
33-36, 592, 778; half-cousin, 645-
46; Irish, 343; in family, 288-89;
international, 74, 907; leader of
after nuclear war, 1033; Mattean,
11; robbers attack village, 10;
schoolboy gang, 245; South American, 11, 219-20, 283, 330, 855,
857, 1076-78; threaten royal family, 918; women, 29-30. *See also*
communists; radicals.
Terry Burch, 184-85
TERRY CHAUNTESINGER, 668, 685-86,
1194
Terry family, 196, 536-37, 904,
1034-35
Terry on the Fence, 52
Terry Timpson, 896

Terry Wooten, 377-79
TESHOO LAMA, 651-54, *1194-95*
TESS BAGTHORPE, 922, *1195*
Tessie, the elephant, 89, 205, 425,
1248-49
tests: by hypnotism, 743; by magic,
743; by ordeal, 739; for membership in club, 490; of inflatable
suit, 225; stolen, 1270; to climb
tree, 490; to lay wreath on Byron's
tomb, 490; to ride milkman's cart,
491
Tewker, Theodore, 333, 853, 1195,
1265-67
Texans, in England, 219
Tey, Mr., 862
Thamar, 522, 658, 737, 829-30, 895
Thames: origin of name, 397; valley,
pre-Arthurian period, 395-97
thanks, told posthumously, 431
Thatcher family, 179, 468-69
Thayli, the rabbit, 95, 1332
Thea Parker, 1191
theaters: eighteenth century, 169-
71; hiding-place, 1090; life in,
169-71, 876; managers, 169-71;
monkey performer, 840; produc-
tions in, 69; scenes in, 84
*Theater Shoes; or, Other People's
Shoes*, 1157
thefts: by weatherman, 1338; bicycle, 156, 164, 704; biscuits for
secret garden, 898; books, 959;
brother's clothes, 790; camera, 877; cheerfully admitted,
142; cigarettes, 518; Circlet of
Deirdre, 216; church keys, 78;
coal, 1277; cookies, 176; diadem,
236; document, 1107, 1108; deer,
544-46; diamond necklace, 183; dog
steals recording equipment, 1420;
doll, 723; dollhouse furniture,
147; domestic animals, 1151-52;
donkey, 675; egg, 954; fire, 65;
food, 73, 74, 1193; food and blanket, 1368; food and file, 492-93;
food for gorilla, 1154; food for
starving children, 53-54, 692;
from clergyman's larder, 272; from
dollhouse, 133; from drowned body,
85;
goblet, 552; harp, 737; horse,
409, 1383; industrial secrets,
984; inheritance, 1114; ivory
chesspiece, 1039-41; jackdaws of
eyeglasses, 931-32; jewels, 195,
541-42, 1397; keys, 552; lead from
church roof, 78; letter, 1318;

life-force, 150; liquor, 843–
44; mannequin's leg, 541; money,
953, 955; monkey, 839; motor car
by Toad, 1383; motorcycle, 951;
mutton, blankets, lamp, 906; nail
scissors knife and hat pin, 135; on
dare, 287; pages from diary, 790;
paper, 730; pearls, 13, 642–43;
Roman Eagle, 349; sheep, 259–60;
ship, 317, 1255; stone face, 1115–
16; table, 556; tape recorders,
286–87, 591, 777, 843;
tarts, 21; teacher's cam-
era, 99, 806; teacher's money,
1270; telescope, 143–44, 186;
tests, 1270; to tease bully, 592;
thwarted, 212; trumpet, 1062–63;
two plums, 718; valuable painting,
797; valuable Chinese treasure,
1105–6; Viking artifacts, 838;
Viking boat, 1101–2; will, suspected, 178; witch's elixir, 1393;
wool, 234, 519, 791, 827, 1402–3;
yacht seized by customs, 764. *See
also* robberies.
theocracies, 121–24
Theoden, King of Rohan, 805
THEODORE TEWKER, 333, 853, *1195*,
1265–67
THEO GREENGRASS, 62, 365, 953–55,
987, *1195–96*
therapists, speech, 826
There, 168, 538, 891
There and Back Again, 550
There's No Escape, 1075
They Raced for Treasure, 1075
thieves: Black Men, 725–26; captured, 30; Elizabethan, 876;
foster girl, 1368; gang, 246, 278,
1352; in Robin Hood tradition,
425; Irish, 186; jewel, 1397; manservant, 218–19; pickpockets,
1087, 1107, 1108, 1186; refugee
children, 1098; schoolboy, 286–
87, 1296–70; seeking pedigree,
758; servant, 428; shoplifter,
640; starving boy, 1417; steal
ransom, 1019; supposed, 1205;
tinkers, 543. *See also* bandits;
burglars; robbers.
Thimbles, 1391
Thing, 117
Thingummy, 1100
third century: B.C., Mesopotamia,
624–27; England, 1088–91
THE THIRD EYE, 573, *1196–
99*
thirst, overpowering, 661

thirteenth century, Ireland, Gal-
way, 215–17
38 Poems, 1257
The Thirty-Nine Steps, 160
Thomas, 1025–26
THOMAS, 162, *1199–202*
Thomas, the cat, 477, 1283
Thomas Egerton, 1199–201
Thomas family, 397–98, 501, 598–99,
667–68
THOMAS FITZAMORY, 916–17, 1137, *1202*
THOMAS HEYWOOD, *1202*, 1351–53
Thomas Hood Raleigh, 558–59
Thomas Kempe, 48–49, 92–93, 451–
52, 595–96, 862
Thomas Piper, 412–14
THOMAS REEVES, 586–87, 828, *1202–3*
THOMAS ROWLEY, 611, 1025–26, *1203*
THOMAS SMITH, 623, *1203*, 1317
Thomas the Knife, 1012–13
Thomas the Rhymer, 411
THOMAS TOREE, 760, 938–39, *1203–4*
Thomas Trumpington, 154
Thomas Venables, 1026, 1203
Thompson family, 314, 334, 514–16,
528, 599–600, 629, 647–48, 838,
1056–57, 1242–43, 1315–16, 1364–
66
THORIN OAKENSHIELD, 95, 552–53, *1204*
Thorkill Fairhair, 1298–1300
Thormod Sitricson, 116–18
thorn, life-restoring, 1093
Thornham, 375
Thornton School, 486
Thoroughbood, Mr., 107
thought control, by capping, 1359
thralls: Saxon, 930; rings, Saxon,
295–96
threats: attached to arrow, 102;
by convict, 492; by Turks, 371–
72; from Christianity, 548; from
witches, 548; of boarding school,
478; of burning barn full of
children, 312; of having dog destroyed, 343; of having to leave
school, 518; of invasion, 509; of
murder, 1293; of murder for lega-
cy, 426; of quick death, 279;
sexual, 603; to blot out sun and
rain, 512; to break boy's back,
656; to destroy Eagle, 350; to kill
several, 615; to make conversation
public, 673; to old people, 289; to
reveal unauthorized home, 466; to
royal family, 918
THE THREE BROTHERS OF UR, 438, 624,
1204–6
THREE LIVES FOR THE CZAR, 984, *1206–8*

The Three Mulla-Mulgars, 302
Three Rainbows, 82
Three Rocks, 258
The Three Royal Monkeys; or, The Three Mulla-Mulgars, 302
THREE TIMES SEVEN, *1208*, 1290
The Three Toymakers, 831
THROUGH THE LOOKING-GLASS, AND WHAT ALICE FOUND THERE, 180, *1208-11*
Thrower family, 497
thrushes, assist hobbit, 552, 1107
thugs: 170, 278, 612, 613, 798, 1380; from Glasgow, 245; Maltese, 401-2, 1177. *See also* hoodlums; Teddy boys; vandals.
Thul, India, late 20th century, 526, 1302-5
THUNDER AND LIGHTNINGS, 771, *1211-13*
THUNDER IN THE SKY, 966, *1213-15*
THUNDER OF VALMY, *1215-18*, 1252
Thursday, Margaret, 560, 694-95, 959, 1220-23
THE THURSDAY KIDNAPPING, 429, *1218-20*
Thursdays, regular, 532
THURSDAY'S CHILD, 1157, *1220-23*
Thursday Street, 359
Thwaite, Sam, 537
Tiberias, 453, 670
Tibet, early 20th century, 333-34, 1265-67
Tibetan language, 1266
Tib Street, 539
"tick," 891
tickets: golden to chocolate factory, 203; won to chocolate factory, 479, 810, 1297, 1305
Tickler, 608
tides, 808, 1105, 1341, 1377
Tiffany Jones family, 722-24
Tiffy, the water rat, 366
Tiger Lily, 957, 961
tigers, talking lame, 11, 630, 1084-85
The Tiger's Bones, 570
"Tiger-Tiger!," 631
The Tiger Who Came to Tea, 647
Tigger, 563
Tiggy Heritage, 155
Tiler family, 1269-70
Till She Stoop, 1164
Tilly Slowboy, 266
Tim Black, 73-74, 520-21, 522
TIM CHARLTON, 160, 281-83, 523, *1223*
Tim Curtin, 1152-53
time: as continuum, 49, 211-13, 564-66, 1140-41, 1234-36, 1288,

1291; backward in, 533; different dimensions, 176; disrupted by candle being moved, 352; examination of, 22; exploration of nature of, 1237-38, 1240-42; machines, boat, 1377; Narnian different from Earth, 712; new dimension, 451; otherworld, different from Earth-time, 875; personified, 22, 753; rabbit worries about, 1362; retreats into past, 264; seen as coil, 367; transferences in, 365; transience of, 199; travels, 307-9, 532, 609, 614, 641, 667; wrong dimension, 472
TIME OF TRIAL, 162, *1223-25*
Tim Hoggart, 599, 1396-97
TIM INGRAM, 821, 883, 944-45, 1024, *1225*, 1237
TIMMO JONES, 50-51, 942, *1225-26*, 1326-27
Timmus, 50, 61, 141-42, 948
Timothy, 606-8
Timothy, the pony, 389
Timperley, Erica, 59
Timperley family, 364, 523-25, 1042, 1283
Timpson family, 836, 883, 896
TIMUR VEN, 214-15, *1226*, 1296
Tina Carson, 243-44
Ti nan Ogoun, 1227
The Tinder Box, 488
The Tingalary Bird, 801
TINKER BELL, 956, 958, 961, *1226*
Tinker family, 449, 1055-56, 1336-38
tinkers, 543-46, 1009-10, 1152-53
Tintagel, 1259
TINY TIM CRATCHIT, 228-29, *1226-27*
tips: anonymous, 182; coal refuse, 1277
TIRIAN, King of Narnia, 377, 603, 687-89, *1227*, 1027
TIR NAN OG, 765-67, *1227*, 642, 643, 830
Tiro, 627-28
Tisroc of Calormen, 43, 561
TITTY WALKER, 972-73, 1047, 1178-79, *1227-28*, 1340-42
TITUS CARVER, Uncle, 399, 601-2, *1228*
Tizzy Alexander, 1149-50
TIZZY RUSSELL, 227, 317, 422-24, 775, *1228-29*
Toad Face, 519, 1402
Toad Hall: 65, 828; invaded by Stoats and Weasels, 1384
Toadhill Flax, the horse, 846, 1190-91

TOAD OF TOAD HALL, 65, 828, 1021, *1229*, 1328-84

Toad of Toad Hall, 812

toads, conceited, 1229

toasts, famous, "God bless us...." 1227

To Be an Author: An Autobiography, 25

Tobias Pennifeather, 153

toboggans, 74

Toby, 1197-98

TOBY GARLAND, 4, 364, 763-64, 1068, *1229*

TOBY OLDKNOW, 16, 211-12, 409, *1229-30*

Toby Trevelyan, 890

Todcaster, England, late 20th century, 752, 824, 835, 874, 1192, 1353-54

Todcaster Palm Orchestra, 518

Todcaster witches, 376

Toft family, 897-99

To Greenland's Icy Mountains: The Story of Hans Egede, Explorer, Coloniser, Missionary, 445

toilets, flush, terrifying, 670

To Kill a King, 986

tollkeepers, 825

TOLKIEN, J(OHN) R(ONALD) R(EUEL), 163, 395, 405, 550, 554, 700, 717, *1230-31*

Tolkien trilogy, 405

TOLLY, 16, 211-13, 217-19, 373-75, 409, 578, 591, 710, 800, 859, 980-81, 1154, 1230, *1231-32*

TOLLY DORKING, 88, 110, 111-13, *1232*

Tom (*Little Plum*), 722

TOM (*Red Shift*), 597, 1025-26, *1232*

Tom (*The Water-Babies*), 363, 851, 853, 1327-30

Tomahawk Club, 13, 193

Tom Ass, 1232-34

TOM ASS; OR, THE SECOND GIFT, 695, *1232-34*

Tom Bombadil, 406

The Tomb of Reeds, 82

Tom Bowman, 738-39

tombs, of St. Cuthbert, 1376

tombstones: 229; inscriptions, 397

TOM DANDO, 42, 529, 996, *1234*, 1356-58

Tom Fell, 818-19

Tom Figgis, 1268

"Tom Fobbled," 1235

TOM FOBBLE'S DAY, 399, 444, 914, *1234-36*, 1281

TOM GOODENOUGH, 49, 61, 134-35, 136-37, 811, 857, *1236*

TOM HENCHMAN, 190-91, 356, 595, 880, *1236-37*

TOM INSKIP, 821, 883, 944-45, 1024, 1225, *1237*

Tomlin, 1301-2

TOM LONG, 59, 532-33, *1237-38*, 1240-42, 1279

TOM LYNN, 412-14, 485, 590, 694, 697, 833, 893, 987-88, 1065, *1238*

Tom Mackenzie, 1049-50, 1058

Tom Meikle, 47

TOM'S MIDNIGHT GARDEN, 949, *1240-42*

TOM MOORHOUSE, 109, 197-200, 264, *1238-39*

TOMMY SEAGRAVE, 787-88, 859, *1239*

Tommy Stubbins, 731, 988, 1309-11

Tom Newsome, 1387

TOM OAKLEY, 467-69, 851, *1239-40*, 1372-73

Tom-o'-Bedlams, 154

Tomorrow Will Come, 26

Tom Piper, 697

Tom Pritchard, 311

Tom Pullen, 85, 1379-80

Tom's Tower, 797

Tom Tiddler's Ground, 1247

Tom Tiddler's Ground: A Book of Poetry for the Junior and Middle Schools, 301

Tom Tit Tot, 1130

"Tom Tit Tot," 393, 1094

TOM TRELOAR, 430-32, 433, 873, *1242*

Tom Twist, 729-30

tone: abstractly mysterious, 1409-11; accusatory, 1187-89; affectionate, 385-86, 486-87, 724-27, 994-96, 1382-85, 1388-89; allegorical, 1002-3; arch, 716-17, 1111-13, 1327-30; bleak, 1276-78; breezy, 416-18; chatty, 912-14, 1094-96; chilling, 307-11; cheerful, 606-08; condescending, 84-85; condescending, 173-75, 1032; cozy, 5-6, 266-69, 713-14; cynical, 339-42; dramatically quiet, 1241; dreamy, 1167-69; dreamy legend, 1409-11; eerie, 824-26; foreboding, 304-6, 645-46, 1187-89; good-natured, 1306-9; grim, 156-58, 1009-12, 1244-45; haunting, 564-66; high-minded, 685-87; high suspense, 1076-78; idyllic, 969, 1169-71; impending danger, 286-87, 287-88, 411-14; improving, 999-1002; intimate, 1114-17, 1196-99; instructive, 1017-20, 1204-6; ironic, 1149-51; jolly, 266-69, 1111-13, 1177-79;

lighthearted, 687-89, 1232-
34; literary, 299-301; "little
girl" story, 818-20; loving, 84-
85; matter-of-fact simplicity,
1145-46; melodramatic, 994-96;
mock-serious, 930-32; moralistic,
786-89, 974-80; naive, 689-92; of
legend, 335-37; often sentimental, 710-13; old fashioned, 382-85;
ominous, 889-91; pessimistic,
156-58; pious, 974-80; playful,
252-54, 395-97, 927-30; playfully
ironic, 847-849;
precious, 1186-87; quietly amusing, 801-4; quietly expectant,
1334-36; sentimental, moralistic, 720-22; sententious, 786-89;
serious, 1206-8; somber, 370-73;
spooky, 1325-27; suspenseful,
1265-67, 1339-40, 1342-45;
tongue-in-cheek, 41-42, 143-
44, 815-16, 829-30, 889, 970-71,
996-99, 1029-31, 1141-43, 1353-
56, 1388-89; upbeat, 79-81;
Victorian, 5-6; well-sustained
suspense, 906-7; whimsical, 1388-
89; wholesome, 724-27. See also
style.
TONY BOYD, 314, 515, 599, 1242-43,
1365-66
Took family, 132, 406-8, 437, 805,
981-82, 1056
"Toomai of the Elephants," 632
Toonits, 733
toothpaste makers, 203
Tooting, mid-19th century, 52-54,
74, 262, 692, 821
Topmeadow, 722
Tops Standish, 236-37, 915, 1268-69,
1412
Torgils Auk, 871, 1243
Tories, 152
Torment, the bloodhound, 815
Torolv the Fatherless, 242
TORQUIL, 44-46, 1087, 1243
TORQUIL MACVINISH, 642-43, 914-15,
1243-44
Torre, Thomas, 1203-4
Torrey, Helen, 1386
torture, 28, 279-81, 465, 711, 1085-
86, 1187-89
Toseland, 211-13, 1231, 1229-30
toshers, 508, 808-9
totalitarianism, 505-9, 1187-89,
1332, 1359-61
To Tame a Sister, 63
Tot Bourke, 61, 474-75
TO TELL MY PEOPLE, 986, 1244-45

totem animals, bear, 279-81
TOTTIE PLANTAGANET, 330-31, 850,
1245-46
Totty Feather, 1168
tourist attractions, 138-39, 369-
70, 411, 837
tourist traps, model village, 138-
39, 837
Tournament, Queen of, 1360
tournaments, 1360
tours, of chocolate factory, 203-4,
865
Tower of the Stars, 531
tower rooms, in castle, 999, 1002
towers: as home, 360; as refuge,
361; church, 272; circular, 724;
defensive, 387; of stone, 1161;
restored Roman garrison, 159, 280
towns, wrecked by dragons, 552
TOWNSEND, JOHN ROWE, 276, 514, 536,
586, 578, 895, 1169, 1246-47, 1364
The Town that Went South, 659
towpaths, back in time, 197
Towser, the dog, 253
toymakers, 267
The Toymaker's Daughter, 831
toys: of dead brother, 7; talking
soldiers, 1274-75
trades, horse for stew by Toad, 1383
traders: ancient wealthy, 624-26;
fur, 733
tradition: of club, 152; protector
of, 1373
Trafalgar, battle of, 190, 356, 1237
Traherne, Michael, 84
The Trailer, 77-78, 753
trainees, wildlife, 1123
trainers: elephant, 632; for circus
children, 205; school rugby, 1363
trains: attacked by wolves, 1400;
dream world, 1209; for school,
497, 994; held up, 1098; night, to
There, 168, 538; out of service,
735; relic of, 1360; Toad rides,
1383; to inner London, 1147; wreck
planned, 354
traitors: 454, 696, 710-11, 848,
965, 1162, 1190, 1213-15; Prioress
to Robin Hood, 717. See also turncoats.
Traitor's Gate: A Historical Play in
Three Acts, 1164
Tramecksan, 509
tramps: eccentric, middle-aged
brothers, 168, 538, 620, 891-92;
grandfather, 955; philosophical,
848
trances: berserk, 746; faked, 557-58

transformations: baby to adult,
417-18; baby to pig, 20, 23; black
man to white, 160; blind fiddler to yellow-haired man, 359;
boy to donkey, 1233; boy to dragon, 377, 1307; boy to giant, 417;
boy to infant, 189; boy to size of
a mouse, 922; boy to water-baby,
1328; by love, 332-33; car to various forms, 221-23; cat to grin, 20,
211; cat to kitten, 189; child to
beautiful woman, 63; children to
mice, 429; children to wrinkled
old people, 462; chimney sweep to
water-baby, 363; dog to King of
Golden River, 661; dog to luminary, 75; evil witch to pile of
clothes, 150; fairy queen as cat,
675;
fat boy to thin boy, 58; frog to
woman, 209; girl to old woman, 568;
girl to water-baby, 363; girls to
kangaroos, 1385; house to castle,
417; humans to mice, 1393; iden-
tities of schoolgirls, 206-7; in
size, 18, 19-21, 22, 1002; in time,
206-8, 287-88; kelpie to black
horse, 642-43; king and retinue
to stalactites, 352; maid to frog,
209; maiden to owl, 932; man to
black stone, 661; miser to generous man, 353; of North Wind, 55-57;
old to young people, 463; old woman to young, 1002; pigskin wallet
to sow, 189; prince to donkey, 562;
queen to kitten, 1024-25; seal to
young man, 1155-56; size and species, 1327-30; skirts to snakes,
208; sailors to thugs, 156-57;
to eagle, 116; to owl, 116; to
stylish appearance, 97; war camp
to cultured court, 760; war leader to gentle king, 760; warrior
to black stone, 115, 754; witch
to coffee table, 836; witch to
tottering woman, 375; various,
325-38, 913, 1001, 1035-36, 1067,
1096, 1354-55
translators, 116, 310
transportation devices, Tripods,
239
transport, farmer of, 532
Tranter family, 483-84, 638-39,
669, 697, 874-75, 1020, 1334-
36
trap doors: over harbor, 401; old
house, 515
trapeze artists, 235

trappers: African black, 743; in
mine, 130; of animals, 716; wicked, 725-26; Yoruba, 1068
traps: animal, 1120; caterpillar,
1042; collossal hole, 584; for army, 1086; for Heffalump, 563; for
Romans, 1162; for tiger, 1085;
lobster, 544; rabbit, 1331; rat,
715
travel agencies, smuggling drugs,
1063
TRAVELERS BY NIGHT, 15, 1247-50
Travels into Several Remote Nations
of the World, by Lemuel Gulliver,
508, 1182
The Travels of Oggy, 695
TRAVERS, P(AMELA) L(YNDON), 779,
781, 783, 784, 1250-51
treachery: against Roman Emper-
or of Britain, 1088-91; among
Arthur's knights, 1037-39; by Ape,
687; by brother, 1205; by celestial companion, 326-28; by Danes,
871; by doctor and butler, 1000-1;
by goblins, 1002-3; by Lombards,
729-30; by neighbors, World War
II, 898-99; by Normans, 1085;
by Prioress, 147, 717; by sailors, 1380; by ship's crew, 256-57;
by uncle, 216, 409, 995; by Viking leader, 91-92, 1298-99; from
within, 333; much, 1114, 1120-
21; of wife, 114-15, 116; planned,
91; political intrigue, 1412-15;
proposed, abandoned, 864; warnings of, 300. See also treason.
Treacle, the pony, 389
treacle: as food, 335; pudding, 1271
TREADGOLD, MARY, 1251-52, 1339
TREASE, (ROBERT) GEOFFREY, 145,
1215, 1252-53
treason: 247, 447, 673, 1405. See
also treachery.
treasure: ancestral, 551-53; boy's,
1087; buried, 89, 100, 172, 282,
1110, 1132, 1147; chest, 1; childhood, 486; Codling jewels, 858;
coining, 463-64; digging for, 334;
discovered, 37, 219, 550; divining
for, 19; dragon's, 396-97; dug
for in back yard, 1147; dwarves',
1204; family, 94, 1058; hidden,
195, 450, 547, 864; hunts, 173,
1268-69, 1412; in abandoned city,
635; in wine jar under roof, 1131-
32; lost, 291, 486; lost family
jewels, 1, 813-14, 862, 1131-32;
of abandoned city, 631; maps, 338;

missing jewels, 615; pirate, 1253-56; recovered family, 817; sought, 486, 486-87, 922, 1132, 1146-47, 1153; stolen by dragon, 1107; stolen jewels, 770; supposed, coveted, 673; voyage for, 1253-56, 1298-1300; witch's, 247. *See also* money.

treasure hunts, novels of, 217-19, 551-53, 812-14, 1146-48, 1253-56

Treasure in Malta, 72

Treasure Island, 1253-56

TREASURE ISLAND, 237, 731, 1138-19, *1253-56*

TREASURE OF GREEN KNOWE, 145, 217. *See THE CHIMNEYS OF GREEN KNOWE, 217-19.*

treasurers, of boy's club, 669

Treasure Trove, 66

Treasure Valley, 659, 661-62

treaties: 213, 217, 1178, 1405. *See also* agreements; bargains; pledges; truces.

Tree and Leaf, 1230

Treebeard, 805

TREECE, HENRY, 119, 335, *1256-58*, 1298

Tree of Life, 756

trees: awakened, 995; campaign to save, 689-92; cotton, cut down, 579; in neighbor's yard, 490; moving, 208; of life, 976; planting, 565; protective apple, 756; silver apple, 756; talking, 687; threatening, 212; yew, sculpted, 710

Treet family, 304-6, 826-27

TREGARTHEN, ENYS, 332, *1258*

Tregeagle family, 1287-90

Tregose, Janey, 1410

Treguddick family, 111-13

Trelawney, Squire, 338, *1132*, 1254-56

Treloar family, 430-32, 1242

trench warfare: wars with Turks, 213-15; World War I, 1214-15

Trennels, 963

Trennels Old Farm, 382, 385

Trent, Cliff, 242, 843, 896

trespass, into swimming pool, 86

TRESASSERS W, 974

Trevelyan family, 890

Trevithic, 224, 1180-81

Trevor, 1115

Trewerry, Jyd, 332-33

trials: arson, 1365; at Vanity, 976-77; by ordeal, 11-12, 673; for treason, 247; for witchcraft, 609;

in Wonderland, 18, 21, 23; mock, 11, 29, 855, 857, 1078; of abusive schoolmaster, 54; of fugitive convict, 494; of Knave of Hearts, 21, 23, 1362; of witches, 554; over ownership of pool, 437; sedition, 338, 859; Toad for stealing car, 1383; witch, 614

triangle, whipping post, 500

tribes: African, 113-15, 123-24, 743, 754, 762, 839, 919, 1189; ancient British, 865; ancient Israel, 895; British, 115, 261, 347-50, 375, 746, 1025, 1089-91, 1117-19, 1171-73, 1244-45; British Bronze Age, 337-38, 1319-22; brutish Red Men, 336-37; Celtic, 245, 681-82, 806, 967-68, 1161-64, 1190; Hiberu, 624-26, Irish, 270-71; lost Yehimelek, 156, 1411; Middle Eastern, found, 1358; New Guinea, 564-66; Pictish, 878, 884, 1299; Scottish, 333, 387, 772-74; South American Indian, 1310; Stone Age, 565; Stone and Bronze age, 336-37; wandering Middle Eastern, 624-26; Yehimelek, 156, 1068, 1357, 1411-12

Tribulation, Aunt, 345

tribunes, Roman, 1119, 1244-45

tributes: annual in gold to Romans, 1118; from Cornwall to Ireland, 1259

tricks: apprentice seamen's, 1064; backfire, 218, 873; black magic, 752; Brownie's, 5-6; uncle's, 755; cutting ice to drown army, 92; female wizard's who is then tricked, 1087; goodhearted, 229; gnome's, 715, 861, 894; housekeeper's, 81; Jacobite's, 13; magic, 844; mean, 208, 225, 262; Mole's, 828; of dog by spirit, 535; pages which disappear, 321; song containing instructions, 12; suspected, 93; Toad's, 1383; to smoke out spy, 402-3; to trap kidnapper, 650-51. *See also* hoaxes; mischief; pranks; scams; schemes.

The Tricksters, 759

tricycles, Yellow Peril II, 959

Trilby (barge), 1213-15

trilogies: Fireball, 232; Flambards, 226-27, 354-56, 421, 424; Ring, 405; Roman, 347-50, 679-83, 1088-91; Sword, 232; Tripods, 231, 237-40, 989-92, 1359-61; Viking,

1298-1300; White Mountains, 231, 237-40, 989-92, 1359-61

triplets, boys on bowl, 782, 783

Triplett, Mr. Tom, 863, 1116

Tripods, 231, 237-40, 989-90, 1359-61

trips: around world, 781; by ship and rackety-pack railroad, 1141-43; down river, 792-93. *See also* journeys; quests; searches; voyages.

TRIS LA CHARD, 1059-60, *1258*

Tristan, 1258-61

TRISTAN AND ISEULT, 1176, *1258-61*

Tristram Treguddick, 1112-13

trolls, 407, 551, 1401

TRON, 121-24, *1261-62*

Trostnikovo, 718-19

Trotter family, 593-95

Trouble Half-Way, 771

TROUBLE IN THE JUNGLE, 514, 1246, 1262. *See GUMBLE'S YARD*, *514-16.*

troublemakers, insect, 246

THE TROUBLE WITH DONOVAN CROFT, 52, *1262*

Trouty, 4

TROY PALMER, 498, 533-34, *1264*

truants, Prince Corin, 561-62

truces: 1038, 1085. *See also* agreements; bargains; pledges; treaties.

trucks: friendly driver, 627; marked for hijackers, 183

Trudy Beech, 468

Truepenny, the mole, 212

Trufflehunter, the badger, 893, 995, 1264

trumpeters, famous, 1061-64

trumpets, stolen, 1062-63

TRUMPKIN, the dwarf, 185, 357, 892-93, 994-95, 1092, *1264-65*, 1306

trunks: hidden under floor, 428; stolen, 428

trustees, of estate, 613, 1115

Tubbs, Uncle Oswald, 922-23, 1267-68

tuberculosis: 735; fear of, 38

Tuck, Friar, 12

Tuckee, Mr., *863*, 1133

Tucker, 1105

Tucker, Mrs., 535, *860-61*, 894

Tudor, Tasha, 22

Tuesdays, Bad, 781

TUG SHAKESPEARE, 335, 525, 606, 917-19, *1265*

Tuileries, 1216

TULKU, 315, *1265-67*

Tulku, unborn child, 1266

Tulku of Siddha Asara, 334

TUMBLEDOWN DICK: ALL PEOPLE AND NO PLOT, 1131, *1267-68*

tumblers: 205, 235, 1351. *See also* players.

Tumnus, Mr., *864*

tumps, 802, 863

tunnels: canal, 197-99; coal mine, 1022; collapsing mine, 1047; entrance to secret at Toad Hall, 1384; entrance to secluded valley, 724; from Crimean War, 1386; hiding place, 290-21; in mountains, 552, 973-74; into castle, 1003; into hill, 352, 388-89, 1344; London, 798; mine, as prison, 34-36; out of dungeon, 1300; secret, 218, 828; to heart of peach, 593; under waterfall, 487; Underland, 1093; used to store explosives, 435-36

Tuppenny, Aunt, 1412

TUPPENNY STANDISH, 236-37, *1268-69*

Tupper, Emma, 27, 29, *368-70*, 411, 992, 1046-47

THE TURBULENT TERM OF TYKE TILER, 643, *1269-70*

The Turf-Cutter's Donkey, 744, 1271

THE TURF-CUTTER'S DONKEY GOES VISITING, 744, *1270-73*

Turkey, 17th century, Istanbul, 213-15

turkey growers, 388

Turkish Delight, 357, 710-11

Turks: besiege Constantinople, 254, 371-72, 633; besiege Vienna, 213-15, 546, 1295-96; in Outremer, 453, 619, 670-71, 968

turncoats: in War of Roses, 102-4, 316-17, 1103; tribesman for Romans, 1190. *See also* traitors.

Turner, Margaret, 1364

TURNER, PHILLIP (WILLIAM), 480, *1273-74*

turnspits, 660

Turska, Krystyna, 1409

turtles: 1186; lachrymose talking, 20-22, 23, 827

Turveytop, 109

Turville, General, 1337

Tussocks, 174

tutors: amoral, 1412; conspirator to overthrow king, 108, 1122; cousin, 718-19; eccentric, 623, 842, 1317-18; ex-violinist, 740; faithful retainer, 637; father, 536; half-dwarf, 185, 323; hermit, 216; inept, 234; mysterious, 807; of blind girl, 616; of prince

of Narnia, 185, 995-96; overly
inquisitive, 1317-18; priest,
102-4, 701, 1103; serious, red-
haired, ex-violinist, 845; 17th
century, 800; summer, 434-35; to
teach blind girl and black boy,
173, 1174; to wealthy boy, 434;
to witch, 208-9; unconventional,
596; witch, 567. See also headmasters; headmistresses; schoolteachers; teachers.
TV addicts: uncle, 1283; boy, 810.
See also television.
TWEEDLEDEE, 1209, 1274
TWEEDLEDUM AND TWEEDLEDEE, 1209,
1274
twelfth century: early, England,
London, 1394-96; Winchester,
1394-96; late, England, 672;
Warwickshire, 738-40; late, Jerusalem, 670-72
Twelfth Night, 288, 964
Twelfth of July, 1286
THE TWELVE AND THE GENII, 241, 1274-
76
Twelves, toy soldiers of Brontes,
1275
twentieth century:
--early:
--Asia: China, 1265-67; Tibet, 1265-
67
--British Isles: England, Bedfordshire, 132-34, 134-36, 136-38,
140-42; Cheshire, 9-10, 1267-68;
Coalgate, 473-75; Cobchester,
276-79; Cornwall, 459-62, 1287-
90; Dartmoor, 1386-88; Essex, 418-
21, 421-24; Kent, 416-18; London,
354-56, 899-902; Manchester,
703-6, 1267-68; Norfolk, 953-55;
seacoast, 1213-15; Staffordshire,
1220-23; village, 206-8, 703-6,
943-45
--British Isles: Ireland, 1270-73;
Inishgallan, 258-61; Barrinish,
1101-3
--British Isles: Scotland, 1123-
25; Hebrides, 588-89; highlands,
1398-99
--Europe: France, Calais, 1213-15;
Russia, 1206-8
--Latin America: Mexico, 601-2
--South Pacific: Halcyon Island,
586-87
--mid:
--British Isles: England, 221-23,
234-36, 381-82, 815-16, 818-20;
Birmingham, 290-91; Canterbury,

223-25, 1180-82; Cobchester,
514-16, 1364-66; Channel, 1339-
40; Cheshire, 1234-36, 1342-45;
city, 77-78, 203-4, 779-81, 781-
83, 783-84, 784-86, 1240-42, 1349;
Colebridge, 382-85; countryside,
193-94, 361-62, 593-95, 710-13;
Devonshire, 389-92; Exeter, 377-
79; farm, 963-65; Garmouth, 400-3,
747-50; Green Knowe, 211-13, 1154-
55; Harwich Harbor, 1340-42;
lake country, 972-74, 1177-79;
Little Barley, 328-30; Little
Weirwold, 467-69; Liverpool,
1064-65; London, 68-71, 84-
85, 173-75, 182-84, 328-30,
330-32, 414-16, 505-8, 667-68,
685-87, 689-92, 722-24, 897-
99, 924-26, 1114-17, 1218-20;
London and Cornwall, 889-91;
Manchester, 359-60; Midlands,
480-82, 1071-74; Midmeddlecum,
1385-86; North Cornwall, 1105-6;
northern marshes, 281-83; Otwell,
385-86; Reedsmere, 495-98; seacoasts, 734-37, 982-84, 1169-71;
Shropshire, 903-4; Somerset, 186-
88; Suffolk, 163-66; Sunny Bay,
923-24;
Sussex, 403-5, 434-36; village,
206-8, 366-68, 812-14, 1167-69;
Warwickshire, 716-17; Withern,
119-21; Yorkshire, 96-99, 351-53,
486-87, 536-38, 801-4, 1021-23,
1274-76
--British Isles: Ireland, 425-27,
713-14; Ballymurry, 1151-54;
Connemara, 543-46
--British Isles: Scotland: Inverness, 642-43; Kilmorah, 79-81;
Skye, 789-91, 1049-50; Skua, 1396-
97; West Highlands, 368-70; West
Lothian, 1196-99
--British Isles: Wales: mining town,
176-77; Penlelig, 558-59; valley,
932-35
--Europe: France, 221-23; Germany,
1096-99, 1348-49; Italy, 662-63;
Norway, 1349-51; Poland, 1096-
99; Sicily, 30-31; Spain, 1366-68;
Switzerland, 1096-99, 1348-49
--high seas, 1064-65
--Latin America: Caribbean, 1064-65
--North America: Canada, 732-
34; New York City, 593-95;
United States, town, 184-
85
--late:

--Africa: Ghana, 248-52; Johannesburg, 627-28
--Asia: India, 1302-5
--Australia: 583-85; Ryan Creek,
620-23; swampy region, 714-16
--British Isles: England, 127-29,
252-54, 949-52, 1004-7, 1058-
60, 1165-67, 1269-70; Berkshire
Downs, 1330-34; Bournemouth,
1392-94; Buckinghamshire, 287-88;
Cheshire, 1025-26; city, 188-90,
465-67, 1363-64; Cornwall, 397-
99, 429-32, 1287-90; countryside,
283-85, 388-89, 523-25, 583-
85, 645-46, 920-22; Cumbrian
fells, 555-57; Darnley, 539-42;
Derbyshire, 917-19; East Anglian
village, 1190-92; farm, 1082-
84; Garmouth, 1325-27, 1389-91;
Ipston, 1334-36;
Kensington, 1076-78; Kent, 248-
52; Lancashire, 876-78; London,
41-42, 519-21, 656-58, 797-99,
1039-41, 1061-64, 1262-64, 1313-
15; Mandover, 891-92; Middleton,
411-14; Midlands, 833-35, 1119-
21, 1322-25; Newcastle, 33-36;
Norfolk, 1211-13; Northend,
85-87; North Oxford, 564-
66; Northumberland, 1376-79;
Oxfordshire, 451-53; school in
city, 286-87; seacoast, 1140-
41; Skirlston, 578-81; suburb,
75-77, 1186-87; Suffolk, 306-9;
Todcaster, 1353-56; village, 318-
21, 325-28, 943-45; Wethershaf,
455-56; Yald Forest, 1247-50
--British Isles: Ireland: Belfast,
1284-87; rural, 1133-36
--British Isles: Scotland:
Edinburgh, 427-28; mountains,
1368-69
--British Isles: Wales, 242-44, 501-
2, 567-69, 847-49, 906-7, 1290-91
--Europe: Netherlands, 1061-64;
Norway, 1392-94
--New Zealand, city suburb, 200-1
--South America: Chile, Santiago,
1187-89
twenty-first century: England,
989-92, 1359-61; France, country-
side, 1359-61; Paris, 1359-61;
Switzerland, 1359-61
The Twenty-Two Letters, 659
Twilight, 336-37
Twilight Fairy, 1096
twins: babies, 779-80; boy and girl,
19, 190, 221-23, 585, 880, 899,

1146-47, 1236; boys, 386, 765-67,
890, 1081, 1117-72, 1381; boys,
princes, 562; boys, black slaves,
1227; contentious, 1274; dolls,
558-59; female witches, 874, 1354;
girls, 179, 383, 468, 963-65;
marionetters, 28, 94, 585; mirror,
1209, 1274; performers, 1187-
89; sons of Usna, 299; toddlers,
781, 783, 785-86
Twiss, Admiral Sir Archibald
Cunningham, 4-5, 318-20, 669
Twite family, 108-9, 344-45, 837,
844, 887-89, 1100, 1141-43
Two Fables, 275
The Two Faces of Silenus, 241
TWOPENCE A TUB, 994, 1276-78
Two Stories, 943
The Two Towers, 1230
Tyburn Hill, 816
Tyburn widows, 110, 111, 113
The Tyger Voyage, 3
Tyke Tiler, 1269-70
Tynemouth, England, 747, 1325
typhoons, 893
Tyrant, the bloodhound, 816
tyrants: barons, 1043; controlled
society, future, 1294-95; form
master, 950-51; French nobles,
1216-17; Masters, 989-91; of
Bombardy, 1386; rabbit dictator,
446; self-appointed, 50; Tisroc of
Calormen, 561; Tripods, 1359-61
Tyson, Kim, 150, 283, 655-56, 1033

U boats, 262-63
Uffington, White Horse of, 1171
Ugandans, in England, 564-65, 613-14
Uglies, 1001-2
Uisneac, sons of: 300. See also Usna,
sons of, 299.
ukelele players, 667
Ukraine: 18th century, 1415; 19th
century, 719
Ukrainians, in England, 501, 599,
667-68
Ulf, 238
Ullathorne family, 129-31, 841, 861
Ulster, ancient, 298-99, 299-301
Umballa, 652
Umbarak, 434-36
umbrella, used as boat, 1388
unbirthdays, 1208-11
Uncle Albert, 780
Uncle Alfie, 16-17
UNCLE ALAN KITSON, 59, 532-33, 1237-
38, 1240-41, 1279

UNCLE ANDREW KETTERLEY, 321, 755-56, *1279-80*
Uncle Aquila, 261, 347-48, 350
UNCLE BEN, 58, 741, *1280*, 1322-24
Uncle Bert Marriot, 1247-48
Uncle Bob, 648
Uncle Bob Lunn, 473
UNCLE CHACHA RAHMTA, 310, 470, *1280*
UNCLE CHARLIE (The Stone Book Series), 9-10, *1280-81*
Uncle Charlie (*The Family from One End Street*), 386
Uncle Crispin Roller, 488
Uncle Davie Dunham, 61-62, 474-75
UNCLE EBENEZER BALFOUR, 13, 289, 648-51, *1281*
Uncle Fred Barnes, 61
Uncle George, 193-94
UNCLE HADDEN, 596, 769, *1281-82*, 1316-19
Uncle Harold Scrubb, 377
UNCLE HAROLD SOWTER, 703-4, 706, *1282*
Uncle Harry, 153
UNCLE HENDREARY, 49, 61, 133, 135, 136-37, 140-42, 560, 811, 1130, 1236, *1282*
Uncle Jack Gowan, 1285-86
Uncle Jagindar, 310
Uncle Jim Turner, 171-72
Uncle John, 1403
Uncle Miheal, 1271-72
Uncle Nicholas Mirkov, 718-19
UNCLE PARKER, 275, 477, 479, 838-39, 920-21, 1195, *1282-83*
UNCLE PETER MYHILL, 364, 523, *1283*
Uncle Pumblechook, 493, 495
UNCLE RON BELL, 476, 900, *1283-84*
UNCLE RUSSELL, 226, 354-55, 419-20, *1284*, 1374
uncles: abstracted, 1281-82; accidentally drowned; 1335; adventurers, 1403; amiable, 278; ardent Ulsterman, 1285; arrested for attempted murder, 474; arrogant, 1279-80; avoid confrontation, 343; bad-tempered, 354-55, 419; barber, 519; bully, 1282, 1284; cheese merchant, 1380-81; children league against, 1178-79; circus clown, 234-36, 516, 962, 1057; complaining, 914; crazy driver, 1283; detested, 703-4, 706; disagreeable, 755-56; dogmatic, 1238; drinker, 474; drowned, 1376; dull, 523, 1283; enchanter, 209, 225; foster father, 635; French, 1020;

garrulous, 601; Grand Master of Hospitallers, 453; great, 68-71, 498-99; guardian, 1364-65; gun runner, 1228; honorary, 97, 532; hymn-singing, 914; ideal, 4, 1147; "idle devil," 1283; Indian, 1148; irresponsible guardian, 1315, 1365-66; lacking in understanding, 1279; lecherous, 900; obnoxious, 610; owner of horse farm, 683; pedantic, 59; pet shop owner, 539, 1267-68; previously unknown, 648-51; produces visions, 733; profligate, 419; rescuer, 916; retired post commander, 347; Roman, 348; roving, 972-74; scheming, 419; sea captain, 112, 1232; Sikh, 886; soldiers, 9-10; stoned to death, 449; treacherous, 408-9; TV addict, 1283; unscrupulous, 321; usurping, 185, 1306, 995; veteran with TB, 422; warden at Oxford, 623, 1316-19; war leader, 113-15, 754; weaver, 914; wicked, 13; writer, 1147
Uncle Tim, 455
Uncle Titus Carver, 315, 399, 629
Uncle Toby Morgan, 425-27
"Uncle Tom-ism," 767
UNCLE TURNER, 610-11, *1284*
Uncle Walter Thompson, 514-16
UNDER GOLIATH, 182, *1284-87*
underground, London, 798
Underland, 1034, 1092-93
Under Plum Lake, 708
understanding: 1264, 1364; intercultural, 248-52, 627-28, 1302-5. *See also* cultures; ethnic customs; rituals.
The Undertaker, 1323
undertakers, greedy, rat-like, 856
Under the Autumn Garden, 771
Under the Orange Grove, 322
underworld, figures, 327, 656-57
unemployment: rife, 876-78, 895; mines closed, 912
Unicorn Gate, 486
Unicorn Inn, 2, 486-87, 960
unicorns: 359-60, 486-87, 687-89, 711, 726, 783; unicorn fights with lion, 1210; watermark, 729
Unicorn Yat, 2
uniforms, school, too small, 540
Uninvited Ghosts and Other Stories, 728
unions: breakers, coal strike, 1276; brother strong advocate of, 1285; coal mine, 1015, 1276-78; in

carpet factory, 808; representa-
tives, 603-4; trade, 805, 876
United Irishmen, 101
United States: mid-19th century,
Nantucket, 887-89; New York City,
593-95; town, 184-85
University College, London, 614
UNLEAVING, 461, 941, *1287-90*
Unwin, David Storr. *See* SEVERN,
DAVID, 1078.
Unwin, Nora S., 332
UP THE PIER, 266, *1290-91*
Upper Folding, 568
"upright men," 246
Ur, on the Euphrates, ancient times,
624-26, 1204-6
urban development, 403-5, 519-21,
1119-21, 1330-34
urban life: 77-78, 276-79, 377--79,
465-67, 514-16, 519-21, 536-38,
606-8, 656-58, 689-92, 703-6,
806-9, 896-97, 1114-17, 1313-15,
1364-66, 1389-91; Bombay, 526,
1302-5; future, England, 895-97.
See also cities.
urban renewal, 77-78, 465-67, 629,
1114-17, 1364-66
Urguk, 280
urns, lettered mysteriously, 412
Ursell, Martin, 1119
Ursula Biddums, 450, 548
Ursula Godman, 459, 582-83, 972,
1033
Ursula Howell, 173, 236, 1412
USAMAH IBN-MENQUIDH, Emir, 671, *1291*
"Useful Boy," starving, 1160
Useful Pot, 1389
Usna, sons of: 298-99. *See also*
Uisneac, sons of, 302.
usurpers: cousin, 672; of Arthur's
throne, 1038; of inheritance, 738,
1103; of estate, 289; of kingship,
185, 806, 995; of kingship, cat,
173, 175; of kingship of Scottish
tribe, 772-74; stepfather, 611;
tutor passes off own son as Duke's,
1122; uncle, 650-51, 994-96
Utrecht, late 17th century, 456-58
Utrillo's Mother, 82
Uttery, Granpa, 33-36, 485-86, 592-
93
Uz, 1205

vaccinations, of monkeys, 1145
VADIR CEDRICSON, 295-96, *1293-94*
vagabonds, assassin, 1012
VAGABONDS ALL, 1076, 1294, 1351.
See WHEN SHAKESPEARE LIVED IN
SOUTHWARK, 1351.
Vagrants, pseudo, 238, 1359
vagrants, arrested, 1009-12
Valhelm, 344
Valiant, the dog, 1395
The Valley of Carreg-Wen, 993
The Valley of Song, 471
Valley of the Shadow of Death, 976,
979
valleys: beautiful, 659, 661-62;
revitalized, 661
Valmy, Battle of, 1217
values: traditional, 105-7, 624,
630-32, 683-84, 747-59, 786-89,
894, 974-80, 1096, 1158-60, 1232-
34, 1374. *See also* virtues.
Val Webster, 205, 656-67
vampires, 200
Vampires, Werewolves and Phantoms
of the Night: Demonic Tales from
Different Lands, 410
vamps, 474
van Bergh, Julius, 1062
THE VANDAL, 1061, *1294-95*
vandals: of church, 78; ruin newly painted red front door, 854;
neighborhood, 1114-15; rampant,
242, 896. *See also* hoodlums; Teddy boys; thugs.
Vanity fair, 976, 979
Van Mierevelt, Maarten, 457
van Stratten family, 15, 662-63
Vanya, 1301-2
Varangian Guard, 118, 371
Vardoe, Zoe, 202, 1280, 1323-24,
1420
varlets, 673
Vasers' barn, 307, 609
VASIF, COLONEL, 214-15, 1226, *1295-*
96
Vaughn, Ann, 1351
Vaughan family, 495-98, 543, 604,
775-76, 786, 866-67
Vaughan-Jackson, Genevieve, 1151
Vavasour, Johanna, 554
Vavasour family, 609, 614
Vavasour house, 303, 307-9
vaudeville shows, 754
vegetables, aunt raises, sells at
stall, 523
vegetarianism, society espouses,
1294
Veikko Kapanen, 1350-51
Velasquez, Eric, 627
Ven, Timur, 1296
Venables, Thomas, 1026,
1203
Venema, Reintje, 606

Venetians, in Constantinople, 371–72, 633

Venezuela, mid-17th century, island, 1043–46

Venice, late 20th century, 15, 662–63, 913

ventriloquists, 551

Venturus, 46, 63, 321, 532, 566

Verger's wife, selfish, foiled, 1160

Verity, Mrs., 92, 452, *862*

VERNEY, (SIR) JOHN, 403, 434, 489, *1296–97*

Vernon-Greene family, 415–16

Versailles, French Revolution, 1216

verses: contain name, 1095; obscure prophecy, 1358. See also poems; rhymes.

VERUCA SALT, 203, *1297*

Very Small Beetle, 563

The Very Special Baby, 1183

veterans: amputee, 469; Boer War, 9–10, 1281; naval officer, 4; of Agincourt, 102; World War I, 210, 1048, 1080; handicapped in World War I, 1123; World War II, 399–400

veterinarians, 307

A Vicarage Family, 1157

vicars: autocratic, 163–66; bad-tempered, 944; complain about plants, 128; Edwardian, 821, 883; father, 153; helpful to poachers, 285; larder raided, 272, 417; manuscript of, 1036; misunderstanding, 690–91; pro-mine owners, 1278; understanding, 387–88; village, 1196; wife of, 852, 1158; "with it," 1024. See also clergymen; curates; ministers; parsons; pastors; preachers; priests; rectors.

Victoria: Queen of England, 529; Golden Jubilee of, 1159–60

Victorian People in Life and Literature, 63

Victorians, 387–88, 532–33, 1143–44, 1316–19

victories, ironic, 715, 894

VICTOR SKELTON, 28–29, 1212, *1297–98*

VICTORY AT VALMY, 1215, 1252. See THUNDER OF VALMY, 1215–17.

Vienna, 17th century, Turkish siege of, 32, 213–15, 546, 1226, 1295–96

The View from the Window, 617

vigil lamps, 667

Vigo, Lord Simon, 613, 863, 1115–16

Vikings: 91–92, 116, 116–19, 725, 733, 1085–87, 1298–1300, 1377–78; artifacts in Ireland, 838

VIKING'S DAWN, 1257, *1298–1300*

Viking's Sunset, 1257, 1300

Vila, 1301–2

VILA, AN ADVENTURE STORY, 82, *1300–2*

Villa, Pancho, 601–2

THE VILLAGE BY THE SEA, 303, *1302–5*

village life: English, 52–54, 266–69, 306–9, 311–12, 318–21, 451–52, 484–85, 549, 578–81, 614, 698, 724–26, 812–14, 874–75, 876, 890, 926–27, 943–45, 970–71, 982–84, 1049–50, 1111–13, 1143–44, 1167–69, 1190–92, 1224–25, 1234–36, 1300–2, 1322–25, 1334–36, 1394, 1396–97, 1402–3, 1404–7, 1409–11; during Great Plague, 938–39; during flood, 495–98, 866–671; Ghana, 250; India, 526, 706, 1302–5; Scotland, 799–800, 1123–25, 1155–57, 1196–99; World War II, 467–69, 1419. See also villages.

The Village of Hidden Wishes, 425

villages: African, devastated by slavers, 743; children's, 1098; destroyed by elephants, 631; dying, 578; English, 366, 604, 1372–73; English, 17th century, 609, 614; English seacoast, 724–26; fishing, 1169–71; flooded, 786, 775; hostile, 470; India, 65–66, 526, 630–31; Iron Age, 802–3; Kent, 482; model, 137, 138–39, 140–41, 822, 837, 856; neolithic, 244; on lake, 1301; prehistoric, in open land, 337; Slav, 280; South African, near Botswana, 627–28; superstitious, 50; Tibetan, 653–54; Wales, 1356. See also village life.

villains: ambivalent, 809–10, 1256; apparent vacationers, 1396; apprehended, 223; attempting flight, 405; attorney, 839; attractive, 790; brother's murderer, 890; caricatured, 1032; Cockle-Snorkle Bug, 432; comic, 688, 1279–80; conspirator against king, 125–26; cousin, 645–46; dwarf, 675; enigmatic, 731–32; escape, 790; fiddler, 1112–13; fishing captain, 85; foiled, 282–83; gets comeuppance, 737–38; girl, 208–9; Greeneyes, 538, 891–92; Grey King, 148, 502; gypsy,

135, 811, 1387; has pet rooster,
725-26; housekeeper, 854, 133-34;
identified, 305-6;
illegally imports explosives,
434-36; imp, 1095-96, 1130-31;
imposters, 1400-1; industrial
spy, 984; lame tiger, 65, 1084-
85; Laurel and Hardy types, 1357;
Lombards, 234, 1402-3; manservant, 195, 218-19; menacing,
833; middle-aged couple, 138-
39, 140-42; mine bosses, 129-31;
mother, 636-37, 638; murdered in
prison, 821; Noah's son, 737; nobles, 146-47; Norman England,
672-75; obvious, 222-23, 237,
284-85, 1379-81, 1398-99, 1412;
one-legged seaman, 884;
pirate, 957-58; queen, 844, 1142-
43; reformed, 858; rabbit, 446;
semi-comic, 856-57; sheriff, 146;
stereotyped American, 1071;
stock, 737-38, 832-33, 858, 1216-
17; talking insect, 246; traitor,
1163, 1190; two-faced, 731-32,
790; two men in brown, 845; uncle,
648-51; various, 738-40; wicked
aunt, 325-27; witch, 752, 1009,
1392-94; wool thieves, 453
Vine Cottage, 138, 140-41
Viner, 39-41
VIOLET BEAUREGARDE, 203, *1305*
Violet Wright, 317, 419-20, 422,
1228
violinists, 485, 786, 807, 845
Vipont, Charles, 1306
VIPONT (FOULDS), ELFRIDA, 685, *1305-
6*
Virage (ship), 262
Viroconium, 294-97, 930, 1029
virtues: knightly feared diminish-
ing, 729-30; personified, 974-80.
See also values, traditional.
Visick family, 397-98
visions: 16, 36, 88, 523, 533, 602,
733, 1001; contrived, 920-21; of
St. Bartholomew, 1016; that curse
is lifted, 625; to build hospital
for poor, 1395
The Visitors, 1247
Voake, Charlotte, 1334
Vogel, Dr., 373
Vogel family, 32-33, 214, 546
voices: ghostly, 533; still, small,
737
Volcano (ship), 237, 1412
volcanos, 236, 586, 828, 1143, 1310
Volunteer Life Brigade, 1325-26

volunteers: in social agency, 242,
896. *See also* social workers; welfare.
Vortrix, 1320-21
vows: to make name famous, 70; to reform, 186; of piety, 491; to start
hospital, 1016
The Voyage Home, 233
THE VOYAGE OF THE "DAWN TREADER",
699, 1091-92, 1265, *1306-9*
voyages: fantasy, 508-14, 1309-
11; hazardous, 1306-8; 1064-65;
sea, 366, 508-14, 887, 1044,
1064-65; to Africa, 210, 1145; to
Australia, 786-87; to find exiled
lords, 376-77; to South America,
1141, 1309-10; to Spidermonkey
Island, 211; treasure, 338, 1268-
69, 1132, 1253-56, 1298-1300;
Viking, to east, 116-19; Viking,
to west, 1298-1300. *See also* journeys; quests; searches; trips.
THE VOYAGES OF DOCTOR DOLITTLE, 731,
1309-11
Voyage to Valhalla, 1183
VRETHIKI, 254, 370-73, 633, *1311-12*,
1136
Vye family, 226, 427, 602-3, 734-37,
823

Waddell, Martin, 1066-67
Wade family, 463-64
Wafango tribe, 114
wagons: covered, 1234, 1357; gypsy,
318, 320, 1009-12
waifs: *See* boys, waifs; children,
waifs; girls, waifs.
Wainganga River, 1084
Wainwright family, 523-24, 363-64,
1283
Wales, David, Prince of, 1357-58
Wales: early 19th century, Pennygaff, 156, 1356-58; mid-20th
century, mining town, 176-79;
Penlelig, 558-59; valley, 518,
574-75, 932-35; late 20th century, Snowden peaks, 242-44, 567-9,
847-49; farm, 501-2; Gwyntfa, 906-
7; Llangolly, 176, 1056, 1290-91;
World War II period, 176-79, 415
Wales, novels of, 176-79, 242-44,
501-2, 558-59, 847-49, 906-7, 932-
35, 1290-91, 1356-58
Walk a Mile and Get Nowhere, 1129
Walker family, 171-72, 614, 972-
74, 1047, 1175, 1177-79, 1227-28,
1340-42

wallet, changed to pig, 189
WALL OF WORDS, 644, *1313-15*
wallpaper, edible, 1376
The Walls of Athens, 941
Walsh, Jill Paton. *See PATON WALSH,
    JILL, 940-41.*
Walsingby, Suffolk, early 19th
    century, 190-91
Walrus (ship), 89, 100, 172
"The Walrus and the Carpenter,"
    1209, 1274
Walters family, 193-94
WALTER THOMPSON, 334, 514-16, 528,
    599, 629, 647, 838, 1056-57, 1242,
    1315-16, 1364-66
Walworth, 1346
Wanda Grieg, 184-85
Wander, 336-37
The Wandering Moon, 1029
WANDERLUST, the dog, 848, *1316*
wands: magic, broken, 712; witch's,
    broken, 357
Want, 228
The Wanton Child, 247
Wanwangeri, 250, 698
Warden Hadden, 1281
wardens: air raid, 415; fire, 1240;
    gnome, 1092; of bear, 158-59; of
    Canterbury College, Oxford, 769,
    1316
THE WARDEN'S NIECE, 63, *1316-19*
War Drobe, 864
wardrobes: apple wood for, 756;
    large, old, passage to otherworld,
    710, 712; made of Narnian wood, 321
wards: girl heiress, 606; of noble
    family, 582-83
warehouses: children live in, 514;
    fire in, 1365
wargs, 439, 551-52
warlocks: 208-9, 225. *See also*
    enchanters; magicians; necroman-
    cers; witches; wizards.
warnings: attempted, 262-63; death-
    bed, 1156; of contemplated murder,
    649; of guards with dog, 521; of
    tall, handsome Irishwoman, 1328;
    of treachery, 300; not to walk
    on farm or near manor house, 455;
    pricked into bank note, 223; time-
    ly, 1380; to get rid of dog, 464;
    to stay away from man, 412. *See
    also* omens; predictions; premon-
    itions; prophecies.
warrens: rabbit, commodious, 1331;
    democratic, 446; destroyed, 418,
    535; on Watership Down, 1331-
    33; overcrowded, 446; poison at,

1332; survivors of destroyed, 557;
    totalitarian, 446, 1332
warriors: elite of tribe, 1319;
    mighty, 1219; noble, 1158. *See
    also* soldiers; women warriors.
Warrior Scarlet, sign of manhood,
    1321
WARRIOR SCARLET, 903, *1319-22*, 1176
war novels: French Revolution,
    1215-17; Haitian Revolution, 765-
    67; Irish Rebellion, 499-501;
    Napoleonic Wars, 190-91; Roman
    Britain, 1117-19; Turks in Europe,
    213-15; World War I, England,
    421-24, 1213-15; World War II,
    England, 377-79, 400-3, 414-16,
    467-69, 734-37, 747-50, 924-26;
    Europe, 1097-99, 1339-40, 1348-
    40, 1349-51
wars: against orcs and wargs, 553;
    Anglo-French, 1405; between
    dwarves and men averted, 553;
    Calormen vs. Narnia, 1174; clan,
    650-51; Crimean, 171; England-
    Spain, 583, 615, 813, 841, 1058;
    English Civil, 307, 611-12, 1025-
    26; fascination with, 252-54;
    Franco-Prussian, 1217; France,
    18th century, 339, 1215-17; harsh
    realities of, 879; Holy War to cap-
    ture Vienna, 213-15; horrors of,
    171, 191, 213-15, 898-99, 1013;
    inhumanity of, 1098-99; Irish
    rebellion of 1798, 445, 879; mock
    sea, 949, 874; Napoleonic, 190-91,
    342, 356, 595; nuclear, 156, 283;
    of Roses, 102-5, 316, 683; over
    treasure, 1204; play, 1178; Russo-
    Japanese, 1207; South American,
    imminent, 907;
    to keep soldiers from mutiny, 213-
    15; with Saxons, 679-83; with
    Scots, 916-17; World War I, 9-10,
    206-8, 227, 421-24, 1123-25, 1374;
    World War II, 31, 37, 60, 176-79,
    253-54, 262-63, 353, 377-79, 400-
    3, 414-16, 467-69, 578, 597-98,
    603, 619-20, 747-50, 924-26, 937,
    1096-99, 1339-40, 1169-71. *See
    also* battles; battle scenes; con-
    flicts; fights; war novels.
war souvenirs, schoolboy, 210
Warsaw, World War II period, 619,
    1096-99
warships, British, anti-slave pa-
    trol, 866
Wars of the Roses, 316, 701
wart removers, 92

Warwickshire: late 12th century, 738-40; late 15th century, 729-30; mid-20th century, 716-17

washerwomen: Mole disguised as, 828; Toad disguised as, 1383

wastelands, reddish, 755

Watcher, Wizard, 1397-98

THE WATCHER BEE, 801, *1322-25*

watches: clue to father's identity, 466; father's gold, 610-11; makers of, 1304; rabbit keeps consulting, 1362; repaired with butter, 753, 767; with hands fixed to jam, 401

Watch House, 33, 50-51, 1225-26, 1325-27

THE WATCH HOUSE, 197, 210, *1325-27*, 1347-48

watchmen: at nursery, 183; church, 1080

water: babies, 363, 851, 853; boy becomes water-baby, 1328; dread of, 1300; river considered magical, 1300; magic, 998

THE WATER-BABIES, 664, *1327-30*

waterfalls: frozen, 476, 556; hiding place, 242-44

watermarks, Unicorn, 729-30

"The Water of Life," 1028

Water Rat, 828, 1382-84

water rats, 1020-21

water reservoir, bombed, 1286

Watership Down, 95, 418, 446, 535, 557, 1331-32

WATERSHIP DOWN, 3, *1330-34*

Water Truce, 631

Water-vole, 716

water-voles, 1120

Watkins-Pitchford, D(enys) J(ames). *See BB, 82-83.*

Watson family (*Hal*), 519-21

Watson family (*Earthfasts*), 351-53

WATSON, JAMES, 1187, *1334*

Watt, the hare, 212

Watt Davie, 428

THE WAY TO SATTIN SHORE, 949, *1334-36*

The Way to Write for Children, 8

weapons: billiard balls, 109; bottle of red wine, 253; blunderbuss, 395; bow, 145-46; crutch, 731; fire, 11; knives, 173; Luger, 749, 887, 1051; machine guns, 197, 210, 245, 656, 747-50, 886, 1051; mirrors, 892; rifles, first among Piegans, 733; rifles, World War I, 9-10; scimitar, 377; smuggled guns, 601-2, 1412; stored in cellar, 108; trans-oceanic cannon, 888

Weasels, 65, 828, 1384

weasels, 365-66, 931-32, 992

Weasel Woods, 432, 1120-21

weather: always winter and never Christmas, 1009; controlled by domes, 1295; extremely cold, 288, 367, 566, 1338, 1344, 1375; magic spells for, 1298; power over, 449

The Weather-Clerk, 1183

weathercocks, golden atop steeple, 1144

Weather Men, 52

weathermonger, community, 1337-38

THE WEATHERMONGER, 309, 315, *1336-38*

Weathertop, 436

WEAVER, STELLA, 1151-54, *1338-39*

The Weaver Birds, 1075

weavers: 684, 914, 1143, 1233-34; of Warrior Scarlet, 1321

Webfeet, 39-40

Web of Violence: A Study in Family Violence, 1031

Webster, Iris, 616, 810

Webster, John, 303, 306-9, 554, 609, *614*, 1174-75

Webster family, 656-58

WE COULDN'T LEAVE DINAH, 1251, *1339-40*

weddings: 329-30, 702, 726, 828, 901, 929, 979, 998, 1001, 1095, 1103, 1113, 1116, 1163, 1172, 1234, 1293, 1323; anvil wedding in smithy, 799-800, 1197; bride jilted on day, 820; cake crumbling to dust, 493; during plague, 939; hobbit, 1056; invitations, refused, 267; of wizard and witch, 1355-56; Quaker, 1201

WE DIDN'T MEAN TO GO TO SEA, 874, 1016-17, *1340-42*

Wegner, Fritz, 1149

Weil, Lisl, 184

Weirdstone of Brisingamen, 414

THE WEIRDSTONE, 443, 1342-45. *See THE WEIRDSTONE OF BRISINGAMEN, 1342-45.*

WELCH, RONALD (RONALD OLIVER FELTON), 670, *1345-46*

welfare: workers, 230, 466; social for starving, 896; unemployment dole, 233. *See also* social workers; volunteers.

Welford, Master, 1233

The Well, 644

Well Hall, 882

wells: dug, 787; home in, 335; poisoned, 157

Welsh persons: 25-26, 148-49, 850, 873-74; in America, 236-37; in England, 285, 358-59, 1180-82, 340; in England, laborers in foundry, 582; prejudice toward, 1047
Welsh language, 1180
Welsh Marches, 672, 968
WEMMICK, JOHN, 495, *1346*
Wemmick family, 1346
WENDY DARLING, 956-58, 961, 1226, *1347*
Wendy Farrar, 73, 896
werewolves, 875, 893
Wesley, John, 464
Wessex, 9th century, 870-72
West, Arnold, 639, 875, 1335
West African Squadron, 1069
WESTALL, ROBERT (ATKINSON), 306, 400, 747, 1058, 1325, *1347-48*, 1376
West Country, 19th century, 1111-13
West Highlands, Scotland, mid-20th century, 368-70
West Indians, in London, 73-74, 77-78, 519-20, 522, 689-92, 1262-64
West Indies, late 18th century, Haiti, 765-67
West Lothian, mid-20th century, 1196-99
Westminster, London, 196, 729
Westminster Abbey, 490
West of Widdershins, 1106
Westward Ho!, 664
West Wind, Blackfeet Piegan, 733
West Wind, takes nanny away, 781
Westwood Estates, 316, 629
Wethershaf, late 20th century, 455-56
Wet Magic, 882
Weymouth: late 18th century, 170, 1337; after Changes, 449
whale oil, as food, 887
whalers, 344
whales: great pink, 887-89, 1048; lured by sweet songs, 889; push island, 1310
Wheal Maid mine, 397-99
wheatfields, hiding place, 190
The Wheaton Book of Science Fiction Stories, 1183
Wheazy-Fidgett, 435
wheelbarrows, tramps employ, 891
wheelchairs, steam, 119
Wheel of Life, 651, 653
wheelwrights, 108
When Darkness Comes, 1183

WHEN HITLER STOLE PINK RABBIT, 646-47, 924, *1348-49*
WHEN JAYS FLY TO BARBMO, 67, *1349-51*
WHEN SHAKESPEARE LIVED IN SOUTHWARK, 1076, *1351-53*
When the Siren Wailed, 1158
When We Were Very Young, 232-33, 812, 989
When Willie Went to the Wedding, 647
Wherton, future, 1359
WHICH WITCH?, 577, *1353-56*
Whigs, 152, 170, 866
The Whinstone Drift, 48
whippings: of apprentice thieves, 1352; of Iceni queen, 1118; of page boy, 1413; for attempted escape, 574; of Vikings, 1300; on triangle, 500; school caning, 129; severe, 672-73. *See also* beatings; floggings.
whiskers, gnome lacks, 1114
The Whispering Knights, 727
Whispering Mountain: 155, 1411; cave in, 1357
THE WHISPERING MOUNTAIN, 8, *1356-58*
A Whisper of Lace, 270
whistlers, 609, 538
White, David Omar, 368
Whitebear farm, 1105
White Boots, 1157
The White Doe, 234
The White Elephant, 241
White family, 125, 477, 1021-23
Whitehead, Nora, 474
White Horse of Uffington, 1171
White House, 416-17
White King, 753, 767, 1210, 1361
WHITE KNIGHT, 1210, *1358-59*
Whitelaw family, 205, 656-57
white light, terrible, 1308
White Mountains, 237, 624, 989, 991, 1359-61
THE WHITE MOUNTAINS, 231, 240, 991, *1359-61*
WHITE QUEEN, 1024, 1210, *1361*
WHITE RABBIT, 19-20, 22, *1361-62*
White Stag, 712
Whitethroat, the dog, 1320-21
White Witch, 710-12, 742, 864, 961-62, 1009
WHITLOCK, PAMELA (FRANCES), 389, 571, *1362*
Whittacker, Polly, 893
Whittacker family, 411-14, 485, 590, 694, 697, 833, 893, 1029, 1065, 1238
WHO LIES INSIDE, 581, *1363-64*
whores, goodhearted, 881

Why Me?, 149
wickedness, widespread, punishment planned, 737, 829
Wicked Winnie, 9
The Wicket Gate, 975
Widdershins Crescent, 648, 1364
WIDDERSHINS CRESCENT, 1246, *1364-66*
Widdison family, 36-37, 450, 547, 548-50, 608, 864, 778
Widdowson, Mr., 314, 599, 1242, 1365
Widdowson Crescent, 629, 838, 1364
Widdowson's Store, 1365
Widford Manor, 450, 547, 548-50, 608
widowers, 1, 79, 190, 259, 342, 455, 587, 636, 846, 971
Widowmaker, 1343
widows: 7, 15, 477, 677, 1018, 1094, 1323; dancer, 678; marrying again, 79, 860, 1058-59; of famous general, 478; of noble, 505; pregnant, 421-22; shunned for adopting bastard, 422; seamstress, 173-75; timid, 163; Tyburn, 110, 111, 113; World War I, 881
Wiggins, the dog, 724
Wight, Isle of, 1403
"The Wild Boar," 214
Wild and Free, 504
Wildcat Island, 1047, 1178-79, 1228
wildcats, tame, 252
Wilde, Dan, 828
The Wild Heart, 504
THE WILD HORSE OF SANTANDER, 504, *1336-68*
Wild Horse Pit, 1276
Wild Hunt, 75, 327, 1042
The Wild Hunt of the Ghost Hounds, 727
The Wild Hunt of Hagworthy, 727
Wild Jack, 232
Wild Lone, 83
Wildsmith, Brian, 129
A WILD THING, 1031, *1368-69*
The Wild Valley, 1078-79
Wild Wood, 65, 828, 1021, 1384
Wilhelm, 422
WILKINS, (WILLIAM) VAUGHAN, 236, *1369-70*
WILL ANDREWS, 53-54, 596, *1370*
WILLARD, BARBARA (MARY), 79, 581, 683, 1009, *1370-72*
Willard family, 582-83
Will Bunce, 583
Will Douglas, 677-78, 814-15, 1412-15
Will Dunham, 61-62, 474
Will Frankland, 637, 63…

WILLIAM (*Danny, the Champion...*), 284-85, 852, 1074, *1372*
William (*John Diamond*), 1066
William (The Stone Book Series), 399, 619, 1234-36
William and Mary, 394
WILLIAM BAGTHORPE, 921, *1372*
WILLIAM BEECH, 179, 467-69, 851-52, 1240, *1372-73*, 1419
William de la Pole, 275
WILLIAM JONAS, 586-87, *1373*
William Jones, 609, 610-11, 1087, 1284
WILLIAM MCSHANE, 1124, *1373-74*
William Ruggles, 386
WILLIAM RUSSELL, 226-27, 319, 335, 354-56, 419-21, 421-22, 1057, 1284, *1374*
WILLIAM SEAGRAVE, 787-88, 859, 1239, *1374*
Williams, Flick, 515
Williams, Foxy, 432
Williams, Garth, 815
Williams, George, 397
Williams, Ursula. *See* MORAY WILLIAMS, URSULA, *830-31*.
Williams family, 290-91
William the Conqueror, 992, 674
Willie Sandowsky, 184-85
Willis, Ben, 235
Will Lawless, 695
Willmay family, 1294-95
Willoughby, Lawrence, 360-61, 361-62, *696*
Willoughby Chase, 1100, 1400-1
Willow family, 14-15, 60, 176-79, 179-80, 543, 826, 842-43, 886
The Willow Pattern Story, 1043
Will Parker, 237-40, 989-92, 1359-61
wills, 178, 430, 477, 543, 557, 704-706, 913, 1282
Will Scarlet, 12
WILL STANTON, 148-49, 287-88, 501-2, 804, 1050, *1375*
Will Swayne, 1010-12
Willum, the dog, 1387
WILLY OVERS, 17, 60, 362, 450-51, 703-6, 872-73, 1132, 1282, *1375*
WILLY WONKA'S CHOCOLATE FACTORY, 58, 203-4, 479, 810, 919, 1297, 1305, *1375-76*
Wilson, Squeak, 1131-32
Wilton school, 1238
Wimbleball, Lorna, 378-79
Winchester, early 12th century, 1394-96
wind, moon makes children naughty, 1385

THE WIND EYE, 1348, *1376-79*
Wind Eye's boat, 1377
WINDFALL, 966, *1379-81*
A Wind from Nowhere, 489
Winding Arrow River, 561
THE WIND IN THE WILLOWS, 472, 812, 885, 932, 1106, *1381-85*
THE WIND ON THE MOON, 709, *1385-86*
windows: church, broken, 359; church, replaced, 480; constructed, 1134
windowseat, Borrower home in, 141, 947
Windruff, the dog, 1386-87
WINDRUFF OF LINKS TOR, 220, *1386-88*
windshields, of Mercedes smashed, 910
The Windswept City, 1257
wine: fine Old Pale Madeira, 489; for instructor's gatherings, 532; jars, contain family treasure, 1131-32; jelly, smashed, 143
Winifred, 70
Winnie, 698
Winnie Ille Pu, 812
Winnie-the-Pooh, 232, 358, 989
WINNIE-THE-POOH, 562, 812, *1388-89*
Winnington, Peter, 225, 983-84
winter: passes in a few hours, 711; perpetual, 710-11
WINTER CARLISLE, 200-1, 692, 815, 1122, *1389*
Winter Holiday, 972, 1016
THE WINTER OF THE BIRDS, 266, *1389-91*
The Winter Princess, 1252
A Winter's Tale, 171
WISEMAN, DAVID, 397, *1391-92*
Wise Woman of Youghal, 1271
wishes: draught grants, 1377-78; granted, 38, 416-18, 570, 598, 785, 1007, 1041, 1042, 1093; for puppy, 1042; for riches, 417; for wings, 417; give dolls power, 819; that everyone wants baby brother, 417; thought granted, 810; three, 725; to be beautiful as day, 417; to seem no cleverer than other people, 999
wishing, power of, 330-31
The Wishing Bone, 1079
witch balls, 374
witchcraft: 150, 568-69, 995, 1342-45, 1416; accusations of, 351; amateurish, 413; executions, 1405; suspected, 200, 1394; 17th century, 303, 306-9, 609
THE WITCHES, 274, *1392-94*

witches: aim to eradicate children, 1392-93; ancestor, 488; assistant to, 698; bad-tempered, 928; bickering, 874; black, 752; blessing, 614; boy, 200-1, 1122-23; broom of, cat of, 173, 174; certified, 208, 225; chief, 1343; comic, 376, 518, 824, 835-36, 874; constantly bickering, 1354; contend for hand of wizard, 845; country, 1354; coven, 505, 637, 638; death of, 567; dedicated to eliminate children, 1392-93; drowning of, 1337; egg, 566; evil, 150, 429, 548, 549, 710-12, 755-56, 742, 1392-94; executed, 554; ex-mermaid, 1354; family of, 815, 1389; forgetful, 1354; daughter of "foreign" woman believed to be, 955, 1396; forest, 1385-86; girl becomes, 692, 1122-23, 1389; good, 543; great-grandmother, 498, 600; has blue light, 246-47; healer, 1019; imagined, 119-21; in Narnia, 321, 356-57, 1009; in Narnia and England, 167; man executed as, 125-26; next door neighbor, 452; of Upper Folding, 568; old and forgetful, 835; old woman rumored to be, 1405; pretend, 230; pretty white, 1354-56; resembling, 297; sea, 824, 17th century, 303, 307-9, 609, 614; shrunk to mouse-size, 1393; speaks with Russian accent, 1392-93; stereotyped, 1392-94; student, 568; substitute, 1354-55; suspected, 13, 351, 449, 454, 642, 799, 830, 915, 1244, 1410-11; the Morrigan, 1067; twins, 1354; unprincipled, 191; water, 1300-2; wears necklace of dead husbands' teeth, 1354; wear gloves and wigs, 1392; white, 614, 642, 864, 961-62, 710-12; wild, troublemaking, 755-56; woman resists, 859; youthful, 208-9, 1264; *See also* enchanters; magicians; necromancers; warlocks; wizards.
witches and wizards, novels of, 200-1, 208-9, 306-9, 1354-56, 1392-94
The Witches' Ride, 151
Witchfinder General, 308, 554
witch hunts, 308, 673-74
Witching Wood, 985, 1094-95, 1130
Witch of the Waste, 568, 1122
witch's alphabet, 374

THE WITCH'S BRAT, 1176, *1394-96*
witch's brooms, 173
THE WITCH'S DAUGHTER, 81, *1396-97*
witch's hats, 174-75
witch's steeple hat, 173
witch trials, 303
Witch Week, 617
Withens Common, 536
Withens family, 196, 536-37, 904,
    1034-35
Withern, mid-20th century, 119-21,
    570
Withishall, 537
Witless family, 140
witnesses, to murder, pickpocket,
    1108
wives: abuse, beating, 1234; afraid
    of husband, 1132; beauty queen,
    762; common-law, 334, 1315, 1364-
    66; deceitful, 114-15, 754;
    departed, of blind professor, 460;
    destructive, 865; discontent-
    ed, 249; intense, determined,
    1053; leaves domineering husband,
    836; loving, 313; manipulative,
    836; murdered, 739, 752, 1105; cf
    parson, 193; overdramatic, 752;
    protective of husband, 728; sec-
    ond, 752; slovenly, 334; socially
    superior to husband, 703-4;
    submissive, 836; treacherous,
    1189-90; unfaithful, 116, 932;
    very beautiful, 1189-90
Wix family, 291-92, 351-53, 641
wizards: 43, 44-47, 63, 96, 132,
    167-68, 407, 408, 439-40, 470,
    532, 551, 553, 566, 568-69, 698,
    805, 932, 1013; black, 752; black
    comic, 376, 518, 824, 835, 874;
    black seeks bride, 1353-56, 1397;
    conjures murderer, 1104; drugged,
    1338; farms music, sports, shops,
    1243; fat, 1087; female, 44-46,
    321, 1087; irresponsible, 567;
    never weep, 1193; ogre of, 697;
    schoolmaster thought to be, 1409;
    secretary of, 845; true discov-
    ered, 1355-56; unexpected, 1192-
    93; Welsh, 116; white-bearded,
    1342. *See also* enchanters; magi-
    cians; necromancers; warlocks;
    witches.
wizards, novels of. *See* witches and
    wizards, novels of.
Wizard Suliman, 569
WIZARD WATCHER, 1356, *1397-98*
Wodensbeorg, 296, 358
Woggle, 490

The Wolf, 530
Wolf, a healer, 11
Wolf, chief of police, 711
Wolf, the Alsatian, 1398-99
WOLFF, Kurt, 1098, 1398
Wolff family, 1398
Wolf Guard, 1321
wolf kill, unsuccessful, 337
*WOLF OF BADENOCH: DOG OF THE GRAMPIAN
    HILLS*, 220, *1398-99*
Wolvercote, 208
wolves: attack, 439, 551-52, 1122,
    1321, 1400; evil, slain, 962;
    fostering infant, 529; kill as
    test, 1320-21; pet, 261; raise
    boy, 630-32, 836-37; ravenous,
    roam countryside, 108, 1400; talk-
    ing, 11, 71, 1084-85
THE WOLVES OF WILLOUGHBY CHASE, 8,
    109, 888, *1399-1401*
the Woman, 525
Woman of Shamlegh, 654
Woman of the Clan, 1171-72
women: appearance conscious, 792;
    butt of village jokes, 821; cat-
    hating, 893-94; die in childbirth,
    1196; exotic, 1420; fear of, 5;
    golden-eyed, 918; green, 1092-
    93; hard-fisted Scottish, 914;
    jilted on wedding day, 820; lead-
    er of Bronze-Age tribe, 336;
    overreligious, 972; market, 1416;
    mysterious, veiled, 887; passive
    characters, 1364; politically
    powerful, 677-78, 881; pregnant,
    cast out by father, 799; remit-
    tance, 853; socially versatile,
    853; strong characters, 1163;
    terrorist, 29-30; terrible-
    tempered, 608; timid, 60; very
    tall, 861; warm-hearted, 275-76;
    warriors, 245, 603, 865, 1086,
    1118-19; young, steals mother's
    lover, 1420
Women of Islam, 747
Women's Institute Rally, 174
Wonder House, 651
Wonderland, 18-19, 19-22, 192, 836,
    1209-11, 1362
Wonka, Mr. Willy, 58, 203-4, *864-65*,
    1297, 1305, 1375-76
Wood, Ann, 980
Woodall family, 1015, 1276-77
Wood between the Worlds, 321, 987
wood carvers, 1205
Wood family, 599, 608-9, 1058-60,
    1100-1, 1258
Woodpecker (ship), 218

Woodpecker Wood, 1120
Woods, Weasel, 432
THE WOOD TROLL, 37, 1350, *1401-2*
Woodward, Hilda, 536-37
Woodwind (boat), 983-84
wool: growers, 791, 1132-33, 1402-3; merchants, 1132-33, 1402-3; packers, dishonest, 1402-3; raising, trading, 884; stolen, 519, 827; used as hiding place, 585
THE WOOL-PACK, 527, *1402-3*
Wooten family, 377-79
Woozle, 974, 1388
Wopsle, Mr., 495
words: power of, 44-46; 2000 in lieu of taxes, 44-46, 321, 566; 2000 sent quarterly, 470
Word to Caesar, 1253
workhouses: 53-54, 74, 596, 692, 728, 821. *See also* poorhouses.
working class, 385-86, 400-3, 427, 536-38, 558, 703-4, 735-36, 876, 911-12, 949, 1143-44, 1276-78, 1234-36
working conditions: exploitive, 1066; factory, dangerous, 807-9; improved, 741
workmen, pygmies, 203
workrooms: secret, 755. *See also* laboratories.
World, End of, 1308
World-Eater, 1183
worlds: aftermath, nuclear war, 155-58; backwards, 1209, 1361; created, 167; devastated by war, 359; end of world feared, 110, 112; medieval, 359-60; mirrors of each other, 359; revived, 360; series of, 755-56; succession of, 1092
World War I: England, 6, 9-10, 206-8, 227, 421-24, 461, 538, 1374; English coast, 1213-15; father killed in, 161; France, 1213-15; post, 1123-25; pre, 354-56, 418-21; Russia, 1207. *See also* war novels.
World War II: aftermath, 1098-99, 1398; channel islands, 175; death in, 841; England, 210, 226, 262-3, 377-79, 400-3, 467-69, 603, 710-13, 734-37, 747-50, 881, 886-87, 937, 1234-36, 1339-40; Europe, 31, 253-54, 353, 597-98, 619-20, 1132, 1348-49; evacuees, 179, 842, 1240, 1372-73; father killed in, 696; fighter planes, 1212; London, 414-16, 897-99, 924-26; Norway, 37, 578, 1349-51; Poland, 152; pre,

969, 1169-71; stories of, 856; Switzerland, 152; Wales, 60, 176-79, 179. *See also* war novels.
The Worm and the Toffee-Nosed Princess, and Other Stories of Monsters, 577
worms, loathly, 929
The Would-be-Goods, 881, 1148
wounds: arm, 74; from boars, 996; from dwarf, 913; from wolf, 1321; gashed arm, 906; hand hurt by terrorist's bullet, 857; head, 866, 1399; healed by cordial, 712; infected, 1361; leg, 768; poisoned arrow in shoulder, 714; rabbit by bullet, 1332; skin on door-scraper, 1384
Woundwort, General, the rabbit, 418, 446, 535, 1332-33
Wrack, Miss, 824, 1354
wraiths, 712
wrappers, metallic papers from toffees, 668
wreaths, to lay on Byron's tomb, 490
Wrench, Zack, 1373
Wrench family, 179, 468-69, 1419
wrens, in song, 1295
Wright family, 226-27, 317, 419-21, 422-24
Wright family, 775, 1228-29
Wrigley, Mrs, 119-21, 230, 570
WRIGHTSON, PATRICIA, 714, *1403-4*
writers: anti-Nazi, 1348-49; beggar, 1268; father, 252-54, 555, 762, 862, 1313-15; hide in bushes to write, 838; Jewish, 937; mother, 838; of book on street people, 449; of children's books, 138, 822; of reading text, 849; of TV scripts, 838; of 2000 words, 1013-14; on Scotland, 588-89, 590; pirates from Agony Columns, 838; tramp, 620, 891; uncle, 171, 1178-79; woman, 823; youthful, 339, 533, 620-23, 635-36, 734-37, 818, 823, 1123-25, 1147, 1185, 1363; illegal, 1294; teaching to, 948
THE WRITING ON THE HEARTH, 527, *1404-7*
Written for Children, 1247
Wroff, the dog, 724
Wyr Geld, 117

The Xanadu Manuscript, 1247

yachts: 184, 433, 1004-5, 1379-81. *See also* boats; canoes; ships.

Yahoos, 513
Yald Forest, 425, 1248-49
YARL CORBIE, 1156, *1409*
Yates, Elizabeth, 332
A YEAR AND A DAY, 794, *1409-11*
The Year of the Stranger, 796
The Year of the Worm, 980
Yeff, the dog, 326
YEHIMELEK tribe, 156, 1068, 1357,
    1411-12
yellow pages, 1315
Yellow Peril, 480, 959
YEMM, CHARLIE, 173, 236-37, *1412*
Yerbut, 524
yew trees, trimmed in shapes, 212,
    710
yokels, 1094
Yolus (Aeolus), 927
Yorkists, 102-4, 317, 615, 683, 701
Yorkshire: 14th century, 717, 915-
    17; 17th century, 636-38; 18th
    century, 169, 463-64; mid-20th
    century, 96-99, 351-53, 486-87,
    536-38, 801-4, 875, 1021-23, 1035,
    1274; late 20th century, 912
Youd, Christoper Samuel, 231. *See*
    CHRISTOPHER, JOHN, *231-32.*
YOU NEVER KNEW HER AS I DID!, 573,
    1412-15
*The Young Fur Traders: A Tale of the
    Far North*, 68
The Young Magicians, 66

YOUNG MARK, 27, *1415-17*
Young Pretender, 648
Young Tilly, the dog, 328-29, 483
Yowncorn Yat, 486-87, 960
Ysabeau, Queen of France, 448, 586

Zabruski family, 214-15
ZACH WRENCH, 179, 468-69, 1373, *1419*
Zachariah, the cat, 724
Zackary Hawkins, 154
Zakyna, 619
zany creatures, 18, 19-22, 22-23,
    41-42, 334-35, 342-43, 505, 572,
    753, 767, 827
zany situations, 19-22, 41-42, 479,
    753, 1208-11
Zapata, Emiliano, 601
Zayid, 434-36
Zepho, 625
Zeppelins, World War I, 1214-15
ZERO, the dog, 838, 921, *1419-20*
Zion, 975-80
"Zoe's summer," 1323
ZOE VARDOE, 202, 741, 1280, 1323-24,
    1420
Zois, 74-5, 325-28
zoos: 798, 1154, 1192; girls land in,
    1385; gorilla escapes from, 525
Zuckerman, General, 1187
Zuckero, General, 585
Zurich, 1348-49
Zwirn family, 1349

About the Authors

ALETHEA K. HELBIG is Professor of English Language and Literature at Eastern Michigan University. She is the co-author, with Agnes Regan Perkins, of *Dictionary of American Children's Fiction, 1859–1959: Books of Recognized Merit* and *Dictionary of American Children's Fiction 1960–1984: Books of Recognized Merit* (Greenwood Press, 1985) and has published articles in *Children's Literature, Children's Literature Association Quarterly, The Alan Review, American Women Writers,* and *Writers for Children.* She compiled *Straight on Till Morning: Poems of the Imaginary World* and *Dusk to Dawn: Poems of Night* (with Agnes Perkins). Professor Helbig is Past-President of the Children's Literature Association (International).

AGNES REGAN PERKINS is Professor of English Language and Literature at Eastern Michigan University. She is co-author, with Alethea K. Helbig, of *Dictionary of American Children's Fiction, 1859–1959: Books of Recognized Merit* and *Dictionary of American Children's Fiction 1960–1984: Books of Recognized Merit* (Greenwood Press, 1985). Her articles have appeared in *A Tolkien Compass, Unicorn, Children's Literature, Children's Literature Association Quarterly,* and *Writers for Children.* In addition, she is co-compiler of *New Coasts and Strange Harbors: Discovering Poems* (with Helen Hill), *Straight on Till Morning: Poems of the Imaginary World,* and *Dusk to Dawn: Poems of Night* (with Alethea Helbig).